The Labor Relations Process

Second Edition

William H. Holley, Jr.
Auburn University

Kenneth M. Jennings
University of North Florida

The Dryden Press
Chicago New York Philadelphia San Francisco Montreal
Toronto London Sydney Tokyo Mexico City Rio de Janeiro Madrid

Acquisitions Editor: Anne Elizabeth Smith
Developmental Editor: Patricia Locke
Project Editor: Ruta S. Graff
Managing Editor: Jane Perkins
Design Director: Alan Wendt
Production Manager: Mary Jarvis

Text and Cover Designer: Harry Voigt
Copy Editor: Loraine Edwalds
Indexer: Bernice Eisen
Compositor: Modern Typographers
Text Type: 9½/12 Helvetica Light

Library of Congress Cataloging in Publication Data

Holley, William H.
The labor relations process.

Includes index.
1. Industrial relations—United States. I. Jennings, Kenneth M. II. Title.
HD8072.5.H64 1983 658.3′15′0973 83-16563
ISBN 0-03-062799-0

Printed in the United States of America
465-039-98765432

Address orders:
383 Madison Avenue
New York, NY 10017

Address editorial correspondence:
One Salt Creek
Hinsdale, IL 60521

CBS College Publishing
The Dryden Press
Holt, Rinehart and Winston
Saunders College Publishing

This book is dedicated to Ali and Bret who found the pencils and to Betty and Jackie who gave them a reason for moving.

The Dryden Press Series in Management

Arthur G. Bedeian, *Consulting Editor*

Albanese and Van Fleet
Organizational Behavior:
A Managerial Viewpoint

Bedeian
Organizations: Theory and
Analysis, Text and Cases
Second Edition

Bedeian and Glueck
Management, Third Edition

Boone and Kurtz
Contemporary Business,
Third Edition

Bowman and Branchaw
Business Report Writing

Chen and McGarrah
Productivity Management: Text and Cases

Compaine and Litro
Business: An Introduction

Gaither
Production and Operations Management: A
Problem-Solving and Decision-Making
Approach, *Second Edition*

Higgins
Organizational Policy and Strategic
Management: Text and Cases, *Second
Edition*

Hodgetts
Management: Theory, Process, and
Practice, Third Edition

Hodgetts
Modern Human Relations at Work, *Second
Edition*

Holley and Jennings
Personnel Management: Functions and
Issues

Holley and Jennings
The Labor Relations Process, *Second
Edition*

Huseman, Lahiff, and Hatfield
Business Communication: Strategies and
Skills

Huseman, Lahiff, and Hatfield
Readings in Business Communication

Jauch, Coltrin, Bedeian, and Glueck
The Managerial Experience: Cases,
Exercises, and Readings, Third Edition

Lee
Introduction to Management Science

Miner
Theories of Organizational Behavior

Miner
Theories of Organizational Structure and
Process

Paine and Anderson
Strategic Management

Paine and Naumes
Organizational Strategy and Policy: Text
and Cases, *Third Edition*

Penrose
Applications in Business Communication

Ray and Eison
Supervision

Robinson
The Internationalization of Business: An
Introduction

Robinson
International Business Management,
Second Edition

Smith
Management System: Analysis and
Applications

Stone
Understanding Personnel Management

Tombari
Business and Society: Strategies for the
Environment and Public Policy

Trueman
Quantitative Methods in Decision Making in
Business

Zikmund
Business Research Methods

Contents

The Labor Relations Process

Preface

A revised book offers several opportunities, including the chance to thank professors and students who helped make this situation possible. We have made many revisions to update the first edition, including new sources, issues (productivity and concession bargaining, employment at will, sexual harassment, and so forth), and cases. Another different feature is the summary *and* implications section which represents an analysis and extension of some points raised in the chapter.

These differences notwithstanding, the objectives, style, and concerns of the first and revised edition are similar. More specifically, *The Labor Relations Process* hopes to accomplish at least three objectives. First, it will provide the reader with an understanding and appreciation of the fundamental principles and concepts of labor relations. Some readers will approach this subject with limited related experience, their attitudes toward labor unions and management having been shaped by their families, associates, and sketchy news coverage of labor-management issues. Yet almost every individual who works or will work for a private or public organization will be either directly or indirectly affected by labor-management relationships. For example, individuals in production positions must administer the agreements; those in finance and accounting departments must calculate the cost of the agreements; sales management personnel must anticipate the effect of a strike on product availability and subsequent price change; and nonunion employees must consider how negotiated agreements will affect their wages and fringe benefits. Thus, this book will provide valuable insights into a topic which contributes to the reader's career development regardless of his or her professional field of interest.

A second objective of this book is to create a continuing interest in the subject matter. In colleges and universities, labor relations courses are often taken as electives. It is hoped that the completion of *The Labor Relations Process* will create in students a lasting interest in the subject. For example, we hope that in the future the reader will take special interest in such occurrences as Dan Rather's assessment of various labor issues, union leaders' testimony before Congress, answers to correspondents on *Meet the Press*, and so on.

Finally, this book is intended to encourage the reader to pursue a career in labor relations. As readers progress through its contents, it will become clear to them that participation in union-management relations will demand all of the behavioral science and managerial skills and theories obtained in academic and management development courses. Not only must one know and be able to interpret accurately legal implications and decisions, but many related issues such as productivity bargaining and unions and minorities have long-term, significant societal implications. Thus, we firmly believe that a career in labor relations is challenging, stimulating, and rewarding, and we hope that *The Labor Relations Process* will influence its readers to share our opinion.

In approaching its topic, our book combines theoretical and practical insights on the assumption that each is insufficient without the contributions of the other. This combination is in part accomplished through numerous practitioner and academic quotations inserted throughout the book. These quotations have been carefully screened and selected for their general applicability. They are an integral portion of the book, providing the inexperienced reader with representative industrial relations insights and the experienced scholar with a provocative means for comparison. Additionally, each section of the book has been subjected to critical academic and practitioner review. From reviewers' suggestions and comments a more balanced academic-practitioner perspective has been provided. We are grateful for the reviewers' time, insights, and efforts; their names are indicated in our acknowledgments.

This book differs from other labor relations books in two major respects. First, its contents relate entirely to the model of the labor relations process which is discussed in Chapter 1. The next twelve chapters explain the various aspects of this process, while the final four chapters enable the reader to apply the labor relations process to different situations, such as those in the public sector, foreign countries, and selected occupations in professional sports, health care, and agriculture.

Second, the book was written with both the beginning student and the professional scholar in mind. For the beginning student, the text has been written in such a way as to explain principles and concepts without confusing them. For the professional scholar, the content is well documented from the best sources that we could find at the time of writing. The rather extensive reference section included at the end of each chapter credits the many contributors for their research in the field of labor relations. More importantly, it is hoped that most readers will regard the references as useful stimuli and starting points for continuing research on the subject.

Any errors of omission and commission are the responsibility of the authors. We have attempted to obtain the most appropriate materials that were available to us. We encourage readers to call any omissions to our attention, and we actively encourage readers to initiate a dialogue with us so that we can improve on this edition in the next one.

Many individuals have enhanced the quality of this book through their contributions to the first and/or second editions. We are most grateful to the following professors who have read the entire book and have made valuable suggestions: William Chase, Adams State College; Milton Derber, University of Illinois; James Dworkin, Purdue University; Geraldine Ellerbrock, California Polytechnic State University; Paul Gerhart, Case Western Reserve University; David Gray, University of Texas at Arlington; Charles R. Greer, Oklahoma State University; Marvin Hill, Jr., Northern Illinois University; Douglas McCabe, Georgetown University; William Maloney, Ohio State University; Pamela Marett, North Carolina State University at Raleigh; Roy Moore, Southern Mississippi University; Thomas Noble, University of Tennessee at Martin; Robert Rodgers, University of Texas at Austin; David Shulenberger, University of Kansas; and William Werther, Arizona State University.

Similar appreciation is extended to many individuals who have read portions of this book and have contributed their expertise in specialized areas: Gwynne Berry, NASA Headquarters, Washington, D.C.; Pat Forbes, University of North Florida; Marc Grossman, United Farm Workers; Alexander Hadden, Office of the Commissioner of Baseball; Dan C. Heldman, National Right to Work Legal Defense Foundation, Inc.; Robert Helsby, University of North Florida; Eileen Hoffman, Federal Mediation and Conciliation Service, New York office; Wayne Howard, the University of Pennsylvania; Truly Kincey, Auburn University; Terry Leap, Clemson University; Jim McCollum, Auburn University; Marvin Miller, Major League Baseball Players Association; Ed Perron, NASA Headquarters, Washington, D.C.; Steve Shapiro, University of North Florida; William Simkin, former director of the Federal Mediation and Conciliation Service; Ron Smith, Union Carbide Corporation; Hans Stadtlander, Morton Salt Company; Roger Wolters, Auburn University; and Albert Zack, AFL–CIO.

We are grateful to A. Dale Allen, Milden Fox, Asa Gardiner, Paul Gerhart, John Remington, Jerald Robinson, and Alex Simon for furnishing an excellent selection of unpublished labor arbitration cases.

Special thanks is extended to those who helped along the way: Achilles Armenakis, Art Bedeian, Ernie Brown, Cliff Carter, Boyd Childress, Kathy Cohen, Anne Davis, Jack Davis, Hubert Feild, Bob Ford, Merian Gay, William Giles, Langston Hawley, Yvonne Kozlowski, Cindy Marcantonio, Frank McLaughlin, Dave Moore, Don Mosley, Jay Smith, Betty Turk, Rudy White, Lorna Wiggins, and Bess Yellen.

Finally, we would like to thank the Dryden staff for their fine work on this book. We are especially grateful to Anne Smith, Jane Perkins, Patricia Locke, Debbie Karaszewski, Doris Milligan, Alan Wendt, and Ruta Graff at Dryden; and to Loraine Edwalds and Robert Beran, for copy editing and proofreading.

William H. Holley, Jr.
Auburn University

Kenneth M. Jennings
University of North Florida
October 1983

ons, including strikes, that could create
ort for tax credit legislation on either the
evels.

MUST overcome their long-felt skepticism of the public schools. "The public wants and we have to help them achieve that,"

"WE'VE GOT TO get out there, righ
said, but she conceded that her memb
some convincing. Many teachers are
have to bear the brunt of the blame
shortcomings, Futrell said, and that the
reform could deteriorate into a campaig
contractual gains made by teachers in
decades.

Dow Chemical Is Ci By EPA for Disposa Of Some Dioxin Wa

MIDLAND, Mich.—Dow Chemic
said the U.S. Environmental Pro
Agency issued a complaint against Do
cerning the disposal of dioxin-contam
waste at its facility here.

ons took place b
ber 1981. Dow
EPA 10 mont
the waste, and
ct to the Toxi
The EPA res
s complaint, w
a fine, Dow

esents the late
between the E
ighly toxic by
cture of certai
ar, Dow came
t was disclos
ficials had pe
and suggest c
repared by the
ago. The draft
from Dow's M
amination in
ichigan.

t the EPA's co
olation of fede
a substantial
spokesman s
"secondary
ed as items s
paper towels t

Unions Offer to Buy Conrail for $2 Billion, But U.S. Sees Serious Problems With Bid

tions. However, the u
ments on the private
stantially offset" by
public sale of 20% to 3
stock.

The government al
that a new Conrail o
keep the road running
that Conrail doesn't r
or financial support.
worry, the unions' off
aimed at speeding a
of the company or its
comes clear that Co
tained as an indepen
the substantial resou
employee actions."

A railroad officia
Conrail issue contends
offer "will drive (g
look for alternatives'
than before.

The unions contend
erous," that Conrail i
without the union con
ernment corporation h
only the unions can k
the current offer, "I
government wanting
piecemeal" to other buyers, Brian Freeman, the group's attorney, said.

The employees want to buy Conrail to "maximize service" and protect their jobs. The jobs would be threatened if the railroad is purchased by other roads, especially piecemeal, that might then seek to abandon big segments, the union association said. Without a union takeover, Conrail "is likely

Hotel Labor Turmoil Is Ended in Las Vegas As New Pact Is Voted

LAS VEGAS—Hotel workers voted overwhelmingly to accept the latest contract offer from the Nevada Resort Association, ending a month-long labor dispute in which 13 hotels locked out hundreds of employees.

A spokesman for Teamsters Local 995 and Operating Engineers Local 501, the two unions representing the employees said the new contract calls for a 16% wage increase over the life of the new four-year pact. It also calls for a six month wage boost freeze and a restrictive strike clause, barring workers from joining other unions' strikes for the first 30 days of such walkouts, the spokesman said.

The previous contract, which covered 3,800 employees, expired April 1.

Employees at the Golden Nugget Hotel

New lab

Better perso

been contaminated with small amounts of herbicide containing traces of dioxin.

The EPA, according to Dow, is simply complaining that Dow failed to notify the agency prior to the disposal. The Dow spokesman said the disposal method was a "common" one, and used the "best available technology." Dow hadn't been sure whether it was supposed to notify the EPA before disposal, he said.

But Thomas Daggett, assistant regional counsel in the EPA's Chicago office, said, "I do not view it as an insignificant violation." Mr. Daggett declined to elaborate, explain-

stands the legal ramifications of doing so. "We feel it's a very positive story in terms of industry regulating itself," the official said.

Dow said it plans to meet "informally" with officials of the EPA's Chicago office to review the EPA's interpretation of the regulations cited in the complaint.

EPA
In San

WASHI
agreed to
vironmenta
Francisco
she was pr
Reagan a
Mrs. Cr
White Hou
William R

ward to se
other capa
said Mrs.
as a speci
haus.
Mrs. Cr
a dozen to
were force
Mr. Rucke
at the EP
tried to fig
the White

Pension funds

Talks Between Ford, UAW Break Down Over Future of Plant

DEARBORN, Mich.—Talks on keeping Ford Motor Co.'s loss-ridden Rouge Steel Co. unit open broke down because the company and the United Auto Workers couldn't agree on wage and benefit concessions.

Ford wouldn't say if it intends to exercise its threat to close the obsolete unit, but the

auto maker h
at the plant. I
ling interest i
nese compani
broke down o
enough conce
The No. 2
say only that
plans" for t
what the alte
stood that one
duction of op
Union offic

approach sou

el relations urged at jo

effective communications and human relations skills, motivating employees, scheduling, manpower planning and teamwork."

misplaced."
Supervisors in
mit to take deliv
rial without te

Part 1
Recognizing Rights and Responsibilities of Unions and Management

Part 1 introduces the labor relations process which will be discussed throughout the book, placing it in historical and legal perspectives. It also examines how employees become unionized and the relationships between the various organizational components of labor.

Chapter 1 Labor-Management Relationships in Perspective

"The American system of industrial relations is characteristic of our free society."
Sumner H. Slichter, James J. Healy, and E. Robert Livernash

Currently, there are approximately 20 million union members and 160,000 collective bargaining agreements in the United States. These statistics are significant for several reasons. They demonstrate the magnitude of labor relations activities in the United States, indicating that these activities are neither rare nor insignificant. They also suggest the difficulty of making generalizations regarding labor relations. In essence, it is nearly impossible to speak of the typical labor agreement, union member, collective bargaining behavior, or union-management relationship.

On the other hand, the magnitude of labor relations activities necessitates the development of a framework (Exhibit 1.1) which will focus on certain related dimensions and allow investigation of similarities and differences in the labor relations process. The labor relations process *is one in which management and the exclusive bargaining agent for the employees (the union) jointly decide upon and enforce terms and conditions of employment (work rules). This framework is needed in order for the practitioner and academician to consistently examine the outcomes of the labor-management relationship. This chapter provides an overview of the labor relations process and introduces those elements which are discussed throughout the remainder of the book.*

Elements in the Labor Relations Process

Exhibit 1.1 provides a framework for the labor relations process and illustrates many elements which are commonly found in this process. These elements can be applied to the labor relations activities at a single manufacturing facility, at some or all of the facilities owned by a single company, or in an entire industry. The exhibit cites three major categories: *the focal point of labor relations*—work rules; *the participants in the process*—union and management organizations,

Exhibit 1.1 Elements in the Labor Relations Process

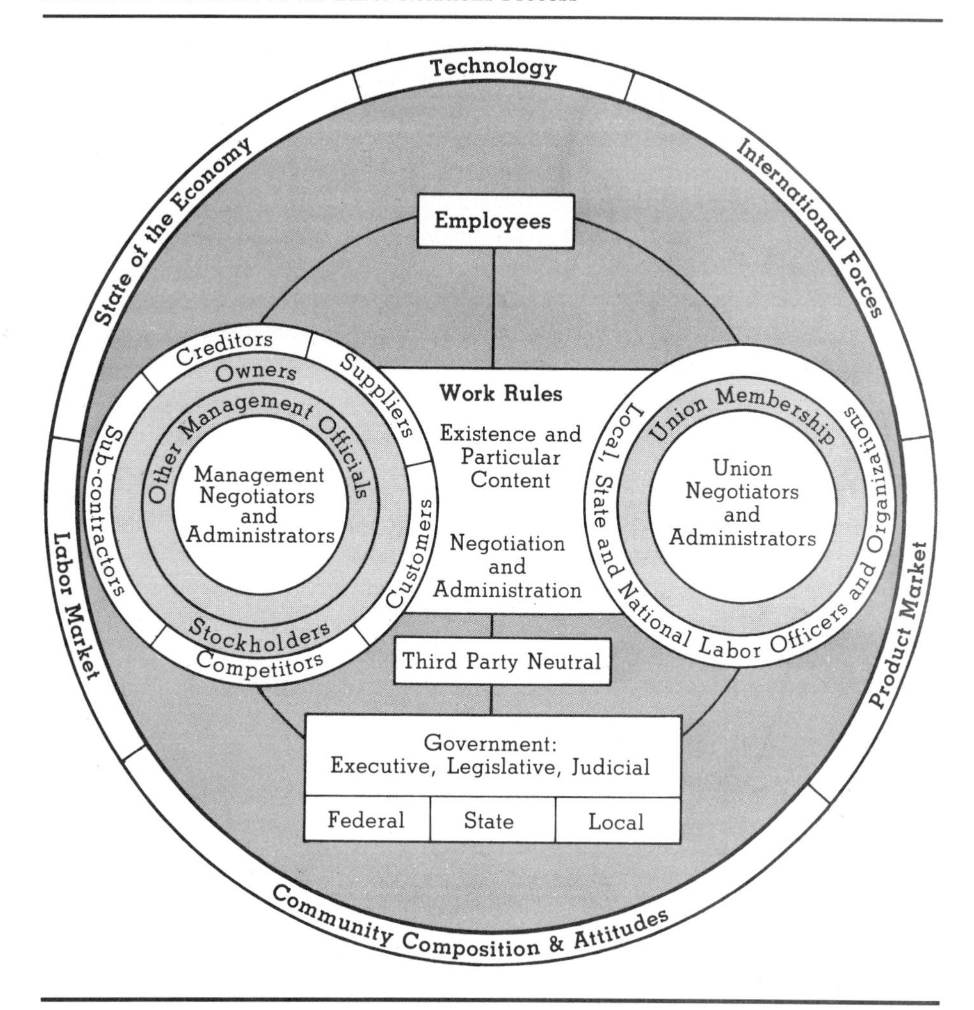

Source: Slightly modified from material supplied by Milton Derber of the University of Illinois.

employees, third party neutrals, and the government; and *constraints or influences* affecting the parties in their negotiation and administration of the work rules.

These categories are interrelated. They will be discussed separately, however, to reflect their unique dimensions and considerations.

The Focal Point of Labor Relations—Work Rules

Any academic discipline needs a focal point so that research, investigation, and commentary can generate applicable insights. "Labor" or "industrial" relations can become a very broad topic including many academic concerns. Sociologists have examined employee alienation, psychologists have investigated causes of job satisfaction, economists have studied wage determination, and political scientists have assessed the structural relationships of the internal union organization and its members and leaders.

In 1958, John Dunlop's book, *Industrial Relations Systems*, provided a useful focal point for the diverse academic approaches. Dunlop suggested that the center of attention in labor relations should be the work rules negotiated between management and union officials. It is important to understand the influences determining whether the rule exists and, if so, its particular content.[1] *Work rules* can be placed in two general categories: (1) *rules governing compensation in all its forms*—overtime payments, vacations, holidays, shift premiums, and so on, and (2) *rules specifying the employees' and employers' job rights and obligations*, such as performance standards, promotion qualifications and procedures, job specifications, and layoff procedures. Additional examples of work rules are furnished in Exhibit 1.2.

Compensation work rules such as negotiated wages are often publicized because they are easily understood by the public. Union and management officials, however, can attach equal or greater significance to the second work rule category, job rights and obligations. Managers, for example, might be most concerned with obtaining a contract provision whereby production employees can be required to perform "minor repairs," instead of requiring higher paid maintenance employees to do them. Also, at least one major union has been successful in negotiating a "justice and dignity" work rule whereby an employee who is suspended or discharged remains on the job until the disciplinary decision is reached (usually by an arbitrator, an individual discussed later in this chapter).[2]

Some work rules, such as the first one in Exhibit 1.2, are common to many occupations or industries. Others may be unique to a particular job classification, such as those for Playboy Bunnies, baseball players, and cemetery employees. Work rules likewise may vary according to their vague or specific nature; for example, consider the "democracy in public college education" provision cited in Exhibit 1.2. This rule at first appears rather insignificant; yet unions and management could easily become heatedly involved over the meaning and intent of the word *democracy*. For example, a professor, discharged because of poor teaching evaluations, might contend this decision violated the "democratic ideal" cited in the labor agreement since he or she also supported an unpopular political cause.

An analysis of work rules regardless of their clarity or scope helps us understand the complex output of the labor relations process. The formal labor agreement in this sense represents a compilation of jointly negotiated work rules. However, as discussed in Chapter 8, labor relations activities are not limited to the mere existence and content of the work rule; it is also appropriate to examine how the particular rule is administered between union and management officials.

Exhibit 1.2 Examples of Work Rules

Work Rule	Job or Industry Classification
After consultation with the Shop Committee, the Corporation shall make reasonable rules in each plant regarding smoking. Any protest against the reasonableness of the rules may be treated as a grievance.	**Auto Assembly**
Discharge and Suspension for Lack of Bunny Image. (1) The parties acknowledge the great importance of Bunny Image and its maintenance to PCI, to the Clubs and to Bunnies, due in part to the established recognition of Bunnies as unique and distinctive Playboy employees. . . . The parties acknowledge the difficulty of defining "Bunny Image" and agree that determination of Bunny Image for purposes of discharge or suspension may include, but is not limited to, the physical appearance of a Bunny and the impression she conveys to customers and others.	**Entertainment—Nightclubs**
An employee reporting for work on his regularly-scheduled shift, unless he is notified by the Company not to report at least sixteen (16) hours prior to the scheduled starting time, shall be given work which is available, but in the event he is not permitted to start work, or works less than one hour, he shall be given four hours' pay. In the event that an employee works more than one hour of his regular shift before being sent home because of lack of work, he will receive eight (8) hours' pay. This provision shall not apply in the event that an employee refused available work which he is physically able to perform or in the event that catastrophes, failures of utilities or acts of a public enemy interfere with work being provided.	**Steel Industry**
Single Rooms on the Road. A Player may elect prior to the commencement of the championship season to have single rooms in the Club's hotels on all road trips. The cost of such rooms shall be paid by the Player except that the Club shall pay a portion of the cost equal to 50% of the Club's usual rate for a double room at the hotels involved.	**Professional Baseball**
Democracy in Public College Education. The Board and the Union recognize and agree that while democratic principles should prevail in every American school system, urban colleges in a city as diverse in population as is Chicago must be exemplary in their expression and practice of the democratic ideal.	**Clerical and Technical Employees at a College**
Gravedigging: In all cases where a grave is dug straight down, a second man shall be assigned to assist the digger after a depth of five feet is reached.	**Cemeteries**

Sources: Various collective bargaining agreements in the United States.

Work rules also respond to changing workplace conditions and societal values over time. For example, the contemporary work rules for airline flight attendants would most certainly differ from the following three work requirements formulated in the 1930s: (a) swat flies in the cabin after takeoff, (b) prevent passengers from throwing lighted cigar butts out the windows, and (c) carry a railroad timetable in case of plane trouble.[3] An example of a change in social values has occurred in the motion picture industry. Today's films often contain explicitly sexual, nude scenes. Related labor agreement provisions concerning actors' rights in this situation have been negotiated to reflect this contemporary working condition.[4]

The Participants in the Labor Relations Process

Management Officials The negotiated and administered work rules involve managers at several different organizational levels and functions. A large corporation is usually divided into several divisions, each having several production facilities or plants. Labor relations managers and representatives are typically found at corporate, divisional, and plant levels. Labor relations objectives are developed and coordinated at the corporate and divisional levels to insure that a particular work rule, such as a wage rate for a particular job classification, does not adversely alter precedents or conditions at another production facility.

Labor relations representatives at the plant level implement these directives, but they must also deal with other managers at the location, particularly first-line supervisors, who direct the daily work activities of hourly employees. As will be further discussed in Chapter 8, management's first-line supervisors typically hear and attempt to resolve employees' grievances on the production floor. In some cases, they are surprised to learn that higher level management officials have overturned their decision on a grievance and have taken an opposite position. Alert union leaders may use dissension among top management officials to influence labor relations activities and the company's position toward unions.

Union Officials Union leaders also do not represent a consensual group since they experience conflict within and between labor organizations. Members and officers do not completely agree on priorities; sometimes conflict occurs over specific tactics to be used in accomplishing commonly shared bargaining objectives.

In some cases different labor relations priorities or beliefs can occur between two labor organizations. PATCO, the Professional Air Traffic Controllers Organization (further discussed in Chapter 15), claimed in its dramatic strike that replacements coupled with extended working schedules would increase the likelihood of aircraft crashes. The president of The Airline Pilots Association, however, declared during this period that "without equivocation the air traffic control system in this country is safe."[5]

The second and third circle surrounding both management and union negotiators (see Exhibit 1.1) demonstrates the pressures and potential influences on the respective managements and unions. Management must be conscious of its competitors, who may challenge the company's product in quality, price, and/or service; at the same time, it must provide a return to the owners (stockholders) by operating in such a way as to retain its customers, pay its creditors, and maintain its supply of raw materials and parts. Unions at each level must operate within the policies and rules of their local and national unions as well as those of the AFL-CIO if the national union chooses to affiliate with this federation. Moreover, since union officers are elected, they must continue to provide those services and benefits that members believe are important. Thus, both union and management negotiators have pressures, policies, and rules that guide their behavior.

Employees Employees represent perhaps the most significant participant category since they often determine whether a union is ever present in an organization (representation elections and union organizing drives are discussed in Chapter 5). Employees also determine whether a negotiated labor agreement is accepted or rejected and whether a threatened strike is actually carried out (Chapter 7). Employees assign different priorities to various working conditions, and have different degrees of commitment to their employers.

Employees are included as a separate category since they can have loyalties to both management and union organizations.[6] This situation is found in both the private and public sectors; for example, public employees such as firefighters, police, and teachers may feel torn between the critical or professional nature of their jobs and the strategic advantages of a strike. Since their desires may shape the existence and content of particular work rules, employees can be considered the third participant in the labor relations process.

In many instances, the employees' racial or ethnic backgrounds may shape their particular work rule preferences. For example, if most of the employees at a facility are black, then there will probably be pressure for a holiday commemorating Martin Luther King's death or birthday. A unique example involves the Navajo Indians working at an Arizona coal mine, who asked that their union's health and retirement fund be used to pay fees charged by Navajo medicine men. While these miners relied on regular physicians to treat most physical injuries, they relied on medicine men to ease aches, pains, and emotional problems.[7]

In other cases, the age of the employees might affect the content of the work rules. If the average age of employees at a facility were fifty, there would probably be more emphasis on pension plan improvements, whereas a younger work force might stress maternity benefits or higher hourly wages.

Third Party Neutrals Often differences of opinion between management and union officials are revealed in contract administration through the grievance procedure (discussed in Chapter 8). An *arbitrator* is a third party neutral selected by union and management officials to resolve a grievance; an arbitrator's decision is binding. Arbitration is discussed in more detail in Chapter 9.

In a very few instances arbitrators might also resolve an impasse during the negotiation of the labor agreement. However, the *mediator* (discussed in Chapters 7 and 14) is the most frequently involved third party neutral if a collective bargaining impasse occurs. The mediator only offers advice and does not have binding decision-making authority.

The Government Traditionally, the federal government has played an indirect role at the bargaining table. A mediator from the Federal Mediation and Conciliation Service can assist union and management officials in reaching an agreement. The mediator's advice, however, can be refused; this individual can also be asked by one or both parties to leave the negotiations. Labor Secretary Raymond Donovan has recently explained,

. . . it is not the government's job to ensure anything when it comes to what I continue to call the miracle of collective bargaining. Industry . . . and labor . . . know better their own needs and their own limits than any Federal Government does. Collective bargaining has served this country well and it will continue to.[8]

While the federal government does not dictate the terms of a negotiated labor agreement, laws, judicial decisions, and administrative agencies (local, state, or federal) can influence or restrict work rules. Union and management officials cannot negotiate a mandatory retirement age of 60 years since this would conflict with the Age Discrimination in Employment Act. To cite another example, coal miners have long believed that if females worked in the mines, bad luck would result. However, union and management officials would be violating the Equal Employment Opportunity Act if they negotiated a provision prohibiting female employees from working in the mines. Perhaps more widespread is the controversy over negotiated seniority provisions which are used for administration decisions, such as promotions and layoffs, and affirmative action programs monitored by the government. This issue will be discussed in more detail in Chapter 12.

Influences Affecting the Participants' Negotiation and Administration of the Work Rules

Thus far we have suggested that the desires and composition of the labor relations participants can affect the development of work rules. However, these participants are in turn influenced by several variables or constraints (see the outer circle of Exhibit 1.1) in their labor relations activities. These influences may relate to the particular firm, the local community, or society in general. The following is not intended to be an exhaustive discussion of these influences but to furnish a few illustrations of how they can affect the existence and content of work rules.

Technology Perhaps the most immediate and persistent influence on the work rules is the technology of the particular workplace. *Technology* is defined to include the *equipment* used in the operation, the *pace and scheduling of work*, and *characteristics of the work environment and tasks to be performed.*[9] Consider, for example, the major equipment found at a steel mill—blast furnaces, which require very high temperatures for operation. These furnaces cannot be simply turned on and off like a household oven. Often several days are required for either reaching these high temperatures or for cooling the furnaces for necessary repairs. This equipment characteristic, in turn, has several implications for the facility's work rules. In essence, steel mills must be operated twenty-four hours a day, seven days a week—a situation prompting related work rules such as wage premiums for working the night shift, weekends, and holidays.

In some cases the introduction of equipment reduces or eliminates employees in a particular job classification.[10] This situation occurs when "robots" (discussed in more detail in Chapter 12) handle tasks formerly performed by employees. A rather common application occurs in the auto industry where mechanically joined arms perform spot welding, spraying, machine unloading, and assembly. Unions faced with membership replacement by robots have increased related bargaining demands (more paid time off, the four day week, etc.) for its members' job security.[11]

The *pace and scheduling* of the workday could also affect the work rules of certain occupations. For example, bus companies optimizing their productivity and revenue would concentrate on rush hour traffic (6:00–9:00 A.M., 3:00–7:00 P.M.), when buses would stand a pretty good chance of being filled with passengers. Problems remain in scheduling work because it is possible that many bus drivers would have a daily work schedule of three hours on, three hours off, one hour on, two hours off, four hours on. Because of the nature of the work, most labor agreements in related industries have provisions pertaining to the permissible number, length, and possible compensation of intervals (times off) between daily work assignments.

Professional sports also experience scheduling problems. Management could conceivably schedule a night game in New York City for one day and then have the baseball team fly to Los Angeles, where it would play two games (a doubleheader) the following day. Of course, many of the baseball players would object to the schedule, an attitude which precipitated the following current labor agreement provision: "(4) (a) A game will not be scheduled to start after 6 P.M. if either Club is scheduled to play a day doubleheader the next day."[12]

Finally, the work environment and tasks to be performed can also influence work rules; for example, particular safety equipment is required on certain jobs in the manufacturing and construction industries. A more specific example relates to actors performing at dinner theatres. The lights in dinner theatres are usually turned off between the acts of a play. Actors retire to their dressing rooms during the intermission, while the stage crew changes the stage scenery for the next act. The actors then return to the stage via aisles which are commonly surrounded by dinner tables before the lights are turned back on for the new act. Those who have attended a dinner theatre might wonder how the actor safely walks to the stage in virtual darkness. This concern has apparently been shared by union officials because the Actors' Equity Association labor agreement governing employment in dinner theatres includes a detailed provision requiring proper spacing and placement of guide-lights.[13]

International Forces The international influence on the labor relations process was most vividly reflected in the United States' involvement in World War I and World War II. The impact of these wars on domestic labor relations activities will be described in more detail in Chapter 2. However, it should be noted that President Franklin Roosevelt, realizing that U.S. production output could not be jeopardized during World War II, established a War Labor Board, which in turn encouraged union and management officials to negotiate provisions in their labor agreement for the administration of work rules.

A more recent example pertains to the Arab oil embargo which increased gasoline prices and consumer preference for fuel efficient automobiles. This situation has resulted in the layoffs of several hundred thousand automotive employees who manufactured large, low mileage cars.

Product Market The *product market* is where the company either sells its product or purchases key elements for its manufacture. Considering the first element, management would be more vulnerable if a strike occurred at the time major customer sales were anticipated. Consider, for example, when a brewery anticipates a peak market demand for its product. Clearly, management at the brewery would not prefer a labor agreement expiring, and possibly leading to a strike, during the summer months. Indeed, one major brewery has been successful in changing the contract expiration date from June 1 to March 1.

The second dimension of the product market is illustrated by the United Auto Workers Union's (UAW's) deep concern that many of the parts for automobiles are being manufactured in foreign countries. If this practice continues, it is likely that a provision in the labor agreement will eventually be negotiated to restrict the number of automobile parts manufactured in foreign countries.[14]

A recent product market development and related strike conducted by the Screen Actors Guild concerned residual payments given to actors if their work is presented or transformed into different product markets such as pay television, or video cassettes. Exhibit 1.3 illustrates the different compensations they negotiated for various product markets.

Community Composition and Attitudes The influence of community composition and attitudes can be examined from two perspectives: (a) influential individuals and/or organizations within the community and (b) cultural values and traditions which are reflected in the community's population. Similarly, the geographical scope of the community can be subject to varying definitions; it can represent the local municipality or a broader geographical region. This variable can even be extended to include societal differences in labor relations patterns (Chapter 16). Consider, for example, the goals of a prominent Japanese union leader outlined in Exhibit 1.4. While the following discussion considers domestic applications of the community influence, it is safe to say that no U.S. union leader would approach the goals outlined in Exhibit 1.4 with management representatives, especially if he or she wanted to be reelected.

The very existence of a labor union can be largely determined by community influences. A company selecting a location for a new production facility often has to contend with a group of influential community citizens. In many cases, these groups, with or without the support of the community's population, have thwarted the efforts of some predominantly unionized, high-wage companies to locate in the area.[15] Attitudes of community citizens and/or potential employees

Exhibit 1.3 Screen Actors Guild Residual Payment Formula for Theatrical and Television Motion Pictures: How It Works

HOW · IT · WORKS

	THEATRICAL FILMS (produced after 10/6/80)	FREE TV (produced after 10/6/80)	MADE-FOR SUPPLEMENTAL (produced after 10/6/80)
When Sold to Pay-Television:	Producer pays SAG 3.6% (including Pension & Welfare) of worldwide gross receipts distributed proportionately among actors according to residual base (salary and time units credited to each performer).	Producer pays SAG 3.6% (including Pension & Welfare) of worldwide gross receipts distributed proportionately among actors according to residual base.	No additional payments due until program has been broadcast for 10 days (within one year from initial exhibition) on each system worldwide. After 10 days or one year, producer pays SAG 4.5% of distributor's worldwide gross, distributed proportionately among actors according to residual base.
When Sold to Videocassette or Videodisc:	Producer pays SAG 3.6% (including Pension & Welfare) of worldwide gross receipts distributed proportionately among actors according to residual base.	Producer pays SAG 3.6% (including Pension and Welfare) of worldwide gross receipts distributed proportionately among actors according to residual base.	Producer pays SAG 4.5% (plus Pension & Welfare) of fees received from sales over 100,000 units, distributed proportionately among actors according to residual base.
When Sold to Free Television:	Producer pays SAG 3.6% (including Pension & Welfare) of worldwide gross receipts distributed proportionately among actors according to residual base.	Rerun formula as set forth in 1977 Television Agreement.	Same formula as Free TV contract of '77, except variety, game, and quiz shows which are covered by AFTRA.
When Sold for Theatrical Release:	Original salary covers theatrical exhibition worldwide, including in-flight use.	Exhibition is divided into two areas: 1. The U.S., its territories and Canada. 2. All other countries. Rights are subject to individual bargaining and payment of not less than 100% of player's total applicable minimum for exhibition in either geographical area. Initial payment for use in one area is 150%, with additional 50% due at time of exhibition in the second area.	Exhibition is divided into two areas: 1. The U.S., its territories, and Canada. 2. All other countries. Rights are subject to individual bargaining and payment of not less than 100% of player's total applicable minimum for exhibition in either geographical area. Initial payment for use in one area is 150%, with additional 50% due at time of exhibition in the second area.
When Sold to Foreign Markets:	Included as theatrical exhibition. No additional payments due to actors.	Payment of 15%-35% of player's total applicable minimum salary, triggered by distributor's foreign gross.	Payment of 15%-35% of player's applicable minimum salary, triggered by distributor's foreign gross.
When Sold to Basic Cable:	Producer pays SAG 3.6% (including Pension & Welfare) of worldwide gross receipts, distributed proportionately among actors according to residual base.	Programs produced after 10/6/80 are paid according to the free television rerun formula established in 1977. Programs produced prior to 10/6/80 which have NOT run longer than three seasons on network, not run in domestic syndication, nor exhibited on non-prime network time require player's consent and payment by producer of 4.5% of distributor's gross receipts, plus Pension & Welfare.	Producer pays SAG 4.5% (plus Pension & Welfare) of worldwide gross receipts, distributed proportionately among actors according to residual base.

Source: Adapted by Mark Locher and Kay Peters for *Screen Actor* magazine (vol. 24, (Summer 1982), p. 4), from the Screen Actors Guild 1980 Theatrical and Television Motion Picture Contract. This formula is a condensation of the three-year SAG contract signed in 1980, effective to June 30, 1982. The contract and residual payment formula are subject to change through collective bargaining with the Alliance of Motion Picture and Television Producers as of June 30, 1983. Information on all current contracts and future contract updates may be obtained through any office of the Screen Actors Guild.

Exhibit 1.4 Japanese Union Leader's Standard of Living Goals for the 1980s

Bachelorhood: A typical factory hand in his early 20s "will live in a small private apartment of one six-mat room and one three-mat room [a mat is 18 square feet]," says Nakamura. "He will work a five-day week, own a refrigerator, color TV, skis and a car and take three domestic trips and a week's vacation abroad every year. He will go to the movies ten times a year and attend five sporting events."

Young Marrieds: After his wedding, at around the age of 25, the typical worker will move into slightly larger quarters—a " 2dk" apartment (two rooms plus a dining room–kitchen) in a company-subsidized housing project. He will buy a sewing machine for his wife and, for the first time, acquire a telephone.

Growing Family: "At 36," Nakamura continues, "the worker buys his own 88-square-meter [947 square feet] house. By then, he has two children. He also has an air conditioner, a piano and golf equipment, and the rooms are carpeted."

The Provider: In middle age, the model employee provides his children with the best possible education. "By the time he is 50, his son has graduated from a private university," says Nakamura. "His daughter has completed junior college."

The Senior Citizen: At 60, the mandatory retirement age, Nakamura's typical union member trudges off, safe and secure, into his sunset years of contentment.

Source: "Five Ages of Man," *Newsweek*, May 24, 1976, pp. 42–43.

can also strongly influence the possibility of a facility becoming unionized. One assessment of white workers in the South suggests that these employees have had the following cultural beliefs: independence, reliance on individual accomplishment, and general distrust of "outsiders." These beliefs can make it difficult for any union organizer who attempts to persuade the employees at a southern industrial facility to join a particular union.[16]

If a facility becomes unionized, community attitudes can shape the subsequent work rules desired by management or union officials. In many cases, this influence occurs when union and management officials reach an impasse over a particular issue. Chapter 7 describes various strategies used by management and labor to resolve a negotiations impasse. One related tactic involves soliciting support from community residents. For example, teachers desiring limitations on the maximum number of students allowed in a classroom might stress to the affected community that increased class size would lower educational quality. Educational administrators, on the other hand, would probably indicate to the community that a teachers' strike over this issue would place educational funding in jeopardy.

The mass media often serve as both generator and conduit of community opinion. Unfortunately, few empirical studies have investigated the effects of the mass media on labor relations participants and work rules in the United States.[17]

One such study examined the editorials of five major newspapers which pertained to the air traffic controllers' strike. Nearly two thirds of the editorials indicated that the strikers were "lawbreakers" who "withheld vital services."[18] The news media are profit-making businesses, and at least one prominent union official contends that this orientation biases the reporting of labor relations activities:

The media tend to cover collective bargaining as if it were a pier six brawl. The intricate moves and tradeoffs that really make up bargaining aren't as newsy as impassioned rhetoric or a picket line confrontation.

Reporters are given little training in covering collective bargaining. They are told to look for the "news"—the fist fight, the walkout, the heated exchange—and, as a result, frequently miss the "story," which is the settlement. . . .

Every union proposal is a "demand," every management proposal is an "offer."[19]

Unions have used two different approaches in resolving negative media attention. Many union officials are beginning to realize that they have to change their former indifferent, even hostile, attitudes toward the media. Long ago, the late George Meany once received the following advice concerning a troublesome reporter, "Why don't you push him down the stairs?"[20] Although union officials of Meany's day would generally have agreed with that advice, many today are receiving training in the skills of holding press conferences and handling hostile reporters' questions.

A second approach towards the media features organized protest toward unfair portrayals of union members and organizations. Recently, for example, the Association of Flight Attendants criticized NBC and a commedienne on the "Tonight Show" for labeling flight attendants "high altitude hookers."[21]

Labor Market The skills and wage levels of employees in the local labor market can affect negotiated work rules. Management is often concerned with the skill levels of employees in the particular community. For example, a firm needing skilled employees from a relatively unskilled labor market would probably wish to negotiate work rules regarding apprenticeship programs. Management under these circumstances would also consider negotiating a probationary period which would give them a relatively free hand in determining whether an employee remains on the payroll during the first ninety days of employment. Within this probationary period, management could terminate an unskilled or nonproductive employee, and the union could not protest the action through the grievance procedure.

Both management and union representatives are also interested in the compensation rates for comparably skilled employees in the labor market. At a minimum, the wages paid by other companies in the local area affect negotiated wage rates. In some cases, particularly in the construction trades, some unions have had to reduce their wages to fight off nonunion competition.

State of the Economy In a sense, the state of the economy can reflect all of the preceding influences discussed in this section, particularly if viewed in microeconomics as well as macroeconomics terms. The rate of inflation, in either local or national areas, will often affect work rules—notably, union insistence that a labor agreement include provisions which will increase the wages if there are increases in the cost of living (see Chapter 13). Similarly, an increase in interest rates could retard home and industrial construction projects. Under these circumstances, work rules might be negotiated to insure that construction workers are not laid off and/or that they receive some compensation for the reduced work load.

The unemployment rate, another key economic indicator of the state of the economy, affects the possible existence and content of work rules which provide job protection. Chapter 6 discusses the various ways in which the unemployment rate can affect the bargaining power of union and management officials. If this and other economic measures pertaining to the Gross National Product, productivity, cost of living, compensation at all employee levels, and exports and imports are unfavorable, their unions will be more likely to accept bargaining concessions (a situation also described in Chapter 6).

Steps in the Labor Relations Process

The labor relations process is comprised of three phases:

1. *Recognition of the legitimate rights and responsibilities of union and management representatives*. This phase includes the legal right of employees to join unions (see Chapter 3), union organizing drives (see Chapter 5), and the rights of management and union officials, as well as their responsibilities to abide by related laws and labor agreement provisions.
2. *Negotiation of the labor agreement, including appropriate strategies and tactics and impasse resolution techniques*. Strikes and mediation are examples of the latter (discussed in Chapter 7). This phase is usually the most publicized by the media, even though phases 1 and 3 are equally essential.
3. *Administration of the negotiated labor agreement—applying and enforcing the terms of the agreement on a daily basis*. This phase of the process (discussed in detail in Chapters 8 and 9) accounts for the most time and energy spent by union and management officials and usually involves a larger number of these officials than the preceding phases.

Clearly, the sequence of the labor relations process is cumulative. Seldom do formal negotiations occur if the parties have not first recognized each other's legitimate rights and responsibilities. Similarly, the first two phases are necessary for the existence of the third phase—administration of the labor agreement. Of course, not all labor-management relationships have focused on these three phases. Indeed, employees and their representative unions at some public and private sector facilities are still striving to accomplish the first phase of the process.

A most important aspect of the labor relations process is the quality of the relationship between management and the union officials. In a general sense, there are probably as many different relationships as there are union and management officials negotiating and administrating labor agreements. Yet these relationships often fall into one or more of the following categories: sympathetic, codified, and power.[22]

Sympathetic relations occur when union and management representatives show sympathetic regard for each other's positions and are guided by such appreciation. This relationship often involves personal sentiments, understandings, and concern for the other party's position.

Codified relations occur when the parties accord each other privileges, prestige, and authority in terms of defining codes—applicable labor laws and the provisions of the negotiated labor agreement. Both parties falling into this relationship category go strictly by the book in dealing with each other; there is little room for modifying or improvising these relationships on the basis of personal experiences and concerns involving the other party.

Power relations are often marked by an opposition of interests, with each party attempting to achieve goals at the expense of the other: "Since action is neither held to an application of a code nor guided by a consideration for the other's welfare, a premium is placed on the successful pursuit of *one's own goal*, thus inevitably introducing egotism and possibilities of ruthlessness that have always made power action morally suspect."[23]

It is possible that the interacting union and management officials develop relationships that fall into all of the previously mentioned categories, depending upon the particular issue involved. For example, union and management officials will likely exhibit sympathetic or problem-solving relationships in dealing with an alcoholic employee, for this employee could harm other employees as well as lower industrial efficiency. The extent to which the union-management relationship shifts from sympathetic to power depends on several factors, such as differing goals and value systems, perceived legitimacy for the other side, past relationships and experiences with each other, and the participants' personalities.[24]

Explanations of Labor Organizations' Existence and Behavior

Thus far this chapter has presented labor organizations or unions as though they are present in every organization. Although the first section suggests that a union might not represent employees at a particular public or industrial facility, a labor organization or group of employees might attempt to organize and represent employees in their interactions with management officials at the facility.

Unions, however, are not always present; in many instances employees have chosen to remain nonunion. Attempts to explain the level and growth of unionization can be conducted at the micro and macro levels. The micro approach, discussed in Chapter 5, attempts to determine what propels employees at a particular facility to join a union.

The macro approach discussed in this section seeks general explanations of employees' collective behavior-protest movements which cut across many organizations even countries. International comparisons are discussed in more detail in Chapter 17. It is important to note, however, that there are many possible forms of worker protest. In other countries workers have formed independent labor political parties and have begun even broader social movements which seek to establish employee rights through a variety of strategies. Related activities in the United States have been confined to collective bargaining, which is an effective but rather limited form of worker protest.

Unions react to and reflect employee protests directed at some institution such as the workplace and economic conditions, distribution of wealth, political ideologies and related forms of government. The macro approach emphasizes that there are basic reasons why employees join unions which go beyond the somewhat simplistic notion that unions cause people to join unions.

Managers at nonunionized facilities should be interested in micro and macro approaches which can help predict the likelihood of their operations becoming unionized. These approaches can also help managers at unionized facilities predict the collective bargaining militancy and direction. Additionally, the macro approach can help in sorting out the many diverse historical events and conditions discussed in the next chapter. The macro explanations can be grouped into two general and overlapping categories: *work and job conditions*, and *employees' social beliefs and desires.*

Work and Job Conditions

Alienation Karl Marx maintained that employees might seek collective action to relieve their feelings of alienation about work conditions. According to Marx, the extensive use of machinery in manufacturing operations under capitalist ownership and control results in the employee being alienated from the work. In essence, the employee becomes an "appendage of the machine," with little skill and knowledge required in his or her performance.[25] The depersonalized nature of work allows no consideration of the individual's needs or concerns. Instead, the employee is completely dominated by the production process and derives neither meaning nor satisfaction from the work. The employee's work performance does not satisfy any work-related need (such as the needs for creativity, self-expression, self-fulfillment, and pride in accomplishment). Work is viewed as being merely a means to satisfy needs external to the work environment (food, shelter, and clothing, for example). According to this theory, employee alienation is compounded as employers increase their exploitation of the wage earners to maximize profits.

The historic inevitability of this pressure would drive capitalists, in the nature of the system of which they were a part, to press down ever lower on wage rates, to extend hours, or to extract more effort, leading to a further and continuous degradation of the working class. These were the 'chains' in which the 'system' held workers in bondage, but which would—inevitably—be thrown off at some point in time when proletarian misery was too great to tolerate.[26]

Marx felt that employees would become aware of their common plight and that their resulting class consciousness would prompt them to overthrow the capitalistic system. Another possible result of class consciousness, neither publicized nor encouraged by Marx, was employees joining a union to alleviate their alienated condition.

To be sure, there is some evidence that U.S. workers are alienated today. For example, several of the employee interviews in Studs Terkel's best seller, *Working*, reflect working conditions and employee concerns similar to those described by Marx.[27] However, two related factors appear to disprove the theory that employees join unions because of their class-conscious attempts to remedy their sense of alienation in work experiences.

First, clear-cut class consciousness, which might compel employees to join a union or to engage in other collective activities to improve their working situation, does not appear to exist in United States history. The presence of geographical, occupational, and social mobility in the United States results in loosely defined social groupings which make membership identification difficult.[28] Consider, for example, the term *middle class* as it is used in the United States. The term is so loosely defined and subject to so many differing interpretations as to make it an impossible predictor of collective action.

A second problem in identifying alienation as the stimulus causing employees to join unions occurs when we assume that the working class (however poorly defined) is more alienated than other employees, who are usually reluctant to join unions. One of the more publicized related studies, *Where Have All the Robots Gone?*, indicates that fewer than 25 percent of the employees have negative attitudes toward their work. Further, negative attitudes toward work do not vary a great deal between blue-collar and white-collar employees, although the latter are often reluctant to join unions.[29] Two observers of the labor movement believe that many employees might either repress or deny their alienation, pursuing instead the more immediate gratifications generated by "the spectacles of the market place" (new cars, attendance at professional sports events, and so on).[30]

As discussed more fully in Chapter 12, there are few if any U.S. unions actively involved in bargaining for more "meaningful" work. However, unions can and do address a possible aspect of employee alienation, namely the employees' desire to speak their minds without fear of management reprisal. Two authors commenting on this aspect suggested in an article written over thirty years ago that "intertwined with the motives for union membership is the almost universal desire to tell the boss to 'go to hell.'"[31] A union typically indicates to its potential members that the employees' rights to voice their opinions regarding a managerial action are protected by negotiated grievance procedures and disciplinary policies (see Chapters 8 and 10).

Finally, employees might be dissatisfied with aspects of their jobs while not being alienated from their work. Some research has shown that employees might join unions if they (a) are dissatisfied with physical characteristics of the workplace, low wages, or lack of benefits and (b) believe that a union will help them achieve the job-related conditions important to them.[32]

Scarcity Consciousness—The Need for Job Security Perhaps a more accurate observation of the union movement was made by Selig Perlman, who suggested that employees are attracted to unions on the assumption that unions will protect their jobs. Perlman suggested that Marx was wrong in thinking the employees will try to overthrow the capitalistic system of which they are a part. According to Perlman, employees are neither particularly alienated nor class conscious. Instead, many employees, particularly manual workers, strongly believe they are living in a country of limited opportunity. Perlman replaces Marx's class consciousness with *scarcity consciousness*—the employees' collective belief that jobs are difficult to obtain and retain. This belief is particularly true today for some industries, as reflected in the contemporary song "Steel Mill Blues."

I used to be a steelworker, I worked in the Midland mill,
'Til my patriotic government imported all the steel.

I used to wear my hard hat with so much dignity inside
And now that I am jobless, it seems I lost my pride.

I got a wife and three children depending on this man
I got a government in Washington who does not give a damn

So please Mr. President, open up a steel mill for me.

I got payments on my house, payments on my car.
But the unemployment checks don't seem to go that far.

Everything I worked for, well it seemed to slip away.
I don't think I'll get no benefits, no compensation pay.

I got a wife and three children depending on my pay.
They say I'm too young to retire, and too old to get hired.

So please Mr. President, open up a steel mill for me.

I used to make my living down in Midland, Pa.
Now I'm just a-dying, for a job to come my way.

What am I to do now that the jobs are hard to find?
I'm so damn sick of standing in the unemployment line.

I got a wife and three children depending on this man.
I got a government in Washington who does not give a damn.

So please Mr. President, won't you Mr. President,
Open up a steel mill for me?

Thus, employees turn to unions to solve these perceived difficulties. The union then

---

asserts its collective ownership over the whole amount of opportunity, and, having determined who are entitled to claim a share in that opportunity, undertakes to parcel it out fairly, directly or indirectly, among its recognized members, permitting them to avail themselves of such opportunities, job or market, only on the basis of a "common rule." Free competition becomes a sin against one's fellows, anti-social, like a self-indulgent consumption of the stores of a beleaguered city, and obviously detrimental to the individual as well. A collective disposal of opportunity, including the power to keep out undesirables, and a "common rule" in making bargains are as natural to the manual group as "laissez-faire" is to the business man.[33]

Unions therefore are attractive to the many employees concerned about job security today, regardless of their skill or occupational level.[34] Consider, for example, the work-related concerns of a college basketball coach. Depending upon the university's size and performance of the basketball team, the coach can receive a multiyear contract with a particular university. The wages and outside interests (for example, television shows) generated by this contract could result in a salary in excess of $100,000 a year. Yet a notably successful basketball coach, Al McGuire, when asked about the major job-related problem facing coaches, responded:

Security, mainly. Your life depends on a 19-year-old, freckle-faced player. Your unity and your whole season can be blown if the cheerleader gets pregnant. Look, I know the fears coaches have. I know how it is when you've lost five or six in a row and the flower of your youth is gone and you're worrying about what you can do next. I know what it's like when the student body is booing and the papers are writing bad things.[35]

Few employees are currently immune from the possibility of a layoff; therefore, employees might join a union in the hope of increasing their job security. The union can in turn strengthen the employees' job security in several ways.

Make-work rules which prescribe certain procedures for performing a job, thereby insuring that a certain number of employees will be assigned work, can be negotiated. One example is the requirement that no more than two floral sprays can be carried with a casket in the funeral hearse. This rule insures in many cases that a second employee will be needed to drive a flower car.

Apprenticeship programs are usually an attempt to insure that qualified people are available for certain skilled jobs. However, these programs can also insure that jobs will be reserved for those individuals who complete the apprenticeship program. For example, a Hollywood property craftsmen union has an apprenticeship program requiring at least two years of prop-making work experience and 1,500 hours of studio training in such techniques as rain making and cobweb construction. This program helps to insure a quality work force, but it also insures that a union member who has completed the program will not be displaced by the son or daughter of a motion picture producer desiring a job during summer vacation from college.

Negotiated seniority and layoff provisions (discussed in Chapter 12) usually do not prevent management from reducing the number of employees at a particular factory. However, most related provisions indicate that those having more job seniority (work years) at a particular facility will be the last to be laid off. Should some of these employees be laid off, they would eventually be called back to work in the order of their seniority; that is, those employees having the most seniority would be called back to work first.

Lobbying for legislation protecting employees' job rights has been a viable alternative used by unions throughout the years. Here, unions attempt to strengthen job security by pressing for restrictions against cheap labor—foreign citizens, child labor, prison labor—quotas or restrictions against imported products[36] and adjustment assistance to employees who are displaced as a result of foreign competition.[37]

Employees' Social Backgrounds and Desires

Employees' social backgrounds and desires are not completely independent from the preceding category in indicating why employees join unions. For example, workers' social backgrounds and desires might strengthen their perceptions of working conditions and affect subsequent decisions about joining a union. Yet the reasons discussed in this section can in most cases be attributed to the potential union member irrespective of the particular working conditions faced by that individual.

Employees' previous experiences with a union can strongly affect their decision to join one. Indeed, many might be influenced by parental attitudes and experiences regarding unions. One active union member stated, "I attended union meetings with my father before I was ever inside a church."[38]

From their social backgrounds employees also bring qualitative assessments of their exposures to union organizations and activities. For example, one union member commented, "My dad was a great union man and that's where I got it—if it wasn't union, it wasn't no good."[39] However, these endorsements can go both ways. Favorable parental comments regarding unions may be offset for some employees by the opposite opinion of a spouse or work associate.

One recent study of over 1,200 employees during union organizing campaigns has partially supported the offsetting nature of personal experiences and the opinions of employees' relatives. For example, the employees' decisions to vote for a union were not significantly correlated with members of their families being union members. Similarly, prior union membership was not significantly associated with a vote for the union in the campaign, suggesting that many members who had been union members elsewhere were not entirely satisfied with union representation. Additional analysis indicated that employees' sex, race, and job seniority did not explain very well their preference for unions.[40] In short, it appears that employees' social backgrounds do not explain group voting behavior; that is, what influences an individual might not be characteristic of the group. This lack of explanation is probably due to a combination of complex, potentially offsetting relationships among all the variables found in employees' social backgrounds.

Unions as well as all formal organizations potentially satisfy the members' needs by providing "a means of developing, enhancing, or confirming a sense of identity and maintaining self-esteem."[41] Thus, unions can appeal to two interrelated social needs of members, the need for *affiliation or belonging* and the need for *status*. One prominent observer of industrial relations has noted that unions restore an employee's social ties to his or her work environment, a situation which also assumes moral significance.

If there is any meaning that can be derived from the persistent grouping of men about their tools or within their industry, it is that work must fill a social and moral as well as an economic role. The vacuum created between the job and the man has proved intolerable; and it cannot be filled by higher wages, shorter hours, better conditions of labor, music in the shops, or baby clinics. Man has to belong to something real, purposeful, useful, creative; he must belong to his job and his industry, or it must belong to him. . . . what gnaws at the psychological and moral roots of the contemporary world is that most urban people, workers and owners, belong to nothing real, nothing greater than their own impersonal pecuniary interests. . . . For the worker the trade-union has represented an unwitting attempt to escape from this dilemma.[42]

The union's possible benefit of social affiliation is strengthened or weakened by the degree of prestige or self-esteem it offers its members. Some employees join a union for the same reason they would join any social organization, namely, to enjoy the responsibility and status associated with being a member of that organization. This feature can be particularly attractive to employees whose jobs are basically interchangeable and carry very few elements of prestige or room for advancement.

Employees who become union officers can often attain prestige or self-esteem in their dealings with management officials:

As a shop steward or union officer or member of the grievance committee, a worker can become "a fellow your buddies look to." Such positions give him the opportunity to win other workers' approval by being "a fellow who stands up to the boss" with impunity. The role of "a fellow who stands up to the boss" is made more significant because the definition of the boss has been enlarged to include not merely the foreman but "the head office in Pittsburgh." He can win prestige as "a guy that gets results" in such matters as the distribution of work, assignment to jobs, seniority policy, and protection from discrimination.[43]

Chapter 8 discusses the notion that union officers and management officials are equals in their day-to-day administration of the labor agreement. However, as the preceding quotation suggests, the union steward can often emphatically disagree with a management official six levels above the steward on the organization chart. This ability to challenge without fear of reprisal is not usually afforded nonunion employees or even management officials when they deal with their organizational superiors.

As discussed earlier in this section, the perceived lack of prestige associated with unions in certain occupations might discourage employees from becoming union members. In some occupations, notably teaching, the union movement progressed slowly at first because employees regarded unions as being unprofessional. Many employees in other occupations (for example, office employees and retail clerks) have tended to identify their career potential more with management and have therefore been reluctant to join unions.

Summary and Implications

Summary

The labor relations process occurs when management and the exclusive bargaining agent for the employees (the union) jointly decide upon and enforce terms of the labor agreement. Work rules constitute the focal point of the labor relations process and pertain either to compensation in all its forms or to the employees' and employers' job rights and obligations.

At first glance, it might appear that union and management officials are the only participants in the labor relations process. Complexities arise with the realization that it is difficult to speak of *the* management or *the* union position on a particular labor relations issue. Instead, union and management officials are members of their respective organizations subject to internal conflicts and external pressures. Employees represent a third participant category in the labor relations process since they can have loyalties to both union and management officials. Various sociodemographic characteristics of the employee group (race, age, and sex) can exert a strong influence on the existence and content of work rules. Also discussed were third party neutrals (arbitrators and mediators) and a fifth participant category, the government, with its executive decisions, legislative action, and judicial decisions. The participants in the labor relations process are influenced in their rule-making efforts by several variables or constraints, such as technology, international forces, the product market, community composition and attitudes, the labor market, and the state of the economy.

The labor relations process consists of three sequential phases: (1) recognition of the legitimate rights and responsibilities of union and management representatives, (2) negotiation of the labor agreement, and (3) applying and enforcing the terms of the agreement on a daily basis. A most important aspect of the process is the quality of the relationship between union and management officials. These relationships can fall into one or more of the following categories: sympathetic, codified, and power.

Additional insights into the labor relations process are found by considering why employees join unions instead of remaining in a nonunion environment. The work environment can prompt the employee to join a union by contributing to feelings of alienation or scarcity consciousness, or related work rules may require union membership. Employees' preferences for unions can also be influenced by their social backgrounds and desires and their general occupational level.

Implications

It should be realized that the labor relations topic cannot be clearly explained by certain all-encompassing generalizations or theories. The more than 160,000 labor agreements are negotiated, interpreted and acted upon by millions of participants, and reflect complex and contradictory external influences.

Union and management officials have to establish some degree of consensus within their respective organizations, a difficult task in the many cases where there are many organizational levels and internal participant groups having different labor relations priorities. This situation results in a variety of labor-management relationships. In some cases the distinction between union and management is slight; union officials sometimes sit on corporate boards of directors.[44] Other relationships might be more adversarial, characterized by the atmosphere of conflict expressed by the president of our country's largest labor organization:

We have come too far, struggled too long, sacrificed too much, and have too much left to do, to allow all that we have achieved for the good of all to be swept away without a fight. And we have not forgotten how to fight.

We are out of step with no one but the cold-hearted, the callous, the avaricious and the indifferent.[45]

The variables associated with varied labor-management relationships and unique labor relations processes have been identified and briefly illustrated in this chapter. The remaining chapters explain and apply these variables.

Discussion Questions

1. Exhibit 1.1 establishes the focal point of the labor relations process and many variables which affect the process. Select an academic discipline such as political science, economics, or sociology, and indicate three specific ways the discipline could add insights into the labor relations process.
2. Discuss the different dimensions of technology, indicating how this variable might contribute to two unique and specific work rules for unionized employees at a grocery store. Also indicate with examples how one other external constraint or influence (see the outer circle of Exhibit 1.1) could affect the work rules at a grocery store.
3. Explain how a management official and a union official can have both sympathetic and power relationships with each other.
4. Compare and contrast the alienation and scarcity consciousness theories of why employees join unions. Which, if either, of these theories would be more appropriate in explaining why professional baseball players would join a union?

References

[1]John Dunlop, *Industrial Relations Systems* (New York: Henry Holt, 1958), pp. 13–16.

[2]"Steelworkers Seek to Extend 'Justice and Dignity' Clause," Bureau of National Affairs Inc., *Daily Labor Report*, no. 202 (October 19, 1982), p. 1. See also Ronald L. Miller, "Worker Privacy and Collective Bargaining," *Labor Law Journal* (March 1982), pp. 154–168.

[3]"Labor Letter," *Wall Street Journal*, November 22, 1977, p. 1.

[4]Screen Actors Guild, *Screen Actor Newsletter*, March 1978, p. 3.

[5]"Skies Are Safe Pilots Declare," Bureau of National Affairs Inc., *Daily Labor Report*, no. 160 (August 19, 1981), p. 1. See also Dale D. Buss, "UAW's Chrysler Canada Strike Creates Further Strains with U.S. Auto Workers," *Wall Street Journal*, November 11, 1982, p. 4.

[6]For an early study of employee dual loyalty, see Theodore V. Purcell, *Blue Collar Man: Patterns of Dual Allegiance in Industry* (Cambridge: Harvard University Press, 1960).

[7]"Labor Letter," *Wall Street Journal*, March 22, 1977, p. 1.

[8]"Excerpts from Interview with Labor Secretary Donovan," Bureau of National Affairs Inc., *Daily Labor Report*, no. 7 (January 12, 1982), G–1.

[9]For an additional discussion of technological dimensions and impacts on negotiated work rules see Dunlop, *Industrial Relations Systems*, pp. 33–61.

[10]See for example Michael Wallace and Arne L. Kallenberg, "Industrial Transformation and the Decline of Craft: The Decomposition of Skill in the Printing Industry, 1931–1978," *American Sociological Review*, 47 (June 1982), pp. 307–324. For further related implications of technology see the entire issue of *Scientific American* (September 1982); and Peter Rachleff, "Working the Fast Lane," *Radical America*, (Spring 1982), pp. 79–96.

[11]See for example, Lee Edson, "Slaves of Industry," *Across the Board*, (July–August 1981), pp. 29–35; and "Robots Next?" *The Economist*, January 30, 1982, p. 64.

[12]*Basic Agreement (1976–1979) between the American League of Professional Baseball Clubs, and the National League of Professional Baseball Clubs, and Major League Baseball Players Association*, p. 4.

[13]*Actors' Equity Association Agreement and Rules Governing Employment in Dinner Theatres (1973–1974)*, p. 24.

[14]John R. Emshwiller, "Looking Homeward: Auto Workers Decry Rise in Foreign Output of Parts for U.S. Cars," *Wall Street Journal*, March 19, 1976, pp. 1, 23.

[15]Douglas Sease, "Yankee Go Home," *Wall Street Journal*, February 10, 1978, pp. 1, 29. See also "Labor Letter," *Wall Street Journal*, August 16, 1977, p. 1.

[16]John Filiatreau, "The White Worker in the South," *Dissent* (Winter 1972), pp. 78–82.

[17]For two related studies pertaining to mass media and the industrial relations process in England, see David Morley, "Industrial Conflict and the Mass Media," *Sociological Review* (May 1976), pp. 245–268; and Paul Hartmann, "Industrial Relations in the News Media," *Industrial Relations Journal* 6 (Winter 1975–1976), pp. 4–18.

[18]Lynne L. Ashmead's unpublished paper, "An Analysis of Editorial Opinion and Public Opinion as Expressed in Letters to Editors Concerning the PATCO Strike" (1981). This study performed a content analysis of 34 editorials from the following papers: *Chicago Tribune, Miami Herald, Washington Post, New York Times*, and *Los Angeles Times*.

[19]Lane Kirkland, "Labor and the Press," *American Federationist* 82 (December 1975), p. 3. See also Albert J. Zack, "The Press Bias on Labor," *American Federationist* 84 (October 1977), pp. 1–7.

[20]Robert S. Greenberger, "Unions Give Leaders Lessons on Dealing with Petulant Press," *Wall Street Journal*, July 23, 1981, pp. 1 and 2.

[21]Bureau of National Affairs Inc., *Daily Labor Report*, no. 196, (October 9, 1981), p. 3.

[22]Herbert Blumer, "Social Structure and Power Conflict," in Arthur Kornhauser, Robert Dubin, and Arthur M. Ross, eds., *Industrial Conflict* (New York: McGraw-Hill, 1954), pp. 232–239.

[23]Ibid., p. 235.

[24]Leon C. Megginson and C. Ray Gullett, "A Predictive Model of Union-Management Conflict," *Personnel Journal* (June 1970), pp. 495–503. For an early examination of divergent industrial relations patterns see Benjamin M. Selekman, "Varieties of Labor Relations," *Harvard Business Review* 27 (March 1949), pp. 175–199.

[25]Karl Marx and Fredrich Engels, "Manifesto of the Communist Party," in H. Beer, ed., *The Communist Manifesto* (New York: Appleton-Century-Crofts, 1955), p. 16.

[26]Neil W. Chamberlain and Donald E. Cullen, *The Labor Sector*, 2nd ed. (New York: McGraw-Hill, 1971), p. 269.

[27]Studs Terkel, *Working* (New York: Random House, 1972). See also Bennett Kremen, "No Pride in This Dust," *Dissent* (Winter 1972), pp. 21–28; and Rick King, "In the Sanding Booth at Ford," *Washington Monthly* 7 (January 1976), pp. 36–44.

[28]Kenneth E. Boulding, *The Organizational Revolution* (Chicago: Quadrangle Books, 1968), pp. 166–167.

[29]Harold L. Sheppard and Neal Q. Herrick, *Where Have All the Robots Gone? Worker Dissatisfaction in the '70s* (New York: Free Press, 1972), p. 193.

[30]Daniel Bell, *Work and Its Discontents* (New York: League for Industrial Democracy, 1970), p. 33; and Stanley Aronowitz, *False Promises: The Shaping of American Working Class Consciousness* (New York: McGraw-Hill, 1973), pp. 409–410.

[31]Clinton S. Golden and Harold Ruttenberg, "Motives for Union Membership," in E. Wright Bakke, Clark Kerr, and Charles W. Anrod, eds., *Unions, Management, and the Public* (New York: Harcourt, Brace, 1948), p. 49.

[32]M. D. Dunnette and W. K. Kirchner, *Psychology Applied to Industry* (New York: Appleton-Century-Crofts, 1965), pp. 199–200; and Henry S. Farber and Daniel H. Saks, "Why Workers Want Unions: The Role of Relative Wages and Job Characteristics" (working paper, Cambridge, Mass.: M.I.T., 1978), pp. 27–28. See also W. Clay Hamner and Frank J. Smith, "Work Attitudes as Predictors of Unionization Activity," *Journal of Applied Psychology* 63 (1978), p. 415; William J. Bigoness, "Correlates of Faculty Attitudes toward Collective Bargaining," *Journal of Applied Psychology* 63 (1978), pp. 228–233; Chester A. Schreisheim, "Job Satisfaction, Attitudes toward Unions, and Voting in a Union Representation Election," *Journal of Applied Psychology* 63 (1978), pp. 548–552; J. G. Getman, S. B. Goldberg, and J. B. Herman, *Union Representation Elections: Law and Reality* (New York: Russel Sage Foundation, 1976); Edward L. Harrison, "Employee Satisfaction and Voting Behavior in Union Representation Elections," in Dennis F. Ray and Thad B. Green, eds., *Toward Renewal of Management Thought and Practice* (State College, Miss.: Southern Management Association, Mississippi State University, 1978), p. 169.

[33]Selig Perlman, *A Theory of the Labor Movement* (1928); reprinted New York: Augustus M. Kelley, 1968), p. 242.

[34]For an assessment of contemporary scarcity consciousness as it applies to employees in the automobile industry, see John R. Emshwiller, "Change in Attitudes: Recalled Auto Worker Finds His Outlook on Life Is Different," *Wall Street Journal*, February 3, 1977, pp. 1, 22.

[35]Larry Keith, "A Conversation with Chairman Al," *Sports Illustrated*, November 28, 1977, p. 36.

[36]See for example "Trade Petition Filed to Preserve Shoe Jobs," Bureau of National Affairs Inc., *Daily Labor Report*, no. 206 (October 25, 1982), p. 2.

[37]See, for example, Bureau of National Affairs, "4,000 More in Steel Given Adjustment Aid," *Daily Labor Report* (Washington, D.C.: Bureau of National Affairs, December 29, 1977), p. 3; and "Labor's New Push for Protection," *Business Week*, December 26, 1977, pp. 31, 32.

[38]Joel Seidman, Jack London, and Bernard Karsh, "Why Workers Join Unions," *Analysis of the American Academy of Political and Social Science* 274 (March 1951), pp. 775–784.

[39]Ibid.

[40]Getman, Goldberg, and Herman, *Union Representation Elections*, pp. 66–68.

[41]Edgar H. Schein, *Organizational Psychology*, 2d ed. (Englewood Cliffs, N.J.: Prentice-Hall, 1965).

[42]Chamberlain and Cullen, *The Labor Sector*, p. 282.

[43]E. Wight Bakke, "Why Workers Join Unions," *Personnel* 22 (July 1947), p. 3.

[44]See for example Brian Hamer, "Serving Two Masters: Union Representation on Corporate Boards of Directors," *Columbia Law Review* (April 1981), pp. 639–661.

[45]"Selected Remarks Presented during Solidarity Day Ceremonies," Bureau of National Affairs Inc., *Daily Labor Report*, no. 182 (September 21, 1981), D–1. These remarks were from Lane Kirkland, president of the AFL-CIO.

Chapter 2 Evolution of Labor-Management Relationships

"The history of the trade union movement has shown that when organized workers were a very, very tiny percentage of the work force, they still accomplished and did things that were important for the entire work force."
George Meany

The American labor movement as we know it today is not new. It has adjusted to changing societal events, employers' attitudes and actions, and employee preferences for more than 100 years.

A historical perspective is necessary to better understand current union behavior and predict how unions might react to sudden and dramatic change. This perspective can give clues to a particular union's current behavior—whether it will support a certain political candidate or accept management's bargaining proposal to reduce the work force by twenty percent in exchange for a "job enrichment" program.

There is no best way to obtain this perspective.[1] *Insights from many academic disciplines (sociology, economics, political science and so forth) have to be considered, and there are many focal points which can be assessed. Our discussion focuses on two interrelated historical dimensions: (1) relationships between labor and management organizations; and (2) organizational characteristics (objectives, structure, and strategies) of labor organizations.*

This second dimension is most important to labor relations' students and practitioners since the current American Federation of Labor-Congress of Industrial Organizations (AFL-CIO, which has millions of affiliated union members) has been historically affected by four major labor organizations: the Knights of Labor (KOL), the Industrial Workers of the World (IWW), the American Federation of Labor (AFL), and the Congress of Industrial Organizations (CIO). These organizations' philosophies and strategies have provided important lessons, both negative and positive, to the AFL-CIO.

The strength of any labor organization depends on four criteria:

- *Its structural and financial stability*
- *Its ability to work within established political and economic systems,*

particularly the wage system where employees work for management and are paid for their services

- *Supportive or disruptive features of the broader social environment such as legislation, media, and public opinion*
- *The ability of union leaders to identify and satisfy members' goals and interests.*

Readers can use these criteria to assess why some labor organizations failed in the past, and predict the likelihood of current unions posing a strong challenge to management.

The historical dimensions are organized into three time periods: 1869 to World War I; World War I to World War II; and World War II to the present.

1869 to World War I

Unions as we know them today were nonexistent before 1800. There were small *guilds*, or joint associations of employers and craftspeople that pressed for professional standards and restriction of outside competition.[2] These guilds pressed for concerns which typically benefited employees and employers alike. By 1820, there were only a few scattered strikes, usually over wages, since only two industries, shoemaking and printing, had even the semblance of collective bargaining. There was also no general labor philosophy or labor movement existing in the United States at this time.[3]

The Civil War (1861–1865) refined and encouraged mass production techniques, concentrating large numbers of semiskilled and unskilled employees under one factory roof—a situation which attracted organized labor.

The period 1869 to World War I saw the formation of three national labor organizations: the Knights of Labor (Knights or KOL), the American Federation of Labor (AFL) under Samuel Gompers, and the Industrial Workers of the World (IWW). Each of these organizations will be discussed in terms of its orientations and goals, organizational structure, and strategies and tactics. Reasons suggested for the demise of the KOL and the IWW and other items discussed apply to the previously mentioned criteria for a labor organization's strength. Three prominent labor episodes of this period are also discussed: the drive for an eight-hour work day (including the Haymarket Riot of 1886), the Homestead strike (1892), and the Pullman strike (1894).

The Knights of Labor

Goals and Organization of the Knights The Knights of Labor was founded by Uriah S. Stephens as a secret society in 1869. Secrecy was maintained until

1882 so that the members would not be discharged by their employers for participating in a labor organization.

There are two major reasons for discussing the Knights. It represented a union national in scope, larger than any previous union in American history. In the early 1880s, it had a steady growth, reaching over 100,000 members in 1885. Between 1885 and 1886, the organization's membership increased sharply to 700,000. The Knights had achieved more power, prestige, and notoriety than any other previous labor organization.[4] The KOL's goals and strategies also deserve consideration since both contributed to its demise as an effective organization. In short, the Knights served as an important negative lesson to the American Federation of Labor and more contemporary labor organizations in establishing and achieving their objectives.

The Knights strongly objected to the method of industrial organization and operation which began during the Civil War. This view led them to establish two major interrelated goals:

1. Change the existing labor-management relationships so that the depersonalized and specialized aspects of mass production can be avoided.
2. Attain moral betterment for employees and society.

The KOL's goals can best be grasped through the views of Terence V. Powderly, its leader and chief spokesman from 1879 to 1883. Mr. Powderly felt that mass production reduced the employees' feelings of pride and personal accomplishment.[5] In previous times, employees could be satisfied with their craftsmanship, a sense of skilled accomplishment in fashioning quality products from beginning to end. Mass production created several specialized employee classifications, each contributing to the completed product. Powderly placed this situation in perspective by considering the shoemaker situation:

The man who was called a shoemaker thirty years ago made shoes; the man who claims to be a shoemaker today makes only part of a shoe. What was once a trade in itself is a multiplicity of trades. Once there were shoemakers, now we have Beaters, Binders, Bottomers, Buffers, Burnishers, Channellers, Crimpers, Cutters, Dressers, Edge Setters . . . and several other workers at the shoe trade, and they all consider themselves shoemakers.[6]

Employees working in these specialized classifications could not obtain meaning or satisfaction from their fragmented work tasks. He also felt that bankers and owners of gold were the villains of industrial society causing higher taxes for employees and the creation of monopolies which further depersonalized the individual employee.[7]

The Knights believed that changing the existing industrial and societal system would help accomplish their second goal, moral betterment and increased dignity for their members. Powderly claimed that members must place their concerns on a "higher" ground than material working conditions, as these physical effects were but stepping stones to "a higher cause, of a nobler nature . . . the more exalted and divine nature of man, his high and noble capabilities for good."[8] The leadership of the KOL was continually concerned that its members would devote too much attention to improving working conditions, a situation which would cheapen their goal of moral betterment—to make every man his own master.[9]

The moralistic overtones of the Knights guided their membership policies, organization structure, and strategies and tactics. Since moral betterment affected all members of society, the Knights encouraged people of all callings to join their organization except professional gamblers, stockbrokers, lawyers, bankers, and those who lived in whole or in part by the sale or manufacture of intoxicating liquors.[10] Employers were also encouraged to join the KOL, the rationale being that they along with employees were being duped by financiers and once educated to this fact would join hands with the employees in improving society.

Thus, the *Local Assembly*, the basic unit in the KOL, could consist of employers and employees from several different trades. There were 1,100 KOL Local Assemblies in 1886; the purpose of these organizations was to educate members on KOL principles. However, authority and power of the Knights was very centralized as it rested with the General Executive Board (national officers and the highest position which was occupied by Powderly).[11] As will be seen later in this section, the structure of the KOL differed dramatically from that of the AFL.

Strategies to Accomplish the Knights' Goals The Knights used at least four strategies to accomplish their goals. *Political action* was viewed as important, particularly since the Knights felt that previous legislation had led society down the wrong road. The Knights believed that politicians were motivated by self-interest and therefore required careful watching. However, the Knights approached this strategy through the existing party. The KOL did actively lobby against importation of foreign labor and for appropriations to public school systems.

A second strategy was the *encouragement of producer and consumer cooperatives*. Unlike the Socialists, the Knights did not want the cooperatives to be owned by the state. Instead, current employees would save enough from their wages to either purchase the operation or establish a new cooperative. Since factories would be owned by the employees, conflict between labor and capital would cease.[12] Cooperatives would also enable the employees to become their own masters; they would have a voice in decision making, including the determination of a fair distribution of profits.

The Knights' leadership believed cooperatives would affect the established wage-profits system most directly; yet they made little attempt to establish a cooperative or to financially aid approximately a hundred cooperatives established at the local or district level during the mid-1880s. Most of the cooperatives failed because of "inefficient managers, squabbles among shareholders, lack of capital, and injudicious borrowing of money at high rates of interest."[13]

The KOL pursued a third strategy when it *actively avoided the use of strikes* to obtain its goals. The Knights' leadership often actively discouraged strikes and, in some cases, demoralized strikers with their statements.[14] Some leaders viewed strikes as a last resort, feeling they would distract members from the major goal of moral betterment and lessen the common interests of employers and employees. Indeed, the General Executive Board set up a complicated procedure that local assemblies had to follow before they could obtain strike funds.[15] Powderly believed that no employees should be able to enter a strike which would result in other employees losing their jobs; therefore, procedure was needed to insure that every employee possibly affected by a strike would have a voice in the strike decision.[16] Yet the red tape involved in obtaining strike funds caused a great amount of dissension between the KOL leaders and members. Local assemblies that conducted strikes were left on their own financially, and the members bitterly resented the lack of support from the board.[17] It became common for the local assembly to conduct strikes without support from the Executive Board—in 1886, there were at least 538 local assemblies participating in either a strike or boycott of an uncooperative employer's products.

The Knights' leadership preferred a fourth strategy to the strike; namely, *education* of the members and citizens as to the evils of the existing industrial system as well as the Knights' goals for societal improvement. Usually the leaders would meet with members of local assemblies in private sessions to inform them of the organization's goals and objectives. The emphasis on education instead of job action efforts (strikes and boycotts) will be further discussed in the next section.

Reasons for the Knights' Failure and Demise Despite tremendous growth, the KOL experienced a sudden demise. One reason for its growth must be the successful strike taken by the local assemblies against Jay Gould's railroads in 1885, in which the Knights showed the public that an aggressive, well-disciplined group could take on one of the most powerful financiers and win. Yet this explanation might be overstated, particularly since neither the Knights nor the newspapers publicized the events. Another reason for the KOL's growth is its identification with the eight-hour work day, an issue which was important to the nation's work force.[18] However, as discussed in the next section, the KOL's endorsement of the eight-hour work day was rather weak.

Faulty assumptions in the KOL's orientation The Knights were reform oriented, interested in changing existing aspects of the society. With the advantages of hindsight, it becomes clear that the KOL erred in assuming that technological advancement could be halted and possibly reversed. The KOL also overestimated the extent to which employers and employees shared common interests. While there are some common grounds, each group is motivated by self-interest. Employers are concerned about increased efficiency and profitability of the operation, while employees are concerned about job security and improvement of working conditions.

The organization's third faulty assumption was that all categories of employees would have identical interests. The KOL was ahead of its time in its attempt to organize unskilled employees—an effort eventually and successfully accomplished by the Congress of Industrial Organizations (CIO) in the late 1930s. However, as further discussed in Chapter 11, employees do not all have the same interests, particularly if they have different skills and work classifications. The *one big union* approach (enrolling nearly anyone who expressed an interest in the Knights) was further complicated by many immigrant members whose differences in race, language, and religion presented barriers.[19]

A lack of protective or supportive legislation governing the rights of employees to join unions and engage in collective bargaining This point will be further discussed in the next chapter. Suffice it to say that the Knights, as well as other labor organizations before 1935, did not have the full force of the law on their side.

Inability of the KOL's leadership (particularly Powderly) to identify with members' goals The Knights insisted upon adopting a middle-class program for the American labor force, which they refused to contemplate in industrial, working-class terms. Many of the members showed little, if any, interest in the Knights after they joined. Almost all local assembly meetings required the members to dress up after a day's work to engage in intellectual discourse. In essence, the members had nothing to do except "ceremonialize, play politics, and study."[20] Powderly felt his position was above the membership. Instead of understanding members' needs, he imposed his goals on his terms:

> **I will talk at no picnics. . . . When I speak on the labor question I want the individual attention of my hearers and I want that attention for at least two hours and in that two hours I can only epitomize. At a picnic where . . . the girls as well as the boys swill beer I cannot talk at all.**[21]

The preference for intellectual deliberation over immediate, gut-level response is perhaps best viewed through Powderly's approach to the eight-hour day movement.

The Eight-Hour Day Movement and the Haymarket Riot One of the more important reforms desired by many employees in the late 1800s was reducing the prevalent ten-hour work day to eight hours. Samuel Gompers, who was a Knights member and an official of other labor organizations (Federation of Organized Trades and Labor Unions, and Cigar Makers' Union), pressed Powderly to support a nationwide general strike (May 1, 1886) for the eight-hour work day. Powderly was receptive to the eight-hour day, as it would give employees more leisure time to pursue intellectual activities. However, he did not join with Gompers since he did not believe the length of the work day was the major problem: "To talk of reducing the hours of labor without reducing the power of machinery is a waste of energy."[22]

Supporters of the eight-hour day believed that this practice, if instituted, would result in more people working, thereby reducing the unemployment problem. On May 3, 1886, some workers striking over this issue in Chicago became involved in a skirmish with the police, with at least four strikers being killed. A leader of this dispute published an inflamatory circular urging "Revenge!" and "Workingmen to Arms!" The circular also indicated that a mass rally would be held the next day at Haymarket Square in Chicago. The stage was set for an event which virtually eliminated the effectiveness of the KOL.

On May 4, 1886, approximately three thousand people attended the scheduled meeting, a meeting that began peacefully, for the police who monitored the meeting were ordered by their chief to return to the station. However, Police Captain Bonfield, whom the governor of Illinois later charged as being responsible for the incident, subsequently ordered the police back to the meeting. During a speech a bomb was thrown into the gathering of police, killing seven and wounding sixty. What happened next is uncertain. The *Chicago Tribune* reported that "anarchists and rioters poured in a shower of bullets before the first action of the police was taken."[23] Yet another report in the same article stated the police opened fire on the crowd immediately after the bomb exploded. Regardless of the order of events, the police did shoot into the crowd, killing several and wounding two hundred.

Eight individuals allegedly responsible for the incident were arrested. Four of the eight were hanged, one committed suicide in prison, and three were eventually pardoned by the governor of Illinois after serving some of their sentence. Their trial was at best shoddy; for example, the hand-picked jury included a relative of one of the bombing victims.[24] The trial never did establish who threw the bomb; however, the accused were judged guilty by the *Chicago Tribune* before the trial took place. More specifically, the paper stressed that the "mob" was led by "two wirey whiskered foreigners,"[25] who were "Nihilistic Agitators."[26]

The Knights were not directly labeled in the immediate press accounts of the strike or in the subsequent series of unsuccessful strikes over the eight-hour day which involved nearly 340,000 employees. However, the strikes contributed to the organization's demise for at least two paradoxical reasons. A substantial body of public opinion labeled the Knights as being involved in the strikes. Yet many of the Knights' members criticized the leadership for not participating enough in the related events during and after Haymarket.[27] Indeed, Powderly strongly discouraged strikes over the eight-hour day, believing instead that members should write essays on the subject. Thus, the Haymarket Riot dramati-

Source: Reproduced from the collection of the Library of Congress.

A mass rally by strikers supporting the eight-hour day movement began peacefully but ended in violence and death in Chicago's Haymarket Square.

cally reflected the split between the KOL and the newly-formed American Federation of Labor, under Gompers, an organization which was to flourish and endure.

The Emergence of the American Federation of Labor

Origin and Goals of the AFL The AFL, an outgrowth of the Federation of Organized Trades and Labor Unions of the United States and Canada, was formed in 1886 after some of its member national unions (most notably the Cigar Makers) were expelled from the Knights.[28] As previously mentioned, Samuel Gompers, a major founder of the AFL, was a member of the Knights but became disenchanted with the leadership's long-range social reform philosophy. Gompers was also upset about KOL activities involving the cigar makers—in particular, KOL's raiding of its members and supplying strikebreakers when the cigar makers struck firms.

He met with the Knights in December 1886 to discuss these problems, but the meeting did not resolve the situation. Indeed, Gompers became incensed when a pamphlet was circulated among KOL representatives that attacked Gompers personally by indicating "the General Executive Board has never had the pleasure of seeing Mr. Gompers sober."[29] Also, in retrospect, KOL leaders blundered when they concentrated on influencing craft employees, a move which resulted in bitter reactions from the trade unions. The Knights would have been better off (and still consistent with their goals) if they had devoted more attention to the unskilled employees where the trades did not have any argument.[30]

Unlike the KOL, the AFL was not established as one big union. (This is discussed more fully in Chapter 5.) It represented a federation or organization which many unions could join while maintaining their separate union status. Craft unions, such as the Cigar Makers, dominated the early stages of the AFL. The AFL influenced its member unions through its services, particularly organizing activities, philosophies, and strategies.

It is impossible to discuss the AFL apart from Gompers, since "in the early years, the A. F. of L. existed only in the person of Gompers and in the annual conventions."[31] With the exception of 1895, Gompers was president of the AFL from its founding in 1886 until his death in 1924. Therefore, much of the discussion of the goals, strategies, and organization of the AFL will be from the perspective of Gompers, a point of view that relates strongly to the current thinking of organized labor; there has been relatively little change in orientation, strategies, and organization since the time of Gompers.

Gompers placed little emphasis on intellectual betterment, and he scorned other union leaders' pretensions to show labor union members the course of action they should pursue.[32] He criticized the KOL as representing "a hodgepodge with no basis for solidarity with the exception of a comparatively few trade assemblies."[33] Gompers believed that the goals and organization of unions should flow directly and naturally from the members' needs, not from the pronouncements of top leaders who structured unions based on their views of what should have been, rather than what was.

Gompers particularly scorned those union leaders who tried to change the existing social system through revolutionary means.[34] Although he was a socialist in his early years, he grew to despise this philosophy, contending that it was economically unsound, socially wrong, and impossible to apply in an industrial setting.[35] He also believed that union members should work for the development of, not the overthrow or destruction of, the society in which they lived and for the most part enjoyed.[36]

Thus, the AFL's major if not sole goal was to *improve the material conditions of members through the existing capitalistic system.* This goal was attacked by the critics of the AFL as representing pure and simple unionism. Gompers embraced this intended insult; indeed, he seemed to devote most of his attention to insuring that the AFL's "pure and simple" approach to collective bargaining successfully differentiated itself from other labor organizations.

There were two major objectives of *pure and simple unionism.* The primary objective was economic betterment of the organization's members; Gompers believed the "truth" or essence of labor unions should be measured in terms of their economic accomplishments:

Economic betterment—today, tomorrow, in home and shop, was the foundation upon which trade unions have been built. Economic power is the base upon which may be developed power in other fields. It is the foundation of organized society. Whoever or whatever controls economic power directs and shapes development for the group or the nation.[37]

Gompers also stressed a second objective of pure and simple unionism—the enhancement of the capitalistic system, which can benefit both groups. Workers can obtain more only if capitalism continues to flourish. Without capitalism neither employees nor employers receive revenues. The AFL therefore believed labor and management shared some similar interests.[38] However, Gompers did not agree with Powderly that this situation would lead to complete employer-employee agreement on all issues. He realized that major differences of opinion would occur over the distribution of revenues and that employees would probably have to pressure employers in order to receive their fair share.

Strategies and Organization of the AFL This realization prompted the AFL to rely on one of its three major tactics—the *strike*. Unlike the Knights, Gompers believed the strike was a viable collective bargaining alternative:

A workman must convince his employer that he is entitled to an advance in wages. . . .

Why should the wage-earner work for less than living wages, which he would have to do if he could not strike? The worker is expected to continue to work at whatever wages his employer is willing to give in order to save the public from inconvenience.[39]

A second AFL strategy (particularly when its headquarters moved to Washington, D.C.) was *involvement in the political arena*. Gompers, an aggressive lobbyist, attempted to translate election votes of AFL members into "rewards" for political friends of labor and "punishments" for political enemies of labor. However, political efforts during Gompers' leadership were neither intense nor widespread throughout the AFL.[40]

AFL political efforts were directed at the existing two-party system instead of forming a third political party. Gompers felt that establishing a third party would divert too much time away from fundamental collective bargaining efforts. He also felt that any new political party would fall into the socialists' control.[41]

The third AFL tactic was *to secure increased status for organized labor and collective bargaining*. Gompers devoted much attention to the National Civic Foundation, formed in 1899 to promote industrial peace through collective bargaining. This organization, comprised of prominent labor, management, and political officials, attempted to guide public opinion toward the positive aspects of collective bargaining. However, at least one observer of industrial relations has questioned the success of this tactic, believing that "its rhetoric surpassed its performance."[42]

The AFL's organizational structure was based on two related principles: *exclusive jurisdiction* and *decentralized authority*. The AFL avoided the concept of "one big union" organization—which proved to be ineffective for the KOL—and insisted on the principle of exclusive jurisdiction. This principle rested on the twofold observation that (a) each craft or trade had unique working conditions and job interests and (b) combining members of different trades into one organization would jeopardize those interests and cause unnecessary dissension. The AFL thus believed in one union representing a particular craft; for example, separate unions would represent carpenters, painters, and cigar makers.

Gompers also strongly believed the AFL was a voluntary organization held together by the mutual self-interests of members. Unlike Powderly, who believed that centralized authority was necessary to achieve the Knights' objectives, Gompers viewed the central AFL as a "rope of sand," dependent entirely on the acceptance of its members. Thus, the real authority rested with various national unions and their member locals. As will be further discussed in Chapter 5, these principles continue to influence contemporary union organizations.

The organizational activity as well as the organizational structure of the AFL must be considered. Gompers was a most active union organizer; he claimed to have helped in organizing twenty-eight unions representing different crafts, such as painters, paper makers, firefighters, and post office clerks.[43] Much of this effort was due to Gompers' view of himself as "one of the boys"—he took pride in his ability to socialize with the members on their own terms.

In spite of Gompers' efforts, the AFL's early growth was not spectacular. Its original membership of 150,000 had increased to only 250,000 six years later. The initial slow growth was due to the counterattack of industry (discussed in the section on World War I to World War II), the generally repressive attitude of the government and the courts, and the difficulties raised by the depression of 1893. Yet Gompers could view these modest membership gains as a tribute to the AFL's powers of "stability and permanency."[44]

From its formation until World War I, the AFL was directly or indirectly involved in three prominent events: the Homestead and Pullman incidents and the formation and demise of the Industrial Workers of the World (IWW).

The Homestead Incident The Carnegie Steel Works, located in Homestead, Pennsylvania, was ironically the scene of one of the more violent episodes in labor history. The founder of these operations, Andrew Carnegie, was a renowned philanthropist who gave every indication of being receptive to organized labor. In one article, written before the Homestead incident, he stated that a strike or a lockout was a "ridiculous affair" since it only represented a test of strength instead of determining what was "fair and just."[45] Carnegie also believed that labor-management problems would occur in large firms run by salaried managers instead of owners, because the former group had no permanent interest in the desires of the workingmen.

Carnegie's remarks proved prophetic in the Homestead incident of July 6, 1892. Although many have labeled the incident a strike, one labor historian has noted that no strike vote was ever taken by the membership,[46] and the employer prohibited the employees from working. During negotiation between the mill and the Amalgamated Association of Iron, Steel, and Tin Workers (an affiliate of the AFL), a fifteen-foot-high solid board fence, topped with barbed wire, was constructed around the building. Andrew Carnegie was vacationing in Scotland during negotiations and had delegated these duties to a management official named Henry Clay Frick. The union labeled the structure around the steel mill "Fort Frick." Members were also undoubtedly aware that Frick was negotiating with Pinkerton detectives while labor-management negotiations were being conducted. Frick intended to use Pinkerton detectives inside the facility to protect the company's property and as strikebreakers.

On June 30, 1892, the company made its last offer, which represented a substantial reduction of previous wages,[47] and locked out its four thousand employees. Workmen then began an around the clock surveillance of the plant. One newspaper account indicated, "The line of pickets covers the river, roads, and railways so tightly that no stranger can enter the town without being known to the strikers."[48] On the morning of July 5, three hundred Pinkertons gathered at Ashtabula, Ohio, and proceeded by rail to Youngstown, Ohio. They then traveled up the Monongahela River by barge. On July 6, word had reached the townspepople that the Pinkertons would be entering the plant from the river. Six thousand people lined the river banks at 2:00 A.M., and employees prepared two small cannons, one on each side of the river, to be used on the Pinkertons.[49]

The Pinkertons attempted to land by the company's beach at 5:00 A.M.; shots were exchanged, and three Pinkertons were killed. Shooting by both sides continued for twelve hours, with an additional seven townspeople being killed and fifty wounded. The Pinkertons surrendered to the townspeople and were forced to run a bloody gauntlet before being locked up for their protection. The townspeople had taken the weapons from the Pinkertons, a situation which resulted in 8,700 National Guard militiamen being sent to secure the town. There were few further incidents, particularly since union leaders believed the troops would discourage further attempts by Pinkertons or strikebreakers.[50] The incident ended for all purposes some five months later (November 20, 1892) when the Amalgamated lifted its prohibition against returning to work.

Homestead has been labeled the Waterloo of unions in the steel industry. National membership in the Amalgamated dropped from 24,000 in 1892 to 8,000 in 1894. On the local level, only 800 of the original Homestead employees were reinstated. Carnegie's mills showed a dramatic increase in profits when the union was eliminated,[51] a message that must have encouraged other employers to take an anti-union stance.

While Homestead represented a victory for management, the AFL and organized labor did benefit to some extent from the situation. First, Gompers demon-

Source: Courtesy of the AFL-CIO.

The bloody confrontation between Pinkerton agents and employees of the Carnegie Steel Works in Homestead, Pennsylvania, in 1892 was one of the most violent in labor history and actually set back the cause of unions in the steel industry.

strated to existing and potential union members his very real concern about the Homestead situation.[52] The funds contributed by the AFL to help defray the workers' legal expenses also demonstrated that the AFL was interested in helping its member unions in a material sense.[53] Finally, the Homestead situation received more sympathetic newspaper accounts than those describing the Haymarket Riot. The press did charge Carnegie with provoking the situation. For example, the *Chicago Tribune* criticized the company's use of Pinkertons strongly and contended that Carnegie's company as well as any large industrial organization "has duties and obligations toward society which it must not forget, and not the least of them is to do all in its power, and make all of the concessions it can, to preserve civil and industrial peace."[54] At a minimum, the press could not continually criticize the involved union or employees in this incident, especially since no individual was found guilty of participating in the incident.

The Pullman Strike Strikes were not uncommon in the railroad industry; for example, the Great Upheaval of 1877 involved independent railroad employee associations protesting wage cuts. It was a bitter and violent confrontation in which more than a hundred employees were killed and several hundred were badly wounded.[55]

Yet the Pullman strike of 1894 assumes significance because of the principal personalities involved (Eugene Debs and George Pullman) and an organization (the American Railway Union or ARU) which had the potential to challenge the AFL for union members. It also approached being the only revolutionary strike in the United States; it became a nationwide strike in one industry and came near to involving all industries.[56]

As a result of the 1893 depression, the Pullman Company laid off 3,000 of its 5,800 employees and cut wages 25 to 40 percent. Both actions were important since they occurred in the milieu of George Pullman's company town. This town represented a social, paternalistic experiment by the owner of the Pullman Palace Car Company. The company owned all of the houses, buildings, and services in the town; employees were not allowed to own their own homes.[57] Pullman did not correspondingly reduce rents and charges for other services; thus the wage cuts resulted in some employees having a net two-week pay of $1 to $6 during the winter of 1893–1894.

This situation generated much hostility among employees, many of whom were members of the American Railway Union (ARU), formed in 1893. The ARU was completely independent from the AFL; indeed, it competed for members with the AFL-affiliated railway brotherhoods. The ARU accepted any white employee, regardless of specific job classification, so that railroad employees could present a unified front to the railroad companies.[58] It was attractive to many employees because employers previously had been able to create dissension among the different craft unions by playing one off against the other in wage negotiations.

The ARU's local unions had sole authority to call a strike, and the Pullman strike began on May 11, 1894. Debs, the union leader, informed the strikers that the strike should represent a protest against philosophical issues instead of mere material betterment: "The paternalism of Pullman is the same as the interest of a slave holder in his human chattels. You are striking to avert slavery and degradation."[59]

At first the strikers followed Debs' orders not to damage railroad property. The ARU instead adopted a strategy of not operating any train which included a Pullman sleeping car—the common practice was to cut these cars from the train and move them to the side tracks. If any employee was discharged for this action, then the entire crew would quit, leaving the train immobilized. This tactic, employed in twenty-seven states and territories, was intended to make railroad carriers put pressure on Pullman to agree with ARU's bargaining position.

However, the railroad employers rallied behind Pullman and countered the union's strategy by hiring strikebreakers. They also decided to include federal mail on nearly every train and were able to obtain an injunction on July 2 (subsequently upheld by the Supreme Court) to prevent any employee from interfering with the delivery of the mail. Employees could no longer engage in their strike strategy of rendering the trains inoperative. Some sixteen thousand troops, dispatched by President Cleveland to enforce the injunction, either delivered the mail and operated the trains or protected strikebreakers so that food and other perishable items could be delivered throughout the country.

The strike then took a particularly ugly turn; employees burned at least seven hundred railroad cars in Chicago on July 7, 1894. Interestingly, management was also criticized for this incident, at the least for failing to take minimum security measures such as guarding or locking the railroad cars. At a maximum, some management officials may have provoked the incident to receive additional support from the government. This second possibility is suggested because all of the burnt cars were old (the more expensive Pullman cars were not on the property), and very few of the cars were loaded with any product.[60]

The resulting negative public opinion and increased action by the federal troops forced Debs to seek Gompers' cooperation. Debs wanted Gompers to call a national strike to enforce Debs' last offer, which was simply management's reinstatement of the striking employees. Gompers refused to support Debs, contending that he did not have authority to call a general strike. Gompers also believed that the proposed settlement would, in effect, admit to the public that the ARU had failed to win material benefits for its members. Much of Gompers' reluctance was due to his view of Debs as being "a leader of irregular movements and lost causes."[61] However, Gompers' inaction might have also been due to his desire to eliminate a potential rival to the AFL and bolster his reputation in the business community.

Debs was eventually convicted and sentenced under the Sherman Antitrust Act of 1890; and the ARU, which had grown to 150,000 members in one year, quickly faded from existence. Organized labor did learn an important lesson from this strike; namely, it would be difficult to alter the existing system against the wishes of a persistent, if not exceptionally stubborn, owner (Pullman), the federal government (troops, injunctions, legislation), the AFL (which supported this system), and negative public opinion (fueled by exaggerated and dramatic newspaper articles).

The Rise and Fall of the IWW The Industrial Workers of the World (IWW) was formed as an alternative to the AFL on June 27, 1905. "Big Bill" Haywood, initial organizer of the IWW, originated the organization's goals in calling the convention of 209 delegates to order with the following remarks:

Fellow Workers . . . We are here to confederate the workers of this country into a working class movement that shall have for its purpose the emancipation of the working class from the slave bondage of Capitalism. . . . The aims and objects of this organization should be to put the

working class in possession of the economic power, the means of life, in control of the machinery of production and distribution without regard to capitalist masters.[62]

The initial goal of the IWW was to overthrow the existing capitalistic system by any means, since it felt that employers and employees had nothing in common. The IWW and the Knights agreed on one point: the existing wage and profit system had to be changed. The Knights, however, stressed that employees and employers had common interests and that change must be peaceful and gradual. The IWW, on the other hand, had no reservations about using any method which would result in the *quick destruction of capitalism.*

The IWW also wanted to remove any societal aspect or group which supported capitalism. This approach placed the IWW into direct opposition with the AFL. The IWW regarded the AFL as an "extension of the capitalist class"[63] since it advocated "pure and simple unionism," which was dependent on capitalism. Haywood believed that Gompers had sold out the ARU when he had not supported Debs in the Pullman strike, and he viewed Gompers as an arrogant, power-hungry leader.[64] Thus, the IWW appeared to have two general enemies: capitalism and the AFL, which did not recognize a working class movement or hourly employees as being a class-conscious group apart from the rest of society. An analysis of the IWW reveals that establishing goals can be an easier task than accomplishing them.

The IWW never did establish an effective organization; in fact, its leaders never made up their minds about precisely what kind of organizational structure it should adopt.[65] Most of the IWW officials agreed with Haywood's objective of organizing "every man that earns his livelihood either by his brain or his muscle."[66] But major differences arose over how to organize one big union into an effective organization. Some members felt that the IWW should work slowly; for example, infiltrate the established AFL unions, and gradually persuade members that the IWW cause was best. Others felt that this temporary acceptance of collective bargaining with the capitalists only made employees "better paid slaves" and would hinder the quick and necessary overthrow of the capitalistic system.[67]

In addition to organizational differences, there were at least four reasons for the demise of the IWW which served as negative lessons for contemporary organized labor.

1. **Lack of permanent membership and financial base.** A large proportion of the IWW consisted of itinerants—individuals who were either unemployed or traveled from job to job, particularly in the agriculture, mining, and lumber industries. The transitory nature of IWW members contributed to an unstable financial base. Many IWW leaders thought the members' dues should not be mandatory; instead, they should be paid out of a voluntary "inner conviction." Apparently, many members did not share this "inner conviction"; for example, in 1907 only 10,000 members out of the total 31,000 members paid any dues.

The lack of revenues resulted in meager strike funds, and by 1909 the organization was deeply in debt.

2. **Inability of the IWW to appeal to members' interests.** The IWW did not consider the short-run material interests of its members. Its major emphasis on long-term philosophical goals and its concern with propaganda as a means to achieve these goals failed to demonstrate tangible signs of success on a continuous basis.[68] The average trade unionist, in or outside the IWW, had no desire to help the underdog. Indeed, it was all he could do to look out for himself.[69]
3. **Identification of the IWW with sabotage and violence.** The relationship between the IWW and sabotage and violence was ambiguous. The IWW in 1914 became the only labor organization to ever officially endorse sabotage at its convention. Yet no local, state, or federal authority could ever establish legal proof of any IWW-instigated violence. The IWW often stated that sabotage does not equal destruction of equipment. For example, employees could "sabotage" the company by "malicious obedience" (following the work rules to the letter, thereby creating a slowdown) and by informing customers that the company's product was of inferior quality. However, at least one article in the IWW's paper, the *Industrial Worker*, indicated how emery dust and ground up glass could cause the destruction of machinery.

   Evidence suggests that the IWW's leadership denounced any type of physical violence.[70] Yet there are also some accounts of incidents where IWW members and leaders pledged a "life for a life" or "an eye for an eye."[71] At a minimum, it appears that the IWW did not actively discourage its link with violence, a situation which is amplified in the following reason for the IWW's demise.
4. **Alienation of the news media and government officials.** The newspapers enhanced the IWW's reputation for violence by labeling members as "desperate villains who set fire to wheat fields, drove spikes into sawmill-bound logs, derailed trains, destroyed industrial machinery, and killed policemen."[72] Part of this negative image was enhanced by leaders of IWW factions who would damn each other in the press. The IWW also engaged in several "free speech fights"—soap box speeches in local communities. This strategy, which has since been copied by various protest groups, including students, relied on there being more participants than there were available jail spaces. City officials, faced with this situation, typically allowed the "unlawful" demonstration to continue.[73] In many of these speeches, the IWW would shout antisocial comments such as "there is no God."[74]

   The press, never enthusiastic about unions in general, reserved a special hatred for the IWW. One editorial against the IWW stated:

They would be much better dead, for they are absolutely useless in the human economy; they are the waste material of creation and should be drained off into the sewer of oblivion there to rot in cold obstruction like any other excrement.[75]

The IWW also remained alienated from the government. It did not actively use the existing political system because many of its transient members could not meet voter registration requirements. It also incurred the wrath of the federal government when it refused to support involvement in World War I, proclaiming instead that the war represented a capitalistic plot. The government responded to the IWW's antiwar stance by arresting over a hundred leaders and sentencing most of them to prison terms ranging from five to twenty years. In effect, the IWW went out of existence in 1918, even though the organization remains today with a handful of members.

The onset of World War I found the AFL on questionably firm ground. It had been the first nationally organized labor movement to withstand a severe economic depression, a hostile press, reluctant or hostile employers, and three rival labor organizations (KOL, ARU, and IWW). Yet the AFL had internal pressures from at least three sources: (a) socialists and other related political groups that advocated independent political action and the organization of unskilled, industrial employees; (b) pacifist members who wanted the AFL to remain neutral or take a stand against the war;[76] and (c) member unions which became involved in jurisdictional problems caused by increased specialization and technological change (for example, the plumber was no longer responsible for the complete installation of the water and heating system for a building). Perhaps the most lingering concern of the AFL was that the largest proportion of the organizable labor force, the unskilled, industrial employees, remained essentially outside the ranks of organized labor.[77] This concern and its eventual resolution are discussed more in the following section.

World War I to World War II

The period from World War I to World War II witnessed several important phenomena:

1. The inability of unions, particularly the AFL, to make substantial membership gains in the 1920s.
2. The development of employer strategies to retard union growth.
3. Increased union concern over organizing the unskilled, industrial employees, which led to a bitter rivalry between the AFL and CIO (Congress of Industrial Organizations).

Some union organizing drives in various industries will be cited briefly to give a further indication of the problems and prospects facing organized labor in this period.

Union Organizing after World War I: Problems and Prospects

The AFL overcame its initial reluctance toward participating in World War I and eventually pledged its cooperation when the United States became directly involved in the war. The government, aware of the necessity of uninterrupted production during wartime, responded by attempting to meet labor's concerns. Governmental agreements with the AFL provided for the enforcement of trade union standards in all government contracts; labor representatives were appointed to all government agencies, including the War Labor Board; and Gompers was made a member of the Advisory Commission of the National Council of Defense. In short, organized labor was elevated to a more prominent status than had heretofore been seen in our society. Accordingly, the AFL had a sizable growth in membership during this period (an increase from 2,370,000 members in 1917 to 3,260,000 members in 1919). Legislative interests were also met; a long-time AFL goal of severely restricting immigrants, a strongly competitive labor source, was accomplished.

The rather sharp increase in the cost of living that followed World War I, coupled with the newly recognized status of labor, resulted in an unprecedented number of strikes. For example, the Seattle General Strike occurred in 1919, along with other strikes by actors, New York waterfront employees, and coal miners. The most widespread strike occurred in 1919 in the steel industry, where some 367,000 employees walked off the job in seventy major cities.

The strike actually resulted in a setback to organized labor in the steel industry. Many possible factors contributed to the setback; some were notably similar to those found in the Homestead and Pullman incidents, while others reflected a typical situation unions faced in the 1920s and early 1930s. Of crucial importance were internal union difficulties: an organizing campaign conducted by twenty-four unions instead of one common industrial union, improvised leadership rather than a consistent union approach to the issue, and poor financial resources. U.S. Steel was also successful in withstanding the strike by using strikebreakers and maintaining strong ties with other companies and social institutions, like the press and the pulpit. Thus the strike was terminated without a labor agreement, and it would take another fifteen years before organized labor would make inroads into the steel industry.[78]

Although the steel industry did not reflect all industrial reactions to collective bargaining, it does appear that many unions were comparatively powerless to organize employers, such as U.S. Steel, which firmly believed unions were not in the firm's best interests. For example, another 1919 strike almost paralyzed the coal industry when no miners returned to work until President Wilson persuaded them to accept a temporary wage increase and submit all other issues to a newly appointed Bituminous Coal Commission. In 1920, the commission awarded increases ranging from 20 to 30 percent; yet this was the last victory for mine workers for several years.

In spite of increased status and militancy, something went wrong for organized labor in the 1920s—the "Golden Twenties" for the majority in the U.S. was a dreary decade for labor. Between 1920 and 1924, total union membership declined from 5,110,000 to 3,600,000; membership in AFL unions dropped from 4,078,000 to 2,866,000. By 1930, total union membership dropped to 3,400,000, and AFL membership dropped to 2,700,000.[79] This decline was due to at least two major factors: (a) aggressive counteractions by employers; and (b) organized labor's inability to overcome anti-union sentiment among potential union members.[80]

Counteractions by employers Concerned with the increased status given labor during the war, employers actively engaged in efforts to roll back gains in union membership. Many tactics, which fall into two general categories—*aggressive opposition toward labor unions* and *formation of an acceptable alternative to unions*—were devised in the 1920s and continued in the 1930s to thwart union growth.

Employers actively opposed unions throughout the open shop movement, which is discussed in more detail in Chapter 11. The alleged purpose of this movement was to insure that employees had the freedom to determine whether they would choose to join a union. Rationale for this movement was found in its companion name, the American Plan—employers felt that employees should adhere to the traditional American value of "rugged individualism" instead of the "foreign," "subversive," and "corrupt" principles of labor unions.

Many employers equated *open shop*—the right to join or not to join unions—with no unionized employees. Several steps were taken to insure that no employee would be able to join a union. For example, some employers would hire industrial spies to determine which employees had pro-union sentiments.[81] These employees would then be discharged and possibly *blacklisted*—their names given to other employers, who would refuse to hire them. Employer violence against participants in union organizing drives was also a potential strategy to counter unions during this period.[82]

A variation of the open shop or American Plan occurred in the 1930s, with the development of the Mohawk Valley Formula. This approach was used when a union attempted to organize or strike a facility in the community. The Mohawk Valley Formula would then be implemented with the following steps:

Form a citizens' committee in the community, label the union leaders as outside agitators, stir up violence or the fear of violence, have a "state of emergency" declared, organize a back-to-work movement, and finally have the back-to-work employees march into the plant protected by armed police.[83]

Employers also countered unions with a second approach, providing an alternative model to unionism. The 1920s saw widespread employer *paternalism*, which assured that the employer had a superior wisdom and knew what was best for the employees. Examples of paternalistic practices included free lunches, baseball fields, vacations, pensions, and employee counseling.[84] Employers felt that employees receiving these benefits would be indebted to the employer and realize that unions would be unnecessary since they could not bargain for what the employees already had.

Employee Representation Plans (ERPs), or company established unions, represented another substitute model for unions. ERPs included as many as 1.5 million employees, and appeared superficially similar to unions since selected employee representatives would discuss working conditions with management officials. But ERPs differed from unions in two major respects. First, *unions had more autonomy than ERPs*. Employers could strongly influence the selection of ERP officers, and could also veto any decision made by the joint labor-management committee. Second *ERPs were usually limited to a single facility and employees under ERPs could neither press for work rules which would remove unfair competition from other facilities nor push for legislation at the local, state, of federal level.*[85]

Labor's inability to overcome anti-union sentiment The lack of organizing gains during the 1920s also has to be attributed to the anti-union sentiment of potential union members and the activities and attitudes of organized labor. Part of this problem may have been due to the relatively good economic conditions that prevailed:

While job insecurity may have deterred some employees from joining unions in the face of employer opposition, many of them apparently felt that unions were no longer as necessary as they had formerly believed them to be. What profit strikes or other agitation for collective bargaining when the pay envelope was automatically growing fatter and a more abundant life seemed to be assured with our rapid approach to the final triumph over poverty?[86]

Many potential members also believed that much of organized labor was corrupt and subject to control by the socialists and communists. Racketeering had become a feature of some local union-employer relationships. For example, in one incident a union official signed a two-paragraph agreement with three major employers which guaranteed no wage increase for three years and required all employees to join the union or be discharged. None of the employees had ever solicited the union, nor did they ever see a union official during the life of the contract. This "sweetheart" arrangement or contract was often coupled with financial kickbacks to the union official, meaning the employer paid the union official a portion of the wage savings.[87]

Some labor unions had also been accused of harboring communists and other political radicals. Many prominent union leaders would occasionally accept help from almost any group that would devote time and effort in organizing employees, believing that they could control these political elements once the local union had been established. However, they overestimated their controlling ability in some instances. One former president of the Steelworkers Union recalled how communists could dominate local union meetings by using the *V technique*, where the leader would find a seat in the center of the auditorium about the second or third row.

A few rows back, two of his associates would locate about ten seats apart, and this same pattern would be followed all the way to the rear of the hall. When the chief spokesman opened debate, his line would then be parroted all the way through the V behind him, giving an illusion of widespread strength. They would also wait until other union members, tired and bored, had gone home before trying to push through their own proposals.[88]

Thus labor, particularly the AFL, devoted much of its attention during the 1920s to overcoming its negative public image.[89] These efforts detracted from active organizing efforts, particularly since Gompers had lost much of his former physical enthusiasm for this activity. In 1924, Gompers died, and his successor, William Green, did not revive any major organizing activities, as he had to maintain the AFL's existing organization in an adverse atmosphere.[90] This situation eventually led to the formation of the Congress of Industrial Organizations (CIO).

Rise of the CIO and Industrial Unionism

There was major disagreement within the AFL over organizing the large ranks of unskilled and semiskilled employees. Tremendous technological shifts occurring during and after World War I reduced the demand for highly skilled employees; hence an increasing percentage of the labor force consisted of production workers. In 1926, for example, 85 percent of the hourly employees at Ford Motor Company required less than two weeks of training.[91] Since craft employees no longer dominated the industrial scene the AFL needed to organize the industrial employees.

Many of the AFL unions did not want to bring industrial employees into their organizations. Some AFL leaders believed these employees were inferior to craft employees and possessed less bargaining power, while others thought the inclusion of these employees would confuse and distort the AFL's organization. William Green himself could not (or would not) view industrial employees as being compatible with the AFL's organizational principle of exclusive jurisdiction.

Some leaders thought that a separate union would be needed for each company's or industry's products—if General Electric had fifty different products, then fifty different AFL unions (each having exclusive jurisdiction over its members' interests) would be needed for effective collective bargaining. Other leaders believed that industrial unionism would at least weaken the AFL's concept of organized labor. The president of one AFL union urged his members to stamp out "the awful serpent of industrial trade unionism that would destroy this International and weaken the entire structure of the Labor Movement."[92]

The issue came to a head in 1935 under the direction of John L. Lewis, president of the AFL's United Mine Workers Union. The AFL rejected the concept of industrial unionism through three separate votes at its 1935 convention.[93] On November 9, 1935, the Committee for Industrial Organizations (CIO) was formed. Its purpose was allegedly "educational and advisory"; in reality, it was intended to promote organizing the unorganized, particularly those in the mass production industries.[94]

In January 1936, AFL leaders were shocked to find that the Committee for Industrial Organizations had been formed in the AFL—they had thought the industrial unionism issue had been buried once and for all at the 1935 convention. The CIO not only discussed the industrial union concept but also requested the immediate granting of industrial union charters to a number of industries such as the rubber workers and the auto workers. The CIO further insisted that an organizing campaign be started at once in the steel industry.

The AFL, confronted with the most serious challenge in its history, ordered the CIO to disband or get out. Personalities intensified the issue. John L. Lewis, a powerful man in voice and action, sought and obtained power and publicity in his union activities.[95] Lewis managed to provoke AFL leaders into a confrontation while at the same time whipping his United Mine Workers members into a "lather of rage" against the AFL.[96] The split over the industrial unionism issue resulted in seven unions with almost a million members forming a rival and completely independent labor federation, the Congress of Industrial Organizations (CIO) in 1938.[97]

The development of the CIO coincided with a significant upsurge in union membership. By November 1937, the CIO's affiliated unions had organized 75 percent of the steel industry, 70 percent of the automobile industry, 65 percent of the rubber industry, and about one-third of the maritime and textile industries.[98] The AFL also saw rapid growth in membership during the late 1930s and the 1940s. It organized the mass production employees into local labor unions and national councils assigned to various craft unions. The steady growth of the AFL during the late 1930s was also aided by employers' preference to deal with the more conservative organization instead of taking their chances with the new and unpredictable CIO.[99]

Why did union membership increase dramatically in the 1930s and 1940s? This question is particularly important since the CIO, like the unsuccessful Knights and IWW before it, organized employees of different crafts into one union for each industry. There appear to be at least five reasons for the growth in unionism during this period.

Strong CIO leadership The aggressive and effective CIO leaders (John L. Lewis, Sidney Hillman, and David Dubinsky, among others) infused new life into a movement previously content with resting on its laurels. Most of the CIO union leaders had extensive organizing experience and prided themselves on keeping in touch with their membership.[100] Union leaders' accomplishments should not be overstated, however, since organizing drives involved the tireless efforts of many individuals who typed up circulars, contacted prospective members, and provided routine services which insured union election victories. In fact, one biographer of John L. Lewis indicated his lack of involvement in the many organizing chores; instead, he preferred "arriving only in time for the triumphant finale."[101]

Realistic goals The CIO shared only a superficial similarity with the KOL in grouping employees with different job interests, believing that organizing along industrial lines would still consider the common interests of employees. More importantly, the CIO dramatically differed from the Knights and the IWW in its goals—short-run gains instead of long-range reform—which paralleled the AFL's "pure and simple" unionism approach, including support of the established economic order, as illustrated in Lewis's remarks,

I think most people have come to realize, that we cannot progress industrially without real cooperation between workers and management, and that this can only be brought about by equality in strength and bargaining power of labor and management. Labor is sincere in its desire to help. It looks forward to an industrial procedure which will increase productive efficiency and lower prices to the consumer.[102]

The effective use of sit-down strikes The CIO also developed a most successful tactic which aided in employer recognition of its unions—the *sit-down strike*, in which employees stayed inside the plant instead of picketing outside. This technique was very successful since employers were reluctant to physically remove the employees from the plant for fear that their equipment could be damaged in the confrontation.

The tactic was initially applied by the IWW at a General Electric facility in 1906, but the most famous of these strikes occurred in December 1936 at a General Motors facility in Flint, Michigan. At one time, 26,000 General Motors employees had belonged to a union; in early 1936, there were only 122 union members, many of whom were management spies.[103] A local grass roots organization was secretly established to build up the union at Flint. The sit-down strike was locally planned; Lewis and the CIO preferred to organize the steel industry before attempting major organizing drives in the automobile industry. The CIO, however, did lend its active support once the strike was under way.[104]

The sit-down strike at Flint lasted forty-four days and received widespread community support, while hindering GM's efforts to reverse its negative profit situation of previous years.[105] The end of the strike resulted in employer recognition of the union, a fact which was noticed by many other employees. Between September 1936 and June 1937 some 500,000 employees in the rubber, glass, and textile industries put the technique to use. Although effective, the sit-down strike was short-lived, because public opinion eventually frowned on this tactic, and a subsequent decision by the Supreme Court declared such strikes illegal.

Passage of the Wagner Act Another (and perhaps the most significant) reason for the increased number of union members was the passage of the Wagner Act in 1935 (discussed in more detail in Chapter 3). The federal government indicated through this law that collective bargaining was in the national interest. More important were the provisions establishing the National Labor Relations Board to administer union representation elections, define employer unfair labor practices, and enforce the legal rights of employees to join unions.

Changes in employees' attitudes Many employees' previously negative attitudes toward organized labor changed dramatically. They had experienced the Great Depression of the 1930s and realized that job security could not be solely achieved through hard work and loyalty to the employer. These employees now viewed unions as a mechanism which could promote job security as well as other material benefits.

By the onset of World War II, organized labor had reversed its membership decline of the 1920s, rising to almost 9 million members in 1940. Yet the rivalry between the CIO and the AFL was intense and violent as AFL and CIO organizers often physically clashed over the right to represent factory employees. James Hoffa, a former president of the International Brotherhood of Teamsters (then an AFL union), recalled violent organizing drives of 1941 between the CIO and his union:

> **Through it all the members wore two pins, putting on a Teamster button when we were around and switching to a CIO button when those guys showed up. They were waiting to see which union was going to win the battle. You couldn't really blame them. They were scared out of their britches because they didn't want to get caught in the bloody middle.[106]**

The CIO-AFL rivalry existed in almost every industry[107] and extended to the local level, where it was common for an employer to have both AFL and CIO unions representing the same employees. Even employers with the best intentions could not build an effective labor-management relationship in this environment.

World War II to the Present

The AFL at first did not want the United States to become involved in World War II; however, this attitude changed after the bombing of Pearl Harbor. Concern over the nation's defense prompted union-management cooperation. For example, both union and management officials participated on War Production Board subcommittees. Such panels weighed employee suggestions which saved 31 million man hours and $44 million during World War II.[108]

The cooperative spirit was not total, particularly from the standpoint of strikes taken during wartime. In February 1943, organized labor complained to President Roosevelt that the cost of living during wartime had increased far beyond wage increases permitted by the government under the 1942 "Little Steel Formula."[109] The United Mine Workers conducted a series of strikes to obtain wage increases of $2 a day in 1943. These actions resulted in President Roosevelt seizing the mines, but eventually a compromise wage settlement was obtained.

The public viewed these and other strikes with anger and alarm, considering them violations of the no-strike pledge announced by organized labor in 1941. Negative public sentiment increased when labor strikes continued and, after 1942, increased every year of the war. The number of employee days lost to strikes was estimated to be the equivalent of no more than one day per year per worker for the four war years.[110] Yet the mere act of participating in a strike was viewed by some as unpatriotic.

Labor's collective bargaining concerns shifted at the end of the war to the issues of full employment and further wage increases in order to sustain national purchasing power and thereby create an expanding market for industrial goods. Labor, remembering World War I's reconversion period, was also concerned about employer policies aimed at restricting union growth and wage gains.

Unions backed their postwar concerns with strikes. "During no period in the history of the United States did the scope and intensity of labor-management conflicts match those recorded in the year following VJ Day, August 14, 1945."[111] In this one-year period, over 4,600 strikes, involving 5 million workers and resulting in almost 120 million man-days of idleness, affected almost every major industry. They were basically nonviolent, representing instead economic tests of strength and endurance. Generally, both labor and management wanted to be free to resolve their differences at the bargaining table without the government interference and wage restrictions which were present during World War II.

Developments in Organized Labor since World War II

Three major developments have occurred in organized labor since World War II: increased concern over new collective bargaining issues, organizing drives aimed at public and white-collar employees, and the merger of the AFL and CIO.

Increased Concern over New Collective Bargaining Issues The return to peacetime after World War II and, particularly, the Korean War saw increased efforts to extend the provisions of the labor agreement to include all aspects of the collective bargaining relationship. In the late 1950s and early 1960s, the relative scarcity of jobs coincided with the need for price stability to ease the deficit in international payments.

Unions directed their collective bargaining efforts toward guaranteeing members job security in the face of possible technological advances, and wages which would compensate for inflation. Organized labor's response toward technological change (discussed in more detail in Chapter 12) brought notable results during this period, including the Automation Fund Agreement between Armour and Company and the Packinghouse Workers and Meat Cutters unions (1959), the Mechanization and Modernization Agreement in the Pacific Coast longshore industry (1960), and the Long-Range Sharing Plan negotiated between Kaiser Steel and the United Steelworkers (1962).

Employee benefits represented a second new bargaining area. Before World War II, labor cost was overwhelmingly straight-time pay for time actually worked.[112] Subsequent bargaining efforts by labor unions (and personnel policies of nonunion firms) have resulted in a substantial increase in employee benefits (pensions, insurance plans and so forth) which are currently estimated at 41 percent of payroll costs.[113]

Finally, the trend in multiyear labor agreements after World War II put pressure on union leaders to safeguard wage increases against the possibilities of inflation. In 1948, General Motors and the United Auto Workers negotiated a long-term agreement with a cost-of-living provision which adjusted wages for inflationary changes during the life of the contract. This contract provision spread to other labor-management negotiations. In 1952, almost 3 million workers (approximately 20 percent of the employees covered by labor agreements) had cost-of-living provisions in their contracts.[114]

Organization of White-Collar and Public Employees The second major development in organized labor occurring since World War II involves the organization of different types of employees. More specifically, white-collar employees (discussed in Chapter 17) and public employees (discussed in Chapters 14 and 15) have received increased attention from union organizers.

Merger of the AFL-CIO Perhaps the most dramatic postwar development in organized labor was the merger of the AFL and CIO. The intense rivalry between the AFL and the CIO did not end with the return to peacetime after World War II. However, the presence of three influences during the 1950s resulted in the eventual merger of these organizations in 1955.[115]

First was the change in the presidents of the AFL and CIO. Phillip Murray became president of the CIO when Lewis resigned in 1940, and continued the verbal feud against the AFL and its president, William Green. In November

1952, however, both Green and Murray died. Their successors (Walter Reuther of the CIO and George Meany of the AFL) had no particular fondness for each other; but unlike Green and Murray, they had not previously gone on record against each other. Therefore, a merger could occur without either president losing face.

Another influence contributing to the AFL-CIO merger was the recognized ineffectiveness of union raiding. The two labor organizations investigated employee representation elections in which the AFL tried to organize CIO employees and vice versa. During a two-year period (1951–1952), 1,245 such elections involved some 366,740 employees, with only 62,000 employees changing union affiliation. This figure overestimates the number affected, because it does not consider the offsetting nature of elections. An AFL union could organize a CIO factory of 1,000 employees only to have a CIO union organize an AFL factory of 1,000 employees—the net change would be zero. In fact, the extensive raiding during 1951 and 1952 resulted in a net gain for the AFL of only 8,000 members or only 2 percent of the total number of employees involved.[116]

Both the AFL and the CIO finally realized that organized labor would benefit if the energies devoted to raiding each other were spent on organizing nonunion employees. Thus many of the AFL and the CIO unions signed a "no raiding agreement" in 1954. Instead of concentrating on disruptive differences emphasized in raiding activities, the two major federations could now look at similar goals which might be more easily attained by a merger.

One similar goal was the desire of both organizations to reward their political friends and punish their political enemies.[117] In many instances, the independent organizations failed to achieve this goal. For example, they were unable to defeat Senator Taft (one of the authors of the Taft-Hartley Act who was perceived as being antilabor) and failed to elect Adlai Stevenson (supporter of organized labor) over Dwight D. Eisenhower. Both organizations felt that a merger might increase their effectiveness in the political arena.

The AFL-CIO merger on December 12, 1955 involved 15,550,000 members, making the new organization the largest trade union center in the world. The president of the AFL-CIO, George Meany, believed this merger would lead to more employees becoming unionized and to a greater political influence for labor within the American two-party system.[118]

The merger resulted in the continued reduction of union raiding. It also reduced the influence of union locals within the national unions—they could no longer threaten to affiliate with another national union in the rival organization.[119] However, as will be further discussed in the next section, the AFL-CIO merger has not resulted in a tremendous increase in union membership or political influence. It did reduce the former divisiveness within organized labor, but it cannot be concluded that the merger was a significant impetus for growth and change.

Aspects of Organized Labor Unchanged since World War II

Organized labor as it existed at the end of World War II compared to its present state appears to have more similarities than differences. The following six similarities are interrelated generalizations that apply to many labor organizations, although there are possible exceptions when individual unions are considered.

Organized labor remains a minority, yet influential, movement in our society[120] Since World War II, the proportion of unionized employees in the civilian work force has never exceeded 28 percent. Yet organized labor's influence on economic and political issues in society can on occasion be pronounced. Clearly, a settlement negotiated between a major corporation and a labor union can have spillover effects on the wage policies of other corporations, union and nonunion.

Also, politicians at least on a superficial basis regard organized labor as an influential force. For example, no president of the United States has made a practice of inviting nonunion employees and/or strikebreakers to the White House for the traditional Labor Day Speech. The vast majority of this audience consists of union leaders or members. Similarly, no political leader in the United States aspiring to the presidency proclaims himself to be anti-union.[121] For example, some political advertisements stressing Ronald Reagan's qualifications for the presidency indicated his past experience as president of the Screen Actors Guild.

Organized labor has had limited effectiveness in the political community At first glance, this generalization appears inconsistent with the one previously discussed. However, there is a difference between having influence and effectively using that influence in rewarding political friends and punishing political enemies. Organized labor has contributed much in time and money in various political campaigns. However, it has seldom, if ever, been able to deliver a large proportion of its members' votes toward any one candidate.

Since World War II, the relationship between organized labor and the Democratic and Republican political parties has been confusing and not always effective.[122]

In 1976, labor's political backing helped President Carter win key political victories in New York and Ohio, although many union officials preferred a "wait-and-see" strategy instead of endorsing Carter.[123] The Carter Administration was less than labor hoped for; ". . . labor greeted the Carter Administration with vague hopes that were transformed into demonstrable disappointment."[124]

Many union leaders and the AFL-CIO endorsed Carter as being the least worst choice over Ronald Reagan in the 1980 presidential election. Even Lane Kirkland, President of the AFL-CIO after Meany's death in 1980, conceded that the union vote for Carter was insufficient.[125]

There are two general barriers to organized labor's political efforts. First, *elected candidates must consider a wide range of programs some of which might ignore or even contradict union goals.* Active political support does not ensure complete cooperation from the elected government official. When President Reagan assumed office, Lane Kirkland expected no problems in communicating with White House officials on labor issues.[126] Subsequent events prompted AFL-CIO officials to feel excluded from the White House, and to believe the Reagan Administration to be "scornful of organized labor."[127]

Perhaps the most dramatic example of problems with politics is found with the Professional Air Traffic Controllers Organization (PATCO), whose president endorsed Mr. Reagan in the 1980 election believing that Mr. Carter was not sympathetic to his union members' concerns. Mr. Reagan informed the PATCO president that he would devote attention to the air controllers.[128] Subsequent events (discussed in more detail in Chapter 15) prompted his administration to fire nearly 12,000 controllers and decertify PATCO. Uncertain or negative reactions of elected government officials will likely chill union leaders' efforts in political campaigns.

Second, *union voters are concerned about more issues than those pertaining to organized labor.* Labor's political strength depends on persuading its members that its self-interest is at stake, and they should act to defend it.[129] However, union members have preferences that extend beyond the work situation.[130] Even George Meany viewed one such issue, support of the Vietnam War, as being significant enough to withhold political support of the Democratic presidential candidate (George McGovern) in 1972. It would be difficult to predict how a union member who was strongly against abortions would vote for a prolabor political candidate in favor of abortions on request. Additional problems in mobilizing political support are found in the third similarity.

There is difficulty in achieving consensus among unions and among members Understandably, agreement among the diverse national unions within the AFL-CIO federation and members within national and local unions is rare. This problem occurs in any large organization, particularly one which grants a large amount of autonomy to its members. The AFL-CIO is always subject to national unions withdrawing from its organization. The federation also realizes that many national unions can get along quite well without its support. For example, the 1957 expulsion of the Teamsters from the federation did not hinder the Teamsters' ability to increase its membership, grow in influence, and engage in collective bargaining. Likewise, the United Auto Workers, who chose to leave the AFL-CIO, fared well before returning to the organization.

Lack of consensus is also found at the local union level, especially when younger employees become members. Most labor unions have had a long tradition of struggle and sacrifice; their leaders have risked physical hardships in order to insure that the employer merely recognized their union. However, in many cases tradition has been forgotten, and many of the younger members are now asking the leaders, "What have you done for me lately?"

Many union leaders have difficulty in understanding the younger union members, particularly those who have identified with social protest groups and/or the rock culture. The possible generation gap in labor unions has been explained by one observer,

---

The labor movement fought for a place for their members in the American Dream; the students seemed to reject the dream most blue collar workers had yet to experience. . . . In 1970, Meany [then president of the AFL-CIO] commented that young people "smoke more pot than we do" . . . and concluded, "I am not going to trust the destiny of the country to that group."[131]

Organized labor has continually pursued short-range material goals instead of long-range reform The Knights of Labor appeared to teach organized labor a permanent lesson—goals should relate to members' needs instead of being abstract attempts to change the existing societal system. The period since World War II has witnessed tremendous economic growth and technological change; therefore, union leaders believe these issues deserve more attention than other societal concerns.[132]

Labor's priorities have been often challenged by members of the academic and intellectual community, who claim that labor should use its strength to press for progressive social change and legislation. Some hostility exists between organized labor and members of the intellectual community. Many intellectuals believe that the labor movement is "facing dynamic new challenges with old leaders and old ideas."[133] Many union leaders reply that intellectuals, in their work and in their surroundings, are out of touch with the everyday struggles faced by union members. Union leaders have also contended that the ivory tower views of academicians have been blurred by their stereotypic view of union members' behaviors and hopes and that academicians need to "get their hands dirty" on the line so they will make a more accurate assessment of unionism.[134] Even when unions make bargaining concessions, as they sometimes might, due to recessionary economic conditions, the concessions are viewed as short-term and material—less wages in exchange for job security, for example.

Collective bargaining tactics and issues remain largely unchanged since World War II Although there has been greater emphasis in *pattern bargaining* (in which a collective bargaining settlement of one company or industry influences subsequent collective bargaining tactics at other locations) since World War II, the basic tactics (strikes, inventory buildups, etc.) remain the same.

Organized labor has had to contend with negative public attitudes No longer viewed as the underdog in U.S. society, labor has in fact become a phenomenon of some public concern. Some are concerned about what they consider excessive wage demands won by labor unions. Labor has been somewhat effective in shaking leftist elements from its organization which long represented a source of negative public opinion. However, the media have consistently presented incidents of corruption in some labor unions[135] and highlighted certain practices where union members seem to receive payment for not working. These restrictive or make-work practices have been publicized in the railroad and construction industries, although elements of them extend to other areas, such as the supermarket industry.[136]

Summary and Implications

Summary

In obtaining a contemporary perspective of organized labor, one must be aware of the evolution of labor-management relationships as well as various labor organizations which have attempted to influence those relationships. Current labor organizations have learned important lessons from their historical counterparts. Criteria for success were suggested as a means of comparing the effectiveness of various labor organizations and were discussed in this chapter. Organized labor did not exert much of an influence before 1869, although employees became increasingly concerned with working and market conditions associated with mass production. The bulk of the chapter is concerned with the active years of organized labor, occurring in the following time periods: 1869 to World War I, World War I to World War II, and World War II to the present.

Three major labor organizations developed in the period from 1869 to World War I: the Knights of Labor (KOL), the American Federation of Labor (AFL) under Gompers, and the Industrial Workers of the World (IWW). These organizations' major goals, strategies, and organizational characteristics were discussed, and, in the cases of the KOL and the IWW, reasons for their demise were given. Also discussed were the Haymarket Riot and the Homestead and Pullman strikes.

The period immediately following World War I saw limited growth in union membership. Many of the factors contributing to this situation were discussed, including several strategies used by employers to counter union organizing campaigns. Internal differences occurred within the AFL regarding the potential advantages of organizing the heretofore nonunion unskilled and semiskilled employees working in the nation's factories. This disagreement led to the formation of a rival union organization, the Congress of Industrial Organizations (CIO), whose major objective was to organize industrial employees. The CIO was effective in achieving substantial membership gains in the late 1930s and 1940s.

Three major developments have occurred in organized labor since World War II. There has been increased concern over new collective bargaining issues; organizing drives have been aimed at public and white-collar employees; and the AFL and the CIO have merged. Although several influences prompted the AFL-CIO merger, the impact of this event on contemporary union-management relationships is difficult to assess. As suggested by the concluding section, there appear to be more similarities than differences when the state of organized labor at the end of World War II is compared to its present state. Organized labor remains a minority, yet influential, movement in our society. It has continued to have a minimal effectiveness in the political community, possibly because of negative public opinion and the difficulty of mobilizing younger union members. Finally, the strategies and tactics of collective bargaining are basically unchanged since World War II.

Implications

An analysis of labor history can encourage speculation as to future union behavior and status in the broader social system. This chapter has indicated that the AFL-CIO has been successful in maintaining itself in a challenging, even adverse environment. This organization has survived aggressive challenges from rival organizations and internal differences of opinion which led to the formation of the CIO. Organized labor has had to face aggressive opposition from some employers, the media, intellectuals, and its younger union members. It has also experienced some disappointment from some of the elected officials who received its sometimes active political support.

This situation has no doubt contributed to a defensive reaction among many labor unions, a reaction which urges preservation of the status quo and a resistance to change. Consider, for example, job enrichment programs which represent current behavioral science solutions to problems of employee dissatisfaction and declining worker productivity. These programs, discussed in more detail in Chapter 12, maintain that employees should have more input into their jobs and working conditions. Yet, many unions are likely to respond to these innovations from a historically learned defensive posture.

They will first question the source of this change, be it academics "with limited real world experience," or employers, "who might use the program as a ploy to get more out of employees and eliminate the union." If unable to dismiss these sources, union officials might question the evidence which supports this innovation. For example, a facility which has benefited from a job enrichment program might also have extremely careful recruiting procedures, wages which are much higher than those found in the area and, unique working conditions such as a newly designed, ultra-modern facility.

If job enrichment cannot be dismissed on these grounds, then some union leaders might use a third defensive tactic: rationalizing the new approach in terms of established union goals and principles. The AFL-CIO has had a tradition of material improvement for members through wage gains and job security measures (such as seniority) and grievance procedures. Union leaders might accept the job enrichment concept, and at the same time indicate that employees already have significant input through collective bargaining, grievances and the opportunity to move to different jobs through existing seniority provisions in the labor agreement.

The historical progress of labor unions also has implications concerning its current usefulness. History has held few promises for organized labor, as witnessed by somewhat consistent and negative media coverage and public opinion. Although many gains have been made by unions, they still represent only a small fraction of the labor force (approximately 20 percent). Furthermore, this proportion has dropped steadily since the 1950s. Unions have also been considered obsolete because they do not push for social issues; organized labor has not become fully involved with automation, unemployment, civil rights, poverty, and the energy crisis.

Union growth and its role in social involvement can be debated. Lane Kirkland contends labor organizations' success cannot be measured solely in membership statistics since unions are not economic institutions competing for market shares.[137] Unions' lack of involvement in social issues has also been contested, since related efforts appear to contradict historical lessons.

Why should American unions turn from the well-understood and tangible goals of collective bargaining for a place in the never-never land of social reform? . . . Unions in America have chosen to define a role for themselves that is intimately tied to the collective bargaining system which, in turn, is concerned with the welfare of employees and the success of management at the workplace.[138]

There is, however, a more difficult argument concerning organized labor's historical progress. Many contend that unions have improved working conditions since the 1800s when the AFL was formed. These improvements and governmental regulations protecting employees' welfare have reduced, if not eliminated, some past employer abuses of employees.

Some believe that this current situation makes unions obsolete; others argue that improvements in working conditions, while impressive, are not complete, and organized labor must remain to press for further gains. It is hard to predict how employers would treat employees if unions vanished from the scene. Organized labor has been compared to the military in peacetime—a strong, countervailing power needed to preserve the existing situation.[139] Management certainly *can* make unions obsolete since they are the ultimate grantor of working conditions in the labor agreement. Whether they would agree to these conditions without the existence and/or threat of labor organizations is uncertain.[140]

Discussion Questions

1. "Strive for the better day" was stated by Gompers (AFL); however, the remark could have just as easily been stated by Powderly (KOL) or Haywood (IWW)—but with entirely different meaning. Explain.

2. Considering the criteria for labor organization strength mentioned on page 28–29, why did the AFL survive and the IWW fade into obscurity?
3. Briefly explain how the Haymarket, Homestead, and Pullman incidents helped as well as hurt the AFL.
4. Discuss the various employer tactics used to thwart union growth in the 1920s and 1930s.
5. Why was the CIO successful in organizing members in the late 1930s when it had the same "one big union" approach which proved most unsuccessful for the KOL in the 1880s?
6. What were several reasons behind the merger of the AFL and the CIO? To what extent will these or other reasons continue this merger into the near future—say, the next ten years?
7. Discuss two similarities of organized labor as it existed at the end of World War II and as it does in the present. Speculate as to how these similarities might be modified in the near future.
8. (From Implications section). Fully assess the following statement: "Unions are obsolete today for many reasons, including their outmoded defensive reactions to social issues and possible innovative working conditions."

References

[1]Robert Ozanne, "Trends in American Labor History," *Labor History* 21 (Fall 1980), p. 521. See also Barry Goldberg, "A New Look at Labor History," *Social Policy* 12 (Winter 1982), pp. 54–63; and, Robert H. Zieger, "Industrial Relations and Labor History in The Eighties," *Industrial Relations* 22 (Winter 1983), pp. 58–70.

[2]Henry Pelling, *American Labor* (Chicago: University of Chicago Press, 1960), pp. 12–13.

[3]Edward B. Mittelman, "Trade Unionism 1833–1839," in John R. Commons et al., eds., *History of Labour in the United States* (1918; reprint ed. New York: Augustus M. Kelly, Publishers, 1966), vol. 1, p. 430.

[4]William C. Birdsall, "The Problems of Structure in the Knights of Labor," *Industrial and Labor Relations Review* 6 July 1953), p. 546.

[5]For a discussion of how the expansion of the markets affected unionization among the shoemakers see John R. Commons, *Labor and Administration* (New York: Macmillan, 1913), pp. 210–264.

[6]T. V. Powderly, *Thirty Years of Labor: 1859–1889* (Columbus, Ohio: Excelsior Publishing House, 1889), p. 21.

[7]Ibid., pp. 58–59.

[8]Ibid., p. 163.

[9]Philip Taft, *Organized Labor in American History* (New York: Harper & Row, 1964), p. 90.

[10]Gerald N. Grob, *Workers and Utopia* (Evanston, Ill.: Northwestern University Press, 1961), p. 35. Powderly was most concerned about the evils of drinking; for example, he spent almost fifty pages of his autobiography, *Thirty Years of Labor*, discussing this issue.

[11]Birdsall, "The Problems of Structure," p. 533.

[12]Melton Alonza McLaurin, *The Knights of Labor in the South* (Westport, Conn.: Greenwood Press, 1978), p. 39.

[13]Joseph G. Rayback, *A History of American Labor* (New York: Macmillan, 1968), p. 174.

[14]Joseph R. Buchanan, *The Story of a Labor Agitator* (1903; reprint ed. Westport, Conn.: Greenwood Press, 1970), pp. 318–323.

[15]For details of these procedures see Taft, *Organized Labor*, p. 91.

[16]Powderly, *Thirty Years of Labor*, pp. 152–157.

[17]It should be noted that local assemblies were somewhat responsible for this situation, as they contributed only $600 to the General Assembly's strike funds in 1885–1886 (McLaurin, *The Knights of Labor*, p. 54). For more details of KOL's strike activities see Norman J. Ware, *The Labor Movement in the United States, 1860–1895* (1929; reprint ed. Gloucester, Mass.: Peter Smith, 1959), pp. 117–154. It should be further noted that the Knights made more effective use of boycotts than any previous union. However, as was true with strikes, the boycott was instigated by the local assemblies and forced on the Knights' national leaders (Grob, *Workers and Utopia*, p. 61).

[18]Donald L. Kemmerer and Edward D. Wickersham, "Reasons for the Growth of the Knights of Labor in 1885–1886," *Industrial and Labor Relations Review* 3 (January 1950), pp. 213–220.

[19]Foster Rhea Dulles, *Labor in America: A History*, 3d ed. (New York: Thomas Y. Crowell, 1966), p. 127.

[20]Ware, *The Labor Movement*, p. 96.

[21]Dulles, *Labor in America*, p. 135.

[22]Powderly, *Thirty Years of Labor*, p. 514. It should also be noted that Powderly believed Gompers misled employees by advocating the eight-hour day without telling them that their wages would be proportionately reduced. Most workers thought they would receive ten hours payment for eight hours of work.

[23]"A Hellish Deed!" *Chicago Tribune*, May 5, 1886, p. 1.

[24]For additional details of the rigged nature of the trial see Samuel Yellen, *American Labor Struggles* (1936; reprint ed. New York: Arno Press, 1969), pp. 60–65.

[25]"A Hellish Deed!"

[26]"Their Records," *Chicago Tribune*, May 5, 1886, p. 1.

[27]Sidney Lens, *The Labor Wars: From the Molly Maguires to the Sitdowns* (Garden City, N.Y.: Doubleday, 1973), p. 67.

[28]It should be noted that the origination of the AFL was changed to 1881 in 1889 to include activities under the Federation of Organized Trades and Labor Unions. At least one historian has claimed that the revised date is regrettable since the parent organization (Federation of Organized Trades and Labor Unions) had little similarity to the AFL in terms of effective organization and broad-based support (Ware, *The Labor Movement*, p. 251). See also Glen A. Gildemeister, "The Founding of the American Federation of Labor," *Labor History* 22 (Spring 1981); and Harold C. Livesay, *Samuel Gompers and Organized Labor in America* (Boston: Little, Brown and Company, 1978), pp. 75–86.

[29]Samuel Gompers, *Seventy Years of Life and Labor* (New York: E. P. Dutton, 1925), p. 266.

[30]Ware, *The Labor Movement*, pp. 70–71.

[31]Norman J. Ware, *Labor in Modern Industrial Society* (1935; reprint ed. New York: Russell & Russell, 1968), p. 262.

[32]Dulles, *Labor in America*, p. 155.

[33]Gompers, *Seventy Years of Life and Labor*, p. 245.

[34]Samuel Gompers, *Labor and the Employer* (1920; reprint ed. New York: Arno Press, 1971), pp. 33–34.

[35]Stuart Bruce Kaufman, *Samuel Gompers and the Origins of the American Federation of Labor: 1848–1896* (Westport, Conn.: Greenwood Press, 1973), p. 173. For details of this relationship see Gompers, *Seventy Years of Life and Labor*, pp. 381–427.

[36]Louis Reed, *The Labor Philosophy of Samuel Gompers* (1930; reprint ed. Port Washington, N.Y.: Kennikat Press, 1966), p. 20. See also an editorial by Gompers in the *American Federationist*, June 1924, p. 481.

[37]Gompers, *Seventy Years of Life and Labor*, pp. 286–287, 381–427.

[38]Max M. Kempelman, "Labor in Politics," in George M. Brooks et al., *Interpreting the Labor Movement* (Ann Arbor, Mich.: Industrial Relations Research Association, 1967), p. 41.

[39]Gompers, *Labor and the Employer*, p. 202.

[40]Marc Karson, *American Labor Unions and Politics: 1900–1918* (Carbondale, Ill.: Southern Illinois University Press, 1968), p. 29.

[41]Reed, *The Labor Philosophy of Samuel Gompers*, pp. 106–110.

[42]Milton Derber, *The American Idea of Industrial Democracy: 1865–1965* (Urbana: University of Illinois Press, 1970), p. 117.

[43]Gompers, *Seventy Years of Life and Labor*, p. 342. For additional details regarding early AFL organizing see Philip Taft, *The AF of L in the Time of Gompers*, (1957; reprint ed. New York: Octagon Books, 1970), pp. 95–122.

[44]Dulles, *Labor in America*, pp. 163–164.

[45]Andrew Carnegie, "An Employer's View of the Labor Question," in *Labor: Its Rights and Wrongs* (1886; reprint ed. Westport, Conn.: Hyperion Press, 1975), pp. 91 and 95.

[46]Yellen, *American Labor Struggles*, p. 81.

[47]For details of the wage package see Ibid., pp. 77–80. See also E.W. Bemis, "The Homestead Strike," *Journal of Political Economy* 2 (1894), pp. 369–396; and LInda Schneider, "The Citizen Striker: Workers' Ideology in the Homestead Strike of 1892," *Labor History* 23 (Winter 1982), pp. 47–66.

[48]"Surrounded by Pickets," *New York Times*, July 4, 1892, p. 1.

[49]"Mob Law at Homestead," *New York Times*, July 7, 1892, p. 1.

[50]"Leader O'Donnell Is Glad," *New York Times*, July 12, 1892, p. 2; "Bayonet Rule in Force," *New York Times*, July 13, 1892, p. 1.

[51]Lens, *The Labor Wars*, p. 77.

[52]"A Talk with Gompers," *New York Times*, July 7, 1892, p. 2; and "Provoked by Carnegie," *New York Times*, July 7, 1892, pp. 2, 5.

[53]Taft, *AF of L in the Time of Gompers*, p. 136.

[54]"Arbitrate the Homestead Strike," *Chicago Tribune*, July 8, 1892, p. 4. See also "The Origin of the Trouble," *New York Times*, July 8, 1982, p. 2.

[55]Yellen, *American Labor Struggles*, p. 3.

[56]Lens, *The Labor Wars*, p. 81.

[57]For additional details about the town see Almont Lindsay, *The Pullman Strike* (Chicago: University of Chicago Press, 1967), pp. 38–60.

[58]For more details regarding ARU's organization see Philip S. Foner, *History of the Labor Movement in the United States*, vol. II (New York: International Publishers, 1955), p. 256.

[59]Lindsay, *The Pullman Strike*, p. 124.

[60]Ibid., p. 215.

[61]Gompers, *Seventy Years of Life and Labor*, p. 403.

[62]*Proceedings of the First Convention of the Industrial Workers of the World* (New York: Labor News Company, 1905), p. 1.

[63]Ibid., p. 143.

[64]Bill Haywood, *Bill Haywood's Book: The Autobiography of William D. Haywood* (New York: International Publishers, 1929), p. 73.

[65]Melvyn Dubofsky, *We Shall Be All: A History of the Industrial Workers of the World* (Chicago: Quadrangle Books, 1969), p. 481.

[66]Haywood, *Bill Haywood's Book*, p. 181.

[67]For additional details pertaining to these differences see Dubofsky, *We Shall Be All*, pp. 105–119; and Joseph Robert Conlin, *Bread and Roses Too* (Westport, Conn.: Greenwood Publishing, 1969), pp. 97–117; and, Lens, *The Labor Wars*, pp. 154–155.

[68]David J. Saposs, *Left-Wing Unionism* (1926; reprint ed. New York: Russell & Russell, 1967), p. 148.

[69]Louis Adamic, *Dynamite: The Story of Class Violence in America* (1934; reprint ed. Gloucester, Mass.: Peter Smith, 1963), p. 174.

[70]Conlin, *Bread and Roses Too*, pp. 97–117. See also Fred Thompson, *The IWW: Its First Fifty Years* (Chicago: Industrial Workers of the World, 1955), pp. 80–87.

[71]Adamic, *Dynamite*, pp. 163–164.

[72]Conlin, *Bread and Roses Too*, p. 96.

[73]Philip S. Foner, ed., *Fellow Workers and Friends: I.W.W. Free Speech Fights as Told by Participants* (Westport, Conn.: Greenwood Press, 1981), p. 15.

[74]Foner, *History of the Labor Movement*, vol. III, p. 465.

[75]Conlin, *Bread and Roses Too* p. 68.

[76]For additional details see Frank L. Grubbs, Jr., *The Struggle for Labor Loyalty: Gompers, the AFL, and the Pacifists, 1917–1920* (Durham, N.C.: Duke University Press, 1968).

[77]James O. Morris, *Conflict within the AFL: A Study of Craft versus Industrial Unionism, 1901–1938* (1958; reprint ed. Wesport, Conn.: Greenwood Press, 1974), pp. 9–10.

[78]Taft, *Organized Labor*, pp. 355–358; and Francis Fox Piven and Richard A. Cloward, *Poor People's Movements* (New York: Pantheon Books, 1977), p. 104. For details of this strike see Lens, *The Labor Wars*, pp. 196–219.

[79]Lens, *The Labor Wars*, pp. 222, 296, and 312.

[80]Derber, *The American Idea*, p. 246. For an application of these reasons to a specific industrial situation during this time period see Stephen L. Shapiro, "The Growth of the Cotton Textile Industry in South Carolina: 1919–1930" (Ph.D. diss., University of South Carolina, 1971), pp. 168–171.

[81]For additional details regarding this tactic see Clinch Calkins, *Spy Overhead: The Story of Industrial Espionage* (1937; reprint ed. New York: Arno Press, 1971).

[82]It should be noted that violence was limited neither to this time period nor to the employer. One of the more publicized episodes of employer violence was the Ludlow Massacre of 1914. The mining camps in Colorado were involved in a strike for union recognition when, on April 20, militiamen opened fire on a tent colony, killing two strikers and one boy. They then set fire to the tents, killing two women and eleven children. For more details of this event see Leon Stein, ed., *Massacre at Ludlow: Four Reports* (reprint ed.; New York: Arno Press, 1971). Perhaps one of the more vivid examples of union violence occurred in Herrin, Illinois (1922), where miners tortured and killed at least twenty-six management officials and strikebreakers. For details of this episode see Saul Alinsky, *John L. Lewis: An Unauthorized Biography* (New York: Vintage Books, 1970), pp. 43–50.

[83]Richard C. Wilcock, "Industrial Management's Policies toward Unionism," in Milton Derber and Edwin Young, eds., *Labor and the New Deal* (Madison: University of Wisconsin Press, 1957), p. 293.

[84]For a case study of paternalism see "Welfare Work in Company Towns," *Monthly Labor Review* 25 (August 1927), pp. 314–321.

[85]Derber, *The American Idea*, pp. 220–221; Morris, *Conflict within the AFL*, pp. 40–41. For more details on ERPs see Ware, *Labor in Modern Industrial Society*, pp. 414–435. For a contemporary assessment of the problems and prospects facing the single-firm, independent union see Arthur B. Shostak, *America's Forgotten Labor Organization* (Princeton: Industrial Relations Section, Department of Economics, Princeton University, 1962).

[86]Dulles, *Labor in America*, p. 245.

[87]This example was drawn from a more detailed account of racketeering during this period found in Sidney Lens, *Left, Right, and Center: Conflicting Forces in American Labor* (Hinsdale, Ill.: Henry Regnery, 1949), pp. 86–108.

[88]David J. McDonald, *Union Man* (New York: E. P. Dutton, 1969), p. 185. See also Max Gordan, "The Communists and the Drive to Organize Steel, 1936," *Labor History* 23 (Spring 1982), pp. 226–245. For further historical insights into the relationship between organized labor and communism, see Harvey A. Levenstein, *Communism, Anticommunism and the CIO* (Westport, Conn.: Greenwood Press, 1981).

[89]James O. Morris, "The AFL in the 1920s: A Strategy of Defense," *Industrial and Labor Relations Review* 11 (July 1958), pp. 572–590.

[90]See for example "William Green: Guardian of the Middle Years," *American Federationist* 88 (February 1981), pp. 24–25.

[91]Bruce Minton and John Stuart, *Men Who Lead Labor* (New York: Modern Age Books, 1937), pp. 14–15.

[92]Morris, *Conflict within the AFL*, p. 216.

[93]For additional details pertaining to the background of this historic convention see Herbert Harris, *Labor's Civil War* (1940; reprint ed. New York: Greenwood Press, 1969), pp. 22–60.

[94]Lens, *The Labor Wars*, p. 284.

[95]Cecil Carnes, *John L. Lewis: Leader of Labor* (New York: Robert Speller Publishing, 1936), p. 299.

[96]David Dubinsky and A. H. Raskin, *David Dubinsky: A Life with Labor* (New York: Simon and Schuster, 1977), p. 226.

[97]The seven unions were: The United Mine Workers; The Amalgamated Clothing Workers; The International Ladies Garment Workers Union; United Hatters; Cap and Millinery Workers; Oil Field, Gas Well and Refinery Workers; and The International Union of Mine, Mill, and Smelter Workers.

[98]Benjamin Stolberg, *The Story of the CIO* (1938; reprint ed. New York: Arno Press, 1971), p. 28.

[99]Milton Derber, "Growth and Expansion," in Derber and Young, *Labor and the New Deal*, p. 13.

[100]See, for example, John Hutchinson, "John L. Lewis: To the Presidency of the UMWA," *Labor History* 19 (Spring 1978), pp. 185–203.

[101]James Arthur Wechsler, *Labor Baron: A Portrait of John L. Lewis* (New York: William Morrow, 1944), p. 71.

[102]S. J. Woolf, "John L. Lewis and His Plan," in Melvyn Dubofsky, ed., *American Labor since the New Deal* (Chicago: Quadrangle Books, 1971), pp. 110–111.

[103]Lens, *The Labor Wars*, p. 295.

[104]Irving Howe and B. J. Widick, *The UAW and Walter Reuther* (1949; reprint ed. New York: De Capo Press, 1973), p. 55.

[105]Sidney Fine, *Sit-Down: The General Motors Strike of 1936–1937* (Ann Arbor: The University of Michigan Press, 1969), pp. 156–177. For another perspective of the sitdown strike see Daniel Nelson, "Origins of the Sit-Down Era: Worker Militancy and Innovation in the Rubber Industry, 1934–38," *Labor History* 23 (Winter 1982), pp. 198–225.

[106]James R. Hoffa and Oscar Fraley, *Hoffa: The Real Story* (New York: Stein and Day Publishers, 1975), p. 65.

[107]For a detailed account of the AFL-CIO rivalries in several industries see Walter Galenson, *The CIO Challenge to the AFL* (Cambridge, Mass.: Harvard University Press, 1960).

[108]Richard B. Morris, ed., *The U.S. Department of Labor Bicentennial History of the American Worker* (Washington, D.C.: U.S. Government Printing Office, 1976), p. 236.

[109]For details of this formula and the extent that cost of living estimates exceeded this formula see Taft, *Organized Labor in American History*, pp. 549–553 and 557–559.

[110]Dulles, *Labor in America: A History*, p. 334.

[111]Arthur F. McClure, *The Truman Administration and the Problems of Postwar Labor, 1945–1948* (Cranburry, N.J.: Associated University Presses, 1969), p. 45.

[112]George H. Hildebrand, *American Unionism: An Historical and Analytical Survey* (Reading: Addison-Wesley, 1979), pp. 36–37.

[113]*Policies and Practices, Personnel Management* (January 1982) 267; 188. Copyright 1982 by The Bureau of National Affairs, Inc., Washington, D. C.

[114]Robert M. MacDonald, "Collective Bargaining in the Postwar Period," *Industrial and Labor Relations Review* 20 (July 1967), p. 568.

[115]For a more detailed discussion of the historical attempts at the merger of the AFL and CIO organizations see Joel Seidman, "Efforts toward Merger 1935–1955," *Industrial and Labor Relations Review* 9 (April 1956), pp. 353–370.

[116]"Document: AFL-CIO No-Raiding Agreement," *Industrial and Labor Relations Review* 8 (October 1954), p. 103.

[117]"A Short History of American Labor," *American Federationist* 88 (March 1981), p. 14.

[118]George Meany, "Merger and the National Welfare," *Industrial and Labor Relations Review* 9 (April 1956), p. 349.

[119]Richard A. Lester, *As Unions Mature* (Princeton, N.J.: Princeton University Press, 1958), p. 25.

[120]Some of the similarities discussed in this section draw from the discussion of Taft, *Organized Labor*, pp. 707–709.

[121]B. J. Widick, *Labor Today: The Triumphs and Failures of Unionism in the United States* (Boston: Houghton Mifflin, 1964), p. 117.

[122]Max M. Kempelman, "Labor in Politics," in George W. Brooks, et al., eds., *Interpreting the Labor Movement* (Ann Arbor, Mich.: Industrial Relations Research Association, 1967), p. 188; and Dick Bruner, "Labor Should Get Out of Politics," in Charles M. Rehmus and Doris B. McLaughlin, eds., *Labor and American Politics: A Book of Readings* (Ann Arbor: University of Michigan Press, 1967), p. 430. For an assessment of organized labor's limited effectiveness in the political arena since the 1930s see Piven and Cloward, *Poor People's Movements*, pp. 161–172; Graham K. Wilson, *Unions in American National Politics* (New York: St. Martin's Press, 1979), p. 36; David Montgomery, *Workers' Control in America: Studies in the History of Work, Technology, and Labor Struggles* (New York: Cambridge University Press, 1979), p. 170; David Brody, *Workers in Industrial America* (New York: Oxford University Press, 1980), p. 243; and Marick F. Masters and John Thomas Delaney, "The AFL-CIO's Political Record, 1974–1980," in Barbara D. Dennis, ed.; *Proceedings of the 34th Annual Meeting of The Industrial Relations Research Association* (Madison: Wisconsin: Industrial Relations Research Association, 1982), pp. 351–359.

[123]Charles W. Dunn, *American Democracy Debated* (Morristown, N.Y.: General Learning Press, 1978), pp. 210–211; and Jong Oh Ra, *Labor at the Polls* (Amherst, Mass.: University of Massachusetts Press, 1978), p. 136.

[124]Arnold R. Weber, "Organized Labor: What Happened to Its Political Clout?" *Dun's Review* 116 (October 1980), p. 12. See also "Labor's Rising Anti-Carter Mood," *Business Week*, August 21, 1978, pp. 22 and 24; "Carter, AFL-CIO Agree to Keep Communicating," Bureau of National Affairs Inc. *Daily Labor Report*, June 19, 1979, p. 2; and Arnold Weber, "What Labor

Expected of Jimmy Carter, the Reality Turns Out to Be Something of a Disappointment," *Across the Board* 15 (May 1978), pp. 56–61.

[125]Lane Kirkland, "Labor and Politics after 1980," *American Federationist* 88 (January 1981), p. 18.

[126]Frank Swoboda, "Reagan Lacks Relations with Labor," *Florida Times-Union*, August 25, 1981, D–5.

[127]"Hard Times for Big Labor," *Newsweek*, September 7, 1981, p. 61. See also "AFL-CIO Aide Says White House Refuses to Consult with Labor Leaders on Issues," *Wall Street Journal*, August 27, 1981, p. 8.

[128]Lindley H. Clark Jr., "Reagan: Labor's Love Lost?" *Wall Street Journal*, June 30, 1981, p. 31.

[129]Patricia Cayo Sexton and Brendan Sexton, *Blue Collars and Hard Hats: The Working Class and the Nature of American Politics* (New York: Random House, 1971), p. 307.

[130]Donald E. Stokes, "Voting Research and the Labor Vote," in Rhemus and McLaughlin eds., *Labor and Amnerican Politics*, pp. 387–389.

[131]Wilson, *Unions in American National Politics*, p. 40.

[132]For a more thorough union perspective of labor's role in social reform see Jack T. Conway, "Ideological Obsolescence in Collective Bargaining," in Walter Fogel and Archie Kleingartner, eds., *Contemporary Labor Issues* (Belmont, Calif.: Wadsworth Publishing Company, 1970), pp. 202–212.

[133]A. H. Raskin, "The Fat Cats of Labor," in David Boroff, ed., *The State of the Nation* (Englewood Cliffs, N.J.: Prentice-Hall, 1965), p. 50. For a further related discussion see Harold L. Wilensky, *Intellectuals in Labor Unions* (Glencoe, Ill.: The Free Press, 1956).

[134]Brendan Sexton, "The Working Class Experience," *American Economic Review* 62 (May 1972), p. 152.

[135]For a fuller discussion of this issue see John Hutchinson, *The Imperfect Union: A History of Corruption in American Trade Unions* (New York: E. P. Dutton, 1972).

[136]Herbert R. Northrup, Gordon R. Stockholm, and Paul A. Abodeely, *Restrictive Labor Practices in the Supermarket Industry* (Philadelphia: University of Pennsylvania Press, 1967), pp. 67–119.

[137]Bureau of National Affairs Inc., *Daily Labor Report*, February 25, 1980, p. E–1.

[138]Tim Bornstein, "Unions, Critics, and Collective Bargaining," *Labor Law Journal* 27 (October 1976), p. 617.

[139]Kenneth A. Kovach, "Do We Still Need Labor Unions?" *Personnel Journal* 58 (December 1979), p. 850.

[140]See for example, Carol Hymowitz, "Labor Muscle: In an Era of Givebacks, Members of One Union Are of No Mind to Give," *Wall Street Journal*, April 28, 1982, pp. 1 and 24; and Lawrence Ingrassia, "Union Rank and File Talk Bitterly of Their Bosses," *Wall Street Journal*, April 12, 1982, p. 22.

Chapter 3 Legal Influences

"Ideally, our labor laws should be closely attuned to the needs of workers and unions in using persuasion and certain economic weapons to organize and bargain effectively, and to the competing interests of employers, employees, and the general public in being free from injurious pressures."*
Theodore J. St. Antoine

Labor relations law serves as the framework for most of our labor relations activities. This chapter is placed early in the book so that a proper foundation can be established for such subjects as organizing unions, negotiating labor agreements, and assuring employee rights. Further, it is essential today not only to know the law but to understand and appreciate the interrelationships between the law and the labor relations process.

This chapter logically follows the historical development of unions in the United States because labor relations law and union development go hand in hand. Law as it pertains to labor is traced from the first court case involving union activities through the development of common law and the use of antitrust legislation that inhibited the growth of unions to the laws that pertain to most private firms: the Norris–La Guardia, Wagner, Taft-Hartley, and Landrum-Griffin Acts. Since these acts cover the major portion of U.S. industries and businesses, a substantial amount of space is devoted to their content. The Railroad Labor Act, which principally covers railroads and airlines, is also explained and assessed. A final section briefly considers several other laws which can affect the labor relations process.

Origin of Labor Relations Law

Labor relations law in the United States is derived from statutory law, judicial decisions and interpretations, and administrative decisions by agencies of the executive branch. Likewise, at the state and local government levels, law is developed and established by analogous documents and actions.

*"The Role of Law," in Jack Stieber, et. al., eds. *U.S. Industrial Relations 1950–1980: A Critical Assessment* (Madison, WI: Industrial Relations Research Association, 1981), p. 196.

Statutory law can be created and amended by legislative enactment at the federal, state, or local levels of government. Congress has enacted numerous labor relations laws in the interest of employees and employers, public welfare, and interstate commerce. Three major ones—the Norris–LaGuardia Act, the National Labor Relations Act, as amended, and the Railway Labor Act—are discussed at length later in the chapter. State legislatures may pass laws and local municipalities pass ordinances to fill voids in the federal laws or to cover issues not covered by federal laws, such as the right of public employees to engage in collective bargaining.

The judicial branch of government, with its accompanying court system at the federal, state, and local levels, functions to determine a law's constitutionality and conformity to legal standards, to assess the accuracy of interpretations by administrative agencies, and to issue injunctions that restrict or require certain activities. In addition, the courts must decide issues not covered by laws and make rulings under the general guides of "equity." Such decisions and rulings constitute case, or common law, which has developed over the years, setting precedents and providing guidance for future decisions.

The executive branch, the administrator of the laws through various governmental agencies, makes rules (sometimes called Executive Orders) and decisions within the framework of the statutes or laws. These decisions are legal and binding although they are subject to appeal to the courts. As long as the decisions are within the authority of the administrative agency and are accurate interpretations of its delegated authority, they have the same effect as law.

In addition, several provisions of the U.S. Constitution have been interpreted as applying to labor relations activities. For example, Article I, Section 8, which authorizes Congress to regulate commerce, has been used to determine the constitutionality of several statutory enactments. The First Amendment, which assures the rights of peaceful assembly and free speech, usually has been interpreted as allowing employees to form and join unions and has provided the justification for union picketing (to communicate information to possible union members and union supporters). The Fifth and Fourteenth Amendments contain due process provisions, and the Fourteenth Amendment provides equal protection under law. These amendments have been used for employment protection in discharge decisions, refusal-to-hire cases, and discrimination cases regarding equal employment opportunity where either state or federal employees are involved.

Some of the more important administrative agencies mentioned throughout the book include:

- **National Labor Relations Board (NLRB):** Administers the National Labor Relations Act as amended by the Taft-Hartley and Landrum-Griffin acts, conducts union representation elections, and adjudicates unfair labor practice complaints.

- **Federal Mediation and Conciliation Service (FMCS):** Provides mediation services to unions and management in collective bargaining and assists these parties in selecting arbitrators in grievance administration.
- **U.S. Department of Labor (DOL):** Performs many labor-related services, such as research and data-collecting functions; administers wage laws, supervises offices under the Occupational Safety and Health Administration, and enforces federal contract compliance under equal employment opportunity requirements. In addition, its secretary serves as the President's cabinet member responsible for labor relations matters.
- **National Mediation Board:** Handles union representation issues under the Railway Labor Act, provides mediation services to parties in negotiations, assists in disputes over contract interpretation, and in cases involving emergency disputes proposes arbitration and certifies the dispute to the President as an emergency.
- **National Railroad Adjustment Board:** Hears and attempts to resolve railroad labor disputes growing out of grievances and interpretation or application of the labor agreements.
- **State and local administrative agencies:** Numerous agencies at the state and local levels of government are responsible for the enforcement and administration of state laws and local ordinances involving labor relations topics.

Early Legal Interpretations Involving Labor-Management Relationships (1806–1931)

As the previous chapter demonstrated, in earlier times labor unions in the United States had to struggle for their existence. With the absence of legislative direction, the judiciary system not only controlled the relationships between labor unions and employers but also played a key role in limiting the organization of unions for many years, especially from the 1800s to the 1930s.

Criminal Conspiracy

The first labor relations case in the United States occurred in 1806, when a group of journeymen shoemakers in Philadelphia were indicted, convicted, and fined $8 each for forming an illegal criminal conspiracy. The shoemakers had joined a combination of workmen in an attempt to raise their wages, and refused to work with nonmembers or at a wage rate less than they demanded. Twelve jurors found the shoemakers guilty of forming an illegal coalition for the purpose of raising their own wages while injuring those who did not join the coalition.[1]

The application of the criminal conspiracy doctrine to attempts by employees to organize unions aroused much public protest, not only from employees but also from factory owners who feared the closing of their factories if the workers' feelings grew too strong. These feelings were undoubtedly considered when the Supreme Judicial Court of Massachusetts *(Commonwealth v. Hunt)* set aside the conviction for criminal conspiracy of seven members of the Journeymen Bootmakers Society who refused to work in shops where nonmembers were employed at less than their scheduled rate of $2 per pair of boots. While not rejecting the criminal conspiracy doctrine, Justice Shaw cut the heart from it by insisting that the purpose of the concerted activity must be considered, not just the fact that the activity occurred. His decision stated that an association of workers could be established for "useful and honorable purposes" as well as for purposes of "oppression and injustice"; however, the means of achieving these purposes could also be legal or illegal. Therefore, to determine its legality, an investigation must be made of the objectives of the particular labor union involved and of the means used to achieve its objectives.[2]

Civil Conspiracy

The *Commonwealth v. Hunt* decision virtually ended the use of the criminal conspiracy doctrine in labor relations. However, the courts developed the civil conspiracy doctrine, which holds that a group involved in concerted activities can inflict harm on other parties even though it is pursuing a valid objective in its own interest.[3] In the *Vegelahn v. Guntner* case, an injunction was issued against a union that was picketing for higher wages and shorter hours. While the court agreed that the purposes were legitimate, it concluded that the picketing and a refusal to work would lead to more serious trouble, and employers could seek injunctive relief.[4]

Breach of Contract

Breach of contract, a common law rule, was used by employers in restricting union membership and union organizing activities. For example, an employer would require its employees to sign a *yellow-dog contract*—an agreement stating that they would neither join a union nor assist in organizing a union. Since this contract would be a condition of continued employment, any violation would allow the company to discharge the employee. More importantly, if any union organizers (non-employees) attempted to solicit union members among those who had signed yellow-dog contracts, they would be interfering with a legal contractual relationship between the employer and its employees. Thus, the employer could go to court and secure an injunction against the union organizers and any union-related activities. Union organizers who violated the court order then could be charged with contempt of court and possibly fined and imprisoned.[5]

Application of Antitrust Legislation to Labor Unions

In the late 1800s, an attempt was made to guard against increasing business monopolies, concentration of ownership, and business combinations that eliminated competition. One such attempt was the passage of the Sherman Antitrust Act of 1890, whose coverage neither specified nor excluded labor unions. Section I states that "every contract, combination in the form of trust or otherwise, or conspiracy, in restraint of trade or commerce among the several states . . . is hereby declared to be illegal."[6] Such wording made it debatable whether Congress had intended labor unions to be covered.

The answer was not given until 1908 in the landmark decision, *Loewe v. Lawlor* (better known as the Danbury Hatters case). The United Hatters of America, having organized seventy of eighty-two firms in the industry, wanted to organize Loewe and Company, a nonunion employer. They sought to have their union recognized and to have only union members employed (a closed shop). When the company refused, the union struck, strikers were replaced, and operations were continued. Recognizing the strike failure, the United Hatters organized a nationwide boycott assisted by the American Federation of Labor and directed toward all retailers, wholesalers, and customers. The boycott was successful; the employer thereupon went to court and eventually appealed to the Supreme Court. The high court ruled that unions were covered under the Sherman Act, that the union owed the company $250,000 (treble damages), and that the membership was responsible for payment.[7]

Once the *Loewe* decision was publicized, organized labor concluded that it must seek changes in the act. An aggressive campaign led to the enactment of the Clayton Act of 1914. Included among its provisions were:

[The] labor of a human being is not a commodity or article of commerce. Nothing contained in the antitrust laws shall be construed to forbid the existence and operation of labor [unions] . . . nor shall such organizations . . . be held or construed to be illegal combinations or conspiracies in restraint of trade.

No restraining order or injunction shall be granted . . . in any case between an employer and employees . . . growing out of a dispute concerning terms or conditions of employment, unless necessary to prevent irreparable injury to property. . . .

No such restraining order . . . shall prohibit any person or persons . . . from ceasing to perform work . . . recommending, advising, or persuading others by peaceful means so to do, . . . peacefully persuading any person to work or abstain from working, . . . peacefully assembling in a lawful manner, and for lawful purposes.[8]

When Samuel Gompers, president of the AFL, read the provisions of the act, he proclaimed it U.S. labor's Magna Charta. Gompers' joy, however, was short-lived; a series of Supreme Court decisions in the 1920s left no doubt that the Clayton Act was not labor's Magna Charta. In fact, the Clayton Act hurt union growth and development more than it helped, because under the act employers could seek injunctions on their own, whereas only the U.S. district attorneys could seek injunctions under the Sherman Act.

The first major case occurred in 1921 and involved the printing press industry. The union had been successful in organizing all of the four major manufacturers of printing presses except Duplex Printing Press. While the three unionized companies operated under an eight-hour day and union wage scale, Duplex continued a ten-hour day and paid below the union scale. Failing to unionize Duplex, the union organized a strike, which was also unsuccessful. Because Duplex was operating at a lower cost than the other companies and posed an economic threat to them, the unions formed a boycott, refusing to install or handle Duplex products and warning users against operating Duplex equipment. The company sued for an injunction under the Clayton Act, and the Supreme Court ruled that unions were not exempt from antitrust legislation when they departed from normal and legitimate union activities. Therefore, the Clayton Act restricted injunctions only when a boycott involved an employer and its own employees. Since many of the boycott activities were conducted by sympathetic union members, not employees of Duplex, the use of the injunction was legal.[9]

Another Supreme Court decision in the same year defined "peaceful picketing" as a single representative at each employer entrance announcing that a strike was occurring and trying to peacefully persuade employees and others to support the strike.[10] With only one person on the picket line, the unions would obviously be unable to demonstrate their strength and unity in the strike.

With injunctions easier to obtain, a series of devastating Supreme Court decisions, absence of favorable labor legislation, use of anti-union tactics such as "goon squads," blackmail, and blacklisting, and the U.S. economy beginning a period of economic prosperity in the 1920, the labor movement entered a comparatively static period. This was a time of regrouping, self-analysis, and establishment of new strategies.

The Norris–La Guardia Act

In the early 1930s, with the beginning of the country's most severe economic depression, political pressure on Congress mounted, and there was general dissatisfaction with judicial restrictions in labor relations. In 1932 Congress passed the Norris–La Guardia Act (also called the Federal Anti-Injunction Act). Marking a change in philosophy in labor relations, the act allowed employees "full freedom of association, self-organization, and designation of representatives of (their) own choosing, negotiation of terms and conditions of . . . employment" and "freedom from employer interference, restraint, or coercion." Further, it recognized employees' right to freedom from employer interference in their efforts of "self-organization and other concerted activities for the purpose of collective bargaining or other mutual aid or protection."[11]

The act restricted the role of the federal courts in labor disputes. Foremost was the restriction of issuance of any injunction, temporary or permanent, in any case involving or growing out of a labor dispute,[12] except where the employer, in open courts and under cross-examination, could prove the following conditions:

1. Unlawful acts had been threatened or committed.
2. Substantial and irreparable injury to the employer's property would follow.
3. Greater injury would be inflicted upon the employer by denial of an injunction than upon the union by granting injunction.
4. Employer had no adequate remedy at law.
5. Public officers were unable or unwilling to furnish adequate protection.
6. The employer had made every effort to settle the dispute through collective bargaining (including mediation, voluntary arbitration, and so on) before going to court.

If and when an injunction was issued, it would stop only specific acts; thereby the general, all-encompassing injunctions that had become customary were prohibited. In addition, individuals held in contempt of court (usually labor leaders who violated a court injunction) would be allowed a trial by jury.

The Norris–La Guardia Act also declared that the yellow-dog contract was unenforceable in federal courts.[13] However, many companies continued the practice of discharging employees for union activities. This provision did allow union organizers more freedom in contacting employees about joining unions with less fear of a breach of contract violation, a tactic that had been used successfully against them.

With no administrative agency under the Norris–La Guardia Act, it was difficult to enforce the act's new policy on behalf of interested employees or unions. Yet two judicial decisions under the act indicated more positive interpretations for organized labor. In both cases, the companies were denied injunctions because of the existence of a labor dispute.[14] A dramatic demonstration of the court's change in viewpoint on labor disputes occurred when the Supreme Court ruled that labor disputes were not covered under the Sherman Act, even though a union had seized a plant, declared a sit-down strike, remained in possession of the plant for nearly a month, and caused over $200,000 worth of damage to the company.[15]

Another case involved a private work dispute in which two unions claimed the right to erect and dismantle machinery at an Anheuser Busch Plant in St. Louis. The union not assigned the work later struck and led a nationwide boycott of Anheuser Busch beer against the producer, who was essentially an innocent bystander in the labor dispute. The union's action was ruled as arising from a labor dispute and was therefore not subject to an injunction, damage suits or criminal proceedings.[16]

Historical Development of the National Labor Relations Act and Its Amendments

In addition to the Norris–La Guardia Act, 1932 witnessed a new president, Franklin Roosevelt, who was backed strongly by labor unions, and a new Congress receptive to labor legislation as a means of ending a long depression. One of the first acts of this new administration was to encourage Congress to pass the National Industrial Recovery Act—a law designed to stabilize economic activity by allowing businesses to form associations drawing up codes of fair competition to standardize marketing, pricing, financial, and other practices. Upon approval of the codes by the National Recovery Administration, firms could display the "Blue Eagle" symbol that supposedly signified compliance and identified firms from which customers should purchase their goods and services. Section 7 of the act required the codes to guarantee employees the right to unionize without employer interference, and a National Labor Board was later established to help settle disputes and to determine violations under Section 7.

Because the act did not require employers to deal with unions and the National Labor Board could not enforce its orders effectively, most employers chose to recognize and develop their own company unions. Prompted by the board's failure, increasing employer resistance, and growing strike activity, in 1934 Congress issued a joint resolution calling for the president to establish a National Labor Relations Board to investigate violations under Section 7 and to hold elections to determine whether the employees would choose a union to represent them.[17] This board, created like its predecessor by executive order of the president, had trouble enforcing its orders and determining employee organizational units for conducting elections. Then, in 1935, the Supreme Court ruled the codes of fair competition unconstitutional, invalidating the National Labor Relations Board.

Senator Robert Wagner, chairman of the National Labor Relations Board and an active participant in labor law matters, in 1935 steered through Congress a separate labor relations law—the Wagner Act or National Labor Relations Act (NLRA). It established that national policy encouraged collective bargaining, guaranteed certain employee rights, detailed specific employer unfair labor practices, and established by law the National Labor Relations Board to enforce its provisions. The board would adjudicate unfair labor practices and conduct representation elections (specific provisions are covered later in the chapter).

For the next two years, significant employer resistance to the act mounted because most employers believed it would be ruled unconstitutional like the National Industrial Recovery Act.[18] However, in 1937 the Supreme Court decided five labor relations cases—the most publicized, *NLRB v. Jones & Laughlin Steel Corp.* [301 U.S. 1(1937)]—and declared the Wagner Act constitutional.

With Supreme Court recognition of the Wagner Act and the improvement of economic conditions in the United States, unions experienced tremendous growth and power.[19] In fact, for the next ten years, union activities caused many to believe that the labor relations pendulum had swung too far toward unions.

Examples that precipitated much public antagonism were strikes over union representation rights between CIO and AFL unions, boycotts that hurt innocent bystanders, union walkouts over bargaining issues, refusal to negotiate in good faith with employers, and pressure on applicants to become members of unions before qualifying for employment.

As a reaction to organized labor's actions, in 1947 Congress amended the National Labor Relations Act by enacting the Taft-Hartley Act, or Labor Management Relations Act. Calling it a "slave labor act," labor groups immediately mounted a successful campaign to have President Truman veto the bill; however, Congress easily overrode Truman's veto. Regaining much balance in labor relations legislation, the act reorganized the NLRB and included union unfair labor practices covering such topics as union membership, bargaining requirements, boycotts by unions not involved in the dispute, and strikes over work assignments.

With the Taft-Hartley Act, unions lost their favorable legal position. Their memberships as a percentage of the labor force began to stabilize, then to decline steadily. (Reasons for the decline are explained in Chapters 2 and 4.)

In the late 1950s, a special senate committee headed by John McClellan vigorously pursued the abuses of power and corruption of union leaders, particularly those of the Teamsters and specifically of Dave Beck and James Hoffa.[20] Exposing shocking examples of corruption and abuses to the U.S. public, Congress reacted in 1959 by passing the Landrum-Griffin Act, also called the Labor-Management Reporting and Disclosure Act. Its first six titles pertain mostly to union internal affairs and government (covered in Chapter 4), and Title VII further amends the Taft-Hartley Act.

Since that time, several serious attempts have been made to further amend the NLRA.

1. In 1965 organized labor mounted a major campaign to amend Section 14(b), a provision which allows individual states to outlaw various forms of union security, such as union shops, in their states (see Chapter 11 for details).
2. Another effort, initially backed by the Nixon administration, was designed to place all transportation under the NLRA. Under its provisions, the president would have alternative courses of action available to stop national emergency strikes in the transportation industry. But when the Teamsters publicly announced their support for Nixon as president in 1972, the administration let its efforts for new legislation quietly die.
3. In 1975 Congress passed the so-called "common situs" picketing bill, which would allow construction unions to picket an entire worksite even though the labor dispute involved only one union and employer. President Ford had agreed with Labor Secretary John Dunlop and labor leaders that he would sign the bill; but under heavy pressure from business, he vetoed it—whereupon, John Dunlop resigned as secretary of labor.
4. Successful legislative attempts have extended the NLRA to the health care industry (see Chapter 17) and the postal service (see Chapter 15).

5. In 1978 an embittered battle for labor law reform was launched. The bill was designed to require representation elections within a month from the date the NLRB received the petition for an election. Also, it called for compensation for employees whose employer refused to bargain in good faith in initial negotiations and included double back pay for employees who were unfairly discharged by employers for union activities. Further, it authorized the withdrawal of federal government contracts from employers who continued to commit flagrant unfair labor practices. Strongly backed by the Carter administration and passed in the House by a strong majority, the bill met its death by a successful Senate filibuster.

The National Labor Relations Act: The Wagner Act of 1935 as Amended by the Taft-Hartley Act in 1947 and the Landrum-Griffin Act in 1959

The National Labor Relations Act is discussed primarily from a contemporary perspective. Less attention is given to indicating the origin of each specific provision to avoid unnecessary confusion.

Statement of Public Policy

The United States was in the midst of its most severe economic depression when the Wagner Act was passed. The Act established a new national labor relations policy of encouraging collective bargaining and gave some indication of the federal government's more active role in national economics. It recognized that employer denials of the employees' right to organize and employer refusal to accept collective bargaining had previously led to strikes and industrial conflicts. It also acknowledged that inequality of bargaining power between employees and employers affected the flow of commerce and aggravated recurring economic depressions by depressing wages and purchasing power and thereby prevented the stability of wages and working conditions. Further, it recognized that protection by law of the right of employees to organize and bargain collectively would promote the flow of commerce, restore equality of bargaining power, and encourage friendly adjustment of industrial disputes.

The Congress declared that the purpose of the new U.S. labor relations policy was

---

to eliminate the causes of certain substantial obstructions to the free flow of commerce and to mitigate and eliminate these obstructions when they have occurred by encouraging the practice and procedure of collective bargaining and by protecting the exercise by workers of full

freedom of association, self-organization, and designation of representatives of their own choosing, for the purpose of negotiating the terms and conditions of their employment or other mutual aid or protection.[21]

After twelve years of experience under the Wagner Act, Congress further defined national labor relations policy with the Taft-Hartley amendments. These acknowledged that industrial strife could be minimized if employees and labor unions, as well as employers, recognized one another's rights and declared that no party had the right to engage in activities or practices that jeopardized the national health or safety.

Rights of Employees

Under Section 7 of the NLRA, employees were assured certain rights: to form and organize their own labor organizations, to become members of labor unions or to refuse to join, to bargain collectively through representatives of their own choosing, and to engage in other concerted activities for the purpose of collective bargaining or other forms of mutual aid or protection, such as strikes, picketing, and boycotts.

However, these rights are not unlimited; they can be restricted. The right to strike can be limited by a strike's objective, its timing, and the conduct of the strikers. For example, if a strike's purpose is to achieve a contract provision forcing the employment of only union members, its purpose is illegal; therefore the strike is illegal. If a strike occurs when there is a no-strike provision in the contract, the timing of the strike is inappropriate, and all striking employees can be disciplined. Further, strikers do not have the right to threaten or engage in acts of violence. For example, neither sit-down strikes nor refusals to leave the plant are protected strike activities. Strikers also exceed their rights when they physically block persons from entering a struck plant or when threats of violence are made against workers not on strike. Picketing and boycott activities are likewise limited. (Limitations on these activities are further explained in Chapter 7.)

Collective Bargaining and Representation of Employees

The NLRA specifies important elements of collective bargaining. (Because representational procedures and elections are nearly always prerequisites to collective bargaining, they are explained in detail in Chapter 5.) Collective bargaining requires both the employer and the representative of the employees to meet at reasonable times and confer in good faith with respect to wages, hours, and other terms and conditions of employment. While the act does not compel either party to agree to a proposal from the other party or to make a concession, it does require the good faith negotiation of an agreement. If an agreement is reached, it must be reduced to writing and executed in good faith.

Other procedural requirements cover those times when either party may desire to change an existing contract. First, the party requesting a change, usually the union, must notify the other party in writing sixty days before the expiration date of the existing agreement of a desire to change it. Upon receipt of the request, the other party, usually management, must offer to meet and negotiate a new contract. Within thirty days after notifying the other party, the initiating party must notify the Federal Mediation and Conciliation Service of the existence of a dispute if no agreement has been reached on the proposed changes. Both parties are required to continue to negotiate without a strike or lockout until sixty days after the first notice or until the contract expires, whichever is later. Only when the contract expires and other procedural obligations have been fulfilled is the union allowed to strike.

Unfair Labor Practices

While unfair labor practices of employers were included in Section 8 of the Wagner Act of 1935 to protect employees from employer abuse, unfair labor practices of labor organizations were added in 1947 and 1959 for employer, employee, and union member protection.

Unfair Labor Practices: Employer First, the employer is forbidden to interfere with, restrain, or coerce employees in the exercise of the rights presented above. Violations include employer threats to fire workers if they join a union, threats to close the plant if the union is organized—especially when other plants owned by the employer are located in the same area—or questioning employees about their union activities. If such violation does occur, the employee or the union may file an unfair labor charge with the NLRB, which then initiates its enforcement procedure (covered later in the chapter). Employees are also protected in pursuing their joint working condition concerns even if they do not belong to a labor organization. [*8(a)(1)*]

The board at first was excessively restrictive in its rulings on employer expressions about unionism and ruled that most employer speeches to employees about unionism were unlawful interference with union activities. However, in 1947 restrictions were eased. Employers were given the right to explain their labor policies, present the advantages and disadvantages of unions, and communicate orally and in writing their arguments and opinions as long as they contained "no threats of reprisal or force or no promise of benefits."[22] (Current application and interpretation of this provision as it pertains to union election campaigns will be covered in Chapter 5.)

Attempting to dominate, interfering with the formation of, and financing and supporting a labor union are all prohibited employer activities. For instance, the existence of a *company union*, one which receives financial help from the company, is illegal. Nor are companies allowed to pressure employees into joining a particular union, to take an active part in organizing a union, to promote one union over a rival union during a representation election campaign, or to otherwise engage in "sweetheart" arrangements with union officials. [*8(a)(2)*]

Employer discrimination against employees in terms of hiring, tenure of employment, or terms and conditions of employment for the purpose of encouraging or discouraging union membership constitutes an unfair labor practice. However, if the labor agreement requires union membership as a condition of employment and the employee does not pay the required union initiation fees and membership dues in accordance with the agreement, the employee may be discharged (see Chapter 11). [*8(a)3)*]

Another unfair labor practice pertains to discharge of or discrimination against an employee because he or she had filed charges or given testimony in an NLRB investigation, hearing, or court case under the act. If employees are refused resinstatement, demoted, or laid off because they have filed charges with the NLRB or testified at NLRB hearings, their employers have committed unfair labor practices. [*8(a)(4)*]

A final employer unfair labor practice covers an employer's refusal to bargain in good faith about wages, hours, and terms and conditions of employment with the representative chosen by the employees. Employer obligations include the duty to supply information, to refrain from unilateral action, and to negotiate with employees after purchasing a unionized plant. (For a more thorough discussion, see Chapter 6.) Refusing to meet the union for purposes of negotiation, refusing to provide cost data concerning an insurance plan, announcing a wage increase without consulting the union, and subcontracting work normally performed by bargaining unit employees without notifying the union that represents the affected employees and without giving the union an opportunity to bargain over the change in the conditions of employment are prohibited practices. [*8(a)(5)*]

Unfair Labor Practices: Labor Union Unfair labor practices committed by unions were included in both major amendments in 1947 (Section 8 [b]) and 1959. The first forbids a union or its agents to restrain or coerce employees in the exercise of their rights guaranteed under the act. Examples include mass picketing that prevents entrance to the plant by nonstriking employees, threats to employees for not supporting the union, refusal to process a grievance because the employee has criticized the union officers, and refusal to refer an employee to a job based on such considerations as race or lack of union activities. [*8(b)(1)*]

A second union unfair labor practice pertains to actions that cause an employer to discriminate against an employee with regard to wages, hours, and conditions of employment or for the purpose of encouraging or discouraging union membership. For example, the company may be forced to assign better jobs to union members. Or, when two unions compete to represent the same workers, the company may side with the less aggressive union by assigning better jobs to its members. Such prohibited practices include causing an employer to discharge employees who circulate a petition challenging a union practice or who make speeches against a contract proposal. [*8(b)(2)*]

A third provision imposes on unions the same duty as employers to bargain in good faith. Refusing to negotiate with the employer's attorney, refusing to process a grievance of a bargaining unit employee, and striking a company to compel it to leave a multi-employer bargaining unit are some activities illegal under the amended act. [*8(b)(3)*]

The fourth unfair labor practice includes four prohibited activities. The union may not force, threaten, require, or induce

- Any employer or self-employed person into joining a union or entering into a *hot-cargo agreement* (signed agreement stating that union members will not be required to handle "hot cargo"—goods made by nonunion labor and workers at a struck plant except in the garment industry).
- Any person from using, selling, handling, and transporting goods of a producer, processor, or manufacturer that is directly involved in a labor dispute (secondary boycott—covered in more detail in Chapter 7).
- Any employer to recognize or bargain with a particular labor organization if another labor organization has already been certified by the NLRB.
- Any employer to assign certain work to employees in a particular labor union, trade, or craft rather than another. [*8(b)(4)*]

Unions are prohibited from charging excessive or discriminatory membership fees. Any illegal discrepancy would be investigated by the NLRB in accordance with the practices and customs of other unions in the particular industry and wages paid to the affected employees. For example, if a union raises its initiation fee from $75.00 to $250.00, an amount equal to four weeks' pay, when other unions charge only $12.50, the practice would be declared illegal. Also prohibited is charging black or female employees higher fees so as to discourage their membership. Labor unions are also forbidden to cause or attempt to cause an employer to pay for services that are not performed or not to be performed; this practice, known as *featherbedding*, is discussed further in Chapter 12. [*8(b(5)*] [*8(b)(6)*]

Enforcement of the Act

National Labor Relations Board Because the rights of employees provided by the act are not self-enforcing and guaranteeing the rights through the court system would be cumbersome and time-consuming, the NLRB—an independent federal agency—was established to administer and enforce them. The NLRB includes a five-member Board that is recommended by the president and confirmed by the Senate; the general counsel; fifty regional and field offices; and staff at each office. While the general counsel has final authority to investigate and issue complaints and general supervisory responsibilities over the regional and field offices, the Board establishes policy and serves as the judge in final appeals within the NLRB structure. In other words, the general counsel's role is like that of a prosecutor, and the Board's more like that of a judge.

The agency has two major functions: (a) supervising and conducting representation elections (covered in Chapter 5) and (b) adjudicating employer and union unfair labor practices. Contrary to some beliefs, the NLRB processes are set in motion *only* when requested in writing and filed with the proper NLRB office. Such requests are called petitions in the case of elections and charges in the case of unfair labor practices.

While the NLRB has authority to enforce the act in all cases involving interstate commerce, it has exercised its discretion and established jurisdictional standards for those cases it will accept and it believes have a substantial effect on commerce. (See the appendix to the chapter, NLRB's Jurisdiction Standards.) For example, a gas station, hotel, retail store, or apartment complex must gross $500,000 in annual volume before the NLRB will accept its petition or charge, whereas gross annual receipts of private colleges and universities must reach $1 million.

NLRB Procedure Regarding Unfair Labor Practices The procedure for an unfair labor practice complaint (see Exhibit 3.1) starts when an employee, employer, labor union, or individual files a charge with an NLRB office. Then the party that is charged is notified that an investigation of the alleged violation will be conducted. The charge is then investigated by an NLRB representative from a nearby regional or field office. Interviews are conducted, documents studied, and other necessary steps taken. At each step the charge may be settled or withdrawn, or the NLRB may dismiss the case due to lack of evidence. (In cases of an unlawful boycott or strike, the NLRB may request a temporary restraining order.) If the investigation confirms the charge, the regional director of the NLRB issues a complaint and provides notice of a hearing. The charged party must then respond in ten days to the complaint.

In many cases, the parties themselves may agree to a resolution before the investigation, and no further steps are needed. However, if no settlement is reached, an unfair labor practice hearing is conducted before an administrative law judge, who makes findings and recommendations to the Board based on the record of the hearing. All parties are authorized to appeal the administrative law judge's decision directly to the Board. The Board considers the information provided and data collected, and if it believes an unfair labor practice has occurred, an order to cease and desist such practices and to take appropriate affirmative action is issued. The decision comes from the Board; parties might appeal the decision, as shown in Exhibit 3.1.

Cease and desist orders simply direct the violators to stop whatever activities were deemed unfair labor practices. The Board exercises some discretion in determining *appropriate affirmative action*, and typical orders to employers include:

Exhibit 3.1 Basic Procedures in Cases Involving Charges of Unfair Labor Practices

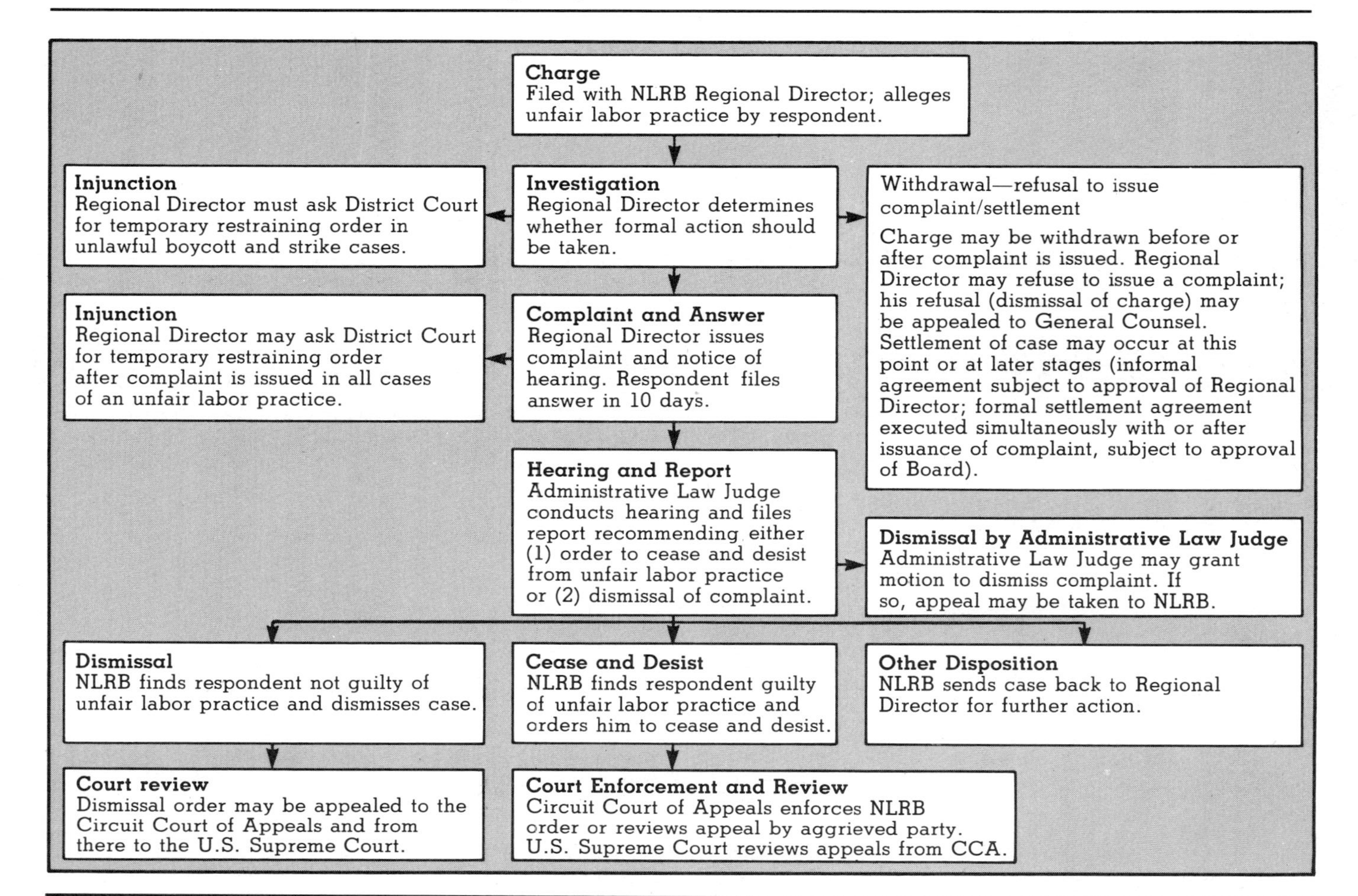

Charge
Filed with NLRB Regional Director; alleges unfair labor practice by respondent.
Injunction
Regional Director must ask District Court for temporary restraining order in unlawful boycott and strike cases.
Investigation
Regional Director determines whether formal action should be taken.
Withdrawal—refusal to issue complaint/settlement
Charge may be withdrawn before or after complaint is issued. Regional Director may refuse to issue a complaint; his refusal (dismissal of charge) may be appealed to General Counsel. Settlement of case may occur at this point or at later stages (informal agreement subject to approval of Regional Director; formal settlement agreement executed simultaneously with or after issuance of complaint, subject to approval of Board).
Injunction
Regional Director may ask District Court for temporary restraining order after complaint is issued in all cases of an unfair labor practice.
Complaint and Answer
Regional Director issues complaint and notice of hearing. Respondent files answer in 10 days.
Hearing and Report
Administrative Law Judge conducts hearing and files report recommending either (1) order to cease and desist from unfair labor practice or (2) dismissal of complaint.
Dismissal by Administrative Law Judge
Administrative Law Judge may grant motion to dismiss complaint. If so, appeal may be taken to NLRB.
Dismissal
NLRB finds respondent not guilty of unfair labor practice and dismisses case.
Cease and Desist
NLRB finds respondent guilty of unfair labor practice and orders him to cease and desist.
Other Disposition
NLRB sends case back to Regional Director for further action.
Court review
Dismissal order may be appealed to the Circuit Court of Appeals and from there to the U.S. Supreme Court.
Court Enforcement and Review
Circuit Court of Appeals enforces NLRB order or reviews appeal by aggrieved party. U.S. Supreme Court reviews appeals from CCA.

Sources: Management & Audit Branch, Division of Administration, NLRB, revised November 1975.

- Disestablish an employer-dominated company union.
- Offer employees immediate and full reinstatement to their former positions, and pay them back their wages plus interest.
- Upon request, bargain collectively with the exclusive bargaining representative of the employees.

Orders to unions include:

- Refund excessive or illegally collected dues plus interest.
- Upon request, bargain collectively in good faith with the prescribed employer.

In the fiscal year 1980, the NLRB handled 42,047 unfair labor practice cases. As shown in Table 3.1, 36.4 percent or 15,301 were dismissed, 31.9 percent were withdrawn, 27.5 percent were resolved by either informal or formal agreement, and 3.1 percent were decided by the Board or courts. Table 3.2 shows the median days taken to process a NLRB charge. For example, an average of

Table 3.1 Disposition of Unfair Labor Practice Cases, Fiscal Year 1980

	Number	Percentage
Total Number of Cases	42,047	100
Dismissals	15,301	36.4
Withdrawals	13,424	31.9
Agreement—Informal	11,357	27.0
Agreement—Formal	174	0.5
Compliance with Board or Court Decision	1,318	3.1

Source: *45th Annual Report of the National Labor Relations Board*, Washington, D.C.: U.S. Government Printing Office, 1980, pp. 256–257.

Table 3.2 Median Days Elapsed in NLRB's Case Processing Stages, Fiscal Year 1980

	Number of Days
Filing of Charge to Informal Disposition before Complaint	40
Filing of Charge to Complaint Issuance	46
Complaint to Close of ALJ Hearing	155
Close of Hearing to ALJ Decision	158
ALJ Decision to Board Decision	133
Filing of Charge to Board Decision	484

Source: Human Resources Division, General Accounting Office, *Concerns Regarding Impact of Employee Charges against Employers for Unfair Labor Practices*, Washington, D.C.: U.S. Government Printing Office, 1982, p. 44.

46 days expire from the filing of the charge to the issuance of a complaint. However, the median amount of time from filing of a charge to a Board decision is 484 days. It is important to note that about 90 percent of unfair labor disputes are settled by informal means in about 40 days.

The Role of the Judiciary The courts under the enforcement provisions of the act serve two major purposes: (a) provide injunctive relief where appropriate and (b) review appealed decisions and orders of the NLRB. As part of the enforcement procedure, the act authorizes the NLRB to petition for an injunction in connection with unfair labor practices where either an employer or a union fails to comply with a Board order. It also provides that any person aggrieved by a Board order may appeal directly to an appropriate court of appeals for a review. Upon reviewing the order, the court of appeals may enforce the order, return it for reconsideration, alter it, or set it aside. The final appeal, of course, is to the U.S. Supreme Court, which may be asked to review a decision, especially where several courts of appeal have differed in their interpretations of the law.

Assessment of the Administration of the NLRB

Overall, the administration of the NLRB, the general counsel, and the regional offices have generally been considered an administrative success. Under delegated authority from the Board and supervision of the general counsel, the regional offices have handled a large number of elections efficiently and economically and have performed their prosecuting functions promptly.[23] In fiscal 1980, the forty-fifth year of the NLRB, the agency closed 55,587 cases, of which 42,047 were unfair labor practices and 13,540 were union representation cases. More than $32.4 million was recovered for 10,033 workers who suffered monetary losses as a result of unfair labor practices, and 8,198 representation elections among 458,114 employee voters were conducted. Since 1935, over 30 million ballots have been cast in over 300,000 representation elections.[24]

Another measure of the success of the NLRB has been its record with the courts. Even though the Supreme Court (as well as the NLRB) has been accused by some of having a pro-union bias, the bottom line for determining the NLRB's compliance with its constitutional powers is the frequency with which its decisions have been upheld or overturned. In this regard, the results are fairly clear; the NLRB has a most supportive record with the high court. In fact, since 1957, about three-fourths of the NLRB cases that have been appealed to the Supreme Court have been upheld.[25]

While the Board has continually faced new problems, such as union officers' failure to carry out the duty of representing their members fairly, deferral to arbitration of certain statutory rights, and preplanned and repetitive violations of the act, the subject that has caused the most criticism has been the inadequacy of the Board's remedial powers. At present, it has no constitutional penal powers; it cannot award damages; it cannot impose severe penalties even when the violations are flagrant and repetitive. For individuals who have been discriminatorily discharged and deprived of employment for improper reasons, reinstatement with back pay plus interest rarely covers the real costs that accompany the period of unemployment.[26]

The Board's record of obtaining reinstatement for unfairly discharged employees has not been impressive either. For example, two studies conducted in different NLRB regions (New England[27] and Texas[28]) revealed distressing results of the NLRB orders for reinstatement. In both studies, not only were less than a majority placed back on the job, but a surprisingly high percentage of those reinstated left their jobs after reinstatement.

In the Texas study, of 217 individuals who had been discriminated against for union activities, 59 percent or 129 refused reinstatement, mostly because they feared company reprisals. Of the remaining 88, 57 were reinstated immediately and 31 others were placed on preferential hiring lists (15 were finally hired). One year after reinstatement, 86.9 percent had left the company, and after eight years, 100 percent had left. The reasons given by 65 percent for leaving was unfair company treatment, while the companies stated that the employees left for unknown reasons in 62.5 percent of these cases.[29]

Nonpartisan analysts have agreed that the Board's remedies for serious unfair labor practices regarding refusal to bargain in good faith in the initial contract have been woefully deficient. Several attempts have been made to broaden the NLRB's authority, but none have succeeded thus far.[30] For example, when the NLRB attempted to assert itself by imposing a checkoff provision on an employer who had not bargained in good faith[31] and requiring the company to compensate its employees for monetary losses incurred as a result of the company's unlawful refusal to bargain with the certified union, the courts overruled the NLRB, stating that it had gone beyond its statutory authority.[32]

Even though these data demonstrate pessimistic findings, it is highly debatable whether stricter, harsher, and costlier remedies would reduce the number of unfair labor practice charges filed. Although several unions, former NLRB members, and at least one circuit court of appeals have endorsed financial reparations to employees in specific refusal to bargain cases, the intent of the act is not to reduce the intake of cases but to promote fair collective bargaining whereby management officials and union representatives are free to jointly determine their particular working conditions.[33] Some have suggested that the Board should press more vigorously to fully realize its present enforcement authority in the courts.

In the case of one employer, J. P. Stevens, who has been cited for many unfair labor practices, the Board devised several extraordinary remedies. They included: posting notices of violations in all 43 plants, mailing these notices to all employees in these plants, providing reasonable access to plant bulletin boards, giving lists of employees in all plants to the union, and providing payment to the NLRB of costs and expenses, counsel fees, and salaries in a civil contempt proceeding.[34] Using this approach in more cases, however, would require more resources for the NLRB since they have a considerable backlog of work. While orders of the NLRB are not self-enforcing, the Board applies to the appropriate court of appeals for enforcement of its order. If the NLRB order is enforced by the court, it becomes a lawful decree of that court, requiring compliance and backed with civil contempt sanctions. If court-enforced orders are violated, the violator can be held in contempt of court and can be subject to more serious penalties.[35] Not to be overlooked is the fact that the members of the NLRB are presidential appointees. This process has a substantial influence on the philosophy and direction of the NLRB and its decisions.

"Interpretations of the facts and law governing union-management relations is . . . dependent in part on the make-up of the Board."[36]

Guy Farmer, former NLRB chairman explains the political influence in his assessment:

"Any decision of the NLRB over the last few years on a significant issue can hardly be considered as etched in stone. Of course, that has always been true to a degree because of the essentially political nature of the Board and the ability of a new administration to change decisions by appointing new members. There is one new member up for appointment every year.

There is, of course, a need for stability and predictability in Board decisions, but the system makes that goal unattainable. We must, therefore, look to the courts and especially to the Supreme Court to supply the consistency that we all desire, and by and large that is what has happened. The great decisions that have shaped the law have come not from the Board and not from the Courts of Appeal, but from the Supreme Court."[37]

Railway Labor Act

The Railway Labor Act, although it applied initially to the railway industry, was actually the first comprehensive labor relations law. Once considered the model labor relations law and hailed as highly successful,[38] the Railway Labor Act has been subjected in recent times to severe criticism. Like other labor laws, the Railway Labor Act did not develop overnight; it resulted from years of union activity and attempts at passing laws accommodating railroad labor relations.[39] The Railway Labor Act relies almost entirely on collective bargaining for settling labor disputes but it has established mandatory mediation by the National Mediation Board (NMB). If mediation fails, the NMB must recommend arbitration. To assist in dispute resolution, the president has authority to appoint an emergency board composed of neutrals to investigate railroad labor disputes and recommend procedures and terms for agreement. This approach was designed to arouse public opinion, which would pressure the parties to arrive at terms of agreement on their own.[40] (More detailed discussion of dispute resolution under the Railway Labor Act can be found in Chapter 7.)

Although the Railway Labor Act has been amended several times,[41] its purposes remain largely the same:

- To avoid interruptions of commerce.
- To forbid any limitation on employees' rights to organize and join labor unions.
- To provide complete independence for both parties in carrying out purposes of the act.
- To provide prompt and orderly settlement of disputes over pay, rules, and working conditions.
- To provide prompt and orderly settlement of disputes over grievances and contract interpretation.[42]

Major tests for the Railway Labor Act came in 1930 and 1937. The first test involved the Brotherhood of Railway Clerks, which presented the Texas and New Orleans Railway with a set of proposed wage increases. In response, the railroad company discharged identified union members and created its own company union. The Brotherhood sought an injunction to restrain the company from interfering with employees' rights granted under the act, and the company responded by declaring that the act should be held unconstitutional in accordance with the First and Fifth Amendments.[43] In 1930 the Supreme Court declared that the Railway Labor Act was constitutional and that the company had no right to interfere with the employees' rights to select their bargaining representative.[44]

The 1937 test came after the Virginia Railway Company had refused to deal with System Federation Number 40, a labor union certified by the mediation board, and continued to deal only with the previously organized company union. The Supreme Court ruled that the purpose of the act was "aimed at securing settlement of labor disputes by inducing collective bargaining with the true representative of the employees and by preventing such bargaining with any who do not represent them."[45] Thus, these two Supreme Court decisions not only upheld the constitutionality of the Railway Labor Act but declared that employers must negotiate with the appropriately certified union and could not interfere with the employees' rights to organize and join unions.

Amendments

As indicated above, the Railroad Labor Act has been amended several times to correct deficiencies or omissions. The first major amendment, occurring in 1934, provided assistance to unions by barring employers from attempting to influence employees in selecting their bargaining representatives. Further, employers were directed to bargain collectively with certified labor representatives, and company-dominated unions and yellow-dog contracts were forbidden.

The 1934 amendment established the National Railroad Adjustment Board, a bipartisan group of eighteen union and eighteen management representatives, to assist in resolving grievances and interpreting provisions of the labor agreements. Where the board could not agree to a settlement, the amendment provided that the grievance be settled by an arbitrator selected by the parties. A three-member National Mediation Board was empowered to conduct representation elections in addition to its role in resolving conflicts over negotiating *new* labor agreements. Two years later, the act was amended again, and coverage was extended to a new and developing industry—air transportation—although the airlines were allowed to continue and maintain their local system boards for grievance resolution.[46]

Administrative Agencies

Two very important administrative agencies under the Railway Labor Act are (a) the National Mediation Board (NMB) and (b) the National Railroad Adjustment Board (NRAB).

The National Mediation Board The National Mediation Board, composed of three presidential appointees with terms of three years, is responsible for representation elections and mediation activities. Representation elections are conducted by the NMB to determine whether the majority of employees want to be represented by a union, and if so, the election will identify the particular union. Its mediation activities involve the reconciliation of differences in negotiating *new* agreements with reference to wages, hours, and working conditions and differences over interpretation of provisions in the agreement. When mediation fails, the mediation board must recommend voluntary arbitration in hopes that an agreement can be reached.

The National Railroad Adjustment Board The National Railroad Adjustment Board, comprised of an equal number of company and union representatives, was created in 1934 to hear disputes growing out of grievances and to interpret provisions in the labor agreements concerning pay, hours, and working conditions.[47] If the NRAB is unable to obtain agreement, the disputes are referred to arbitration.

Assessment of the Railway Labor Act

Faced with such problems as changing markets for freight transportation, severe competition, government regulation, and public interest in uninterrupted railroad service, labor relations in the railway industry are unique. Complicating the situation further are the chronic financial instability of the numerous independent railroads, the presence of strong, competing craft unions, and tradition-bound work rules. These factors affect labor relations in the following ways: 1.) Because the public depends on railroad transportation for many essential goods, there has been much effort to avoid strikes (five interventions by Congress). 2.) With the "fractionated" craft unions (20 or more different unions), the labor relations process takes much time and creates many opportunities for disputes. 3.) The tradition-bound work rules of the operating crafts strictly control not only how a particular job will be performed, but also which craft will be assigned the job. These work rules postpone the introduction of new technology and magnify the problems of a declining industry.[48] Any assessment of the Railway Labor Act must be kept in proper perspective. There are over 7,000 labor agreements in the railroad and airline industries, and about 1,000 railroad and 200 airline agreements (mostly local) are involved in negotiations during any given year.[49] Further, any measure of its effectiveness must be made with reference to the act's objectives—to promote free collective bargaining and protect the public from interrupted flows of commerce.[50]

Regarding negotiations, mediation has been the most important method of intervention under the act; however, very few nationwide railroad wage cases have been settled by mediation since 1936. Its greatest success has been in settling minor controversies after the major issues have been resolved. This does not mean that mediation is unimportant—minor disputes left unresolved could easily lead to major strikes in future negotiations.

One problem continually facing the NMB is that the parties involved often do not genuinely attempt to settle the issues on their own. Perhaps the mere presence of a special agency established solely to serve at no additional cost and assist in resolving disputes encourages its overuse. On the other hand, disputants have been accused of using it as a means of preparing for the emergency board intervention instead of actually negotiating with the other party.

Between 1926 and 1934, the act was highly effective: only two minor strikes occurred; only ten emergency boards were needed. And from 1934 until 1941 only one dispute was presented to an emergency board. During this time the Railway Labor Act was proclaimed the "model law," but then the case results began to change. By 1970, 176 cases (almost 5 per year) were taken to emergency boards. Not only were emergency boards quite common, but the procedures severely inhibited collective bargaining, and recommendations of the boards at critical times were handled with political expediency.[52]

With increasing support from the federal government for the railway industry, decline in employment, changing technology, and less than optimistic projections for the railroad carriers, the period from 1971 to 1976 brought faint evidence that the administration of the Railway Labor Act and union-management relationships under the act had improved. Only nine emergency boards were appointed during this time (well below the long-term average). The low number is deceptive and prematurely optimistic, however, because Congress became heavily involved in resolving labor disputes in the railroad industry by enacting ad hoc legislation.[52]

The Railway Labor Act has been frequently criticized because the parties that seek its help fail to use voluntary arbitration. Under the act, the NMB must request that the parties arbitrate their disputes if mediation should fail. However, because either may refuse this request without penalty, a number of major disputes have been referred to the emergency boards rather than voluntarily arbitrated.[53]

Actual data, however, may alleviate these criticisms. Parties in conflict have actually accepted voluntary interest arbitration 350 times between 1935 and 1975, involving 60 different labor unions, 152 railroad companies, and 26 airlines. (Pan American World Airways alone has been involved in 30 such arbitration cases.) Thus, while not widely publicized, voluntary interest arbitration has played a far more important role in maintaining industrial peace between rail and air carriers and the unions representing employees than is generally realized. While its importance should not be overstated, neither should the extent of its use go unrecognized.[54]

The operations of the NRAB and other special boards have not been very successful. Since 1934, over 70,000 cases have been filed with the board.[55] By the end of 1975, there were over 21,000 grievances pending before it, special adjustment boards, and public law boards. Many of these possessed little merit, and most neutral observers have concluded that the problem with such a high number of grievances cannot be alleviated until both parties are forced to pay for their own arbitration costs—the practice in all other industries.[56] While these procedures cost the unions and companies only the salaries and fees of their own representatives, taxpayers' support of the NRAB and its referees amounts to over $900,000 per year.[57]

Promising Developments

Several events and developments that have occurred recently provide the basis for some optimism:

1. The most recent national railroad agreements have included a fixed term, a no-strike clause, and common expiration dates. These changes have moved collective bargaining closer to the pattern common in other industries and in effect have reduced the opportunities for conflict.
2. Recent negotiations have also been characterized by union-management cooperation, which has resulted in fewer conflicts and outside interventions.
3. Emergency board procedures have been drastically improved, and excessive ritualism and legalism so prevalent in the 1960s have been reduced.
4. Encouraging progress has been made on some long-standing manning and work-rule issues, such as the fireman on diesel trains, combined road and yard service, and interdivisional runs.
5. New leadership has had a positive influence on both management and unions, and neutrals and governmental officials have provided capable assistance in the bargaining and dispute resolution processes.

Critical issues remain to be resolved: work rules in some agreements that are more restrictive than others, intercraft wage structure problems, crew size, and others.[58] But there is still reason to be optimistic if the recent trend can be sustained. As one authority has said:

> **No labor law can ensure peaceful and constructive labor relations. Although specific amendments to the Railway Labor Act may be desirable—notably, in connection with representational questions—we should be careful about casting into oblivion a law that both parties, on balance, seemingly want to retain.[59]**

Other Laws That Affect Labor Relations

Other statutes and executive orders, more narrow in scope, influence labor relations either directly or indirectly. The following section only highlights their major provisions; however, practitioners find that detailed knowledge of them is essential to most business operations. (Related legislation is summarized below; its specific implications for labor relations activities and unions are discussed in Chapters 11 and 12.)

Employment Discrimination Laws and Executive Orders

The *Equal Employment Opportunity Act of 1972*, which amended Title VII of the Civil Rights Act of 1964, prohibits any form of employment discrimination by companies, labor unions, and employment agencies on the basis of race, color, religion, sex, or national origin. Creating the Equal Employment Opportunity Commission, the act provides an enforcement procedure that includes investigations, attempts at conciliation, and suits filed on behalf of the complainant.

The *Age Discrimination in Employment Act of 1967*, as amended in 1978, prohibits employment discrimination against those who are between the ages of forty and seventy, forbids forced retirement based on age before age seventy, permits compulsory retirement for executives who are entitled to pensions of $27,000 per year or more, and authorizes jury trials in covered cases.[60]

Executive Order 11246, as amended by Executive Order 11375, prohibits employment discrimination in the federal government and by federal government contractors and subcontractors receiving $50,000 or more. Those having contracts of $50,000 or more and employing 50 people or more are required to establish affirmative action plans that prescribe specific goals and procedures for increasing the percentage of minority employees. Firms that fail to comply could lose part or all of their contracts.[61]

The *Vocational Rehabilitation Act of 1973* (Section 503) requires holders of federal government contracts in excess of $2,500 to take affirmative action to employ and advance in employment qualified physically and mentally handicapped individuals. Further, if any handicapped individual believes that any federal contractor has failed to comply with the act or refuses to do so, such individual may file a complaint with the Department of Labor, which will investigate the complaint and take such action as the facts and circumstances warrant. In addition, Section 504 extends coverage to organizations receiving federal financial assistance and is enforced by the Department of Health and Human Services.[62]

Other Labor Relations-Related Laws

The Military Selective Service Act of 1967 requires employers to restore veterans (those whose total military service time does not exceed four years) to the positions they held before entering the armed services or to similar positions of like seniority, status, and pay.

Also, the *Vietnam Era Veteran Readjustment Assistance Act* requires employers with governmental contracts of $10,000 or more to take affirmative action to employ and advance disabled veterans and qualified veterans of the Vietnam War.

The *Social Security Act of 1935*, as amended, established two national systems of social security for protection against loss of income due to unemployment, old age, disability, and death: (1) retirement, survivors and disability insurance, and health insurance for persons over 65, and (2) unemployment insurance, which operates under a state-administered, federal-state plan whose operating costs are paid by the federal government.[63]

Other rather important laws include the Wage Laws and Employee Retirement and Income Security Act of 1974 (covered in Chapter 13), the Occupational Safety and Health Act (covered in Chapter 12), and the various state laws and local ordinances which pertain to public sector labor relations, and equal employment opportunity.

Summary and Implications

Summary

This chapter has included the major provisions of federal labor relations laws in the United States. The knowledge and understanding of these legal influences are imperative for the full appreciation of the remaining chapters in this book, because nearly all issues in labor relations are either directly or indirectly influenced by labor relations law.

While many think of law in terms of statutes passed by the U.S. Congress or various state legislatures, labor relations and other types of law proceed not only from statutes but also from the U.S. Constitution, judicial decisions, and administrative decisions of government agencies. Similar laws and decisions develop at the state and local government levels.

Developing the legal influences historically, this chapter began with the early struggles of labor unions to exist as they faced unsympathetic judiciary and lack of any permissive legislation. Several hurdles included the criminal conspiracy and civil conspiracy doctrines as well as the breach of contract rulings. Then the Sherman Act, passed primarily to control business monopolies, was applied to labor unions also. With support of labor, the Sherman Act was amended by the Clayton Act; however, this act also proved unfavorable to unions.

While the 1920s did bring passage of the Railway Labor Act, little legislative action occurred in other sectors. However, the 1930s, with the country's most severe economic depression, brought about major changes. The enactment of the Norris–La Guardia Act changed the public policy toward labor relations. Not only did it recognize employees' rights to various freedoms, such as freedom of association and self-organization, it also restricted the role of the federal courts in labor disputes.

Recognizing several deficiencies in the Norris–La Guardia Act, Congress passed the National Labor Relations Act in 1935. This act dealt with employer unfair labor practices, established an administrative agency—the NLRB—and guaranteed a number of employee rights, such as the right to form and join unions and to participate in concerted actions. Then, in 1947 and again in 1959, Congress amended the National Labor Relations Act, with passage of the Taft-Hartley and the Landrum-Griffin Act, respectively. The 1947 amendments added union unfair labor practices and restrictions on union security clauses, and the 1959 act added regulations of government and internal operations of unions and amended strike, picketing, and boycott activities.

Starting in 1863, union activity in the railroad industry played a key role in the legislative arena. The Railway Labor Act of 1926, whose major purpose is to provide for stable and effective labor relations without major interruptions in commerce, established procedures for resolving labor disputes and created the National Mediation Board and National Railroad Adjustment Board to accomplish the act's purposes. While the assessment may seem less than optimistic, several recent developments that give some evidence of success have been recognized: acceptance of negotiations and responsibilities by the parties, recent no-strike clauses, improved employer-union cooperation on important issues, new leadership in both unions and management, and improved emergency board procedures.

The final section related to other laws that affect labor relations. While some of these laws affect labor relations more than others, each is important to those organizations and/or unions which it covers.

Implications

This chapter explained the basic content of the National Labor Relations Act, as amended, which has established the legal framework for labor relations in the United States for nearly half a century. Like most laws, it has deficiencies, such as the inadequacy of the remedy for many situations and the inordinate delay in securing a remedy in contested cases. As explained in the chapter, one of the purposes of the NLRA was to protect employees from employer unfair labor practices, such as discrimination against employees who are encouraging union membership or attempting to form a union. In fact, 58.6 percent or over 18,000 charges filed against employers in fiscal year 1980 alleged such discrimination. The General Accounting Office studied a sample of 400 of these cases and found the following:

- 57 percent of the complainants were fired during union organizing campaigns.
- Employees discharged were out of work for an average of 20.2 weeks before reinstatement or finding new employment.
- Most employees who had been reinstated were no longer working for their former employers.
- The firings made it difficult for the employee to find new employment.
- Most employees revealed that their financial situation had worsened as a result of their discharge.
- The firings had a chilling effect on the employees' selection of a union to represent their interests.
- Unions were less successful in organizing when employers committed unfair labor practices.[64]

The NLRB has authority to require the employer to reinstate the discharged employee if an unfair labor practice has been committed by the employer. Cases take so long to process, however, that the requirement is rarely effective. NLRB officials suggest that stronger penalties be authorized, such as requiring double backpay to unfairly discharged employees, or denial of federal government contracts to flagrant violators. Another suggestion is the immediate reinstatement of employees after a formal complaint of an unfair labor practice has been issued against the employer. These suggestions would deter employers from committing unfair labor practices by increasing the costs of such actions and would relieve the discharged employees of some of their burdens.[65]

Another possibility is the creation of a specialized labor judiciary or the appointment of an adequate number of federal district judges who specialize in labor law. These judges would be empowered to enforce the NLRA by issuing cease-and-desist orders, ordering reinstatement with backpay, and issuing injunctions as well. This alternative would eliminate the delays at the Circuit Court of Appeals level (which can take as much as one year) and would allow greater flexibility in the adjudication of the NLRA.[66]

As noted in the chapter, over ninety percent of the cases are informally resolved in about forty days; however, the time between the issuance of formal complaints and decisions of the administrative law judges (ALJ) has steadily increased. One reason for this increase is the lack of a sufficient number of ALJs for the increasing number of cases. For example, between 1974 and 1981, the number of cases scheduled for hearing before ALJs increased eighty-five percent and the number of ALJs increased only twenty percent. The imbalance is further complicated by budget cuts at the federal level, inability to offer competitive salaries to qualified individuals, and a fairly constant number of decisions rendered by ALJs averaging twelve per year. Suggestions on improving the process include giving the ALJs discretion to issue oral decisions in clear-cut cases, hiring recent law school graduates to assist ALJs in their work, locating ALJs closer to their work to avoid unnecessary travel, and permitting ALJs to become involved in the cases earlier.[67]

One researcher who investigated the effectiveness of the remedial power under the NLRA concluded:

It is sad that guaranteed rights cannot truly be guaranteed. It may be doubtful that such a condition could ever exist. But one fact looms large for us all, whether union member or company executive or observing American. When one suffers from injustice, so do we all.[68]

Discussion Questions

1. How have the major labor relations laws helped or hindered the development of unions?
2. How were "yellow-dog" contracts used against union organizers? How were they used to slow union growth?
3. Why did the 1914 Clayton Act, called by AFL president Samuel Gompers U.S. Labor's Magna Charta, prove to be less than a benefit to unions?
4. What was missing in the Norris–La Guardia Act (regarding administration of the law) that was present in the National Labor Relations Act? Why was its absence important?
5. Although the National Labor Relations Act gives employees certain rights, these rights are not unlimited. Discuss.
6. The NLRB has been criticized for its lack of success in the actual reinstatement and continued employment of discharged employees under the NLRA. What could be changed in the NLRA or its administration that would improve the record on reinstatement?
7. The Railway Labor Act, once called the "model labor law," has been criticized by many. What are the reasons underlying this criticism? Why has the act lost its favorable status?
8. Why is it essential that there be a separate labor relations law for the railway and airline industries?

References

[1]J. R. Commons and E. A. Gilmore, *A Documentary History of American Industrial Society* (Cleveland, Ohio: A. H. Clark, 1910), p. 68.

[2]*Commonwealth v. Hunt*, 45 Mass. 4 (1842).

[3]E. E. Herman and G. S. Skinner, *Labor Law* (New York: Random House, 1972), p. 21.

[4]*Vegelahn v. Guntner*, 44 N.E. 1077 (1896). See Herbert L. Sherman, Jr., and William P. Murphy, *Unionization and Collective Bargaining*, 3d ed. (Washington, D.C.: Bureau of National Affairs, 1975), p. 3.

[5]*Hitchman Coal & Coke Company v. Mitchell*, 245 U.S. 229 (1917).

[6]26 Stat. 209 (1890).

[7]*Loewe v. Lawlor*, 208 U.S. 274 (1908).

[8]38 Stat. 731 (1914).

[9]*Duplex Printing Press Co. v. Deering*, 254 U.S. 443 (1921).

[10]*Truax v. Corrigan*, 257 U.S. 312 (1921).

[11]47 Stat. 70 (1932).

[12]A labor dispute was defined as "any controversy concerning terms or conditions of employment, or concerning the association or representation of persons in negotiating, fixing, maintaining, changing, or seeking to arrange terms or conditions of employment regardless of whether or not the disputants stand in the proximate relation of employer and employee." 47 Stat. 70 (1932).

[13]Ibid.

[14]*Lauf v. E. G. Shinner & Co.*, 303 U.S. 315 (1938); *New Negro Alliance v. Sanitary Grocery Co.*, 303 U.S. 552 (1938).

[15]*Apex Hosiery Co. v. Leader*, 310 U.S. 467 (1940).

[16]*United States v. Hutcheson*, 312 U.S. 219 (1941).

[17]Alvin L. Goldman, *The Supreme Court and Labor-Management Relations Law* (Lexington, Mass.: D.C. Heath, 1976), pp. 26–28; and Sherman and Murphy, *Unionization and Collective Bargaining*, pp. 7–9.

[18]Goldman, *The Supreme Court*, pp. 28–31.

[19]Sherman and Murphy, *Unionization and Collective Bargaining*, p. 9.

[20]Goldman, *The Supreme Court*, pp. 31–39.

[21]This section was taken from the Wagner Act, 49 Stat. 449 (1935); Labor Management Relations Act, 61 Stat. 136 (1947); Landrum-Griffin Act, 73 Stat. 519 (1959); Office of General Counsel, National Labor Relations Board, *A Guide to Basic Law and Procedures under the National Labor Relations Act* (Washington, D.C.: Government Printing Office, 1976), unless otherwise noted.

[22]Cindy M. Hudson and William B. Werther, Jr., "Section 8(c) and Free Speech," *Labor Law Journal* 28 (September 1977), pp. 608–614.

[23]Edward B. Miller, *An Administrative Appraisal of the NLRB* (Philadelphia: Industrial Research Unit, University of Pennsylvania, 1977), p. 130.

[24]National Labor Relations Board, *45th Annual Report of the NLRB, 1980* (Washington: D.C.: Government Printing Office, 1981), pp. 3–4.

[25]Roger Handberg, Jr., "The Supreme Court and the NLRB," *Labor Law Journal* 26 (November 1975), pp. 737–739.

[26]John H. Fanning, "We Are Forty—Where Do We Go?" *Labor Law Journal* 27 (January 1976), pp. 5–6.

[27]Les Aspin, "Legal Remedies under the NLRA," in G. G. Somers, ed., *Proceedings of the Annual Meeting of the Industrial Relations Research Association* (Madison, Wis.: Industrial Relations Research Association, 1970), pp. 265–267. A study in the 1960s revealed that in seventy-one New England companies where 194 workers were unfairly discharged, only 85 were actually placed back on the job, and 23 others placed on preferential hiring lists. The reasons given by employees for not going back to their jobs were fear of company retaliation (39 cases) and possessing a better job (28 cases). Surprisingly, of the 85 who were actually reinstated, 60 had left their companies within two years.

[28]Elvis C. Stephens and Warren Chaney, "A Study of the Reinstatement Remedy under the National Labor Relations Act," *Labor Law Journal* 25 (January 1974), pp. 31–46. This study was conducted in 1971–72 and involved 86 companies and 43 unions.

[29]Warren H. Chaney, "The Reinstatement Remedy Revisited," *Labor Law Journal* 32 (June 1981), pp. 357–361.

[30]Frank W. McCulloch and Tim Bornstein, *The National Labor Relations Board* (New York: Praeger Publishers, 1974), p. 180.

[31]*H. K. Porter Co. v. NLRB*, 73 LRRM 2561 (1970).

[32]*Auto Workers v. NLRB*, 76 LRRM 2573 (1971); *Ex-Cell-O Corp. v. NLRB*, 77 LRRM 2547 (1971).

[33]Bernard Samoff, "The Case of the Burgeoning Load of the NLRB," *Labor Law Journal* 22 (October 1971), pp. 264–265.

[34]William B. Gould, *A Primer on American Labor Law* (Cambridge, Mass.: The MIT Press, 1982), p. 22.

[35]Douglas S. McDowell and Kenneth Huhn, *NLRB Remedies for Unfair Labor Practices* (Philadelphia: Industrial Research Unit, University of Pennsylvania, 1976), pp. 245–246.

[36]William N. Cooke and Frederick H. Gautschi III, "Political Bias in NLRB Unfair Labor Practice Decisions," *Industrial and Labor Relations Review* 35 (July 1982), p. 549.

[37]"Remarks of former NLRB Chairman Guy Farmer at Federal Bar Association Labor Law Seminar," *Daily Labor Report*, September 9, 1982, p. E–1.

[38]Sherman and Murphy, *Unionization and Collective Bargaining*, p. 6.

[39]Charles M. Rehmus, "Evolution of Legislation Affecting Collective Bargaining in the Railroad and Airline Industries," in Charles M. Rehmus, ed., *The Railway Labor Act at Fifty*, (Washington, D.C.: Government Printing Office, 1977), p. 4.

[40]Rehmus, "Collective Bargaining," p. 9.

[41]1934, 1936, 1940, 1951, 1964, 1966, and 1970.

[42]44 Stat. 577 (1926), as amended.

[43]Rehmus, "Collective Bargaining," p. 11.

[44]*Texas & New Orleans R.R. V. Brotherhood of Railway and Steamship Clerks*, 281 U.S. 548 (1930).

[45]*Virginia Ry. v. System Federation No. 40*, 300 U.S. 515 (1937).

[46]Rehmus, "Collective Bargaining," pp. 14–15. The remaining amendments were comparatively minor; the 1940 amendment clarified the coverage of rail operations in coal mines; 1951, the closed shop was prohibited, but the union shop was allowed; 1964, the terms of office for members of the National Mediation Board were classified; 1966, special adjustment boards were authorized to hear and resolve grievances on local properties; 1970, membership on the National Railroad Adjustment Board was reduced to 34—half management-appointed and half union-appointed.

[47]45 U.S.C. Sections 154–158.

[48]Douglas M. McCabe, "The Railroad Industry's Labor Relations Environment: Implications for Railroad Managers," *ICC Practitioners' Journal* 49 (September–October 1982), pp. 592–602.

[49]Charles M. Rehmus, "The First Fifty Years—And Then," in Rehmus, ed., *Railway Labor Act at Fifty*, p. 246.

[50]Beatrice M. Burgoon, "Mediation under the Railway Labor Act," in Rhemus, ed., *Railway Labor Act at Fifty*, p. 23.

[51]Herbert R. Northrup, "The Railway Labor Act: A Critical Reappraisal," *Industrial and Labor Relations Review* 25 (October 1971), p. 7.

[52]Donald E. Cullen, "Emergency Boards under the Railway Labor Act," in Rhemus, ed., *Railway Labor Act at Fifty*, pp. 175–176.

[53]Northrup, "A Critical Reappraisal," p. 8.

[54]Rehmus, "First Fifty Years," pp. 250–251.

[55]Northrup, "A Critical Reappraisal," pp. 17–22.

[56]Rehmus, "First Fifty Years," pp. 248–249.

[57]*44th Annual Report of National Mediation Board* (Washington, D.C.: U.S. Government Printing Office, 1980), p. 53.

[58]Cullen, "Emergency Boards," pp. 176–183. Also see "The Railroads Lose Their Bargaining Unity," *Business Week*, April 10, 1978, pp. 31–32.

[59]Mark L Kahn, "Labor-Management Relations in the Airline Industry," in Rehmus, ed., *Railway Labor Act at Fifty*, p. 128.

[60]Bureau of National Affairs, *1978 Age Discrimination Act Amendments* (Washington, D.C.: BNA Books, 1978), pp. 3–12.

[61]*Fair Employment Practice Manual* (Washington, D.C.: Bureau of National Affairs, 1981) p. 401: 283.

[62]Public Law 93–112, 1973.

[63]Employment Standards Administration, *Federal Labor Laws and Programs* (Washington, D.C.: Government Printing Ofice, 1971), pp. 100–138.

[64]Human Resources Division, General Accounting Office, *Concerns Regarding Impact of Employee Charges against Employers for Unfair Labor Practices* (Washington, D.C.: Government Printing Office, 1982), pp. 1–7.

[65]Theodore J. St. Antoine, "Proposed Labor Reform: 'Brave New World' or 'Looking Backward?'" *Proceedings of the 30th Annual Winter Meeting, IRRA* (Madison, Wis.: Industrial Relations Research Institute, 1978), p. 165.

[66]Edward B. Miller, *An Administrative Appraisal of the NLRB*, Rev. Ed., (Philadelphia, PA: The University of Pennsylvania, 1980), pp. 132–133.

[67]Human Resources Division, General Accounting Office, *Concerns Regarding Impact of Employee Charges*, pp. 3–7.

[68]Chaney, "The Reinstatement Remedy Revisited," p. 365.

Appendix to Chapter 3

The NLRB's Jurisdictional Standards

The board's standards in effect currently are as follows:

1. **Nonretail business.** Direct sales of goods to consumers in other states, or indirect sales through others (called outflow), of at least $50,000 a year; or direct purchases of goods from suppliers in other states, or indirect purchases through others (called inflow), of at least $50,000 a year.

2. **Office buildings.** Total annual revenue of $100,000, of which $25,000 or more is derived from organizations which meet any of the standards except the indirect outflow and indirect inflow standards established for nonretail enterprises.
3. **Retail enterprises.** At least $500,000 total annual volume of business.
4. **Public utilities.** At least $250,000 total annual volume of business, or $50,000 direct or indirect outflow or inflow.
5. **Newspapers.** At least $200,000 total annual volume of business.
6. **Radio, telegraph, television, and telephone enterprises.** At least $100,000 total annual volume of business.
7. **Hotels, motels, and residential apartment houses.** At least $500,000 total annual volume of business.
8. **Privately operated health care institutions.** At least $250,000 total annual volume of business for hospitals; at least $100,000 for nursing homes, visiting nurses associations, and related facilities; at least $250,000 for all other types of private health care institutions defined in the 1974 amendments to the act. The statutory definition includes: "any hospital, convalescent hospital, health maintenance organization, health clinic, nursing home, extended care facility, or other institution devoted to the care of the sick, infirm, or aged person." Public hospitals are excluded from NLRB jurisdiction by Section 2(2) of the act.
9. **Transportation enterprises, links and channels of interstate commerce.** At least $50,000 total annual income from furnishing interstate passenger and freight transportation services; also performing services valued at $50,000 or more for businesses which meet any of the jursidictional standards except the indirect outflow and indirect inflow standards established for nonretail enterprises.
10. **Transit systems.** At least $250,000 total annual volume of business.
11. **Taxicab companies.** At least $500,000 total annual volume of business.
12. **Associations.** These are regarded as a single employer in that the annual business of all association members is totaled to determine whether any of the standards apply.
13. **Enterprises in the territories and the District of Columbia.** The jurisdictional standards apply in the territories; all businesses in the District of Columbia come under NLRB jurisdiction.
14. **National defense.** Jurisdiction is asserted over all enterprises affecting commerce when their operations have a substantial impact on national defense, whether or not the enterprises satisfy any other standard.
15. **Private universities and colleges.** At least $1 million gross annual revenue from all sources (excluding contributions not available for operating expenses because of limitations imposed by the grantor).
16. **Symphony orchestras.** At least $1 million gross annual revenue from all sources (excluding contributions not available for operating expenses because of limitations imposed by the grantor).

17. Day care centers. At least $250,000 total annual volume of business.
18. Law firms. At least $250,000 total annual volume of business.

Through enactment of the 1970 Postal Reorganization Act, jurisdiction of the NLRB was extended to the United States Postal Service, effective July 1, 1971.

In addition to the above-listed standards, the board asserts jurisdiction over gambling casinos in New Jersey, Nevada and Puerto Rico, where these enterprises are legally operated, when their total annual revenue from gambling is at least $500,000.

Ordinarily if an enterprise does the total annual volume of business listed in the standard, it will necessarily be engaged in activities that affect commerce. The board must find, however, based on evidence, that the enterprise does in fact affect commerce.

The board has established the policy that where an employer whose operations affect commerce refuses to supply information concerning total annual business, the board may dispense with this requirement and exercise jurisdiction.

Finally, Section 14(c)(1) authorizes the board discretion to decline to exercise jurisdiction over any class or category of employers where a labor dispute involving such employers is not sufficiently substantial to warrant the exercise of jurisdiction, provided that it cannot refuse to exercise jurisdiction over any labor dispute over which it would have asserted jurisdiction under the standards it had in effect on August 1, 1959. In accordance with this provision the board has determined that it will not exercise jurisdiction over racetracks; owners, breeders, and trainers of racehorses; and real estate brokers.

In addition to the foregoing limitations, the act states that the term *employee* shall include any employee *except* the following:

Agricultural laborers.

Domestic servants.

Any individual employed by a parent or spouse.

Independent contractors.

Supervisors.

Individuals employed by an employer subject to the Railway Labor Act.

Government employees, including those employed by the U.S. Government, any government corporation or federal reserve bank, or any state or political subdivision such as a city, town, or school district.

Supervisors are excluded from the definition of employee and, therefore, are not covered by the act.

Chapter 4 Union Organizations

Unions' external relations express their reason for being and their uniqueness as organizations. . . . Internal relations are concerned in large measure with creating the organizational conditions which maximize their effective power vis-à-vis the enterprise.

Arnold S. Tannebaum, "Unions," in *Handbook of Organizations*, 1965.

A key actor in the labor relations process is the union. To understand the operations of unions, we can compare the union to government. There are executive, legislative, and judicial activities at various levels. The local union meetings and national conventions are the legislative bodies; the officers and executive boards compose the executive bodies; and the various appeal procedures serve a judicial function. A union can also be compared to a private organization because it is a specialized institution having a primary purpose of improving the economic conditions of its members.

Unions claim the democratic ideal; but realistically they must rely on a representative form of government. On the whole they do not seem to be any less democratic than local, state and federal governments. In fact, the membership probably has more to say about the way the union operates than citizens have a say in their governments or stockholders in their corporations.[1]

To appreciate unions as organizations, one must recognize their wide diversity, the organizational relationships of the various levels, the functions of the officers, and the varying degrees of control. This chapter presents an explanation of the craft and industrial union characteristics, the functions of local union officers, and local union government and operations. The national or international union (the terms are considered interchangeable in the chapter), which is composed of the local unions within a craft or industry, is explained in a similar framework. Not to be overlooked are the various intermediate levels of union organizations which provide specific functions for their affiliated unions. A fourth level for many union organizations is the federation, or the AFL-CIO, whose organization structure, functions, and officer responsibilities are also discussed. The chapter concludes with a section on the status of union membership and growth in the United States, and reasons for the slowing growth are explained.

Organizational Levels of Unions

The Local Union

Although there are generally four levels of unions—local, national, intermediate (or international), and the federation of unions—the local union is the main point of contact for the individual employee. The typical union member often identifies more closely with the local union than with the other union levels. He or she attends and sees local officers at the local meetings and workplace. When the union member has a grievance, the local union officers are the first to assist. When a strike occurs, the local union officers are the ones who make continuous contact with the strikers on the picket line. Although the national union may negotiate the master labor agreement under which the local union member works and the AFL-CIO may deal with the president and Congress on vital issues facing the nation, the local union serves as the vital link between the individual union member and the national union which in turn might link with the AFL-CIO.

Organizationally, the local union is a branch of the national union. It receives its charter from the national union, and it operates under the national union's constitution, bylaws, and rules. The constitution of the national union prescribes the number and types of officers, their duties and responsibilities, and the limits of their authority. Although union constitutions vary in length and content, they often mandate certain financial reports and require that a certain number of meetings be held, that the local labor agreement conform to the master labor agreement negotiated by the national union if there is industrywide bargaining, and that approval to call a strike be obtained by the local union. With the trend toward greater centralization of authority by the national union, the local union over the years has lost much of its operational flexibility.

Local Craft versus Industrial Unions The operation of the local union in large part depends on the nature and type of workers and membership. Although there is not a clear-cut division between them, unions can be divided generally into two groups: craft and industrial.

Differing union organizations Craft unions are composed of members who have been organized in accordance with their craft or skill, for example, bricklayers, electricians, carpenters, or ironworkers. Industrial unions have been organized on an industry basis, for example, the Steelworkers, Autoworkers, Rubber Workers, Mine Workers, Textile Workers, and so on. This, of course, does not mean that there are no skilled workers in the steel, auto, rubber, or textile industries; but it does mean the electricians and bricklayers in a steel plant or a coal mine operation would likely be members of the Steelworkers and United Mine Workers, respectively.

Differing scope of the labor agreement The craft and industrial unions differ in other ways that have an effect on their operations at the local, regional, and national levels. First, the craft unions, which frequently represent the building trades, usually negotiate short labor agreements (supplemented by detailed agreements on special topics, such as apprenticeship programs and safety) which cover a small geographic region, and each has considerable independence from the national union compared to industrial unions. Because of the nature of their work, craft union members may work on several different job sites for several different employers in a given year, still working under the same labor agreement. The labor agreement covers the various construction companies in the area and a number of the building trades unions for the particular geographic area.

The industrial union, on the other hand, may be covered by a national labor agreement negotiated between the company and the national union, which covers all of the company's unionized plants. For example, General Motors plants in Atlanta, Detroit, and Los Angeles are covered by the same master agreement. Well over 100 pages long, it explains in detail the wage plan, transfers, pensions, layoffs, etc. A local agreement is negotiated to cover matters of concern to the specific local plant and its employees, and must be consistent with the master agreement.

Differing skills Types of skills help demonstrate another difference in local union operations. The craft members are highly skilled artisans who have completed formal training, usually in a formal apprenticeship program. Many industrial employees, on the other hand, do not require much prior job training. Therefore, the craft union members often feel that they have higher status than their industrial counterparts. The training programs available for the industrial union members are usually offered by the company, whereas the training received by members of craft unions is jointly controlled and operated by the unions. So craft unions select those who will be offered the apprenticeship training, while companies alone select the trainees in the plants. Such an arrangement has allowed the craft unions to limit the numbers in the craft, sometimes only to their families and friends. In addition, the administration of these apprenticeship programs may adversely affect minority group members, a situation discussed in Chapters 11 and 12.

Differing job characteristics The nature of work also creates a unique opportunity for craft unions to operate under conditions that approximate a closed shop. Since many of the work assignments last only a short period, the craft members, such as electricians on a building project, return to the union hiring hall for their next assignment after their part of a project is completed. Upon receiving the assignment, the union members could report to another job site and work, possibly for another company. Usually, these arrangements are worked out in advance by the business agent of the craft union and the companies who agree to operate under the existing labor agreement. In other words, the union hiring hall serves as a clearinghouse or placement office for the construction companies as well as the union members. Since the hiring hall must be operated in a nondiscriminatory manner, nonunion workers may also use its services; however, use by nonunion employers is still quite rare. In comparison, the typical member of the industrial union is hired by the company and will work for the same employer—usually at the same facility—until employment is terminated.

Differing leadership roles The last difference pertains to the roles of the business agent and shop stewards of the craft union and the local union officials of the industrial unions. The *business agent*, the full-time administrator of the local craft union, provides many of the same services as the local union president of a large industrial union. They are both considered the key administrative officials of their respective local union halls and they lead the local union negotiations and play a key role in grievance administration. However, the business agent has additional duties, such as administering the union hiring hall, serving as the chief "watchdog" over the agreement at the various work sites and appointing an employee on each job site to serve as the shop steward. The *shop steward*, who may be the first person on the job or a senior employee, will handle employee grievances, represent the business agent on the job, and contact the business agent if anything goes wrong.

In local industrial unions, the president may or may not be full-time. If the job is full-time, the salary comes from union dues. If the job is part-time, the president is compensated from the union treasury only for the time that is lost off the job (at the regular rate of pay). The presidential duties include participating in local negotiations, maintaining the local lodge, assisting in grievance administration, and assuring that management abides by the agreement. On many occasions, a staff member of the national union (usually the international union representative) assists local officers in negotiations and in administering the labor agreement and makes sure that the local's activities conform to the national constitutions and directives. The shop steward, the elected representative in each department in the plant or facility, represents the members at local union meetings, handles grievances at the shop level, and collects dues, if necessary.[2] (See Exhibit 4.1 for shop steward's organizational relationship.)

Government and Operation of the Local Union The government of the local union is affected by its periodic meetings and by the constitution of its national union.

Participation in meetings Attendance at local union meetings often varies between 5 and 10 percent; attendance is higher, however, among union members who perceive a potential payoff for participation.[3] When the union is confronted with important business or a crisis, such as during negotiations or when a strike seems certain, attendance also rises. Unions and their members have been criticized for their lack of attendance, but formal attendance cannot be taken as the

Exhibit 4.1 An Example of the Organizational Relationship between Union Officials and Management Officials at Local Plant

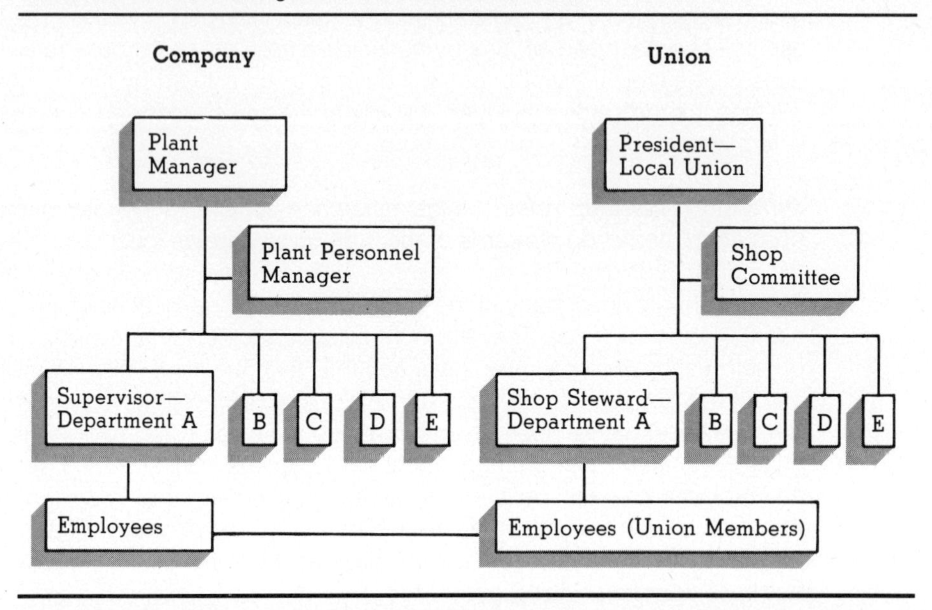

real measure of membership participation. Much membership participation takes place on an informal basis at the plant level between employees, among friends during lunch, or between shop stewards and members during rest breaks. Concerns are channeled to the union leadership through these stewards who regularly attend local meetings. The influence of these informal channels over union policies and actions should not be underestimated.[4]

Research into union member participation has helped to explain attendance patterns and identify characteristics of active union members. Participation is higher among those who feel a sense of community with the union (close friends involved), have influence in decision-making processes, and identify with the union's positions. Union members who believe the union is effective and believe they have influence over union decisions are more involved. On the other hand, those members who believe the union is ineffective (either because they are alienated from the union or apathetic) do not participate because they think it would be a waste of time. Further, union members become active when such participation helps to fulfill their social and psychological needs.[5]

Those who actively participate in the union usually have jobs higher in pay, skill, seniority, and job status than those who don't. As far as personal characteristics are concerned, they are more likely to be older, male, and married and tend to be well integrated in social life, for example, to belong to organizations, fraternal groups, sports teams, or veterans' organizations outside the plant. Finally, they have a higher degree of job satisfaction, a favorable feeling toward the union as well as the company (discussed in Chapter 1 as *dual loyalty*),[6] and higher order needs, such as growth, accomplishment, and decision making.[7]

The union leaders and their followers almost always attend local union meetings, as do departmental representatives, "hard core" members, pressure groups, social groups, and aspirants to union leadership positions. Locals have tried a number of techniques to increase attendance of regular members, such as providing beer and sandwiches, showing movies, fining members who miss a specified number of meetings or refusing to let them seek an elected office, and providing door prizes. While some gimmicks may increase the attendance in the short run, many members still feel the meetings are "long, boring, and frustrating affairs."[8]

Local meetings are held at a time that meets the approval of the majority. While they often start late and last too long, the average length is about two hours. The content inspires little attendance because much of the time is devoted to reading reports from the treasurer, project leaders, and committee chairpersons. Opportunities are provided for members to discuss these reports, but this procedure itself takes time, especially when a grievance involving someone in attendance is presented or when a controversial issue is raised before the meeting as a whole. Parliamentary procedure is used, at times to excess by quasi-parliamentary experts who may want to tie up the meeting. Although the meeting may stray from the ideal, generally the business of the local is accomplished.[9]

Functions of the meeting While the local union meeting may seem boring and not well-attended, it serves several vital functions in the local union government. First, the meeting is the union's single most important governmental activity, and all authority at the local level is derived from it. Second, the meeting provides an opportunity for members to communicate with union leaders, express gripes directly, and call attention to their concerns. Likewise, it is an opportunity for leaders to give information to members, present results of activities, seek union support, and give direction to the membership. Last, the meeting is the supreme legislative body; this is where decisions are made on such items as disposition of grievances and approval of expenses and constitutional changes, election of officers, and ratification of the contract.[10]

The National (International) Union

The national or international union[11] in the United States occupies the "kingpin" position in organized labor "because of its influence in collective bargaining—the core function of American unions"[12] Size alone (See Table 4.1) indicates the magnitude of the influence of national unions—millions of members work under labor agreements that are directly or indirectly the result of national union actions. The local union operates under its constitution and directives, and the federation (AFL-CIO) derives its influence, prestige, and power from the affiliated national unions.

Table 4.1 International Unions

Unions	Membership
Teamsters[a]	1,891,000
Auto Workers	1,357,000
National Education Association[a]	1,684,000
Steelworkers	1,238,000
United Food and Commercial Workers	1,300,000
Electricians (IBEW)	1,041,000
Machinists	754,000
Carpenters	769,000

[a]Not affiliated with the AFL-CIO.

Source: Preliminary data from U.S. Department of Labor, Bureau of Labor Statistics, *News*, September 1981, p. 2.

The national union operates under a *constitution* adopted in a convention by representatives from locals. These constitutions have evolved over time through three stages: first, the locals were initially careful to restrict the power of the national union; second, as national unions became more active in collective bargaining, political action, and so on, the locals became subordinate bodies; and third and presently, the constitution includes provisions that not only authorize the major national union functions but also protect individual rights and rights of locals in relation to the national union.[13]

The Convention The supreme governing body of the national union is its *convention*, which is usually held annually or biennially.[14] It serves the national union in many ways; as the constitutional assembly, the legislature of the national union, the final court for union decisions, and the means for nominating officers (and the election in many cases). The convention provides the time and place for national officers to report to the members their accomplishments and disclose their failures. It provides the agenda for policy formulation, program planning, and rule making. It represents the time in which the voice of the membership holds leaders accountable for their actions. However, not all activities are official; the convention provides a reward for drudgery work at the local, an opportunity for politicking and public relations, and a time and place for the members to "let their hair down."

The convention makes use of the *delegate system* in which the number of delegates allowed depends on the number of members in the local. Since even the smallest union is allowed one delegate, the number of delegates is not in direct proportion to the size of the local, although larger locals usually have more delegates. The convention conducts its business similarly to Congress and various state legislatures in that much committee work (including the possible holding of hearings) is performed prior to debate and vote on the convention floor. However, much discussion takes place in the convention hotel bars and smoke-filled rooms.[15]

Although many subjects may go before the convention, several continue to emerge year after year.

- Internal government: dues, financial matters, authority of the president, executive board, and locals.
- Collective bargaining: problems with current agreements, membership requests for future negotiations, establishing bargaining priorities, determination of strategy for next negotiations.
- Resolutions in support of or against domestic and international public policies: labor law reform, inflation, interest rates, unemployment, international balance of payments, loss of jobs to foreign countries.[16]

Leadership and Administration Between conventions, the national union is led by its executive board, whose members are elected by the membership. In some cases, executive board members are elected on a regional basis, and they are responsible for regional intermediate organizations that maintain contact between the locals in the region and the national. The relationship between the executive board and the national union president is usually specified in the constitution. For example, some national union presidents primarily carry out the policies of the executive board; others direct the affairs of the national union, subject to the approval of the board. However, the largest group of presidents have virtually unrestricted authority to appoint their staff, regulate locals, and direct the activities of the national union. The rationale for allowing such great authority to be vested in the chief executive is that the union frequently finds itself in struggles with employers or other situations where it must act decisively and quickly. Thus, a strong executive is needed and a single spokesperson for the union is required. However, the concentration of power creates opportunities for misuse of power, and an internal system of checks and balances must be devised to assure democracy and adequate representation. Experiences that brought on the passage of Titles I to VI of the Landrum-Griffin Act have shown that internal control often does not work effectively, and governmental regulation is essential.

A major and difficult reason for abuse of leadership is member apathy. For example, only 33 percent of 275,000 members of the International Union of Electrical Workers (IUE) voted in one of its last elections of national union officers, and only 193 of the 600 local unions were represented at the national union convention. In response to this apathy and lack of participation, the delegates to the convention voted to have the officer elections conducted at the convention rather than by direct vote of the rank-and-file, further removing the individual member from a role of active participation in union decisions.[17]

One slight sign of improved democracy and active participation by members has been the increased turnover rates of national union presidents. The period of 1973–1975 witnessed fifty changes in national union leaders, up from thirty-six during the 1971–1973 period. This higher turnover rate is misleading, however, because only three of these cases resulted from an election defeat; eighteen were caused by death of the incumbent and fifteen by retirement. High turnover continues to occur more frequently in the smaller unions and at the local levels than at the national level.[18] The president's tenure in office tends to be longer in larger unions, with formalized communication networks, centralized bargaining, and heterogeneous rank and file members.[19]

The operational departments of nationals may vary in kind and number, but the typical national union will have at least the following departments: (1) executive and administration; (2) financial and auditing; (3) organizing and servicing; and (4) technical staff, which includes research, education, economics, law, publications, and public relations.

The executive and administrative group includes the president, vice-president(s), secretary-treasurer, and their assistants. This group will be chiefly responsible for the activities of the overall union. In some cases the vice-president may concentrate on organizing or collective bargaining, whereas the secretary-treasurer naturally will focus on financial matters.

The organizing and service functions are usually handled by international union representatives employed by the national but assigned to a regional office to assist the locals in that geographic area. In addition, if there are unorganized workers in the area, this representative usually devotes some efforts to organizing these workers. The technical staff departments may be one-person shops that provide expert assistance to locals on a broad range of subjects, such as selecting arbitrators, carrying out economic research, and writing news releases.[20]

National unions have traditionally selected their staff through political processes by rewarding demonstrated leadership and loyalty at the local level. Union officers traditionally have been suspicious of college-educated persons and believed that the staff should work their way up the ranks. More recently, national unions are using personnel practices used by business and government. With the election of more college educated persons to national offices, much of the resistance to college education has declined. For example, both the president and secretary-treasurer of the AFC-CIO have college degrees and an attorney was elected president of the United Mineworkers. Today, it is still common to employ international union representatives and organizers from the ranks, but almost all unions fill their technical positions with college-educated outsiders. Another personnel activity within unions which is growing is training and staff development. There are labor education centers at many universities; over 3,000 union staff members from nearly 100 national unions took courses from the George Meany Center for Labor Studies, and a college degree program has been established with the cooperation of Antioch College.[21]

Services to and Control of Locals As indicated earlier, the locals are constitutionally subordinated to the national union, but the degree of subordination varies with the union. The national provides services to the local union in several ways while at the same time controlling local union leaders. For example, where a national product market exists, a master labor agreement with one firm might be negotiated to cover all its facilities (such agreements have been negotiated in the steel, auto, rubber, aircraft, and electrical appliance industries). Also a union, such as URW may negotiate an agreement with a company like Uniroyal at the national level, and this agreement may establish a pattern for negotiating with other rubber companies such as Goodyear, Goodrich, and Firestone. Following the negotiations of the master agreement between the national and each company, the local union will negotiate a local agreement with officials at each plant, covering local rules, policies, and benefits. Deviations from the master agreement are possible, but they must be okayed by the national union. (See Chapter 6 for further coverage.)

The national union assists locals in collective bargaining, grievance administration, strike activities, and internal financial administration. These services also provide an opportunity for national union staff members to assure that the local unions are conforming to national policies.

The international union representative, in addition to organizing new unions, also helps the local unions in grievance administration and labor arbitration. The national supports the local in strike situations, but the local must get approval in order to qualify for strike benefits. The national union provides counseling and consultation for internal financial administration (bookkeeping, dues collection, purchases, financing union lodges, and so on), but trusteeship (receivership) procedures are available whereby the national union can set aside the local for abuses such as malfeasance, corruption, and misuse of funds in favor of a trustee under national direction.[22]

Dues, Fees, and Distribution of Funds Although all union members pay dues or fees to their national unions, the amount and form vary considerably. Such fees are the chief source of revenue for unions, and some national unions receive less than $6 per member monthly while others receive more than $16. Some unions set a single rate, but most allow the local some flexibility in making the final determination. Frequently, dues are collected via a dues checkoff system (discussed in more detail in Chapter 11). The member agrees to a payroll deduction of union dues, which are collected by the employer and paid directly to the union.

Initiation fees in most cases are less than $40 per member; however, several specialized unions with small membership, such as Director's Guild, Football Players, Mineworkers, and Ironworkers, charge over $100, and the Radio Association charges $2,000. Usually when dues are high the payments often include premiums for insurance, pension payments, and other benefits.

The local unions forward a portion of the monthly dues for each member to the national union. Table 4.2 presents the results of a study of 169 national unions in which about one-third of the unions representing nearly 50 percent of the

Table 4.2 Portion of Monthly Dues Forwarded to National Unions

	169 National Unions (21,426,000 Members)	
Amount of Dues	Number of Unions	Membership (in thousands)
Less than $1.00	11	474
$1.00 to 1.99	26	2,077
$2.00 to 3.99	55	10,689
$4.00 to 5.99	32	3,237
$6.00 and above	27	1,757
Undetermined	18	3,192

Source: Charles W. Hickman, "Labor Organizations' Fees and Dues," *Monthly Labor Review* 100 (May 1977), p. 22.

members require the local to pay between $2.00 and $3.99 per month per member to the national union.

The nationals use these funds for various purposes beneficial to the membership. While the largest percentage of funds goes to the general fund, which covers administrative and operational costs and salary expenses, allocations are made to other accounts such as a strike fund, a convention fund, union publications, educational activities, and a retirement fund.[23]

Use of union dues and fees for political purposes and non-collective bargaining activities has come under fire in the last few years. Union members who disagree with the manner in which their unions contribute or use their funds have challenged their respective unions. Recent court decisions have caused several unions, such as the Machinists, Auto Workers, and American Federation of State, County, and Municipal Employees, to adopt dues rebate plans. These plans allow a rebate of a portion of member dues spent on political activities if the member requests it in advance (usually annually).

A district court judge in California has ruled that if a union uses dues and fees of protesting employees for non-collective bargaining activities and purposes, "it breaches its fiduciary duty of fair representation."[24] In addition, the judge listed twelve activities, including political ones, that were considered non-collective bargaining activities.[25] If such decisions are allowed to stand, it may alter significantly the role of unions in the political arena. While unions can continue to solicit volunteer contributions through such units as the AFL-CIO Committee on Political Education (COPE), the Auto Workers' Community Action Program (CAP), and the Mine Workers' Coal Miners' Political Action Committee (COMPAC), collections may be more difficult.

Mergers of National Unions Encouraged by the AFL-CIO merger but mostly spurred by rising costs, the need for stronger bargaining positions, expensive jurisdictional disputes, decline of some U.S. industries,[26] avoidance of external controls, and the need for self-preservation,[27] mergers of national unions have occurred at a quickening pace. There were one hundred and forty-three mergers between 1900 and 1978; sixty of those have occurred in the last twenty years.[28] In recent years, important union mergers have occurred in the paper, clothing and textiles, railroad industries, the postal service, and state government employees. The merger of the Retail Clerks and Meat Cutters and Butchers created the United Food and Commercial Workers with 1.3 million members—one of the largest unions in the United States.

These mergers occur through amalgamation, which is the joining together of two or more unions, or through absorption, which is a large union taking over a much smaller union. These mergers do not always produce a complete fusion or a total submergence of the absorbed unions. Occasionally there is a strong membership resistance to the merger, and the larger union may establish a division within its union to allow members of the former union to have a separate voice in the policy of the larger union after the merger. Other causes of resistance stem from membership interest in preserving their craft identity, desire to carry on their union's historical traditions, and membership identity with a small geographic region.[29]

Typically, mergers have not succeeded immediately in welding together functions, organization units, and staff members. They have required the time, patience, and good will of all parties, as officers and staff members who have different personalities and modes of operation have been meshed. The local unions must be accommodated as well as the employers and the collective bargaining relationships. Mergers have been particularly difficult when one of the unions feels a loss of its autonomy and when the merger occurs between unions whose prior dealings have been characterized by intense rivalry. Often members' pride is hurt, and fear surfaces when they find out that their union may be submerged by another.

In a more positive vein, the resulting larger unions gain more clout with industrial giants and can negotiate more as equals. The greater size generates resources to provide better training in collective bargaining, grievance administration, and steward leadership; to offer greater strike benefits; to lobby more effectively for legislation; and to maintain a staff to combat unfair labor practices. Moreover, successful mergers reduce the risks to smaller unions from technological change, economic recessions, declines in membership, unemployment, and financial strains.[30] The potential advantages of a merger coupled with the risks of not merging suggest that mergers of national unions will be continued in the future.[31]

Intermediate Organizational Units

Within the union structure between national headquarters and the locals lie the intermediate organizational units—regional or district offices, trade conferences, conference boards, and joint councils. These units usually operate under the guidance of their various national unions, but their activities are important to the union members and employers in their areas.

The *regional* or *district offices* house the regional or district officers, the staff, and the international union representatives for the geographic area served. For example, Michigan has a number of Auto Workers' district offices; the Steel Workers have district offices in Pittsburgh, Birmingham, and elsewhere. The offices are established to better serve locals from their respective national unions.

Trade conferences are set up within national unions to represent a variety of industrial groups. For example, the Teamsters' Union has established eleven trade conferences for such groups as freight, laundry, airlines, and moving and storage. These groups meet to discuss various mutual problems and topics of interest.

Conference boards are organized within national unions in accordance with the company affiliation to discuss issues that pertain to the union and the particular company. For instance, each of the national unions within the steel, auto, rubber, and electric industries has established conference boards which meet to discuss negotiations and related problems. Delegates are chosen from the local unions to represent the interests of their constituents at meetings, to plan the next negotiations, and then to relay these plans to the local union members.

Joint councils involve groupings of local unions which have common goals, employers, and interests. Examples are the building trades councils established in most metropolitan areas in the United States. They negotiate with the association of construction employers in the area, coordinate their activities, and assist in resolving jurisdictional disputes between unions.

The American Federation of Labor and Congress of Industrial Organizations (AFL-CIO)

The American Federation of Labor and Congress of Industrial Organizations (AFL-CIO), while not including all U.S. labor unions, is composed of 101 national and international unions that have more than 49,400 local unions and 15,000,000 members. In addition, there are 78 directly affiliated local unions having 57,000 members.[32] Members represent a wide diversity of occupations, such as actors, construction workers, barbers and hairdressers, steel workers, bus drivers, railroad workers, telephone operators, newspaper reporters, sales clerks, garment workers, engineers, school teachers, and police.[33] These AFL-CIO affiliates maintain day-to-day relationships with several thousands of employers and administer more than 160,000 labor agreements. Most (over 98 percent) of these agreements are negotiated without strikes or other forms of conflict and serve as the basis of employment conditions under which many work.

Established in 1955 when the American Federation of Labor and the Congress of Industrial Organizations merged, the AFL-CIO recognized the principle that both craft and industrial unions are an appropriate, equal, and necessary part of U.S. organized labor. The federation accepts the principle of *autonomy*—each affiliated union conducts its own affairs; has its own headquarters, offices, and staff; decides its own economic policies; sets its own dues; carries out its own contract negotiations; and provides its own services to members.

No national union is required to affiliate with the AFL-CIO. About sixty unions, including one of the largest—Teamsters—remain outside the AFL-CIO. Member unions are free to withdraw at any time; however, their voluntary participation plays an essential role that advances the interest of every union. National unions continue their membership because they believe that a federation of unions serves purposes their own individual unions cannot serve as well.

Examples of the AFL-CIO services include:

- Speaking for organized labor before Congress and other branches of government.
- Representing U.S. labor in world affairs, keeping in direct contact with labor unions throughout the free world.
- Coordinating activities such as community services, political education, lobbying, and voter registration with greater effectiveness.
- Helping to coordinate efforts to organize nonunion workers throughout the United States.

Another vital service enhances the integrity and prestige of AFL-CIO unions—they must operate under established ethical practice codes covering union democracy and financial integrity. The federation also assists in keeping down conflicts that cause work interruptions by mediating and resolving disputes between national unions, such as organizing disputes and conflicts over work assignments.[34]

Organization Structure The AFL-CIO organization structure, shown in Exhibit 4.2, illustrates the importance of the *convention*. Meeting every two years and at times of particular need, delegates decide on policies, programs, and direction for AFL-CIO activities. Each national union (international) is authorized to send delegates to the convention. Each union's representation of delegates at the convention is determined by the number of dues paying members. In addition, other affiliated organizations, such as state labor councils, are represented by one delegate each.

Between conventions, the governing body is the Executive Council, comprised of the president (currently Lane Kirkland), secretary-treasurer (currently Thomas R. Donahue), and thirty-three vice-presidents elected by majority vote at the convention. The Executive Council meets at least three times a year and handles operational duties involving legislative matters, union corruption, charters of new internationals, and judicial appeals from member unions.

Between meetings of the Executive Council, the president, who is the chief executive officer, has authority to supervise the affairs of the federation and to direct its staff, and the secretary-treasurer handles all financial matters. To assist in his administration, the president has appointed fifteen *standing committees* on various subjects and with the assistance of the AFL-CIO staff provides related services to member unions. The staff, located at headquarters in Washington, D.C., corresponds closely to these standing committees in order to better serve the member unions. (See Exhibit 4.2 for a listing of standing committees and staff divisions.) The *General Board*, composed of the Executive Council and one officer from each member union, is available to act on matters referred to it from the Executive Council.

The AFL-CIO has established fifty *state central bodies* (plus one in Puerto Rico) to advance the statewide interests of labor through political, lobbying, and organizing activities, which involve attempts to elect friends of labor, to have favorable legislation passed, and to organize nonunion workers, respectively. Each local union of AFL-CIO affiliated unions in a particular state may join the state organization and participate in and support its activities. In addition, 746

Exhibit 4.2 Structural Organization of the American Federation of Labor and Congress of Industrial Organizations

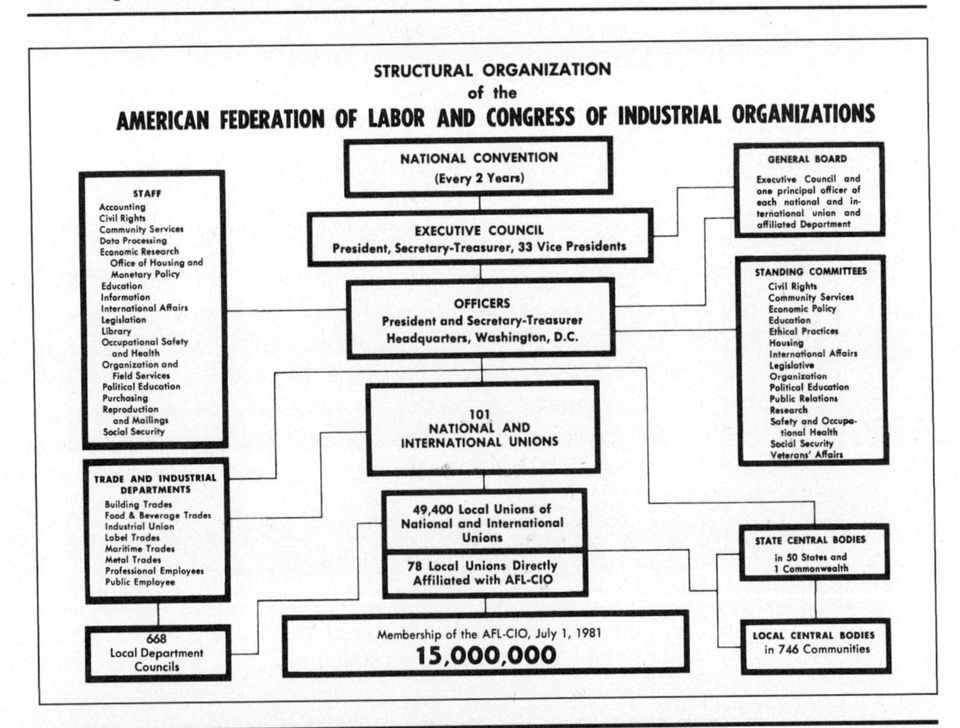

Source: *American Federationist*, the official monthly magazine of the AFL-CIO.

local central bodies have been formed by local unions of the national affiliates to deal with civic and community problems and other matters of local concern.

To accommodate and serve the interests and needs of various trade and industrial unions, the AFL-CIO has established eight *trade and industrial departments*. The Industrial Union Department represents the interests of industrial unions, mostly members of the former CIO. Another department, the Union Label Department, promotes the purchases and sales of union-made goods and services. The remaining departments represent the interests of such union groups as the building trades, food and beverage trades, maritime employees, metal trades, public employees, and professional employees. In addition, throughout the United States where there is sufficient interest and support, 668 *local department councils* have been organized.[35]

The AFL-CIO's operations are financed through regular member dues, called *per capita taxes*, which are paid by affiliated unions on behalf of their members. Currently, the per capita tax is $.19 per month or $2.28 per year for each member. Thus, the AFL-CIO's operating budget is $27.8 million, of which $25.1 million covers regular operating expenses. A major portion of the budget goes to the salaries of the staff. For example, AFL-CIO President Lane Kirkland's salary was $110,000 in 1982, and Secretary-Treasurer Thomas R. Donahue's was $88,000. (These seem high until they are compared to the highest paid U.S. executives. For example, the average annual total compensation for 21 U.S. executives was over $1.5 million in 1981, and 14 of these earned over $2 million.)[37] The detailed financial report of the AFL-CIO is submitted to the delegates at each convention.

Other AFL-CIO activities are educational and informational, presenting the federation's stance on a variety of issues. For example, the AFL-CIO publishes a weekly *AFL-CIO News* that keeps members up-to-date on current events that pertain to them, and various reports on problems and policies of organized labor. The AFL-CIO maintains the George Meany Center for Labor Studies, offering short courses in union leadership development, a Speaker's Bureau to provide labor speakers for high school and college classes, and makes available educational films to interested groups for a nominal fee.[37]

In the political arena, the AFL-CIO receives much attention. The representatives of organized labor, it serves as the focal point of political activities. Not only does it lobby aggressively for favorable legislation, but it publishes the voting records of each senator and representative at both federal and state levels. It attempts to influence appointments, such as Supreme Court judges, Secretary of Labor, and National Labor Relations Board members, who are important to organized labor.[38] Its policy of "Reward Your Friends, Punish Your Enemies" has not changed much since Samuel Gompers' days. The AFL-CIO's Committee on Political Education (COPE) has a network in each state and in most large communities. COPE seeks voluntary contributions to provide funds for its activities, which include voter registration, "get-out-the-vote" campaigns, preparation of leafflets and posters, and research on behalf of its candidates.[39] Although the Federal Election Campaign Act of 1971, amended in 1974, has restricted financial contributions to federal candidates, the AFL-CIO, COPE, and state and local bodies can still amass amazing support to help their candidates for office, especially when the candidate is clearly the choice of organized labor.[40]

While organized labor has played a major role in U.S. politics, it retains the independence of a national political party. Over the years it has been more closely aligned with the Democratic Party, both philosophically and politically. It has become perhaps the single most important political force that has supported government programs to help the socially and economically disadvantaged. It has supported consumer and environmental protection and safety and health legislation which has benefited all workers, not only union members.

Organized labor has accumulated much power and influence through its own established network and has also been instrumental in organizing other politically active groups with socially oriented objectives, such as minorities and senior citizens. However, organized labor's overall political strength and actual effectiveness should not be exaggerated. In some states and municipalities, union membership is so negligible that its influence is inconsequential. In others, where union membership is high, its influence is significant, and political candidates must actively solicit its support.[41]

New Leadership Style Lane Kirkland, AFL-CIO president, is projecting a new, modern style of directing the federation. He participates in discussions at regional meetings with rank and file union members, projects an image of an intelligent, articulate leader, and directs the AFL-CIO's Executive Council by consensus with every member being given an opportunity to express himself.[42]

As A. H. Raskin, long-term labor analyst for the *New York Times* has stated:

In Kirkland the Federation has a leader of supreme intelligence and sophistication, who has also shown subtlety and skill in building consensus. His command is firm, his recognition of the need for change clear. If anyone can restore the movement to its indispensable place as an effective countervailing force in the American economy and public life, he is the one to do it.[43]

Union Corruption and the Landrum-Griffin Act

Corruption, racketeering, and embezzlement have been discovered in some local and national unions. Union abuses of power were exposed by the McClellan hearings of the late 1950s.[44] Large amounts of Teamster pension funds have been allegedly misused;[45] its president and four others have been indicted for conspiracy to bribe a U.S. Senator.[46] A review of public documents from 1973 to 1980 revealed that only 300 of the 75,000 local unions—less than one-half of one percent—are involved in illegal activities.[47] In fact, unions compare favorably with other sectors of the U.S. society. They certainly fare better than the banking industry, which in a single year reported 100 bank presidents, 65 vice-presidents, 145 managers, 345 cashiers, and 490 other employees on embezzlement charges. Therefore one must conclude that:

The overwhelming majority of labor leaders are honest men who take seriously their obligations to represent the interest of the members who have elected them to office.[48]

The AFL-CIO established the Ethical Practices Committee in its efforts to control corrupt practices and racketeering of its member unions, and its Executive Council was given the authority to suspend any affiliated union with corrupt practices.[49] Then, in 1959, the U.S. Congress showed its concern with union abuse and the potential misuse of union power by amending the National Labor Relations Act through passage of the Landrum-Griffin Act (the Labor-Management Reporting and Disclosure Act) which has several provisions governing union operations and government. For example, it governs:

- Disclosure by union officers and employees (and employers and their agents) about financial dealings, trusteeships, and any private arrangements made with any employees,
- Regulation of union trusteeships, including rules for their establishment and maintenance, and the protection of the rights of members of unions under trusteeship, and
- Fiduciary responsibilities of union officers and representatives. It also disqualifies criminals and former Communists from holding union offices, and requires certain union officers to be bonded to assure the faithful discharge of their duties and responsibilities.[50]

More recently, the AFL-CIO and the Reagan Administration have supported the Labor Management Racketeering Act of 1982, which would prohibit union officers guilty of accepting payoffs from employers from holding office for up to 10 years, increase the penalty for buying and selling labor peace from a misdemeanor to a felony subject to a $15,000 fine and up to five years imprisonment, and require union officers to resign their positions upon conviction of a crime.[51] (The act failed to pass in 1982.)

Status of Union Membership

Trends and Possible Explanations for Union Stagnation

Union membership continued to increase during the 1970s; however, this increase accounts for a smaller percentage of the labor force. Table 4.3 shows an increase in membership from 20.7 million in 1960 to 22.3 million in 1980. However, the table also reveals that membership in unions has declined from 30.5 to 24.7 percent of the total nonagricultural labor force. Some of the variation can be explained by the definitions used. For example, the total labor force used in Table 4.3 as the basis for comparing trends in membership includes persons not normally eligible to become union members, such as supervisors, unem-

Table 4.3 National Union and Employee Association Membership, Totals and Proportion of Labor Force and Nonagricultural Employment, 1958–1978

Year		Total Labor Force		Nonagricultural Employees	
Unions and Associations	Union Membership (in Thousands)	Number (in Thousands)	Percent Members	Number (in Thousands)	Percent Members
1968	20,721	82,272	25.2	67,951	30.5
1970	21,248	85,903	24.7	70,880	30.0
1972	21,657	88,991	24.3	73,675	29.4
1974	22,809	93,240	24.5	78,265	29.1
1976	22,662	96,917	23.4	79,382	28.3
1978	22,757	102,537	22.2	86,697	26.3
1980	22,366	106,821	20.9	90,657	24.7
Unions					
1960	17,049	72,142	23.6	54,234	31.4
1962	16,586	73,442	22.6	55,596	29.8
1964	16,841	75,830	22.2	58,331	28.9
1966	17,940	78,893	22.7	63,955	28.1
1968	18,916	82,272	23.0	67,951	27.8
1970	19,381	85,903	22.6	70,920	27.3
1972	19,435	88,991	21.8	73,714	26.4
1974	20,199	93,240	21.7	78,413	25.8
1976	19,634	96,917	20.3	79,382	24.7
1978	20,238	102,537	19.7	85,762	23.6

Source: U.S. Department of Labor, Bureau of Labor Statistics, *News* (Washington, D.C.: Government Printing Office, September 18, 1981).

ployed persons seeking work, self-employed persons, and unpaid family members. According to the AFL-CIO, if the term "total labor force" was defined to include only those eligible for union membership, unions would represent 32.5 percent of the work force.[52]

These percentages seem low, but they average those in industries that are heavily unionized, such as transportation, manufacturing, mining, and contract construction, and others that are less unionized, such as banking, agriculture, and insurance. Table 4.4 demonstrates the broad percentage categories of thirty-five industries by the degree of unionization. In addition, the degree of unionization is not equal geographically—the North and Northeast are heavily organized and the South and Southwest less so than the average (see Table 4.5).

A number of researchers have attempted to identify the reasons for the decline in union membership as a percent of the labor force or, more descriptively, "union stagnation." While there seems to be no single reason for this lack of growth,[53] a number of explanations have been given. The reasons below may

Table 4.4 Industry Classification by Degree of Unionization

75 percent and over	25 percent to 50 percent
Transportation	Printing, publishing
Contract construction	Leather
	Rubber
50 percent to 75 percent	Furniture
Electrical machinery	Machinery
Transportation equipment	Lumber
Food and kindred products	Electric, gas utilities
Primary metals	State governments
Mining	Local governments
Telephone and telegraph	
Paper	**Less than 25 percent**
Petroleum	Nonmanufacturing
Tobacco manufacturers	Instruments
Apparel	Textile mill products
Fabricated metals	Chemicals
Manufacturing	Service
Stone, clay, & glass production	Trade
Federal government	Agriculture, fisheries
	Finance

Source: U.S. Department of Labor, Bureau of Labor Statistics, *Directory of National Unions and Employee Associations, 1977* (Washington, D.C.: Government Printing Office, 1979), p. 70.

For additional information concerning the extent of union membership by industry name (SIC Code), and SMSA, see Richard B. Freeman and James L. Medoff, "New Estimates of Private Sector Unionism in the United States," *Industrial and Labor Relations Review* 32 (January 1979), pp. 143–174.

overlap to some extent; each attempts to explain the causes for the lack of union growth:

- Structural changes in employment are occurring, with the heavily unionized industries (such as manufacturing, railroads, and mining) either declining or growing at a lesser rate than less unionized industries (such as services, finance, and trades).[54]
- Shifts in the product and labor markets have affected organized firms; for example, some firms have folded, plants have closed, plants have moved to less organized sections of the U.S. (the West and South), and organized companies have lost business to nonunion firms.
- Interindustry shifts in employment to newer, high-technology industries, such as computers, technical equipment, and scientific instruments, also affect union growth, for the employees in these industries have always been difficult to organize.
- The occupational mix is changing toward more professional, technical, and service (white-collar) employees—also traditionally difficult to organize.

Table 4.5 Distribution of Membership of National Unions and Employee Associations by State

State	Percent Nonagricultural Employee Union Members	Rank	State	Percent Nonagricultural Employee Union Members	Rank
Alabama*	24.0	26	Montana	29.5	18
Alaska	36.0	7	Nebraska*	19.4	36
Arizona*	20.6	33	Nevada*	27.5	22
Arkansas*	18.5	38	New Hampshire	17.9	39
California	32.2	14	New Jersey	29.9	17
Colorado	21.7	30	New Mexico	22.1	29
Connecticut	30.3	16	New York	44.8	1
Delaware	24.2	25	North Carolina*	11.1	49
Florida*	14.8	46	North Dakota*	17.7	40
Georgia*	17.0	43	Ohio	35.8	8
Hawaii	40.1	3	Oklahoma	17.3	42
Idaho	20.6	34	Oregon	31.3	15
Illinois	34.3	9	Pennsylvania	39.7	4
Indiana	33.4	11	Rhode Island	34.1	10
Iowa*	22.3	28	South Carolina*	9.1	50
Kansas*	18.6	37	South Dakota*	13.2	47
Kentucky	28.0	21	Tennessee*	21.7	31
Louisiana*	17.6	41	Texas*	14.8	45
Maine	24.5	24	Utah*	19.9	35
Maryland–D.C.	25.4	23	Vermont	23.2	27
Massachusetts	28.1	20	Virginia*	16.7	44
Michigan	36.6	6	Washington	39.7	5
Minnesota	28.7	19	West Virginia	42.6	2
Mississippi*	13.2	48	Wisconsin	32.3	13
Missouri	33.0	12	Wyoming*	21.7	32

*Right-to-work state (see Chapter 10).

Source: U.S. Department of Labor, Bureau of Labor Statistics, *Directory of National Unions and Employee Associations, 1977* (Washington, D.C.: Government Printing Office, 1979), p. 74.

- More organizations are learning how to operate their businesses on a nonunion basis through enlightened management, double breasting (see Chapter 5), anti-union campaigns, and so on. In other words, management has become more sophisticated in understanding the reasons workers organize unions and more aggressive within the legal framework in presenting its viewpoint to the employees.
- Changing demographics in the work force have helped to slow union growth; women, the better educated, and the younger employees who are new entrants have traditionally been more difficult to organize.
- Surprisingly, the rapid expansion in legal rights through the Equal Employment Opportunity Act, Occupational Safety and Health Act, Employee Retirement and Income Security Act, and other legislation has helped make union organizing more difficult. The legal rights give employees a free ride in areas

for which the union once was the primary protector and provider, and the incrasing costs of these programs to the employers have caused them to stiffen their resistance to unions, to be more cost conscious, and to increase their level of managerial sophistication in personnel practices.[55]

- Union officials place much blame on deficiencies in the labor relations laws. Preelection time delays, contested elections, lengthy appeals, and stalled negotiations are possible under the National Labor Relations Act. They claim that companies are allowed to frustrate the objectives of the NLRA and negate the results of free employee choices through secret-ballot elections.[56]
- It appears that unions are committing more of their resources to servicing the needs of their current members, rather than organizing new unions. As unions mature and have organized a major portion of the workers within their jurisdiction, such as in manufacturing, mining, construction, and transportation, their expenditures, time and efforts focus on representation services, such as negotiating contracts, research on wages and benefits, preparation for arbitration, processing grievances, and so on. In fact, organizing new members may not be in the interests of the present membership, if the union would have to divert funds from services for its members to organizing efforts. Because unions are political organizations and the leaders are elected by the membership, the incentive to organize new members is frequently less than the incentive to provide services to current members.[57]

Other reasons given for union stagnation have been: (a) faulty unionization strategies where unions have neglected the high-growth, low-union density markets; (b) the declining image workers and the public have of organized labor due to the advanced age of most labor leaders and the absence of young, aggressive, and imaginative leaders; (c) recent political setbacks, such as the failure of Congress to amend the NLRA by passing the Labor Law Reform Bill, (d) budget cuts in the public sector where union growth has been substantial in recent years,[58] and (e) an economic recession which has lowered the number of persons employed.

Questions for Unions in the 1980s

With these declines, organized labor is faced with significant challenges and important questions:

1. Can organized labor develop new techniques that appeal to the needs of workers in the less unionized sectors (such as health-care, white-collar, textile, service, finance, and agriculture workers) and in the South, West, and Southwest?[59]
2. Will union leaders be able to renew the direction of organized labor and regain lost prestige and influence? A 1980 public opinion poll revealed that

only 15.4 percent expressed a great deal of confidence in the leadership of organized labor, lower than any other institution listed, including business and Congress.[60]

3. Will organized labor be able to appeal to groups of employees now entering the labor market in large numbers for the first time, such as women? Can it accommodate their interests regarding such issues as flexible hours, seniority lists, pension benefits, desire for challenging work, and more leisure time? Can it deal with the new breed of workers—the overqualified placed in blue-collar jobs, workers who don't trust management or the union?[61]
4. Can it continue to mobilize what some people consider the best political machine in the country to elect public officials?[62] (Unions have recently been taking new initiatives in political actions; the AFL-CIO will get involved in party primaries for the first time in 1984. They have taken steps to consummate a new partnership with the Democratic National Committee and have fifteen seats, 14 percent of the total. In 1981, organized labor raised nearly 15 percent of the funds raised by the Democratic party.)[63]
5. Can organized labor combat and deal with employers who have hired expert labor relations consultants and attorneys to keep unions out of companies[64] or who have designed personnel programs that create a work climate not conducive to unionization?
6. Will unions be able to take advantage of the predicted labor market glut of highly educated persons within the age range of 25 to 44 (which will reach 50 percent of the labor force by 1990)?[65] Much depends on the employer's reaction to this labor market glut and the way white-collar employees are treated in terms of employer practices (such as promotions, job security, career opportunities, and wage increases). Will the unions be able to react positively to employer practices unacceptable to employees?
7. Will the various unions have the resources to service their membership through negotiations, arbitration, etc., to ward off attempts at decertification?
8. Will unions be able to take advantage of opportunities for increased membership, problems of inflation and unemployment, decline in job satisfaction, and latent interest in unionism by the unorganized?[66]

Summary and Implications

Summary

Unions are usually part of a larger unit of organized labor. A local union becomes part of a national union, and most national unions affiliate with a federation of unions called the AFL-CIO. Because these unions vary so widely in structure, interest, and function, this chapter attempted to identify the general purposes, activities, and operational matters which are pertinent to most unions. Much of the discussion related to the governance of the various levels of unions as set up in the local union meetings and the conventions of the national unions and the AFL-CIO. Other topics of importance to union government and operations include duties and responsibilities of union officers, union finances, and political and lobbying activities.

With the exposure of union corruption and abuses of power by the McClellan committee in 1958–1959, Congress reacted by passing the Landrum-Griffin Act (or the Labor-Management Reporting and Disclosure Act) to guarantee union members certain rights of participation in union affairs, to regulate union elections and trusteeships, and to assure financial and reporting compliance.

Patterns of union membership have shown a stagnant growth in recent years, and a long-term trend of lower union membership as a percentage of the labor force has been noted. Experts who have studied the issue of union stagnation attribute it to a variety of causes; for example, a lessened growth rate in industries which are heavily unionized and interindustry shifts in employment to newer, high-technology industries whose employees are difficult to unionize. Organized labor's ability to overcome its present decline will depend upon its ability to adapt its techniques to needs of the changing work force and of employees currently not being reached, to regain lost prestige and influence with the public, and to effect political moves advantageous to unions.

Implications

The answers to the questions posed in this chapter must come in part from within the unions themselves. An important issue here is the degree to which the unions are responsive to their members and operate their organizations as democratic institutions within society. The more the union is controlled by those governed, the greater the degree of democracy; the less control by those governed, the lesser the democracy.[67]

The degree of democracy within each union can be determined by assessing the legal framework—examining the constitution, elections, regularity of meetings and opportunities for opposition to develop. The participation rates in elections and attendance at meetings can also be examined, as well as reactions to opposite views and leader responses in close elections. Studying the means of obtaining member input and the responses given to suggestions can also determine whether leaders reflect the values of the members.[68]

Unions have at least three reasons for remaining democratically controlled:

1. Democratic procedures permit members to exert pressure on the leaders to respond to the members' needs when formulating policies and programs.
2. Employees value the sense of participation they derive from helping to select union officials and influence their decisions.
3. The public has a stake in assuring the unions are democratic so that corruption and strikes are minimized.[69]

While democracy is important, it is difficult to achieve for several reasons:

1. Most members are apathetic about the day-to-day affairs of union government, and care only about elections, strike votes, etc.

2. The larger the union, the more distant the leaders are from the members, due to the many layers of organization.
3. Union leaders frequently have to act quickly in negotiations and during strikes; there is not enough time to call for a vote among all members.[70]

Any assessment of union democracy must not overlook the importance of union stewards. Union stewards regularly attend meetings because the members whom they represent expect it. Members elect their union stewards to represent their interests within the union. The degree to which the unions encourage stewards to mirror the aspirations, interests, and opinions of their constituencies in large part determines the degree of union democracy.[71]

Employers frequently find it easier to deal with authoritarian unions because their leaders make decisions quickly and can better control the membership, making it easier to achieve a contract acceptance or stop an illegal strike. On the other hand, democratic unions are slow to make decisions and often appear to behave irrationally because so many members have an opportunity to give their input. Thus, employers have little incentive to help facilitate union democracy.[72]

Congress, through the Landrum-Griffin Act, has attempted to strengthen union democratic processes and gave power to union members to protect themselves against irresponsible leaders. Unions at every level are required to hold elections at stipulated intervals; members are guaranteed a reasonable opportunity to nominate candidates and seek office; officers are prohibited from using union funds to promote their favored candidate. Unions are required to file reports, such as financial affairs, constitution, names and salaries of union officers, and financial transactions with potential conflicting interests with the Department of Labor. Further, the Secretary of Labor can investigate elections to assure compliance with the regulations.[73]

By and large, the Landrum-Griffin Act has significantly advanced the cause of union democracy while doing little, if any, damage to the structure of organized labor. Still, as one author has claimed:

Unions are not merely debating societies. They are militant organizations that must act quickly and decisively in times of crisis. Real friends of the worker would not insist that every union decision be argued out and voted upon in town-meeting fashion. At the same time, however, both management and the public arguably stand to suffer from the irresponsibility in collective bargaining which is a possible side-effect of a massive injection of democracy into labor organizations.[74]

The U.S. Supreme Court has approved the Secretary of Labor's approach for determining "reasonable" qualifications for elections of union officers. By this approach, if too many members (perhaps two-thirds) are disqualified by a rule, the rule may be considered invalid. For example, a requirement of attendance at one-half of union meetings during three years prior to the election was considered unreasonable because its application would disqualify 96.5 percent of 660 members.[75]

With many efforts made to assure more democratic union,

> **The question should be, not whether any given change will make the union more democratic, but whether it will serve the ends of the modern union—to respond to the interests of the membership, to promote them effectively, to deal fairly with individuals and minorities within its ranks, and to exhibit a due regard for legitimate interests of those beyond its walls.[76]**

Discussion Questions

1. Select a craft union and an industrial union and point out differing characteristics of these two types of unions.
2. Compare the government of the local union to student governments and municipal governments, with special attention to participation by members.
3. Explain why and how national union presidents have been able to accumulate so much authority and power.
4. Differentiate among the business agent of a local union, a shop steward, and an international union representative. How do their roles differ?
5. Since the AFL-CIO does not negotiate labor agreements on behalf of national unions, how can it claim to be the "spokesman for organized labor" in the United States?
6. Considering the reasons given to explain union stagnation, what are your predictions for union growth in the 1980s? Why?
7. Compare the requirements for union democracy to any student organization with which you are familiar. (Materials from Implications section provide help.)

References

[1] Alice H. Cook, *Union Democracy: Practice and Ideal* (Ithaca, New York: Cornell University, 1963), pp. 19–26.

[2] Allan Nash, *The Union Steward: Duties, Rights and Status* (Ithaca, N.Y.: New York State School of Industrial and Labor Relations, 1977), pp. 20–22.

[3] John C. Anderson, "Local Union Participation: A Re-examination," *Industrial Relations* 18 (Winter 1979), p. 30.

[4] Arnold S. Tannenbaum, "Unions," in James G. March, ed., *Handbook of Organizations* (Chicago: Rand McNally, 1965), pp. 745–748.

[5] Anderson, "Local Union Participation," pp. 29–31. See also Nigel Nicholson, Gill Ursell, and Jackie Lulsboch, "Membership Participation in a White-Collar Union," *Industrial Relations* 20 (Spring 1980), pp. 162–177.

[6] Tannebaum, "Unions," pp. 745–747.

[7] William Glick, Phillip Mirvis, and Diane Harder, "Union Satisfaction and Participation," *Industrial Relations* 16 (Spring 1977), p. 145.

[8] Leonard R. Sayles and George Strauss, *The Local Union*, rev. ed. (New York: Harcourt, Brace & World, 1967), pp. 96–100.

[9] Ibid., pp. 93–96.

[10] Ibid., pp. 100–105.

[11]National and international unions are nearly synonymous; the small difference is that internationals may have locals outside the United States. Thus, in this book, the terms will be used interchangeably.

[12]Jack Barbash, *American Unions* (New York: Random House, 1967), p. 69.

[13]Ibid., pp. 71–72.

[14]The Landrum-Griffin Act requires a convention at least every five years, and some unions, such as the Teamsters, take the limit of five years.

[15]George Strauss, "Union Government in the U.S.: Research Past and Future," *Industrial Relations* 16 (Winter 1977), p. 234.

[16]Barbash, *American Unions*, pp. 76–80.

[17]John Hoerr, "Union Democracy and Apathy Don't Mix," *Business Week*, October 2, 1979, p. 28.

[18]U.S. Department of Labor, Bureau of Labor Statistics, *Directory of National Unions and Employee Associations, 1975* (Washington, D.C.: Government Printing Office, 1977) p. 55.

[19]J. Lawrence French, David A. Gray, and Robert W. Brobst, *Political Structure and Presidential Tenure in International Unions: A Study of Union Democracy* (Detroit: paper presented at the annual meeting of the Academy of Management, 1980), p. 16.

[20]Barbash, *American Unions*, pp. 81–88.

[21]Lois S. Gray, "Union Implementing Managerial Techniques," *Monthly Labor Review* 104 (June 1981), pp. 3–8.

[22]Barbash, *American Unions*, pp. 89–93.

[23]Charles W. Hickman, "Labor Organizations' Fees and Dues," *Monthly Labor Review* 100 (May 1977), pp. 19–24.

[24]Nels E. Nelson, "Union Dues and Political Spending," *Labor Law Journal* 28 (February 1977), pp. 109–119.

[25]Examples include recreation, social and entertainment activities, organization and recruitment of new members, convention attendance, general news publications, support of pending legislation, and contributions to charity. Ibid., pp. 117–118.

[26]Charles J. Janus, "Union Mergers in the 1970s: A Look at the Reasons and Results," *Monthly Labor Review* 101 (October 1978), p. 13.

[27]John Freeman and Jack Brittain, "Union Mergers Process and Industrial Environment," *Industrial Relations* 16 (Spring 1977), pp. 173–174.

[28]Janus, "Union Mergers," p. 13.

[29]Gary N. Chaison, "Union Mergers and Integration of Union Governing Structures," *Journal of Labor Research* 3 (Spring 1982), p. 139.

[30]Janus, "Union Mergers," pp. 13–15.

[31]Ibid., p. 22.

[32]*This Is the AFL-CIO* (Washington, D.C.: American Federation of Labor and Congress of Industrial Organizations, 1981), p. 1.

[33]Ibid.

[34]Ibid., pp. 1–3.

[35]U.S. Department of Labor, Bureau of Labor Statistics, *Directory of National Unions and Employee Associations, 1975* (Washington, D.C.: Government Printing Office, 1977), pp. 1–4.

[36]"Annual Survey of Executive Compensation," *Business Week*, May 18, 1982, p. 79.

[37]*This Is the AFL-CIO*, pp. 8–10.

[38]Marvin Caplan, "What Washington Labor Lobbyists Do," in Charles M. Rehmus, Doris McLaughlin, and Frederick H. Nesbitt, eds., *Labor and American Politics*, rev. ed. (Ann Arbor: University of Michigan Press, 1978), pp. 225–229.

[39]*This Is the AFL-CIO*, pp. 10–12.

[40]Edwin M. Epstein, "Labor and Federal Elections: The New Legal Framework," *Industrial Relations* 15 (Summer 1976), pp. 257–274. Also see Philip Taft, "Internal Union Structure and Functions," in Gerald G. Somers, ed., *The Next Twenty-five Years of Industrial Relations* (Madison, Wis.: Industrial Relations Research Association, 1973), pp. 1–9.

[41]J. David Greenstone, *Labor in American Politics* (Chicago: University of Chicago Press, 1977), pp. xiii–xxix.

[42]Robert S. Greenberger, "Kirkland Alters Style at AFC-CIO, Stresses Politics, Organizing Moves," *Wall Street Journal*, June 18, 1982, p. 27.

[43]A. H. Raskin, "The Road to Solidarity: Labor Enters a New Century," *The New Leader*, November 30, 1981, p. 13.

[44]Herbert L. Sherman and William P. Murphy, *Unionization and Collective Bargaining* (Washington, D.C.: Bureau of National Affairs, Inc., 1975), p. 12.

[45]"Dissidents in the Teamsters Are Gaining Clout," *Business Week*, November 13, 1978, pp. 136–139.

[46]"How Williams' Case Will Punish Labor," *Business Week*, March 29, 1982, p. 32.

[47]"Union Corruption: Worse than Ever," *U.S. News and World Report*, September 8, 1980, p. 33.

[48]Derek Bok and John T. Dunlop, *Labor and the American Community* (New York: Simon & Schuster, 1970), pp. 67–69.

[49]Woodrow Ginsburg, "Review of Literature on Union Growth, Government, and Structure: 1955–1969," *A Review of Industrial Relations Research*, vol. 1 (Madison, Wis.: Industrial Relations Research Association, 1970), pp. 232–233.

[50]George W. Bohlander and William B. Werther, Jr., "The Labor-Management Reporting and Disclosure Act Revisited," *Labor Law Journal* 30 (September 1979), pp. 582–589.

[51]"Racketeering Measure Due for Senate Vote," *Daily Labor Report*, July 27, 1982, p. A–5.

[52]Rudy Oswald and Rick Krashevski, "Union Structure," in James C. Stern and Barbara D. Dennis, eds., *Trade Unionism in the United States: A Symposium in Honor of Jack Barbash* (Madison, Wisc.: Industrial Relations Research Institute, 1981), pp. 17–19.

[53]Albert A. Blum, "Why Unions Grow," *Labor History* 9 (Winter 1968), pp. 39–41.

[54]Leo Troy, "Trade Union Growth in a Changing Economy," *Monthly Labor Review* 92 (September 1969), pp. 3–5.

[55]Myron Roomkin and Hervey A. Juris, "Unions in the Traditional Sectors: The Mid-Life Passage of the Labor Movement," in Barbara D. Dennis, ed., *Proceedings of the Thirty-first Annual Meeting: Industrial Relations Research Association* (Madison, Wis.: Industrial Relations Research Association, 1979), pp. 213–222.

[56]Richard Prosten, "The Longest Season: Union Organizing in the Last Decade, a/k/a How Come One Team Has to Play with Its Shoelaces Tied Together?" in Dennis, *Proceedings of the Thirty-first Annual Meeting: Industrial Relations Research Association*, pp. 240–249.

[57]Richard N. Bloch, "Union Organizing and the Allocation of Union Resources," *Industrial and Labor Relations Review* 34 (October 1980), pp. 101–112.

[58]James B. Dworkin and Marian Extejt, "Why Workers Decertify Their Unions: A Preliminary Investigation," paper presented at the Annual Meeting of the Academy of Management, August 1979; and Ronald Berenbeim, "The Declining Market for Unionization," *Conference Board Information Bulletin*, no. 44, August 1978, pp. 2–11.

[59]Alan Kistler, "Trends in Union Growth," in James L. Stern and Barbara D. Dennis, eds., *Proceedings of the 1977 Annual Spring Meeting: Industrial Relations Research Association* (Madison, Wis.: Industrial Relations Research Association, 1977), pp. 541–544.

[60]Seymour M. Lipset and William Schneider, "Organized Labor and the Public: A Troubled Union," *Public Opinion* (August-September 1981), p. 52.

[61]"Labor's Big Swing from Surplus to Shortage," *Business Week*, February 20, 1978, pp. 75–78.

[62]"Are Unions Losing Their Clout?" *U.S. News & World Report*, October 4, 1976, pp. 29–32.

[63]"Labor Digs in to Elect Its Friends," *Business Week*, February 15, 1982, p. 122.

[64]Kistler, "Trends in Union Growth," p. 540.

[65]Roomkin and Juris, "Unions in the Traditional Sectors," pp. 220–222.

[66]Jerome M. Rosow, "American Labor Unions in the 1980s," *IRRA Newsletter*, November, 1979, p. 1.

[67]Arthur Hochner, Karen Koziara, and Stuart Schmidt, "Thinking about Democracy and Participation in Unions," in Barbara D. Dennis, *Proceedings of the thirty-second Annual Meeting of the Industrial Relations Research Association* (Madison, Wis.: Industrial Relations Research Association, 1980), p. 15.

[68]George Strauss, "Union Government in the U.S.: Research Past and Future," *Industrial Relations* 16 (May 1977), pp. 239–241.

[69]Bok and Dunlop, *Labor and the American Community*, pp. 70–71.

[70]Ibid., p. 84.

[71]Nash, *The Union Steward*, pp. 17–19.

[72]Doris B. McLaughlin and Anita W. Schoomaker, *The Landrum-Griffin Act and Union Democracy* (Ann Arbor: The University of Michigan Press, 1979), p. 186.

[73]Bok and Dunlop, *Labor and the American Community*, p. 65–66.

[74]Theodore J. St. Antoine, "The Role of Law," in Jack Stieber, Robert B. McKensie, and D. Quinin Mills, eds., *U.S. Industrial Relations 1950–1980: A Critical Assessment*, (Madison, Wis.: Industrial Relations Research Association, 1981), pp. 191–192.

[75]Ibid., p. 192.

[76]Bok and Dunlop, *Labor and the American Community*, p. 91.

Chapter 5 How Unions Are Organized

Unions are here to stay. . . . Some among even the best of employers might occasionally fall into short-sighted or careless employee practices if it were not for the presence or distant threat of unions.

Lemuel Boulware, *Statesman in Industrial Relations*, 1964.

The United States has a wide variety of unions. They range from single independent local unions which group members for the purpose of negotiating employment conditions with a single employer, to large international unions representing nearly 2 million members and negotiating with several hundred different employers.

This chapter focuses on some of the most essential elements of unionization: (1) How employees are organized into unions, with explanation of the NLRB procedure, the determination of an appropriate bargaining unit, the election campaign, and the election, and (2) employer activities designed to maintain nonunion status or prevent union formation.

How Employees Are Organized into Unions

Much recent research has focused on unionization of employees and on voting patterns. Employees mainly consider whether forming and joining a union will improve their wages and benefits, promotional opportunities, and job security. Can the employees expect to satisfy their job-related goals and needs by forming or joining a union? Will the union provide the means for achieving these goals?[1] If employees perceive that a union will help them attain their goals, they will likely vote for it in an election and support its activities afterwards. If they are not convinced, they will not vote for the union and, if subsequently required to join it, will not support its activities.

The union's campaign to secure employee support may contribute to a union vote, especially among those who are familiar with the union's positions and who attend union campaign meetings. Employees who are satisfied with the working conditions are less likely to attend union campaign meetings, but those who do attend often become more favorable toward the union.

The company's campaign can indirectly affect the vote because it affects employees' belief in the anticipated influence of the union. If the company campaigns hard, some employees will believe that the employer has "seen the light" and will now improve conditions without the union. Further, a strong antiunion campaign may convince some employees that the employer is so antiunion that the union cannot improve working conditions.[2]

While there may be many explanations for the reasons a particular group of employees votes for or against the union in a specific election, several influences have been identified that affect union votes generally. Exhibit 5.1 helps to provide a framework for showing the relationship that exists among the general influences on employees. The *work context* includes specific work-related influences, such as supervisory effectiveness and style, job dissatisfaction, working conditions, pay, and benefits. *Attitudes toward unions* include the beliefs that employees have prior to the vote about unions as institutions and their role in society and in organizations.[3] *Economic considerations* include such external factors as wage levels of other firms, level of unemployment in the industry, economic activity and forecasts, and growth rates.[4] These influences interact with *union instrumentality* which is the employees' perception of whether or not the union will be instrumental in attaining desired outcomes, such as higher wages, improved working conditions, job security, and protection from arbitrary treatment by management.[5] In general if these interactions are positive, the em-

Exhibit 5.1 Influences on Employees on Whether to Vote For or Against Unions

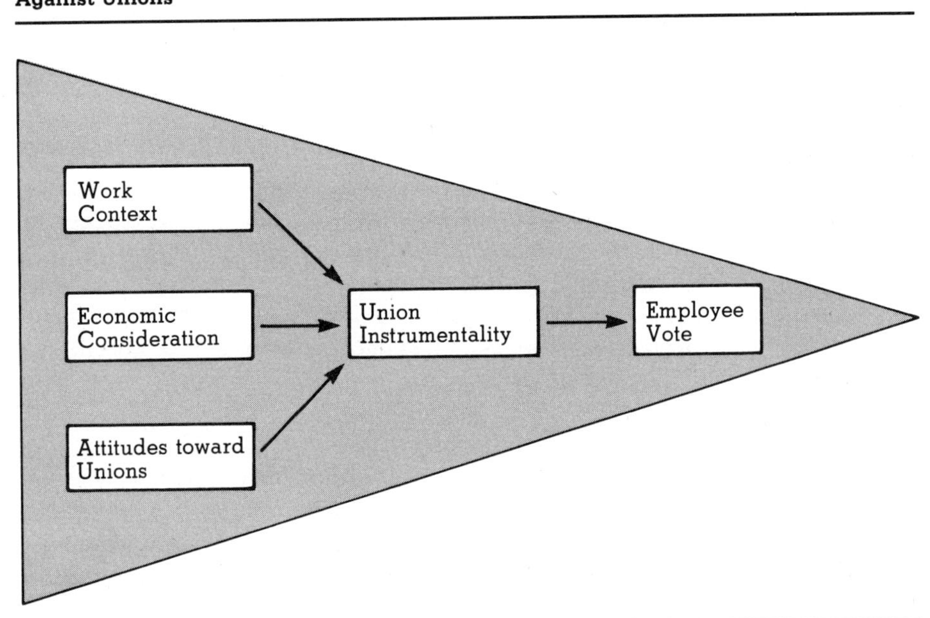

ployee will vote for the union; if not, the employee will vote against union representation.[6] For the individual worker, any one of the influences may cause the employee to vote a certain way. For example, if an employee believes his supervisor is considerate and supportive, this belief may be enough to cause him to vote against union representation.[7]

Another explanation of individual behavior of union voting is that an individual's decision on whether to vote for union representation depends on his or her subjective assessment of the expected benefits to be obtained as weighed against the subjected assessments of the costs.[8] If the expected benefits of being represented by the union are higher than the cost, the employee will vote for the union. Otherwise, the vote will be against representation. If employees have a good chance of promotion, can expect a higher wage based on their present level of effort, and are pleased with their supervisor, they probably will not vote for representation.[9]

Role of the Union in Organizing

Employees' initial interest in unionization is usually based on their dissatisfaction with some work-related situation coupled with a feeling that they can't change the situation. Most managers of nonunion companies incorrectly believe that labor unions initiate union organization drives; however, it is usually the employees themselves that begin the process. For example, one employee or a small group becomes disenchanted with management and makes contact with the union. This contact with union organizers usually occurs after employees believe that there is support for the union and the union's external structure and expertise will help.[10]

The union organizer does not create job dissatisfaction but assists in transforming this employee dissatisfaction into collective action, through formation of a union. The union organizer tailors the organizing approach to the concerns and problems of the prospective members and focuses on the special needs of various groups, such as skilled workers, female or minority workers, or white collar workers. The organizer tries to sell the idea that group action via the union provides the instrument through which employee concerns and dissatisfaction can be most effectively addressed.[11]

Union organizers should never be underestimated by the company. The union organizer is usually first seen distributing handbills to employees as they leave the company parking lots. They dress like the workers so that the workers will identify with them. While their dress may result in a negative impression with management, management should never lose sight of the fact that union organizers are professionals at organizing a union.[12]

Contemporary union organizers, like their counterparts in management, must understand the psychology of the workplace, the workers' needs and goals, and the labor relations climate in which employees work. To be successful, they must be able to diagnose each of these elements at particular sites and at particular time periods. Because conditions change and employee needs may change, the diagnosis must be timely and accurate. As indicated in Chapter 1, unions are formed for a variety of reasons—alienation, job security, dissatisfaction with wages, benefits, physical environment of the workplace, and so on. However, recognition of the reasons does not make unionization campaigns a reality or guarantee their success. The union organizers must be able to (a) sort out these complex factors for the employees on a group or individual basis and (b) operationalize in the employees' language how the union can fulfill their needs in the specific work environment.

Many union organizers are becoming more sophisticated and knowledgeable about employee interests, job expectations, and work-related concerns. As an example, Exhibit 5.2 lists a number of work-related concerns and problems determined by a national survey of the Survey Research Center of the University of Michigan.[13] To the right of each is a possible course of action the union could take to satisfy the concern or alleviate the problem. The union organizer would bring to the employees' attention outcomes which could result from such activities by the union on their behalf.

Although the items listed pertain to national data, experienced and professional union organizers would be able to relate them to employee concerns at a particular facility, explaining what the union could do to help employees resolve job-related problems and achieve individual goals. Companies, knowing full well that the unions' strategies and activities are becoming more sophisticated, likewise expend considerable effort in explaining that the employees can achieve goals and resolve problems through the company alone, without any need for a union. (The company effort to remain nonunion will be explained later in the chapter.)

Union organizers and management both must be aware that job-related needs, interests, concerns, and goals may differ among individual employees, employees of different employers, occupational groups, and so on. For example, teachers at a particular school may be primarily interested in job security; professional white-collar employees may be most concerned about starting salaries of inexperienced employees and promotion opportunities; older factory employees may be more concerned about pensions and retirement policies, and young workers more concerned about wages.

While the union and company must be aware of these differences, the fact generally remains that all employees have some identifiable needs which can be either gratified or frustrated on the job. The main question the union organizer (and the management personnel who may be trying to remain unounion) must ask is: Can the union and its activities facilitate the gratification of employee needs or alleviate employee frustration? The answers to this question on an individual and group employee basis go far in determining whether employees will choose to elect a union as their bargaining representative.

Exhibit 5.2 Union's Strategy and Courses of Action to Achieve Employee Goals and Resolve Job-Related Problems

Examples of Work-Related Problems and Employee Concerns	What the Union Could Negotiate with the Company
Desire for improvement of present fringe benefits	Negotiate better benefits for bargaining unit employees
Desire for additional fringe benefits	Negotiate new benefits, such as dental insurance and legal aid, which would not be provided on the company's initiative
Earns less than deserved compared to others doing similar work	Emphasize comparable wages (local, regional, national, industry); provide data from other unions, Department of Labor, and wage surveys
Exposed to one or more safety and health hazards	Highlight the role of union safety committees and the responsibilities of the company and rights of the union under OSHA
Difficult to get work days and hours changed	Negotiate work schedule procedures with rules and policies which are administered fairly and in accordance with the contract
Inconvenient or excessive hours	Negotiate hours and days of work with advance notice to employees when they work at inconvenient times, call-in pay, overtime, flexitime systems, and so on
Difficult to get duties changed	With job content declared as a *mandatory* negotiable issue, the union could present alternative job descriptions, combine tasks, and so on
Inadequate time for leisure activities	Attempt to obtain shorter hours and workweek, more holidays, and longer vacations for time worked
Skills underutilized in present job	Negotiate promotion policies and procedures; institute a job bidding plan
Unpleasant work environment	Negotiate working conditions and transfer opportunities; institute safety and health committee

Source for work-related problems: Graham L. Staines and Robert P. Quinn, "American Workers Evaluate the Quality of Their Jobs," *Monthly Labor Review* 102 (January 1979), pp. 3–12. Survey data courtesy of the Center for Political Studies, University of Michigan.

Alternative Methods for Establishing Unions

In most cases, a union attains exclusive bargaining agent status through a secret ballot representation election.[14] While the NLRB considers secret-ballot elections superior, it has discretionary authority to allow alternative methods, such as authorization cards (see Exhibit 5.3). In its *Gissel* decision the Supreme Court upheld the NLRB's authority to order employers to bargain with the union when authorization cards have been used under the following conditions:[15]

Exhibit 5.3 Examples of Union Authorization Card

United Food & Commercial Workers International Union

Affiliated with AFL-CIO-CLC

AUTHORIZATION FOR REPRESENTATION

I hereby authorize the United Food & Commercial Workers International Union, AFL-CIO-CLC, or its chartered Local Union(s) to represent me for the purpose of collective bargaining.

(Print Name) (Date)

(Signature) (Home Phone)

(Home Address) (City) (State) (Zip)

(Employer's Name) (Address)

(Hire Date) (Type Work Performed) (Department)

(Hourly Rate) (Day Off) Day Shift ____ Night Shift ____ Full Time ____ Part-Time ____

Would you participate in an organizing committee? Yes ____ No ____

Source: Courtesy of the United Food & Commercial Workers International Union

1. Evidence reveals that a fair, impartial election would have been *impossible* at the time that the election was held because of flagrant employer unfair labor practices.
2. Authorization cards were clear and unambiguous.
3. Employee signatures were obtained without threat or coercion.
4. A majority of employees in the bargaining unit had signed the cards.[16]

In essence, the NLRB and the courts concluded that holding another election where the employer had made a fair and impartial election impossible would not be a realistic remedy because a reurn election would favor the party that had committed unfair labor practices, interfering with the first election.[17]

In 1982, the NLRB ordered an employer to bargain with a union even though the union had not established its majority status because the employer had committed "outrageous" and "persuasive" unfair labor practices. It concluded that these violations were so serious that they precluded any reasonable possibility of holding a free and uncoerced election. (The NLRB was split 3–2 on this election and this decision is on appeal to the courts.)[18]

In a few cases the union may request employer recognition and then offer to prove that a majority of employees want to join the union. The union may offer to submit signed authorization cards to an impartial third party (arbitrator, mediator, or clergyman) who will check the signatures on the cards against payroll signatures. If the employer agrees to this process, the majority status can be affirmed and union recognition be extended.[19] (Employers may choose this approach if they agree with conclusions of a research report based on 146 NLRB elections showing that the cost per employee in a representation election was $126.60.)[20]

Generally, there is strong employer opposition to granting union recognition without an election. There have been strong allegations that employees were pressured or forced into signing cards. Examples of extreme cases include the refusal of union organizers to leave employees' houses until the cards are signed, obtaining signatures after drinking parties, and threatening injury to or perpetrating violence against employees who refuse to sign. These extremes reveal obvious violations of employees' rights, but they occur in very few cases.[21] Another reason for opposition to union recognition without elections is that signed authorization cards are relatively poor predictors of union success in elections. In a study of 1,174 elections, where over 75 percent of the employees had signed the cards, the union won only 70 percent of the elections.[22]

Initiation of Organizing Campaigns

Representation Election Procedure The union pre-election campaign is not a simple process of exchanging letters and handbills and then holding an election. The campaign usually goes through several stages:

1. Identifying the target organization by initiating contacts with employees at the workplace (handbilling) or receiving notification from disgruntled employees.
2. Determining interest by calling meetings, visiting homes, and counting responses to handbills.
3. Setting up an organizing committee by identifying leaders and educating them as to the benefits and procedures of the union, the law, and the issues likely to be raised by management.
4. Building interest by soliciting signatures on authorization cards. (Most organizers will wait to announce that the union represents a majority until over 50 percent and usually 60 to 80 percent, have signed cards.)[23]

During this time the union discovers and highlights employees' problems, compares wages at their facility to wages at unionized facilities, and explains the role of the union in helping to satisfy their job-related needs. In other words, the union will attempt to convince the workers of a need for the union, then to sign union authorization cards[24] (see Exhibit 5.2), and to support the forthcoming organizing campaign by wearing union buttons, attending meetings, and signing up others.[25] While various means are available to gain support, research indicates that one-to-one contact, peer contact and persuasion, and high quality, professionally designed written communication are most effective.[26] Other efforts used by unions include television and radio advertising, "hotline" telephone numbers, group meetings, and handbilling.

Organizing new unions is costly. Leaflets and literature must be printed and mailed, office space rented, staff hired, and legal expertise retained. Such efforts usually take time from the union staff that could be devoted to providing services to present union members (handling grievances, arbitration, and negotiating). Because present members pay dues and unions are democratic institutions, the union's priority is to provide services to its membership, then to attempt to organize new members when it promises a return on its investment. In other words, organizing new unions may not be a high priority item for unions when the costs do not justify the expected returns to the union.[27]

Companies often learn of union organizing attempts from supervisors or rank and file employees and through actual observation before they receive official notification (by letter or telegram) from the union demanding recognition. Some companies react vigorously, while others do little to acknowledge any union's attempt to organize the employees. Some employers tell their employees about their opposition and urge them not to sign union authorization cards. Because the cards may specifically state that the signee favors union representation, any employee signature assists the union in establishing itself in the company. Other employers publish no-solicitation rules[28] that apply to all nonemployees and are specifically designed to curtail unionization efforts. If posted, these rules must have been in effect prior to the organizing campaign.[29]

Filing a petition for the election Prior to 1935, in order to obtain recognition the union had to show its strength and employee interest in representation by such actions as strikes. The Wagner Act and the NLRB changed this situation by developing procedures and guidelines for peacefully determining the majority interest of employees through elections or some other comparable demonstration. The procedure is initiated when the potential bargaining representative for the employees files a petition for an election.

The NLRB is authorized to conduct an election only when such a petition has been filed by an employee, group of employees, an individual or labor organization, or an employer. Usually the petition is filed after a union has requested union recognition from the employer and the request is denied. If filed by an employee or on behalf of employees, the petition must be supported by evidence (usually by authorization cards) that a substantial interest in union representation (30 percent of the bargaining unit) exists. Further, it must show that the employer has declined a request by the union to organize it as the employee representative.[30] The employer cannot petition for an election until the union seeks recognition. If the employer could, it would petition at the time when the union's support was weakest.

After receiving a petition, the NLRB will first determine whether it has jurisdiction (see Chapter 3). If so, it will promptly notify the company and request a listing of employees. Companies are not required to submit a list but usually comply with the request as an act of good faith. Next, the NLRB will arrange a conference with the company and union to discuss the possibility of a consent election. Here, both sides may agree to the appropriate bargaining unit, voter eligibility, ballot, date, time and place for the election, and a consent election will be held. If either party refuses to agree on any of these items, a formal hearing to settle these matters will be requested and conducted.[31]

Election investigation and hearing If the union and management officials do not agree to a consent election, the NLRB must investigate the petition, hold a hearing if necessary, and then direct an election if it finds that there is a question of employee representation. This investigation will secure answers to the following questions:

1. What is the appropriate bargaining unit?
2. Does substantial interest in representation (30 percent) exist among employees in the unit?
3. Are there any barriers to an election in the form of existing unions, prior elections, or present labor agreements?[32]

Appropriate bargaining unit The appropriate bargaining unit is a grouping of jobs or positions in which two or more employees share common employment interests and conditions (community of interests) and which may reasonably be grouped together for collective bargaining purposes. Determination of the appropriate bargaining unit is left to the discretion of the NLRB, which decides in each representation case how employee rights can best be protected under the act. The board's discretion has, however, been limited in several ways.

- Professional employees cannot be included in a unit composed of both professional and nonprofessional employees, unless a majority of the professional employees vote to be included in a mixed unit.
- A proposed craft unit would not be ruled inappropriate simply because a different unit has been previously approved by the board unless a majority of employees in the proposed craft unit vote against being represented separately.
- Plant guards may not be included in any bargaining unit which has nonguard employees in the unit.
- Supervisors and managers are not considered employees under the Act and may not be in any bargaining unit.
- Excluded are agricultural laborers, public employees (except postal employees), and independent contractors, although some of these may be covered in separate state statutes.[33]

The NLRB's determination of bargaining unit strongly influences whether the union will win the election, whether one union will prevail in an interunion contest, whether craft employees will have their own union or be included in a plant-wide unit, or whether the union will include key employees who could give direction and leadership for the bargaining unit employees. The composition of the bargaining unit is important to the employer as well as to the public. Should a plant have several small bargaining units, the employer may face different unions in negotiations several times throughout the year, which could cause continuous instability in labor relations. Separate units concerned with similar jobs may cause disputes over rights to jobs, leading to strikes or slowdowns. Should a small bargaining unit be merged with a nationwide bargaining unit, any confrontation that resulted in a strike could cause a nationwide shutdown and complications for customers in need of the companies' products.[34]

The bargaining unit itself may cover employees in one plant, in two or more facilities of the same employer, or in some industries (coal mining, construction, and trucking) of several different employers. The NLRB considers a number of relevant factors in determining the composition of the appropriate bargaining unit:

- Interests of employees and employers.
- Community of interests, such as wages, working conditions, training, and skill.
- History of collective bargaining either at the location in question or another facility owned by the company.
- Transfers of employees among various facilities.
- Geography and physical proximity of the workplaces.
- Employer's administrative or territorial divisions.
- Degree of separation (or distinctiveness) of work or integration (or interrelatedness) of work.[35]

Where the relevant factors do not give a clear indication for the composition of the appropriate bargaining unit, an election (commonly called a *Globe* election, from the original NLRB case) may be held to determine employee interests. For example, one group of electricians in a steel plant might wish to be represented by the International Brotherhood of Electrical Workers (IBEW) instead of the United Steelworkers of America (USWA). The USWA wants to include all electricians in a bargaining unit composed of all production and maintenance workers in the plant. Under such circumstances, the electricians' vote will determine whether they will be members of the Steelworkers, a separate electricians' union (IBEW), or no union.[36]

Election Bars There are several rules that make a petition for a representation election untimely. The first is a legal requirement which prohibits any NLRB representation election where one has been held in the last twelve months and where a petition for election covers a group of employees who are already covered by an existing contract and already members of a legally certified union.[37]

The second barrier to elections is an administrative determination that was made in the interest of stable and effective labor relations. The NLRB rule, called the *contract bar doctrine*, specifies that a valid, signed agreement for a fixed period of three years or less will bar any representation election for the life of the agreement (a longer contract is still limited to three years). Thus, the contract bar doctrine could extend the twelve-month statutory limitation on elections to three years. To do otherwise would be unfair to union and management officials who have negotiated a multiyear labor agreement in good faith.[38]

Eligibility of voters Before an election is conducted, voter eligibility must be determined. Usually, those employees on the payroll just before the date of the election are eligible. While the employee must be employed in the unit on the date of the election, exceptions are made to allow employees who are on sick leave, on vacation, temporarily laid off, or on temporary leave, such as military duty, to vote in the election. In addition, the NLRB will occasionally consider irregularity of employment, such as in the construction, food processing, and longshoring industries. Also, economic strikers who have been replaced by permanent employees are allowed to vote in any election within twelve months after the strike begins. This policy insures that management does not provoke a strike and hire replacements who could vote out the union.[39]

***"Names and addresses"* rule** Within seven days after the regional director of the NLRB has approved a consent election or after an election has been directed, the employer must file a list of names and addresses of all eligible voters with the regional director. This information is then made available to the union. Refusal to comply could be identified as a bad faith act on the part of the employer and cause the election to be set aside or the NLRB to seek the names and addresses by subpoena.[40] The purpose of this disclosure rule is to give the unions the same right of access to employees that management already possesses.[41]

The election The representation election, acclaimed as "one of the great innovations of American labor law,"[42] is conducted by NLRB officials. Eighty percent are consent elections and are held within 45 days (median) of the initial request. After a preelection hearing, elections are held in about 75 days.[43] NLRB data show that 90 percent of the eligible voters in NLRB elections, as compared to 50 percent in major political elections, choose to vote.

The high voter turnout in union representation elections might be due to the convenient voting procedure (usually carried out on company property) and the belief of many employees that their vote more directly affects their lives (at least their working conditions) than political elections at the local, state, and national levels. Finally, both unions and management realize that an employee could express union preference to a union representative and an opposite preference to the management representative to avoid a confrontation during the election campaign. Neither side is sure of employee voting preferences when faced with a secret ballot; therefore, union and management officials actively work to get out the vote.

Voter participation tends to decline the longer it takes for the NLRB to conduct the elections. Thus, some employers are motivated to refuse to consent election in hopes of increasing the changes of the union losing the election. Also, because most single-unit elections are close, the non-participants affect the outcome of many elections.[44] The number of pre-election days has also been linked to union losses. During the first six months of delay, there is an average drop-off in union victories of 2.5 percent per month. Consent elections have the highest union victory rate; however, there has been a decided downward trend in these types of elections.[45]

Using a ballot with the appropriate company and union designations (see Exhibit 5.4), a secret-ballot election is usually conducted under NLRB supervision during working hours at the employer's location. However, the NRLB has discretionary authority to conduct it by mail ballot if a regular election is not fair and reasonable. For example, if it is physically impractical for eligible voters to cast their ballots at a centralized location for such reasons as widely scattered work, adverse weather conditions, or excessive travel required, the regional director of the NLRB may conduct the election by mail balloting.[46]

The NLRB must determine whether the majority of the employees in an appropriate bargaining unit want to be represented for collective bargaining purposes. It defines *majority* as the simple majority rule generally accepted in democratic elections, which means that those choosing not to vote in the election have decided to assent to the wishes of the majority who did vote. Therefore, a majority of the employees who vote (50 percent plus one of those voting) in the election must favor representation before a union will be certified by the NLRB.[47]

If two or more choices are placed on the ballot, a runoff election may be necessary between the choices receiving the two highest numbers of votes in the initial election. If the majority votes "no union," no representation election can be held for twelve months. If a union receives the majority of the votes, the NLRB will certify it as the exclusive bargaining agent of the employees in the bargaining unit.

After the votes have been counted, either party has five days to file objections alleging misconduct or to challenge the ballots of voters whom one party believes should not have voted in the election.[48] This part of the representation process receives considerable criticism because the delay in assessing the ballot challenges and objections concerning misconduct seems excessive. Although only 15 percent of the elections require post-election proceedings, the time can be considerable,[49] and if decisions are appealed to the courts, it could take years before the final outcome is determined.

Duties of the exclusive bargaining agent and employer The bargaining representative chosen by the majority of the employees in the appropriate unit has the duty to represent equally and fairly *all* employees in the unit regardless of their union membership. The employer has a comparable obligation, that is, to bargain in good faith with the exclusive bargaining agent and to refuse to bar-

Exhibit 5.4 Examples of Secret Ballots for Union Representation Elections

UNITED STATES OF AMERICA

National Labor Relations Board

OFFICIAL SECRET BALLOT

FOR CERTAIN EMPLOYEES OF

CONTAINER CORPORATION

Do you wish to be represented for purposes of collective bargaining by -

METAL PRODUCTS, MACHINERY AND RELATED EQUIPMENT WORKERS OF AMERICA, AFL-CIO

SAMPLE

MARK AN "X" IN THE SQUARE OF YOUR CHOICE

YES	NO
☐	☐

DO NOT SIGN THIS BALLOT. Fold and drop in ballot box.
If you spoil this ballot return it to the Board Agent for a new one.

UNITED STATES OF AMERICA

National Labor Relations Board

OFFICIAL SECRET BALLOT

FOR CERTAIN EMPLOYEES OF

CONTAINER CORPORATION

This ballot is to determine the collective bargaining representative, if any, for the unit in which you are employed.

SAMPLE

MARK AN "X" IN THE SQUARE OF YOUR CHOICE

[Name of Union A]	NEITHER	[Name of Union B]
☐	☐	☐

DO NOT SIGN THIS BALLOT. Fold and drop in ballot box.
If you spoil this ballot return it to the Board Agent for a new one.

gain with another union seeking to represent the employees. Further, any negotiated labor agreement covers all employees in the bargaining unit, regardless of their union membership status.[50]

Decertification Procedure

Whenever employees believe that the union is not representing the interests of the majority, a *decertification procedure* is available. In recent years, decertification elections have been on the increase; researchers have identified a variety of reasons for this:

- Fairer treatment of employees by employers.
- Poor job by unions (especially smaller unions) in providing services to members.
- Inability of unions to negotiate an effective first contract after winning bargaining rights.[51]
- Striking employees having skills that can be readily replaced,[52] so that when a strike occurs, the employer hires replacements.

Any employee, group of employees, or employee representative may file a petition for a decertification election twelve months after the union has been certified or upon expiration of the labor agreement. This petition must be supported by at least 30 percent of the bargaining unit employees.[53]

While employers cannot petition for a decertification election, they can question the union's majority status and petition the NLRB for a representation election. This petition must be supported by objective evidence, such as absence of a labor agreement, to show that the union no longer represents the majority of the bargaining unit employees.[54] If the employees choose to decertify their union, there cannot be another representation election for twelve months.[55] However, after a valid petition is filed with the NLRB but before the election, the employer must still bargain with the union until the question of union representation is resolved.[56]

Although employers must be careful of their role in the decertification process, they have exhibited growing interest in it.[57] For example, a one-day seminar offered for $450 per person is designed to teach management representatives about the entire process of decertification.[58] Many employers have concluded that they should become more involved, especially since they are becoming aware that they do not necessarily have to play a passive role in the decertification process.

When management chooses to become involved in the decertification campaign, it usually relies on four major tactics:

1. Meetings with employees, either one-to-one, in small groups, or with the entire unit.

2. Use of legal or expert assistance for advice in the campaign.
3. Letter campaigns to employees at their homes.
4. Improvement of the employment climate at the workplace by developing more effective performance appraisal, personnel development programs, and improved communication.[59]

The number of decertification elections has increased fivefold (872 in 1980) since the 1950s and the number of eligible voters has tripled. Unions are losing as much as 75 percent of the elections. Nevertheless, substantially less than one percent of the estimated 15 or more million union members under the NLRB's jurisdiction participate in any decertification election in any given year. Thus, while the trends appear to be drastic for the unions, decertification actually has not been a significant burden to most unions.[60]

Factors that have influenced the outcome of decertification elections are:

- Decertified units tend to be small. Here, managers and employees are closer. Also, unions find it difficult and costly to service smaller locals.
- Chances of decertification are greater when the workforce is homogeneous.
- Decertification elections are more common in manufacturing and the retail and wholesale trades than other industries.
- Seven national unions were involved in 45 percent of the decertification elections. The largest national union, the Teamsters, was involved in the most.
- Votes to decertify occur most often after the first year of representation, and decline thereafter.
- Decertification is more likely when the union-management relationship is extremely good (employees are happy with management) or when it is extremely bad (numerous strikes occur).
- The vote for decertification declines when union involvement is intense. The percentage of employees who vote to decertify is directly related to the percentage of employees who had signed the decertification petition.[61]

Important factors that influence the outcome of decertification votes are:

- The presence of an active, credible, informed leader or leaders who are able to convince the membership to support the union or to vote for no union representation.
- The presence of a salient issue, such as pension payments by younger employees, union security or unsafe working conditions.
- The occurrence of an event or series of events, such as a strike or a number of grievances not processed, that causes employees to start the decertification process.
- The use of direct contact between trustworthy, credible managers and members of the bargaining unit.[62]

While management must consider the economic costs of a decertification campaign, it must also consider the implications of both possible election outcomes and legal issues involved in its participation. For example, if management campaigns vigorously for decertification but the union wins, what type of labor-management relationships will result? If the results are close, will the relationships be unstable in the future? Should the union lose, will a more militant union seek representation after a year? These factors and others should play an important role in determining the specific strategy of the employer.[63]

Any members of a company's management staff, from first-line supervisors upward, must be wary of committing unfair labor practices. In fact, the NLRB reviews very carefully any aid provided employees by employers in any decertification effort. However, the employer may provide aid in some areas:

- Answer employee inquiries on how to decertify unions by referring the employees to the NLRB.
- Respond to specific employee questions about the decertification process in a manner which conveys no coercion or other unfair labor practice.
- Furnish an employee or any representative of a group of employees with a current list of employee names and addresses.[64]

Yet the employer must be aware of related unlawful activities, such as:

- Obtaining NLRB forms for employees who may be interested in union decertification.
- Providing services such as typing, assistance in phrasing the petition for decertification, and use of company stationery to employees who are interested in launching a decertification campaign.
- Initiating discussions on how or whether to decertify the union.
- Allowing supervisors or any other persons identified with management to promote the decertification process.[65]

As employers become more active in the decertification processes, unions should begin to monitor union members' attitudes toward the company and union. They should observe levels of competence, self-esteem, job satisfaction and role stress because these attitudinal measures may help determine the possibility of a decertification campaign.[66]

The employees, like the employer, must be aware of possible consequences of their activities attempting to decertify the union. Decertification advocates must be prepared for pressure from union officials, ostracism from fellow employees who may be pleased with the union and involved in its activities, and expulsion from the union. The NLRB has upheld the union's right to discipline union members who actively participate in the campaign to decertify the union, as long as the disciplinary action does not affect the employees' employment status.[67]

Conduct of the Representation Election Campaign

All elections are conducted according to NLRB standards, which are designed to assure that employees in the bargaining unit can indicate freely whether they want to be represented for collective bargaining purposes. However, election campaigns differ substantially, and the strategies of individual unions and employers vary widely. For example, handbills similar to those in Exhibit 5.5 are frequently used in addition to speeches, informal talks, interviews, and films. Thus, the election campaign, one of the most interesting and controversial activities in labor relations, has led to a body of doctrines and rules.

Campaign doctrines and the NLRB The *totality of conduct doctrine*, although confusing and controversial, guides the NLRB interpretations of unfair labor practice behavior. This doctrine essentially means that isolated incidents, such as campaign speeches, must be considered within the whole of the general circumstances of the campaign and with the possibility that other specific violations have occurred.[68] The best description of *totality of conduct* may have come from Judge Learned Hand, who wrote:

Exhibit 5.5 Examples of Handbills Distributed during Representation Election Campaigns

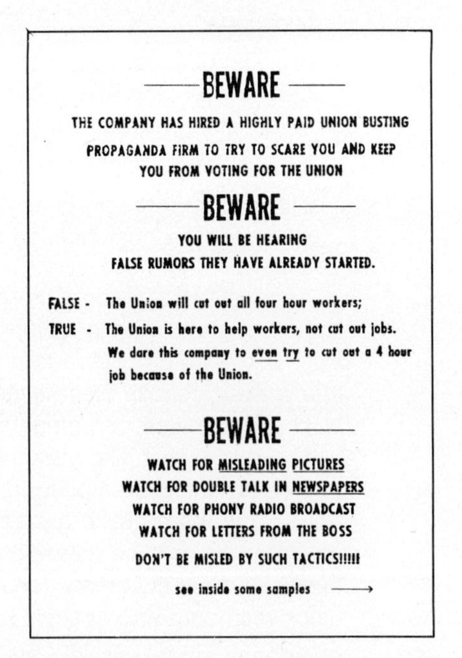

Words are not pebbles . . . ; they have only a communal existence; and not only does the meaning of each interpenetrate the other, but the aggregate take their purpose from the setting in which they are used, of which the relation between the speaker and the hearer is perhaps the most important part.[69]

One of the more enduring doctrines has been the *laboratory conditions doctrine* established in the *General Shoe* decision in 1948. In this case, the NLRB clearly specified that its function was

to provide a laboratory in which an experiment may be conducted, under conditions as nearly ideal as possible, to determine the uninhibited desires of the employees. It is our duty to establish these conditions; it is our duty to determine whether they have been fulfilled. . . . [If] the standard drops too low [and] the requisite conditions are not present, . . . the experiment must be conducted over again.[70]

In 1962 the NLRB established further campaign standards concerning preelection campaigns and held that it would overturn an election whenever an unfair labor practice occurred during a critical phase of the campaign. It concluded that conduct that interferes with the employees' exercise of "a free and untrammeled choice" in an election is cause to set aside the outcome of an election.[71] In the same year, the NLRB, in setting aside an election, established guidelines that stood for fifteen years and were used to determine whether employer or union speeches constituted sufficient interference with employee rights to a fair election.[72] Subjects covered in these guidelines included:

1. Misrepresentation of material facts or other similar company trickery.
2. Presentation of information by a person known by employees to have special knowledge about the information presented.
3. Presentation of information so close to the election that the other party or parties have no opportunity to make an effective reply.
4. A reasonable probability that the misrepresentation may have a significant effect upon the election.
5. Lack of qualification to evaluate the statements.[73]

The NLRB has emphasized that "absolute precision of statement and complete honesty are not always attainable in an election campaign, nor are they expected by the employees." It has also recognized that both union and management have the right to conduct "free and vigorous" campaigns and that "exaggeration, inaccuracies, half-truths, and name-calling, though not condoned, [would] not be grounds for setting aside elections."[74] Thus, the NLRB has concentrated on misrepresentations that are *substantial* departures from the truth.[75]

In 1982, the NLRB rejected "laboratory of conditions" doctrine as unrealistic in response to research showing that employees *are* able to assess misleading campaign propaganda. In a 3–2 vote, the majority stated:

We will no longer probe into the truth or falsity of the parties' campaign statements, and that we will not set elections aside on the basis of misleading campaign statements. We will, however, intervene in cases where a party has used forged documents which render the voters unable to recognize propaganda for what it is. Thus, we will set an election aside not because of the substance of the representation, but because of the deceptive manner in which it was made, a manner which renders employees unable to evaluate the forgery for what it is. . . .

American employees may be better educated, in the formal sense, than those of previous generations, and may be in certain respects more sophisticated. We do not honor them by abandoning them utterly to the mercies of unscrupulous companies, including the expert cadre of professional opinion molders who devise campaigns for many of our representation elections.[76]

The NLRB was influenced by a significant study by Getman, Goldberg, and Herman, who had interviewed over 1,000 employees in thirty-one elections in five states. Their findings cast doubt on the previously held assumption that employees are unsophisticated about labor relations and are swayed easily by campaign propaganda. In fact, votes of 81 percent of the employees could have been predicted from their pre-campaign intent and their attitudes toward working conditions and unions in general. The study concluded that employees' votes appeared to be the product of attitudes that resulted from their everyday experiences in the industrial world and not from the campaign itself.[77]

Captive Audience—"Twenty-four Hour Rule" One approach, usually taken by management, includes presenting "captive audience" speeches, which are delivered to employees during working time. Whereas the NLRB earlier required the company to offer the union equal time during working hours, its rule has been altered significantly. For example, now neither the union nor management may make a captive audience speech within twenty-four hours of the election; however, the employer may deny any union request to reply to a company speech on the company premises during working hours as long as the union has another means by which to effectively communicate with the employees.[78] But if the union has no acceptable means of communicating with the employees, as in the lumber and logging industry where employees live on company property, and if the employer's unfair labor practices have created a serious election campaign imbalance, the NLRB and the courts may grant the union access to plant bulletin boards, parking lots, and entrances so that it may communicate with the employees.[79]

Polling or questioning employees Polling employees or asking questions about their interests in unions was considered unlawful interference with employee rights in earlier days. This rigid position on employer inquiry has become more flexible. The present NLRB rule states that activities regarding polling of employees by an employer will not be an unlawful interference if each of the following safeguards is taken:

- The purpose of the inquiry is to determine the accuracy of the union's claim that it represents a majority of the employees and this purpose is clearly communicated to the employees.
- The employees are polled by secret ballot and assurances are given against any employer reprisal.
- The employer has not otherwise committed any unfair labor practices.[80]

Distribution of union literature on company property The NLRB and the courts have long held that except in special circumstances employees may not be prohibited from distributing union organizing materials in nonworking areas on their own time[81] *unless* the employer can show that such activity would disrupt production, employee work, and plant discipline. For example, employees of restaurants and retail establishments cannot distribute union materials in customer areas, and employees of health-care institutions cannot distribute materials in areas designated strictly for patients.[82] However, distributing materials in such places as hospital cafeterias predominantly patronized by hospital employees cannot be prohibited.[83] In addition, the employer cannot prohibit distribution of union material if the basis for the prohibition is that part of its content includes political issues, such as right-to-work laws and minimum wages.[84]

Showing of films during election campaigns Films presented to discourage workers from joining unions have taken on new dimensions, especially since the 1950s, by production of the movie *And Women Must Weep* by the National Right to Work Committee. This movie portrays union violence, strikes, vandalism, phone threats, a house bombing, and even the shooting of a baby of a dissident union member. Frequent use of the film by employers prompted the International Association of Machinists to produce a rebuttal film, entitled *Anatomy of a Lie*, which projects no evidence of a connection between the shootings and other misconduct and the union's activities. On-site interviews with persons involved in the strike are shown to reveal an exact opposite view of the employer film, and the president of the union is filmed stating that nearly 99 percent of the union members voted to strike. The NLRB's position regarding the showing of these films has varied; its current position is that their showing does not constitute an unfair labor practice and alone is not sufficient cause to have the results of an election set aside.[85]

The Nonunion Firm

Employer Attempts to Maintain Nonunion Status

The fact that less than one-fourth of nonagricultural workers are union members is in part due to employers' actions aimed at maintaining a union-free work environment. Employers have attempted to maintain nonunion status through many methods, ranging from effective personnel programs to the use (or misuse) of related legal procedures. Obvious and substantial interest by nonunion employers is evident in a multitude of programs, such as *How to Maintain Nonunion Status,*[86] *Winning Union Organizing Campaigns,*[87] and related publications.[88]

These efforts have elicited strong union reactions, as evidenced by recent caustic articles in the AFL-CIO publication, *American Federationist:* "Peddling the 'Union Free' Guarantee"[89] and "The Consultants Who Coach the Violators."[90] Yet, some believe that it is only the unenlightened employers who should be classified as "union busters"; the "smart" nonunion employers are attempting to operate without a union because they believe it is a "sound business decision."[91]

It is impossible to state one single motive for employer actions. Some employers are openly anti-union and would seriously consider almost any method that would keep their organizations free from unions. Other employers sincerely believe that their effective personnel programs and policies render unions unnecessary. Regardless of the motive, many nonunion employers believe that "management that gets a union deserves it. . . . No labor union has ever captured a group of employees without the full cooperation and encouragement of managers who create the need for unionization."[92]

Today, some major corporations (IBM, Texas Instruments, Eastman Kodak, Delta Airlines) remain largely or totally nonunion, and a multitude of small companies carry nonunion status. Some of these companies clearly state their position on unions. For example, Texas Instruments' position is stated in the company handbook which is given to all employees:

TI believes a union would be detrimental to TI and to TIers because it would reduce the operational flexibility and efficiency that have contributed greatly to both TI's success and the growth goals of individual TIers. Most TIers apparently agree, since historically they have not felt the need for a union in their quest for job security, job satisfaction and good economic benefits. As a result, TI is one of the largest non-union companies in the U.S. TI hopes that TIers will continue to feel the same way and, in turn, expects to continue its pledge to make company and employee goals as compatible as possible.

TI has instituted many personnel programs, such as Success Sharing, including a profit sharing plan, a pension plan and an employee stock option purchase plan, that are designed to relate your personal goals for financial security to TI's own goals for growth, productivity and profitability.[93]

In addition, it has a brochure entitled "TI and Unionism" which is also distributed to employees.

Other companies likewise have their position on unionism published for employee consideration. Excerpts similar to that below are frequently included:

Our company does not believe it necessary for our employees to organize unions in order to deal directly with management. In addition, it is not necessary now nor do we believe it ever will be necessary to join a union in order to work at our company.

We believe our employees would rather deal with management directly, rather than through a union. We also believe that our employees value their freedom to handle their own affairs and to speak on their own behalf, rather than being dictated to and controlled by an outside union which knows nothing about their jobs and is interested more in the union dues than their job interests. We believe that where there are unions there is trouble, strife, and discord; therefore, we intend to oppose unionism by every proper means.

As President of ______ and one who is vitally interested in your welfare, I want you to know that you have the right to reject the union and to refuse to sign these union cards. Union organizers will tell you that these cards will be kept confidential, but they must be shown to the National Labor Relations Board if the union pursues an election. I am calling this to your attention because I don't want you to be tricked into signing a card which may be used against your interest.[94]

While these statements clearly indicate that the employer would rather not deal with the union, they are within the rights of the employers to express their opinion on unionism.

Some nonunion companies concentrate on developing a sound personnel program instead. For example, Foulke's study of large nonunion companies identified nine common factors:

- The absence of symbols of rank and status such as parking spaces, company cars, or country club memberships for managers.
- Carefully considered surroundings—locating where quality high schools and universities are near, and keeping individual facilities small.
- Overall corporate strength—high profits, fast growth, high technology, or dominant market position.

- Programs to promote employment security, such as work sharing or overall reduction in pay to avoid layoffs in hard times.
- Promotion from within—job posting, career development, training and education programs.
- Influential personnel programs, for example, having the personnel director report directly to top management.
- Competitive pay and benefits, especially having compensation that is equitable externally and internally and comparable to the pay at unionized companies.
- Management that listens—using systematic approaches such as attitude surveys and open-door policies appeal procedures.
- Careful grooming of managers—focusing on long-term results, using assessment centers, and appraising in terms of competence and employee relationships.[95]

Other, more extreme tactics used by some companies to avoid unionization are:

- Developing a spy network (tattle-tales) to identify union supporters.
- Refusing to hire former employees of unionized companies (but giving the applicant a reason other than prior union affiliation for employment denial).
- Establishing a case for discharge (including documentation) of known union advocates.
- Seeking to determine prospective employees' attitudes toward unions from interviews, references, and so on, then refusing to hire them (again giving another reason) if they are pro-union.
- Giving psychological tests (job interest questionnaires) to determine the likelihood that an applicant will be interested in a union.
- Locating new plants in areas where union membership is low and expanding the company's nonunion plants.[96]
- Using a standard application form of a State Employment Service that asks applicants whether they have been a member of a union and using the application form as part of the pre-employment inquiry.[97]

Some employers facing union organizing campaigns have committed unfair labor practices deliberately, with the expectation of economic returns to them. A recent research study demonstrated that "under realistic conditions it is economically feasible for employers to secure economic gains by violating the National Labor Relations Act,"[98] Even more disappointing was the conclusion that

in the past, the compliance system [of the National Labor Relations Act] has been inadequate to the extent that some employers have found it profitable to commit unfair labor practices in order to forestall unionization. Those employers obeying the law because "it's the law" have faced a greater probability of incurring costs of unionization and may have been at a competitive disadvantage to employers who violated the law. Such inequities do not encourage compliance with the law and provide evidence of the need for labor law reform.[99]

The unfortunate reasons behind these activities are simply that the risks of this approach are relatively low. Violations are not criminal; no one is imprisoned or fined for violating the National Labor Relations Act. Social costs are not high because most of the public is unaware of the employers who flagrantly violate the law. Too, the potential gains for these employers include not only the possibility of forestalling unionization but also of employees losing interest in unions after a long period of judicial appeals.[100]

Employee committees Another tactic is the use of employee committees. Although the NLRA has outlawed company unions and unlawful assistance to unions affiliated with national organizations, some companies have organized and supported employee committees for the purpose of discussion and resolving grievances.[101] Even though these committees differ from traditional unions in their discussions with employers because they do not negotiate labor agreements, they could subsequently come under the provisions of the National Labor Relations Act if their discussions over wages and employment conditions are interpreted as negotiations by the NLRB. Further, the employer could be directed to recognize and bargain with committee members as a labor union.[102]

Double-breasted construction companies In the construction industry, where an estimated one-third of the nonresidential work is performed by nonunion construction firms and the percentage has been growing in the last few years, nonunion firms have been successful. They have been able to pay less per hour than the union scale, to employ people at different wage scales, and to save on fringe benefits, while having a flexible and strike-free work environment.[103]

Some unionized construction companies have established nonunion subsidiaries in order to compete in the construction market (called *double breasted* companies).[104] While the building and construction trade unions strongly contend that these firms are in reality only one firm and should recognize the union, the employers maintain their separate corporate identity.[105] A determination of their legal separateness for labor relations purposes involves investigations of the following by the NLRB and court: commonality of management and supervision, commonality of personnel and labor relations policies, commonality of ownership and financial control, and interrelationship of operations.[106]

New Union Strategies Countering Employers' Efforts to Maintain Nonunion Status

In response to nonunion employers' strategies in maintaining nonunion status, unions have been forced to return to the drawing board to design new strategies. One example is the use of a telephone taped speech in which an employee may call a well publicized number and receive the "union message" for the day or week during an organizing campaign.[107] These messages range from benefits of joining unions and anticompany messages to personal testimony of popular, well-known plant employees.

Other new approaches include:

- Publicly embarrassing firms that have close business ties to the anti-union firm by refusing to do business with retail or wholesale firms or threatening to withdraw money from banks.
- Attending stockholder meetings and making stockholders aware of managerial attitudes toward employees and unions in hopes that adverse publicity and embarrassment will change management's behavior.
- Withholding use of union pension funds from investment in companies whose behavior is deemed anti-union and which restrict organizing efforts.
- Attempting to develop acceptance of unions in the community by allying with church groups or civil rights organizations as a way to address social, economic, and personal needs of the people.
- Coordinating organizing activities and combining resources of several groups in large metropolitan areas to promote unionization in that area.[108]
- Negotiating a neutrality agreement which includes a clause stating that if the union seeks to organize employees in nonunion plants, management will remain neutral and a statement defining the limits of acceptable union organizing behavior. If management signs the agreement, the union will have to behave in a manner that neither demeans nor ridicules the company or its management.[109]

Summary and Implications

Summary

This chapter discussed how unions are organized and how employers try to avoid unionization. Starting with the employees' perceived needs and job-related concerns, the role of unions in fulfilling these needs and concerns was discussed.

Unionization efforts progress from first contacts with employees to the signing of authorization cards, petition for election, hearings, determination of the appropriate bargaining unit, and the eventual representation election. Within this framework numerous rules, regulations, and legal requirements govern the union certification process. In addition, the duties of the union—the exclusive bargaining agent—to represent the bargaining unit employees are explained. If employees do not believe that the union is representing the majority interest, decertification procedures are available.

Noting that less than one-fourth of the nonagricultural labor force is unionized, the next section highlights a number of ways employers attempt to maintain nonunion status—some focusing on positive personnel practices and programs, but others involving tactics which could be considered unfair labor practices. In response to companies' efforts to remain nonunion, new union strategies such as the use of union financial clout and neutrality pacts have been devised and implemented.

Implications

More recently, nonunion companies have been faced with the expansion of employee rights under common law and the National Labor Relations Act. Under common law (and potentially statute) an emerging labor relations issue is the application of the principle of "employment at will." Employment at will (or termination at will) means that if an employee can quit for any reason, the employer can discharge for any reason. In other words, the employment relationship should not be forced on either party.[110]

Until recently, courts and state legislatures have refused to tamper with employer rights to terminate employees "at will." However, thirteen state courts have now taken the position that company manuals, handbooks or employment interviews constitute implied contracts to which the employer is legally bound. For instance, if the handbook states that employees will be discharged for just cause only, the employer may be required to prove just cause if taken to court. Three states, Michigan, Wisconsin, and Pennsylvania, have legislation pending that would alter the rights of employers to terminate employees at will.[111]

Unions in the United States have provided workers (members of bargaining units) a guarantee of due process involving discipline and discharge for job behavior through collective bargaining and appeal through grievance procedures. Since only about one-fifth of all employees are covered, there are over 50 million workers who are not covered by the labor agreements and can be discharged at the will of their employer (unless protected by other laws). Using estimates for unionized settings, this means that about 2.3 million employees are discharged each year without protection from union representation.[112]

While employers obviously will resist such legislation and the unions will passively support it, the end result will probably be improved personnel policies, overall better management, cautious construction of employee manuals and handbooks, and honest, informative feedback on performance appraisals.

On another front concerning nonunion settings, the caseload of the NLRB concerning protected concerted rights of nonunion employees under the National Labor Relations Act has been growing and it is predicted that this growth will continue. Section 7 of the Act guarantees to both union and nonunion employees the right to engage in concerted activities for the purpose of collective bargaining or other mutual aid or protection. Such activities must be of common interest to a group of employees and must concern wages, hours and conditions of employment.

Nonunion employees have had these rights since 1960, when the Supreme Court upheld a seven-employee walkout over cold working conditions. The Court stated that since these employees had no bargaining rights and no grievance procedure by which to resolve their claim, they had no alternative but to walk off the job. Later cases have been extended to employee claims over safety, refusal to work overtime, pay differences, and discharge of fellow employees. While employees may be replaced during the walkout and are not entitled to wages and benefits during the walkout, the employer may not discharge them for their concerted activities. A controversy which still is not settled is whether one employee who claims to act on behalf of other employees when he walks off the job is involved in a protected concerted activity. Thus far, the courts have generally concluded that the employee acts on his own behalf, although the Board has shown some tendency to protect the employee.[113]

In 1982, the NLRB extended the *Weingarten* rights to nonunion employees, that is, ruled that an employee is entitled to representation in an interview which he reasonably believes may result in his discipline. In the specific case, disciplinary action had been taken against members of a group who had encouraged group discussions about changes in work rules. Later, when a member of the same group was directed to attend a meeting about the incident, the employee asked for representation because he believed that the subject for the meeting was his previous actions involving the discussions over work rules.[114]

Discussion Questions

1. By referring to the reasons why employees become members of unions given in Chapter 1, assess the *means* used by union organizers to meet these needs.
2. Select an organization with which you are familiar, and determine the number of possible bargaining units which would be appropriate for collective bargaining in its structure.
3. Explain the contract bar doctrine. How would it influence the negotiation of the first labor agreement?
4. Discuss the shifting position of the NLRB regarding representation election campaigning. Appraise each position.
5. Prescribe a "do" and "don't" list for supervisors involved in unionization campaigns so they will not commit any unfair labor practices.
6. Why do you believe employers are becoming more interested in decertification elections?
7. Explain the following statement: "It is not the union that organizes the workers; it is management."

8. What new strategies have unions used to counter employer efforts to maintain nonunion status? Appraise the effectiveness of these strategies.

9. What effect will the courts' rulings on "employment at will" and the NLRB's extension of protected concerted activities to nonunion employees have on nonunion employees? Explain. (The Implications section may be helpful)

References

[1]Victor H. Vroom, *Work and Motivation* (New York: Wiley, 1964), p. 30.

[2]J. M. Brett and T. J. Hammer, "Organizational Behavior and Industrial Relations," in T. A. Kochan, et al., eds., *Industrial Relations Research in the 1970s: Review and Appraisal* (Madison, Wis.: Industrial Relations Research Association), pp. 245–251.

[3]Thomas A. DeCottis and Jean-Yves Le Lovarn, "A Predictive Study of Voting Behavior in a Representation Election Using Union Instrumentality and Work Perceptions," *Organizational Behavior and Human Performance* 27 (February 1981), pp. 103–118.

[4]Thomas Hyclak, "Union-Nonunion Wage Changes and Voting Trends in Union Representation Elections," in Barbara D. Dennis, ed., *Proceedings of the Thirty-Fourth Annual Meeting of the Industrial Relations Research Association* (Madison, Wis.: Industrial Relations Research Association 1982), p. 350.

[5]DeCottis and Lovarn, "A Predictive Study of Voting Behavior," p. 109.

[6]Stuart A. Youngblood, William H. Mobley, and Angelo S. DeNisi, "Attitudes, Perceptions, and Intentions to Vote in a Union Certification Election: An Empirical Investigation," in Barbara D. Dennis, ed., *Proceedings of the Thirty-Fourth Annual Meeting of the Industrial Relations Research Association* (Madison, Wis.: Industrial Relations Research Association, 1982), pp. 244–253.

[7]Edward L. Harrison, Douglas Johnson, and Frank M. Rachel, "The Role of the Supervisor in Representation Elections," *Personnel Administration* 26 (September 1981), pp. 69–70.

[8]Orley Ashenfelter and John H. Pencaval, "American Trade Union Growth: 1900–1960," *Quarterly Journal of Economics* 83 (August 1969), pp. 434–448.

[9]Henry S. Farber and Daniel H. Saks, "Why Workers Want Unions: The Role of Relative Wages and Job Characteristics," *Journal of Political Economy* 88 (April 1980), pp. 349–369.

[10]John J. Hoover, "Union Organization Attempts: Management's Response," *Personnel Journal* 61 (March 1982), pp. 214–215.

[11]James A. Craft and Marian M. Extejt, "New Strategies in Union Organizing," *Working Paper Series* (Pittsburgh, PA: University of Pittsburgh, 1982), p. 304.

[12]Hoover, "Union Organizing Attempts," pp. 214–215.

[13]Graham L. Staines and Robert P. Quinn, "American Workers Evaluate the Quality of Their Jobs," *Monthly Labor Review* 102 (January 1979), pp. 3–12.

[14]National Labor Relations Board, *A Guide to Basic Law and Procedures under the National Labor Relations Act* (Washington, D.C.: Government Printing Office, 1976), pp. 10–11.

[15]Robert E. Williams, Peter A. Janus, and Kenneth C. Huhn, *NLRB Regulation of Election Conduct* (Philadelphia: Industrial Research Unit, University of Pennsylvania Press, 1974), pp. 371–372.

[16]NLRB v. Gissel Packing Co., 395 U.S. 575 (1969).

[17]Herbert L. Sherman, Jr., and William P. Murphy, *Unionization and Collective Bargaining*, 3d ed. (Washington, D.C.: Bureau of National Affairs, 1975), pp. 69–70.

[18]Conair Corp., 110 LRRM 1161 (1982). See Robert P. Hunter, "Conair: Minority Bargaining Order Ushers in 1984 at NLRB," *Labor Law Journal* 33 (September 1982), pp. 571–575.

[19]Stephen I. Schlossberg and Frederick E. Sherman, *Organizing and the Law* (Washington, D.C.: Bureau of National Affairs, 1971), pp. 97–99.

[20]Woodruff Imberman, "How Expensive Is an NLRB Election?" *MSU Business Topics* 23 (Summer 1975), pp. 13–18.

[21]Robert Lewis, "The Law and Strategy of Dealing with Union Organizing Campaigns," *Labor Law Journal* 25 (January 1974), p. 45.

[22]Marcus H. Sandver, "The Validity of Union Authorization Cards as a Predictor of Success in NLRB Certification Elections," *Labor Law Journal* 28 (November 1977), pp. 698–701.

[23]William E. Fulmer, "Step by Step through a Union Campaign," *Harvard Business Review* 59 (July-August 1981), pp. 94–95.

[24]An authorization card signifies that the employee desires to be represented by the union in collective bargaining. The employee thereby authorizes the union to represent him with his employer. The signed card may be used later by the union as proof of majority representation, as support to demand recognition, and as evidence that there is "substantial interest" among the bargaining unit to support a petition to the NLRB for representation election. Schlossberg and Sherman, *Organizing and the Law*, p. 50.

[25]Ibid., pp. 41–42.

[26]David B. Stephens and Paul R. Timm, "A Comparison of Campaign Techniques in Contested Faculty Elections: An Analysis of the Florida Experience," *Journal of Collective Negotiations in the Public Sector* 7 (1978), pp. 167–177.

[27]Richard N. Block, "Union Organizing and the Allocation of Union Resources," *Industrial and Labor Relations Review* 34 (October 1980), pp. 101–113.

[28]This rule must be applied equally to all forms of solicitation, such as politicians seeking votes and charitable organizations seeking contributions.

[29]Lewis, "Law and Strategy," pp. 42–48.

[30]National Labor Relations Board, *Guide to Basic Law*, pp. 11–16.

[31]Lewis, "Law and Strategy," pp. 45–47.

[32]National Labor Relations Board, *Guide to Basic Law*, p. 11.

[33]Ibid., pp. 9–11.

[34]Schlossberg and Sherman, *Organizing and the Law*, p. 60.

[35]John E. Abodeely, *The NLRB and the Appropriate Bargaining Unit* (Philadelphia: Industrial Research Unit, University of Pennsylvania, 1971), pp.7–86.

[36]Sherman and Murphy, *Unionization and Collective Bargaining*, pp. 60–61.

[37]National Labor Relations Board, *Guide to Basic Law*, pp. 13–14. There are exceptions, such as when the agreement is not in writing, has not been signed, or has not been ratified.

[38]Ibid.

[39]Ibid. However, permanent replacements are also eligible to vote in the same election.

[40]*Excelsior Underwear, Inc.*, 156 NLRB 1236 (1966).

[41]Sherman and Murphy, *Unionization and Collective Bargaining*, p. 39.

[42]William P. Murphy, "Reforming the National Labor Relations Act," in Barbara D. Dennis, ed., *Proceedings of the Thirtieth Annual Meeting: Industrial Relations Research Association* (Madison, Wis.: Industrial Relations Research Association, 1978), p. 157.

[43]Ibid., pp. 158–159.

[44]Richard N. Block and Myron Roomkin, "Determinants of Voter Participation in Union Certification Elections," *Monthly Labor Review* 105 (April 1982), pp. 45–47.

[45]Marcus H. Sandver and Herbert G. Heneman III, "Union Growth through the Election Process," *Industrial Relations* 20 (Winter 1981), pp. 109–115.

[46]Williams, Janus, and Huhn, *NLRB Regulation*, pp. 371–372.

[47]Ibid., pp. 391–395.

[48]National Labor Relations Board, *Guide to Basic Law*, p. 17.

[49]Murphy, "Reforming the National Labor Relations Act," p. 161. For example, if the regional director proceeds to an investigation, the median time is 41 days; if a hearing is held, the time extends to 58 days; if the issue goes to the board, another 87 days are required.

[50]National Labor Relations Board, *Guide to Basic Law*, p. 8.

[51]James B. Dworkin and Marian Extejt, "Why Workers Decertify Their Unions: A Preliminary Investigation," paper presented at the Annual Meeting of the Academy of Management, August 1979.

[52]I. Chafetz and C. R. P. Fraser, "Union Decertification: An Exploratory Analysis," *Industrial Relations* 18 (Winter 1979), p. 68.

[53]Mark Z. Sappir, "The Employer's Obligation Not to Bargain When the Issue of Decertification Is Present," *Personnel Administrator* 27 (February 1982), pp. 41–45.

[54]Kenneth C. McGuiness, *Silverberg's How to Take a Case before the National Labor Relations Board*, 3d ed. (Washington, D.C.: Bureau of National Affairs, 1967), p. 179.

[55]Ibid.

[56]Dresser Industries, 111 LRRM 1436 (1982).

[57]Ibid., p. 10; and Woodruff Imberman, "How to Win a Decertification Election," *Management Review* 66 (September 1977), pp. 26–28, 37–39.

[58]Executive Enterprises, *The Process of Decertification.*

[59]William E. Fulmer, "When Employees Want to Oust Their Union," *Harvard Business Review* 56 (March–April 1978), pp. 163–170. Also see William T. Downey, "The *Mar-Jac* Rule Governing the Certification Year," *Labor Law Journal* 29 (September 1978), pp. 608–614.

[60]Joseph Krislov, "Decertification Elections Increase but Remain No Major Problem to Unions," *Monthly Labor Review* 102 (November 1979), pp. 30–31.

[61]William E. Fulmer and Tamara A. Gilman, "Why Do Workers Vote for Union Decertification?" *Personnel*, 58 (March–April 1981), pp. 29–32.

[62]John C. Anderson, Gloria Busman, and Charles A. O'Reilly III, "The Decertification Process: Evidence from California," *Industrial Relations* 21 (Spring 1982), pp. 193–195.

[63]Fulmer, "When Employees Want to Oust Their Union," pp. 167–169.

[64]William A. Krupman and Gregory I. Rasin, "Decertification: Removing the Shroud," *Labor Law Journal* 30 (April 1979), pp. 234–235.

[65]Ibid., p. 236.

[66]Charles A. Odewahn and M. M. Petty, "A Comparison of Levels of Job Satisfaction, Role Stress, and Personal Competence between Union Members and Nonmembers," *Academy of Management Journal* 23 (January–February 1981), pp. 150–155.

[67]*Tawas Tube Production, Inc.*, 151 NLRB 9 (1965).

[68]Sherman and Murphy, *Unionization and Collective Bargaining*, pp. 39–40.

[69]*NLRB v. Federbush Co.*, 121 F.2d 957 (1941).

[70]*General Shoe Corp.*, 77 NLRB 124 (1948).

[71]*Dal-Tex Optical Co.*, 137 NLRB 1782 (1962).

[72]*Hollywood Ceramics*, 140 NLRB 221 (1962).

[73]Cindy M. Hudson and William B. Werther, Jr., "Section 8 (c) and Free Speech," *Labor Law Journal* 28 (September 1977), p. 611.

[74]*Hollywood Ceramics*, 140 NLRB 221 (1962).

[75]"NLRB Member Truesdale on *General Knit* Decision," *News and Background information*, 99 LRR 307 (1978).

[76]Midland National Life Insurance Company, 110 LRRM 1489 (1982).

[77]*Shopping Kart Food Market*, 94 LRRM 1705 (1977). Julius G. Getman, Stephen B. Goldberg, and Jeanne B. Herman, *Union Representation Elections: Law and Reality*, (New York: Russell Sage Foundation, 1976).

[78]Hudson and Werther, "Section 8 (c)," pp. 612–613. Also see *Peerless Plywood Co.*, 107 NLRB 427 (1953); and *Livingston Shirt Co.*, 107 NLRB 400 (1953).

[79]Max Zimny, "Access of Union Organizers to Private Property," *Labor Law Journal* 25 (October 1974), p. 624.

[80]Hudson and Werther, "Section 8 (c)," p. 613. Also see *Blue Flash Express, Inc.*, 109 NLRB 591 (1954); and *Struknes Construction, Inc.*, 165 NLRB 1062 (1967).

[81]*Republican Aviation Corp. v. NLRB*, 324 U.S. 793 (1945).

[82]"Justices Twice Back Right to Distribute Union Literature on Company Property," *Wall Street Journal*, June 23, 1978, p. 6.

[83]*Beth Israel v. NLRB*, 46 U.S.L.W. 4765 (June 22, 1978).

[84]*Eastex, Inc. v. NLRB*, 46 U.S.L.W. 4783 (June 22, 1978).

[85]Joseph A. Pichler and H. Gordon Fitch, "And Women Must Weep: The NLRB as Film Critic," *Industrial and Labor Relations Review* 28 (April 1975), pp. 395–410.

[86]"Fair Plant, 'Easy Task,' Keeps Union Door Shut," *Kansas City Star*, July 21, 1977.

[87]Executive Enterprises, New York, N.Y.

[88]Scott Myers, *Managing without Unions* (Reading, Mass.: Addison-Wesley Publishing, 1976); Louis Jackson and Robert Lewis, *Winning NLRB Elections* (New York: Practising Law Institute, 1972); and I. Herbert Rothenberg and Steven B. Silverman, *Labor Unions, How to: Avert Them, Beat Them, Out-Negotiate Them, Live with Them, Unload Them* (Elkins Park, Pa.: Management Relations, 1973).

[89]Charles McDonald and Dick Wilson, "Peddling the 'Union-Free' Guarantee," *American Federationist* 85 (April 1979), pp. 12–19.

[90]Phillis Payne, "The Consultants Who Coach the Violators," *American Federationist* 84 (September 1977), pp. 22–29.

[91]Peter J. Pestillo, "Learning to Live without the Union," in Barbara D. Dennis, ed., *Proceedings of the Thirty-first Annual Meeting: Industrial Relations Research Association* (Madison, Wis.: Industrial Relations Research Association, 1979), pp. 233–239.

[92]Charles L. Hughes, *Making Unions Unnecessary* (New York: Executive Enterprises Publications, 1976), p. 1.

[93]*TI and You . . . the TIer's Handbook* (Dallas: Texas Instruments Incorporated, 1978), p. iv. Reprinted by permission of Texas Instruments.

[94]Paraphrased from a company which shall remain anonymous.

[95]Fred K. Foulkes, "How Top Nonunion Companies Manage Employees," *Harvard Business Review* 59 (September–October 1981).

[96]Techniques told to authors by employers and union organizers.

[97]Alan Balfour, "The Unenforceability of the UAW's 'Neutrality Pledge' from General Motors," Paper presented at the Second Annual Meeting of the Southern Industrial Relations Association, 1981.

[98]Charles R. Greer and Stanley A. Martin, "Calculative Strategy Decisions during Organization Campaigns," *Sloan Management Review* 19 (Winter 1978), p. 73.

[99]Ibid.

[100]Ibid., pp. 61–74.

[101]Sherman and Murphy, *Unionization and Collective Bargaining*, p. 47.

[102]*NLRB v. Cabot Cargon Co.*, 360 U.S. 203 (1959). The union challenged a General Foods job enrichment program that divided employees into work groups for the purpose of working job assignments, scheduling overtime, and discussing job-related concerns with a consultant (with management representatives in attendance on occasion). While the NLRB ruled that no union existed, it could raise interesting issues in the future. *General Foods Corporation and American Federation of Grain Millers, AFL-CIO and Its Local 70*, 231 NLRB 122 (1977).

[103]"Open-Shop Construction Picks Up Momentum," *Business Week*, December 12, 1977, p. 108.

[104]Robert V. Penefield, "The Double-Breasted Operation in the Construction Industry," *Labor Law Journal* 27 (February 1976), pp. 89–93.

[105]Tim Bornstein, "The Emerging Law of the 'Double-Breasted' Operation in the Construction Industry," *Labor Law Journal* 28 (February 1977), pp. 77–79.

[106]Joseph F. Canterbury, Jr., "Dual Shops in the Construction Industry," in Bernard J. King and Donald W. Savelson, eds., *Construction Industry Labor Relations 1977* (New York: Practising Law Institute, 1977), pp. 459–462.

[107]Used by the International Brotherhood of Electrical Workers in a campaign to organize clerical workers of Alabama Power Company, Birmingham, Alabama, fall 1978.

[108]James A. Craft and Marian M. Extejt, "New Strategies in Union Organizing," *Working Paper Series* (Pittsburgh, PA: University of Pittsburgh, 1982), pp. 5–17.

[109]James A. Craft, "The Employer Neutrality Pledge: Issues, Implications, and Prospects," *Labor Law Journal* 31 (December 1980), pp. 753–754.

[110]Stuart A. Youngblood and Gary L. Tidwell, "Termination at Will: Some Changes in the Wind," *Personnel* 58 (May–June 1981), p. 25.

[111]Labor Special Projects Unit of the Bureau of National Affairs, *The Employment-at-Will Issue*, (Washington, D.C.: The Bureau of National Affairs, Inc., November 19, 1982), pp. 3–8.

[112]Jack Stieber, "The Case for Protection of Unorganized Employees against Unjust Discharge," in B. D. Dennis, ed., *Proceedings of the Thirty-Second Annual Meeting of the Industrial Relations Research Association* (Madison, Wis.: Industrial Relations Research Association, 1980), pp. 150–160.

[113]George W. Bohlander, "Employee Protected Concerted Activity: The Nonunion Setting," *Labor Law Journal*, 33 (June 1982), pp. 344–351.

[114]"NLRB Extends *Weingarten* to Unrepresented Workers," *Daily Labor Report* 143, July 26, 1982.

AS PART OF the contract negotiated last year with the railroad industry, the union agreed to submit to arbitration a proposal that the railroads be allowed to eliminate 25 percent of the cabooses on through freight trains.

James Martin, operating vice president

man crews and no cabooses. Martin said those trains operated safely.

Simmons said the union's campaign for mandatory caboose laws was spurred by the railroad industry's attempt to renege on provisions of the 1982 contract.

"We had settled in our national contract for the railroads to eliminate 25 percent of the cabooses on trains of 35 cars or less," Simmons said. "Now they want all

on fights U.S. Steel import plan

m Sun-Times Wires

l Corp. and British Steel reported close to agree- controversial joint venture the United Steelworkers formal unfair labor prac- in an attempt to stop the

eel spokesman confirmed mpany's chairman, David

The USW says the plan would cost 3,000 jobs at Fairless and thousands more nationwide.

fended its proposal at its Fairless Works near Philadelphia as the only way to keep the aging mill open.

But the USW charges the plan would cost 3,000 jobs at Fairless and thousands more nationwide if other steelmakers follow U.S. Steel's lead.

UFW adopts boycott strate

SAN JOSE, Calif. (AP)—The United Fa has launched a slick, direct-mail campaign boycott of a supermarket chain, and the stor back by dropping leaflets into every bag of

A far cry from the rallies and picketing o against stores d the $1 million c technologies ava businesses," saic

"We cannot c 1980s with the . . . or even the 1960s," Chavez said in a mem the new tactics.

"While we will not abandon our time-honor picketing and leafleting, we must also incorpo technologies in our boycott campaigns," he

In the campaign's first mailing last week, chures urged residents near 15 Lucky grocery San Diego to San Francisco to shop at oth Another mailing to homes near another planned later this summer. Eventually, 75,00 targeted to receive mailings.

Business Must L

In Current 'Em

aymment utlawed

itives are said to be anx- plete the deal before Mac- ches jobs Sept. 1 to be- nan of Britain's National

The union said U.S. Steel's refusal to furnish data "is a violation of its duty to bargain with the USW." A U.S. Steel spokesman refused to comment. The giant steelmaker has de-

vernment workers

The board then would deter- the employees are essential ding public health and safety ld bar certain groups from

Part 2
Negotiating and Administering the Labor Agreement

Part 2 pertains to key activities in the labor relations process: the negotiation and administration of the work rules. These topics are approached from the vantage point of legal and quasi-legal (labor agreement) proscriptions on related behavior as well as with an eye to the practical realities forged out of the relationships between union and management officials.

THE DOMINANT company, IBP Inc., was founded in 1960 by Currier Holman and Andy Anderson. Formed originally as Iowa Beef Processors and now a subsidiary of Occidental Petroleum Corp., IBP controls about 20 percent of the nation's cattle slaughter through its ultramodern plants.

The late Holman once expressed his philosophy of meatpacking: "Business, as we pursue it here at IBP, is much like waging war."

It was an appropriate comparison. The successful slaughtering and selling of meat depends on a collection of variables. But for the companies that find the best way to meet those variables—prices paid to farmers, wages paid to labor, demand in the marketplace—the rewards are substantial, as IBP has proven.

While old-line packers were busy shutting down their big-city plants and contemplating building new ones in rural areas, Holman and Anderson were moving aggressively into the business. Their first plant opened in Denison, Ia., in 1961.

AFTER BUYING a second Iowa plant, IBP constructed a sprawling, single-story factory in 1966 in Dakota City, Neb. Workers standing elbow to elbow along the disassembly line cut up the beef and put it into boxes for shipping to retailers around the country.

...ore to Upgrade Schools

...ncy,' Task Force Says

sidered a "company union" and voted in the meat cutters.

The strike that followed lasted for eight months. There were bombings and shootings. It also set a pattern for bitter strikes that would follow at IBP plants. Today, only 4 of Iowa Beef's 13 plants are unionized.

There was a clear-cut purpose behind IBP's labor strategy. It allowed the company to enter the business with labor costs that ran about half the amount paid by its competitors.

While IBP was busy cementing its position in the late 1960s, the old-line packers were

Chapter 6 Negotiating the Labor Agreement

Despite recent glamorization of the practice or art of collective bargaining, the collective-bargaining process is little known and widely misunderstood. To some, it is a mystical ritual of legal mumbo jumbo. Others regard it as a closed society which transcends mere labor and management roles and practitioners' labels. Whatever the viewpoint, the lack of commonality is apparent.

George E. Constantino Jr., "Defining Line and Staff Roles in Collective Bargaining," *Personnel Journal* 58 (October 1979), p. 689.

Negotiation is a common feature of everyday life. Newspapers and other media vividly document international negotiations (such as Egypt and Israel's and the nuclear weapons disarmament) as well as dramatic confrontations between government officials and terrorist organizations. Negotiations are also a central feature of our interpersonal activities—we continually make deals or exchange favors with our friends and work associates. While this chapter covers negotiations between union and management officials over conditions of employment, many aspects of negotiations have broader applications to other bargaining activities in our society.

This chapter first defines collective bargaining or its interchangeable term "contract negotiations" and explains initial influences affecting this activity. Subsequent sections consider pre-negotiation activities and collective bargaining behaviors. The final section places these diverse collective bargaining approaches in a perspective by describing "the bargaining power model," a likely resolution framework.

Collective Bargaining: Definition and Initial Influences

Collective bargaining is an *activity whereby union and management officials attempt to resolve conflicting interests in a manner which will sustain and possibly enrich their continuing relationships.* There are legal, administrative and attitudinal implications of this definition.

Some legal guidelines discussed later in this chapter and in chapter 7 pertain to the negotiation of the labor agreement which reflects the *interests*, obligations and expectations of labor and management officials and bargaining unit employees. However, the agreement is often vague and/or inapplicable to some working conditions which occur during its duration.

Consequently, *administrative* considerations occur in negotiating the labor agreement, so it can be fairly interpreted on a daily basis. The newly negotiated contract provisions can significantly affect workplace operations. For example, a provision which lets employees refuse overtime assignments can affect work-scheduling policies, and might restrict management's ability to produce materials for a key customer's deadline. Related considerations also occur in interpreting and administering the labor agreement on a daily basis (employee grievances over the "*rights*" aspect of collective bargaining discussed in chapter 8).

Attitudes of union and management officials toward collective bargaining and the negotiated settlement influence their relationships during the length of the labor agreement.[1] A successful collective bargaining settlement occurs when both parties believe they have gained something[2] even though a "gain" for management might mean maintaining the status quo, and a "gain" for the union might be only a tradeoff (wage reductions for guaranteed employment) in recessionary times. Contract negotiations, should reinforce the following attitudes:

First, each side needs the other. The union needs jobs for its members at acceptable wages and conditions; the employer needs an efficient work effort at a minimum cost. Second, each side is capable of withholding for a time something the other side needs. The union withholds labor by striking or imposing other sanctions; the employer can say no to union demands and/or actually withhold employment.[3]

Collective bargaining is more easily defined than explained. Exhibit 6.1 establishes a framework for the complete collective bargaining process. The tone and result of collective bargaining are initially influenced by the negotiating parties' structure and bargaining objectives, and the structure of the negotiation unit.

Union and Management Bargaining Objectives and Bargaining Range

Union and management officials each have general bargaining objectives which are determined by the constraints in the labor relations process (See Exhibit 1.1). For example, management does not want the negotiated settlement to put the company at a competitive disadvantage, and the union wants the best possible conditions for its members.

There are a wide variety of bargaining objectives. In some cases management might be out to "break the union," as was alleged in the 1982 negotiations to end the football players' strike. On the other hand, a superordinate goal or

Exhibit 6.1 Dimensions of Collective Bargaining

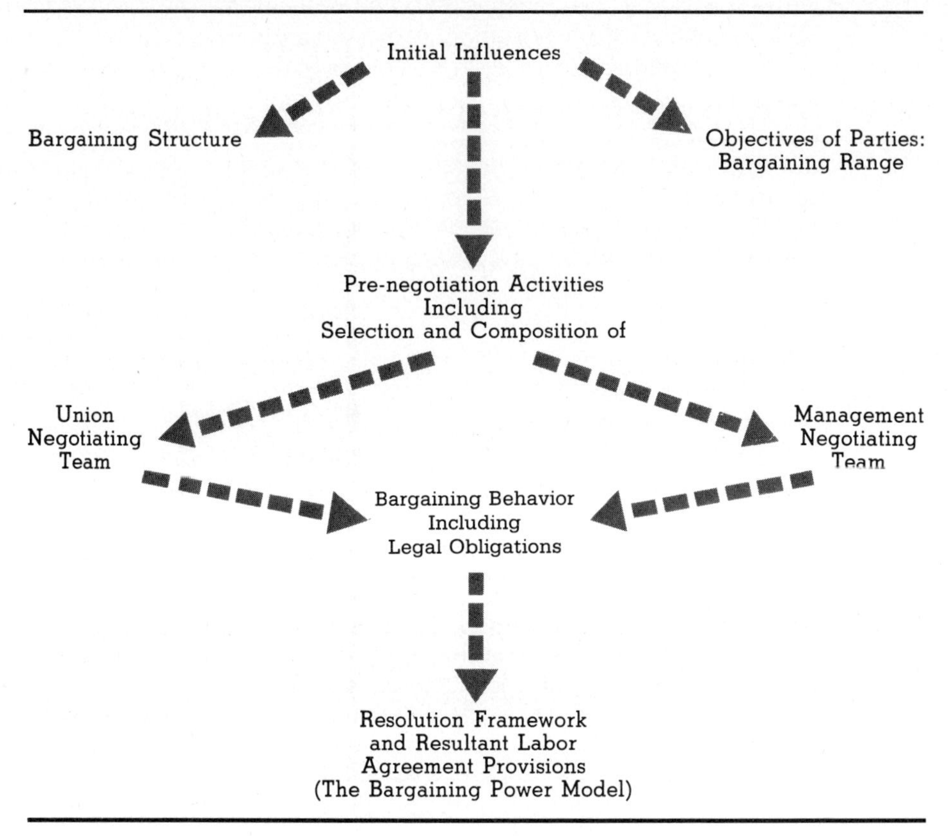

objective commonly shared by management and the union can pervade collective bargaining; the drive to save Chrysler Corporation from bankruptcy, for example. Although bargaining objectives are unique to the negotiating parties, there are some objectives that usually apply when management and the union formulate the upper and lower limits of their bargaining ranges.

Bargaining Ranges Union and management officials both enter collective bargaining with their own ideas of an acceptable settlement, although both parties know the other will not agree entirely with their position. Therefore, both parties usually enter negotiations with a variety of acceptable positions, which gives them some room for maneuvering.[4]

These positions are given priorities and grouped into two *bargaining ranges*, one for management, the other for the union. (See Exhibit 6.2 for an illustration.) The bargaining ranges represent a multitude of priorities for union and management officials. Exhibit 6.2 contains only a few issues for illustrative purposes; however, it is common for the parties to negotiate a hundred or more bargaining

Exhibit 6.2 Bargaining Ranges for Union and Management Negotiators

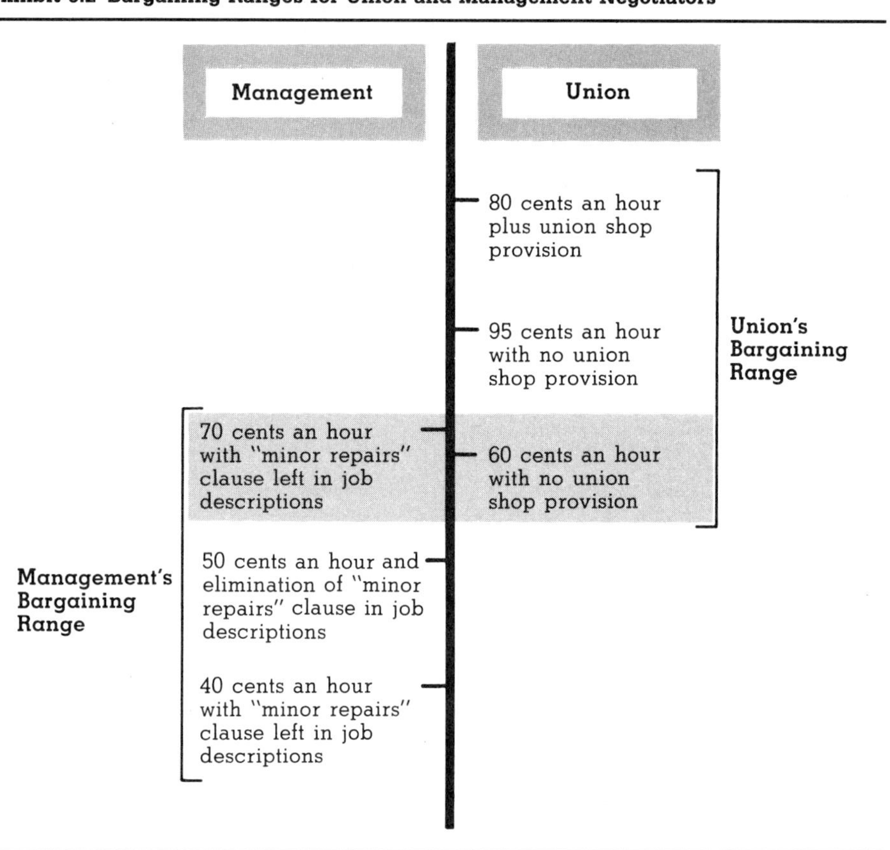

issues. (See Exhibit 6.3 for a general list of issues which may appear in a collective bargaining agreement and be included in the bargaining range.)

Both management and union representatives have upper and lower limits on their respective ranges. Management's upper limit is usually determined by its objectives (profitability, growth, and so on). A settlement above this perceived upper limit would be incompatible with the company's objectives.[5] For example, management would close, move its operations, or bring new employees into its existing facility rather than agree to a settlement that would make operating unprofitable. On the other hand, management would not like to be known as the cheapest employer in the area, nor would it want to be unable to recruit, retain, and reward its employees. These concerns help place a lower limit on management's bargaining range—a point management feels is necessary to maintain current employee morale and output.

The union's upper limit is usually shaped by two factors: (a) employment levels and (b) ability to promote and sustain a strike. The union realizes that there can be a tradeoff between a high economic settlement and total number

Exhibit 6.3 Representative Issues Which Might Appear in a Collective Bargaining Agreement and/or Bargaining Range

Ability, Definition of
Absence
Reporting of
With Leave
Without Leave
Arbitration
Bargaining Unit, Definition of
Benefits, Employee
Funeral Pay
Glove, Hat, and Shoe Allowance
Jury Duty
Layoff Allowance
Nonoccupational Disability Pay
Occupational Disability Pay
Pension and Insurance
Vacation
Bidding
Bulletin Boards
Call-out
Definition of
Holiday
Regular
Seventh Consecutive Day, in P/R
Sixth Day Worked in Holiday Week
Change of Rate
Permanent
Temporary
Company Service Credit Rules
Contract
Duration
Purpose of
Termination
Differentials, Shift
Disability Pay Plans
Nonoccupational
Occupational
Discipline
Discharge
Unsatisfactory Attendance
Dues Deduction
Authorization Form
Duration
Withdrawal, Method and/or Date of
Funeral Pay
Glove Allowance
Grievances
General Committee
Procedure—General
Other
Discharge and Suspension
Job Rate Establishment
Handicapped Employees
Hat Allowance
Health and Safety
Holidays and Holiday Pay
Hospitalization Agreement
Hours of Work
Insurance Plan
Interchange of Work
Job Classifications and Rate Schedule
Job Rate Establishment
Job Sequence Charts
Jury Duty Allowance
Layoff
Allowance Plan
Procedure
Recall after
Seniority Rights during
Temporary
Leave-of-Absence
General
Military
Seniority, Accumulation of
Service Credit, Accumulation of
Union Business
Lunch, Overtime
Maintenance of Union Membership
Management Rights
Master Overtime Agreement
Military Service
Nonoccupational Disability Pay
Occupational Disability Pay
Overtime
Daily
Distribution of
Lunch
Pyramiding of
Weekly
Pay
Call-out
For Grievance Meetings
Hiring
Holiday
Overtime
Progression
Rate Schedule
Report-in
Seventh Consecutive Day in Workweek
Shift Differential
Sixth Consecutive Day in Workweek
Sunday Premium
Pension Plan
Probationary Period
Progression
Rate Schedule
Recall
Recognition, Union
Rehire and Reinstatement
Company Service Credit
Rate of Pay
Seniority Rights
Vacation Eligibility
Safety and Health
Safety Shoes
Seniority
Application of
Bidding in
Curtailment in
Definition of
Departmental
Equality of
Handicapped Employees
Layoff during
Loss of
Plant
Recall after
Rehire after
Reinstatement after
Strike Notice during
Supervisors
Ties of
Veterans
Seventh Day, Overtime Pay for
Shift Differential
Shoe Allowance
Sixth Day, Overtime Pay for
Stewards
Strikes and Lockouts
General Provisions

Exhibit 6.3 (Continued)

Suspension
Temporary Change of Rate
Termination of Contract
Time and One-Half Pay
Transfers (Vacancies)
Out of Bargaining Unit
Pay Changes Because of Temporary
Within Bargaining Unit
Transportation

Union
Bulletin Boards
Officials, Leave-of-Absence
Plant Visit of Business Representative
Recognition
Security
Vacancies
Permanent
Temporary
Vacation Plan

Voting Time
Wages (Pay)
Hiring Rate
Progression
Rate Schedule
Work
Conditions
Day, Basic
Hours of
Supervisors
Week, Basic

Source: Union contract.

of jobs at a facility—employers might offset their newly negotiated labor costs by laying off some employees. To some extent, the union's upper limit is governed by its desire to maintain the existing labor force or dues-paying membership.

The union also realizes that its members might want to strike over an unrealistic, pie-in-the-sky proposal presented by the union. Some individuals believe that unions do not have upper limits on their bargaining range, that union leaders will press for outrageous proposals on the rationale that "it does not hurt to ask," and " nothing ventured, nothing gained." These unrealistic proposals can backfire on the union leaders if they raise membership desires for an appropriate settlement. Assume, for example, that the union anticipates the employer's upper limit represents a total settlement cost of 75 cents an hour per employee. The union could hold firm to its upper limit of $1.50 an hour per employee; however, it would incur tremendous risks. First, it would be difficult to motivate employees to go out on strike, particularly if they were satisfied with the 75 cent package. Even if it succeeded in calling a strike, the union would have difficulty convincing employees to return to work on terms similar to management's prestrike offer. Union leaders who raised members' expectations would be placed in the awkward position of having to convince their members that the strike had not been in vain.

On the other hand, the union realizes that there is a lower limit and that a settlement below this limit would result in membership dissatisfaction. Because union leaders are strongly influenced by their desire to assure the survival of the union and their continued roles as union officers,[6] they would never accept a settlement below their minimum, except in extreme cases. If members accepted such a settlement, they could subsequently express their dissatisfaction in one or more of the following ways: (a) voting in new union officers; (b) withdrawing their membership from the union; (c) reducing their support for the current officers through wildcat strikes or the formation of uncontrollable factions[7] or (d) voting out the existing union. To avoid such consequences, union negotiators rarely accept below their minimum (lower limit).

The bargaining ranges, while bounded by upper and lower limits, represent a multitude of priorities for union and management officials. The assigning of priorities to these issues and their possible combinations produces bargaining ranges of an almost infinite number of possibilities. Bargaining ranges can also change over time, usually becoming finalized as the contract expiration date approaches. During the course of negotiations, management and union officials may receive additional information causing them to alter their own upper and lower limits.

Collective Bargaining Structure

Meaning and dimensions Bargaining structure has two general meanings: (1) *employee groupings which can affect the collective bargaining outcome*; and, (2) *the employees and employers who are subject to the provisions of the negotiated labor agreement.*

Unions are responsive to several groups within and outside their organization. Every organization has *informal work groups* (the night shift crew or the company bowling team, for example) which have unique preferences and place pressures on union officers to achieve their preferences in collective bargaining.

In some cases union and management officials are influenced by other collective bargaining settlements. For example, a labor settlement between city government and the police might influence subsequent negotiations between city government and the fire fighters. In the private sector, the United Rubber Workers union has on occasion struck for cost-of-living labor agreement provisions similar to those obtained previously by the United Auto Workers union.

A related concept is *pattern bargaining* which can take the following forms:

- Unions focus their bargaining and strike threats on one company (Ford Motors, for example) then attempt to negotiate a similar settlement with another company (General Motors) that manufactures a similar product.
- A settlement obtained for one segment of the industry (interstate truck drivers, for example) is passed on to related companies, such as local delivery and food wholesaling concerns.

Pattern bargaining strongly influenced wage settlements in the 1970s, although this activity appears to be less popular in the 1980s. Two factors have accounted for this reduction:

1. The market power of concentrated, highly unionized industries is diminishing. Increased foreign competition prevents companies from increasing prices to cover higher labor costs, so management is looking at company operating costs and bargaining accordingly.
2. The capacity of some heavy industries is contracting; production facilities are closing. These industries and companies are the very ones that were once the center of union power and the pattern setters for the entire economy.[8]

The negotiating unit The second dimension of bargaining structure, the negotiating unit, refers to the employees and employers who will be bound by the negotiated labor agreement. There are three possible negotiation units:

1. The negotiation unit is the same as the appropriate bargaining unit (ABU), determined by the National Labor Relations Board for representation election purposes, and is the *minimal* collective bargaining component.
2. The negotiation unit represents more than one ABU, or *centralized bargaining*, of which there are two major types.

   Single employer–multiplant bargaining. For illustrative purposes, assume one company has three separate facilities, each having a separate ABU. The employer and union representatives at these three facilities might combine into one negotiating unit for collective bargaining purposes.

   Multi-employer bargaining. More than one employer and the corresponding union or unions form one negotiation unit each at the bargaining table. This type of centralized bargaining is common in the trucking, construction, longshore, and newspaper industries.

3. A combination of the preceding arrangements. ABUs might be combined for certain issues (pension plans, for example) which are equally applied to employees throughout the industry, while working conditions specific to the individual ABU are resolved at the local facility.

Centralized bargaining One or both parties might consider centralized bargaining because of *product interdependence*, *market factors*, and *legal considerations*.

Assume, for example, a company has three manufacturing facilities, each having a separate ABU. Further, products at these facilities are independent of each other—each facility can produce a completed product without parts or products from other facilities. Examples of product independence would be three steel mills, each completing a similar product, or three facilities having unrelated products (say Facility A produces baseball gloves, Facility B produces cereal, and Facility C produces marbles). The parties must determine whether they want to negotiate separately, which would probably result in three separate contract expiration dates.

The other option would be centralized bargaining—combining the three facilities into one negotiation unit—which would probably result in a common contract expiration date. In this situation, management would prefer the first option, particularly in the steel mill example. If one facility is out on strike, management could transfer some of the orders from that facility to the other two facilities where the contracts have not expired. The union prefers centralized bargaining in this situation, realizing that a strike could effectively shut down the company's entire operations, thereby increasing union bargaining strength.

If the products at the facilities in our example are interdependent (Facility A's product is needed for Facility B, whose product is in turn completed with products at Facility C), then management would probably prefer centralized bargaining—a common expiration date and one possible strike at all facilities—instead of three different contract expiration dates and possible separate strikes at each of the facilities. The second alternative could in effect shut down manufacturing operations three times compared to one shutdown under centralized bargaining.

Market factors also influence the degree of centralization of the bargaining unit. In a highly competitive market, a multi-employer (centralized) negotiation unit would be desirable to employers who fear that their firms would be placed at a competitive disadvantage if other employers subsequently negotiated lower wage rates. Combining with other employers into a multi-employer negotiation unit alleviates this fear while minimizing another problem—the loss of customers to competitors during a strike.

Unions are also concerned about market problems in some industries (construction, coal, trucking, ladies' garment, longshore, and so on) and attempt to extend the negotiating unit to include the entire geographical area in which the product is competitively produced. This is to prevent a few employers from separately negotiating lower wages, which would allow production at lower costs, thereby attracting customers from the other firms and resulting in employee layoffs. In essence, the unions are attempting to standardize wages, hours, and other terms of employment in order to exclude them as a competitive factor and force the employers to compete on the basis of other factors, such as product design, service, marketing, and so on.

Multi-employer bargaining offers some additional advantages and disadvantages. Both labor and management can pool their respective negotiation expenses by hiring a few experts to negotiate an agreement covering several firms. Yet a corresponding disadvantage of centralized bargaining is that the hired negotiators usually do not have extensive knowledge of the parties' attitudes and strategies. Centralized bargaining tends to become more formal and less flexible in terms of meeting employee and employer concerns at the individual workplace.[9] Finally, multi-employer bargaining can create tensions among the member employers, as evidenced in a recent coal negotiation—an employer might pull out of the association if it feels it can get a better deal negotiating separately with the union.[10]

The decision to engage in centralized bargaining can also be affected by legal guidelines. Currently, the union can have representatives from other unions (desiring a centralized negotiation unit) at the bargaining table as negotiating team members. If the employer only desires to negotiate with the single union, then that union cannot delegate its authority to accept or reject the employer's settlement to the representatives of the other unions sitting at the bargaining table. "Moreover, the courts have ruled out as unlawful a 'lock-in' agreement between unions, which deprives individual unions of the right to sign a contract until all other unions have agreed to sign."[11]

Pre-Negotiation Activities

Selection of the Negotiating Team and Related Bargaining Responsibilities

Union and management negotiators often prepare well in advance of contract negotiations[12] although many of the activities discussed below continue throughout collective bargaining. Several considerations face the union and management chief negotiators in the selection of their respective negotiating teams. Personal attributes are a major factor in the selection process. Both chief negotiators desire members who can keep their emotions and opinions in check. An indiscreet negotiating team member can unintentionally reveal confidential settlement points and strategies to the other team. While the chief negotiator is the principal figure in negotiations, there are some occasions when the two teams divide into joint labor-management subcommittees to resolve particular proposals and review contract language. Hence, interpersonal skills are essential requisites for team members.

The individual's experience and background are also considered in the selection process. Management wants at least one line manager who supervises bargaining unit employees on its team to either interpret or answer related negotiating issues. Unions also prefer to select team members from a variety of operating departments to insure membership representation and the discussion of working concerns which might be uniquely related to a particular department.

Finally, political-organizational considerations are also involved in the selection of negotiation team members. In many cases, the union negotiating team is elected by the members, and the union's chief negotiator has little input into the selection process. If discretion is allowed, the chief negotiator will at least think twice before appointing a political rival or member of an opposing faction to the negotiating team.

Management's chief negotiator in single plant bargaining is often the labor relations manager at the plant level, although in a large, multiplant organization, this individual might be another management official in the organization. One study of several hundred organizations determined which management official had final approval authority and responsibility for the following collective bargaining practices and items:

- wages and benefits
- the outside limits (upper and lower limits) of the bargaining range
- the strike point or issues
- approving the package as a whole

This study found that the plant labor relations manager has very little approval authority or responsibility for these items. The individuals who usually assume this responsibility are: Executive Officer, Division or Group Executive, and Corporate or Divisional Vice-President of Labor Relations.[13]

Exhibit 6.4 Priority of Factors Used in Evaluating Labor Relations Performance in Unionized Companies

	Number of Times Item Was Ranked:				
	First	Second	Third	Fourth or Lower	Not Considered
Effect of negotiations on labor cost	281	104	53	76	9
Size of settlement compared with industry settlement	92	148	69	160	54
Attitudes and morale	72	101	133	200	17
Cooperative relations with union	31	71	120	273	27
New union organizing	50	57	52	257	107
Unexpected strikes during negotiations	21	39	45	299	119
Wildcat strikes during contract	5	12	28	315	163

Source: Audrey Freedman, *Managing Labor Relations* (New York: The Conference Board, 1979), p. 73.

This situation can place the chief management negotiator on uncertain grounds, particularly when the success of the labor agreement (See Exhibit 6.4) hinges on the performance, if not responsibility and authority, of the chief negotiator. Management's chief negotiator therefore needs to directly confer with other officials, although they usually are not present at the bargaining table. This gives the chief negotiator a way out when confronted with a union's request. Often, this individual will inform the union that "I have to see my boss on this issue." This ploy is eliminated when the negotiator's boss is there at the bargaining table.

Proposal Determination and Assessment

Management relies on several sources in anticipating what the union will seek in collective bargaining. A review of recent contract settlements negotiated by the company's competitors and other firms located in the same geographical area may suggest issues desired by the union. The company and union may have negotiated settlements at other facilities which might also be used as a starting point in the current negotiations. Some management officials obtain bargaining insights by reviewing the proceedings of the national union's convention.[14]

A review of the local bargaining situation at the facility is essential in anticipating union bargaining issues. Much attention is given to the previous negotiation, particularly to those issues that the union actively sought and reluctantly dropped. Compromise settlements on previous issues also generate valuable clues since compromise does not mean permanent resolution of the issue.

An analysis of previous grievances at the facility can also illustrate certain trouble spots. General Motors, for example, uses a computerized analysis of number, type, and resolution status of grievances in their negotiations preparation. However, caution has to be taken not to overemphasize these grievances. As mentioned in Chapter 8, unions often step up grievance activity just before negotiations to dramatize widespread concern over certain bargaining issues—a concern perhaps more tactical than real.

Formulating Proposals Many management negotiators, unlike their union counterparts, do not formulate bargaining proposals to discuss with the union. One study found that a large majority of employers

> **does not see the development of management proposals as desirable or practical. Although productivity trade-offs are raised during negotiations as counterproposals, they are not introduced as initial bargaining demands. If proposals are initiated at all by these employers, they tend to be 'throw aways.'**[15]

Managers might be reluctant to formulate proposals because that will "tip their hand" to the union—reveal management's weaknesses. A recession, however, might prod management to formulate proposals and bargain accordingly.

Managers who do formulate proposals often perform a close analysis of the labor agreement to determine desirable changes in contract language. Management will attempt to change the contract language in order to reduce labor costs and give itself more discretion in operations. Assume, for example, that the current provision restricts supervisors entirely from performing any bargaining unit work. Since this provision makes no exceptions, management would probably seek to change this language to allow supervisors to perform bargaining unit work under at least three conditions: (a) when training new employees, (b) in emergency situations (usually interpreted to mean when employees' lives or production equipment are jeopardized), and (c) when experimental production efforts are involved.

Both management and the unions are concerned about the legal implications of current contractual language, particularly in terms of recent decisions by the National Labor Relations Board and the courts. Management and union officials would also like to nullify the impact of adverse arbitration decisions. This can be accomplished by inserting contract language contradictory to the arbitrator's decision into the subsequent labor agreement.

Both parties would also be interested in knowing if various administrators of the labor agreement (union stewards and first-line supervisors) have difficulties in implementing certain labor agreement provisions on the shop floor. Efforts will also be made to research data from government reports and various labor relations services (Bureau of National Affairs, Commerce Clearing House, and Prentice-Hall). Data from these and other sources give both parties substantial information with which to prepare for negotiations.

Unions often have an added consideration in proposal formulation—their members' expectations. The union generally encourages its members to present issues they feel are important in the upcoming negotiations. Some of these issues are contradictory; others are irrelevant to the union leaders' bargaining goals. One of management's goals during negotiations is to determine whether the goals stressed by union negotiators are sincere concerns or merely artificial recitals of union members' superfluous suggestions.

Costing Proposals Management's overriding concern in negotiation preparations is the eventual cost of the union's proposals. Related activities occur both before and during negotiations. Costing proposals can become a very involved process. Unfortunately, there has been little published research into costing practices. One notable exception has suggested that many management officials do not use sophisticated costing practices in labor-management negotiations, because management negotiators fail to take into account:

- The precise financial impact of the labor agreement on corporate profits, as well as operating costs.
- The opportunity costs of new contract provisions in terms of lost production (for example, the effect of a proposed ten-minute cleanup time provision).
- Expertise and figures from financial managers, because they usually do not sit in on formal negotiations and do not consult with industrial relations managers on a regular basis.[16]

Yet, management negotiators include at least some costing considerations in their labor negotiations efforts. Two such methods are preparation of employee background data and the calculation of the cost of a cent-per-hour wage increase. Management usually obtains statistical summaries of employees cross-tabulated by several variables (age, sex, marital status, seniority, job classifications). These summaries provide immediate information necessary to cost out a variety of union negotiation proposals such as vacations, funeral pay, and pensions.

A most significant calculation pertains to the cost of a cent-per-hour wage increase. Since wages are inevitably discussed in negotiations, a cost figure is needed to formulate management's bargaining range and to determine whether a union's wage proposal is excessive. An illustrative calculation of a cent-per-hour wage increase for a bargaining unit of 1,000 employees is presented below:

$20,800	Straight time pay (1,000 employees × 40 hours a week × 52 weeks × $.01)
900	Premium pay related to wages (1,000 employees × estimated 60-hours-per-year overtime, holiday, and call-out premium worked × $.015)
5,200	Benefits directly affected by the wage increase (profit sharing, pensions, life insurance, employer contributions to social security, and so on) estimated for illustrative purposes at 25 percent of the straight time wage rate
$26,900	Cost of a cent-per-hour wage increase

The wage total calculated above does not take into account opportunity costs or the spillover effect on wages of nonunion company employees, who will probably receive the negotiated wage increase as a minimum in their subsequent salary increases.[17] Additionally, many cost categories, such as overtime and holidays worked, have to be estimated from past payroll records and future production and manning requirements.

Unions often pursue two general negotiating strategies to counter management's costing activities. Union officials often submit proposals which are difficult to cost, thereby weakening management's related statistical objections during negotiations. Assume, for example, a current contract provision provides a Sunday work premium of 75 cents an hour if the employees have no absences during their regularly scheduled work week. The union proposes that employees working on Sunday receive this premium regardless of their attendance record during the week. Management can examine past payroll records to estimate the added cost of this proposal, a difficult task if there are thousands of employees involved and an uncertain indicator of extra absences that might occur if this proposal is accepted.

Other proposals are almost impossible to cost out because no records have been kept and there is no way to obtain accurate data, as in the case of a union's proposal to include deaths of employees' first cousins for the three-day paid funeral leave provision. Management should maintain accurate and separate cost categories on benefits paid during the previous year.

Unions also formulate proposals which provide costly benefits to members and save management money at the same time. This is difficult, and depends on the abilities and imagination of union negotiators. One example of this approach is a proposal which allows police to keep a squad car for personal use after their work day. This practice appears costly; however, it can deter potential crimes and thereby reduce crime statistics and related expenses.

Another example is paid time off (sabbaticals) for public university professors. Say, for example, a university agrees to pay half of the professor's salary and benefits ($48,000), and the professor is released from teaching obligations (six courses) for the nine-month period. It appears, at first glance, that the university pays $24,000 to the professor and receives nothing in return. However, a closer examination reveals the university has received funding from the state for the $48,000 salary, and retains $24,000 after paying the professor for his or her sabbatical. The six courses can be assigned to "adjunct" (part time) professors or to teaching assistants for a total cost of $12,000. This often means that the university can divert the $12,000 salary savings to other expenses, and both administration and faculty have received financial benefit from this proposal.

Bargaining Behavior

Negotiating Atmosphere and Tactics

It is impossible to describe a "typical" labor-management negotiation since there are over 160,000 labor agreements in the United States. The particular negotiating atmosphere is influenced by the familiarity of the parties and the extent to which their bargaining relationship has been viewed as being mutually acceptable.[18] Both chief negotiators realize their counterpart is an influential if not determining force in the eventual settlement. In many cases, they realize that they will have to live with each other long after the contract has been signed. Finally, each knows that the other has to deal with conflicting goals of other members on the negotiating team.

Most negotiations are conducted in an atmosphere which features *respect and honesty*,[19] *rationality*, and *rituals*. Respect is an interpersonal variable seldom researched by academicians. It is not synonymous with friendship—one can dislike and respect an individual at the same time. Management and labor negotiators seldom socialize with each other; however, they can respect each other for their technical competence and experience. They also can respect the negotiators' personal qualities, such as the ability to go out on a limb in standing up for what is right, admitting when they are wrong, and perhaps most important, *credibility*, or keeping their word when they have taken a concrete position.

Closely related to respect is honesty. It permits each party to rely on the statements of the other. There is, however, a thin line between dishonesty and withholding the truth—union and management officials are not going to volunteer items which could damage their respective bargaining positions.[20] Successful negotiators are skilled in asking the correct questions and interpreting omissions from the other party's remarks.

Rationality is also found in most collective bargaining situations. Contrary to popular beliefs, negotiations are not usually characterized by emotional outbursts and random thinking. Instead, union and management officials are ". . . conscious decision makers, who think about what they are doing and act in accord with their perceptions."[21]

Many bargaining sessions also have ritualistic elements such as the elaborate charts and tables which are ignored after serious negotiations begin. In some cases, irrelevant material or propaganda parade as facts or, as contended by one union research director, "a fact is as welcome at a collective bargaining table as a skunk at a cocktail party."[22] Similarly, one management negotiator has suggested that his union counterpart approaches him at the start of negotiations and whispers, "We'll get together privately and talk about what we are really going to do to make a deal as soon as this show is over."[23]

The negotiating atmosphere between particular management and union bargaining teams is uniquely shaped by the decision to include or exclude certain *bargaining tactics* (see Exhibit 6.5). These tactics are conveyed through various communication styles, and are influenced by different collective bargaining strategies.

Exhibit 6.5 Number of Negotiators Reporting Use of Specific Tactic in Recent Negotiation, in Order of Frequency of Use (N = 61)

Specific Tactic	Used	Didn't Use
Making information available to the other side	60	1
Identifying problem situation	59	2
Persuading other side of joint need for focusing on problem	59	2
Probing for other side's target and resistance points	56	5
Using clear hints and signals	56	3
Remaining flexible on team's position	54	7
Focusing upon long-term bargaining relationship	53	7
Allowing other side to "save face"	51	10
Withholding commitment while discussing problems and exploring solutions	51	10
Having frequent contact between bargaining teams	49	12
Persuading other side of minimal cost to them of your proposal	44	16
Holding back on responses to other side's proposals	26	33
Holding information close to the belt	24	36
Reminding the other side of your side's bargaining power	24	37
Maintaining freedom from constituents	22	34
Holding off final offer until deadline	21	39
Taking an early firm commitment	21	39
Keeping the other side off balance	21	38
Presenting a large number of bargaining demands	18	43
Withholding information from the other side	16	45
Using overt threats in bargaining	15	46
Dominating discussion of agenda items	14	46

Source: Richard B. Peterson and Lane Tracy, "Preferences, Bargaining Tactics and Goals of Union and Management Negotiators," paper presented at the 1981 Academy of Management Meeting (San Diego, California), p. 7.

Communication Style

Management and union negotiators spend a major portion of their time communicating messages to each other. Most of this communication can be channeled into three general directions: *language analysis*; *package discussion of proposals*; and *argumentation*.

Language Analysis In many cases union and management negotiators have to convey their preferences and positions to each other while at the same time giving their fellow bargaining team members a slightly different impression. For instance, consider the following situation. The chief union negotiator discusses the company's latest negotiation proposal with the union members, who, in turn, feel that he or she should go back to the table and press management for a more favorable settlement. Believing that the company's proposal was reasonable, the union negotiator must communicate this preference to management and at the same time convince the bargaining committee she fought for their rights. Confronted with this difficult situation, the union negotiator might open the next bargaining session by forcefully stressing to management: "'The membership disagreed' with the company's economic proposal. 'The present contract will not extend beyond 12:00 tonight.'"

At first glance, the union negotiator's statement seems strong and unyielding. However, a skilled management negotiator would analyze it through three questions.[24]

1. How *final* is the statement?
2. How *specific* is the statement?
3. What are the *consequences* associated with this statement?

At second glance, the statement appears neither final nor specific. In fact, management could interpret it to mean the union negotiator is relatively satisfied with the proposal, particularly if no specific recommendations for improvement follow. Finally, the union negotiator, by stating "the present contract will not extend," does not give a clear indication that a strike will occur if the offer is not changed.

Package discussion of proposals Since maintaining communications between parties during negotiations is essential to the bargaining process, negotiating several issues (a *package*) at the same time is preferable to the item-by-item, or "yes-no," approach. The item-by-item negotiations technique does not allow the parties to communicate their preferences realistically and at the same time maintain flexibility in their decision making.

In using the *package approach*, each party combines several bargaining issues for discussion purposes. For example, the union might propose dropping issues 2 (union shop), 7 (birthday off), and 9 (voluntary overtime) from its bargaining list if management would agree to issues 3 (eliminating subcontracting) and 10 (optional retirement after thirty years). Management might then present the following counterproposal: agree to issues 3 and 10 if the union drops issues 2, 7, 9, and 11 (free dental care). This process would be repeated until the parties eventually resolved the issues in dispute.

The advantage of this approach is that both parties indicate which issues they will concede (for the union, issues 2, 7, and 9; for management, issues 3 and 10); and, if agreement is not reached, these issues are still considered negotiable. Moreover, both parties keep track of these proposals because they offer insights into their opponent's bargaining preferences.

Argumentation In essence there are three bargaining positions: "Yes," "Maybe—keep on talking," or "No." When one negotiator has adopted either the second or third position, the other negotiator has to use arguments which have several forms and uses.

Arguments are the justifications, explanations, rationalizations, or legitimizations that parties give for the positions they take in bargaining. Arguments are an instance of tactical dramaturgy, directed at recasting the opponent's definition of the bargaining situation. The objective validity of any redefinition is irrelevant as long as the opponent accepts its validity.[25]

Closely related to arguments are threats and promises. *Threats* carry the intent of one negotiator to harm the other negotiator's position or organization, while *promises* offer rewards for the other party's concessions. Both are not always explicit or clear since they are often hinted, not stated.

Complicating matters is the often thin line between promises and threats. For example, the union negotiator might promise the management negotiator that he will recommend the proposed settlement to the membership if management agrees to the remaining bargaining item. This promise carries an implicit threat that the settlement will not be recommended if the final proposal is not resolved to the union leader's liking.[26]

Collective Bargaining Strategies

Collective bargaining's atmosphere and tactics are strongly influenced by the various strategic approaches which are used by management and union negotiators. One study has identified four such approaches: *distributive bargaining*, *integrative bargaining*, *attitudinal structuring*, and *intra-organizational bargaining*.[27]

Distributive bargaining occurs over some issues when one party's goals conflict with those of the other party. Certain issues, particularly wages, heighten conflict of interest in that one party tends to gain at the other party's expense. Each negotiator tries to obtain and modify the opponent's position and values assigned to these issues. This approach encourages threats, bluffs, and secrecy as each party tries to keep the upper hand.[28]

Integrative bargaining occurs when both parties attempt to resolve a common problem or concern to their mutual benefit. Many of the administrative issues discussed in Chapter 12 are resolved by integrative or problem-solving bargaining. An illustrative issue is alcoholism among bargaining unit employees. Management is concerned about the alcoholic employee's higher absentee rate and poorer work performance. The union fears that this employee could pose a safety hazard to other employees. Therefore, both union and management officials attempt to resolve this issue in a mutually beneficial manner.[29] This approach is often characterized by trust in the other party, open sharing of information, and active consideration of the other party's suggestions.[30]

Attitudinal structuring involves activities aimed at attaining a desired relationship between the parties. This subprocess does not pertain to particular issues; instead, each party attempts to change the opponent's attitudes and the relationships which affect the negotiation process and subsequent administration of the labor agreement. This activity often assumes that a good relationship influences concessions. Related dimensions typically include

. . . behaving in a warm and friendly fashion, doing favors for the other so as to enhance the other's liking of and dependence on oneself, seconding the other's attitudes, behaving in accordance with the other's values, sending a representative who is similar to the other, encouraging the other to engage in role reversal, and choosing a pleasant setting (such as a bar or nice restaurant) for the conduct of business.[31]

At first glance, attitudinal structuring and integrative bargaining appear similar since both are rather pleasant situations. Yet, attitudinal structuring can be used to accomplish both integrative (problem solving) or distributive (competitive) bargaining, and can contribute to "intra-organizational" bargaining.

Intra-organizational bargaining refers to activities employed by management and union negotiators to achieve consensus within their respective organizations. However, bargaining teams are seldom unified; in fact, union and management negotiators often have more difficulty with members of their respective negotiating teams than with each other.[32]

Management's chief negotiator sometimes takes a back seat to other management officials, particularly lawyers, at the bargaining table. When a settlement is reached, it is also subject to second guessing by other officials, who contend that management negotiators could have obtained a better deal with a tougher negotiation philosophy.[33] The union is not exempt from internal disputes either, particularly since its chief negotiator is seldom given a free hand in selecting the negotiating committee. In many cases, at least one member of the union's negotiating team is a political rival of the union's chief negotiator. More prevalent are factions which attempt to obtain various bargaining demands regardless of the chief negotiator's preferences.

Management and union negotiators spend much time resolving differences within their respective organizations. One observer of labor-management negotiations has maintained that

a large share of collective bargaining is not conflict but a process by which the main terms of the agreement, already understood by the negotiators, are made acceptable not to those in charge of the bargaining but to those who will have to live with its results![34]

Legal Considerations Affecting Bargaining Behavior— The Good Faith Bargaining Requirement

Union and management officials are not completely free to shape bargaining behavior and approaches. There are several legal considerations (laws, National Labor Relations Board decisions and judicial interpretations) which must be taken into account. These considerations center on the dimensions of "good faith" bargaining, including successor employer bargaining obligations and the legal consequences associated with a violation of the collective bargaining obligation.

The Legal Requirements Concerning Good Faith Bargaining The National Labor Relations Act requires that the parties negotiate in *good faith*—that they demonstrate a sincere and honest intent to consummate a labor agreement and exhibit reasonableness in their bargaining position, tactics, and activities. However, *good faith* represents a state of mind difficult to define precisely.

The NLRB and the courts deal with this concept in their interpretation of the following provisions of the Labor Management Relations Act:

8(a)(5) **It shall be an unfair labor practice for an employer . . . to refuse to bargain collectively with representatives of his employees, subject to the provisions of Section 9(a).**

8(b)(3) **It shall be an unfair labor practice for a labor organization or its agents . . . to refuse to bargain collectively with an employer, provided it is the representative of his employees subject to Section 9(a).**

8(d) **[Collective bargaining entails] the performance of the mutual obligation of the employer and the representative of the employees to meet at reasonable times and confer in good faith with respect to wages, hours, and other terms and conditions of employment, or the negotiation of an agreement, . . . incorporating any agreement reached if requested by either party . . .**

The good faith bargaining obligation is imposed equally on union and management; either will be guilty of an unfair labor practice if it fails to live up to its bargaining obligation. However, this obligation does not specifically require that a party must agree to the other's proposal or make a concession to the other party.[35] Violations of good faith bargaining can come from four sources: *the nature of the bargaining issues*, *specific bargaining actions* (called per se violations), *totality of conduct*, and *successor employer bargaining obligations*.

Nature of Bargaining Issues Over the years, the NLRB and the courts have categorized bargaining issues as illegal, mandatory, or voluntary. *Illegal* subjects are not bargainable, and the parties cannot insert them into the labor contract even if they are in agreement over the issue. Examples of illegal subjects include a closed shop, a "whites only" employment clause, mandatory retirement at sixty-two, and compensation arrangements which violate the provisions of the Fair Labor Standards Act (for example, not paying bargaining unit employees overtime for work in excess of forty hours per week).

Mandatory subjects are related to wages, hours, and other conditions of employment. Examples of mandatory subjects are wage systems, bonus plans, pensions, profit sharing, vacations, holidays, plant rules, grievance procedures, and management rights.[36] These subjects must be bargained, and the party advancing these subjects may insist on their inclusion to a point of impasse. However, failure to reach agreement does not automatically constitute a bargaining violation.

Union and management officials can also negotiate *voluntary* (also called permissive or nonmandatory) subjects like industry promotion plans, strike insurance, interest arbitration clause, and benefits for retired employees. Unlike mandatory issues, these do not require either party to bargain. In fact, insisting on their bargaining and inclusion in the labor agreement would be an unfair labor practice.

Specific Bargaining Actions In some cases a specific, single action by an employer constitutes an unfair labor practice in bargaining. Examples of per se violations for union and management are presented below.[37]

Management commits a per se violation whenever it:

- refuses to meet with the union to negotiate its proposals.
- insists to a point of impasse on a provision requiring that a secret ballot election be held before a strike can be called,
- refuses to supply cost and other data relating to a group insurance plan, or
- announces a wage change without consulting the union.

A union commits a per se violation when it:

- insists on a closed shop or discriminatory hiring,
- refuses to meet with a legal representative of the employer about negotiations, or
- refuses to negotiate a management proposal involving a mandatory subject.

Totality of conduct Sometimes the NLRB and the courts have determined that one activity alone does not constitute a bargaining violation; however, a combination of activities, *totality of conduct*, might reflect a violation of the duty to bargain. A prominent and controversial example of this legal consideration involved General Electric's bargaining approach, *Boulwarism*, named after the vice-president of General Electric, Lemuel Boulware.

General Electric contended that it simply approached bargaining in a manner similar to its product marketing—by finding out what the employee desired, and, on the basis of employee survey results, formulating a bargaining proposal. G.E. contended that this approach was not capricious, but "fair and firm," as management's bargaining position was based on a careful examination of the "facts" and was capable of being altered if the union presented new and significant information at the bargaining table. Some contended that this approach represented a sincere bargaining effort, one that was not aimed at destroying the union, but rather at eliminating a time-consuming and unnecessary ritual from collective bargaining (for instance, initial unrealistic offers which both parties know will not be accepted).[38]

However, General Electric's totality of conduct was found violative of good faith bargaining, primarily because it went directly to the employees rather than working through the employees' exclusive bargaining agent (the union). The NLRB found several bargaining activities which contributed to General Electric's "take it or leave it" bargaining approach. These activities included: refusals to supply cost information on an insurance program, vague response to the union's detailed proposals, prepared lecture series instead of counter offers, and a "stiff and unbending patriarchal posture" even after it was apparent that the union would have to concede to the employer's terms.[39]

Other factors involving employer or union conduct have provided indicators of good and bad faith bargaining. The following factors, while they probably would not individually constitute bad faith bargaining, might be considered so if many of them were committed together.[40]

- **Surface bargaining:** The party is willing to meet at length and confer but merely goes through the motions of bargaining. It includes making proposals which cannot be accepted, taking an inflexible attitude on major issues, and offering no alternative proposals.
- **Concessions:** Although the LMRA does not require the making of concessions, the term *good faith* certainly suggests a willingness to compromise and make a reasonable effort to settle differences.
- **Proposals and demands:** Advancing proposals which open the doors for future discussions indicates good faith, whereas proposals that foreclose future negotiations and are patently unreasonable are reflectors of bad faith.
- **Dilatory tactics:** Refusal to meet, unreasonable procrastination in executing the agreement, delay in scheduling meetings, willful avoidance of meetings, evasive tactics, delay in providing data for bargaining, and similar tactics are evidence of bad faith.
- **Imposing conditions:** Attempts to specify conditions on bargaining or the administration of the agreement will be scrutinized closely to determine whether such conditions are onerous or unreasonable (for example, insisting that all grievances be resolved before collective bargaining can start). In addition, the requirement of agreement on a specific item as a prerequisite to negotiating other issues reflects bad faith bargaining.
- **Unilateral changes in conditions:** Such actions as changing the compensation or fringe benefits plan unilaterally during bargaining is a strong indicator of bad faith bargaining. Unilateral changes per se may not be illegal, but justification must be reasonable and accurate.
- **Bypassing the representative:** Since the collective bargaining agreement supersedes the individual employee contract, the employer must not refuse to

negotiate over mandatory issues. The duty to bargain is essentially equivalent to the duty to recognize the exclusive bargaining representative of the employees. Attempts to bypass this representative are evidence of bad faith.

- **Commission of unfair labor practices:** Committing unfair labor practices (such as threatening to close the plant, promoting withdrawal from the union, reducing working hours, and engaging in discriminatory layoffs) during negotiations is indicative of conduct inconsistent with good faith bargaining.

In addition, the NLRB and court rulings have been consistent in deciding that unions should have sufficient information to understand and intelligently discuss the issues raised in collective bargaining. Without such information, the union would be unable to properly perform its collective bargaining and contract administration duties. This information is, however, subject to the following prerequisites.[41]

1. The union must make a good faith demand or request for the information.
2. The information sought must be relevant to the bargaining relationship.
3. When the employer alleges that it is financially unable to meet a union wage demand, financial information relevant to the negotiations must be supplied to the union.[42]
4. The information must be supplied to the union promptly and in a form reasonably useful for negotiation purposes.

Successor Employer Bargaining Obligations When a new employer takes over a plant which has an exclusive bargaining representative, the bargaining unit may remain intact unless sufficient change occurs whereby majority status is lost. The test of *successor employer bargaining obligations* depends on a number of factors: the degree of change brought about by new ownership, whether the company's operations or products change, whether most employees remain, and whether the plant remains in the same location.[43]

The employer violates its legal obligations to bargain in good faith if after purchasing another business it continues operations intact and with predecessor employees and refuses to bargain after notifying the employees that previous benefits will not be continued.[44] The union has a similar obligation because it cannot force the successor employer to bargain if the successor willingly adopts the contract already negotiated between the union and the predecessor employer.[45]

The *Burns International Detective Agency Inc.* case is a prominent illustration of the successor employer's obligation to bargain. Burns, the employer, bid successfully on a contract to provide guard services at an aircraft manufacturer's installations but refused to honor the contract between the predecessor employer and the certified bargaining units, and further refused to bargain with the same union. The Supreme Court held the successor employer violated good faith bargaining since Burns hired a majority of its work force from the former employees of the predecessor, continued the former operations substantially intact, knew in advance that the union was the certified bargaining representative with a contract, and provided essentially the same working conditions and services. Burns had to honor the contract and negotiate with the union.[46]

Other decisions have provided further insights into the application of the successor employer bargaining obligation. In one case, the employer violated its bargaining obligation when it took over a franchise, retained all the employees, and made unilateral changes in the wages and employment conditions.[47] In another case, the successor employer did not violate its bargaining obligation when it hired a majority of the predecessor's employees and established unilateral wages and employment conditions but agreed to later negotiations.[48] A subsequent decision indicated that the successor employer, who hired substantially all of the predecessor's employees, could legally establish the initial wages and employment conditions but must be willing to negotiate further over these issues.[49]

Legal Remedies Associated with Violations of Good Faith Bargaining In 1980, 32 percent (9,866 of 31,280) of NLRB cases alleging employer violations involved employer refusal to bargain in good faith, and 7.3 percent (913 of 12,628) of NLRB cases alleging union violations involved similar union activities.[50] Although there are many cases to be handled, the NLRB is limited in its remedial powers. As one NLRB member illustrates this situation: "The Board under the act is constituted as the midwife of the bargaining relationship. It oversees the birth of that relationship and attempts to prevent any miscarriage."[51]

Once a violation is found, the board orders the violator to cease and desist bad faith bargaining and to take affirmative action. These actions include bargaining upon request, posting notices pledging to bargain in good faith, and notifying offices of the NLRB of steps being taken to comply with the order.[52]

Union officials have contended that the lack of significant remedies makes correction of good faith bargaining violations a farce. Since NLRB decisions can be appealed to the courts, it might take three or more years for a final determination. If the final decision finds the company guilty, affected employees are not entitled to any make-whole remedies.

Attempts to expand the NLRB's remedial power have failed. In the *H. K. Porter* case, the NLRB granted the union a contract clause which allowed checkoff of union dues after the employer repeatedly refused to bargain in good faith on the checkoff issue. The Supreme Court concluded that the bargaining obligation "does not compel either party to agree to a proposal or require the making of a concession," and "it is the job of Congress, not the Board or the courts, to decide when and if it is necessary to allow governmental review of proposals for collective bargaining agreements and compulsory submissions to one side's demands."[54] In addition, the NLRB cannot currently order an employer to compensate employees for monetary loses incurred as a result of an employer refusal to bargain until it has obtained a court test of the validity of certification.[55]

Resolution Framework (The Bargaining Power Model) and Resulting Labor Agreement Provisions

Dimensions and Applications of the Model

Thus far the various bargaining behaviors and legal considerations have been described. A framework is needed to provide direction and place these behaviors in perspective. One such framework suggests both parties arrange their strategies and tactics in a manner that will enhance their *bargaining power* and eventual settlement.

One of the better known bargaining models was suggested by Chamberlain and Kuhn,[56] a model further expressed in two equations presented in Exhibit 6.6. These equations can apply to individual issues or to the eventual package settlement, and reflects

> **. . . the simple and obvious notion that bargainers compare the costs and benefits of no agreement with the costs and benefits of particular settlements. These costs and benefits ostensibly determine the concession behavior of the parties and also the nature of the ultimate settlement.[57]**

There are at least two major assumptions of the bargaining power model:

1. Union and management negotiators are rational individuals.
2. If it costs more for a party to disagree than to agree with the other, then the party will agree to the other's position.

Therefore, each side can increase its bargaining power by reducing the cost to the other of agreement or increasing the cost to the other of disagreement.

Exhibit 6.6 Bargaining Power Equations for Union and Management

$$\text{Union's Bargaining Power} = \frac{\text{Management's Cost of Disagreeing with the Union}}{\text{Management's Cost of Agreeing with the Union}}$$

$$\text{Management's Bargaining Power} = \frac{\text{Union's Cost of Disagreeing with Management}}{\text{Union's Cost of Agreeing with Management}}$$

Source: Equations are modified slightly from Allan M. Cartter and F. Ray Marshall, *Labor Economics*, rev. ed. (Homewood, Ill.: Richard D. Irwin, 1972), p. 283.

This strategic framework can be illustrated with a union bargaining proposal for ten minutes cleanup time before the end of the work shift. Management would probably refuse this item unless the union presented arguments relating to the bargaining power model. First, the union could reduce management's cost of agreeing with the cleanup time proposal by eliminating some of its original bargaining proposals—if management agrees to cleanup time, the union will drop four bargaining items. The union negotiator might also reduce management's agreement costs with an argument along the following lines:

There are currently many different cleanup practices at our facility. Some departments do not have cleanup time while other departments let their employees stop work a half hour early for cleaning up. If you calculated the total cleanup time in the plant, it would probably amount to fifteen minutes per employee. Worse yet, you cannot currently discipline employees who are abusing cleanup time since there are so many different practices in the plant. This contract provision would enable management to wipe the past practice slate clean. Management could instruct the supervisors to rigidly enforce this provision, which could actually save the company money.

In case management does not accept the above argument, the union could follow the second strategic approach—increasing management's cost of disagreeing with the union. The ultimate related argument would be to threaten a strike unless the cleanup time provision was granted. This threat might carry some weight, particularly if management knew there was widespread dissatisfaction over this issue. However, chances are that management would view this as an idle threat and would not believe its disagreement cost had increased.

There is a related threat, however, which could raise management's cost of disagreeing with the union over this issue. The union could make related arguments regarding safety hazards at the facility and suggest two alternatives: management can allow cleanup time before the end of the shift or the union can lodge a safety complaint with the Occupational Safety and Health Administration (OSHA). Management negotiators would prefer the first alternative over the second since they know that it would not cost the union anything to file the complaint, and an OSHA investigation might uncover other safety problems whose correction would be more expensive.

Several variables can affect the bargaining power equations in Exhibit 6.6 (discussed in detail in Chapter 7 as strike decision criteria); however, three variables will be briefly discussed here to illustrate the bargaining power model's function.

Timing of Negotiations has a significant impact on the bargaining power model. The backlog of customer orders to be filled after the contract expiration date adds a major dimension. One facet of negotiations timing illustrating the effect on bargaining power concerns the time at which profit-sharing checks are mailed. If the company mails them to employees one day before the labor agreement expires, management's bargaining power is reduced. Then union members have added money to spend, and their costs of disagreeing with management are reduced.

In some situations, it is difficult to determine the other party's disagreement costs associated with the timing of negotiations. In at least one situation, a management negotiator appears to have been taken by the union in timing of negotiations. This management official was approached by the union's negotiator, who stated that if the contract expiration date was pushed ahead, the union would work for wages under the old agreement until the new contract expiration date arrived. The official carefully considered the union's request and agreed, after determining that the new contract expiration date would not increase the union's bargaining power.

However, much to the management negotiator's chagrin, the new contract expiration date coincided with the opening day of hunting season. Thus management's bargaining power and the union's disagreement costs were dramatically reduced, particularly since the employees at the facility were avid hunters. With the new contract expiration date, the union leaders could give the membership two alternatives: (a) accept the company's offer and forget about the hunting season, or (b) strike and go hunting without angering their spouses, since employees could use their subsequent vacation time for family outings. It would not take an exceptionally skilled orator to persuade the union members to accept the second option.

Unemployment can affect both bargaining power equations presented in Exhibit 6.6. High unemployment increases the union's cost of disagreeing with management since potential strikers would find it difficult to find employment at other firms. And it reduces management's disagreement costs since high unemployment tends to make it easier for management to find strike replacements.

Company Characteristics Union officials are more likely to increase their bargaining power by reducing management's disagreement costs when management can pass on increased labor costs to the consumer without incurring reduced product sales, or receive productivity increases to offset the cost of the labor settlement.[58] Union officials seldom have influence on the first characteristic since price levels are often affected by consumer preferences. Union negotiators can and have affected the second characteristic by giving up previously obtained work rules so that management has more discretion in determining and scheduling work assignments.[59]

A problem occurs when management cannot lower its agreement costs through either method, a situation which has become increasingly common. Union bargaining power on at least some issues becomes difficult to increase since

---

Bargaining and obtaining real wage gains in the face of declining productivity is most difficult. Sooner or later even the most tenacious and effective union will learn the wisdom of John L. Lewis's remark that 'bankrupt companies aren't good employers.'[60]

This situation, labeled *concession bargaining*, occurs when unions bargain for no wage increases in an attempt to continue or increase job security.[61] Concession bargaining is often limited in both scope and permanence. One reseacher has concluded that this situation currently applies to only four percent of the total workforce. Also, it appears to be a reaction to temporary economic conditions, and should not be viewed as a permanent union bargaining stance.[62]

Limitations of the Bargaining Power Model

The bargaining power model is a theory which tries to explain real world situations. It cannot predict bargaining behavior and related settlements with complete accuracy. There are two general and related limitations; namely, *uncertainty-imprecision*, and *dramatic, sudden change.*

There are many factors which contribute to bargaining uncertainty. First, a negotiator cannot always assess the behavior and thought processes of the other negotiator. In some cases, one negotiator appears "irrational" from the other negotiator's perspective. There can be some "low cost issues" (providing employees with an additional pair of safety gloves each month, for example) which assume distorted importance.

Second, it is difficult to determine bargaining "costs." Consider, for example, a union's proposal for eliminating a previously agreed-upon contract provision that all employees can be required to perform "minor repairs." It is difficult to determine the cost of removing this provision, although management will probably have to assign more overtime and possibly hire more employees if maintenance employees have to repair items which were formerly repaired by production employees. Even if the cost of this item could be measured in economic terms, this figure might be complicated by "political costs"—the union negotiator determines that failure to eliminate the "minor repairs" clause will result in political defeat in the next election of union officers. A single item or bargaining proposal can become a matter of moral principle. "Costs" therefore assume economic, political, and moral dimensions; the combination of these varied components results in a confusing sum.

Finally, cost calculations are derived from estimates based on future events. The usual, ultimate threat to management is a strike. Management must then estimate both the likelihood and length of a strike. Other uncertain, future events which surround the negotiation of labor agreements are the economic and political environments.[63]

Another limitation of the bargaining power model is that it is subject to rapid and sudden change. Governmental wage-price controls or guidelines can be suddenly announced, forcing unions to agree to wage settlements comparable to the limits set by the government.

On the other hand, management could receive a sudden influx of rush orders from a major customer near the contract expiration date. Management's disagreement costs are then sharply increased, particularly if the customer indicates he or she will take unfinished orders to a competitor.

The limitations of the bargaining power model do not eliminate its usefulness. Union and management officials do assign costs, however crudely, and direct their strategies toward increasing the other party's disagreement costs relative to agreement costs.

Summary and Implications

Summary

This chapter has examined collective bargaining's characteristics. Two initial influences on collective bargaining are the priority arrangement of bargaining issues for each negotiator and the bargaining structure, including the negotiating unit.

Management and union negotiators are involved in two general pre-negotiation activities; namely, selecting the negotiating team, and determining and assessing proposals. The atmosphere surrounding most labor-management negotiations typically features three general elements: respect, honesty, and rituals.

The negotiating atmosphere between particular management and union bargaining teams is uniquely shaped by the decision to include or exclude certain bargaining tactics. These tactics are influenced by four bargaining strategies; distributive bargaining, integrative bargaining, attitudinal structuring, and, intra-organizational bargaining. These behaviors are shaped by legal considerations such as good faith bargaining and successor employer bargaining obligations.

A resolution framework, the bargaining power model, was discussed to place the varied collective bargaining behaviors into a proper perspective. In essence, union and management negotiators try to manipulate each other's agreement and disagreement costs on the assumption that if it costs more to disagree than to agree, then agreement will be reached.

Implications

Collective bargaining is a significant activity, and has therefore drawn the attention of many academic researchers. One book devoted to analyzing these research efforts lists over a thousand studies in its bibliography.[64] There are three general approaches which are often used to explain bargaining behavior:[65]

- The *psychological* approach focuses on negotiatiors' personalities and their perceived use of interpersonal strategies to modify each other's attitudes.[66]

- The *economic* approach views unions and employers as economic agents trying to maximize wages and profits respectively.[67]
- The *game theory* focuses on strategic interactions between two or more parties in interdependent decision making.[68]

Each approach offers insights into collective bargaining, although all are narrowly focused,[69] and methodologically difficult. This second problem occurs largely because practitioners—people actively involved in contract negotiation—often exclude academicians from their bargaining sessions. This is in part because union and management negotiators fear the potentially disruptive presence of an academic third party in their negotiations. There is also a possibility that "real bargaining" occurs between the management and union negotiators away from the bargaining table. The secrecy and trust necessary for these discussions would be hampered, if not destroyed, by the addition of another individual.

Many academicians have responded to this situation by trying to replicate bargaining situations with students, an activity which seldom reflects real world practice because the students do not have to live with the terms of the agreement at the conclusion of their "negotiations." It has been mentioned that honesty and respect characterize most labor-management negotiations. It is hoped that these variables will become more prevalent in interactions between academicians and practitioners so that both groups can benefit from collective bargaining research.

Discussion Questions

1. What are some situations in which management or the union would prefer centralized bargaining? In what instances might both prefer centralized bargaining? Discussion should take into account specific legal considerations affecting centralized bargaining.
2. Our discussion of bargaining power touched on only three variables: timing of negotiations, unemployment and company characteristics. Relate three other variables (from either Exhibit 1.1 or your own experience) to the bargaining power model, indicating how they could affect the equations.
3. Assume that you are a management negotiator and the union presents the following negotiation proposal: Any overtime assignment will be guaranteed a minimum of two hours at time and one-half the base hourly rate for the classification. Previously, employees working overtime received time and one-half payment for the hours they worked but no two-hour guarantee. Indicate in some detail how you would cost out this proposal. Also discuss some arguments the union might use to make it easier to accept this proposal (to reduce your agreement costs).

4. Good and bad faith regulations might be easier to define than implement. Discuss problems management and unions believe they face in attempting to bargain in good faith. (Boulwarism and legal remedies, for example, are considered problems by management and unions, respectively.) What recommendations would you suggest for improving these situations?
5. Assume you are establishing a research project to investigate an aspect of collective bargaining. Indicate (a) a rather specific, narrow topic for investigation, (b) hypotheses or key questions you would examine, (c) and how you would operationalize or measure the key variables. Also discuss some limitations of your research effort as well as the particular academic discipline(s) influencing your project. (Exhibit 6.1 and material in the Implications section might provide a useful starting point.)
6. Fully assess the following statement, qualifying it when appropriate: "Communication plays a very small role in labor management negotiations since this activity is largely determined by established rituals."
7. Explain how "attitudinal structuring" can relate to the three other collective bargaining strategies discussed in the text.

References

[1]Gary G. Whitney, "Before You Negotiate: Get Your Act Together," *Personnel* 59 (July–August 1982), p. 14.

[2]Hjalmar Rosen and R. A. H. Rosen, "The Union Bargaining Agent Looks at Collective Bargaining," *Personnel* 33 (May 1957), p. 541; David L. Cole, "Focus on Bargaining: The Evolving Techniques," *American Federationist* 81 (May 1974), p. 15; and Otomar J. Bartos, *Process and Outcome of Negotiations* (New York: Columbia University Press, 1974), p. 15.

[3]Jack Barbash, "Price and Power in Collective Bargaining," *Journal of Economic Issues* 11 (December 1977), p. 847.

[4]Carl M. Stevens, *Strategy and Collective Bargaining Negotiations* (New York: McGraw-Hill, 1963), p. 34.

[5]Richard E. Walton and Robert B. McKersie, *A Behavioral Theory of Labor Negotiations* (New York: McGraw-Hill, 1965), pp. 19, 23.

[6]Wallace N. Atherton, *Theory of Union Bargaining Goals* (Princeton, N.J.: Princeton University Press, 1973), p. 4.

[7]Jeffrey Z. Rubin and Bert Brown, *The Social Psychology of Bargaining and Negotiation* (New York: Harcourt Brace Jovanovich, 1975), p. 50.

[8]Audrey Freedman and William E. Fulmer, "Last Rites for Pattern Bargaining," *Harvard Business Review* 60 (March–April 1982), p. 31.

[9]See for example, Frances Bairstow, "The Structure of Bargaining: International Comparisons—A Story of Diversity," *Labor Law Journal* 31 (August 1980), p. 561; James L. Perry and Harold L. Angle, "Bargaining Unit Structure and Organizational Outcomes," *Industrial Relations* 20 (Winter 1981), p. 57; and Wallace E. Hendricks and Lawrence M. Kahn, "The Determinants of Bargaining Structure in U.S. Manufacturing Industries," *Industrial and Labor Relations Review* 35 (January 1982), p. 191.

[10]"Multiemployer Bargaining Called Failure in Coal," Bureau of National Affairs Inc., *Daily Labor Report* 78 (April 23, 1981), pp. 1–2. See also, Robert B. Hoffman, "The Trend Away From Multiemployer Bargaining," *Labor Law Journal*, 34 (February 1983), pp. 80–93.

[11]Abraham Cohen, "Coordinated Bargaining Structures of Collective Bargaining," *Labor Law Journal* 26 (June 1975), p. 385. For a detailed review of the literature pertaining to centralized bargaining, including its history as well as related union-management attitudes, see the preceding article as well as the same author's "Union Rationale and Objectives of Coordinated Bargaining," *Labor Law Journal* 27 (February 1976), pp. 75–82; George H. Hildebrand, "Cloudy Future for Coalition Bargaining," *Harvard Business Review* 46 (November–December 1968), pp. 114–128; Herbert J. Lahne, "Coalition Bargaining and the Future of Union Structure," *Labor Law Journal* 18 (June 1967), pp. 356–359; William N. Chernish, *Coalition Bargaining: A Study of Union Tactics and Public Policy* (Philadelphia: University of Pennsylvania Press, 1969); and Kenneth O. Alexander, "Union Structure and Bargaining Structure," *Labor Law Journal* 24 (March 1973), pp. 164–172.

[12]Meyer S. Ryder, Charles M. Rehmus, and Sanford Cohen, *Management Preparation for Collective Bargaining* (Homewood, Ill.: Dow Jones-Irwin, 1966), p. 9.

[13]Audrey Freedman, *Managing Labor Relations* (New York: The Conference Board, 1979), pp. 8–9.

[14]Bruce Morse, *How to Negotiate the Labor Agreement* (Detroit: Trends Publishing, 1974), p. 19.

[15]Ronald L. Miller, "Preparations for Negotiations," *Personnel Journal* 57 (January 1978), p. 36.

[16]Michael H. Granof, *How to Cost Your Labor Contract* (Washington, D.C.: Bureau of National Affairs, 1973), pp. 5, 19. For another costing approach see W. D. Heisel and Gordon S. Skinner, *Costing Union Demands* (Chicago: International Personnel Management Association, 1976).

[17]For a review of several considerations affecting the costing process see Gordon S. Skinner and E. Edward Herman, "The Importance of Costing Labor Contracts," *Labor Law Journal* 32 (August 1981), pp. 497–507.

[18]For a rich, detailed account of the variety of collective bargaining relationships see Frederick H. Harbison and John R. Coleman, *Goals and Strategy for Collective Bargaining* (New York: Harper & Bros., 1951), pp. 4–6.

[19]Paul Diesing, "Bargaining Strategy and Union-Management Relationships," *Journal of Conflict Resolution* 5 (December 1961), p. 369.

[20]Rosen and Rosen, "The Union Bargaining Agent," p. 540.

[21]Samuel B. Bacharach and Edward J. Lawler, *Bargaining Power: Tactics and Outcomes*, (San Francisco: Jossey-Bass, 1981), p. x.

[22]Albert A. Blum, "Collective Bargaining: Ritual or Reality?" *Harvard Business Review* 39 (November–December 1961), p. 65. See also the discussion of ritualistic elements (such as "snow job") in Frank L. Acuff and Maurice F. Villere, "Games Negotiators Play," *Business Horizons* 19 (February 1976), pp. 70–76.

[23]Ryder, Rehmus, and Cohen, *Management Preparation for Collective Bargaining*, p. 61.

[24]Walton and McKersie, *A Behavioral Theory*, p. 96.

[25]Bacharach and Lawler, *Bargaining Power*, p. 157.

[26]Dean G. Pruitt, *Negotiation Behavior* (New York: Academic Press, 1981), pp. 77–79.

[27]Walton and McKersie, *A Behavioral Theory*, pp. 4–6. For an empirical study of union and management negotiators which lends some support to the independent nature of these processes see Richard B. Peterson and Lane Tracy, "Testing a Behavioral Theory Model of Labor Negotiations," *Industrial Relations* 16 (February 1977), pp. 35–50.

[28]Robert W. Johnston, "Negotiation Strategies: Different Strokes for Different Folks," *Personnel* 59 (March–April 1982), p. 38.

[29]For a discussion of various union-management efforts in this area see Gordon H. Cole, "Alcoholism: Tragedy on the Job," *American Federationist* 83 (May 1976), pp. 1–4.

[30]Johnston, "Negotiation Strategies," p. 38.

[31]Pruitt, *Negotiation Behavior*, p. 80.

[32]David L. Cole, *The Quest for Industrial Peace* (New York: McGraw-Hill, 1963), pp. 9–13.

[33]George J. Berkwitt, "Industrial Relations Is Nowhere," *Dun's Review* 99 (February 1972), pp. 58–60.

[34]Blum, "Collective Bargaining: Ritual or Reality?" p. 65.

[35]National Labor Relations Board, *A Guide to Basic Law and Procedures under the National Labor Relations Act* (Washington, D.C.: Government Printing Office, 1976), p. 7.

[36]Bureau of National Affairs, *Labor Relations Expediter*, pp. LRX87–LRX99. It should be noted that the NLRB's right to categorize collective bargaining subjects as mandatory, voluntary, and illegal was upheld by the Supreme Court, *NLRB v. Wooster Division of Borg-Warner Corporation*, 356 U.S. 342 (1958).

[37]National Labor Relations Board, *Guide to Basic Law*, pp. 28, 36.

[38]For management's position in General Electric's bargaining see Virgil B. Day, "Bad Faith Bargaining?" in Walter Fogel and Archie Kleingartner, eds., *Contemporary Labor Issues* (Belmont, Calif.: Wadsworth Publishing, 1968), pp. 388–392; and Lemuel R. Boulware, *The Truth about Boulwarism* (Washington, D.C.: Bureau of National Affairs, 1969).

[39]*NLRB v. General Electric*, 72 LRRM 2530 (1969); *General Electric v. NLRB*, 397 U.S. 965 (1970). See also Thomas P. Brown IV, "Hard Bargaining: The Board Says No, the Courts Say Yes," *Employee Relations Law Journal* 8, No. 1 (Summer 1982), pp. 37–51.

[40]Charles J. Morris, *The Developing Labor Law* (Washington, D.C.: Bureau of National Affairs, 1971), pp. 286–309. See also the 1973, 1974, and 1976 supplements to this volume for an updated legal consideration of these activities.

[41]Ibid., pp. 309–316.

[42]For organizational implications of the financial disclosure requirement see James A. Craft, "Information Disclosure and the Role of the Accountant in Collective Bargaining," *Accounting Organizations And Society* 6, No. 1 (1981), pp. 97–107; Richard A. Beaumont, "The Risks of Opening the Corporate Books to Unions," *Wall Street Journal*, October 18, 1982, p. 34; and, James T. O'Reilly, *Unions' Rights to Company Information* (Philadelphia: University of Pennsylvania, The Wharton School, 1980).

[43]Bureau of National Affairs, *Labor Relations Expediter*, LRX102.

[44]*Overnite Transportation Company v. NLRB*, 64 LRRM 2307 (1967).

[45]*Kota Division of Dura Corp.*, 182 NLRB 51 (1970).

[46]*Burns International Detective Agency Inc.*, 80 LRRM 2225 (1972).

[47]*Howard Johnson Co.*, 80 LRRM 1769 (1972).

[48]*Emerald Maintenance, Inc.*, 80 LRRM 2801 (1972).

[49]*Wayne Convalescent Center, Inc.*, 81 LRRM 2129 (1972). For additional insights into this legal bargaining obligation see Saul G. Kramer and Aaron J. Schindel, "Bargaining Obligations and Corporate Transformations," in Richard Adelman, ed., *Proceedings of New York University's Thirty-Third Annual Conference on Labor* (New York: Matthew Bender, 1981), pp. 223–262; William A. Krupman and Roger S. Kaplan, "The Stock Purchaser after *Burns*: Must He Buy the Union Contract?" *Labor Law Journal* 31 (June 1980), pp. 328–334; and, Jules I. Crystal, "Successor and Assigns Clauses: Do They Actually Require That a Purchaser Adopt the Seller's Contract?" *Labor Law Journal* 33 (September 1982), pp. 581–585.

[50]National Labor Relations Board *Forty-fifth Annual Report* (Washington, D.C.: Government Printing Office, 1980), p. 243.

[51]Peter D. Walther, "The Board's Place at the Bargaining Table," *Labor Law Journal* 28 (March 1977), p. 131.

[52]B. M. Schieber, "Honesty in Bargaining," *American Federationist* 82 (April 1975), p. 20.

[53]For a more detailed discussion of these remedial problems see Elliot Bredhoff, "The Scope of 'Good Faith Bargaining' and Adequacy of Remedies," in Somers, *Industrial Relations Research Association: Proceedings of the Twenty-sixth Annual Winter Meeting*, pp. 109–118.

[54]*H. K. Porter*, 73 LRRM 2561 (1970).

[55]*Ex-Cello Corp.*, 74 LRRM 1740 (1970).

[56]Neil W. Chamberlain and James W. Kuhn, *Collective Bargaining*, 2nd ed. (New York: McGraw Hill, 1965), pp. 162–190.

[57]Bacharach and Lawler, *Bargaining Power*, p. 4.

[58]Charles Craypo, "The Decline of Union Bargaining Power," in Michael J. Carter and William H. Leahy, eds., *New Directions in Labor Economics and Industrial Relations* (London: University of Notre Dame Press, 1981), p. 109.

[59]"Concessionary Bargaining: Will the New Cooperation Last?" *Business Week*, June 14, 1982, p. 66.

[60]Joseph Krislov and J. Lew Silver, "Union Bargaining Power in the 1980s," *Labor Law Journal* 32 (August 1981), p. 482.

[61]William J. Lanouette, "Recession Brings Labor, Management Closer Together on Union Contracts," *National Journal* 14 (March 16, 1982), p. 422.

[62]"Concession Pacts Seen not Having Wide Impact," Bureau of National Affairs Inc., *Daily Labor Report* 155 (August 11, 1982), p. 2.

[63]William Earle Klay, "Contending with Uncertainty in Collective Negotiations," *Journal of Collective Negotiations in the Public Sector* 11 no. 3 (1982), pp. 189–200.

[64]Rubin and Brown, *The Social Psychology of Bargaining*. See also Milton Derber, *Research in Labor Problems in the United States* (New York: Random House, 1967), pp. 301–341.

[65]William Zartman, "Negotiation as a Joint Decision-Making Process," *Journal of Conflict Resolution* 21 (December 1977), pp. 623–625.

[66]For an example of this approach, see Bertram I. Spector, "Negotiation as a Psychological Process," *Journal of Conflict Resolution* 21 (December 1977), pp. 607–618.

[67]See, for example, Oran R. Young, *Bargaining: Formal Theories of Negotiation* (Urbana: University of Illinois Press, 1975), pp. 131–242; John G. Cross, *The Economics of Bargaining* (New York: Basic Books, 1969), and Allan M. Cartter and F. Ray Marshall, *Labor Economics* (Homewood, Ill.: Richard D. Irwin, 1972), pp. 242–243.

[68]R. D. Luce and H. Raiffa, *Games and Decisions: Introduction and Critical Survey* (New York: Wiley, 1957).

[69]For an example of how this problem can be minimized see Terrence A. Oliva and Terry L. Leap, "A Taxonomy of Bargaining Models," *Human Relations* 34 (November 1981), pp. 935–946.

Chapter 7 Resolving Negotiation Impasses and Developing Cooperation

In today's more sophisticated environment of worldwide competition, both labor and management know that the best way to move forward is together. Open combat was yesterday's agenda. Today's world calls for a fundamental reordering of our relationship, a reordering so far-reaching that it will alter the shape of the organizations themselves.

Roger B. Smith, Chairman and Chief Executive Officer, General Motors Corporation, "Toward a New Alliance with Labor," lecture as Robert S. Hatfield Fellow at Cornell University, April 7, 1982.

How often have you seen headlines declaring "99 Percent of Employees' Time Did Not Involve Strikes Last Year"? Probably never! More than likely you have read: "Railway Strike Causes Massive Layoffs in United States."

Media coverage of labor-management activities often overemphasizes labor conflicts, even though a very high percentage of unions do not strike to obtain a negotiated agreement. In fact, most relationships between union and management are peaceful, with only minor, resolvable conflicts.

This chapter discusses the ratification of the negotiated labor agreement and explains the impasse resolution procedures involving third parties, such as mediation, varieties of contract arbitration, and fact-finding. It also examines strikes, pickets and boycotts in terms of their administrative and legal considerations. A concluding section briefly illustrates the potential of various cooperative efforts aimed at avoiding union-management conflicts.

Contract Ratification

Negotiators, after resolving their differences and agreeing on tentative contract language, submit the proposed agreement to the union members for ratification; this usually requires a favorable majority vote.[1] Although a vote by the members is not legally necessary, some affirmation via referendum or delegated authority is normally used in the ratification process. For example, the United Auto Workers and United Mine Workers have a direct referendum, whereas the Steelworkers have delegated authority for ratification to a bargaining committee. In recent years, union members have shown increasing interest in greater participation, and more ratification elections have been held.

The ratification process determines whether members can live with the proposed agreement, even though they may not be completely satisfied with all of its provisions. Acceptance by the membership gives management some assurance that the employees will comply with the letter and spirit of the agreement. A vote to accept, therefore, is considered a commitment or willingness to be bound by the agreement.[2] When and if union members find the agreement unacceptable, they may vote to reject it, as they have in about eleven percent of the cases between 1972 and 1981.[3]

Reasons for Rejection of Tentative Agreements

The rejection of tentative agreements is an often debated subject. There has been disagreement over the reasons behind and the significance of contract rejections. One study of 1,973 related cases attempted to determine the reasons for tentative contract rejections by the membership. The most frequent reason given for rejection was that employees felt that they were shortchanged in comparison to other agreements in their vicinity. Members will reject contracts if they feel the provisions would make them "second-class citizens." Internal union politics was given as the second most frequent reason mentioned for contract rejection. Sometimes union leaders are elected by slight majorities; their rivals will campaign against any labor agreement negotiated by the incumbent leaders.

Other factors contributing to contract rejections relate to other types of internal union problems, such as feelings of inequity and lack of upward communication within the union itself. For example, in industrial unions, skilled workers usually represent a minority of the membership, having little bargaining strength. These members might vote to reject the contract when their wages do not compare favorably with those of highly-paid skilled tradesmen in the building and construction industry.

Other groups (women, racial minorities, younger workers, and so on) continue to claim intraplant inequities. Although equal employment opportunity laws have been passed, wage differentials continue to exist for racial minorities and women. Moreover, young employees with low seniority view pensions and layoffs, which are usually based on seniority or retirement age, differently from the older employees, causing additional internal friction. Unless any of these subgroups feels that the agreement reflects its own personal needs, it assuredly will vote to reject the entire agreement.[4]

Another study found that the primary cause of rejection is union members' economic concerns—rejection percentages generally corresponded to a downturn in economic activity. In over half of the cases studied, high employee expectations coupled with reasons for union members to question the employer's wage offer led to rejection of the tentative contract. To confirm their conclusions, the researchers followed up on the agreements that were ultimately accepted and found that 65 percent included an increase in the wage package above that of the initial tentative settlement.[5]

A third study of about a thousand contract rejections concluded that the definition of contract rejection in previous studies had been too broad, overestimating the number of contract rejections and overemphasizing their problematic nature. These researchers found considerably lower rejection rates after redefining the term *contract rejection*. For example, less than 2 percent of the tentative agreements were rejected when all members of the bargaining committee recommended acceptance, and less than 3 percent were rejected when a majority of the bargaining committee recommended acceptance. Therefore, their conclusion was that contract rejection should be defined as the membership's rejection of the union bargaining committee's contract acceptance recommendation, not management's final contract proposal.[6]

Although issues involving contract rejection will be debated, other interesting possibilities need consideration. These are:

1. Whether union negotiators may involve contract rejection as part of their bargaining strategy. For instance, rejection of a tentative agreement may indicate to management that the members want a more favorable package. When the bargaining committee presents the proposed agreement for a vote without any endorsement, it can return to the bargaining table after a contract rejection with renewed confidence and commitment from the membership.
2. Whether contract rejection reflects underlying problems of communication within the union, upward and downward. For example, members may not understand the terms of the agreement and their implications; the leaders may have misjudged the needs and wishes of the membership.
3. Whether contract rejection indicates a weakness in the union leadership because union members rarely give their leaders full authority to negotiate a contract without a ratification vote.
4. Whether factionalism within a union—young versus old, black versus white, male versus female, craft versus production workers, personality differences, political differences, and so on is really the reason for rejection, thereby reflecting a lack of unity within the union.[7]

Impasse Resolution Procedures Involving a Third Party Neutral

Usually both parties attempt to resolve impasses, which can occur either before or after the contract's expiration date. In some cases, union and management officials need third parties either to facilitate the negotiation process or to resolve the bargaining difference with finality. There are five impasse resolution procedures involving third parties: mediation, conventional contract arbitration, mediation-arbitration (med-arb), final offer selection arbitration, and fact-finding.

Mediation

Many union-management impasses are resolved with help from neutral third-party mediators, obtained either from the Federal Mediation and Conciliation Service (FMCS) or from state agencies. Mediators perform a number of functions: they assist in scheduling meetings, keeping the parties talking, carrying messages back and forth, and making suggestions. The mediator has no authority to make binding decisions and must rely on persuasion and recommendations; the negotiators make the final decisions.[8] The mediator is the "invited guest" who can be asked to leave. However, acceptance of mediators is an indicator of the effort of one or both of the parties to bargain in good faith.

The FMCS was involved in 21,346 cases in 1981,[9] and the trend toward using mediation in dispute settlement continues upward. Added to this number should be the activities of separate mediation agencies in some eighteen states and Puerto Rico that assist parties in their own jurisdictions.

The mediation process is much more an art than a science. There is no general theory of mediation; rather it has been described as a process that "has been helpful in a haphazard way largely because of the talents of certain individuals who themselves would find it difficult to say why they had been successful."[10] Because there are no set rules, different mediators are able to obtain equally good results by different methods; therefore, mediation does not permit much generalization.

One analytical approach to the process focuses on personal qualities of the mediator—quickness of mind, evenness of temper, sense of humor, and knowledge and understanding of the industry. William E. Simkin, former director of the FMCS, developed a list of sixteen qualities sought in a mediator—all of which would be difficult to find in any one individual. Among the appropriate qualities are the patience of Job, the wit of the Irish, the broken-field dodging abilities of a halfback, the physical endurance of the marathon runner, the hide of a rhinoceros, and the wisdom of Solomon.[11]

Carl Stevens' study of mediation focusing on the mediator's functions and tactics has identified several causal factors that lead to negotiated settlements—the bottom-line criterion of successful mediation. Timing of the mediator's involvement was identified as one of the most important considerations. The mediator should enter before the parties become too fixed in their positions but not so early as to upset the power balance between the parties, causing them to harden their bargaining positions.

In some instances, the mere entrance of the mediator may be sufficient for dispute settlement. For example, assume that one of the chief negotiators leaves an active negotiation in a temper tantrum, vowing never again to return to the bargaining table. Upon subsequent reflection, the negotiator realizes a mistake was made but feels that calling the opposing negotiator would be embarrassing and perhaps indicate weakness. A common tactic used in such situations would be to call the mediator who could schedule another meeting. Thus, mediation in this sense represents a very potent face-saving device.[12]

In other cases, the parties do not desire any specific help from the mediator, but the availability of that mediator and the very existence of the mediation forum facilitates the bargaining process.[13] Mediation can be analyzed in terms of roles, behaviors, and styles of the mediators and the parties. For example, one mediator described his role as a third party:

My role is to help the parties reach a settlement. I am just a third party, another forum to talk about your differences. I want to develop a dialogue on these open issues and hopefully reach an agreement but the burden of reaching that agreement rests with the union and management.[14]

Another mediator explained her role as a more direct participant:

I am here to make a deal. Negotiations are over as far as I am concerned. I refuse to play a passive role and just let the parties talk. I will not be a messenger either. First they have to convince me and then we will see what I can do with it.[15]

A successful mediator is frequently an interpreter and clarifies perceptions of the bargaining climate and possible costs of impasse. For instance, if the parties disagree on data about cost of living, comparative wage rates, and productivity, the mediator could assist in reaching agreement on the statistical data. When negotiators tend to underestimate the costs of a strike or lockout or to overestimate the cost of an agreement, the mediator may be able to provide insights enabling them to evaluate their positions more realistically. Frequently a mediator will hold separate meetings with each group before calling for a joint meeting.

Helping each party to understand the tactics or intentions of the other can also aid the bargaining process. If management bluffs about its willingness to accept a strike or to allow an ongoing strike to continue indefinitely, the mediator may attempt to diagnose management's true intentions and then advise the union. On the other hand, if the union threatens a strike to obtain an excessive bargaining demand, the mediator could attempt to diagnose what the union is "really trying to say" and so inform the company negotiator. The mediator, in determining the true intentions of one party, may advise the other, who may realistically believe the mediator, but not the other party. By holding private caucuses with each, the mediator is privy to much confidential information. While no mediator would reveal this information to the other party, he or she can determine the magnitude of the real differences and encourage the parties that a settlement may be near if they continue bargaining.

The mediator also may facilitate the bargaining process by proposing alternate solutions to the parties. There can be little effective bargaining without an overlap of at least some of the issues. Therefore, the mediator must create and propose alternate solutions, compromised settlements, and definitions of the respective bargaining positions.[16]

The parties, however, play the dominant role in shaping the mediation process. For example, in cases where experienced negotiators have a clear understanding of their bargaining objectives and strategies, the mediator is primarily the servant of the parties. But where less sophisticated negotiators have not clearly defined their bargaining objectives, the personal qualities and actions of the mediator have their greatest impact. Here, an aggressive mediator may be able to gain the trust of the parties and create the type of negotiating atmosphere that achieves a settlement.[17]

In addition to mediating activities, mediators must be conscious of the perceptions of the parties and his or her own position. Not only must the mediator be uninvolved in any actions or tactics of deception and coercion, he or she must also retain the qualities of neutrality, objectivity, and professionalism.

Conventional Interest (or Contract) Arbitration

Conventional interest or contract arbitration involves the selection of a neutral person or panel to hear the bargaining positions of the parties and make a final and binding decision on what should be included in the negotiated agreement. This process differs from grievance or rights arbitration (see Chapter 9), which is concerned mostly with interpreting and applying the terms of the existing labor agreement. Interest arbitration is less used in the private sector than the public, but it makes up in relevance what it lacks in numbers because each decision is significant. (A more thorough discussion is included in Chapter 14.)

Although interest arbitration is not common (less than one percent of the negotiations)[18] in the private sector, many parties consider it an alternative procedure for impasse resolution. They realize that strikes are costly to both union and management personnel and also strain relationships. But with the trend toward longer contracts and away from wage reopener clauses, the opportunities for contract arbitration are reduced, and the risks of arbitration are increased. In other words, longer contracts require fewer negotiation times but extend the length of time that the parties may have to live with an arbitrator's decision.

Management and unions in the private sector have varied opinions on interest arbitration. Both parties prefer the arbitrator's decision when it reflects their own final position and avoids a strike. On the other hand, both parties have concerns about the delay in scheduling an arbitrator and the extra cost involved. In addition, management becomes particularly concerned if the arbitrator fails to take into account the economic effect of the decision or if the award is above the norm for the industry.[19]

Others criticize interest arbitration for having a "chilling" effect on negotiations. They believe that if one of the parties thinks it can get a better contract by delaying and presenting its proposals to an arbitrator, it will. Also, arbitrators have been accused of "splitting the difference" between parties' proposals, causing both parties to make more extreme proposals rather than genuinely negotiating by the usual "give and take" and compromise.

Mediation-Arbitration (med-arb)

Med-arb occurs when the parties agree in advance that contract language, whether reached by mediation or arbitration, will be final and binding. Usually no decisions on the contract language will be sent back to the parties—either the board or directors of the union membership—for ratification. Once the parties agree to med-arb, those issues that cannot be resolved by mediation will be resolved by arbitration. The neutral will wear the mediator's hat at first, but if no agreement is reached by a predetermined date, he or she will become the arbitrator and decide the remaining unresolved issues. Under this procedure, most issues will be resolved by the parties because, in addition to the traditional pressures, there will be the pressure of knowing that the mediator-arbitrator will make a final and binding decision, if the parties do not.

An example of med-arb in the private sector involved a San Francisco printing company that published two local newspapers and had bought new automated equipment called scanners. The scanners required numerous changes in the work and the collective bargaining agreement over such issues as loss of jobs, seniority, and newly assigned work. These issues were important to both parties and perhaps would have been too complicated for a traditional arbitration hearing. Such wide differences could have resulted in a strike; however, the flexibility of the med-arb procedure resulted in a successful resolution of the issues.[20] Med-arb was also used in the 1978 postal negotations, in which Professor James Healy of Harvard University served as mediator-arbitrator (see Chapter 15).

Final Offer Selection Arbitration

Final offer selection (FOS) arbitration is a type of interest arbitration which gives the arbitrator the authority to select one of the proposals made by the parties. Procedurally, union and management present their separate final proposals to the arbitrator, who selects only one proposal, making no change in any of the provisions. Since the parties know in advance that the arbitrator cannot make a compromise decision, they will try to present to the arbitrator an acceptable proposal. Theoretically, if both parties attempt to present acceptable proposals, their positions will converge, and will possibly settle their differences without third-party intervention. (Variations of FOS arbitration will be discussed in Chapter 14).

FOS arbitration has some shortcomings, particularly if standards for arbitration decisions are not supplied. More importantly, the labor negotiations usually involve several issues, making FOS arbitration a very complex process. If the parties do not change or compromise their initial positions on some or all of these issues, the offers will not converge. The arbitrator must then select one of the extreme proposals, possibly heightening union-management tensions during the life of the contract and causing future difficulties in negotiating subsequent contracts.[21]

Another criticism of FOS arbitration is that it tends to lead to compromised settlements over the long run where arbitrators appear to make awards to both management and unions in equal proportions, thus balancing the winners and losers over time. However, preliminary analysis of data from FOS arbitration has found rather meager support for this criticism.[22]

Fact-Finding

Somewhere between the extremes of mediation and interest arbitration lies *fact-finding.* This is a semijudicial process in which the major focus is placed on gathering the facts and using some of the principles of mediation and arbitration. The fact finder's purpose is to assess the facts presented and gathered and to organize and display them publicly in the hopes that the parties will feel an obligation to settle their differences.

Fact-finding may be used in major disputes under the National Labor Relations Act and Railway Labor Act and fact-finding reports are useful to presidents in determining what actions to take in national emergency disputes, such as when to seek an injunction or recommend legislation. Because of its distant involvement and its lack of finality, this process does not have a good record in resolving disputes. Mediation, arbitration, and fact-finding all involve a third party, who either assists or directs union and management officials in resolving a negotiation impasse. As is discussed in the following section, management and union officials might prefer not to use a third party in this situation, but to rely instead on economic tests of strength.

The Strike and Related Activities between Union and Management

Work stoppages include both strikes and lockouts that cause a business to stop production, distribution, and sales of its goods or any organization to cease its operations. Generally a *strike* is a temporary stoppage of work by a group of employees for the purpose of expressing a grievance or enforcing a demand. The counterpart to the strike is the *lockout* which is an act by an employer of withholding or denying employment during a labor dispute in order to enforce terms of employment on a group of employees.[23]

Within this general framework there are a number of different types of strikes, usually labeled in accordance with their cause, purpose, nature, or accompanying activities:

- **Economic strikes** are worker stoppages to gain economic goals such as higher wages, improved pensions, and vacations.
- **Wildcat strikes** are strikes that occur without approval from higher union officials.
- **Unfair labor practice strikes** are worker stoppages that occur as a reaction to an employer's unfair labor practice. Examples include strikes in response to an employer's refusal to bargain or its discharge of a union member for engaging in union activities.
- **Secondary strikes** are worker stoppages by employees who have no dispute with their own employer but are striking to support another union.
- **Jurisdictional strikes** occur when two unions conflict over work assignments (for example, plumbers strike when laborers are directed to unload a truck full of plumbing materials).
- **Recognition strikes** occur when employees interested in a union strike an employer to gain recognition of the union.

Usually accompanying the strike, especially the economic strike, are pickets and boycotts. *Picketing* refers to the outside patrolling of the employer's premises, usually using placards and handbills to achieve a specific objective. For example, *recognitional picketing* is used to gain recognition of the union as the employees' bargaining representative. Recognitional picketing is limited for a period of up to thirty days, at which time the union must petition for an election. Also, recognitional picketing is illegal where a certified union exists or where an election has been held within the last twelve months.

Informational picketing occurs when the union attempts to inform the public that a labor dispute exists between the workers and their organization. *Product or consumer picketing* attempts to persuade customers to refuse to purchase products from the employer with whom the union has a labor dispute. Often the employees and their supporters also *boycott* the employer, or refuse to purchase products made by the employer with whom they have the dispute.

Table 7.1 shows that work stoppages between 1973 and 1980 continued at a low rate in terms of workers involved and days idled as compared to work stoppages between 1940 and 1970. The last three years average less in percent of working time lost and percent of workers involved than any other three year period. Table 7.2 attempts to display the major issues involved in work stoppages, but experience has cautioned against arbitrary labeling. Work stoppages are not caused by one factor alone, but usually by many factors. Even so, there can be little argument that the main issue is wages, followed by plant administrative issues.

An analysis of strike activities over the last 30 years shows the following:

- Annual number of strikes fluctuated between 3,000 and 6,000
- Average number of workers involved ranged from 1 to 3.5 million
- Average duration ranged between 15 and 27 days
- Lost time at work ranged from one-tenth to one-half of 1 percent
- A few large strikes usually accounted for most of the workers involved and most of the time lost

Table 7.1 Work Stoppages in the United States, 1930–80

			Workers Involved		Days Idled	
Years	Number	Duration (Mean Number of Days)	Number (Thousands)	Percent of Total Employed	Percent of Working Time	Per Worker
1930–1939 (Average)	2,015	21.2	911	4.1	NA[a]	17.4
1940–1949 (Average)	3,893	16.5	2,311	5.4	.31	12.2
1950–1959 (Average)	4,248	19.9	2,198	4.3	.50	17.4
1960–1969 (Average)	4,104	23.5	1,809	2.8	.22	19.9
1970	5,716	25.0	3,305	4.7	.37	20.1
1971	5,138	27.0	3,280	4.5	.26	14.5
1972	5,010	24.0	1,714	2.3	.15	15.8
1973	5,353	24.0	2,251	2.9	.14	12.4
1974	6,074	27.1	2,778	3.5	.24	17.3
1975	5,031	26.8	1,746	2.2	.16	17.9
1976	5,648	28.0	2,420	3.0	.19	15.6
1977	5,506	29.3	2,040	2.4	.17	17.6
1978	4,230	33.2	1,623	1.9	.17	22.8
1979	4,827	32.1	1,727	1.9	.15	20.1
1980	3,885	35.4	1,366	1.5	.14	24.4

[a]NA = not available.

Source: U.S. Department of Labor, Bureau of Labor Statistics, *Work Stoppages, 1980* (Washington, D.C.: Government Printing Office, 1981), p. 3.

Table 7.2 Work Stoppages According to Major Issues, 1980–1981

	Stoppages			
	1980		1981[a]	
Major Issue	Number	Percent	Number	Percent
General Wage Changes	2,601	66.9	1,442	65.8
Supplementary Benefits	79	2.0	43	2.0
Wage Adjustments	52	1.3	27	1.2
Hours of Work	9	0.0	6	0.3
Other Contractual Matters	204	5.3	101	4.6
Union Organization and Security	205	5.3	139	6.3
Job Security	202	5.2	117	5.3
Plant Administration	383	9.9	259	11.8
Other Working Conditions	55	1.4	25	1.1
Interunion or Intraunion Matters	65	1.7	27	1.2
Not Reported	30	0.8	5	0.2
Total	3,885		2,191	

Source: Bureau of Labor Statistics, *News*, Washington, D.C.: The U.S. Department of Labor, January 29, 1982, p. 6.

- Wages were consistently (40 to 65 percent of cases) the major issue
- There were considerable variations across industries, occupations, and regions.[24]

Explanation of Strikes

There have been numerous studies designed to explain why strikes occur. The decision to strike or cause a strike is conditioned by the *total* environment—the bargaining structure, the security of the organizations, the power resources of the parties, and the economic climate. A change in any one aspect of this environment will, in turn, affect the level of strike activity. One review of strike activity since 1948 showed that not only have strikes declined but there is less variation in strike activity from year to year. This study attributed the change to the greater stability in the economic climate and the organizational and political framework governing the practice of collective bargaining.[25]

At a single location, strikes occur not only to enforce a demand, but because of the parties' misconceptions about collective bargaining and their lack of information about the positions of their bargaining counterparts. The nature of the bargaining process causes each party to hold back on its "real" position. Thus, strikes frequently occur when one party misperceives the other's position. Then, when the strike occurs, both parties gain more information about the negotiations because they know more about what the other party considers unaccept-

Source: Courtesy of Wide World Photos.

Striking employees may picket the struck firm to inform the public of the dispute and to gain recognition for their goal or union.

able. Thus, strikes often improve the information exchange between the parties.[26] For example, if the union is asking for a 10 percent increase in wages and the company negotiators believe that the union will accept an 8 percent increase, the union may have to strike in order to show the company that it was serious in its demand of 10 percent. When the strike starts, the company negotiators know that an 8 percent increase in wages was not the union's acceptable minimum and its demand for 10 percent was not a "bluff."

Although strikes have traditionally been viewed as economic or legal conflicts, the psychological aspects have received more attention recently. Psychologically, strikes can be categorized as a protest, or a group process for organizational change. Protest strikes include actions by the membership of walking off their jobs without the approval of their leadership (called *wildcat strikes*). These spontaneous protests may be in reaction to a unilateral change by management in introducing production quotas or working conditions, or even in lowering thermostats in winter months.

As a group process, strikes require an issue around which to revolve, as well as the machinery to mobilize the membership and adequate strike resources. The union leadership is critical, as the leaders must instill unity among the membership, control courses of action, respond to the feelings of the group, and maintain communication with management.

A strike can be a process for change for the individual as well as the working environment. An issue, such as a wage increase, may remain at the center of the dispute; however, other elements that enter the bargaining process subsequently change. Strikes can have traumatic effects on the parties' attitudes; they can temper the militants with realism and radicalize the conservatives. Strikes may cause the members to question the credibility of their leaders or management. Furthermore, once the strike is over, much rebuilding must occur.[27]

Criteria Involved in Union-Management Strike Decisions

When negotiators have failed to reach an agreement by the time the previous labor agreement expires, both union members and officers and management officials have to seriously consider whether a strike is in their best interests. In most cases union members return to work after the negotiators agree temporarily to a tentative settlement but postpone a final decision on whether to strike until the ratification vote is taken. In some cases, as with the United Mine Workers, union members will not work without an agreement fully ratified by the membership. In other cases, such as the 1982 Chrysler-UAW negotiations, the contract may be extended for a short time if negotiators believe they are close to agreement.

Regardless of the approach used, each union must consider a number of factors before the members will vote to approve and commit themselves to a strike. Likewise, management must analyze its own situation to determine whether to take a strike. In addition, each party attempts to assess the position of the other party in order to determine the relative strength of each factor considered. For example, if management can operate at nearly 100 percent capacity during a strike, this would certainly be a positive factor for management and a negative one for the union.

Although the factors that unions consider in their determination to strike are fairly easy to identify, the uncertainties and relative importance of these factors will vary with the particular circumstances of each case. For example, union members may know in advance how much income they will lose each day of a strike but be unable to predict its length. More difficult to weigh is the balance between income lost due to the strike and the expected income increase gained as a result of the strike. Both parties must take into account imprecise data in their strike decision. These data can be grouped into four broad categories: financial considerations; goodwill, public image, and government intervention; strategic purposes of the strike; and previous strike experience.

Financial Considerations While employees consider their lost wages and other accompanying costs of a strike, management looks at its own figures to compute how much a strike will cost. These include fixed costs like rent, interest on loans, payments for equipment, and salaries. Also, customers may be lost, unless there is significant customer loyalty, and the costs of stockpiling and building inventories and preparing for the strike can cost millions of dollars. Or, when the employer prepares by stockpiling and building inventories and no strike occurs, then the employer has other complicated problems—whether to continue full operation, who to lay off, and how to temporarily or permanently retrench—all long-run cost factors.[28]

Operating the plant during a strike with management personnel and nonstriking employees must be considered. But such operation is more difficult than anticipated in some cases because it is occasionally accompanied by violence on the picket line and operating a plant during a strike with non-union employees certainly strains the labor-management relationship. Thus management's decision to operate during a strike involves many uncertainties.

Employer costs may also depend on the durability or perishability of the product or the substitutability of goods or services offered by the company. A strike for a short period at a large automaker having a large stockpile of autos would be only a small inconvenience; in fact, it could even save the automaker money if inventories were excessive. However, a farmworker strike of two weeks during harvest season could cause enormous damage, and the cost to the farmer would be prohibitive. A strike by a local bus service that transports only a small percentage of the commuters might be inconsequential, especially if these commuters will be able to find alternative means of getting to work. But if the bus service transports a large percentage of commuters, serious and time-consuming traffic problems could develop, leading to poor public relations for the employer and the union.

While many of the effects and costs of a strike rest with the immediate employer and the union, strikes against employers producing basic materials that are used by other industries extend the effects and the costs of the strike to other employers and union members.[29] A steel strike would be felt throughout the country. With so much interdependence in the industrial sector, few strikes can occur that will not have an impact on operations and employees in other industries.

One financial consideration that is associated with union *and* employer behavior during strikes is shareholder return (such as dividends, capital gains). For short strikes of ten days or less, shareholders' returns appear to be below market levels. Also returns decline prior to the strike with the anticipation of the strike, and decline further after the strike. Thus, the low shareholder return reflects a less favorable financial position and indicates the firm's weakened ability to withstand a long strike and the union's reluctance to endanger the life of the firm. For strikes of thirty or more days, the shareholders' returns appear to be above the market returns and increase prior to the strike. These relatively high returns reflect a more favorable financial position for the firm, a better position to resist the union's demand, and an increased ability to sustain a strike.

These higher returns increase the union's determination to obtain a more favorable settlement and press its demands to the point of striking longer to obtain a better settlement. After longer strikes, shareholder returns decline, indicating lengthy strikes are perceived unfavorably by shareholders and implying that managers should avoid lengthy strikes.[30]

Strike Benefits and Public Aid for Strikers The strike benefits received by many union members, usually less than $50 per week, often determine whether union members will vote to strike as well as how long they will strike. Although the amount that each union member receives during a strike is minimal, the total amount of annual strike payments can be large.[31]

Unions use several approaches in the design of their strike benefit plans and the manner in which the benefits are disbursed. Some unions earmark a certain proportion of their total per capita receipts, some levy temporary assessments as needed, and others have no separate funds but pay from the union treasury. The United Rubber Workers once used a special assessment of $5 per member to replenish its strike funds, and the Chemical Workers activates its crisis strike plan when the balance in the strike fund falls below $50,000. Most unions pay strike benefits when funds are available and the strike has been sanctioned by the national union leadership, but there are often additional stipulations: that the member be in good standing, complete a waiting period, and establish a need for the payments.[32]

When the strike is settled, the strike benefits usually end. In other cases, the benefits stop or the payments are reduced before the strike is over. Some unions set a minimum for their strike fund balance, and payments cease when the minimum is reached. Other unions will either terminate or reduce the benefits for individual members who work for other employers or cannot perform their strike duties.[33]

One controversial source of funds for strikers is public aid. Related striker assistance programs include aid to families with dependent children (AFDC), medical assistance, general assistance, and unemployment insurance.[34] Some of these programs are federal and strikers must meet the program's qualifications; others are administered only within an individual state and only residents qualify. Welfare relief is based solely upon the criterion of need, and in some cases, each state decides for itself the level of need required, the form of public aid, and the circumstances of qualifications. In fact, no two welfare programs are likely to define need exactly the same and even within certain states, there may be different interpretations of the qualifying considerations. In addition, most states require "good faith" attempts to obtain employment or that the need for public aid arose from an uncontrollable cause. Thus, public aid has strict qualifications and public administrators have considerable leeway in determining whether strikers qualify.[35]

Strikers rights to unemployment compensation may be limited by state law. For example, New York has extended the qualifying period for unemployment compensation from one week to eight weeks in the event employees are off their jobs due to a strike or lockout. In one case involving a strike of seven months, striking employees began collecting unemployment compensation after an eight-week waiting period. Because unemployment compensation is primarily financed by employer contributions, critics argue that the laws require employers to support the employees on strike and therefore alter the balance in the collective bargaining relationship. Advocates would counter that these legal requirements provide greater incentives for employers to settle their differences with the union.[36]

Public support programs for strikers date back to the New Deal era of the 1930s. Public support for strikers during the 1976 Rubber Workers and Auto Workers strikes and the coal strike of 1977–1978 caused political controversy and led to a bill to deny strikers food stamps. When public aid is available, rigorous requirements must be met.[37]

Advocates of public aid and assistance for strikers make several arguments for their availability:[38]

- Strikers are taxpayers who pay their taxes when they work. When they don't work, they should receive aid.
- Tax dollars are used to feed hungry people in other countries and prisoners in this country. Strikers who are needy should receive the same consideration.
- Even though some persons may be against public aid for strikers, they should not be against public aid for the families—those who are directly affected.
- If providing public aid to strikers is subsidizing a strike against a company, letting new federal contracts or failing to cancel existing contracts while a strike is in effect subsidizes the company's position against the union.
- Eligibility for public support is based on need as determined by law, not on whether a person is on strike.

Opponents to public support to strikers argue that:

- Legislatures never intended to provide public aid to strikers, particularly since strikers have refused bona fide employment by refusing to go back to work.
- Giving public aid to strikers violates a traditional policy of governmental neutrality in labor-management relations.[39]
- If strikers' attitude—"others are entitled to it, so I am"—spreads to the general public, it would modify many peoples' attitudes toward work, reduce workers' incentive, increase the rolls of public aid recipients, increase welfare costs, and waste government funds.[40]
- Collective bargaining as a process depends on a viable strike mechanism to insure a proper balancing of the costs of disagreement and the costs of

agreement at the negotiations table. Therefore, availability of public support for strikers increases the propensity of unions to strike and causes the strike to be longer.

- There is no reason to think public assistance would make strikers less bitter or violent in their strike activities.[41]

Strike Insurance— Mutual Aid Pacts (MAPs) Employers can mitigate strike costs by establishing strike insurance and *mutual aid pacts* (MAPs). These arrangements include "an agreement by which competing employers contract that, if one of them is struck, the others will indemnify it by some predetermined amount of money to help withstand the impact of the strike."[42] Although a number of industries—for example, newspaper publishing, rubber, air and rail transportation, Hawaiian sugar cane, and California fruits and vegetables—have had experience with these agreements, only a few industries have characteristics that are conducive to strike insurance and mutual aid pacts: homogeneous, time-sensitive product; high fixed production costs; multiple unions; and labor atmosphere with high incidence of strife.[43]

The most publicized MAP was formed in 1958 when several airlines entered an agreement to provide cash payment to any struck airline from other members of the pact. These payments were designed to approximate the additional profits to the nonstruck airlines that resulted from increased income due to the strike and to approximate 50 percent of the company's operating expenses during the first two weeks, 45 percent during the third week, 40 percent during the fourth, and 35 percent therefter. Each member company's contributions would equal 1 percent of its operating revenue from the previous year.[44]

However, the Airline Deregulation Act of 1978 made some modifications of the industry's MAP and in effect destroyed the airlines' incentive to establish these plans.[45]

Goodwill, Public Image, and Government Intervention Goodwill, public image, and possible government intervention are factors that influence the decision to strike or to take a strike. *Goodwill*, especially important in small plants, pertains mostly to internal relationships. For instance, neither management nor the union wants antagonistic attitudes to develop that linger after the strike. Neither wants plant relations to deteriorate or trust between the parties to decline. Therefore, careful attention must be given to goodwill throughout the process. *Public image* involves mostly the attitudes and opinions of people external to the particular strike. Union and company officials certainly do not want their activities labeled irresponsible or heedless of the public interest.[46] Possible government intervention for vital industries must be considered, especially if management or the union believes government intervention will weaken its respective bargaining position.

Strategic Purposes of a Strike While the main purpose of the strike is to secure a contract, it serves other purposes. For example, it may be part of an overall union strategy to help resolve internal problems. It may have a cathartic effect on the union members, removing accumulated tensions and releasing frustrations resulting from monotonous jobs. In fact, strikes under these conditions might improve productivity when the strikers return to work. A strike might also help to unify union members—rallying the diverse prestrike membership factions to work toward a common goal.

In some cases, the union calls a strike just to show management it can unify the membership over a collective bargaining issue. Over a period of time, threats of a strike lose their effectiveness. If such threats are not carried out, management views the union leader as "the boy who cried wolf." Therefore, union leaders are sometimes forced to carry out a bluff or threat in order to substantiate future threats.

Union leaders might also believe that their members would be more willing to accept a slightly modified final offer if they have not received wages during a brief strike. In this sense, strikes are used to "roll the steam" out of employees and their initially unrealistic expectations.[47]

Unions also have to consider the effects of a strike on their institutional security. During the strike, some union members might accept jobs elsewhere and decide not to return after the strike. Sometimes employers hire permanent replacements for union strikers, and the negotiations are never consummated. Possibly rival unions are waiting on the sideline for the legally recognized union to falter.[48] With these considerations, the union must be aware that a concerted decision to strike may be a risk to its own survival.

A strike may serve a strategic purpose for management as well. While management cannot call a strike, it can take actions that it knows will likely result in a strike. For example, management can demand that the union collect dues rather than have management deduct them from worker paychecks (checkoff). Unions view this demand as a threat to their security and will most often strike. Management's demand to subcontract at will or to change the wage system will be protested vehemently and the union will almost certainly strike. Thus, management may make these demands when causing a strike is to its relative advantage, such as when inventories are high and customer demand is low. If non-union workers can produce at a sufficient level to maintain acceptable production, the union is weak or management knows that all employees will not support the strike, it may secure a more favorable contract.

Previous Strike Experiences An assessment of previous strike experiences unique to the particular situation must be considered by unions and management. Strikes can range from very peaceful conflicts of short duration to outrageous, unlawful conflicts of months, even years. They have no uniform sequence, although strikers are usually most enthusiastic during the early days of the strike. Indeed, the first few days on a picket line often draw a large proportion of union members in an almost carnival-like atmosphere. After several weeks, it may be difficult to recruit members to walk the picket line.

Frustrations, antagonisms, and anxieties usually increase as the strike continues, with increased membership pressure being placed on union leaders to resolve the impasse.[49] The relative peacefulness of a strike is influenced by the attitudes of community citizens, particularly merchants and creditors, toward the dispute. The striker's spouse is perhaps the most influential individual in shaping the striker's behavior and attitudes. It is of course much easier for a striker to sustain a long strike if her or his spouse lends moral and, in some cases, financial support to the cause. On the other hand, tensions created by the strike can create permanent divisions among family members, friends, and other groups in the community as the strike endures and as individuals are asked for their support.[50]

Tensions can be heightened if the company continues to operate the business with either supervisory personnel or strike replacements. Bernard Karsh has described several possible striker responses to this situation in his detailed account of one industrial strike:[51]

- Mill supervisors hung in effigy on lampposts around the mill.
- Bedroom sized mirrors brought to the picket line to reflect the sunrays on the nonstriking workers to annoy them while they tried to work.
- Setting up circular saw blades mounted on wooden horses for strikers to pound with automobile axles as hammers (the noise is deafening).
- Setting fire to fifty-gallon oil drums filled with old tar and tar paper, then placing them in an alley directly in front of a loading dock and shipping entrance so that the odor from the flames would be drawn into the mill every time the door opened.
- Throwing rocks through windows, tacks in driveways, and egg shells filled with colored paint on cars.

Preparing for a Strike

Both parties must prepare for a possible strike before the contract expiration date, whether a strike is called or a settlement is reached. Union leaders must be certain of the extent to which members will actively participate during a strike and present a unified front against the employer. Division within the ranks causes much difficulty and dilutes the union's bargaining strength.

As the strike date approaches, union officers must schedule pickets, assure appropriate support for those on the line, and properly prepare the pickets for various situations, such as what to do when strike replacements cross the picket line. The union also has to determine qualified recipients of strike benefits as well as to inform the members of appropriate procedures for obtaining any available public aid. Finally, communication channels (telephone hot lines) must be established to inform members of the negotiations' progress.

Management often spends much time in its strike preparations, particularly if it is essential that the employer continue to operate during a strike, as public utilities must do. Many organizations have emergency strike manuals that provide specific and detailed plans in the event of a strike. The manual typically has two major components: (a) specific job assignments for nonstriking employees, professional personnel, and managers and (b) checklists of appropriate strike activities, such as notifying customers and suppliers, contacting law enforcement officials, and providing food and housing for those staying on the job.[52] Management might also seek professional assistance from employer colleagues, such as members of the American Society for Personnel Administration, which has published a *Strike Preparation Manual*.[53]

Although union and management officials carefully consider the advantages and disadvantages of strikes, lockouts, and pickets, they are not entirely free to implement these activities as they please. Various legal considerations can raise additional problems and prospects.

Legality of Strikes and Related Activities

The Right to Strike The right to strike has long been subject to philosophical debate. Opponents of the right to strike usually cite examples of violence and civil disobedience which have occurred in strike activities. In the history of the United States, many violent strikes have resulted in significant damage to property and loss of lives. (see Chapter 2).

Strike opponents also contend that strikers infringe on employers' property rights. One critic of strikes has noted the strike

---

is not even merely the simultaneous and collective act of a large group of workers in "withholding their labor." The strikers have not simply given up their jobs. On the contrary, they not only contend that they are still employees of the company at the jobs at which they are refusing to work, but that they are the only legitimate employees.

They claim an *ownership* of such jobs. They mean to prevent the struck company from offering—and anybody else from taking—the jobs that they have themselves abandoned. They also physically prevent existing employees from continuing their work.[54]

Yet advocates of the right to strike contend that such rights must be preserved.

. . . the right to strike is preferable to a compulsory settlement system. It does not follow that the government should never move to protect the public against strikes which create serious hardships, but it does follow that any move to prohibit the use of the strike in the private sector

should be made cautiously and only to the extent that is clearly required. Any broad prohibition of strike freedom would prove to be very costly in itself and also lead to major government controls over other parts of the economy. Free collective bargaining, which includes the right to strike and the right to lock out, constitutes the outer defense of the private enterprise system.[55]

In this sense, strikes are basic to the industrial relations system—inseparable from collective bargaining because they cannot be severed without hurting both.[56] Strikes are usually not entered into lightly; both parties realize that the strike can hurt as well as help their respective positions.[57]

The potential or actual occurrence of strikes is an inherent aspect of labor-management relationships where the parties seek to obtain their preferences over their opponent's disagreement.[58] Unions that *always* agree with management over the years cease to be unions; similarly, management will reduce its effectiveness if it *always* agrees with the union. Therefore, conflict is apparent, possibly inherent, in collective bargaining, and strikes are sometimes viewed as a necessary alternative for expressing this conflict.

Legal guidelines have been formulated which attempt to minimize the controversy over the right to strike by balancing employee and employer rights during a strike. The *Commonwealth v. Hunt* decision (1842)—discussed in Chapter 3—was the first judicial act that recognized employees' right to participate in concerted activities for their own economic welfare. The National Labor Relations Act guarantees employee rights to engage in "concerted activities for the purpose of collective bargaining or other mutual aid or protection." Section 13 also states: "Nothing in this Act, except as specifically provided for herein, shall be construed so as to interfere with or impede or diminish in any way the right to strike or to affect the limitations or qualifications on that right."

The right to strike is not absolute; there are restrictions on national emergency strikes, secondary strikes, jurisdictional strikes, and recognitional strikes. Yet current legislation implicitly assumes that most strikes occur only after months of intensive negotations under the rules established by the NLRB and the courts. While both parties are required by law to negotiate in good faith, they do not always reach agreement and strikes do occur, but usually only after authorization from the national office and a strike vote by the membership.[59]

Many legal questions concerning strikes, pickets, and boycotts involving the employees' immediate, or *primary*, employer have been resolved over the years by statute or judicial decisions. Other activities concerning employers not directly involved in the labor dispute (*secondary* employers) are usually subject to much more complex legal interpretation. While secondary activities often have narrow applications, their significance is especially pertinent to those unions and employers that frequently face these issues.

Strikes and Related Activities Involving the Primary Employer When the union and management fail to reach an agreement upon the expiration of their labor agreement, the union normally calls an economic strike accompanied by picket lines and a boycott of the product. If only the immediate employer and the union are involved, the strike, picket, and boycott are considered primary. The overwhelming majority of strikes, pickets, and boycotts that occur in the United States in any given year are of this type.

Employers may permanently replace the economic strikers with other employees during a strike and attempt to continue their operations during the strike. Once the negotiations are complete, these employees usually return to their former positions. However, the employer is *not* legally obligated to remove any permanent replacements in favor of returning strikers even though retaining the replacements instead of the returning strikers will obviously strain relationships between the union and management.[60] Practical considerations can prevent the employer from exercising the legal right to replace strikers. It is not easy to replace all of the striking employees, particularly if the firm requires a large number of replacements. This problem is compounded when the operations are somewhat complicated, since many employees will have to be trained in a short period of time. Finally, extreme tensions can occur between strikers and strike replacements at the picket line, possibly resulting in violence and community disorder.

If the strike resulted from an employer's unfair labor practice, strikers may be replaced only for the duration of the strike, but *must* be reinstated to their former (or substantially equivalent) positions when the negotiations are complete. In addition, any employees unfairly discharged for union activities will be returned to their former positions with back pay.[61] However, if strikers participate in activities classified as unacceptable striker misconduct, they lose their reinstatement rights. Such misconduct includes: calling nonstrikers vulgar names, making obscene gestures at nonstrikers, preventing entry to the plant, jumping in front of moving cars, following nonstrikers by car as they leave work, and throwing rocks, eggs, and tomatoes while on the picket line.[62]

Wildcat strikes include work stoppages that involve the primary employer-employee relationship and that are neither sanctioned nor stimulated by the union, although union officials might be aware of them. They can vary in length and number of affected departments in the facility. They may also take the form of heavy absenteeism for several days, especially under no-strike pledges and contracts.[63] These stoppages might be caused by membership dissension and factionalism[64] or may have the union leader's tacit support in order to gain a particular management concession.

Since most labor agreements provide for arbitration as the final step in the grievance procedure and such agreements to arbitrate are usually accompanied by a no-strike clause, a wildcat strike represents a violation of the labor agreement. Employers can respond to wildcat strikes in several ways: (a) requesting informally and formally that strikers return to work, (b) contending that employees have voided their labor agreement, (c) disciplining or discharging the strikers, and (d) bringing suit against the union for damages suffered.[65] Two Supreme Court decisions discussed in Chapter 9 (*Boy's Market* and *Buffalo Forge*) suggest that employees can be legally enjoined from continuing a wildcat strike under certain conditions.

Lockouts Additional activities involving the primary employer include lockouts. The right of single employers to lock out employees is the analogue of employees' right to strike. *Lockouts* can be used legally by employers after an impasse has been reached over a mandatory bargaining issue. They have also been approved by the NLRB to prevent seizure of a plant by a sit-down, to forestall repetitive disruption in plant operations by "quickie strikes," to avoid spoilage of perishable materials, and to avert the immobilization of automobiles brought in for repairs.

Yet the right to lock out employees is qualified, particularly since the NLRB maintains that the employer already has the power to counterbalance the strike by permanently replacing the strikers, stockpiling, subcontracting, maintaining operations with nonstrikers, and unilaterally instituting working conditions once the contract has expired.[66] However, this power is limited by the fact that primary economic strikers are authorized to vote in any representation or decertification elections for twelve months, and if the employer commits an unfair labor practice, the strikers may be reinstated with full back pay.

The NLRB and courts have been more lenient in situations in which the union attempts to "whipsaw" by striking individual employers in a multi-employer bargaining association to force a more favorable agreement. In the Teamsters' strike of 1979, nonstruck members of the association temporarily locked out their employees in reaction to the Teamsters' strike against only a selected number of trucking companies. The association legally claimed that "a strike against one is a strike against all." Failure to cease operations by all companies would imperil the employers' common interest in bargaining on a group basis and significantly dilute their bargaining strength.

Because unions often strike members of a multi-employer association one at a time, hoping to put pressure on the struck firm while the others operate, the NLRB and the courts have allowed temporary lockouts to preserve the association's unity. In addition, nonstruck firms in a multi-employer bargaining association have been allowed to hire temporary replacements to preserve the bargaining unit structure and to maintain operations. Because the struck firm can hire permanent replacements in order to continue operations, the courts have reasoned that it would be unfair to require that the nonstruck firms be shut down completely while the struck firm operates.[67]

Strikes and Related Activities Involving Secondary Employers Secondary parties are those who are not directly bound by the terms of the labor agreement in dispute. They are not at the bargaining table; however, they become involved when the union attempts to persuade them to influence the primary employer to agree with the union's proposals.

Activities involving product boycotts and picketing, common situs picketing, the ally doctrine, and hot cargo agreements are discussed below to illustrate the point that it is not always easy to distinguish between a primary and secondary party to a negotiations impasse.

Product (consumer) boycotts and picketing include handbilling, carrying placards, and urging customers to refuse to purchase products from a particular retail or wholesale business. For example, the striking employees of a clothing manufacturer might legally boycott and picket a nearby retail clothing store owned by the manufacturer, say, the factory outlet. But if these employees travel considerable distance to picket a retail clothing store that sells many items—one of which is bought from the manufacturer—the legal issue becomes more complex.[68] Picketing in front of a retail clothing store in another city (a secondary employer) violates the NLRA *if* the picketers attempt to convince customers to refuse to shop at the store. But if the picketers make an appeal to the customers to refuse to buy only the struck product (clothing items produced by the primary employer), the picket is legal.

A leading case, *Tree Fruits*, involved a strike against some fruit packing firms that were members of a multi-employer bargaining association and that sold Washington State apples to Safeway, a retail grocery chain. As part of the boycott effort, the union picketed and handbilled forty-six Safeway stores, appealing to the customers to refrain from buying Washington State apples. The union carefully avoided making appeals to employees at the stores, closely instructed the individuals on the picket line not to interfere with employees and made certain there was not a general appeal to request that potential customers not patronize the store. As a result, the picketing was peaceful, the employees continued to work, no obstructions occurred, and the courts upheld the legality of the picketing activities.[69] Product boycotts also may involve larger multi-plant operations and subsidiary operations. In one case, the union had a dispute with a wholly owned subsidiary manufacturer of Pet, a diversified, billion-dollar conglomerate with plants and retail stores located throughout the United States. Because of the nature of Pet's operations, in which one facility provides support for and contributes to others, and because the struck manufacturer produced products sold by Pet, the union's publicity urging a total consumer boycott of Pet's products was protected and legal.[70]

Common situs and reserve gate picketing *Common situs picketing* involves both the primary and secondary neutral employers who share the same physical work premises, as is the case at construction sites and shipping docks. The problem arises when the union that is picketing the primary employer also adversely affects the work or business of the neutral employer located at the same site. The union has the right to picket the primary employer with whom it has a labor dispute and to bring economic pressure on its immediate employer.

Yet the neutral or secondary employer has a right to be free from economic pressure from unions with whom it has no bargaining relationships.[71]

Unions argue that the employers who occupy the same work site (*common situs*) are so intertwined that a labor dispute with one employer is a labor dispute with all; therefore, unions allege that there are no neutral employers on the site. Employers argue they are independent operations and should be legally protected from picketing. The Supreme Court ruled on a case involving a general contractor on a construction project who subcontracted some electrical work to a nonunion subcontractor who paid less than the union scale.[72] When the nonunion employees arrived at work, the union set up pickets on the entire work site, and other union employees honored the picket line and refused to work. The union's strategy was to force the nonunion subcontractors off the job, and the general contractor complied with the union demands. Although the contractor complied, it took the case to the NLRB, and appealed eventually to the Supreme Court. The Court ruled that general contractors and subcontractors on a building site were separate business entities and should be treated separately with respect to each other's labor controversies.[73]

In another *common situs* case, the union had a dispute with a restaurant employer which was located on the 46th floor of a 50-story office building. In support of its contract demands, it struck and stationed pickets on public sidewalks at every entrance and distributed leaflets in the foyer of the 46th floor which was under the exclusive control of the employer. The restaurant employer alleged trespassing by those distributing leaflets, demanded they leave, and threatened them with arrest. Thus, the NLRB had to reconcile protected rights of employees and property rights of employers. The Board found that

restricting strike-related activity to the public sidewalks would excessively hinder the unions' efforts to communicate a meaningful message to its intended audience (and) . . . the property rights of the neutral employer must yield to the right of the union to publicize its disputes with the primary (employer).[74]

Unions have been limited further in their flexibility in applying economic pressure via picketing at work sites from another case in which the company (General Electric) used independent contractors for constructing a new building, rearranging operations for a new product, and performing general repair work. In order to minimize contact between GE employees and employees of the contractor, a separate gate (*reserve gate*) was set aside for employees of the contractor. The union called a strike and picketed all gates, including the separate gate, and most of the employees of the contractor honored the picket line. The NLRB found that picketing at the separate gate was designed to enmesh employees of a neutral employer in the labor dispute and was therefore illegal. The

Supreme Court agreed to sustain the NLRB order unless the NLRB found through further investigation that the separate gate was established for the purpose of entry by employees who performed work that was necessary for the normal operations of the plant—work normally performed by GE employees.[75] Once the neutrality of the reserve gate has been breached, such as when the reserve gate is used to deliver electrical fixtures for installation by the struck electrical contractor, the union can lawfully picket the gate. Thus, any gate used by the primary employer to deliver materials essential to its normal operations is subject to a lawful picket.[76]

Alliance between employers If a secondary employer is closely associated with the primary employer and its labor dispute with the union, neutrality is lost, and the secondary employer should be treated as a primary party to the labor dispute. For example, a secondary employer would lose its neutrality by accepting a subcontract to do work that would normally be done by workers on strike.

This work performed by the employees of the secondary employer can be classified as *struck work*, which includes "work, that but for the strike would be performed by the employees of the primary employer."[77] Another situation occurs in cases where the business relationship of the primary and secondary employer is so intertwined as to almost create a co-employer relationship.[78] Close business relations can easily be so intertwined within conglomerated manufacturing or insurance companies that picketing the secondary employer is permissible.[79]

Yet the courts have determined that single employers can be protected when distance between facilities is great and the operations are autonomous. For example, when union members having a labor dispute with the *Miami Herald* went to Detroit to picket the *Detroit Press* (both owned by Knight Newspapers), the board found the common ownership *alone* did not create an allied relationship. In fact, more recently the board has concluded that separate divisions of the same corporation may also be able to claim protection from secondary picketing if the dispute exists at only one division.[80]

Hot-cargo agreements Designed to promote union-made products and support union members on strike, *hot-cargo agreements* were negotiated in labor agreements to specify that employees may refuse to use or handle products of certain employers, such as nonunion companies and companies experiencing strikes. Before the enactment of the Landrum-Griffin Act in 1959, these clauses were not illegal and were considered loopholes in the provisions of the Labor Management Relations Act, which dealt with secondary boycotts. While they had the same effect as secondary boycotts, they adversely affected neutral employers. In 1959, they were made unfair labor practices,[81] although the 1959 amendments included a special provision for the apparel, clothing, and construction industries.[82]

Where labor disputes develop to the stage in which they are regarded as having an adverse effect on the U.S. national interest, they assume a special significance. Legal procedures discussed in the following section are available for these occasions.

Resolution Procedures for National Emergency Disputes Occasionally, strikes occur which have an adverse impact on national economic or defense interests; these are classified as *national emergency strikes.* A number of research studies have shown that the economic effects of such strikes often have less impact than a casual observer may believe. Furthermore, it has been extremely difficult to estimate all the effects of a particular strike, even after it is over. After years of debate, there is still no consensus on what constitutes an emergency strike or on the actual number of emergency strikes that have occurred in our nation's history.[83]

The federal government uses three methods in dealing with national emergency strikes: presidential actions including seizure, procedures under the Railway Labor Act, and procedures under the Labor Management Relations Act.

Presidential intervention and seizure *Presidential seizures* or attempts at seizure occurred seventy-one times under four presidents—Lincoln, Wilson, Franklin D. Roosevelt, and Truman—in the interests of maintaining production when actual strikes or threatened strikes caused national emergencies. They have been used mostly during wars (World War I, 3 times; World War II, 51 times; Korean War, 3 times), although declared war has not been an essential requisite. In more recent years, presidents have confined their intervention to exceptional cases, chosen carefully, given the possibility of a legislative or judicial resistance.

A more common presidential approach is the application of pressure and inducements on the parties to resolve the strike without compulsion.[84] Well-known "arm-twisting" maneuvers of then Vice-President Nixon in the 1959 steel strike and of President Johnson on several occasions were well publicized. Involvement of officials in the Reagan Administration in the 1982 railway negotiations were viewed by millions on television.

Procedures under the Railway Labor Act The Railway Labor Act provides a procedure for resolving national emergency work stoppages in the railroads and airlines which includes the following steps:

1. The parties to a labor agreement give a 30-day notice of a desire to change the agreement.
2. The National Mediation Board (NMB) attempts to mediate the dispute.
3. If mediation fails, the NMB recommends voluntary interest arbitration.
4. If arbitration is rejected, the NMB gives notice that it has failed, and for 30 days the wage rates, working rules, working conditions, etc., remain the same.

Exhibit 7.1 National Emergency Procedure under LMRA

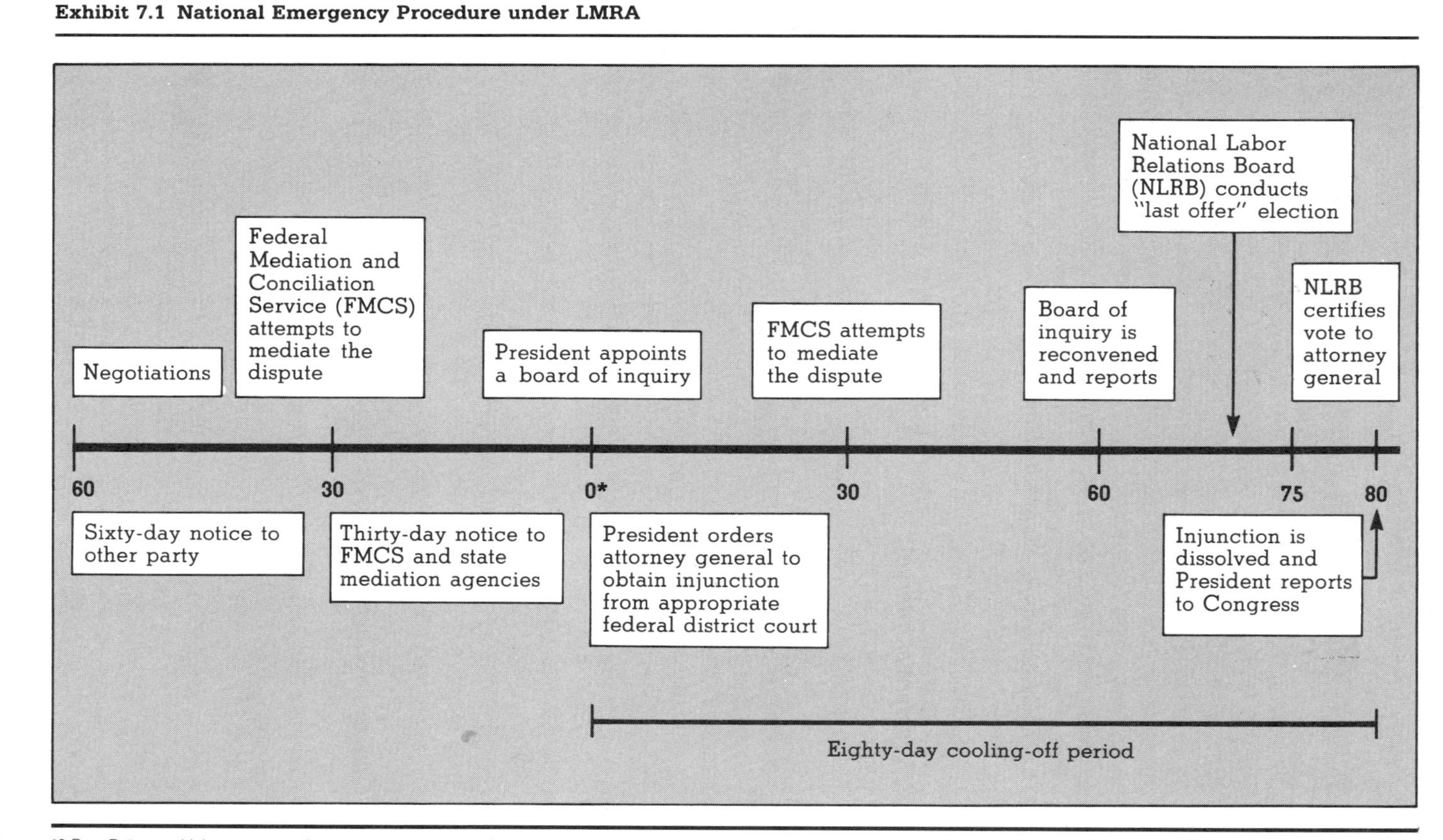

*0 Day: Date on which contract expires—may or may not be first day of planned strike; date of injunction if president invokes the LMRA procedures.

Source: Diagram created by Dr. Roy Moore, Chairman, Management Department, University of Southern Mississippi, Hattiesburg, Mississippi.

5. If the dispute threatens to substantially interrupt interstate commerce in any section of the country and deprive it of an essential transportation service, the president is notified and an emergency board is appointed.
6. The emergency board investigates the disputes and reports, with recommendations, within 30 days. During this time, the status quo is maintained.[85]

Since the act's passage in 1926, its emergency provisions have been invoked nearly 190 times, an average rate of four times per year, and work stoppages have occurred at the end of the sixty-day period at a rate of one per year since 1947.[86] Before 1941, the parties never refused the recommendations of the emergency boards. However, since a 1963 congressional decision regarding firemen on diesels, it has become quite common for one of the parties to pursue its interest to the fullest extent by relying more on third-party intervention and ad hoc legislation than on its own negotiations.[87] Congress intervened eight more times between 1963 and 1975, then not again until 1982, when it imposed a settlement on the Brotherhood of Locomotive Engineers.

Procedures under the Labor Management Relations Act The enactment of the Labor Management Relations Act in 1947 authorized the president to invoke its national emergency provisions, Sections 206 to 210, in labor disputes of the national emergency magnitude. These provisions provide a step-by-step procedure to halt the strike for eighty days and provide the parties assistance in resolving their disputes.

Exhibit 7.1 displays the steps in the national emergency procedure of the Labor Management Relations Act. It includes the requirements specified for all parties: the sixty-day notice to the other party that a change in the present agreement is desired and the thirty-day notice to the Federal Mediation and Conciliation Service and state agencies that the negotiations are in process and a settlement has not been reached.

The first step for the president is the appointment of a board of inquiry when the strike or the threat of a strike is believed to be of sufficient severity to imperil the national health or safety. Because of the urgency of the matter, the board will investigate the issues in dispute, gather relevant facts, and make a report to the president in a very short time—usually in about one day.

When the report is received and studied by the president, he *may* direct the attorney general to secure an eighty-day injunction from an appropriate federal district court to prevent or end the strike. Once the injunction is issued, the board is reconvened and after the first sixty days of the injunction period will be asked to report to the president on the employer's last offer and any other relevant factors. During the interim period, the FMCS continues to assist the parties in reaching a settlement. After the board reports the final employer offer, the NLRB will conduct and certify a secret ballot election (between the sixtieth and eightieth days of the injunction period) to determine whether the employees will accept this offer. If they refuse, the attorney general must ask the federal district court to dissolve the injunction at the end of eighty days, and the union may legally strike. The last step involves a full and comprehensive report by the president to Congress, accompanied by any recommendations that he may have.

Some examples Although the national emergency strike provisions have been invoked, on the average, once per year during the last thirty years, national emergency strikes have involved some of the more interesting personalities of the labor movement—for example, John L. Lewis and David McDonald. In the 1948 coal miners' strike, United Mine Workers President John L. Lewis was found guilty of both criminal and civil contempt of court and was fined $20,000; his union was fined $1,400,000 for criminal violations. Neither fine was ever paid.

The 1959 steel strike, lasting 119 days and involving 12 basic steel producers, also received considerable national attention because it affected other industries—auto, construction, and coal. The negotiations took place at very high levels and involved not only top company and union officials but also the president, vice-president, and secretary of labor.[88]

The 1977–1978 coal strike, coinciding with public concern over the energy crisis and high utility bills, probably received more day-to-day media coverage and national attention than any previous strike. Daily broadcasts and interviews with company and union officials educated millions about the processes of collective bargaining during crisis periods and informed many about national emergency strikes and the Taft-Hartley injunction. Interestingly, the Taft-Hartley Act was invoked and a temporary injunction was obtained. However, the district court judge lifted the injunction ten days later when the attorney general failed to prove that a national emergency existed, the strikers refused to return to work, and the federal government refused to enforce the temporary injunction.

Throughout the years, every time there has been a major strike, critics have become vocal about the inefficacy of the procedures for dealing with national emergency strikes. One critic wrote:

When all the people have to suffer because of the willfulness and ineptitude of economic power blocs, the establishment of improved governmental machinery for breaking deadlocks is an affirmation—not a denial—of democracy.

In general, the mechanics of bargaining require recasting to get rid of the explosive notion that the world stops on the date the contract runs out. The existence of an expiration deadline ("no contract, no work") has become the single most powerful element in the deification of force as the determinant of equity in industrial relations.[89]

Other critics have been more specific. For example, the strongest criticism has been directed toward the rigidity and predictability of the procedures. When each step is predicted, either party may include the issuance of the injunction as part of its bargaining strategy. Another area of criticism is the secret-ballot election on the employer's last offer, which has often solidified the union position rather than facilitating the bargaining process toward settlement. Lastly, because the presidential boards of inquiry are prohibited from proposing settlements, their effectiveness in securing the necessary public support and pressure to move the parties toward settlement is limited.[90]

Cooperation between Union and Management to Reduce Conflicts

Preceding sections of this chapter have emphasized impasse resolution procedures and conflict. However, there is growing support for greater union-management cooperation.

A 1982 survey of 500 opinion leaders in the United States by Opinion Research Corporation revealed 70 percent (76 percent of the business leaders surveyed and 86 percent of the union leaders) strongly favor a more cooperative relationship between labor and management. Reasons given for these opinions include the need for increased productivity and the threats posed by international competition, slower economic growth, and automation.[91]

Although there is still support for the belief that we cannot have free collective bargaining without reliance on the strike, management and labor have learned that many basic common interests outweigh the use of the strike.[92]

Labor-management cooperation has met some resistance from both sides. Employers fear cooperative efforts might give unions increased prestige and reduce managerial prerogatives. Other employers question the value of the individual worker's contributions toward cooperative efforts.[93] Some union officials are also reluctant to participate in cooperative efforts if they believe these efforts' sole goal is to increase productivity, which can ultimately reduce the size of the work force. Other union leaders believe that these projects might result in a "happier" work force, thereby adversely affecting membership allegiance.[94]

A major influence in delaying cooperative efforts is the absence of signals upward from the rank-and-file for involvement in these projects. In fact, unions continue to focus their efforts and interests in collective bargaining on the traditional issues—wages, job security, economic supplements, and so on[95]—and overall there has been limited interest in union-management motivational programs via collective bargaining.[96] Only 3.9 percent of 1,550 labor agreements studied by the Bureau of Labor Statistics in 1980 included labor-management study committees that examined such sensitive issues as subcontracting, seniority, and wage incentives and made appropriate recommendations to the negotiators. On the other hand, there were more joint committees which periodically met separately from negotiations to improve safety conditions (these existed in 36.8 percent of the 1,550 agreements).[97]

There have been some successful examples of labor-management cooperation programs that have received national attention: Relations by Objectives, joint labor-management committees, and Experimental Negotiating Agreements.

Relations by Objectives

In 1975, the FMCS introduced a new program—Relations by Objectives (RBO). This program was designed to eliminate factors that cause breakdowns in negotiations and prolong strikes. RBO focuses on intergroup team building, intragroup image clarification and diagnosis, confrontation meetings, coaching, and other developmental approaches. The program consists of four phases:

1. Problem solving and goal setting.
2. Action planning and programming.
3. Implementation of plans and programs.
4. Periodic review and evaluation of progress toward goal accomplishment.

Phases one and four take place at a neutral, off-site location for three intensive days. Ten to fifteen members of the union and management attend sessions with federal mediators. Separate and joint sessions are held until neutral problems and goal statements are clarified, covering such subjects as communication, grievance handling, supervisor and steward training, and attitudes and positions of both the union and management.[98] Since its inception, 87 RBO programs have been initiated with favorable success. Positive results include improved stability in the parties' relationship, less grievance activity, improved production and plant morale, and smoother contract negotiations after the program.[99]

Joint Labor-Management Committees

Hundreds of joint labor-management committees have been established on the parties' own initiative and with the assistance of the FMCS. These committees provide labor and management with an opportunity to discuss problems without the pressures of the bargaining table.[100]

The committees attempt to resolve problems between contract negotiations and through cooperative efforts develop trust and a spirit that carries over to the bargaining table. Examples of neutral problem-solving in the retail food industry include a study of working conditions, such as exposure to hazardous materials, particularly in the wrapping of meat, use of protective gloves and aprons, and using knives and other cutting equipment.[101] In the health care industry, joint committees explored the alternatives to strikes for achieving peaceful settlements, treatment of registered nurses by physicians and hospital administrators, use of temporary employment agencies, work shifts, and quality of care and staffing.[102] These committees, thus far, have no long list of tangible achievements; however, they do explore sensitive issues that would deter effective collective bargaining.[103]

Automobile Industry's Programs The automobile industry has received much attention for its cooperative labor-management programs. General Motors and the UAW began Quality of Working Life programs in 1969 and have them in over 50 facilities. Ford and the UAW have a joint national committee on employee participation but the committee was inactive until recently. Now employee participation is used in Ford's TV and magazine advertisements.

One noted example of achievement is the General Motors car assembly plant in Tarrytown, New York. In 1970, the plant had the worst labor relations and production records in the company. It suffered from high absenteeism and turnover; operating costs were excessive; frustration, fear, and mistrust characterized labor relations; as many as 2,000 labor grievances had been filed at any given time. Facing a serious consideration for a shutdown, the union and management launched a collaborative approach to resolve their problems.[104]

After about 15 months of the collaborative program, it was declared a success. Quality of performance improved, absenteeism declined from 7¼ percent to 2–3 percent, grievances were reduced to 32, and relations between management, union and the workers were positive.[105]

Then in 1982, faced with layoffs, plant shutdowns, and operating losses, General Motors and the UAW entered a historic agreement which included several elements of labor-management cooperation:

- A wage freeze accompanied by the establishment of a profit sharing plan for the employees.
- More job security provided through income guarantees and job protection.
- A $120 million training program established to assist displaced employees.
- Joint councils formed to address problems of excessive absenteeism.

As Roger Smith, Chief Executive Officer of General Motors, stated:

. . . our new agreement with the UAW encompasses much more than improvements in job security and modifications in cost containment, important as they are. It also initiates significant changes in the way we handle the union-management relationship. It moves us in a new direction—away from confrontation and toward cooperation, away from our adversarial past and toward a new alliance aimed at the future . . . This opens a new chapter in American labor relations, but at the same time it builds on the previous text. Cooperation in working toward mutual goals has long been an objective of GM's and the UAW's.[106]

Experimental Negotiating Agreement (ENA)

Having experienced several years of strikes and government intervention when negotiations were unsuccessful, the United Steelworkers and the major steel companies negotiated an Experimental Negotiating Agreement (ENA) in 1973 that was considered a major breakthrough for labor-management cooperation. This agreement formulated a structure for arbitrating unsolved issues by a specific date prior to expiration of the labor agreement, which eliminated the possibility of a national steel strike in 1974.[107] While the union did agree to abandon the strike weapon on a national scale, it agreed only under certain preconditions.[108]

1. A 3 percent annual wage increase plus continuation of the cost-of-living clause (1 cent increase for each 0.3 rise in Consumer Price Index).
2. A bonus of $150 for each employee, available from company savings due to strike avoidance.
3. Allowing local unions to strike over local plant issues and excluding certain fundamental issues, such as union shop and checkoff, from arbitration.

Negotiations were successfully completed without strikes under ENA in 1974, 1977, and 1980, but in 1982 management informed the union that it wanted changes in ENA. It claimed that the automatic wage increase and the cost of living adjustment clause had boosted steelworker wages without comparable productivity increases. In 1982, the total employment cost, including wages and benefits, averaged over $23.00 per hour for each employee. Unable to agree on modifications, management refused to renew ENA.[109]

On another front, the major steel companies and steelworkers were establishing labor-management participation teams at the plant level to reduce conflict between workers and supervisors. Jones & Laughlin and Bethlehem Steel had adopted such programs in a few plants after the 1980 negotiations and showed dramatic gains in productivity. The participation teams consist of workers and supervisors and have twin goals making work more productive by improving product quality, reducing absenteeism, increasing efficiency and making work more satisfactory by improving the work environment, safety and health, and incentive pay plans.[110]

Paul Thayer, Chief Executive Officer of LTV Corporation, owner of Jones & Laughlin Steel, called for a new partnership:

Americans from every walk of life are now recognizing the devastating effect that uncooperative feelings between unions and management have on national productivity. Some are calling for "new" partnerships to be forged to overcome the difficulties many U.S. companies are facing. No meaningful partnership between management and unions will be achieved, however, until we deal with several basic issues that unions tend to overlook.

Primary among these is the need to recognize that each company is unique. Each has its own peculiar problems and its own set of opportunities. Each has differing resources to bring into action for the long-term good of the company and its employees. Union leaders—particularly at the international level—need to be more sensitive to individual

company situations and to long-term solutions to problems. Where this is not the case, the results can stifle growth and even bring about unnecessary job losses and business failures. . . .

. . . The sharing of ideas, criticisms, suggestions and knowledge of the task at hand is the key to intelligent, effective decisions that will benefit everyone. Management must have this input from all employees, union represented or not, and labor leaders equally must seek information if their advocacy is to be informed and appropriate to the local situation.

In the final analysis, management and workers have a mutual interest. Each of us is an employee and each of us has a stake in the success of a common venture: the company for which we work.[111]

While in some areas the desired cooperative efforts seem to be making progress, in 1982, with 50 percent of the steelworkers on layoff, the union rejected a company proposal of cost savings of $8 billion through wage reduction of 11 percent, postponed wage increases. The company rejected a $2 billion counter-offer by the union.[112] Then, in March 1983, the union accepted a new 41-month contract which cut wages about 9 percent and should allow U.S. firms to be more competitive with foreign steelmakers whose workers earn considerably less (for example, Japanese workers earn about 50 percent that of U.S. steelworkers).[112]

Summary and Implications

Summary

This chapter focused on the efforts of unions, management, and third parties to resolve negotiation impasses, activities surrounding conflicts, and cooperative efforts by union and management. A discussion of contract ratification and membership rejection was highlighted. Earlier research has led to the conclusion that contract rejection is relatively high; however, more recent research finds a lower rate when contract rejection is redefined as rejection of the bargaining committee's recommended labor agreement.

Third-party procedures to assist the parties in resolving negotiation impasses were presented. These range from mediation—where the third party attempts to facilitate resolution by keeping the parties bargaining, acting as a go-between, and offering alternatives—to arbitration, a quasi-judicial procedure in which the bargaining positions are presented to the arbitrator, who makes a final and binding decision. Within this range are the med-arb procedure (which attempts mediation first and then arbitration if mediation fails) and fact-finding, (in which the parties present their positions to the fact-finder, other facts are collected, and a report, which includes a recommended resolution of the impasse, is written and presented).

Not all bargaining issues are resolved through negotiations; strikes, boycotts, pickets, and related activities do occur. However, both parties have to seriously consider their positions and the consequences of their actions before taking any actions. Each hurts the costs, profits, and production of the companies and the income and public image of the union. While both parties may prepare for employee job actions, a high percentage of strikes, boycotts, and pickets have taken their toll in terms of costs to both parties.

The right to concerted actions by employees is an intricate part of the labor relations process and is guaranteed by law. On the other hand, possession of a right to strike does not mean that it should be exercised frequently. The data show that strikes occur very infrequently, but those that do occur can be damaging economically and are well publicized by the media.

Most strikes and related activities involve primary employers, but often secondary employers (not directly involved in the employer-employee relationship) are affected. A complex body of law and judicial decisions covers such activities as consumer boycotts and picketing; common situs and reserve gate picketing; employer-ally relationships; and hot-cargo agreements.

Strikes and related activities that have an adverse effect on the national interest may be declared national emergency strikes. In this regard, resolution procedures are available in the Railway Labor Act and the Labor Management Relations Act to facilitate their resolutions. While such impasses occur infrequently, they are significant when they do occur.

Efforts by unions and management to organize and develop cooperative efforts to reduce the possibility of conflicts are still a relatively infrequent occurrence. However, several unions and companies have spent much time and money and put forth much effort to minimize conflicts.

Implications

The issue remains whether union-management cooperation can become the rule rather than the exception. Since the roles of the union and management in the labor relations process have been characterized as adversary and the right to strike is considered fundamental to the system, what conditions are conducive to labor-management cooperation? While conflicts and strikes will no doubt occur, cooperation can be enhanced by the presence of *superordinate goals*—goals desired by both the union and management.[113] For example, economic survival of the company and job protection for the workers go hand in hand.

Other prerequisites for successful labor-management cooperation are *shared participation, increased responsibility of the work force*, and *development of trust between the parties.*

[There must be] a willingness on the part of management to leave its authoritative hat at the door and talk eyeball to eyeball and gut to gut across the table and hear what those people really feel. Let them lay it out to you without feeling hostile, without having elements of reprisal.

On the union side, are you willing to go in there and make suggestions to improve the quality of work and reduce the inefficiency of that plant that you and your people walking around in that plant see every day? Are you willing to take the initiative in this crisis situation that this American economy finds itself in?[114]

Success of labor-management cooperation also requires the *support of the union and management.* If supervision resists employees' influences on decision making and the union refuses to support the cooperative efforts, the program will fail. To overcome this resistance, management can:

- Involve the union in program planning.
- Share gains with employees.
- Negotiate a contractual agreement committing both parties to the program.
- Determine causes of negative attitudes.
- Evaluate superior-subordinate relationships.[115]

A final factor for success is *progressive development of the program and patience to wait for results.* Because those cooperative programs usually are foreign to most union-managment relationships, they should be well-planned, involve the union, gain support of the parties, receive support from top management and union officials, and proceed with deliberation. Goals should be set by the participants and progress recorded.[116] The final evaluation may be seen in better attitudes toward each other, higher productivity and fewer grievances.

Discussion Questions

1. What are the chief reasons for rejection of tentative agreements by union members?
2. What problems may be caused as a result of contract rejection?
3. Define the major types of third-party interventions. How do they differ, and how do they appear similar?
4. What specific qualities should a mediator possess? Why do these qualities facilitate impasse resolution?
5. Why is interest arbitration used so infrequently in the private sector?
6. Think of a strike that has occurred recently and itemize the costs to the employer as well as to the employees on strike.
7. What are your political and philosophical views of public aid to strikers?
8. Discuss the following statement: "Strikes are an intricate and essential element of the collective bargaining process."
9. Define and discuss the various types of secondary activities of unions that may occur during impasses.
10. Explain the alternatives which could be made available for resolving national emergency strikes.

11. List the issues in which both management and the union can cooperate to their mutual advantage. Do you know of other cooperative efforts by union and management to reduce conflict? List the strong and weak points of these efforts.

References

[1]Clyde W. Summers, "Ratification of Agreements," in J. T. Dunlop and N. W. Chamberlain, eds., *Frontiers of Collective Bargaining* (New York: Harper & Row, 1967), pp. 82–83.

[2]Ibid., p. 83.

[3]Federal Mediation and Conciliation Service, *Thirty-Fourth Annual Report* (Washington, D.C.: Government Printing Office, 1982), p. 21.

[4]William E. Simkin, "Refusal to Ratify Contracts," *Industrial and Labor Relations Review* 21 (July 1968), pp. 528–529.

[5]Charles Odewahn and Joseph Krislov, "Contract Rejections: Testing the Explanatory Hypothesis," *Industrial Relations* 12 (October 1973), pp. 289–296.

[6]D. R. Burke and Lester Rubin, "Is Contract Rejection a Major Collective Bargaining Problem?" *Industrial and Labor Relations Review* 26 (January 1973), pp. 832–833.

[7]Summers, "Ratification of Agreements," pp. 88–98.

[8]William E. Simkin, *Mediation and the Dynamics of Collective Bargaining* (Washington, D.C.: Bureau of National Affairs, 1971), pp. 25–28.

[9]Federal Mediation and Conciliation Service, *Thirty-Fourth Annual Report*, p. 18.

[10]Carl Stevens, "Mediation and the Role of the Neutral," in Dunlop and Chamberlain, *Frontiers of Collective Bargaining*, p. 271.

[11]Simkin, *Mediation*, p. 53.

[12]Stevens, "Mediation and the Role of the Neutral," pp. 280–284.

[13]Joseph Krislov and Amira Ealin, "Comparative Analysis of Attitudes Towards Mediation," *Labor Law Journal* 30 (March 1979), p. 173.

[14]Quote by a federal mediator in Deborah Kolb, "Roles Mediators Play: State and Federal Practice," *Industrial Relations* 20 (Winter 1981), p. 4.

[15]Ibid.

[16]Stevens, "Mediation and the Role of the Neutral," pp. 280–284.

[17]Thomas A. Kochan and Todd Jick, "The Public Sector Mediation Process," *Journal of Conflict Resolution* 22 (June 1978), p. 236.

[18]Jack Stieber, "Voluntary Arbitration of Contract Terms," in G. G. Somers and B. D. Dennis, eds., *Arbitration and the Expanding Role of Neutrals* (Washington, D.C.: Bureau of National Affairs, 1970), pp. 71–76. Also see Irving Bernstein, *Arbitration of Wages* (Los Angeles: University of California Press, 1954), p. 4; and R. U. Miller, "Arbitration of New Contract Wage Disputes: Some Recent Trends," *Industrial and Labor Relations Review* 20 (January 1967), pp. 250–264.

[19]Stieber, "Voluntary Arbitration," pp. 92–94.

[20]Sam Kagel, "Combining Mediation and Arbitration," *Monthly Labor Review* 96 (September 1973), pp. 62–63.

[21]David E. Fuller, "The Impetus to Contract Arbitration in the Private Area," *Twenty-fourth Annual NYU Conference on Labor* (New York: Matthew Bender, 1972), pp. 95–98.

[22]Peter Feuille and James B. Dworkin, "Final Offer Arbitration and Intertemporal Compromise, or It's My Turn to Win," in B. D. Dennis, ed., *Proceedings of the Thirty-first Annual Meeting: Industrial Relations Research Association* (Madison, Wis.: Industrial Relations Research Association, 1979), pp. 87–95.

[23]U.S. Department of Labor, Bureau of Labor Statistics, *Analysis of Work Stoppages, 1975* (Washington, D.C.: Government Printing Office, 1977), p. 78.

[24]Peter Feuille and Hoyt N. Wheeler, "Will the Real Industrial Conflict Please Stand Up?" in Jack Stieber et al., eds., *U.S. Industrial Relations, 1950–1980: A Critical Assessment* (Madison, Wis.: Industrial Relations Research Association, 1981), pp. 260–261.

[25]Bruce E. Kaufman, "The Determinants of Strikes in the United States, 1900–1977," *Industrial and Labor Relations Review* 35 (July 1982), p. 490.

[26]Martin J. Mauro, "Strikes as a Result of Imperfect Information," *Industrial and Labor Relations Review* 35 (July 1982), pp. 536–538.

[27]N. Nicholson and J. Kelly, "The Psychology of Strikes," *Journal of Occupational Behavior* (October 1981), pp. 275–284.

[28]Albert Rees, *The Economics of Trade Unions* (Chicago: University of Chicago Press, 1962), pp. 34–37.

[29]Ibid., pp. 277–279.

[30]Charles R. Greer, Stanley A. Martin, and Ted A. Reusser, "The Effects of Strikes on Shareholders Returns," *Journal of Labor Research* 1 (Fall 1980), pp. 217–229.

[31]Sheldon M. Kline, "Strike Benefits of National Unions," *Monthly Labor Review* 98 (March 1975), p. 17.

[32]Ibid., pp. 21–22.

[33]Ibid., p. 22.

[34]The Supreme Court upheld New York's law authorizing the payment of unemployment compensation after eight weeks. *New York Telephone Co. et al. v. New York State Department of Labor et al.*, Supreme Court of the United States, Slip opinion, No. 77-961, March 21, 1979.

[35]Armand J. Thiebolt and Ronald M. Cowin, *Welfare and Strikes: The Use of Public Funds to Support Strikers* (Philadelphia: Industrial Research Unit, University of Pennsylvania, 1972), pp. 207–208.

[36]*New York Telephone Co. v. New York Department of Labor*, 100 LRRM 2896 (1979).

[37]Thiebolt and Cowin, *Welfare and Strikes*, p. 3.

[38]G. C. Pati and L. G. Hill, "Economic Strikes, Public Aid, and Industrial Relations," *Labor Law Journal* 23 (January 1972), p. 32.

[39]Marc E. Thomas, "Strikers' Eligibility for Public Assistance: The Standard Based on Need," *Journal of Urban Law* 52 (August 1974), pp. 115–154.

[40]Pati and Hill, "Economic Strikes," p. 37.

[41]Thiebolt and Cowin, *Welfare and Strikes*, pp. 217–219.

[42]John S. Hirsch, Jr., "Strike Insurance and Collective Bargaining," *Industrial Labor Relations Review* 22 (April 1969), p. 399.

[43]Ibid., p. 400.

[44]Marvin J. Levine and L. W. Helly, "The Airlines Mutual Aid Pact: A Deterrent to Collective Bargaining," *Labor Law Journal* 28 (January 1977), pp. 44–55.

[45]S. Herbert Unterberger and Edward C. Koziara, "The Demise of Strike Insurance," *Industrial and Labor Relations Review* 34 (October 1980), pp. 82–88. The new requirements are:

1. No airline may receive payments greater than 60 percent of its direct operating expenses
2. No airline may receive payments for more than 8 weeks
3. No airline may receive payments for losses incurred during the first 30 days of any strike,
4. Every party to the Mutual Aid Agreement must agree to submit the issue(s) in conflict to binding agreement.

[46]R. E. Walton and R. B. McKersie, *A Behavioral Theory of Labor Negotiations* (New York: McGraw-Hill, 1965), pp. 31–32.

[47]William Serrin, *The Company and the Union* (New York: Knopf, 1973), p. 4.

[48]Walton and McKersie, *Behavioral Theory*, pp. 31–32.

[49]George Getschow, "Strike Woes Pile Up for Leader of Local That Started It All," *Wall Street Journal*, August 8, 1977, pp. 1, 17.

[50]John R. Emshwiller, "Strike Is Traumatic for a Quiet Village in Michigan Woods," *Wall Street Journal*, July 30, 1977, pp. 1, 24.

[51]Bernard Karsh, *Diary of a Strike* (Urbana: University of Illinois Press, 1958), pp. 70–73.

[52]L. L. Helmer, "Facing Up to a Strike," in E. Marting, ed., *Understanding Collective Bargaining* (New York: American Management Association, 1958), p. 323.

[53]American Society for Personnel Administration, *Strike Preparation Manual* (Berea, Ohio: American Society for Personnel Administration, 1974). Also see L. C. Scott, "Running a Struck Plant: Some Do's and Don't's," *SAM Advanced Management Journal* 38 (October 1973), pp. 58–62; and John G. Hutchinson, *Management under Strike Conditions* (New York: Holt, Rinehart and Winston, 1966).

[54]Henry Hazlitt, untitled, in Harold Hart, ed., *The Strike: For and Against* (New York: Hart Publishing, 1971), p. 64.

[55]Thomas Kennedy, "Freedom to Strike Is in the Public Interest," *Harvard Business Review* 48 (July–August 1970), p. 57.

[56]Theodore W. Kheel, "Is the Strike Outmoded?" *Monthly Labor Review* 96 (September 1973), pp. 35–37.

[57]For a discussion of strike costs see James Stern, "The Declining Utility of a Strike," *Industrial and Labor Relations Review* (October 1964), pp. 60–72.

[58]Lloyd G. Reynolds, *Labor Economics and Labor Relations* (Englewood Cliffs, N.J.: Prentice-Hall, 1970), pp. 440–442.

[59]Kheel, "Is the Strike Outmoded?" pp. 35–37.

[60]Stephen J. Cabot and Jerald R. Cureton, "Labor Disputes and Strikes: Be Prepared," *Personnel Journal* 60 (February 1981), pp. 122–123.

[61]Ibid.

[62]John R. Erickson, "Forfeiture of Reinstatement Rights through Strike Misconduct," *Labor Law Journal* 31 (October 1980), pp. 602–616.

[63]K. C. Miller and W. H. Form, *Industrial Sociology*, 2d ed. (New York: Harper & Row, 1964), pp. 385–388.

[64]Alvin W. Goldner, *Wildcat Strikes* (Yellow Springs, Ohio: Antioch Press, 1954), p. 95.

[65]Morrison Handsaker and Marjorie Handsaker, "Remedies and Penalties for Wildcat Strikes: How Arbitrators and Federal Courts Have Ruled," *Catholic University Law Review* 22 (Winter 1973), pp. 279–323. Summarized in *Industrial Relations Law Digest* 16 (July 1973), pp. 49–68.

[66]*American Shipbuilding Co. v. NLRB*, 380 U.S. 300 (1965).

[67]Walter E. Oberer and Kurt L. Hanslowe, *Labor Law* (St. Paul, Minn.: West Publishing, 1972), pp. 482–483. See *Buffalo Linen Supply Company*, 353 U.S. 85 (1956): and *Brown Food Store et al.*, 380 U.S. 278 (1965).

[68]Ralph M. Dereshinsky, Alan D. Berkowitz, and Phillip A. Miscimarra, *The NLRB and Secondary Boycotts* Rev. ed. (Philadelphia: Industrial Research Unit, University of Pennsylvania Press, 1981), pp. 191–195.

[69]*Tree Fruits*, 377 U.S. 58 (1964).

[70]*Forty-Fourth Annual Report of the NLRB* (Washington, D.C.: U.S. Government Printing Office, 1979), pp. 150–151. For thorough discussion, see Robert C. Castle and Richard Pegnetter, "Secondary Picketing: The Supreme Court Limits the *Tree Fruits* Exception," *Labor Law Journal* 33 (January 1982), pp. 3–16.

[71]Dereshinsky et al, *NLRB and Secondary Boycotts*, pp. 9–11.

[72]*NLRB v. Denver Building Trades Council*, 341 U.S. 675 (1951).

[73]Stephen J. Cabot and Robert J. Simmons, "The Future of Common Situs Picketing," *Labor Law Journal* 27 (December 1976), p. 775. A law allowing *common situs* picketing was passed by Congress but vetoed by President Ford. Another attempt was made in 1977 when President Carter said he would sign the bill; however, the House of Representatives refused to pass the law.

[74]*Forty-Fourth Annual Report of NLRB*, p. 147.

[75]Ibid.

[76]Ibid., pp. 149–150.

[77]Dereshinsky, et al., *NLRB and Secondary Boycotts*, p. 128.

[78]Ibid.

[79]*Forty-Fifth Annual Report of the NLRB* (Washington, D.C.: U.S. Government Printing Office, 1980), p. 158.

[80]Robert J. Deeny, "Secondary Boycotts," in Walter B. Connolly, Jr., ed., *Strikes, Stoppages, and Boycotts, 1978* (New York: Practising Law Institute, 1978), pp. 128–135.

[81]Dereshinsky, et al., *NLRB and Secondary Boycotts*, pp. 237–239.

[82]Edward B. Robin, "Secondary Boycotts in the Construction Industry," in B. T. King and D. W. Savelson, eds., *Construction Industry Labor Relations, 1977* (New York: Practising Law Institute, 1977), pp. 101–103. This provision has been amended by a subsequent Supreme Court decision: *Connell Construction Co. v. Plumbers and Steamfitters Local Union No. 100*, 421 U.S. 616 (1975).

[83]Donald E. Cullen, *National Emergency Strikes* (Ithaca, N.Y.: NYSSILR, Cornell University, 1968), pp. 45–48.

[84]John L. Blackman, Jr., *Presidential Seizure in Labor Disputes* (Cambridge, Mass.: Harvard University Press, 1967), pp. 1–21.

[85]Charles J. Morris, "The Role of Interest Arbitration in a Collective Bargaining System," *Industrial Relations Law Journal* 1 (Fall 1976), pp. 515–516.

[86]U.S., Congress, House, House Document No. 91–266, *Congressional Record* 116, no. 30, 91st Cong., 2d. sess., March 2, 1970, p. H1385.

[87]Morris, "Role of Interest Arbitration," p. 516.

[88]U.S. Department of Labor, Bureau of Labor Statistics, *National Emergency Disputes* (Washington, D.C.: Government Printing Office, 1969), pp. 1–31.

[89]A. H. Raskin, "Collision Course on the Labor Front," *Saturday Review*, February 25, 1967, pp. 32–35.

[90]Oberer and Hanslowe, *Labor Law*, pp. 901–902.

[91]"LTV Corp. Survey on Outlook for Labor-Management Cooperation," *Daily Labor Report*, September 7, 1982, p. E-1–E-2.

[92]David L. Cole, "The Search for Industrial Peace," *Monthly Labor Review* 96 (September 1973), p. 37.

[93]Sumner H. Slichter, James J. Healy, and E. Robert Livernash, *The Impact of Collective Bargaining on Management* (Washington, D.C.: Brookings Institution, 1960), p. 842.

[94]Ted Mills, "Human Resources: Why the Concern?" *Harvard Business Review* 53 (March–April 1975), pp. 127–129.

[95]Raymond Katzell et al., *Work Productivity and Job Satisfaction* (Chicago: Psychological Corporation, 1976), p. 95. Also see E. E. Lawler and J. A. Drexler, Jr., "Dynamics of Establishing Cooperative Quality-of-Work-Life Projects," *Monthly Labor Review* 101 (March 1978), pp. 25–27.

[96]A. A. Blum, M. L. Moore, and B. P. Fairly, "The Effect of Motivational Programs on Collective Bargaining," *Personnel Journal* 52 (July 1973), pp. 633–641.

[97]U.S. Department of Labor, Bureau of Labor Statistics, *Characteristics of Major Collective Bargaining Agreements, July 1, 1980*, Bulletin 2095 (Washington, D.C.: Government Printing Office, 1981), p. 32.

[98]David A. Gray, Anthony V. Sinicropi, and Paula Ann Hughes, "From Conflict to Cooperation: A Joint Union-Management Goal-Setting and Problem-Solving Program," in Barbara D. Dennis, ed., *Proceedings of the Thirty-Third Annual Meeting of the Industrial Relations Research Association, 1981* (Madison, Wis.: IRRA, 1982), pp. 26–28.

[99]*Thirty-Third Annual Report, Federal Mediation and Conciliation Service* (Washington, D.C.: U.S. Government Printing Office, 1981), pp. 29–31.

[100]Ibid., p. 29.

[101]Phillip E. Ray, "The Retail Food Industry," in Dennis, ed., *Proceedings of the Thirty-Fourth Annual Meeting of the Industrial Relations Research Association* (Madison, Wis.: IRRA, 1982), pp. 146–149.

[102]Laurence P. Corbett, "The Health Care Experience," Dennis, ed., *Proceedings of the Thirty-Fourth Annual Meeting of the Industrial Relations Research Association* (Madison, Wis.: IRRA, 1982), pp. 156–157.

[103]Ben Burdetsky, "Discussion," in Dennis, ed., *Proceedings of the Thirty-Fourth Annual Meeting of the Industrial Relations Research Association* (Madison, Wis.: IRRA, 1982), pp. 159–160.

[104]Robert H. Guest, "Quality of Work Life—Leaving from Tarrytown," *Harvard Business Review* 57 (July–August 1979), pp. 77–79.

[105]Guest, "Quality of Work Life," p. 85.

[106]Roger B. Smith, "Toward a New Alliance with Labor," Speech at Cornell University, April 7, 1982.

[107]James A. Craft, "The ENA, Consent Decrees, and Cooperation in Steel Labor Relations: A Critical Appraisal," *Labor Law Journal* 27 (October 1976), p. 633.

[108]BNA Editorial Staff, *Labor Relations Yearbook: 1973* (Washington, D.C.: Bureau of National Affairs, 1973), p. 46.

[109]"U.S. Steel's Get-Tough Policy," *Business Week*, August 30, 1982, pp. 73–74.

[110]"Steel Seeks Higher Output via Workplace Reform," *Business Week*, August 18, 1982, pp. 98–103.

[111]Paul Thayer, "How LTV Is Involved," *Wall Street Journal*, August 3, 1982, p. 23.

[112]"Steeling for Some Givebacks," *Time*, March 14, 1983, p. 64.

[113]Leon C. Megginson and C. Ray Gullett, "A Predictive Model of Union-Management Conflict," *Personnel Journal* 49 (June 1970), pp. 495–503.

[114]William L. Bott, Jr. and Edgar Weinberg, "Labor-Management Cooperation Today," *Harvard Business Review* 56 (January–February 1978), pp. 103–104.

[115]George W. Bohlander, "Implementing Quality-of-Work Programs: Recognizing the Barriers," *MSU Business Topics* 27 (Spring 1979), pp. 33–40.

[116]Richard P. Nielsen, "Stages in Moving Toward Cooperative Problem Solving Labor Relations Projects and a Case Study," *Human Resource Management* 18 (Fall 1979), pp. 2–8.

Chapter 8 Contract Administration

The grievance procedure constitutes the central focus of day-to-day union-management activity.
David A. Peach and E. Robert Livernash, *Grievance Initiation And Resolution: A Study in Basic Steel* (Boston: Harvard University Press, 1974), p. 1.

Labor agreement negotiation is usually the most publicized and dramatic aspect of labor relations. Strike deadlines, negotiators in shirt sleeves working around the clock to avert a possible strike, and the economic settlement of the labor agreement receive attention from the news media. The day-to-day administration of the labor agreement, on the other hand, receives little if any recognition beyond that given by the involved parties. Yet contract administration is an important part of collective bargaining. Chapter 6 indicates that Section 8 (d) of the National Labor Relations Act defines collective bargaining in such a way that good faith bargaining extends from negotiating the agreement to resolving questions arising from the agreement (contract administration).

Contract administration transforms the negotiated labor agreement because grievance settlements over a period of time will establish interpretative principles or common laws that supplement or even modify the terms of the negotiated labor agreement. Administration of the negotiated contract gives dynamic meaning to its rather skeletal terms.

This chapter first defines employee grievances, then explores their sources and significance. The next section examines the grievance procedure: its typical steps, the relationships among grievance participants, and theoretical as well as practical concerns involved in contract administration. The final section discusses a legal ("fair representation") requirement in the grievance procedure.

Grievances: Definition, Sources, and Significance

The core of contract administration consists of *employee grievances*, which can be defined as any employee's concern over a perceived violation of the labor agreement which is submitted to the grievance procedure for eventual resolution. Thus a grievance is distinguished from an employee's concern or complaint which is expressed, independent of labor agreement provisions, during the course of a typical work day.

Most grievances are reduced to writing, a factor which has several advantages for management and/or union officials:

1. Both union and management representatives need a written record of their daily problem resolutions. This record generates precedents which can guide future actions while also saving time in deciding similar grievances in the future.
2. Written grievances tend to reduce emotionalism present in many employee concerns. As the reader can recall from experience, an immediate verbal confrontation with someone by whom one feels he or she has been wronged allows the individual to blow off steam. However, the possible name-calling and obscenities at best blur real issues and facts and at worst irreparably harm the relationship between the parties. Consequently, writing the grievance can be viewed as necessary for its rational discussion.
3. Having the concern written out allows management representatives to focus on the employee's original grievance. As will be dicussed further in the chapter, a grievance can proceed through several steps which involve many more individuals than the aggrieved employee. Union officials may alter an employee's initial concern into a broader philosophical issue. (For example, a complaint over the company's unilateral selection of candy bars for the vending machine could conceivably be magnified in subsequent steps to protest the company's arbitrary and capricious actions in other working conditions.) Management always has the option of returning to the concern(s) expressed in the original grievance.
4. Written grievances can benefit management in cases where the employee is apprehensive about signing a written protest. Even though most labor agreements permit a union officer to file a grievance on behalf of the grievant, requiring grievances to be written probably reduces the total number that management representatives must administer.

Our definition of a grievance is extremely broad and hinges on the employee's perception that he or she has a grievance. Assume, for example, that Employee A protests Employee B's "immoral" behavior. This protest could take the form of an oral complaint without reference to the grievance procedure, or the same employee could insist the complaint represents a violation of the terms of the labor agreement. The supervisor can attempt to convince the employee that the complaint is unrelated to the terms of the labor agreement, indicating that there is no provision pertaining to the exact behavior of any particular employee, especially off the job.

Yet what happens if the employee insists that the concern is a grievance and should be processed as such? Further, the employee cites a vague and probably unrelated contractual provision in the argument such as an article stressing the "company's obligation to maintain a work environment in as safe a condition as possible." After unsuccessfully discussing the issue with Employee A, the supervisor has two options: (a) to refuse to accept the employee's grievance or (b) to accept the employee's grievance and deny it in the written grievance answer on the basis that there is no contractual violation. Not wishing to risk a time-consuming unfair labor practice charge, the supervisor will probably take the second alternative.

The broad definition of a grievance realizes, then, that there is a difference between *accepting* an employee's grievance and *deciding the merits* of an employee's grievance. The broader definition safeguards against unfair labor practice charges and at the same time preserves management's right to deny the grievance in its written answer.

Reasons for Employee Grievances

In order to better understand the reasons behind employee grievances, the following hypothetical example is given. A first-line supervisor administers a labor agreement which has the following provisions pertaining to management's rights and the scheduling of work to be performed on a holiday:

Article III: Management Rights

Section 1. The company's right to hire, fire, and direct the working force, transfer or promote is unqualified as long as this right is not used in any conflict with any provision of this contract.

Article IX: Holiday Scheduling

Section 1. When less than a normal crew is required to work on a holiday, the following procedure will apply:

(a) The senior employee working in the classification desired will be given the opportunity to work.

(b) Employees assigned holiday work will be paid a minimum of eight hours at time and one-half the contract rate of pay.

(c) If an employee works out of classification on the holiday, the senior employee in the appropriate classification will also be paid a minimum of eight hours at time and one-half his or her contract rate of pay.

With these provisions in mind, consider the following chain of events. A crane operator is needed to work the July 4 holiday. The senior employee in this classification starts work on this shift; however, after he has worked one-half hour, the crane breaks down and can no longer be operated. Further, management believes the maintenance department will be able to repair the crane within three hours. It should be noted that all job classifications typically perform some minor housekeeping and cleanup work, such as dusting and picking up debris around the work station; however, there is also a janitor's classification in the labor agreement.

The first-line supervisor has three options. First, the employee can be sent home. However, according to Section 1 (b) of the labor agreement, management will have to pay that employee eight hours at one and one-half times the employee's hourly pay rate and the same amount to another employee who is called to work once the crane is repaired. Consequently, option one is not attractive to management.

Option two would have the employee remain at work and in effect do nothing until the crane is repaired. Since management is already obligated to pay the employee for the entire shift, it does not cost any additional money to have the employee sit in the work shed until crane operations can be renewed. This, however, is not a pleasant option for the first-line supervisor, particularly if higher level management officials and other hourly employees see this individual being paid for not performing work.

Thus, option three, having the crane operator perform minor housekeeping chores until the crane is repaired, appears most beneficial to management. Yet there is a good possibility that this action would result in a grievance from the senior employee in the janitorial classification, asking payment for eight hours at time and a half since Section 1 (c) would apparently have been violated. The aggrieved employee could file this grievance for one or more of the following reasons.

1. *To protest a contractual violation.* When labor and management officials negotiate a labor agreement, they are mainly concerned with agreement over the major issues. The negotiations are not concerned with determining the precise meaning of every word in the labor agreement, particularly if there have been few or no previous problems arising from the contract language. Similarly, these officials cannot possibly anticipate all of the unique situations which could potentially distort or add to the negotiated terms of the labor agreement. Consequently, union and management negotiators often gloss over the "unimportant" provisions, leaving potential interpretational problems to those who must live with and administer the labor agreement on a daily basis.

In the crane operator example, local union officials could contend that the crane operator did "work out of classification"—a clear violation of Section 1 (c). Management, on the other hand, could contend that the needed holiday work was within the scope of a crane operator's job. Moreover, it had no intention of paying an employee an amount equal to twelve hours contract rate of pay simply to dust or straighten up the workplace. Another management contention could be that minor housekeeping chores are performed by all employees; therefore, the crane operator did not work out of classification on the day in question. Hence, Article III, Management Rights, would prevail in this situation.

Thus, the interpretational differences over the terms of the labor agreement are magnified when the inevitable contractual gaps or areas in which the contract is silent surface (here, on appropriate procedures to follow when the equipment is temporarily out of order on holidays).

2. *To draw attention to a problem in the plant.* Some grievances do not protest violation of the labor agreement; instead, they stress that management has obligations beyond the scope of the labor agreement. Most grievances over alleged safety hazards fall into this category, as few labor agreements specify management's obligation in this area. The employee might realize that there is no contractual violation but still files the grievance to communicate concern to management over a safety issue. In our example, the grievance over holiday scheduling might have been filed, not over receiving payment for the senior janitor in the classification, but in order to give union officers the forum in which to stress the inadequate number of maintenance employees for equipment repair.

Unions quite often draw attention to a problem in the hopes of setting the stage for future labor agreement negotiations. A common union tactic is to file several grievances over a particular issue to buttress and document its demands during negotiation of the subsequent labor agreement.

For example, labor unions adhering to the job protection philosophy discussed in Chapter 1 do not want supervisory personnel performing their members' work since these activities could reduce overtime opportunities or even result in employees being laid off. In the course of a work day, supervisors may perform several chores which could be classified as bargaining unit work. A union wishing to obtain a contractual restriction against supervisors performing bargaining unit work might encourage employees to file a grievance whenever the foreman engages in this practice no matter how minor that physical activity may be (for example, changing a light bulb). Armed with several grievances, in formal contract negotiations the union can dramatize its concerns that: (a) supervisors performing bargaining unit work is a widespread problem and (b) a contractual provision restricting foremen from performing bargaining unit work would save the company time and money by eliminating related grievances.

3. *To get something for nothing.* Some managers believe that a few employees file grievances to receive pay related to their skill in formulating and writing grievances instead of their work efforts. The janitor in our crane operator example might not have been inclined to file a grievance at the time the work was denied. Indeed, he or she may have had previously scheduled holiday plans and refused to work if management had made the initial offer. However, assuming the janitor's classification paid $4 an hour, the janitor might have felt that time and one-half for eight hours ($48) worth the effort to file a grievance. This payment could be particularly attractive to an individual who did not have to alter holiday plans to obtain it.

Employees filing grievances for this reason find opportunities in the area of overtime administration. A common labor agreement provision requires management to equalize overtime opportunity among qualified bargaining unit employees desiring overtime. Additionally, management is often contractually required to pay the employee for the overtime worked by another employee if an administrative error was made. For example, assume the following list represents the names of employees in the electrician's classification who signed the daily overtime list, thereby volunteering to work overtime if the assignment occurs after the completion of their normal work shift.

Name of Employee	Number of Overtime Hours Worked and/or Refused since January 1
A. Jones	89 hours
T. Grant	76 hours
B. Simms	43 hours

The figure to the right of the employee's name represents the number of overtime hours worked by the employee to date and also includes any overtime assignments refused by the employee—if Jones refused to work an eight-hour overtime assignment eventually worked by Grant, both employees are charged the eight hours for administrative purposes. If an overtime assignment for electricians is needed on the day in question, the supervisor checks the overtime list and determines that Simms is lowest in overtime hours. Consequently, the supervisor would give Simms the first opportunity to accept or refuse the overtime assignment.

Suppose, however, that Simms desires the overtime payment without actually having to work the overtime assignment. There are several rather dubious strategies Simms could use in this situation. Perhaps the best alternative would be to actively avoid (in some cases hide from) the supervisor. Confronted with an overtime emergency, the supervisor has to offer the assignment to Grant, the employee next lowest in overtime. The next day, Simms could file a grievance on the "administrative error" and be paid the equivalent of Grant's overtime assignment for no corresponding work effort. Needless to say, this reason for filing a grievance draws management's ire, particularly since some employees appear to make a contest out of acquiring grievance "freebies," or payment for time not worked.

4. *To make the grievant and union feel important.* In nonunion settings, the authority of managerial policies and actions often goes unchallenged. However, the grievance procedure permits, and in some cases encourages, an employee to protest an alleged wrong committed by management officials. Some employees bolster their perceived status in the organization by calling their organizational superiors on the carpet for an explanation of their actions. This motiva-

tion for filing a grievance is particularly likely in the case of a supervisor who flaunts authority unnecessarily, thereby creating tensions and grievances which protest the supervisor's personality as well as actions.

Similarly, some union officials wish to emphasize their importance and self-interests through grievance involvement. Those falling into this category use grievances and contract administration problems to advance to higher political office in the union or to bring themselves to management's attention for possible promotion in the management organization.

Grievances in these cases provide a forum where the union steward can demonstrate his or her verbal and intellectual capabilities to other management and union officials. Other union officials might wish to strengthen the union as an institution through the grievance procedure. Here, the union's (not the union official's) importance is stressed; the union is safeguarding its members from management's arbitrary and capricious actions. One union steward reflecting this reason has commented:

Every so often you'd hear a couple of guys really lambasting the foreman in the washroom—that's where you can really hear the gripes. But when I'd write up the grievance and take it to the fellows, they'd say it was too small. I'd say "the hell with you" and push it anyway.

Soon the company would be coming to me and saying, "Those guys don't have a grievance. They're perfectly satisfied." And I'd say, "The hell they don't. If you don't want to recognize it, I'll take it to the next step." I didn't care if the guys supported me, I went through with it.[1]

There are other, miscellaneous reasons employees file grievances. Motives are as varied and complex as the employees' personalities and life experiences.[2] For example, an argument with the employee's family, friends, or work associates might provoke a grievance. Other motives, such as poor employee/job match or a generally poor managerial climate, are perhaps more easily rectified by subsequent managerial action. Uncovering the motive behind a grievance may be helpful to management. However, it must be stressed that management must process the grievance even if it feels the employee's motives are illegitimate or improper.

Significance of Employee Grievances

Unresolved employee grievances or concerns can significantly affect both nonunion and union firms. In some cases, unsettled employee grievances or concerns have prompted successful union organizing drives.[3] In unionized firms, employees often have unique concerns which are neither addressed in collective bargaining nor explicitly covered in the labor agreement. Union officials therefore demonstrate their intent to represent members' particular job interests against conceivable arbitrary managerial actions through the use of the grievance procedure. A union not demonstrating its interest in union members through an effective grievance procedure runs the risk of law suits (see the chapter's final section on "fair representation") or severe membership dissatisfaction with union leaders.[4]

Employee grievances can also serve two important organizational functions: *conflict rationalization* and *communication*. Unions often present different challenges and perspectives to managers; thus,

The employer-employee relationship is wrought with inevitable conflict. This conflict, however, can be managed in ways that are beneficial to employers and employees alike. The most common conflict management tool available to employers is the formal grievance procedure. Organizations that do not provide such complaint processing mechanisms for their employees may suffer debilitating consequences.[5]

Grievances when processed through established procedures both indicate potential areas of disagreement and provide an orderly way of resolving differences of opinion.

Grievances can also clarify labor agreement provisions and communicate suggestions to management. Although managers can communicate to employees in a variety of ways, they cannot be assured that employees will in turn generate concerns and suggestions to them. Employee silence does not always equal satisfaction;[6] grievances and the grievance procedure offer the potential for open discussion.

The Grievance Procedure

Steps of the Grievance Procedure

The process for resolving employee grievances is specified in approximately 99 percent of existing labor agreements.[7] However, the procedures themselves are as varied as the labor agreements found in U.S. industry today. Some consist of only one step, whereas others contain as many as nine. While there is no one grievance procedure applicable to all labor-management relationships,[8] the four-step procedure illustrated in Exhibit 8.1 and discussed below is fairly representative.

First step This stage actually consists of two phases. First, the employee (with or without the union steward) discusses the concern with his or her first-line supervisor. If agreement is not reached, then a written grievance is filed by the grievant or the union steward acting on the grievant's behalf. The supervisor then answers the employee's grievance in writing.

Exhibit 8.1 Example of a Typical Grievance Procedure

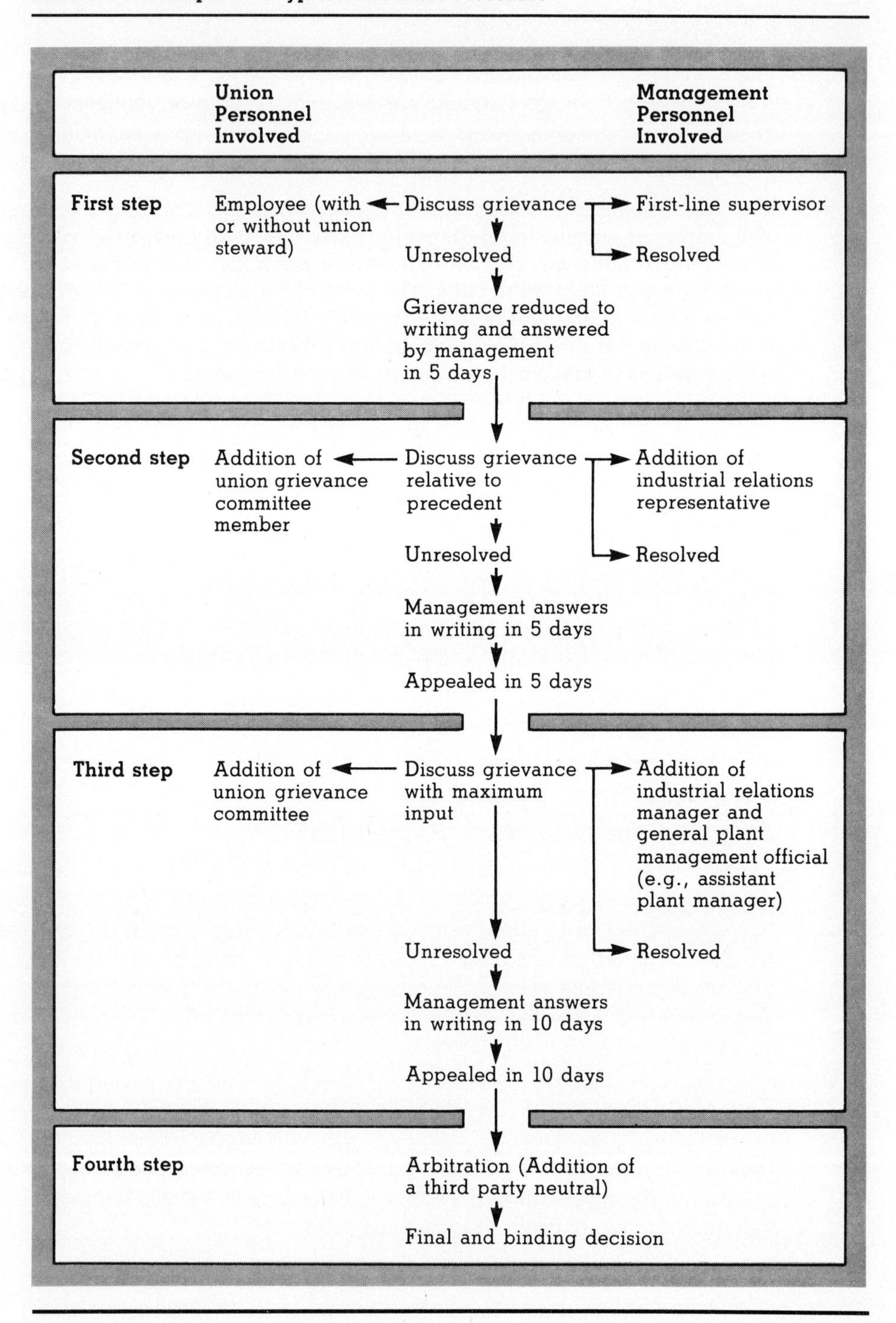
Union Personnel Involved
Management Personnel Involved
First step
Employee (with or without union steward)
Discuss grievance
First-line supervisor
Unresolved
Resolved
Grievance reduced to writing and answered by management in 5 days
Second step
Addition of union grievance committee member
Discuss grievance relative to precedent
Addition of industrial relations representative
Unresolved
Resolved
Management answers in writing in 5 days
Appealed in 5 days
Third step
Addition of union grievance committee
Discuss grievance with maximum input
Addition of industrial relations manager and general plant management official (e.g., assistant plant manager)
Unresolved
Resolved
Management answers in writing in 10 days
Appealed in 10 days
Fourth step
Arbitration (Addition of a third party neutral)
Final and binding decision

The purpose of the discussion is to resolve the grievance as early and as informally as possible. However, in some cases, the oral discussion is *pro forma*—the employee initiates this step with a written grievance on the assumption that no amount of discussion will change his or her mind. As is true with the next two steps of the grievance procedure, if the employee accepts management's answer to the written grievance, then the grievance is considered resolved and subsequent steps are unnecessary.

Second step In addition to the individuals in the first-step grievance meeting, the union grievance committeeperson and management's industrial relations representative are brought in to discuss the foreman's first-step grievance answer. Both of these individuals are aware of administrative precedent throughout the entire shop; their main role is to determine whether the grievance should be resolved at this stage on the basis of this precedent.

For example, say Employee A files a grievance protesting management's unilateral action in reducing wash-up time in her work area. The grievance committeeperson might be aware, however, that (a) the contract does not have a provision pertaining to wash-up time and (b) employees in other departments do not receive any time before the end of the shift to clean their hands. Therefore, he or she would probably encourage the grievant to accept the reduction in wash-up time rather than risk losing the privilege entirely in subsequent steps of the grievance procedure.

On another issue—for example, an employee working out of his or her normal work classification and demanding an upgrade in pay for the time worked—the industrial relations representative might reverse the foreman's first-step answer to avoid sending the grievance to the third step, where it might affect employees with similar work experiences in other departments. The second-step written grievance answer is furnished by the industrial relations representative, and any precedent resulting from this answer usually applies only to the particular work department instead of the entire facility.

Third step The third-step meeting involves the same individuals as the second step but in addition includes the industrial relations manager and another management official (such as a general foreman, superintendent, or assistant plant manager) and members of the union's grievance committee (see Chapter 4). These individuals are added because the grievance answer at this level could affect the entire industrial operation, and both management and union representatives wish to obtain as much input as possible before making the decision.

These additional individuals serve other purposes, particularly from the union's standpoint. First, the third-step meeting can be used as a training or educational device for relatively new union officers. Since many labor agreements require paid time off for grievance meetings, a new union official can learn the often complex issues and strategies involved in grievance resolution at the company's expense. The union grievance committee can also serve tactical purposes and political functions because the sheer number of individuals on the committee can impress upon the grievant that the union is forcefully representing his or her interests.

Also, the committee can serve as a buck-passing device for the union steward or committeeperson who informs the grievant that he or she did all that was possible to win the grievance but was turned down by other members on the committee. Buck passing is not restricted to union personnel, since supervisors can claim to their managerial counterparts that they were not wrong, merely "sold out" by higher level management officials in subsequent steps of the procedure.

This step can also function as a therapeutic device for the grievant, who simply wishes to express concern to many levels of management officials. Perhaps the most important function of the third-step meeting is the inclusion of additional union and management officials who are not personally involved in the grievance outcome and can assess its merits with relative objectivity. The third-step grievance answer is usually written by the industrial relations manager because the decision probably will have plantwide implications and applications.

Fourth step—arbitration The final step in the procedure, particularly in the private sector, involves the same individuals as step three and adds a selected third-party neutral who hears the grievance and makes a final decision resolving the issue. The arbitration process of "rights" disputes over existing terms of the contract is of such significance and complexity that it warrants a more thorough discussion in a separate chapter (see Chapter 9); however, it should be mentioned that this process terminates the typical grievance procedure.

Even though they may vary in terms of steps, time limits for the processing of each step, and participants, grievance procedures represent a progression of the initial grievance to higher level management and union officials for consideration. Such procedures written in labor agreements have the drawback of being formal instead of tailored to an individual's personality and concerns. Yet this formality insures that any bargaining unit employee can have his or her grievance heard. While many procedures may appear inflexible, they merely serve as the arena for dynamic social relationships and interactions among management and union officials.

Grievance Participants and Their Relationships in the Grievance Procedure

The most frequent interaction in grievance resolution takes place between the first-line supervisor and the union steward. These relationships can be classified along dimensions presented in Chapter 1, as *codified, power,* or *sympathetic.*

Codified Relationships The rights and privileges of foremen and union stewards often stem from a defining code established through the labor agreements and various union and management publications. Union steward handbooks emphasize mutual rights and respect.

The Foreman is the key man in the company's collective bargaining setup just as you, the Steward, are the key man in the union setup. There is a small area of decision that the Foreman does make interpreting policy, and it is in this area that the union can gain by establishing a cooperative relationship.[9]

Generally, every effort should be made to settle a grievance as close to the source of the dispute as possible. The representatives of both groups have to live with any settlement reached. If they can arrive at one, rather than having it imposed on them from above, both parties will be better off. In addition, the further the grievance travels up the procedure the more difficult it becomes to settle, because it becomes a matter of pride or prestige. Therefore, both sides tend to back up their subordinates even when they feel they may have been wrong originally.

It is absolutely essential that the steward talk to the foreman after getting the worker's story. He can probably evaluate the complaint only after hearing both sides. The foreman may provide certain facts that were not available to the worker or the steward.[10]

Exhibit 8.2 stresses the union's obligation to state the grievance in an objective, rational manner, basing it on contractual violations instead of personality clashes.

Similarly, excerpts from American Management Association publications presented below emphasize the appropriate codes of conduct the foremen should follow when dealing with union stewards:

In labor management relations, there is no room for prejudice toward union representatives. The presence of the union organization in the plant effects a union-management marriage, and a corresponding obligation to observe the vows of recognition and good faith. In their grievance relationships, the foremen and the stewards are co-equals.[11]

Supervisors should be thoroughly informed about the rights and responsibilities of shop stewards under the contract and should take care to respect the steward's role. If the steward has the contractual right to investigate grievances, he should not be hampered in doing so, and if an employee requests a shop steward to assist in processing his grievance or to be present during disciplinary action, the supervisor should acquiesce promptly.[12]

Exhibit 8.2 Union Instructions Regarding Grievance Processing

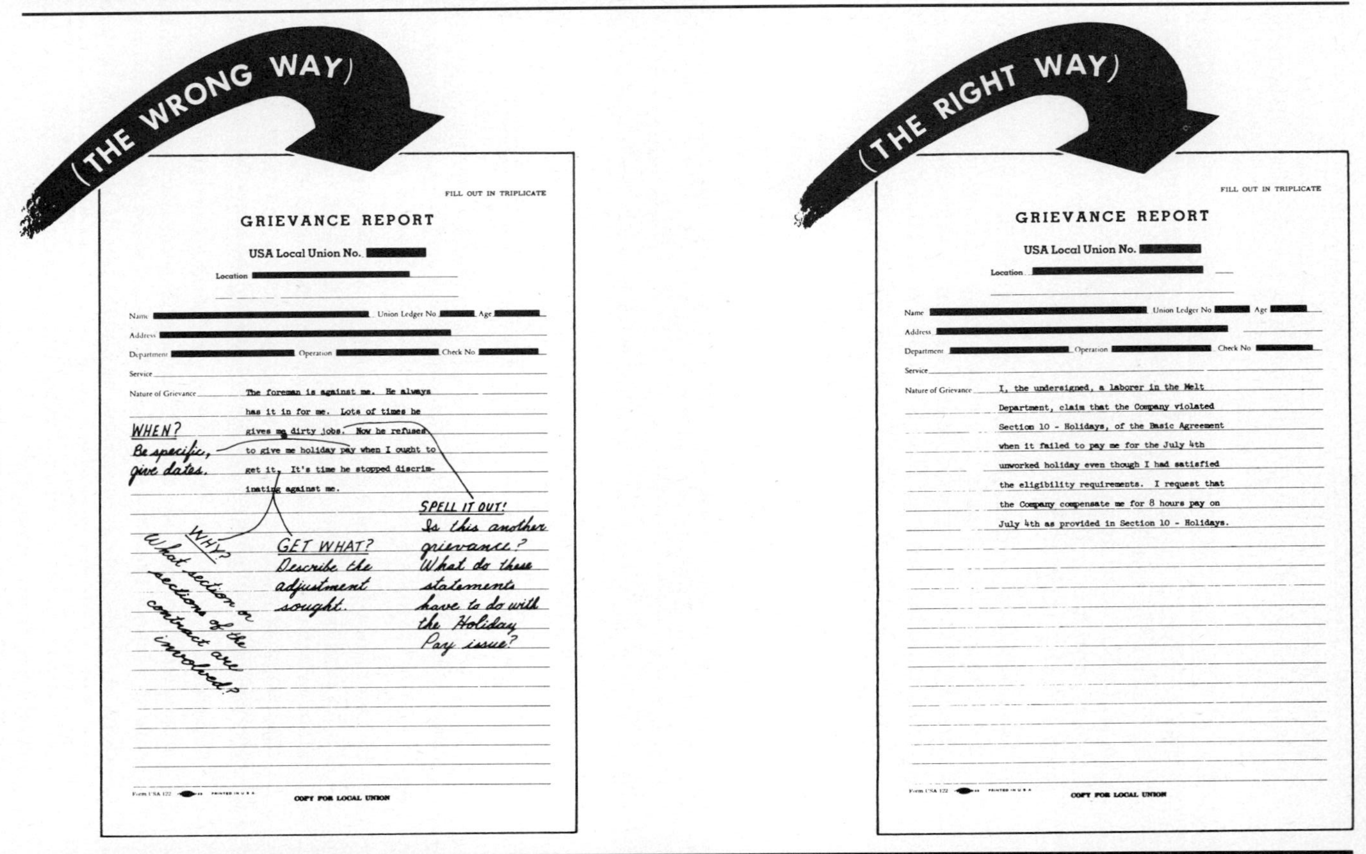
(THE WRONG WAY)

FILL OUT IN TRIPLICATE

GRIEVANCE REPORT

USA Local Union No.

Location

Name Union Ledger No Age

Address

Department Operation Check No

Service

Nature of Grievance The foreman is against me. He always has it in for me. Lots of times he gives me dirty jobs. Now he refuses to give me holiday pay when I ought to get it. It's time he stopped discriminating against me.

WHEN? Be specific, give dates.

WHY? What section or sections of the contract are involved?

GET WHAT? Describe the adjustment sought.

SPELL IT OUT! Is this another grievance? What do these statements have to do with the Holiday Pay issue?

Form USA 122 COPY FOR LOCAL UNION

(THE RIGHT WAY)

FILL OUT IN TRIPLICATE

GRIEVANCE REPORT

USA Local Union No.

Location

Name Union Ledger No Age

Address

Department Operation Check No

Service

Nature of Grievance I, the undersigned, a laborer in the Melt Department, claim that the Company violated Section 10 - Holidays, of the Basic Agreement when it failed to pay me for the July 4th unworked holiday even though I had satisfied the eligibility requirements. I request that the Company compensate me for 8 hours pay on July 4th as provided in Section 10 - Holidays.

Form USA 122 COPY FOR LOCAL UNION

Source: Reprinted by permission from United Steelworkers of America. *The Grievanceman's Handbook* (n.p.,n.d.), pp. 14, 15.

Foremen and union stewards may be aware of the preceding normative philosophies and codes but often do not take them into account when interacting.[13] For example, the *AFL-CIO Manual for Shop Stewards* strongly urges union stewards to present their grievances directly to the first-line supervisor in the first step of the grievance procedure.

It is important to observe the steps in the grievance procedure even if the foreman has limited authority. Leapfrogging to a higher step may have undesirable effects. The lower level of management will resent this and will be more difficult to deal with the next time, or the company may seek to get the grievance thrown out because the proper steps were not followed.[14]

Yet some research has shown that many first-line supervisors believe union stewards violate this aspect of a codified relationship[15]—the supervisors maintain that they are often completely bypassed by the union steward in the grievance process.

Power Relationships Conflicting power relationships develop in situations where the foremen and union stewards pursue differing interests or goals. For example, both are encouraged by their respective superiors to be attentive to problems in the department. The foreman is encouraged to discover problems before they become grievances,[16] whereas the steward is encouraged to talk to the potential grievant before that employee talks to the foreman.

A steward has the responsibility of enforcing the contract in the best interests of all the workers. He should encourage workers who have grievances to come directly to him, not to the foreman. A worker who does not know the contract thoroughly may let the foreman talk him out of a just grievance. Or he may agree to a settlement that weakens the contract and limits the whole union.[17]

Another type of power relationship results from the union steward's knowing the labor agreement better than does his counterpart, the foreman. Union stewards can concentrate on particular provisions of the labor agreement and their application to the shop. The foreman, on the other hand, has major responsibilities for production scheduling, meeting departmental quality and quantity standards, participating in cost reduction programs, and so on, which reduce the amount of time available for grievance and labor agreement analyses.

The steward's relatively superior knowledge of the labor agreement provides the union with at least two strategic advantages over the foreman. First, stewards might be more able to turn a labor relations problem not covered by the labor agreement into a bona fide grievance. For example, guidance given to union stewards in a typical union steward's manual contends:

Almost every grievance is covered by some sections of the contract. An able grievanceman will know how to make the contract fit the case, as the contract should be more than just a piece of paper.[18]

Second, the union steward can directly put his or her labor agreement knowledge to advantageous use, given the chance to discuss the problem one-to-one with the foreman. One steward emphasizes the results of this practice: "Any steward who knows his stuff can talk rings around a foreman. If he says the foreman's wrong and talks enough, whether he's entirely accurate or not, he's apt to buffalo him."[19]

Intimidation is another power relationship strategy which can be employed by both the union steward and the foreman to obtain their respective objectives. In some situations the union steward anticipates that the foreman is vulnerable when he or she receives an excessive number of grievances—the foreman will be concerned with how management officials will react to this apparent inability to resolve labor relations problems. Of course, the grievances might not be valid, and other management officials might consequently consider the foreman to be defending the best interests of the company. But, as the following notation indicates, some management officials might hold the opposite opinion:

The good foreman doesn't have to have grievances. He has enough discretion to be able to settle most complaints—*if* he handles himself well. Many things—for example, pay for overtime work—he is able to adjust if the worker has been wronged. Other things, beyond his scope—for example, where company rules or policies are involved—can be settled if the foreman uses tact and diplomacy. There's no question that even when he can't begin action himself, he can settle the fellow's complaint.[20]

Consequently, a union steward can use the threat of additional grievances (bogus or real) to persuade the foreman to concede to the particular grievance in question or to alter the foreman's overall approach to industrial relations. The practice is explained by a union official:

A short time ago we had a lot of trouble with a certain foreman. . . . He was making them toe the line . . . no quitting early, work from whistle to whistle, no sitting down, no horseplay, this and that. I told the committeeman there, "You do the same thing. Every time he does any work, even if he picks up a box, write a grievance. . . ." The first thing you know grievances started mounting—finally had a pile like that.

Things got so bad . . . this foreman was removed from that department. He was moved to our department and it's his last chance. If he doesn't do good in this department, out he goes. So I went to the guy and told him, "It's your last chance here and you know it. You cooperate with us and we'll cooperate with you. If you don't we'll put the screws on you and out you go." Things are working out pretty good so far.[21]

If the foreman believes that there is a strong possibility of his being returned to the bargaining unit, the steward's intimidation can be particularly effective.

I've been broken four or five times [returned to the bargaining unit], and that's a big scare right there for the simple reason that I've been previously warned regarding tussles with the union steward. [He said] "I'll remember this when you come back down to production." In other words, when we get out of salary and back down to production we have to be OK'd by the union in order to get back to our job again. So you're in the middle there and you don't know what you are going to do. I may be here a day, a month, a year, I don't know, and all of a sudden they don't need me any more, and I go back to production, and the union don't want me. That's not only with me, but a lot of supervisors are shaky on that point . . . we have no backing; whereas the workmen have the union to back them up, the foreman has nothing. You're either a good Joe or you're just out.[22]

Intimidation tactics are not always one-sided; a clever foreman can make industrial life very difficult for the union steward, probably without incurring an unfair labor practice charge. For example, many job classifications have a wide variety of work assignments, with some of these assignments being less desirable than others. A foreman could assign undesirable work assignments to the union steward, who would have little recourse as long as they were within his or her job classification. The foreman can also undermine the steward's formal position in the union by: (a) restricting the amount of freedom and time necessary for the steward to investigate the grievance and (b) refusing to resolve any grievance in the first step whenever the union steward is present with the grievant. It should be noted that these tactics are only successful if the union steward is inexperienced.

Regardless of the "success" of such actions, a grievance relationship governed by power and intimidation tactics distorts the primary purpose of contract administration—namely rational decision making.

Sympathetic Relationships Sympathetic relations occur between individuals when each is aware of the other's situation and is guided by an understanding appreciation. An example of this appreciation comes from a union steward's comment:

You can't have industrial relations without giving and taking on both sides. You'll always win more cases by getting along with supervision than by being tough. You've got to swap and make trades. . . . Sometimes I have to talk like hell to explain some of the deals I make with them and sometimes I keep what I'm doing to myself if I see a chance to get something good later on. The thing some grievers never get through their heads is that a lot of bosses are on the spot themselves. If you go a little easy on them when they're on the pan, by God—you make friends—they'll stand by you sometime when you're back of the eight ball. Sometimes when I have a rotten grievance, I'll take the case up to the soop [superintendent] and let him know I won't push it hard.[23]

In some extreme examples, union stewards have led (or offered to lead) wildcat strikes when their foremen did not receive a promotion to a higher position.[24]

Sympathetic relationships are aided when the foreman and the union steward realize that they both occupy marginal positions within their own organization. For example, many foremen do not have full authority to resolve grievances at the first step because other management officials, concerned with the precedential impacts of grievance decision, like to be continually informed of related supervisory activities.

In some cases, higher level managers second guess the initial handling of the grievance, and might overturn the foreman's decision.[25] This practice typically makes the foreman look foolish and weakens his or her authority in the organization.[26]

Union stewards have also experienced this situation in contract administration. On the other hand, constituents expect their union steward to actively press every grievance, reasoning that the union's sole purpose is to represent its members. Consequently, it is difficult for the union steward to accept the foreman's first-step rejection of the grievance, even if he or she feels the foreman is correct. On the other hand, union officials receiving the grievance in subsequent steps of the grievance procedure tend to view the union steward as either ignorant of the labor agreement or gutless.

The preceding varieties of interpersonal relationships reveal how the *real* grievance procedure varies from that typically outlined in labor agreements.[27] Individual objectives, strategies, and personalities force the contractual procedure to be more flexible in practice. More importantly, as discussed in the following section, the process's numerous interacting relationships and human elements make it difficult to process grievances in accordance with theoretical industrial relations principles.

Effective Grievance Procedures: Theory versus Practice

The Clinical Approach Some students and practitioners of labor relations feel that a clinical rather than a legalistic approach to grievance resolution is most appropriate. The former approach attempts to uncover all of the causes of the employee's grievance, whereas the latter approach goes strictly by the labor agreement in determining whether a contractual violation has occurred. To be sure, the clinical approach can be regarded as more humane and fair. However, it has several limitations.

First, the labor agreement seldom considers issues of fairness and equity. For example, a provision found in most labor agreements allows management to require the junior employee (one having the least amount of seniority) in the work classfication to work an overtime assignment if it is refused by the senior employees. But if the junior employee had previous plans for the evening of the overtime assignment, he or she might refuse to work. Refusal may mean suspension, say for two days, for failure to follow reasonable work orders. This same employee could then file a grievance protesting the suspension.

The clinical approach to grievance resolution would attempt to uncover any unique motivations for the employee's refusal and might even resolve the grievance in his or her favor. However, current managers, being justifiably concerned with precedent, would be reluctant to allow the employee's insubordination to go unnoticed, particularly since the employee acted in clear violation of the labor agreement.

The clinical approach also implies that management's grievance answer will be thorough and specifically tailored to the employee's unique grievance. Any employee who files a grievance after careful deliberation and personal soul-searching expects more than the following three-word grievance answer: "No contract violation." However, management officials have long since learned that the time for a lengthy discussion is in the grievance meeting, not in the written grievance answer. The rationale for this belief is that a wordy grievance answer can often give the union ammunition not only for the specific grievance in question but for other grievances as well. Thus, while few individuals would argue with the principles and objectives of the clinical approach, its limitations have caused industrial grievance administration to become more legalistic.

Adherence to Procedures and Participants' Roles A second principle of effective contract administration requires that the grievance procedures and roles of participants be clearly defined and followed. Each party to a grievance should know the others' corresponding roles and responsibilities, and the time limits for grievance resolution should be clearly spelled out and honored. Practical obstacles to fulfilling this requirement occur when the labor agreement requires the first-line supervisor to treat the union steward as an organizational equal in the grievance process. It is difficult for a foreman, accustomed to giving daily work orders to the union steward, to turn around in a grievance meeting and consider the union steward as a peer. Some foremen can accept this situation; others, subscribing to one or more of the following beliefs, have problems:

This guy, Walker (union steward) here, doesn't realize that the gang is kidding him. They haven't got anything to kick about. All the stuff he is bringing up is old stuff. We've gone over it before with the other representatives. The other representative was sick of the job and gave it up. So the gang decided to elect this squirt because nobody else wanted the job. This fellow doesn't know anything about the department. He's only been there three months. He's only a kid and doesn't know what it's all about. I haven't got time to rehash this all over again. . . . He's not qualified to talk about anything that happens in my department, and I haven't got time to waste with him. He brings up all this stuff and nonsense just so he can be a big shot.[28]

This principle also suggests that first-line supervisors should have authority for resolving grievances at the first step of the procedure in order to give the employee a prompt, responsive answer.[29] In addition to promptness, supervisory resolution of grievance at the first step can help prevent the plantwide precedents that are established in the third step of the grievance meeting. However, other management officials, who prefer to be kept informed on employee grievances, instruct the supervisors to inform the industrial relations representative of the situation before taking any action. Being alert to this situation, the union steward will often bypass the supervisory middleman, taking the grievance directly to the industrial relations representative. Thus the advantages of supervisory resolution of grievances go untried.

Unfortunately, for various reasons, many first-line supervisors are quite willing to abdicate their supervisory authority in this area. Realistically, they see little direct reward (like pay increases) for effectively resolving grievances at the first step. Conversely, if a production problem occurs on the shop floor when the supervisor is in the office discussing an employee's grievance, he or she often faces a managerial reprimand.

Grievance procedures usually indicate the time limits in which an employee can file the grievance after discovering the alleged infraction and require a timely answer by management officials. In addition, appeal to each higher grievance step must be within prescribed time limits. For example, the employee may have five days in which to file a grievance, and management may have to furnish its first-step grievance answer within five days after receiving it. Upon receiving management's first-step answer, the grievant might have five days to appeal to the second step. If it isn't sent to the second step within that contractually specified time period, the grievance is considered resolved.

Adhering to time limits benefits the union as well as management. The grievant desires a prompt resolution. However, one related study found that the length of time elapsing between an employee's initial grievance and the arbitrator's decision averages 242 days.[30] Similarly, grievances that are ignored or grievance procedures that contain no time limits could hurt management—the union could hold or delay grievances until it thought management was more vulnerable. However, time limits are difficult if not impossible to realize because the number of individuals who must be present at any one of the grievance steps poses extreme scheduling problems (for example, around vacations and different work shifts).

Individual, Objective Consideration of Each Grievance The third and final principle of effective grievance procedures requires that each grievance be considered on its individual merits. The grievant wishes to receive an answer uncolored by any political or tactical concerns, but the union must consider political influence and overall strategy in its determination of which grievances will be filed and pursued. Not all grievances are clear-cut issues; in fact, many involve rather confusing and somewhat opposing interpretations of the labor agreement. In these cases, management has two options—decide the grievance in the employee's favor or appeal the grievance to arbitration. The latter alternative is not always very attractive, particularly if management realizes there is little contractual guidance in the issue (as in the example on the holiday scheduling of a crane operator) and insufficient past practice or precedent to support the decision. There are many gray areas in contract administration which are open to interpretation. This uncertainty is compounded when the parties solicit a neutral party to resolve the issue in binding arbitration. Also, the arbitrator's decision might refute management's action in terms that further erode management's discretion in future matters. Unions also tend to use arbitration only as a last resort because several arbitration cases can drain the union's treasury.

In these instances, flexibility may be possible with the addition of an informal *third and one-half step* in the grievance procedure. This step is not found in the grievance procedure specified in the labor agreement. It occurs after management's "final" third-step decision but before the arbitrator hears the grievance. During the third and one-half step meetings, management and union representatives meet to discuss and trade grievances, dispatching several cases originally scheduled for arbitration. Usually the grievances involved in the negotiated package are settled without prejudice to either party's position in future related issues. This statement preserves management's discretion on these issues and the union's right to file future related grievances.

Opponents of this practice contend that valid employee grievances are bargained away for an expedient settlement. Grievance trading in the third and one-half step can also discourage first-line supervisors from actively trying to resolve grievances if they believe their efforts will be overturned in a mass grievance settlement. For example, the following remarks were made by a foreman who had sent an employee home for repeated tardiness. The employee filed a grievance with the foreman's supervisor, who sent the employee back on the job.

I went over to O'Brien's (the superintendent's office) to find out why he had overruled me. He handed me a line of salve about "having to do it." Said "it was a small item after all" and that he "might want a big favor from the union sometime in the future." He said, "We have to trade back and forth. Sometimes we give in; sometimes they give in. That's why we never have any big trouble!" Then he said he might have to reverse some of my decisions again sometime, but if he did, not to get sore about it, because he wouldn't mean no offense by it. Well damn that noise! If O'Brien wants to make me look like a fool every time I make a decision, why by God, he can make all the decisions. You know two can play that game. I can give the boys (workers) every damn thing he can give them. Then when they come up with a big one that I know damn well he can't give them, I'll tell 'em to take it up to him.[31]

As a result of management using the third and one-half step in the grievance procedure, unions might be encouraged to file more grievances in the belief that they can obtain more from a trade involving fifty fabricated grievances than they can from five legitimate ones. Furthermore, those settlements "without prejudice" can result in more grievances of the same sort since the issues are not considered jointly resolved by management or union officials.

Advocates state that this process merely represents another legitimate cooperative effort between labor and management officials in efficiently dealing with day-to-day administrative problems. These individuals indicate that the union's and management's organizational self-interests require considerations and possible use of the third and one-half grievance trading session.

The Legal "Fair Representation" Obligation in the Grievance Procedure

Thus far we have discussed grievance procedures from the perspectives of the union, management, and employee participants. As is true with most labor relations activities, grievance resolution can be strongly influenced by the fourth participant, the government. The union is legally obligated to represent fairly all of the bargaining unit employees, union members and non-union members alike. This section focuses on the extent of the union's obligation, particularly when some of the bargaining unit employees believe the union has acted in an unsatisfactory manner.

The fair representation issue is one of the most difficult to resolve. On the one hand, there must be some sacrifice of individual freedom if the union organization wishes to effectively represent its members. However, the individual member's right to dissent must also be protected, and all employees represented must be safe from negligent or corrupt representatives.[32] The Railway Labor Act and the National Labor Relations Act add to this issue's complexity, since they do not contain any explicit provisions obligating the union to represent fairly all bargaining unit employees.[33]

Fair representation has been subsequently interpreted by the courts. Related decisions have reasoned that the purpose of labor legislation, industrial peace, imposes on the union the duty of fair representation.[34] While unions cannot completely ignore certain bargaining unit employees, the following question remains: How far must the union go in representing employees whose interests or claims could potentially disrupt union goals and policies? The importance of this question is magnified when we consider that there are many decisions which help some members while hurting others. However, if unions were required to process contradictory claims, nothing would be accomplished.

One such double-edged issue is seniority. Union actions pertaining to this issue (such as merging seniority rosters and calculating seniority credits for employees returning from the armed services) will hurt some bargaining unit members while helping others. Not surprisingly, two Supreme Court cases involving fair representation concerned the seniority issue.[35] These decisions indicated that the union must consider all employees and make an honest effort to serve the interests of all members without hostility to any.[36] However, the decisions also realized that unions cannot effectively operate if they must press every unit member's concern to the fullest:

Inevitably, differences arise in the manner and degree to which the terms of any negotiated agreement affect individual employees and classes of employees. The mere existence of such differences does not make them invalid. The complete satisfaction of all who are represented is hardly to be expected. A wide range of reasonableness must be allowed a statutory bargaining representative in serving the unit it represents, subject always to complete good faith and honesty of purpose in the exercise of its discretion.[37]

Thus, the union satisfies its fair representation obligation in collective bargaining and enforcing the labor agreement if it considers all members and takes its ultimate position honestly, in good faith, and without hostility or arbitrary discrimination.

These rather broad guidelines were also applied in another landmark Supreme Court decision, *Vaca v. Sipes*, which considered the union's fair representation obligation in the grievance procedure. A bargaining unit employee claimed that the union "arbitrarily, capriciously and without just or reasonable reason or cause" refused to take his grievance to arbitration. The employee, a long-term high blood pressure patient, returned to work after a sick leave and was judged by the company's doctor as being unfit for reemployment. The employee's personal physician as well as a second doctor indicated that the employee was fit for work; therefore, the employee asked the union to seek his reinstatement through the grievance procedure. The grievance was processed; however, the union, in attempting to strengthen its case before going to arbitration, sent the employee to a third doctor. The third doctor did not support the employee's position; therefore, the union refused to take the employee's case to arbitration.

The Supreme Court decided that the union, in this case, acted in good faith and was neither arbitrary, nor discriminatory.[38] It also indicated (in this and in another case):

- ☐ The employee has the burden of proof in establishing that the union breached its fair representation obligation.
- ☐ Fair representation does not require the union to take every grievance to arbitration, since this would create an intolerable expense for union and management, and would destroy the effectiveness of the lower steps in the grievance procedure.[39]

Currently, fair representation poses two difficult questions to the union and employer. First, *what are specific types of conduct that constitute violation of the fair representation duty?* As previously noted, the Supreme Court has given only broad bench marks ("arbitrary," "bad faith," "dishonest," and so on). Sometimes these guidelines can be rather easily applied; for example, a union refusing to process grievances of any black, female, or nonunion employees.[40] Other cases can become more complicated. The union, while not obligated to take every grievance to arbitration, has an obligation to consider the merits of the grievance[41] and effectively use the grievance procedure. In some cases the courts have determined that union "negligence" or "perfunctory conduct" (simply going through the motions) makes the union liable for breach of fair representation.[42] Related actions include:

- Providing inadequate defense of the grievant at an arbitration hearing.
- Delaying grievance processing until the time limits in the grievance procedure have expired.
- Failing to inform the grievant that the union accepted a different remedy than that asked for by the grievant.[43]

The judicial interpretation of "negligence" in grievance administration is often subjective which might place an unrealistic burden on the union organization.

. . . to suggest that union representation should approximate the standard of a lawyer to a client, is asking more than can be reasonably expected in a system of industrial self-government generally carried out by employees and laymen not trained in law.[44]

A typical union steward lacks legal training and is a working department member who is usually elected by other departmental employees. In many cases, stewards are elected on their popularity, not on their ability to interpret and process grievances. Any attempt by the union leaders to appoint union stewards on the basis of their competence will probably be strongly resisted by the employees, who maintain that they have the right to select their own work group representatives.[45]

A second question is *What can the employer do to avoid liability when the union breaches fair representation?* Employees currently can sue the union and the employer for breach of the labor agreement including fair representation under Section 301 of the National Labor Relations Act. Assume, for example, that an employee is discharged, then later establishes that the union breached its duty of fair representation. The employer can also be liable under this suit and might have to reinstate the employee with back pay, even though the union was responsible for bungling the grievance.[46]

Needless to say, employers do not like this situation. To avoid subsequent liability, the employer has to closely monitor the union to make sure that it presents a competent case. Managers believe that they should not be held accountable for the union's errors, particularly since management is legally prohibited from dealing in the internal affairs of the union.[47]

Summary and Implications

Summary

Employee grievances and grievance administration extends collective bargaining by giving dynamic meaning to the negotiated terms of the labor agreement. Grievances are broadly defined as any employee's concern over a perceived violation of the labor agreement which is submitted to the grievance procedure for eventual resolution.

An employee might file a grievance for any of various reasons, such as to protest a contractual violation, to draw attention to a problem in the plant, to get something for nothing, or to feel more important. Regardless of motives for filing grievances, management must process them through the grievance procedure specified in the labor agreement.

Although no one grievance procedure applies to all labor-management relationships, a representative four-step grievance procedure was presented. Two of its important aspects are inclusion of higher level management and union personnel at each successive step and, particularly in the private sector, a final step involving binding arbitration by a third-party neutral.

The grievance procedure as actually carried out involves a variety of social relationships (codified, power, and sympathetic) enacted among the grievance participants in resolving the grievance according to appropriate contractual provisions. The variety of personalities and motives of the participants also makes it difficult to effect three rather lofty principles of grievance procedures: a clinical rather than a legalistic approach should be followed, the grievance participants' roles and grievance procedures should be clearly spelled out in the labor agreement, and each grievance should be decided on its own merit.

Unions have a legal obligation to fairly represent their members in the grievance procedure. While unions do not have to take each grievance to arbitration they must consider and process grievances in an effective, "good faith" manner. Legal complications can arise when the courts determine whether the union was "negligent" in grievance handling, and whether the employer should be financially liable for this activity.

Implications

Grievances are of great concern to employees and unions because of the time and emotions involved, and the possibility that grievances will modify labor-management relationships as well as provisions in the labor agreement. However, concern over grievances and related research should not focus solely on various grievance statistics such as number of grievances filed in a year. While these figures can be translated into costs such as time spent on grievance resolution, they give little insight into supervisory effectiveness or the quality of labor management relationships.

. . . it is possible to conceive, for example, of a seriously disturbed department having a low grievance rate simply because the parties ignored the formal procedure. It is also possible to imagine a low rate in which management had largely abdicated, leaving little or nothing for the union to grieve. The interpretation of any given grievance rate or any given grievance rate difference requires analysis in depth and not a glance at the figures.[48]

It is unrealistic to compare grievance statistics when there can be much qualitative variation among grievances.

. . . the kinds of issues which may be called an employee grievance are extremely varied in content and significance for the organization concerned. At one extreme they may affect only a single individual, have nothing to do with union-management agreements and have no implications for general company policies. The whole process consists of no more than the raising of a question and the provision of a satisfactory answer. At the other extreme is the opposite of all these conditions: groups of workers, a challenge to the interpretation of a prior union agreement or management decision manifesting itself in a process which grows to include increasing numbers of people and results in highly disruptive actions before being settled.[49]

There do appear to be two potentially valuable research areas into employee grievances. One might focus on *grievance impact* on union and management officials and on subsequent labor agreement negotiations. The impact of grievances can be measured in terms of the number and types of employees who are aware of the grievance, and the behaviors and attitudes of the parties involved in resolving the grievance. This impact can also be assessed in terms of subsequent grievance outcomes, such as defeat of a union official in an election or new language in the labor agreement.

Another research area concerns the *factors associated with effective grievance resolution*. Effective grievance resolution depends on the organization, leadership, and policies of management and the union.[50] Conceivably, investigation into this area might result in innovative grievance resolution procedures which operate to the satisfaction of managers, union representatives, and employees.[51]

Discussion Questions

1. There is a thin line differentiating employee grievances and employee complaints. Discuss the problems involved in defining a grievance, indicating why a broad definition of employee grievances is both confusing and necessary.
2. Discuss two reasons grievances might be filed, furnishing examples of these reasons other than those found in the text.
3. Why does a grievance procedure have so many steps, since the employee is either right or wrong, and a one- or two-step procedure would save time and money? In your answer, discuss the various functions, opportunities, and problems each of the grievance steps can offer.
4. Formulate three rather specific ways the "real" grievance procedure can differ from the grievance procedure established in the labor agreement.
5. Why is it difficult for union and management officials to resolve each grievance on its own merits?
6. Briefly discuss the broad judicial guidelines concerning unions' fair representation obligations to members. Also discuss the reasoning behind these guidelines, furnishing some appropriate examples.

References

[1]Leonard R. Sayles and George Strauss, *The Local Union*, rev. ed. (New York: Harcourt, Brace & World, 1967), p. 50.

[2]W. W. Ronan et al., "Three Studies of Grievances," *Personnel Journal* 55 (January 1976), pp. 33–38.

[3]Joseph Kovner and Herbert Lahne, "Shop Society and the Union," *Industrial and Labor Relations Review* 7 (October 1953), p. 6. See also Joel Seidman et al., *The Worker Views His Union* (Chicago: University of Chicago Press, 1958), pp. 182–183.

[4]George Getschow, "Aggrieved over Grievances: Revised Complaint System Raises Tension in Coal Mines, Will Be Issue in 1977 Talks," *Wall Street Journal*, March 4, 1977, p. 30.

[5]Steven Briggs, "The Grievance Procedure and Organizational Health," *Personnel Journal* 60 (June 1981), p. 471.

[6]H. A. Enochs, "Essentials of Labor Agreements," *Personnel Journal* 14 (January–February 1936), p. 247.

[7]Bureau of National Affairs Inc., *Basic Patterns in Union Contracts* (Washington, D.C.: Bureau of National Affairs, 1979), p. 11.

[8]For insights into the variety of grievance procedures, see A.W.J. Thomson and V. V. Murray, *Grievance Procedures* (Westmead, England: Saxon House, 1976).

[9]United Automobile Workers, *Shop Steward Manual* (n.p., n.d.), pp. 10–11.

[10]*AFL-CIO Manual for Shop Stewards* (Washington, D.C.: AFL-CIO, March 1971), p. 36.

[11]Walter E. Baer, *Grievance Handling: 101 Guidelines for Supervisors* (New York: American Management Association, 1970), p. 53.

[12]William Karpinsky, "Front-Line Contract Administration," *Personnel* 33 (January 1957), p. 384.

[13]William F. Dowling, Jr., and Leonard R. Sayles, *How Managers Motivate: The Imperatives of Supervision* (New York: McGraw-Hill, 1971), p. 350.

[14]*AFL-CIO Manual for Shop Stewards* (n.p., n.d.), p. 37.

[15]John A. Patton, "The First Line Supervisor: Industry's Number One Problem," *Business Management* 40 (September 1971), p. 38. See also Ken Jennings, "Foremen's Views of Their Involvement with the Union Steward in the Grievance Process," *Labor Law Journal* 25 (September 1974), p. 541.

[16]Delbert C. Miller and William Form, *Industrial Sociology*, 2d ed. (New York: Harper & Row, 1964), p. 401.

[17]International Chemical Workers' Union, *Handbook for Union Stewards* (n.p., n.d.), pp. 31–32.

[18]United Glass and Ceramic Workers of North America, *So You're a Grievanceman!* (n.p., n.d.), p. 15.

[19]James W. Kuhn, *Bargaining in Grievance Settlement* (New York: Columbia University Press, 1961), p. 29.

[20]Sayles and Strauss, *The Local Union*, p. 16.

[21]Miller and Form, *Industrial Sociology*, pp. 401–402.

[22]Robert Kahn et al., *Organizational Stress* (New York: Wiley, 1964), p. 61.

[23]Melville Dalton, "Unofficial Union-Management Relations," *American Sociological Review* 15 (October 1950), p. 613.

[24]Ibid.

[25]Kuhn, *Bargaining*, p. 19; and, Charles Myers and John Turnbull, "Line and Staff in Industrial Relations," in Joseph Litterer, ed., *Organizations: Structure and Behavior* (New York: Wiley, 1966), p. 313.

[26]Ross Stagner and Hjalmar Rosen, *Psychology of Union Management Relations* (Belmont, Calif.: Wadsworth, 1965), p. 62.

[27]Sayles and Strauss, *The Local Union*, p. 22.

[28]Paul Pigors, "The Old Line Foreman," in Austin Grimshaw and John Hennessey, Jr., eds., *Organizational Behavior* (New York: McGraw-Hill, 1960), p. 98.

[29]Robert McKersie and William M. Shropshire, Jr., "Avoiding Written Grievances: A Successful Program," *Journal of Business* 24 (April 1962), pp. 135–152. See also William B. Werther, Jr., "Reducing Grievances through Effective Contract Administration," *Labor Law Journal* 25 (April 1974), p. 212.

[30]Pearce Davis and Gopal C. Pati, "Elapsed Grievance Time: 1942–1972," *Arbitration Journal* 29 (March 1974), p. 21.

[31]Melville Dalton, "The Role of Supervision," in Arthur Kornhauser, Robert Dubin, and Arthur Ross, eds., *Industrial Conflict* (New York: McGraw-Hill, 1958), pp. 183–184.

[32]Harry H. Wellington, *Labor and the Legal Process* (New Haven, Conn.: Yale University Press, 1968), p. 129.

[33]Edward H. Nakamura, "The Duty of Fair Representation and the Arbitral Process," in Joyce M. Najita, ed., *Labor Arbitration for Union and Management Representatives* (Honolulu: Industrial Relations Center, University of Hawaii, 1976), p. 87.

[34]See for example, *Steele v. Louisville and N. R. R.* 323 U.S. 200; and Wellington, *Labor and the Legal Process*, p. 146. For a more detailed account of jurisdictional issues between the NLRB and the courts over fair representation cases see Benjamin Aaron, "The Duty of Fair Representation: An Overview," in Jean T. McKelvey, eds., *The Duty of Fair Representation* (Ithaca, N.Y.: Cornell University, 1977), pp. 8–16; and, Timothy J. Boyce, *Fair Representation: The NLRB and the Courts* (Philadelphia: The University of Pennsylvania, 1978).

[35]*Ford Motor Co. v. Huffman et al.*, 345 U.S. 320 (1953); and *Humphrey v. Moore*, 375 U.S. 335 (1964).

[36]*Ford Motor Company v. Huffman*, p. 338.

[37]Ibid. See also *Humphrey v. Moore*, p. 349.

[38]*Vaca v. Sipes*, 386 U.S. 191 (1967).

[39]*Amalgamated Association of Street, Electric Railway and Motor Coach Employees of America v. Wilson P. Lockridge*, 403 U.S. 294 (1971); and Robert J. Rabin, "The Impact of the Duty of Fair Representation Upon Labor Arbitration," *Syracuse Law Review* 29 (Summer 1978), p. 857.

[40]For an example of a relatively straightforward breach of fair representation see *Hines v. Anchor Motor Freight Inc.* 424 U.S. 554 (1976).

[41]Marvin J. Levine and Michael P. Hollander, "The Union's Duty of Fair Representation in Contract Administration," *Employee Relations Law Journal* 7 (Autumn 1981), p. 203.

[42]Jeffrey A. Swedo, "*Ruzicka v. General Motors Corporation:* Negligence, Exhaustion of Remedies, and Relief in Duty of Fair Representation Cases," *Arbitration Journal* 33 (June 1978), pp. 6–15. For a discussion of varied judicial interpretations of fair representation see Aaron, "Duty of Fair Representation: Overview," pp. 18–21; and Clyde W. Summers, "The Individual Employee's Rights under the Collective Agreement," in McKelvey, ed., *Duty of Fair Representation*, pp. 60–83.

[43]Robert W. Kopp, "The Duty of Fair Representation Revisited," *Employee Relations Law Journal* 5 (Summer 1979), pp. 6–10.

[44]Martin Wagner, "Have the Courts Extended a Sound Doctrine Too Far?," *Labor Law Journal* 33 (August 1982), p. 492.

[45]Judith P. Vladeck, "The Conflict between the Duty of Fair Representation and the Limitations on Union Self-Government," in McKelvey, ed., *Duty of Fair Representation*, p. 45.

[46]*Hines v. Anchor Motor Freight*, 424 U.S. 554 (1976), at 556. For a more detailed account of the dimensions of this activity see Paul H. Tobias, "The Plaintiff's View of '301-DFR' Litigation," *Employee Relations Law Journal* 6 (Spring 1980), pp. 510–533. For further insights see also a recent Supreme Court decision, Charles V. Bowen v. United States Postal Service et al, Bureau of National Affairs Inc., *Daily Labor Report*, no. 7 (January 11, 1983). p. 1.

[47]For a more thorough discussion of employer liability in fair representation cases see C. Paul Barker, "The Employer's Stake in the Union's Duty of Fair Representation: A Form of Liability without Fault—The Employer's Duty to Police the Handling of Employee Grievances," in Martha L. Langwehr, ed., *Labor Law Developments* (New York: Matthew Bender, 1978), pp. 61–87; Charles A. Edwards, "Employer's Liability for Union Unfair Representation: Fiduciary Duty or Bargaining Reality?" *Labor Law Journal* 27 (November 1976), pp. 686–692; and, Tracy H. Ferguson and Elia M. Desruisseaux, "The Duty of Fair Representation: Exhaustion of Internal Union Remedies," *Employee Relations Law Journal* 7 (Spring 1982), pp. 610–618.

[48]David A. Peach and E. Robert Livernash, *Grievance Initiation and Resolution: A Study in Basic Steel* (Boston: Harvard University Press, 1974), p. 145.

[49]Thomson and Murray, *Grievance Procedures*, p. 18.

[50]Peach and Livernash, *Grievance Initiation*, pp. 60–129. For possible related insights into this area, see Richard B. Peterson and David Lewin, "A Model for Research and Analysis for the Grievance Process," in Barbara D. Dennis, ed., *Proceedings of the Thirty-Fourth Annual Meeting of the Industrial Relations Research Association* (Madison, Wis.: Industrial Relations Research Association, 1982), pp. 303–312; and, Dan R. Dalton and William D. Tudor, "Antecedents of Grievance Filing Behavior: Attitude, Behavioral Consistency and the Union Steward," *Academy of Management Journal* 25 (March 1982), pp. 158–169.

[51]For insights into related procedures see Steven Briggs, "Innovative Approaches to Complaint/Grievance Resolution," *Labor Law Journal* 33 (August 1982), pp. 454–459; Mollie H. Bowers, Ronald L. Seeber, and Lamont E. Stallworth, "Grievance Mediation: A Route to Resolution for the Cost-Conscious 1980s," *Labor Law Journal* 33 (August 1982), pp. 459–466; Gordon A. Gregory and Robert E. Rooney, Jr., "Grievance Mediation: A Trend in the Cost-Conscious Eighties," *Labor Law Journal* 31 (August 1980), pp. 502–508; and, S. B. Goldberg and J. M. Brett, "An Experiment in the Mediation of Grievances," *Monthly Labor Review* 106 (March 1983), pp. 23–30.

Chapter 9 Labor Arbitration: A System of Industrial Jurisprudence

Arbitration is too important an institution to be taken for granted. We may not be able to control the future development of arbitration, but we should at least be aware of the existing state of affairs and possible future dangers.

J. Joseph Lowenberg, "An Arbitration Timebomb?" *The Arbitration Journal* 37 (March 1982), p. 53.

The previous chapter illustrated how employee grievances affect labor-management relations. In some cases, grievances that are resolved by an arbitrator have an even greater influence on labor-management relationships since the arbitrator's decision often establishes a binding precedent for similar issues.

This chapter will only consider grievance or "rights" arbitration (which interprets provisions of the existing contract); interest arbitration over terms of a new contract is discussed in Chapters 7 and 14. Arbitration is first discussed from a historical perspective; then elements of a typical arbitration proceeding and arbitrator's decision are described. Current jurisdictional issues involving the arbitrator and various government agencies are also discussed, and, finally, the process is appraised.

Development of Labor Arbitration

1865 through World War II

Arbitration was first used in the United States in 1865, but was used rarely before World War II, when it was used by the War Labor Board. In many cases employee grievances were resolved through sheer economic strength. For instance, a union desiring resolution of a particular grievance often needed to mobilize the entire work force in a strike against the employer—a difficult task—before the company would attempt to resolve the grievance. Union and management officials were legally free to ignore the arbitrator's decision if they did not agree with it.

Other factors limiting the early growth of arbitration were the relatively few unionized facilities and the vague language found in labor agreements, which gave little contractual guidance for the arbitrator's decision. Consequently, the early arbitration process combined elements of mediation and humanitarianism in an effort to reach a *consensus decision*, one that would be accepted by both parties to a grievance. The arbitrator under these circumstances had to draw on diplomatic and persuasive abilities to convince the parties the decision should be accepted.

Arbitration's popularity increased during World War II, when President Roosevelt's Executive Order 9017 provided for final resolution of disputes interrupting work that contributed to the war effort. Essential features of this order included a no-strike, no-lockout agreement and a National War Labor Board (NWLB) comprised of four management representatives, four union representatives, and four representatives of the public—all presidential appointees. The board was to encourage collective bargaining and, if necessary, resolve disputes over the terms of the agreements.

The advent of World War II encouraged the role of arbitration in several ways. Many union and management officials realized that uninterrupted wartime production was essential and that grievance resolution was more effectively accomplished through arbitration than through strikes.[1]

The NWLB urged labor and management officials to resolve their own disputes and encouraged the parties to carefully define the arbitrator's jurisdiction in the labor agreements. Thus, the board gave any negotiated restrictions full force when deciding cases and denied arbitration where it was reasonably clear that the arbitration clauses meant to exclude a subject from arbitral review. It further defined grievance arbitration as a judicial process, thereby limiting a decision solely to the evidence presented at the hearing.[2]

Results of the NWLB's activities further popularized and enriched the arbitration process, as the board resolved some 20,000 disputes during its tenure.[3] Additionally, these efforts served as a training ground for many arbitrators, who could apply their acquired skills to the arbitration process after the war effort.

The Postwar Years

Although the use of arbitration increased during World War II, the relationship among arbitrator, management, and union officials was far from resolved. Both parties still remained legally free to ignore the arbitrator's award. In 1957, however, the Supreme Court declared in its *Lincoln Mills* decision that an aggrieved party could legally bring suit against a party that refused to arbitrate a labor dispute for violation of the labor agreement, under Section 301 of the Taft-Hartley Amendments. Thus, grievance procedures including arbitration could be subjected to judicial review, although much confusion remained over the court's role in these activities.

Either party could refuse to submit the grievance to arbitration if the labor agreement did not cover the issue in question. Some state statutes that made the agreement to arbitrate enforceable resulted in attempts to persuade the court to compel arbitration of the issue. Many courts then became involved in assessing the merits of a particular grievance and whether it should be arbitrated. These actions, of course, contradicted arbitral belief that arbitrators alone should rule on the merits of the grievance. Confusion resulted when labor and management representatives played the courts against the arbitrators in their attempts to obtain favorable decisions.

In 1960, the Supreme Court clarified and strengthened the arbitrator's role with three decisions commonly referred to as the "Trilogy." Because of their significant relationship to the arbitration process, these cases will be individually summarized.

United Steelworkers of America v. American Manufacturing Company In this case, the union brought suit in district court to compel arbitration of a grievance involving an employee who was awarded 25 percent disability pay on a permanent basis. Two weeks after this determination the union filed a grievance charging the employee was eligible according to the seniority provisions of the labor agreement to return to the job. Management contended that the grievant was physically unable to perform the job and that this type of dispute was not arbitrable under their labor agreement. After reviewing the merits of the grievance, both the district court and court of appeals upheld management's action. However, the Supreme Court noted that there were no explicit restrictions placed on arbitration in the labor agreement; therefore, the grievance procedure should be given "full play" in the resolution of the dispute. Accordingly, the Supreme Court reversed the lower courts' decisions with the following reasoning:

The function of the court is very limited when the parties have agreed to submit all questions of contract interpretation to the arbitrator. It is confined to ascertaining whether the party seeking arbitration is making a claim which on its face is governed by the contract. Whether the moving party is right or wrong is a question of contract interpretation for the arbitrator. . . .

The courts, therefore, have no business weighing the merits of the grievance, considering whether there is equity in a particular claim, or determining whether there is particular language in the written instrument which will support the claim. The agreement is to submit all grievances to arbitration, not merely those which the court will deem meritorious. The processing of even frivolous claims may have therapeutic values of which those who are not a part of the plant environment may be quite unaware.[4]

United Steelworkers of America v. Warrior and Gulf Navigation Company Here, the union grieved over employee layoffs which were in part due to management's contracting out work previously performed by bargaining unit employees. The collective bargaining agreement did state that "matters which are strictly a function of management shall not be subject to arbitration." Again, both the district court and court of appeals reviewed the merits of the grievance and decided against the union on the reasoning that contracting out was within management's discretion. However, the Supreme Court decision noted that the employment relationship generates a common law born out of the experiences of a particular industrial facility. The experiences and precedents shaping this common law also clarify the often vague terms and conditions expressed in the labor agreement. The reliance on common law suggests that the labor arbitrator is more effective than the courts in interpreting and resolving a dispute over the terms of an existing labor agreement.

The labor arbitrator's source of law is not confined to the express provisions of the contract, as the industrial common law—the practices of the industry and the shop—is equally a part of the collective bargaining agreement although not expressed in it. The labor arbitrator is usually chosen because of the parties' confidence in his knowledge of the common law of the shop and their trust in his personal judgment to bring to bear considerations which are not expressed in the contract as criteria for judgment. The parties expect that his judgment on a particular grievance will reflect not only what the contract says but, insofar as the collective bargaining agreement permits, such factors as the effect upon productivity of a particular result, its consequence to the morale of the shop, his judgment whether tensions will be heightened or diminished. . . . The ablest judge cannot be expected to bring the same experience and competence to bear upon the determination of a grievance, because he cannot be similarly informed.[5]

In assessing the exclusion from arbitration provisions, the Supreme Court interpreted "strictly a function of management" to mean that in which the contract expressly "gives management complete control and unfettered discretion." This issue would not have been arbitrable had there been an explicit statement excluding contracting out from the arbitration process. Since there was no related contractual language, the Supreme Court believed the arbitrator (not the lower courts) should resolve the contracting out issue.

United Steelworkers of America v. Enterprise Wheel and Car Corporation The preceding two decisions underscored the arbitrator's role in interpreting the labor agreement, particularly in determining whether the grievance should be arbitrated. However, the role of the arbitrator in fashioning an appropriate grievance remedy remained unsettled. This decision concerned a grievance over management's dismissal of a group of employees who walked out of the plant to protest the discharge of another employee. Management refused to arbitrate the grievance; however, the district court, considering the union's suit under Section 301, ordered the case arbitrated. Eventually, the arbitrator determined that the employees should be reinstated to their jobs with back pay for all but ten days (to be considered as a disciplinary suspension). Management, noting that the labor agreement had expired before the arbitrator's decision was rendered, challenged the arbitrator's authority to fashion the reinstatement remedy. While the district court compelled compliance with the remedy, the court of appeals furnished advice as to what would constitute an appropriate remedy. Justice Douglas, in writing the Supreme Court's opinion, drew upon the previous decision and indicated the relatively superior knowledge arbitrators have in resolving industrial disputes:

A mere ambiguity in the opinion accompanying an award, which permits the inference that the arbitrator may have exceeded his authority, is not a reason for refusing to enforce the award. Arbitrators have no obligation to the court to give their reasons for an award. To require opinions free of ambiguity may lead arbitrators to play it safe by writing no supporting opinions. This would be undesirable for a well reasoned opinion tends to engender confidence in the integrity of the process and aids in clarifying the underlying agreement. Moreover, we see no reason to assume that this arbitrator has abused the trust the parties confided in him and has not stayed within the areas marked out for his consideration. It is not apparent that he went beyond the submission.[6]

In summary, the Supreme Court Trilogy greatly enhanced the authority and prestige of the arbitrator in interpreting the terms of the labor agreement and determining whether the issue is appropriate for arbitration. It also endorsed the arbitrator as most qualified to fashion an appropriate grievance remedy, with the qualification that the arbitrator has the express obligation to base the decision on the essence of the labor agreement. The courts remain available to a party contesting the arbitrator's jurisdiction, but doubts about the scope of the arbitration clause are usually resolved in favor of the arbitrator. To justify judicial intervention, the parties' intentions to exclude a matter from arbitration must be expressed in clear and unambiguous language in the labor agreement or a supplemental agreement.

Some Recent Court Decisions The Supreme Court has recently determined that the obligation to arbitrate a grievance cannot be nullified by the termination of a labor agreement. Management representatives in this case argued that arbitration is a feature of the contract which ceases to exist when a contract terminates; therefore, a grievance cannot be processed to arbitration if the labor agreement is no longer in effect. Consequently, management representatives felt that the issue of severance pay was not subject to arbitration since the labor agreement had expired and management had decided to permanently close its operations. However, the Supreme Court indicated that arbitration was still appropriate:

While the termination of the collective-bargaining agreement works an obvious change in the relationship between employer and union, it would have little impact on many of the considerations behind their decision to resolve their contractual differences through arbitration. The contracting parties' confidence in the arbitration process and an arbitrator's presumed special competence in matters concerning bargaining agreements does not terminate with the contract. Nor would their interest in obtaining a prompt and inexpensive resolution of their disputes by an expert tribunal. Hence, there is little reason to construe this contract to mean that the parties intended their contractual duty to submit grievances and claims arising under the contract to terminate immediately on the termination of the contract; the alternative remedy of a lawsuit is the very remedy the arbitration clause was designed to avoid.[7]

Another issue resolved by the Supreme Court in recent years concerns how far the courts are willing to go in enforcing the role of the arbitrator. More specifically, what happens when one party is willing to arbitrate a grievance while the other party prefers to use the strike or lockout in order to resolve a dispute? As previously mentioned, a strike was a plausible alternative in resolving a grievance in the early years of arbitration. Also, the Trilogy did not specifically consider this alternative in its conclusions.

The award enforceability issue was brought before the courts in 1969 when a union protested a work assignment given to non-bargaining unit personnel. The union expressed its concern by striking even though the labor agreement contained a provision for arbitrating disputes over the terms of the agreement. In federal district court, management officials stressed that the union should use the contractually specified arbitration procedure and be enjoined from striking the employer. In its *Boy's Market* decision, the Supreme Court enforced injunctive relief in spite of the contrary philosophy of the Norris–La Guardia Act:

Indeed, the very purpose of arbitration procedures is to provide a mechanism for the expeditious settlements of industrial disputes without resort to strikes, lockouts, or other self-help measures. This basic purpose is obviously largely undercut if there is no immediate, effective remedy for those very tactics that arbitration is designed to obviate. . . .

. . . the central purpose of the Norris–La Guardia Act to foster the growth and viability of labor organizations is hardly retarded—if anything, this goal is advanced by a remedial device that merely enforces the obligation that the union freely undertook under a specifically enforceable agreement to submit disputes to arbitration.[8]

Elements of a Typical Arbitration Proceeding

Selection and Characteristics of Arbitrators

The Supreme Court has encouraged the use of arbitration, contending that this essentially private process is best suited to labor relations issues and to the unique needs of the parties at a particular facility. This means there are no universally applicable rules concerning arbitration hearings. For example, the number of participants (even arbitrators) can vary; also, the location of the hearing might be at the production facility, a hotel room, or a courtroom. There are, however, some considerations and procedures which are common to most, if not all, arbitration hearings.[9]

First, the number of arbitrators needed to resolve a grievance must be determined. Sometimes the labor agreement specifies a three-member arbitration board or panel with management and the union each nominating a member and these two individuals selecting the third member (the impartial arbitrator). Most decisions are made by the impartial arbitrator since the other two members of the panel are influenced by their respective management and union constituents. The most common method is to avoid the panel approach—the impartial arbitrator selected by management and union officials is solely responsible for the decision and obtains no help from other individuals in formulating the written decision. In either case, the arbitrator's decision is final and binding unless, in extremely rare circumstances, both management and the union agree to disregard or set aside the arbitrator's award.

About 6 percent of the labor agreements in the United States provide for a *permanent arbitrator* or umpire to resolve all disputes during the life of the labor agreement.[10] Usually, this provision applies to large companies or industries, in which it is anticipated that a large number of grievances will be filed. Presumably, the permanent arbitrator can better allocate and schedule time to meet the grievance load of the union and employer, so that settlements can be reached more promptly. This type of selection arrangement also allows the permanent arbitrator to become more knowledgeable of the rather complex and unique terms of the parties' labor agreement and industrial operation. Assume, for example, that an arbitrator is hearing a grievance in the railroad industry for the first time. How long would it take for the arbitrator to accurately interpret the meaning of the following witness's testimony?

At 3 P.M. Mott Haven Yard was a busy place. A crew of gandy dancers tamped methodically on a frong near the switching lead. L.S. 3 was all made up and ready to be doubled over. She had forty-six hog racks on the head end and sixty-five empty reefers on the hind end. Her crew were all new men on the run. Mike Madigan, the hog-head, had just been set up. Bill Blanchard, the fire-boy, was a boomer who had recently hired out. Jack Lewis, the brains of the outfit, had been a no bill since he was fired out of the Snakes for violating Rule "G." Brady Holms, the

flagman, used to work the high iron in a monkey suit, and J. B. Wells was a "stu" brakeman, right off the street. Over on the hump lead, the yard rats were riding 'em in the clear and typing 'em down. The east side switcher was kicking loaded hoppers around, despite the violent washouts of the yardmixer who had discovered a hot box. Two Malleys were on the plug and three more were at the coal pocket. Our train, Number B.D. 5, was all ready to pull out.[11]

A permanent arbitrator saves time and expense since the parties do not have to repeatedly explain the unique meaning and implications of these terms in the arbitration hearing. Greater consistency can be attained where one individual applies the same decision-making criteria to all of the arbitrated grievances. Consistent decisions aid union and management officials in the day-to-day administration of the labor agreement. They also should enable the parties to better predict the permanent arbitrator's subsequent decisions on similar issues, perhaps decreasing the number of frivolous grievances referred to arbitration as the parties become more certain of the arbitrator's reasoning. On the other hand, a retainer paid to the permanent arbitrator might encourage the parties to increase the grievance case load so that they can "get their money's worth."

Most labor agreements indicate that the arbitrator will be selected on an *ad hoc*, or case-by-case, basis; union and management representatives choose an arbitrator for a specific grievance, then select other arbitrators for subsequent grievances arising during the life of the labor agreement.[12] Particularly in the case of an established collective bargaining relationship, management and the union often reach an informal agreement regarding the appropriate arbitrator for a particular grievance. However, if they cannot agree, they usually obtain a list of arbitrators' names from either the Federal Mediation and Conciliation Service or the American Arbitration Association. In some cases, the parties request that these organizations select the particular arbitrator.

Clearly, for unions and companies having few grievances, ad hoc arbitrators are less expensive than permanent arbitrators. Regardless of the grievance load, ad hoc arbitration offers the advantage of flexibility. Permanent arbitrators usually are appointed by the parties for a specified period of time; neither side can discontinue the appointment alone if it views the permanent arbitrator's decisions with disfavor. There is no obligation to retain the ad hoc arbitrator in future grievances if one or both sides are displeased with the award.

Since some ad hoc arbitrators specialize in particular categories of grievances, such as job classification or wage incentives, they should be better informed than the permanent arbitrator on such issues. Permanent arbitrators may be more familiar with the parties, but may have seldom encountered a particular issue in their arbitration experience. Since both types of arbitrators have comparative advantages and disadvantages, management and union officials should carefully assess their particular situation before agreeing to either selection method.

Arbitrators have many different characteristics. For example, one recent study of nearly 600 arbitrators found a wide range of arbitrators' ages (27 to 85 years). The same survey, while noting wide variations, compiled the following profile of labor arbitrators:

The profile that emerges reveals that the average arbitrator is a male in his 50s. He is likely to have several degrees, with both law and economics as areas of specialization. In the profession, part-time arbitrators predominate; the mean years of experience is 14.2. Roughly a third are educators and a fourth are attorneys. They handle about 20.3 cases a year and a majority divide their cases between the public and private sectors.[13]

Approximately 52 percent of the arbitrators in this survey had law degrees and 17 percent of the individuals had Ph.D.s[14]

Arbitrators' characteristics can be significant for at least two reasons. First, union and management officials might select an arbitrator possessing certain characteristics which, according to one study, included:

- Name recognition
- Reputation for integrity
- Geographic location[15]

Second, there is a possibility that the arbitrators' decisions could be influenced by certain characteristics, such as age of the arbitrator.[16]

Elements of the Arbitration Hearing

Prehearing briefs, highlighting the issues and positions of the parties, can be filed by management and the union representative before the arbitrator arrives at the hearing. These optional briefs, which are infrequent, vary in length from a one-page letter to an extensively footnoted document. Some arbitrators see value in the prehearing brief, but others prefer to enter the hearing in a completely unbiased manner—the only information they would like to know in advance is the general subject matter of the grievance—whether it involves discipline, work assignment, or overtime payment, for example.

The prehearing brief might backfire for the presenting party, who is subject to challenges on the assumed facts and inconsistencies that may surface in the witnesses' testimonies.[17] On the other hand, prehearing briefs can be viewed as keeping the parties honest—they must approach their contentions thoroughly and are forced to adhere to them during the arbitration proceedings.[18]

Perhaps more arbitrators would agree to the value of *prehearing stipulations*—joint union-management statements as to the issues involved and certain applicable grievance "facts." They save time in the arbitration hearing, for neither party feels obligated to repeat what the other has either previously said or agreed to in principle. Additionally, through the process of working together to stipulate the issues and facts, the parties may be able to resolve the disputes without arbitration.

The arbitration hearing, held on a date convenient to the arbitrator and parties, varies in length from one-half hour to ten or more hours. Variations also occur in the extent to which courtroom procedures and behaviors are used or required during the hearing. Usually, the union and management representatives initiate the proceedings with opening statements which establish their respective issues and contentions on the issues. They attempt to focus the arbitrator's attention on points that will be proved to the satisfaction of the arbitrator in the subsequent discussion.[19]

The *grievance issue* (or submission agreement) to be resolved in the arbitration hearing is often complex, although it may be stated with deceptive simplicity. It is usually a one-sentence question to be answered by the arbitrator's award. Typical examples are:

- Did the company violate Section VI, Part 3 of the labor agreement when it transferred S———— S———— from position of leadman to welder III?
- Was B———— B———— discharged for just cause? If not, what shall be the remedy?
- Did the duties of machinist A's job undergo a significant change, thereby allowing the company to change the wage scale?
- Did J———— J————'s off-the-job activities have a significantly adverse effect on the company to justify dismissal?

Unfortunately, the issue is not always agreed upon by union and management representatives. The holiday scheduling grievance example in Chapter 8 can illustrate the problems surrounding issue formulation. Assume, for example, that the labor agreement has two provisions pertaining to arbitration:

Article XX: Arbitration Procedures

Section 1. The arbitrator's authority is solely derived from the clear and unequivocal terms of the labor agreement.

Section 2. The arbitrator may not add to, subtract from, or otherwise modify the express terms of the labor agreement.

In this situation, the union would claim that the issue pertains to the senior janitor's entitlement to holiday pay for the time involved due to the violation of Section 1 on the day in question. Management would contend that the issue of arbitrability is at stake or, more specifically, question whether the arbitrator has the authority to hear the case and fashion a remedy in accordance with the union's desires. The determination of the specific grievance issue could take a lot of time but is important, for the nature of the issue often determines whether the grievance is upheld or denied.

The remainder of the hearing is devoted to the presentation of: (a) the opening statement by each party's spokesperson, in which the major issues are presented to the arbitrator, (b) union and management witnesses for testimony and cross-examination, (c) related evidence to support union and management contentions (such as pictures of a job site, warning letters, performance ratings, and so on), and (d) union or management exhibits and those exhibits jointly recognized (if not entirely accepted) by both parties (such as the collective bargaining agreement and the employee's written grievance). The hearing is concluded with summaries and closing statements made by the union and management representatives, which stress why their respective positions must be accepted by the arbitrator. However, closing arguments and summaries are usually not presented when the parties submit posthearing briefs.

The posthearing brief One or both parties can file a written *posthearing brief* after the arbitration proceedings have ended. This device (used approximately 42 percent of the time according to one study)[20] can be helpful when the arbitration case is very technical or complicated or includes statistical data which are difficult to explain in an oral argument.[21] In many cases, however, a posthearing brief is unnecessary if the parties have prepared and presented their cases well during the hearing.[22]

This summary of arbitration procedings does not do justice to the dynamics and reality of the hearing. Assume for example that you are an industrial relations manager charged with proving an employee deserved discharge for smoking marijuana on company premises. Related concerns are:

- How do you prove the employee actually smoked the marijuana, since the evidence was destroyed, and it is the employee's word against supervisory observations?
- Will the grievant's testimony be strengthened or broken under cross examination?
- How long can the supervisor remain calm under union cross-examination, without losing his temper?
- What if the arbitrator gives little weight to the circumstantial evidence presented by the company and a great deal of weight to the grievant's previous long and exemplary work record with the company?
- Will the union introduce a surprise contention or witness not previously discussed in the grievance proceedings (for example, that the grievant's discharge was due to the racial bias of the supervisor)?

Exhibit 9.1 Gamesmanship in Labor Arbitration

In its broadest sense, Gamesmanship may perhaps be defined as the art of winning games without seeming to indulge in unfair tactics.

As the parties assemble for the hearing, there are numerous opportunities for ploys. Let us review only a handful of the more obvious.

The Geographical Ploy

The first may be called the geographical ploy, often of no great utility but sometimes telling. The alert Gamesman will scout the hearing room carefully in advance, and if there appears to be any advantage to be gained by seating his legions on one side of the table rather than the other, he will of course arrive early for the hearing and occupy the favorable side for his *entourage*. Such items as the sun shining brightly into the opposition's eyes, or placing them in a draft, or next to hot radiators, may be involved. The opponent may have a superstitious preference for facing the arbitrator from one particular side of the table; if so, the Gamesman will of course arrange things otherwise.

The Greeting-the-Arbitrator Ploy

The arrival of the arbitrator at the hearing is a sensitive moment in some circumstances. If the Gamesman knows the arbitrator from earlier cases (and he will probably have assured himself that he does, in making his selections), he should fashion his greeting carefully.

If he knows his opponent to be a stranger to the arbitrator, and especially if the opponent is the jittery and suspicious type, there is much to be said for the Gamesman greeting the arbitrator casually by his first name.

This should not be overdone, lest the *arbitrator* get the impression that some advantage is being taken of their relationship. All that is needed is to get across to the nervous opponent the impression that the Gamesman and the arbitrator are well acquainted, accustomed to working together amicably.

Other ploys can drive the point home, always keeping in mind that blatant overtures are likely to backfire. A reference to the weather is innocuous enough, and the Gamesman may follow up with a remark to the arbitrator, in friendly and open fashion, to this effect: "This is almost as nice (or lousy) a day as we had on the case up in Wilkes-Barre; by the way, Jim and the boys on the committee send their regards."

If the opponent's eyes begin to betray signs of panic, the Gamesman may press the point a bit further, with a ploy of this sort to the arbitrator:

"We may have an interesting case coming up for you at the Zilch Metals plant next month; I sent the list back today."

The Additional Cases Ploy

This last example brings to mind a controversial subject among practicing gamesmen in the field. It has to do with what is known as the "Additional Cases Ploy." The tactic is simplicity itself—at the opening of the hearing, the would-be Gamesman loudly proposes the following:

"We have four more cases in this plant ready for arbitration. Why don't we agree right now to have Scotty Crawford here be the arbitrator on those cases too?"

Source: Lewis M. Gill, "Gamesmanship in Labor Arbitration," in Edwin R. Teple and Robert B. Moberly, eds., *Arbitration and Conflict Resolution* (Washington, D.C.: Bureau of National Affairs Inc., 1979), pp. 78–79.

Management and union officials often enter arbitration hearings emotionally charged and uncertain. They are usually skillful in establishing their respective positions to the arbitrator's satisfaction, and damaging their opponents' case by exploiting the opponents' weaknesses and uncertainties (see Exhibit 9.1). The arbitrator must also display many skills in keeping an orderly hearing while, at the same time, objectively understanding and recording all of the facts presented by the union and management representatives.

Arbitration and Judicial Proceedings Compared

The arbitration proceedings share some similarities with judicial proceedings, but their differences are profound. Many arbitration hearings differ from courtroom proceedings in that testimony of witnesses is not taken under oath and transcripts of the proceedings are also not taken. Except in a few states, arbitrators do not have the power to subpoena witnesses, and arbitrators nearly always have much more latitude than judges in determining admissibility of evidence, including, for example, hearsay testimony.

The most significant difference between the two proceses is the arbitrator's reliance on *common law of the shop* principles in the resolution of disputes. Arbitrators, unlike judges, are selected by the parties to the dispute; thus, the arbitrator's major responsibility is to resolve a dispute in a manner that the parties can live with. Unlike judicial decisions in lower courts, the arbitrator's decision is usually final and not subject to further appeals. Consequently, the arbitrator must be concerned with the subsequent effects of his decision on union-management relationships. A judge has no such allegiance to the particular parties, the major responsibility being adherence to the statute in question, to established courtroom and legal procedures, and to precedent resulting from other applicable cases.

The common law of the shop thus often narrows the scope of arbitral decision making to the labor agreement language, intent, and past practices of the union and management officials at a particular industrial facility:

A proper conception of the arbitrator's function is basic. He is not a public tribunal imposed upon the parties by superior authority which the parties are obliged to accept. He has no general charter to administer justice for a community which transcends the parties. He is rather part of a system of self-government created by and confined to the parties. He serves their pleasure only, to administer the rule of law established by their collective agreement. They are entitled to demand that, at least on balance, his performance be satisfactory to them, and they can readily dispense with him if it is not.[23]

But a good arbitrator is more than an "ad hoc judge . . . expert in analyzing issues, in weighing evidence, and in contract interpretation." He must do that in the specialized context of labor relations, in the special community of an industrial plant and a local union. To be meaningful and convincing to the parties, his decisions should impart an understanding and comprehension of that atmosphere and should convey to them the conviction that their controversy is being decided not with reference to abstractions remote from their ken but with reference to the realities which govern their day-to-day in-plant lives.[24]

The distinction between judicial reasoning and common law of the shop principles can be shown through the following example. Assume that an employee has been discharged at Company A for drinking alcohol on the job. After the arbitral decision upholding the discharge has been reached, another employee at Company B is also discharged for drinking alcohol on the job. Strict adherence to judicial principles would uphold the second employee's discharge for drinking on the job. More specifically, the judicial principle of *stare decisis* (letting the decision at Company A stand in Company B's situation) would probably disregard the differences in work environments of the two companies.

However, the common law of the shop principles governing arbitration could lead the arbitrator to render an opposite decision at Company B than that reached at Company A. For example, supervisors at Company B may have been condoning this behavior and other employees at this company may have been caught drinking on the job without being discharged for the infraction. Consequently, the arbitrator recognizes the two companies are independent, with potentially unique circumstances, and therefore deserve mutually exclusive decisions.

It is also important to note that arbitrators are much more liberal than the courts in the types of evidence permitted at the hearing.[25] Rationale for this practice is based on the notion that the parties are seeking a solution to their perceived unique problem. In addition, some arbitrators maintain that arbitration performs a therapeutic function, that the parties are entitled to air their grievances regardless of the eventual decision. Arbitrators may allow aggrieved employees to digress from the pertinent subject or "tell it like it is" in order to serve this therapeutic function.

Occasionally, evidence unknown to the other party is introduced in the arbitration hearing (either or both of the parties may introduce evidence which was not previously introduced in the pre-arbitral grievance steps). The arbitrator may accept or reject this new evidence, depending upon the weight attached to the following sometimes conflicting considerations: (a) the arbitrator's desire to learn of all the pertinent facts surrounding the grievance; (b) the need to protect the integrity of the pre-arbitral grievance machinery; and, (c) general concepts of fairness.[26] Since union and management officials and their designated arbitration panels are entitled to receive all evidence presented at the hearing, it may be necessary to allow the opposing party additional time to review and respond to new evidence.

Offers of compromise settlements before the hearing are given no weight by the arbitrator. Management officials, for example, might compromise their third-step discharge decision before arbitration by offering the grievant reinstatement with no back pay. A union could use this evidence to indicate to the arbitrator that management admitted being wrong by revising its original decision. However, arbitrators maintain that the parties should make every effort to resolve their disputes internally instead of going to arbitration. Thus, a compromise settlement between the parties is viewed by the arbitrator as a genuine attempt to accommodate differences, not an admission of guilt.

Other types of evidence are subject to varying arbitral consideration. As previously cited, hearsay testimony is usually admitted; however, it is typically given little or no weight, particularly if it is deduced that the witness has self-serving motives for testifying. Many of the more controversial sources of evidence are presented in discipline cases, which are further discussed in Chapter 10.

The Arbitrator's Decision

Characteristics and Scope

The *arbitrator's decision* is a written document submitted to the management and union officials. Its components include:

1. A statement of the issue(s).
2. A statement of the facts surrounding the grievance.
3. Pertinent provisions of the labor agreement.
4. A summary of the union and management contentions.
5. A discussion and opinion of the validity and relative weight of the facts and contentions.
6. The arbitrator's award (grievance upheld, grievance denied, or a compromise between union and management contentions.)[27]

Few proscriptive guidelines govern the form and content of the arbitrator's decision. However, the arbitrator should demonstrate through the decision a thorough understanding of all the facts and contentions raised in the arbitration hearing. Some arbitrators address the decision to the losing party in the arbitration hearing because the winner does not have to be convinced he is right.

The necessity of the arbitrator's opinion has been subjected to considerable controversy. At least one labor lawyer has suggested that the arbitrator's decision is important, not the opinion explaining the reasoning behind the decision.

I am told by arbitrators that they write opinions because parties want an explanation. As a frequent party, my response is that this is often not true. I can tell you as a practitioner in this field that . . . I turn to the award and find out whether I won or lost. If I won, I really am not concerned with why I won. If I lost, I may read the opinion in order to confirm my conviction created by the award that the arbitrator was, is, and undoubtedly will continue to be as blind as a bat and as ignorant as an ass.[28]

The contrary view maintains that the arbitrator's opinion performs a necessary function for the arbitrator and others who may read his or her decision.

Not only is an arbitrator's writing style on display in the usual opinion, but far more important is the exposure given his analytical skills, the fairness he demonstrates in evaluating the arguments of the parties, and his knowledge of the subtleties and unusual equities involved. . . . The writing of an opinion is also of tremendous value to the arbitrator. Only too often initial impressions, and even what we would consider well thought-out decisions have been modified or dramatically changed under the potent rigors involved in the discipline of writing an opinion.[29]

Additionally, the reasoning embodied in the arbitrator's opinion can serve as an instructional guideline for labor-management relationships. One arbitrator has stated:

Parties do not spend many days of preparation, three days of hearings, and thousands of dollars worth of time of important officers and attorneys, for the purpose of finding out whether one girl should or should not have gotten a trivial promotion. They are interested in principles.[30]

In some cases, the arbitrator's opinion can even be more important than the award. Assume, for example, the union grieves management's assignment of work normally performed in Job Classification A, loading trucks on Saturday, to an employee in Job Classification B, a laborer. Further, the union seeks a remedy of eight hours at overtime rate of pay for the appropriate employee in Job Classification A, the senior employee in the shipping department, on the reasoning that the company's violation of the contract had deprived a Classification A employee from the overtime opportunity. However, the arbitrator denies the grievance and stresses the following in his opinion: "The various job classifications are for pay purposes only and do not restrict management's prerogative to assign work across different job classifications." This statement significantly harms the union in related matters, particularly if the language was not expressly stated in the labor agreement. Now the union will have a difficult time in grieving any work assignment controversy, even though the above decision pertained to one specific situation.

In other situations the arbitrator's gratuitous advice in the opinion may harm one or both of the parties.[31] There is often a thin line between "consulting" management and union practitioners on more effective and humane ways to run the operation and arbitrating the grievance solely on the merits of the case. The latter approach does not advise, merely determines if management's action was justifiable under the terms of the labor agreement and applicable past practice.

Decision-Making Criteria Used by Arbitrators

There are few consensually defined principles applicable to arbitrators' decisions, as arbitrators do not follow precise or identical methods in making decisions.[32] Nonetheless, generally accepted guidelines have developed and serve as focal points subject to interpretation, consideration, and application by arbitrators in resolving grievances.

Provisions of the Labor Agreement reflect the collectively bargained rights of union and management officials. Adherence to common law of the shop principles stresses that the major function of the arbitrator is the interpretation of the labor agreement's provisions. Indeed, many arbitrators adhere at least in part to the *parol evidence rule*, which in its classic form holds that evidence, oral or otherwise, cannot be admitted for the purpose of varying or contradicting written language recorded in the labor agreement. Rationale for this rule is that the parties have spent many hours in negotiating standardized employment conditions; thus, disregarding negotiated terms would damage stable labor-management relationships and communicate to the parties that there is little or no point in reducing contract terms to writing. The *parol evidence* rule is applicable when the parties "intend that the written agreement is the final and complete integration of all the terms of the contract."[33]

A problem remains when the labor agreement language is ambiguous. For example, such terms as "reasonable," "make every effort," "minor repairs," and "maintain the work environment as safely as possible" might have resolved negotiation impasses but still pose interpretive problems for the arbitrator.

Some contract provisions which appear clear on the surface can cause differences of opinion among union and management officials as well as arbitrators. Consider the following two examples and related questions.[34]

Example 1: "The company will provide required safety equipment." Does the company have to pay for safety equipment or merely make it available for employees to purchase?

Example 2: "An employee must work on the scheduled day before and after the holiday in order to receive holiday pay." What happens when the employee works three hours the day before the holiday, goes home because of sickness, and works the full eight hours the day after the holiday?

Arbitrators prefer to approach the ambiguity problem initially in terms of the labor agreement, and ambiguous language or provisions of the labor agreement would be construed so as to be compatible with the language in other provisions of the agreement. Thus, the contract should be viewed as a whole, not in isolated parts, and any interpretation which would nullify another provision of the contract should be avoided. When ambiguity remains, the arbitrator must seek guidance from sources outside the labor agreement.[35]

Intent of the Parties refers to what union and management officials had in mind when they (1) negotiated the labor agreement or (2) engaged in an action that resulted in a particular grievance. Intent is entirely subjective; however, arbitrators consider observable behavioral manifestations of the intent to determine what a reasonable person would conclude from that behavior. For an example of the first intent, consider the previously cited holiday pay situation. To demonstrate that it intended for holiday pay to be given only to those individuals who worked a full eight hours the day before and the day after the holiday, management might supply the arbitrator with negotiation notes.

An example of the second intent might occur when a supervisor believes an employee has stolen some company property. The supervisor approaches the employee stating:

You and I both know you were caught stealing. Therefore, you have two options. You can file a grievance which will be denied in arbitration and the discharge on your record will make it difficult for you to find a job elsewhere. Or you can sign this resignation slip, quit, and we won't tell any other companies about the stealing incident.

The employee hastily signs the slip and leaves the company premises. However, the next day she returns, informing management that she wants to work, since she never really quit. If the company refuses the employee's request and a subsequent grievance is filed, the arbitrator would have to determine the grievant's and management's intent. Observable behaviors of an employee intending to quit are cleaning out the locker, saying good-bye to colleagues, and asking management for the wages earned for that week. An employee usually resigns only after giving the decision careful thought and consideration. Since none of the behaviors were operative in this case, the arbitrator might attempt to determine management's intent in this action. Possibly, the supervisor was simply trying to do the employee a favor by letting her off the hook. However, management may have given the employee the alternative of quitting to avoid subsequent arbitration of the discharge and the risk of their discharge decision being overturned. The latter intent is viewed by arbitrators as being *constructive discharge*.

Under this principle, the arbitrator would view the termination of employment as being subject to the employee discipline provisions of the labor agreement. These provisions usually call for union representation and written explanation at the time of the employee's discharge. Since these procedures were not followed, many arbitrators would reinstate the grievant with full back pay. Sometimes, union and management officials attempt to convince the arbitrator of their specific intent by producing written notes of previous discussions so that there will be documentation of their related past behaviors.

Past Practice demonstrates to the arbitrator how the parties have carried out the labor agreement.

Much of what is considered a part of the labor agreement is unwritten. As with any working relationship, the parties to a labor agreement do not specify every detail and understanding in their interactions, but rely on implicit acceptance of certain practices that have been developed over the years.[36]

This consideration has been used by both management and the union, depending upon the particular situation. Management is usually more concerned about past practice, since it administers the labor agreement through various supervisory directives to the hourly employees. Since established contractual provisions place restrictions on managerial discretion, management attempts to avoid further reductions on supervisory decision making by pressing for a past practices clause to be included in the labor agreement, similar to the following:

Article XXVIII: Other Agreements
Section 2. The parties do hereby terminate all prior agreements heretofore entered into between representatives of the company and the unions (including all past understandings, practices, and arbitration rulings) pertaining to rates of pay, hours of work, and conditions of employment other than those stipulated in this agreement between the parties.[37]

However, this clause does not guarantee that management does not add to its contractual restrictions by repeatedly handling a situation in a similar manner. For example, one arbitrator agreed with the union that a prevailing practice should be compelling in interpreting the labor agreement's ambiguity or silence on a particular issue.

The repeated execution of collective bargaining agreements which contain exclusive agreement provisions cancelling "all previous agreements" *has no magical dissolving effect* upon practices or customs which are continued in fact unabated and which *span successive contract periods.* Although not verbalized in the current agreement, such practices may nonetheless comprise a part of it *as any of its written provisions.*[32] [Emphasis added.]

Thus, a continued managerial practice of unilaterally giving employees a Christmas bonus might become a binding, implied term of the labor agreement. Further, management will likely have to negotiate a labor agreement provision to the contrary (even if the current labor agreement is silent on the subject) if they wish to discontinue the Christmas bonus in subsequent years.

In addition to interpreting ambiguous language or resolving problems not covered in the agreement, past practices may even alter clear and convincing contractual provisions. At one company, it had been a practice for many years to require clerks to perform cleanup operations at the end of their work day and to pay them no money for up to ten minutes work, fifteen minutes straight time for eleven to fifteen minutes' work, and time and one-half for work of more than fifteen minutes in duration. There was clear contractual language specifying that work in excess of eight hours per day would be computed at time and one-half overtime premium. The union eventually filed a grievance stating that clear contractual language compelled overtime payment for any amount of daily work exceeding eight hours. However, the arbitrator maintained that past practice was more significant than the express terms of the labor agreement in this case.

The written contract is, of course, the strongest kind of evidence of what the parties willed, intended or agreed upon. An arbitrator will not ordinarily look beyond its *unambiguous* language. Where, *however*, as here, the parties have *unmistakably* demonstrated *how they themselves* have read and regarded the meaning and force of the language, and *where the meaning varies* from its normal intendment, the arbitrator *should not*, indeed, *cannot* close his eyes to this demonstration.[39]

Past practice represents a specific and identical action which has been continually employed over a number of years to the recognition and satisfaction of both parties. Moreover, since there are no uniform standards of time, it is very difficult to determine for certain how long or how frequently an action must be continued before it is considered a binding past practice.

De minimis refers to a technical but insignificant violation of the labor agreement. Arbitrators using this principle might deny a grievance because of its trivial, inconsequential nature. In one related situation, the union claimed that a contractual provision prohibiting supervisors from performing bargaining unit work was violated. The supervisor in this instance adjusted the prongs of a fork lift mechanism so that it could pick up an object. The supervisory effort took no more than two seconds, as he simply kicked one of the prongs with his foot to make the distance between the prongs wide enough to pick up the object. Therefore, the arbitrator denied the grievance, stating that the union was "scratching with the chickens" on such a small and insignificant issue. To award the union this grievance would be to encourage the filing of more trivial grievances, making a mockery of the labor-management relationship.

As is true with past practice, *de minimis* is not easily defined. This principle would probably be applicable if the supervisor changed one light bulb. The union might have a legitimate grievance, however, if the supervisor changed eight light bulbs (for a time period of fifteen minutes), and if the act deprived a union member of a call-out or overtime opportunity.

Previous Arbitration Awards are frequently introduced by either party when they have been decided at the same property or at different locations and could bolster either's position in the arbitration case. Similarly, the arbitrator may cite these awards to refute the parties' contentions or to illustrate the divergent arbitral opinion over the issue. However, one study analyzing the role and effectiveness of prior arbitration awards found that arbitrators tend to either ignore or refute them in their decisions.[40] Prior arbitration awards involving other facilities are at best illuminating but they do not overide contract language or past practices at the facility in question. However arbitrators will consider other awards which focus on important principles that can be applied to the immediate case.

Thus, the common law of the shop diminishes the weight of prior arbitration awards from other properties, as arbitrators recognize the uniqueness and autonomy of a particular operation. In fact, arbitrators might negatively regard the introduction of prior arbitration awards into a current arbitration hearing:

Unwillingness to present a case solely on its own merits may come to be interpreted as a sign of weakness. Also it may be considered that citation of prior arbitration awards indicates either a lack of confidence in the judgment of an arbitrator or a belief that he may be swayed by irrelevant considerations. An attempt to induce an arbitrator to follow some alleged precedent may come to be recognized as at least bad etiquette.[41]

Prior arbitration awards presented at the same location carry more weight, particularly if the situation and contractual language are similar. Of course, few prior arbitration awards contain these elements, since the parties would be extremely reluctant to arbitrate the same issue a second time, given the first arbitrator's decision.

In summary, arbitration hearing procedures approximate courtroom behavior but depart from judicial procedures and principles in several ways. As is discussed in the next section, these differences can raise potential jurisdictional problems for various governmental agencies which are also charged with enforcing an employee's job rights.

Current Issues Affecting Arbitration: Legal Jurisdiction and Appraising Arbitration's Effectiveness

Legal Jurisdiction

Although the current role of labor arbitration has been clarified and enhanced through judicial decisions, jurisdictional problems still remain when a case heard by an arbitrator is also covered by related legislation. Consider a case in which a black union steward who filed a safety complaint, is discharged for insubordination. A subsequent grievance is filed and proceeds to arbitration under the terms of the labor agreement. However, the employee claims that the discharge was due not only to racial bias but also to the fact that the grievant filed a safety complaint in his capacity as a union steward. Conceivably, the discharge grievance could claim the attention of a number of persons—the arbitrator and representatives from the Equal Employment Opportunity Commission (EEOC), the Occupational Safety and Health Administration (OSHA), and the National Labor Relations Board (NLRB). The problem involves untangling the various jurisdictional squabbles which could arise over this one grievance.

The passage of the 1964 Civil Rights Act (amended by the Equal Employment Opportunity Act of 1972) and subsequent judicial decisions have emphasized that management's well-meant intentions are not sufficient to preclude a possible charge of racial discrimination. Indeed, in administering this aspect of public law, the EEOC holds that employers must actively devise and implement employment procedures which remove present as well as possible residual effects of past discrimination. Hiring and promotion procedures may be carefully scrutinized by the EEOC to protect minority employees from arbitrary and discriminatory practices. In a unionized facility, arbitrators also often assume a related decision-making role, particularly in grievances protesting discipline of a minority employee. This situation poses at least two questions:

1. Should management, the union, and the employee turn to the arbitrator, the EEOC, or both in resolving a minority employee's grievance?
2. How do the courts and the EEOC view the arbitrator's decision in terms of Title VII of the 1964 Civil Rights Act?

The first question was answered by a 1974 Supreme Court decision, *Alexander v. Gardner-Denver Company.* In this case, a discharged minority employee claimed racial discrimination; however, management's action was upheld by the arbitrator. Following the EEOC's subsequent determination that there was not reasonable ground to believe that a violation of Title VII of the 1964 Civil Rights Act had occurred, the employee sought relief from the alleged discriminatory action in the federal district court. This court (subsequently upheld by the court of appeals) dismissed the employee's action since the petitioner, having voluntarily elected to pursue his grievance under the nondiscrimination clause of the collective bargaining agreement, was bound by the arbitral decision and thereby precluded from suing his employer under Title VII. However, the Supreme Court reversed previous judicial decisions, finding that Title VII does not expressly permit deferral and that the arbitrator's major concern is to interpret the labor agreement, not federal law. Additionally, the Court found that the intent of Congress was to have the federal courts exercise final responsibility for the enforcement of Title VII, particularly since the arbitrator's expertise (as outlined in the previously discussed Trilogy) pertains to the interpretation of the labor agreement.

Arbitral procedures, while well suited to the resolution of contractual disputes, make arbitration a comparatively inappropriate forum for the final resolution of rights created by Title VII. This conclusion rests first on the special role of the arbitrator, whose task is to effectuate the intent of the parties rather than the requirements of enacted legislation. Where the collective-bargaining agreement conflicts with Title VII, the arbitrator must follow the agreement. To be sure, the tension between contractual and statutory objectives may be mitigated where a collective-bargaining agreement contains provisions facially similar to those of Title VII. But other facts may still render arbitral processes comparatively inferior to judicial processes in the protection of Title VII rights. Among these is the fact that the specialized competence of arbitrators pertains primarily to the law of the shop, not the law of the land. . . .

Moreover, the factfinding process in arbitration usually is not equivalent to judicial factfinding. The record of the arbitration proceedings is not as complete; the usual rules of evidence do not apply; and rights and procedures common to civil trials, such as discovery, compulsory process, cross-examination, and testimony under oath, are often severely limited or unavailable.[42]

Consequently, a minority employee is almost encouraged to pursue the arbitration process as well as appropriate judicial procedures. Arbitration (particularly cases resolved in the grievant's favor) could reduce unnecessary litigation. Also,

. . . the federal policy against discriminatory employment practices can best be accommodated by permitting an employee to pursue fully both his remedy under the grievance-arbitration clause of a collective-bargaining agreement and his cause of action under Title VII. The federal court should consider the employee's claim *de novo*. The arbitral decision may be admitted as evidence and accorded such weight as the court deems appropriate.[43]

Similar reasoning is prevalent in the Department of Labor, where an Occupational Health and Safety Administration was created to enforce Public Law 91-596, the Occupational Safety and Health Act of 1970. Section 11 (c) of the act indicates that no employer shall discharge or in any manner discriminate against any employee because such employee has either filed a safety complaint or caused a proceeding related to the Act. Thus, the secretary of labor is empowered to investigate related disciplinary action, the arbitral decision of the case notwithstanding.

Perhaps the most frequent supplements to arbitral decisions have come from the NLRB, because the grievant could have been discharged for reasons pertaining to provisions of the labor agreement which are similar to laws, such as engaging in union activities on the job or acting overly aggressive in the capacity of a union official. Section 10 (a) of the National Labor Relations Act provides that the NLRB "is empowered . . . to prevent any person from engaging in any unfair labor practice (listed in Section 8) affecting commerce. This power shall not be affected by any other means of adjustment or prevention that has been or may be established by agreement, law, or otherwise."

Although it has the power, the board does not ignore arbitration awards covering unfair labor practice issues. In fact, it often withholds its jurisdictional determination and investigation pending the arbitrator's decision. In 1955, the NLRB's deferral to arbitration policy was formulated in the *Spielberg Manufacturing Company* case. In that case, the board honored an arbitration award that denied reinstatement to certain employees guilty of strike misconduct. Resulting deferral guidelines stressed that the arbitration proceedings must be fair and regular, there must be adequate notice and representation, the arbitrator must approach the issue of the alleged unfair labor practice, and all parties must agree to be bound by the arbitration award.[44] However, the board will disregard the arbitrator's award if it is ambiguous or if the board obtains pertinent evidence not presented in the arbitration proceeding.

The NLRB's deferral to arbitration policy was enhanced in the 1971 *Collyer* case, in which the NLRB trial examiner had found that the company had committed an unfair labor practice when it made certain unilateral changes in wages and working conditions.[45] The company maintained that the issues should be resolved through existing arbitration proceedings instead of the NLRB. The board in essence agreed with the company's position. While reserving the right to investigate the merits of the issue, the board maintained that:

1. Related disputes can be better resolved through the special skills and experiences of the arbitrators.
2. The objectives of the National Labor Relations Act, industrial peace and stability, can be significantly realized through adherence to arbitration procedures established in the labor agreement.

Under *Collyer*, the employee was obligated to use the arbitration procedure before the NLRB would review the merits of the case.

Recent NLRB decisions, however, have modified the broad deferral policy established in *Collyer*.[46] More specifically, the NLRB will defer to arbitration only if the issue does not involve a dispute alleging interference with employees' Section 7 rights. Thus, the NLRB will not currently defer an issue involving discipline for union activity even if the labor agreement specifies discipline for just cause is subject to arbitration. The employee, however, has to elect the remedy, going either to arbitration or to the NLRB for relief. The NLRB has indicated in another decision (*Suburban Motor Freight*) that it "will give no deference to an arbitration award which bears no indication that the arbitrator ruled on the statutory issue of discrimination in determining the propriety of an employer's disciplinary actions."[47]

In summary, the Supreme Court has recognized the ability of arbitrators to interpret the labor agreement provisions and has even encouraged parties to arbitrate the issue before proceeding to the NLRB.[48] However, this encouragement is not given to the same extent in Title VII disputes. Additionally, governmental agencies such as EEOC, OSHA, and NLRB retain jurisdiction of a related issue and can modify an arbitrator's decision if it conflicts with their conception of public policy.

The issue of arbitral consideration of federal policy is still inconclusive. Some arbitrators believe they should only interpret labor agreements and let appropriate government agencies and the courts resolve legal aspects of their decisions. Other arbitrators believe they have an obligation to consider appropriate judicial decisions in their awards.

Appraising Labor Arbitration's Effectiveness

Although the courts have praised the effectiveness of arbitration, some critical assessments have come from the participants—union and management officials and even some arbitrators. There appear to be two general areas of criticism: the capability and ethics of the arbitrator, and potential procedural problems in the arbitration process.

The Capability and Ethics of the Arbitrator It has been contended that the arbitrator's decisions are adversely linked with financial dependence on the parties:

A proportion of arbitration awards, no one knows how large a proportion, are decided not on the basis of the evidence or of the contract or other proper considerations, but in a way which in the arbitrator's opinion makes it likely that he will be hired for other arbitration cases. It makes no difference whether or not a large majority of cases is decided in this way. A system of adjudication in which the judge depends for his livelihood, or for a substantial part of his livelihood or even for substantial supplements to his regular income, on whether he pleases those who hire him to judge is per se a thoroughly undesirable system. In no proper system of justice should a judge be submitted to such pressures. . . .

We know that a large proportion of the awards of arbitrators are rendered by incompetents, that another proportion—we do not know how large but are permitted by the circumstances to suspect that it is quite large—is rendered on the basis of what award might be best for the arbitrator's future.[49]

In some instances, union and management practitioners believe that the arbitrator "owes them one" due to their support (financial and otherwise). One arbitrator, who expressed surprise to union and management officials at being selected to replace another prominent arbitrator, was given the following reason why the previous arbitrator was fired:

"I'll tell you why we fired him. The last case he had ended here at about 4:00. Mr. ________ expressed considerable concern since he had to make a plane for New York and was running late. I assured him that he would have no problem. I carried his bags to his car, drove in excess of all the speed limits, went through back roads, even proceeded through changing traffic lights. After a hectic ride and at considerable risk, I got him to the airport just in time to make the plane. I parked my car in a no parking zone. I even carried his bags to the gate. After all this, you know, that son-of-a-bitch ruled against me."[50]

Yet other participants or students of arbitration maintain that the arbitrator's indebtedness to the parties is a necessary ingredient of dispute resolution. They maintain that the arbitrator owes allegiance to both union and management and thus is accountable rather than indebted to the parties:

The arbitrator functions in a glass bowl. The conduct of the hearing is closely observed by sophisticated, knowledgeable advocates. An arbitrator who exhibits a lack of understanding of the process and who fails to conduct a hearing in an orderly fashion will usually find himself unacceptable to the parties for a subsequent hearing. The *ad hoc* arbitrator has no tenure; an umpire has limited tenure, and nothing is so impermanent as the permanent arbitrator. . . . His decisions are read and reread, not only by the parties, but by hundreds of company and union representatives who have access to his awards through their own systems of distribution. Awards that are not based upon logical, sound interpretation of the provisions of the agreement will very quickly make the arbitrator responsible unacceptable to companies and unions alike.[51]

Other criticisms have focused on the quality of the arbitrator's decision. The arbitrator's written opinion and award dissatisfy the parties if they do not reflect the original expectations and understandings of one or both regarding the nature or scope of the grievance. But many arbitral decision problems may be attributed in large part to the union and management officials instead of the arbitrator. For example, some union and management officials ask the arbitrator to isolate and define the issues from the presentations of the case and then resolve the issue on the basis of that haphazard record. Under this situation, the officials must share the greater burden of blame if the arbitrator's decision doesn't directly and concisely resolve the particular problem.

Management and union representatives might also obtain poor arbitration awards under the *garbage in, garbage out theory*. Since the arbitrator's decision is based on the merits of the grievance, a sloppy grievance formulation and presentation might result in a relatively lackluster arbitral decision. Sometimes, union and management officials present the arbitrator with poorly conceived grievances which one of the parties could and should have resolved before going to arbitration. Such grievances are often prompted by political considerations[52]—the union or management officials take the grievance to arbitration to show support for their constituents (union stewards or first-line supervisors) even though they know them to be wrong. Arbitration in this sense serves as a buck-passing device; the errant union steward or supervisor is apparently given support but in reality is provided an education through the arbitrator's decision.

One almost inescapable concern arises from the finality of the arbitrator's award. While the Supreme Court has encouraged single-person resolution of an industrial dispute, opponents of this practice suggest that an arbitrator has more authority than a judge, whose decision may be overturned through judicial appeal. Unfortunately, there would be many problems if arbitration awards were subjected to an appeals procedure. Any such procedure would be time consuming and expensive. If the arbitrator's award were reversed by a second arbitrator in the appeals procedure it would be impossible to determine which arbitrator wrote the "correct" decision. Also, the "arbitrator as judge of last resort" situation might beneficially place pressure on the arbitrator to produce high quality opinions.[53]

Procedural Problems There are two general categories of procedural problems: *time lag* and *expense of the arbitration proceedings.* One study found the length of time from request for arbitration to the arbitrator's award averages 168 days.[54] Clearly, this delay affects employees who rightfully maintain that their complaint should be resolved in a prompt and efficient manner. Similarly, management equates the arbitral decision-making delay in many grievance issues, such as discipline and reclassification of a particular job, with unnecessary expense, since adverse awards can also include remedies for back pay retroactive to the date the grievance was filed.

Many times this delay is due to a rather limited supply of experienced arbitrators, who hear a large proportion of the cases. Accepted arbitrators tend to belong to a select group, with little opportunity for newcomers to join. If grievance resolution is limited to a relatively small number of arbitrators, then time delays are inevitable. However, the causes for this short supply of arbitrators appear mainly attributable to union and management practitioners, many of whom candidly admit that they will wait months for the "old hands" instead of taking their chances with "newcomers."

. . . it is reassuring and convenient to present one's case before an arbitrator with whom you've worked before, one who knows the ropes, who goes quickly to the heart of the case, and whose evidentiary rulings and written opinions have a track record of acceptability to the parties.[55]

In some cases experienced arbitrators have assumed responsibilities for training new arbitrators. In this situation, often called *internship*, the intern progresses from merely observing hearings and discussing cases to drafting awards for the arbitrator's use and sitting as a hearing officer.[56]

Time delay is only one of several expenses associated with arbitration. Other expenses include: the arbitrator's daily fee, normally around $300 (and in some cases exceeding $500); the arbitrator's travel and study time, normally paid at the daily rate; the fees for the parties' attorneys, which usually exceed the arbitrator's fee; wage payments to plant personnel who take part in the proceedings; and stenographic transcription costs, if a record of the hearing is desired. While most labor agreements provide for sharing of arbitral expenses, excluding the expenses associated with the parties' attorneys and witnesses, the cost of a one-day hearing could run as high as $1,000 for each of the parties.[57]

Whereas arbitral fees have increased over the years, this situation, adjusted for inflation, does not appear unreasonable. In many cases, management and union officials bring added expenses upon themselves when they insist that the arbitrator review unnecessary materials, such as testimony, transcripts, prior arbitration awards, superfluous union and management witnesses, and pre- and posthearing briefs. They may also insist on expensive frills, such as the renting of a hotel suite for a neutral arbitration site, which do not materially affect the quality of the decision.[58]

Some union and management officials have reduced expenses by using *expedited arbitration procedures*. These procedures are varied, although the most basic form of expedited arbitration has occurred with the ten major steel producers (the Coordinated Steel Companies) and the United Steelworkers of America. They adopted an expedited arbitration procedure whereby some two hundred relatively inexperienced arbitrators decide routine (non-precedent-setting) grievances. This process requires a brief (one- or two-page) decision within two days after the hearing.[59] The use of this experimental approach illustrates two fundamental issues concerning arbitration:

1. This process, while not perfect, appears to offer great advantages over alternative methods of grievance resolution, such as "pulling the pin" through sudden strike activity.[60]
2. Union and management officials created the arbitration process and are charged with controlling it in accordance with their jointly determined needs. They must monitor the process as well as their related actions and attitudes[61] to insure a relatively inexpensive, efficient, and objective means of dispute resolution.

Summary and Implications

Summary

The arbitration process was little used during the period from 1865 to World War II; however, during World War II the National War Labor Board encouraged its widespread use. While the increased reliance upon arbitration continued after World War II, a major problem of enforcing the arbitrator's decision remained. Either party could have refused to abide by the arbitrator's decision, with uncertain consequences from the courts. This problem was initially approached by the *Lincoln Mills* decision, which provided a judicial avenue for enforcement, and the Supreme Court Trilogy, three cases which established the superiority of the arbitration process relative to the courts in resolving industrial grievances. Subsequent Supreme Court decisions have indicated that termination of the labor agreement does not eliminate the possibility of arbitration and injunctive relief might be granted when one party refuses to arbitrate according to grievance procedures established in the labor agreement.

Before the arbitration hearing, arbitrators must be selected either on an ad hoc or permanent basis. Each of these selection techniques has unique advantages, depending on the particular circumstances. The same can be said of prehearing and posthearing briefs. Other elements of an arbitration hearing include the grievance issue, presentation of witnesses for testimony and cross-examination, and presentation of separate and joint exhibits.

The hearing scene is a dramatic one; union and management officials display their skills in attempting to convince the arbitrator their positions are correct. The arbitration hearing shares many similarities with a judicial trial but differs in several ways. Perhaps the most significant difference is the arbitrator's reliance on the common law of the shop.

In determining the common law of the shop, arbitrators give particular weight to the provisions of the labor agreement, the intent of the parties, and past practice. Arbitrators may also consider the *de minimis* principle and, to a much lesser extent, prior arbitration awards in arriving at their decisions. Since arbitration procedures differ in some respects from those used in a courtroom, various jurisdictional disputes can occur regarding interpretations of contract provisions by arbitrators and the legal interpretation of federal policy. For example, a discharge case decided by the arbitrator could be subsequently considered by the Equal Employment Opportunity Commission, the Occupational Safety and Health Administration, and the National Labor Relations Board.

Some criticisms directed toward arbitration pertain to the capability of the arbitrator and potential procedural problems in the arbitration process. Certain arbitral problems such as expense, time lag, and excessive formality may be due to labor and management preferences rather than any characteristics inherent in the arbitration process. Management and union officials have reduced some of these problems by using expedited arbitration and new arbitrators.

Implications

The advantages and special expertise of arbitrators pertain to interpreting the labor agreement in an informal manner which best suits the labor-management relationship at the particular facility. This situation has been endorsed by the Supreme Court, although there have been numerous challenges raised when the arbitration issue is also the subject matter of legislation, such as racial discrimination. Also, as noted in Chapter 8, the parties have a legal obligation (fair representation) concerning the processing of employee grievances.[62]

Legal challenges to arbitration decisions have increased over the years,[63] making arbitrators consider grievance aspects which are broader than the common law of the shop. "The confidence of parties in the continued national recognition of effective collective bargaining as a 'cherished national goal' may suffer yet another sharp jolt if arbitration in a substantial portion of the labor/management community becomes yet another level of decision making subjected to scrutiny on the merits by a review level."[64]

These pressures place management and union officials in a tough bind.[65] Do they enter arbitration with a legalistic attitude, or do they continue to rely upon the intended purpose of the mechanism? The future of arbitration, and labor-management relationships as well, depends on eventual answers to these questions.

Discussion Questions

1. How did World War II and the National War Labor Board greatly expand the use of arbitration?
2. "The Supreme Court Trilogy greatly enhanced the arbitrator's authority when compared to previous years, yet did not give the arbitrator final jurisdiction over certain issues." Thoroughly discuss the preceding statement in terms of the specific features of these judicial decisions; also consider current jurisdictional issues arbitrators face in terms of governmental agencies.
3. Discuss the similarities and differences of arbitration and judicial hearings, with particular emphasis on the common law of the shop, admission of evidence, and the role of the arbitrator versus that of the judge.
4. Why are arbitrators' decisions usually lengthy, since one sentence could indicate who was right and wrong? Your discussion of this question should include the purposes of arbitration and advantages as well as disadvantages of an extensive arbitral decision.
5. Discuss two decision-making criteria used by arbitrators, furnishing rather specific examples (not mentioned in the text) of how these criteria can come into play.
6. Cite and defend three specific methods you would use to make the typical arbitration procedure more effective. Also indicate the advantages and disadvantages of your suggestions. (Material from Implication section may be of some help.)

References

[1]See for example William P. Witherow, "Labor Arbitration in Wartime," *Arbitration Journal* 6 (Spring 1942), pp. 11–12; and Matthew Woll, "Labor Arbitration in Wartime," *Arbitration Journal* 6 (Spring 1942), pp. 94–95.

[2]Brook I. Landis, *Value Judgments in Arbitration: A Case Study of Saul Wallen* (Ithaca, N.Y.: Cornell Studies in Industrial and Labor Relations, Cornell University, 1977), pp. 5–6.

[3]Frank Elkouri and Edna Asper Elkouri, *How Arbitration Works*, 3d. ed. (Washington, D.C.: Bureau of National Affairs, 1973), p. 15.

[4]*United Steelworkers of America v. American Manufacturing Company*, 363 U.S. 566–567 (1960).

[5]*United Steelworkers of America v. Warrior and Gulf Navigation Company*, 363 U.S. 582 (1960).

[6]*United Steelworkers of America v. Enterprise Wheel and Car Corporation*, 363 U.S. 598 (1960).

[7]*Nolde Brothers, Inc. v. Local No. 358, Bakery and Confectionary Workers Union AFL-CIO*, 430 U.S. 254 (1977).

[8]*The Boys Market, Inc. v. Retail Clerk's Union, Local 770*, 398 U.S. 249, 250, 252–253 (1970). It should be noted that injunctive relief applies only when one party refuses to arbitrate issues which are subject to grievance procedures specified in the labor agreement. For additional details, see *Buffalo Forge Company v. United Steelworkers of America*, 428 U.S. 397 (1970); and John Hoerr, "Why a Labor Pact Won't End Steel's Problems," *Business Week*, September 26, 1977, p. 56.

[9]Edwin R. Teple and Robert B. Moberly, *Arbitration and Conflict Resolution* (Washington, D.C.: Bureau of National Affairs Inc., 1979), p. 62.

[10]Bureau of National Affairs, *Basic Patterns in Union Contracts* (Washington, D.C.: Bureau of National Affairs, 1979), p. 39.

[11]Delbert C. Miller and William Form, *Industrial Sociology*, 2d ed. (New York: Harper & Row, 1964), p. 264.

[12]Bureau of National Affairs, *Basic Patterns*, p. 16.

[13]John Smith Herrick, "Profile of a Labor Arbitrator," *Arbitration Journal* 37 (June 1982), p. 18.

[14]Ibid., p. 20.

[15]Eric W. Lawson Jr., "Arbitrator Acceptability: Factors Affecting Selection," *Arbitration Journal* 36 (December 1981), pp. 25–26. For related research, see Steven Stambaugh Briggs and John C. Anderson, "An Empirical Investigation of Arbitrator Acceptability," *Industrial Relations* 19 (Spring 1980), pp. 163–174.

[16]Nels E. Nelson and Earl M. Curry Jr., "Arbitrator Characteristics and Arbitral Decisions," *Industrial Relations* 20 (Fall 1981), pp. 312–317.

[17]Benjamin C. Roberts and G. Allan Dash, Jr., "How to Get Better Results from Labor-Management Arbitration," *Arbitration Journal* 22 (1967), p. 4.

[18]Samuel H. Jaffee, "It's Your Money! Cutting the Costs of Labor Arbitration," *Arbitration Journal* 26 (1971), p. 170.

[19]For a detailed discussion of the arbitration hearing see Sam Kagel, *Anatomy of a Labor Arbitration* (Washington, D.C.: Bureau of National Affairs, 1961).

[20]Maurice S. Trotta, *Arbitration of Labor-Management Disputes* (New York: American Management Association, 1974), p. 102.

[21]Jaffee, "It's Your Money! Cutting the Costs," p. 176.

[22]Harold Davey, "Restructuring Grievance Arbitration Procedures," *Iowa Law Review* 54 (February 1969), p. 560.

[23]Harry Shulman, "Reason, Contract, and Law in Labor Relations," *Harvard Law Review* 68 (1955), p. 1016.

[24]Byron Yaffe, ed., *The Saul Wallen Papers: A Neutral's Contribution to Industrial Peace* (Ithaca: New York State School of Industrial Relations, Cornell University, 1974), p. 32.

[25]See for example, Daniel T. Dennehy, "The Status of Lie Detector Tests in Labor Arbitration," *Labor Law Journal* 31 (July 1980), pp. 430–440.

[26]Elkouri and Elkouri, *How Arbitration Works*, p. 258.

[27]For a complete discussion of arbitrators' remedial powers and remedial alternatives for a variety of grievance subjects see Marvin Hill Jr., and Anthony V. Sinicropi, *Remedies in Arbitration* (Washington, D.C.: Bureau of National Affairs Inc., 1981).

[28]Stephen C. Vladek, "Comment: The Use and Abuse of Arbitral Power," in Barbara D. Dennis and Gerald G. Somers, eds., *Labor Arbitration at the Quarter-Century Mark* (Washington, D.C.: Bureau of National Affairs, 1973), p. 84.

[29]Hyman Cohen, "The Search for Innovative Procedures in Labor Arbitration," *Arbitration Journal* 29 (June 1974), pp. 112–113. For related insights see Peter Seitz, "The Arbitrator's Lot," *Arbitration Journal* 38 (March, 1983), pp. 51–55.

[30]Whitley P. McCoy's comments in an arbitration decision (Southern Bell and Telegraph Co., January 29, 1951), cited in Harry J. Dworkin, "How Arbitrators Decide Cases," *Labor Law Journal* 25 (April 1974), p. 208.

[31]See, for example, Anthony V. Sinicropi and Peter A. Veglahn, "Dicta in Arbitration Awards: An Aid or Hindrance?" *Labor Law Journal* 23 (September 1972), pp. 560–566.

[32]Harold Davey, "How Arbitrators Decide Cases," *Arbitration Journal* 27 (December 1972), p. 277.

[33]Marvin Hill Jr., and Anthony V. Sinicropi, *Evidence in Arbitration* (Washington, D.C.: Bureau of National Affairs Inc., 1980), p. 50.

[34]Examples from Allan J. Harrison, *Preparing and Presenting Your Arbitration Case: A Manual for Union and Management Representatives* (Washington, D.C.: Bureau of National Affairs Inc., 1979), pp. 23–24.

[35]Owen Fairweather, *Practice and Procedure in Labor Arbitration* (Washington, D.C.: Bureau of National Affairs Inc., 1973), pp. 166, 167, and 169. See also Peter Seitz, "Communications: Value Judgments in the Decisions of Arbitrators," *Industrial and Labor Relations Review* 21 (April 1968), p. 429.

[36]C. Ray Gullett and Wayne H. Goff, "The Arbitral Decision-Making Process: A Computerized Simulation," *Personnel Journal* 59 (August 1980), p. 666.

[37]This provision on past practice taken from Walter E. Baer, *Practice and Precedent in Labor Relations* (Lexington, Mass.: Lexington Books, 1972), p. 8.

[38]Ibid., p. 9.

[39]Ibid., p. 38.

[40]Ken Jennings and Cindy Martin, "The Role of Prior Arbitration Awards in Arbitral Decisions," *Labor Law Journal* 29 (February 1978), pp. 95–106.

[41]William H. McPherson, "Should Labor Arbitrators Play Follow the Leader?" *Arbitration Journal* 4 (1949), p. 170.

[42]*Harrel Alexander, Sr., v. Gardner-Denver Company*, 415 U.S. 60 (1974).

[43]Ibid., p. 57. For an analysis of this case's implications for the arbitration process see Sanford Cohen and Christian Eaby;, "The Gardner-Denver Decision and Labor Arbitration," *Labor Law Journal* 27 (January 1976), pp. 18–23. It should be noted that the dual options available to the employee are concurrent—the employee is almost obligated to pursue both options at the same time, as the time required for arbitral decisions is credited to the statute of limitations imposed by the EEOC. See Marvin Hill, Jr., "Grievance Procedures and Title VII Limitations," *Labor Law Journal* 28 (June 1977), pp. 339–343.

[44]*Spielberg Manufacturing Company*, 112 NLRB 1080 (1955).

[45]*Collyer Insulated Wire and Local Union 1098, International Brotherhood of Electrical Workers*, 192 NLRB 150, (August 20, 1977).

[46]*Ray Robinson, Inc., and International Association of Machinists and Aerospace Workers, Local Lodge 1224, AFL-CIO*, 228 NLRB (March 20, 1977); and *General American Transportation Corporation and Perry Soape, Jr.*, 228 NLRB No. 102 (March 20, 1977). Both cases cited in Bureau of National Affairs, *Daily Labor Report*, No. 53 (March 18, 1977). It should be noted that these cases reflect the NLRB's split over Collyer's deferral guidelines over the years.

[47]"NLRB Tightens Deferral to Arbitration Policies," Bureau of National Affairs Inc., *Daily Labor Report*, No. 10 (January 15, 1980), p. 1. It should be noted, however, that the NLRB's decisions are subject to judicial review. For an example of one judicial modification of this policy see "NLRB Improperly Overruled Arbitration in Discharge Case Ninth Circuit Says," Bureau of National Affairs Inc., *Daily Labor Report*, No. 220 (November 16, 1981), pp. 1 and 2.

[48]*James B. Carey v. Westinghouse Electric Corporation*, 375 US 261–276 (1964). See also Raymond L. Britton, *The Arbitration Guide* (Englewood Cliffs, New Jersey: Prentice Hall, 1982), p. 180.

[49]Paul R. Hays, *Labor Arbitration: A Dissenting View* (New Haven, Conn.: Yale University Press), pp. 112–113.

[50]Dworkin, "How Arbitrators Decide Cases," p. 203.

[51]Burt L. Laskin, "Arbitration and Its Critics," in Charles M. Rehmus, ed., *Proceedings of the Twenty-first Annual Meeting, National Academy of Arbitrators* (Washington, D.C.: Bureau of National Affairs, 1968), p. 134. For details concerning legal accountability of arbitrators see Leslie Alan Glick, "Bias, Fraud, Misconduct, and Partiality of the Arbitrator," *Arbitration Journal* 22 (1967), pp. 161–172.

[52]One related empirical study has suggested that almost one out of every four grievances taken by the union to arbitration was for a political goal, not necessarily directly related to the issue or merit of the case. Donald J. Peterson, "Why Unions Go to Arbitration: Politics and Strategy versus Merit," *Personnel* 48 (July-August 1971), pp. 44–49.

[53]"Arbitrating Labor Disputes Said Superior to Litigation," Bureau of National Affairs Inc., *Daily Labor Report*, No. 107 (June 3, 1982), p. 2.

[54]W. J. Usery, Jr., "Some Attempts to Reduce Arbitration Costs and Delays," *Monthly Labor Review* 95 (November 1972), pp. 3–4. A more recent study has found that the average time from grievance date to the receipt of the arbitration award is over 220 days. Peter A. Veglahn, "Arbitration Costs/Time: Labor and Management Views," *Labor Law Journal* 30, (January 1979), p. 49.

[55]Arnold M. Zack, "Who Is Responsible for the Development of Arbitrators—the Parties or the Arbitrators?" *Arbitration Journal* 36 (June 1981), p. 12.

[56]John Van N. Dorr III, "Labor Arbitrator Training: the Internship," *Arbitration Journal* 36 (June 1981), p. 6.

[57]Usery, "Some Attempts to Reduce Arbitration Costs and Delays," p. 3. These expenses pertain to the arbitration hearing. Another potentially significant expense could arise in subsequent litigation of the arbitrator's award.

[58]Jaffee, "It's Your Money! Cutting the Costs," pp. 168, 172. For a thorough discussion of several ways union and management officials can reduce arbitration costs see William B. Werther, Jr., and Harold C. White, "Cost Effective Arbitration," *MSU Business Topics* 26 (Summer 1978), pp. 57–64.

[59]For a discussion of various types of expedited arbitration and related successes see Marcus H. Sandver, Harry R. Blaine, and Mark N. Woyar, "Time and Cost Savings through Expedited Arbitration Procedures," *Arbitration Journal* 36 (December 1981), pp. 11–21.

[60]This attitude was generally expressed in the following survey of 239 union officials: Harry E. Graham, Brian P. Heshizer, and David B. Johnson, "Grievance Arbitration, Labor Officials' Attitudes," *Arbitration Journal* 33 (June 1978), pp. 21–24.

[61]For an example of varied participant attitudes toward arbitration see Kent F. Murrmann and Bruce S. Cooper, "Attitudes of Professionals Toward Arbitration: The Case of Unionized School Administrators," *Arbitration Journal* 37 (June 1982), pp. 12–17.

[62]For an application of fair representation to the arbitrator's role in grievance resolution see James A. Gross and R. Daniel Bordoni, "Reflections on the Arbitrator's Responsibility to Provide a Full and Fair Hearing: How to Bite the Hands That Feed You," *Syracuse Law Review* 29, (Summer 1978), pp. 877–899.

[63]Thomas W. Jennings, "The Crossroads of the Future," *Labor Law Journal* 31 (August 1980), p. 499; and Joseph Antonio Raffaele, "Lawyers in Labor Arbitration," *Arbitration Journal* 37 (September 1982), pp. 14–23.

[64]Eva Robins, "The Presidential Address: Threats to Arbitration," in James L. Stern and Barbara D. Dennis, eds., *Arbitration Issues for the 1980s* (Washington, D.C., Bureau of National Affairs, Inc., 1982), p. 17.

[65]See for example, Alvin R. Rubin, "Arbitration: Toward a Rebirth," in James L. Stern and Barbara D. Dennis, eds., *Truth, Lie Detectors, and Other Problems in Labor Arbitration* (Washington, D.C.: Bureau of National Affairs Inc., 1979), pp. 30–39.

Jim Koerlin, a Lucky spokesman, said the chain's position is "neutral. It's a dispute between a lettuce grower and a union. Sadly enough, the issue is being argued on our premises."

After staging sporadic rallies and picketing for four years, the union decided to infuse its lackluster boycott with techniques that Chavez called "a new era . . . for our union."

earning histori
nover. In addi
could use th
cows" by not
plants and equ

The old-line
losing their sh
ket. In the ear
more aggressi

REFERENCE CHECKS get tightened a
more concerns use outside services.

Such services typically charge from $
to $250 per check. They cater to employe
worries over applicants' false credential
ed to match ca
ter LeVine Ass
s., posts a 25
sting referenc
ential Insuranc
uses similar services for about 20% of i
jobs, usually where money is handled.

Fidelifacts, New York, will even com
court files; a "serious" problem, such as
criminal record, turns up in about 4%
checks. Phone interviews with reference
led Barada Associates, Rushville, Ind.,
conclude a man wasn't ready to be hired b
a client as a senior internal auditor. He wa
hired for a lower-level post instead.

Yet, Barada says "a number of companies" don't check applicants' claims at all.

* * *

UNION DRAMA: A producers' union i
sists its members aren't in managemen

The Producers Guild of America's 8
members push to negotiate over certain pe
sion and working conditions with the maj
movie and TV studios; they haven't had
pact with any studio since 1981. The PG
says its members, who earn up to $50,000 f
coordinating projects, don't make manag
ment decisions. But the National Labor R
lations Board's regional office disagree
The PGA is appealing because manage
aren't subject to certain bargaining laws.

A group representing the studios asser
that producers have the authority to hi
and fire and make budget and other ma
agement decisions. The union places a
warning other workers, such as art directo
and writers, that the precedent of the lab
board's decision also could affect their ba
gaining rights.

* * *

CONGRESSIONAL CURE? Chances im
prove for an occupational disease bill.

House hearings begin Monday on a bill
bolster compensation for workers exposed

)Ks teacher strikes

Lucky, concerned over the effect the mailings may have, has begun distributing leaflets in grocery bags, posting a letter titled "Our Position" in stores and mailing it to nearby homes.

"We've never seen anything of this sort," Koerlin said. "Of course we take threats to damage our reputation . . . seriously."

market. They

But at about
was pursuing
a bid to incre
The plot was
introduced in
Rapids, Ia., la

Perry Haine
School gradua
president in c
tions, wrote t
dressed the sul

Sales could
wrote, by cutti

"THE PRIC

nakers on edge

steel

Bayou on
the deal
npetitive.
an of the
teee, said
d formal
deal with
a variety

s because
and the
drive.
osenheim

GM.
ns are being
GM may be
ce the num-

manager of

Bethlehem Steel Corp.'s Burns Harbor plant, said in an interview last month that he expects GM to begin narrowing its suppliers by turning increasingly to single sources for individual products.

And the chief executive of another major steel company said recently that he expects GM's two-year-old bidding system to be replaced next year with longer-term contracts containing volume guarantees.

Such a step wouldn't necessarily be bad for steel companies, who could use the assurance of future business to justify investing in the modern equipment needed to make steel that meets the auto industry's increasingly exacting standards.

"We would like to be able to look out a little and anticipate where our business is going," Penny said.

But the process of reducing suppliers is bound to be painful for those companies left behind, and some industry observers believe GM is wrestling with the anticipated fallout from such a move.

Other companies try to save on labor, too. They can slash wages and benefits in times of high unemployment because jobs in their plants are at a premium.

John Morrell Co., a subsidiary of United Brands, Inc., recently reopened a pork plant in Arkansas City, Kan., at starting wages of $5 an hour.

But some industry executives believe their competitors have gone too far, that slashing wages and benefits to improve profits or position in the marketplace could backfire.

"We have more leverage today than the union, but that will
el President Wil-
of his company's
ized, and starting
$6.14 to $8.75 an
insurance cover-

eople will work in
$5 an hour is just
"It's tough manu-
environment. It's
the sunshine."

ıgshoremen Union
·eatens to Strike
ts in Three Months

V YORK—The International Long-
en's Association threatened to strike
·om Maine to Texas in three months
sing its latest battle to regain control
ie handling of containerized cargo.
union filed a 60-day notice of its in-
terminate its contract with the ship-
'he union said that would allow a
n three months.
ıwhile, the union said it will try to
:e a new agreement on the loading
oading of cargo containers.
ɔattle over the handling of container-
go has been waged in the courts, be-
National Labor Relations Board and
ocks for many years. Shipping goods
: containers reduces the labor re-
o load and unload ships.
'atest action came earlier this year
e NLRB struck down certain restric-
'k rules favoring the longshoremen's
'he NLRB action was upheld by a
court in New Orleans.
ınion said it wants to renegotiate
terms covering containerized cargo
the federal court ruling indicates
judicial solution of the rules contro-
; unlikely in the foreseeable fu-

Part 3
The Outcomes of the Labor Relations Process: Collective Bargaining Issues

Part 3 examines the variety of work rules which represent the outcomes of the labor relations process. Employee discipline is a significant factor in establishing work rules as well as the basis for much arbitration. Next, institutional issues pertaining to the rights and responsibilities of unions and management, including their responsibility to minorities and women, are explored. A discussion of many administrative and economic issues which are resolved through collective bargaining concludes this section.

Chapter 10 Employee Discipline

Management must have the power to discipline employees or to discharge them. Most executives think that the power to discipline workers is crucial. Without that right, they believe that it would be impossible to run a business. . . .

An employer needs to provide an orderly and sufficient work place. It would be nice if employees could work under a system of self-restraint. But human nature being what it is, rules are necessary.

Robert Coulson, *The Termination Handbook* (New York: The Free Press, 1981), p. 7.

Employee discipline, perhaps more than any other collective bargaining issue, reflects the arbitration process across the spectrum of labor-management agreements. Many other issues, such as work assignments or computation of overtime pay, usually depend on unique work experiences and related labor-agreement provisions found at a particular facility. Disciplinary principles, however, tend to be more broadly applied. Most arbitrators feel that effective employee discipline has common elements which should be familiar to all parties to labor agreements.[1]

Because discharge of employees and other disciplinary issues represent the most frequent grievance topics resolved by arbitrators,[2] *general disciplinary principles have been developed. This chapter approaches employee discipline by discussing its changing significance over time and its elements and how they affect labor-management relations.*

The Changing Significance of Industrial Discipline

Nature and Significance of Discipline

Employee discipline is a fundamental element of any industrial organization, particularly when viewed as a state of employee commitment, motivation, and self-regulation.[3] In this sense, discipline is both a condition and an attitude—a "disciplined" work group willingly accepts management's directives and behavioral standards.

On the other hand, discipline represents an action taken by management against an employee who has violated organizational rules.[4] This chapter focuses on the action rather than the conditional component of employee discipline by examining situations in which management has either been successful or unsuccessful in disciplining employees. The premise is that, while it cannot solve all industrial problems, discipline is nonetheless a significant option when used with other alternatives or when other approaches have failed.

Management regards the right to discipline its employees as an important element of its broader prerogative to direct its working force. The significance of discipline becomes apparent when it is either neglected or poorly administered. If management does not deal effectively with those who violate organizational rules, then the disrespect from them will spread to other employees. For example, if a few employees are permitted to line up at the time clock before quitting time, then each day the number will grow, until nearly all of the work force are in line.[5]

Employee discipline occurs at unionized and nonunionized firms alike; improperly administered discipline can have significant consequences for both kinds of organizations. Nonunion firms might discover that disciplining employees in an arbitrary or capricious manner prompts employees to join unions.[6] Also, nonunion employees who feel they have been discharged unfairly might challenge management's actions in the courts. Related legal actions could allege employment discrimination (the employee claims she was fired because of her sex or race, for example) or challenge the "employment at will" concept discussed in Chapter 5.[7]

Management and union officials as well as employees at unionized firms are also strongly affected by disciplinary actions and arbitrators' decisions concerning these actions. An arbitrator has two general options regarding the discharged employee. He or she can (1) uphold management's discharge decision, or (2) reinstate the employee to work with either no, some, or all back pay for wages which were lost due to the employee's forced absence.

The second alternative modifies management's decision, a situation which according to one study of 400 discharge cases occurred 58 percent of the time.[8] From a statistical perspective, management generally loses in arbitration of discipline grievances, a situation which becomes more apparent when the reinstated employee is brought back to the shop floor. "Nothing is more frustrating—more humbling—for a company than to have its discharge of an employee reduced to a suspension, or even a mere warning, with back pay awarded the offender.[9]

Reinstatement of the employee with back pay represents a financial loss to management (for example, one Playboy Club Bunny received $15,000 for being improperly discharged), and supervisory authority may also be lost, for it is a rare supervisor who, upon experiencing the return of one disciplined employee to his work group with a large back pay check, will pursue subsequent disciplinary action with as much vigor and initiative.[10]

Arbitral reversal of management decisions can also create tensions between different levels of management officials. As noted in Chapter 1, management participants in the labor relations process do not constitute a unified group. The first line supervisor is often the most involved official in employee discipline: he or she has typically trained the employee, created past practices in the department which might influence the arbitrator's decision, and witnessed, reported, and in some cases participated in the events resulting in discipline. The supervisor also actually disciplines employees for their incorrect work behavior.

Other management officials such as industrial relations representatives monitor these activities to make sure that supervisory actions are consistent with company policy, reversing them if they are not to avoid adverse arbitration.[11] This reversal can cause tensions, as indicated in the following remarks of a first line supervisor:

I had this one troublemaker. He was a solid goldbricker. He couldn't cut the buck on any job. I tried everything, but he was lazy and he was a loud-mouth. I caught him in the toilet after being away from his machine for over an hour. I told him he was through and to go upstairs and pick up his check. And damn. Do you know what those college boys in personnel did? He gives them some bull about being sick and weakly and the next day he is sitting at a bench in the department next to mine. He says to me, "Well wise guy, you don't count for nothin' around here. Every time I see you, I'm going to call you Mr. Nothin."[12]

What management loses in arbitration hearings appears to be the union's gain. Most if not all union members believe the union should be responsive to problems arising from their day-to-day working conditions that remain after the formal labor agreement has been negotiated. There is no more dramatic example of union concern for its members than "saving" an employee's job. Almost every union newspaper contains at least one article per issue which describes (along with appropriate pictures of union representatives, the grievant, and the back pay check) how the union successfully defended an employee against an unjust act of management. A representative article from one union newspaper proclaimed in bold headlines: "Worker Wins $5,895 in Back Pay When Fired for Opening Beer Can."[13]

Perhaps a disciplinary action carries the most significance for the affected employee. Some writers have contended that discipline is well received by employees, for "it is part of discipline to encourage employees to develop their talents and skills and to acquire attitudes and build patterns of behavior that earn self-respect."[14] On the other hand, discharge, the ultimate disciplinary act, has been viewed by many arbitrators as *economic capital punishment*, for it deprives the employee of presently earning a livelihood and at the same time (with the discharge on his or her work record) makes it difficult to find future employment elsewhere.

Discharge can also have powerful psychological consequences for the employee.

When you are fired, you have no place to go. You have . . . no function. You reach out for friends, but find that they are busy and have no time for you. Suddenly, you know you are a failure. Unemployment shatters the worker's self-image as a valuable, productive person.[15]

At the least, any form of discipline represents an embarrassment to individuals who do not like being told they are wrong and, in some instances, have to explain a disciplinary layoff or discharge to their friends and family.

Historical Overview of Employer Disciplinary Policies

During the eighteenth and nineteenth centuries, the employer exercised "uncontrolled discretion" in directing the work crew. Discipline during this time period was sometimes harsh—common law considerations allowed the employer to administer severe bodily punishment to employees who refused to follow orders. Hence, employees who were verbally "insolent" to their superiors could expect to have their tongues burned with a hot iron. Public humiliation was another popular form of discipline, with the guilty employee either being whipped in the town square or subjected to wearing a sign indicating that he or she was an unsatisfactory employee.[16]

As society became more humane, the courts frowned on physical punishment. Yet management's right to discharge the employee for any reason was typically upheld until the 1930s, since the employment contract was legally interpreted to mean "freedom for the organization to hire at will, with either party free to terminate the employment relationship at any time, with or without cause."[17]

During the early 1900s, however, employers began to recognize employees as an investment that involved recruiting, development and turnover costs.[18] To arbitrarily dismiss an employee without regard to this investment was considered unwise. Frederick Taylor's *scientific management*, popular by 1920, also shaped modern disciplinary attitudes and procedures in several ways. The scientific management approach stressed management's obligation to provide its employees with clear and detailed work rules, along with scientifically designed work equipment and appropriate training. Management, according to Taylor, had obligations to train employees to obtain the desired job behavior and correct (instead of discharge) the employee who deviated from managerial standards. Interestingly, as will be demonstrated later in the chapter, all of these elements help to formulate contemporary discipline administration.

The Wagner Act of 1935 legally shaped management's disciplinary policies. A primary feature of this legislation was the prohibition of discriminatory discipline of employees because of their union preferences or membership. An independent agency, the National Labor Relations Board (NLRB) was created, in part, for enforcement purposes. Management often had to defend disciplinary actions against appeals to this agency, with a potential remedy being reinstatement with back pay. This was the first time that management was legally held accountable for employee discipline, a situation that encouraged further development of corrective disciplinary principles and policies. The NLRB also affected organizational discipline procedures in an indirect fashion when it ruled that discipline and grievance procedures were mandatory issues subject to collective bargaining. As a result of this NLRB decision, over 95 percent of existing collective bargaining agreements now have both a provision regulating discipline and a grievance procedure which enables the submission of discipline issues to arbitration.[19]

From the 1940s to the present, managerial policies regarding employee discipline were greatly influenced by the growth and development of labor arbitration. Currently, arbitrators have three broad powers regarding discipline:

1. To determine what constitutes "just cause" for discipline.
2. To establish "standards of proof and evidence."
3. To review and modify (or eliminate entirely) the penalty imposed by management.[20]

Because the arbitrator has a significant role in formulating principles of contemporary employee discipline, the following section examines arbitral reasoning in discipline cases by indicating those situations and considerations which typically lead arbitrators to either uphold or deny management's disciplinary action.

Principles and Elements of Discipline

Discipline for Just Cause

Most labor agreements contain a statement indicating that management retains the right to discipline employees for *just cause* or simply *cause*; for example, one survey found 80 percent of 400 separate labor agreements contained this provision.[21] Arbitrators consider this concept in any discipline grievance, their rationale being that just cause is an implicit, necessary prerequisite for the collective bargaining relationship.[22] Unfortunately, the arbitrator receives little help from the union and management representatives in defining just cause. Lacking contractual guidelines, the arbitrator must fashion a definition out of his or her own experience and consideration of the individual merits of the case. One arbitrator has suggested, "Whether an employee was discharged for just and proper cause is a matter to be decided from the nature of the employee-employer relationship, from contract provisions, from proper rules of conduct and from established and accepted practices."[23]

There is no uniform, precise definition of just cause which applies to all companies or even all circumstances within one company; instead, what constitutes just cause depends upon the particular combination of circumstances present in each individual case.[24] Arbitrators tend to accept two broad principles of just cause in guiding their consideration of the individual case:

1. There is clear and convincing evidence that a disciplinary offense was committed by the grievant.
2. The disciplinary action taken by management was appropriate for the offense committed.[25]

In following these principles, arbitrators apply several tests or guidelines. Exhibit 10.1 represents a schematic diagram indicating the approximate progression of these considerations. Each consideration will be discussed in terms of its significance for employee discipline.

Although these considerations are useful and important they are not set in concrete. There are many variations within each element, due to differences at the work place and among arbitrators. Consider, for example, an employee who is an alcoholic or who has a serious drinking problem. Many arbitrators view this situation in narrow terms—managers who discharge the employee according to the steps in Exhibit 10.1 will likely have their decision upheld in arbitration. However, some arbitrators feel that,

---

. . . management has a continuing obligation to try to rehabilitate alcoholic employees regardless of how long this problem persists. This position is predicated on the belief that because alcoholism is a 'disease,' a person so afflicted is entitled to as much time as is necessary to recover.[26]

Legitimate Purpose of Employee Discipline

Arbitrators have long held that management has the right to direct the work force and manage its operations efficiently. Indeed, inefficient operations harm both the employer and employees since subsequent reduced profits can result in employee layoffs. Discipline can improve efficiency through the following interrelated purposes:

- *Set an example of appropriate behavior.* For example, management impresses upon its employees the seriousness of being tardy by giving one tardy employee a five-day suspension.
- *Transmit rules of the organization.* As illustrated in the previous purpose, management has transmitted a rule of the organization—lateness will not be accepted.
- *Promote efficient production.* Discipline those employees who either cannot or will not meet production standards.

Exhibit 10.1 Schematic Diagram Indicating Elements of Discipline

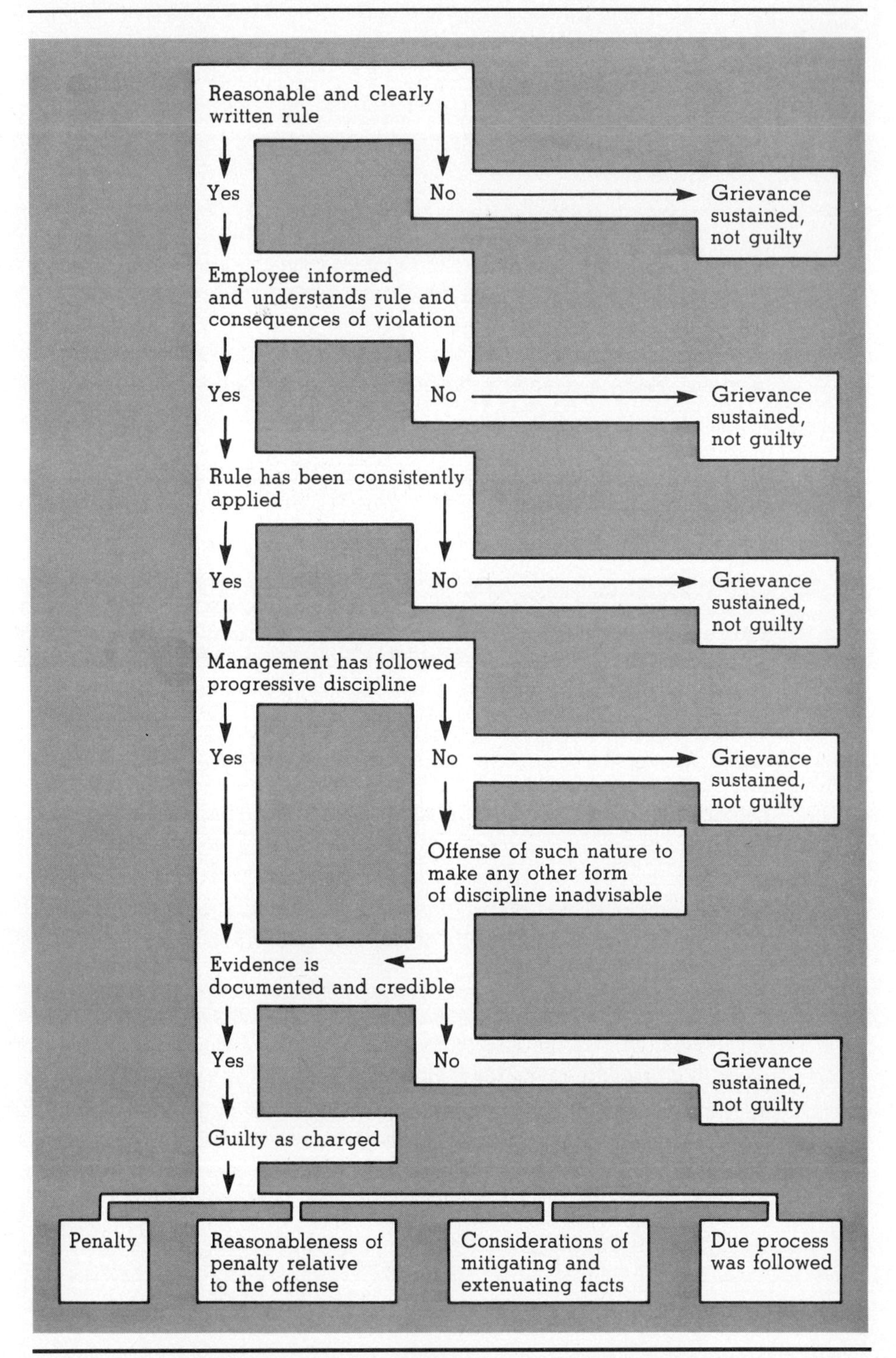

Sources: Modified from Floyd S. Brandt and Carroll R. Daugherty, *Instructor's Manual for Conflict Cooperation: Cases in Labor-Management Behavior* (Homewood, Ill.: Richard D. Irwin, 1967), p. 6. © 1967 by Richard D. Irwin, Inc. Used by permission.

- *Maintain respect for the supervisor.* In a sense, discipline shows the employee who is the boss. A supervisor who does not discipline poor employees weakens managerial authority.
- *Correct an employee's behavior.* Indicate what is expected, how he or she can improve, and what negative consequences might result in the future if the behavior does not change. The assumption here is that most employees have good intentions and will improve if management will simply show them the error of their ways.

Discipline can accomplish all these purposes, but labor arbitrators primarily recognize the last purpose, *correction*, as the legitimate disciplinary objective. Arbitrators usually view discipline as corrective rather than punitive in purpose; their corrective emphasis influences the following dimensions of just cause.

Nature of the Work Rules

The right of management to establish (even without initially advising the union) and administer work rules is generally acknowledged as fundamental to efficient plant operations:

The rules and regulations of a modern company are designed to promote a constructive working environment, protect the health and welfare of personnel, and assure individual employees full protection from capricious or arbitrary decisions of management. Sensible rules are essential to organizational effectiveness, and if they are understood and accepted by the members of the organization as an intelligent guide to cooperative endeavor, they will be supported.[27]

Yet managerial administration of work rules also assumes some fundamental responsibilities and obligations which, if not followed, may affect management's disciplinary efforts.

A first question that arises is: What happens if management has no rule governing the alleged offense committed by the employee? This situation is not uncommon since employers cannot possibly anticipate the endless variety of employee misbehaviors.[28] Arbitrators, for example, have upheld the discharges of an employee who watched a fire develop and destroy a portion of company property over a lengthy period of time without notifying the company,[29] and another employee who made telephone calls to several management officials in the early morning hours with no messages other than belching sounds.[30] Needless to say, management had no previously established work rules covering these subjects. Arbitrators have also upheld management's right to discipline employees for those offenses that are commonly regarded as unwritten laws—prohibitions against stealing or striking a supervisor, for example.

Employees can also be disciplined for activities occurring off job time and away from company property, situations which seldom have applicable written work rules. For example, an employee was disciplined for drunkenly threatening and swearing at his plant manager at a picnic,[31] as was an employee whose off-the-job behavior caused demonstrable bad publicity for the company.

However, in most disciplinary situations, particularly those cases which are somewhat common in industry (poor performance, absenteeism, insubordination and so forth) management is on weak ground with the arbitrator when it does not have established work rules. Further, written work rules must have several characteristics if they are to be effective. A written rule must be *reasonable, clear,* and *state the possible consequences of its violation.*

A *reasonable* rule is one that is job related and intended to promote safe and efficient work efforts. A rule prohibiting employees from wearing wedding rings at work would be unreasonable unless there was a safety hazard, such as employees working close to machines.[32] Usually, a rule which subjects an employee to humiliation or personal embarrassment (for example, requesting supervisory permission to go to the washroom) will be labeled unreasonable unless it can be shown that the technology of the workplace necessitates an employee remaining at a work station at all times. For example, an automobile assembly line relies on continual production; therefore, it is normally reasonable to require supervisory permission for restroom breaks so that a temporary replacement can be found.

Hence, the reasonableness of an industrial work rule can vary according to industrial or company differences. A unilateral ban on *moonlighting* (working a second shift with another employer) is regarded as reasonable in the utility industry, which often needs emergency work performed during off shifts. Other industries not having emergency-related concerns might have a difficult time in establishing the appropriateness of this rule. Rule reasonableness can also vary within an industrial production facility. For example, an employer might reasonably require a long-haired employee working in the cafeteria to wear a hair net (for sanitary reasons); it would be unreasonable to request the same compliance if he worked in the shipping department.

The clarity of a work rule is also an important issue in corrective discipline, the rationale being that employees cannot adequately perform or correct behavior if they do not know what is expected. Work rules can only serve as guidelines and cannot be applied to every problem. Management officials can, however, create a problem when they discipline employees for infractions of a vague and sometimes confusing work rule. For illustrative purposes, the following examples of work rules are presented:

- Horseplay can inflict serious physical harm on other employees and therefore will not be tolerated in any form by the company.
- Any individual found guilty of gambling on company premises will be subject to immediate discharge.[33]

These rules may, at first glance, appear clear and conclusive; however, their vagueness becomes very apparent to the first-line supervisor who tries to enforce them. Horseplay can take place without physical touching. For example, a group of employees puts a dead fish in a "lazy" inspector's testing pan, giving her equipment a lasting smell before she actually performs inspection duties. Yet a question arises as to whether this is actually a form of horseplay. A fine distinction between relatively harmless practical jokes and horseplay may haunt management when it discharges the employees on the rationale that such behavior was indeed horseplay.

A problem also arises with the term *gambling*, particularly when management discharges employees caught at a card game, while at the same time a management representative was sponsoring a World Series pool with hourly employee participants. Also, does gambling occur when employees are playing cards during their lunch break for matches or a numerical score which management (perhaps correctly) assumes will be converted into cash payments once the employees are off the company premises?

The existence of work rules carries the implicit if not explicit obligation for management to inform its employees of the rules as well as the consequences of their violation. In some instances, an employee disciplined for violating a rule contends that he or she was unaware of the directive. In these cases, management usually has to prove that the employee was indeed informed of the rule, a difficult task. Some arbitrators have even suggested that a card signed by an employee indicating he or she has read the rules is insufficient since it is signed in haste as part of the employee's orientation, and the signed card does not indicate that management has actively and patiently explained each rule to the employee, allowing time for questions and explanation.

Rule Violations Little has been written on the managerial obligation to inform the employee of the consequences of rule violation, although many arbitrators appear to give this item serious weight in their decisions. The training or corrective element in discipline should include a discussion of which rules are most important; a related feature of employee orientation would be informing the employee what type of penalty could be expected for violation of a particular work rule. Returning to the work rule examples, it can be easily seen that the admonition "will not be tolerated in any form" fails to inform the employee of the punishment for engaging in horseplay. The employee could interpret the vague penalty to mean a stern, oral reprimand, which he or she would accept in view of successfully completing a practical joke. Knowing in advance that the activity would likely result in a suspension or discharge, the employee would probably think twice before committing the offense.

Management's statement that rule-breakers are "subject to discharge" is qualified. This qualification is necessary in order that the unique, mitigating circumstances of each offense be given consideration, thereby avoiding arbitrary disciplinary measures. Yet management should be advised that arbitrators regard the phrase *subject to discharge* as carrying explicit potential for disciplinary measures other than discharge; the burden of proof is on management to establish why it chose discharge as opposed to the lesser penalty options.

Finally, management must administer the rules consistently for those employees violating the rules under similar circumstances. In assessing the degree of consistency, arbitrators place particular emphasis on past practice, which refers to the "customary way of dealing with given classes of rule violations and covers both methods of handling and the relationship of penalties to offenses."[34]

Some companies seek to impose consistent discipline by including a *price list* in the labor agreement; it cites specific rules and furnishes uniform penalties for single or repeated violations (see Table 10.1). This form of rule making has advantages: (a) the employee is clearly informed of the specific rules and consequences of violations, (b) the standardized penalties suggest consistent disciplinary action is implemented, and (c) if agreed to by the union, the price list assumes more legitimacy than a unilateral work rule posted by management. However, some individuals contend that the price list represents a mechanical imposition of discipline which runs counter to the corrective philosophy, since it does not consider each case on its individual merits. Say, for example, management finds two employees fighting—one a short-term, the other a long-term employee with a fine work record. According to the price list approach, management is obligated to discharge both employees; yet it is likely that the arbitrator will reinstate the senior employee, who, because of his past record, will typically respond to corrective measures in order to retain job seniority investments.

Table 10.1 Example of Disciplinary Price List

Type of Offense	First Offense	Second Offense	Third Offense	Fourth Offense	Fifth Offense
1. Abusive Language toward a Supervisor	3-day Suspension	Discharge			
2. Failure to Punch In and Out on Time Clock	Oral Warning	Written Warning	3-day Suspension	5-day Suspension	Discharge
3. Failure to Report an Absence	Oral Warning	Written Warning	3-day Suspension	5-day Suspension	Discharge
4. Stealing Company Property	Discharge				
5. Sleeping on the Job	Written Warning	3-day Suspension	5-day Suspension	Discharge	
6. Damage of Company Equipment or Property	Written Warning	5-day Suspension	Discharge		
7. Gambling or Engaging in a Lottery on Company Premises	5-day Suspension	Discharge			
8. Striking a Supervisor	Discharge				

Progressive Discipline

Progressive discipline refers to increasingly severe penalties corresponding with repeated, identical offenses committed by an employee. It relates to correction in at least two ways: (a) by impressing upon the employee the seriousness of repeated rule infractions and (b) by furnishing the employee additional chances to correct his or her behavior before applying the ultimate penalty of discharge. Management typically has to give an oral warning, a written warning, and at least one suspension before it can discharge an employee for repeatedly committing a similar offense, such as failure to wear safety equipment.

An *oral warning* represents an informal effort to correct and improve the employee's work performance. The informality of this reprimand is for corrective training purposes; however, the oral warning can be prejudicial to the employee if it is entered as evidence in arbitration hearings. This disciplinary action, however, is subject to the following employee defenses: (a) the employee might have thought the supervisor's remarks were instructional and been unaware of the disciplinary aspects or consequences of the warning; and (b) an oral warning given in private can lead to conflicting testimony—the employee can state that the supervisor never gave him or her an oral warning. However, because of its relatively harmless nature, the union seldom contests this form of discipline.

A *written warning* is a much more serious matter because it summarizes previous oral attempts to correct the employee's behavior and is entered in the employee's work record file. More official than an oral reprimand, it brings disciplinary actions into focus by warning the employee of future consequences of rule violation.

Suspensions are disciplinary layoffs without pay given by management to impress upon the employee the seriousness of the offense. Oral and written reprimands might also achieve this purpose, but they do not involve a financial sacrifice on the part of the employee. A suspension serves as an example of the economic consequences associated with discharge and at the same time indicates that management is willing to retain the employee who will comply with directives and change errant ways. Management initially imposes a mild (one- to three-day) suspension and will seldom impose a suspension greater than ten days for a repeated offense. Under these circumstances, arbitrators are reluctant to reduce the suspensions, unless it can be shown that other employees were given lesser penalties for identical offenses under similar circumstances.[35]

Discharge is not a corrective measure, since it means the employee is permanently released from the company.

Although commonly used, this retrospective and punitive approach [discharge] is not satisfactory. Discharge should not be viewed as punishment for misconduct. Rather, an employee is discharged because his past actions are indicative of what he may do in the future, and the company considers that prospect so unappealing (in a business sense) that it no longer wishes to employ the worker.[36]

As mentioned earlier, arbitrators have attached tremendous significance to the effects of discharge upon the employee, regarding it as a last resort to be used sparingly when all other corrective attempts have failed and the employee's usefulness to the firm is totally lacking. An exception to this procedure occurs when the nature of the offense is so heinous (stealing, striking a supervisor, setting fire to company property, sexual assault of another employee) as to make other forms of corrective discipline unnecessary.

Progressive discipline also implies a *statute of limitations.* For example, it would be difficult to discharge an employee who has previously received two suspensions for failing to report his or her absence to management if the worker has worked for a fairly long period of time (say, three to five years) before committing a similar, present offense. Management is usually not obligated to return to the first step, that is, an oral warning; however, discharge (the next step after the second suspension) is not warranted—the employee's offense-free performance for the three- to five-year period indicates that corrective measures did have some effect and should be tried again before separating the employee from the firm.

How long a period of offense-free employment should justify an alteration of the progressive discipline procedure? One company has explicity answered this question with the following labor agreement provision:

With regard to discipline imposed for any cause other than those set forth above, the company will not refer to any disciplinary notices received by an employee more than five years prior to the current situation for which the employee is being disciplined.[37]

This provision is advantageous to management since it furnishes the arbitrator specific guidelines to be applied in progressive discipline. Furthermore, the five-year statute of limitations is longer than that imposed by most arbitrators. One possible disadvantage of this strategy is that its specific inclusion in the labor agreement subjects the time period to collective bargaining—the union will be encouraged to negotiate a reduced statute of limitations, perhaps a time period shorter than most arbitrators would regard as being appropriate.

Finally, it should be noted that a discipline price list does not take statute of limitations into account—its penalties are for repeated infractions regardless of the intervening time period. In these circumstances, should management negate its own price list by returning to a suspension even though discharge is the next step in the procedure? Or proceed with the discharge, knowing that many arbitrators, employing a statute of limitations, would reinstate the employee because of the commendable performance for a period of time between his or her previous and recent offenses? Both courses of action have risks: In the first case, management might establish precedent which can adversely affect other cases; in the second, management might appear arbitrary in its discipline administration.

Degree of Proof and Nature of the Evidence

The burden of proof for all disciplinary actions rests with management; however, the degree of proof necessary varies among arbitrators. There are two schools of thought regarding the degree to which a person should be proven deserving of discipline. One arbitral attitude is that an employee must be shown guilty beyond reasonable doubt. This high degree of proof is usually required in discharge cases for criminal offenses (stealing or assault) rather than in discharge cases for noncriminal offenses (absenteeism, sleeping on the job, and so on), because it would be much more difficult for the employee to obtain employment with a work history that includes a discharge for criminal offenses.[38]

The second approach, used by a majority of the arbitrators, is that the preponderance of the evidence must establish the employee's guilt. The testimony and evidence must be adequate to overcome opposing presumptions and evidence; the grievance decision is influenced by who presents the best case instead of an absolute standard. A common problem facing management and union representatives is that neither party knows for sure how much evidence the arbitrator will require to uphold the disciplinary penalty.

Additional problems occur over the type of evidence that is used to support management's contentions and disciplinary action. Management can usually enter the grievant's past work record as evidence that corrective discipline was imposed. This issue becomes more complex when the company offers the employee's past record for the purpose of suggesting the likelihood that the employee has committed the present offense. Assume, for example, a bus driver is disciplined for negligent driving, and he denies the charge. The company then shows the grievant's past record to show that he has had three accidents of a similar nature during the past year and must now be considered "accident prone." Arbitrators do not regard this evidence in a uniform manner; however, "a large majority will admit the evidence and give it weight when the present offense has a functional relationship to the past offense."[39] As can be seen from the following quotation, some arbitrators accept the grievant's past work record as evidence even when it is not functionally related to the present offense:

The existence of "proper cause" for discharge reasonably may be based upon any significant and relevant record of prior disciplinary actions, and it is not necessary that specific prior infractions relied upon involve the same misconduct.[40]

However, in submitting unrelated offenses to the arbitrator, management runs the risk (either through direct challenge by the union or arbitral interpretation) of demonstrating that it is out to get the employee by any means possible.

Another controversial aspect of evidence occurs when management uncovers the evidence while using search and seizure techniques. Few arbitrators deny the employer's right to impose, as a condition of employment, an inspection of the employee's clothes and packages on entering and leaving the plant; however, a problem arises when company officials search an employee's locker or, in some cases, home, with or without the employee's permission. Many arbitrators permit evidence obtained without the employee's knowledge if it is from company property, even if the property (such as locker or tool chest) is momentarily under the control of the employee. On the other hand, few, if any, arbitrators believe evidence should be accepted if management obtained the evidence by forcibly breaking into the employee's personal property, even if the property is located on company premises.[41]

Evidence obtained through alleged entrapment techniques poses an additional problem for the arbitrator. Some arbitrators recognize the legitimacy of evidence obtained by company-hired undercover agents, particularly if it is corroborated by other employees and management officials. Problems can arise, however, when a management representative entraps an employee. An illustrative arbitration decision involved a foreman having several discussions regarding marijuana with an hourly employee. On one occasion, the foreman approached several employees standing near the grievant's car, whereupon the foreman said, "I know what you fellows are up to. You better be in shape for work tomorrow." The grievant then asked the foreman if he wanted some and handed the foreman two marijuana cigarettes when the foreman replied, "Yes." After conferring with legal authorities, the foreman was advised to arrange a sale of marijuana. He asked the grievant if he could purchase $5 worth, with the grievant responding in the affirmative. The foreman then notified a representative of the county prosecutor's office, who in turn searched the grievant's automobile at the end of the shift and found a quantity of marijuana. The employee was arrested for possession, pleaded guilty, and received a $25 fine. In discharging the employee, management contended that it could not have an acknowledged pusher on its premises. However, the arbitrator believed that the evidence did not establish the employee as being a pusher and that the foreman provoked the employee to distribute the substance on company premises.

The critical question is whether the record establishes that X acted as a pusher or supplier. There is no proof that he ever sold marijuana. His general statements to Porter [the foreman] that he had done so, in the course of friendly and casual conversation, do not establish that he actually sold the drug on any specific occasion. That he knew the prices of marijuana and was familiar with the language associated with its distribution is also not sufficient to prove that X was a pusher.

While X did give Porter two cirgarettes, Porter initiated the conversation and, in earlier talks, had asked for marijuana cigarettes and had just indicated to the employees he suspected they were smoking marijuana and his only concern was that they report to work in good shape the following morning. X's act in giving the foreman two of his

cigarettes was not a sale or form of distribution under the circumstances, particularly in view of the foreman's expressed interest in using marijuana and their friendly discussions of the subject.

Quite apart from the foregoing, we are impressed by the union's theory that management has an obligation to deter potential violators. The record is clear that instead of cautioning X during April against engaging in marijuana possession and activity on company property, Porter persisted in approaching him and prodding him on to commit a wrongful act. We do not condone the practice by a supervisor of preying upon an employee's weakness in order to subject him to discipline.[42]

Finally, arbitrators are often faced with the issue of credibility of the witnesses and the accompanying dilemma of how to resolve a grievance when testimony of union and management representatives is completely contradictory. Two general tests appear applicable, the first being an evaluation of the witnesses' behaviors on the stand and their ability to hold up under cross-examination. Arbitrators also attach particular significance to a party's silence in the face of opposing testimony. Arbitrators regard the silence as an implicit acceptance of the other's testimony.

In the second test arbitrators ask themselves what each party stands to gain by lying. The supervisor who does not like the grievant and wants him or her discharged at any cost stands to benefit from lying. Similarly, the foreman does not wish to have the grievant reinstated at the expense of his or her reputation as an efficient management official. However, grievants stand to gain much more by lying—their jobs. Generally, the grievants are in trouble in cases featuring contradictory testimony. This is especially true if the arbitrator is not able to award the first test in his or her favor, because the second test, with rare exceptions, is decided in management's favor.

Nature of the Penalty

In some instances, management establishes that the employee was guilty of the offense but not that the penalty was appropriate. Arbitrators consider the reasonableness of the penalty relative to the offense, particularly if the employee was discharged. Few offenses merit discharge for their single commission, even if management regards the offense as being exceptionally serious. For example, termination might be too severe a penalty for an employee who loses $500 of company money.[43] Arbitrators, while reluctant to modify suspensions, have no reservations about reducing a discharge penalty to a suspension. They reason that arbitrary or capricious discharge is a total waste to the employee was well as the firm, which incurs employment costs in hiring a replacement.

Some cases make one wonder why management wanted to enforce a rule in such a silly way. . . . ten electricians at a nuclear construction project had been dismissed by the . . . Company for refusing to remove American flag decals from their hard hats. The reason? They were accused of defacing company property, a violation of the published work rules. One worker said, "I'm so damned proud of being fired for this that I'd do it again tomorrow." Another proclaimed, "The flag's a symbol of our country. We've been promoting patriotism on the job and thought it would help boost morale . . . The decals don't damage or deface the hat, interfere with the quality of our work or slow down production." If you were chief executive of that company, how would you regard the judgement of your project manager?[44]

In determining whether the penalty is appropriate, arbitrators look to previous practices in the company or, in some instances, rely on precedents established by other arbitrators when management has never encountered the particular disciplinary situation. Arbitrators also scrutinize the disciplinary proceedings to see whether mitigating circumstances were involved and due process was followed.

Mitigating Circumstances If certain mitigating circumstances have influenced the offense, then arbitrators will tend to reduce a disciplinary penalty under one of two assumptions:

1. Management contributed to a problem and must therefore assume part of the responsibility for this wrongdoing.
2. The circumstances of the case were so unusual as to give great doubt that it will occur again, particularly if management uses corrective techniques instead of discharge.

An example of mitigating circumstances under the first arbitral assumption occurs when management has provided the employee with faulty tools and equipment and subsequently disciplines the employee for low production output.

A more common example of mitigating circumstances occurs when a management representative provokes the employee into committing physical or verbal abuse. In a representative discharge grievance, a fellow employee made vulgar and apparently misguided remarks about the fidelity of the grievant's wife. Later in the shift, another employee reported to the grievant that the foreman was asking other employees about the grievant's wife. The grievant thereupon confronted the foreman, who responded by treating the situation as a joke. The arbitrator reinstated the grievant on the basis that the foreman's poor judgment contributed to the grievant's subsequent physical attack on the supervisor.[45] In essence, arbitrators maintain that management must make every effort to avoid continuing an argument with the employee in order that the argument will not turn into a serious breach of industrial discipline.

Management might also contribute to a disciplinary infraction by condoning (either openly or tactily) offenses committed in the shop. This situation is illustrated in a brief summary of an arbitration case from the *Wall Street Journal*:

Humiliating the boss isn't grounds for dismissal, an arbitrator rules.

On the night before his wedding day, a plant supervisor for International Harvester Co. was seized on the factory floor by six male workers. They removed some of his clothes and held him while a female worker put grease on his body. The company fired all seven employees, charging that the pre-wedding prank amounted to "physical abuse of the most degrading and humiliating form."

The union agreed the prank was wrong, but argued that dismissal was an overly severe penalty. Agreeing with the union, arbitrator Louis Crane ordered the workers rehired, reducing the penalty to an unpaid suspension. He reasoned that the workers' "crude joke" wasn't physically harmful and was tacitly condoned by other supervisors who saw it happen.[46]

In some cases the foreman might encourage employees to break rules. Sometimes this encouragement is unintentional (a supervisor who forgets to wear specified safety equipment might encourage his or her employees to do likewise). In some instances the foreman might actually encourage the employee to violate the rules in order to maintain or increase productivity. Perhaps the most vivid documented example of this situation occurred at an airplane manufacturing facility. One of the most serious offenses (resulting in automatic discharge) is the use of a tap to rethread unaligned bolt holes. The use of a tap is strictly prohibited by Air Force regulations; however, the alternative is disassembling and reassembling previous installations to make sure the holes line up for bolt insertion.

In most instances, the supervisor cannot afford to have a large amount of down time recorded for the department. Therefore, many supervisors condoned and encouraged serious rule infractions in the name of efficiency, and the following remarks made to their employees were not uncommon:

Now fellas, there's a big drive on taps. The Air Force just received a special memo. For God's sakes, don't use a tap when I'm around. If somebody sees it while I'm in the area, it'll be my ass. Look around first. Make sure I'm gone.[47]

A thorough discussion of the numerous mitigating circumstances suggested by the second arbitral assumption is beyond the scope of this chapter, but an example is given for illustrative purposes. An employee has been repeatedly warned and suspended for failure to report his absence to management when he is unable to work a production shift; the last suspension informed the grievant that another infraction would result in discharge. One month after suspension, the employee again fails to report his absence to management and is discharged when he reports to work the following morning. The employee contends (and adds evidence in the form of a doctor's slip) that his wife became suddenly, unexpectedly, and seriously ill and that his concern for his wife, coupled with no telephone in the apartment, resulted in his failure to report his absence to management. Here, management has followed all of the principles of progressive discipline; however, the employee's discharge might be set aside if the arbitrator maintains the circumstances were so unusual as to give management no reason to think it will happen again in the future.

Arbitrators often consider the mitigating effects of the grievant's role as a union officer. Compared to other employees, union officials usually have special rights and privileges, particularly when conducting union business. Many arbitrators regard the union steward and foreman as organizational equals in discussion of union matters. Arbitrators therefore give the union steward leeway if harsh words are exchanged in these meetings, while other employees might be successfully charged with insubordination for identical actions.

Union officers can also have greater responsibilities that correspond to their rights. For example, arbitrators have upheld more serious disciplinary action for union officers who failed to prevent a wildcat strike than for employees who actually participated in the strike.[48] This differential penalty implies that union stewards should be more knowledgeable about contractual prohibition against a wildcat strike and uphold their contractual obligation to maintain uninterrupted production during the term of the labor agreement.

Perhaps the most commonly considered mitigating circumstance in discharge cases is the employee's work record. An arbitrator will likely consider reinstating a discharged employee who violated a work rule (one that prohibits insubordination, for example) if that employee has a long and good work record with the company. The arbitrator in this situation realizes the potential of the employee returning to previous work habits, and might reinstate the employee with no back pay, which would represent a suspension.

Due Process and the Weingarten Decision

Due process has both its substantive and procedural aspects. Substantive due process focuses on the purpose or rationale of the work rules to ensure that an employee has not been arbitrarily disciplined or discharged.[49] This aspect is reflected in the previously discussed purpose and elements of discipline. The following procedural aspects of due process are usually found and acted upon in labor agreements:

1. The discipline process will follow certain time limits specified in the labor agreement.

2. The employee will be entitled to union representation when discipline is being administered.
3. The employee will be notified of the specific offense in writing.[50]

The second due process procedure, union representation, has been influenced by NLRB decisions and by the Supreme Court in its *Weingarten* decision. This situation will be discussed in detail because it illustrates the model of the labor relations process presented in Chapter 1 (Exhibit 1.1) and because it illustrates the impact of the fourth participant, the government, on labor-management relations.

The *Weingarten* decision pertained to an employee who was believed to have paid only a fraction of the required price of food she took out of the store. During the interview with management representatives she repeatedly asked for a union representative to be present but was denied. Management subsequently found her version of the incident to be supported, but in her emotional state she admitted that over a period of time she had taken several free lunches (totaling approximately $160) from the store, something a management official and other employees had also done. She was not disciplined for her actions; however, she informed her union representatives of the events, and an unfair labor practice was filed. The NLRB decided that management did commit an unfair labor practice (violating Section 8(a)1 of the National Labor Relations Act mentioned in chapter 3) by denying the employee union representation.

Union representation must be given to the employee when the employee requests this representation in situations where the employee reasonably believes the investigation will result in disciplinary action. Employers, however, have no legal requirement to bargain with any union representative who attends the interview; managers may insist that they are only interested in hearing the employee's own account of the matter under investigation.

The NLRB's *Weingarten* decision was appealed through the courts, and eventually upheld by the Supreme Court. Rationale for this decision was in part based on the union official's potential contribution to the disciplinary investigation:

A single employee confronted by an employer investigating whether certain conduct deserves discipline may be too fearful or inarticulate to relate accurately the incident being investigated, or too ignorant to raise extenuating factors. A knowledgeable union representative could assist the employer by eliciting favorable facts, and save the employer production time by getting to the bottom of the incident occasioning the interview. Certainly his presence need not transform the interview into an adversary contest.[51]

This decision also refuted the company's contention that union representation is only necessary after the company has made its discipline decision. The Supreme Court contended that this practice would diminish the value of union representation, thereby making it increasingly difficult for the employee to vindicate himself or herself in the subsequent grievance proceedings.

The written notice element of due process has caused some problems for management and is a major reason for the involvement of industrial relations representatives in the discipline process. Say an employee gets into a heated argument with the supervisor, refuses to work the assignment, and shouts an obscenity at the supervisor. The foreman could discipline the employee for "directing obscene and profane language toward a management representative." Once the charges are in writing, management must convince the arbitrator that this charge warrants discipline, a task which is not easy given the usual arbitral recognition that obscene language is regarded as common shop talk in an industrial facility. In this instance, management would have been wiser to have disciplined the employee for a more serious offense: "insubordination: refusal to follow supervisory orders." However, management can seldom change the offense once it is in writing and handed to the grievant. Consequently, a member of the industrial relations department is usually present for consultation (or in some cases direction) before the charges are reduced to writing.

Another related element of due process is *double jeopardy*—assigning an employee a more severe penalty than the one originally given. The rationale against double jeopardy is "since management is held to any desicion which purports to be final, it is important that it acts only after ascertaining all relevant facts and determining the magnitude of the offense."[52] Management can avoid the problem of double jeopardy if it makes clear to the grievant that the action taken in the first instance is temporary, pending further investigation by higher company officials. Usually, this takes the form of an indefinite suspension which, pending a subsequent investigation, can be converted to discharge without arbitral disapproval. A final element of due process is the keeping of secret records on the employee, which most arbitrators maintain are worse than no records at all.

One arbitrator notes three alternative positions that the arbitrator can take regarding procedural or due process irregularities:

---

(1) that unless there is strict compliance with the procedural requirements, the whole action will be nullified; (2) that the requirements are of significance only where the employee can show that he has been prejudiced by failure to comply therewith; or (3) that the requirements are important, and that any failure to comply will be penalized, but that the action taken is not thereby rendered null and void.[53]

Arbitrators tend to favor the third alternative, reasoning that management should suffer the consequences of its errors, but not to the point of exonerating an employee who is guilty of a serious offense (particularly if it has not prejudiced the employee's case).

Summary and Implications

Summary

In many respects, employee discipline represents the most significant day-to-day issue in administering the labor agreement. For the union and management organizations, administration of discipline is a key factor related to control and production; the supervisor and the affected employee are even more directly and personally affected.

Management had a unilateral right to discharge or discipline employees until the 1930s, although psychological reform and efficiency movements in the early 1900s urged management to critically examine its disciplinary policies. Some managers realized that an employee represented an investment which could be unnecessarily lost due to whimsical disciplinary actions. These individuals realized that they had an obligation to provide employees with clear work rules and proper training, which would minimize the number of discipline problems and lead to increased productivity. The establishment of the NLRB further refined employers' disciplinary policies, as employees discharged for their union activities could be reinstated to their jobs with back pay.

Discipline in unionized settings must be for just cause, a concept consisting of several dimensions. While discipline can accomplish several purposes for the organization, management may have to prove that its actions were taken to *correct* an employee's behavior. Correction suggests that an employee must be aware of work rules which are clear in their content as well as consequences for their infraction. The work rules must also be reasonable—that is, related to the job—and consistently applied to all employees under similar circumstances.

Discipline's corrective emphasis also suggests progressive or more severe penalties be given to an employee for repeating a similar offense. Progressive discipline impresses upon the employee the seriousness of repeated rule infractions while giving the employee additional chances to correct work behavior. Usually, management has to give an employee an oral warning for the first offense, then a written warning and suspension for subsequent, similar offenses. Discharge is a last resort—used only when all other attempts at correction have failed or the nature of the offense is so unacceptable as to make corrective efforts unnecessary.

Arbitration of discipline grievances places the burden of proof on management to establish that the employee committed the offense. Arbitrators may require the company to prove the employee guilty "beyond a reasonable doubt" or by establishing a "preponderance of the evidence." Additional dimensions of evidence can occur when the company attempts to enter the employee's work record into the hearing or uses search and seizure techniques, or when contradictory testimony is entered into the hearing. Management must also establish that the penalty fits the crime and that it considered all possible mitigating circumstances before imposing discipline.

Management must also provide the employee with due process in the disciplinary procedure—insure that the appropriate contractual provisions are upheld. The employee usually has the right to union representation and the right to be notified of the offense in writing.

Implications

Emotions and strong feelings surround the discipline issue; many managers contend that arbitrators often exceed their powers in reinstating disciplined employees.

. . . Published arbitration opinions reveal an ever-increasing trend among arbitrators to invade the priesthood. Indeed, in divining the judgment to be meted out in discipline cases they have assumed the role not only of clergymen, but trial judges and psychiatrists. . . . In far too many cases the arbitrators' opinions demonstrate that the touchstone for evaluating the appropriateness of disciplinary penalties is simply the subjective views and personal prejudices of the arbitrators.[54]

Arbitrators, the NLRB, and the courts have no doubt on occasion interpreted a particular situation more broadly than managers would prefer. In some cases this is due to the extremely vague discipline clause in the labor agreement. "Just cause," without further contractual guidance, can have many definitions and implications. Sometimes arbitral reversal is due to the notion that management must follow *intent* as well as *content* of discipline procedures.

Some managers regard progressive discipline as a mechanical process ending in termination.

Little or no thought is given to how the procedure might be used to improve poor performance as it was meant to. [Managers contend] "If I just follow the steps, I won't have any problems, and personnel will let me fire this employee."[55]

Holders of this attitude believe that discharge is the only objective instead of dealing with the employee and the problem.

One indication of the effectiveness of arbitral reversals of management decisions to discharge should be the reinstated employees' subsequent job behavior. One recent study found mixed results. Managers believed that reinstated employees (who were still employed by the company) had made "normal progress" in twenty-eight out of the forty-seven cases. However, only twenty-three of these individuals had no subsequent disciplinary problems—eight employees repeated the same offense and sixteen employees engaged in different disciplinary offenses.[56]

The debate over the prudence of arbitrators in discipline cases is not resolved and will continue. Employee discipline will also continue to represent a most significant aspect of day-to-day labor relations activities on the shop floor.

Union and management officials and the affected employees have rather large investments in the outcome of disciplinary actions. All of the participants need to approach this topic in a rational manner to strengthen labor-management relationships and minimize the possibly far-reaching implications of an arbitrator's award.

Discussion Questions

1. Why is discipline a most significant issue for the union and management organizations? Describe how this significance has shifted over time.
2. One union newspaper indicated how it saved an employee's job. The employee was in the mechanic's classification and was discharged for refusing to comply with management's sudden, unilateral rule that mechanics perform janitorial duties. Given this sketchy situation, discuss the many possible reasons for the disciplinary action, indicating why the arbitrator might not have been convinced that management's discipline was for a "legitimate purpose." (You are free to make assumptions in your answer.)
3. Explain in some detail the difficulties management would have in administering the following work rule in accordance with the disciplinary principles established in the chapter: "Any employee reporting to work under the influence of alcohol will be subject to discharge."
4. Indicate the comparative advantages and disadvantages of the checklist of disciplinary prerogatives in the labor agreement and a one-sentence contractual provision indicating "management has the right to discipline or discharge an employee for cause."
5. While not subject to judicial scrutiny, evidence in an arbitration hearing still has its complexities. Discuss the complexities which could be involved in an arbitration hearing involving an employee who was discharged for smoking marijuana on the job.
6. Assume you are in charge of establishing a training program for supervisors in administering discipline. Based on the supervisor's potential role in the disciplinary process, formulate and discuss three major principles you would stress in this session.

References

[1]Clyde W. Summers, "Protecting All Employees Against Unjust Dismissal," *Harvard Business Review* 58 (January-February 1980), p. 106.

[2]See for example Bureau of National Affairs Inc., *Daily Labor Report*, August 5, 1982, p. A–2; and, Perry A. Zirkel, "A Profile of Grievance Arbitration Cases," *Arbitration Journal*, 38 (March, 1983), p. 37.

[3]William P. Anthony and Philip Anthony, "More Discipline, Less Disciplinary Action," *Supervisory Management* 17 (September 1972), p. 18.

[4]Orme Phelps, *Discipline and Discharge in the Unionized Firm* (Berkeley: University of California Press, 1959), p. 1.

[5]Earl R. Bramblett, "Maintenance of Discipline," in Paul Pigors, Charles A. Meyers, and F.T. Malm, eds., *Management of Human Resources*, 3d ed. (New York: McGraw Hill, 1973), p. 470.

[6]James Menzies Black, *Positive Discipline* (New York: American Management Association, 1970), p. 60.

[7]See for example Theodore A. Olsen, "Wrongful Discharge Claims Raised by At Will Employees: A New Legal Concern for Employers," *Labor Law Journal* (May 1981), pp. 265–297; and, "The Growing Cost of Firing Nonunion Workers," *Business Week*, April 5, 1981, pp. 95–98.

[8]Ken Jennings and Roger Wolters, "Discharge Cases Reconsidered," *Arbitration Journal* 31 (September 1976), pp. 164–180. For an earlier study see J. Fred Holly, "The Arbitration of Discharge Cases: A Case Study," in Jean McKelvey, ed., *Critical Issues in Labor Arbitration* (Washington, D.C.: Bureau of National Affairs, Inc., 1957), p. 15.

[9]Joseph P. Wollenberger, "Acceptable Work Rules and Penalties: A Company Guide," *Personnel* 40 (July-August 1963), p. 23.

[10]For a discussion of other reasons for supervisory apathy see Wallace Wohlking, "Effective Discipline in Employee Relations," *Personnel Journal* 54 (September 1975), p. 489. For an empirical study examining supervisory apathy in enforcement see William B. Boise, "Supervisors' Attitudes toward Disciplinary Actions," *Personnel Administration* 28 (May-June 1965), pp. 24–27.

[11]Charles Myers and John Turnbill, "Line and Staff in Industrial Relations," in Joseph Litterer, ed., *Organizations: Structure and Behavior* (New York: Wiley, 1966), p. 313. For further insights, see Norman R. F. Maier and Lee E. Danielson, "An Evaluation of Two Approaches to Discipline," *Journal of Applied Psychology* 40 (October 1956), p. 323; Peter B. Schoderbeck, "The Changing Role of the Foreman," *Personnel Journal* 44 (August 1970), pp. 680–687; and David Kipnis and Joseph Cosentino, "Use of Leadership Powers in Industry," *Journal of Applied Psychology* 53 (December 1969), pp. 460–466.

[12]D. C. Miller, "Supervisor: Evolution of a Forgotten Role," in Floyd Mann, George Homans, and Delbert Miller, eds., *Supervisory Leadership and Productivity* (San Francisco: Chandler, 1965), p. 113.

[13]"*Oil, Chemical, and Atomic*" *Union News*, July 1970, p. 9.

[14]Black, *Positive Discipline*, p. 28.

[15]Robert Coulson, *The Termination Handbook* (New York: The Free Press, 1981), p. 7. See also, John Herrick, "Labor Arbitration As Viewed by Labor Arbitrators," *Arbitration Journal*, 38, (March, 1983), p. 42.

[16]Lawrence Stessin, *Employee Discipline* (Washington, D.C.: Bureau of National Affairs Inc., 1960), pp. 2–3.

[17]Dallas L. Jones, *Arbitration and Industrial Discipline* (Ann Arbor: Bureau of Industrial Relations, University of Michigan, 1961), p. 5.

[18]See for example, Mangus W. Alexander, "Hiring and Firing: Its Economic Waste," *Annals of the American Academy of Political and Social Science* 45 (May 1916), p. 128.

[19]For a discussion of how the NLRB and other governmental agencies such as EEOC and OSHA have influenced company discipline policies, see Charles A. Edwards, "Protection of the Complaining Employee: How Much Is Too Much?" *Employee Relations Law Journal* 6 (Autumn 1980), pp. 207–227.

[20]Robert Skilton, *Industrial Discipline and the Arbitration Process* (Philadelphia: University of Pennsylvania Press, 1952), pp. 22–23; Lawrence Stessin, "Is the Arbitrator Management's Friend in Discipline Cases?" *Monthly Labor Review* 72 (April 1959), p. 373. It should be noted that arbitrators' decisions can be modified by subsequent court decisions. See for example, Walter Fogel, "Court Review of Discharge Arbitration Cases," *Arbitration Journal* 37 (June 1982), pp. 22–33.

[21]Bureau of National Affairs, *Basic Patterns in Union Contracts* (Washington, D.C.: Bureau of National Affairs, 1979), p. 6.

[22]Stessin, *Employee Discipline*, p. 36.

[23]*Alden's Inc.*, 61 LA 665 (D. Dolnick, 1973).

[24]*Huron Forge and Machine Company*, 75 LA 88 (G. Roumell Jr., 1981).

[25]*Hoosier Panel Co., Inc.*, 61 LA 983 (M. Volz, 1973).

[26]Michael Marmo, "Arbitrators View Alcoholic Employees: Discipline or Rehabilitation?" *Arbitration Journal* 37 (March 1982), p. 24.

[27]Black, *Positive Discipline*, p. 52.

[28]Lewis Yagoda, "The Discipline Issue in Arbitration: Employer Rules," *Labor Law Journal* 15 (September 1964), p. 573.

[29]*Buick Youngstown Company*, 41 LA 570–573 (H. Dworkin, 1963).

[30]A. B. Chance Company, 57 LA 725–731 (P. Florey, 1971).

[31]"Picnic Misbehavior Warrants Discharge," Bureau of National Affairs, Inc., *Daily Labor Report*, May 12 1980, pp. 2–3.

[32]*General Foods Corporation*, 76 LA 532–535 (F. Denson, 1981).

[33]For an arbitral example of the problems of clarifying a work rule pertaining to insubordination see *General Electric Company*, 75 LA 118–120 (J. Larkin, 1981).

[34]Phelps, *Discipline and Discharge*, p. 48.

[35]Roland P. Wilder, "Discharge in the Law of Arbitration," *Vanderbilt Law Review* 20 (December 1966), pp. 124–125.

[36]Roger I. Abrams, "A Theory for the Discharge Case," *The Arbitration Journal* 36 (September 1981), pp. 24–27.

[37]*Inmot Corporation*, 58 LA 18 (J. Sembower, 1972).

[38]Maurice C. Benewitz, "Discharge Arbitration and the Quantum of Proof," *Arbitration Journal* 28 (June 1973), p. 103.

[39]R. W. Fleming, *The Labor Arbitration Process* (Urbana: University of Illinois Press, 1965), p. 222.

[40]*U.S. Steel Corporation*, 61 LA 1201 (H. Witt, 1973).

[41]Fleming, *Labor Arbitration Process*, p. 189.

[42]*New Jersey Bell Telephone*, 61 LA 255–256 (H. Weston, 1973).

[43]Bureau of National Affairs Inc., *Daily Labor Report*, August 2, 1982, p. A–3.

[44]Coulson, *The Termination Handbook*, p. 91.

[45]*Gindy Manufacturing Company*, 58 LA 1038–1040 (M. Handsaker, 1972).

[46]"Labor Letter," *Wall Street Journal*, August 30, 1977, p. 1. Reprinted by permission of *The Wall Street Journal*, © Dow Jones & Company, Inc., 1977. All rights reserved.

[47]Joseph Bensman and Israel Gerver, "Crime and Punishment in the Factory: The Function of Deviancy in Maintaining the Social System," *American Sociological Review* (August 1963), p. 593. For positive aspects of the supervisor's role in discipline see R. Dirk Van Horne, "Discipline: Purpose and Effect," *Personnel Journal* 48 (September 1969), pp. 728–731.

[48]W. H. Leahy, "Arbitration, Union Stewards, and Wildcat Strikes," *Arbitration Journal* 24 (1969), pp. 50–58. For a discussion of the employee's race as a possible mitigating circumstance see Harry Seligson, "Minority Group Employees, Discipline, and the Arbitrators," *Labor Law Journal* 19 (September 1968), pp. 544–554. It should be noted, however, that a recent judicial decision upheld the NLRB's contention that union stewards should not receive more discipline than other employees committing a similar offense unless there is a contractual provision specifying higher duties and responsibilities for union stewards. Bureau of National Affairs Inc., *Daily Labor Report*, August 19, 1982, p. 1.

[49]John D. Aram and Paul F. Salipante Jr., "An Evaluation of Organizational Due Process in the Resolution of Employee/Employer Conflict," *Academy of Management Review* 6 (1981), p. 200. See also Raymond L. Hogler, "Industrial Due Process and Judicial Review of Arbitration Awards," *Labor Law Journal* 31 (September 1980), pp. 570–576.

[50]In some cases, arbitrators and the courts have contended that due process procedures, such as the rights of employees to be heard before management's discharge decision is reduced to writing, are implied from the "just cause" provision. An employer might therefore be responsible for due process procedures even though they are not specified in the labor agreement. John S. Irving and Carl L. Taylor, "Pre-Disciplinary Hearings: An Unbargained Procedural Trap in Arbitration," *Employee Relations Law Journal* 6 (1980–1981), pp. 195–206.

[51]*NLRB v. J. Weingarten, Inc.*, 420 U.S. 262, 1974. It should be noted that this decision recognized several qualifications to the employee's right of union representation. For example, the employee must request the representation; the exercise of the right to representation may not interfere with legitimate employer prerogatives; the employer has no duty to bargain with any union representatives during the meeting. For a discussion of subsequent NLRB cases which appear to expand the principles expressed in *Weingarten* see Bruce Stickler, "Investigating Employee Misconduct: Must the Union Be There?" *Employee Relations Law Journal* 3 (Autumn 1977), pp. 255–265; Lewis H. Silverman and Michael J. Soltis, "*Weingarten*: An Old Trumpet Plays the Labor Circuit," *Labor Law Journal* 32 (November 1981), pp. 725–736; Paul N. Erickson Jr. and Clifford E. Smith, "The Right of Union Representation During Investigatory Interviews," *Arbitration Journal* 33 (June 1978), pp. 29–36.

[52]Wilder, "Discharge in the Law of Arbitration," p. 96.

[53]Fleming, *Labor Arbitration Process*, p. 139. See also Harry T. Edwards, "Due Process Considerations in Labor Arbitration," *Arbitration Journal* 25 (1970), p. 145.

[54]William M. Saxton, "Discipline and Discharge Cases," Address before the National Academy of Arbitrators, Dearborn, Michigan, *Daily Labor Report* (Washington, D.C.: Bureau of National Affairs Inc., 1979), cited in Arthur Anthony Malinowski, "An Empirical Analysis of Discharge Cases and the Work History of Employees Reinstated by Labor Arbitrators," *Arbitration Journal* 36 (March 1981), p. 32.

[55]Ira G. Asherman, "The Corrective Discipline Process," *Personnel Journal* 61 (July 1982), p. 529.

[56]Malinowski, "An Empirical Analysis," p. 39.

Chapter 11 Institutional Issues: Managerial Prerogatives, Union Security, and the Rights of Minority and Female Employees

"Today, because of the majoritarian bias inherent in collective bargaining—its commitment to democratic and egalitarian values—there must be some sacrifice of individual freedom. . . . But within the collective framework, the dissenting individual must be protected, and all those represented must be saved from negligent or corrupt representatives."

Harry H. Wellington, *Labor and the Legal Process*, 1968.

A major collective bargaining issue pertains to the rights and obligations of the labor and management organizations. Management's major institutional issue concerns its managerial prerogatives, or right to manage. The union has a corresponding institutional concern of union security, or its ability to preserve its organization—mainly by enrolling and retaining employee members. These two concerns are discussed in the chapter, as is the relationship between organized labor and minority and female employees.

Managerial Prerogatives

Background and Extent of Managerial Prerogatives

Before the advent of unions, or, more precisely, the passage of the National Labor Relations Act in 1935, management prerogatives and discretion in operating facilities were seldom questioned, and managers were virtually free to run their operations as they saw fit. In many cases unions were considered "intruders" into managerial prerogatives, since there were few laws regulating managers' actions toward employees. Consider for example the following managerial quotation, which could have been widely applicable in the early 1900s, but is out of date today due to employment laws:

Who but a miserable, craven-hearted man would permit himself to be subjected to such rules, extending even to the number of apprentices he may employ, and the manner in which they shall be bound to him; to the kind of work which will be performed in his own office, at particular hours of the day, and to the sex of the persons employed. . . . For ourselves, we never employed a female as compositor, and have no great opinion of apprentices; but sooner than be restricted on these points, or any other, by a self-constituted tribunal outside of the office, we would go back to the employment of our boyhood and dig potatoes.
. . . It is marvelous to us how any employer having a soul of a man within him can submit to such degradation.[1]

Although unions have become more accepted today, managers remain concerned over the gradual erosion of their rights in the labor relations process. Two questions which help us assess this concern are:

1. Does management have inherent rights regarding its employees?
2. To what extent does the union desire to assume managerial discretion?

Under common law, management officials were relatively free to manage their businesses and their employees. In unilaterally running the operation, the employer drew from the concepts of property rights and the laws of agency as well as the legal and social acceptance of "private enterprise," "ingenuity," and the "profit motive." Hence, management assumed the right to manage derived from the property rights of the owners or stockholders. The authority of these owners is delegated to management, which in turn directs the employees in achieving the goals of the company. Following this line of reasoning, management contends it cannot share its prerogatives with employees or any other group, as that would represent a dereliction of legal responsibility to the stockholders.

There is no question that management can organize, arrange, and direct the machinery, materials, and money of the enterprise; however, at least one author contends that managers have no comparable right to direct the employees. Indeed, the employee-employer relationship is similar to a continuing buyer-seller relationship in which the employer purchases the employee's services. In the absence of a written or terminal agreement between the manager and the employee, both parties are free to terminate the relationship if not satisfied with the conditions. Property rights carry no duty on the part of others to be managed—they can quit or be discharged without regard to the employer's property rights. *Thus, management's property rights have never extended over the employees. "What has happened is that, through the union, the employee has acquired sufficient power to exercise the legal right that he has always possessed."*[2]

Unions have typically expressed reluctance to become involved in management's rights pertaining to machinery, materials, and money of the enterprise. For example, two surveys found that most union officials believe management has the right to determine layout of equipment, financial policies and practices, source of materials, and determination of products and services to be rendered.[3] The following comments of a union official place the survey's findings in perspective:

The union doesn't want to run the business. It doesn't want to take over management. At the same time, while we don't attempt to usurp management's prerogatives, we do attempt to mitigate them so that their exercise cannot endanger the security and well-being of the workers.[4]

Unions' reluctance to become partners with management is subject to qualification, particularly if managerial actions affect employee job content and opportunities. Generally, the union's interests are restricted to protecting its members' job interests and itself as an institution. The distinction between the employer's property rights and the union's interests is not clear-cut. For example, new machinery or arrangement of production equipment might affect employees' wages and job tenure. Managerial discretion in running operations might be challenged and limited by unions if management's actions affect union members. This lack of clear-cut distinction is further illustrated by related provisions of the labor agreement.

"Reserved Rights" and the Collective Bargaining Agreement

Management does not have any inherent rights over employees and employees can sometimes alter working conditions through collective bargaining and the negotiated labor agreement. Yet problems sometimes occur when managment claims it has full discretion to administer issues which are not covered in the labor agreement. There is a "reserved rights" doctrine which in its simplistic, unqualified form holds

. . . that management's authority is supreme in all matters except those it has expressly conceded in the collective agreement and in all areas except those where its authority is restricted by law. Put another way, management does not look to the collective agreement to ascertain its rights; it looks to the agreement to find out which and how many of its rights and powers it has conceded outright or agreed to share with the union.[5]

Although the reserved rights doctrine gives management full discretion to act on any item not covered in the labor agreement, in reality, it can be diluted by three general factors:

- *Legal obligations* placed on management to negotiate "mandatory" collective bargaining issues with the union. In some cases, the NLRB has determined that matters which are subject to collective bargaining cannot unilaterally be altered by management even when it is acting on a specific right to alter the terms of the labor agreement.[6] (See Chapter 3.)
- *Arbitrators' decisions* which often interpret labor agreement provisions differently from management (consider the implications of "just cause" for discharge, for example). Arbitrators also consider past practices, which can add to the terms of the labor agreement. (See Chapter 9.)
- *Attitudes of some arbitrators and management officials* that the labor agreement is a "living document" which reflects the dynamics of labor-management relationships. Holders of this attitude tend to view the labor agreement in flexibile terms. Management, for example, might prefer to establish "mid-contract bargaining" with the union, particularly when the firm is unstable due to changes in the economy or when there is a need for productivity improvements.

Thus management cannot rely too strongly on the reserved rights doctrine. In fact, management officials usually negotiate either a long or short form "management prerogatives" or "rights" provision in the labor agreement. The following management rights provision illustrates the *short form*:

Employer retains all rights to manage, direct and control its business in all particulars, except as such rights are expressly and specifically modified by the terms of this agreement or any subsequent agreement.

Some managers prefer this all-encompassing provision on the assumption that it guarantees management complete discretion in those matters not cited in the labor agreement. Originally, managers felt this provision could justify their refusal to go to arbitration over an issue not specifically stated in the labor agreement. However, as discussed in Chapter 9, the Supreme Court (*United Steelworkers v. Warrior and Gulf Navigation Company*) stated that the arbitrator should determine whether an issue is a managerial prerogative if it is not specifically included in the labor agreement.

Many management officials responded to this decision by adopting the *long form* management rights provision—indicating several specific areas where management rights are unqualified (see Exhibit 11.1). Presumably, arbitrators, upon seeing these prerogatives clearly stated in the labor agreement, would rule in management's favor on whether the grievance is subject to arbitration. However, the long form managerial prerogatives clause is not without its problems:

1. It is difficult to list items which clearly specify management's unilateral discretion.

Exhibit 11.1 Example of a Long Form Management Rights Clause

Except as otherwise specifically provided in this Agreement, the Employer has the sole and exclusive right to exercise all the rights or functions of management, and the exercise of any such rights or functions shall not be subject to the grievance or arbitration provisions of this Agreement.

Without limiting the generality of the foregoing, as used herein, the term "Rights of Management" includes:

a. the right to manage the plant;
b. the right to schedule working hours;
c. the right to establish, modify or change work schedules or standards;
d. the right to direct the working forces, including the right to hire, promote, or transfer any employee;
e. the location of the business, including the establishment of new plants or departments, divisions or subdivisions thereof, and the relocation or closing of plants, departments, divisions or subdivisions thereof;
f. the determination of products to be manufactured or sold or service to be rendered or supplied;
g. the determination of the layout and the machinery, equipment or materials to be used in the business;
h. the determination of processes, techniques, methods, and means of manufacture, maintenance or distribution, including any changes or adjustments of any machinery or equipment;
i. the determination of the size and character of inventories;
j. the determination of financial policy, including accounting procedures, prices of goods or services rendered or supplied, and customer relations;
k. the determination of the organization of each production, service maintenance or distribution department, division or subdivision or any other production maintenance, service or distribution unit deemed appropriate by the Employer;
l. the selection, promotion, or transfer of employees to supervisory or other managerial positions or to positions outside of the bargaining unit;
m. the determination of the size of the working force;
n. the allocation and assignment of work to employees;
o. the determination of policy affecting the selection or training of new employees;
p. the establishment of quality and quantity standards and the judgment of the quality and quantity of workmanship required;
q. the control and use of the plant property, material, machinery, or equipment;
r. the scheduling of operations and the determination of the number and duration of shifts;
s. the determination of safety, health, and property protection measures for the plant;
t. the establishment, modification and enforcement of plant rules or regulations, which are not in direct conflict with any of the provisions of this Agreement;
u. the transfer of work from one job to another or from one plant, department, division or other plant unit to another;
v. introduction of new, improved or different production, maintenance, service or distribution methods or facilities or a change in existing methods or facilities;
w. the placing of production, service, maintenance or distribution work with outside contractors or subcontractors;
x. the determination of the amount of supervision necessary;
y. the right to terminate, merge or sell the business or any part thereof; and
z. the transfer of employees from one job to another or from one plant, department, division or other plant unit to another.

It is agreed that the enumeration of management prerogatives above shall not be deemed to exclude other management prerogatives not specifically enumerated above.

Source: Reprinted by permission of the publisher from Walter E. Baer, *Practice and Precedent in Labor Relations* (Lexington, Mass.: D. C. Heath and Company, Copyright 1972 by D. C. Heath and Company).

2. Management may overlook an item and fail to include it in the labor agreement. Arbitrators view a detailed management rights provision as expressing managerial intent to define all its perogatives. Since it is impossible for management to express all of its felt prerogatives, a problem may arise when management omits a particular item from the long form. Most arbitrators reviewing this omission would conclude that management should not view the omitted issue as being within its exclusive domain.

Both long and short forms of management prerogative clauses can cause additional problems. Most of the items cited in these provisions are subject to union involvement. Items in the short form are usually qualified by the terms of the agreement, whereas items in the long form can become eventual collective bargaining topics. By insisting on including the management rights clause in the labor agreement, management runs the risk of stirring up ideological differences with the union. The items in the management rights provision might also influence the union's bargaining goals in subsequent negotiations.

Management apparently believes the advantages of the management rights clause offset potential risks. Approximately 70 percent of the labor agreements contain management rights clauses which help remind arbitrators, union officials, and other managers (particularly first-line supervisors) that management never gives up its administrative initiative to establish the status quo.[8]

The union likewise seeks contractual language to strengthen its security. This issue is discussed in the following section.

Union Security

Inclusion of a union security clause in the labor agreement makes it easier for the union to enroll and retain members. Unions must be concerned about their security for at least two reasons. First, they are often only granted a one-year existence upon NLRB union certification under the National Labor Relations Act. As noted in Chapters 3 and 5, representation or decertification elections may be legally held one year after the union is recognized as the exclusive bargaining agent. Although existing union members are seldom approached ("raided") by other unions for representation purposes, the possibility of a rival union seeking recognition for these employees still exists. A union security provision does not eliminate this possibility but can make it easier for the current union to enroll members, which is an initial step in winning their loyalty.

Second, union security provisions tend to strengthen the union's financial resources by increasing the number of dues-paying members. Unions would like to recoup their initial time and money investments spent on organizing employees at an industrial facility by subsequently obtaining dues from the eligible members. Union leaders also feel they are morally justified in asking employees to pay for services provided by the union, since it is legally obligated to represent all bargaining unit employees regardless of their union membership.

Union security provisions are therefore sought to strengthen the union, a situation which can offer possible benefits to the employer as well as the union. Many might contend that employers prefer dealing with a weak instead of a strong union. Weak unions might aid the employer who wishes to terminate the union-management relationship, but they frustrate an employer who earnestly tries to resolve working condition disputes through an established union-management relationship. It is commonly the union, not the employer, who sells the collective bargaining agreement to the membership. A union has difficulty in accomplishing this objective when there are non-union member factions which vocalize their dissent about the collective bargaining process and the resulting outcomes.

Union officials contend that union security provisions offer other advantages to the employer. They contend that less time will be spent in recruiting new members and collecting dues of existing members during the workday. However, management officials counter that this time saving will not result in more production, since union officials might use the extra time to police the labor agreement and formulate additional grievances. Unions also maintain that morale would be improved if all employees were union members. Tensions arise when some people do not pay for the same services shared by all. However, a counterargument could be made that tensions are not reduced by union security, merely redirected. The possible anger of union members working with nonunion employees is replaced by the anger of forced members who feel they have to pay for unwanted services.[9]

With these potential advantages and disadvantages in mind, union security provisions have taken one or more of the following forms:

Closed shop. In order for an employee to obtain a job in a closed shop, he or she must first become a member of a union. The closed shop was made unlawful by the Taft-Hartley Act of 1947.

Union hiring hall. According to the union hiring hall provision, employers must hire employees referred by the union if the union can supply a sufficient number of qualified applications.[10] This provision is usually found in the construction trades, where a union provides the employer with qualified employees for a relatively short-term project. This provision has been supported by the Supreme Court, with the provision that the union hiring hall does not discriminate between union and nonunion applicants.[11]

Union shop. Under a union shop contract provision, the employee does not have to be a union member in order to be hired by the company. However, he or she must become a union member *after* a probationary period of not less than thirty days in order to remain employed by the company. Under a union shop provision, the company does not always have to discharge an employee who is not a union member if: (a) the employer believes union membership was not offered the employee on the same terms as other employees or (b) membership was denied for reasons other than the failure to tender dues. The union shop provision does not give the union the right to reject certain employees for membership and then seek their discharge for not being union members.

Agency shop. An agency shop provision does not require the employee to join the union; however, in order to remain employed by the company, the employee must pay to the union a sum equal to membership dues. This provision is based on two principles: (a) all employees who are represented by the union should help defray the bargaining and grievance costs, and (b) employees should not be forced to join a union.[12] The Supreme Court has upheld the validity of the agency shop in both the private[13] and public sectors, although nonmembers may have to pay only the portion of dues that are related to collective bargaining and contract administration (not funds which are used for political expenditures).[14] Under agency shop provisions, nonunion employees may continue to work during a strike and refuse to participate in other strike-related activities without being penalized by the union.

Maintenance of membership. A maintenance of membership provision does not require all employees to become members of a union as a condition of employment. However, an employee who joins the union must remain a member for a specified period of time, such as the duration of the labor agreement. Maintenance of membership provisions also contain an escape period (usually fifteen days) after the subsequent labor agreement becomes effective. Employees who do not leave the union during the escape period must remain members until the next escape period.

"Quasi-union shop." It is illegal to require the union shop provision in right-to-work states and areas having similar public sector bargaining statutes. However, union and management officials sometimes get around these legal restrictions by inserting "quasi-union shop" provisions in the labor agreement. Usually, the first page of the agreement states that employees will have to join the union as a condition of employment—a union shop provision. The union steward shows the new employee this provision, which usually results in that employee joining the union. A second provision, usually buried in some footnote elsewhere in the labor agreement, states, "Any provision found in this agreement which conflicts with local, state, or federal law is considered null and void." These provisions have the same effect as a union shop (particularly since the new employee will seldom research the labor agreement when confronted by the union steward) and at the same time comply with anti-union shop legislation.

Contingency union shop. Some labor agreements in right-to-work states (where union membership is not a condition of employment) have a provision which states that union shop provisions will apply if and when the state's right-to-work laws are repealed.

Dues checkoff. A dues checkoff provision can be used in connection with any of the previously cited union security provisions or can stand alone in the labor agreement. It is not a union security clause in the strict sense of the word, as it does not guarantee that some or all employees will become union members. However, dues checkoff allows the union members to have their dues automatically taken out of their payroll checks (as for any other payroll deduction) and transferred to the union. This provision is most important to the union; indeed, most unions given an either/or choice would prefer dues checkoff over any other union security provision, because it assures the union of an uninterrupted flow of income. Without a systematic dues deduction, union officers would have to spend a great deal of time with recalcitrant members who kept delaying their dues payments. In many cases, the employer automatically agrees to this provision in the first contract negotiation on the assumption that every other labor agreement contains it. Often an administrative fee is charged the union for the collection of dues and other paperwork. In negotiations, astute management officials usually bargain for something in return for this provision, such as flexibility in making work assignments, subcontracting, and writing job descriptions.

Union security provisions are found in 83 percent of the labor agreements reviewed in a recent survey. Union shop provisions are by far the most common (63 percent of the surveyed agreements) followed by agency shop (7 percent) and maintenance of membership provisions (3 percent).[15] Likewise, over 86 percent of the agreements provide for checkoff procedures for dues, assessments and initiation fees.[16] In many cases, however, the parties are not free to negotiate a particular union security provision. Right-to-work laws which restrict this discretion are discussed in the next two sections.

Right-to-Work Laws: Meaning and Controversy

Employers, some employees, and the courts have long been concerned with union security provisions. In 1943 the Associated Industries of Florida successfully obtaining the first right-to-work amendment to the state constitution. The Taft-Hartley Act in 1947 gave federal permission to right-to-work laws. More specifically, Section 14(b) of the act remains in force today and states:

Nothing in this Act shall be construed as authorizing the execution or application of agreements requiring membership in a labor organization as a condition of employment in any State or Territory in which such execution or application is prohibited by State or Territorial law.

Under this provision, states may initiate legislation prohibiting union membership as a condition of employment. However, continuing lobbying efforts must be made by individuals or organizations to pass such a state law, a none too simple task since there are corresponding attempts by others to oppose right-to-work legislation. Current efforts are mainly conducted by the National Right to

Work Committee, founded in 1955. Both employees and individuals have joined this committee, whose stated purpose is to protect the employee's right to determine whether to join unions. The committee does not regard itself as being against unions, merely union security provisions which compel employees to become members. However, it has been alleged that the committee's "pro-union, anti-union security" stance has been modified to a flat "anti-union" approach in recent years.[17] A related but separate organization, the National Right to Work Legal Defense Foundation, provides legal representation in right-to-work cases.

The arguments concerning right-to-work laws can be intense, provocative, and varied. (See Exhibit 11.2 for both sides of this controversial issue.) These arguments fall into four groups:

1. The meaning of right-to-work.
2. The morality of right-to-work laws.
3. The relationship of right-to-work laws and union democracy.
4. The effect of right-to-work laws on employees' economic status.

"Meaning of "right-to-work." Supporters of right-to-work laws contend the underlying definition affirms the right of every U.S. citizen to work for a living, whether or not he or she belongs to a union. In their view, compulsory unionism in any form (union shop, agency shop) contradicts a fundamental human right—freedom to join or not to join a union. Even Samuel Gompers, at least on occasion, stressed the necessity for "voluntarism" in labor unions:

The workers of America adhere to voluntary institutions in preference to compulsory systems which are held to be not only impractical but a menace to their rights, welfare, and their liberty.[18]

Opponents of "right-to-work" contend this term represents a gimmicky public relations slogan designed to restrict union security and related bargaining power.[19] They argue that unions do not deny anyone the fundamental freedom to seek work. Union security represents one of many negotiated working conditions such as work schedules, type of work performed or wages. If an employee does not like a particular working condition, he or she is free to seek employment elsewhere. This argument can also be supported by a quotation from Samuel Gompers (which shows that quotations from a prominent individual can often be used to support both sides of an issue).

[T]he union shop, in agreement with employers, mutually entered into for the advantage of both employees and unions and the maintenance of industrial peace . . . is to the economic, social and moral advancement of all our people.[20]

Exhibit 11.2 Attitudes Concerning Right-to-Work

Should nonunion teachers be required to pay agency shop fees?

YES

Whoever thought up the slogan "right to work" was a master of public relations. Even though the slogan caught on, it is very misleading. The issue is not whether anyone has a right to work. It is whether there is any justification in requiring employees who do not wish to join the union which represents them, to pay union dues or an amount equal to union dues, commonly called an agency fee.

For teachers and other public employees, the constitutional issue has been settled. In *Abood v. Detroit Board of Education*, the United States Supreme Court ruled last spring that the agency fee was constitutional. Why did the Court reach this conclusion?

Under our labor laws, employees themselves decide whether or not to be represented by a union. In a typical situation, a union claims to represent the employees and produces evidence. One or more other unions may then also claim to represent the employees. An election is held and one of the ballot choices is "No Union." If there is no clear majority on the first ballot, there is a runoff between the two top choices. When a union is selected it is the choice of the employees and that union is required under law to represent *all* the employees in the bargaining unit, whether they are members or not. Unions resemble governments, providing services for all in their territory. Police and fire protection, pollution control, defense, and other services are provided for *all* residents—not just those who want the services and not merely those who vote.

A union chosen to be the bargaining agent must negotiate salaries, pensions, holidays, and other conditions of employment for all. It is illegal to negotiate them for members only. Furthermore, even after benefits have been negotiated, the union is required to administer and police the contract on a day-to-day basis. It must provide for legal, grievance, and arbitration costs. It must employ a lobbyist or pay dues to state and national affiliates to insure that what was won is not taken away.

How should all these services be supported? In society at large, services provided for all are not paid for on a voluntary basis. We do not allow Mr. Smith to say that if he does not believe in or need police or fire protection, he will not pay for them. Those who have fought against unions

NO

The question could also ask, "Should eminently qualified teachers be required to pay a private organization for the privilege of keeping jobs they obtained on their own initiative and retained by their own merit?"

The answer, of course, is a resounding "No!"

Yet, teacher union officials are demanding that educators all over America be fired if they refuse to pay union dues and fees. And the demands are being met. Literally tens of thousands of teachers in 19 states would be fired if they chose to stop paying dues. Experience, dedication, qualifications—even tenure—are irrelevant.

The "agency shop" *is* legal in those 19 states. There is no argument about that. But the overriding question is not whether it's legal—but whether it's morally right.

Union officials base their demand for payment of fees in lieu of membership (agency shop) on the premise that they *have* to represent all members in a bargaining unit: therefore, all should pay. They claim those who don't are "riding free." That simply isn't true.

What they don't say is that they *demanded* that the government give them the privilege to represent all members of a bargaining unit. (They call it "exclusive representation"—though "monopoly bargaining" is a much more accurate description.) Because lawmakers gave in to that demand, teachers who want to represent themselves are not allowed to do so.

Now union officials claim that monopoly bargaining (exclusive representation) is a burden on dues-paying members. Therefore, they insist, teachers who refuse to pay up should be fired from their jobs.

If union officials are serious about the representation of nonmembers being a burden, then the equitable solution is to let teachers who reject union membership fend for themselves. Require unions to bargain only for those persons who *want* their services. After all, if a union is able to show its benefits to be attractive—if it does the best job—then teachers will want to join, and the so-called "free rider" problem will be solved.

We don't believe anyone should be denied the right to join a union. But we also don't believe anyone should be forced to join or pay a union not of his or her own choosing. So we'll work with *any* union to re-

Exhibit 11.2 (Continued)

YES	NO
under the slogan "the right to work" are now fighting against the agency fee. They know that without adequate financing for the work of unions, unions are weakened, and so is their ability to deliver for all employees. The "right to work" is a misnomer. It really means the right to work without union protection, the right to work for lower wages, the right to work under conditions of exploitation. Teachers, who only recently gained a real voice in their own professional destiny, know this. They will not be fooled. **Albert Shanker** is president of the American Federation of Teachers and a vice-president, AFL-CIO.	move the unfair "burden" of representing everyone. Teachers must wake up to prevent this ruin of individual liberty. It is absolutely untrue that those of us who oppose coercive unionism are antiunion. There is a difference. It's the same distinction as between being against unresponsive and inadequate school officials and being against all school management. We aren't *against* teachers, we're *for* teachers—every single, individual one. **Susan Staub** is staff director of Concerned Educators Against Forced Unionism, a division of the National Right to Work Committee.

Source: Concerned Educators Against Forced Unionism (CEAFU).
Reprinted from Instructor, copyright March, 1978, used by permission.

The morality of right-to-work laws. Supporters of right-to-work contend that no individual should be compelled to join a private organization, particularly if that organization uses the individual's dues to support causes which the individual believes are morally unjust or contrary to his or her religious beliefs. "No other private organization in America insists on having the power to force membership on an unwilling people."[21] The government alone should have the right to tax the citizen or require compliance to its rules.

This attitude has been reinforced by a 1980 amendment to the National Labor Relations Act and actions by the Supreme Court which have in effect stated that employees may refuse to pay union dues because of religious objections.[22]

Opponents believe, for moral reasons, that right-to-work laws should be abolished. A person is more than an individual; he or she is also a member of society with responsibility for contributing to the common good. Industrial society's common good might demand that individuals conform to norms (for example, a union security provision) for the good of all.[23]

The relationship of right-to-work laws and union democracy. Right-to-work advocates contend voluntary union membership insures that unions will be responsible to that membership. With compulsory union membership, the members cannot express their dissent—they must remain "captive passengers" of the union if they wish to keep their jobs. Union leaders can become indifferent or even corrupt, since members have no economic way of voicing their displeasure. Union leaders should have to earn their dues through their responsive, diligent actions. "Good unions don't need compulsory unionism—and bad unions don't deserve it."[24]

Opponents stress that under the National Labor Relations Act, unions are responsible for representing all bargaining unit employees. Also, unions may be sued for lack of fair representation by bargaining unit employees who are nonmembers. Those individuals who do not join the union are regarded by union members as being free riders—ones who never go near the kitchen but always show up for dinner.[25] Unions expect that all employees represented should pay their fair share, just as citizens pay taxes for public services.

Democracy means abiding by the will of the majority. Employees do have voting rights regarding a representation election and must live with the outcome of the majority vote. Thus, to be fully represented and involved in the democratic processes (voting, attending meetings to formulate bargaining proposals, and so on), employees should join the union and represent their interests in the union government processes.

The effect of right-to-work laws on employees' economic status. Advocates claim these laws benefit the employees from several economic standpoints. First, firms are attracted to right-to-work states which creates new jobs for employees in these states.[26] Second, in attempting to obtain a union security clause, unions might conduct a strike to pressure the employer. Since there can be no union security clause in right-to-work states, no strike can result over negotiating this issue, and employees do not needlessly lose income.

However, these arguments can be challenged. For example, the additional jobs in right-to-work states are caused by "runaway" firms from non-right-to-work states seeking workers at low wages. Almost all the right-to-work states have a lower per capita income than states that do not have such laws. Also, very few strikes result from union requests for union security provisions in the contract;[27] indeed, some evidence suggests that strike activity in right-to-work states is no different from that in non-right-to-work states.[28]

The Institution and Effects of Right-to-Work Laws

Currently, twenty states have right-to-work laws.[29] Their passage has required procedural and political maneuvering of legislators as well as the skills of business lobbyists and other community interest groups.[30] Some believe that right-to-work laws have had little if any influence on the unions' strength and bargaining power. One author contends that this inconclusive relationship might be due to loopholes which negate the impact of right-to-work laws and the fact that right-to-work laws only apply when the union wins a representation election. Regarding the second factor, there is no reason to think that a union will be reluctant to initially organize employees simply because it will be legally unable to require them all to join.[31]

There are also several legal and quasi-legal loopholes which minimize the effects of right-to-work legislation, particularly since these laws seldom have an effective enforcement mechanism to insure that union security provisions do not exist. For example, the Indiana right-to-work provision allowed a grace period for employers and employees to resolve their differences over this issue. Many labor agreements were reopened before their expiration dates and before the effective date of the right-to-work legislation in order to take advantage of this grace period. Union security clauses were extended along with provisions for wage increases in the subsequent years of the "new" contract.[32]

Other legal loopholes depend on court sanctions. In Indiana, for example, agency shop provisions were deemed legally permissible in this state's right-to-work legislation. As stated earlier in the chapter, agency shop provisions do not require union membership; instead, the employee is obligated to pay the equivalent of a service charge to the union. After the Indiana right-to-work law was passed in 1955, an estimated 91 percent of the collective bargaining agreements in the state included an agency shop provision. When Indiana repealed the right-to-work law in 1965, the agency shop provision was dropped from all but 37 percent of the collective bargaining agreements.[33] Union-management cooperation to circumvent right-to-work legislation can result in related contract provisions (such as the "quasi-union shop"). In another right-to-work state it was common to include *contingent union shop clauses*—provisions indicating that management and the union would automatically include the union shop arrangement if and when the state's right-to-work law were eliminated. This type of clause performed a psychological function: it told employees that management backed the union's efforts to enroll all employees as members. On some occasions, management gives more direct encouragement to employees to join the union. One union official has commented:

We've found that in the right-to-work states, some of the big nationwide corporations which have the union shop elsewhere, will often cooperate with us in getting new employees to join. The plant supervisor just has a little chat with the man when he's hired and says a few kind words about the union, and the worker usually gets the point.[34]

On the other hand, some evidence exists that right-to-work laws can reduce existing union membership by 6 to 15 percent. Further, this reduction can result in a cutback of union services and staff personnel. The prospect of not obtaining all employees as members might also discourage unions from organizing smaller and automated facilities, particularly since overhead costs for negotiation and contract administration tend to remain the same regardless of the number of dues-paying employees.[35]

Thus, the effects of right-to-work laws on number of union members, union organizing drives, and labor-management relationships are subject to debate. However, related investigations usually agree on one point: it is difficult if not impossible to measure specific impacts of right-to-work laws. States having these laws have a significantly smaller percentage of their work force unionized, but this difference often reflects preferences and attitudes of the affected states' populations instead of the impact of the laws themselves.[36]

Thus far, we have discussed institutional issues that affect the union and management organizations in their relationships with each other. However, there are also intra-institutional issues, such as the relationship between labor unions and black and female employees, which are discussed in the next section.

Unions and Minority Groups

Unions and Black Employees

Historical Overview There is tremendous variation both historically and currently in the union response toward black employees. A prominent report on this subject has noted that trade union policies regarding black employees have varied from outright exclusion to full acceptance with all privileges of membership.[37] Most of the generalizations in this section focus on the extent to which the union movement has discriminated against black employees. Such discrimination has had two general dimensions: exclusion (through constitutional provisions, initiation rituals, or tacit agreements) and segregation (in either separate locals or separate job classifications).[38]

The Knights of Labor (KOL) actively recruited black members and attempted to treat them in an equalitarian manner.[39] Much of the KOL's enthusiasm was due to its social reform philosophy (discussed in Chapter 2). However, pragmatic reasons also prompted this organization's recruiting efforts because employers during the late 1800s and early 1900s often used black employees as strikebreakers to put pressure on white strikers to resolve their differences.

A typical handbill distributed by strikebreaker recruiting agents during an 1896–1897 strike read:

WANTED! COLORED coal miners for Weir City, Kan., district, the paradise for colored people. Ninety-seven cents per ton, September 1 to March 1; 87½ cents per ton, March 1 to September 1 for screened coal over seven-eights opening. Special train will leave Birmingham on the 13th. Transportation advanced. Get ready and go to the land of promise.[40]

The presence of black employees working while white employees were on strike increased tension and thwarted the KOL's goals of social betterment. One way to stop this disruption was to bring black employees into the union membership.

The American Federation of Labor (AFL) assumed the KOL's equalitarian racial attitude almost from its inception. The AFL's president, Samuel Gompers, proclaimed a firm antidiscrimination policy regarding black employees. He initially effected this policy by refusing to grant an AFL charter to national unions whose constitutions formally excluded blacks from membership. One such membership qualification clause was found in the Order of Sleeping Car Conductors' Constitution: "The applicant for membership shall be a white male, sober and industrious, and must join of his own free will. He must be sound in mind and body."[41]

Gompers quickly found out that stating a policy is much easier than subsequent enforcement. His first departure from his anti-exclusionary clause stance indicated that unions would be refused a charter only if they had an explicit racial exclusion clause in their constitution. In essence, the AFL was unconcerned if national unions resorted to less explicit practices in denying membership to black employees.[42] For example, the International Association of Machinists dropped its constitutional provision prohibiting black members and was granted an AFL charter in 1895. However, the union excluded blacks from its initiation ritual—in effect, excluding them from membership—until 1948.[43] Indeed, eleven unions affiliated with the AFL had formal race bars as late as the 1930s.[44]

Gompers rationalized accepting unions which discriminated against black employees on the basis that the AFL would have no power to effect change if the unions were outside its jurisdiction. Presumably, once in the AFL, national union leaders would see the errors of their ways and accept black members. This belief was not supported by facts, as a 1902 study found that (a) forty-three international unions did not have any black members and (b) there were only 40,000 black members in the AFL unions, with half of this total belonging to one union, the United Mine Workers.[45] A second strategy to increase black membership while not offending national unions was the AFL's granting of charters to segregated black locals, a policy which continued until 1939.[46]

As early as 1905, the AFL's policy became less enthusiastic and aggressive. Gompers, obviously recalling black strikebreaking activities, expressed only qualified support for racial membership integration:

Tis true that some men have been angered at the introduction of black strike breakers. I have stood as champion of the colored man and have sacrificed self and much of the labor movement that the colored man should get a chance. But the caucasians are not going to let their standard of living be destroyed by Negroes, Chinamen, Japs, or any others.[47]

In essence, Gompers informed black employees that they had to earn consideration by the AFL by not engaging in efforts which could hurt their potential union brothers and by obtaining requisite job skills.[48] This self-help emphasis for black employees continued for several decades. In 1941, William Green, Gompers' successor, and two other AFL officials expressed their attitudes toward black membership along the following general lines: "[a] discrimination existed before the AFL was born and human nature cannot be altered . . . [b] the AFL, per se, does not discriminate because it gladly accepts Negro workers into its directly affiliated federal locals . . . and [c] . . . Negroes should be grateful for what the AFL has done for them."[49]

At least two forces have influenced a more progressive union stance for black employees: a prominent black labor leader, A. Philip Randolph, and the emergence of the Congress of Industrial Organizations (CIO). Randolph, president of the Brotherhood of Sleeping Car Porters, became involved in the AFL's racial betterment activities when his union received a national charter from the federation in 1936; his 35,000 members comprised one-half of the total black AFL membership at the time. Randolph's initial skepticism of the AFL's attitude toward minorities did not appreciably change over the years. Indeed, his verbal battles with AFL leadership on civil rights often became quite heated. In 1961 he was censured by the AFL's Executive Committee for getting close to "militant groups," thereby creating a "gap between organized labor and the Negro community."[50] It is difficult to measure the precise success of Randolph's efforts; however, at the least, he continually insured that the AFL's leadership could not forget the black employee.

The independent CIO also pressured the rival AFL to enroll black employees. Unlike the AFL craft unions, the CIO's unions had no control over employment. Therefore, they had to organize all existing employees, black and white, at a facility if they were to be successful.[51] The CIO also needed broad-based support in pressing its legislative goals of minimum wages, unemployment insurance, and social security. The AFL, on the other hand, usually having higher wage earners as members, could not see similarities between their craft jobs and lower wage classifications which were populated largely by black employees.

The Relationship between Unions and Black Employees since 1955

Since the AFL-CIO merger in 1955, unions have attempted to further racial equality in one or more of the following ways:[52]

1. *Avoid expulsion of the national unions where discrimination exists.* As Gompers earlier contended, the AFL can only achieve success if the offending union is within their organization, subject to the federation's sanctions. By retaining these unions, the AFL-CIO, particularly through its Civil Rights Committee and other organizations of black union leaders,[53] can continue to apply pressure for equal opportunity. It should also be noted that the national union can place its local union affiliates under trusteeship if the local union has engaged in discriminatory practices.[54]
2. *Set a favorable example for national and local unions to follow.* The AFL-CIO has on occasion publicly and financially helped civil rights groups such as the NAACP. However, on at least one major occasion—the 1963 civil rights march on Washington—The AFL-CIO was conspicuously absent from the list of sponsors, leaving such preferences, if any, to "individual union determination."[55]

3. *Urge that civil rights legislation be passed at the local, state, and federal levels.* George Meany stressed the need for this type of legislation because, ". . . the labor movement is not what its enemies say it is—a monolithic, dictatorial centralized body that imposes its will on the helpless dues payers. We operate in a democratic way, and we cannot dictate even in a good cause. So in effect, we need a federal law to help us do what we want to do—mop up those areas of discrimination which still persist in our own ranks."[56]

Unions have also lobbied for another solution to the civil rights issue—more jobs. This position has consistently been taken by union leaders; for example, in 1963 Walter Reuther commented:

Does anybody in his right mind believe we can solve the civil rights social revolution in the framework of mass unemployment? . . . There must be a job for every able bodied worker in America whether he is white or black or brown or yellow.[57]

A recent study has found that economic gains of black U.S. citizens are tied to full employment.[58] Some, however, contend that unions, insisting that unemployment is the problem, are passing the racial discrimination buck to the employers. Yet, particularly in the nonconstruction sector, there is some merit to the unions' notion that they cannot be blamed for something they cannot control—the hiring of additional black employees.

Some evidence suggests that unions have been relatively successful in removing racial discrimination. Studies have found, for example, that: (a) unionized black employees have higher wages than black nonunion employees and (b) the average wage of black workers relative to white workers is consistently higher in unionized than in nonunion labor markets.[59] Yet even these figures suggest two possible areas of discrimination. First, black union workers have lower wages than their white counterparts, an observation possibly stemming from past union policies of segregating black employees in lower wage classifications. Second, unions discriminate against black nonunion employees when they determine they will organize all-white facilities before organizing all-black facilities.[60]

Discrimination also occurs within the union in terms of *the day-to-day attitudes of white union members, the number of black members who are union officers,* and the *quality of union services given to black employees.* Workplace tensions have been increased because white employees feel economically threatened by black employees, with whom they compete for the same jobs, promotions, and job security possibilities. Tensions can also be attributed to racism, irrespective of the underlying cause.[61]

In a number of cases, the racist attitudes of local union members place union leaders in an almost helpless situation—a price of union democracy is the union leader's obligation to abide by the will of the majority. This situation prompts minority union members to solidify their ranks around racial concerns. One black vice-president of the UAW has commented,

---

Many local unions in urban areas are dominated by blacks. Blacks go to the union meetings because the halls are in urban areas. Blacks don't have boats or summer cottages, so they go to the union meetings on weekends.[62]

In some cases, all-black organizations have been formed within the local or national union to monitor or change the union's policies toward minority members. Coordinated efforts across national unions have been made through the Coalition of Black Trade Unionists (CBTU) which was formed in 1972. The mission of the CBTU states,

---

[A]s black trade unionists, it is our challenge to make the labor movement more relevant to the needs and aspirations of black and white workers. The CBTU will insist that black union officials become full partners in the leadership and decision making of the American labor movement.[63]

White union leaders are also reluctant to press for an increased number of black members because these individuals might vote along racial lines. One study of United Auto Workers local union officers' elections found that the racial composition of the leadership clearly reflects the racial composition of the membership.[64] Consequently, the established white union leaders are fearful that increased numbers of black members would vote them out of office.

The number of black union leaders can be also limited by the reluctance of blacks to seek such positions. Black union leaders usually have a difficult time reconciling union and racial priorities. This difficulty is reflected by one black union leader, who indicates, "If I moved into the White House, I wouldn't paint it, but I also wouldn't forget that I'm black—I can't."[65] The contradictory pressures on black union leaders are increased by age differences.

Usually, black union leaders have had more union experience than their black constituents. They believe they have paid their dues in dealing with union pressures and recoil at the urgings of "young, black upstarts" for "more now." One such black union official has reacted directly to criticisms of "Uncle Tomism" in these terms: "An Uncle Tom is a Negro who has a job that a nigger wants."[66] Perhaps similar pressures have discouraged some blacks from running for office. Regardless of the reason, very few blacks currently hold union leadership positions. (The United Auto Workers, United Steelworkers, and the American Federation of State, County, and Municipal Employees represent notable exceptions.)

The lack of black union leaders coupled with antagonism of white and black members influences the quality of union services provided black members. This potential source of discrimination has been discussed in Chapter 8. However, there are additional legal possibilities for black employees who charge discrimination.

Legal Considerations Affecting the Rights of Minority Employees at the Local Union Level In Chapter 9 we noted that under the *Gardner-Denver* decision minority employees can file a grievance over alleged discriminatory action while also filing charges with the Equal Employment Opportunity Commission (known as having "two bites at the apple"). Likewise, Chapter 12 will discuss legal remedies for minority employees who successfully contend that seniority systems discriminatorily affect their job progression and retention. The Equal Employment Opportunity Act subjects the union as well as the employer to liability for back pay awards, court costs, and the attorney fees of the plaintiffs,[67] particularly when the employer's discrimination arises from a collective bargaining agreement that the union signed.[68] Unions can also be legally liable for discrimination if they do not fairly represent minority and female employees (discussed in Chapter 8), or if unions actively discriminate (or cause employers to discriminate) against an employee.[69]

Minority employees can also seek legal recourse if they believe that the proposed union discriminates racially. A 1973 court of appeals decision, (*NLRB v. Mansion House Center*) upheld the National Labor Relations Board's contention that unions engaging in racial discrimination or sexism should be denied initial certification and that employers could invoke the discriminatory practices of a union as a reason for refusing to bargain with that union. However, the quantity and type of evidence needed for this action has not yet been specifically established by the NLRB.[70]

The extent to which minorities can engage in self-help techniques to prevent discriminatory actions has been before the Supreme Court. The 1975 *Emporium* decision concerned several black employees who believed the grievance procedure in the labor agreement was an inadequate forum to resolve racial discrimination issues. Over the objections of their union officers, these employees picketed the allegedly discriminatory employer instead of processing a related grievance and were eventually discharged for their picketing activities. The Supreme Court addressed itself to the following question: Are such attempts to engage in separate bargaining protected by the National Labor Relations Act? The Supreme Court concluded that the employees' actions were not protected by the act; employees can be discharged for engaging in these unprotected activities. The Court further reasoned:

The potential for conflict between the minority and other employees in this situation is manifest. With each group able to enforce its conflicting demands—the incumbent employees by resort to contractual processes and the minority employees by economic coercion—the possibility of strife and deadlock is high; the likelihood of making headway against discriminatory practices would be minimized.[71]

Thus, the *Emporium* decision suggests minority employees are on weak ground when they take discrimination issues into their own hands, particularly if the labor agreement has a no-discrimination clause and a grievance procedure which encompasses discrimination issues.

Construction industry. Concentrated legal and governmental efforts to promote equal employment opportunity have taken place in most industries, the construction industry being a prominent example. The Equal Employment Opportunity legislation passed in 1964 did not initially accomplish much in improving the number of black or female union members in the construction industry. For example, three local craft unions in Philadelphia (Sheet Metal Workers, Electricians, and Plumbers) had over 4,000 journeymen members in 1967; of this total, 16 were nonwhite.[72] The lack of minority representation in the construction trades has been in part attributed to one or more of the following union recruiting practices:[73]

- Requirements for admission based on endorsement by present members, relationship by blood or marriage to present members, or election by members.
- Nonvalidated tests and interview practices containing subjective material. (One union is purported to ask applicants for their views on "law and order.")[74]
- Work referral preferences based on a worker's membership in a labor organization, seniority within the union, or length of experience in a trade.
- Selections from waiting lists compiled when the union was excluding minority workers.
- Word-of-mouth recruiting of members and apprentices.

Most of these practices were not specifically designed to discriminate against minority members, but their application and continuance in an all-white, male union perpetuates discrimination, regardless of intent.

Tangible governmental concern over this issue was first expressed in Executive Order 11246 issued by President Johnson in 1965. It required all contractors, producers, and servicers doing business ($10,000 or more annually) with the federal government to be equal opportunity employers; firms guilty of discrimination could have their federal projects cancelled and be debarred from future government projects.

Currently, under affirmative action plans employers seek to employ minority workers at the same rate they are represented in the labor force.[75] Related affirmative action programs can be either imposed by the government (as was the 1967 Philadelphia Plan, revised in 1969)[76] or be voluntary hometown programs (employed in at least seventy geographical areas in the United States).[77]

Success of these affirmative action programs has been qualified. The Philadelphia Plan resulted in a notable increase in the number of hours worked by minority employees, particularly in 1972. However, these plans can also be subjected to one or more of the following problems:

- Lack of enforcement by government agencies, such as the Office of Federal Contract Compliance Programs.[78]
- The fact that many of the hometown plans are signed by *umbrella organizations* (union building trade councils and contractors' associations) which have little or no authority to force compliance with the plan.
- Lack of qualified black and/or female employees to assume construction positions.

The government has recognized this last problem and, along with private organizations, has focused much attention on the recruitment of black apprentices. A hopeful note is the upward trend in the number of black and female apprentices.[79]

Unions and Female Employees

Many of the issues confronting female employees are similar to those discussed in the previous section on black employees. This is especially true of legal remedies, since both groups are covered by the Equal Employment Opportunity Act. Yet some differences in relationships of women and unions emerge when the history of female union workers is considered.

Historical Overview One difference is that female employees, unlike their black counterparts, were involved in collective action including strike activities in the early 1800s. The first major strike conducted by females occurred in 1828. The dispute was not over wages; rather, it protested paternalistic work rules prohibiting gambling, drinking, or other "debaucheries" and requiring church attendance.[80] A woman who became known as Mother Jones was one of the more fiery and energetic figures of the U.S. labor movement from the 1880s through the 1920s. Her role in mine workers' strikes and in helping to form the IWW reached legendary proportions. However, female unions during the 1800s were usually short-lived—the organizations were formed prior to a strike and lasted only for its duration.

From its formation until World War I, the AFL felt that the woman's place was in the home—allowing women to work would be contrary to its public principles supporting motherhood and the family. In addition to the lack of support from the AFL, union leaders faced many difficulties in organizing female employees into permanent union organizations, such as,

- Low wages of female employees made it difficult for women to pay union dues.
- Many female employees' belief that they would only be working for a short period of time.
- Strong employer opposition to unions.
- Lack of female union organizers.

The AFL increased its attention toward female workers when it appeared likely that the United States would enter World War I. Gompers was initially concerned about women's ability to do work traditionally performed by men.[81] However, he was also concerned that women who might be employed during the war could pose a threat to the unionized male employees returning from the war. Trained, experienced female employees who would work for lower wages could place higher-salaried male union members at a competitive disadvantage.[82] Hence, the AFL—perhaps out of organizational necessity rather than ideological commitment[83]—became interested in the prospects of enrolling female union members.

The AFL's encouragement of female unionization continued through World War II, although some maintained the AFL was long on words and short on action. The number of female union members increased from 800,000 at the time of Pearl Harbor to 3,000,000 in 1945; however, only one out of five working women belonged to a union. Many male union leaders and members contended that female union members were basically unenthusiastic, even hostile to union principles and efforts, following World War II. Some of this hostility was due to the fact that many of the female employees working in the factories during the war were summarily sent home to stay following Armistice Day.

Relationships between Organized Labor and Female Employees after World War II The situation for women in unions has remained unpromising in the years following World War II.[84] Related measures are *the lack of women in union leadership positions* and *the large number of female employees that do not belong to unions.*

Exhibit 11.3 indicates the broad-based underrepresentation of female leaders in National Labor organizations. (The American Nurses' Association and the National Education Association are exceptions.) There are several possible reasons for this situation.

Exhibit 11.3 Female Union Membership and Leadership Statistics for Selected National Labor Organizations

	Membership			Officers & Governing Board Members		
Organization	Total	Women	Percent Female	Total	Women	Percent Female
Amalgamated Clothing & Textile Workers Union	501,000	330,660	66	41	6	15
American Federation of Government Employees	266,000	130,000	49	18	0	0
American Federation of State, County, and Municipal Employees	1,020,000	408,000	40	29	1	3
American Federation of Teachers	500,000	300,000	60	32	8	25
American Nurses' Association	187,000	181,390	97	15	14	93
Communication Workers of America	508,063	259,112	51	17	0	0
Hotel, Restaurant Employees & Bartenders Union	430,000	180,600	42	22	1	4
International Association of Machinists & Aerospace Workers	920,735	118,775	13	11	0	0
International Brotherhood of Electrical Workers	1,011,725	303,518	30	24	0	0
International Brotherhood of Teamsters	1,923,896	480,974	25	21	0	0
International Ladies' Garment Workers	348,380	278,704	80	26	2	7
International Union of Electrical, Radio & Machine Workers (IUE)	255,427	102,171	40	25	1	4
National Education Association	1,696,469	1,239,500	75	9	5	55
Service Employees International Union	625,000	312,500	50	46	7	15
United Auto Workers	1,499,425	164,937	11	26	1	3
United Food & Commercial Workers	1,235,500	480,105	39	55	2	3
United Steel Workers of America	1,285,740	162,500	13	29	0	0

Source: Bureau of National Affairs, Inc., *Daily Labor Report*, No. 171 (September 2, 1980), A–4 and A–5.

Many women have two jobs, one paid and the other at home. Also, although the number of women with careers interrupted by childbearing is declining, women are more likely than men to have interrupted careers. The time when women leave the labor force is also the time when people interested in union office generally take their first positions. Women are also less likely than men to be in the high status, visible positions from which union officers are generally selected, and at least some men and some women see women as inappropriate for union office.[85]

Many male union members' perception that women are not capable of leading unions might be changing if the following remarks of one male union member are representative: "For too long we have looked cynically at the problems of women in industry, only wanting to send them home in order to solve the unemployment problem. But now we realize we can't replace women, and we might as well accept that."[86]

The absolute number of female union members has increased over the years; indeed, one estimate indicates that women have accounted for about 50 percent of the growth in union membership since 1960.[87] However, female union membership lags far behind the growth in female employment. One reason for this situation is the lack of union organizing activity in female-dominated occupations. For example, approximately 90 percent of all office workers do not have union representation; and, approximately 80 percent of these individuals are female.[88]

Recent Responses of Organized Labor to Female Employees There are at least three current and interrelated union initiatives toward female employees; (1) *addressing issues relevant to women*; (2) *organizing efforts directed at female employees*; and (3) *development of female organizations within the AFL-CIO*. Lane Kirkland placed these initiatives into proper perspective when he indicated,

The federation reaffirms its commitment to strive for eliminating discrimination against women, especially in the workforce. AFL-CIO officials should "push forward" to organize, secure quality child care service, address the issues of pay equity and affirmative action, eliminate sexual harassment and remove any inequities that may remain in collective bargaining agreements.[89]

However, addressing a particular issue is often easier said than done, particularly since some issues can compound the traditional labor relations process. Consider, for example, the "sexual harassment" issue which, in one form or another, affects many female employees.[90] Some unions have proposed specific actions, such as

1. Educate members as to the reality and dimensions of the issue.
2. Determine the extent of sexual harassment at the workplace, possibly through questionnaires sent to employees.
3. Indicate how union members should conduct themselves when they are sexually harassed.[91]

Unions might also attempt to negotiate a labor agreement provision pertaining to sexual harassment (see Exhibit 11.4 for a related example). This provision has several implications for the union. For example, the union might be subjected to rather vague legal liabilities (fair representation, as discussed in Chapter 8, and sexual discrimination) if a female union member unsuccessfully presents her sexual harassment claim directly to management officials.

There is also a possibility that sexual harassment can be initiated by either managers or male union members. One recent study found that "leering and pornography are most often directed against female employees by co-workers, while touching and proposition complaints arise most often from the behavior of supervisors. . . ."[92] The question becomes: Does a sexual harassment provision in the labor agreement (Exhibit 11.4, for example) apply when this activity is committed by fellow union members? If so, who is the grievance filed against? Obviously, this situation can cause internal problems within the union.

There have been recent efforts to organize workers in occupations traditionally staffed by women. To help promote the organization of office workers, for example, the Service Employees International Union and Working Womens National Association of Workers created District 925, named after a recent movie ("9 to 5"). District 925 addresses issues of particular concern to women such as equal pay, child care, maternity leave, and promotional provisions in bargaining agreements.[93]

Attention to certain issues along with legal counseling and education concerning the advantages of unions for female employees can aid union organizing efforts. These activities are currently performed by the Coalition of Labor Un-

Exhibit 11.4 Sample Labor Agreement Provision Concerning Sexual Harassment

Article ____
Sexual Harassment

The employer recognizes that no employee shall be subject to sexual harassment. In this spirit a statement of commitment to this principle will be posted in all work areas. Reference to sexual harassment includes any sexual attention that is unwanted. In the case of such harassment, an employee may pursue the grievance procedure for redress. Grievances under this Article will be processed in an expedited manner. If, after the grievance is settled, the employee feels unable to return to his/her job, the employee shall be entitled to transfer to an equivalent position at the same salary and grade as soon as a vacancy exists for which he/she is qualified.

Source: *Sexual Harassment* (Washington, D.C.: American Federation of State, County and Municipal Employees, n.d.), pp. 25–26.

ion Women (CLUW), formed in 1974, which is largely staffed by female officers from AFL-CIO affiliated unions as well as the International Brotherhood of Teamsters. There are an estimated 8,000 members which is slightly more than 1 percent of eligible female union members.[94] The CLWU works with other women's organizations in carrying out the previously mentioned activities. It also supports research and encourages the advancement of women into union leadership positions.

Summary and Implications

Summary

Management and union officials want to maintain and strengthen their respective organizations through the collective bargaining process. Management has been long concerned about maintaining its prerogatives to run the organization. While union officials do not appear to be particularly concerned about management's property rights pertaining to the machinery, materials, and money of the enterprise, management's prerogatives regarding its employees have been weakened or eroded through decisions by arbitrators, the NLRB, and the courts, as well as collective bargaining. Management prerogatives are usually specified in the labor agreement in either the long or short form.

Unions are also concerned about their organizations when they attempt to negotiate a union security provision (such as union shop, union hiring hall, or agency shop) into the labor agreement. However, certain union security provisions cannot be negotiated in states having right-to-work laws, permitted under Section 14(b) of the National Labor Relations Act. Arguments for and against these laws have economic and moral dimensions, as do those about whether union security provisions represent an inappropriate working condition.

A variety of relationships occurs between unions and minority employees. Although there have been exceptions, blacks have not been well received by organized labor. At least three forces have influenced a more progressive union stance for black employees: a prominent labor leader, the emergence of the CIO, and civil rights legislation. Although female employees became active in labor relations earlier than blacks, women have not been as well integrated into the labor-management relationship in terms of the percentage of unionized female employees. Unions have recently attempted to correct this situation by addressing relevant issues, organizing occupations which are dominated by women, and developing female organizations within the AFL-CIO.

Implications

Institutional issues, perhaps more than other collective bargaining issues, are subject to ethical ironies. Consider for example the management prerogatives issue from the perspectives of two collective bargaining observors,

---

The ethical principle underlying the concept of collective bargaining as a process of industrial governance is that those who are integral to the conduct of an enterprise should have a voice in decisions of concern to them. We may call this the "principle of mutuality."[95]

Most union and management officials would agree with this statement, although wide differences could occur in applying it to specific workplace operations. Unions, while not wishing to become partners with management, still want to be involved in managerial decisions which could adversly affect their membership (technological change which could result in employee layoffs, for example). In general, management prefers a narrow interpretation of this statement which limits choices made by employees and union representatives.

Yet, many managers take an opposite view when the union security issue is raised—employees should have the freedom of choice to determine whether they will join the union.[96] Union officials on the other hand pride themselves on leading democratic organizations; however, they often seek to compel membership regardless of the employees' preferences. Compounding this irony is the rather limited meaning of "right-to-work." Right-to-work laws enable employees to decline union membership and dues payments; however, an employee can do this in any state if he or she claims that union membership would be against religious beliefs. The employee in either situation is still subject to working conditions negotiated between management and the union; "right-to-work" does not mean the nonunion member can establish his or her own terms of employment.

The union's relationship with minority and female members completes the circle of ethical irony. In many instances unions indicate that lack of minority and female participation is due to factors beyond their control: preferences of union members and managerial employment decisions. Union officials claim that the first factor represents "the price of democracy"—unions must be responsive to the desires of their members who are often white males. Many union officers also claim that they are powerless to alter the second factor; since it is management's prerogative to select and hire employees.

Since institutional issues often involve people's beliefs and prejudices, they can complicate the labor relations process. The underlying logic is of human psychology, since labor-management relations are interpersonal relations.

Discussion Questions

1. What are the comparative advantages of the long and short forms of managerial prerogative clauses?
2. Discuss how managerial prerogatives can be eroded, even though most unions have no desire to "run the business."

3. Formulate a one- or two-sentence argument for or against the right-to-work philosophy. Fully defend your statement from arguments which could be made against your position.
4. Discuss the similarities and differences between black and female employees in their experiences with unions.
5. Discuss the various approaches unions have taken toward improving the situation of minority employees, indicating which alternatives have been met with the least resistance from union members.
6. (From Implications section.) Describe the "ethical ironies" surrounding institutional issues. Also furnish a logical explanation or rationale for these ironies.

References

[1]George A. Stevens, *New York Typographical Union No. 6, Annual Report of the Bureau of Labor Statistics* (New York: State Department of Labor, 1911), part 1, pp. 240–241; cited in Neil W. Chamberlain, "The Union Challenge to Management Control," *Industrial and Labor Relations Review* 16 (January 1963), pp. 185–186.

[2]Stanley Young, "The Question of Managerial Prerogatives," *Industrial and Labor Relations Review* 16 (January 1963), p. 243.

[3]Martin M. Perline, "Organized Labor and Managerial Prerogatives: An Empirical Study," *California Management Review* 14 (Winter 1971), pp. 46–50; and Milton Derber, W. E. Chalmers, and Milton T. Edleman, "Union Participation in Plant Decision Making," *Industrial and Labor Relations Review* 15 (October 1961), pp. 83–101.

[4]Neil W. Chamberlain, *The Union Challenge to Management Control* (New York: Harper & Bros., 1948), p. 90.

[5]Paul Prasow and Edward Peters, *Arbitration in Collective Bargaining; Conflict Resolution in Labor Relations* (New York: McGraw Hill Book Company, 1983), pp. 33–34.

[6]Robert A. Gorman, *Labor Law* (New York: West Publishing Company, 1976), pp. 455–480. We are grateful to Paul Gerhart for suggestions in formulating these factors.

[7]Gene Huntley, "Diminishing Reality of Management Rights," *Public Personnel Management* 14 (May–June 1976), p. 176.

[8]Paul Prasow, "The Theory of Management Reserved Rights—Revisited," in Gerald G. Somers, ed., *Industrial Relations Research Association Series; Proceedings of the Twenty-sixth Annual Winter Meeting* (Madison, Wis.: Industrial Relations Research Association, 1974), p. 84.

[9]Written correspondence from Dan C. Heldman, Studies Coordinator, the National Right to Work Legal Defense Foundation, Inc., December 28, 1978.

[10]Gerald J. Skibbins and Carolina S. Weymar, "The Right-to-Work Controversy," *Harvard Business Review* 44 (July-August 1966), p. 8.

[11]James N. Wilhoit, III, and Jonathan C. Gibson, "Can a State Right-to-Work Law Prohibit the Union Operated Hiring Hall?" *Labor Law Journal* 26 (May 1975), p. 302.

[12]George W. Cassidy, "Equity Consideration in Public Sector Union Security Arrangements: Should 'Free Riders' Pay?" *Journal of Collective Negotiations in the Public Sector* 5 (1976), p. 37.

[13]*Retail Clerks International Association Local 1625 AFL-CIO v. Schermerhorn et al.*, 373 U.S. 746 (1963). It should be noted that this decision stated that state laws prohibiting compulsory unions (right-to-work states) can also prohibit agency shops.

[14]*D. Louis Abood et al. v. Detroit Board of Education*, 431 U.S. 209 (1977). See also, Charles M. Rehmus, "The Agency Shop after *Abood*: No Free Ride, but What's the Fare?" *Industrial and Labor Relations Review* 34 (October 1980), pp. 92–100.

[15]"Agency Shop Clauses Gain Increased Favor," Bureau of National Affairs Inc., *Daily Labor Report* No. 123 (June 25, 1982), p. 1.

[16]"Dues Checkoff Clauses Increase Substantially," Bureau of National Affairs, Inc., *Daily Labor Report* No. 124 (June 28, 1982), p. 3.

[17]Labor Letter, *Wall Street Journal*, September 13, 1977, p. 1.

[18]"The Voluntarism of Samuel Gompers," National Right to Work Committee (Fairfax, VA.: n.d.), p. 1. For a fine discussion of many of these controversial dimensions see *Journal of Labor Research* 1 (Fall 1980), pp. 285–415.

[19]Norman Hill, "The Double Speak of Right-to-Work," *American Federationist* 87 (October 1980), p. 13.

[20]*The Truth About 'Right-to-Work' Laws* (Washington, D.C.: American Federation of Labor and Congress of Industrial Organizations, January 1977), p. i.

[21]"The Right-to-Work Issue: Questions and Answers," National Right-to-Work Committee, n.p., n.d.

[22]See for example, "Supreme Court Revives Objection to Agency Fee," Bureau of National Affairs Inc., *Daily Labor Report* No. 85 (May 3, 1982), pp. 2 and 3.

[23]Very Rev. Andrew J. McDonald, "The Moral Case against Right-to-Work," *American Federationist* 82 (August 1976), p. 20.

[24]Reed E. Larson, "Are Right-to-Work Laws Desirable? Yes," in Walter Fogel and Archie Kleingartner, eds., *Contemporary Labor Issues* (Belmont, Calif.: Wadsworth Publishing, 1968), p. 272.

[25]Mike LaVelle, "Half a Loaf Better Than Right-to-Work," *Chicago Tribune*, July 27, 1976, Section 2, p. 4.

[26]For additional statistics supporting this argument see a brochure published by the National Right to Work Committee, "Some Things You Just Can't Ignore! Right-to-Work States Lead Nation in Creating New Jobs," (November 1978).

[27]AFL-CIO, *Union Security: The Case against the Open Shop* (Washington, D.C.: AFL-CIO, p. 7.

[28]John M. Kuhlman, "Right-to-Work Laws: The Virginia Experience," *Labor Law Journal* 6 (July 1955), p. 460.

[29]These states include Alabama, Arizona, Arkansas, Florida, Georgia, Iowa, Kansas, Louisiana, Mississippi;, Nebraska, Nevada, North Carolina, North Dakota, South Carolina, South Dakota, Tennessee, Texas, Utah, Virginia, and Wyoming. It should be mentioned that this citation applies to private sector employees. The list would be greater if states having similar legislation for the public sector were considered.

[30]For a detailed examination of this particular political process see Fred Witney, "The Indiana Right-to-Work Law," *Industrial and Labor Relations Review* 11 (July 1958), pp. 506, 515; and Glenn W. Miller and Stephen B. Ware, "Organized Labor in the Political Process: A Case Study of the Right-to-Work Campaign in Ohio," *Labor History* 4 (Winter 1965), pp. 51–63. For a study which attempts to quantify the relationship between certain variables (percentage of urbanized population, per capital income, and so on) and the existence of right-to-work legislation see William J. Moore, Robert J. Newman, and R. William Thomas, "Determinants of the Passage of Right-to-Work Laws: An Alternative Interpretation." *Journal of Law and Economics* 17 (April 1974), pp. 197–211.

[31]Frederic Meyers, "Effects of Right-to-Work Laws: A Study of the Texas Act," *Industrial and Labor Relations Review* 9 (October 1955), p. 78. See also "Right-to-Work Laws Don't Curb Unionizing," *Nation's Business* 68 (December 1980), pp. 16–17; and, Robert Swidinsky, "Bargaining Power under Compulsory Unionism," *Industrial Relations* 21 (Winter 1982), pp. 62–72.

[32]Witney, "Indiana Right-to-Work Laws," p. 516.

[33]Mitchell S. Novit, "Right-to-Work: Before and After," *Business Horizons* 12 (October 1969), p. 64.

[34]"The Right-to-Work Laws," *Fortune* 56 (September 1957), p. 236.

[35]James W. Kuhn, "Right-to-Work Laws: Symbols or Substance?" *Industrial and Labor Relations Review* 14 (July 1961), pp. 592–593.

[36]Keith Lumsden and Craig Petersen, "The Effect of Right-to-Work Laws on Unionization in the United States," *Journal of Political Economy* 83 (December 1975), p. 1248. For a review of related research methods and problems concerning this topic see Walter J. Wessels, "Economic Effects of Right-to-Work Laws," *Journal of Labor Research* 2 (Spring 1981), pp. 55–75.

[37]Herbert R. Northrup, *Organized Labor and the Negro* (New York: Harper & Bros., 1944), p. 1.

[38]Ray Marshall, *The Negro Worker* (New York: Random House, 1967), p. 57.

[39]For a more detailed account of blacks and the Knights of Labor see Sidney H. Kessler, "The Organization of Negroes in the Knights of Labor," *Journal of Negro History* 37 (July 1952), pp. 248–275.

[40]Herbert G. Gutman, "The Negro and the United Mine Workers of America," in Julius Jacobson, ed., *The Negro and the American Labor Movement* (Garden City, N.Y.: Doubleday, 1968), p. 99.

[41]Herbert Hill, *Black Labor and the American Legal System*, vol. 1 (Washington, D.C.: Bureau of National Affairs, 1977), p. 20.

[42]Marc Karson and Ronald Radosh, "The American Federation of Labor and the Negro Worker: 1894–1949," in Jacobson, *Negro and the American Labor Movement*, pp. 155–156.

[43]Ray Marshall, *The Negro and Organized Labor*, (New York: Wiley, 1965), p. 16.

[44]Derek C. Bok and John Dunlop, *Labor and the American Community* (New York: Simon and Schuster, 1970), p. 119.

[45]Karson and Radosh, "AFL and the Negro Worker," p. 156. For more details of the role of blacks in the United Mine Workers see Herbert Gutman, *Work, Culture, and Society in Industrializing America* (New York: Alfred A. Knopf, 1976), pp. 121–208.

[46]Bok and Dunlop, *Labor and the American Community*, p. 119.

[47]Samuel Gompers, "Talks on Labor," *American Federationist* 12 (September 1905), p. 636.

[48]For a more detailed account of this shift in philosophy see Bernard Mandel, "Samuel Gompers and the Negro Workers: 1866–1914," *Journal of Negro History* 40 (January 1955), pp. 34–60.

[49]Northrup, *Labor and the Negro*, p. 13.

[50]Herbert Hill, "The Racial Practices of Organized Labor: The Contemporary Record," in Jacobson, ed., *Negro and the American Labor Movement*, p. 288. For additional details concerning Mr. Randolph and his union see William H. Harris, *The Harder We Run: Black Workers Since the Civil War* (New York: Oxford University Press, 1982), pp. 77–94.

[51]Summer M. Rosen, "The C.I.O. Era: 1935–1955," in Jacobson, ed., *Negro and the American Labor Movement*, p. 202. For a detailed account of the CIO's efforts to mobilize black employees' support in organizing the steel industry see Horace R. Cayton and George S. Mitchell, *Black Workers and the New Unions* (1939; reprint ed. Westport, Conn.: Negro Universities Press, 1970), pp. 190–224.

[52]These alternatives to further racial equality were formulated by Gus Tyler in "Contemporary Labor's Attitude toward the Negro," in Jacobson, ed., *Negro and the American Labor Movement*, pp. 363–364.

For a provocative and well researched discussion of the negative impact of the AFL–CIO merger on black employees see Herbert Hill, "The AFL-CIO and the Black Worker: Twenty-Five Years after the Merger, " *The Journal of Intergroup Relations* X (Spring 1982), pp. 1–78.

[53]For a discussion of these organizations see Kenneth A. Kovach, "Blacks in the U.S. Labor Movement," *Michigan State University Business Topics* 25 (Autumn 1977), p. 12.

[54]For examples of this sanction see Farrell E. Bloch, "Discrimination in Nonreferral Unions," in Leonard J. Hausman et al., eds., *Equal Rights and Industrial Relations* (Madison, Wis.: Industrial Relations Research Association, 1977), pp. 111–112.

[55]Julius Jacobson, "Union Conservatism: A Barrier to Racial Equality," in Hausman et al., eds., *Equal Rights*, p. 13.

[56]*Civil Rights: Hearings Before Subcommittee No. 5 of the House Committee on the Judiciary, 88th Congress, 1st Session (1963)*, p. 1791, statement of George Meany cited in H. Hill, "AFL-CIO," p. 35.

[57]Walter P. Reuther, *The Values We Cherish* (Washington, D.C.: Industrial Union Department, AFL-CIO, n.d.), p. 15.

[58]Barbara Becnel, "Black Workers: Progress Derailed," *American Federationist* 85 (January 1978), p. 8.

[59]Ibid. See also Orley Ashenfelter, "Racial Discrimination and Trade Unionism," *Journal of Political Economy* 80 (May-June 1972), p. 461; and, "Study Sees Unionization Hurting Nonunion Blacks," Bureau of National Affairs, Inc., *Daily Labor Report* No. 54 (March 20, 1981), p. 2.

[60]Bloch, "Discrimination in Nonreferral Unions," p. 105.

[61]For an example of racist attitudes of some union members see Scott Greer, *Last Man In: Racial Access to Union Power* (Glencoe, Ill.: The Free Press, 1959), pp. 149–150.

[62]Everette J. Freeman, "Blacks and Labor: From Union Periphery to Union Leadership," *Perspectives* 12 (Summer-Fall 1981), p. 37.

[63]Hill, p. 9.

[64]B. J. Widick, "Black City, Black Unions?" *Dissent* 19 (Winter 1972), pp. 138–145.

[65]Roger Lamm, "Black Union Leaders at the Local Level," *Industrial Relations* 14 (May 1975), pp. 228–229.

[66]Bernard Rosenberg, "Torn Apart and Driven Together: Portrait of a UAW Local in Chicago," *Dissent* 19 (Winter 1972), p. 64.

[67]For more discussions of this liability see Robert H. Sand, "Back Pay Liability under Title VII," in James L. Stern and Barbara D. Dennis, eds., *Proceedings of the Twenty-seventh Annual Winter Meeting: Industrial Relations Research Association* (Madison, Wis.: Industrial Relations Research Association, 1975), pp. 225–230; David C. Hershfield, "Labor Relations Pressures for Equal Opportunity," *Conference Board Record* 10 (September 1973), pp. 44–46; and Arthur B. Smith, Jr., "The Impact on Collective Bargaining of Equal Employment Remedies," *Industrial and Labor Relations Review* 28 (April 1975), pp. 376–394.

[68]"Union Liability for Employer Discrimination," *Harvard Law Review* 93 (February 1980), pp. 702–724. For further insights into the relationship between collective bargaining and the EEOC see "EEOC Background Paper and Resolution to Encourage Voluntary Affirmative Action in Collective Bargaining," Bureau of National Affairs Inc., *Daily Labor Report* No. 65 (April 2, 1980); and, Peter Feuille and David Lewin, "Equal Employment Opportunity Bargaining," *Industrial Relations* 20 (Fall 1981), pp. 322–334.

[69]Barbara N. McLennan, "Sex Discrimination in Employment and Possible Liabilities of Labor Unions: Implications of *County of Washington v. Gunther*," *Labor Law Journal* 33 (January 1982), p. 30.

[70]Hill, *Black Labor*, pp. 159–160.

[71]*Emporium Capwell Co. v. Western Addition Community Org.*, 420 U.S. 68–69 (1975). For additional details regarding the rights of minority employees when they picket over an alleged racial injustice see Kenneth M. Schwartz and Martin Simone, "Civil Rights Picketing," in Walter B. Connolly, Jr., ed., *Strikes, Stoppages and Boycotts: 1978* (New York: Practising Law Institute, 1978), pp. 397–419. The potential for racial discrimination issues being resolved through arbitration is discussed in Lawrence R. Jauch, "The Arbitration of Racial Discrimination Cases as a Result of Employment Practices," *Labor Law Journal* 24 (June 1973), pp. 367–375.

[72]R. L. Rowan, "Discrimination and Apprentice Regulation in the Building Trades," *Journal of Business* 40 (October 1967), pp. 435–447.

[73]Benjamin W. Wolkinson, "The Effectiveness of EEOC Policy in the Construction Industry," in Gerald G. Somers, ed., *Proceedings of the Twenty-fifth Annual Meeting: Industrial Relations Research Association* (Madison, Wis.: Industrial Relations Research Association, 1973), p. 363.

[74]William B. Gould, *Black Workers in White Unions* (Ithaca, New York: Cornell University Press, 1977), p. 285.

[75]"Minority Construction Goals Become Effective Next Month," Bureau of National Affairs, Inc., *Daily Labor Report* No. 187 (September 24, 1980), pp. 1 and 2.

[76]For additional details regarding the Philadelphia Plan see Robert W. Glover and Ray Marshall, "The Response of Unions in the Construction Industry to Antidiscrimination Efforts," in Hausman, et al., eds., *Equal Rights and Industrial Relations*, pp. 130–132; and Arthur A. Fletcher, "Whatever Happened to the Philadelphia Plan?" *Business and Society Review/Innovation* 5 (Spring 1978), pp. 24–28.

[77]For a further discussion of voluntary and imposed plans to place minorities in the construction industry see Gould, *Black Workers in White Unions*, pp. 297–315.

[78]For a more detailed discussion of bungling enforcement efforts of the EEOC and OFCC see Arthur Fletcher, *The Silent Sell-Out: Government Betrayal of Blacks to the Craft Unions* (New York: The Third Press, 1974), pp. 47–75; and Benjamin W. Wolkinson, *Blacks, Unions and the EEOC* (Lexington, Mass.: Lexington Books, 1973).

[79]For example, the Department of Labor indicated that in 1975, 18.4 percent of construction apprentices were minority members. Glover and Marshall, "The Response of Unions," p. 124; and Bureau of National Affairs, *Daily Labor Report*, October 27, 1976, p. 2.

[80]John B. Andrews and W. D. P. Bliss, *History of Women in Trade Unions* (New York: Arno Press, 1974), p. 24.

[81]Samuel Gompers, "Don't Sacrifice Womanhood," *American Federationist* 24 (August 1917), pp. 640–641.

[82]Samuel Gompers, "Women Workers Organize and Win," *American Federationist* 23 (March 1916), p. 201. It should also be noted that the rise of female unionists in the women's and men's garment industries preceded World War I.

[83]It should be noted, however, that the AFL did evidence at least a retrospective concern with the ideological side of women's place in the labor movement during World War I. See "Labor and Woman's Suffrage," *American Federationist* 27 (October 1920), pp. 937–939.

[84]See for example, Nancy Gabin, "Women Workers and the UAW in the Post-World War II Period," *Labor History* 21 (Winter 1979–1980), pp. 5–30.

[85]Karen S. Koziara and David A Pierson, "The Lack of Female Union Leaders," *Monthly Labor Review* 104 (May 1981), pp. 30 and 31. See also, "Women Workers: Gaining Power, Seeking More," *U.S. News & World Report*, November 13, 1972, p. 106; Joann S. Lublin, "Getting Organized: More Women Enroll in Unions, Win Office and Push for Changes," *Wall Street Journal*, January 15, 1979, pp. 1, 32.

[86]Lucretia M. Dewey, "Women in Labor Unions," *Monthly Labor Review* 94 (February 1971), p. 48.

[87]"Women Underrepresented in Union Hierarchy, Women's Group Asserts," Bureau of National Affairs Inc., *Daily Labor Report* No. 171 (September 2, 1980), p. A–3.

[88]Walter M. Klimschurd, "9 to 5 Wasn't Much; Will 925 Do Better?" *Administrative Management* 42 (April 1981), p. 21.

[89]"Kirkland Pledges AFL-CIO Support of Women's Rights as ERA Is Defeated," Bureau of National Affairs Inc., *Daily Labor Report* No. 126 (June 30, 1982), p. A–8.

[90]For insights into legal complications of sexual harassment see Robert W. Schupp, Joyce Windham, and Scott Draughn, "Sexual Harassment Under Title VII: The Legal Status," *Labor Law Journal* 32 (April 1981), pp. 238–252; and, Robert H. Faley, "Sexual Harassment: Critical Review of Legal Cases with General Principles and Preventive Measures," *Personnel Psychology* 35 (Autumn 1982), pp. 583–600.

[91]Modified from material in American Federation of State, County, and Municipal Employees, *Sexual Harassment* (Washington, D.C.: n.d.), pp. 9–10.

[92]*Sexual Harassment and Labor Relations* (Washington, D.C.: Bureau of National Affairs Inc., 1981), p. 32. See also, Carol Hymowitz, "*In the Pits*: Women Coal Miners Fight for Their Rights to Lift, Shovel, Lug," *Wall Street Journal*, September 10, 1981, pp. 1, 20.

[93]"Coalition Gears Up to Organize Women," *Industry Week*, March 23, 1981, p. 136.

[94]Mim Keller, "AFL-CIO for Men Only?" *The Nation* 228–229 (November 17, 1979), pp. 490–492.

[95]Neil W. Chamberlain and James W. Kuhn, *Collective Bargaining* 2d ed., (New York: McGraw Hill, 1965), p. 134.

[96]Kuhn, "Right-to-Work Laws," p. 587.

Chapter 12 Administrative Issues

"Collective bargaining can help democratize labor-management relations and humanize the work-place and work itself, including the impact of innovation and new technology on workers' jobs and earnings."

Markley Roberts*

Several important administrative issues can cost as much as or more than negotiated wage increases. This chapter focuses on four broad administrative issues: (a) technological change and its impact on labor relations issues; (b) personnel changes and their relationship to subcontracting, work assignments and jurisdiction, job structuring and work scheduling, and the role of seniority; (c) employee and job development, including job enrichment issues; and (d) safety and health.

Most of these issues involve conflicting priorities. Management wishes to have complete discretion in arranging its work content and schedules in order to maximize efficiency. Unions seek to protect employees' jobs and job rights in cases of new job assignments. The attempts of management and labor to achieve their respective priorities are discussed throughout this chapter.

Technological Change and Job Protection

Technical change refers to changes in the production processes which result in the introduction of labor-saving machinery and changes in material handling and work flow. *Automation*, a type of technological change, goes one step further in that machines perform tasks formerly performed by humans, and the human operator is replaced by automatic controls.[1]

Annual investments in automation are currently estimated at $5 billion, triple the amount of 1981. These investments will include purchases of computer-aided design systems (the first step towards computer-aided manufacturing systems), minicomputers, numerical controls, programmable controllers, and robots.[2]

The following are estimates of the use of robotics technology:

- 20 percent of final assembly of automobiles by 1985

*Markley Roberts, "Harnessing Technology: The Workers' Stake," *AFL-CIO American Federationist* 86 (April 1979): 20.

- 15 percent of all assembly systems by 1987
- 50 percent of small component assembly by 1988
- development of sensory techniques that enable robots to approximate human capability in assembly lines by 1990.

For individual companies, General Motors had 2,000 robots in place or on order in 1981, and will have 5,000 by 1985 and 14,000 by 1990.[3] At the new Nissan Motor plant in Tennessee, 176 robots are utilized in the most highly automated car assembly lines in the world. The robots work both day and night shifts and stop only when their human supervisors take lunch and coffee breaks.[4]

A major reason for the fast development of robotics is that two decades ago a typical assembly-line robot cost about $4.20 an hour to operate, just slightly under the average wage of a factory worker. Today however, the robot can still be operated at less than $5.00 per hour, but the factory worker's wages and benefits have increased significantly (between $15 and $20 per hour in auto companies).

The most common uses of robots are in materials handling, welding, spray painting and assembly. About half of the robots in the U.S. are used in the auto industry for spot welding and spray painting. Most of those remaining are used in the electric component industry for assembly of electric motors and printed circuit boards.

Like all factors of production, robots have advantages and disadvantages. Their advantages are that they perform consistently with high quality, operate in work environments dangerous to humans, operate for two or three shifts with less than 5 percent "down time," and perform monotonous, boring work. Their disadvantages include their difficulty translating two-dimensional images into three-dimensional reality. Robots can be programmed to perform only the simplest of tasks and will perform only what they are programmed to perform. Also, they have relatively high start-up costs: $150,000 for a typical robot, plus 60 to 75 percent more for programming, engineering, and maintenance during the first year.[5]

Thus, a realistic conclusion is that robots are definitely coming. They're profitable. They're productive, and American industry's survival may depend on them.

The main cost of this possible dependence on robots is the probable displacement of large numbers of employees in some industries. This cost can be reduced through cooperation between labor and management. . . .[6]

Although there are advantages for management in using robots, Joseph Engleberger, president of Unimation, the largest U.S. robot manufacturer has dismissed grave predictions of robots replacing most workers. He estimates that replacement of only 5 percent of the blue-collar workers in the Western industrialized nations would require investments of $3 billion per year for the next forty years. Also reassuring are the results of a poll of 100 users and manufacturers of robots who concluded that robots are likely to replace 440,000 workers by 1990 (not a million as predicted by some) and that all but 5 percent of the displaced workers will be retrained rather than dismissed.[7]

In general, technological progress in the U.S. has resulted in higher productivity, the elimination of many menial and dangerous jobs, higher wages, shorter hours, and a higher standard of living.[8] Technological advances have brought about numerous positive effects: more wealth is produced with less effort; machinery that either performs tasks that humans cannot or performs them with more reliability and efficiency has lowered the costs of production and allowed products to be sold at lower prices; better working conditions prevail; backbreaking work assignments are minimized; and skill levels of workers have increased, with consequent increases in pay. While the vast majority of technological changes have had no direct effect on labor relations, some related changes have been most influential: power-driven equipment substituted for hand labor; use of faster, more adaptable equipment, such as the printing press; use of automatic controls; use of conveyors and automatic loading and unloading equipment; use of computers to process, compute, and record data at phenomenal speeds; and substitution of factory production for on-the-job fabrication, such as prefabricated housing units.

Advances in technology have increased the demand for skilled labor and created new occupations, such as computer programming and digital machine operating. Technological advances have also necessitated significant adjustment within industries and have also caused shifts among industries; for example, growth in the television industry has resulted in a decline in movie production, and development of plastic products for milk bottles and fruit juice and paper products for towels and napkins have adversely affected the glass and textile industries, respectively.[9]

Reactions to Technological Change

Union leaders and members have been far from unanimous in their views on technological change. Some have ranked it as the foremost problem of our age; others welcome advances with open arms as long as the workers share in the rewards and benefits. Union leaders have generally accepted the inevitability of technological change but want to protect their members and negotiate protective clauses to assure job security.

Rank-and-file members' opinions about technological change vary in accordance with the advances made in their particular occupations and industries. For example, in fast-growing industries, such as electronics, union attitudes are quite positive, because the rate of expansion offsets the unfavorable effects on employment. In those industries that have not been penetrated greatly by automated technology, union members are either indifferent or experience some anxiety (due mostly to unfavorable publicity about automation found in labor publications).[10] Others view management as pressing for labor-saving technological changes to improve production efficiency and lower costs. These changes strike hard at one of the union's primary functions: to protect the jobs of its members. Thus, unions tend to view technological change as they do subcontracting, moving operations away from union influence, and other management actions that cause a reduction in jobs.[11]

Such defensive union responses to technological change seem to evolve in three stages:

1. Unions first attempt to negotiate provisions designed to maintain the existing jobs at existing earnings, such as prohibiting layoffs, seniority preferences in layoffs and job assignments, work sharing, supplemental unemployment benefits, guaranteed hours of work, and retraining for automated jobs.
2. The union recognizes that job and earnings changes cannot be entirely resisted; therefore, its position shifts toward attempts to cushion the problems of worker displacement. The strategy shifts from maintenance of jobs and earnings to moderating the impact of displacement to ease the transition. Unions seek to broaden the use of seniority to interplant, intercompany, and interarea transfers; to negotiate retraining and relocation allowances; to serve in an advisory or joint research capacity in adjustment planning, and so on.
3. The final stage usually indicates the inevitability of technological change and involves the union assertion that any loss of jobs should be compensated in return for employer freedom to maneuver. This strategy assumes that employees have a vested right in their jobs, and any loss of these job rights would justify compensation to the employees via severance pay, dismissal pay, or terminal payments (for accumulated vacations and sick leave) and payment of any accumulated supplemental unemployment benefit accounts.[12]

While union reaction to technological change ranges from one extreme to another, the majority of cases involve compromise, working together to introduce technological change with a minimum of adverse effect on employees. Both unions and management attempt to soften the impact of automation on workers, but naturally the union's requests are higher than the employer's willingness to consent. For example, the union will frequently request that technological change be scheduled during periods of high employment, that attrition be permitted to reduce the work force, that results of increased productivity be shared, that the workweek be reduced, that seniority be used in decisions, that preferential hiring be considered on other jobs, and so on.[13] Because these union proposals are felt to be either too costly or too restrictive on management's freedom to make changes, they are frequently resisted by management and cause temporary conflicts.

Examples of Various Unions' Reactions to Technology An extreme example of outright resistance occurred in England 160 years ago; Luddite workers, fearing massive unemployment, attempted to prevent the use of any labor-saving machinery by breaking the machines, burning the factories, and resorting to various forms of sabotage and work slowdowns.[14]

Other unions have responded positively. For example, the United Mine Workers have accepted advanced technology for years because John L. Lewis, its long-time president, believed: (1) it is better to have fewer miners at higher wages than many at low wages, and (2) high productivity is essential for high wages.[15] In construction, the building trades unions accommodated their employers' demands and accepted work rule changes to increase productivity and promote labor stability. In meatpacking, in the face of plant closings due to modernization, joint union-management teams were established to adjust to mechanization, recommend training, and assist displaced employees in adjusting. In the longshore industry, automation and containerized shipping have replaced manual loading in exchange for guaranteed work or income and early retirement for those affected by technological change.[16] In the railroad industry, technological advancement has improved safety, introduced faster, longer, heavier trains, affected the job content, work requirements, pay scales, and responsibilities of work crews.[17]

American Telegraph and Telephone and the Communication Workers of America have set up twenty-five joint committees to help introduce new equipment. General Electric and Westinghouse negotiated provisions with the International Union of Electrical Workers that require advance notification of technological change, joint technology committees, retraining, and safety measures for people who work with robots.[18]

There are other specific company and union efforts to make technological change easier for employees to accept. General Motors and the United Auto Workers have agreed to set up experimental programs at four plants guaranteeing protection from layoff for up to 80 percent of the workforce.[19] Ford Motors has agreed to a lifetime pay guarantee program covering workers with fifteen years or more service. If these employees are laid off, they will continue to receive pay until they retire or reach sixty-two years of age. With such guarantees of employment or income, employees will more likely accept technological change and employers will be motivated to make training available so employees can adjust to new technology.

Job Security and Personnel Changes

A primary concern of unions is insuring that members' jobs are protected from elimination due to technological change or managerial decision making. Unions have been able to protect jobs by negotiating clauses about job security, subcontracting, work assignments and jurisdiction, work scheduling, and use of seniority in personnel changes.

During the early 1980s, some unions have been successful in attaining greater job security for their members by postponing plant closing and ceasing outsourcing (purchasing parts and services from outside firms) in exchange for wage concessions or postponement of contractual wage increases (covered in Chapter 13) and changes in work rules.[20] Some unions, mostly at the local level, have changed long-standing work rules to increase productivity and profits in order to help their ailing employers. Examples include:

- Truck drivers have agreed to eliminate costly rehandling of certain freight.
- Aluminum workers agreed to a reduction in their craft groups from eighteen to twelve and expanded the types of jobs each worker do.[21]

Job Security Work Rules

Job security work rules are provisions that attempt to make jobs more secure, such as spreading the workload by placing limits on the load that can be carried, restricting the duties of employees, limiting the number of machines one operator can tend, prohibiting modern tools or equipment, and requiring standby crews.[22] Such practices carried to an extreme are known as *featherbedding*, which exhibits "unreasonable limits to the amount of work employees may do in a given period, . . . payment for unneeded workers, unnecessary tasks, work not performed, or jobs duplicating those already done."[23] It is viewed negatively by the public, since it is associated with an economic waste of resources.

Work load restrictions lie at the foundation of many labor relations conflicts. From an overall (macro) viewpoint, union leaders agree that change is necessary for economic progress, but from an individual (micro) view, where significant adjustment would be necessary, change is resisted.[24] Congress attempted to help reduce featherbedding practices when it amended the National Labor Relations Act in 1947 and included Section 8 (b) (6), which prohibits a labor union from causing or "attempting to cause an employer to pay or deliver or agree to pay or deliver any money or other thing of value, in the nature of an exaction, for services which are *not performed or not to be performed.*"

After two Supreme Court decisions involving newspapers, Section 8 (b) (6) lost much of its potential for restricting featherbedding practices. In one case, the Supreme Court agreed that some of the work practices at issue were wasteful, but the NLRB had found that the work was actually performed and employees had been hired by the employer to perform the work required, some of which was not necessary.[25] Thus the courts have given fairly specific direction to unions and management to resolve these featherbedding practices in collective bargaining. Recognizing that there may be some value to this approach rather than a purely legalistic one, the NLRB and the courts have set ground rules for these issues. The same means by which unions seek to improve wages, hours, and working conditions are available to maintain or establish job security provisions. Employers can resist these union demands, but they may also have to give up or trade something in return.

This trade-off is the essence of collective bargaining. Resolving such employment security issues through collective bargaining enables the parties themselves to deal with the problem in a manner suited to their specific needs and situation (see Chapter 13 on productivity bargaining). Moreover, in some cases, the unions help to minimize the impact on the workers.[26] Abolishing featherbedding and make-work practices in one stroke by legislative decree would abruptly increase the burdens of unemployment dangerously, with serious economic and social consequences.[27]

Recently, unions have shown their willingness to assist management in remaining competitive by adjusting long-standing work rules. General Motors placed a high priority on work rule concessions in the 1982 negotiations. In fact, changes in the following work rules have the potential of increasing productivity by as much as 25 percent:

- reduction of relief time (forty-six minutes)
- alteration or elimination of production quotas in nonassembly plants
- broadening job classifications so that employees perform a wider variety of tasks
- penalizing employees whose "controllable absences" exceed 20 percent of the available work hours during a six-month period by reducing their vacation pay and supplemental unemployment benefits.[28]

Continental Airlines anticipated an increase of 15 to 20 percent in pilot productivity by negotiating the following work rule changes:

- scheduling pilots for 78 hours per month, up from 75
- a reduction from 20 to 15 percent of total pilots kept on reserve at each of its bases for emergencies, such as substituting for sick pilots.[29]

Subcontracting

Subcontracting occurs when a firm determines that it cannot perform all the tasks that are necessary to operate its business successfully or that another firm can perform the needed tasks (janitorial and cafeteria services, equipment repair, parts production, and so on) at a lower cost. In either case, the firm may contract with others to assume responsibility for certain work requirements. The subcontracting process, apparently a normal economic practice, is a volatile

Exhibit 12.1 Example of Subcontracting Clause

The Company agrees that it will not contract normal routine maintenance work, excluding dryer, coagulation, recovery unit cleaning and the cleaning of any other equipment which has normally been contracted or requires special cleaning equipment, so long as it has the necessary manpower and equipment to timely and properly perform such work. On occasions when it is necessary to contract such work, such contracting shall not result in the displacement of bargaining unit employees. Before such work is contracted, the Union will be given advance notice. Such contract is to be for specific work of a definite duration and shall not be for the purpose of performing any such work on a full-time basis for the sole purpose of eliminating work from the bargaining unit. If it should become necessary to contract such work under this condition, the Company will determine whether such a job will be contracted to an outside contractor, to the Company's Roving Crew, or through another source and the Union will be so notified. (Phillips Chemical Company and Oil Workers)

Source: *Collective Bargaining Negotiations and Contracts* (Washington, D.C.: Bureau of National Affairs, 1982), p. 65:183.

and complicated collective bargaining issue. From management's view, subcontracting raises issues of managerial flexibility, the firm's ability to progress economically, and its right to pursue its economic goals free from union interference. From the union's perspective, subcontracting raises problems of job security, challenges from competing groups of workers, and undermining of contract standards.[30]

Unions have increasingly attempted to influence management's decisions to subcontract. These decisions usually are motivated by the company's need to reduce production costs. Unions generally try to limit management's freedom to subcontract in order to protect and maximize work and economic opportunities for their members, to prevent the firm from escaping from the union, and to protect the members' jobs against competition from nonunion firms. The example of a subcontracting clause in Exhibit 12.1 shows how employers' actions can be limited.

Since subcontracting has been declared a mandatory issue of collective bargaining,[31] unions have made significant inroads on this issue in collective bargaining. It is now limited or prohibited in nearly half of the labor agreements, and inclusion of these clauses has increased significantly in the last ten years. Labor agreements seldom strictly prohibit subcontracting, but often limit it in one or more of the following ways: they require advance consultation with the union, prohibit subcontracting if layoffs would occur from such decisions, allow subcontracting only if the necessary skills and equipment are not available, or require use of skilled workers for maintenance and construction jobs within the bargaining unit.[32]

Arbitration likewise has played an increasingly important role in the subcontracting issue. This role has usually involved such aspects as determining whether subcontracting is an arbitrable issue without explicit contractual language on the subject. Arbitrators are commonly asked to interpret the recognition clause and any accompanying bargaining unit work and appraise commonly specified criteria, such as "good faith," proof of "sound business practices," and "no harm to members of the bargaining unit."[33]

Subcontracting has been frequently arbitrated under the management rights clause of the agreement (see Chapter 11). When agreements do not explicitly provide management the right to subcontract, the unions seek to bargain over the subject. When and if management refuses, the union will frequently petition the NLRB, alleging that the employer has committed an unfair labor practice by refusing to bargain in good faith. Where a management rights clause is written in generalities, not specifically alluding to subcontracting, the union challenge will more likely be decided in arbitration.

Work Assignments and Jurisdiction

Management can assign individual duties and tasks to employees on the job more easily than it can assign employees to jobs that have permanent job classifications. While assignments of workers to such jobs are usually limited by contract provisions covering seniority or fitness, labor agreements sometimes contain direct restrictions on the right of management to assign specific duties and tasks to workers. In grievance administration and arbitration, it is usually held that, unless the agreement provides otherwise, employees are not allowed to select only those duties or tasks within their classification which they particularly prefer.[34]

On the other hand, assignment of work to employees often gives rise to union-management confrontations, especially where changes in operations, job descriptions, and technology occur and where more than one union represents employees. While the National Labor Relations Act prohibits unions from engaging in or inducing strike action to force an employer to assign work to a particular union or craft, disputes do occur.[35] Such disputes occur usually under three types of circumstances:

1. When two or more unions claim jurisdiction over specific work assignments.
2. When bargaining unit employees believe their work is being assigned to other employees outside the bargaining unit, such as supervisors.
3. When disagreement occurs within a union over particular work assignments.

Conflicts between unions over work assignments occur more commonly in industries having craft unions, such as the building and construction industries. Each craft union believes it should have exclusive jurisdiction over some phase of construction work, and the work is performed on job sites for only a short time with frequent movement from place to place. Each craft guards its rights to perform a specific task, and so no intercraft relationship develops between craft unions and their members which could help moderate any disputes over work assignments. To complicate the situation further, the work is characterized by an infinite variety of similar materials and equipment. For example, the plasterers' union will probably claim jurisdiction when carpenters who commonly install accoustical ceilings start using a spray gun to blow materials on a surface that looks like plaster.[36] The disputes can be resolved through procedures established by the NLRB. To avoid going before the NLRB, the Building and Construction Trades Department and several national contractors' associations have agreed to establish a national joint board to consider and decide cases of jurisdictional disputes in the building and construction industry.[37]

Most of the time the work-jurisdiction lines are distinct, but in research and technical jobs (such as laboratory heads, engineers, draftsmen, and chemists), work jurisdiction frequently overlaps. For example, if professionally certified engineers are difficult to hire, companies may resort to assigning engineering tasks to draftsmen or technicians. These assignments may be acceptable when jobs for professional engineers are plentiful, but during a recession, when jobs are scarce, these same engineers may resist any assignment of "their" work to others they believe less qualified.

Some labor agreements require that bargaining unit work be performed only by bargaining unit employees except in instructional, experimental, or emergency situations. In instructional situations, there must be a clear, direct, and immediate connection between members of management and instructions given to bargaining unit employees. Experimental work includes the introduction of a new technique, method, or procedure, and emergency conditions occur as the result of unforeseen circumstances, such as a tornado, fire, or power outage, which calls for immediate action.[38] Although most companies do not resist these clauses, several interesting issues regarding this matter must be addressed:

- Is a clear division between hourly employees and management in the best interest of effective labor relations?
- With more college graduates becoming first-line supervisors, how can they realistically get a feel for their subordinates' jobs if they are precluded from working on these jobs?
- If challenged over a production standard or promotion, how can management prove that the jobs can be done a certain way and within a certain time?

Intra-union work assignment problems, although not as critical and dramatic as the previous ones, often are very sensitive to local union leaders. Various individuals or group interests of members of the same union over work assignments can cause problems, especially in industrial unions having craft and semiskilled employees as members. Whenever production processes are automated, assignment of work from skilled employees to semiskilled production workers causes emotional conflicts within the union. For example, having pipefitters do welding tasks when welding is not included in their job description gives rise to disputes.

To resolve these conflicts, unions favor specific, written job descriptions and would like to refuse to perform work outside their jurisdiction. However, companies prefer general job descriptions, which include phrases such as "perform related duties" and "make minor repairs," in order to provide flexibility in making work assignments.[39] Whether detailed or vague, the particular duties included in a job description often result in disagreements between management and union officials.[40]

Work Scheduling

Collective bargaining agreements frequently deal with *work scheduling*, such as regulating shifts and fixing the workday or workweek. Management also has the right to schedule work unless restricted by the agreement. For example, it usually has the right to suspend operations temporarily, reduce the number of shifts, and change the number of days to be worked. Moreover, it can usually make unscheduled and emergency changes in the work schedule if such changes are made in good faith and for reasonable cause, such as extreme weather conditions, bomb threats, and civil disturbances.[41]

Unions and management continue to negotiate the workday and workweek issues. While the five-day, forty-hour workweek has been standard since 1938 when the Fair Labor Standards Act was passed, unions have continued their attempts to reduce the hours of work. In 1978, a group called the All Unions Committee to Shorten the Work Week, composed of such unions as the United Auto Workers, United Steelworkers, Machinists, Electrical Workers, and Meatcutters, was established. Recognizing that an across-the-board reduction in the forty-hour week is unlikely, their attention has been directed to retirement policies of *thirty and out* (thirty years of work, then retirement with full benefits), longer vacations, sick leaves, and more holidays.[42]

Individual unions continue to attempt to adjust the workweek. The United Auto Workers inched closer to the four-day workweek with its "paid personal holiday," which allowed auto workers with one year's seniority seven personal holidays per year.[43] However these were essentially eliminated by the concessions made in the 1982 negotiations.

Unions in the United States and elsewhere have shown increasing interest in *flexitime programs*, which allow an employee to start and finish work at his or her discretion, as long as the specified total number of hours per week or per day are worked and the employee is present at work during the core-hour period (for example, 9:00 A.M. to 11:00 A.M. and 1:30 P.M. to 3:30 P.M.).[44] These programs are designed to fit together job requirements and personal needs of individual employees. There is proof that flexitime has accommodated such personal needs as avoiding heavy traffic in commuting to work, working during the time of day of peak efficiency, shopping during a two-hour lunch period, and finishing work by the time children are out of school. There is also some evidence that attitudes toward work and production are improved or at least maintained.[45] While flexitime has much potential for meeting employee needs, some operations require all workers on the job at the same time, and work schedules cannot be altered unless the entire group accepts the alternative work schedule.

The Role of Seniority in Personnel Changes

Employers usually have a free hand in selecting those employees who best fit the needs of their organizations and who best meet the prescribed job requirements. However, once any employee has been selected and placed on a job within the bargaining unit, the employer must abide by provisions of the labor agreement regarding personnel decisions such as promotions, transfers, and layoffs. This section highlights issues involving administrative determination and presents the concept of seniority, including its legal complications.

Seniority is usually measured by the length of an employee's continuous service. Seniority is considered

---

. . . an integral part of the institutionalized web of rules that affect the administration of human resources in the internal labor market. Specifically seniority has come to represent an enforceable priority under a collective bargaining agreement which qualifies an employee for benefits from the employer and provides a common basis for employees to estimate their relative status in terms of job security and opportunities for advancement.[46]

Seniority can be divided into two categories of employee rights:

1. *Job rights* (also called competitive rights) apply in decisions on promotion, layoff-recall, transfers, work assignments, shift preference, selection of days off, overtime, and vacation date selection. The most senior employee usually will be given preferential treatment—will be laid off last, recalled first, and offered a shift preference and overtime first.
2. *Benefits rights* concern eligibility for certain employee benefits, such as vacations, pensions, severance pay, sick leave, and insurance. These rights are not competitive with those of other employees and begin to accumulate immediately upon employment with the organization.[47]

Seniority provisions, found in nearly 90 percent of all labor agreements,[48] show how seniority accrues over an employee's continuous service and, in some cases, how it can be lost for a variety of reasons (layoff, failure to respond to recall, unauthorized absences, or taking a job elsewhere during leave of absence).[49]

Job seniority may be measured in a number of ways: total length of time with an employer (employment, mill, or plant seniority), length of service in a line of progression (progression line seniority), and length of service in a job classification (job seniority). While the particulars of the seniority system may vary greatly, some type of preference is usually accorded the more senior workers.[50]

Seniority is considered "sacred" by most union members,[51] yet it is doubtful that any other concept of labor relations has been as "influential, persuasive, and troublesome in collective bargaining."[52] Management seldom objects to providing some sense of security to long-service employees,[53] and unions and management generally agree that senior employees should be entitled to greater security and superior benefits as a matter of equity and fairness. However, for other reasons, seniority has played an increasingly important role in the labor relations environment. For example, it serves as an important objective measure for making personnel decisions—the concept dictates that length of service, not managerial discretion, determines who will be promoted or laid off. In addition, the number and types of employee benefits tied to seniority have increased dramatically.[54]

Seniority can be very costly to the company as well as to union members. For example, Lockheed has claimed that it lost $15 million in two years as a result of its complicated seniority system, which allows layoff-threatened employees with more than six years' service to take junior employees' jobs. A study of Lockheed's seniority system, which had been in effect for fifteen years, showed that one layoff caused an average of five job changes—which caused serious problems with employee training.[55] It is difficult to compute the specific costs of other problems caused by seniority systems, such as an aging work force, the possibility of lessening ambition and motivation of younger workers, and the loss of key personnel low in seniority.[56]

Union and management representatives carefully negotiate the seniority provisions of their agreements in anticipation of future negotiation issues and in accordance with rules of clarity, equity, and simplicity. Seniority provisions usually include such items as the seniority unit (company, plant, department, job), how it is used (promotion, transfer, layoff, recall), and how it accumulates (effect of interruptions of service such as military leave or layoff); rules on loss of seniority (voluntary quit, discharge for cause, failure to report from layoff, unexcused absence, and misuse of leave of absence); administration of the seniority list (posting requirements, supplying lists to the union, and keeping lists up to date); special arrangements (mergers, acquisition of firms, and succession); and special exemption of certain employees.[57] In some cases, unions and management include a seniority provision called *superseniority*, which exempts highly skilled technical employees and union officials from layoffs—a move which allows the company to retain essential skills and at the same time promote stable labor relations.

Promotions and Transfers *Promotions* are personnel changes within an organization, advancing the employee to a position of more responsibility, usually accompanied by a wage increase. Appearing in the majority of the collective bargaining agreements,[58] promotion provisions usually state that seniority and ability are the deciding factors. While seniority can be easily measured by several indicators, determination of ability is more complex.[59] *Transfer* provisions, appearing in slightly less than the majority of agreements, cover personnel changes from one position to another with relatively equal authority, responsibility, and compensation. Seniority and ability are also usually the determining factors used in making the transfer decision.[60]

Four basic types of seniority clauses are used in promotion and transfer decisions:

1. Seniority as the sole factor.
2. Seniority used after ability to perform the job is demonstrated.
3. Seniority and ability as two determining factors.
4. Relative ability used before seniority.

Straight seniority is the easiest to administer for determining eligibility for promotions and transfers. However, there is a possibility that the eligible senior employee is unfamiliar with the job and will need extensive training for the new assignment.

Seniority with minimum ability simply means that the more senior employee gets the job if minimum qualifications can be demonstrated. Such provision requires that the employer promote or transfer not the most competent candidate nor the most superior one, but the most senior employee among the qualified candidates.

When seniority and ability are given equal weight as determining factors in the agreements, arbitrators have concluded that when seniority is relatively close, it is reasonable to use relative ability, but when seniority differs extensively, ability must be substantially greater to justify equal consideration.[61] Clauses that prescribe the use of relative ability before seniority use seniority as the determining factor only if management determines that all the candidates for a vacancy have approximately the same qualifications for the job.[62]

Ability, the measure usually accompanying seniority, includes "some combination of skill, knowledge, attitudes, behavior, performance, pace, and production and perhaps talent."[63] While the employer has the right to establish any criteria for assessing ability, it must comply with the standards negotiated and written in the collective bargaining agreement[64] and "Uniform Guidelines on Employment Selection Procedures"[65] covering race, sex, national origin, and religious discrimination. These guidelines, used by the Equal Employment Opportunity Commission, Office of Personnel Management, and Departments of Labor and Justice, specify requirements covering employment decisions defined broadly as "tests and other selection procedures which are used as a basis for any employment decision. [These] decisions include but are not limited to hiring, promotion, demotion, . . . selection for training, or transfer."[66] Moreover, the provisions of the labor agreement itself must not be discriminatory or perpetuate past discriminatory practices.

Employers may design selection techniques to determine employees' qualifications for promotions and transfers. Techniques most commonly used are tests,[67] experience, education, production records, performance ratings,[68] personality traits, and absence, tardiness, and discipline records. Because each of these criteria may be limited in its specific relationship to the needs of particular jobs, the determination of employee qualifications is usually based on several criteria, not one. Where superior qualifications are identified, the determination may be clearcut. However, where the criteria themselves produce conflicting results, the burden is on the employer to assure accurate determination.[69]

Transfer procedures are basically the same as those for promotion, except that employee requests are used more frequently. An employee dissatisfied in his or her present job and requesting transfer to more pleasant working conditions or work group, or to a more favorable line of progression, is generally granted the transfer if the employee qualifies and a vacancy occurs.

Other provisions affecting personnel decisions in collective bargaining agreements are included to prevent problems that often emerge. For example, agreements should prescribe whether an employee carries his or her seniority to a new position or whether seniority will be retained only after a predetermined period of time. Other provisions should specify whether an employee who transfers out of the bargaining unit or is promoted to supervision will be allowed to retain seniority or will lose it.[70]

Layoffs and Recall Layoff provisions included in most contracts consider seniority first in retaining employees during layoffs. Increasingly, seniority has become the sole factor in layoff determination; however, some contracts consider seniority as the determining factor only if employees are qualified for available jobs. In others, seniority is given consideration only when factors such as ability and physical fitness are equal.

Of course, there are exceptions to these general rules. For example, union stewards and local union officers might be given superseniority and will be the last ones laid off in their respective departments. Unions sometimes desire this provision to encourage members to run for the many positions available in the union. In some cases, superseniority can be a strong incentive, if not the only one, to become a union steward. To protect the organization from having unqualified employees, some contracts stipulate that the union representatives must be qualified for the jobs available if they are to be exempt from layoff.

Advance notice of impending layoffs to the employees and the union is often required, and some agreements specify one to four days' notice. Frequently, employees scheduled for layoffs are permitted to displace or "bump" less senior employees, although they usually must qualify beforehand for the jobs in order to do so. While nearly a majority of agreements allow companywide or plantwide bumping, others confine bumping to the employee's own classification or work group, to former job classification, or to the department or division. Most agreements provide for recall of employees after layoff. These provisions usually specify that employees be rehired in reverse order of layoff, but only if they show that they are qualified for the open position.[71]

Legal Issues Involving Seniority in Administrative Determinations Job rights guaranteed by the labor agreement may conflict with employee rights guaranteed by the U.S. Constitution and Equal Employment Opportunity Act of 1972. Use of seniority in administrative determinations such as promotions and layoffs has been the focus of much legal attention. In some cases it has been shown that minorities have been locked in departments or jobs with unfavorable lines of progression, and these practices tend to perpetuate past employment discrimination. The following are examples of discriminatory seniority practices:

- Separate seniority lists for black and white employees doing the same work.
- Black and white employees holding similar jobs, while only whites are eligible for promotion.
- Separate seniority lists from which blacks are hired for less desirable jobs and whites for more favorable jobs.
- Refusing employment to minorities after the Civil Rights Act went into effect, then, after losing several EEOC cases, starting to hire minorities but maintaining seniority lists that continue to place minorities at the bottom.[72]

In resolving these cases, the courts would probably void the practices of using separate departmental seniority lists or seniority for personnel decisions[73] and might order one or more of the following forms of affirmative action:

- Change departmental seniority to plantwide or company seniority, possibly merging seniority lists.
- Restore those persons who have suffered under the discriminatory seniority plans to their "rightful place" (a place where they would have been if they had not been discriminated against), thereby awarding retroactive seniority.
- Modify seniority rights of the majority and minority, taking into account restored job rights and the merged seniority lists.[74]
- Remove any barriers to transferring from previously segregated departments.
- Allow a reasonable time for minorities who have been bypassed on promotions because of their seniority status to request consideration—failure to request consideration would constitute a waiver.
- Allow minorities who were victims of discriminatory seniority systems to use their plant or employment seniority to bid for vacancies and present their qualifications.
- Allow *red-circling* (pay above the rate specified for the particular job) for previous victims of discrimination so that they may move to better lines of progression. Red-circling the wage rate would allow such a move without jeopardizing previously earned seniority credits used in wage determination.[75]

- Abolish job residency requirements, except in those jobs where experience is essential to advance up the occupational ladder and equivalent experience cannot be attained by working elsewhere.
- Examine the qualifications necessary to perform all jobs, remove all unrelated and artificial promotion prerequisites built into the job structure, develop objective criteria for advancement, and formally spell out these policies and procedures in the labor agreement.[76]
- Allow companies and unions to negotiate an affirmative action plan in which a prescribed percentage of the craft trainee openings is reserved for minority applicants until the in-plant percentage of minority craft workers approximates that of the local labor force.[77]

Not only are employers and unions being taken to court over work assignments, promotions, and transfers, but layoff-recall decisions based on seniority have become important issues. Assuming that employers have been hiring minorities recently at a greater rate than in the past, the company seniority list would consist of white males toward the top and minorities toward the bottom. At times when product demand is low, the employer may face the probability of laying off the newly-hired minority employees in accordance with the "last hired, first fired" provision in the labor agreement.[78] In those cases where plant, department, or job seniority is used, the layoffs would erase much of the employer's progress in its affirmative action plan and affect minority employment disproportionately.

Minority groups have attacked these seniority and layoff practices on the basis of two theories:

1. The last hired, first fired layoff practice perpetuates past discrimination, since it takes the minority ratio of the work force back to the days when employment discrimination was practiced.
2. As an employment criterion having a disparate effect on minority employees, the last hired, first fired layoff rule can be justified only on the grounds of its "business necessity" or as a "bona fide occupational qualification" (conditions which minority groups feel are not present).[79]

Seniority issues have arisen on transfer rights of black employees to departments with better lines of progression, and layoff-recall procedures during reductions-in-force. The existing seniority systems did not credit time spent in all-black jobs or departments toward opportunities available in previously all-white jobs and departments. Blacks who transferred were unable to carry forward their accumulated seniority, and would have to start at the bottom of the job and department seniority when transferred to a better line of progression. In 1977 the U.S. Supreme Court upheld the legality of bona fide seniority systems which tended to perpetuate the effect of pre-Act (1964) discrimination, but it ruled that individuals could seek relief (sue) for any employer's post-Act discrimination.[80]

In *Franks v. Bowman Transportation*, the Supreme Court ruled that minority employees are entitled to retroactive seniority to the date in which they were improperly denied employment opportunities. Without such restoration of seniority, those who had been discriminated against would never obtain their rightful place in the seniority hierarchy.[81] Then in 1982, the Supreme Court stated that EEOA affords broad immunity and latitude to seniority systems that are adopted and applied without the intent to discriminate.[82]

Another issue involving use of seniority for promotion and transfer and EEO matters was the conflict between contractual provisions and affirmative action plans negotiated between companies, unions, and government agencies. The courts agreed that seniority systems may be modified to meet affirmative action goals, and minority members are permitted to "leap frog" incumbents with greater seniority and/or qualifications as a remedial measure to correct past underutilization of women and minorities. However, this policy did not affect use of seniority with respect to layoffs and recall.

These decisions led some companies and unions to include commitments to resolve prior discriminatory practices in their labor agreements. Kaiser Aluminum and United Steelworkers agreed to establish a program for training craft workers wherein 50 percent of each class would be reserved for minority and/or female employees. Brian Weber, a white employee who had more seniority and better qualifications than some minorities selected for a training class, alleged reverse discrimination. The U.S. Supreme Court recognized collective bargaining as a means for accommodating diverse interests in the workplace and upheld the union-company plan because it was temporary, corrected prior discrimination, and was negotiated with the union which represents the interests of the bargaining unit employees under the principle of exclusive bargaining representation.[83]

Employee and Job Development

Apprenticeship Programs

Many employees receive on-the-job training from management officials. Unions tend to become much more involved in a particular form of training—*apprenticeship programs.*

Apprenticeships refer to formal, supervised programs of training and experience, often supplemented by off-the-job instruction. About 46 percent of the labor agreements have provisions governing apprenticeship programs although certain industries have considerably more (printing and publishing, 85 percent; rubber and plastics, 91 percent; primary metals, 88 percent; fabricated metals, 64 percent; transportation equipment, 85 percent; construction, 67 percent).[84]

Labor and management officials become more deeply involved in the administration of apprenticeship programs than other types of training. Apprenticeship represents a particular interest to craft unions. Over forty international unions deal with apprenticeship programs in their constitutions and bylaws. For example, the constitution may set the ratio of apprenticeships to journeymen, length of the apprenticeship, requirements for admission and completion and admission to journeymen status.

The labor agreements often control apprenticeship programs in five ways:

- Determine conditions of entry, such as age, education, and test score.
- Establish joint apprenticeship committees composed of an equal number of union and employer representatives.
- Determine the number of apprentices per journeyman and the duration of the apprenticeship program (usually four to five years).
- Set standards for training, which is divided between on-the-job and classroom work.
- Establish employment rules, such as wages, probationary period, supervision by journeymen, and certification.

Craft unions have a particular interest in apprenticeship programs because these programs allow their members to maintain high wages while protecting members' job from being taken by nonapprentices. They also combine with union hiring halls to preserve the union's power to provide services to the employers in their areas. Employers don't have to recruit and train apprentices alone, because the unions work with the employers in training and then, through the union hiring halls, provide placement services for construction companies who employ union journeymen and apprentices.

Industrial unions also have an interest in apprenticeship training, but because they do not operate union hiring halls and the employers do their own recruiting, selection, and placement, their interest is not as strong. Industrial unions deal with apprenticeship programs through collective bargaining and union-administered training programs funded by employers and/or government. Such provisions of the labor agreement include:

- Protecting the wage standards of journeymen.
- Providing rights to training for incumbents as a way to minimize wage and job loss caused by technological change, mergers, relocation, and shifts in demand.
- Providing training opportunities in the form of wage supplements or fringe benefits to support the employee on outside job-related training.[85]

Enrollment in registered apprenticeship programs in 1981 was a record 395,000 or 0.3 percent of the civilian labor force, and 130,000 of this number were new apprentice registrations. While this number may appear high, if the proportion of apprentices in the United States equaled that of Austria, Germany, or Switzerland, there would be 7 million American apprentices.[86]

Because craft unions have played a vital role in training and have greatly influenced the labor supply, their *nepotism* (practice of hiring relatives) and discriminatory practices that have prevented minorities from entering skilled occupations have made them prime targets of civil rights suits. Since labor unions are now covered under the Equal Employment Opportunity Act, they too must be conscious of EEOC regulations. Through union hiring halls and apprenticeship programs, craft unions have an important role in selecting apprentices and assigning union members to jobs. Therefore, the EEO (equal employment opportunity) agencies have been very interested in their operations.

The EEO agencies and the courts have significantly affected the internal affairs of craft unions through affirmative action plans, conciliation, consent decrees, and court cases. The following policies are the result of EEO regulations and interventions:

1. Acceptance for apprenticeship training based on valid testing and licensing procedures, legitimate experience requirements, and standard initiation fees.
2. Union advertising of vacancies with the time and place for tests.
3. Policies abolishing nepotism (long a tradition with craft unions).
4. "First-in, first-out" referral procedures continued, but master referral registers, which include names, addresses, sign-in books, and availability sheets, maintained and operated in a nondiscriminatory fashion.
5. Craft unions and construction companies agreeing to an affirmative action plan, including goals, timetables, and specific actions which will increase minority employment in the specific crafts.[87]

Job Enrichment

Worker job dissatisfaction has been the focus of much national publicity as well as academic research. The 1973 report *Work in America* alarmed management and unions when it concluded that large numbers of workers found their jobs devoid of meaning, dignity, and prestige and that work-related problems contributed to unstable family and community relations, alcoholism, drug abuse, and delinquent behavior.[88] Employees at a Lordstown, Ohio, General Motors plant struck over what many described as the dehumanizing work of the assembly line.[89] The prevailing attitudes of employees involved in the strike became known as the Lordstown Syndrome. These events led to significant interest in redesigning jobs to make them more challenging, more responsible, and less monotonous and to provide opportunities for advancement, feedback on performance, and participation in the work process. Programs that have incorporated such job elements have been labeled job enrichment programs.[90]

The Reluctance of Unions to Accept Job Enrichment Programs With few exceptions, successful ventures with such programs have occurred in nonunion companies under very accommodating conditions (for example, in new plants with hand-picked employees). In those few cases where unions and management have cooperated, management has usually been the initiator of the experiments.[91] By and large, labor unions have been either uninterested in or extremely suspicious of job enrichment programs.[92] Still, with much attention being given to job design today, unions have found that they either must be involved or must defend themselves from attacks for not being involved. Unions' reluctance about job enrichment programs is due primarily to the following factors.

Previous experiences with management Some union leaders recall the era of scientific speed-up schemes and other anti-union devices, some of which date back to the early 1900s. They perceive job enrichment programs as "ideologically and institutionally unfriendly to trade unions and collective bargaining"[93] and believe such programs are "devices (1) to increase effort norms without compensating increases in effort value, (2) to move workers from job to job without reference to job rights, and (3) to upgrade skill and responsibility without paying for it."[94] Although this belief has not been universally adopted by unions, it does explain in part their reluctance to involve themselves.

Perceptions of the union's role in labor relations Management has generally considered determination of job content and assignments managerial prerogatives and has been hesitant to enter negotiations with unions over these subjects.[95] Furthermore, it is unclear whether management is required by law to negotiate over the content of job enrichment programs, even if unions press for negotiation of the issues. Labor unions have traditionally left to management the problems of increasing worker satisfaction and have perceived their role as concentrating their efforts on the gut issues of money and job security.[96]

Interpretations of membership needs by the union leadership Some union leaders do not believe that there is sufficient support from the rank-and-file union members for negotiating job enrichment issues. As William W. Winpisinger, president of the Machinists Union and outspoken critic of job enrichment, has said:

In my years as a union representative and officer, I've negotiated for a lot of membership demands. I've been instructed to negotiate on wages . . . noise . . . seniority clauses; health and welfare, . . . and everything else you find in a modern labor-management contract. But never once have I carried into negotiations a membership mandate to seek job enrichment.[97]

For union leaders to insist vigorously on job enrichment in negotiations with management, they would have to believe that a majority of workers feel that such changes are important, in some cases even worth striking for.[98] Most union leaders and members rank these issues behind the bread-and-butter issues and do not view collective bargaining as a particularly effective method for enriching a job.[99] To improve worker attitudes and employee motivation, union officials have traditionally placed more emphasis on job security, high wages, and improved working conditions[100] and have given little emphasis to those subjects commonly associated with job enrichment: opportunities for advancement, more feedback to employees on how well they are doing, more interesting and challenging work, job redesign and enlargement, and more autonomy on the job.[101]

Union leaders appear to have a fairly accurate perception of what their members want from collective bargaining. In fact, surveys of union members reveal that job enrichment ranks behind wages, fringe benefits, working conditions, and job security as priority items in collective bargaining.[102] Moreover, union members seem to prefer joint union-management programs to deal with job enrichment subjects, while using collective bargaining to focus on traditional bargaining topics.[103]

One study of union members' bargaining preferences revealed that job content demands (more interesting work and greater participation) were relatively unimportant. This finding indicates either that job satisfaction that results from job content has a lower priority than traditional issues, such as wages and job security, or that union members do not view the unions as instrumental in changing job content.[104]

Winpisinger, expressing the views of many unionists, firmly believes that the way to gain job satisfaction is to pay wages commensurate with skill:

If you want to enrich the job, enrich the paycheck. The better the wage, the greater the job satisfaction. There is no better cure for "blue-collar" blues. If you want to enrich the job, begin to decrease the number of hours a worker has to labor in order to earn a decent standard of living. . . . The time has come to translate the increased productivity of automated processes into the kind of enrichment that comes from shorter work weeks, longer vacations, and earlier retirements.[105]

He also believes that employees have a say in their job content through the grievance procedure and the use of seniority, which enables them to transfer to jobs more to their liking.

Other union leaders have not been as harsh in their view; George Nestler of the Amalgamated Meatcutters' International has a somewhat contrasting opinion:

What do workers want? They want to identify with the company, the union, the product, and the group they work with. They want responsibility, they want communication and they want to contribute. They want to participate in their jobs, to have input. These things are meaningful to workers. They want to care about people. They want a

share of the aims and goals, and of the financial rewards. Initially, financial rewards are what everyone looks at. This diminishes after a period of time. They are looking for new skills in their work, and for training. They want job security. And they want the right to question what's going on in their environment, in their workplace.[106]

The Potential of Job Enrichment Programs in a Unionized Environment

The rather dim picture thus far presented for job enrichment programs appears even worse when (a) union and management officials have had little experience with these programs and (b) administrative issues pertaining to job enrichment, such as specific objectives of the program and payment for training time, have to be negotiated.[107]

Yet, all is not lost for these programs. Contract rejections, employee job dissatisfaction, and prolonged negotiations might stimulate union and management officials to believe "there must be a better way." Thus, out of disenchantment, fatigue, or possibly boredom, both parties might become attracted to an approach that has some potential for providing relief from the adversarial relationship while serving the mutual interests of the respective parties.[108]

Safety and Health: The Occupational Safety and Health Act

Safety and health provisions now are quite common in labor agreements;[109] however, these provisions vary considerably from general statements of safety responsibility to specific items,[110] such as:

- Guards for machines.
- Safety goggles and boots.
- Joint union-company investigation of accidents.
- Employee obligation to follow safety rules.
- Right to refuse hazardous work.
- Rules and procedures for joint safety and health committees, such as periodic meetings and inspections, payment for time spent, and authority to resolve safety disputes by use of grievance procedure and arbitration.

Many of these provisions have resulted from governmental legislation,[111] namely, the Occupational Safety and Health Act (OSHA), passed in 1970[112] in an attempt to improve industrial safety statistics.[113]

The employer's overriding duty under OSHA is to furnish each employee with conditions free from recognized hazards that may cause illness, injury, or death and to comply with all occupational safety and health standards adopted by the Department of Labor. Further, employers must permit inspectors to enter their establishments without delay and at reasonable times to conduct inspections.

Exhibit 12.2 Many safety and health hazards, commonplace in the past, have been eliminated through the use of safety equipment. Yet safety remains an issue in current collective bargaining.

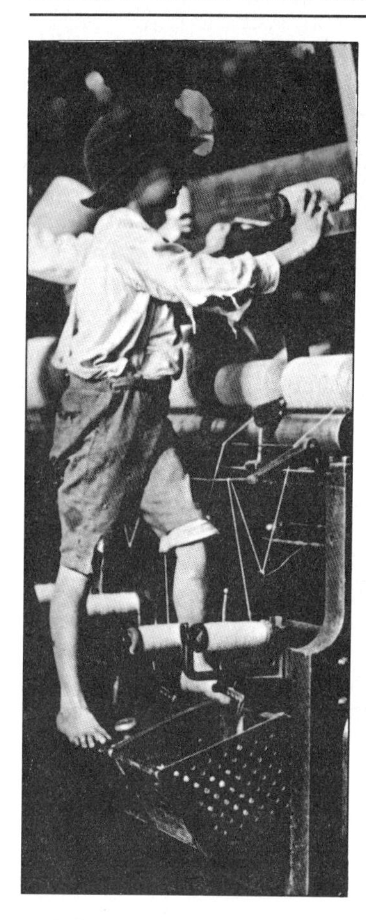

Sources: Photo on left reporduced from the collection of the Library of Congress. Photo on right by Bohdan Hrynewyvch, Stock, Boston.

They must place appropriate notices, provide protective equipment when necessary, and maintain designated records of illnesses.

The act has been praised by some and criticized by others. An objective, comprehensive assessment of the entire OSHA program in terms of cost-benefit analysis has yet to be conducted,[114] although preliminary findings indicate a level of effectiveness ranging from limited[115] to pronounced.[116]

Management and union representatives have not been reluctant to criticize the act and its administration. One management official has concluded that

a principal goal of the Act, the protection of worker health, is lost sight of as OSHA presses its regulations upon us, regardless of whether or not those regulations make good sense. Instead of allowing industry flexibility in achieving health protection, the government has attempted to compel industry to do things only one way—the way prescribed by armchair governmental experts and lawyers.[117]

Another, a management official and former president of the Industrial Relations Research Association, Douglas Soutar, has been equally critical:

The Act [has become] as much a labor-management act as one of safety and health, and this has become excruciatingly the case. Hardly a day goes by, even in my own company, without some disturbance in our labor-management relations because of OSHA. Its abuse has produced bitter confrontations and consequences over such matters as rate retention, walk-arounds, alleged discrimination, refusal to work protected by the "smoke screen" claim of unsafe conditions, "calling in the Feds" (or state agencies) in retaliation against employer's direction of the workforce, and generally obtaining through OSHA and the Act what normally should be subject to collective bargaining. Also, as predicted, the health aspects of the Act are having a far greater impact than the safety side even though the latter produces about 95 percent of the reportable incidents.[118]

Unions also have been critical in their assessment of OSHA. One international union criticized the act primarily because of its lengthy appeals procedure and the time it takes to reach a consensus on various safety standards.[119] Congress was criticized because of budget cuts and underfunding of OSHA functions. Unions have also expressed some concern about discharge of employees who file safety complaints. While the act prohibits such action, unions allege that employers find "other reasons" for these discharges.

OSHA had made some attempts to adjust to union and management concerns. It has, for example, eliminated some of its former "nitpicky" standards and has issued regulations concerning possible cancer-causing elements (such as cotton dust, lead, benzene, and acrylnitrate). In addition, OSHA indicated that workers removed from their jobs because of excessive lead in the body would be protected against loss of pay, seniority, and other job rights. The regulations' aim is to encourage workers to take medical exams without the fear of losing their jobs.[120]

Another OSHA-related controversy has developed in the chemical industry over voluntary sterilization. On certain jobs, female workers are exposed to chemicals which could cause fetal damage. To reduce the risks, companies are restricting certain jobs to men and to women workers who are not capable of having children. Insurance carriers for the companies are worried about potential liability; unions are threatening the companies with sex discrimination suits; OSHA is claiming that the companies are not controlling and monitoring the conditions under which the women work. To these conflicting concerns is added the inconclusiveness of the existing research on fetal damage caused by the chemicals used in production.[121]

New Administration—New Direction

With the introduction of the Reagan Administration, OSHA, like many other federal agencies, took a new direction. OSHA now inspects companies based on whether the industry is designated as "high hazard"—a new targeting system. This means that upon arrival at a high-hazard workplace, inspectors will review the log of injuries and illnesses. If the lost days are higher than the industry average, the inspection will continue. If the firm's record is lower than the average, the inspector will leave. Under this new plan, OSHA doubles its visits to high-hazard work sites.

OSHA has also taken the initiative toward a less legalistic approach to violators. When employers are cited for violations, they may contest the violation through several appeals. The new emphasis is toward settlement of any dispute with the employer's assistance and without litigation. Under this cooperative approach, contested violations have dropped nearly two-thirds. Also, when inspectors find a violation, they provide abatement information for correction. The intent is to focus on correction, not legal suits.

Several cooperative efforts are being initiated by OSHA. For example, OSHA has sought cooperation with officials in the twenty-four state-operated safety and health programs. OSHA has developed a pilot program to help employers where workers are protected through existing programs, and safety and health matters are handled through established procedures, such as joint union-management committees and grievance procedures. OSHA will assist trade associations so these groups may help their members comply with safety and health regulations.[122]

AFL-CIO records indicate that OSHA enforcement has declined under the Reagan Administration in 1982–1983. For a comparable period in 1981–1982, total inspections dropped 25 percent; complaint inspections, 58 percent; and follow-up inspections, 87 percent. The AFL-CIO found an 11 percent decline in initial inspections with citations; penalties were down 70 percent; and serious citations were down 51 percent.[123]

Contemporary Issues

Occupational safety and health regulations have raised other issues. One issue is the right of employees to refuse to perform hazardous work. While none of the provisions of the Occupational Safety and Health Act (the Act) explicitly protect employees who refuse to perform work because of safety and health reasons, employees are protected from discipline under certain circumstances. For example, when two employees refused to remove debris from an overhead wire mesh screen one week after an employee fell to his death through the screen, the employer sent them home with a loss of wages for six hours. The Secretary of Labor, on behalf of the employees, contended that the suspension was a discriminatory act under the Act and on appeal, the Supreme Court agreed.[124] However, the Court placed two cautions on employees who refused work:

The employees have no power under the regulation to order their employer to correct the hazardous condition or to clear the dangerous workplace of others. Moreover, any employee who acts in reliance on the regulations runs the risk of discharge or reprimand in the event a court subsequently finds that he acted unreasonably or in bad faith.[125]

In a related matter, employees who walk off their jobs in an expression of concern over unsafe working conditions are protected by the National Labor Relations Act. Under the NLRA, when employees act as a group, they are protected for their concerted activities, if they believe in good faith that they are exposed to a safety risk. In such cases, they may protest exposure to the dangerous condition without being subjected to subsequent discipline or discrimination by the employer.[126]

A second issue is the controversial OSHA rule that allows employees, their designated representatives, and OSHA inspectors the right to examine on-the-job medical records as well as company records of exposure to hazardous conditions. Employers are not required to measure exposure to toxic substances or to conduct medical surveillance of employees. However, if an employer conducts these activities and records the results, this information must be accessible to employees, their representatives, and OSHA inspectors. Refusal by the employer or occupational physician to provide such information is allowed only when the information would be detrimental to the employee's mental health, such as information about the employee's psychiatric state or a diagnosis of terminal illness.[127]

A third issue is the controversy over the employees' right to know the toxic substances to which they are exposed on the job. Eight states already have "right to know" laws and legislation is pending in twenty other states. Advocates want toxic substances labeled as dangerous so that workers may take the necessary precautions. They want companies to provide employees with information sheets that describe the toxic substances used on the job, the symptoms of exposure, and the procedures to follow in emergencies. OSHA has a "hazardous communication program" but lets the companies decide for themselves which chemicals to identify for employees. While some companies, such as DuPont, already have information programs, many small and nonunion companies do not. Further, many business groups are against legislation mandating the release of information because the bureaucratic burdens would be placed on business and trade secrets concerning use of certain chemicals could be compromised.[128]

Summary and Implications

Summary

The four general categories of administrative issues—technological change, personnel changes, employee and job development, and safety and health—have many important facets which may be negotiated and often end up in labor agreements.

Technological change, an essential ingredient of a dynamic economic system, is broadly defined to include such activities as introduction of labor-saving machines, power-driven tools, and automatic loading equipment. While unions generally accept these changes as inevitable, they attempt to negotiate provisions in labor agreements to protect members' present jobs and establish the means for assuring future protection. Collective bargaining has provided avenues for working together to resolve complicated problems emanating from technological changes; significant examples have occurred in various industries, such as the railroad, construction, and meatpacking industries.

Two interrelated issues, job security and personnel changes, raise questions about employee protection. Often, unions will seek to protect their members by negotiating work load restrictions, limiting management's rights to subcontract, demanding specific work assignments and jurisdiction, and structuring jobs and scheduling work to the advantage of the employees. When personnel changes are made, seniority becomes a key issue. Likewise, where firms are growing and opportunities for advancement are present, seniority and merit are key considerations. Employers and unions must consider EEOC regulations and court rulings in addition to labor agreement factors in deciding courses of action on personnel adjustment.

Employee and job development incorporate employee training, emphasis on apprenticeship, and job enrichment programs. Unions and employers alike place great emphasis on and expend much effort in apprenticeship programs. Job enrichment efforts are often initiated by management, but union cooperation is essential to complete success of such programs. While some unions are reluctant to become involved with them, major breakthroughs have been identified in selected unions, such as the United Auto Workers.

Safety and health issues have become important since the passage of the Occupational Safety and Health Act of 1970. Criticism of the act's administration has led to reevaluation, elimination of nitpicking rules, and a focus on major problems. Much progress has been made in its administration, but vital issues remain: clarification of operations, rules concerning regulation of chemicals which may cause cancer, and coverage and obligations of small businesses. On the positive side, considerable progress has been made by employers and unions toward cooperative programs and toward meeting the objectives of the act. In additon, new directions of OSHA, such as focusing on "high hazard" industries, reducing legalism, and developing greater cooperation, were discussed. Finally, employee rights, which include the right to refuse hazardous job assignments, to examine records, and to know about exposure to toxic substances, were explained.

Implications

In studying the labor relations issues, it appears that unions place a high priority on economic issues (wages) and job protection (use of seniority in personnel decisions). However, it may appear that administrative issues are slow to change over time. This is not true. These issues do change and are influenced by several factors mentioned in this chapter: the bargaining climate, the job, and the employees.

The bargaining climate is influenced enormously by national economic conditions and related factors, such as low productivity, international competition, high unemployment and legal rules and regulations. Low sales cause loss of jobs; outdated methods of production, as well as restrictive work rules, cause lower productivity. Because unions are expected to protect their members, they are learning that they cannot protect them unless employers are able to sell their products competitively. This means that unions have had to adapt by changing work rule practices in order to protect their members from job loss. While unions originally negotiated work rule restrictions to protect jobs, they are now accepting change in these restrictions for the same reason.

Technological advancement and its introduction in the workplace will inevitably change job content. New skills must be developed and displaced employees must be accommodated. Technology, skill training, and increased productivity go hand and hand and increased productivity will allow for a higher standard of living, better quality of jobs, and improved job satisfaction. As A. H. Raskin, labor expert, predicts:

[T]he workplace of the twenty-first century will be a more congenial place to work if only because many of the more disagreeable jobs will have been taken over by machines, and these, in general, will be quieter and cleaner. . . .[129]

From the standpoint of (workers') feeling of self-worth: (they) want to feel that their boss and their union respect the ideas they have about how their own work could be done better, how the plant or office can be made more efficient and pleasant, and what is good or bad about certain equipment, lighting, work flow, or methods of compensation. The benefits to the enterprise of involving workers in decisions on such matters go far beyond having a more satisfied work force; their involvement provides a basis for cooperative relationships indispensable to the welfare of employer and employee and to social stability.

Autonomous work teams, the opportunities of rotated leadership, two-way communication on everything important to the worker in his job, plus a widening list of joint policy decisions at the shop level are inevitable.[130]

Finally, administrative issues, especially seniority and safety, have been influenced greatly by legislation and administrative rules and regulations. Both the equal employment opportunity and occupational safety and health issues will continue to develop; administrative and court decisions that have affected labor relations in the past will do so in the future. As has been discussed in Chapters 1 and 3, the government as representative of the public interest will continue to play an important part in the labor relation process and in administrative issues, such as use of seniority, promotions, and safety.

Discussion Questions

1. Why do unions' reactions to technological change vary in accordance with their industry affiliation?
2. Think of an industry or company with which you are familiar and assume that you are the local union president. What types of clauses regarding technological issues would you attempt to negotiate with your employer?
3. Explain why unions place priority on seniority in personnel decisions, while employers seek to identify other determining factors.
4. Compare the legal restrictions that apply in selecting applicants for apprenticeship programs and promoting employees in the bargaining unit.
5. Since many experts in organization behavior and industrial psychology are strong advocates for job enrichment programs, why are some union leaders still reluctant to join the campaign?
6. Why are many unions critical of OSHA, whose purpose is to protect the physical well-being of their members?

References

[1]Julius Rezler, *Automation and Industrial Labor* (New York: Random House, 1969), pp. 5–6.

[2]"The Speedup in Automation," *Business Week*, August 3, 1981, p. 59.

[3]John Dodd, "Robots: The New 'Steel Collar' Workers," *Personnel Journal* 60 (September 1981), pp. 690–691.

[4]Joseph Albright, "Assembly-line Automations Common in Japanese Plants," *Atlanta Constitution*, November 28, 1982, p. 1E.

[5]Dodd, "Robots," pp. 688–690.

[6]Dodd, "Robots," pp. 694–695.

[7]Sar A. Levitan and Clifford M. Johnson, "The Future of Work: Does It Belong to Us or to the Robots?" *Monthly Labor Review* 105 (September 1982), p. 13.

[8]Richard W. Riche, "Impact of New Electronic Technology," *Monthly Labor Review* 105 (March 1982), p. 37.

[9]Sumner H. Slichter, James J. Healy, and E. Robert Livernash, *The Impact of Collective Bargaining on Management* (Washington, D.C.: Brookings Institute, 1960), pp. 343–345.

[10]Rezler, *Automation and Labor*, pp. 140–141.

[11]It should be noted that only about 17 percent of the collective bargaining agreements restrict technological change, and most of these are job protective clauses, such as guarantees of retraining displaced employees. Editors of Collective Bargaining Negotiations and Contracts, *Basic Patterns in Union Contracts* (Washington, D.C.: Bureau of National Affairs, 1979), p. 64.

[12]Jack Barbash, "Union Response to the Hard Line," *Industrial Relations* 1 (October 1961), pp. 25–29.

[13]Edward B. Shils, *Automation and Industrial Relations* (New York: Holt, Rinehart and Winston, 1963), pp. 130–132.

[14]B. S. Kirsh, *Automation and Collective Bargaining* (New York: Central Book, 1964), pp. 15–16.

[15]Slichter, Healy, and Livermash, *Collective Bargaining*, p. 349.

[16]Joseph P. Goldberg, "Bargaining and Productivity in the Private Sector," in Gerald Somers, ed., *Collective Bargaining and Productivity* (Madison, Wis.: Industrial Relations Research Association, 1975), pp. 22–42.

[17]Douglas M. McCabe, The Crew Size Dispute in the Railroad Industry (Washington, D.C.: U.S. Department of Transportation, 1977), pp. 6–8.

[18]"Changing 45 Million Jobs," *Business Week*, August 3, 1981, pp. 66–67.

[19]"General Motors and UAW Pick Fourth Plant for Establishment of Lifetime Jobs Program," Bureau of National Affairs, *Daily Labor Report*, November 22, 1982, p. A–12.

[20]George Ruben, "Collective Bargaining in 1982: Results Dictated by Economy," *Monthly Labor Review* 106 (January 1983), p. 29.

[21]Robert S. Greenberger, "Work Rule Changes Quietly Spread As Firms Try to Raise Productivity," *Wall Street Journal*, January 25, 1983, p. 35.

[22]Slichter, Healy, and Livernash, *Collective Bargaining*, pp. 317–335.

[23]Robert D. Leiter, *Featherbedding and Job Security* (New York: Twayne Publishers, 1964), pp. 32–33.

[24]William Gomberg, "The Work Rules and Work Practices," *Labor Law Journal* 12 (July 1961), pp. 643–653.

[25]Benjamin Aaron, "Government Restraint on Featherbedding," *Stanford Law Review* 5 (July 1953), pp. 687–721.

[26]Aaron, "Governmental Restraint."

[27]Kirsh, *Automation and Collective Bargaining*, pp. 16–17.

[28]"The Work Rule Changes GM Is Counting On," *Business Week*, April 5, 1982, pp. 30–31.
[29]"The Airlines Lighten Their Labor Load Again," *Business Week*, December 20, 1982, pp. 22–23.

[30]Slichter, Healy, and Livernash, *Collective Bargaining*, pp. 280–285.

[31]*Fibreboard Paper Products v. NLRB*, 379 U.S. 203 (1964).

[32]Eds. of Collective Bargaining Negotiations and Contracts, *Basic Patterns*, p. 63; U.S. Department of Labor, Bureau of Labor Statistics, *Characteristics of Major Collective Bargaining Agreements July 1, 1976* (Washington, D.C.: Government Printing Office, 1979), p. 75.

[33]Slichter, Healy and Livernash, *Collective Bargaining*, pp. 309–312.

[34]Frank Elkouri and Edna A. Elkouri, *How Arbitration Works*, 3d ed. (Washington, D.C.: Bureau of National Affairs, 1973), p. 458.

[35]NLRB, *42nd Annual Report of the National Labor Relations Board* (Washington, D.C.: Government Printing Office, 1977), p. 133.

[36]Slichter, Healy, and Livernash, *Collective Bargaining*, pp. 244–266. Also see Robert B. Hoffman, "The Representational Dispute," *Labor Law Journal* 24 (June 1973), pp. 323–339; and Stephen J. Cabot, "How Not to Get Caught in the Middle When Labor Unions Start Squabbling with Each Other," *Labor Law Journal* 24 (September 1973), pp. 626–628.

[37]NLRB, *42nd Annual Report*, p. 113. This board uses two procedural rules that are worthy of note:
1. A request for a decision in a specific case does not have to wait until the dispute occurs. Once the contractor makes the initial work assignments, a request for a decision can be made. Thus, time is saved by facilitating the dispute resolution process.
2. Decisions of the board are not precedent setting. This does not mean that similar decisions within an area are not based on patterns; it means that conditions vary from region to region, union to union, even agreement to agreement. Therefore, the board is not bound completely by precedent, but past practice. Custom in the industry, and skills, training, and job content are important elements that are considered.

[38]Elvis C. Stephens, "A Supervisor Performs Bargaining Unit Work: Is the Contract Violated?" *Labor Law Journal* 31 (November 1980), pp. 683–688.

[39]Slichter, Healy, and Livernash, *Collective Bargaining*, pp. 266–276.

[40]Ronald Wiggins, *The Arbitration of Industrial Engineering Disputes* (Washington, D.C.: Bureau of National Affairs, 1970), pp. 2–4.

[41]Elkouri and Elkouri, *How Arbitration Works*, pp. 469–487.

[42]"Unions Campaign to Shrink Work Time," *Business Week*, April 24, 1978, pp. 30–31.

[43]"Detroit Inches Closer to a Four-Day Week," *Business Week*, February 13, 1978, pp. 85–86.

[44]J. Carroll Swart and Robert A. Quakenbush, "Union's Views Concerning Alternative Work Schedules and Proposal to Alter Federal Overtime Pay Legislation," in Barbara D. Dennis, ed., *Proceedings of the Thirtieth Annual Meeting: Industrial Relations Research Association* (Madison, Wis.: Industrial Relations Research Association, 1977), p. 378.

[45]Jeffrey M. Miller, *Innovations in Working Patterns* (Washington, D.C.: Communication Workers of America and German Marshall Fund of the United States, 1978); and W. H. Holley, A. A. Armenakis, and H. S. Feild, "Employee Reactions to a Flexitime Program: A Longitudinal Study," *Human Resource Management* 15 (Winter 1976), pp. 21–23.

[46]James A. Craft, "Equal Opportunity and Seniority: Trends and Manpower Implications," *Labor Law Journal* 26 (December 1975), p. 750.

[47]George Cooper and Richard B. Sobol, "Seniority and Testing under Fair Employment Laws: A General Approach to Objective Criteria of Hiring and Promotion," *Harvard Law Review* 82 (June 1969), pp. 1601–1602.

[48]Eds. of Collective Bargaining Negotiations and Contracts, *Basic Patterns*, p. 73; and U.S. Department of Labor, Bureau of Labor Statistics, *Characteristics of Collective Bargaining*, p. 69.

[49]Eds. of Collective Bargaining Negotiations and Contracts, *Basic Patterns*, p. 73.

[50]Cooper and Sobol, "Seniority and Testing," p. 1602.

[51]"Why Lockheed's Strike Is a 'Holy War,'" *Business Week*, December 19, 1977, p. 31.

[52]Slichter, Healy, and Livernash, *Collective Bargaining*, p. 104.

[53]C. W. Randle, "The Pros and Cons of Seniority," in E. W. Bakke, C. Kerr, and C. W. Anrod, eds., *Unions, Management, and the Public* (New York: Harcourt Brace Jovanovich, 1976), p. 422.

[54]Slichter, Healy, and Livernash, *Collective Bargaining*, pp. 104–105.

[55]"Lockheed's Strike," p. 31.

[56]Randle, "Pros and Cons of Seniority," pp. 423–424.

[57]U.S. Department of Labor, Bureau of Labor Statistics, *Administration of Seniority* (Washington, D.C.: Government Printing Office, 1972).

[58]Eds. of Collective Bargaining Negotiations and Contracts, *Basic Patterns*, p. 74.

[59]Elaine F. Gruenfeld, *Promotion: Practices, Policies, and Affirmative Action* (Ithaca, N.Y.: New York State School of Industrial and Labor Relations, Cornell University, 1975), p. 12.

[60]Eds. of Collective Bargaining Negotiations and Contracts, *Basic Patterns*, p. 75.

[61]Thomas J. McDermott, "Types of Seniority Provisions and the Measurement of Ability," *Arbitration Journal* 25 (1970), pp. 101–105. Also see W. E. Howard, "The Interpretation of Ability by Labor-Management Arbitrators," *Arbitration Journal* 14 (1959), pp. 122–123.

[62]McDermott, "Seniority Provisions," p. 106.

[63]Gruenfeld, *Promotion*, p. 12.

[64]McDermott, "Seniority Provisions," p. 110.

[65]"Uniform Guidelines on Employee Selection Procedures," *Government Employee Relations Reporter*, August 28, 1978.

[66]Ibid., p. 2.

[67]George Hagglund and Duane Thompson, *Psychological Testing and Industrial Relations* (Iowa City: Center for Labor and Management, University of Iowa, 1969); R. E. Biddle and L. M. Jacobs, "Under What Circumstances Can a Unionized Company Use Testing for Promotion?" *Personnel Psychology* 21 (Summer 1968), pp. 149–177; Dale McConkey, "Ability versus Seniority in Promotion and Layoff," *Personnel* 37 (May–June 1960), pp. 51–57.

[68]William H. Holley, Jr., "Performance Ratings in Arbitration," *Arbitration Journal* 32 (March 1977), pp. 8–25.

[69]McDermott, "Seniority Provisions," pp. 110–124.

[70]U.S. Department of Labor, Bureau of Labor Statistics, *Seniority in Promotion and Transfer Provisions* (Washington, D.C.: Government Printing Office, 1970), pp. 15–21, 42.

[71]Eds. of Collective Bargaining Negotiations and Contracts, *Basic Patterns*, p. 53.

[72]Bernard J. Offerman et al., "Legal Update: Seniority and Affirmative Action," working paper, Cleveland State University, Cleveland, Ohio, January 27, 1977. Also see *Quarles v. Phillip Morris Inc.*, 179 F. Supp. 507 (1968); *United Paperworkers v. U.S.*, 416 F.2d 980 (1969); *U.S. v. Bethlehem Steel Corp.*, 446 F.2d 652 (1971); *Bing v. Roadway*, 485 F.2d 441 (1973); and *Franks v. Bowman Transportation Co.*, 12 FEP 549 (1976).

[73]Cary D. Thorp, Jr., "Racial Discrimination and Seniority," *Labor Law Journal* 23 (July 1972), pp. 401–403.

[74]Bernard J. Offerman, "Legal Update: Seniority and Affirmative Action," *Labor Studies Journal* 2 (1978), pp. 202–214.

[75]Thorp, "Racial Discrimination," pp. 412–413.

[76]Richard D. Sibbernsen, "A Review of Job and Seniority Structures in Light of EEO Liability," *Labor Law Journal* 26 (October 1975), p. 674.

[77]*United Steelworkers of America, AFL-CIO, v. Brian F. Weber et al.*, 47 LW 4851, *U.S. Law Week* (Washington, D.C.: Bureau of National Affairs, June 28, 1979).

[78]William H. Holley, Jr., and Hubert S. Feild, "Equal Employment Opportunity and Its Implications for Personnel Practices," *Labor Law Journal* 27 (May 1976), p. 285.

[79]Barbara Linderman Schlei and Paul Grossman, *Employment Discrimination Law* (Washington, D.C.: Bureau of National Affairs, 1976), pp. 458–459.

[80]Phyllis Wallace and James Driscoll, "Social Issues in Collective Bargaining," in Jack Stieber et. al., *U.S. Industrial Relations 1950–1980: A Critical Assessment* (Madison, Wis.: Industrial Relations Research Association, 1981), pp. 217–218.

[81]Michael E. Gordon and William A. Johnson, "Seniority: A Review of Its Legal and Scientific Standing," *Personnel Psychology* 38 (Summer 1982), pp. 259–260.

[82]Thomas Bagby, "The Supreme Court Reaffirms Broad Humanity for Seniority Systems," *Labor Law Journal* 33 (July 1982), p. 416.

[83]Wallace and Driscoll, "Social Issues in Collective Bargaining," pp. 219–221.

[84]Bureau of Labor Statistics, *Major Characteristics of Collective Bargaining Agreements, January 1, 1980* (Washington, D.C.: U.S. Government Printing Office, 1981), p. 105.

[85]Jack Barbash, "Union Interests in Apprenticeships and Other Training Forms," in Norman F. Duffy, ed., *Essays on Apprenticeship* (Madison, Wis.: The University of Wisconsin, 1967), p. 36.

[86]Vernon M. Briggs, Jr., "Conference Summary and Critique," in Vernon M. Briggs, Jr. and Felician F. Foltman, eds., *Apprenticeship Research* (Ithaca, NY: Cornell University, 1981), p. 218.

[87]Bureau of National Affairs, *EEOC Compliance Manual* (Washington, D.C.: Bureau of National Affairs, August 1977), p. 660:0001.

[88]U.S. Department of Health, Education, and Welfare, *Work in America: Report of a Special Task Force to the Secretary of Health, Education, and Welfare* (Cambridge, Mass.: MIT Press, 1973). A 1977 survey by the Survey Research Center, University of Michigan, revealed a decline in job satisfaction from 1969 to 1973 and 1973 to 1977. Graham L. Staines and Robert P. Quinn, "American Workers Evaluate the Quality of Their Jobs," *Monthly Labor Review* 102 (January 1979), p. 4.

[89]Allan Nash, *Quality of Worklife* (Chicago: Roosevelt University, 1977), pp. 3–12.

[90]William F. Giles and William H. Holley, Jr., "Job Enrichment versus Traditional Issues at the Bargaining Table: What Union Members Want," *Academy of Management Journal* 21 (December 1978), p. 727.

[91]Mitchell Fein, "Job Enrichment: A Reevaluation," *Sloan Management Review* 15 (Winter 1974), p. 70; Mitchell Fein, "The Myth of Job Enrichment," in R. P. Fairefield, ed., *Humanizing the Workplace* (Buffalo: Prometheus Books, 1974), pp. 71–78.

[92]Neal Q. Herrick and Michael Maccoby, "Humanizing Work: A Priority Goal of the 1970's," in L. E. Davis and A. B. Cherns, eds., *The Quality of Working Life* (New York: The Free Press, 1975), p. 71; William Gomberg, "Job Satisfaction: Sorting Out the Nonsense," *American Federationist* 80 (June 1973), pp. 14–20; T. R. Brooks, "Job Satisfaction: An Elusive Goal," *American Federationist* 79 (October 1972), pp. 1–7.

[93]Jack Barbash, "The Union as a Bargaining Organization: Some Implications for Organization Behavior," *Proceedings of the Twenty-eighth Annual Meeting: Industrial Relations Research Association* (Madison, Wis.: Industrial Relations Research Association, 1975), p. 152.

[94]Ibid.

[95]Sam Zagoria, "Policy Implications and Future Agenda," in Jerome Rosow, ed., *The Worker and the Job* (Englewood Cliffs, N.J.: Prentice Hall, 1974), p. 181.

[96]Albert Blum, "Union Prospects and Programs for the 1970s," *Proceedings of the Twenty-second Annual Winter Meeting: Industrial Relations Research Association* (Madison, Wis.: Industrial Relations Research Association, 1969), pp. 136–141.

[97]Fein, "Job Enrichment," p. 79.

[98]Sar Levitan and William B. Johnston, *Work Is Here To Stay, Alas* (Salt Lake City: Olympus Publishing, 1973), p. 137.

[99]Lee Dyer, D. B. Lipsky, and T. A. Kochan, "Union Attitudes toward Management Cooperation," *Industrial Relations* 16 (May 1977), pp. 163–172.

[100]Giles and Holley, "Job Enrichment versus Traditional Issues," pp. 225–230; and T. A. Kochan, D. B. Lipsky, and Lee Dyer, "Collective Bargaining and the Quality of Work: The Views of Local Union Activists," *Proceedings of the Twenty-seventh Annual Meeting: Industrial Relations Research Association* (Madison, Wis.: Industrial Relations Research Association, 1974), pp. 150–162.

[101]Raymond A. Katzell et al., *Work, Productivity and Job Satisfaction* (Chicago: Psychological Corporation, 1976), p. 95.

[102]Giles and Holley, "Job Enrichment versus Traditional Issues," pp. 728–729.

[103]William H. Holley, Jr., Hubert S. Feild, and James C. Crowley, "Negotiating Quality of Worklife, Productivity, and Traditional Issues: Union Members' Preferred Roles of Their Union," *Personnel Psychology* 34 (Summer 1981), pp. 316–318.

[104]Craig A. Olson, "The Relationship Between Union Member Preferences for Bargaining Outcomes, Union and Job Satisfaction," in Barbara D. Dennis, ed., *Proceedings of the Thirty-fourth Annual Meeting: Industrial Relations Research Association* (Madison, Wis.: Industrial Relations Research Association, 1982), p. 243.

[105]William W. Winpisinger, "Job Satisfaction: A Union Response," *American Federationist* 80 (February 1973), pp. 8–10. See also *Proceedings of the Twenty-fifth Annual Meeting: Industrial Relations Research Association* (Madison, Wis.: Industrial Relations Research Association, 1972), pp. 154–159.

[106]Bernard J. White, "Innovations in Job Design: The Union Perspective," *Journal of Contemporary Business* 6 (Spring 1977), pp. 24–25.

[107]Edward E. Lawler III, and John A. Drexler, Jr., "Dynamics of Establishing Cooperative Quality-of-Worklife Projects," *Monthly Labor Review* 101 (March 1978), pp. 24–26.

[108]Ibid., p. 26; John A. Drexler, Jr., and Edward E. Lawler III, "A Union-Management Cooperative Project to Improve the Quality of Worklife," *Journal of Applied Behavioral Science* 13 (July–September 1977), p. 386.

[109]Ninety-four percent of labor agreements include such provisions. U.S. Department of Labor, Bureau of Labor Statistics, *Major Collective Bargaining Agreements: Safety and Health Provisions* (Washington, D.C.: Government Printing Office, 1976), p. 49.

[110]Eds. of Collective Bargaining Negotiations and Contracts, *Basic Patterns*, pp. 109–111.

[111]T. A. Kochan, Lee Dyer, and D. B. Lipsky, *The Effectiveness of Union-Management Safety and Health Committees* (Kalamazoo, Mich.: W. E. Upjohn Institute for Employment Research, 1977), p. 5.

[112]84 Stat. 1590 (1970).

[113]The year that OSHA of 1970 was passed, the following statistics were presented to Congress:
14,500 killed—average of 55 per workweek.
2.2 million injured.
390,000 disabling occupational diseases (lung cancer, asbestos, and so on).
250 million man-days lost, ten times that lost from strikes.
$1.5 million lost in wages.
$8 billion lost to GNP.
Benjamin L. Brown, "A Law Is Made: The Legislative Process in the Occupational Safety and Health Act of 1970," *Labor Law Journal* 25 (October 1974), p. 597.

[114]A study of three industries—aerospace, chemicals, and textiles—was conducted. See Herbert R. Northrup et al., *The Impact of OSHA* (Philadelphia: Industrial Research Unit, University of Pennsylvania, 1978).

[115]Nicholas Ashford, *Crisis in the Workplace* (Cambridge, Mass.: MIT Press, 1976), p. 13.

[116]Lawrence P. Ettkin and J. Brad Chapman, "Is OSHA Effective in Reducing Industrial Injuries?" *Labor Law Journal* 26 (April 1975), p. 242; Wayne Wendling, "Industrial Safety and Collective Bargaining," in B. D. Dennis, ed., *Proceedings of the Thirtieth Annual Winter Meeting: Industrial Relations Research Association* (Madison, Wis.: Industrial Relations Research Association, 1978), p. 435.

[117]Kenneth W. Nelson, quoted by Douglas Soutar, "A Management View," in B. D. Dennis, ed., *Proceedings of the 1978 Annual Spring Meeting: Industrial Relations Research Association* (Madison, Wis.: Industrial Relations Research Association, 1978), p. 495.

[118]Ibid., p. 493.

[119]*Occupational Safety and Health Act 1970: A Trade Union Review and Analysis* (Kansas City, Kans.: International Brotherhood of Boilermakers, Iron Shipbuilders, Blacksmiths, Forgers, and Helpers, 1978), pp. 19–21. Also see John Zalusky, "The Worker Views the Enforcement of Safety Laws," *Labor Law Journal* 26 (April 1975), p. 235.

[120]Leon Bornstein, "Industrial Relations in 1978: Some Bargaining Highlights," *Monthly Labor Review* 102 (January 1979), pp. 63–64.

[121]Gail Bronson, "Issue of Fetal Damage Stirs Women Workers at Chemical Plants," *Wall Street Journal*, February 9, 1979, pp. 1, 33.

[122]Thomas G. Auchter, "OSHA: A Year Later," Labor Law Journal 33 (April 1982), p. 195.

[123]"AFL-CIO Statistics Show Decline in all OSHA Compliance Indicators," *Daily Labor Report*, November 5, 1982, p. A–11.

[124]*Whirlpool Corp. v. Marshall*, Secretary of Labor, Slip Opinion, Supreme Court of the United States, No. 78–1870, February 26, 1980.

[125]Ibid.

[126]"Taft-Hartley Act Held to Protect Workers Who Protest Unsafe Conditions," *Daily Labor Report* (Washington, D.C.: Bureau of National Affairs, Inc.), November 26, 1982, p. A–5 to A–6.

[127]Mary Hayes, "OSHA Final Rule Gives Employees the Right to See Their Exposure and Medical Records," *Personnel Administrator* 27 (March 1982), pp. 71–75. A federal district court in Louisiana upheld this rule in November, 1982; Bureau of National Affairs, *Daily Labor Report*, November 12, 1982, p. A–7.

[128]Frank Allen, "Battle Building Over 'Right to Know' Laws Regarding Toxic Items Used by Workers," *Wall Street Journal*, January 4, 1983, p. 31.

[129]A. H. Raskin, "Toward a More Participative Work Force," in C. S. Sheppard and D. C. Carrol, eds., *Working in the Twenty-First Century* (New York: John Wiley & Sons, 1980), p. 94.

[130]Ibid., p. 97.

Chapter 13 Economic Issues

A responsible wage policy "provides a *modus operandi* and keeps the peace, . . . creates a measure of certainty and a basis of planning for a year or two ahead, . . . strengthens the fealty of the union toward the private-ownership system of production."

Arthur M. Ross, "What Is a Responsible Wage Policy?" *Southern Economic Journal*, 1948.

Wages and other economic benefits are vitally important to everyone in the labor relations process. They represent income to the employee, cost to the organization, and a basis for taxes to the government. In addition, wages serve important economic functions: they serve as a factor in the allocation of resources; they influence the selection of an individual's occupation and movement from one firm, industry, or location to another; they influence decisions on plant location and investments in machinery and capital equipment, and affect employment and unemployment. More importantly, if wages become exorbitantly high, employees may price themselves out of particular labor markets. Thus, wages are both economic indicators and determinants.[1]

Unions and management are required by the National Labor Relations Act to bargain in good faith with respect to wages. As a result of NLRB and court decisions, wage-related topics such as pensions, overtime, shift differentials, job evaluation, and incentive systems must be bargained over if either party presents such topics during negotiations.

Scholars have spent much time studying and explaining wage theories and the effects of wages on the economy, and thousands of union and management negotiators spend many hours annually bargaining over wages, wage-related issues.[2] *While both activities are important to an understanding of labor economics as well as labor-management relationships, this chapter does not deal with the theory of wages and the economics of labor markets. Rather it focuses on the methods of wage determination and factors used by negotiators in determining the wage package—wages and other economic benefits.*

Wage Determination

Union and management officials have to agree on what the term *wages* means before they can successfully bargain over this issue. For instance, wages may mean the basic wage rate, average gross hourly earnings, average weekly earnings, or incentive pay (payment per product completed). Basic wage rates for each job class are usually listed in the labor agreement; however, other wage payments (overtime, incentive pay, shift differentials, and other compensation earned in the regular work-week) may have to be computed in accordance with provisions in the labor agreement.[3]

After agreeing on the language for the basis of wage negotiations, the parties determine those wage rates and related terms of employment.[4] In this process, the parties will consider various factors and will conclude with numerous wage rates, job classes, and wage ranges. As most readers have already experienced, jobs with varying duties and responsibilities are assigned different wage rates. Besides these occupational differentials within a firm there are regional, industry, and shift differences that cause an employer to pay different combinations of wage rates. Textile workers in the South generally earn less than those in the North; electricians and laborers in the building trades generally have higher wage rates than electricians and laborers in factories.

Wage differentials among individuals, jobs, industries, or regions can be explained in a variety of ways. However, any explanation must look at the interrelationships between labor and capital as factors of production and as contributors to productivity. For example:

It is sometimes said that if productivity rises by "x" percent and the workers receive an "x" percent increase in compensation, then the workers are getting all of the productivity increase, leaving nothing for others. This is incorrect. If productivity rises, say 10 percent, and output increases commensurately, then each factor of production—labor-management, capital—can receive a 10 percent increase. If output does not rise commensurately . . . then total compensation of input factors and rates of return to those factors will depend on the difference between the output increase and the productivity increase, the size of the hourly compensation increase, and the cost of new capital investment.[5]

Industrial Wage Differentials

Industrial wage differentials may be explained in terms of three interrelated factors: (a) the degree of competition or monopoly in the product market, (b) the value added by workers in a particular industry, and (c) the percentage of total costs that labor costs represent.

Competition in the product market First, if a firm has a monopoly or near monopoly (the product is essential, with no available substitute), then increased labor cost can be easily passed on to the consumer. In such cases, the employer will resist higher wages less rigidly in negotiation. For example, if a private or public utility agrees to a 12 percent increase with cost-of-living adjustments, it then can add the increased cost to its customers' bills (unless the utility is heavily regulated). Consumers in this situation frequently have little choice but to pay the higher prices. Thus, in those industries where the firm controls the pricing without competitive threats, wages tend to be proportionately higher.

Value added by employees *Value added* refers to the contribution of factors of production to the value of the final product. Comparing labor's contribution for different industries helps to explain industrial wage differentials. For example, the value added by labor in sawmills, cotton weaving, clothes manufacturing, and the mobile home industry is significantly lower than corresponding figures in the steel, petrochemical, and tire industries. However, because employees must use machines, which represent capital investments, and because there is such a close interrelationship between labor and capital investments in machinery and equipment, exact determination of labor's contributions has become a complicated process. In unionized settings, negotiations between union and management representatives determine labor's share in the amount of value added.

Labor costs as percentage of total costs The relationship between labor costs and total costs must also be considered in determining the industrial wage rate. Highly interdependent with capital investment per worker and the product market, this relationship is important in wage negotiations. For example, labor intensive organizations, such as health care facilities, textile firms, and government, have high labor costs in relation to total costs. On the other hand, petroleum and chemical firms and electric-generating plants have relatively low labor costs as a percentage of total costs.

Usually, firms with a high ratio of labor costs to total costs are more likely to resist wage increases. For example, if a hospital where labor costs are 60 percent of total costs grants a 10 percent wage increase, it must raise prices about 6 percent. A petroleum processing plant where labor cost is 5 percent of total cost would have to raise its price about 0.5 percent to cover a 10 percent increase in wages. We would therefore expect to find workers in the same job classifications receiving higher wages in chemical and petroleum companies than in hospitals or textile firms. Of course, there are many qualifications to this conclusion in specific incidents—for example, consumers may not accept a higher price and a company may choose to cover the wage increase out of its profits. Nonetheless, the relation of labor cost to total cost can be an important factor in industrial wage differentials.

Occupational Wage Differentials and the Role of Job Evaluation and Wage Surveys

Within a company or industry, maintaining a proper and rational wage relationship among various jobs is important. The relationships are often maintained under job evaluation programs but in other cases are determined by individual or collective bargaining.[6] The process of determining the relative importance of each job to the organization helps in understanding occupational wage differentials; therefore, the following steps in a job evaluation program are presented.[7]

How Jobs Are Evaluated within the Organization The first step in *job evaluation* is an organization analysis[8] which appraises and examines the organization's objectives, structure, and authority and responsibility relationships. The findings from this analysis help insure that the job content is up-to-date.

The second step is the selection and measurement of job factors which are found at least to some extent in all of the organization's job classifications. Job factors vary substantially depending on the organization, but skill (education and training), effort, responsibility (for people and equipment), and working conditions (hazards, surroundings) are typically selected. Management must consider the minimum amount of each job factor or qualification necessary to adequately perform the particular job. For example, it may be nice to employ a typist who can edit, interpret, and make complex economics subjects understandable, but few organizations can find or are willing to pay wages needed to attract such a qualified person.

Next, an appropriate job evaluation system for appraising jobs according to the established job factors is selected. There are four job evaluation methods available: ranking, classification, factor comparison, and point system. The *ranking* and *factor-comparison* methods compare jobs non-quantitatively in terms of one or more job factors; the *classification* and *point system* methods compare jobs to predetermined numerical rating scales designed to measure one or more job factors about each job. Firms' job evaluation systems may use ten to fifteen different job factors, with these factors often divided into subfactors. For example, effort may be divided into physical and mental effort.[9]

The fourth step involves *job analysis*, a process of systematically securing information and facts about the jobs to be evaluated. (Throughout the job evaluation process, it is the jobs, not employees in the job classification, that are being analyzed.) The job classifications resulting from job analysis will receive the same rating whether the employee holding the job has a master's degree or high school diploma, is lazy or ambitious, or is a high or low performer.

Commonly used methods of job analysis include the method of the U.S. Department of Labor,[10] the critical incident method,[11] and the position analysis questionnaire (PAQ).[12] These techniques use observation, interviews, and questionnaires in gathering data about the jobs which will be used to formulate job descriptions and job specifications. The *job descriptions* include written summations of the duties and responsibilities; the *job specifications* include the personal characteristics a worker must possess to qualify for the job. Both will be used in the job evaluation process. As firms try to relate wages to various degrees of duties and responsibilities, they must also pay more to employ workers who have high qualifications, such as education, training, and skills.

Management often prefers to conduct its job evaluation independent of the union. Management may prefer not to share its weightings of the job factors, particularly when it believes certain factors (such as training, skill, and responsibility for equipment) should receive more compensation than others, such as working conditions. By withholding the weightings, management may avoid confrontations with the union. On the other hand, unions do not want to be totally excluded from the job evaluation process.

Union leaders generally view job evaluation with disfavor, because it tends to limit bargaining and freeze the wage structure.[13] Three surveys of union officials over a ten-year period have revealed that unions prefer to establish wage scales through collective bargaining, although their resistance to job evaluation has declined. While unions reserve the right to file grievances to resist or express dissatisfaction with job evaluation, they seldom show strong opposition unless firms attempt to use job evaluation as the sole criterion for wage determination or try to substitute it for collective bargaining.[14] In fact, some unions regard job evaluation techniques not only as useful guides in negotiating wages but as a means by which they can more effectively explain the negotiated wage settlements to their members.[15]

Regardless of the job evaluation method, the objective is to develop a wage structure that prices jobs with less skill, effort, and responsibility at lower wage rates and jobs with greater skill, effort, and responsibility at higher wage rates. Table 13.1 presents an example wage structure for a firm, which includes job

Table 13.1 Typical Wage Structure for a Manufacturing Firm

Job Titles	Labor Grade	Points	Starting Hourly Wage Rates
Janitor	I	200–249	$6.20
Material Handler	II	250–299	6.55
Shipper	III	300–349	6.90
Tool Room Keeper	IV	350–399	7.24
Machine Operator B	V	400–449	7.57
Machine Operator A	VI	450–499	7.88
Maintenance B	VII	500–549	8.23
Tool Grinder B	VIII	550–599	8.57
Maintenance A	IX	600–649	8.88
Tool Grinder A	X	650–699	9.23
Electrician A	XI	700–749	9.52
Tool and Die Maker A	XII	750–800	9.95

Source: Adapted (adjusted for increase in cost of living) from U.S. Department of Labor, Bureau of Labor Statistics, *Major Collective Bargaining Agreements: Wage Administration Provisions* (Washington, D.C.: Government Printing Office, 1978), p. 2.

titles, labor grades, point ranges, and starting wage rates for each labor grade. Since a numerical score should indicate the relative value of the job, the greater the score, the higher the labor grade and the hourly wage rate. Table 13.2 shows job classes and the effective wage rates at different dates during the agreement.

Table 13.2 Hourly Wage Structure for a Steel Company

Job Class	Effective Through 7/31/80[a]	Effective 8/1/80[b]	Effective 8/1/81[c]	Effective 8/1/82[d]
1–2	8.725	8.725	8.925	9.075
3	8.852	8.852	9.062	9.222
4	8.979	8.979	9.199	9.369
5	9.106	9.106	9.336	9.516
6	9.233	9.233	9.473	9.663
7	9.360	9.360	9.610	9.810
8	9.487	9.487	9.747	9.957
9	9.614	9.614	9.884	10.104
10	9.741	9.741	10.021	10.251
11	9.868	9.868	10.158	10.398
12	9.995	9.995	10.295	10.545
13	10.122	10.122	10.432	10.692
14	10.249	10.249	10.569	10.839
15	10.376	10.376	10.706	10.986
16	10.503	10.503	10.843	11.133
17	10.630	10.630	10.980	11.280
18	10.757	10.757	11.117	11.427
19	10.884	10.884	11.254	11.574
20	11.011	11.011	11.391	11.721
21	11.138	11.138	11.528	11.868
22	11.265	11.265	11.665	12.015
23	11.392	11.392	11.802	12.162
24	11.519	11.519	11.939	12.309
25	11.646	11.646	12.076	12.456
26	11.773	11.773	12.213	12.603
27	11.900	11.900	12.350	12.750
28	12.027	12.027	12.487	12.897
29	12.154	12.154	12.624	13.044
30	12.281	12.281	12.761	13.191
31	12.408	12.408	12.898	13.338
32	12.535	12.535	13.035	13.485
33	12.662	12.662	13.172	13.632
34	12.789	12.789	13.309	13.779

[a]Includes 25¢ general increase with a job class increment increase of 1¢ and 44¢ Cost-of-Living Adjustment which became effective February 1, 1980.

[b]Each Job Class rate will be adjusted by adding the Cost-of-Living Adjustment effective 8/1/80 excluding the Cost-of-Living Adjustment which would have become effective May 1, 1980.

[c]Each Job Class rate will be adjusted by adding the Cost-of-Living Adjustment effective 8/1/81.

[d]Each Job Class rate will be adjusted by adding the Cost-of-Living Adjustment effective 8/1/82.

Table 13.3 Typical Results from a Wage Survey

	Firms						
Job Title	A	B	C	D	E	F	Average
Janitor	5.98	6.11	6.76	5.46	5.98	6.11	6.07
Assembler	6.24	6.63	6.89	7.80	7.02	7.15	7.05
Shop Clerk	7.93	7.80	8.71	7.93	7.80	7.67	8.00
Welder	9.10	9.23	9.75	9.10	9.10	9.10	9.23
Machinist I	8.45	8.32	9.10	8.45	8.58	8.45	8.55
Machinist II	8.97	8.84	9.62	9.10	8.97	9.10	9.10
Machinist III	9.62	9.75	10.40	9.75	9.49	9.75	9.79
Electrician	11.18	11.05	11.96	10.92	11.05	11.18	11.25
Tool and Die Maker	11.70	12.02	13.39	11.18	11.96	12.35	12.10

Surveys to Compare Firms' Wage Structures *Wage surveys* are conducted to assure that external labor market considerations, such as comparable wages, are included in the wage structure. While firms attempt to rationalize their wage structure internally through job evaluation, they must also maintain competitive wages externally to insure that the firm can recruit qualified employees and retain productive ones. Usually a wage analyst either visits, sends questionnaires to, or conducts a telephone interview with the wage analysts of similar organizations or comparable firms. The one conducting the survey provides the responding firms with titles, descriptions, and specifications of the jobs in the wage survey. Participating firms will supply the starting wage rate and the appropriate economic benefits paid individuals in these job classifications (see Table 13.3). After the wage survey is complete, the firm must determine how the data will be used. For example, does it want to lead the industry, compete with Firm C, or pay the industry average?

These wage surveys may be conducted by the firm or the union, or obtained from trade groups, employer associations or the Bureau of Labor Statistics, which periodically publishes industry, area, occupational, and national wage survey data.[16] From such abundant data, union and management officials sometimes have difficulty determining which are most appropriate for their particular situation. (This problem is further discussed in the section on wage comparability.)

The wage plan concludes with a certain number of wage classes, wages for each job or job class, wage ranges (starting to top wages) for each class, policies and procedures for wage adjustments (seniority, merit, and so on), procedures for job changes to a different class, temporary job changes, procedures for jobs that pay above or below their wage range (*red-circled* wage rates), and policy on union involvement.

After the wage plan and policies are established, individual wage adjustments are made on the basis of merit and seniority. A study of 600 labor agreements by the Bureau of Labor Statistics revealed that 65 percent provide for automatic wage increases at fixed intervals without reference to merit. Another 11.6 percent relied completely on merit while the remainder used some combination of an automatic increase plus merit.[17]

Production Standards and Wage Incentives

Unions and management sometimes negotiate provisions in the labor agreement that cover wage-related issues, such as production standards, time studies, and incentive wage payments. *Production standards* refer to the expected employee output which is consistent with workmanship quality, operational efficiency, and reasonable working capacities of normal operators. These standards are often determined by time studies which involve analyses of time and motions of workers on the job, and the resulting standards are used to assess performance and determine the wage incentives for individual workers or groups of workers.[18]

Wage incentive plans Where *incentive plans* are negotiated, the structure and design are included in the contract, although specific details may not be included. The role of the union in setting and protesting production standards and rate changes and its right to be consulted on related issues are also usually included. Some contracts include provisions about time studies and the involvement of unions. A small number permit a union observer during the time study, and a few go as far as to provide special training for the union time study representative. Other provisions include procedures used for timing a worker, specification for the meaning of *normal employee*, advance notice to the employee holding the job being studied, and specification for fatigue and personal allowances in setting production standards.[19]

While wage incentive plans vary in structure and specific content, their goals are essentially the same: (a) to increase employee productivity, (b) to attract prospective employees to the company, and (c) to reward employees monetarily for their increased productivity. A typical individual wage incentive plan is one in which workers are paid for the number of pieces or jobs completed. Others pay bonuses or premiums to employees for production above the standard. Many varieties of these incentive plans exist, but, while they are numerous and sometimes confusing to employees, they are similar in concept.

Until recently, when many companies and unions began to investigate gain-sharing plans, interest in wage incentive plans as a way to stimulate worker productivity had declined. In fact, the great majority (82 percent) of production workers continue to be paid time rates. The major reasons for time-based compensation plans are that plant jobs are usually machine-paced, workers have little control over their pace of work. In only six industries—men's and children's hosiery, women's hosiery, leather footwear, men's and boy's suits and coats, men's and boy's shirts, and basic steel and iron—are a majority of the workers paid by incentive plans. In these six industries, machines are controlled by the operators, workers exercise considerable discretion over the pace of work, and output is identifiable and measurable.[20]

In 1982, profit-sharing plans that provided for cash bonuses based on the company's profit to partially or totally take the place of wage increases were negotiated with several companies, including Ford, General Motors, Pan Am, Uniroyal, International Harvester, and the New York *Daily News*. The concept was introduced twenty-five years ago by Walter Reuther, then president of the United Auto Workers, but the auto industry denounced it as "socialistic." Although interest in profit sharing may last only as long as the recession, experts have concluded that for profit sharing to work, employees, their unions, and management must develop a "common fate" or "we are all in this together for good or for ill" attitude, and management must be willing to provide job security, job training, and a structure for genuine worker participation.[21]

In recessionary times, there have also been incidents where workers have abandoned their traditional wage scales in order to be paid according to their productivity. In exchange, management has agreed to allow workers to have more input in managing their work. For example, Crown Zellerbach and the International Woodworkers of America have agreed to a compensation plan that pays loggers by the measured cubic feet of logs cut. Joint labor-management committees decide the number of crews, which job functions are needed, and how to organize the work. An experimental plan of this sort resulted in worker earnings of $3.00 more per hour than straight wages.[22]

Group incentive plans are designed so that companies make monetary payments to a specific group or groups of employees for producing more than expected. Incentives include group bonuses, group piece rates, profit sharing, production sharing, and cost sharing. In some cases, the plans are limited to a few employees, to specific departments, or to other organizational divisions; in others, the entire company work force is covered. While group incentives aim to increase production and reduce costs, they are also designed to increase teamwork, provide greater job security, and achieve greater acceptance of new technology.

There are a variety of group incentive plans. One of the most popular is the *Scanlon Plan*, a plan for saving labor costs that was developed by former union leader Joseph Scanlon in the late 1930s. It provides bonus payments based on a computed ratio of total labor costs (TLC) to total production values (TPV), which typically equal monthly sales, plus or minus inventory adjustments. This means that if the TLC/TPV ratio is 50 percent, a reduction in the ratio would be a labor cost savings. For example, if the workers were to reduce costs by working harder, producing more efficiently, and saving on wastes and the TLC/TPV ratio declined to 40 percent, the 10 percent labor savings would be shared with the workers in relation to their basic wages.[23]

The *Rucker Plan* is based on a change in the ratio between dollar payroll and dollar value added. The value added equals sales less purchased materials.

Under this plan, if employees lower the ratio between payroll costs to dollar value added, the productivity gains are shared.

Improshare is a plan derived from improved productivity through sharing. Improshare productivity measurements use traditional work measurement standards for a selected base period. However, productivity gains are divided evenly between employees and company. A study of thirty-four Improshare programs in unionized companies showed an average productivity gain of 26.9 percent after the first year, whereas the average gain for thirty-eight nonunion plants was 21.5 percent.[24]

Arguments Used by Management and Union Officials in Wage Determination

Unions and management have recognized that there is no single causal influence on wage determination; however, both parties will use any identifiable influence to support their arguments for or against wage increases. The most common influences are: differential features of the work (usually determined by job evaluation), wage comparability, ability to pay (financial condition of the organization), productivity, cost of living and legal requirements.[25] Union and management officials do not always accept the same criteria. Moreover, each might emphasize different criteria at different times. During prosperous times unions tend to emphasize the ability to pay; during recessions management presents its poor financial position. Similarly, during periods of rapid inflation, unions emphasize cost-of-living adjustments; when prices are stable, management places much weight on the lack of necessity for cost-of-living adjustments. Certainly, these influences cannot be entered into a computer that will yield a precise solution to the wage determination, but they do provide a framework within which the parties present their data and arguments in order to resolve their differences over wage issues through collective bargaining.[26]

Differential Features of the Work: Job Evaluation and the Wage Spread

The job evaluation process described in the preceding section can influence the wages assigned to various job classifications in an organization. The relative influence of job evaluation can be seen in the *wage spread*, which represents the internal distribution of the proposed or actual negotiated wage increase to the bargaining unit employees (see Table 13.4).

At first glance, the wage spread appears to be a formality, determined after the average hourly rate increase per employee is resolved. Yet the particular

Table 13.4 Three Examples of Internal Wage Spreads

Examples	Number of Employees	Employee Classification	Total of Plant's Employees (In Percent)	Increase (in Cents per Hour)
1	184	A	16	57.0
	197	B	18	50.0
	165	C	15	48.0
	237	D	21	46.0
	149	E	13	44.0
	193	F	17	42.0
	1,125			
2	381	A&B	34	60.0
	402	C&D	36	44.0
	342	E&F	30	34.0
	1,125			
3	1,125	A,B,C,D,E,&F	100	47.2

wage spread can determine whether the parties ever reach an agreement. For example, the union might refuse the first and second wage spreads and accept the third wage with no spread (see Table 13.4) even though the total wage costs of the three spreads are nearly identical.

The six employee job classifications in Table 13.4 range in skill and pay from Classification A (highest) to Classification F (lowest). The A through F ranking also conforms to management's job evaluation procedure. Consequently management prefers the second wage spread, since it gives higher skilled employees higher wages that could maintain or increase their wage differential over unskilled employees. This wage differential is important to management for two reasons:

1. It ensures that present skilled employees do not leave because of higher wages offered by other firms.
2. It offers some motivation to employees in lower paid classifications to train for higher level classifications in the company.

Unions are not always concerned with job evaluation as a wage determination factor. The union officer's main concern is to ensure that the negotiated wage spread will result in sufficient votes to ratify the agreement. Satisfied union members will also be likely to vote for reelection of union officers. Assume, for example, that Classification C represents a politically influential group of employees. The union officers would not prefer the second wage spread as it stands (44.0 cents per hour increase). Instead, they would prefer the first (48.0 cents per hour increase) or third (47.2 cents per hour increase) wage spread shown in the table. The union might even propose a different wage spread (there are an almost infinite number of possible arrangements) which would give the employees in Classification C a much higher wage increase.

Management is also concerned that employees ratify the agreement. Consequently, it might agree to an across-the-board, cents-per-hour increase (the third in the table) which would give the same cents per hour to all employees regardless of their particular job classification. This wage spread might generate enough votes to ratify the collective bargaining agreement, but it will narrow the wage differential between skilled and unskilled employees. However, over a longer period of time, management cannot continually grant this type of increase if it wishes to attract and retain skilled employees.

One of the principal goals of unions has been to reduce dispersion of wages. Their goal is to obtain "equal pay for equal work" across establishments and to reduce differentials based on personal characteristics rather than specific job tasks. Unions seek this goal by negotiating a single rate of pay for each occupational group and a seniority-based progression of rates up to a maximum level. Single rates (one pay level for all workers in a given job category) eliminate wage dispersion and seniority plans control overall wage rates by requiring similar treatment to workers who have the same seniority. Because of the "spillover" effect of union wage practices, even nonunion companies experience less wage dispersion than one would expect.[27]

Wage Comparability

A common argument in wage negotiations is that wage rates in one bargaining unit should be equal to or related to the wage rates in comparable bargaining units.[28] Wage comparisons are given considerable weight in wage determination, although these comparisons can become quite complicated. Wage surveys can be helpful, but do not measure how the job content, method of payment, regularity of employment, supplemental unemployment benefits, vacations, pensions and holidays vary from company to company. Fundamental considerations such as the size of the appropriate labor market and occupational and geographic differentials must be recognized. At first glance, it appears that bus drivers in Miami would have duties identical with those of bus drivers in Chicago. However, many differences in these similar jobs can exist: weather conditions, number of scheduled stops, location of scheduled stops, number of passengers, and so on. Further, a major difference could arise in situations where the bus drivers are required to make change. In such cases, the union would claim that this job responsibility creates a safety hazard by increasing the likelihood of robberies. Thus, in negotiations the union would seek adequate compensation for this additional safety hazard.

As with industrial wage differentials, the relative importance of wages to total costs is an important factor in wage comparability. For example, if a modern, highly automated textile mill pays wages that account for 30 percent of total costs, a 10 percent increase in wages would equal a 3 percent change in the sales price. But in an old textile mill with out-of-date machinery, where wages account for 65 percent of total costs, a 10 percent increase in wages would equal a 6.5 percent change in sales price. Even though wage data are either largely fragmented[29] or deficient,[30] negotiators still have to rely on wage comparability in arguing for or against certain levels of wages. Therefore, both parties continue to look for commonalities (other companies, local firms, similar jobs) which can provide a base from which to present their proposals.

Ability to Pay

The *ability to pay* (or the financial condition of the organization) is a commonly used standard for wage determination. Given much weight by unions during periods of high profitability, it is advanced more frequently by management as the "inability to pay."[31]

Ability to pay has limited usefulness in the wage determination process, for a number of reasons:

1. Wages based solely on ability to pay would create a chaotic wage structure and would cause a change in the wage-costs-price-profit relationships that have evolved over time.
2. Unions would not want to apply this criterion uniformly and consistently. To be applicable, it must work both ways, leading to wage reductions when profits are nonexistent or inadequate. Such an approach would be generally unacceptable to unions.
3. It is extremely difficult to determine what part of profits should be used for wage increases. If the profit is distributed to employees in terms of higher wages and none of the profit is shared with stockholders, there will be no incentive for investment, and growth and expansion will be limited.
4. Wages supposedly are paid to workers in accordance with their relative value to the firm, their contribution to its goals, and the relative importance of their services. If ability to pay is the major factor, the relationships between actual pay and actual value could become disproportionate.
5. Wages are negotiated for future application, and there is no necessary relationship between profits of the past and ability to pay in the future. Profits are the result after past costs have been deducted from past sales; they are most volatile and fluctuate greatly in good and bad times. If wages are dependent upon profits, they too will fluctuate erratically.[32]

Poor economic conditions in the early 1980s resulted in many companies claiming their inability to pay and unions agreeing to wage concessions or "give-backs" in order to preserve employment. The most highly publicized pay concessions involved the United Auto Workers and Teamsters. Both Ford's and General Motors' agreements called for a freeze on general wages for the term of the labor agreement, an eighteen-month deferral of cost-of-living adjustments, and the elimination of nine paid personal holidays. The savings to Ford were estimated from $600 million to $1 billion, and General Motors saved as much as

$3 billion. With 20 percent of the driver members (60,000) on layoff, the Teamsters agreed to a freeze on general wages and a reduction in their cost-of-living adjustments. Other concessions were made in the rubber, meatpacking, steel, airline, and newspaper industries. There were ninety-one collective bargaining situations between January 1 and March 31, 1982, and in thirty-one cases some form of giveback was approved.

Even though there was much publicity about wage concessions, acceptance was not automatic. The United Steelworkers on two occasions rejected wage concessions, before agreeing to concessions, and the United Auto Workers rejected Chrysler's request for further concessions in 1982 after they had already granted concessions in two previous negotiations.[33] Then in 1983, when Chrysler reported record earnings, the UAW requested reopening negotiations.

Productivity

While no argument has been advanced with more conviction or sophistication than that wages should vary with changes in productivity, the principle has grave difficulties when applied to specific negotiations. For example, the rate of change in productivity varies widely from industry to industry, firm to firm, even plant to plant. Not only is productivity itself difficult to measure accurately, but any change in productivity (usually measured in output per employee-hour) results from many causes, only one of which is labor.[34]

Those who study productivity have generally agreed that new capital investment and mechanization have been the primary causes for greater productivity, but there are still important issues to reconcile: Who shall share the results from increased productivity? the workers, stockholders, consumers? What are the relative advantages of higher wages, increased dividends, and lower prices? What is the proper balance among the contributing factors of production—labor and capital investments?[35] Any use of the productivity criterion must be handled carefully because the available data are only approximate. Output per employee-hour often over-states gains attributed to labor, and hourly earnings data fail to account for the relative contributions of advanced technology, improved methods, better machines, and so on.[36]

Productivity Sharing Some union and management officials have undertaken cooperative efforts to bring productivity issues directly into collective bargaining. Labeled as *productivity sharing*, management and unions seek ways to achieve greater productivity while providing employees a comparable share of the resulting savings in the form of higher wages. Traditionally, labor agreements have provided protection to workers who are subject to loss of employment (in such forms as advance notice, use of attrition in work reduction, early retirement, guaranteed wages, and severance pay),[37] and unions have often resisted speed-up efforts or productivity improvement campaigns.

However, one advocate of cooperative efforts in productivity explains:

Productivity Sharing is not an incentive plan; it is a philosophy of managing that encourages employees to become involved in productivity improvement. Productivity sharing creates a work environment in which employees see improved productivity as beneficial to them. Under the philosophy of productivity sharing, worker productivity goals and management goals became congruent. . . .

. . . In sharing productivity gains, employees accept management's productivity goals. The we-they adversary relationship changes so both gain together as they cooperate to produce more product or services in fewer man hours. . . . We now know that the missing link (involving workers in improving productivity) has been trying to get workers involved with no reward; it does not work. Give workers a piece of the action, a stake in the outcome, and their response is tremendous. Productivity in this country can be raised appreciably by putting to use techniques and concepts that were developed by Americans and are suited to our culture and way of life.[38]

The General Accounting Office estimates that there are about 1000 productivity sharing programs. Its researchers obtained financial data from twenty-four firms and found that plans over five years old experienced a 29 percent labor savings in the last five-year period and plans less than five years old averaged savings of 8.5 percent. Nonmonetary benefits were also reported: 80.6 percent reported improved labor management relations; 47.2 percent, fewer grievances; 36.1 percent, less absenteeism; and 36.1 percent, reduced turnover.[39]

Productivity has become a national concern. Although the United States still leads the industrial world in productivity in absolute numbers, it now lags all other industrialized countries in productivity growth.[40] In fact, it is projected that at current productivity growth rates, four countries—Canada (2.2 percent), France (3.8 percent), Germany (4.0 percent), and Japan (6.3 percent)—will overtake the United States (1.5 percent) in absolute terms of productivity per employee by the year 1990.[41]

Congress has indicated its concern about low productivity in the United States and has authorized a White House Conference on productivity. The conference is designed to bring together individuals who are experts on productivity, labor relations, and management. The result will be a report to the President and the President will then report his recommendations to Congress.[42]

Problems with Productivity Sharing Although productivity sharing offers an innovative approach for mutual gain-sharing and cooperative activity, it, too, has its problems. Foremost is the determination or measurement of productivity, because there are many possible measures. Some jobs just do not lend themselves to measurement of output. It is much easier to measure bricks laid than letters taken by dictation and typed, particularly since letters vary in complexity and length. Many jobs are not routine or repetitious; therefore, exact measures are impossible.

Another problem is locating and organizing productivity data in such a manner that it may be useful to a firm. Serious arguments over the contribution of specific factors to increased productivity can inhibit the success of any productivity bargaining. What is the chief contributor to productivity gains? Is it the skill, efforts, and attitudes of the employees? Or the advanced technology of the machinery and equipment, efficiency of the operations, or scale of operations? Or the interaction between these sets of factors?[43] Since productivity gains will be shared under the productivity bargaining concept, they will certainly give rise to rigorous and complicated negotiations, particularly when bargaining unit employees are accustomed to receiving comparable wages.

One successful experience with productivity sharing has occurred at an Esso refinery. The following principles derived from this experience could possibly be applied in other situations:

1. Management accepted the necessity for change as fundamental and invested time, energy, and patience to make it happen.
2. Personnel motivated to pursue the issues to a workable compromise or conclusion—specifically, Esso managers and directors with a drive for recognition and leadership—were involved.
3. It assumed that the only way to break the status quo and achieve widespread reforms was to accept full responsibility and initiative.
4. It set a course of give-and-take negotiations and responded throughout to ideas, needs, and desires of workers, stewards, and union leaders.
5. It offered real incentives to the workers—sharply reduced hours and much higher pay—in exchange for flexibility and elimination of obsolete practices.
6. It met the workers' psychological need for job security.
7. It shared credit for the accomplishments with the trade union leaders who were vital to the agreement and to the application of the written word to actual practice.[44]

Other examples of bargaining for productivity improvement have occurred in the construction industry. Negotiations there have resulted in understandings to reduce work stoppages and provisions covering jurisdictional disputes, inefficient work rules, illegal feather-bedding, and nonworking stewards have also been negotiated. Interestingly, the stimulus for productivity bargaining in the construction industry was the loss of work that increasingly went to nonunion and open-shop contractors and the desire of union members to protect or expand their employment opportunities, particularly during unfavorable economic conditions.[45]

Joint advisory committees in the steel industry have been formed in plants to deal with productivity problems. The retail food industry has established a joint labor-management committee that aids collective bargaining settlements and technological change. The shipping industry has been involved in joint programs to promote productivity in exchange for improving wages and benefits for longshoremen and their unions. These agreements basically have involved "buy out" of restrictive provisions and practices, which allowed a reduction in the "work gang" size and increased flexibility in manpower use. To obtain these agreements, attractive early retirement provisions and guaranteed work have been included in the labor agreements.[46]

Effect of Unions on Productivity Recently, there has been considerable debate and research about the effect of unions on productivity. On the positive side, William Winpisinger, President of the International Association of Machinists, has identified several ways that collective bargaining has contributed to greater productivity:

1. Unions' continuing pressure for higher wages and benefits makes union workers expensive, so management must seek better methods, such as technological improvements, to maintain lower unit labor costs.
2. Unions' success in reducing the average number of hours worked per week has actually increased worker productivity because the effort is greater in the fewer hours.
3. An orderly and equitable procedure for settling grievances helps resolve employee problems and therefore improves productivity.
4. Collective bargaining involves negotiating subjects related to industrial accidents and diseases. Accident prevention saves time and consequently increases productivity.
5. Union apprenticeship programs help train employees in critical skills and allow them to produce more.[47]

Some labor economists concur that unions can have a positive effect on worker productivity because they influence training, morale, turnover and interaction between workers and management.

On the other hand, unions can also have a negative effect on productivity because of work rule restrictions, such as limits on workloads, restrictions on tasks performed, requirements for unneeded standby crews or crews of excessive size, and interference with the introduction of technological change.[48]

In some settings, unions have resulted in higher productivity because of greater capital intensity, higher labor quality, and presence of institutional grievance procedures. This is most likely to occur where management uses the collective bargaining process to learn about ways to improve the operations of the workplace and the production processes. However, if management reacts negatively to collective bargaining, or if unions try to prevent the reorganization of the workplace, the effect of unions on organizational performance will be negative.[49]

Critics of unions' effect on productivity have indicated that unions are not the reason that productivity in unionized plants is higher. In fact, higher wages in unionized settings encourages managers to substitute capital (technology) for labor, and this technology advancement increases the productivity per worker. Also, higher wages in unionized plants motivate the employers to seek out the "better quality" employees; likewise, the "better quality" employees of nonunion plants tend to look for work in the higher paying unionized plant. In other words, productivity in unionized plants may be higher; however, this higher productivity may not be caused by unions, but several other intervening factors.[50] One analysis of unions' effects on productivity concludes:

[O]ne cannot conclude from the evidence (far less the theory) that unions are good for productivity. Moreover, productivity as measured is not the same as efficiency. We do not observe unit cost reductions in unionized settings![51]

Cost of Living

During periods of rising prices, unions support their wage demands by referring to the cost of living. Union negotiators advance the argument that a rise in the cost of living without a commensurate wage increase is equivalent to a cut in real wages or a drop in purchasing power. Thus, the proposition that wages be raised at least in proportion to the rise in living costs seems quite fair and reasonable. But the complete reliance on use of this criterion needs careful appraisal.[52]

Unions and management must come to an agreement on the meaning of cost of living. *Cost of living* usually refers to the consumer price index (CPI) as determined by the Bureau of Labor Statistics; its computation includes such items as housing, food, and automobiles which may not be purchased regularly by employees in a specific plant or community. The parties must also negotiate the base period, the starting date, and the CPI most appropriate for use (the Bureau of Labor Statistics publishes an all-cities CPI plus CPIs for most major cities).

Automatic increases in general wages present problems in their effect on the cost-price-profit mechanism.[53] In other words, costs of labor which are automatically increased throughout the economy can increase total costs and sales prices unless there is a commensurate productivity increase. The increases in wages are passed on to the consumer; large firms, having some monopolistic control, simply raise their prices. Thus, the market economy is restricted and does not function effectively as a determiner of prices and an allocator of resources—two of its most important functions.

Perhaps management's greatest concern over cost of living is that it receives nothing in return for this wage increase, granted on the basis of factors over which it has no control. The cost-of-living argument seldom if ever considers employees' productivity at a particular facility. Additional considerations of cost of living are discussed in the section on wage adjustments.

Legal Influences

Wage negotiations occur within a legal framework which either directly or indirectly affects the outcome. The National Labor Relations Act requires the union and management to negotiate in good faith over wages and other economic issues such as pensions, insurance, vacations and holidays. Other laws, such as the Davis-Bacon, Walsh-Healy, and Fair Labor Standards Act, deal more directly with specific requirements. The remaining laws affecting wages can be categorized as equal employment opportunity legislation.

Davis-Bacon Act The Davis-Bacon Act of 1931 was passed to help maintain wages at a level that would allow workers to purchase products, thereby putting more money in circulation and helping to end the existing economic depression. This law requires federal government contractors performing construction work for $2,000 or more to pay *prevailing wage* (which includes fringe benefits) of the labor market in which the construction takes place. It authorizes the Secretary of Labor to determine in advance the wages acceptable on federal projects. The Department of Labor determines the prevailing wage by determining the wage paid to the majority of workers in various job classifications. Since wage data are maintained by labor organizations, critics of this law contend that unions are able to keep wages high because they represent the largest number of construction workers in most areas and are able to send wage data on short notice to the wage specialists in the Department of Labor. Since the law's enactment, forty-one states have passed "little Davis-Bacon Acts," and seventy-seven federal laws now require Davis-Bacon Act wage determination.[54]

There have been four major criticisms of this Act:

1. The Labor Department tends to select union wage rates as the prevailing wage rates.
2. The law discourages bids from nonunion contractors.
3. The law raises construction prices paid by the federal government by preventing the use of lower-paid nonunion workers.
4. The administrative burdens on the contractors and federal agencies add to the overall costs.

In response to the criticism, proponents of the law contend that productivity improvements offset the increased cost. Proponents also claim that the Labor Department does not always select the union wages and when it does, it picks out-of-date wages which are lower than the current union rate.[55]

Walsh-Healy Act The Walsh-Healy Act of 1936 extended the authority of the Secretary of Labor to determine the prevailing wage in all industries having federal government contracts for goods and services worth $10,000 or more. The prevailing wage rates were to be determined much as under the Davis-Bacon Act; but this law further requires that employers pay all employees time and one-half for working over eight hours in any work day.

Fair Labor Standards Act In 1938, Congress passed the Fair Labor Standards Act, which regulates wages as well as hours (and also regulates child labor). This act covers most firms in interstate commerce. It requires the payment of overtime (one and one-half the regular wage) for any hours over forty per week and the payment of a minimum wage of $3.35. The law is administered by the Wage and Hour Administration in the Department of Labor and receives complaints from workers as well as initiating its own investigations of employers' records and practices.

Laws Administered by the EEOC Three laws, the Equal Pay Act of 1963, Title VII of the Civil Rights Act of 1964 (now Equal Employment Opportunity Act of 1972), and the Age Discrimination in Employment Act of 1978, are now administered by the Equal Employment Opportunity Commission. The Equal Pay Act of 1963 prohibits pay discrimination between men and women who perform jobs that require equal skills, effort, and responsibility and who work under similar conditions. The Equal Employment Opportunity Act is broader in that it prohibits employment discrimination (including compensation discrimination) related to race, color, religion, sex, and national origin. The Age Discrimination in Employment Act prohibits employment discrimination (including compensation discrimination) against employees between the ages of forty and seventy.

Wages of women and minorities average about 60 percent those of white males, and the wage gap has not shown any improvement over the last twenty years. In a public EEOC hearing on job segregation and wage discrimination in April 1980, then-Chairperson Eleanor Holmes opened by stating:

Wage discrimination is likely to be one of the central legal and industrial relations issues of the 1980s. It clearly affects both minorities and women, although its most obvious effects have been on women who hold jobs in a very few categories of work that have most often never been held by any other group of workers.[56]

In addition to federal laws, fourteen states have passed laws requiring equal pay for work of equal value (also known as comparable worth). While four states' laws apply to the public sector only, most do not limit application. Thus far, the laws have not been tested in courts. Unions are also becoming involved in the comparable worth issue. The Communications Workers of America and the International Brotherhood of Electrical Workers have entered into a joint job evaluation study to resolve the conflict of having mostly female operators, traffic, billing and office personnel, while line and installation work is performed primarily by males.[57]

Some unions, such as the International Union of Electrical Workers (IUE) have sued employers, in this case, Westinghouse. The company had properly evaluated the jobs of men and women; however, the rate for women's jobs thereafter was less than men's of equal value in the job evaluation plan. This resulted in most females being placed three to four labor grades below the janitor and other unskilled common laborers.

In San Jose, the American Federation of State, County, and Municipal Employees (AFSCME) and the city engaged in a joint job evaluation study which showed that salaries of jobs held predominantly by females averaged 15 percent less than salaries of male jobs although the value by points was the same. This caused the study team to ask the following questions:

1. Why do librarians receive less pay than men with jobs requiring less than an eighth grade education?
2. Why do female M.A.'s and Ph.D.'s who supervise as many as twenty-five people earn less than street sweepers and gardners?
3. Why do nurses earn less than tree trimmers, painters, and parking lot attendants?
4. Why do male toll collectors earn more than medical stenographers?

The city and the union met for over a year and were not able to resolve their differences. A nine-day strike—supported by both male and female employees—occurred before a settlement was reached.[58]

Economic Stabilization Act In 1970, Congress passed the Economic Stabilization Act, which authorizes the president to establish wage and price controls or guidelines. This authority was used by President Nixon, who placed a ninety-day freeze on wages, followed by a 5.5 percent limit on pay increases, and then by a voluntary compliance period, which was lifted in 1974.[59] President Carter established a voluntary pay and price program in 1978, placing the pay standard at 7 percent. Exceptions for pay inequities, acute labor shortages, and productivity-improving work-rule changes were created for special incidents, and the Carter administration later adjusted the pay standard to permit increases up to 10.5 percent in any year as long as the increases averaged 9.5 percent.[60]

These guidelines can cause negative consequences for companies adhering to them. For example, when the inflation rate is higher than the wage increase allowed by the guidelines, employees are displeased. If competitive firms do not abide by the guidelines, then external equity becomes a problem.[61]

Wage Adjustments during the Life of the Labor Agreement

In addition to wage determination during negotiations, labor and management will likely agree to provisions that will allow adjustment of wages during the life of the contract—usually cost-of-living adjustments (or COLA, also called escalator clauses), deferred wage increases (also called annual improvement adjustments), and contract reopeners that allow for wages to be negotiated at a predetermined date. While annual wage improvements are specified in nearly 90 percent of the contracts, COLA provisions are included in about half, and reopener clauses are written in just over 20 percent of 1,550 agreements covering 1,000 or more employees each.[62]

COLA, or escalator, clauses first appeared after World War I in the printing and clothing industries, but they were eliminated during the late 1920s. Immediately after World War II they were renewed, as employees tried to keep up with rapid inflation.[63] These clauses imposed "a contractual obligation upon an employer to change rates of pay in accordance with a formula embodied in a collective bargaining agreement."[64] Their present popularity (estimates range from 5.6 to 9.0 million employees covered by these clauses)[65] owes much to the long-term contracts pioneered by the United Auto Workers and General Motors in 1948. Since then, not only has the number of agreements having COLA provisions grown, but the average length of contracts has been extended.[66]

Coverage by escalator clauses is concentrated in various industries. Nearly 90 percent of the employees in communications, primary metals, rubber, electrical machinery, and transportation industries have COLA provisions.[67] The majority of the workers under COLA provisions are affiliated with the United Auto Workers, Teamsters, Steelworkers, Communication Workers of America, Retail Clerks, and Machinists.[68]

When negotiating the COLA provisions, union and management representatives usually consider a number of matters:

1. Selection of the particular price index and base point. Usually the all-cities consumer price index (CPI) is selected in nationwide agreements, and the beginning date of the contract is specified.
2. Frequency and timing of the wage adjustment. Half of the agreements call for adjustments every quarter; one-fourth every year; the remainder semi-annually.
3. Formula for adjustment. The most common is cents per hour for each point increase in the CPI; the remainder require a percentage change in wages in accordance with a percentage change in the CPI. The most common arrangement is to have wages adjusted 1 cent for each 0.3 rise in the CPI. (See Table 13.5 for Cost-of-Living Schedule.)
4. Effect of COLA on other elements of the compensation package. There is little uniformity in this matter. Some agreements adjust the gross hourly earnings after incentives; others adjust only the base wage rate. Still other pay-

Table 13.5 Cost-of-Living Schedule

The Consumer Price Index for Urban Wage Earners and Clerical Workers—United States—All Items (C.P.I.-W) (1967 = 100) published by the Bureau of Labor Statistics, United States Department of Labor.

262.7—262.9	76¢	266.6—266.8	89¢
263.0—263.2	77¢	266.9—267.1	90¢
263.3—263.5	78¢	267.2—267.4	91¢
263.6—263.8	79¢	267.5—267.7	92¢
263.9—264.1	80¢	267.8—268.0	93¢
264.2—264.4	81¢	268.1—268.3	94¢
264.5—264.7	82¢	268.4—268.6	95¢
264.8—265.0	83¢	268.7—268.9	96¢
265.1—265.3	84¢	269.0—269.2	97¢
265.4—265.6	85¢	269.3—269.5	98¢
265.7—265.9	86¢	269.6—269.8	99¢
266.0—266.2	87¢	269.9—270.1	100¢
266.3—266.5	88¢		

Source: Agreement between U.S. Steel Corp. and United Steelworkers of America, 1980–1983.

ments, such as overtime, call-in pay, night work, and differentials, must be considered.

5. Limitations on the adjustment. About one-fourth have formulas with CAPS (limits on the amounts that may be received from cost-of-living provisions within a given period). On the other hand, some agreements specify that wages will not be reduced in the event of a CPI decline.[69]

COLA provisions are becoming more common not only in labor agreements but also outside the collective bargaining arena. For example, 31 million Social Security recipients and 2.5 million military and civil service retirees are now covered. It has been estimated that over 50 million U.S. citizens now have their incomes adjusted by some automatic cost-of-living adjustment.[70]

Wage reopener clauses are usually written in such a way that wages may be renegotiated at a specified time during the length of the agreement or when the CPI has risen by a specified amount. Some of the agreements allow only wages to be renegotiated, whereas others allow nonwage items or do not specify the items. Deferred wage increases, annual improvement factors, and productivity increases enjoy a broad acceptance in most contracts, and many of these are included with cost-of-living adjustments as well as contract reopeners.[71]

Yet cost-of-living adjustments and wage reopeners have their problems. Cost-of-living adjustments are very difficult to negotiate out of a contract, because union officers and members assume the COLA will continue in subsequent contracts. This situation makes it difficult for either union or management to receive credit for the contract. Assume, for example, that management anticipates that COLA will cost 60 cents per employee per year. If the negotiated wage settlement costs 70 cents per employee, then employees will receive only a 10-cent-an-hour increase plus continuation of the COLA. The union officer will have a difficult time selling the labor agreement to the members, particularly since they probably take the established COLA clause for granted. It might be easier to sell the labor agreement if there were not any COLA and the wage package were publicized as an annual improvement increase of 70 cents an hour.

Wage reopeners are also subject to problems, particularly when the union wishes to extend negotiated items to noneconomic items. While this is not allowable in theory, the distinction between economic and noneconomic discussion becomes blurred in practice. Some practitioners have suggested that a wage reopener is similar to an entirely new contract negotiation as the parties bring noneconomic items into the discussion.

Employee Benefits

In 1981, U.S. employers paid an average of $6,627 per employee in benefits, or 37.3 percent of payroll costs, up from 19.2 percent in 1953. These benefits included 12.7 percent of payroll costs for pensions, insurance, and other agreed-upon payments, 10 percent as payments for time not worked (such as vacations, sick leave, and holidays), 9 percent for legally required payments for unemployment and workers compensation, 3.4 percent for paid rest and lunch breaks, and 2.2 percent for profit sharing and bonuses.[72] It has been estimated that over $150 billion is contributed annually to employee benefits.[73] The following sections present major areas of employee benefits, relying largely on studies of 1,570 agreements by the Department of Labor[74] and 400 agreements by the Bureau of National Affairs.[75]

Insurance

Insurance provisions have been substantially expanded. More than 90 percent of the contracts provide life and hospitalization insurance, and the majority include coverage for major medical expenses, surgery, maternity care, doctor's visits, accidental death and dismemberment, and nonoccupational sickness and accidents. Most contracts continue coverage to employees after retirement but reduce the amount of coverage. Hospitalization and surgical insurance for dependents of employees are covered in over 83 percent of the contracts, and premiums are paid by the company in the majority of cases. There are also increasing numbers of medical-related plans covering new areas: prescription drugs (24 percent), dental care (41 percent), optical care (10 percent), and supplements to Medicare (21 percent). It is expected that these areas of coverage will show significant growth.

Income Maintenance

Income maintenance provisions that provide income protection for employees are now found in nearly one-half of the labor agreements. Such provisions usually involve work or pay guarantees, severance pay (separation or termination pay), and supplemental unemployment benefits (SUB) plans. Just over 11 percent of the agreements contain work or pay guarantees, with the majority of those providing a weekly guarantee of forty hours of work.

Severance pay plans providing for lump sum payments upon termination are included in 34 percent of the agreements. In most cases, severance pay is extended only to workers whose jobs have been terminated as a result of permanent shutdown, to those whose layoffs continue beyond a minimum length of time, or to those who have no prospect for recall. The amount of severance pay varies with the length of service—each year of service allows for increased benefits. Severance payments are usually restricted for a particular time period or until the worker is reemployed.

Supplemental unemployment benefit plans, included in 14 percent of the agreements, are usually classified as pooled fund systems (benefits are allowed only in the event of lack of work). A few SUB plans provide individual accounts in which the employee has a vested right and from which he or she may withdraw money for reasons other than lack of work. The most common method provides payment of an amount equal to a percentage of the employee's take-home pay. Plans involving the United Auto Workers are the most lucrative for the workers, with SUB payments and unemployment compensation equalling 95 percent of take-home pay minus $7.50 in work-related expenses. Other plans range from $20 per week minimum to 90 percent of take-home pay. Other considerations, such as duration of benefits, length of service requirements, and employer financial requirements, must also be included in the composition of the plan.

Premium Pay—Overtime and Other Supplements

Most labor agreements specify daily or weekly work schedules and provide premium pay for hours worked beyond the normal hours. Most agreements call for eight-hour days and workweeks of forty hours—Monday through Friday. Overtime premiums are usually paid for work over eight hours per day at a time-and-a-half rate, which is more beneficial to the worker than the Fair Labor Standards Act requirement of time-and-a-half payments for work in excess of forty hours in a week. (Workers on a four-day, forty-hour workweek would receive eight hours of overtime pay.) A few agreements provide sixth-day and seventh-day premiums, but the majority of agreements prohibit pyramiding of overtime (combining a number of different premium payments, allowing overtime duplication).

Many labor agreements also contain provisions for overtime administration. For example, overtime assignments may be restricted to employees within a job classification or a given department, to a particular shift, to qualified personnel, and so on. In some cases, where management has had difficulty getting employees to work overtime, provisions that make overtime mandatory have been negotiated. Some agreements have gone so far as imposing penalties for refusing overtime work and specifying a loss of claim to the number of hours reduced. Likewise, unions have sought provisions in the labor agreement which would enable their members to better plan their off-the-job activities: advance notice, relief from mandatory overtime if not notified by a certain time, and others.

Various forms of supplementary pay are included in most contracts. For instance, shift differentials (premium payments for working the night shift, for example) are provided in 64 percent of the agreements. Other forms, such as reporting pay (employees who report for scheduled work, but find no work, are still paid) and call-back pay (pay to employees who are called back to work at hours other than normal), are also usually included. Reporting pay guarantees range from one hour to eight hours, except with some maritime firms that provide one full week. Call-back or call-in pay guarantees are most frequently for four hours. Other supplements include pay for temporary transfer, hazardous work, travel, work clothes, tools, and bonuses other than production.

Payments for Nonwork—Holidays, Vacations, and Rest Periods

While many agreements provide for such nonwork activities as rest periods, cleanup time, time lost to job-related injury, waiting time, standby time, travel time, and voting time, payments for nonwork involving the most money are holidays and vacations. The median number of holidays provided is ten; the range is from five to fifteen. Nearly all agreements provide holidays for Labor Day, Independence Day, Thanksgiving, Christmas, New Year's Day, and Memorial Day. Good Friday, Christmas Eve, and the day after Thanksgiving appear in less than 50 percent of the agreements. Most agreements have eligibility requirements, for example, specified length of service (usually four weeks) before being given a paid holiday, or working the day before and after the holiday. More complicated provisions involve issues such as holidays falling on Saturday, Sunday, or a day off or during vacation, and premium pay for work on holidays.

Nearly all agreements provide for vacations for covered employees; the latest data show sharp increases in agreements allowing five- and six-week vacations and slight reductions in amount of service to qualify for nearly all types of vacations. Somewhat surprisingly, vacations for one week only are now less frequent than two- and three-week vacations. In most cases, vacation entitlement is linked to length of service.[76]

Nearly all agreements have provisions that pertain to the administration of vacations. The majority contain specific work requirements, such as a minimum number of hours, days, weeks, or years necessary to qualify for various lengths of vacation. Vacation scheduling provisions appear in 88 percent of all agreements; they cover such items as annual plant shutdowns and consideration of employee seniority and employee preference. These provisions are essential in organizations employing large numbers of employees, not only to reduce friction between employees but to allow management to properly plan its production schedules.

Pensions

Nearly all labor agreements make some reference to pension plans, whether in the form of a general statement mentioning the plan or a fully detailed provision. Items usually mentioned include age for retirement (normal and early), disability retirement, benefits available and requirements for qualifying, vesting provisions, administration procedures, and financial arrangements.[77] Most plans stipulate a mandatory retirement age of 70 because the 1978 amendment to the Age Discrimination in Employment Act prevents any mandatory retirement before age 70.[78]

Most plans guarantee the retired employee a flat monthly dollar amount for each year of service ($10.50 is the median; they range from $4.05 to $27.50) or a percentage of earnings times years of service. Special provisions are usually included for employees forced to retire due to total or permanent disability. In addition, voluntary early retirement is allowed in 97 percent of the plans.

Frequently, early retirement plans offer several options to the employee. For example, the United Auto Workers' agreements provide three options: retirement at age 60 after ten years of service; retirement at age 55, but only when the combined age and service years equal eighty-five; and retirement after thirty years of service, without regard to age. The financial arrangements in 92 percent of the agreements show that the employer finances the pension plan entirely (that is, it is noncontributory); where plans are contributory, labor agreements include very specific provisions about the amounts that the employer and the employees contribute.

Although 89 percent of the contracts contain *vesting* provisions (an employee whose service is terminated continues to be entitled to earned benefits), the Employer Retirement Income Security Act of 1974 (also known as either ERISA or the Pension Reform Act) has very specific regulations governing vesting requirements of pension plans. Although management and labor may negotiate provisions covering pensions which are more favorable than the law requires, most agreements for the time being will no doubt closely correspond to the legal minimum.[79] Under any of these options, an employee must be at least 50 percent vested after ten years of service and 100 percent vested after fifteen years of service, regardless of age.[80]

Prepaid Legal Services

Only fifteen years ago, prepaid legal services did not exist. In fact, any attorney who contracted with a group to provide legal services for a predetermined fee would have been disbarred.[81] Now legal assistance is available to organized group members who have pooled prepaid amounts. By January 1978, 3,500 prepaid plans covering 2 million families had been filed under ERISA.[82]

These group plans began after a 1971 Supreme Court decision that declared that a United Transportation Union's legal service plan was an exercise of First Amendment rights. One year later, a highly publicized experiment involving the Laborers' International in Shreveport, Louisiana, and the American Bar Association was established. Two other actions have helped in the growth of these plans: (a) legal services were recognized as a valid subject for collective bargaining in which unions and employers negotiated the financial arrangements for the plans,[83] and (b) the Tax Reform Act of 1976 clarified the tax status of prepaid plans (neither employer contributions nor employee benefits were taxable).[84]

By 1983, twenty-eight unions had negotiated prepaid legal plans in their labor agreements.[85] These plans vary in terms of whether the parties will set up open panels (the client chooses the attorney) or closed panels (legal services are provided by a law firm retained under the plan or by an attorney staff).[86] Some plans offer a full array of services, ranging from counsel for criminal offenses to routine matters (such as wills, divorces, house closings, and landlord-tenant problems). Most believe prepaid legal services will become more common; these projections are supported by a recent American Bar Association study that predicts that prepaid legal service plans will be as common in ten to fifteen years as medical insurance is today.[87]

Union Effects on Wages and Benefits

The degree to which unions influences wage and benefit levels is a frequently debated subject among labor economists. In a 1963 classic, *Unionism and Relative Wages in the United States,*[88] Greg Lewis concluded union wages ranged between 10 and 15 percent higher than nonunion wages. Further analysis reveals a greater impact on wages of blue-collar workers, younger workers, and less educated workers.

Unions also have a greater effect on fringe benefits than wages. Blue-collar employees covered by labor agreements receive fringe benefits that average 28 to 36 percent higher than those of blue-collar employees in nonunion settings.[89]

Unions also contribute to wage equalization by decreasing the differential between unionized blue-collar workers and nonunion white-collar workers, as well as reducing wage dispersion (covered earlier in this chapter). This union contribution frequently results in less turnover, because seniority-based wage increases, promotion possibilities, and other benefits cause employees to stay with their employers longer.[90]

Some studies have shown that the wage differences between union and nonunion workers are the products of other interrelated influences, such as higher occupational skills, fewer females, lower quit rates, larger organizations and greater capital intensity of production in unionized industries.[91] Other studies have even contended the union-nonunion wage differential is an illusion, because the higher paid workers tend to unionize in order to obtain union services.[92] In other words, workers who share a beneficial wage and benefit differential will form unions to protect their advantageous positions.

Unions also have an effect on wages and benefits in nonunion companies. Union wage and benefit changes "spill-over" into nonunion companies because nonunion employers who want to maintain their nonunion status will respond to union wage increases by raising wages of their workers. Such increases are provided not only to reduce the threat of unions, but to provide equity and maintain morale and productivity.[93]

Although there have been cases where unions respond to nonunion wages in order to remain competitive, craft unions, which have recently been heavily damaged by job losses, have not reduced their wage premium over the nonunion craft employers. Thus far, these unions have apparently been willing to tolerate even higher unemployment to avoid lowering their wage demands.[94]

Summary and Implications

Summary

Economic issues pertain to wages and the variety of economic benefits which make up what is commonly called the wage package. The discussions focused on reasons for wage differentials—industrial, occupational, and regional. A more specific presentation on job evaluation began with an organizational analysis and concluded with a wage structure which includes job classes, wage rates, and wage ranges.

In addition to the basic wage structure, some firms provide either individual or group wage incentives. Negotiators use certain wage-determining criteria in arriving at an acceptable wage structure; commonly accepted criteria include: differential features of jobs, comparable wages, ability to pay, productivity and cost of living.

Since labor agreements usually are negotiated for periods greater than one year, provisions are commonly negotiated to adjust wages during the life of the contract. A common form of wage adjustment is the cost-of-living adjustment (COLA), or escalator clause, which adjusts wages in accordance with the consumer price index or cost of living. Another form of wage adjustment less frequently included in agreements is the wage reopener clause, providing that wages be renegotiated at a predetermined time during the life of the agreement.

Employee benefits have now increased to consume 37.3 percent of the company's total payroll. Numerous types of benefits exist. The major ones include: insurance, income maintenance, premium pay, payments for nonwork, and pensions. One type of benefit, prepaid legal services, has recently come into existence and has growth potential and interest among employees.

Implications

The chapter concluded with the acknowledgment that unions have an influence on wages, benefits, tenure, and wage dispersion. In the early 1980s, a depressed economy, with high unemployment, made many employers unable to compete nationally and internationally. Concessionary bargaining became a practical reality for both unions and management.[95]

There is no doubt that recent wage and other concessions by unions have attracted much public attention. While these adjustments are in part a counterreaction to the long-term trend of a widening difference between union and nonunion wages, the more immediate causes of these concessions were plant closings, layoffs, and bankruptcies.

While union concessions are not a new phenomenon, they are unusual and occur only during difficult economic conditions. During recessions, management frequently hardens its bargaining positions and the unions seem more receptive to cooperative efforts, such as worker participation teams, profit sharing, and quality circles.

While some observers have quickly labeled the recent union concessions as a "turning point" in union-management relations, it is more important to distinguish between a temporary period of low wage settlements and a fundamental change in the way union wages are established. There is a little evidence to suggest that long-term labor arrangements and escalator clauses will be permanently abandoned. During 1981–1982, unions in such industries as petroleum refining, petrochemicals, and electrical equipment manufacturing, which were not facing crisis situations, did not agree to wage concessions. In other words, concessions did not spill over into sectors where crises did not exist.[96]

Unions are resisting further concessions to employer demands. In 1982, a conference was held of 750 union leaders from 45 international unions to debate the concession issue. Several arguments were presented against concessions. First, evidence was presented that wage concessions did not save jobs. Second, once concessions are granted, unions assume it will be difficult to win back what they had conceded because there is nothing automatic about restoring the concessions. Third, concession bargaining often pits workers in one plant against workers in another and this competition destroys the union's solidarity and eliminates the standardized wage structure for the industry. Companies are asking their employees to compete against each other in order to preserve their jobs. History will tell whether concession bargaining is a short-term phenomenon or a long-term factor in collective bargaining.[97]

Discussion Questions

1. List the main factors that help explain the wage differentials for five jobs in an organization with which you are familiar.
2. Explain why job evaluation plans must take into consideration not only internal factors but also external factors, if they are to be successful.
3. Assume that labor and management are negotiating a labor agreement and the wage spread becomes an issue of disagreement—management wants a wider wage spread, and the union wants a smaller wage spread. Why should management be cautious about the union's proposal, even though the total costs may be the same?
4. For each of the wage criteria given in the chapter, state the union's expected arguments and management's expected counterarguments, given the following conditions:
   a. High profits, a growing firm, a healthy economy, and the cost of living rising at 8 percent per year.
   b. Low profit, no anticipation of growth, questionable economic conditions, and the cost of living adjusting upward but by wide variations each month.
5. Assuming that a firm's costs of employee benefits are 37.3 percent of payroll, why doesn't the firm just let the union determine the manner in which the amounts are apportioned to the variety of benefits, such as insurance, holidays, and vacations, without negotiating each specific clause, especially since the overall costs probably would be the same?
6. Of the employee benefits explained in this chapter, which do you expect to grow in the future? Which do you expect to decline? Why?

References

[1]Jules Bachman, *Wage Determination: An Analysis of Wage Criteria* (Princeton, N.J.: D. Van Nostrand, 1959), pp. 1–7.

[2]Ibid., p. 14.

[3]Ibid., pp. 20–21.

[4]George W. Taylor, "Wage Determination Process," in George W. Taylor and Frank C. Person, eds., *New Concepts in Wage Determination* (New York: McGraw-Hill, 1957), p. 84.

[5]Leon Greenberg, "Definitions and Concepts," in Gerald Somers, ed., *Collective Bargaining and Productivity* (Madison, Wis.: Industrial Relations Research Association, 1975), p. 12.

[6]Bachman, *Wage Determination*, p. 58.

[7]For further reference, see David W. Belcher, *Compensation Administration* (Englewood Cliffs, N.J.: Prentice-Hall, 1974); J. O. Dunn and F. M. Rachel, *Wage and Salary Administration: Total Compensation Systems* (New York: McGraw-Hill, 1971); Richard Henderson, *Compensation Management* (Reston, Va.: Reston Publishing, 1976); Allan N. Nash and Stephen J. Carroll, Jr., *The Management of Compensation* (Monterey, Calif.: Brocks/Cole Publishing, 1975); M. L. Rock, *Handbook of Wage and Salary Administration* (New York: McGraw-Hill, 1972); Robert E. Sibson, *Compensation* (New York: American Management Association, AMACOM, 1975); T. A. Mahoney, *Compensation and Reward Perspectives* (Homewood, Ill.: Richard D. Irwin, 1979).

[8]Approach developed and advocated by L. T. Hawley and H. D. Janes.

[9]David W. Belcher, "Wage and Salary Administration," in Dale Yoder and H. G. Heneman, Jr., eds., *Motivation and Commitment* (Washington, D.C.: Bureau of National Affairs, 1975), p. 6–95.

[10]U.S. Department of Labor, *Handbook of Analyzing Jobs* (Washington, D.C.: Government Printing Office, 1972).

[11]W. K. Kirchner and M. D. Dunnette, "Identifying the Critical Factors in Successful Salesmanship," *Personnel* 34 (September–October 1957), pp. 54–59; and M. D. Dunnette, *Personnel Selection and Placement* (Belmont, Calif.: Wadsworth Publishing, 1966).

[12]E. J. McCormick, D. R. Jeanneret, and R. C. Mecham, "A Study of Job Characteristics and Job Dimensions as Based on the Position Analysis Questionnaire (PAQ)," *Journal of Applied Psychology* 56 (April 1972), pp. 347–368.

[13]Harold D. Janes, "Issues in Job Evaluation: The Union View," *Personnel Journal* 51 (September 1972), p. 675; also see Research Department, International Association of Machinists, *What's Wrong with Job Evaluation?* (Washington, D.C.: International Association of Machinists, 1954).

[14]Harold D. Janes, "Comparative Issues in Job Evaluation: The Union View, 1971–1978," *Personnel Journal* 58 (February 1979), pp. 80–85.

[15]Sibson, *Compensation*, p. 120.

[16]Belcher, *Compensation Administration*, pp. 6–98 to 6–103. Also see footnote 7.

[17]U.S. Department of Labor, Bureau of Labor Statistics, *Characteristics of Major Collective Bargaining Agreements, January 1, 1980* (Washington, D.C.: U.S. Government Printing Office, 1981), p. 45.

[18]Ibid.

[19]Herbert G. Zollitsch, "Productivity, Time Studies, and Incentive-Pay Plans," in Yoder and Heneman, eds., *Motivation and Commitment*, pp. 6–61.

[20]Norma W. Carlson, "Time Rates Tighten Their Grip on Manufacturing Industries," *Monthly Labor Review* 105 (May 1982), pp. 15–16.

[21]John Hoerr, "Why Labor and Management Are Both Buying Profit Sharing," *Business Week*, January 13, 1983, p. 84.

[22]"Loggers Tie Pay to Productivity", *Business Week*, November 29, 1982, p. 35.

[23]Zollitsch, "Productivity," pp. 6–66. Also see J. Kenneth White, "The Scanlon Plan: Causes and Correlates of Success," *Academy of Management Journal* 22 (June 1979), pp. 292–312.

[24]Mitchell Fein, "Improved Productivity through Workers Involvement," *Hearings before the Subcommittee on General Oversight of the Committee on Small Business* (Washington, D.C.: U.S. Government Printing Office, 1982), pp. 118–123.

[25]Irving Bernstein, *Arbitration of Wages* (Berkeley: University of California, 1954), pp. 26–27; Craig Overton, "Criteria in Grievance and Interest Arbitration in the Public Sector," *Arbitration Journal* 28 (1973), pp. 159–166; Howard S. Block, "Criteria in Public Sector Interest Disputes," in G. G. Somers and B. D. Dennis, eds., *Arbitration and the Public Interest* (Washington, D.C.: Bureau of National Affairs, 1971), pp. 161–193.

[26]Bachman, *Wage Determination*, pp. 14–15.

[27]Richard B. Freeman, "Union Wage Practices and Wage Dispersions Within Establishments," *Industrial and Labor Relations Review* 36 (October 1982), pp. 3–21.

[28]John Dunlop, "The Economics of Wage-Dispute Settlements," *Law and Contemporary Problems* 12 (Spring 1947), p. 282; and Bernstein, Arbitration of Wages, pp. 26–27.

[29]Bachman, *Wage Determination*, pp. 18–32.

[30]J. Fred Holly and Gary A. Hall, "Dispelling the Myths of Wage Arbitration," *Labor Law Journal* 28 (June 1977), p. 346.

[31]Sumner Slichter, *Basic Criteria Used in Wage Negotiation* (Chicago: Chicago Association of Commerce and Industry, January 30, 1947), p. 25.

[32]Bachman, *Wage Determination*, pp. 251–258.

[33]The BNA Staff, *Labor Relations in an Economic Recession: Job Losses and Concession Bargaining* (Washington, D.C.: Bureau of National Affairs, Inc., 1982), pp. 9–15.

[34]Dunlop, "Wage-Dispute Settlements," pp. 286–289.

[35]Bachman, *Wage Determination*, p. 174.

[39]Ibid., pp. 202-203.

[37]Greenberg, "Definitions and Concepts," p. 2.

[38]Fein, "Improved Productivity," pp. 117–129.

[39]General Accounting Office, *Productivity Sharing Programs: Can They Contribute to Productivity Improvement?* (Washington, D.C.: U.S. Government Printing Office, 1981).

[40]The Decline of Productivity and the Resultant Loss of U.S. World Economic and Political Leadership (Dearborn, Mich.: Robot Institute of America, 1981).

[41]Keith E. McKee, *Manufacturing Productivity Centers* (Dearborn, Mich.: Society of Manufacturing Engineers, 1980), pp. 4–5.

[42]News from Congressman John J. LaFalce, October 2, 1982.

[43]Jerome Rosow, "Productivity and the Blue-Collar Blues," *Personnel* 48 (March–April 1971), pp. 8–10.

[44]Jerome M. Rosow, "Now Is the Time for Productivity Bargaining," *Harvard Business Review* 50 (January–February 1972), p. 85.

[45]William F. Maloney, "Productivity Bargaining in Contract Construction," *Proceedings of the 1977 Annual Spring Meeting: Industrial Relations Research Association* (Madison, Wis.: Industrial Relations Research Association, 1977), pp. 533–534.

[46]Joseph P. Goldberg, "Bargaining and Productivity in the Private Sector," in Gerald Somers et al., eds., *Collective Bargaining and Productivity* (Madison, Wis.: Industrial Relations Research Association, 1975), p. 28–42.

[47]William W. Winpisinger, "Output: Collective Bargaining and Productivity," in F. J. Havelich, ed., *Collective Bargaining: New Dimensions in Labor Relations* (Boulder, Colo.: Westview Press, 1979), pp. 25–28.

[48]Charles Brown and James Medoff, "Trade Unions in the Production Process," *Journal of Political Economy* 86 (June 1980), pp. 355–359.

[49] Richard B. Freeman and James L. Medoff, "The Two Faces of Unionism," *Public Interest* 57 (Fall 1979), pp. 69–93.

[50]J. T. Addison and A. H. Barnett, "The Impact of Unions on Productivity," *British Journal of Industrial Relations* 20 (July 1982), pp. 145–149.

[51]John T. Addison, "Are Unions Good for Productivity?" *Journal of Labor Research* 3 (Spring 1982), p. 137.

[52]Slichter, *Basic Criteria*, pp. 14–15.

[53]Dunlop, "Wage-Dispute Settlements," pp. 289–290.

[54]John P. Gould and George Bittlingmayer, *The Economics of the Davis-Bacon Act* (Washington, D.C.: American Enterprise Institute for Public Policy Research, 1980), pp. 5–9, 84–89.

[55]Robert J. Flanagan and Daniel J. B. Mitchell, "Wage Determination," in Thomas A. Kochan, et. al., Industrial Relations Research in the 1970s," Madison, Wis.: Industrial Relations Research Association, 1982, p. 74.

[56]Equal Employment Opportunity Commission, *Hearings before the United States Equal Employment Opportunity Commission—on Job Segregation and Wage Discrimination* (Washington, D.C.: Government Printing Office, 1980), p. 4.

[57]Alice H. Cook, "Comparable Worth, Background, and Current Issues," *Reports* (Honolulu, Hawaii: University of Hawaii, Industrial Relations Center, 1982), pp. 5–6. For an examination of the Chairman of the EEOC's view of the comparable worth issue, see Clarence Thomas, "Pay Equity and Comparable Worth," *Labor Law Journal* 34 (January 1983), pp. 3–12.

[58]Winn Newman, "Pay Equity: An Emerging Labor Issue," In James L. Stern and Barbara D. Dennis, eds., *Proceedings of the Thirty-fourth Annual Meeting of the Industrial Relations Research Association* (Madison, Wis.: Industrial Relations Research Association, 1982), pp. 167–170.

[59]Bruce R. Ellig, "Compensation Management: Its Past and Its Future," *Personnel* 54 (May/June 1977), pp. 32–34.

[60]Lucretia D. Tanner and Janice D. Murphy, "The Voluntary Pay Standard: A Review," *Labor Law Journal* 32 (March 1981), pp. 158–163.

[61]Mitchell L. Marks and Phillip H. Mirvis, "Wage Guidelines: Job Attitudes and Behavior," *Industrial Relations* 20 (Fall 1981), p. 295.

[62]U.S. Department of Labor, Bureau of Labor Statistics, *Characteristics of Major Collective Bargaining Agreements*, p. 40.

[63]John Zalusky, "Cost of Living Clauses: Inflation Fighters," *American Federationist* 83 (March 1976), p. 1.

[64]H. L. Douty, "Escalator Clauses and Inflation," *Collective Bargaining Negotiations and Contracts* (Washington, D.C.: Bureau of National Affairs, December 1975), p. 16:1.

[65]Douglas R. LeRoy, "Scheduled Wage Increases and Escalator Provisions in 1978," *Monthly Labor Review* 101 (January 1978), pp. 3–8; Beth A. Levin, "Scheduled Wage Increases and Escalator Provisions in 1979," *Monthly Labor Review* 102 (January 1979), pp. 20–27; Victor Sheifer, "Cost-of-Living Adjustments Keeping Up with Inflation?" *Monthly Labor Review* 102 (June 1979), p. 14.

[66]The average length increased from 26 months in 1972 to 32.5 months in 1977. Those with COLA averaged 36.1 months; without COLA, 27.4 months. Janice D. Murphy, "Wage Developments during 1977," *Monthly Labor Review* 101 (April 1978), p. 5.

[67]William M. Davis, "Collective Bargaining in 1983: A Crowded Agenda," *Monthly Labor Review* 106 (January 1983), p. 10.

[68]LeRoy, "Scheduled Wage Increases," pp. 5–6.

[69]Audrey Freedman, "Cost-of-Living Clauses in Collective Bargaining," *Compensation Review* 6 (third quarter 1974), pp. 11–19; Robert H. Ferguson, *Cost-of-Living Adjustments in Union Management Agreements* (Ithaca, N.Y.: Cornell University, 1976), pp. 15–27; and LeRoy, "Scheduled Wage Increases." pp. 7–8.

[70]Robert J. Thornton, "A Problem with the COLA Craze," *Compensation Review* 9 (second quarter 1977), pp. 42–44.

[71]U.S. Department of Labor, Bureau of Labor Statistics, *Measures of Compensation* (Washington, D.C.: Government Printing Office, 1977), pp. 46–47.

[72]"Chamber Says Employee Benefits Averaged 37.3 Percent of Payroll in 1981," *Daily Labor Report*, November 22, 1982, p. A-1.

[73]Colman S. Ives, "Benefits and Services—Private," in Yoder and Heneman, eds., *Motivation and Commitment*, p. 6–186.

[74]U.S. Department of Labor, Bureau of Labor Statistics, *Characteristics of Major Collective Bargaining Agreements.*

[75]Editors of Collective Bargaining Negotiations and Contracts, *Basic Patterns in Union Contracts* (Washington, D.C.: Bureau of National Affairs, 1979).

[76]Ibid., pp. 18–40, 88–96. For example, the media length-of-service requirement for one week's vacation is one year, two weeks after two years, three weeks after ten years, four weeks after seventeen years, five weeks after twenty-four years, and six weeks after thirty years. Some of the United Steelworkers' agreements allow extended vacations up to thirteen weeks; however, these vacations are provided only in intervals of five years to senior employees.

Ibid., p. 68.

[78]Age Discrimination in Employment Act, as amended in 1978 by Public Law 95–256.

[79]Eds. of Collective Bargaining Negotiations and Contracts, *Basic Patterns*, pp. 70–71.

[80]U.S. Department of Labor, Office of Employee Benefits Security, *Often-Asked Questions about the Employee Retirement Income Security Act of 1974* (Washington, D.C., Government Printing Office, 1976), pp. 16–17. Also see Ian D. Lanoff, "Civil Enforcement and Criminal Penalties under the Employee Retirement Income Security Act of 1974," in Virginia S. Cameron, ed., *Labor Law Developments* (New York: Matthew Bender, 1976), pp. 1–31.

[81]Sandy DeMent, "A New Bargaining Focus on Legal Services," *American Federationist* 85 (May 1978), pp. 7–10.

[82]"Pay Now, Sue Later," *Time*, September 4, 1978, p. 71.

[83]T. J. St. Antoine, "Growth Patterns in Legal Services," *American Federationist* 83 (February 1976), pp. 19–21.

[84]DeMent, "New Bargaining Focus," p. 7.

[85]Robert S. Greenberger, "Legal Service Plans Emerge as a Growing Fringe Benefit for Union Workers," *Wall Street Journal*, April 26, 1983, p. 1.

[86]Ibid.

[87]"Pay Now, Sue Later," p. 71.

[88]Greg Lewis, *Unionism and Relative Wages in the United States* (Chicago: University of Chicago Press, 1963).

[89]Richard B. Freeman and James L. Medoff, "The Impact of Collective Bargaining: Illusion or Reality?" in Jack Stieber, et al., eds., *U.S. Industrial Relations 1950–1980: A Critical Assessment* (Madison, Wis.: Industrial Relations Research Association, 1981), pp. 53–54.

[90]Jacob Mincer, "Union Effects: Wages, Turnover, and Job Training," *Working Paper Series* (Cambridge, Mass.: National Bureau of Economic Research, Inc.), p. 42.

[91]Daniel J. B. Mitchell, "Collective Bargaining and the Economy," in Steiber, et al. eds., *U.S. Industrial Relations 1950–1980*, pp. 1–44.

[92]Robert J. Flanagan and Daniel J. B. Mitchell, "Wage Determination and Public Policy," in T. A. Kochan, et al., eds., *Industrial Relations Research in the 1970s: A Review and Appraisal* (Madison, Wis.: Industrial Relations Research Association, 1982), p. 74.

[93]Susan Uroman, "The Direction of Wage Spillovers in Manufacturing," *Industrial and Labor Relations Review* 36 (October 1982), pp. 102–103.

[94]David E. Shulenburger, Robert A. McLean, and Sarah B. Rosch, "Union-Nonunion Wage Differentials: A Replication and Extension," *Industrial Relations* 21 (Spring 1982), p. 254.

[95]George Ruben, "Collective Bargaining in 1982: Results Dictated by Economy," *Monthly Labor Review* 106 (January 1983), pp. 28–37.

[96]Daniel J. B. Mitchell, "Recent Union Contract Concessions," *Working Paper Series* (Los Angeles: UCLA Institute of Industrial Relations, 1982).

[97]"Union Dissenters Deplore Concession Bargaining Trend as Counter-Productive," *Daily Labor Report*, November 19, 1982, p. A-3.

found that posi-
ilar effort paid
male-dominated

As an example of unequal pay for equal work, Currie cited the jobs of an electrician and a nurse. The study ranked the nurse's job at 534 "value

y here to call attention
blems of black business

Filing
1 Roils
orkers

Page 25

ent of Motor Inn
Wilson employ-
ritable organiza-
e United Way of
ifth of its annual
n employees. "If
l hurt the whole
a Butler, direc-

s he sympathizes
rstand the hard-
this or lose the
bying with local
foreclosures and
n says.

ces

filing go far be-
away at the hog-
h, buyer Gilbert

black business growth include access to capital and credit and the enforcement of federal programs to aid black contractors, according to the NAACP's national director of economic development, Fred Rasheed.

"No one on the national level is an advocate for the cause of black business development," said Rasheed. "We were approached about this problem last year by a group of black business persons who felt the NAACP could play this role."

Rasheed maintained that black businesses still have difficulty obtaining credit. "To put it bluntly, banks discriminate against minorities, particularly when it comes to investment purposes," he said.

Another problem, Rasheed said, is

that the Reagan administration has refused to expand a special "set-aside" program that earmarks certain federal contracts for small minority firms.

Local NAACP Director Frank Williams, a South Side Realtor, said the conference represents a "partnership between the nation's oldest civil rights organization and black businesses to improve their [businesses'] gross receipts."

Another objective, Williams said, is to increase black employment at major white-owned firms. "We want major white corporations to tighten up their employment practices. We want to see more blacks on boards of corporations and in managerial posi-

TACTFUL about being too gleeful over
turnabout in seeking their counsel.
reful about stepping on the toes of the
man while scouting in his territory and
the limits of their assignments.
day at the bat," Hitchner explained. He
etirement in early 1982 rather than move
n the company was centralizing regional

ressman clash

> 66 State and federal officials charac
> intervention on behalf of Velsicol as

The lagoons cover 18 acres and contain an estimated 300,000 cubic yards of hazardous sludge, said Robert Cowles, Superfund coordinator for the Illinois EPA.

can un
the co
the co
Rich

Labor asks tou
to protect agai

WASHINGTON (UPI)—A labor group Wednesday called on the government to protect employees who work in public buildings that contain the carcinogen asbestos, saying employees "should not have to risk cancer just to earn a living."

The Public Employee Department of the AFL-CIO said tougher safety standards are needed to protect workers against the potentially deadly insulating material.

The department, which represents more than 200,000 federal, state and local workers, convened a national

eventually have
enough to do n
say no asbestos i
John Leyden, d
director.

Asbestos was
homes and ship
years before th
mined in the
caused cancer.

Although asb
new buildings i
an untold numb
as thousands of

An estimated

Part 4
Applying the Labor Relations Process to Different Work Arrangements

Part 4 gives the reader an opportunity to apply the previous chapters' discussions of the labor relations process to various labor relations situations. Collective bargaining in the public sector at all governmental levels is discussed, and a discussion of foreign labor relations processes is presented for comparative purposes. A concluding chapter describes labor relations activities in the white-collar employees, professional sports, health care, and agricultural industries.

Chapter 14 Labor Relations in State and Local Government

"Collective bargaining in the public sector is . . . still developing. It is, therefore, much too soon to pronounce it a success or a failure."
Benjamin Aaron
U.C.L.A.

The public sector has grown to become an important factor in the U.S. labor scene. As the number of public employees has increased, so has the number of these employees joining unions. This chapter presents an overview of labor relations in the public sector and provides a brief summary of the similarities and differences found in public and private sector labor relations. It also examines public sector bargaining at the state and local levels and concludes with a discussion of one of the affected groups—educators.

The Significance of Public Sector Labor Relations

Public sector labor relations has developed from a time when public employees were required to lobby their respective legislators for favorable employment terms to one in which bona fide collective bargaining occurs. It has moved from a generation of rapid growth, management's inability to react to collective bargaining, and a horror of strikes to a generation characterized by slow union growth, few states passing enabling public sector legislation, and a willingness to take strikes.[1] With many state legislatures becoming interested in legislation to cut taxes, many public employees have become more concerned about their job security and welfare. Thus, union leaders are showing increased attention to public sector employees, hoping that gains in membership in this area will offset the lack of membership gains in the private sector.[2] Although unions received a setback in a 1976 Supreme Court decision which led many to believe that a national public sector labor relations law would be declared unconstitutional, their optimism was furthered by passage of state and local legislation and positive (if qualified) public opinion favoring public sector bargaining.[3]

The tremendous growth in government employment at all government levels (see Table 14.1) affects not only government agencies but the organized labor community (AFL-CIO) as well. The precise strength of this influence on AFL-CIO

Table 14.1 Governmental Employment by Levels of Government 1971–1980

	Numbers of Employees (in Thousands)				
Year	Total	Federal (Civilian)	Total State and Local	State	Local
1971	13,316	2,872	10,444	2,832	7,612
1972	13,759	2,795	10,964	2,955	8,002
1973	14,139	2,786	11,353	3,013	8,339
1974	14,628	2,874	11,754	3,155	8,599
1975	14,986	2,890	12,097	3,268	8,829
1976	14,948	2,733	12,215	*	*
1977	15,195	2,727	12,468	*	*
1978	15,470	2,758	12,712	*	*
1979	15,688	2,771	12,917	*	*
1980	16,156	2,789	13,367	*	*

*data not reported

U.S. Department of Labor, *Employment and Training Report of the President* (Washington, D.C., U.S. Government Printing Office, 1976–1981).

policies is currently undetermined. However, at least some public employee union officials maintain that their unions are not given enough consideration in the AFL-CIO; they charge that the AFL-CIO is dragging its feet regarding unionized public employees' concerns and the desires of other public employees to form unions. Some of this dissension prompted Jerry Wurf, former president of the American Federation of State, County and Municipal Employees (AFSCME), to consider pulling his organization out of the AFL-CIO.[4] Perhaps AFSCME's stance has been modified with the recently developed Public Employee Department of the AFL-CIO. The relative degree of influence exerted by public employee unions on the AFL-CIO's structure and policies in the near future remains an interesting and speculative topic for labor relations students.

Private and Public Sector Labor Relations Compared

Although labor relations in the private and public sectors have much in common, there are at least five general differences that aid in obtaining a full appreciation of the public sector's labor relations process.

Differences in Private and Public Sector Bargaining

1. The nature of the public service One difference between the public and private sectors can be explained in terms of the economic systems and the market economy. Unlike the private sector, many of the services in the public sector (such as public education and police and fire protection) are supplied to the citizens at little or no additional cost (beyond taxes). The market economy therefore does not operate in the public sector and cannot act as a constraint on the labor union and management negotiators.

Moreover, monopolistic conditions often exist in the public sector, and public organizations often control the services rendered or the products offered. For example, the police and fire departments are the primary organizations that provide certain types of security protection. Public education has very little real competition from the private sector, and even that is usually among only the more affluent families. Thus, products and services provided by the government cannot be readily substituted if they become more costly.[5]

The lack of substitute goods or services distinguishes public sector collective bargaining from related activities in the private sector and adds to the critical nature of public services. For example, citizens usually take garbage collection services for granted; yet a strike by city garbage collectors would be regarded by the public as a crisis, since there is no immediate alternative means for garbage disposal. The lack of substitute services also eliminates one of management's strike costs: loss of business to a competitor. In fact, some union leaders contend that municipal leaders use a strike to their advantage—the payroll savings during a strike are transferred to other governmental budgetary accounts.

Finally, the relatively vague aspects of the particular public service institutions make productivity bargaining difficult. Clear and precise productivity measures are a necessary first step in productivity bargaining (although many private sector companies have these figures and do not engage in productivity bargaining). Most public sector bargaining parties do not have specific productivity measures at their disposal and could not engage in productivity bargaining even if they desired this approach. Many public services are provided regardless of customer use. Policemen and bus drivers can legitimately contend that they should not be financially punished for nonuse of their services—their salaries should not be a direct function of the number of crimes detected and punished or riders served if the service is available to all. Hence, much of the public sector wage determination process is based on comparisons with similar jobs in the public and private sectors rather than on employee performance records.[6] Because the market does not act as a moderator in the public sector, budgetary limitation, public attitudes, and administrative discretion must operate to successfully maintain order, equity, and balance in collective bargaining relationships.[7]

2. The relationship between the budget and public sector bargaining processes The budget usually tends to have a more conspicuous if not significant role in public sector collective bargaining. Most municipal budgets are posted in advance before public hearings and subsequent adoption. Although many citizens ignore public hearings, key taxpayers such as local companies give close attention to the budget in terms of its implication for increased property taxes. The anticipated salaries for public employees are recorded as separate line items on the budget, something not done in the private sector. Thus, the opportunity exists for concerned taxpayers to pressure city officials in the hopes of keeping the budget and subsequent taxes at a minimum.

The specific influence of the budget on the public sector collective bargaining process remains uncertain. Some suggest that there is a great deal of flexibility in the budget-bargaining relationship in terms of budget padding, transfer of funds among line items, and supplemental or amended budgets that can often be filed after the final approval date.[8] In these cases, the governmental officer in charge of labor relations may have little concern with the agency's financial activities. The following related comments were expressed by a former director of the budget for New York City:

The director of the budget is less a part of a unified management team than a part of the problem, an adversary not unlike the union leaders themselves. . . . Underlying the situation is the belief held by most labor negotiators that they know "what it takes" to effect a settlement and that, in the large complex public body, alleged or actual limits on available resources have no effect upon the ultimate settlement. And they are, in fact, largely correct.[9]

Similarly, as illustrated by one union official's comment, public sector unions seldom allow the budget to influence their collective bargaining strategies and settlements:

The budget does not mean too much to me—if we based our bargaining demands on the budget, we would never get any money. The union is never cognizant as to the amount [in the budget] because there never is enough money. We are aware of the dire need for money and campaign politically [to obtain additional funds], but when we go into negotiations we don't discuss the budgetary problems.[10]

Their major concern pertains to securing benefits for their members; it is up to management to find sufficient funds for an equitably negotiated settlement. Thus, there is little union-management agreement over the budget's significance in contract negotiations; few if any public sector collective bargaining agreements have provisions specifying the role the budget will assume in the collective bargaining process.

This situation poses a dilemma. On the one hand, if the budget were a controlling factor in contract negotiations, unilateral managerial decision making would render collective bargaining a farce. On the other hand, if collective bargaining were entirely removed from budgetary constraints, fiscal responsibilities would be abated at taxpayer expense. Some degree of union involvement in the budget-making process might be needed in instances of severe fiscal constraints. A hopeful note is reflected in the observations of a New York City Emergency Financial Control Board member: "I have found the municipal labor unions to be the most practical people in this [financial] crisis. They understood the problem more quickly than the city administration."[11]

3. Collective bargaining structures and decision-making processes It is more difficult to define the appropriate bargaining unit in the public sector than in the private sector.[12] Private sector legislation and related administrative enforcement agencies provide direction for determining the appropriate bargaining unit. For example, plant guards in the private sector are required to be in separate bargaining units, and supervisors are not eligible for membership in the bargaining unit. The public sector, especially at the state and local levels, experiences many different combinations of appropriate bargaining units. Depending on the particular applicable state law or administrative determination, public sector supervisors can be prohibited from joining unions, they can be in the same bargaining units as other employees, or they can join unions in separate bargaining units. All these combinations can be found in states having no statutory regulations.[13]

Another organizational difference applies to the chief negotiator in the public sector, who often lacks authority to reach a final and binding agreement with the union on behalf of the public organization. The doctrine of sovereignty makes it difficult to delegate decision-making authority to specific administrative officials. Many elected officials still refuse to give up their legislative authority to make final decisions on matters that they believe are important to effective governmental operations, since they feel responsible directly to the electorate. They do not want appointed negotiators to bind them to wage settlements and other provisions of collective bargaining agreements which they believe are unworkable.[14] For example, unionized school teachers might encounter a variety of managers in collective negotiations—the school principal, the superintendent of schools, the school board, and possibly state education officials. The problem of determining "who is management?" can negatively affect the negotiations process in two ways.

a. Management can pass the buck to other management officials in the bargaining process. Union officers are often shuffled off to a variety of governmental officials in collective bargaining on the premise that another individual has specific authority for a particular issue or a portion of available funds. Often, political rivalries prompt certain government officials to either intervene or pass the buck in the hopes of looking good at another official's expense.[15] This situation can result in a more confusing collective bargaining relationship than is typically found in the private sector. In some cases, it can almost entirely prevent serious collective bargaining efforts between management and the union.[16]

b. The unwillingness of some government agencies to delegate sufficient authority to a labor relations representative can result in a lack of labor relations understanding on management's side of the negotiation table. In some cases, taxpayers are affected if unions take advantage of the inexperienced management negotiators. Perhaps in other cases a public strike could have been avoided if the parties had had a more realistic understanding of the collective bargaining process.

4. Negotiable issues and bargaining tactics Exemption by statute of many of the traditional collective bargaining subjects from negotiations is another difference between private and public sector labor relations. Under the Civil Service Reform Act of 1978, wages and position classifications of federal employees cannot be negotiated. (The postal service is covered under another law.) In many states operating under merit system rules and regulations, related subjects such as promotion, pension plans, and layoff procedures cannot be negotiated.[17]

A problem arises if public sector negotiation topics are restricted to those already found in the labor agreement. One study found that some public sector labor agreement provisions are not actually negotiated between the parties, while other decisions are jointly determined but not included in the formal labor agreement.[18] Thus, relatively few generalizations can be made regarding collectively bargained items in the public sector.

Sometimes the public sector's bargaining tactics differ from those in the private sector. Certain bargaining practices allowed in the public sector would probably be considered unfair labor practices in the private sector. Negotiations in the private sector stem from a bilateral relationship—management and union representatives negotiate the terms of the labor argreement with little involvement from outside groups. Public sector bargaining, particularly at the state and local levels, is multilateral, involving various groups of community citizens and government officials as well as the formally designated negotiators. Thus, it often becomes an exercise in politics—who you know and what you can do to help or hurt the government official's political career can play a decisive role. Public sector unions therefore often have opportunities to *end-run* the negotiations before, during, or after their occurrence; that is, they make a direct appeal to the legislative body that will make final decisions on the agreement in the hope that they will gain a more favorable agreement. For example, one mayor made concessions to the police association in return for its endorsement in the gubernatorial primary. He changed the regular police work schedule from five days on and two off to four days on and two off (increasing annual days off by 17), guaranteed two patrolmen in all cars, and agreed that 50 percent plus one of the patrol cars in each police district would be on the street during night hours.[19] Because public labor unions in many settings are politically potent, elective officials are generally more receptive to this end-run process than a corporation president, members of the board of directors, or majority stockholders of a corporation would ever be in the private sector.[20] In fact, such attempts by the union to bypass the management negotiators of a private sector organization would probably result in an adverse NLRB determination of refusal to bargain in good faith.

Occasionally, the media aid the end-run tactic—management and the union present their positions to the press rather than to the other party at the bargaining table. Public sector bargaining is usually given more press coverage than similar activities in the private sector since more related information is typically furnished to the press and the eventual settlement will have a more direct impact on the government's constituents. The end-run to the news media can harm the collective bargaining approach, as evidenced by a union leader's account of the one-contract negotiations between New York City and the uniformed forces:

All of this [bargaining issues] should have been brought to the bargaining table. It would have given both labor and management a chance to work out of these very difficult trouble spots. . . . But, almost nothing was done at the table; instead both sides took to the television, advertising, and the loud and dramatic press releases. . . .

Experts . . . know the best way to insure trouble is to bring collective bargaining into the public arena. Instead of labor and management representatives talking to each other, they will talk to the public and to their principals only. Invariably, the wrong things will be said.

Management will talk of the "irresponsibly high demands" of the workers, and about how services will have to be cut back or taxes raised. . . .

The labor leader now has to talk tough. The strike threat becomes almost obligatory, because he is now put in an impossible squeeze. When the union leader goes public he first must talk to the people he represents, and retain their confidence. Understandably, the public responds not to the facts of the situation but to the militant rhetoric. Everybody loses in the process, a process that has little or nothing to do with collective bargaining.[21]

Accompanying the upsurge of collective bargaining in the public sector have been efforts to open negotiations to citizen observation and participation through "sunshine bargaining" legislation. The rationale for this approach is that citizens can provide more input into how tax dollars are spent by their involvement, and openness reduces public distrust. Twelve states have passed "sunshine bargaining" laws; however, interpretations by enforcement agencies and courts have concluded that collective bargaining sessions need not be open to the public.[22]

The open approach to public sector bargaining differs widely from the private sector, as a private enterprise's owners (stockholders) are excluded from collective bargaining sessions. Also, flexibility and honesty are necessary prerequisites of successful labor-management relationships, and these qualities are often lost if union and management negotiators have to posture their efforts before a public audience.

5. The right-to-strike controversy The right to strike, considered by many a vital instrument for successful collective bargaining, is usually prohibited by statute in the public sector. The federal government and most state governments prohibit strikes. The basic argument given for legislative prohibition of strikes is that the services provided by public organizations are essential to the general welfare of the citizens, and work stoppages or refusals to work would adversely affect the delivery of these vital services and create disorder in the community. As is true with many industrial relations concepts, the words *essential services* are subject to many diverse interpretations. Some maintain that all public services are essential, while others suggest that many public employee classifications (such as clerks, mechanics, and motor pool personnel) are no more essential than their counterparts in private industry. Police and firefighters are almost always viewed as crucial for public safety; however, at least one police strike saw no increase in the area's crime rate. One police official, believing that criminals fear irate citizens more than they fear the police, commented, "Hoods have no rights without police protection. Shop owners will use their shotguns."[23]

The right to strike in the public sector has other debatable dimensions. Some would prohibit public sector strikes because they would place too much power in the hands of the unions relative to the taxpayers. Also, unions would unnecessarily benefit at the expense of other groups that are dependent on government revenues but that do not strike or participate in power ploys with public officials.[24]

George Taylor further elaborates on the effect of the right to strike on political processes:

It is ultimately the legislative and the political processes which have to balance the interests of public employees with the rest of the community. The balancing involves considering the relation of the compensation of public employees to tax rates, an appraisal of the extent and quality of public service desired by the taxpayer, and an evaluation of the efficiency of the performance of public employees. . . . Methods of persuasion and political activity, rather than the strike, comply with our traditions and with the forms of representative government to which we are dedicated as the appropriate means for resolving conflicts of interests in this area. . . . Strikes are not the answer, new procedures are.[25]

One research project found that successful bargaining gains in the public sector occur when unions either use the threat of a strike despite its illegality or intertwine themselves closely with their employers through patronage-political support arrangements. If this assessment is correct, prohibiting strikes would lead to changes in patterns of political decision making which would subvert the "normal" political processes.[26]

Some contend that prohibiting public sector strikes distorts the collective bargaining process:

The conclusion is inescapable that collective bargaining cannot exist if employees may not withdraw their services or employers discontinue them. This is not a statement of preference, but a statement of fact. But it is now also evident that collective bargaining is the best way of composing differences between workers and their employers in a democratic society even though there is much room for improvement in the process. So, if we believe public employees should have bargaining rights, we must accept the possibility of a strike and consider how best to guard against it. If we believe the case against strikes by public employees is so overwhelming that all such strikes must be prohibited, let us then say frankly that public employees cannot be given bargaining rights and that the use of such euphemisms as collective negotiations cannot alter the basic structural differences the strike ban entails.[27]

Yet others believe that the right to strike in the public sector is not essential to collective bargaining, since public sector unions are already influential interest groups and effectively use their lobbying and political support techniques to obtain collective bargaining goals.[28]

Regardless of the arguments for or against the right to strike or statutory penalties assigned to strikers, significant strikes have occurred in the public sector in recent years, involving teachers, firefighters, police, and sanitation workers in many large cities and postal employees in the federal sector. In fact, since 1960 there has been a considerable increase in public employee strikes, not only in number but in the number of employees involved and in working-days lost as a result of the strikes. In 1960, there were only 36 public sector strikes, causing 58,400 lost working-days.

In 1980 state and local governments experienced 502 work stoppages, (about 9 percent fewer than in 1979) involving 233,095 employees and 2,406,708 days of worker idleness. The largest number of strikes occurred in education, and seven states, California, Illinois, Michigan, New Jersey, New York, Ohio, and Pennsylvania, accounted for 90 percent of the idle days.[29] Moreover, strikes are often prolonged until all strikers or discharged employees have been granted amnesty or reinstatement to former positions. Thus, laws have not prevented strikes; they have not been invoked against all employees who have participated in strikes, and, when invoked, the law has not been applied with like effect to all strikers. Some believe that laws prohibiting strikes may have deterred some strikes and injunctions may have had a sobering effect on some strikers, but prohibiting strikes by passing a law has not realized a great degree of success.[30]

Similarities in Private and Public Sector Bargaining

While there are differences between private and public sector labor relations, there are also similarities. First, many of the participants in public sector bargaining are trained and gain their experience in the private sector. They tend to mold the emerging institutions in the public sector in a familiar image, using NLRB criteria for appropriate bargaining units, subjects for collective bargaining, use of labor injunctions, and standards for arbitration. Also, some of the unions, such as the Service Employees International Union and the Teamsters, have much experience in the private sector. Other unions, such as the National Education Association, the American Federation of Teachers, the AFSCME and civil service employee groups, hired their professional staffs from the private sector.[31]

One major similarity shared by public and private sector negotiations is that the collective bargaining settlement will often be influenced by the personalities of the union and management negotiators and their respective abilities to increase their bargaining power relative to the other party (the bargaining power model has been discussed in Chapter 6). To reiterate briefly, each party increases bargaining power over the opponent by either increasing the cost to the opponent of disagreeing or reducing the cost to the opponent of agreeing.

Public opinion represents a most significant cost item in public sector labor relations—both union and government officials often structure their tactics in a manner that gains public support for their position, which places pressure on their opponents to concede negotiation items.

A former president of a major public employee union frequently appealed to public opinion (see Exhibit 14.1), contending that public opinion often translates into election votes—government officials approach labor relations with their political careers uppermost in mind.[32] He further believed that public opinion usually prompts government officials to take a hard-line approach regarding union proposals and strategies:

[I]f we're [public unions] so powerful, why does every mayor and governor try to make his political reputation by fighting our union? If you sat in this office all day, you'd get the impression that every public official in the United States thinks he can win his epaulets by declaring war on our members.[33]

Exhibit 14.1 Attempt by a Public Employee Union to Align Public Opinion with Its Goals

"One of these could educate every kid in Cincinnati."

"One brand-new B-1 bomber costs $87 million.

Enough to wipe out the cost of public education in Cincinnati. With enough left over to fund the libraries in the District of Columbia.

A single B-1 could pay for fire protection in Los Angeles for one year. Or finance the entire budget for the city of Atlanta.

Or pay all yearly expenses for streets, parks, and sanitation for Indianapolis, St. Louis, Pittsburgh, Hartford, and Milwaukee. *Combined.*

But what about the military benefits of the B-1?

According to a host of experts, there aren't any.

A Brookings Institution study found: 'No significant military advantages [are] to be gained by deploying a new penetrating bomber such as the B-1.'

Yet, two weeks ago, Congress voted full speed ahead on the most expensive weapon in U.S. history – a 244-plane system that could cost $100 billion.

Our union wants to stop the B-1 funding.

And we urge the Democratic Convention to join us.

We support a military strong enough to deter any aggressor foolish or venal enough to attack us.

But what good is it to be able to destroy Moscow ten times over if our own cities die in the meantime?"

– **Jerry Wurf,** President
American Federation of State,
County and Municipal Employees

American Federation of State, County, and Municipal Employees, 1625 L Street, N.W., Washington, D.C. 20036 Jerry Wurf, President William Lucy, Secretary-Treasurer.

In New York City, AFSCME Is The Parent Organization of The 105,000 Municipal Employees Who Belong To District Council 37, AFSCME; And 10,000 Members of District Council 1707, The Community And Social Agency Employee Union.

Source: *Columbia Journalism Review* 15 (November–December 1976), p. 41. Courtesy of the AFSCME.

To be sure, some municipal and state officials have taken a stern approach toward public union strikers. For example, government officials in West Virginia and Atlanta, Georgia, discharged striking state and municipal employees and started hiring their replacements.

However, public opinion and political support can be a double-edged sword in the bargaining power model. Public unions can use at least three general strategies to increase management's cost of disagreeing with the union's position.[34] The first technique is the union's threat to "blow the whistle" on a questionable practice unless the government agency agrees with the desired negotiated settlement. Examples of such strategy include an announcement by union officials releasing information on the unpublicized practice of dumping raw sewage in a river or on the dollar amount of government officials' liquor bills, which are paid by the taxpayers. Of course, the union is hoping that government officials will capitulate rather than risk potential vote loss in subsequent elections due to the public revelation of a particular incident. Management's cost of disagreeing can be more directly increased by the union's threat of withdrawing political support.[35] The success of this tactic depends on the number of union members and the ability of the union to mobilize a cohesive voting bloc.

Finally, the union can use various job action techniques to raise management's cost of disagreeing. As mentioned earlier in the chapter, a complete withdrawal of service is usually prohibited by statute, but strikes by public employees have occurred frequently in spite of these legal sanctions. Perhaps these actions are taken under the assumption that most public sector strikes have been eventually resolved without fines or other sanctions, even though their activity runs counter to the established laws. However, some other job actions that have been used are outside the law or proscribed by the job requirements (for example, government employees in New York raising the toll bridges at rush hour when walking off the job), while others are marginally outside the law or job requirements (for example, all public employees calling in too sick to work).[36]

From the union standpoint, a most promising job action is working within the law while at the same time placing pressure on management to resolve the dispute. Job slowdowns fall into this category marginally, since most public sector labor agreements give management the right to discipline employees for poor production performance. Yet there is a thin line between a job slowdown and *malicious obedience* (also called work-to-rule), by which the employees follow the agency's rules to the letter. For example, a fingerprint technician is charged with verifying an individual's address during his criminal booking. This can be done by simply telephoning the individual's purported residence. However, fingerprint technicians desiring to follow the malicious obedience technique might personally visit the individual's residence for a more accurate verification. Needless to say, this approach creates an assignment backlog. Other public employees can also use bureaucratic rules to their advantage. For example, toll booth employees could check paper currency serial numbers against a list of counterfeited bills, and postal workers could check each item to insure a proper zip code. Malicious obedience has the tactical advantage of cutting back services. More importantly, employees continue to receive wages under this tactic while being relatively immune from disciplinary actions.

The variety of job action techniques depends on the creativity and resourcefulness of the union leaders. New York City's police and firefighters announced that off-duty personnel would distribute a pamphlet at the city's airports, railroad stations, bus terminals, and hotels. The cover of the pamphlet featured a human skull in a shroud with the caption, "WELCOME TO FEAR CITY." Union officials contended that this pamphlet represented an educational "survival guide" for tourists, since the city was contemplating police and firefighter layoffs. Included in the pamphlet were the following helpful hints:

- Stay off the streets after 6 P.M.
- Avoid public transportation.
- Do not walk.
- Beware of fire hazards.

Job actions of this nature, although not initially illegal, run the risk of an eventual restraining order. This occurred in the aforementioned New York City pamphlet example when the New York supreme court at least in part accepted the city's contention that such conduct endangers the citizens' lives and threatens the economic well-being of the city.

Public sector unions can also reduce management's cost of agreeing with the union by campaigning for referendums to fund the negotiated labor settlement or eliminating some of their initial proposals. They can also push for certain issues that contribute significantly to their economic well-being at little cost to the political incumbents. Employee pensions usually fall into this category since they can be increased without immediate cost implications; indeed, the bulk of pension costs will be incurred by some unhappy politician in the distant future.

Management can reduce its political cost of agreeing on wages by publicizing a rather low across-the-board settlement along with general improvements in the pay step plan. This plan usually gives progressive salary increases to each job classification. For example, an employee in one particular classification might receive a 5 percent wage increase after three years' service in that classification. Management can improve the employee's situation by either raising the percentage increase or reducing the number of service years needed for a step wage increase. However, it is difficult to determine and report the precise cost of these changes. Most news media presentations are limited to specific reports on the average wage gain of public employees and ignore the more detailed cost implications of the modified pay plan.

In summary, the form of public sector collective bargaining is generally similar to that found in the private sector. In both situations, the parties are trying to increase their bargaining power relative to their opponent's by increasing the cost to the opponent of disagreeing with the party's position or by reducing the cost to the opponent of agreeing with the party's position. This section also highlighted some differences in public and private sector bargaining processes. Once these differences are acknowledged and understood, one can better appreciate the public sector as it fits into the overall framework of labor-management relations in the United States.

Development of Labor Relations in State and Local Governments

Background and Membership Status

Union activities in local governments predate the twentieth century; however, they were spontaneous reactions, usually strikes, and not collective bargaining as we know it today. Initially, unions promoted merit systems to prevent political firings, increase job security, and obtain equitable wage administration. Unions allied themselves closely with political parties and provided human resources and financial support for their candidates. As a result, they were rewarded with jobs and equitable wages.

In the late 1950s the demand for public services and labor increased dramatically. As a result, a greater number of younger workers who were more aggressive and militant became public employees. Political interests turned to the passage of laws enabling collective bargaining, and patience with ineffective merit systems and their comparatively low wages waned. Wisconsin was the first state to pass a statewide law in 1959; others followed in the sixties. As a means for protection and improvement of their economic situation and with a growing public acceptance of public employee unions, public employees increasingly turned to unions.[37]

Although the states of New York and Wisconsin showed the most activity in the legislative area in the early sixties, most states today and many of the larger cities have now passed legislation that sets up a legal framework for labor relations in their state or city. Twenty-four states have passed comprehensive legislation which enables most state and local government employees to gain bargaining rights. These laws include the duty to bargain, unfair labor practices, administrative agencies, and impasse resolution procedures, such as mediation and arbitration. (See Table 14.2).

Employees in states having no legislation setting up a labor relations framework still have the legal right to be members of unions or employee associations as a result of the *AFSCME, AFL-CIO v. Woodward* (406 F.2d 137 [1969]) decision, which stated that the right of employees to join unions is protected by the First and Fourteenth Amendments and public administrators who

Table 14.2 States Having Comprehensive Laws Covering *Most* State and Local Employees (Duty to Bargain, Unfair Labor Practices, Administrative Agencies, and Impasse Procedures)

Alaska	Massachusetts	North Dakota
California	Michigan	Oregon
Connecticut	Minnesota	Pennsylvania
Delaware[a]	Montana	Rhode Island
Florida	Nebraska	South Dakota
Hawaii	New Hampshire	Vermont
Iowa	New Jersey	Washington
Maine	New York	Wisconsin

[a]No unfair labor practices listed.

Source: U.S. Department of Labor, Labor-Management Services Administration, *Summary of Public Sector Labor Relations Policies* (Washington, D.C.: U.S. Government Printing Office, 1981).

Ohio governor signed a new law that will go into effect April 1, 1984.

deny these rights are subject to court action for damages under the Civil Rights Act of 1871.[38]

State and local governments had 5,030,564, or 48.4 percent of all full-time employees, who were members of labor unions or employee organizations in 1980, an increase of 0.6 percent from 1975. There were 14,302 state and local governments that either engaged in collective negotiations or participated in meet-and-confer discussions with representatives of the employees. School districts are the most organized, followed by municipalities and state governments.[39] Table 14.3 demonstrates that the percentage of union membership is higher in local governments than in state governments, with the exception of employees in highway departments and hospitals. Overall, in both state and local government, the highest percentage of membership is in education, fire protection, and police protection. Yet, collective bargaining in state and local governments is far from universal; only 17.9 percent of the 79,928 state and local units engage in collective negotiations and hold meet-and-confer sessions with employee representatives.[40]

State and Local Government Labor Relations Policies, Statutes, Executive Orders, and Ordinances

State and local government units and labor units may establish their labor relations framework in several ways: by policy, statute, executive order, or ordinance. By 1975, 15 percent of the local governments had labor relations policies or related guidelines, whereas 88 percent of the state governments and 48 percent of the nation's school districts had policies.

An analysis of the existing laws and policies suggests that favorable legislation is concentrated in the states located in the Northeast, North, Midwest, West Coast, Alaska, and Hawaii. The so-called sunbelt states, located in the lower Atlantic Coast, Southeast (except the state of Florida), Southwest, and lower Rocky Mountains, generally do not have labor relations legislation that compre-

Table 14.3 Percentage of Full-Time Employees Organized by Function and Level of Government, 1980

Function	State and Local Governments	State Governments	Local Governments
Total	48.8	40.5	51.9
Education	55.4	29.6	61.3
Highways	45.0	52.9	37.6
Public Welfare	41.8	41.2	42.4
Hospitals	40.0	49.8	29.4
Police Protection	52.7	51.9	52.8
Local Fire Protection	70.6	—	70.6
Sanitation Other Than Sewerage	40.2	—	40.2
All Other Functions	39.4	41.4	38.3

Source: U.S. Department of Commerce, Bureau of the Census, Labor-Management Relations in State and Local Governments: 1980 (Washington, D.C.: Government Printing Office, 1981), p. 2.

hensively covers the public sector (that is, covering administrative agency, bargaining rights, scope of bargaining, impasse provisions, unfair labor practices, and strike provisions).[41]

Thirty-eight states and the District of Columbia have statutes or executive orders that provide for collective bargaining for at least one group of employees. However, *de facto* bargaining occurs in the other states or cities.[42] Most states prescribed bargaining over wages, hours, terms of employment, and working conditions for some or all public employees. However, a majority of the states have statutory limitations on the scope of collective bargaining, such as management rights.[43]

Another important element of labor legislation is unfair labor practices. Although these vary somewhat from state to state, most states (thirty-five) have legislation defining unfair labor practices for some or all public employees. The existing legislation typically prohibits strikes. Exceptions to outright prohibition are twofold: either they are not mentioned in the statute, or the states (Alaska, Hawaii, Idaho, Minnesota, Montana, Oregon, Pennsylvania, Vermont, and Wisconsin) allow strikes only under specific circumstances.

In eight states, Delaware, Georgia, Indiana, Maryland, Minnesota, New York, Oklahoma, and Virginia, mandatory penalties are levied against striking government employees.[44] For example, New York's Taylor Law prohibits work stoppages and provides penalties against both the strikers—loss of two days pay for each day on strike, loss of tenure and job security protections—and the union—suspension of dues checkoff.[45]

Many states have sanctions varying from injunctions to dismissals, jail sentences, substantial fines, and loss of union recognition when a strike occurs. An investigation of teacher strikes revealed that increasing the level of sanctions against strikers reduces strike activity up to a point, but beyond that point, more strikes, not fewer, occur. The reason for this occurrence seems to be that severe sanctions are seldom enforced, but more moderate ones are. Thus, it seems that strikes can be reduced if moderate, enforceable sanctions are provided.[46]

Municipal and county policies tend to have similar provisions and coverage. The bargaining obligation is enforced by an administrative agency and includes either the duty to bargain or to meet and confer over such topics as wages, hours, and terms of employment. Strikes are usually prohibited, and procedures have been established in the event an impasse occurs.

Without legislation enabling collective bargaining, unions have difficulty maintaining their membership, collecting dues, and entering into agreements with public officials. Some unions survived adverse court decisions and the lack of favorable enabling legislation by representing their members in grievance procedures and becoming involved in political activities.[47] The absence of a clear, easily applied recognition procedure frequently leads to much unproductive and unnecessary bickering among the parties. Unfortunately, this bickering "spills over" into other areas, causing high absences and distrust between parties when bargaining finally occurs.[48]

Provisions in Collective Bargaining Agreements—State, County, and Municipal Employees

Unions representing state, county, and municipal employees generally negotiate collective bargaining agreements similar to those negotiated in the private sector. These agreements in the public sector fall into two categories: (a) contractual agreements and (b) memoranda of understanding. A Census Bureau study reported 27,274 agreements in effect between state and local governments and their respective employee organizations in 1980 and 7,477 memoranda of understanding.[49] Although specific bargaining items, such as merit system subjects, are often excluded by statute, most issues are quite similar to those negotiated in the private sector.[50]

Many bargaining issues cut across public employee job classifications. Wages, for example, are a concern of state, local, and county employees regardless of their particular job duties. However, as indicated in Chapter 1, the technological features of the workplace can generate certain unique work rules and concerns. For example, firefighters and police are often more concerned than other public employees about safety provisions. In 1975, nearly 50 percent of all firefighters were injured on the job.[51] Labor and management officials have explored technological advances (improved fire hose nozzles, fire coats, chemicals, and so on); however, many of these improvements require rather large expenditures. For example, one company has introduced "Rapid Water," a chemical additive that reduces friction in the fire hoses, resulting in 50 percent more flow with the same pump pressure. Yet only a few of the nation's approximately 25,000 fire departments spent funds to obtain this system.[52]

Police are also concerned about safety problems; a recent demand by a Washington, D.C., policemen's union sought two related proposals: (a) better marksmanship training and (b) deadlier, "all-lead semi-wadcutter" bullets, which are used in other cities.[53] In some cases, safety issues can involve broader issues of management's right to schedule and direct the working force. One of the more emotional issues in police negotiations concerns one-person versus two-person squad cars. Management wants the freedom to assign one-person cars on the basis of crime data reported for various areas and shifts. The unions want two-person cars to maximize patrolman safety under unsafe street conditions.[54] Police are also concerned about other job-related issues, for example, the benefit of "false-arrest" insurance.[55]

Types of Impasse Procedures: Description and Effectiveness

Although statutes usually prohibit public employee strikes, policy makers recognize that neither no-strike legislation nor related penalties for striking are sufficient for obtaining labor peace. Consequently, impasse procedures are established in many states and localities as a substitute for the strike alternative.[56] These procedures normally involve a third party who assists the parties in reaching an agreement without interrupting services or endangering the public interest.

Public sector impasse procedures are controversial and have received considerable attention; they have been instituted in thirty-eight states. The most popular impasse procedure combines mediation, fact-finding, and arbitration (available in twenty states); a variety of other forms also exist: arbitration only (eight states), fact-finding only (seven states), mediation and fact-finding (nine states).[57]

Mediation The oldest and most common public sector impasse procedure, *mediation* works much like the process in the private sector in that a neutral attempts to persuade the parties to a labor dispute to settle their own differences. In these efforts, the mediator keeps the talks going, translates and analyzes positions and proposals, helps identify what is important and what is expendable, assists each party's evaluation of a particular issue, influences the bargaining climate, makes suggestions, exerts pressure where and when necessary, and remains even-handed and neutral.[58]

Parties, rather than mediators, play the dominant roles in shaping the mediation process, especially when the negotiators are experienced, and have a clear understanding of their interests and bargaining objectives. Where the parties are less experienced and somewhat unsophisticated, the personal qualities and strategies of the mediator have greater influence.[59]

The advantages of public sector mediation are also similar to those found in the private sector[60] (discussed in Chapter 7). Mediation has worked well in those disputes where the parties were inexperienced in labor relations and unsure of themselves, lacked knowledge of contract language, and were susceptible to personality conflicts. It has been less successful where strong pressures from constituents were present, resources were scarce, and sophisticated negotiators who could manipulate the procedures to their own tactical advantage were involved. This can be especially true when mediation is followed by another impasse procedure, such as by fact-finding or arbitration.[61] In comparison, mediation works better when followed by arbitration than by fact-finding, especially when the type of arbitration is final offer selection.[62]

The style of the mediator can have an effect on the results of a negotiation. Where disputes are difficult or subject to another impasse resolution procedure after mediation, intense mediator behavior is critical for success; low-intensity mediators are of little use. In tough disputes, high-intensity mediation tends to result in lower negotiated settlements, whereas in easy disputes, mediation appears to increase the settlement. While mediation is not the only answer to public sector impasses, intense mediator behavior appears to be effective in difficult negotiations or ones subject to impasse procedures beyond mediation.[63]

Mediation has been used quite often in local and state government negotiations. For example, the Federal Mediation and Conciliation Service (FMCS) has reported dramatic increases in numbers of cases closed. Because the FMCS will generally defer to state and local agencies if they are available, the largest percentage of cases for this agency have occurred in states having either new public collective bargaining laws or active unions but no applicable laws.[64] However, there are other indications of the success of mediation as a process of dispute resolution. In New York, 30 percent of all negotiations eventually resulted in an impasse, and half of these (or 15 percent of the total) were settled by mediation. This percentage does not include all those disputes settled prior to impasse with the assistance of mediators.[65]

Fact-Finding and Arbitration Fact-finding and arbitration are separate impasse resolution procedures; however, they are discussed and assessed jointly because of their many similarities. *Fact-finding*, the second most used type of impasse procedure, is a process in which a neutral (a fact finder) conducts a hearing where management and the union define the issues in dispute and each party proposes its own resolutions supported with evidence and justifications. The fact finder then studies the materials provided and in many cases structures a position on the basis of what management and union should accept.[66] However, these recommendations are not binding, and the parties may accept them or not.[67]

This procedure is similar in many respects to arbitration: both procedures are quasi-judicial in that both management and the union have similar obligations in preparing and proving their respective cases, and both parties are bound by similar concepts of conduct and evidence in defending their positions. Also, the neutrals have similar roles in that they must objectively assess the evidence and in many cases develop rationales for their eventual decisions. The fundamental difference between the two processes is that arbitration is final and binding and by definition terminates the impasse, whereas fact-finding is terminal only if both parties agree to conform to the fact finder's report and recommendation.[68] Because of its lack of finality, fact-finding has been criticized as an impasse resolution procedure. It has, in fact, been used to delay genuine negotiations.

Arbitration of negotiation impasses (interest arbitration) can be classified as voluntary or compulsory and as conventional or final offer selection.[69] In *voluntary arbitration*, the parties voluntarily agree to submit issues to a third party neutral for dispute resolution, whereas in *compulsory arbitration* the parties are required by statute, city ordinance, or court decree to submit unresolved issues to arbitration. *Conventional interest arbitration* involves submitting the issues in dispute to the arbitrator, who will make a settlement, based on the proposals presented by the parties, within the extremes of the public employer's and the union's last offers. Often, interest arbitrators have been accused of compromising or splitting the difference between these offers in an attempt to please everybody.

Final offer selection (FOS) arbitration is a relatively new procedure in which the union submits its final demand for settlement and management submits its final offer to the arbitrator, who selects the most reasonable final offer without modifications.[70] It attempts to make the failure to agree more expensive by eliminating the arbitrator's discretion and avoiding any arbitral compromise whatsoever. The theory on which this type of arbitration is based is that each party will develop a more realistic final position, hoping their positions will converge because they both want their position accepted by the arbitrator. Both parties bargain in earnest up to the point of arbitration, increasing the chances that they will resolve or at least reduce their differences.[71]

There are two types of FOS arbitration. The first requires each party to submit its last best package and the arbitrator chooses from one of these offers. Four states (Wisconsin, Massachusetts, Nevada, and New Jersey) allow the use of this approach. The second type allows the parties to submit their last best offer, but the arbitrators *may* select one of the offers or make a settlement on an issue by issue basis from the last best offers. Four states (Connecticut, Iowa, Michigan, and New Jersey) allow this form of settlement.[72]

Fact-finding and arbitration share several basic advantages that help to show why they have gained acceptance in the public sector:

1. Both help to conclude the negotiations process, which could otherwise drag on indefinitely, since they give the parties deadlines for resolving their differences.
2. The neutrals in both processes provide fresh viewpoints and approaches to the unresolved issues. Because of their experience in similar situations, many are able to provide insights to the issues not available from the parties themselves.

3. These processes can offer the parties political advantages in resolving their impasses. Both the public employer and the union can use the neutral as a buck-passing device for the eventual settlement—they can blame the fact finder or the arbitrator instead of themselves if they don't receive a completely desirable settlement. In some cases, the union and management negotiators are in close agreement; however, they need to persuade their constituents that the settlement is equitable. Fact-finding can help structure public opinion and prepare the public for the negotiated settlements.
4. The mere possibility of these procedures may encourage the parties to resolve the dispute on their own. This would particularly be the case if one or both of the parties feared the neutral outsider would not understand its position. Thus, fact-finding or arbitration may serve to keep the parties "honest" in attempting to resolve their differences.[73]

Fact-finding and arbitration also have their disadvantages. Although they may resolve issues for the short run, both procedures have been accused of leaving the two parties in disharmony.

1. If either party is not receptive to the fact finder's report or the arbitrator's decision, the basic causes of their differences have not been resolved—much negotiation remains to settle the real differences. A related concern is that neither process can guarantee that there will be no strike, slow-down, sick-in, blue flu, or similar tactic. Fact finders have no binding authority over the parties, and arbitrators usually do not have access to information that accurately sets priorities for the true interests and preferences of the parties.
2. Fact-finding and arbitration tend to cement positions, because the parties believe that there is a possibility of getting a better deal from the arbitrator or a more favorable report from the fact finder.[74] Instead of earnestly attempting to resolve their differences in the final negotiations, the representatives focus their time and thoughts on preparing for the fact finder or arbitrator.
3. The role of the fact finder or arbitrator has often been challenged, since these individuals are not held accountable for their decisions. Neither is elected by the taxpayers, and often the official comes from a different town or state. Many politicians have claimed that they do not want to give the keys to the government's treasury to an "outsider" or a "limousine liberal," who makes the decision and then leaves town.[75]

Variation in Procedures In the public sector few jurisdictions have the same arbitration scheme. Within the FOS approach there are several variations. In some cases, the parties are permitted to submit several final offers. Another variation specifies the number of steps that may be used. For example, the State of Iowa mandates the intermediary step of fact-finding between mediation and FOS arbitration. Where mediation and fact-finding fail, the dispute proceeds to FOS arbitration at either party's request. Further, the FOS arbitrator may select the fact finder's recommendation or one of the final offers from union or management.[76] Other variations include use of a single arbitrator or a panel, selection on an ad hoc or permanent basis, different criteria to be used by arbitrators and fact finders, and the range of issues subject to arbitration.[77]

Effectiveness of fact-finding and arbitration Describing impasse procedures is much simpler than assessing their effectiveness for two main reasons: (1) there are problems in obtaining relevant operational data, and (2) it is difficult to control for the many variables that influence the bargaining process and outcomes.[78] Generally, it can be concluded that:

An effective impasse procedure raises the cost to at least one of the parties of continuing to disagree and, perhaps, at the same time, lowers the cost to the other party of agreeing voluntarily.[79]

Union and management officials are likely to push disputes to the last step of an impasse procedure when one or both parties:

- Are uncertain of future costs of continued collective bargaining (a situation which particularly applies to inexperienced negotiators).[80]
- Expect to receive a better settlement through the impasse procedure.
- Need to pass the blame for an "unfavorable" settlement to a third party neutral instead of accepting personal responsibility for the results.[81]

Assessing fact-finding is particularly difficult. Its effectiveness does not hinge on the fact finder's ability; this individual is presented facts by the parties in hopes that he or she will agree with their respective positions. The success of such a procedure is based on the assumption that the fact finder's report will structure public opinion, which will in turn place pressure on the parties to resolve their differences in accord with published recommendations. Thus far, there is no concrete evidence to show that public pressure has noticeably affected public sector management and union officials. Indeed, one experienced fact finder has observed:

I do not view fact-finding as being quite the exact science your administrative agency believes (or hopes) it to be. For these [*sic*] of you who have visions of becoming cultural heroes as a result of your peacemaking efforts, you are probably in for a disappointment. In most instances such status will be rudely denied you—by the parties, by the public, and most grievously, by your fellow fact finders. Fact-finding, in short, is not an endeavor that flatters the ego. As for the distinctive contribution of your carefully wrought analysis, most of you, I suspect, will eventually come around to the view, as I have, that aside from poison [pen] letters and ransom notes, there is probably no literary form in which there is less pride of authorship than a fact-finding report.[82]

Studies conducted in two states (New York and Wisconsin) found that both labor and management officials have rejected relatively high proportions of fact finders' recommendations (39 percent and 51 percent respectively).[83] A similar, more recent observation of Florida's experience found an even higher rate of fact finder rejections.[84] Over the years, acceptance of fact-finding as a dispute resolution procedure dwindles, especially when there is a high percentage of rejection and where parties incorporate fact-finding into their bargaining tactics (primarily to postpone a settlement).[85]

Overall, interest arbitration in the public sector seems to have passed the test, at least in the short run; most of the participants as well as the analysts have been satisfied with the process. It has not substantially lessened serious negotiations despite its availability. Also, the number of strikes has been reduced substantially in cases where employees have been covered by compulsory arbitration legislation. Even though some management officials feared arbitration, arbitrators have not stripped them of their rights and authority. The settlements have not been significantly greater than the parties would have reached themselves in similar circumstances, and the public in general has not openly indicated displeasure with the process. Most significantly, arbitration has been increasingly adopted as an impasse resolution procedure in the public sector, and the parties express satisfaction with the initial experience.[86]

One of the bigger concerns about public sector interest arbitration is its *chilling effect* on the parties' incentives to reach their own agreement. If either believed that it could get a better settlement from an arbitrator than from negotiation, there would be an incentive to maintain excessive demands in hopes that the arbitrator would "split the difference" and make a favorable award. When one side acts in such a manner, the other side has no realistic choice but to respond similarly, widening the gap between the parties.[87]

Research into this arbitral aspect has produced mixed results. An analysis of arbitral decisions regarding police impasses found that some management officials are reluctant to negotiate their best offer before arbitration on the assumption that the arbitrators will use management's final offer as a starting point in their decisions.[88] Yet this concern is somewhat dampened by a study of several arbitration awards of firefighter interest disputes, which revealed that a large majority of arbitrators take an intermediate or compromise stance between the union's and management's stance on a few negotiation issues, such as wages and clothing allowances. However, arbitration settlements did not compromise the other issues; they either supported management's or the union's final position. It seems that there is no guarantee that arbitrators will compromise any or all of the issues presented for their decisions.[89]

Another concern about public sector interest arbitration is that the mere existence of impasse procedures could create a *narcotic effect.* That is, once the parties start using the procedures, they become increasingly reliant upon them in subsequent negotiations. In New York, the impasse procedure covering police and firefighters changed from fact-finding with recommendations followed by hearings to fact-finding terminating in conventional compulsory arbitration.

This switch to arbitration in the first year resulted in an increased probability of going to impasse and to the final step of the procedure by approximately 16 percent. Research revealed a definite narcotic effect pattern of reusage of impasse procedure.[90] However, researchers found no more of a chilling effect under arbitration than under fact-finding in New York.[91]

Several states (Iowa, Massachusetts, Michigan, Minnesota, and Wisconsin) and at least two municipalities (Indianapolis and Eugene, Oregon) have had experience with final offer selection arbitration. Experiences in these settings as compared to conventional interest arbitration have been analyzed closely by Peter Feuille, who concluded:

Final offer arbitration does a reasonably good job of protecting the parties' incentives to negotiate but . . . it does not operate as effectively as its theoretical rationale suggests it could. . . .

However, over time there seems to be a general tendency for the parties to increase their reliance upon the final-offer procedures either as a forum for continued negotiations or as a source of an imposed settlement. This increased usage may be related to the lack of costs attached to declaring impasse and using the early steps of the impasse procedure.[92]

After examining data from the city of Eugene, Oregon, and the states of Wisconsin and Massachusetts, Feuille and James Dworkin found little support for the criticism that final offer arbitrators tend to balance the winners and losers over a longer period of time.[93] Permanent FOS arbitrators have been criticized of "flip-flopping" their awards—awarding the decision to one party the first time and to the other party the next time—so that they can be reasonably assured of receiving future assignments.[94]

The multi-step procedure in Iowa was studied over a five-year period, and it was concluded that the parties modify their positions only slightly from fact-finding to FOS arbitration and that FOS arbitrators are likely to affirm the recommendation of the fact finder. Two criticisms are that the availability of fact-finding delays serious bargaining until after the fact-finding procedure is complete and that compromise-oriented fact finders' recommendations create a new negotiating floor above which the union attempts to settle.[95]

Arbitrator Fred Witney concluded from his experiences in Indianapolis, Indiana, that final offer arbitration is successful in that it has been accepted by the parties, prevented strikes, and resulted in no subsequent work slowdowns or interruptions of services. Yet he also felt that arbitration would be more effective if arbitrators were given more flexibility in which to rule on the merits of the multitude of issues to be decided.[96]

Flexibility, however, is relative, and arbitrator Theodore Kheel believes at least some guidance is needed to insure that the arbitration award is realistic and appropriate. He found when he served as the first arbitrator to be appointed under the applicable 1968 statute in Pennsylvania that there were no guidelines regarding wage determination. The union contended that the arbitrator should determine what a policeman is worth in today's society. Management, on the other hand, argued that the arbitrator should be guided by the fiscal responsibilities and limitations of the deficit-ridden municipal government. Without guidelines, the arbitrator's award could have been grossly out of line with either management's or the union's legitimate concerns.[97] The degree of arbitral flexibility should possibly depend on the nature of the issues to be resolved. For example, a study in Eugene, Oregon, found that certain "yes-no" positions, such as the union's insistence on agency shop (a worker does not join the union but pays a service fee equal to dues) versus the city's proposal for maintenance of membership shop (once joining the union, a member must continue membership for the duration of the contract), are difficult to resolve through final offer selection arbitration.[98]

Referendum Another impasse resolution procedure places the unresolved issues on a taxpayer referendum or vote. The following item, for example, might be placed on a ballot: "Do you approve of granting a wage increase of 'X' cents per hour to our police officers at an estimated additional annual cost to property taxpayers of 'Y' millions?"[99]

This procedure would avoid the problems of an outsider (fact finder or arbitrator) determining the cost of a negotiated settlement. Citizens could not complain if the union's settlement was achieved in a democratic manner. Similarly, the union's integrity would be at stake if it refused to abide by the "will of the public." Yet, this procedure could turn collective bargaining into a public relations campaign directed at a body of individuals (citizens) largely unfamiliar with labor relations' complexities. Further, the procedure has no precedent in private sector labor relations, since no company submits labor agreement proposals to a stockholder vote.

Referenda, or direct submission to the electorate for final and binding settlement of labor-related issues, have been used in several Texas cities for over thirty years. Employees have won over two-thirds of the elections involving civil service and bonus issues, but lost 56.6 percent where the issue was pay parity.[100] Other cities have used this method, but assessment of this approach has not been favorable. First, the electorate has little understanding of the law and the issues and are highly susceptible to propaganda compaigns by both parties. Second, the referendum appears to help make the strong stronger and the weak weaker without regard for what is equitable or reasonable for all the parties involved.[101]

Additional Options While mediation, arbitration, and fact-finding remain the most commonly used procedures, various states have started to experiment with other forms of impasse procedures. For example, Massachusetts provides mediation followed by final offer selection arbitration. Hawaii and other states allow some strikes after mediation and/or fact-finding have been tried. The New Jersey law that covers police and firefighters allows the parties to choose from a variety of options: final offer package, final offer issue by issue, final offer on some issues, conventional arbitration, and so on. Iowa allows parties to negotiate their own impasse procedures for local use. While there are many options, there is no single best way to resolve labor disputes. However, the multiple objectives remain the same: to avoid strikes, to minimize dependence on outsiders, to maximize "good faith" bargaining between parties, to protect the public interest, and to build a commitment to accountability and mutual problem solving.[102]

This section on labor relations in state and local governments included a brief description of historical development; status of union membership; labor relations policies, statutes, executive orders, and ordinances; the subjects in collective bargaining; and the variety of impasse procedures. While labor relations in state and local governments is rapidly developing and offers unique complexities for students to consider, the following section provides specific application to a sector of society with which students should immediately identify—the academic community.

Labor Relations Application to the Academic Community: Teachers and Professors

In this labor relations application, teachers at the elementary and high school levels and professors at the college level are treated as one occupational group, because they share many common working conditions. However, some characteristics and working conditions unique to different educational levels will be discussed when appropriate. Collective bargaining has also involved students, research and graduate student assistants, and college administrators at some campuses, but space limitations do not allow discussion in this section.

Development and Growth of Unions in the Teaching Profession

While teachers' unions date back to the late nineteenth century, it was not until the 1960s that many teachers turned to collective bargaining to resolve issues in education. One of the early attempts for union recognition and negotiation involved the Norwalk, Connecticut, teachers in 1946. The school board refused to recognize and negotiate with the teacher organization, which in turn appealed to the state supreme court. The court decided that the board could negotiate if it so desired but the teachers could not force the board to negotiate. Furthermore, it ruled that the board had full authority to make decisions concerning school matters and this authority could not be delegated. The court agreed that the board could bargain collectively over wages, hours, and employment conditions but only the school board had authority to make decisions.[103] However, teachers through collective bargaining could provide useful inputs for these decisions.

The Norwalk decision publicized teacher unionization, but the major breakthrough occurred in New York City in 1961. After considerable negotiations and a strike, the board of education accepted collective bargaining and agreed to an election for choosing a bargaining agent. The United Federation of Teachers—a local of the American Federation of Teachers (AFT)—won an overwhelming victory for its members, representing over 30,000 teachers.

The increasing acceptability of collective bargaining resulted in professional teacher associations changing their emphasis to traditional union concerns. The National Education Association (NEA)—an AFT rival—had begun as a general advocate for public education and emphasized professionalism. For 100 years, it considered itself a professional organization, not a proponent for such issues as higher teacher salaries. Slowly the AFT, a more militant, teacher-centered union, began attracting NEA members who were interested in improving their economic situation. In response to the growing threat from the AFT, the NEA shifted its priorities to advocate collective bargaining and to accept the strike as a legitimate means of resolving negotiation impasses.[104] AFT and the NEA had by 1977 grown to be among the largest employee organizations in the United States, with 441,000 and 1,679,689 members, respectively.[105]

The success of secondary and elementary school teachers prompted college and university faculty members to become more interested in engaging in collective bargaining activities. By 1982, 157,000 faculty members were covered by collective bargaining agreements.[106] In 1981, unions had been chosen to represent the faculty on 737 campuses; on only 94 had they been rejected.[107] The biggest successes have been at two-year community colleges, but key victories have also occurred at some of the largest and most respected schools in the country (State University of New York, University of Hawaii, Temple University, Rutgers University, State University System of Florida, University of Massachusetts, and University of Illinois). In several states (Massachusetts, New Jersey, Connecticut, Rhode Island, New York, Delaware, and Hawaii) most public institutions of higher education are organized. Similarly, with the exception of large research-oriented universities, most institutions of higher education in Michigan, Pennsylvania, and Minnesota are organized.[108] However, unionism in higher education has remained mostly in public institutions where state laws permit collective bargaining.

Most organizable units have been unionized in those states which have supporting legislation. It seems improbable that major research universities in states with supporting legislation will vote for union representation, as suggested by union rejection at UCLA, Berkeley, University of Minnesota, and Michigan State University.[109]

In the private sector, the Supreme Court rejected the NLRB's position regarding faculty representation rights under the National Labor Relations Act in 1980, and ruled that faculty at Yeshiva University were managerial employees.[110] The controlling consideration by the Court was whether the Yeshiva faculty exercised authority which would be considered managerial. It claimed that the decision-making authority of faculty at Yeshiva was typical of a mature university and this authority qualified them for managerial status, therefore excluding them from coverage under the National Labor Relations Act.[111]

Since the *Yeshiva* decision, about forty private colleges and universities—about one-half of the private institutions where faculties engage in collective bargaining—have claimed that their faculty have managerial status. In addition, thirty of these institutions have cases pending before the NLRB and are claiming that the faculty should not be covered under the National Labor Relations Act and therefore have no bargaining rights. In these cases, the NLRB used the following guideline questions to determine whether faculty members are entitled to bargaining rights:

1. Does the faculty formulate, determine, and effectuate managerial decisions, such as curriculum development, selection of administrators, and promotion and tenure decisions?
2. Do the faculty members act in the interest of the employer?
3. Are the faculty members held accountable for conforming with managerial policies?
4. What percentage of faculty time is spent on exercising authority?[112]

By 1982, five cases had been decided by the NLRB. The faculty at three institutions (Ithaca College, Thiel College, and Duquesne University's law school) were considered managerial, and two (Bradford College and Montefiore Hospital and Medical Center) were determined to be employees under the Act, therefore having rights to union representation.[113] Thus, NLRB post-*Yeshiva* decisions have formed a clearer definition of employer and employee and resulting bargaining units in private higher education. Consequently, academic collective bargaining will come closer to the industrial model.[114]

When the NLRB decided in 1970 to assert jurisdiction over private, nonprofit colleges and universities, it admitted openly that it was venturing into uncharted areas.[115] The same could have been said about public education institutions in various states with no statutory guidance or with state laws widely varied in content.[116] Whether they will continue to grow as in the past few years will depend on the following factors:

- Salary levels keeping up with prices.
- Success in organizing areas that have been difficult to organize, for example, the South and Southwest.[117]

- Increases in the number of states having public employee bargaining laws, since collective bargaining tactics depend on having established and recognized unions.[118]
- Improvements in union organizing efforts, such as more funds, reduction in union rivalry, and possible merging of efforts.
- Continuing reductions in educators' positions and relative salaries caused by falling student population and shifting public interests and attitudes.
- Continuing attacks on tenure and other forms of job security and protective policies by administrators.[119]
- The extent to which NLRB decisions affect jurisdiction over private colleges and universities.

Bargaining Units

Deciding the appropriate bargaining unit in elementary and secondary schools has not been as complex as in higher education, but it has been complicated by the ambiguous role of the principal. The principal represents the board of education and school superintendents in many situations and then joins the teachers in other situations. Principals' status is further complicated by the failure of most state laws to prescribe whether they should be included with the teachers, organize a union of their own, or remain separate from the teachers and represent the board and superintendents. Whatever the situation, they have a key role in any negotiations that affect the policies, programs, and working climate of their schools.[120]

Defining the appropriate bargaining unit in higher education is often a complex task given the collegial decision-making process and relatively active role played by faculty members in the government of the institution.

Collective bargaining in higher education is governed by twenty-four separate laws. Some 75 percent of the established bargaining units are multi-campus; 90 percent contain personnel in addition to full-time teaching and research faculty. Part-time instructors and graduate students are usually excluded from the bargaining units of faculty, and the department heads' status varies. Also, professional schools, such as law and medicine, are usually allowed to form separate bargaining units.[121] In some cases, unions represent only the nonprofessional staff and employees.

While faculty unions have direct influence on specific issues in collective bargaining, they also have an effect on the institutions in other areas: more staff positions to accommodate collective bargaining, more training for administrators to develop expertise in dealing with unions, closer coordination between various administrative functions and implementation of personnel policies and procedures, and greater centralization of benefits.[122]

Issues

The provisions of labor agreements in education are similar to those in other occupations in many ways; nonetheless, some provisions (for instance, those on faculty governance, types and duties of committees, selection and duties of administrators, content and access to personnel files, faculty reduction, overload, compensation for extra courses, academic freedom, office space, and professional development[123]) are unique to educators. In elementary and secondary schools, additional issues may include definition of the school day and year, number and duration of after-school meetings, nonteaching duties such as bus duty and selling tickets at athletic events, competency testing, rotation of classes, selection of textbooks, class size and teaching loads, curriculum development, student discipline, preparation time, use of free time, use of automated teaching methodologies, access to personnel files, and teacher evaluation.[124]

In the early 1980s, teachers' unions were fighting just to keep what they had gained over the years. The climate of declining enrollments, diminishing tax bases, and federal education cutbacks changed negotiated settlements drastically. School districts attempted to gain concessions from teachers in the form of pay freezes, benefits reductions, and even salary cuts. With such limited resources available, strikes also became an unattractive option. While there were 242 strikes in 1979–1980, there were 191 in 1980–1981, and only 65 in fall 1982.[125]

Discipline One of the more significant employment concerns of elementary and secondary teachers relates to student discipline and violence. One estimate of expenditures to repair school vandalism ($590 million) exceeded the total amount spent on textbooks that year.[126] Student violence and vandalism might reflect more permissive parental and administrative attitudes that in turn can make it more difficult for teachers to adequately perform their duties. Comments from teachers tend to reflect this frustration:

Once you are in that classroom you're all alone. Lots of discipline problems go unreported: verbal assaults, a teacher gets shoved. Sometimes it's just easier to forget it all. If you complain or report it, there's always the implication that maybe you're incapable of handling your own problems. . . .

I taught one high school reading class where I could look out my window and watch kids getting high behind the trunk of one of the pine trees. When I complained about it, I was told that the kids hadn't been caught smoking marijuana and so nothing could be done. But all the principal had to do was come up to my classroom and look out the window; the principal couldn't be bothered to do that.[127]

Job Security Another issue confronting educators at all levels is job security. Academicians in higher education who are renowned consider job security irrelevant, since they are eagerly sought by many colleges and universities.[128] But most faculty members are not in this position, particularly those in disciplines supplying more applicants than available jobs. Recently, for example, there have been over 400 applications for one college-level English professorship, and some prestigious schools have received 5,000 applications for a similar position.[129]

As the school population has declined and the labor market changed, job security has been affected in other ways. First, institutions have rapidly increased use of part-time or adjunct instructors, who usually receive less money and need few if any supporting services such as office space or student assistants. Part-time instructors also contribute to administrative flexibility because they can be hired for specific courses and dismissed after the course is completed.[130]

Second, more schools appear to be restricting new faculty positions and the number of instructors who can receive tenure.[131] Tenure has been criticized by some as a device that locks an inept professor into a job for life with no possibility of removal, whereas it is supported by advocates as the only way to provide true academic freedom. Actually, tenured faculty members *can* be removed for incompetency or unprofessional conduct (but only for just cause) and only after due process procedures are fulfilled. In such cases, the discharge of a tenured faculty member places the burden of proof on academic administrators to justify their decisions.[132]

The tenure and just cause concepts have long been challenged in the courts by both tenured and nontenured teachers (for example, single, female teachers who were discharged because they were pregnant) who believe they have inherent rights to their jobs.[133] Judicial decisions on such cases appear to be contradictory; however, teachers continue to seek due process redress in the courts. Unions continue to approach the tenure issue in collective bargaining by seeking formal justification in cases where tenure is denied[134] and by clarifying the peer review process.[135]

Lately, faculty member first amendment rights have become critical issues; in fact, there were more cases involving these rights in 1981 than any year since the McCarthy era of the 1950s. Because many colleges were considering or executing reductions in force, courts were faced with the issue of balancing an institution's authority to deny tenure and discharge or discipline faculty members with the teacher's right to academic freedom and the right to keep confidential his or her vote on the granting or denial of tenure to another faculty member.[136]

Negotiations

Although the inclusion of these issues in a labor agreement formalizes the policies and procedures, many teachers and administrators have found that collective bargaining is time-consuming and costly, particularly in terms of negotiators' preparation. Some factors influencing the length of negotiations are the scope of prior agreement, the degree of impasse, the bargaining itself, team changes during negotiations, and the extent to which professionals are used in the bargaining process.[137] Negotiations might be prolonged over issues such as compensation for extra duty, teacher work loads, length of the school day, association and union rights, grievance procedures, salary, fringe benefits, paid leaves, and roll-back of previous rights.[138]

Collective bargaining might also be delayed when unions are unable to locate the appropriate managerial decision maker—as frequently happens in the bargaining process. In some cases, the union negotiates with administrators who do not have authority to sign a bargaining agreement; in others, it is prohibited from negotiating with officials who do have the authority to approve the agreement. A recent Supreme Court decision has held that a school board meeting open to the public cannot exclude teachers from presenting their opinions on the collective bargaining sessions and agreement.[139] Therefore, teachers can go directly to the board and present their bargaining demands.

Strikes and Teacher Militancy

Strikes are infrequent in education, although the ones that occur receive much publicity. For example, the 152 strikes in 1977–1978 represented less than 1 percent of the total teacher bargaining relationships.[140] There have been a number of attempts to identify predictors and causes of strikes and teacher militancy. Research suggests that the propensity to strike is influenced by personal characteristics of the strikers. For example, support for strikes has been greatest among male teachers, younger teachers, teachers with advanced degrees, and junior and senior high school teachers.[141] Other studies, however, question whether the teacher's personal characteristics explain strike activity.[142] This research suggests that more general environmental factors (such as general labor market conditions, consumer prices, and a permissive bargaining climate[143]) help explain the frequency of teacher strikes.

The relatively few strikes in higher education have involved mostly the two-year community colleges represented by the American Federation of Teachers. Generally, the difficulties in reaching agreement can be traced to either the lack of experience of the negotiators on the first contract or the wage issue. Most of these strikes have been brief and have caused little loss in enrollment or faculty salary; they have occurred mostly at the beginning of the fall term, some causing a postponement of fall opening, temporary closing of college dormitories and food services, and rescheduling of classes to compensate for lost time; but thus far no fall sessions have been cancelled by strikes.[144]

This new militancy and aggressive behavior in negotiations and organizing efforts have generally resulted from a number of factors. One significant factor is the attitude of university administrators toward faculty unions. Some evidence suggests that administrators tend to view them in negative terms, although a more positive administrator response tends to be found at universities with collective bargaining experience.[145]

In many cases, initial labor-management relations in this occupation do not differ from similar relationships in the private sector. Administrators become upset when employees express dissatisfaction by joining a union, and union leaders have to take a strong antimanagement stance to prove their mettle. Thus, the initial negotiations are often conducted in an atmosphere of bitterness. For example, in one such incident, the union leader called the university president the "Idi Amin of Higher Education." The university president responded by asking the professors, "Do you want to be guided by degenerate fools?"[146]

Militancy and hostile collective bargaining attitudes among teachers may also be affected by one or more of the following interrelated factors:

- Teachers' beliefs that unions will help them achieve better salaries and economic benefits.
- Demographic changes among teachers.
- Teachers' desire to have a stronger voice in formulating rules and policies that control their work lives.
- More favorable legislation concerning collective bargaining.
- Better training and educational preparation and increased emphasis on professionalism among teachers.
- AFT-NEA rivalry, causing each organization to become more aggressive and militant.
- Defensive reaction by teachers to the continuing and widespread ciriticism of public education at all levels.
- Changes in the climate of and attitudes toward collective actions and political activism, which have become both effective and fashionable.[147]
- Teacher reaction to tax reducing legislation and other tax-cutting measures.[148]

Effects of Collective Bargaining

Two areas of teacher collective bargaining that have had pronounced impact are wages and collegiality (shared administrative activities).

Wages Unions have had mixed success in increasing wages in education at a single location. Some studies have shown that academic unions have had little[149] or no[150] success in increasing wages, while others have reflected a markedly positive union influence on higher wages.[151] One study of teachers' wages in grades K through twelve revealed that wage differentials between union and nonunion teachers had reached between 12 and 20 percent by the late 1970s and during the 1974–1980 period real wages of unionized teachers increased while those of nonunion teachers declined. Attempting to identify the reasons for this wage differential, the researchers concluded that a combination of inflationary pressures, excess teacher supply, growth in legislation favorable to teacher bargaining, and maturity of teacher unions resulted in a significant increase in the union/nonunion wage differential in the 1970s.[152]

Collective bargaining has notably affected teachers' wage structure, if not total wages.[153] In some cases, proportionately higher wage increases have gone to the higher ranked and more senior faculty members.[154] In other cases, negotiated wage settlements have emphasized across-the-board increases that tended to deemphasize differences in teacher competency, experience, and academic discipline.

Union emphasis on across-the-board increases may pose problems for managements and unions, particularly in higher education. For example, some higher educational disciplines, such as medicine, business, engineering, and law have relatively few available applicants, particularly since academicians in these areas command much higher salaries in related private sector endeavors. While across-the-board increases may benefit the greatest number of union members, academic unions' long-term success will depend on the degree of membership consensus. Thus, the extent to which the market-privileged groups can influence the unions' egalitarian wage policies is still subject to speculation. There is a strong possibility that these groups will feel their wages proportionately lessened by across-the-board wage settlements, and their dissatisfaction may lead to internal union squabbles that could in turn undermine the success and existence of academic unions. Further, it could cause professors in high-demand disciplines to form separate unions to protect their privileged status.

Faculty Governance and Collegiality Faculty governance is a multi-level process that includes departmental, school, and college-wide participation, but faculty members participate primarily at the departmental level. The faculty senate, which has representatives from each department, usually carries out its tasks through departmental subgroups.[55] Collective bargaining has altered traditional forms of faculty governance. Many schools, particularly at the university level, have emphasized *collegiality*—an attitude that faculty should have input into administrative decisions (for instance, those involving course content, graduation requirements, and promotion of faculty members) because they have professional expertise and concerns. Collegiality has been traditionally fostered through two mechanisms: (a) faculty senates and (b) faculty committees (for example, the promotion and tenure committee).

Some maintain that collegiality is more symbol than substance,[156] since most if not all faculty recommendations can be vetoed by an administrative official such as the university president. Following this line of reasoning, administrators can use collegialty to their own benefit. Assume, for example, that the faculty promotion and tenure committee recommends that a particular faculty member not be promoted. The administrative official who has the final say on the matter can either overturn or support the committee's position. In either instance, the administrator's task is made easier. In overturning the committee's recommendation, the administrator will be a "good guy" in the eyes of the faculty member. The administrator can also absolve himself or herself of blame if he or she supports the committee's position by informing the faculty member that the decision to deny promotion was made by fellow faculty members.

Regardless of its actual usefulness, collegiality affects unions and vice versa. It can be contended that unions enhance collegiality, particularly if a grievance is subject to a neutral arbitrator (not the university administrator) for a final decision. Yet faculty unions, accepting the traditional union model, also realize that administrators are managers and the faculty members are employees. A strong union needs to present a unified protest of a particular administrative decision or action. Returning to our promotion example, assume the union grieves the promotion denial of the particular member. Its case is weakened or ruined if fellow union members on the promotion and tenure committee recommended that promotion be denied. Also, internal union dissension is increased when some members aid in an adverse managerial action taken against other union members.

Thus, unions may need to virtually eliminate the use of collegiality if they are to be successful.[157] If collegiality remains, then members can continually be played off against each other. A major problem arises when faculty members place a higher value on their continued collegial roles as quasi-managers than on potential gains offered by the union. Apparently, this situation has occurred at the State University of New York (SUNY) system, where fewer than 4,500 people of some 15,000 in the bargaining unit are dues-paying members.[158] The success of university unions will largely depend on their ability to resolve the collegiality issue in a manner satisfactory to most members and traditional union principles.

While it seems clear that the economic, political, and demographic conditions within a given state have more effect on the quality of education than does collective bargaining,[159] there are reasons for caution in pursuing negotiations. Collective bargaining, which is usually conducted in closed meetings, may raise the level of suspicion among students, parents, and the public and cause problems to all concerned with education. Furthermore, it could create an adversarial relationship between the administration and faculty, one which may not be suitable for dealing with complex and delicate education matters such as curriculum design, credits required for graduation, professional conduct, and grade inflation.[160]

The complexities of labor relations, requiring procedures and policies that must be administered accurately and carefully, could also lead to an increase in administrative bureaucracy. Because all personnel decisions must be fully documented and justified, labor agreements will become larger over time and the red tape will grow in length, breadth, and width. The burgeoning bureaucracy will mean additional costs, such as more time in preparation and negotiations, attorney fees, and training costs,[161] none of which are particularly attractive to an institution with limited resources.

Organizational Effectiveness

A controversial study of organizational effectiveness measures in 41 institutions of higher education in the northeastern United States revealed that unionized institutions were less effective at acquiring resources (donations and grants) from external sources than nonunion institutions. Further, institutions already receiving adequate resources were less likely to unionize. Student education satisfaction, faculty and administrator job satisfaction, and organizational health at the nonunion institution were high, low at the newly organized institution, and mid-ranged at the older unionized campus. This finding supports the belief that low satisfaction is associated with the faculty's desire to unionize. However, once the union is established, unionism is not associated with low morale and dissatisfaction.

The researcher concluded that nonunion institutions were considered highly effective academically; newly unionized institutions, less so; those unionized longest, least effective. Several reasons were given for this evaluation: (1) the presence of unions complicates the decision-making process and takes faculty time away from other activities; (2) research-oriented institutions tend to remain nonunion; (3) unions tend to emphasize economic and satisfaction issues in their negotiations; and (4) collegiallity among faculty after unionization is reduced, thereby inhibiting cooperative, scholarly work.

Thus, it is suggested that institutions high in effectiveness on academic dimensions, satisfaction indices, and ability to acquire resources tend to remain nonunion. When the institution is low in these dimensions, the faculty is motivated to unionize. After unionization, morale dimensions and ability to acquire resources improve, but not academic dimensions.[162] It will be interesting to observe whether faculty unions will counter these findings.

Summary and Implications

Summary

This chapter presented an overview of public sector labor relations and collective bargaining at the local and state levels, as well as specific coverage of a public sector segment with which college students can identify—academic unions.

Public and private sector labor relations differ in numerous ways: (a) in its very nature, public service differs economically and demand-wise; (b) the effect of the budget on bargaining processes differs; (c) the bargaining structure differs, affecting decision-making processes; (d) negotiable issues and bargaining tactics tend to be less predictable; and (e) the right to strike is usually prohibited by law. Public and private sector similarities include areas like the role of personalities and skills of negotiators and the interplay of bargaining power model variables such as public opinion, political support, and various forms of job actions.

Developing first in the major metropolitan areas in the Northeast and North, unionization in state and local governments spread throughout the country. While unions struggled against unfavorable public opinion and publicity and adverse state legislation in the early days, the early sixties brought permissive legislation, favorable judicial interpretations of constitutional rights, and an increasing interest among public employees in joining unions. Such events coupled with union efforts culminated in organizational representation for a majority of employees in education, police protection, and fire protection in state and local governments.

Permissive state labor relations legislation or policy generally developed according to geography. Alaska and Hawaii passed favorable legislation as did states located on the West Coast and in the Northeast, North, and Midwest. Most of the lower Atlantic Coast, Southeast (except Florida), Southwest, and lower Rocky Mountain states have no comprehensive legislation. In states having laws, the legislation typically specifies the administrative set-up, bargaining rights, impasse procedures, unfair labor practices, and strike provisions. Within this framework, the parties attempt to negotiate labor agreements covering permissible subjects.

The impasse procedures often established as the substitute for the strike alternative include mediation, fact-finding, arbitration, and various combinations of these; the latter seem to be most popular. Such terms as *splitting the difference, chilling effect*, and *narcotic effect* have become common in assessing effectiveness of these procedures. Definitive conclusions about impasse procedures have not been made, and further research into their effectiveness is needed. However, some promising results, such as serious negotiations and low evidence of strikes, have been identified in many states. In some states, chilling effects and narcotic effects have been identified.

As an example of application, the chapter concluded with coverage of the academic community. Teachers in elementary and secondary education and professors in higher education share many common employment concerns, but different salient concerns exist at the two levels: shared governance and collegiality in higher education and student discipline in elementary and secondary schools. Further developments and problems may well stem from the decline in enrollments, scarcity of jobs, and increasing numbers of qualified graduates.

Implications

The most significant contemporary developments have been the tax cuts at state levels, the Reagan Administration's budget cuts, and a recessionary economy. At the state level, reductions in government expenditures have resulted in layoffs as high as 1.5 percent of the workforce; at the local level, cities have laid off employees at record rates, some as high as 20 percent.[163] While elected officials and public administrators were cutting costs, unions were attempting to protect the economic and noneconomic issues that have been negotiated into their agreements. Thus, the economic conditions have strained the relationships between unions and public managers. One survey of labor relations professionals in California revealed that none believed Proposition 13 (a tax cut bill) had strengthened the relationship between unions and management, 22 percent believed the relationship had grown to be very negative, and 39 percent perceived the effects as negative.[164] In other areas, collective bargaining agreements in state and local governments established personnel policies concerning promotions, transfers, vacations, and discipline where no written policies had existed. It also eliminated or diminished the effects of nepotism, favoritism, and cronyism.[165]

While economic conditions reveal a rather pessimistic outlook for public sector labor relations, there are some optimistic conclusions. First, only a few years ago many contended that collective bargaining did not belong in the public sector; today, however, most states have adopted some form of bargaining as essential. Second, collective bargaining will continue to take place within a political arena and both parties must seek political approval by the appropriate legislative body, elected by the citizens. Third, employers are increasingly more willing to accept strikes as an alternative to compulsory and binding arbitration. Traditionally, many public employers viewed strikes as tantamount to anarchy. Now with so many public employers facing financial crises, strikes are more feasible alternatives. Finally, interest arbitration is becoming more acceptable to the parties. Twenty-two states have some form of compulsory arbitration for essential employees and interest arbitration seems to be a feasible alternative to "trial by combat" along with the emotional confrontations that accompany strikes.[166] As one expert has concluded:

---

in those very difficult, emotional situations there is a *better opportunity to achieve some reasonable semblance of equity for both* of the parties involved by some carefully trained, competent, disinterested and detached neutral who can cut through the emotional rhetoric and reach some appearance of equity.[167]

Discussion Questions

1. Think of a public organization with which you are familiar. Explain how it differs from a private company in terms of the following:
   a. nature of its service
   b. relationship between its budget and collective bargaining processes

c. bargaining structure and decision-making processes
d. negotiable issues and bargaining tactics
e. its right to strike

2. Using the same public organization (as in 1 above), discuss the similarities between collective bargaining in this organization and a typical negotiation between a private company and its union.

3. Give reasons why unions developed later in the public sector than in the private sector, especially at the local level.

4. Public sector labor relations legislation differs on a geographic basis. Explain why this might have occurred.

5. Describe the different types of impasse procedures used in the public sector and discuss the relative effectiveness of each.

6. Compare the chilling effect and the narcotic effect as they pertain to negotiations and impasse procedures in the public sector.

7. How does shared governance or collegiality affect collective bargaining in higher education? For what reasons do administrative officials in higher education prefer shared governance over collective bargaining?

8. Considering the predicted decline in school enrollment, a growing scarcity of faculty positions, and an increasing number of available instructors, what are the prospects for increased unionization and collective bargaining in public educational institutions? Explain.

9. At the school that you attend, are faculty members "managerial employees" as described by the U.S. Supreme Court in its Yeshiva University case (see footnote 114)?

References

[1]David Lewin, Peter Feuille, and Thomas Kochan, *Public Sector Labor Relations: An Analysis and Readings*, 2d ed. (Glen Ridge, N.J.: Thomas Horton & Daughters, pp. 1–5. The reader may wish to refer to a position essay against public employee collective bargaining in R. S. Summers, *Collective Bargaining and Public Benefit Conferral* (Ithaca, N.Y.: Cornell University, 1976).

[2]Bureau of National Affairs, *Government Employee Relations Reporter*, September 19, 1977, p. 726:24. Government employee membership in unions is 20.1 percent of the total government employment and 39.2 percent if employee organizations are counted. See John F. Burton, Jr., "The Extent of Collective Bargaining in Public Sector," in Benjamin Aaron, Joseph R. Grodin, and James L. Stern, eds., *Public Sector Bargaining* (Washington, D.C.: Bureau of National Affairs, 1979), p. 3.

[3]B. V. H. Schneider, "Public-Sector Labor Legislation—An Evolutionary Analysis," in Aaron, Grodin, and Stern, *Public Sector Bargaining*, p. 222. See also *National League of Cities, et al., v. Usery et al.*, 426 U.S. 833 (1976).

[4]Walter Mossberg, "The Labor Movement's Maverick," *Wall Street Journal*, October 14, 1974, p. 14.

[5]Harry H. Wellington and Ralph K. Winter, Jr., *The Unions and the Cities* (Washington, D.C.: Brookings Institution, 1971), pp. 10–17.

[6]Walter Fogel and David Lewin, "Wage Determination in the Public Sector," *Industrial and Labor Relations Review* 27 (April 1974), pp. 410–431. It should be mentioned that productivity bargaining has been approached in some public sector collective bargaining situations. For a discussion of productivity considerations in public sector negotiations see Rudy Oswald, "Public Productivity Tied to Bargaining," *American Federationist* 85 (March 1976), pp. 20–21; Walter L. Balk, "Why Don't Public Administrators Take Productivity More Seriously?" *Public Personnel Management* 3 (July–August 1974), pp. 318–324; Paul D. Staudohar, "An Experiment in Increasing Productivity of Police Service Employees," *Public Administration Review* 35 (September–October 1975), pp. 518–522; and Marvin Friedman, *The Use of Economic Data in Collective Bargaining* (Washington, D.C.: Government Printing Office, 1978), pp. 53–56.

[7]Michael Moskow, J. J. Loewenberg, and E. C. Koziara, *Collective Bargaining in Public Employment* (New York: Random House, 1970), pp. 14–18; and H. H. Wellington and R. K. Winter, Jr., "Structuring Collective Bargaining in Public Employment," *Yale Law Journal* 79 (April 1970), pp. 806–822.

[8]Milton Derber et al., "Bargaining and Budget-Making in Illinois Public Institutions," *Industrial and Labor Relations Review* 27 (October 1973), pp. 49–62; and Kenneth M. Jennings, J. A. Smith, and Earle C. Traynham, Jr., "Budgetary Influences on Bargaining in Mass Transit," *Journal of Collective Negotiations in the Public Sector* 6, no. 4 (1977), pp. 333–339.

[9]Frederick O'R. Hayes, "Collective Bargaining and the Budget Director," in Sam Zagoria, ed., *Public Workers and Public Unions* (Englewood Cliffs, N.J.: Prentice-Hall, 1972), p. 91.

[10]Derber et al., "Bargaining and Budget-Making," p. 58.

[11]Arvid Anderson, "Local Government-Bargaining and the Fiscal Crisis: Money, Unions, Politics, and the Public Interest," in James L. Stern and Barbara Dennis, eds., *Proceedings of the 1976 Annual Spring Meeting: Industrial Relations Research Association*, p. 518. It should be mentioned that this board was formed to alleviate the recent fiscal crisis in New York City.

[12]William H. Holley, Jr., "Unique Complexities of Public Sector Labor Relations," *Personnel Journal* 55 (February 1976), p. 75.

[13]Stephen L. Hayford, "An Empirical Investigation of the Public Sector Supervisory Bargaining Rights Issue," *Labor Law Journal* 26 (October 1975), pp. 641–652; Alan Balfour, "Rights of Collective Representation for Public Sector Supervisors," *Journal of Collective Negotiations in the Public Sector* 4, no. 3 (1975), pp. 257–265; and William H. Holley, Jr., J. Boyd Scebra, and William Rector, "Perceptions of the Role of the Principal in Professional Negotiations," *Journal of Collective Negotiations in the Public Sector* 5, no. 4 (1976), pp. 361–369.

[14]George Hildebrand, "The Public Sector," in John T. Dunlop and Neil Chamberlain, eds., *Frontiers in Collective Bargaining* (New York: Harper & Row, 1967), pp. 126–127; Louis V. Imundo, Jr., "The Federal Government Sovereignty and Its Effect on Labor-Management Relations," *Labor Law Journal* 26 (March 1975), pp. 145–152; Louis V. Imundo, Jr., "Some Comparisons between Public Sector and Private Sector Collective Bargaining," *Labor Law Journal* 24 (December 1973), pp. 810–817. For an excellent discussion on the issue of "who is management?" in the public sector, see Milton Derber, "Management Organization for Collective Bargaining in the Public Sector," in Aaron, Grodin, and Stern, *Public Sector Bargaining*, pp. 80–117.

[15]For a vivid example of political considerations affecting collective bargaining, see A. H. Raskin, "Politics Up-ends the Bargaining Table," in Zagoria, *Public Workers*, pp. 122–146; and A. H. Raskin, "Mayor and Governor: Knee-Deep in Trouble," in Robert T. Woodworth and Richard B. Peterson, eds., *Collective Negotiation for Public and Professional Employees* (Glenview, Ill.: Scott, Foresman, 1969), pp. 288–292.

[16]For a case study example of this situation see Arnold R. Weber, "Paradise Lost: Or Whatever Happened to the Chicago Social Workers?" *Industrial and Labor Relations Review* 22 (April 1969), pp. 323-338.

[17]I. B. Helburn and N. B. Bennett, "Public Employee Bargaining and the Merit Principle," *Labor Law Journal* 23 (October 1972), p. 619; and I. B. Helburn, "The Scope of Bargaining in Public Sector Negotiations: Sovereignty Reviewed," *Journal of Collective Negotiations in the Public Sector* 3 (Spring 1974), pp. 147–166.

[18]Paul F. Gerhart, "The Scope of Bargaining in Local Government Negotiations," *Labor Law Journal* 20 (August 1969), pp. 545–552.

[19]Peter Feuille, "Police Labor Relations and Multilateralism," *Journal of Collective Negotiations in the Public Sector* 3 (Summer 1974), p. 216.

[20]Lee C. Shaw and R. Theodore Clark, Jr., "The Practical Difference between Public and Private Sector Collective Bargaining," *UCLA Law Review* 19 (August 1972), p. 885.

[21]Victor Gotbaum, "Collective Bargaining and the Union Leader," in Zagoria, *Public Workers*, pp. 83–84.

[22]Marvine J. Levine, "The Status of State 'Sunshine Bargaining' Laws," *Labor Law Journal* 31 (November 1980), pp. 709–713.

[23]"Crime Rate Is Same Despite Police Strike," *Miami Herald*, July 20, 1975, p. 15-A.

[24]Wellington and Winter, "Structuring Collective Bargaining," pp. 822–851.

[25]George W. Taylor, "Public Employment: Strikes or Procedures?" *Industrial and Labor Relations Review* 20 (July 1967), p. 636.

[26]John F. Burton and Charles Krider, "The Role and Consequences of Strikes by Public Employees," *Yale Law Journal* 79 (January 1970), pp. 418–440.

[27]Theodore Kheel, "Resolving Deadlocks without Banning Strikes," *Monthly Labor Review* 91 (July 1969), pp. 62–63.

[28]Wellington and Winter, "Structuring Collective Bargaining," pp. 822–825.

[29]U.S. Department of Commerce, *Labor-Management Relations in State and Local Governments: 1980* (Washington, D.C.: U.S. Government Printing Office, 1981), pp. 4–5 and p. 101.

[30]Bonnie G. Cebulski, "Analysis of Twenty-two Illegal Strikes and California Law," *California Public Employee Relations* 18 (August 1973), pp. 2–17.

[31]Tim Bornstein, "Legacies of Local Government Collective Bargaining in the 1970s," *Labor Law Journal* 31 (March 1980).

[32]Henry B. Burnett, Jr., "Interview with Jerry Wurf," *Skeptic*, May–June 1976, p. 13.

[33]Ibid., p. 54.

[34]These techniques were formulated in various discussions with Paul Gerhart of Case Western Reserve University.

[35]See, for example, Raymond D. Horton, *Municipal Labor Relations in New York City: Lessons of the Lindsay-Wagner Years* (New York: Praeger Publishers, 1973), p. 134; Michael Marmo, "Public Employee Unions: The Political Imperative," *Journal of Collective Negotiations in the Public Sector* 4, no. 4 (1975), p. 371; and Jay F. Atwood, "Collective Bargaining's Challenge: Five Imperatives for Public Managers," *Public Personnel Management* 5 (January–February 1976), p. 29.

[36]For a discussion of the variety and legal interpretations of these strikes, see Paul D. Staudohar, "Quasi-Strikes by Public Employees," *Journal of Collective Negotiations in the Public Sector* 3 (Fall 1974), pp. 363–371.

[37]Paul Gerhart, "The Emergence of Collective Bargaining in Local Government," *Public Personnel Management* 4 (1980), pp. 287–294.

[38]Benjamin J. Taylor and Fred Witney, *Labor Relations Law*, 2d ed. (Englewood Cliffs, N.J.: Prentice-Hall, 1975), pp. 557–570.

[39]U.S. Department of Commerce, Bureau of the Census, *Labor-Management Relations in State and Local Governments, 1980* (Washington, D.C.: Government Printing Office, 1981), p. 1.

[40]Ibid., p. 2.

[41]For analysis of public collective bargaining situations in southern states, see John R. Stepp, "The Determinants of Southern Public Employee Recognition," *Public Personnel Management* 3 (January–February 1974), pp. 59–69.

[42]Roger E. Dahl, "Public Sector Bargaining Issues in the 1980's: A Management View," *Proceedings of New York University Thirty-Third Annual National Conference on Labor* (New York: Matthew Bender, 1981), p. 288.

[43]Schneider, "Public-Sector Labor Legislation," pp. 192–212.

[44]Michael Grace, "The Chaos in Public Sector Bargaining," *AFL-CIO American Federationist* 88 (July 1981), pp. 9–12.

[45]Joel M. Douglas, "Injunctions under New York's Taylor Law: An Occupational Analysis," *Journal of Collective Negotiations in the Public Sector* 10, no. 3 (1981), p. 249.

[46]Alan Balfour and Alexander B. Holmes, "The Effectiveness of No Strike Laws for Public School Teachers," *Journal of Collective Negotiations in the Public Sector* 10, no. 2 (1981), pp. 133–143.

[47]James K. McCollum, "Decertification of the Northern Virginia Public Sector Local Unions: A Study of Its Effect," *Journal of Collective Negotiations in the Public Sector* 10, no. 4 (1981), pp. 345–353; James K. McCollum, "Politics and Labor Relations in Virginia: The Defeat of Public Sector Unionism," *Employee Relations Law Journal* 7, no. 3 (1981), pp. 414–431.

[48]Alan Balfour and Sandra Jennings, "Chaos in Union Recognition Procedures: A Case History of Oklahoma's School Teacher Bargaining Law," *Journal of Collective Negotiations in the Public Sector* 11, no. 1 (1982), pp. 82–83.

[49]U.S. Department of Commerce, Bureau of the Census, *Labor-Management Relations*, p. 4.

[50]U.S. Department of Labor, Bureau of Labor Statistics, *Municipal Collective Bargaining Agreements in Large Cities* (Washington, D.C.: Government Printing Office, 1972); and U.S. Department of Labor, Bureau of Labor Statistics, *Collective Bargaining Agreements for State or County Government Employees* (Washington, D.C.: Government Printing Office, 1976).

[51]"Labor Letter," *Wall Street Journal*, December 7, 1976, p. 1.

[52]Jeffrey A. Tannenbaum, "Frustrated Firemen: Fire Fighting Gear Improves, but Cities Can't Afford to Buy It," *Wall Street Journal*, January 30, 1975, pp. 1, 21.

[53]"Labor Letter," *Wall Street Journal*, April 8, 1975, p. 1.

[54]Hervey A. Juris and Peter Feuille, *Police Unionism* (Lexington, Mass.: Lexington Books, 1973).

[55]Thomas J. Hilligan, "Police Employee Organizations: Past Developments and Present Problems," *Labor Law Journal* 24 (May 1973), p. 298.

[56]David Lewin, Peter Feuille, and Thomas Kochan, *Public Sector Labor Relations: An Analysis and Readings* (Glen Ridge, N.J.: Thomas Horton & Daughters, 1977), p. 222.

[57]U.S. Department of Labor, Labor-Management Services Administration, *Summary of Public Sector Labor Relations Policies, 1976* (Washington, D.C.: Government Printing Office, 1976), pp. 1–126. Totals are greater than 38 because some states have different impasse procedures for different types of employees; for example, Connecticut has mediation, fact-finding, and arbitration for state employees; fact-finding and arbitration for municipal employees; and mediation and fact-finding for teachers.

[58]Eva Robbins and Tia S. Denenberg, *A Guide for Labor Mediators* (Honolulu: Industrial Relations Center, University of Hawaii, 1976), pp. 3–4; and Paul D. Staudohar, *Public Employment Disputes and Disputes Settlement* (Honolulu: Industrial Relations Center, University of Hawaii, 1972), p. 41.

[59]Thomas A. Kochan and Todd Jick, "The Public Sector Mediation Process," *Journal of Conflict Resolution* 447A 22 (June 1978), p. 236.

[60]Thomas P. Gilroy and Anthony Sinicropi, "Impasse Resolution in Public Employment: A Current Assessment," *Industrial and Labor Relations Review* 25 (July 1972), pp. 500–501.

[61]Ibid., p. 499.

[62]James L. Stern et al., *Final Offer Arbitration* (Lexington, Mass.: D. C. Heath, 1975), p. 175.

[63]Paul F. Gerhart and John E. Drotning, "Dispute Settlement and the Intensity of Mediation," *Industrial Relations* 19 (Fall 1980), pp. 352–358.

[64]Federal Mediation and Conciliation Service, *Twenty-ninth Annual Report* (Washington, D.C.: Government Printing Office, 1977), pp. 18–20.

[65]Lewin, Feuille, and Kochan, *Public Sector Labor Relations*, p. 225.

[66]Robert E. Doherty, "Fact-Finding: A One-Eyed Man Lost among the Eagles," *Public Personnel Management* 5 (September–October 1976), p. 366.

[67]Arnold Zack, *Understanding Fact-Finding and Arbitration in the Public Sector* (Washington, D.C.: Government Printing Office, 1974), p. 1.

[68]Ibid., p. 3.

[69]Also called final-offer arbitration, last-offer arbitration, and last best-offer arbitration.

[70]Nels E. Nelson, "Final Offer Arbitration: Same Problems," *Arbitration Journal* 30 (March 1975), p. 51.

[71]Lewin, Feuille, and Kochan, *Public Sector Labor Relations*, p. 230.

[72]Daniel H. Kruger and Harry E. Jones, "Compulsory Interest Arbitration in the Public Sector: An Overview," *Journal of Collective Negotiations in the Public Sector* 10, no. 4 (1981), p. 359–360.

[73]Zack, *Understanding Fact-Finding and Arbitration*, p. 4.

[74]Ibid., p. 5.

[75]For a further discussion of related concerns and possible remedial alternatives see Joseph R. Grodin, "Political Aspects of Public Sector Interest Arbitration," *California Law Review* 64 (May 1976), pp. 678–701.

[76]Daniel B. Gallagher and M. D. Chaubey, "Impasse Behavior and Tri-Offer Arbitration in Iowa," *Industrial Relations* 21 (Spring 1982), p. 129.

[77]John C. Anderson, "The Impact of Arbitration: A Methodological Assessment," *Industrial Relations* 20 (Spring 1981), p. 129–130.

[78]Lewin, Feuille, and Kochan, *Public Sector Labor Relations*, p. 223.

[79]Paul F. Gerhart and John E. Drotning, "Do Uncertain Cost/Benefit Estimates Prolong Public-Sector Disputes?" *Monthly Labor Review* 103 (Sept. 1980), pp. 26–30.

[80]David E. Bloom, "Is Arbitration *Really* Compatible with Bargaining?" *Industrial Relations* 20 (Fall 1980), pp. 233–244.

[81]Henry S. Farber, "Role of Arbitration in Dispute Settlement," *Monthly Labor Review* 104 (May 1981), p. 34.

[82]Doherty, "Fact-Finding," p. 367.

[83]William R. Word, "Fact-Finding in Public Employee Negotiations," *Monthly Labor Review* 95 (February 1972), pp. 60–64. Also see James L. Stern, "The Wisconsin Public Employee Fact-Finding Procedure," *Industrial and Labor Relations Review* 19 (July 1966), p. 8.

[84]William McHugh, Seminar for Special Masters, Tallahassee, Florida, Spring 1978.

[85]Lucian B. Gatewood, "Fact-Finding in Teacher Disputes: The Wisconsin Experience," *Monthly Labor Review* 97 (October 1974), pp. 47–51. For earlier and somewhat more optimistic assessments of fact-finding see Robert G. Howlett, "Comment," in G. S. Somers and B. D. Dennis, eds., *Arbitration and the Expanding Role of Neutrals* (Washington, D.C.: Bureau of National Affairs, 1970), pp. 181–182; and Byron Yaffe and Howard Goldblatt, *Fact-Finding in Public Employment Disputes in New York State: More Promise than Illusion* (Ithaca, N.Y.: Cornell University, 1971), p. 62.

[86]J. Joseph Loewenberg, "Compulsory Arbitration in the United States," in J. J. Loewenberg et al., eds., *Compulsory Arbitration* (Lexington, Mass.: D. C. Heath, 1976), p. 166. Also see Hoyt N. Wheeler, "An Analysis of Fire Fighter Strikes," *Labor Law Journal* 26 (January 1975), pp. 17–20; and Charles M. Rehmus, "Legislated Interest Arbitration," *Proceedings of the Annual Meeting: Industrial Relations Research Association, 1974* (Madison, Wis.: Industrial Relations Research Association, 1975), pp. 307–312.

[87]Lewin, Feuille, and Kochan, *Public Sector Labor Relations*, p. 229; and Charles M. Rehmus, "Public Employees: A Survey of Some Critical Problems on the Frontier of Collective Bargaining," *Labor Law Journal* 27 (September 1976), pp. 588–599.

[88]Craig E. Overton and Max S. Wortman, "Compulsory Arbitration: A Strike Alternative for Police?" *Arbitration Journal* 28 (March 1974), p. 40.

[89]Hoyt N. Wheeler, "Is Compromise the Rule in Fire Fighter Arbitration?" *Arbitration Journal* 29 (September 1974), pp. 176–185.

[90]Thomas A. Kochan and Jean Baderschneider, "Dependence on Impasse Procedures: Police and Fire Fighters in New York State," *Industrial and Labor Relations Review* 31 (July 1978), pp. 431, 447.

[91]Thomas A. Kochan et al., *Dispute Resolution under Fact-Finding and Arbitration: An Empirical Evaluation* (New York: American Arbitration Association, 1979), p. 158.

[92]Peter Feuille, "Final-Offer Arbitration and Negotiating Incentives," *Arbitration Journal* 32 (September 1977), pp. 203, 220.

[93]Peter Feuille and James B. Dworkin, "Final-Offer Arbitration and Intertemporal Compromise, or It's My Turn to Win," in Barbara D. Dennis, *Proceedings of the Thirty-first Annual Meeting: Industrial Relations Research Association* (Madison, Wis.: Industrial Relations Research Association, 1979), pp. 87–95.

[94]Kruger and Jones, "Compulsory Interest Arbitration," p. 359.

[95]Gallagher and Chaubey, "Impasse Behavior and Tri-Offer Arbitration," p. 146; also see Daniel Gallagher and Richard Pegnetter, "Impasse Resolution Procedure under the Iowa Multistep Procedure," *Industrial and Labor Relations Review* 32 (April 1979), pp. 327–328.

[96]Fred Witney, "Final-Offer Arbitration: The Indianapolis Experience," *Monthly Labor Review* 96 (May 1973), pp. 20–25. It should be noted that Witney, unlike Feuille (footnote 93), found no substantial evidence to conclude that final offer arbitration either encouraged or discouraged the parties from resolving their differences on their own.

[97]Theodore W. Kheel, "Strikes and Public Employment," *Michigan Law Review* 67 (March 1969), pp. 939–940. It should also be noted that vague guidelines, such as "public interest," have often plagued at least one fact-finder; see Doherty, "Fact-Finding," p. 366.

[98]Gary Long and Peter Feuille, "Final-Offer Arbitration: Sudden Death in Eugene," *Industrial and Labor Relations Review* 27 (January 1974), p. 203.

[99]J. H. Foegen, "Public Sector Strike-Prevention: Let the Taxpayer Decide," *Journal of Collective Negotiations in the Public Sector* 3 (Summer 1974), p. 223.

[100]I. B. Helburn and J. L. Matthews, "The Referendum as an Alternative to Bargaining," *Journal of Collective Negotiations in the Public Sector* 9, no. 2 (1980), pp. 93–105.

[101]Donald T. Barnum and I. B. Helburn, "Influence the Electorate Experience with Referenda on Public Employee Bargaining," *Industries and Labor Relations Review* 35 (April 1982), pp. 330–342.

[102]Thomas Kochan, "Dynamics of Dispute Resolution in the Public Sector," in Aaron, Grodin, and Stern, *Public-Sector Bargaining*, pp. 155–189.

[103]Robert L. Walter, *The Teacher and Collective Bargaining* (Lincoln, Nebr.: Professional Educators Publications, 1975), pp. 14–15.

[104]Marvine J. Levine and Katherine G. Lewis, "The Status of Collective Bargaining In Public Education," *Labor Law Journal* 33 (March 1982), pp. 177–179.

[105]U.S. Department of Labor, *Directory of National Unions and Employee Associations, 1977* (Washington, D.C.: U.S. Government Printing Office, 1979), p. 64; Bureau of National Affairs, *Government Employee Relations Reporter*, August 29, 1977, p. 723:17.

[106]"Faculty-Union Membership at an All-time High," *Chronicle of Higher Education*, April 28, 1982, p. 2.

[107]"Faculty Bargaining Agents at 600 Campuses," *Chronicle of Higher Education*, June 26, 1978, p. 8. The American Association of University Professors has organized 55 campuses; the AFT, 213; the NEA, 244; AAUP-NEA, 11; others were independent.

[108]Joseph Garbarino and John Lawler, "Faculty Union Activity in Higher Education, 1977," *Industrial Relations* 17 (February 1978), pp. 117–118.

[109]John J. Lawler, "Faculty Unionism in Higher Education: The Public Sector Experience," *Labor Law Journal* 33 (August 1980), p. 476.

[110]*NLRB v. Yeshiva University*, 444 U.S. 672 (1980).

[111]Edward L. Suntrup, "NLRB v. Yeshiva University and Unionization in Higher Education," *Industrial Relations Law Journal* 4, no. 2 (1981), pp. 288–291.

[112]John A. Gray, "Managerial Employees and the Industrial Analogy: *NLRB v. Yeshiva University,*" *Labor Law Journal* 33 (July 1982), p. 392.

[113]Beverly T. Watkins, "NLRB Rules Professors at 3 Private Institutions Are Managers. Those at 2 Others May Bargain," *Chronicle of Higher Education*, May 12, 1982, p. 1.

[114]Joel M. Douglas, "Distinguishing *Yeshiva*: A Troubling Task for the NLRB," *Labor Law Journal* 34 (February 1983), p. 118.

[115]Ralph E. Kennedy, "NLRB and Faculty Bargaining Units: The Charting of an Uncharted Area," in Thomas M. Mannix, ed., *Collective Bargaining in Higher Education* (New York: National Center for the Study of Collective Bargaining in Higher Education, City University of New York, 1975), pp. 35–50.

[116]For an illustration of divergent state statutes regarding a most significant academic working condition, tenure, see L. H. Schramm, "Is Teacher Tenure Negotiable? A Review of Court Decisions," *Journal of Collective Negotiations in the Public Sector* 6, no. 3 (1977), pp. 245–257.

[117]William J. Moore, "An Analysis of Teacher Union Growth," *Industrial Relations* 17 (May 1978), pp. 204–214.

[118]Robert J. Thornton and Andrew R. Weintraub, "Public Employee Bargaining Laws and the Propensity to Strike: The Case of Public School Teachers," *Journal of Collective Negotiations in the Public Sector* 3 (Winter 1974), p. 35. As of April 1978, thirty-two states had collective bargaining legislation for teachers allowing negotiations on pay and other working conditions.

[119]Joseph W. Garbarino and Melvin W. Aussieker, "Faculty Unionization in Institutions of Higher Education," *Monthly Labor Review* 97 (April 1974), pp. 48–51.

[120]Holley, Scebra, and Rector, "Perceptions of the Role," pp. 361–369; Charles T. Schmidt, Jr., "The Question of the Recognition of Principal and Other Supervisory Units in Public Education Collective Bargaining." *Labor Law Journal* 19 (July 1968), pp. 283–291.

[121]Julia Newcomer and Elvis C. Stephens, "A Survey of Patterns of Unit Composition at Public Higher Education Institutions Involved in Collective Bargaining," *Journal of Collective Bargaining in the Public Sector* 11, no. 2 (1982), pp. 109–111.

[122]Carol B. Gilmore, "The Impact of Faculty Collective Bargaining on the Management of Public Higher Educational Institutions," *Journal of Collective Negotiations in the Public Sector* 10, no. 2 (1981), p. 145.

[123]H. B. Means and P. W. Semans, eds. *Faculty Collective Bargaining*, 2d ed. (Washington, D.C.: Editorial Projects for Education, 1976), pp. 11–20.

[124]Charles R. Perry and Wesley A. Wildman, *The Impact of Negotiations in Public Education* (Worthington, Ohio: Charles A. Jones Publishing, 1970), pp. 137–214.

[125]"Little Room to Negotiate," *Time*, October 18, 1982, p. 83.

[126]Birch Bayh, "School Violence and Vandalism: Problems and Solutions," *American Educator* (Summer 1978), p. 5; and David L. Manning, "Discontent in Teaching Ranks," *Wall Street Journal*, January 9, 1978, p. 12.

[127]"Teacher to Teacher: Interviews on Discipline Policy and School Violence," *American Educator* (Summer 1978), p. 10.

[128]Rich Jaroslovey, "Bidding for Brains: Despite Glut of Teaching Applicants, Colleges Raid Other Schools for Distinguished Faculty," *Wall Street Journal*, June 28, 1976, p. 24.

[129]Miami Herald, *Tropic Magazine*, August 7, 1977.

[130]"Labor Letter," *Wall Street Journal*, March 7, 1978, p. 1.

[131]"Labor Letter," *Wall Street Journal*, January 24, 1978, p. 1.

[132]Walter S. Griggs and Harvey W. Rubin, "Legal Ramifications of the Tenure Cases," *Journal of Collective Negotiations in the Public Sector* 6, no. 2 (1977), p. 123.

[133]Jim Montgomery, "Breaking the Mold: Teachers Fight Effort to Remove Them for Personal Conduct," *Wall Street Journal*, January 28, 1978, pp. 1, 24.

[134]Paul D. Staudohar, "Negotiation and Grievance Arbitration of Teacher Tenure Issues," *Labor Law Journal* 29 (July 1978), pp. 413–419.

[135]Joseph W. Garbarino and Melvin Aussieker, *Faculty Bargaining* (New York: McGraw-Hill, 1975), pp. 257–258; and A. W. J. Thomson, *An Introduction to Collective Bargaining in Higher Education* (Ithaca, N.Y.: Cornell University, 1974).

[136]The Staff of the Bureau of National Affairs, *Labor Relations in Higher Education, 1981* (Washington, D.C.: Bureau of National Affairs, Inc., 1982), p. 2.

[137]Robert F. Cook and Barbara W. Doering, "Negotiating a Teachers' Contract," *Arbitration Journal* 32 (September 1977), pp. 145–179.

[138]Barbara Doering, "Impasse Issues in Teacher Dispute Submitted to Fact-Finding in New York," *Arbitration Journal* 27 (March 1972), pp. 1–17; Willis J. Nordlund, "A Critique of Teacher Negotiations in 1974–1975," *Labor Law Journal* 26 (February 1975), pp. 119–124; and Bureau of National Affairs, *Government Employee Relations Reporter*, July 17, 1978, p. 768:14.

[139]*City of Madison Joint School District 8 v. Wisconsin Employment Relations Commission*, 97 Supreme Court Reporter, December 12, 1977, pp. 421–429.

[140]Bureau of National Affairs, *Government Employee Relations Reporter*, July 17, 1978, p. 768:14.

[141]Charles Winick, "When Teachers Strike," *Teachers College Record* 64 (April 1963), pp. 563–604; Don Hellriegel, Wendell French, and Richard B. Peterson, "Collective Negotiations and Teachers: A Behavioral Analysis," *Industrial and Labor Relations Review* 23 (April 1970), pp. 380–396; and William S. Fox and Michael H. Wince, "The Structure and Determinants of Occupational Militancy among Public School Teachers," *Industrial and Labor Relations Review* 30 (October 1976), p. 50.

[142]Roy R. Nasstrom and Robert L. Belsford, "Some Characteristics of Militant Teachers: A Reassessment Based on an Indiana Study," *Journal of Collective Negotiations in the Public Sector* 5, no. 3 (1976), pp. 247–256; J. A. Alutto and J. A. Belasco, "Determinants of Attitudinal Militancy among Nurses and Teachers," *Industrial and Labor Relations Review* 27 (July 1974), pp. 216–227; and C. Mushel, "Teacher and Administrator Attitudes toward Collective Negotiation Issues," *Education and Urban Society* 1 (May 1974), pp. 216–227.

[143]Andrew R. Weintraub and Robert J. Thornton, "Why Teachers Strike: The Economic and Legal Determinants," *Journal of Collective Negotiations in the Public Sector* 5, no. 3 (1976), p. 205.

[144]Melvin Aussieker, "The Incidence and Impact of Faculty Union Strikes," *Labor Law Journal* 28 (December 1977), pp. 777–784.

[145]Charles A. Odewahn and Allan Spritzer, "Administrators' Attitudes toward Faculty Unionism," *Industrial Relations* 15 (May 1976), pp. 206–215.

[146]Lynn Langway, "Union Problems," *Newsweek*, June 12, 1978, p. 73. Also see John E. Cooney, "Stevens Tech Professors' Strike Disturbs Campus Tranquility; Outcome Watched," *Wall Street Journal*, February 11, 1977, p. 10.

[147]Perry and Wildman, *Impact of Negotiations*, pp. 13–14; and Marshall J. Donley, Jr., *Power to the Teacher* (Bloomington: Indiana University Press, 1976), pp. 193–202.

[148]"Proposition 13's Impact on Collective Bargaining," *PERS Information Bulletin* 1 (June–July 1978), pp. 1–2; and Beverly T. Watkins, "The Budget Cutting Begins in California Community Colleges," *Chronicle of Higher Education*, June 26, 1978, p. 5.

[149]Hirshel Kasper, "Reply," *Industrial and Labor Relations Review* 25 (April 1972), pp. 417–423. Also see Robert H. Baird and John H. Landon, "Comment: The Effects of Collective Bargaining on Public School Teachers' Salaries," *Industrial and Labor Relations Review* 25 (April 1972), pp. 410–416; Robert J. Thornton, "The Effects of Collective Negotiations on Relative Teachers' Salaries," *Quarterly Review of Economics and Business* 11 (Winter 1971), pp. 37–47; Hirshel Kasper, "The Effects of Collective Bargaining on Public School Teachers' Salaries," *Industrial and Labor Relations Review* 24 (October 1970), pp. 57–72; and W. Clayton and Norman Carroll, "The Effects of Teachers' Organizations on Salaries and Class Size," *Industrial and Labor Relations Review* 26 (January 1973), pp. 834–841.

[150]David B. Lipsky and John E. Drotning, "The Influence of Collective Bargaining on Teachers' Salaries in New York State," *Industrial and Labor Relations Review* 27 (October 1973), pp. 18–24; and G. A. Balfour, "More Evidence That Unions Do Not Achieve Higher Salaries for Teachers," *Journal of Collective Negotiations in the Public Sector* 3 (Fall 1974), pp. 289–303.

[151]Charles Rehmus and Evan Wilner, *The Economic Results of Teacher Bargaining: Michigan's First Two Years* (Ann Arbor: University of Michigan and Wayne State University Research Papers, No. 6, 1968).

[152]William H. Baugh and Joe A. Stone, "Teachers, Unions, and Wages in the 1970s: Unionism Now Pays," *Industrial and Labor Relations Review* 35 (April 1982), pp. 368–376.

[153]Trevor Bain, "Collective Bargaining and Wages in Public Higher Education: The Case of CUNY (New York City)," *Journal of Collective Negotiations in the Public Sector* 5, no. 3 (1976), pp. 207–214; Bureau of National Affairs, "PSRC Finds Bargaining Laws Limit Teachers Pay Gains, Foster Strikes," *Government Employee Relations Reporter*, September 25, 1978, pp. 778:11–778:12, 778:33–778:35.

[154]*Salaries under Unions* (Washington, D.C.: Academic Collective Bargaining Information Service, March 1978), p. 1. For an excellent discussion see F. R. Kemerer and J. V. Baldridge, *Unions on Campus* (San Francisco: Jossey-Bass Publishers, 1975).

[155]Stanley J. Schwartz, "Governance: Another View," *Labor Law Journal* 31 (October 1980), pp. 645–650.

[156]Alfred Loewenthal and Robert Nielsen, "Unions in Academia: A Bargaining Frontier," *American Federationist* 80 (April 1977), pp. 18–23.

[157]John E. Dougherty, "Collegiality, Governance, and Collective Bargaining in the Multi-Campus State University of New York," *Labor Law Journal* 28 (October 1977), pp. 645–650.

[158]Dougherty, "Collegiality, Governance, and Collective Bargaining," p. 646.

[159]Victor E. Flango, "The Impact of Collective Negotiations in Education Policies," *Journal of Collective Negotiations in the Public Sector* 5, no. 2 (1976), pp. 133–155.

[160]George LaNoue and Marvin R. Pilo, "Teacher Unions and Educational Accountability," in Robert H. Connery and William V. Farr, eds., *Unionization of Municipal Employees* (New York: Academy of Political Science, 1970), p. 157.

[161]Kemerer and Baldridge, *Unions on Campus*, pp. 166–195.

[162]Kim Cameron, "The Relationship between Faculty Unionism and Organizational Effectiveness," *Academy of Management Journal* 25 (March 1982), pp. 18–24.

[163]"Layoffs, RIFs, and EEO in the Public Sector," *Government Employee Relations Reporter*, February 8, 1982, p. 3.

[164]Virginia Ermer-Bott and Alan Saltzstein, "The Impact of Proposition 13 on Labor-Management Relations in California," *Public Personnel Management* 10 (Summer 1980), pp. 203–206.

[165]Comment from James McCollum, Auburn University.

[166]Robert D. Helsby, "Public Sector Unionism in the 80s," *The CERL Review* 2 (Spring 1980), pp. 20–22.

[167]Ibid., p. 22.

Chapter 15 Collective Bargaining in the Federal Government

"There are many questions to be answered and procedures to be worked out and this will require a joint effort, and the best efforts, of all involved in federal sector labor-management relations. We have a big challenge before us."

Henry B. Frazier, III, Member of the Federal Labor Relations Authority

The preceding chapter presented an overview of labor relations in the public sector, highlighting comparisons and contrasts with corresponding activities in the private sector and focusing on state and local governments. While many similarities can be found within public sector bargaining units, there are differences across the governmental levels. The purpose of this chapter is to examine labor-management relationships at the federal government level, concentrating on federal executive orders and the 1978 Civil Service Reform Act. One area of the federal government not covered under the Civil Service Reform Act, the postal service, is presented. Also, because the air traffic controller strike of 1981 affected so many U.S. citizens and received such notoriety, this chapter presents a more detailed coverage of the negotiations, the resulting strike, and the union's subsequent decertification.

Federal Sector Labor Relations

Historical Developments

The historical development of unions in the federal government can generally be considered in three phases: (1) prior to 1960, from the time unions were actively discouraged by the administration to the time employee and union rights began to be recognized; (2) 1962 to the 1970s, when a series of presidential executive orders established an operational framework for labor relations in the federal sector and formalized unions' rights; and (3) the current period, during which statutory rights were provided to federal employee unions, starting with the Postal Reform Act of 1970 and continuing with the passage of the Civil Service Reform Act of 1978.

Early union activity in the federal government appeared first in 1835 and 1836, when work stoppages occurred at the Washington and Philadelphia navy yards. Workers at these sites sought a ten-hour workday and general redress of their grievances. Union members at this time were primarily laborers and mechanics who belonged to the same unions as private employees. In fact, it was not until the postal employees began to organize in the 1860s that the federal government showed any marked resistance to union organizational efforts. President Theodore Roosevelt followed his predecessor's (President Cleveland) policy of opposing union activity of federal employees and proclaimed that the federal government had special status as an employer and union actions would interfere with his presidential authority to manage the government.

These early unions did not negotiate labor agreements, but were vigorously involved in lobbying and petitioning members of Congress for better wages, job security, and improved working conditions. It was these activities that led to a series of gag orders from Presidents Roosevelt and Taft and orders from the postmaster general that prohibited federal employees from visiting Congress in efforts to influence favorable legislation.

The authoritarian position of the administration resulted in low employee morale, work interrruptions, defiance of orders, and threats of formal strikes. Congress reacted to this strained situation by passing the Lloyd-La Follette Act of 1912, which guaranteed employees the right to join unions, secure a trial for suspension or discharge, and communicate directly with Congress without interference. In addition, Congress attempted to eliminate anti-union activities of federal government officials.

In the 1930s, a rapid expansion of government programs to improve economic and social conditions brought increased federal government employment, and unions showed tremendous growth. Franklin Roosevelt resisted any extension of full collective bargaining rights to federal employees, so unions continued to rely on Congress for any improvement in their employment conditions. The election of President John Kennedy (a Democrat who was heavily supported by organized labor in 1960) generated legislative and administrative interest in changing the rules of federal sector labor relations.

In 1961, President Kennedy appointed a Task Force on Employment-Management Cooperation to review the status of labor relations in the federal sector and to make any appropriate recommendations. On the basis of the task force report and its recommendations, President Kennedy on January 17, 1962, signed two executive orders: (a) Executive Order 10987, which set up federal agency appeal systems for appeals of adverse job actions and (b) Executive Order 10988, which set up the framework for labor-management relations in the federal government.[1]

Executive Order 10987 required each federal agency to establish a procedure for the appeal of administrative decisions that adversely affect employees and to communicate these procedures to the employees. The Civil Service Commission was given the authority to issue appropriate regulations for these appeal procedures.[2] Executive Order 10988 gave significant impetus to unionization in many federal agencies. For the first time, employees were given the protected right to join or refrain from joining labor organizations, and federal agencies were required to recognize unions. Unions designated as exclusive bargaining units were required to represent all employees in the unit without discrimination and without regard to their union membership. The executive orders enabled unions to obtain greater recognition, to grow numerically, and to gain influence with management.

Although the executive order exempted certain decision-making areas from negotiations, such as selecting employees and directing employee activities, it allowed negotiation of certain subjects such as promotion procedures. However, management retained the right to decide which employee would be promoted. It further stated that the agency must confer with representatives of the employees regarding negotiable issues. Any negotiated agreement *could* contain a grievance procedure, but arbitration was only allowed for the interpretation or application of the agreement. Another provision, disliked by unions, allowed federal agencies themselves to determine whether a labor organization was to be granted exclusive recognition.[3]

Executive Order 10988 did not offer many substantive benefits to organized labor and the management rights section gave public administrators considerable discretion in labor relations activities.

Regardless of its specific impact, Executive Order 10988 provided the framework for labor relations in the federal government for eight years before it was amended by Executive Order 11491 in 1970, the same year in which the Postal Reorganization Act was passed. Executive Order 11491 was amended three times, by Executive Orders 11616, 11636, and 11838.[4] Then, the Civil Service Reform Act was passed in 1978, making major changes in labor relations in the federal government.

Current Federal Labor-Management Relations under the Civil Service Reform Act of 1978

While the Civil Service Reform Act (CSRA) has retained many provisions of previous executive orders, the following discussion centers on the provisions of the CSRA as they currently exist. The act's ramifications extend beyond the labor relations function—it deals with other functions, such as merit system principles, civil service functions, performance appraisal, adverse actions, staffing, merit pay, and senior executive service. Its Title VII, entitled "Federal Service Labor-Management Relations," is the primary focus here.

The CSRA establishes a new Federal Labor Relations Authority (FLRA),[5] an independent, neutral agency that administers the federal labor relations program and investigates unfair labor practices. The FLRA oversees the creation of bargaining units, supervises elections, and assists federal agencies in dealing with labor relations issues. It is headed by a chairperson and two members, appointed on a bipartisan basis for five-year terms. Its structure provides for a General Counsel, who prosecutes unfair labor practices and incorporates the existing Federal Service Impasse Panel (FSIP), which provides assistance in resolving negotiation impasses.[6]

The FLRA's leadership responsibilities include determining appropriate bargaining units, supervising and conducting elections, prescribing criteria for determining national consultation rights, conducting hearings and resolving complaints on unfair labor practices, and resolving exceptions to arbitrator awards.[7] The General Counsel investigates any alleged unfair labor practices, prosecutes complaints under the act, and exercises such powers as the FLRA may prescribe.[8]

The *Federal Service Impasse Panel* within the FLRA structure consists of at least six president-appointed members and one chairperson. It investigates any negotiation impasse presented to it and is authorized to take any action that it considers necessary to settle the dispute. Although the Federal Mediation and Conciliation Service (FMCS), the federal agency established in 1947 by the Taft-Hartley Act, is required to assist the parties in resolving negotiation impasses, either party may request that the FSIP consider the matter or pursue binding arbitration. The panel must investigate the impasse and recommend a procedure for resolution or assist the parties through whatever means is necessary, including fact-finding and recommendations. If these actions fail, it may conduct a formal hearing and take whatever action is necessary and legal to settle the dispute.[9]

Of the thousands of negotiations that took place in the federal government between 1970 and 1978, 415 cases were sent to the FSIP; however, over 200 were handled by the FSIP in 1979 and 1980. Before 1978 the panel had issued a decision and ordered settlement in only twenty-seven cases; in the last two years, forty-five cases have been resolved in a similar manner.[10] The FMCS was able to assist the parties in settling impasses in 393 cases in 1981, involving such issues as union security, seniority, grievance procedures, arbitration, guarantees, hours (overtime), management prerogatives, duration of the contract, job classification, and working conditions.[11]

Appropriate Bargaining Units and Union Recognition in the Federal Sector The appropriate bargaining units for exclusive recognition may be established on an agency, plant, installation, functional, or other basis in order to assure a clear and identifiable community of interests among employees and to promote effective dealings and efficiency of the agency operations. The criteria used for determining community of interests are similar to those which have been used by the National Labor Relations Board in the private sector. These include common duties and skills, similar working conditions, and common supervision and work site. Similarly, certain positions are generally excluded from the bargaining unit, such as confidential employees, management and supervisory personnel, personnel employees, and professionals from the employee unions unless they vote in favor of inclusion.[12]

Under CSRA, federal agencies may give either exclusive recognition or national consultation rights to unions that meet the appropriate requirements. The granting of *national consultation rights* indicates that the union is the representative of a substantial number (10 percent or 5,000) of the civilian employees in the specified federal agency. This recognition only allows the union to be notified of proposed substantive changes in conditions of employment and provides a reasonable opportunity for the union to present its views and recommendations on any proposed changes.[13]

A federal agency accords *exclusive recognition* to a labor union if the union has been selected as the employee representative in a secret ballot election by a majority of the employees in the appropriate unit who cast valid ballots.[14] The current popularity of exclusive recognition in the federal government is demonstrated by the fact that the majority (61 percent or 1,234,256) of federal civilian (nonmilitary) employees are currently in bargaining units bearing this designation.

Eighty-eight percent of the blue-collar employees and 45 percent of the white-collar employees are represented by unions. Table 15.1 indicates the number of exclusive recognitions, agreements, and employees under agreement for the twelve largest federal agencies. Federal employees are reported to be

Table 15.1 Exclusive Recognitions and Agreements by Agency, 1981 (Twelve Largest Federal Agencies in Terms of Number of Exclusive Unions)

Agency	Employees under Agreements	Percentage of Employees under Agreement
Treasury	98,769	82
Army (nonmilitary)	209,109	66
Navy (nonmilitary)	203,010	65
Air Force (nonmilitary)	155,772	75
Defense Logistics Agency	34,742	77
National Guard Bureau	32,476	63
Interior	25,553	33
Agriculture	31,654	26
Health and Human Service	97,162	58
Transportation	42,267	42
General Services Administration	22,414	66
Vetrans Administration	164,693	71

Source: Office of Personnel Management, "Analyses of Data and Report on Union Recognition in the Federal Service," *FPM Bulletin* 711–86, June 24, 1982, pp. 9–10.

members of a number of different international unions, although the American Federation of Government Employees (AFL-CIO) leads by far, with 1,093 exclusive recognitions and 692,225 employees. Table 15.2 shows the number of recognized units, employees represented, units under agreement, and employees covered by each of the major unions in the federal sector.

Negotiable Subjects in the Federal Sector As in the private sector, the federal agency and the exclusively recognized union must meet at reasonable times and confer in good faith with respect to *mandatory* subjects of collective bargaining, such as certain personnel policies and practices and working conditions, to the extent that appropriate laws and regulations allow such negotiations. The parties are allowed to bargain over subjects that are *permissible*, but the CSRA does not require negotiation over permissible subjects—one party can legally refuse to negotiate these issues. Permissible subjects include numbers, types, and grades of positions assigned to any organizational unit, work project, or tour of duty; technology of the workplace; and methods and means of performing the work. Subjects *prohibited* from negotiations include wages and various management rights:

- To determine the mission, budget, organization, number of employees, and internal security practices.

Table 15.2 Exclusive Recognitions and Agreements by Major Unions, November 1981

Union	Recognition Units	Employees Represented
American Federation of Government Employees (AFGE)	1,093	692,225
National Federation of Federal Employees (NFFE)	423	136,323
National Treasury Employees Union (NTEU)	28	106,747
National Association of Government Employees (NAGE)	232	75,635
Metal Trades Council (MTC)	49	65,628
International Association of Machinists and Aerospace Workers (IAM)	88	35,596

Source: Office of Personnel Management, "Analysis of Data and Report on Union Recognition in the Federal Service," *FPM Bulletin* 711–86, June 24, 1982, p. 11.

- ☐ To hire, assign, direct, lay off, and retain employees in accordance with applicable law.
- ☐ To suspend, remove, reduce in grade or pay, or take other disciplinary action.
- ☐ To assign work, subcontract, and select personnel for promotion from properly ranked and certified candidates and other appropriate sources.
- ☐ To take whatever actions may be necessary to carry out the agency mission during emergencies.[15]

Although the CSRA limits the negotiable subjects, the parties have ample opportunity to negotiate many issues,[16] as illustrated in Table 15.3. However, it should be noted that federal unions and management representatives do not have a totally free hand in negotiating these items and either party may run the risk of committing an unfair labor practice by refusing to negotiate their mutual working conditions concerns in good faith.

Unfair Labor Practices in the Federal Sector The Civil Service Reform Act specifies unfair labor practices in order to protect the rights of individual employees, labor organizations, and federal agencies. The General Counsel investigates charges of unfair labor practices and prosecutes them before the three-member FLRA. Employee grievances over matters concerning adverse action, position classification, and equal employment opportunity are issues covered by other laws, statutes, or agency rules, and cannot be raised in the forum of an unfair labor practice hearing.

Table 15.3 Potential Negotiation Issues in the Federal Sector

- Procedures and standards to determine which employee(s) from a group of employees will be selected to perform work
- Merit promotion procedures and union participation on promotional panels
- Reduction-in-force procedures and management's obligation to notify employees and the union
- Procedures on job assignments
- Dues withholding
- Union rights regarding office services and space
- Safety considerations, including inspection, equipment, clothing, and union representation
- Discipline procedures
- Union participation in wage surveys
- Overtime distribution
- Meal and rest periods
- Excused time, including training and sick leave
- Travel time and transportation

Source: Source: A survey of 2,418 labor agreements by the Office of Personnel Management, published in *The Federal Labor-Management Consultant* (Washington, D.C.: Office of Personnel Management, July 31, 1981), p. 3. For analysis of FLRA cases, see H. H. Robinson, *Negotiability in the Federal Sector* (Ithaca, N.Y.: Cornell University, 1982).

Unfair labor practices under the act are very similar to those covered under previous executive orders, the National Labor Relations Act, and the Labor Management Relations Act. For example, prohibited management activities include restraining and coercing employees in the exercise of their rights; encouraging or discouraging union membership; sponsoring, controlling, or assisting the labor organization; disciplining union members who file complaints; and refusing to recognize or negotiate with a designated labor organization. The labor organization is prohibited from interfering with, restraining, or coercing employees in the exercise of their rights; attempting to induce agency management to coerce employees; impeding or hindering an employee's work performance; calling or engaging in job action; and discriminating against employees or refusing to consult, confer, or negotiate with the appropriate federal agency. In such cases, the FLRA can issue cease-and-desist orders and/or require reinstatement with back pay.

The CSRA makes it an unfair labor practice to refuse or fail to cooperate in impasse procedures and decisions. Moreover, an agency cannot enforce regulations that conflict with a negotiated agreement, and the union cannot picket if it interferes with the agency's operation.

The FLRA has authority to revoke recognition of a union which commits an unfair labor practice or encourages a strike or slowdown. As will be discussed later, the FLRA revoked the Professional Air Traffic Controller Organization's (PATCO) status as the exclusive bargaining agent for 18,000 air traffic controllers. It can also require the parties to renegotiate a labor agreement in accordance with an FLRA decision and seek temporary restraining orders in unfair labor practice cases.[17] In fiscal year 1980, 4,955 unfair labor practices were filed with FLRA, 96 percent against federal agencies.[18]

The CSRA requires that all negotiated agreements in the federal sector include a grievance procedure with binding arbitration as its final step. A grievance is broadly defined to include *any* complaint by any employee or labor organization relating to employment with an agency and any claimed violation, misinterpretation, or misapplication of any law, rule, or regulation affecting conditions of employment. Certain issues are exempt from the grievance procedure, such as employee appointment, certification, job classification, removal for national security reasons or political activities, issues concerning retirement, and life and health insurance.[19] However, the scope of grievance procedure coverage has been extended considerably. In fact, *all* matters within the allowable limits of the CSRA shall be *within* the scope of any grievance procedure negotiated by the parties, unless the parties have specifically agreed to exclude certain matters from coverage. Thus, departing from previous practices and private sector practices, the parties will *not* be negotiating matters into coverage; they will, however, be negotiating them out of coverage.

Negotiated grievance procedures now serve as the exclusive forum for bargaining unit employees in most cases; however, in cases of adverse action and removals and demotions for poor performance, the employee may choose *either* the negotiated procedure or the statutory procedure, but not both. Moreover, in discrimination cases, the grievant may proceed to arbitration and then appeal to the EEOC or the Merit System Protection Board, an independent agency established to hear federal employee grievances under CSRA.

Arbitration awards may be reviewed by the FLRA, but appeal to the courts is allowed only for adverse action and equal employment opportunity cases. Between January, 1979, and October, 1980, there were 1,045 federal sector arbitration awards, the FLRA decided 130 awards on appeal, and less than 1 percent were not upheld.[20]

Conflict over whether a grievance is arbitrable can be decided by arbitration and then reviewed by the FLRA. Remedial action can include back pay and attorney fees in discrimination and adverse actions cases where the federal agency's action is clearly without merit.[21]

Operational Assessment

An assessment of labor relations in the federal sector reveals growing pains of adjusting to a law allowing collective bargaining and a recognition that negotiators on both sides are more often novices in labor relations than trained, experienced professionals. Because management traditionally dominates its employees and unions lack the authority to strike, management is prone to "dally at the bargaining table because it sees little advantage in pressing for a contract."[22]

Federal labor relations are further complicated by rules and regulations from the Office of Personnel Management, the non-negotiability of wages and fringe benefits, active lobbying in Congress, and decisions by the Comptroller General affecting employment. Identifiable problems include:

- The parties reach negotiation impasses, refer the issues to the FLRA or FSIP to gain time in avoiding a disliked settlement and then place the decision in the hands of the FSIP or FLRA.
- The parties waste time and effort dealing with numerous small bargaining units.
- Management negotiators continue to claim issues are non-negotiable in hopes that the union will withdraw them or avoid bargaining.
- There is no pressure on the parties to come to an agreement principally because there is no threat of a strike.
- Management negotiators often lack the authority to make decisions; negotiators appear to be errand boys running between the bargaining table and those in command.

- There appears to be a lack of sophistication in bargaining due to lack of training and absence of mature bargainers.[23]

The General Accounting Office (GAO) found that the number of unfair labor practice charges has more than doubled since 1978 and the cost to process the 6,448 cases in 1981 was estimated at $25.9 million. GAO concluded that the disputes, many of which are allegations that managers fail to negotiate changes in working conditions, could be resolved informally, thereby avoiding the high costs of formal unfair labor practice procedures. GAO recommended that the FLRA require the parties to discuss the issues before filing an unfair labor practice charge, increase training in labor relations, assess the labor relations performance of managers, and implement systems to monitor and evaluate the unfair labor practice process.[24]

Application: The Postal Unions

The U.S. Postal Service was covered under executive orders until 1970, when separate legislation was enacted to govern labor relations in this important public service area. While there are a number of reasons for the passage of the Postal Reorganization Act of 1970, a major impetus came from the 1970 postal strike.

The Postal Strike of 1970

Even before the 1970 negotiations, postal employees, who were heavily unionized, believed they were grossly underpaid, especially those in the large metropolitan, high-cost areas. For example, members of the National Association of Letter Carriers (NALC) received a 1970 starting annual salary of $6,176; employees with twenty-one years' service earned $8,442.[25] The mass media recognized the discrepancies, and President Nixon agreed there were wage disparities and inequities. At the same time, postal employees were aware that far higher salaries had been achieved by sanitation workers and others at local levels through illegal strikes.

The economic considerations were reinforced by rather outdated working conditions; for example, restroom facilities were often shared by female and male employees. The assistant postmaster general reflected on working conditions at the time of the strike:

For years, the government has been telling the private sector how to treat its personnel, how to run a safety program, how to do everything better. When I came down here, I thought I was coming straight to the Messiah. I found just the opposite. I found an operation that's back in the 19th century. The Post Office doesn't begin to approach the progressive practices industry found pay off long ago.[26]

Accidents in this occupation were above the nation's average due to the working conditions in facilities and on deliveries. In heavy crime areas, postal employees secretly packed pistols to ward off muggers.[27]

In the 1970 negotiations the parties were unable to reach a settlement. The strike started in New York City and spread quickly to cities in New Jersey and Connecticut, then to Philadelphia, Cleveland, Chicago, Milwaukee, and San Francisco. Virtually the entire postal service came to a halt as an estimated 200,000 postal employees went on strike.[28] Although the Post Office Department secured an injunction, strikers did not return to work, and much of the mail service was paralyzed. Federal officials and the postal administrator negotiated with postal union leaders to end the strike. Twenty-five thousand U.S. Army soldiers were called out to perform the tasks of the striking postal employees in the New York City area; however, 90 percent of the strikers returned to work fairly soon, and serious collective bargaining began (a historic event in the federal sector). The negotiations resulted in a memorandum of agreement, a general wage increase, a change in the wage schedule, a joint commitment to postal reform, establishment of a system of collective bargaining similar to the private sector's, and, most importantly, amnesty for postal strikers. For the first time, leaders of federal employee unions sat with administration officials and negotiated a collective bargaining agreement.[29] While the strike was declared illegal,[30] its effect had been legitimized by the passage of the Postal Reorganization Act of 1970.

The Postal Reorganization Act of 1970

The Postal Reorganization Act (PRA), signed by President Nixon on August 12, 1970, fulfilled the desires of the postal unions to have their labor-management relations programs established by statute. Under Kennedy's executive orders, the Post Office Department never fully accepted collective bargaining, even though it was the largest single employer in the United States and had the largest proportion of employees belonging to unions.

The act created the U.S. Postal Service (USPS) as an independent establishment within the executive branch of the federal government. The office of postmaster general, previously a position in the cabinet, was made independent of Congress and the president. The postmaster general was to be selected by an eleven-member board of governors. Further, under the PRA many new policies of vital importance to the postal unions, such as an 8 percent retroactive pay increase, attainment of the highest wage rate in job classifications in eight years instead of twenty-one, acceptance of the concept of federal-civilian pay comparability, and establishment of self-supporting postal service by 1984, were adopted.

Under the PRA, the national labor rules that have evolved over the years under the National Labor Relations Act apply to the USPS. Wages, hours, benefits, and terms and conditions of employment are to be determined through collective bargaining. Grievances, adverse actions, and arbitration procedures are subject to negotiations. The NLRB supervises representation elections and prosecutes unfair labor practices. Although the right to strike was prohibited, a fact-finding–arbitration procedure was made available if a bargaining impasse persisted longer than 180 days after bargaining began.

Since the PRA was passed, contracts have been negotiated without major disruptions of postal services. Each negotiation, however, has been accompanied by serious threats of work stoppages by urban postal employees, who believed that their wages did not compare with other urban wage earners of similar skills and responsibilities.[31]

The 1978 agreement, which reflected the postal employees' major concerns, was successfully negotiated with only minor walkouts but was rejected by the membership. Both parties had made extensive preparations for a possible national strike, and after seventeen weeks of negotiations, a tentative agreement was reached on the last day before the old contract expired. The rejected agreement included a 19.5 percent wage and cost-of-living increase over three years (average annual salary would be about $19,000 by 1981) and a no-layoff clause. Although the agreement was deemed noninflationary, it would have pushed the average pay of postal employees to $7.58 per hour as compared to $5.62 for private nonfarm workers,[32] a wage differential that researchers took to task.[33]

After the contract was rejected and under the threat of a national mail strike, the postal union leaders insisted upon further negotiations; however, Postmaster General William Bolger would accept no alternative except arbitration, as outlined by law.[34] Then, under an unusual agreement worked out by the FMCS, James Healy was asked to serve as mediator while the negotiations were resumed for fifteen days. If no agreement was reached by negotiation, Healy would impose an arbitrated settlement that would be final and binding on both parties.[35]

Because the parties were unable to reach a settlement on the issues themselves, Healy issued an arbitration award. The wage and cost-of-living payments over three years were projected at 21.3 percent (based on estimated 6.5 percent inflation rate); however, the *cap* (ceiling on the cost-of-living adjustments) was removed. The no-layoff provision included in the rejected contract, which would have expired in three years and would have reemerged as a critical issue in future negotiations, was also changed. Healy's award protected current postal employees from layoffs for the rest of their working lives; however, the no-layoff provision does not apply to new postal employees until they have worked for the postal service for six years. After that, they too will have the same protection from layoffs.[36]

Thus, the 1978 negotiations introduced a new era for collective bargaining in the federal government. While the arbitrated settlement was unusual, it demonstrated that the impasse procedure can be applied peacefully and the settlement can be rendered with considerations given to future problems, such as inflation and layoffs caused by technological change.

The 1982 negotiations occurred in an adverse climate: two union presidents accused the postal service of treating collective bargaining as a sham. The postal service countered by showing that postal employees, for their education and skill, earn more than comparable workers in every sector of the private economy except miners. The postal service announced that it would not tolerate a strike and sent letters to all employees, warning them that strikers would be fired and would forfeit their rights to any future government employment.[37]

The final agreement boosted wages 10 percent over three years before cost-of-living adjustments and provided for a productivity bonus of at least $350 and a one-time $150 for ratifying the agreement. In addition, workers within six years of retirement received cost-of-living adjustments for the years 1979–1982 totalling $3,619, and this amount was added immediately to their pay for computing retirement benefits.[38] This agreement was negotiated without a strike, which challenged the previous power tactics of the unions. One major factor explaining this settlement was the timing of the 1982 negotiations, which occurred shortly after the air traffic controllers' strike (discussed later in the chapter). Public opinion was against any disputes in the federal government; it was probably influenced by the mass media which had provided daily coverage of the controllers' strike and included many negative editorials about strikes by federal employees.

Assessment

Collective bargaining in the USPS has not evolved as many expected. It has not followed the private sector model despite adopting many of its procedures. Lobbying with Congress continues to be an important part of the process not only for terms of the labor agreement but for working conditions outside the scope of negotiations and appeal of managerial decisions. Given that this system of labor relations was introduced into such a large, multi-faceted public organization only a decade ago, collective bargaining has been absorbed well. There have been no major disputes despite changes in staffing patterns, mechanization, and organization structure. Sometimes arbitrary authority of local postmasters has been curbed; there have been no damaging strikes in five negotiations; and the existence of unions and collective bargaining is now accepted as a way of life.[39]

PATCO–FAA Negotiations— A Study of Miscalculation

Negotiations and Strike

One of the most dramatic events in the history of federal government labor relations occurred on August 3, 1981, when 12,000 members of the Professional Air Traffic Controllers Organization (PATCO) struck against the Federal Aviation Administration (FAA).

Like other employer-union conflicts, the PATCO strike was not a sudden incident. For some time PATCO had been unsuccessful in bringing about change under the Carter administration. In fact, as noted in Chapter 2 PATCO was one of the few unions that endorsed Ronald Reagan for president. Soon after Reagan's inauguration PATCO President, Robert Poli, and other PATCO officials met with the President, and he promised to consider their views in his budget proposals. In his order to freeze federal hiring, the air traffic controllers were exempted.

Soon after PATCO and FAA began negotiations, the union announced that its principal collective bargaining goal was to have FAA support for pending legislation which would boost top salaries to $73,420 per year (the 1981 average was about $30,000). The PATCO proposal included a four-day, 32-hour workweek and a more liberal pension plan than for other federal employees. The Secretary of Transportation announced that the cost of the union proposal would be $1.1 billion in the first year. PATCO President Poli countered that the cost would only be $1.7 billion over three years. In March, the union conducted informational pickets to publicize its goals and the fact that its contract with FAA had expired.

PATCO held a convention in May and a cheering delegation approved a leadership decision to set a strike deadline of June 22. The FAA informed the air traffic controllers that federal law prohibited work stoppages and also directed its managers to review the FAA strike contingency plan. Ninety minutes before the strike deadline, however, the negotiators for the FAA, Department of Transportation, and PATCO announced a tentative agreement that would have boosted air traffic controllers' total pay $40 million. President Reagan supported the settlement, but the PATCO executive board unanimously recommended rejection.[40] The tentative agreement would have raised the average salary to $38,000, enabled controllers to receive forty-two hours of pay for forty hours of work, provided income differentials for night and overtime, and allowed fourteen weeks of salary for controllers who are retired for medical reasons.[41]

On July 29, 1981, 90 percent of the 15,000 PATCO members rejected the tentative agreement. The issues that were still disputed were union participation in management decisions on selection of technology, a more liberal early retirement plan, levels of pay, sick leave accumulation, and a thirty-two-hour workweek.

On Friday, July 31, Poli announced that he would return to the bargaining table, but unless an agreement was reached by 7:00 a.m. Monday, August 3, a national walkout would occur. When no agreement was reached by the deadline, the union struck. The result was a wholesale disruption of the nation's air transportation system. President Reagan became personally involved and warned that unless strikers returned to work within forty-eight hours, they would be fired.[42] As one writer contended:

The President's timing couldn't have been worse; strikers' resolve runs the highest on the first day of a walkout.[43]

One government official claimed that if the President had given the strikers ninety-six hours, there would have been more time for maneuvering and face-saving. Another observed that once the President had taken his position, there was no one in the federal government who could have taken another position that would perhaps have resulted in the controllers return.

With 12,000 PATCO members on strike and the President's decision to discharge the strikers, it appeared that the union had miscalculated the President's tough stance and overestimated support from the public, who would be inconvenienced by the strike.

After the strike began, behind-the-scenes efforts to start negotiating again were attempted. However, Poli insisted on an agreement before cancelling the strike. Secretary of Transportation Drew Lewis maintained that he would not negotiate until PATCO announced plans to end the strike. With both parties maintaining fixed positions, there was no room for compromise.

Meanwhile, the President's order was modified, and fired controllers were given up to a week to prove that they were not strike participants. Also, it was announced that strikers had the right to appeal their dismissal to the federal court. The FAA announced that it would take nearly two years to recover from the massive firing; at twenty-one airports flight schedules were reduced 50 percent. Nonstrikers, supervisors, and military air traffic controllers worked ten to twelve hour days, six days a week. Five union officials were jailed, and the Justice Department obtained back-to-work orders in fifty-seven federal courts. Criminal complaints were filed against thirty-nine union members in fourteen cities, and PATCO was fined $1 million a day.[44]

PATCO had assumed that a complete controller strike would bring the nation's air traffic system to a halt, causing such economic damage that the government would yield to the union's demands. However, the FAA's contingency plan worked better than expected, military controllers became acclimated quicker than predicted, and support for PATCO from the public and other unions was not forthcoming. Two reports were released in August that hurt the PATCO position: one by the Commerce Department that predicted the long-term effect of the strike would not be great and a research report that revealed controller "burnout" was not as severe as claimed by PATCO.

The federal government then proceeded to have PATCO decertified for violating the no-strike provisions of the Civil Service Reform Act. The Federal Labor Relations Authority in October 1981, ordered PATCO decertified as the air traffic controllers' representative. PATCO protested the decision, but Secretary Lewis called it sound and responsible. He then announced that he would send legislation to Congress similar to the settlement rejected by PATCO.

While immediate monetary costs to the airlines amounted to millions, their other costs included the loss of many well-trained, experienced air traffic controllers, air travelers inconvenienced by disrupted service, significant airline layoffs, and loss of funds spent to train replacements and rebuild the air traffic controller system.[45]

Post-Decertification Activities

Congress debated the proposed legislation and questioned the effect of singling out one group of federal employees for special treatment. Several Congressmen critized the FAA for negotiating economic issues because these were not permissible bargaining subjects under the Civil Service Reform Act. Two reports from Congress indicated that air travel was not as safe as before the strike and that the FAA was overly optimistic about its ability to rebuild the air traffic control system within its timetable. Private groups, such as the Airline Passengers Association, came out in favor of rehiring the air traffic controllers, and the AFL-CIO convention called on President Reagan to end his brutal punishment of the strikers. Even the Soviet delegates to the International Labor Organization in Geneva called the U.S. government's action against PATCO a violation of the elementary rights of trade unions.

In late October, 1981, PATCO offered to call off its strike if its members could return to work; however, no reaction came from the government. In December, President Reagan offered to permit strikers to apply again for other federal jobs—not with the FAA—but this offer did not extend to strikers who had engaged in violence or misconduct. The Merit Systems Protection Board began hearing appeals from air traffic controllers on a case-by-case basis. A federal judge dismissed contempt indictments against PATCO strikers because the government had already fired them, and contempt charges would have been punitive. PATCO President Poli announced his resignation, and PATCO filed for bankruptcy.

In 1982, the Merit System Protection Board upheld the firing of striking controllers in its first case. Some federal judges allowed community service to be used as punishment for criminal contempt of court by former PATCO leaders who defied the order to return to work. Still Congress had not approved the proposed pay increases recommended by Secretary Lewis after the strike. A three-member task force was named to study labor relations in the air traffic control system and it reported:

1. a need to select skilled managers who are more sympathetic to worker complaints,
2. low morale, with factors that caused problems in the past reasserting themselves,
3. automatic, impersonal, and by-the-book management.[46]

While all parties share part of the responsibility for the incident, critics have blamed the Federal Labor Relations Authority and the Federal Service Impasse Panel for their lack of action. However, the FLRA and the FSIP had questionable authority to act because PATCO and the FAA were negotiating over wages, a subject prohibited under the Civil Service Reform Act—the act which gives authority to both the FLRA and the FSIP.[47] Because the law is silent as to whether the FSIP can enter a negotiation without a request from either party, the FSIP lacked authority to bring the dispute to a conclusion.[48]

In late 1982, one report indicated that relations between air traffic controllers and their bosses were reverting to the open hostility evidenced before the strike. Examples of complaints include working twenty-five to thirty planes at once, up from twelve to fifteen before the strike; forty-eight-hour workweeks; and work for four straight hours without a break; outspoken controllers sent for medical and psychiatric exams. FAA management reacted by having all managers attend management development programs, appointing a human relations specialist in each region, and emphasizing human relations considerations in promotion decisions. The FAA has estimated that by July, 1985, the system will be fully recovered, but many controllers remain skeptical. Likewise, without a union for protection, many of the controllers are skeptical about the employer-employee relationships.[49]

Summary and Implications

Summary

This chapter presented the historical development of unionism in the federal government and the effect of the executive orders of the president and the Civil Service Reform Act of 1978. While legislation and executive permission to allow federal employee unions was absent for many years, unions still developed, even under adverse conditions. Executive Order 10988 did not offer many substantive benefits to federal employee unions but provided the framework for a labor relations system in the federal government and gave tremendous impetus to union organization and growth. Each subsequent executive order added new features, and federal employees were eventually given many rights similar to those of employees under many state statutes and the National Labor Relations Act.

The administrative agencies under the Civil Service Reform Act include the Federal Labor Relations Authority, the General Counsel, and the Federal Service Impasse Panel. Also available for assistance are the Federal Mediation and Conciliation Service, labor arbitrators, and fact finders, who provide important services for the parties. Since the CSRA has only been in effect since early 1979, directions and many interpretations remain for the future.

Two important segments of the federal government, the postal service and air traffic control system, were discussed. The postal unions have a critical effect on the operations of the postal service. Although no major strike has occurred since the enactment of the Postal Reorganization Act of 1970, such a strike could drastically affect commerce and create emergency conditions in many sectors of our economy. Thus, continuing efforts by the postal unions and the U.S. Postal Service are essential to assure successful labor relations. A summary of major events of the PATCO-FAA negotiations and the subsequent PATCO strikes were also highlighted.

Implications

With over a decade of experience with the Postal Organization Act of 1970 and over two decades with the various executive orders and subsequent Civil Service Reform Act of 1978, questions arise as to the future direction of federal government labor relations. Several alternatives are present for improving the federal system of labor relations. First, the role and authority of the Federal Service Impasse Panel must be clarified so as to avoid conflicts such as the PATCO-FAA conflict. Second, because federal employees cannot legally strike, methods for resolving impasses must be introduced to encourage the parties to conscientiously attempt to resolve disputes on their own. If they are unable to resolve their disputes, methods for resolution, possibly arbitration, should be available. Third, a procedure must be designed for parties to obtain quicker answers to questions of negotiability. In the present system, federal managers too often use non-negotiability as a bargaining tactic to delay the negotiations. Finally, a genuine effort must be made by both parties to upgrade the sophistication and qualifications of the negotiators and representatives.[50] While much can be achieved over time, the parties can speed up the process by committing resources to improving the skills and abilities of professionals who are involved in the bargaining process.

Discussion Questions

1. Do you see any similarities between the development of labor unions in the federal sector and those in the private sector (outlined in Chapter 2)? Describe these.
2. What were weaknesses in the three types of union recognition allowed under Executive Order 10988?
3. What are the administrative agencies under the Civil Service Reform Act? What are their responsibilities?
4. Considering the multitude of subjects that are bargainable in the federal sector, list some of the more important ones that are not.
5. Compare and contrast the negotiated grievance procedures under the CSRA with most found in the private sector.

6. What type of impasse resolution procedure was used in the 1978 postal negotiations? Why do you think this procedure was used? (See Chapter 7.) How effective was it?
7. Assess the union's strategy in the air traffic controllers' strike. Assess the president's actions.

References

[1]Murray B. Nesbitt, *Labor Relations in the Federal Government Service* (Washington, D.C.; Bureau of National Affairs, 1976), pp. 6–17; and Richard J. Murphy, "The Federal Experience in Employee Relations," in Richard J. Murphy and Morris Sackman, eds., *The Crisis in Public Employee Relations in the Decade of the Seventies* (Washington, D.C.: Bureau of National Affairs, 1970), pp. 1-2.

[2]K. L. Hanslowe, *The Emerging Law of Labor Relations in Public Employment* (Ithaca, N.Y.: Cornell University, 1967), p. 40.

[3]Ibid., pp. 41–43.

[4]United States Federal Labor Relations Council, *Labor-Management Relations in the Federal Service* (Washington, D.C.: Government Printing Office, 1975), p. 28.

[5]This agency assumes many of the responsibilities of the Federal Labor Council and Assistant Secretary of Labor for Labor-Management Relations.

[6]U.S. Civil Service Commission, Office of Labor-Management Relations, *Introducing the Civil Service Reform Act* (Washington, D.C.: Government Printing Office, 1978), pp. 1–4.

[7]92 Stat. 1212–1213 (1978).

[8]92 Stat. 1196–1197 (1978).

[9]92 Stat. 1208–1209 (1978).

[10]"Impasse Panel Report for 1980," *The Federal Labor-Management Consultant* (Washington, D.C.: Office of Personnel Management, October 23, 1981), p. 4.

[11]Federal Mediation and Conciliation Service, *Thirty-fourth Annual Report: 1981* (Washington, D.C.: Government Printing Office, 1982), p. 13 and 29.

[12]United States Federal Labor Relations Council, *Labor-Management Relations*, p. 11.

[13]92 Stat. 1201 (1978).

[14]92 Stat. 1199 (1978).

[15]92 Stat. 1198 (1978).

[16]92 Stat. 1194 (1978). Section 7103 (a) (14) states that "conditions of employment means personnel policies, practices, and matters, whether established by rule, regulation, or otherwise, affecting working conditions, except that such term does not include policies, practices, and matters—(A) relating to political activities . . . ; (B) relating to the classification of any position; or (C) to the extent such matters are specifically provided for by Federal statute."

[17]92 Stat. 1204–1205 (1978).

[18]*Federal Labor Relations Authority and the Federal Service Impasse Panel* Second Annual Report (Washington, D.C.: U.S. Government Printing Office, 1980), p. 45.

[19]92 Stat. 1204–1206 (1978).

[20]Francis J. Loevi, Jr., and Roger P. Kaplon, *Arbitration and the Federal Sector Advocate* (New York: American Arbitration Association, 1982), p. 43. For a legal analysis of the remedial authority of the arbitrator, see S. L. Hayford, "The Impact of Law and Regulation upon the Remedial Authority of Labor Arbitrators in the Federal Sector," *Arbitration Journal* 37 (March 1982), pp. 28–37.

[21]92 Stat. 1211–1214, 1216 (1978).

[22]Douglas M. McCabe, "Problems in Federal Sector Labor-Management Relations Under Title VII of the Civil Service Reform Act of 1978," *Labor Law Journal* 33 (August 1982), p. 561.

[23]Ibid., pp. 561–563.

[24]U.S. General Accounting Office, *Steps Can Be Taken to Improve Federal Labor-Management Relations and Reduce the Number and Costs of Unfair Labor Practice Charges* (Washington, D.C.: U.S. General Accounting Office, 1982), pp. 1–22.

[25]"The Strike That Stunned the Country," *Time*, March 3, 1970, p. 11.

[26]"Federal Workers March to a New Drummer," *Business Week*, March 28, 1970, p. 91. For a visual and descriptive depiction of working conditions, the reader is also referred to pp. 86–87 and pp. 90–92.

[27]Ibid., p. 91.

[28]S. C. Shannon, "Work Stoppage in Government: The Postal Strike of 1970," *Monthly Labor Review* 101 (July 1978), pp. 15–17.

[29]Nesbitt, *Labor Relations in the Government*, pp. 8–90.

[30]*United Federation of Postal Clerks v. Blount*, 325 F. Supp. 879 (1971); 404 U.S. 802 (1971).

[31]Nesbitt, *Labor Relations in the Government*, pp. 316–347.

[32]"A Stop-the-Clock Postal Pay Deal Aids the Battle against Inflation," *Time*, July 31, 1978; p. 50.

[33]Sharon Smith, "Are Postal Workers Overpaid or Underpaid?" *Industrial Relations* 15 (May 1976), pp. 168–176.

[34]"Postal Strike Threat Apparently Averted as Two Sides Agree to Resume Talks," *Wall Street Journal*, August 29, 1978, p. 2.

[35]"Postal Labor Uncertainty Will Linger Despite Arbitrated Settlement of Dispute," *Wall Street Journal*, September 18, 1978, p. 7.

[36]Ibid. Also see Leon Bornstein, "Postal Accord Retains 'No Layoffs' Clause," *Monthly Labor Review* 101 (September 1978), p. 13; and Leon Bornstein, "Arbitration Awards Higher Pay to Postal Employees," *Monthly Labor Review* 101 (November 1978), p. 44.

[37]Robert S. Greenberger, "Mail Service May Continue Past Deadline for Contract Monday if Pact Seems Near," *Wall Street Journal*, July 16, 1981, p. 8.

[38]Robert S. Greenberger, "Postal Service, 2 Major Unions Set 3-Year Pact," *Wall Street Journal*, July 22, 1982, p. 3.

[39]J. Joseph Loewenberg, "The U.S. Postal Service," in Gerald G. Somers, ed., *Collective Bargaining: Contemporary American Experiences* (Madison, Wis.: Industrial Relations Research Association, 1980), pp. 483–484.

[40]"PATCO Members Voting on Contract; Overwhelming Rejection Is Expected," *Government Employee Relations Report* (Washington, D.C.: Bureau of National Affairs, Inc., July 13, 1981), pp. 920:16.

[41]"Air Controllers Strike Stands Out among 1981's Top Federal Developments," *Government Employee Relations Report* (Washington, D.C.: Bureau of National Affairs, Inc., January 4, 1981), 944:5–7.

[42]*Annual Report of the Federal Mediation and Conciliation Service, 1981* (Washington, D.C.: U.S. Government Printing Office, 1982), pp. 15–16.

[43]Joann S. Lublin, "Both Sides Made Mistakes in Controllers' Strike," *Wall Street Journal*, September 15, 1981, p. 29.

[44]Joann Lublin, "Firings of Air Traffic Controllers Begin as Efforts to Resume Talks Stall," *Wall Street Journal*, August 6, 1981, p. 1

[45]Government Employee Relations Report, January 4, 1981, pp. 940:5–8.

[46]"U.S. Panel Suggests FAA Pick Supervisors More Sympathetic to Workers' Complaints," *Wall Street Journal*, March 18, 1982, p. 7.

[47]"FSIP Role in PATCO Strike," *Government Employee Relations Report* (Washington, D.C.: Bureau of National Affairs, Inc., July 26, 1982), pp. 972:12.

[48]"Statement of Ronald W. Haughton," *The Arbitration Journal* 37 (September 1982), pp. 56–60.

[49]"Tower Turbulence: Labor Friction Returns to Air-Traffic System a Year After the Strike," *Wall Street Journal*, October 4, 1982, p. 1 and p. 27.

[50]McCabe, "Problems in Federal Sector Labor-Management Relations, pp. 563–565. Also see Ronald W. Haughton, "The Need for Urgency in Federal Sector Bargaining," *Journal of Collective Negotiations in the Public Sector* 10 (Third Quarter 1981), pp. 201–208.

Chapter 16 Foreign Labor Movements and Transnational Collective Bargaining

The interdependency of nations is a powerful fact of life in the world economy . . . the activities of multinational corporations are an important aspect of economic relations between nations . . . the large increase in the number of multinationals and the growth of their share of world output since the early 1960s has greatly expanded their importance and visibility in both industrialized and developing countries.

Robert F. Banks and Jack Stieber, "Introduction," in Robert F. Banks and Jack Stieber, eds., *Multinationals, Unions and Labor Relations in Industrialized Countries* (Ithaca, N.Y.: Cornell University, 1977), p. 1.

Growing interdependency among nations, major improvements in communication and travel between countries, and the increasing role of multinational corporations (MNCs) have all led to the need to learn more about labor relations systems in other parts of the world. Books have been written about many of the specific topics in this chapter, and no attempt will be made to present detailed descriptions or analyses of labor relations systems in the countries mentioned. The chapter presents a number of unique and interesting features of a variety of countries with the hope of encouraging the readers to pursue more serious investigations in the future. Its coverage ranges from the developing countries of Latin and South America to the countries nearest our borders—Mexico and Canada—to the major trading partners of the United States such as Japan and the Western European countries. From these discussions, specific attention is directed toward multinational corporations and transnational collective bargaining.

Unions in Other Countries

Many U.S. residents tend to view the rest of the world in terms of their own patterns of living. The fact is that virtually no country has labor relations like ours; even the most similar country, Canada, has several major departures from typical U.S. labor relations practices. Unions of Eastern and Western Europe have much closer ties to political parties; Japanese unions are organized on the enterprise level; Latin American unions are split along ideological lines. By contrast, the United States' industrial relations system is based on majority rule, exclusive representation for bargaining agents, and political independence.[1] Table 1 presents an overview of distinguishing features of foreign labor relations systems; the following discussion briefly explains these systems.

Table 1 Overview of Distinguishing Features between U.S. and Other Labor Relations Systems

United States	Exclusive bargaining representation Majority rule Political independence
Canada	Influence by unions and companies from U.S. Two major linguistic and cultural groups Decentralized and fragmented collective bargaining Legal influence within provinces
Latin and South America	Wide variation in the degree of sophistication in labor relations systems Close connection between trade unions and political parties Voluminous labor codes and government regulations that cover wages and terms of employment Predominantly negotiations at plant level only
Western Europe	Exclusive bargaining representation nonexistent Much negotiation between employer association and union confederation with individual bargaining under the resulting agreement Many fringe benefits established by law Worker participation mandated in many countries
Japan	Lifetime employment in large firms Enterprise unions Wage system with much weight on seniority
Australia	Arbitration tribunals Wage boards Compulsory arbitration
Eastern Europe	Government controlled unions Lack of collective bargaining No labor agreements

Canada

Canada's labor relations system is affected by a number of variables: foreign influences, climate, natural resources, and two major linguistic and cultural groups. Its economy is subject to cyclical fluctuations resulting from harsh winters, seasonality of its industries, and foreign influences (mostly the U.S.). In addition, Canada's geographical spread and regional concentration of resources and production have led to decentralized and fragmented collective bargaining. The penetration of United States corporations into Canada has had a significant effect on Canadian labor relations due to the fact that many major decisions still are made in the United States. The French- and English-speaking division of Canada has produced two distinct labor movements; further, relationships between management, which is primarily unilingually English-speaking, and the predominantly French-speaking work force have not been ideal.[2]

In Canada, governments within the provinces (similar to the various states in the U.S.), not the federal government, have established the legal framework for 90 percent of the collective bargaining.[3] These laws are similar to the United States' in many ways and cover such topics as appropriate bargaining units, prohibition of work stoppages during tenure of agreements, and guidelines for workers voting for representation rights.[4] On the other hand, the emphasis on provincial determination has resulted in many different legal frameworks for Canadian collective bargaining (much the way it has in the public sector in the United States).

More recently, because there has been significant union activity in the public sector (for example hospital, postal and teacher strikes), the Canadian federal government has been asserting itself more and accumulating more centralized authority to produce a stronger national government with respect to labor relations and standards. In response, the Canadian Labour Council (CLC), a labor federation similar to the AFL-CIO in the U.S., has more and more become the central voice for organized labor. As the federal government continues to gather more power over collective bargaining, the provincial governments will lose control, and the CLC will gain power in its role.[5]

Probably the most controversial issue in Canadian labor relations grows out of the alleged domination by U.S. unions and corporations. Over 35 percent of Canada's industry is foreign owned, but this segment accounts for 70 percent of the business activity.[6] Of the twelve largest labor unions (representing over 50,000 members), eight are affiliated with major U.S. labor unions, such as the United Auto Workers and Teamsters, and the remaining ones are AFL-CIO affiliates.[7] Forty-five percent of union members belong to international unions based in the United States.[8] This means there is a potential for undermining Canadian sovereignty if foreign-based unions and companies are not sensitive to Canada's needs. For instance, Canadians have serious concerns over decisions that are made by U.S.-based unions and corporations but implemented in Canada.

Collective bargaining in Canada remains highly localized with the predominant bargaining unit, the single establishment-single union. This bargaining arrangement prevails in over 60 percent of the contracts covering 500 employees or more and covering over 50 percent of Canada's union members. Corporation-wide bargaining occurs in railways, communications, airlines, and broadcasting due to the highly integrated technology in these industries.[9]

Latin and South America

Collective bargaining in Latin America is far less extensive and sophisticated than corresponding activities in the United States; however, the number of agreements have been increasing. While the percentage of workers covered by labor agreements is greater in Mexico, Venezuela, and Argentina than in the United States, this amount reflects more a government extension of contract terms than actual industry-wide bargaining patterns. The extent of development of collective bargaining may be illustrated in three categories:

1. The advanced group, as exemplified by Mexico and Argentina.
2. A much larger middle group in which bargaining ranges from advanced collective bargaining with larger firms to very simple or no bargaining in smaller firms, as in Chile and Brazil.
3. A large third group in which collective bargaining is not widespread, as in Costa Rica, Ecuador, and Nicaraugua.[10]

Negotiations between unions and employers take place primarily at the plant level. Only Argentina, Venezuela, and Mexico have widespread industry-wide bargaining. The principal reason for this arrangement is that legislation in the various countries typically does not require employers to bargain except on a plant-level basis.

An interesting departure from most of the world is the important role of collective bargaining between employers and nonunion workers. In fact, over 25 percent of the labor agreements in Columbia and Venezuela are negotiated without trade unions. Obviously, the unions look with disfavor on this arrangement because employers use the nonunion groups as a means to bypass trade unions.[11]

In the more industrialized countries of the world, people interpret labor-management relations activities to mean the wide nature of the relationships between employers and employees. However, people of Latin American countries tend to define labor relations in terms of the voluminous labor codes and governmental regulations.[12]

Labor relations vary widely among the countries in Latin America, but one common thrust is present: the close connection between trade unions and political parties. For example, in Mexico unions constitute a large section of the ruling political party and therefore are assigned a quota of candidates on the party's ticket for office. Thus, unions have some assurance of having a voice in the party's program and on its council.[13] Some unions have been very effective in gaining relatively high wages for members. For example, the electrical workers in Mexico earn two to three times more than the urban working class.[14] Likewise, unions have been criticized because they have made gains for their own members while neglecting the interests of the great mass of people, including the peasants, who are terribly poor.[15]

Labor agreements vary in content both within countries and among countries. In Argentina, labor agreements include provisions that set forth in some detail the employment conditions and establish a highly developed shop steward system to administer grievances and assure that employers abide by the agreements. In Chile, labor agreements are more general, but they do establish certain minimum rules and include a grievance machinery to enforce the agreement. In Brazil, where unions have struggled since 1945 to have a greater say in determining employment rules and conditions for their members, they have achieved more through labor legislation than by engaging in collective bargaining.

In these countries, political parties maintain close ties with unions for their support, votes, and influence. Likewise, trade unions depend on the politicians for laws to protect their members, to legalize their organizations, and to regulate their relations with employers.[16] On the other hand, political parties have appealed to organized labor to favor their own policies, and in some cases, they have accommodated organized labor in hopes that they will remain temporarily satisfied and continue to support the existing economic and political system.[17]

Western Europe and Great Britain

Unionization in Western Europe is significantly greater than in the United States, with the exception of France and Italy. The range is from 42 percent in Germany to over 80 percent in Sweden. Unions have been able to use this membership strength to accumulate political influence at the national level. Further, they have been able to coordinate their efforts with large, well-established labor parties in government to achieve their goals. Unions have achieved significantly greater worker participation in the operation of the firm—many times through legislative mandate and sometimes through management reaction to wildcat strikes and worker dissatisfaction.[18] In addition, public opinion in these countries strongly supports the idea that worker participation enhances production, fosters harmony, and enriches the worker's personally.[19]

The labor relations system in Western Europe can be contrasted with that of the United States in a number of ways:

1. In the United States, unions are selected by the majority of the appropriate bargaining unit, whereas in Western Europe exclusive representation is not a common concept.
2. In the United States, the exclusive bargaining representative has a monopoly over all employee bargaining, and the employer is required to bargain only with the legally certified union. In Western Europe, the employer often bargains with a number of unions in addition to councils elected by the workers.
3. In Western Europe, negotiations take place between representatives of employer associations and those representing a confederation of unions; in the United States, this bargaining arrangement is adopted only in a few industries.
4. The number of fringe benefits established by law is greater in Europe; therefore, trade unions have found that they can obtain benefits more quickly through the political arena and have tied themselves more closely with political parties.[20]

Great Britain The traditional system in Great Britain is characterized by voluntary collective bargaining, implemented without legal compulsion through unenforceable labor agreements that have been negotiated by a large number of multi-union-multi-employer negotiating committees.[21] There are nearly 600 labor unions in the United Kingdom, over three times the number in the United States, and a manufacturing firm typically negotiates with about seven unions. Over the years there has been little labor relations law; thus a wide diversity in the collective bargaining arrangements developed. One of the most important negotiations involved the Engineering Employers' Federation, representing 4,500 plants, and the Confederation of Shipbuilding and Engineering Unions, representing thirty-four unions and over 2 million employees. This agreement sets forth general guidelines that establish the floor for additional bargaining at the plant. Labor agreements are administered at the plant level; however, they are not enforceable by law and grievances are not privately arbitrated.

Shop stewards, unlike their U.S. counterparts, are volunteers serving without pay and cannot be removed by union executives. Often, they accumulate much authority and influence at the plant and have more control over local union affairs than any national union official. Steward councils composed of union stewards from various unions and works councils representing members of the various departments are important in the labor relations system.

Labor agreements at the plant level are often negotiated by representatives of the national union, steward councils, and works councils. These agreements usually have no fixed term and include letters of understanding, minutes of meetings, and oral understandings. While there is no legal obligation to negotiate, unions have gained extensive power and control over jobs, refusing to work with any employer whom they find in bad standing and maintaining strict membership discipline.[22]

In 1979, a shift occurred from Labor Party majority in Parliament to the Conservative Party with Margaret Thatcher as Prime Minister. Proposals to reduce strikes, make it more difficult to organize workers, and cut the bargaining leverage of unions were introduced in Parliament. By 1982, this legislation had not been enacted, but Prime Minister Thatcher believes that she has an electorate mandate to restrict union rights and activities.[23]

Co-determination Policies One unique feature of Western European labor relations is the interest in and wide implementation of co-determination concepts. These concepts include the policies of shared authority on personnel matters, protected employee rights, guarantees of worker participation, and appeal of alleged unfair personnel decisions. West Germany has moved further in co-determination than other European countries, but Denmark, The Netherlands, Luxembourg, France, Austria, Norway, and Sweden all have some sort of legal requirements for worker representation on company boards—generally in the form of works councils that vary greatly in authority. Other countries (for example, Belgium, England, Italy, and Switzerland) have no laws requiring worker participation on boards, but forms of worker participation are present in various stages of development, and are frequently discussed.[24]

A look at West Germany's co-determination system Co-determination in West Germany can be traced back to 1920, but formulated principles were not legally established until the Co-determination Law of 1952, applicable to the iron, coal, and steel industries was passed. This law provided for a labor director on the executive committee and a parity agreement in the supervisory board (half representing the owners and shareholders, half representing employees, plus a neutral chairperson).

Formalized co-determination after World War II can be attributed to some degree to union reaction to the Nazi era, during which unions were dissolved and industrialists amassed tremendous power. Co-determination developed at least in part to allow worker involvement at a level in organizations where any possible extremism among industrialists and government officials could be monitored.[25]

Enacted in 1972, the Labor-Management Relations Act (of West Germany) redefined the functions of the works councils and specified rights of the individual worker. The council functions were oriented toward increased worker participation in the immediate labor environment. Workers' rights include the right to be informed about matters pertaining to their jobs, to make suggestions about their jobs, to see all of their work-related files, and to appeal management decisions that are considered unfair. Works councils were established at the plant level in such a way that they could guard and monitor these rights. They also serve as useful instruments of conflict resolution and a means of communication between management and the worker.

Co-determination expands the voice of labor in the two governing boards of large corporations: the supervisory board and board of executive directors.[26] While the supervisory board concerns itself with overall strategic business issues, the board of executive directors runs the daily business operation. The Co-determination Act of 1976 extended codetermination coverage to all companies which employ more than 2,000 workers (smaller companies remain under the 1952 law). The supervisory boards continued to have equal representation between capital and labor; however, the labor side was divided into three distinct groups: (a) union representatives, (b) white- and blue-collar employees, and (c) executives (see Exhibit 16.1).

Employee members of the supervisory boards are elected by a direct vote by employees or by a vote of electors who themselves have been elected to represent the employees. Employees in the firms decide by direct vote which election approach they will use, even though the law suggests that direct vote be used in small firms and election by employee representatives in larger ones. Union leaders tend to favor the indirect approach, and conservatives prefer the direct. The chairperson and vice chairperson are elected by two-thirds vote; if this two-thirds vote is not obtainable, the shareholders elect the chairperson, and labor the vice-chairperson. The chairperson's position is important because he or she casts the deciding vote on all issues that the supervisory board cannot resolve in the first round.[27]

Since the 1952 act, the works councils have been involved in regulating personnel and industrial relations practices and policies. These include daily hours, breaks, remuneration, leave schedules, discipline, welfare services, job and piece rates, new methods of compensation, vocational training, and review of major alterations that could involve substantial disadvantages for the company employees. Then, in 1972, the powers of the works councils were increased. They now also police union contracts, handle employee grievances, and co-determine personnel forms, wage plans, training, and related programs.[28]

Co-determination has had both advocates and critics. It has been labeled a "social partnership" that has brought about "social harmony" between unions and employers.[29] It has been credited as the main reason for relative labor peace in West Germany for the last twenty years, when compared to nearby countries like England, France, and Italy.[30] West German Chancellor Helmut Schmidt acclaimed it as the key to his country's postwar economic recovery and the competitive economic advantage which West Germany has held internationally.[31] One authority has said, "The fact that those countries with industrial democracy are some of the more successful economies is no coincidence."[32]

Criticism of these worker participation models has come from unions, management and the public. Unions have accused the top management of manipulating the regulations by delegating decision-making authority to lower management so that the supervisory boards will not be given the opportunity to discuss expenditures and investments. Management has accused the union representatives of disclosing corporate secrets, slowing the decision-making process, and

Exhibit 16.1 Selection Model of Co-determination Membership for Large Corporations

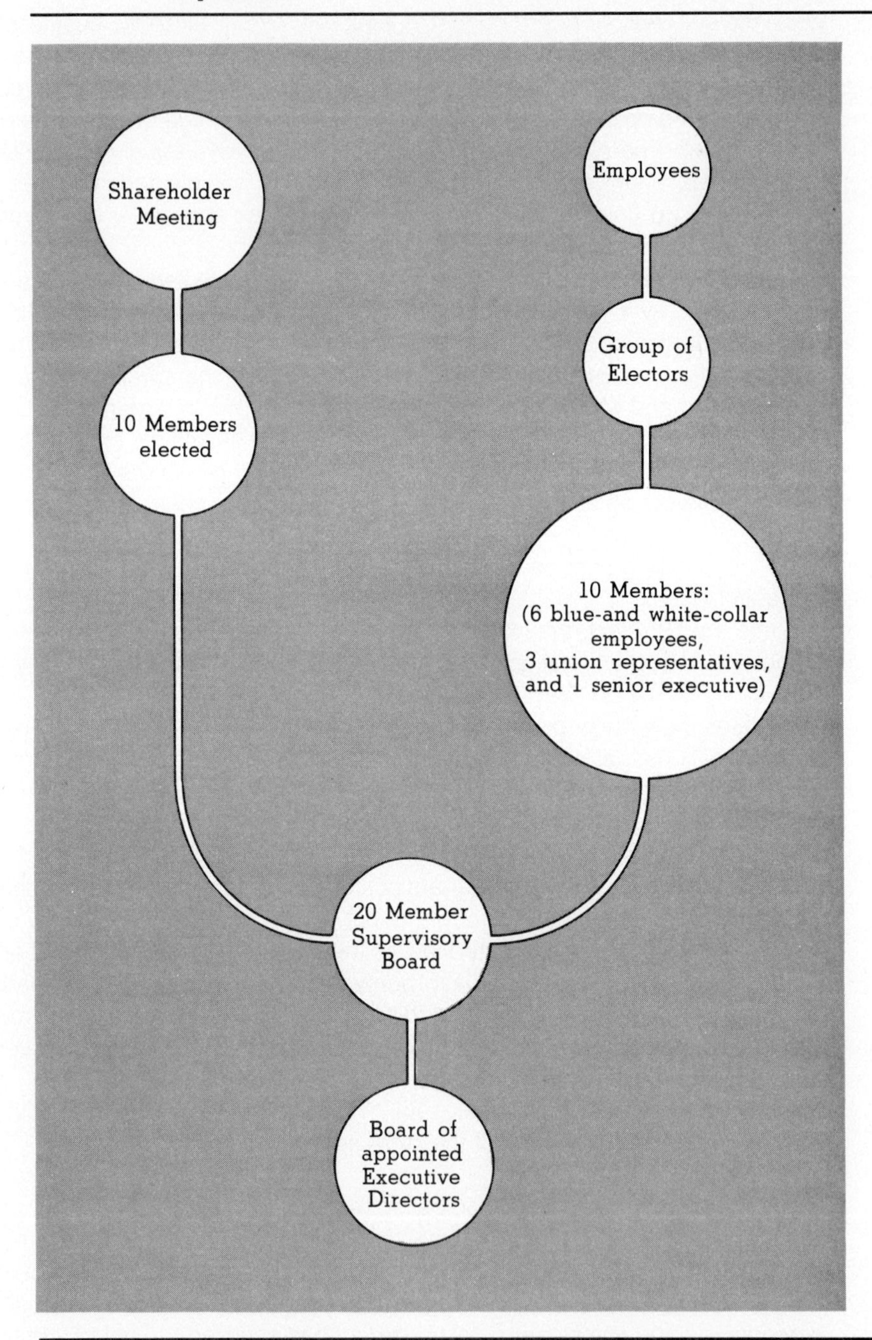

Source: Adapted from David T. Fisher, "Worker Participation in West German Industry," *Monthly Labor Review* 101 (May 1978), p. 61.

distributing confidential information, such as wage data, to the union membership. Outside observers have contended that joint decision making on the supervisory board favors the mutual interests of labor and management at the expense of the consumer.[33]

Japanese Industrial Relations

Japan's industrial relations system has three distinguishing characteristics: lifetime employment, a unique wage system, and the enterprise or "company" union. *Lifetime employment* simply means that an employee, after joining the company, will remain employed until retirement and only in extreme circumstances will a company terminate an employee. This benefit is provided mostly by large firms (over 500 employees) and considerable employee loyalty is given in return.[24]

The *wage system* in Japan has several distinguishing characteristics:

1. Salaries paid monthly, even though the employee may be absent (with justification) from work.
2. Small wage differentials between regular line employees and staff personnel, all of whom are members of the same union.
3. Wage distinctions between amounts earned for one's work (for example, efficiency output) and amounts earned for just being an employee (such as allowances for housing, transportation, and dependents).
4. Wages accepted as permanent and lasting for the employee's entire career, including a minimum annual increase and lump sum at retirement.

The *enterprise union* is composed of employees working for a single employer at a single location. These unions comprise nearly 90 percent of all union organizations in Japan and include all categories of skills among employees of a company. The development of the enterprise union has been aided substantially by the system of lifetime employment and a heavy reliance on seniority. Thus, the individual employee identifies more closely with the company than the typical employee in many Western countries does.

Labor unions do have national organizations in the textile, electricity, shipbuilding, automobile, steel, appliance, and chemical industries, that hold conferences to discuss industrial policies. However, they do *not* consider such topics as wages, working conditions, and other employment policies. These topics are discussed within the enterprise union. At the national level, they discuss industrial problems in a more general context (for example, economic growth, employment forecasts, retirement ages, and improved communications).[35]

As a result of high oil prices, rising protectionism abroad, heavy dependence on exports, lowering trade barriers, and slower economic growth, several Japanese firms have recently been considering abandoning their policies of lifetime job security. Compounding these economic problems have been the gradual aging of the work force, automatic wage increases based on seniority, and higher labor costs. Some firms have offered "sayonara" (the Japanese word for goodbye) premiums to encourage early retirement; some have set up special units for older workers at reduced pay; others have taken a harsher approach of laying off the older workers.[35]

Since 1973, one of Japan's largest unions, the Japanese Federation of Synthetic Chemical Workers' Union, has lost 8 percent of its members through firings and layoffs. Some have concluded that lifetime employment as a policy has begun to expire and that Japanese employers will begin laying off workers during recessions and linking pay raises more closely to skill than seniority. If employers abandon the security of a lifetime employment system, they will have to adjust to job-hopping by employees and to a more adversarial type of labor relations system.[37] Moreover, the government will probably become more involved with problems of unemployment and industrial conflicts. For example, almost 700 man-days per 1,000 workers were lost in larger establishments due to strikes in 1974, and the strike participation rate of employees was a rather high 10 percent—both figures exceeding U.S. statistics for most years since 1950.[38] However, total work days lost average one-third of the U.S.[39]

The spring of each year brings on the annual labor offensive or "shunto" (twenty-seven consecutive years as of 1982). The unions participate in nationwide demonstrations, singing labor songs, wearing red armbands, and refusing to work for short periods. While these demonstrations may be mistaken by an outsider as an indication of deteriorating labor-management relations, it actually is a time for labor to voice its views and to allow workers to let off steam. For example, in 1981, the major labor demand was bigger pay raises and lower taxes to increase disposable income and to revive a sluggish economy.[40]

In the final analysis, Japanese employers and unions eventually will have to face a number of critical issues that may cause a break with the traditional system: early retirement, higher unemployment, elimination of automatic pay increases and promotions, introduction of labor-saving devices, union emphasis on job security rather than wage hikes, decline of worker loyalty to the firm, and declining competitiveness with rapidly developing countries, such as Brazil, South Korea, Singapore, and Taiwan.[41]

Australia

Australia has developed a compulsory arbitration system at the federal level and in four of its six states,[42] and while the system relies mostly on negotiation and conciliation, it is very legalistic.[43] Two of the states have established wage boards that are quasi-legislative, tripartite bodies for the direct regulation of wages and conditions. For labor agreements to be legal under Australian law, unions must register them with the appropriate arbitration tribunal. This form of compulsory arbitration is designed to restrict the number of strikes and lockouts, although these activities do occur at a moderate rate after the rather complicated arbitration procedures are followed.[44] The arbitration tribunals are required to take into account the criterion labeled "the public interest." Government officials may present evidence to the tribunals for consideration. In practice the tribunals have considered the public interest to be the effect of their awards on the economy, especially inflation and unemployment.[45]

In recent years, labor and management have faced several key issues: wage indexation, strikes, and government intervention. The wage indexation controversy began in 1974 when labor unions claimed that wage increases should be automatically adjusted to the rise in the consumer price index (CPI). While wages were adjusted in relation to the CPI for the following two years, wage increases have fallen behind the CPI since 1976. Despite the arbitration system, the number of strikes in recent years is nearly as great as in the United States. For example, from 1972 to 1977 the days annually lost per worker averaged 0.19 and amounted to 2.7 million.[46] The number of days lost in 1979, however, rose to 4 million.[47] The final problem is government involvement, which stems from labor unions' heavy involvement with the Australian Labor Party. As with other labor-oriented political parties, changes in personnel on boards and commissions affect the labor relations climate as the different parties achieve and lose control of Parliament.[48]

Eastern Europe—Soviet Bloc Countries

Firmly entrenched in the U.S.S.R. since 1917, Communists took power in most of the East European countries after World War II and began transforming their political, economic, social, and cultural systems to the Soviet model. Institutions and social systems became formalized and bureaucratic and were controlled and directed by the Communist Party. The result has been increased similarity in the industrial relations systems among the various countries.[49]

In these countries, trade unions represent all employed persons, white- and blue-collar alike, and are authorized to represent both their members and nonmembers. Thus, trade unions represent nearly 90 percent of the populations. Theoretically, they are independent organizations, and nobody can interfere with their internal affairs. Realistically, they are directed by the party and their autonomy is low. Unions are governed in accordance with principles of democratic centralism, where each member may vote in a democratic manner; however, the organization structure centralizes authority at the top. The union members have only meager rights and very extensive duties, and they can be punished for failing to perform their duties according to union statutes.[50] Under the Soviet-type system the party "elite" will not allow trade union members to associate and dissociate at will. If such freedom were allowed, party officials believe that articulation of group interest would increase, unity of the official trade unions would be endangered, and the party "elite" would lose control over them.

In Eastern Europe, trade unions have two major functions:

1. Production promotion, which includes promoting the state plan, strengthening work discipline, and raising productivity.
2. Political indoctrination, which includes fostering the political consciousness, dedication to the public interest, and education of trade unionists on party matters.

Other proclaimed functions include defending the workers' interests, complying with labor legislation, administering social insurance, and promoting opportunities for physical training, sport, and recreation. Unions have attempted to perform these functions through only a small number of trade unions. For example, there were nineteen in Hungary in 1966, thirty in Czechoslovakia in 1969, twenty-five in the Soviet Union in 1970, and twenty-three in Poland in 1976.

To accomplish these functions, workers have been granted rights ranging from the right to make suggestions to the right to make decisions. These include the right to consummate a collective bargaining agreement that enumerates the rights and obligations of employees. But the agreements are not the result of collective bargaining as in the United States; their content is more the result of legal and political directives. Therefore, the labor agreements differ greatly in content, character, and role when compared to those in the West even though they may be labeled identically.[51]

The Soviet labor system has many critics, including Vladimir Bukovsky who alleges:

Soviet trade unions do not protect the workers against hunger, persecution or exploitation. Labor unions in the USSR are part of the party-government machine, which addresses itself not to defense of the interests of working people, but only to the implementation of party-government projects. Even the Soviet Supreme Court, having looked into the practice of court cases involving illegal firings, was forced to point out that the labor union organizations are not observing labor legislation and do not defend the workers actively enough. Workers' complaints to labor union organizations are handed over to the KGB [Soviet secret police].[52]

Further, Bukovsky contends that Soviet union members are prevented from using instruments of industrial conflict which many countries have accepted. He states:

The rare, desperate strikes in the Soviet Union do not occur in the demand of better working conditions or a raise in pay—but only when the workers and their families literally have nothing to eat.

The weavers in Ivanovo struck in 1970 when food ceased to be supplied to the city. As the USSR Helsinki Accords Monitoring Group in-

forms us, four port workers in Riga were arrested in May 1976 and in August sentenced to 1½ to 3 years deprivation of freedom after a strike which took place because of the absence of meat in the food stores.

The Soviet Union has signed various international conventions recognizing the right of workers to strike. But it has not bothered to formulate this right in its own legislation. Moreover, strikes are regarded as a "rude, group violation of social order," for which one can be deprived of freedom for up to three years. This is for a completely peaceful strike—merely a refusal to work. When it comes to other forms of struggle—such as sit-down or picketing—these are punishable under the article entitled "mass disorders," by deprivation of freedom, up to 15 years in jail or by the death penalty.

In the West, the decision to strike is usually taken for granted by the labor union. In the Soviet Union, this is beyond imagination.[53]

Poland's Challenge of Solidarity Although Poland's Solidarity union has received much international attention, worker opposition to the Soviet model is not a new phenomenon. In the past there were worker revolts in East Germany in 1953, Hungary in 1956, Poland in 1956, Czechoslovakia in 1968, and Russia in 1972. In every case, the revolts were short-lived and were suppressed by military force. The Solidarity movement in Poland in the 1980s, although it brought about the imprisonment of Lech Walesa, its leader, and many other Solidarity leaders, has been designed to bring about sweeping changes. Solidarity's demand can be summarized as:

It wanted free unions, in accordance with the eighty-seventh convention of the International Labour Organization, which had been ratified by Poland; the right to strike, and safety for strike participants and their helpers; freedom of speech, as guaranteed by the Polish constitution; restoration of jobs to employees dismissed for participating in earlier strike actions; liberation of all political prisoners; full publicity for Solidarity; the appointment of managers on the basis of competence; the abolition of privileges for the party apparatus, the police, and the internal security police; and a number of improvements in economic and social services.[54]

Obviously, these demands ran counter to the fundamental principles of the Soviet model, which allowed the Communist Party to control trade unions. These principles include:

- The Party's supremacy over unions through its power to name, dismiss, promote, train, and educate officials in the unions.

- The Party's supremacy over all workers from unskilled laborers to directors of factories (workers were not allowed to establish separate unions).
- The supremacy of top union officials over local unions with union branches permanently placed under supervision and control of officials outside their enterprise.[55]

At its October, 1981, convention, Solidarity issued its goals and proposals. They included:

1. Civil liberties and the rule of law.
2. Self-managed enterprises.
3. Improvement in current economic conditions.

While the proposals for civil liberties, rule of law, and improvement in economic conditions were general proposals, the proposed self-managed enterprise accompanied by self-financing, freedom from government control, and profit-orientation advocated using the market as the price regulator and resource allocator and called for the abolition of privileges and social inequality, all of which went against the core of the Soviet model.[56] Two years after its inception, the independent trade union was suspended; its leader, Lech Walesa, and 637 others were placed in detention, its printing presses were stopped, most of its activities were declared criminal and the hopes of a genuine democratic union died.[57] At the beginning of 1983, Walesa was released but was refused his former job until April 1983, and was not permitted to make any public speeches. The Polish Government established a union, but most Solidarity members refused to join. Because the Solidarity union was declared illegal, its members' activities went underground.

Efforts at Cooperation among Unions across National Boundaries

Any discussion of foreign labor movements would be incomplete without mentioning efforts made by unions in different countries to develop some type of cooperative activities. One of the earliest efforts in this regard was the creation of the International Labor Organization (ILO). Founded in 1919 under the auspices of the League of Nations by a small group of social innovators, among whom was Samuel Gompers, president of the American Federation of Labor, the ILO was established to help raise the standards of life and work around the world by adopting uniform standards. In its early years, the organization established such norms as the eight-hour day, limits on child labor, freedom to form unions and strike, and a score of others.

In 1954, the Soviet Union rejoined the ILO after twenty years of absence, and by 1980 the ILO's membership had increased to 142 nations. Gradually, it became more political, taking such stances as condemning Israel in 1974 for discriminating against Arab workers and seating the Palestine Liberation Organization (PLO) as one of its members. Such actions provoked the United States to withdraw its membership and support (25 percent of the organization's operational budget) from the ILO.[58]

The United States returned to the ILO after two years and the ILO seems to be turning toward issues, rather than politics. Recent resolutions adopted by ILO conventions include the promotion of collective bargaining in all branches of economic activity, standards for occupational safety and health, and corporate responsibility for termination of employment.[59]

Other efforts have been made by international trade secretariats, which are union coordinating bodies on an international scale designed to counteract the multinational firms. While these organizations have achieved only limited success in fostering collective bargaining, coordinating strikes and boycott activities, and enacting laws regulating companies' activities, they have been successful in exchanging data and providing information useful to their memberships. The sixteen international trade secretariats vary in size; their affiliated membership ranges from 11,000 to more than 13 million and represents unions in four to ninety countries.[60] The role of these organizations will be discussed further in the next section.

Multinational Corporations and Transnational Collective Bargaining

The growing interdependency among nations and the activities of multinational corporations (MNCs)[61] have become important facets of economic life. Although multinational firms have existed for more than 150 years, their numbers and share of world output have expanded their importance and visibility. They have expanded consideration of the production phase of business to include marketing and distribution activities which cut across countries' borders.[62] MNCs are now producing as well as marketing their products in several countries instead of producing only at the home base and selling abroad, and they are doing so with increasing impact. For example, U.S. firms invested $53.3 billion in foreign production facilities in 1982, an increase of 6 percent over 1981,[63] and sales by U.S. MNCs have reached over $2 trillion.[64] Interestingly, foreign direct investment in the United States reached $65.5 billion in 1980, an increase of 20 percent, following a 28 percent rise in 1979.[65] More startling is the fact that of the world's hundred largest economic units fifty are MNCs, and the other fifty are countries.[66] While U.S.-based multinationals still dominate the world economy, increasing numbers are operating from Western Europe and Japan.

Some union leaders view multinational firms as the root cause of American economic troubles. They contend that unemployment has resulted from the exportation of U.S. jobs to foreign countries and that the balance of payment deficits stem from the increase in the dollar outflow caused by U.S. investments abroad.[67] They further believe that the MNC "owes its allegiance to no one and has no interests above its goals of maximizing profits."[68] Therefore, the MNCs will move to those countries "where overhead and labor costs are lowest, where tax advantages are highest and where transportation facilities can be made available to transport goods and equipment."[69] One union leader believes that the MNC has "power to influence, if not dictate, national policies . . . [because of] . . . its readiness to locate capital, technology, administration, manufacture, merchandising, and other vital business operations where it pleases and to remove these resources from lands where it is displeased."[70]

Unions have advanced several arguments alleging that MNC activities have upset the power relationship in collective bargaining across a broad front. These include:[71]

1. **MNCs reduce employment** in the parent country while establishing production facilities in foreign markets, thereby reducing the size of the bargaining unit. Often cited as an example is the Litton Corporation's orchestration of its movement of Royal typewriter production from Missouri and Connecticut to England and Germany. The company manipulated the union to accept proposals concerning pensions and severance pay settlements after strikes, then never paid these benefits. One account of the Litton situation was:

Litton transferred overseas the jobs of about 2,500 unionized workers without having to incur severance or termination payments, improved pension benefits, worker relocation and retraining benefits, or any of the other compensations often obtained by unions in negotiations accompanying plant relocations. The impact of conglomerate, multinational structure on collective bargaining is to give the employer, under certain conditions, the capacity to make the institutionalized bargaining system an ineffective method of resolving industrial disputes.[72]

2. **If there is a strike** in the parent company country, the union does not shut down the flow of financial resources to the corporation. Operations in other countries continue to operate and generate profits, thereby relieving management of much pressure in negotiations. Thus far, there is little empirical evidence to support this conclusion.
3. **MNCs have an internal source of products** from facilities in several countries and use this position as leverage to bargain down wages, benefits, and other conditions of employment to its least-cost production (called "whipsawing" the union). If there should be a strike at one facility, the MNCs increase production at other units, destroying the potency of the strike.[73] Many specific examples of whipsawing can be identified. General Motors was able to expand the workweek from thirty-seven and a half hours to forty hours by convincing the unions in West Germany that they must increase hours to retain

competitiveness. In 1982, General Motors considered increasing its auto production in Brazil and Mexico as part of the "wage concession" demands, and when Canadian unions resisted wage concessions, GM considered shifting production back to the United States.[74] While there are specific examples of using production shifts in bargaining, it does not appear that firms locate production facilities overseas for the major purpose of discouraging strikes in their home country.[75]

4. **MNCs with complex tiers of management** do not delegate authority to make labor relations decisions to local management, thereby complicating the negotiation process because unions do not know who is in charge.[76] Empirical evidence indicates that most unions have not encountered different behavior between domestic and foreign-owned MNCs, but there seems to be a wider variation in behavior among the MNCs in terms of grievance settlement prior to arbitration, amount of local autonomy in negotiations, and difficulty in negotiating the first agreement.[77] However, because budget and investment decisions are made at the home office, local negotiations are certainly affected.
5. **MNCs shift profits to different facilities,** manipulate prices on internal transactions, and change marketing emphasis, confusing the unions in negotiations when they seek the facts necessary to address and resolve collective bargaining issues.

Because U.S. unions are accustomed to bargaining on "ability to pay" and are entitled to wage and financial information that allows them to conduct informed negotiations, they are frustrated when MNCs furnish only information that is required by law. Such information as locating plants in foreign facilities and operating data on these plants may be refused by the MNCs with the approval of the NLRB.[78]

Union Approaches to Multinational Bargaining and Employer Reactions

To combat the power of the MNCs and to seek objectives that are mutually beneficial to the unions and their members, union leaders have tried two main approaches: (a) collective bargaining and (b) legislative enactment. Through collective bargaining, unions have either attempted to directly bargain with the MNCs or coordinate their bargaining activities with unions in other countries by sharing information and supporting each other's activities. Legislative approaches typically have involved protective national legislation: regulations on foreign investments; international codes of conduct (fair labor standards) for the MNCs, such as minimum wages and full employment;[79] tax measures and regulatory schemes to limit outflow of capital and technology; and reporting requirements that provide unions information on MNCs.[80]

Furthermore, unions from developed countries have intervened on behalf of unions in developing countries. The International Metalworkers Federation has rallied international political pressure for jailed labor leaders in Brazil. The United Auto Workers has represented workers in disputes with General Motors in Australia, South Africa, Denmark, and Mexico.[81]

In addition to the main approaches, unions have proposed *Guidelines on Multinational Companies* to regulate their modes of operations. Thus far, through the Organization for Economic Cooperation and Development, a Paris-based clearinghouse for economic policy makers in twenty-four industrial democratic countries, unions in most countries have adopted the guidelines. These guidelines include certain rights: the right to organize and bargain collectively, to have access to data for negotiations, to be trained as a member of the work force, and to be given advance notice for changes in operations. Further, subsidiaries of MNCs are expected to observe employment standards comparable to those in the host countries; MNCs are expected not to threaten to shift production to other countries to influence negotiations or to prevent unionization; and local management representatives should be authorized to negotiate on behalf of the MNCs.[82]

Although there have been efforts toward developing multinational union activities in the chemical, food, flat glass, metal working, and other industries,[83] MNCs have not accepted the unions' preferences for realistic transnational collective bargaining. Extension of collective bargaining from a national scale to an international scale would require a major change in the present attitudes of corporation management. Although some form of transnational industrial relations seems to be inevitable, most MNCs generally consider it a distant prospect and one which will not be lightly entertained by management.[84]

Part of management's opposition stems from the unions' potential for shutting down production on an international basis. Further, multinational bargaining would introduce a trilevel structure of bargaining which would include multinational negotiations, followed by national ones, then local. This additional level would increase the complexity of negotiations as well as companies' vulnerability to strikes at the international level without a comparable reduction in vulnerability at the national and local levels.[85]

In some cases, countries themselves are not encouraging investments by MNCs; taxation policies, building limitations, requirements for local partners, the possibility of nationalization and expropriation of facilities, and the risks of political uncertainties are factors deterring MNC investment.[86] Less developed countries seek additional investments by MNCs for economic stimulus to the countries' development, income, employment programs, and so on, and MNCs find these countries attractive because of the low wage structures, tax incentives, and political guarantees. Such advantages are particularly appealing to the MNC, which must operate in a very competitive product market.[87] But when unions press via transnational bargaining for improved wages, benefits, and working conditions—all socially desirable goals for the populace—they become a force running counter to the short-run national economic goals of the country.[88] The economic boost MNCs can give a developing nation will not occur if firms fail to locate there; MNCs might well decide to avoid countries with the high wages and benefits that transnational bargaining has instituted.

Obstacles for Unions in Bargaining with MNCs

Unions face formidable tasks in their efforts to arrange transnational bargaining because they must be successful in mediating and balancing the conflicting interests of different groups encompassed by the MNC's employees, labor leaders, companies, and governments.[89] In fact, unions themselves provide some of the more important obstacles to transnational bargaining, and only when these are overcome can their attention be turned to external factors.

Absence of a central authority Unions lack a strong, centralized decision-making authority regarding transnational affairs, and most national union leaders are reluctant to allow an international body to make decisions that affect their unions and members.

Cultural differences Another complicating factor is the differences in ideological and religious beliefs among, for example, free trade unions and socialist- or communist-linked unions. Such differences have made it almost impossible for joint undertaking between unions in the free world and elsewhere.[90]

Lack of coordination of activities Unions have not been very successful in coordinating their international bargaining, boycott, and strike activities. An excellent example occurred in the 1976 rubber strike of Goodyear, Uniroyal, B. F. Goodrich, and Firestone. (Each has extensive overseas operations; for example, Goodyear has thirty and Firestone has twenty-five non-U.S. operations.) Support for the U.S. strikes was to come from a multinational union, the International Federation of Chemical and General Workers Unions (ICF), which has affiliates in Europe, North America, and Japan. The ICF Rubber Division approved a ban on overtime by employees of nonstrike companies and a system of monitoring and preventing shipments to the United States. At the end of the strike—the longest rubber strike in U.S. history—the ICF claimed that its efforts had had a significant effect on the bargaining outcome; however, the facts seemed to contradict this claim. A study by Northrup and Rowan of the 1976 strike did not reveal a single instance of interference with tire shipments from Europe, Japan, or North America; in fact, they found that imports jumped substantially in anticipation of the strike and never fell below the prestrike level. Furthermore, even Canadian imports were significantly increased during the strike, reversing what had occurred several years before, when U.S. rubber workers refused to support a strike by Canadian rubber workers.[91]

Differing national priorities The existing economic, social, legal, and political differences between countries serve as yet another obstacle to transnational bargaining. Few if any countries would subvert their national needs on behalf of and in the interests of developing an international system of industrial relations.

Employer resistance Employer resistance is less obvious than other obstacles at this time, mostly because of the inability of the unions to overcome the other hurdles that they face.[92] No doubt once the initial hurdles are overcome, employers' true opinions and attitudes concerning transnational collective bargaining will emerge, but in the meantime MNCs may sit idly by until the unions get their own houses in order.

Activities of Multinational Unions

Although much of what unions have accomplished in achieving international cooperation and coordination is considered by some a "public relations coup,"[93] there have been some tangible activities among unions. The International Conference of Free Trade Unions and International Trade Secretariats have proposed that the United Nations adopt charters for MNCs, specifying their obligation to recognize trade unions, observe fair labor standards, observe prevailing wage rates, attempt betterment of social conditions, reinvest profits made from less developed countries in those countries, establish work councils worldwide, and use labor-intensive technology when possible. In Western Europe, unions have backed the European company statutes that require worker participation and works councils' agreement on such issues as rules for recruitment, career advancement, dismissal, training, health and safety, welfare and social programs, pay methods, and holidays.

In addition, four multinational labor organizations have been quite active in international activities: International Federation of Chemical and General Workers Unions (ICF), International Metalworkers Federation (IMF), International Federation of Petroleum and Chemical Workers (IFPCW), and International Federation of Air Line Pilots Associations (IFALPA). Their activities thus far have essentially included gathering information about MNCs, providing education programs, and coordinating collective bargaining activities (although the federations themselves do no actual collective bargaining).[94] Each of these organizations believes that it must establish a firm foundation upon which to develop more penetrating actions in the future.

Effects of Unions on MNCs

Research conducted mostly in European countries has indicated that unions have had little direct effect on investment and production allocation policies of MNCs. However, they have had considerable effect indirectly because union relations with employers help shape the investment climate of a country.

Thus far, MNCs rarely have been able to afford to switch production to other countries as a bargaining or union intimidation tactic because of the costs involved. They no doubt would shift production to another country in cases where a labor dispute stops production and the move is economically and practically possible. However, such decisions are considerably limited because companies must have the necessary excess production capacity available and management must expect the labor dispute to last sufficiently long to justify any shift in production before it would be feasible.

Overall, there is little evidence of substantial negative effects of MNCs on industrial relations in countries in which they operate. They usually offer prevailing or superior wage standards and provide comparable working conditions for several reasons. The strengths of unions in the respective countries, the highly integrated and institutionalized nature of industrial relations systems, and the socioeconomic-political climate of the countries have clearly constrained the potential for direct adverse effect.[95]

Conclusions and Predictions on Transnational Bargaining

Systematic investigations of transnational collective bargaining reveal that it does not yet exist in any realistic form and will not likely occur in the near future. MNCs are generally opposed to it, and trade unions are not of a single mind regarding its desirability. While there have been several cases of information exchange between multinational unions and MNCs and a few instances of union-management consultation, only one trade union secretariat—the International Transport Workers Federation (ITF)—has actually negotiated an agreement with shipping companies. Further, only in the unique U.S.-Canadian environment does much transnational bargaining occur.[96]

There has been no identifiable trend toward transnational collective bargaining by companies and unions in the U.S., Europe, or Japan.[97] Some believe that there will be no effective transnational collective bargaining in the near future.[98] However, others believe that such collective bargaining is inevitable.[99] It will probably develop first in either North America, the European community, or Central America and deal initially with general topics, such as employment protection, investment policies, and codes of fair practices, before broadening into other bargaining topics.[100]

Summary and Implications

Summary

This chapter first presented the substantive elements of labor unions in other countries and then discussed the multinational corporation (MNC) and union activities related to transnational collective bargaining. The extensiveness of discussion of each country's labor relations system was determined by its proximity to the United States; its trade, economic, and political relationships with the United States; and its uniqueness among the world's labor relations systems.

Discussion of the labor relations system of Canada revealed concern over the United States' economically dominant role in North America and its influence in the internal affairs of that country. Latin and South American unions were also discussed. Western European coverage focused on co-determination and worker participation. West Germany's system of co-determination was described in some detail.

A view of the labor movements in some East European, Soviet bloc countries revealed the major influence of the Communist Party on the labor unions of these countries. In fact, their trade unions seemed to serve as tools of the party, unlike those in most of the free world. Special attention was given to Poland's Solidarity union.

Unique features of the Japanese system include a lifetime employment policy, a unique wage system, and the enterprise union. However, international money exchange rate fluctuations, trade agreements, rising oil prices, and slower economic growth could quickly alter these special union-management relationships of the Japanese system. The Australian system, which involves mediation, conciliation, and arbitration procedures, was also briefly presented.

Brief mention was made of the international labor organizations which have been established across national boundaries to represent the interests of their constituents. While none of these plays a major role in collective bargaining, their informational assistance to their members is important.

Implications

Multinational corporations and transnational collective bargaining are becoming increasingly important topics of labor relations. While multinational corporations continue to grow in sales volume, capital investments, and economic influence, they have also aroused trade unions in various countries to combine their energies, skills, and power in an effort to negotiate on an equal footing. Thus far, little success has been achieved, because of legal, political, social, economic, and organizational obstacles. However, one must clearly appreciate the fact that transnational collective bargaining could have a tremendous impact on the world's economy if the obstacles can be eliminated. Time will tell whether unions will be able to overcome the obstacles.

Discussion Questions

1. While we share a common border with Canada, its labor relations system is affected by a number of variables that do not greatly affect the United States. Enumerate and explain these variables.

2. Explain why labor unions in many of the Latin American countries have developed more slowly than those in the United States.

3. Western Europe seems to be uniquely involved with various forms of worker participation. What are some reasons that these worker participation systems have developed so fully there instead of elsewhere?
4. What are the three special features of the Japanese system? Why haven't they been adopted in the United States?
5. While multinational corporations seem to be growing in size and influence, what must occur before transnational collective bargaining can be effectively carried out?
6. How does the Polish government's position on Solidarity compare with the U.S. government's position on the PATCO strike?

References

[1]David C. Hershfield, *The Multinational Union Challenges the Multinational Company* (New York: Conference Board, 1975), pp. 4–5.

[2]"Report of the Task Force of Labour Relations," *Canadian Industrial Relations* (Ottawa: Information Canada, 1968), pp. 14–16.

[3]John Crispo, "Multinational Corporations and International Unions: Their Impact on Canadian Industrial Relations," in Robert J. Flanagan and Arnold R. Weber, eds., *Bargaining without Boundaries* (Chicago: University of Chicago Press, 1974), p. 106.

[4]Arthur Kruger, "The Direction of Unionism in Canada," in R. U. Miller and Fraser Isbester, eds., *Canadian Labor in Transition* (Ontario: Prentice-Hall, 1970), pp. 88–90.

[5]Ronald Lang, "Labour's Manifesto for Canada: A New Independence?" in J. L. Stern and B. D. Dennis, eds., *Proceedings of the Twenty-ninth Annual Winter Meeting: Industrial Relations Research Association* (Madison, Wis.: Industrial Relations Research Association, 1977), pp. 91–99.

[6]Crispo, "Multinational Corporations and International Unions," pp. 103–104. It should be noted that 15 to 20 percent of foreign ownership is outside the United States.

[7]"Unions Grow," *Labor Gazette*, October 1974, pp. 687–688.

[8]I. A. Litvak and C. J. Maule, "U.S. Union Domination of Canadian Labor," *Columbia Journal of World Business* 7 (May–June 1972), pp. 57–63.

[9]Kevin Quinn, "Canadian Labor Seeks Greater Autonomy From Unions Dominated by U.S. Workers," *Wall Street Journal*, April 29, 1982, p. 56; Mark Thompson "Canada," in Albert A. Blum, ed., *International Handbook of Industrial Relations* (Westport, Conn.: Greenwood Press, 1980), p. 86.

[10]James O. Morris, "Latin American Collective Bargaining Agreement: An Illustration," in Stanley M. Davis and Louis W. Goodman, eds., *Workers and Managers in Latin America* (Lexington, Mass.: D.C. Heath, 1972), p. 209.

[11]Arturo S. Bronstein, "Collective Bargaining in Latin America: Problems and Trends," *International Labour Review* 117 (September–October 1978), pp. 590–593.

[12]International Labour Office, "Labor Legislation and Collective Bargaining," in Davis and Goodman, eds., *Workers and Managers in Latin America*, pp. 217–229.

[13]Everett M. Kassalow, *Trade Unions and Industrial Relations: An International Comparison* (New York: Random House, 1969), pp. 302–303.

[14]Howard Handelson, "Oligarchy and Democracy in Two Mexican Labor Unions: A Test of Representation Theory," *Industrial and Labor Relations Review* 30 (January 1977), pp. 205–218.

[15]Kassalow, *Trade Unions*, p. 303. For a current discussion see James L. Schlagheck and Nancy R. Johnson, *The Political, Economic, and Labor Climate in Mexico* (Philadelphia: Industrial Research Unit, University of Pennsylvania, 1977).

[16]Robert J. Alexander, *Labor Relations in Argentina, Brazil, and Chile* (New York: McGraw-Hill, 1962), pp. 11–13. For a specific discussion of Brazilian labor relations see James L. Schlagheck, *The Political, Economic, and Labor Relations Climate in Brazil* (Philadelphia: Industrial Research Unit, University of Pennsylvania, 1977).

[17]Hobart A. Spaulding, Jr., *Organized Labor in Latin America* (New York: Harper & Row, 1977), p. x. For excellent discussions on Peru and Venezuela see Nancy R. Johnson, *The Political, Economic, and Labor Climate in Peru* (Philadelphia: Industrial Research Unit, University of Pennsylvania, 1978); and Cecilia M. Valente, *The Political, Economic, and Labor Climate in Venezuela* (Philadelphia: Industrial Research Unit, University of Pennsylvania, 1979).

[18]Everett M. Kassalow, "Conflict and Cooperation in Europe's Industrial Relations," *Industrial Relations* 13 (May 1974), pp. 156–163.

[19]Milton Derber, "Cross Currents in Workers' Participation," *Industrial Relations* 9 (February 1970), p. 123.

[20]Owen Fairweather, "Western European Labor Movements and Collective Bargaining: An Industrial Framework," in Alfred Kanan, ed., *Western European Labor and the American Corporation* (Washington, D.C.: Burean of National Affairs, 1970), pp. 69–72.

[21]John F. B. Goodman, "Great Britain: Toward the Social Contract," in Solomon Balkin, ed., *Worker Militancy and Its Consequences, 1965–75* (New York: Praeger Publishers, 1975), pp. 39–81.

[22]Fairweather, "Western European Labor Movements," pp. 71–74. Also see "Britain's Renegade Stewards," *Business Week*, February 19, 1979, pp. 92–95.

[23]"Thatcher Reins in Labor's Legal Rights," *Business Week*, December 14, 1981, p. 25.

[24]Robert Ball, "The Hard Hats in Europe's Boardrooms," *Fortune* 93 (June 1976), p. 189; and Robert J. Kuhne, "Co-determination: A Statutory Restructuring of the Organization," *Columbia Journal of World Business* 11 (March–April, 1976), pp. 17–25.

[25]Heinz Hartman, "Co-Determination Today and Tomorrow," *British Journal of Industrial Relations* 13 (March 1975), p. 54. Also see Wolfgang Heintzler, *The Codetermination Problem in Western Germany* (London: Aims of Industry Publications, 1974).

[26]David T. Fisher, "Worker Participation in West German Industry," *Monthly Labor Review* 101 (May 1978), pp. 59–63; and Kuhne, "Co-determination," pp. 17–25.

[27]Kuhne, "Co-determination," pp. 18–19.

[28]G. David Gaison, "The Codetermination Model of Workers' Participation: Where Is It Leading?" *Sloan Management Review* 18 (Spring 1977), pp. 63–78.

[29]B. C. Roberts, "Industrial Relations and the European Economic Community," *Labor Law Journal* 24 (August 1973), pp. 484–490.

[30]Neil Ulman, "The Workers' Voice: Giving Employees a Say in Firm's Management Seen Gaining in Europe," *Wall Street Journal*, February 23, 1973, p. 21.

[31]Gaison, "Codetermination Model," p. 63.

[32]"Setbacks Spur German Unions to New Militancy," *Business Week*, March 9, 1981, p. 73.

[33]Ibid.; Bill Paul, "Directors' Conflict: Germany's Requiring of Workers on Boards Causes Many Problems," *Wall Street Journal*, December 30, 1979, p. 29.

[34]Katsumi Yakabe, *Labor Relations in Japan* (Tokyo: International Society for Educational Information, 1974), pp. 1–14; Hisashi Kawada and Ryuji Komatsu, "Post-War Labor Movements in Japan," in Adolph Strumthal and James G. Scoville, eds., *The International Labor Movement in Transition* (Urbana: University of Illinois Press, 1973), pp. 122–148; and Tadashi A. Hanami, "The Multinational Corporation and Japanese Industrial Relations," in Duane Kujawa, ed., *International Labor and Multinational Enterprise* (New York: Praeger Publishers, 1975), pp. 183–185.

[35]"An Aging Work Force Strains Japan's Traditions," *Business Week*, April 20, 1981, pp. 72–85.

[36]"Japan: The End of Lifetime Jobs," *Business Week*, July 17, 1978, pp. 82–83.

[37]Solomon B. Levine and Kaji Taira, "Japanese Industrial Relations—Is One Economic Miracle Enough?" *Monthly Labor Review* 101 (March 1978), pp. 31–33.

[38]Solomon B. Levine, "Japan," *Country Labor Profile* (Washington, D.C.: Bureau of International Labor Affairs, U.S. Department of Labor, 1979), p. 7.

[39]Masayoshi Kanabayashi, "Japan's Unions Try a New Approach," *Wall Street Journal*, February 18, 1982, p. 33.

[40]"An Aging Work Force," pp. 72–85.

[41]R. C. Simpson, "The Significance of Legal Status of Trade Unions in Britain and Australia," *Journal of Industrial Relations* 18 (September 1976), pp. 229–242.

[42]J. W. Mohony, "Decisions Affecting Industrial Relations in 1977," *Journal of Industrial Relations* 20 (March 1978), p. 72.

[43]Kenneth F. Walker, *Australian Industrial Relations System* (Cambridge, Mass.: Harvard University Press, 1970), pp. 13–14.

[44]Normal F. Duffy, "Australia," in Albert A. Blum, ed., *International Handbook of Industrial Relations* (Westport, Conn.: Greenwood Press, 1980), pp. 13–14.

[45]Ibid., pp. 22–25.

[46]"Australia Clamors for a 35-hour Work Week," *Business Week*, December 15, 1980, p. 83.

[47]Duffy, "Australia," pp. 25–31.

[48]J. L. Porket, "Industrial Relations and Participation in Management in the Soviet-Type Communist System," *British Journal of Industrial Relations* 16 (March 1978), pp. 70–71.

[49]Ibid., pp. 72–73.

[50]Ibid., pp. 73–74.

[51]Vladimir Bukovsky, "We Have Looked with Hope at the West," *American Federationist* 84 (March 1977), pp. 20–21.

[52]Ibid.

[53]Horst Brand, "Solidarity's Proposals for Reforming Poland's Economy," *Monthly Labor Review* 105 (May 1982), p. 43.

[54]Thomas Lowit, "The Working Class and Union Structures in Eastern Europe," *British Journal of Industrial Relations* 20 (March 1982), pp. 67–69.

[55]Brand, "Solidarity's Proposals," pp. 43–45.

[56]Serge Schmemann, "'Suspended,' Solidarity Thrives as a Symbol," *New York Times*, August 8, 1982, p. E-2.

[57]Lane Kirkland, "A Time for Testing at the ILO," *American Federationist* 83 (August 1976), pp. 11–15.

[58]Tadd Linsenmayer, "ILO Conference Focuses on Bargaining, Worker Safety, Rather Than Politics," *Monthly Labor Review* 104 (October 1981), pp. 44–46. See also Walter Galenson, *The International Labor Organization* (Madison, Wis.: The University of Wisconsin Press, 1981).

[59]John P. Windmuller, *The Shape of Transnational Unionism: International Trade Secretariats* (Washington, D.C.: Bureau of International Labor Affairs, U.S. Department of Labor, 1979), pp. 20–34.

[60]"There is no agreed definition of the multinational enterprise. Some find its determining characteristics in the organization of its activities; that is, the extent to which its operations in different countries are actually co-ordinated by a corporate centre, or the degree of 'global outlook' to be found in the enterprise's decision making. Others use as criteria the number and types of its subsidiaries, the number of countries in which these subsidiaries operate, and the proportion of foreign sales, assets, and employment in the enterprise's total sales, assets, and employment. Still others look to the nationality mix of its management or to its ownership characteristics." International Labour Office, *Multinational Enterprises and Social Policy* (Geneva, Switzerland: International Labour Office, 1973), p. 3.

[61]Robert F. Banks and Jack Stieber, "Introduction," *Multinationals, Unions, and Labor Relations in Industrial Countries* (Ithaca: New York State School of Industrial and Labor Relations, 1977), p. 1.

[62]Jeffrey H. Lowe, "Capital Expenditures by Majority-owned Foreign Affiliates of U.S. Companies, 1981 and 1982," *Survey of Business* 61 (October 1981), p. 58.

[63]Betty L. Barker, "A Profile of U.S. Multinational Companies in 1977," *Survey of Business* 61 (October 1981), pp. 38–39.

[64]William K. Chung and Gregory G. Fouch, "Foreign Direct Investment in the United States in 1980," *Survey of Business*, 61 (August 1981), p. 40.

[65]International Labour Office, *Multinational Enterprises*, p. 4.

[66]William J. Curtin, "Multi-National Corporate Bargaining," *Collective Bargaining: Negotiations and Contracts* (Washington, D.C.: Bureau of National Affairs, 1972), p. J-2. Little mention is made by union leaders of the relatively high wage rates in the United States and other foreign nations.

[67]Andrew C. McLellan and Michael D. Baggs, "Multinationals: How Quick They Jump," *American Federationist* 80 (September 1973), pp. 22–24.

[68]Ibid., p. 22.

[69]Gus Tyler, "Multinationals: A Global Menace," *American Federationist* 79 (July 1972), pp. 1–7.

[70]Duane Kujawa, "Collective Bargaining and Labor Relations in Multinational Enterprise: A U.S. Public Policy Perspective," in Robert G. Hawkins, ed., *Research in International Business and Finance* (Greenwich, Conn.: JAI Press, Inc. 1979), p. 27; John Shearer, "Fact and Fiction Concerning Multinational Labor Relations," *Vanderbilt Journal of Transnational Law* 10 (Winter 1977), pp. 51–82.

[71]Charles Craypo, "Collective Bargaining in the Conglomerate, Multinational Firm: Litton's Shutdown of Royal Typewriter," *Industrial and Labor Relations Review* 29 (October 1975), p. 19.

[72]Kujawa, "Collective Bargaining and Labor Relations."

[73]"Canada's UAW Thumbs Its Nose at Concessions," *Business Week*, July 26, 1982, p. 23.

[74]Charles R. Greer and John Shearer, "Do Foreign-owned U.S. Firms Practice Unconventional Labor Relations?" *Monthly Labor Review* 104 (January 1981), pp. 45–47.

[75]Kujawa, "Collective Bargaining and Labor Relations," pp. 36–37.

[76]Greer and Shearer, "Do Foreign-owned U.S. Firms Practice Unconventional Labor Relations?" p. 47.

[77]Kujawa, "Collective Bargaining and Labor Relations," pp. 37–38.

[78]Banks and Stieber, *Multinationals, Unions, and Labor Relations*, p. 11.

[79]Curtin, "Multi-National Corporate Bargaining," p. J-2.

[80]Robert L. Simison, "UAW and Foreign Unions Plan Strategies to Confront World-Wide Firms Like GM," *Wall Street Journal*, June 24, 1981, p. 56.

[81]Hermian Rebhan, "Building a Counterforce to Multinational Corporations," *Monthly Labor Review* 100 (March 1977), pp. 46–47.

[82]See Richard L. Rowan, Herbert R. Northrup, and Rae Ann O'Brien, *Multinational Union Organizations in the Manufacturing Industries* (Philadelphia, Penn.: University of Pennsylvania, 1980).

[83]B. C. Roberts and Jonathan May, "The Response of Multinational Enterprises to International Trade Union Pressures," *British Journal of Industrial Relations* 12 (November 1974), pp. 403–416.

[84]Northrup and Rowan, "Multinational Bargaining Approaches in the Western European Flat Glass Industry," *Industrial and Labor Relations Review* 30 (October 1976), pp. 32–46.

[85]George B. McCulloch, "Transnational Bargaining—Problems and Prospects," *Monthly Labor Review* 101 (March 1978), pp. 33–34.

[86]Arnold R. Weber, "Bargaining without Boundaries: Industrial Relations and the Multinational Firm," in Flanagan and Weber, eds., *Bargaining without Boundaries*, pp. 233–249.

[87]McCulloch, "Transnational Bargaining—Problems and Prospects," p. 33.

[88]Weber, "Bargaining without Boundaries," pp. 233–249.

[89]Banks and Stieber, *Multinationals, Unions, and Labor Relations*, pp. 11–12.

[90]Herbert R. Northrup and Richard L. Rowan, "Multinational Union Activity in the 1976 U.S. Rubber Tire Strike," *Sloan Management Review* 18 (Spring 1977), pp. 17–28.

[91]G. B. J. Bomers, *Multinational Corporations and Industrial Relations* (Amsterdam, The Netherlands: Van Gorcum, Assen, 1976), pp. 179–195.

[92]Richard L. Rowan and Herbert R. Northrup, "Multinational Bargaining in Metals and Electrical Industries: Approaches and Prospects," *Journal of Industrial Relations* 17 (March 1975), pp. 1–29.

[93]Hershfield, *Multinational Union Challenges Multinational Company*, pp. 4–5.

[94]Banks and Stieber, *Multinationals, Unions, and Labor Relations*, pp. 15–16; and Bomers, *Multinational Corporations and Industrial Relations*, pp. 179–185.

[95]Herbert R. Northrup, "Why Multinationals Bargaining Neither Exists Nor Is Desirable," *Labor Law Journal* 29 (June 1978), pp. 330–331.

[96]Owen Fairweather, "Trends in International Collective Bargaining with Multinationals and the Respective Strategies," *Proceedings of the Twenty-sixth Annual Winter Meeting: Industrial Relations Research Association* (Madison, Wis.: Industrial Relations Research Association, 1973), pp. 145–154.

[97]McCulloch, "Transnational Bargaining—Problems and Prospects," p. 34.

[98]Paul A. Heise, "The Multinational Corporation and Industrial Relations," *Labor Law Journal* 24 (August 1973), pp. 480–483; Betty S. Murphy, "Multinational Corporations and Free Coordinated Transnational Bargaining: An Alternative to Protectionism?" *Labor Law Journal* 28 (October 1977), pp. 619–632.

[99]Hershfield, *Multinational Union Challenges Multinational Company*, pp. 4–5.

Chapter 17 Nontraditional Labor Relations Sectors: White-Collar Employees, Professional Sports, Health Care, and Agriculture

"The opera ain't over til the fat lady sings."*

This chapter is intended to pose the reader with a very real challenge—the application of the previous material to four nontraditional areas of labor-management relationships: white collar employees, professional sports, health care, and agriculture. While the four sections in this chapter are independent, they should be read with two issues in mind: (a) the extent to which these areas share similarities and differences, and (b) their respective applications to the elements in the labor relations process portrayed in Exhibit 1.1 of Chapter 1.

White-Collar Employees: Trends and Potential Union Optimism

White-collar employees fall into job classifications which cut across companies and industries. We have previously discussed white-collar employees in the public sector (Chapters 14 and 15), union attempts to organize female office employees (Chapter 11), and health care employees (later in this chapter); therefore, little emphasis to these areas will be given here. Exhibit 17.1 presents some representation election statistics reported by the National Labor Relations Board for private sector white-collar employees including clerical, professional, sales, and technical personnel. The following trends and implications are suggested by this exhibit:

- Unions have consistently won a majority of the representation elections, an indication that their organizing drives and tactics have been basically successful.

*Attributed to a nineteenth century ranch foreman who was explaining what signals the end of an opera.

Exhibit 17.1 Trends in White-Collar Representation Elections

								Winning Elections	
Year	Elections	Won	Number in Units	Lost	Number in Units	Total Number of Employees	Average Employees per Election	Percentage of Total Elections	Percentage of Total Employees
1961	395	177	4,660	218	6,845	11,505	29	45	40
1962	462	273	5,880	189	8,460	14,340	31	59	41
1963	443	255	6,495	188	15,250	21,745	49	58	30
1964	471	268	6,730	203	9,225	15,955	33	57	42
1965	514	318	7,600	196	10,125	17,725	34	62	43
1966	579	352	9,085	227	9,990	19,025	33	61	48
1967	868	567	15,090	301	11,940	27,030	31	65	56
1968	808	422	11,175	386	15,900	27,075	33	52	41
1969	752	422	10,695	330	14,885	25,580	34	56	42
1970	809	428	11,110	381	17,895	29,005	36	53	38
1971	825	437	12,085	388	22,305	34,390	42	53	35
1972	1,010	574	21,780	436	26,000	47,780	47	57	46
1973	1,031	548	15,965	483	28,375	44,340	43	53	36
1974	1,281	725	22,790	556	29,925	52,715	41	57	43
1975	1,219	706	23,885	513	28,745	52,630	43	58	45
1976	1,187	648	24,450	539	33,375	57,825	49	55	42
1977	1,173	613	23,820	560	35,435	59,225	50	52	40
1978	1,078	595	21,910	483	25,550	47,460	44	55	46
1979	1,055	622	23,890	433	34,515	58,405	55	59	40
1980	1,134	616	26,595	518	43,105	69,700	61	54	38

Source: The first six columns furnished by Bureau of National Affairs Inc., *Daily Labor Report*, No. 70, April 12, 1982, B-4.

- Representation election victories have only accounted for a minority of eligible employees. The proportion of white-collar employees covered by union representation is higher than the unionized proportion of the labor force; however, this does not automatically mean that every employee covered by a union representation election victory will become a union member.
- The total number of representation elections in any given year is relatively small. Also, the average number of white-collar employees involved in a representation election, while increasing, has remained low. This might prompt some unions to think twice before becoming involved in a representation election of white-collar employees since the potential bargaining unit membership dues might not justify organizing drive expenses.

There are, however, some grounds for union optimism in organizing white-collar employees, particularly when these employees are concerned with traditional issues such as wages, working conditions, and job security[1] as well as with emerging issues such as disenchantment with merit-based promotion systems,[2] limited opportunity for advancement, lack of career progression programs, shift work, and routine and uninteresting jobs. Indeed, two-thirds of the executives polled by the Conference Board believed that white-collar unions were on the upswing, and some even believed that by 1990 most white-collar employees would be union members. The accuracy of these predictions depends on a number of variables:

- The extent of union organizing efforts.
- Reactions of white-collar employees to the continuing depersonalization and routinization of their jobs.
- Gains in negotiated wages and fringe benefits of blue-collar relative to white-collar employees.
- The extent to which white-collar employees view unions as a means of bettering their conditions of employment.[3]

Collective Bargaining in Professional Sports

The total number of unionized athletes in professional baseball, basketball, hockey, football and soccer is less than the number of unionized employees at one medium-sized manufacturing facility. Although there are few participants, professional sports generate a tremendous interest among the American public. Anyone who has been to a professional baseball stadium has experienced the excitement of the game:

The lack of violence but the sense of menace in the thrown ball, the slashing spikes, the swing of the bat; the sudden splendid bursts of action—a runner going from first to third, or even home, on a single, sliding in inches ahead of or behind a perfect peg; the suspense of pitcher vs. hitter in a late-inning rally, with the winning runs on base; . . . the power and the glory of an overwhelming pitcher in his prime; the art and cunning of an experienced pitcher past his prime; the swagger of a big hitter at the plate.[4]

Behind the scenes union-management relationships seldom are as exciting as on-field action; yet a consideration of these unique activities can serve as an interesting application of the labor relations process. This subject is divided into four areas, which represent differences between unionized sports[5] and other industries, including health care and agriculture, which are discussed later in the chapter.

Lack of Traditional Guidelines for Wage Determination

In other industries, union and management officials often rely on certain common variables for their wage arguments. One of these variables, completed formal education or apprenticeship training, is not relied upon in professional sports. Indeed, one forty-year-old golfer who won more than $300,000 in 1982 passed his high school equivalency tests and commented, "Now that I'm a high school graduate, all kinds of opportunities should open up for me next year."[6] Other traditional variables such as job classification and seniority are also not relied upon in wage discussions, although the National Football League Players Association (NFLPA) was successful in obtaining (after a strike in 1982) bonus and severance payments to players based on their length of service.

There are two major reasons for this difference. First, professional sports replaces traditional variables with a wide variety of performance-based statistics,[7] such as passes completed, number of tackles, and earned run average. At first glance, accurate performance statistics would suggest a straight forward approach to wage determination; however, this is seldom the case.

Several studies have attempted to determine the extent player salaries have been tied to team performance (athletic and financial).[8] It is difficult to establish this relationship in precise terms; to determine, for example, a player's specific contribution to team attendance. In many cases owners' egos contribute toward exorbitant bidding for free agents and/or player salary increases regardless of statistical evidence. There might also be some variables which are statistically associated with team revenues which would be inappropriate, and possibly illegal for salary consideration. One study, for example, found that baseball team revenues are positively associated with population size and negatively associated with the percentage of black baseball players on a team, the latter appearing to be a result of racial discrimination by baseball fans.[9] Players will not agree to be judged on factors beyond their control, particularly on a factor which contradicts laws preventing employment discrimination on the basis of race.

In baseball, final offer arbitration considers a variety of performance statistics in resolving salary disputes between a player and his present team. As previously indicated in chapters 7 and 14, the third party arbitrator makes a binding decision on which either the final salary offered by the owner or by the player will be accepted (there is no compromise between the two offers).

This straight forward practice can become complicated when the arbitrator considers the significance of various objective but sometimes offsetting performance statistics. For example, management can present data showing a pitcher had a poor won-lost record. The pitcher, however, might present additional data indicating that he gave up few runs in those lost games but his team hit for a lower percentage in those games than for the entire season. The arbitrator must then determine the relatively vague contribution of team performance to the pitcher's success. Similarly, a hitter could explain his relatively low runs batted in (RBI) total with the fact that he was assigned to a lower position in the batting order, for which fewer runners were on base to score with a hit. In short, the arbitrator maintains that, while statistics are helpful, salary decisions are also affected by imponderables less objective and susceptible to measurement than traditional statistical categories.[10]

A second reason for this difference is that players negotiate their wage contracts individually with the owners, a situation which can result in rather large salaries (multiyear contracts for one baseball and one basketball player are $20 million and $13 million respectively). Individual player contracts have also resulted in unique clauses such as incentive payments for team victories in basketball; also, one baseball player (Reggie Jackson) received fifty cents a head for every California Angel admission over 2.4 million in 1982. Union officials could not negotiate these contracts for all of their members; therefore, they negotiate minimum salary levels paid for professional athletes.

Additional Participants in Collective Bargaining

As in other industries, labor relations activities in professional sports are primarily conducted by union and management officials or their representatives. There are, however, some unique considerations of sports owners; also, there are five additional categories of participants which can directly affect the labor relations process.

Owners Professional sports owners likely represent a more diverse group than other employer associations, and have not often presented a unified front in collective bargaining. They can be differentiated along several dimensions: experience with and knowledge of the professional sport, extent that the sport represents their entire financial investments, financial wealth, and conservative vs. liberal philosophies regarding game rules and player involvement in managerial decisions.[11] Many of these differences have resulted in public name-calling among owners.[12] More important are the publicized owner differences regarding the game's financial aspects and related collective bargaining issues.

Professional sports represent large revenues and expenditures. Many of the so-called "trivial" expenses can add up. For example, the negotiated meal allowance for baseball players ($42 a day in 1982) cost a club $18,540 for a fourteen day road trip.[13] Of course, a major cost item is player salaries, a subject of disagreement among owners. One baseball owner recently commented,

Years ago, . . . ballplayers had to accomplish something to get paid. These days they don't have to do much . . . I hate to think what it will be like in five years if owners don't start realizing that they're dishing out too much money.[14]

However, another baseball owner during the year of this quotation had ten outfielders at an annual cost of approximately $8 million.[15]

Expenses can strongly influence the atmosphere and results of collective bargaining. For example, it has recently been estimated that only one-third of professional basketball teams are either in a break-even or money-earning situation,[16] a factor which could restrict subsequent negotiating gains for the union. Yet many owners prefer not to discuss finances with other owners. According to one football owner,

My biggest surprise was at the owners' meetings, the financial aspects are very seldom talked about. It's more on the competitive rules. We spent two days on when the national anthem should be sung and when the coin toss should be made.[17]

Perhaps some of this care-free attitude toward managerial finance is explained by the belief that money can be made in professional sports regardless of team performance. This situation has possibly occurred in professional basketball.

Where once there had been real economics based on real attendance and real payrolls, now there were illusory economics of owner ego and tax writeoffs and television checks and endless new suckers always waiting to get in. In the early sixties a franchise was worth perhaps $200,000; in 1980 Dallas bought in for $12 million. Every time the buy-in rate went up, every other owner could claim that his franchise was worth at least that much, because he of course had a few years of tradition and a few valuable players. It was a dangerous and unreal time. No

one could lose. If professional basketball moved into a city which was not ready for it, New Orleans, for example, there were so many others wanting to get in that the present owners, having taken their tax deductions, could always sell at a much higher price to newer owners in another city. There was a goose and it laid golden eggs and every year the eggs would get bigger and the goose would live forever. . . .[18]

Owner differences can be compounded when each of the owners or their designated management officials interpret and administer the negotiated labor agreement. Each team can have a different labor relations climate, with some players not being able to appreciate administrative problems occurring on another team. For example, the NFL players' strike in 1974 met with some player resistance. One player representative for the Los Angeles Rams stated, "It's difficult to resist an [adverse managerial] attitude when you haven't been affected by it."[19]

It is therefore difficult to speak of *the* management side in professional sports' collective bargaining activities. This situation is further complicated by the presence of another individual in each sport, the commissioner.

Commissioners These individuals have an uncertain, confusing status in professional sports. The commissioner is supposed to coordinate managerial policies and actions affecting the teams in the league; however, the commissioners of at least three sports (hockey, football, and baseball) have fined some owners for various infractions, such as indicating the team should finish last in order to receive a top draft choice.

Equally uncertain is the commissioner's role in collective bargaining. Most union officials regard this individual as a paid management representative instead of a third party neutral. However, the commissioners of baseball and football were criticized in some quarters for not helping to resolve the 1981 baseball and 1982 football strikes.

Agents A second additional participant category, agents, represent players in individual salary and contract negotiations. This situation can complicate the traditional union-management relationship.[20] Indeed, a rash of successful contract negotiations conducted by the independent agents can result in players questioning the value of union membership.

Team managers and coaches These individuals are often involved in the daily activities of sports competition, and can affect the quality of the labor-management relationship and the possibility of grievances. Their activities comprise a part of one of the most perplexing occupations in the United States. The manager's success or failure is often due to factors beyond his control (player injuries, the relative success of other teams in the division, and so on). This individual is also charged with maintaining harmony among many players having different backgrounds and aspirations. In many situations, young rookies are on the same team with players old enough to be their fathers. It is difficult to imagine this as a harmonious situation, particularly since the rookie is competing for the older player's job. Some players also resent the large salaries given to other players on the team. A player earning $30,000 a year might acknowledge that another player earning $600,000 is a better performer. Yet few if any players aware of the salary differences and comparative performance statistics would believe another player is twenty times better. In some cases, tension is created between racial or ethnic factions on the team. Finally, the manager must be able to motivate the nonplayer, who sits on the bench believing he is as good as the starting player on the field.

Managers also have to contend with owners who usurp their authority in front of their players,[21] a situation which can result in discipline problems. One former manager suggests that very high player salaries also create disciplinary problems:

It isn't the game I used to know. In the first place there are the players. They're a different breed. . . . You can't tell them what to do. They have to be consulted; they want to know why. Not *how* but *why*. The battle cry to today's player is: *I don't have to.*

And do you know something? He doesn't. What are you going to do with a guy making [a very high salary], fine him? He'll laugh at you. . . .

The other slogan of the day is *I'll do it my way*. The prevailing attitude is that they've got everything coming to them. Not by accomplishment but just cause they're alive.[22]

Media The media are significant participants in the labor relations process.[23] Television networks can pay and receive substantial fees for sporting events. For example, CBS received the following amounts for a thirty-second advertising spot shown during the 1982 Super Bowl: $345,000 during a game time spot, $130,000 during the pregame show, and $190,000 during the locker room wrap-up.[24] Naturally, professional sports teams receive revenues from the television's broadcast of sporting events. The 1982 football players' strike was at least partially influenced by a five-year $2 billion contract (each team receives $14 million annually) signed by the television networks and the National Football League. The NFLPA hoped to obtain 55 percent of the gross revenues;[25] however, they were unsuccessful in their efforts. One argument used by the union (and other sports unions) was that they are media entertainers and should be paid wages similar to other media entertainers.

Media financial arrangements can also pose scheduling problems as the media balances professional sports with other programs. This can put limits on when games can be played or if they can be made up after a delay caused by a strike. One television commentator of baseball games suggested, "If television wanted a game played in six inches of snow, it just might be aired."[26] It has also been disclosed that a television station, mindful of increased ratings and revenues, made it financially possible for the Philadelphia Phillies to obtain Pete Rose from the Cincinnati Reds.[27]

The media can also indirectly influence collective bargaining through reportage of collective bargaining and strike activities. Professional sports seem to receive a disproportionately large amount of media coverage in bargaining efforts, given the rather small number of employees and effects on the economy. A comment made by a disgruntled union member about poor union leadership receives little media attention in most industries; however, an entire newspaper article or television interview might be given to a professional athlete-celebrity who expresses the same attitude. Marvin Miller, former head of the Major League Baseball Players' Association (MLBPA) and a former official with the Steelworkers Union commented during the 1981 baseball strike,

The steelworkers' union negotiations always had a far greater impact on the economy of the country than the baseball negotiations. But it probably got five percent of the attention that the baseball strike has received. I'm well aware of the kind of focus and artificial spotlight that is placed on baseball.[28]

Sports fans The media audience and/or paying customers represent the final (albeit indirect) participant in the labor relations process, since owners and unions have to consider the collective bargaining settlement's potential effects on fan support and related revenues. However, this influence is not uniformly perceived by sports owners. The owner of the New York Yankees indicates his public criticism of players is conducted from the fans' (and possibly his own) perspective,

People get on me for blasting players in public . . . But some of them are making hundreds of thousands of dollars for playing a kid's game. I mean, the game should be fun but it is also serious work. Look at [one highly paid player]. The other night in Milwaukee he makes us an error that costs us the game. You've got to produce for these people—. . . these construction guys and cab workers—they deserve the best. This is their recreation after a grueling day. [The particular player] makes $440,000 a year, this is after I rescued him from the scrap heap at Toronto, where he was making $100,000. And as soon as he comes to New York he takes me to arbitration and wins with some garment-district arbitrator who knows nothing about baseball. And if [he] doesn't do well is he gonna return the money to me? Hell no. It's a new age, and these players are making more than some big corporate executives. So I've got a platform where the little guy doesn't, and I use it.[29]

Another baseball team owner, on the other hand, took his team's baseball games, which were previously shown on free television, to a pay TV system where individual households pay about $22 a month.[30] One basketball team owner guaranteed season ticket holders partial refunds if the team failed to win thirty games in the season,[31] while the ticket prices to attend another basketball team's games were increased substantially (from $12 to $30 for best seats and from $10 to $20 for next best seats) in a single season.[32]

These contradictory activities might be partly due to uncertain fan reaction to activities such as strikes and higher ticket prices. One estimate indicates that three-fourths of the baseball fans attend five or fewer games a season regardless of their team's won-loss record.[33] Also, many baseball fans strongly disapproved of the 1981 baseball strike which shortened the baseball season and altered the traditional championship playoff system; yet, 1982 baseball attendance figures were higher than any previous year. There were many "no shows" (empty stadium seats) after the 1982 football players' strike was ended during the season; it will be interesting to see if this situation continues.

Players' Careers Are Typically Short and Restricted

One study found the average career for professional athletes was seven and a half years in hockey, seven years in basketball, four and a half years in football, and four years in baseball.[34] Short careers can affect union leader-member relationships, and can structure certain collective bargaining issues. A head of the MLBPA once observed, "I am neither the smartest, most skilled, nor ablest person alive, but if I were, it would cut no ice if I had no support from the players. The owners would pay no attention unless they were convinced there was a unified group.[35] However, other sports' union leaders have not appeared as fortunate, as noted by an executive director of the NFLPA,

Football players are young, but they have limited careers. It's harder to get them to fight for causes that may not bring them immediate benefits. They're playing now; what do they care about the rights of players in the future?[36]

A relatively short career coupled with intense competition for few playing positions creates a tense situation for many athletes.

There is a special kind of fear, a fear without fright, that is part of every athlete's burden. In few walks of life does one do his work extemporaneously and in the public view, and since the quality of an athlete's performance is rendered in numbers, he is obliged to live each day in the crucible of final judgment.[37]

This situation is compounded when some players realize they are not prepared for another career once their sports participation is over. This situation might have prompted some athletes to have drug and/or alcoholism problems. Drug and alcohol rehabilitation programs have been established in baseball, basketball, and football, although the executive director of the NFLPA commented that managerial "concerns" about drug abuse and solutions were timed to weaken the football players' bargaining position in 1982.[38] Other bargaining issues pertain to increasing a player's job security or tenure. For example, the NFLPA cooperated with football owners, who reduced the number of exhibition games in a season. The smaller number of exhibition games translates into fewer opportunities for rookies to prove they should replace veteran performers.[39]

Another problem facing professional athletes is that they do not have complete flexibility in selecting their employer.[40] Most players enter sports through a "draft" where only one team offers employment for their services. Once on a team, players are restricted in moving to another team. This situation has been described by a former baseball player who felt

A salesman reluctant to transfer from one office to another may choose to seek employment on the sales force of a different firm. A plumber can reject the dictates of his boss without relinquishing his right to plumb elsewhere. At the expiration of one contract, an actor shops among producers for the best arrangement he can find. But the baseball monopoly offers no such option to the athlete. If he elects not to work for the corporation that "owns" his services, baseball forbids him to ply his trade at all. In the hierarchy of living things, he ranks with poultry.[41]

Unions have attempted to remove some of these restrictions. The Major League Baseball Players Association negotiated perhaps the strongest contract provision regarding player rights to move from one team to another (after an arbitrator ruled in the union's favor on this matter).[42] In essence, a baseball player with six years of service who has not executed a contract for the next succeeding season can become a "free agent" (negotiate with other teams for his services) after notifying his club.

Several empirical studies have demonstrated that free agency has been associated with increased player salaries;[43] however, they are limited to the relatively few years that free agency has existed. There are two other potential implications of free agency which might exhibit a downward effect on salaries. First, free agency might reduce player trades (and potential for reopening the existing contract for higher wages), since a team might be reluctant to obtain a player who could become a free agent the next season. Second, free agency might increase the number of multiyear player contracts. While this results in large initial amounts, there is some chance that a player could undervalue himself in the later years of a contract.

Success of Collective Bargaining

Collective bargaining in professional sports has been relatively uneven, and has been affected by outside sources. Unions representing hockey, football, and basketball players were formed in the late 1950s,[44] but collective bargaining gains for these sports were sporadic. For example, hockey players achieved early collective bargaining gains only after agreeing that they would drop litigation against management for refusing to recognize the union's existence.[45] In essence, the hockey players "won" when they agreed that management did not have to recognize their union.[46]

The NFLPA's early bargaining gains came mostly from "outside sources," namely judicial decisions which supported players' concerns regarding mobility to other teams. In essence, the Rozelle Rule (named after the commissioner of football) governing compensation for traded players, as well as the arbitrary assignment of a player to only one team in the entry draft, was found to be illustrative of a "group boycott," or a per se violation of antitrust laws. This decision directed the owners to negotiate a new method for free agents in 1977; however, gains were not made in free agency, since the union used the opportunity to negotiate a compulsory union membership clause.[47]

In baseball, another outsider's (arbitrator's) decision motivated serious collective bargaining over player mobility issues. Finally, strikes, despite heavy media attention, have occurred only five times in professional sports—in baseball in 1972 and 1981, and in football in 1970, 1974, and 1982.

Health-Care Employees

Most of us have personal recollections of hospitals and health care through direct involvement as patients or through related experiences of friends and relatives. There are at least three labor relations differences between health care and professional sports or agriculture: *several different job classifications*; *unique labor legislation* (Taft-Hartley amendments in 1974 and public sector legislation): and *unique bargaining issues and concerns*. The implications of these are discussed below.

Legislative and Administrative Influences on Health-Care Bargaining

Legal guidelines Prior to 1935, the health-care industry was relatively unaffected by labor legislation. The Wagner Act of 1935 did not specifically exempt hospital organizations; thus the NLRB and the courts determined whether certain hospitals came under its coverage.[48] In 1947, Section 2 (2) of the Taft-Hartley Act exempted voluntary, nonprofit hospitals from federal labor relations laws.[49] Employees working in veterans' hospitals of the federal government were eventually granted organizational and collective bargaining rights under the

1962 Executive Order 10988 and are now covered under the Civil Service Reform Act of 1978. Employees working in state administered hospitals (for example, mental institutions) usually had to rely upon applicable state statutes in attempting to engage in collective bargaining activities.

Because voluntary, nonprofit hospitals constitute the largest single sector of the health-care industry in terms of number of hospitals, admissions, payroll expenses, and union activity, their omission from federal labor legislation coverage greatly blunted collective bargaining prospects in the industry for many years. Unions seeking to organize these hospitals could not rely on procedures found in the National Labor Relations Act due to the industry's exemption. Therefore, rights to form unions would have to be found in state statutes. Most state statutes either prohibited collective bargaining in hospitals or had no provisions regarding the subject.

This situation changed in 1974 with the Taft-Hartley amendments extending federal labor relations coverage to all private sector hospitals, including convalescent hospitals, health maintenance organizations, health clinics, and nursing homes. These amendments were controversial. Opponents maintained that they would encourage collective bargaining and possible strikes which would interrupt continued and critical health care.

Supporters of the 1974 amendments contended that the service provided by voluntary hospitals is no more critical than that performed by proprietary or profit-making hospitals included under Taft-Hartley, that in fact

there have . . . been instances of proprietary hospitals becoming nonprofit hospitals. This can happen without any visible signs. The employees may not even be aware of this change in status. The patients in the beds would not be aware. There would be no change in any function, service, or cost to the patients. The only difference would be a nondiscernible change in the type of ownership.[50]

There was also disagreement over the effects of these amendments on increased strike activity. Union officials have repeatedly maintained that most strikes have been over union recognition, a situation which would be eliminated by the orderly election procedures established and monitored by the NLRB. Yet other individuals anticipated that these amendments would eliminate the previously established strike prohibitions in many state labor relations laws and lead to an increase in the number of strikes.

The 1974 amendments recognized that strikes could cause serious problems in the health-care industry, and established unique collective bargaining and strike guidelines. Management and/or union officials in health care (unlike their counterparts in other private sector industries) have to[51]

- Submit a notice to modify or terminate existing labor agreements to the Federal Mediation and Conciliation Service (FMCS) sixty days before the expiration of the existing labor agreement (a thirty-day notice is required in other industries).
- (Union representatives) submit a ten-day intent to strike notice in writing to the hospital and FMCS specifying the exact date and time the strike is to occur.
- Be involved in a fact-finding procedure through a Board of Inquiry (BOI) which can be appointed by the director of the FMCS if a threatened or actual strike or lockout affecting a health care operation would substantially interrupt the delivery of health care in the local community. The reports of the BOI range from a detailed assessment of bargaining issues to a simple statement that "we met, we bargained, we settled."[52]

Thus, strikes are legal in the private health-care industry but only after complying with several unique legislative provisions.

The passage of the 1974 amendments caused a substantial increase in union organizing activities and employee representation elections. There are now forty-four national and international unions which have organized health-care employees. Unions which represent the largest number of hospital employees include Service Employees Union, District 1199 National Union of Hospital Health Care Employees, American Federation of State, County and Municipal Employees, and the Teamsters.[53] The wide variety of unions potentially reduces the number of employees who can belong to one particular union; union raiding of another union's members might therefore occur, a situation which can divert union and management attention away from substantive bargaining issues.[54]

Administrative Considerations of the National Labor Relations Board

Representation elections in the health-care industry (private sector) are conducted by the NLRB, which has unique legislative and administrative considerations regarding election solicitation and bargaining unit determination.

A current problem concerns areas in the hospitals *where unions may solicit employees.* One court of appeals has decided that employers have a legitimate interest in barring union solicitation of employees in areas accessible to patients.[55] Another has contended that unions are "common entities" on the American scene and that only an "extraordinary patient" would be so dismayed at witnessing a solicitation effort that his or her health would be impaired.[56] The Supreme Court partially resolved some of the controversy in a case where solicitation was prohibited in areas accessible to patients (such as the cafeteria). Its decision in effect indicated that the NLRB has the proper expertise to determine appropriate places for union solicitation. The Court also reasoned that there was no congressional intent in the 1974 amendments to restrict solicitation. Indeed, Congress determined that improvements in health care might result from unions and possibly even from strike activity.[57]

The issue of where employees can or cannot solicit during a union representation election is not completely resolved. The Supreme Court has indicated that a broad rule prohibiting solicitation is likely unreasonable, and that union solicitation can occur in areas where patient care will not be jeapordized. However, specific solicitation areas at particular hospitals often rest on contradictory interpretations of related evidence by the NLRB, lower courts, and the Supreme Court.

The NLRB is also charged with determining appropriate bargaining units (ABUs) in private hospitals, and must consider the provision in the Taft-Hartley amendments that "due consideration should be given by the Board to preventing proliferation of bargaining units in the health care industry."[58] In other words, too many ABUs could jeapordize efficient health care. However, the definition of "proliferation" is subject to controversy among the NLRB and the courts.[59]

Roughly speaking, the NLRB believes the following classifications are appropriate units or groupings of hospital employees for union representation elections:

1. A unit of professional employees.
2. A separate unit for registered nurses.
3. A separate unit for office and clerical employees (for example, switchboard operators and employees in the billing and credit departments).
4. A separate unit for technical employees (for example, licensed practical nurses and X-ray and lab technicians).
5. A unit of service and maintenance employees.[60]

Collective Bargaining Activities by Hospital Employees and Related Bargaining Issues

Collective bargaining in the health-care industry first started in the San Francisco Bay area in 1919, although it did not spread to many hospitals in that area until the middle 1930s. During World War II, the few advances in collective bargaining were primarily limited to San Francisco, Seattle, and Minnesota.[61] Active unionization of health care personnel occurred during the period of 1959–1972, particularly in New York City.

The success of many hospital organizing drives depends on various factors such as:

- *Characteristics of the hospital*—unions appear to be more successful in proprietary hospitals than nonprofit hospitals, larger hospitals, and non-church-related hospitals.
- *High voter turnout* usually reduces chances of a union election victory.[62]
- *Employee characteristics*—employees who receive higher pay and better working conditions, and have more investments in their work (seniority, education, and so forth), are least likely to join a union.[63]
- *High proportion of the non-agricultural workforce which is unionized in the community* is often positively associated with union election victories.[64]

Successful representation elections also depend on effective union efforts, such as those employed by District 1199, which has organized hospital employees throughout the country. Two successful organizing tactics of this union have been appealing to the racial or ethnic pride of hospital employees and mobilizing other unions to sway community opinion in favor of hospital representation elections.[65]

Nurses The American Nurses Association (ANA), while having less than 30 percent of all employed nurses as members, is the major organization representing nurses.[66] Since its inception in 1897, the ANA has been concerned with economic protection of its members. The organization avoided direct involvement with collective bargaining; however, in 1946 it encouraged state nurses' associations to actively implement collective bargaining programs aimed at economic benefits and participation of nurses in the planning and administration of nursing services. Under this arrangement, the state nurses' associations negotiate with employers when authorized to do so by the membership. The ANA believes that its state affiliates have more direct knowledge about actual and desired working conditions, and it will not become involved in a dispute from a financial or advisory standpoint unless requested to do so by the appropriate association.

This program has continued, although it was modified in 1950 when the ANA adopted a no-strike policy and formulated a *nurses in dispute policy*, which contended that because nurses have direct legal and ethical obligations to patients they should take a neutral position if their facility is involved in a labor-management dispute.[67] Hence, the ANA emphasized that nurses were not to strike; instead, they should tend to their patients during employee-employer negotiations.

Throughout the 1950s the ANA economic program had limited application, with very few job actions or strikes. As was true in other health-care occupations, union activity of nurses increased dramatically in the 1960s and 1970s. In spite of ANA's no-strike and nurses in dispute policies, several strikes have taken place since 1965 (1966 and 1974 San Francisco strikes, the 1975 Ohio Nurses' Association strike, and others, such as the 579-day strike by nurses in Ashtabula, Ohio, which ended in 1982). Other state nurses' associations (in Connecticut, Iowa, Massachusetts, and so on) have had active collective bargaining roles in recent years.[68]

Nurses have received a surprising amount of public support during their strike activities. Few people directly blame them for dislocations during a strike.[69] In most strike situations, ample time has been given to transfer already admitted patients or to stop accepting patients for elective surgery.[70] Also, the public has begun to view hospitals as big business concerns rather than charitable institutions.[71]

As is true with other employee classifications, nurses have varying attitudes toward collective bargaining.[72] Differences of opinion can be due to relative emphasis given to two bargaining objectives: professional nursing standards and economic gains.[73] For example, "the Ohio Nurses' Association insisted that the ANA Code of Ethics for nurses be incorporated into the collective bargaining agreement, thus ensuring from their point of view that management will adhere to the highest standards for nursing care given to patients." [74] Another recently negotiated contract provision obligated management to purchase fresh rather than canned fruit for inpatient consumption.[75] Factions could develop within the ANA when one bargaining objective is stressed over another.[76]

Other attitudinal differences may cause divisiveness among nurses—for example, the degree of career satisfaction nurses found with their present positions (see Exhibit 17.2). One study found that nurses who are dissatisfied with their careers view themselves as having few professional advancement opportunities; there are few if any organizational promotions available in a hospital. Furthermore, career dissatisfaction has been one of the major contributors to militancy—belief in collective bargaining and strikes. Another factor contributing to attitudinal differences among nurses has been age. Younger nurses tend to view strikes and unions more favorably than do their older colleagues.[77]

House Staff Graduates from medical schools have not been immune to collective concerns and actions. House staffs consist of hospital-based interns, residents, and fellows in training programs who, according to a recent U.S. Court of Appeals decision, are protected by the 1974 amendments in labor relations activities.[78] These individuals, in many cases, have to participate in hospital training programs, since nearly all medical practices are specialties which require hospital training for certification.

Labor relations concerns arise over the various working conditions that house-staff personnel face—for example, low wages and extensive working hours, averaging in some cases a hundred hours a week, often for consecutive periods ranging from thirty-six to seventy-two hours.[79] Additionally, training necessary for certification makes house-staff officers particularly vulnerable; they are subject to arbitrary actions by medical supervisors. In some cases, the training program is designed to eliminate a specified number of personnel before completion. Those completing the program still have to depend on the good will of their supervisors and other hospital administrators for further hospital privileges and recommendations for other positions.[80]

Currently, two organizations represent the house staff: (a) New York City Committee of Interns and Residents (CIR) and (b) the Physicians' National Housestaff Association (PNHA). Both pursue collective bargaining activities, yet neither is chartered by a national union, and both are headed by house staff officers actively engaged in a training program.

Exhibit 17.2 Example of Career Problems Which Might Propel Nurses to Join a Union

If you had to list the job attributes that separate the professional from the tradesman, laborer or merchant, you probably would begain to check off such items as

- control over the scope and exercise of duties
- some control in selecting work hours
- ability to decide what "safe working conditions" are based on
- training
- compensation in line with education and responsibility

Perhaps you would also add a few terms like "self-respect" and "feeling capable" as well.

Now prepare for a shock. According to that definition, nurses are not professionals. Do you know any staff nurses who have the power to order new equipment for their unit because the old has broken down and is unsafe? How many nurses can take a "personal" day off, without pretending to be sick? What do you do if you have a child at home, too ill to be left alone? Who can do any of these things without feeling they are putting their job security on the line? With all this to think about as well, what nurse thinks her salary matches her professional responsibilities?

In truth, nurses have not yet fulfilled their potential as professionals and the answer is not more training. Rather, it is learning a simple lesson in power, which doctors and hospital administrators have known so long: it is not in the financial interest of hospitals to volunteer to pay nurses more, nor to hire more staff, nor to grant them seniority or time off, or any other privileges. If you have been depending on the benevolence and the essential fairness of administrators to better your lot, reconsider. Regardless of how "nice" he is, a hospital administrator is not going to make any changes in the status quo, unless his hand is forced. After all he has the hospital board looking over his shoulder, judging him by his books and by his ability to manage—his future jobs depend on their evaluation and that of fellow administrators in the area. He is not going to risk all that unless you come up with compelling evidence that salaries are below the local norm, and remind him that nurses are not hospital property. He certainly will not do it even then if he thinks you do not mean business. Expressed like that, you can see why one nurse complaining about conditions, or five nurses trying to better their lot, cannot wield enough influence to force hospital administrators to make changes. Nurses are too easily replaced, unless the facility is very small or very rural.

But if the nurses in a hospital unify, set reasonable goals for a collectively bargained contract, and are determined—"here I stand, I can do no other"—they have the ability to exert financial and moral pressure and can win some changes. How many hospitals have you heard of that voluntarily changed their staffing patterns, granted continuing education time, or significantly raised salaries without the presence of a nurses' union?

Along these lines, beware of the pay-off approach, used at some facilities when it becomes obvious that nurses are talking about forming a union. The hospital administrator becomes concerned and friendly, and appears on wards he has scarely been seen on before. Sometimes all problems are heaped on the head of the nursing services' director, and the administrator fires her and promises better policies are on the way. Sometimes the facility "evaluates" pay scales and hands out increases, and nurses are foolish enough to believe all their problems revolve around money and forget their union discussions. Within months after the let's-go-union enthusiasm ends, nurses wake up to find the halls may have been painted a different color and they may have a new coffee machine, but it is still the same hospital with the same understaffing, poor health insurance and/or sick leave policy, and they have allowed themselves to be manipulated once again.

Source: Karen A. O'Rourke and Salley Reynolds Barton, *Nurse Power: Unions and the Law* (Bowie, M.D.: Robert J. Brady Co., 1981), pp. 6–7.

The CIR has had rather limited success in strikes conducted over working conditions and patient care. Although strikes have not occurred on a frequent basis, the CIR organized the first major interns and residents strike in 1975. Three thousand employees struck several New York City hospitals so that no member would be required to work more than eighty hours in a week or fifteen hours consecutively in a twenty-four-hour period. The four-day strike was ended with a promise to formulate a joint house staff and management committee to look into the problem.[81] In 1981, the CIR struck for better patient care standards; they returned without receiving their bargaining objectives.[82]

Physicians Apart from house-staff personnel, there are some 16,000 physicians belonging to twenty-six organizations committed to some form of collective bargaining. It should be noted that only four of fourteen of these organizations responding to a survey had negotiated labor agreements.[83] Some of this inactivity is no doubt due to the rather strong anti-union positions taken by the American Medical Association and American Dental Association. While the American Medical Association gave some support to the concerns of house-staff personnel involved in the 1975 New York strike,[84] the organization has long maintained that unions would harm the physician-patient relationship.

However, physicians have become more militant in recent years because of issues that threaten their economic and professional positions. Related issues include:

- Increases in malpractice insurance, which prompted California physicians to engage in a coordinated work slowdown to protest perceived unjust actions by insurance companies.[85]
- Potential legislation, such as national health insurance, which could result in a near employee-employer relationship with a federal agency responsible for administering the program.[86]
- Reduced patient loads,[87] in part caused by a surplus of doctors in some areas,[88] which have prompted some physicians to sue hospitals for staff privileges as competition rises.[89]

Additional efforts at collective action and the possibility of altered attitudes by the American Medical Association remain interesting, speculative topics of labor relations.

Union Impact on Health-Care Work Rules Unions have historically been associated with wage increases in the hospital industry. For example, when District 1199 started organizing hospital employees in 1959, income ranged from $26 to $28 per forty-four-hour week. Between 1959 and 1975, wage levels at these hospitals increased almost 800 percent ($181 per thirty-seven-hour week).[90] Other studies have supported the union's impact on wages;[91] however, two recent studies[92] have shown:

1. Union officers representing hospital nonprofessionals tend to obtain higher wage gains than union officers representing nurses.
2. The union's impact on wages increases with the length of time collective bargaining has been in effect in hospitals.

The first finding seems reasonable in view of the historically non-militant stance of the American Nurses Association, which has stressed professional issues instead of economic job actions such as strikes. The second finding can be partially explained by a shift in union goals over time. Unions, after winning a representation election, first concentrate on union security issues, then in subsequent negotiations focus on economic issues. This situation might change if the federal government reduces payments (Medicare and Medicaid) for hospital services, thereby increasing hospital deficits.[93] Unions also have impact on hospital administrative issues. Exhibit 17.3 shows hospital managers' perceptions of the effects of unions.

Exhibit 17.3 Hospital Managers' Perceptions of the Strength and Direction of Union Impact in Selected Areas

Impact Areas	Mean Response[a]	Percent Negative		No Impact	Percent Positive	
		Strong	Weak		Weak	Strong
General						
Centralized Policy Making	4.04	07.7	03.5	11.6	32.0	45.2
Wage Levels (union employees)	3.53	24.7	08.9	02.6	16.6	47.2
Ability to Retain Employees	3.52	08.2	11.3	25.7	30.0	24.9
Overall Quality of Care	2.86	10.9	22.3	42.0	19.7	05.0
Productivity of Employees	2.80	19.9	23.5	26.3	17.5	12.7
Financial Standing of Hospital	2.65	39.8	16.6	06.2	13.3	24.1
Hospital Management						
Overall Quality of Management	3.70	05.8	05.8	27.4	35.1	25.9
Ability to Run Hospital Effectively	2.97	15.8	25.8	19.2	23.8	15.4
Authority of Supervisors	2.93	22.8	33.6	09.3	26.6	17.8
Employee Attitudes and Behavior						
Interest in Long-Term Employment	3.62	05.4	09.3	28.3	32.2	24.8
Turnover	3.30	07.7	15.1	34.7	25.1	17.4
Interest in Promotion	3.28	08.2	14.0	31.1	34.6	12.1
Morale	3.12	11.5	23.0	20.3	33.0	12.3
Absenteeism	2.79	17.6	26.1	25.3	21.8	09.2
Commitment to Goals of Hospital	2.75	15.6	25.9	33.8	17.1	07.6
Willingness to Perform Extra Work	2.40	30.3	27.3	21.1	12.7	07.6

[a]Items are Scaled
1 = Strong Negative Impact 2 = Weak Negative Impact 3 = No Impact
4 = Weak Positive Impact 5 = Strong Positive Impact Total Number of Responses Was 292.

Source: Charles Maxey, "Hospital Managers' Perception of the Impact of Unionization," *Monthly Labor Review* 103 (June 1980), p. 37.

Farm Workers

Instead of describing agriculture labor relations activities across the nation, this section focuses on union efforts in California, a state which has experienced significant union activity and has farm working conditions similar to those throughout the United States. California labor relations activities have been pronounced, directly involving more employees and related research efforts than those of any other state. This state has also witnessed a comprehensive labor relations law as well as the emergence of a charismatic union leader, Cesar Chavez. Finally, Chavez's union, the United Farm Workers, provides vivid examples of problems and prospects that all farm worker unions face.

Overview of Farm Laborer Working Conditions and the Rise of Cesar Chavez

Statistics on the number of farm workers often vary because of the rapid mobility of migrants. There are an estimated 3 million farm workers in the United States;

Source: Photo by Paul Fusco, Magnum.

Cesar Chavez, the powerfully charismatic leader of the United Farm Workers, has successfully organized migrant workers to gain wage increases and contracts. His nonviolent approach, based on worker loyalty to "La Causa," usually relies on boycotts of products.

almost 200,000 are seasonal migrant laborers. Migrant working and living conditions have often been described as brutal.[94] For example, one study found that a typical agricultural laborer had eight and one-half years of education and worked an average of eighty-eight days a year at $13.20 a day, for an annual wage of $1,160. Further, this occupation is dangerous; at least for one year, there were more fatal accidents in agriculture than in any other industry.

Four unique working conditions further illustrate the migrant worker's plight.

1. *"El Cortito."* The dreaded, common piece of equipment, "El Cortito," or "the short hoe" used in crop tending, has a handle less than three feet long. The migrants have to stoop in the fields to use it, so that their backs are practically parallel to the ground. Governor Jerry Brown outlawed the use of this equipment in California; however, "El Cortito" still remains in other states.[95]
2. *Transitory nature.* Another unpleasant aspect of this job is its transitory nature, necessitating frequent relocations to find work. Cesar Chavez's recollection of his typical work year is presented in Exhibit 17.4 to illustrate a representative work schedule.
3. *Employer attitudes.* It is, of course, impossible to identify the growers as having a common attitude regarding their employees. Yet the following quotations from growers illustrate employment philosophies ranging from indifference to paternalism to racism:

The class of labor we want is the kind we can send home when we are through with them.[96]

It wasn't fair for Chavez to strike my ranch. . . . My workers were simple people, good people, and I liked them and took good care of them. If a man and his family worked hard, I gave them a low-rent room and sold them groceries at only slight markups. Once, I even paid for the funeral of the daughter of one of my workers.

These people were made to suffer; some of them even enjoy the work. God made the Mexicans with stubby legs and greasy hair. So, you see, they can lean low and tolerate the sun in the fields. Chavez made those people think they're something better.[97]

---

4. *Exemption from labor relations laws.* Finally, agricultural employees continue to be specifically exempted from federal labor relations laws, and this lack of federal labor relations coverage has made it most difficult for farm workers to organize.[98] Without federal legislation, legal emphasis shifts to appropriate state laws and judicial interpretations of legal organizing and collective bargaining tactics (for example, picketing and boycotts of farm products). Only seven states (Arizona, Idaho, Kansas, Michigan, California, Wisconsin, and Hawaii) currently have laws covering farm workers.[99]

It should be noted that at least one farm workers' union has reservations about being included under the National Labor Relations Act. Under this act, most migrant workers could be denied voting rights in union elections since employers could request elections during the off season, when a handful of steady, company-dominated workers would decide the representation issue for the

Exhibit 17.4 Cesar Chavez's Recollections Regarding His Work Year

We did not pick the same crops every year, but there was a pattern. Most winters we spent in Brawley where there were carrots, mustard, and peas. I did cabbage and lettuce in January, picking or working it, tying or loading it on a trailer. Then a little later we capped cantaloupe and watermelon, putting a wax paper over the plant to keep it from freezing and to keep the ground warm, just like an individual hothouse for every plant. When it got warmer, we came back, took the cap off, worked the ground around the plants, and thinned them, using a short-handle hoe.

Probably one of the worst jobs was the broccoli. We were in water and mud up to our necks and our hands got frozen. We had to cut it and throw it on a trailer, cut and throw, cut and throw. We slipped around in the mud, and we were wet. I didn't have any boots, just shoes on. Those crops were in December through March. In January to March there also were the cauliflower, mustard greens, onions, carrots, cabbage, and lettuce.

Then we worked in the watermelon, just picking up the vines which grew in the irrigation ditches and training them away from the ditches. The melons started in May, and I would work in the sheds for a labor contractor who was related to us.

In late May we had two or three options, Oxnard for beans, Beaumont for cherries, or the Hemet area for apricots, places that no longer have much or any of those crops. I think we did all at one time or other. Most of the time my dad would leave it up to us. "Do you think you'll like it?" he would ask.

We started making the apricots in Moorepark where they pick them up from the ground, just like prunes. In San Jose, on the other hand, we had to climb a ladder.

That would be the early part of summer. From there we had all kinds of options. We never did asparagus, and we only did figs once. The milk of the fig eats through your skin like acid. Some people put grease on their hands, but we couldn't do that. It was just awful.

We worked in lima beans, corn, and chili peppers, picked fresh lima beans for fifty cents a basket. Then in August we had grapes, prunes, cucumbers, and tomatoes. Those go into September and part of October. We would go before those crops started and wait in a camp until they were ready. For example there were raisin grapes about ten miles beyond Fresno. We had to be there at least a week in advance, or we couldn't get a job. That was a week of lost time, sometimes more, with no pay whatsoever.

Then we did cotton from October through Christmas. I just hated it. It was very hard work, but there was nothing else. After the cotton, just like ducks, we usually went back to Brawley to start with the crops in January.

So we traveled from the Imperial Valley in the south as far north as Sacramento and San Jose.

Source: Selection is reprinted from *Cesar Chavez, Autobiography of La Causa,* by Jacques E. Levy, with the permission of W. W. Norton & Company, Inc.

majority of seasonal workers. "Only the California Agricultural Labor Relations Act guarantees peak season elections."[100]

Early Organizational Attempts In 1905, the Industrial Workers of the World attempted to organize farm workers; however, union organizing successes until 1962 were sporadic because of the lack of membership base and labor legislation.[101]

Another major obstacle to union organization has been the *bracero program,* which allowed legal importation of Mexican farm workers *(braceros)* under war emergency agreements between the United States and Mexico during World War II. Almost overnight, the haphazard system of recruiting farm labor was replaced by a highly organized recruiting process. This method insured growers a plentiful supply of cheap labor, while allowing Mexico to send its restless unemployed to another country. The two countries continued this program after World War II until Congress officially terminated it in 1964.

The ending of the bracero program may have helped farm worker organizing, as unions might have had a more stable base of potential members. However, some research has shown that the program's elimination has neither significantly reduced the number of foreign farm workers nor increased the wages of domestic farm workers. These findings might be due to increases in the number of alien workers illegally crossing the border.[102]

Chavez's Formation of a Union Forming a union in 1962 enabled Chavez to approach the farm worker's employment conditions more directly. Using the approaches proposed by Ghandi, Chavez relied on nonviolence in union activities. He viewed nonviolence as necessary to obtain favorable public opinion; the concept also had pragmatic value—a nonviolent act (a boycott, for example) on a supermarket hurts the employer economically, while a violent act (such as arson) enables the employer to collect insurance and receive a refund on taxes. Chavez was also influenced by another aspect of Ghandi's movement, the loyalty of followers which allows an insistence that many rules be obeyed.[103] As will be discussed later in this section, Chavez's reliance on loyalty might blunt his union's collective bargaining effectiveness.

The first strike conducted by Chavez occurred in the rose fields in the spring of 1965. This dispute lasted four days, with employees receiving a wage increase but no labor agreement. The growers were eager to resolve the dispute since skilled rose grafters were in short supply.

The most publicized activities of this union were the 1965 Delano strike and the grape boycott. These efforts were initially successful in that longshoremen refused to load "scab" grapes on ships. However, the boycott became somewhat difficult when the growers increased the number of different labels from 6 to 100, thereby confusing the pickets. Thus, the boycott was enlarged to include all California-grown grapes.[104]

The grape boycott received national attention, particularly in the 1968 presidential campaign, during which it was endorsed by candidates Kennedy, McCarthy, McGovern, and Humphrey. On the other hand, Nixon denounced the boycott while eating grapes at a press conference in Fresno, California.[105] The Nixon administration later gave more tangible support to the grape growers during the Vietnam War. The Defense Department countered reduced consumer interest in grapes by increasing 1968–1969 grape shipments to the troops some 350 percent (2.5 million pounds) over the previous year.[106]

Two major companies recognized the union in the relatively early stages of the grape boycott: Schenley, which experienced Teamster refusal to deliver its products from a major warehouse, and the DiGorgio Corporation. The later agreement included several important provisions, such as an employer-financed health and welfare fund, layoffs and promotions based on seniority, holiday pay, and vacation benefits. By mid-July 1970, five years after the initial dispute, the Delano growers agreed to the principle of collective bargaining and signed labor agreements which raised economic benefits and established grievance procedures. Delano could be termed a success for the farm workers, yet the labor settlement increased jurisdictional battles among unions for the right to represent farm workers.

Jurisdictional Problems among Farm Worker Unions and Current Issues Facing Farm Labor Organizations

The union formed by Cesar Chavez was originally independent from the AFL-CIO, which had been conducting its own organizational drives with farm workers. After extensive negotiations, Chavez merged his union with the related AFL-CIO organizing committee during the grape boycott. This merger culminated in an AFL-CIO charter in 1972. The union, after numerous name changes, became the United Farm Workers (UFW).

Teamster-UFW Conflict While jurisdictional problems were somewhat peacefully worked out with the AFL-CIO, serious problems remained with an independent union, the Teamsters. A discussion of these disputes helps explain the internal problems of the UFW and the emergence of related labor legislation and also enables an examination of a rather rare impediment to the contemporary labor relations process—intense union rivalry for the same employees.

Although at least one Teamster local provided assistance to the UFW during the grape boycott, cooperation between the two unions was the exception rather than the rule.[107] The 1970 UFW victory in Delano heightened jurisdiction problems, for it prompted other growers to resolve labor relations in an expedient manner. In fact, 170 labor agreements were signed with Salinas and Santa Maria growers one day before Chavez announced the Delano settlement.

The UFW intended to switch its attention to the lettuce and vegetable fields of the Salinas and Santa Maria valleys after the Delano settlement. Growers in these valleys realized that unions were inevitable, and their concern shifted to minimizing their losses. They had previously approached the Teamsters, who were initially reluctant to break a 1966–1967 jurisdictional treaty with the UFW. Yet a Teamster-grower settlement was reached when Teamster drivers, who were on a brief strike, agreed to return to work only if their jobs were not disrupted by field hand strikes. This rationale prompted the Teamsters to push for (and quickly receive from the growers) extension of truck driver agreements to include the farm workers.

The UFW was predictably outraged by this turn of events, charging that the Teamsters had "sweetheart contracts" with the growers and the agreements were secured without asking the employees to vote for their union preference. The UFW countered with a strike (involving some 10,000 employees) to put pressure on the growers; violence often occurred between UFW and Teamster employees. Although this effort and the related lettuce boycott hurt the growers, problems continued to exist between the Teamsters and the UFW.

Teamsters made huge inroads into the UFW's bargaining victories. In 1973, the UFW held agreements with approximately 300 growers, involving some 60,000 employees. In 1974, this number was reduced to 12 agreements covering only 5,000 employees, while the Teamsters held some 350 collective bargaining agreements with the growers. A large part of this turnaround was due to the eager reception given to the Teamsters by the growers. To be sure, employees under these sweetheart arrangements were not able to vote their particular union preference (Teamsters or UFW). When this situation changed in California, many of the farm workers indicated their preference for the UFW.

Yet there might be other reasons for the Teamsters' success, as illustrated by the following remarks of a farm worker on Chavez's "La Causa."

La Causa is good, and its time will come again. When I hear the cry of 'Huelga' I want to, you know, walk out of the fields, to screw the grower right at Harvest time, to help Cesar in this hard time he has. But look around you at all these open mouths to feed. We will keep thinning the lettuce because we need the dollars. I like the Chavez union most, but they made some mistakes. The Teamsters are not as bad as he says. They helped me get food stamps in January when there was no work.[108]

The Teamsters' traditional approach to collective bargaining clashed with the UFW's broader social goals. The Teamsters' use of much greater financial resources and of skilled staff personnel in their collective bargaining efforts may have raised doubts among some farm workers as to the appropriate method of union representation and the most efficient method of attaining these goals.[109] As suggested by the preceding quotation, many farm workers still revere Chavez as a hero; however, their concerns are shifting to bread and butter issues.

Part of the tactical difference between the unions is due to Chavez's formulation of the UFW as a social movement:

I once said you couldn't organize farm workers in conventional ways. . . . It has to be a movement. . . . What happens is the people get to feel that the idea, the movement, belongs to them. It's theirs, not ours. No force on earth, including the Teamsters and the growers can take that away from them. The more the people get beaten, the more they'll fight. The more persecution, the more strength they have. . . . When you learn about your movement, . . . you get to love it.[110]

Viva la huelga! can be roughly translated as meaning strike; yet its Spanish meaning carries a much more social connotation, particularly when associated with the UFW flags symbolizing hope, aspiration, and sacrifice. The movement for which the cry is the catchword has also had strong religious overtones since its inception—religious officials of many denominations have historically lent their efforts to farm workers in general.[111]

As previously noted, Chavez has always considered loyalty to the movement a prerequisite for participation. Most of the UFW's staff have been volunteers, paid $5 a week. The lack of full-time, experienced personnel placed the UFW at a disadvantage to the Teamsters. The administration of the UFW became somewhat haphazard—terms and records of negotiations were either slipshod or nonexistent. Also, with few exceptions, negotiators could not make binding agreements with the growers on even routine matters without Chavez's personal approval. Turnover among volunteers further added to haphazard administration.[112]

Chavez countered the Teamster invasion with at least two approaches. First, he promoted a boycott of all crops, especially lettuce and grapes, grown by nonunion growers and growers who had signed agreements with the Teamsters. He repeatedly attempted to persuade George Meany to endorse a secondary boycott of all the products at stores selling affected produce. Mr. Meany, however, cognizant of the implied illegality of this boycott as well as the concerns of an AFL-CIO affiliate (Retail Clerks), refused. While Mr. Meany eventually endorsed a product boycott, public support of these boycotts was considerable but not complete. For example, a 1975 nationwide Harris Survey found that 12 percent (17 million adults) had stopped buying grapes and 11 percent (14 million) had stopped buying lettuce.[113]

The California Agricultural Labor Relations Act In addition to continuing organizing activities and administering the UFW, Chavez also pressed for farm labor legislation. After years of lobbying efforts and negotiations with various legislative officials, the California Agricultural Labor Relations Act (CALRA) went into effect on August 28, 1975.[114] This act has several provisions which strengthen farm worker unions in general and the UFW's position relative to the Teamsters in particular. Two major provisions of CALRA require secret ballot elections before union certification at times when the employer's payroll reflects at least 50 percent of the peak agricultural employment. Also, elections are to be held within seven days after the receipt of the election petition. "Under the law, a union may not conduct a secondary boycott against an employer that handles the products of a company where the union has lost an election conducted under the Act." However, consumer boycotts of a particular struck product remain legal.[115] Recently, CALRA has adopted a make-whole remedy for employees when the employer has been found not to have bargained in good faith.[116] The AFL-CIO has long desired that this remedy for bad faith bargaining be included in the National Labor Relations Act; however, they have to date been unsuccessful.

In the first five months after the act was passed, over 32,000 farm workers voted in 429 elections. The pro-union sentiment of these elections was evident (84 percent of the workers voted for union representation), as was the pro-UFW sentiment. The UFW once again became the major bargaining representative, winning 198 elections during this five-month period.[117]

The implementation of the CALRA and the voting results prompted the UFW and the Teamsters to resolve their jurisdictional differences. On March 10, 1977, the unions signed a pact. The UFW would organize all employees in elections conducted by CALRA's Agricultural Labor Relations Board, and the Teamsters would organize all employees in NLRB elections. In essence, the UFW will represent the field workers, and the Teamsters will represent cannery workers and most agricultural truck drivers.[118]

The Future The future of unionized farm workers, particularly of the UFW, seems to be subject to at least two related factors.

The first factor represents *the extent to which the UFW will modify its current goals and administrative procedures to reflect those found in more traditional unions.* Chavez has taken steps in that direction, noting, "Now we have to get the workers, especially the younger ones, to learn the mechanics of operating the union. . . . We want to train them to be professionals, to negotiate and administer the contracts we've already won."[119] Mexican farm laborers comprise the largest employee category, yet their numbers still represent an ethnic minority of farm laborers in California. The UFW, on the other hand, is dominantly Mexican in both leadership and ethos. Ethnic pride and heritage have been successful building blocks of the UFW; however, this organization will need to rely on traditional union goals to attract non-Mexican laborers.[120]

Currently, the UFW's base is being questioned in some quarters. Its total membership has been reduced, even though it has won certification of nearly forty new locals in a two-year period (1979–1981).[121] Criticism has focused on Chavez, who has tightened the union's leadership, isolating the UFW from mainstream union philosophies and strategies.[122] Boycotts of farm products have continued although without the public support evidenced in past years.[123]

Mechanization A second factor concerns the potentially devastating impact of mechanization on farm workers. For example, Libby, McNeil and Libby countered a successful union organizing drive of Wisconsin cucumber workers by mechanization. Within one year of the union's *(Obreros Unidos')* successful election, harvesting machines rendered the bargaining unit nonexistent.[124] In view of mechanization advances, farm worker unions will face a difficult dilemma: do they fight mechanization as a job destroyer, or do they attempt to win higher wages for a smaller number of workers? The UFW appears to favor the first approach, contending

The taxpayer pays twice for state-supported farm research. He pays, first, when public funds are used to develop the machines with no thought for the men and women whose jobs are wiped out; he pays again when these once gainfully employed workers turn to the state for support and the public is forced to absorb the social costs of mechanization.[125]

Agricultural employment has steadily decreased since the 1970s although it has decreased less quickly than predicted. It was expected that a larger decline would occur because productivity would rise more than demand. Foreign agricultural exports, which have doubled in the past ten years, coupled with the effects of agricultural demand and mechanization, will affect the UFW's future growth.[126]

Summary

This chapter first briefly assessed trends of white-collar employees' representation elections as well as potential bases for union optimism in these occupations. Also discussed were labor relations activities in various professional sports, particularly those arrangements and influences which are different from corresponding activities found in other occupations.

Until recently, collective bargaining in health-care organizations has been hindered by a lack of labor legislation. This situation changed in 1974 with the Taft-Hartley amendments that extended federal labor relations coverage to all private-sector hospitals. Yet subsequent labor relations activities (such as union organizing and strikes) are differentiated from other occupations because of the critical nature of work in the health-care fields. Similarly, nurses, house staff, and physicians often modify their collective bargaining concerns with the concept of "professionalism."

While many of the conditions found in the agricultural industry are described as "brutal," collective bargaining in this sector was virtually nonexistent until 1962, when Cesar Chavez founded a union (subsequently called the United Farm Workers). This union faced several obstacles, such as rival union activity, opposition from the growers, and absence of federal labor legislation. One of its major concerns is the effect mechanization can have in reducing the agricultural work force.

Discussion Questions

1. Considering the variables shown in Exhibit 1.1 (elements in the labor relations process), discuss two differences that professional sports, health care, and agriculture have when compared to the others. Also indicate two general similarities of all three sectors, qualifying your answer when appropriate.
2. Select one nontraditional sector and present a detailed discussion of how this sector relates to all of the variables in Exhibit 1.1. You might have to engage in some speculation and outside research to complete this question.
3. Considering the occupational portrayals expressed by a baseball player (page 534), nurse (Exhibit 17.2), and farm worker (Exhibit 17.4), discuss two similarities these occupations might share. Also indicate the specific strategies a union organizer could use to approach these similarities.

References

[1] *Edward R. Curtin, White-Collar Unions* (New York: National Industrial Conference Board, 1970), pp. 71–72.

[2] Claude Edwards, *Some Reflections on White-Collar Collective Bargaining* (Kingston, Canada: Queens University, 1977), p. 3.

[3] Edward R. Curtin, "The Facts About White-Collar Unionization," *Conference Board Record* 6 (June 1969), pp. 11–13.

[4] Tom Wicker, "Baseball," *Esquire*, December 1975, p. 135.

[5] For additional insights into collective bargaining activities in a variety of major sports see James B. Dworkin, *Owners Versus Players: Baseball and Collective Bargaining* (Boston: Auburn House, 1981), pp. 229–286.

[6] "Scorecard," *Sports Illustrated*, December 20, 1982, p. 12.

[7] For a consideration of the potential complications of these statistics see Thomas Boswell, "Dwight Evans Should Have Been MVP," *Inside Sports*, February 1982, pp. 19–23.

[8] See, for example, Marshall H. Medoff, "On Monopolistic Exploitation in Baseball," *Quarterly Review of Economics and Business* 16 (Summer 1976), pp. 113–121. For an approach to this problem and discussion of related research see Gerald V. Scully, "Pay and Performance in Major League Baseball," *American Economic Review* 64 (December 1974), pp. 915–931. For an earlier conceptual approach to wage determination see Simon Rottenberg, "The Baseball Players' Labor Market," *Journal of Political Economy* 64 (June 1956), pp. 242–258.

[9]Scully, "Pay and Performance," p. 920. For a discussion of this reason as it applies to another sport, basketball, see John Papanek, "There's an Ill Wind Blowing for the NBA," *Sports Illustrated*, February 25, 1979, pp. 22, 27.

[10]Peter Seitz, "Footnotes to Baseball Salary Arbitration," *Arbitration Journal* 29 (June 1974), pp. 100–101.

[11]Arthur A. Sloane, "Collective Bargaining in Major League Baseball: A New Ball Game and Its Genesis," *Labor Law Journal* 28 (April 1977), pp. 205–206. For Additional insights into the background of some owners see Don Kowet, *The Rich Who Own Sports* (New York: Random House, 1977); CBS Reports, "The Baseball Business" (as broadcast over the CBS television network, Tuesday, April 26, 1977), transcript, p. 4; Philip Taubman, "Caroll Rosenbloom's Obsession," *Esquire*, January 21, 1978, p. 112; Geoffrey Norman, "The Dallas Cowboys' Art of Hiring Winners," *Esquire*, September 12, 1978, pp. 69–72, 74–75; Hal Lancaster, "Baseball's Big Hit: Los Angeles Dodgers, Again Seeking Pennant, Keep On Winning Fans," *Wall Street Journal*, October 5, 1978, pp. 1, 35; and William Oscar Johnson, "Jerry Is Never behind the Eight Ball," *Sports Illustrated*, June 18, 1979, pp. 22–24, 29; and Gregory Stricharchuk, "Ted Stepien Learns Pro Basketball Is an Expensive Hobby," *Wall Street Journal*, February 16, 1983, pp. 1 and 21.

[12]See, for example, Douglas S. Looney, "OK, What's the Pitch?" *Sports Illustrated*, March 8, 1976, p. 46; and "Name Tiff Leads to Name-Calling," *Miami Herald*, February 16, 1978.

[13]Gordy MacKenzie, "Cubs' Meal Money Adds Up—$18,540," *Times Union and Journal*, May 16, 1982, p. D-4.

[14]Lawrence Ingrassia, "Minnesota Slims," *Wall Street Journal*, July 22, 1982, p. 1.

[15]"Scorecard," *Sports Illustrated*, December 20, 1982, p. 4.

[16]H. L. Klein, "Sports Business," *Wall Street Journal*, August 27, 1982, p. 3.

[17]Judy Moore, "Buc Owner's Strategy: Keep Costs Low," *Jacksonville Journal*, October 24, 1978, p. 17.

[18]David Halberstram, *The Breaks of the Game* (New York: Alfred A. Knopf, 1981), p. 13.

[19]Ron Reid, "It's One Big Happy Family, But," *Sports Illustrated*, August 26, 1974, p. 20.

[20]For insights into this situation see Bill Brubaker, "The No. 1 Headache for Last Year's No. 1 Pick," *Inside Sports* 4 (April 1982), pp. 65–67; Jerry Kirshenbaum, "Sports Agents: Raising Ethical Questions That Run from A (Armas) to Z (Zadora)," *Sports Illustrated*, April 12, 1982, pp. 21–23; "The Fearsome Onesome," *New Times*, December 9, 1977, pp. 69–74; and Allen S. Keller, "Pinch-Hitting at the Bargaining Table," *Wharton Account* 18 (Winter 1978), pp. 14–18.

[21]See, for example, Milton Richman, "Martin Gets Reprieve from Steinbrenner, but He's Not Safe Yet," *Los Angeles Times*, June 21, 1977, part III, p. 1; Reggie Jackson, *Reggie: A Season with a Superstar* (Chicago: Playboy Press, 1975), pp. 66, 68–69; Larry Keith, "A Bunt That Went Boom," *Sports Illustrated*, July 31, 1978, pp. 14–19; and Ed Linn, *Inside the Yankees: The Championship Year* (New York: Random House, 1978). One of the more publicized situations involving owner-manager frictions occurred when Billy Martin left the New York Yankees in 1978 only to return in 1979. The following articles describe events leading to Martin's departure and subsequent return: Murray Chass, "Martin Resigns; Bob Lemmon to Manage Yankees," *New York Times*, July 25, 1978, pp. A-1, B-11; and Pete Axthelm, "Stars in Their Eyes," *Newsweek*, July 2, 1979, p. 55.

[22]Leo Durocher, *Nice Guys Finish Last* (New York: Simon and Schuster, 1975), pp. 410–411.

[23]Glenn Dickey, "The T.V. Tail Wags the Dog," *San Francisco Chronicle*, June 24, 1977.

[24]"Tropic Magazine," *Miami Herald*, February 28, 1982, p. 4.

[25]"Labor Letter," *Wall Street Journal*, February 2, 1982, p. 1. For additional considerations affecting this strike see Kenneth A. Kovach, "Professional Football Penalized for Delay of Game: The Coming Strike in the National Football League," *Labor Law Journal* 33 (May 1982), pp. 306–310.

[26]Richard O'Connor, "Will Free Agents Kill Baseball?" *Sport*, April 1978, p. 42.
[27]William Oscar Johnson. "The Greenbacking of Pete Rose," *Sports Illustrated*, January 22, 1979, p. 38.

[28]Gary Pomerantz, "Marvin Miller," *Times Union and Journal*, June 28, 1981, p. D-3.

[29]Ira Berkow, "King George," *Times Union and Journal*, September 27, 1981, p. D-3.

[30]Frederick C. Klein, "A Big Bucks Blue Print for the White Sox," *Wall Street Journal*, April 2, 1982, p. 23; and, William Taaffe, "Tooting His Own Einhorn," *Sports Illustrated*, September 6, 1982, pp. 48–49.

[31]"Scorecard," *Sports Illustrated*, October 4, 1982, pp. 11–12.

[32]Frederick C. Klein, "Fun and Folly in the National Basketball Asylum," *Wall Street Journal*, October 28, 1982, p. 30.

[33]Ray Kennedy, "More Victories Equals More Fans Equals More Profits, Right? Wrong, Wrong, Wrong," *Sports Illustrated*, April 28, 1980, pp. 34–45.

[34]*Face Off*, September 1971, p. 2.

[35]Robert H. Boyle, "This Man Miller Admits He's a Grind," *Sports Illustrated*, March 11, 1974, p. 21.

[36]Bob Rubin, "Dolphin's Disinterest? Maybe It Was the Sun?," *Miami Herald*, June 5, 1977.

[37]Stanley Cohen, "A Monkey on the Back, A Lump in the Throat," *Inside Sports* (April 1982), p. 20.

[38]For related insights into this issue see Don Reese and John Underwood, "I'm Not Worth a Damn," *Sports Illustrated*, June 14, 1982, pp. 66–82; Bob Welch and George Vessey, *Five O'Clock Comes Early* (New York; William Morrow and Company, 1982); and Douglas S. Looney, "A Test with Nothing but Tough Questions," *Sports Illustrated*, August 9, 1982, pp. 24–26 and 29.

[39]"A Bidding War Product, Neely Advocates the Draft," *Miami Herald*, January 23, 1977.

[40]For a thorough discussion of how this issue applies to professional sports see James B. Dworkin and Thomas J. Bergmann, "Collective Bargaining and the Player Reservation/Compensation System in Professional Sports," *Employee Relations Law Journal* 4 (Autumn 1978), pp. 241–256. For a recent explanation of free agent compensation rules from the 1982 hockey player agreement see H. L. Klein, "Sports Business," *Wall Street Journal*, August 27, 1982.

[41]Curt Flood, *The Way It Is* (New York: Trident Press, 1970), pp. 14–15. See also. *Curtis C. Flood v. Bowie Kuhn et al.*, 407 U.S. 258 (1972). For additional details regarding this decision see Phillip L. Martin, "The Labor Controversy in Professional Baseball: The Flood Case," *Labor Law Journal* 23 (September 1972); pp. 567–571.

[42]Professional Baseball Clubs 66 LA 110 (P. Seitz, 1975).

[43]James B. Chelius and James B. Dworkin, "Free Agency and Salary Determination in Baseball," *Labor Law Journal* 33 (August 1982), pp. 539–545; Paul D. Staudohar and Edward M. Smith, "The Impact of Free Agency on Baseball Salaries," *Compensation Review* 13 (Third Quarter 1981), pp. 46–55; Paul M. Sommers and Noel Quinton, "Pay and Performance in Major League Baseball: The Case of the First Family of Free Agents," *Journal of Human Resources* 17 (September 1982), pp. 426–436; and James Richard Hill and William Spellman, "Professional Baseball: The Reserve Clause and Salary Structure," *Industrial Relations*, 22 (Winter, 1983), pp. 1–19.

[44]"Football Players Form Pro Bargaining Group," *New York Times*, November 29, 1956, p. 45; "National Hockey Players Organize, Name Lindsay Head of Association," *New York Times*, February 12, 1957, p. 34; "Cousy to Discuss Union with Labor Executives," *New York Times*, January 13, 1957, sec. 5, p. 9.

[45]"Hockey Players Win Concessions," *New York Times*, February 6, 1958, p. 35. For background information see "Hockey Clubs Hit in Antitrust Suit," *New York Times*, October 11, 1957, p. 38.

[46]For a discussion of the reorganization of the hockey players' union see "Hockey League Players Look to Teamwork, Union Style," *IUE News*, July 20, 1967, p. 10.

[47]"NFL Owners Get Tackled," *Business Week*, October 11, 1976, p. 36. For a historical development of the Rozelle Rule's judicial implications see Leonard Koppett, "Development of Rozelle Rule Is Traced from Owen's Case," *New York Times*, December 31, 1975, p. C-28. See also, "Inside Track: Gene Upshaw," *Inside Sports*, (July 1982), pp. 8–10.

[48]For a discussion of some of these cases see Dennis D. Pointer, "The Federal Labor Law Status of the Health Care Delivery Industry," *Labor Law Journal* 22 (May 1971), pp. 279–280.

[49]The application of Taft-Hartley to profit-making hospitals and nursing homes remained uncertain until 1969, when the NLRB indicated it would retain jurisdiction if the hospitals and nursing homes exceeded $250,000 and $100,000 gross annual revenues, respectively. Emil C. Farkas, "The National Labor Relations Act: The Health Care Amendments," *Labor Law Journal* 25 (May 1978), p. 259; Harry E. Graham, "Effects of NLRB Jurisdictional Change on Union Organizing Activity in the Proprietary Health Care Sector," in Gerald G. Somers, ed., *Proceedings of the Twenty-fourth Annual Winter Meeting: Industrial Relations Research Association* (Madison, Wis.: Industrial Relations Research Association, 1972), pp. 273–283.

[50]U.S., Congress, Senate, Committee on Labor and Public Welfare, *Coverage of Nonprofit Hospitals under National Labor Relations Act, 1973*, hearings before the Subcommittee on Labor, S.794 and S.2292, 93rd Cong., 1st sess. 1973, pp. 5, 479–480.

[51]Lucretia Dewey Tanner, Harriet Goldberg Weinstein, and Alice L. Ahmuty, "Collective Bargaining in the Health Care Industry," *Monthly Labor Review* 104 (February 1980), p. 50.

[52]Ibid. For additional insights into the BOI see Scott A. Kruse, "Boards of Inquiry in Health Care Disputes: New Options for the Parties," *Labor Law Journal* 30 (October 1979), pp. 603–610.

[53]For additional insights into some of these unions see Richard N. Block, "Unionism in the Health Care Industry: An Overview," Journal of Health and Hospital Administration (August 1979), pp. 41–59; and Richard U. Miller, "Hospitals," in Gerald G. Somers, ed., *Collective Bargaining: Contemporary American Experience* (Madison, Wis.: Industrial Relations Research Association, 1980), pp. 394–414.

[54]Felix A. Nigro, "Introductory Note," *Journal of Health and Hospital Administration*, (August 1979), p. 9.

[55]Bureau of National Affairs, *Daily Labor Report*, July 21, 1977, pp. 2, 3.

[56]Bureau of National Affairs, *Daily Labor Report*, October 14, 1977, p. 2.

[57]*Beth Israel Hospital v. National Labor Relations Board*, 98 S.C. 2468 (1978).

[58]Don A. Zimmerman, "Trends in National Labor Relations Board Health Care Industry Decisions," Bureau of National Affairs Inc., *Daily Labor Report* No. 223 (November 17, 1980), p. D-1.

[59]For additional insights into this controversy and related cases see Stephen P. Pepe and Calvin L. Keith, "Health Care Labor Relations Law—Understanding the Issues," *Employee Relations Law Journal* 7 (Autumn 1978), pp. 235–250; and George W. Bohlander and Kevin C. O'Neil, "Health Care Bargaining Unit Determination: Congressional Intent and National Labor Relations Board Decisions," *Labor Studies Journal* (Spring 1980), pp. 25–41.

[60]Peter Nash, "Impact of the Amendments on the Law—NLRA and NLRB Changes," in A. Eliot Berkeley, ed., *Labor Relations in Hospitals and Health Care Facilities* (Washington, D.C.: Bureau of National Affairs, 1975), p. 27.

[61]Norman Metzger and Dennis D. Pointer, *Labor-Management Relations in the Health Services Industry* (Washington, D.C.: Science and Health Publications, 1972), pp. 22, 23.

[62]John Thomas Delaney, "Union Success in Hospital Representation Elections," *Industrial Relations* 20 (Spring 1981), pp. 149–161.

[63]Robert B. McKersie and Montague Brown, "Nonprofessional Hospital Workers and a Union Organizing Drive," *Quarterly Journal of Economics* 77 (August 1973), p. 35.

[64]Frank A. Sloan and Bruce Steinwald, *Hospital Labor Markets* (Lexington, Mass.: Lexington Books, 1980), p. 145.

[65]A. H. Raskin, "A Union with 'Soul,'" *New York Times Magazine*, March 22, 1970, pp. 24 and 39. For a research effort which examines the racial impact on collective bargaining issues see Ken Demarko, James W. Robinson, and Ernest C. Houck, "A Pilot Study of the Initial Bargaining Demands by Newly-Organized Employees of Health Care Institutions," *Labor Law Journal* 29 (May 1978), pp. 275–291.

[66]Archie Kleingartner, "Nurses, Collective Bargaining, and Labor Legislation," *Labor Law Journal* 18 (April 1967), p. 237.

[67]Daniel H. Kruger, "Bargaining and the Nursing Profession," *Monthly Labor Review* 84 (July 1961), p. 702.

[68]John M. Boyer, Carl L. Westerhaus, and John H. Coggeshall, *Employee Relations and Collective Bargaining in Health Care Facilities*, 2d ed. (St. Louis: C. V. Mosby Company, 1975), p. 240.

[69]Kleingartner, "Nurses, Collective Bargaining, and Labor Legislation," p. 243.

[70]Martha Belote, "Nurses Are Making It Happen," *American Journal of Nursing* 67 (February 1967), p. 287.

[71]Philip D. Rutsohn and Richard M. Grimes, "Nightingalism and Negotiations—New Attitudes of Health Professionals," *Personnel Journal* 56 (August 1977), p. 399.

[72]See, for example, Anne B. Mahoney, "Bargaining Rights: Convincing the Membership," *American Journal of Nursing* 66 (March 1966), pp. 544–548.

[73]William G. Scott, Elizabeth K. Porter, and Donald K. Smith, "The Long Shadow," *American Journal of Nursing* 66 (March 1966), p. 539.

[74]Sally T. Holloway, "Health Professionals and Collective Action," *Employee Relations Law Journal* 1 (Winter 1976), p. 414.

[75]"Employee Relations Are Changing Rapidly in Health Care Industry, Conference Told," Bureau of National Affairs Inc., *Daily Labor Report* no. 142, July 24, 1981, p. A-2.

[76]For additional insights into nurses' bargaining issues see Allen M. Ponak, "Unionized Professionals and the Scope of Bargaining: A Study of Nurses," *Industrial and Labor Relations Review* 34 (April 1981), pp. 396–407; and, Joan R. Bloom, G. Nicholas Parlette, and Charles A. O'Reilly, "Collective Bargaining by Nurses: A Comparative Analysis of Management and Employee Perceptions," *Health Care Management* 5 (Winter 1980), pp. 25–33.

[77]Joseph A. Alutto and James A. Belasco, "Determinants of Attitudinal Militancy among Nurses and Teachers," *Industrial and Labor Relations Review* 27 (January 1974), pp. 212–217.

[78]"Court Overturns NLRB's Interns, Residents Ruling," Bureau of National Affairs, Daily Labor Report, April 3, 1979, p. 1.

[79]Murray A. Gordon, "Hospital Housestaff Collective Bargaining," *Employee Relations Law Journal* 1 (Winter 1976), p. 419. For a detailed analysis of one intern's working conditions see Barry Newman, "Calling Dr. . . . For an Intern, the Life Is Intense, and A 'Day' Can Last for 36 Hours," *Wall Street Journal*, April 17, 1975, pp. 1, 75. For a different viewpoint of house staff officials' economic conditions see "Socialized Medicine Still Means a Lot of Friendly Doctors at a Party," *New Times*, February 20, 1978, p. 23.

[80]Gordon, "Hospital Housestaff Collective Bargaining," p. 420.

[81]Peter Kihss, "Pact Ends Doctor Strike; Staffs Return to Hospitals," *New York Times*, March 21, 1975, p. 42.

[82]Bureau of National Affairs Inc., *Daily Labor Report* No. 60 (March 1981), p. 3.

[83]Mario F. Bognanno, James B. Dworkin, and Omotayo Fashoyin, "Physicians' and Dentists' Bargaining Organizations: A Preliminary Look," *Monthly Labor Review* 98 (June 1975), p. 34.

[84]"Doctors Hit the Streets with a New Strike Law," *Business Week*, March 31, 1975, p. 19; and "A.M.A.'s Militancy," *New York Times*, March 22, 1975, p. 30.

[85]"When Doctors Went Out on Strike," *U.S. News & World Report*, May 26, 1975, p. 34.

[86]Jon A. Klover, David B. Stephens, and Vincent P. Luchsinger, "Contemporary Perceptions of Unionization in the Medical Profession: A Study of Unionized and Non-Union Physicians," *Journal of Collective Negotiations in the Public Sector* 9 no. 2 (1980), p. 108.

[87]"Labor Letter," *Wall Street Journal*, March 13, 1980, pp. 1 and 32.

[88]Marilyn Chase, "City of Doctors," *Wall Street Journal*, March 13, 1980, pp. 1 and 32.

[89]Doron P. Levin, "Health-Care Battle," *Wall Street Journal*, September 29, 1981, pp. 1 and 9.

[90]Harry Weinstock, "The Organized Hospital Worker's View," in Berkeley, *Labor Relations in Hospitals*, p. 55.

[91]It should also be noted that one empirical study has found that unions have had a statistically significant impact on wages, although the difference is not particularly high in dollar terms. Myron Fottler, "The Union Impact on Hospital Wages," *Industrial and Labor Relations Review* 30 (April 1977), pp. 342–355.

[92]Sloan and Steinwald, *Hospital Labor Markets*, pp. 105–121; and, Richard Feldman and Richard Scheffler, "The Union Impact on Hospital Wages and Fringe Benefits," *Industrial and Labor Relations Review* 35 (January 1982), pp. 196–206.

[93]William M. Bulkeley, "Failing Health," *Wall Street Journal*, February 9, 1982, pp. 1 and 14.

[94]For a detailed analysis of social and economic conditions confronting migrant labor in the Northeast see William H. Friedland and Dorothy Nelkin, *Migrant* (New York: Holt, Rinehart and Winston, 1971).

[95]Personal correspondence from Marc Grossman, assistant to the president of the United Farm Workers of America, November 13, 1978.

[96] Sam Kushner, *Long Road to Delano* (New York: International Publishers, 1975), p. 95.

[97]Winthrop Griffith, "Is Chavez Beaten?" *New York Times Magazine*, September 15, 1974, p. 24. © 1974 by The New York Times Company. Reprinted by permission.

[98]Pros and cons of this exemption can be found in Stephen Jacobson, "Labor Legislation and The Agricultural Laborer," *Industrial and Labor Relations Forum*, 11 (Summer, 1975), p. 135; Karen S. Koziara, "Collective Bargaining in Agriculture: The Policy Alternatives," *Labor Law Journal* 24 (July 1973), pp. 424–435; and Sylvester Petro, "Agriculture and Labor Policy," *Labor Law Journal* 24 (July 1973), pp. 24–51; and Harriet E. Cooperman and Marc P. Gabor, "Legal Implications of the Farmworker Exemption," *Industrial and Labor Relations Forum* 11 (Summer 1975), pp. 154–184.

[99]For additional insights of these laws see Karen S. Koziara, "Agricultural Labor Relations Laws in Four States—A Comparison," *Monthly Labor Review* 100 (May 1977), pp. 14–18; Harold C. White and William Gibney, "The Arizona Farm Labor Law: A Supreme Court Test," *Labor Law Journal* 31 (February 1980), pp. 87–99; and Ronald W. Haughton, "The Influence of Labor Management Relations on the Settlement of Agricultural Disputes," *Arbitration Journal* 35 (June 1980), pp. 3–7.

[100]Grossman, personal correspondence, November 13, 1978.

[101]For a detailed history of labor relations activities during this period see S. M. Jamieson, *Labor Unionism in American Agriculture* (Washington, D.C.: Government Printing Office, 1946); and Ernesto Galaza, *Farm Workers and Agri-business in California, 1947–1960* (Notre Dame, Ind.: University of Notre Dame Press, 1977).

[102]Lamar B. Jones and G. Randolph Rice, "Agricultural Labor in the Southwest: The Post Bracero Years," *Social Science Quarterly* 61 (June 1980), pp. 86–94.

[103]Jacques E. Levy, *Cesar Chavez: Autobiography of La Causa* (New York: W. W. Norton, 1975), pp. 92-93.

[104]Ibid, p. 267.

[105]Mark Day, *Forty Acres* (New York: Praeger Publishers, 1971), p. 89.

[106]Dick Meister and Anne Loftis, *A Long Time Coming* (New York: Macmillian, 1977), p. 157.

[107]See, for example, "The Rape of the Farm Workers," *Steel Labor*, September 1973, pp. 8–9.

[108]Griffith, "Is Chavez Beaten?" p. 18.

[109]For an example of this consideration see Joel Solkoff, "Can Cesar Chavez Cope with Success?" *New Republic*, May 22, 1976, p. 14.

[110]Griffith, "Is Chavez Beaten?" p. 18.

[111]See, for example, Joan London and Henry Anderson, *So Shall Ye Reap* (New York: Thomas Y. Crowell, 1970), pp. 79–98; and Day, *Forty Acres*, pp. 53–60.

[112]Michael Yates, "The Trouble with Chavez: A Union Is Not a Movement," *Nation*, November 19, 1977, p. 520.

[113]Harry Bernstein, "UFW Leads in Farm Balloting and Opinion Poll," *Los Angeles Times*, October 30, 1975, part 2, pp. 1–2.

[114]For details of the early implementation of CALRA and voting procedures (for example, bargaining unit determination and voter eligibility) see Joseph R. Grodin, "California Agricultural Labor Act: Early Experience," *Industrial Relations* 15 (October 1976), pp. 275–294. See also William Wong, "California Votes Farm-Labor Election Bill, Presaging a New Unionizing Drive in the Fall," *Wall Street Journal*, May 30, 1975, p. 30; and "Farm Turmoil from a Model Labor Law," *Business Week*, October 13, 1975, p. 88. For a more current assessment of California's Agricultural Labor Relations Board see Bureau of National Affairs, *Daily Labor Report*, May 2, 1978, pp. 1–2.

[115]Grossman, personal correspondence, November 13, 1978; and Refugio I. Rochin, "New Perspectives on Agricultural Labor Relations in California," *Labor Law Journal* 28 (July 1977), p. 398.

[116]Bureau of National Affairs, *Daily Labor Report*, May 19, 1978, pp. 1-2. See also "ALRB Make Whole Remedy," *National Farm Worker Ministry Newsletter 7* (September 1978, p. 5.

[117]W. H. Segur and Varden Fuller, "California's Farm Labor Elections: An Analysis of the Initial Results," *Monthly Labor Review* 99 (December 1976), p. 29. See also "Chavez versus the Teamsters: Farm Workers' Historic Vote," *U.S. News & World Report*, September 22, 1975, pp. 82–83.

[118]Rochin, "New Perspectives," p. 400. For additional details of this pact see "Questions and Answers about Teamster-UFW Agreement," *National Farm Worker Ministry Newsletter* 6 (Spring 1977), p. 2.

[119]William P. Coleman, "Chavez, UFW in the Midst of Changes," *Oakland Tribune*, March 27, 1978.

[120]Varden Fuller and John W. Mamer, "Constraints on California Farm Worker Unionization," *Industrial Relations* 17 (May 1978), p. 51.

[121]"What Happened to Chavez's Union?" *Newsweek*, December 14, 1981, pp. 22 and 24.

[122]Erik Larson, "Internal Strains Split United Farm Workers as a Movement Changes into a Trade Union," *Wall Street Journal*, May 17, 1982, p. 29.

[123]Derek T. Dingle, "Farm Workers' Chicago Office Keeps the Faith," *Wall Street Journal*, July 7, 1981, p. 19. However, some feel that boycotts or their threat can still influence a company's labor relations policies. Chester Goolrick, "Life on the Job," *Wall Street Journal*, May 18, 1981, pp. 1 and 25.

[124]Phillip L. Martin, "Harvest Mechanization and Agricultural Trade Unionism: *Obreros Unidos* in Wisconsin," *Labor Law Journal* 28 (March 1977), pp. 166–173; see also Al Meyerhoff, "Big Farming's Angry Harvest," *Newsweek*, March 3, 1980, p. 11. One other issue involving recent UFW attention is the effects of pesticides on farm workers and their children. See Linda C. Majka, "Labor Militancy among Farmworkers and the Strategy of Protest: 1900–1979," *Social Problems* 28 (June 1981), pp. 533–547.

[125]Cesar Chavez, "The Farm Workers' Next Battle," *Nation*, March 25, 1978, p. 331.

[126]Patricia A. Daly, "Agricultural Employment: Has the Decline Ended?," *Monthly Labor Review* 104 (November 1981), p. 16.

Table of Cases

Case 1

Appropriate Bargaining Unit

Background

The company operates seven retail women's apparel shops in Detroit, Michigan. In June and July 1979, the union filed three election petitions with the NLRB, asking for separate elections at the company's Dearborn, Livernois, and Woodward Avenue stores. These petitions called for three separate bargaining units and each unit would consist of all full- and part-time employees at each store. The company opposed the petitions and contended that an appropriate bargaining unit would be all seven stores and the central office.

Company Position

First, the company pointed out that the seven stores and the central office are within an eighteen-mile radius. Second, it argued that the company's organizational structure is highly centralized. For example, management at the central office controls all aspects of merchandising, shipping and receiving, credit and accounting, advertising, data processing, and personnel and employee benefits throughout the network of stores. All supplies are purchased and distributed centrally. Each store must report to the central office daily. Representatives frequently visit each store without forewarning.

Third, the company presented evidence that authority over matters of personnel and labor relations rests exclusively with the company personnel director who controls the number of employees at the seven stores. The controller establishes the maximum number of hours permitted at each store. Hiring authority rests with the central office; the store manager may not fire any employees. Store managers suggest wage increases but the central office makes the final decision. New employees are trained at the central office before they are sent to the stores.

Fourth, the company offered a history of employee transfers from store to store by presenting evidence that thirty-two current employees have transferred at least once. Also, the company stated that employees are frequently transferred between stores temporarily when there are special sales, holidays, or inventory compilation.

B. Siegel Company and Retail Store Employees, Local 876, United Food and Commercial Workers International Union, AFL-CIO-CLC

Source: 109 LRRM 2843(1982) 250 NLRB No. 112(1980)

Union Position

The union argued that the separate stores were sufficiently autonomous to comprise individual bargaining units. Store managers at their respective stores are more closely involved in employees' daily work than are central office personnel. Each store manager schedules working hours and handles schedule complaints. Each store manager enforces all company rules and policies and reports any infractions. Each store manager evaluates employees and recommends wage increases and promotions. In other words, store managers have discretion to act unilaterally in areas of daily importance to employees. Therefore, there should be separate units for each store.

Questions

1. What are the possible reasons (perceived advantages) behind the union's and management's arguments in this case?
2. What guidelines should be used by the NLRB to determine an appropriate bargaining unit?
3. How should the NLRB decide this case? On what grounds?
4. If the Company or Union disagrees with the NLRB's decision in this case, what alternatives are available to them?

Case 2

Employer Interference with Elections

Facts and Background

In early 1978, the company comptroller, Victor Feildson, asked William Williamson how he was planning to vote in the upcoming union election. When Williamson told him that he did not know, Feildson told Williamson that he would discharge him unless he voted for District 1199. Right before the election, when it looked as though Local 144 would win, Feildson ordered Williamson to "get on the ball" and "urge others to vote for 1199."

In addition, the chief administrator of Greenpark, Simon Pell, called a meeting of all employees and explained his position regarding the upcoming election. He said that he would rather deal directly with employees, not through a union, and urged them to vote no in the election. Further, he promised all bargaining unit employees new Blue Cross and Blue Shield benefits if they rejected the union.

Greenpark Care Center and Service Employees Local 144 AFL-CIO, and District 1199, Retail, Wholesale, and Department Store Union, AFL-CIO

This case is taken from 236 NLRB No. 68(1978). The names of the people involved have been changed.

The election took place on March 31, 1977, and 104 ballots were cast (11 for Local 144, 20 for an independent sales service union, 72 for District 1199, and 1 for no union). Upon the count of the election ballots, the officials of the independent sales service union filed objections to the election.

Questions

1. Have the election results been affected by either Feildson or Pell?
2. What should be the remedy if the company is found to have committed an unfair labor practice?
3. What arguments could District 1199 offer against the NLRB setting aside the election results?

Case 3

Discharge of Employee—Concerted Activities

Background

Jacob Reed was a ten-year employee at Timet and worked as a departmental metallurgist at the time of the discharge. The day before his discharge on June 23, 1978, Reed's supervisor told him that he would receive a 4 percent salary increase. Reed vigorously expressed his displeasure with the amount.

The supervisor asked: "What do you think you can do about it?"

Reed responded: "I can organize."

The supervisor said: "I'm going to tell the plant manager about this."

On the same afternoon, Reed drafted a letter to all salaried personnel criticizing the merit salary increase and volunteering to act as their representative before upper management with regard to pay issues. This letter was typed and shown to several others for their advice and consideration. At 10:30 a.m. the following morning, Reed was discharged.

Reed's Position

The General Counsel of NLRB argued on Reed's behalf that he was entitled to protection under the National Labor Relations Act for concerted activities. He was unlawfully discharged for his complaints and for drafting and

---

Timet versus Jacob Reed

Source: 109 LRRM 2937 (1982); 251 NLRB No. 157 (1980)

circulating a letter in which he offered to represent employees to upper management with regard to wage issues. It is an unfair labor practice for an employer to interfere with, restrain, or coerce employees in the exercise of their Section 7 rights. Because the company had violated the law by discharging Jacob Reed, the General Counsel argued that Reed should be reinstated and made whole for such unlawful action.

Company Position

The company argued Reed's actions were not protected by the National Labor Relations Act. It also argued that Reed was *not* covered under the Act because he was a professional with a college degree and had substituted as a foreman on two occasions in the past. While he did not supervise employees, he did on occasion give them instructions and had authority to recommend discipline. Further, all salaried personnel had been told about their salary increase and all, but Reed, graciously accepted. Reed was "furious," called the increases "ridiculous," and said the company was "putting it to us." The reason for the 4 percent increase was that Reed had not been "on the floor enough . . . not having full command of the job . . . made several errors because he did not yet have full command of the job." The plant manager stated that he had decided to terminate Reed on the night of June 23, 1978, and called Reed's supervisor to discuss the possibility. Early the next morning, company officials sought a replacement for Reed to be sure that the job would be filled. When they located a replacement, Reed was terminated, independent of any of his letter-writing activities.

Questions

1. Are salaried employees covered by the National Labor Relations Act? Why? Why not?
2. Does an employee have to be affiliated with a union to be protected under the NLRA?
3. Were Reed's actions protected concerted activities?
4. How should the Board rule? Why?

Case 4

Discharge of Employee—Organizing Union

Background

Pat Patrick was employed as a waiter by Rusty's from June 1977 until his termination in May 1979. In December 1978, Patrick and a co-employee, Joe Blue, initiated a union organizing campaign.

In early 1979, Don Mang became the new night floor manager. One of his first acts was to hold a meeting with all employees to give his views of management and to tell them how he would "run the ship." His theme was "Return to the Basics." During this meeting on May 22, he went through the employee manual which included the following passage:

No employee will be allowed to drink while on duty. Furthermore, under no circumstances can an employee come to work under the influence.

Additionally, the Pittsburgh facility had a waiter's manual which provided, "No smoking or drinking during duty." He spoke about service, morale, and uniforms and specifically emphasized the rule of no eating, smoking, or drinking during working hours. He warned that violations would lead to termination.

Later that night, Mang observed two other employees, Pitts and Fulgham, with beers in their hands. Mang reminded them that they had work to do and told them to sign out before he saw them drinking on the job.

Two days later, Patrick invited another employee, Marie Spellings, to meet two customers who had been pleased with Patrick's service. The customers asked Spellings and Patrick to have a seat and have a drink. Smith and Patrick did so and drinks were ordered. At that moment, Patrick had no immediate duties to perform. While Patrick, Spellings and the customers sat and drank, a group of patrons who had been served by Patrick paid their check and left a tip. Patrick had already completed his required twenty-five set-ups (placing silverware into the napkin and then into a glass) and had filled out his tip income information paperwork. Spellings, however, had customers at two tables waiting on their meals. Further, she also had cleanup duties assigned to her after the restaurant closed. What occurred next is a matter in considerable dispute. According to Spellings, she left the table to retrieve the order from the kitchen and ran into Mang. She informed him that Patrick and she were having a drink with two customers.

Rusty's Restaurant versus NLRB

Source: 110 LRRM 2799, 251 NLRB No. 134

Mang replied that it was all right as long as she informed him of her activities. Mang then questioned her about Patrick's activities and she requested that any comments be directed at Patrick. Spellings returned to the table and told Patrick that he should talk with Mang.

Patrick claimed that he approached Mang and told him that he had completed his duties and needed to be signed out. He also told him that he was now seated with two customers having a drink. Mang supposedly replied that it was all right as long as he was informed.

Mang's version differs from Spellings' and Patrick's. He asserted that he was eating dinner when he observed Spellings and Patrick sitting at a table drinking and smoking. As he approached the table, Spellings walked toward him and said that she hoped that he didn't mind what she was doing. Mang stated that he was very upset and reprimanded Spellings. She apologized and did not return to the table with Patrick. Mang was then approached by Patrick, and Mang asked him whether or not the May 22 meeting had any effect on him. Before receiving an answer, Mang reprimanded Patrick.

Mang made an entry in his daily report of May 24, 1979, that Patrick had been caught drinking on the job and was reprimanded. The notation made was: "Next strike three—out."

On May 26, Mang summoned Patrick to his office to meet with James Lowrey and Grace Jackson, Rusty's owners. According to Patrick, he was told that management did not like his attitude and that he was being terminated. When Patrick pressed for a reason, Jackson alluded to the drinking incident. When Patrick asserted that it was customary to drink with customers and that Spellings was also there, Jackson replied that she did not care and subsequently uttered: "I got rid of Joe Blue and now I'm rid of you." At the NLRB hearing, all company representatives denied that Jackson said anything like this.

Questions

1. Which party should have the burden of proof in this case? Rusty's or the NLRB as the representative of Patrick? Why?
2. Of what importance are the consistency of treatment and the provisions of the employee handbook?
3. What should be the ruling in this case?

Case 5
Bargaining in Good Faith

Background

The Teamsters had represented the bargaining unit employees for some time. The latest contracts had expired on March 31, 1979, at which time the union went on strike. Prior to March 31, union and management representatives had engaged in eight bargaining sessions without reaching an agreement.

On May 17, 1979, a bargaining session had been held between union representative Dick Parramore and company industrial relations manager Frank Brooks. The company, considering poor economic conditions, proposed a two-year extension of the present agreement except for two changes:

1. A no-strike clause and the inclusion of a provision which called for the discharge of any strikers in violation of the no-strike clause and
2. A proposal to discontinue the union's welfare and pension plan and provide similar coverage under a company plan.

After some bargaining, the parties met separately and thereafter communicated through a mediator. The mediator told Parramore that there was no problem with having the no-strike clause removed, but the company was holding firm on the welfare and pension plan proposal. Parramore concluded that the company would not accept the union's proposed changes to the agreement and was, in effect, withdrawing its proposals. At the NLRB hearing, Brooks claimed however that he had never withdrawn or deleted any proposals.

On May 23, Parramore contacted Neal Worthington, a company vice-president (superior to Brooks), and sought his assistance in preserving the union's pension plan. Later that day, Parramore called Worthington and said that he would schedule a ratification vote on the company proposal but wanted to confirm that the company's proposal for a no-strike clause had been dropped. Worthington said that he did not know about the no-strike clause and would get back with Parramore. Without receiving any confirmation from Worthington either way, Parramore proceeded to conduct a ratification vote on the company's proposed agreement, but without the no-strike clause. The vote was favorable.

Parramore asked the company to prepare drafts of the agreement for execution. The company included the no-strike clause with the provision

---

Pittsburgh-Des Moines Corporation versus NLRB

Source: 253 NLRB 86 (1980)

which called for discharge of strikers in violation of the no-strike clause, and mailed copies to the union on June 10.

When Parramore received the agreement, he immediately called Worthington and protested the inclusion of the no-strike clause. Worthington denied any understanding that the no-strike clause was dropped and suggested that the parties might enter discussions toward a trade-off in contract language. Parramore refused any discussions and asserted that an agreement had been reached and that the no-strike clause had been deleted. Parramore marked through the no-strike clause, signed the agreement, and mailed it to the company.

Worthington responded that there was no agreement to delete the no-strike clause and refused to execute the altered agreement.

On July 12, after hearing nothing from the union, Brooks wrote Parramore the following:

It is clear that we are in disagreement regarding certain essential contract terms and have not been able to consummate an agreement.

By this letter, we hereby withdraw our last contract proposal and suggest that we get together in the immediate future to continue negotiations to reach an agreement. We will review all matters and have a new proposal for your consideration.

I hope to hear from you as soon as possible regarding the scheduling of a meeting for negotiations.

On July 16, the union filed an unfair labor practice charge against the company, alleging that since June 21 the company had refused to execute the collective bargaining agreement which had been agreed on by the parties and ratified by the union. The NLRB investigation revealed no complaint would be issued and the union withdrew the charge.

The union contended that it had secured copies of the ratified agreement, signed them, and forwarded copies to Brooks. A few days later, Brooks responded by letter:

This contract proposal embodies terms of an offer which was unconditionally withdrawn by the Company by a letter dated July 12, 1979. Accordingly, the proposal we received is rejected by the Company. Enclosed is your copy of this rejected proposal which we have not signed.

The Company remains ready and willing to meet with you to bargain in good faith in order to reach an acceptable agreement. I will be preparing a counter proposal from the Company which I will forward to you shortly.

After further exchanges with each party adhering to its position, the company drew up a new contract and mailed it to Parramore on September 11.

The company stated:

You will note that while certain language changes have been made, the Company's proposals contain the same economic provisions which were included in our previously withdrawn proposal.

In the new proposal, the economic provisions remained the same; however, there were substantial changes in clauses concerning union membership, check-off of dues, management rights, and grievance procedures. On September 17, Brooks wrote Parramore a letter urging a negotiations session. He states:

At this meeting, I hope to explain further the Company's current proposals and the circumstances which have contributed to those proposals. The Company will certainly consider any counter proposals the Union may have.

Parramore refused and Brooks expressed regrets over the union's position and stated:

The Company is anxious to meet with you for the purposes of negotiating the contract. Although we apparently have some differences, I believe that through negotiations, these differences can be resolved. We are ready to move in good faith to reach an agreement. You have not even given us a chance to explain our proposal, or to hear any counter proposals you may have.

The Company remains ready and willing to negotiate with the Union at a time and place of your choice. We want to reach an agreement with you.

This letter brought a response from Sam Mason, union attorney, who claimed that negotiations are not in order because a contract already existed. On September 25, Brooks wrote again and denied any existence of an agreement. On October 10, the union finally agreed to negotiate, but to discuss only minor variations of the June 10 proposal. A meeting was held and neither party changed its position.

On October 23, Brooks wrote to Parramore and offered to substitute the union's proposed grievance procedure for the company's last proposal and to include a provision respecting the crossing of picket lines which was desired by the union but eliminated from the company's last proposal. Then Mason responded:

> **Your company has consistently ignored our proposals. The Union is not and will not enter into any negotiations with your company other than on the basis of a compromise for an existing contract.**

With this response from Mason, the union again filed an unfair labor practice charge against the company.

Questions

1. What is meant by surface bargaining? Is either party involved in surface bargaining?
2. What are the consequences of committing an unfair labor practice by refusing to bargain in good faith?
3. What should be the decision in this case?
4. Assess the strategies of both union and company negotiators in this case.

Case 6

Refusal to Bargain—Union Recognition

Facts and Background

The union conducted an employee-initiated organizational drive among production and maintenance employees on February 28 and March 2, 1977. By March 3, 1977, the union had secured thirty-three authorization cards out of a bargaining unit of forty-five employees. On March 3, the union representative, Nancy Gant, visited the company and requested union recognition from the company president, Mr. Pauley. As support, she presented the thirty-three signed authorization cards. Mr. Pauley examined the cards and replied "You got them all." In response, Ms. Gant said that the company should grant recognition and negotiate a contract. Mr. Pauley asked whether the union expected him to sign a contract at that time, and Ms.

Jerr-Dan Corp. and Meat Cutters Local 72, AFL-CIO

Source: 237 NLRB 49 (1978)

Gant replied that it did not, but that collective bargaining would commence at a later date.

The parties agreed to meet on March 7, 1977, for the purpose of engaging in collective bargaining. However, before the March 7 meeting, Mr. Pauley retained legal counsel and sent a telegram to Ms. Gant cancelling the meeting. In his telegram, he also indicated that:

1. He doubted the union majority status.
2. He doubted the appropriateness of the unit.
3. He refused to recognize the union without an NLRB election.

On March 7, 1977, when the company president, Mr. Pauley, did not meet with the union, the thirty-three employees went out on strike in protest of Mr. Pauley's action in repudiating his March 3 agreement. The strike lasted until April 19, 1977. Upon the commencement of the strike, the union also petitioned the NLRB for an unfair labor practice charge against the company for refusal to bargain.

Questions

1. Can collective bargaining take place without an NLRB election?
2. What are the conditions under which a union can be recognized without an election?
3. If you had been Mr. Pauley on March 3, what would you have done?
4. What do you believe was the NLRB decision and order? Why?

Case 7

Refusal to Bargain—Mandatory Bargaining Issues

Facts and Background

The management at the Chicago Stamping Plant, Ford Motor Company, refused to bargain and supply information to the United Auto Workers Local 588 in regard to the plant's vending machine and cafeteria prices and services.

The company provides its employees with two air-conditioned cafeterias and five air-conditioned vending areas. These are serviced by ARA Services, pursuant to a 1972 agreement. Under the agreement, ARA furnishes food and machines and is reimbursed for all direct costs of food and vending

---

Ford Motor Company and Automobile Workers, Local 588

Source: 230 NLRB 101 (1977)

machine operations, plus a general administrative cost of 4 percent net receipts and a service fee of 5 percent net receipts. Should the net receipts exceed costs plus the 9 percent surcharge, the excess funds are returned to the company. If revenues are less than costs plus the 9 percent surcharge, the company makes up the difference, a situation which the company has faced in recent years.

The company has in the past at all times refused to bargain over prices set by ARA but has bargained over the quality of the service provided. Since 1967, the local contract has included provisions dealing with vending and cafeteria services such as service lines, machine repairs, and menu variety.

The employees have a thirty-minute lunch break and two twenty-two-minute rest breaks. They are not allowed to leave the plant during the rest breaks, and it is not feasible to leave during the lunch breaks. Employees are permitted to bring their own food into the plant, and lockers are furnished. Usually only a small number ever leave the plant during lunch.

On February 6, 1976, the company reviewed its financial situation concerning cafeteria and vending machine prices and, hoping to break even, decided to raise prices on items from 5 to 10 cents per item. The union responded by letter a week later, asking to meet with the company in order to bargain over the prices and services. The company refused to bargain, and the union began a boycott of the food service operations (over half of the bargaining unit employees participated). On March 23, 1976, the union requested information concerning the company's role in cafeteria and vending operations in order to administer the present agreement and to prepare for the upcoming negotiations. The company refused to provide the information. The case was sent to the NLRB for a determination.

Questions

1. Should cafeteria and vending prices be considered "wages, hours, and other terms of employment"?
2. What are the consequences of the company's refusal to bargain?
3. If the company should lose, what alternatives are available to it?

Case 8
Discharge for Theft

Issue

1. Was Laura Kuller (called Bunny Mary) discharged for just cause?
2. If not, what should the remedy be?

The grievant, Laura Kuller, was employed under the name of Bunny Mary at the Central City Playboy Club for four years. No disciplinary action had been taken against her prior to her discharge on August 2, 1977. Then she was terminated for allegedly changing the server's name on a customer's check on July 19, 1977, so that she could obtain the $7.64 tip rather than the employee who provided the service. The following paragraphs present the key events that transpired on that evening.

On July 19, 1977, the grievant was one of four Bunnies working the evening shift in the Living Room section of the Central City Playboy Club. Her station was located in the club's disco dancing area. At approximately 10:00 P.M., one of the Bunnies, Terri James, who was working in the same room away from the dance floor, wanted to leave early for the night, a practice allowed when business was slow. She obtained permission from management to leave after her customers moved forward to tables closer to the disco dancing area, which left her without anyone to serve. Among the customers moving on the night in question was a party of three women who moved to a table in the grievant's area.

Customers at the Central City Playboy Club are charged a 17.5 percent serving charge. This money is given to the Bunny whose name appears on the check, and it is her primary source of earnings. When the party in question moved forward, Ms. James closed out the check with her name on it (included on the check were the cover charge and the cost of dinner and a round of drinks prior to and after dinner). It was undisputed that she had served these items, for which her tip was $7.64. She then opened a new check with the grievant's name on it, got the guests another round of drinks, and left. A second cover charge was not imposed, and the grievant continued to serve drinks to the party as requested between 10:00 and 12:00; her total service charge was $2.27.

Feeling that Ms. James had "skimmed the cream" by serving the customers dinner and including the cover charge on her bill, the grievant expressed unhappiness with her leaving early, causing the grievant to have to provide the customers the less lucrative part of their service. There was no

---

Playboy Club of Central City

This case has been adapted with the permission of the Bureau of National Affairs from its publication *Labor Arbitration Reports*. 70 LA 304 (Stuart P. Herman), 1977. The names of the people involved have been changed. The name of the particular Playboy Club has also been changed.

dispute that the grievant informed the other Bunnies and the assistant Bunny trainer of the actual facts and what she intended to do. It was not disputed that before closing that night she retrieved the first check with Ms. James's name on it and crossed it out, inserting her own name. The grievant made no attempt to hide what she had done, made the changes in front of other employees, and told several other Bunnies what she had done. While the grievant never informed Ms. James about what she did, the other Bunnies did tell her. Although there was disagreement as to whether any conversation took place between the grievant and Ms. James later that night or within a few days thereafter, there was agreement that Ms. James was informed within a week of the incident. She chose not to discuss it with the grievant but instead reported it to the union shop steward, who informed management of the situation.

No written policy was presented by the employer concerning the changing of a server's name on checks or the signing of someone else's name on them, but shortly after the termination of the grievant, the employer posted a written memo informing the Bunnies such practices were prohibited.

On August 2, 1977, the club supervisor, Janet Thomas, upon being informed of the incident of July 19, 1977, called a meeting with the grievant and her union representative. At that meeting, the grievant admitted changing the check to get the tip for herself and that she had never subsequently discussed the matter with Ms. James. Upon conclusion of the meeting, the decision was made to terminate the grievant.

Pertinent Contract Provisions

Article VII (q) (1):
No Bunny will be discharged, suspended or otherwise disciplined without just cause.

Article VII(x):
Pertaining to Bunnies: **Except as limited and restricted by this Agreement, PCI has and shall retain the right of management and the direction of the Clubs, as it pertains to Bunnies. Such rights of management include, among other things, but are not limited to: the right of PCI to plan, direct, control, increase, decrease or diminish operations in whole or in part; to remove any Club or any portion thereof to another location; to hire, suspend, discharge or discipline employees for just cause or lack of Bunny image, subject to grievance and arbitration procedures as herein provided; and to determine the number of employees that it shall employ at any time and the qualifications necessary to any of the jobs, provided it is not inconsistent with this Agreement; to adopt and from time to time modify, rescind or change reasonable safety and work**

rules and regulations so long as such rules are not inconsistent with a provision of this Agreement and to enforce such rules; and to select and assign such work and duties not covered by this Agreement as it deems appropriate to supervisory and other categories of employees excluded from this Agreement, as specified in this Agreement.

Article IX(g):
The arbitrator shall have no authority to alter or amend the terms of this Agreement.

Positions of the Parties

Company The employer argued that it is undisputed that the grievant altered a check in order to get a tip belonging rightfully to another Bunny. The employer further contended that it was undisputed that the policy among the Bunnies, through custom and practice, if not formally reduced to specific writing, that checks should not be altered without the knowledge and consent of another Bunny entitled to receive a tip based on a portion of that check.

Based on the above, the employer contended in its presentation that what the grievant did actually constituted theft from another employee. It presented supporting cases that theft was an adequate ground for discharge, regardless of the value of the item or the employee's work record. (S.A. Shenk, 26 LA 395; Franz Food Products, 28 LA 543; Plough, Inc., 57 LA 369; Borg-Warner, 47 LA 903; United Hosiery Mills, 22 LA 573; Hawaiian Telephone Co., 43 LA 1218.) Therefore, the employer contended that the discharge of Laura Kuller (Bunny Mary) was for just cause pursuant to the provisions of the current collective bargaining agreement.

Union It was the position of the union that the conduct of Laura Kuller (Bunny Mary) did not constitute just cause for discharge within the meaning of Article VII (q) (1) of the current collective bargaining agreement, and that she should be reinstated to her former position with full back pay. The union further argued that the supporting cases named by the employer were unlike the present case in both facts and issues.

Questions

1. Assume you are the union representative. Formulate the best, most thorough case that you could present before the arbitrator. Repeat the process, assuming that you are a management representative. On the basis of both sets of formulated contentions, how would you decide the issue as an arbitrator? Why?

2. Who has the burden of proof in this case?
3. To what extent should the arbitrator consider and use the supporting cases referenced by the employer in making the decision?
4. Should the grievant, Laura Kuller, be reinstated? If so, what should be the remedy? What is your reasoning?
5. Where did the employer fail in its managerial practices in this case?

Case 9

Discharge for Insubordination, Safety, Management Rights

Background

ABC company is engaged in the mining, processing, and smelting of iron ore and the production of steel at its plant in Bessemer, Alabama. The United Metal Workers is the collective bargaining representative for the production and maintenance employees.

On April 12, 1983 the grievant was cut on the right wrist while working at his company job. Per normal procedure, the grievant reported to the company doctor who in turn sent him to the Hospital-in-the-Pine for examination and treatment of the cut. Dr. Andy Fingers examined the cut and placed three sutures in it plus bandaging it. On April 13, 1983 the grievant had the wound redressed. On April 20, 1983 the grievant reported to the company clinic and requested that the duty nurse remove the sutures. They were removed and an impervious type paper tape bandage (similar to a Bandaid) was applied to the wound. At that time the duty nurse made a medical entry which indicated that ". . . there was a little redness along the line of his (grievant's) wound." The company doctor testified at the arbitration hearing that this type of reaction, that is, the redness along the line of wound closure, was normal for the type of injury the grievant had sustained. The grievant was told by the nurse to return the next day and have his dressing changed. It was left to the grievant's option as to when he was to return during his shift the next day for the dressing change. The medical department did not put any restrictions on the work activity of the grievant.

The incident in question took place on the first shift which commenced at 11:30 p.m. on April 20, 1983 and extended over into April 21, 1983. During this shift the grievant was assigned to work as a crane follower in the specialty tubing department.

ABC Steel Company and United Metal Workers*

*The authors wish to express our appreciation to Dr. Milden J. Fox, (Jr.), Arbitrator and Professor (Industrial Engineering), Texas A&M University, for this case.

According to the grievant's foreman, Tom Stepstone, the grievant arrived at 11:35 p.m., April 20, in the mill office. Not only was the grievant's arrival some five minutes after the official shift started, he was fifteen to twenty minutes late with respect to the unofficial relief time customary among bargaining unit employees. The foreman then questioned the grievant about reporting late for work. According to the foreman, the grievant said he had to hitch-hike to work due to car trouble. According to the foreman, the grievant was told that he would have to start reporting to work on time or else the foreman would have to take disciplinary action. The foreman further stated that the grievant had been checking in late for ". . . a couple of months." Following the consultation meeting, the grievant proceeded to his work station. Shortly thereafter, the foreman made a routine check of the work area, including the grievant's work station, whereupon the grievant told the foreman the nurse wanted the grievant or the foreman to contact her that night about the grievant's wound. The foreman called the nurse and she reportedly informed him she just wanted to check the grievant's wound. The foreman further stated that he asked the nurse if she wanted to see the grievant right away. The nurse supposedly replied that she did not want to see the grievant right away, just some time during the shift.

According to the grievant, when the nurse removed his three sutures the morning of April 20, she was hesitant, as she wanted a doctor to see the wound. Furthermore, the nurse allegedly told him there was ". . . possible infection." The grievant further stated that the nurse wanted him to report to the clinic at the beginning of his next shift so that the wound might be checked. According to the grievant, he told the nurse that he would have his foreman call her and, he, the grievant, would come in for the wound check after his foreman called her.

According to the grievant, on the night in question, he got to work about 11:25 p.m. He then signed his time card and on the way to his job another employee asked him a question. He then allegedly proceeded to his job when he met his Foreman "close to 11:30 p.m." The grievant testified that the foreman questioned him as to his tardiness whereupon the grievant said "I explained I was late because of the car trouble and things." The foreman gave him a work order and the grievant proceeded to his job.

Shortly after commencing work the grievant claimed that he informed his foreman as to what the nurse had told him and requested permission to go to the clinic. The grievant further testified the bandage on his wound was "loose and filthy." The grievant also testified that on four other occasions, he had asked Foreman Stepstone for permission to go to the clinic. According to the grievant, he told his foreman that the cut was irritating him and that he felt it was hazardous to his health. The grievant further stated that the fumes from the acid vat were irritating his wound. The grievant's job that night was to place tubes in the degreaser vat and then into a sulfuric acid vat.

Following the initial contact between the grievant and his foreman at the grievant's work station, the foreman returned to his office where he allegedly told another foreman, James Lowrey, that he would send the grievant to the clinic as soon as possible during the shift. A few minutes later the grievant came into the office and said, "If you're going to go by the book, I'm going to go by the book. I want to go right now." The foreman stated that he told the grievant "I will get you up there as soon as I can; go back to work." The grievant made a few comments and then returned to his work station.

A few minutes later, according to the foreman, the grievant returned with another employee, Bob Stanford. The grievant allegedly removed his gloves and glasses and told his foreman "I'm not going back to work until I go to the clinic, it's a hazard to my health." According to the foreman, he reiterated to the grievant that he would get him to the clinic as soon as he could. At this point the foreman allegedly gave the grievant a direct order to leave the office and return to work. The grievant supposedly told his foreman again that he was not going to return to work because "it's a hazard to my health." The Foreman then said "I'm going to give you a direct order to leave the office and go back to work." The grievant still refused.

The testimony of the grievant and his witness, Bob Stanford, fairly well substantiates the foreman's testimony in that the grievant kept saying that the cut was irritating him, and hazardous to his health, and that he (the grievant) would like to go to the clinic at that time. The grievant admitted the foreman told him that he, the foreman, was giving him a direct order to return to work.

The foreman twice repeated his order to the grievant directing him to return to his job, and each time the grievant refused on the grounds of work hazardous to his health. The foreman then called the guard to escort the grievant out of the plant. Before leaving the plant, the grievant was taken to the clinic where the dressing (paper tape) was changed on his cut wrist.

The grievant was charged with a violation of Group III, Rule 3 of the general plant rules and terminated from employment. The grievant appealed his discharge, and the case has been processed in accordance with the grievance procedure and appealed to arbitration.

Pertinent Contract Provisions

Section 3 Management

The management of the business and plant and the direction of the working forces, including, but not limited to, the right to hire, suspend or discharge for just cause, assign or transfer employees, adopt new or

changed methods of performing the work, prescribe reasonable general plant rules and the right to relieve employees from duty because of lack of work, or for other legitimate reasons, and to contract out work, is vested exclusively in the Company, and the Company retains all rights that it legally had, subject to the restrictions of law or a specification provision of this Agreement.

In the exercise of its right, however, whether here enumerated, or here or elsewhere retained, the Compny agrees not to discriminate against any member of the Union and to exercise its prerogatives for legitimate business reasons. The Company in the exercise of its rights shall observe the provisions of this Agreement.

Section 13 Safety and Health
Any employee or group of employees who believe that they are being required to work under conditions which are unsafe or unhealthy beyond the normal hazard inherent in the operation in question shall first report such conditions to their immediate supervisor and then shall have the right to:

1. **File a grievance in the third step of the grievance procedure for preferred handling in such procedure and arbitration; or**
2. **Relief from the job or jobs without loss to their right to return to such job or jobs, and at management's discretion, assignment to such other employment as may be available in the plant; provided, however, that no employee, other than communicating the facts relating to the safety of the job, shall take any steps to prevent another employee from working on the job. Should it be determined through the grievance procedure that an unsafe condition existed as claimed by the employee, the employee will be compensated for any time lost.**

The General Plant Rules (JE-3) revised February 11, 1982, are relied upon as follows:

Group III: Major Offenses
Violation of any rule in this Group will result in discharge unless major extenuating circumstances exist.

3. **Insubordination, failure or refusal to carry out a work assignment (except as permitted by Section 13, paragraph C of the contract).**

Positions of the Parties

Company Position The company contended that there is no proof of any new or "abnormal" hazard to which the grievant was exposed, as is required under Section 13. It appeared ludicrous to believe that the grievant perceived any real threat to his health. When asked if the cut burned while he was working, the grievant had replied "No, but it was stinging." The company maintained that minor discomforts are not "abnormal hazards" and certainly not real threats to health. On the contrary, heat, minor cuts and abrasions, and dust are all accepted as normal hazards or physical inconveniences of this type of job, and the grievant was fairly compensated specifically for such hazards. Furthermore, the medical evidence presents no existence of any health hazard to the grievant.

The Company is, therefore, faced with an employee who, with a spirit of malevolence toward his supervisor, committed insubordination and was properly terminated, but who now looks to the Arbitrator to reward his misbehavior with amnesty. His attitude in this act reflects contempt for authority and an incorrigible nature which would not be improved by his return to the Company's employment. Vindication of this Grievant would be a signal to others that insubordination is a safe pursuit, so long as one deviously invokes the magic words: "Section 13," and points to a hangnail or chipped tooth.

Simply stated, the Company asks the Arbitrator to make a common-sense interpretation of the Contract, and to base his construction of it upon the realities of human nature and the legitimate business needs and traditional prerogatives of the Company's production-conscious heavy industry. The plain truth is that a mill cannot operate in an environment where any employee can with impunity ignore his supervisor's orders and shut down his job, knowing that nobody can question his claim of safety or health hazard. The Union's position would subvert the intent of Section 13 and, after abuse by some malicious employees, poison the heretofore generally cooperative spirit between labor and management on legitimate safety and health matters. At stake here are issues of management rights and future business viability that transcend a mere discharge case. The Company therefore asks the Arbitrator to answer both of its stated issues in the *negative*.

Having shown that its discharge of the grievant was reasonable under the circumstances, the company earnestly requested the arbitrator to rule the grievance denied.

Union Position The union argued that the grievant was unjustly discharged on April 22, 1983 for alleged violation of General Plant Rules, Group III (3) which states:

---

3. Insubordination, failure or refusal to carry out a work assignment (except as permitted by Section 13 paragraph C of the contract).

It was the union's position that Section 13(C) clearly gives an employee the right to request relief from his/her job for unsafe or unhealthy conditions. Furthermore, Section 13(C)2 states that the only penalty, if the job is found to be safe and healthy, is that the employee loses whatever time off was involved surrounding the situation in question.

The Company has attempted to imply that Section 3, Management, somehow overrides Section 13, Safety and Health. This false allegation is seen in the last sentence of Section 3 which says "The Company in the exercise of its rights shall observe the provisions of this Agreement."

Since there is no past practice clause in the Contract, any attempt on the part of the Company to imply some type of past practice involving Section 13 would of necessity not be controlling.

Under other contracts in this industry, an employee who believes that he/she is being required to work under conditions beyond the normal hazards of his/her job may file either a grievance or claim (request) relief from the job. If the employee requests relief and the Company does not agree that relief is warranted, the Company may attempt to impose disciplinary penalties on the employee. However, the Union argued that Arbitrators have consistently held, under these contract provisions, that if the employee acted in good faith with the request, the employee is not guilty of insubordination and hence may not be subject to discipline.

In the instant case the Grievant's concern for his arm arose as a result of the nurse having told him that his arm looked red and was possibly infected. Furthermore, the nurse told him to return that evening and let her check his wound and redress it. Following the Grievant's third request to be sent to the clinic so his wound could be attended by medical personnel, the Grievant invoked Section 13 stating the cut was irritating him and he felt the working environment and wound combined were hazardous to his health. At no time did the Grievant refuse to perform his job. He merely kept telling his Foreman that he felt there was a hazard to his health.

It is the Union's opinion that the evidence clearly shows the Grievant had a good faith belief that he was being required to work under conditions hazardous to his health. Even if the Arbitrator were to find the job not to be hazardous to the Grievant's health, the only penalty should be the loss of pay for the balance of the involved eight-hour shift.

The Union requests that the Arbitrator instruct the Company to reinstate the Grievant with full seniority and full back pay.

Questions

1. Does an employee have the right to refuse work which the employee believes is injurious to his/her health?
2. Would it have been more appropriate for the grievant to have contacted his union steward when the foreman refused to send him to the clinic?
3. What is meant by insubordination?
4. Does the principle, "follow supervisor's orders; grieve later" apply to this case?
5. Of what importance is industry practice and other arbitrator decisions?
6. You be the arbitrator: how would you decide this case?

Case 10

Discharge for Inefficiency

Background

The Exquisite Cigar Company manufactures cigars in one of its plants in Asheville, North Carolina. The production employees are represented by the United Cigar Makers Union.

The grievant, 62 years of age, was employed initially in 1960 as a tobacco stripper (tears tobacco apart) and worked in this job until 1976, when the stripping department was eliminated. The company and union negotiated an agreement that allowed these employees to bump into other departments. The grievant was successful in her bid to become a carrier cleaner and then, in 1977, a machine tender operator—the position held at the time of discharge.

In 1977, the grievant was trained and given the assistance of an experienced operator. At that time each operator was responsible for two machines and the production standard of 6,600 cigars per machine per day was not strictly enforced. During this period, there were no quality standards, although reclaims (cigars not meeting sufficient standards to be sold as "Exquisite" cigars) were taken out by the operators. Operators were not disciplined for failing to meet standards; however, any operators who failed to produce 6,600 cigars per machine per day would have a "red card" placed on their machines.

Because the cigar industry had been declining in previous years, the company added an automatic tray loader to each machine to improve efficiency and productivity. Since the workload of each operator was re-

Exquisite Cigars and United Cigar Makers Union*

*This case is written by W. H. Holley, Jr.

duced, each operator was assigned four machines instead of two. The union had filed a grievance over this change and contended that the operators were entitled to higher wages, but an arbitrator ruled that the overall workload had not been "radically" increased to warrant a higher wage.

In late 1979, both the union and company became concerned about the quality of the cigars that were being produced. This was magnified by the general decline in the industry and a decline in the company's best selling product, the "Exquisite." The company then employed an industrial engineering consulting firm to study productivity and it studied the position of the machine tender operator. The consultants reported that the production standard should be 7,182 cigars per machine per day with a reclaim percentage (number of faulty cigars divided by total cigars produced) of 1.5.

To institute these standards, the company began servicing all 104 machines in February, 1980, to assure that they were in peak operating condition. In June, 1980, the program started and a four-step disciplinary procedure was to be used. Below-standard performance was considered less than 6,804 per machine per day or reclaims above 2 percent.

Between June, 1980, and October, 1980, the slower operators were assigned a teacher to assist them in becoming more productive and efficient. A teacher worked with the grievant during the week of September 22, 1980. Then in October and November, 1980, teachers were assigned to sections and helped operators who needed additional assistance on their machines.

Between June 1, 1980, and October 1, 1980, warnings were issued to most employees for either low production or excessive reclaims, but no one was discharged. The company continued to be concerned because production did not increase and the percentage of reclaims did not decrease. On the first of October, 1980, the company held meetings with each production section and the grievant attended the meeting in her section. At this meeting, Plant Manager Charlie Atkinson and three vice-presidents discussed production problems and employee complaints about the quality of the filler (cigar ingredients) and tape (outside wrappings). The company committed itself to correcting the problem and told the employees that all previous warnings would be voided. Also, the first two weeks of October would be a "grace period" when no form of discipline would be administered; however, failure to meet standards after the "grace period" would initiate the disciplinary procedure. All employees were informed that the minimum standards would remain at 6,804 units at 2 percent reclaim for the remainder of 1980; however, the ultimate standard of 7,182 and 1.5 percent would go in effect on January 2, 1981. During the two-week period of October 17, 1980 to October 31, 1980, several warnings were given, but the management and employees agreed that the filler and tape had improved.

From October 17, 1980, on, the grievant had no problem with production, but experienced difficulty with reclaims. The grievant received a verbal warning on November 5, 1980, a written warning on December 16, 1980, a suspension on January 20, 1981, and a discharge on February 3, 1981. During this time, the grievant was able to meet the reclaim standard in only one period. On February 2, 1981, the grievant requested to transfer to the night shift and worked one night in which her reclaim percentage was 4.1 and her production was above standard. The following day the two-week report for the period ending on January 30, 1981, was released and it showed that the grievant's reclaim rate had been higher than standard. She was discharged on February 3, 1981, for the following reason:

Discharge for high reclaims after verbal warning, written warning, and suspension.

The grievant filed a grievance on February 5, 1981, which stated:

"I was discharged for high reclaims when I went to night shift to improve and was given one night. The next day I was called in and discharged. Past practice was to give you a chance. This did not happen in my case."

The grievance was denied and appealed through the next steps and finally to arbitration.

Pertinent Contract Provisions

Article 2 Management's Rights

Section 1. The management of the Plants and the direction of the working forces, including the right to direct, plan and control Plant operations, sub-contract work, close or remove the location of the Plant for economic reasons, the right to hire, promote, demote, suspend or discharge employees for just cause, or to relieve employees because of lack of work, or for other legitimate reasons under this Contract, or to establish work schedules and make changes therein essential to the efficient operation of the Plant, or the right to introduce new improved methods, new machines, machinery or facilities, or to change existing production methods or facilities, is vested exclusively in the COMPANY; provided, that in the exercise of these rights, the COMPANY agrees that it will not conflict with the other provisions of this Contract.

Article 9 Terms of Employment

Section 1. The COMPANY shall decide as to the ability and efficiency of the workers to be employed or to be retained in its employment; but shall at no time discriminate on account of UNION activities.

Section 2. (a) The COMPANY, upon discharging or suspending regular employees for cause, shall give notice to the UNION that such actions have been taken with reasons for same.

(b) When an employee is charged only with inefficiency such employee and the UNION shall have ten (10) work days written notice thereof. If the inefficiency shall not have been corrected within thirty (30) work days from the period of said notice, such employee may be subject to discharge. This discharge shall be subject to the grievance procedure. After sixty (60) work days from the date of the written notice, if no further action has been taken, such notice shall expire and become void.

Company Rules

You will be given at least a verbal warning for violation of these rules. Depending upon the nature and circumstances of the violation, you are subject to a written warning, suspension, or discharge.

3. Inefficiency . . . lack of ability or negligence on the part of the employee to perform his/her job.

Positions of the Parties

The company contended that it not only had the contractual right to set reasonable production standards and enforce these standards through discipline, but it had the right to tighten work standards and require better performance than in the past.

Second, the company argued that it had the right to set standards even though its position in a 1979 arbitration case was that no production standards or quotas were to be met by operators. Before June, 1980, the company had a goal of 6,600 cigars per machine per day, but this goal was used as an incentive and not as a standard. During this time there was no standard for reclaims, and operators were not fully charged with the responsibility of quality control. This responsibility still essentially resided with the press feeders in the finishing department.

Next, the company, concerned about competing in a declining industry, became increasingly concerned about efficiency and productivity. The union itself had expressed concern about the quality of the cigars being produced. Meetings were held, a study was conducted by industrial engineers, and production and reclaim standards were established. Then standards were announced and implemented in June and October, 1980; no grievance was filed over their reasonableness.

The company contended the union members' testimony concerning "stress and hardship" placed on employees attempting to meet the production standards is not relevant; neither is the testimony that employees have to work through their breaks to meet production standards. The evidence of employees quitting and retiring early because of the pressure to meet standards was presented by witnesses as second-hand evidence or as "hearsay." Further, the grievant did not testify that she felt any pressure or stress. In addition, working through breaks is not essential to meet the production standard because production on a plant-wide basis now is above standard. Plant Manager Atkinson testified that if employees want to work through breaks, they do so voluntarily.

The company claimed that,

Any attempt by the union to argue that the standards are difficult for "older employees" to meet or there was an attempt to weed out older employees (or at least had this effect) would not be viable.

The company submitted an exhibit which showed a number of employees who were older and had more seniority than the grievant but who were meeting the standard. Also, it claimed that her replacement had no difficulty meeting the standard.

The company claimed that the real issue in the case is:

Whether the Company acted fairly in regard to the Grievant's ability to meet the *reclaim standard* and, in accordance with the wording of the grievance itself, whether she was given an adequate opportunity to meet the standards.

The company presented several guidelines that had been established in previous arbitration cases:

1. The standard must be clearly defined and communicated to the employees. *Adel Precision Products*, 8 LA 282 (Cheney, 1947).
2. The charge of inefficiency must be investigated or substantiated. *Royal Industrial Union*, 51 LA 642 (D.E. Johnson and V.J. Sirabella, 1968).
3. The standard must be reasonable.
4. The employees must be specifically warned that their performance is inadequate. *West Chemical Products, Inc.*, 63 LA 610 (Dykstra, 1974).
5. Employees with equally poor records must be treated the same.
6. The question of ability and the availability of another job must be considered. The grievant met the standards during the weeks November 17th to 29th and the grievant failed to bid for transfers when other jobs were available and when other machines were available. *Weber Aircraft Corp.*, 26 LA 598 (Jones, 1956); *Bell Aircraft Corp.*, 20 LA 551 (Shister, 1953).

7. The employee must have received adequate training and have been given an opportunity to meet the standards. *Weber Aircraft Corp. supra.*
8. The employee must be provided with proper equipment and operating conditions. *Fruehauf Trailer Co.*, 20 LA 854 (Wilson, 1953).

The company responded to the union's position that the grievant could not meet the reclaim standard for several reasons: impossibility of employees to operate all four machines, lack of cooperation of supervisor and mechanics, poor materials, and poor machines, by presenting evidence that the majority of employees had reached the standard by November and December, 1980, and that nearly all were meeting the standard presently. No evidence was presented that proved that the supervisors and mechanics were not cooperative. Since the other operators were meeting the reclaim standards, it was the company's position that the grievant's reasons for not meeting the reclaim standard must be something other than poor materials.

Regarding the machinery, the company argued that even though machines were different, it is common practice to establish standards of performance. Furthermore, a good operator would stop a machine that is having trouble and ask for help or solve the problems herself. She should keep her machine clean and this would go a long way toward preventing a machine malfunction. The company claimed that the operators who worked on the second shift (Holmes and Pittman) met the standards and the grievant's replacement also met the standard. A company witness testified that:

. . . the Grievant did not keep her machinery clean, that she often left the machines jammed, that she did not use materials correctly and that she would not call her supervisor or a mechanic when it was necessary.

The company responded to the union's contention that standards were relaxed after the grievant's discharge. The company admitted it relaxed the standard regarding "loose tucks on the cigar tip" in December and "in regard to grease" in February, but major changes did not occur. A company witness testified:

Both of these changes were made prior to the grievant's departure so that she should have benefited from these changes.

While one union witness, Roberts, testified that she believed the standard was relaxed, Bing, her supervisor, stated that there was no relaxation regarding the established standards. Although the cigars were softer and "lighter," the standards did not change.

The company argued that it used the correct procedure of progressive discipline in this discharge. It complied with Article 9 and notified the grievant's union steward at each step. Article 9 allows a discharge if not corrected within thirty days of the notice of inefficiency. Instead, the company used the four-step procedure which gave the grievant ample opportunity to correct her performance.

Based on these arguments and response to the union, the company requested that this grievance be denied.

The union argued that the machines that were operated differed and these differences resulted in variation in quality of the cigars produced. When a machine produces unacceptable cigars, the machine operator contacts her supervisor who will then contact a mechanic. In rare cases, the machine operator will shut down a machine if the quality is extremely bad. In line with the quality of production, the union argued that employees were not responsible for quality per a previous arbitration case between the parties. It presented the arbitrator's opinion and award which included the following passages:

There are no production standards or quotas to meet." ". . . the operators are not fully charged with the responsibility of quality control. Of course, if an operator sees a bad cigar then it should be replaced. The primary responsibility, however, for quality control lies in the Finishing Department.

The union contended that it was concerned about quality of product after the operators were assigned four machines and asked for meetings with management. When the company established and implemented the production and reclaim standards, the union had no input and was not consulted.

The union maintained that the new standards placed enormous pressure on the operators. Union witnesses testified that they had been told by other workers who had retired early that they could not keep up the pace.

The union pointed out that the discharge of the grievant for inefficiency was the first ever. There existed no past practice for such discharge of an operator, especially a long-time employee. The union further argued that the company did not use the proper procedure in the discharge. The company did not inform the union at each step in the discipline procedure and Atkinson, the plant manager, signed the discharge form instead of the grievant's supervisor.

The union responded to the company position that the grievant had been offered other machines and positions. It claimed that the other machines that were offered were not any better than hers—as evidenced by the fact that the former operators had pending warnings of excessive reclaims or inadequate production. The positions offered in other departments were those which paid lower wages and the grievant should not be expected to bid for a job at a lower wage.

Finally, the union claimed that the quality standards were administered inconsistently. Both press feeders testified that the company was more rigorous in identifying reclaims before the grievant was discharged. Both testified that they heard their supervisor tell at least one other press feeder to lower standards. The union argued also that the company has changed the standard officially at least twice: once in December when looser tucks were accepted and in February when the operator was not charged with grease and oil on the cigars.

Based on these arguments and evidence, the union contended that the discharge was not for just case and the grievant should be reinstated.

Table 1 Average Production and Reclaims for Shifts 1 and 2

	First Shift		Second Shift	
Dates of Two-Week Periods	Production (4 machines)	Percent Reclaim	Production (4 machines)	Percent Reclaim
10/6–10/17	27,544	2.2	(unclear)	1.8
10/17–11/3	27,772	2.5	26,698	2.0
11/3–11/14	28,081	1.7	27,856	1.8
11/14–11/29	27,960	1.5	27,680	1.6
12/1–12/12	28,225	1.6	28,315	1.6
Christmas Break				
1/5–1/16	28,712	1.47	28,942	1.31
1/19–1/30	28,974	1.4	29,117	1.5
(Discharge)				
2/2–2/13	28,639	1.6	28,930	1.5
2/16–2/27	28,345	1.7	28,920	1.3
Union alleges standards were loosened				
3/2–3/13	28,704	1.2	29,059	1.2
3/16–3/27	29,072	1.1	29,068	1.2
3/30–4/18	28,875	1.1	29,203	1.1
4/20–5/1	29,318	0.9	29,380	1.0

Table 2 Number of Operators *Not* Meeting the Reclaim Standard

Dates of Two-Week Periods	First Shift	Second Shift
10/6–10/17	12	10
10/17–10/31	18	12
11/3–11/14	8	6
11/17–11/29	3	3
12/1–12/12	6	3
Christmas Break		
1/5–1/16	4	0
1/19–1/30	4	2
(Discharge)		
2/2–2/13	5	1
2/16–2/27	5	0
Union alleges standards were loosened		
3/2–3/13	0	0
3/16–3/27	0	0
3/30–4/18	0	0
4/20–5/1	0	0

Table 3 Reclaim Records on Grievant, Her Replacement, and Second Shift Operator on Same Machines

Dates of Two-Week Periods	First Shift Operator	Percent of Reclaims on Grievant's Machine	Second Shift Operator	Percent of Reclaims on Grievant's Machine	Percent of Reclaims on Other Machines Operated by Grievant's Replacement (Cox)
10/6–10/17	Grievant	3.6	Holmes	1.3	1.8
10/17–10/31	Grievant	4.1	Holmes	2.6	3.1
11/3–11/14	Grievant	2.2	Holmes	2.2	1.5
(Verbal Warning)					
11/17–11/29	Grievant	2.0	Holmes transfers	1.4	1.0
12/1–12/12	Grievant	3.3	Pittman	2.3	2.8
(Written Warning)					
1/5–1/16	Grievant	2.5	Pittman	1.7	1.3
1/19–1/30	Grievant	2.2	Pittman	1.7	1.6
(Suspension) 1/21–1/23					
(Discharge)					
2/2–2/13	Cox (see below)	2.2	Pittman	1.4	
2/16–2/27	Cox transfers back to former machines	Open	Pittman	1.4	1.4
Union contends standards were loosened					
3/2–3/15	Walker	1.3	Pittman	1.3	1.1
3/16–3/27	Walker	1.2	Pittman	1.1	1.2
3/30–4/18	Walker	1.3	Pittman	1.4	1.2
4/20–5/1	Walker	1.1	Pittman	1.3	.6

Table 4 Reclaim Records on Grievant's Machine Immediately after Grievant's Discharge

Date	Operator	Percent of Reclaims on Grievant's Machine
2/2	Cox	3.82
2/3	Cox	2.59
2/4	Cox	1.1
2/5	Cox	1.88
2/6	Cox	1.49
2/9	Burkett	2.32
2/11	Cox	1.83
2/12	Cox	2.47
2/13	Cox	1.8

Summary

Holmes' average (part of time with teacher) on the Grievant's machines was 1.96 percent reclaims during 10/6–12/12. Her reclaim average from 1/19–5/1 on other machines was 1.15 percent.

Pittman's average on all machines from 10/6–12/12 was *1.92* percent reclaims.

Burkett's average on other machines from 10/6–5/1 was 1.4 percent reclaims.

Walker's average on the grievant's machines from 3/2–5/1 was 1.2 percent reclaims.

Cox's average on other machines from 10/6–1/30 was 1.87 percent reclaims; on the grievant's machines from 2/2–2/13 was 2.2 percent; and on other machines from 2/16–5/1 was 1.1 percent.

Questions

1. To what extent was progressive discipline properly applied in this case?
2. Because the grievant did not testify on her behalf, how should the arbitrator treat her lack of testimony?
3. Of what relevance is hearsay evidence? Should it be accepted by the arbitrator?
4. Of what relevance and use are the arbitration cases cited by the company?
5. How would you, as the arbitrator, decide this case? Give your reasoning.

Case 11
Bidding on Bus Routes

Provisions of the Contract

Article 31 Bus Drivers

Section 1 *Vacancies*

(a) On or before November 15th of each year all bus routes will be open for bids on the basis of seniority. All bidding shall be completed within four (4) work days.

(b) The following procedure shall be used:
1. The bus drivers shall be divided into three groups, by seniority, as equal in number as possible and routes posted on the first day.
2. The upper third will, on the second day, be given first opportunity to bid and their bidding will be frozen at the end of that day.
3. The second third will, on the third day, be given the opportunity to bid and their bidding will be frozen at the end of that day.
4. The remaining third will, on the fourth day, be given the opportunity to bid and their bidding will be frozen at the end of that day.
5. Thereafter any routes unbid may be assigned by the District to drivers without routes.

(c) No seniority shall be given for substitute or probationary employees.

Section 2 *Work Year*

Bus drivers' schedules will be set each year according to the needs of the children. The statements in this Article shall not be considered as a guarantee of hours per day or week.

Statement of Grievance

On June 6, 1978, the employer posted all bus runs for bidding except Special Education runs. This is a direct violation of the contract, Article 31, Section 1, (a) and (b). The intent of the language at the negotiating table was that the runs would be bid after the start of each school year on or before November 15. The drivers were not given ample time to review the runs and the runs were not complete as to the changes when the drivers went in to bid on them.

Portland Community Schools (School Board) and Local 555, International Union of Bus Drivers*

*Special appreciation is extended to Dr. A. Dale Allen, (Jr., labor arbitrator and) Professor of Behavioral Management and Labor Relations, Hankamer School of Business, Baylor University, for providing this case.

The Union requests that all runs including the Special Education runs for the 78–79 school year be reposted and be rebid after September, 1978, prior to November 15, 1978.

Position of the Union

The union contended that the board violated Article 31, Section 1 (a) when bus routes were posted for bids on two occasions within one school or fiscal year—in November 1977 and again in June 1978. The disputed article stated that "on or before November 15th *of each year all* bus routes will be open for bids on the basis of seniority." (Emphasis added.) Regardless of whether one uses a fiscal year or a school year, the language clearly states that bids are made only once each year.

The union presented testimony that the board had no unilateral right to move the bidding period to June, some three to four months prior to the opening of the school year. Requiring drivers to bid on bus routes in accordance with seniority this early forces them to request runs which may change considerably before they finally go into effect by the next fall. Thus, senior drivers may end up with less desirable routes than they might have been entitled to.

The union pointed out that the words "on or before November 15th" were placed in the contract to indicate that route bidding would take place sometime after the commencement of a new school year but not later than November 15. Veteran drivers wanted to start the routes because they would be familiar with the old stops, children, and directions, thereby avoiding a lot of confusion created by having a new driver and bus number. Once the veteran drivers had worked out any changes in the route, then they could record these alterations on the route sheet and more efficiently pass this information on to new drivers. In contrast, if new drivers started at the beginning of the year, it would be very confusing for drivers and children alike. When, several years ago, it was decided to bid the routes before school started, chaos was the result. For example, one driver picked up the wrong load of children and took them to the wrong school district. Thus, that idea was dropped; it was revived again this year by the board, however, in spite of contract language and established past practice.

The union also noted that the board could have requested a change in language of Article 31 in the last negotiations if it had wanted to move the bidding to June. However, no such demand was made by the board. Therefore the board cannot after the fact unilaterally alter the contract's intent and a past practice of ten years or more without consulting with the union.

The union also contended that *all* bus routes were supposed to be posted for bid per Article 31, including special education runs. These latter routes had not been posted along with regular ones. Since the language does not exempt special education routes, they must also be posted each year.

The board charged that only a few bus drivers were interested in the present grievance; the union countered this notion by submitting a list of names of twenty-five drivers who were present when this complaint was presented orally to Mr. Morehouse, Director of Transportation. Hence a majority of the drivers in the bargaining unit were upset with the change in bidding procedure.

For these reasons, the union requested that the grievance be upheld.

Position of the School Board

The board maintained that Article 31, Section 1 (a) merely required that route bids be posted "on or before November 15th." Hence this language does not preclude the possibility of bidding in June. The board further contended that Article 31 does not state that posting must occur after school has commenced, nor is that the intent of the provision. The posting of November 1977 was for school year 1977–1978 and the June 1978 posting was for school year 1978–1979. Since the two postings were for different school years, they were not violations of Article 31, Section 1 (a).

The board chose to move the bidding period to June because of several resulting advantages. First, drivers would begin with a given route and stay with it throughout the year, avoiding the confusion of mixing drivers about after school had been in session several weeks. Second, there would be less uncertainty among the students and school administrators. Third, the board pointed out that with the stabilizing school enrollment more accurate predictions concerning school bus routes could be made at an earlier time than in previous years, when enrollments fluctuated. Thus the board contended that there was merit to altering the past practice.

The board maintained that the desire to retain posting of bids in the fall had been the wish of only a few in the bargaining unit, that the majority of the drivers were not concerned one way or another. Thus, the board should not be constrained from moving to an earlier posting time simply because a few stubborn members were opposed. No drivers lost any wages as a result of this change.

Finally, the board noted that the issue regarding posting of special education runs had been the subject of another grievance already presented under arbitration, but that no decision had been rendered.

Questions

1. Of what relevance is the intent of the parties when they negotiated the labor agreement in this arbitration case?
2. Discuss the political implications or internal union rivalries which could possibly underlie the grievance.

3. What should be the arbitrator's decision after thoroughly considering union and management contentions, the facts, and the evidence.
4. List the possible effects of your decision in Question 3 on the following:
   a. internal union affairs
   b. political maneuvering by officers
   c. future negotiations

Case 12

Work Assignments

Pertinent Provisions of the Agreement

Article II, Management Rights

1. **The Union recognizes that the management of the Employer's business, including but not limited to, the assignment and direction of the working force; the determination of the numbers to be employed or retained by the Employer; the right to make reasonable rules and regulations; the right to hire, suspend, discharge, discipline, promote, demote, or transfer employees; and the release of employees because of lack of work or for other proper reasons is vested exclusively in the Employer. It is understood that rights granted in this paragraph shall not be arbitrarily exercised and that the Union shall have the right, under grievance procedure set forth in this Agreement, to question any action deemed unjust.**
2. **. . .**
3. **The Union agrees that its officers, agents, and members shall not oppose or interfere, directly or indirectly, with the inherent right of the Employer to train employees, to improve the skill and ability of the employees, to make operational improvements, to maintain reasonable and proper discipline and efficiency, and to make economies in the operation of its business.**

Article IV, Workweek and Overtime

1. **Forty hours constitute the regular workweek. The Employer may require employees to work overtime, but so far as reasonably possible the work shall follow a regular schedule.**
2. **. . .**
3. **All regular full-time employees who are available and able to work shall be guaranteed forty (40) hours per week. The Employer shall have the option of scheduling such forty (40) hours: (a) in five 8-hour days or (b) four 10-hour days. One and one-half (1½) the employee's**

Ringgold Materials Corporation and Unified Workers of North America (UWNA)*

*The authors thank Dr. John Remington, (labor arbitrator, Director and Associate Professor, Center for Labor Research and Studies), Florida International University, (Miami) for providing this case.

regular rate shall be paid for all hours worked in excess of nine (9) hours per day on a 5-day schedule; or ten (10) hours per day on a 4-day schedule; or forty (40) per week; whichever is more advantageous to the employee.

Letter of Intent

Management Trainees

The Union recognizes that the Employer has a management trainee program, a portion of which includes work normally performed by bargaining unit personnel. Such training shall be accomplished so that bargaining unit personnel shall not be displaced by management trainees.

Background

The Ringgold Materials Corporation is engaged in the distribution of ready-mix concrete and concrete products. The company distributes its products from various plants located throughout the state. Company employees working as truck drivers, equipment operators, yard workers, and general laborers are represented for purposes of collective bargaining by the UWNA. The company and the union entered into a collective bargaining agreement covering employees working in four plants located in Florida on June 12, 1980. This agreement was to be in full force and effect through 1983. On July 2, 1980, representatives of the company and the union signed a "Letter of Intent" which was subsequently incorporated into the collective bargaining agreement. One of the provisions of this "Letter of Intent," hereinabove cited, pertains to the company's "pre-management training program.

The company has maintained a pre-management training program since the 1960s and revised said program at least twice. The most recent revision became effective October 2, 1972. The program, as it has been constituted since 1972, provides for five stages or "steps" of training over a maximum period of fifty-two weeks. While considerable flexibility exists in the implementation of the program, approximately thirteen weeks cover training in warehouse work; four weeks include training for driving a mechanical unloader; nine weeks deal with the training in a company steel yard; thirteen weeks cover training as a batchman; and thirteen weeks are reserved for training for driving a ready-mix truck. All of the above training is in work normally performed exclusively by bargaining unit members. The company promotes extensively from within and views the pre-management training program as a crucial element in the development of management personnel.

On Friday, July 24, 1981, the company laid off three bargaining unit members from its Lake Front plant due to lack of work. All three employees were thereby forced to exercise their seniority rights and "bump" into jobs at another plant in order to work the following week. On Monday, July 27, 1981, the company utilized two trainees, William Ikerd and Larry Tate, as mixer-truck drivers in the Lake Front plant. Both trainees worked in excess of five hours driving a mixer-truck. On Tuesday, July 28, the company again utilized Ikerd and Tate as mixer drivers and assigned another trainee, Bob Boyce, to drive a third mixer truck. Tate drove for approximately five hours, while Ikerd and Boyce drove for approximately four hours apiece. On Wednesday, July 29, Ikerd and Tate again drove mixers, with Ikerd driving for four hours and Tate driving in excess of six hours. On Thursday, July 29, and Friday, July 30, trainee Tate drove a mixer truck for approximately six and nine hours, respectively. In summary, it is readily apparent that the company utilized trainees to do approximately forty-eight hours of bargaining unit work in its Lake Front plant during the week of July 27, 1981.

On July 20, 1981, Union Steward Charles Hastings filed an employee grievance form which alleged that the company was in violation of Item #3 of the "Letter of Intent," dated July 2, 1980, through its use of trainees to perform bargaining unit work. Specifically, the grievance contends that, with regard to the period July 27–29, 1981:

There was sufficient work, which could have been done by displaced union personnel. . . . The Union recognizes that the Employer has a management trainee program, a portion of which includes work normally performed by bargaining unit personnel. Such training shall be accomplished so that bargaining unit personnel shall not be displaced by management trainees.

In remedy, the grievance seeks to "stop trainees from replacing union personnel." The grievance was subsequently discussed by representatives of the company and the union and, finding themselves unable to resolve the dispute, the parties submitted the matter to arbitration.

Positions of the Parties

The Union takes the position that the company has displaced bargaining unit members through the use of trainees; that such displacement is evident, based on the layoff of July 24, 1981, at the Lake Front plant coupled with the assignment of trainees to replace the laid-off employees on the next regularly scheduled workday (July 27); and that such displacement is in violation of the "Letter of Intent." The union argues that the company is abusing the pre-management training program and objects to trainees being assigned to bargaining unit work which is not supervised by a bargaining unit member serving as trainer.

The Company takes the position that the pre-management training program is a necessary and valuable operational procedure of benefit to both the company and the union; that trainees are permitted, under the terms of the collective bargaining agreement, to perform bargaining unit work as trainees; that this training work is a longstanding and established practice; and that the assignment of trainees which occurred at the Lake Front plant is permitted under both the Management Rights clause of the contract and the "Letter of Intent." In this connection, the company contends that the "Letter of Intent" was negotiated to prevent use of trainees while active bargaining unit members were off-the-clock rather than to prohibit the use of trainees working alone or during layoffs. The company argues that "brief surges" in the demand for its products or "scheduling requirements" will sometimes necessitate the use of trainees, as was the case at the Lake Front plant in July.

Questions

1. What is the union's purpose in having the "Letter of Intent" incorporated in the agreement?
2. Does it matter whether or not management trainees are included in the bargaining unit? Why? Why not?
3. Reconcile any differences between management rights, past practice and the "Letter of Intent."
4. You be the arbitrator. What is your decision? What reasons can you offer to support your decision?

Case 13
Assignment of Teacher Aides

Background

The Port Clampton School Board is a citizen-elected body that manages the school district of Port Clampton. The Port Clampton Federation of Teachers (PCFT or federation) is the collective bargaining representative for the teachers in the district. In January, 1980, the federation and board entered into a master agreement containing new language on the matter of non-teaching duties (Article VI, Section 13).

Port Clampton Federation of Teachers (PCFT) and Port Clampton School Board*

*The authors wish to express our appreciation to Dr. Paul F. Gerhart, Arbitrator and Professor, Case Western (Reserve) University for this case.

In the spring of 1980, a teachers' committee from the junior high school met with the principal to let him know how the teachers wanted the aide or aides used. They indicated to the principal that a poll of all members of the bargaining unit who were employed at the junior high school indicated the top priority for aide use to be afternoon bus duty.

After some delay, which extended into the fall term, an aide was finally hired and placed on bus duty on October 13, 1980. According to a bus duty roster, the grievant, J. W. Walker, was scheduled for bus duty on October 17. When he appeared, he discovered that an aide was present. The grievant advised the principal that since an aide was now available, the grievant should not have to continue taking bus duty. At a meeting between the grievant and the principal on October 20, there was a disagreement on the interpretation of the master agreement provision here involved. The grievant contended that the agreement and the information conveyed by the teachers' committee concerning the use of aides relieved him of any further obligation to perform bus duty. The principal, nonetheless, instructed the grievant to continue with bus duty on October 21, 22, and 23.

Pertinent Provisions of the Agreement

Article VI, Section 13,
(in relevant part)

Assignment to lunchroom and restroom duty at the high school shall first be on a volunteer basis. If sufficient volunteers are not available, the administration will notify the PCFT. The PCFT will attempt to provide the additional volunteers. If the PCFT is unsuccessful, the administration shall have the right to appoint the additional staff.

Teachers in each school building shall have the services of an aide or aides to take care of nonteaching duties, such as: lunchroom, bus, study hall, recess, morning supervision, restroom, clerical, money collecting, etc. The Principal shall assign the aide or aides to perform such duties after working cooperatively with the teachers to determine what duties they want assigned to the aide or aides.

It is the purpose and intent of this section to provide aides to meet the needs of the teachers. Each building shall have the services of an aide or aides at the rate of one hour times the number of teachers assigned to the building per week. . . .

Article IV, Section 2,
(in relevant part)

---

(4) The arbitrator shall have no power to alter, add to, or subtract from the terms of the Master Agreement or make any decision contrary to law.

Positions of the Parties

The Federation contended that educational aides are to be employed and assigned to meet the needs of the teachers, according to Article VI, Section 13. The Federation maintained that the board's contention that the agreement language merely provides for teacher input on the assignment of aides is incorrect, for three reasons:

1. The language specifies that aides will "take care of" non-teaching duties; it does not say that aides will merely help with such duties.
2. The second sentence of the second paragraph of Article VI, Section 13 states, "The Principal shall assign the aide or aides to perform such duties after working cooperatively with teachers to determine what duties they want assigned to the aide or aides." It is clear—the Principal shall assign the aide or aides to perform the duties that the teachers want assigned.
3. The language of the next sentence in the agreement, "It is the purpose and intent of this section to provide aides to meet the needs of the teachers."

The teachers further made it clear to the principal that their number one priority was to "get rid" of bus duty. They wanted bus duty "taken care of." The record shows that all parties clearly understood the desires of the teachers on this matter. The principal preferred to assign one teacher and one aide to bus duty, but the teachers did not accept this idea.

The board had claimed that one aide and one teacher were assigned to bus duty because it had been the past practice to assign two people to bus duty. By special arrangement, the grievant had been assigned to permanent bus duty as the principal's surrogate during the 1979–1980 school year. Although two other teachers were assigned, on a rotating basis, to bus duty at the same time, Ms. Flippo, another teacher, testified that about one-third of the time the grievant was alone on bus duty. Furthermore, during the period of the 1980–1981 school year prior to the aide's being hired, only one teacher had been assigned to bus duty. The argument that two people are necessary in order to assure the safety of students is without merit. Half of the students walk home over the same street upon which the buses are parked. No one supervises the walkers. Further, bused students arrive at the same point in the morning without direct supervision.

The Federation argued that if the principal wants two people to observe bus loading, he can accomplish this without violating the teacher agreement. The formula provides for more than enough aide time at the junior high school to provide two aides for the 3:00 to 3:15 bus loading period. Other means for assuring pupil safety could be developed. There is no board policy on bus loading, so the principal has within his purview the power to develop other procedures for bus loading which do not conflict with the master agreement.

The federation took issue with the board's argument that to sustain the grievance would be an infringement on management's rights. The grievance clearly relates to working conditions. By the terms of the contract, the parties agree that the performance of nonteaching duties by classroom teachers is undesirable. Language governing the hiring of aides is in the contract because the parties have agreed to change the past practice concerning the assignment of nonteaching tasks to classroom teachers. That language is specific and calls for the hiring and assignment of aides to take care of nonteaching duties determined by the teachers. The language does not hint at, allude to, or suggest that teachers are only to make suggestions or recommendations.

Finally, the federation stated that the agreement provides, in Article IV, Section 2, "The arbitrator shall have no power to alter, add to, or subtract from the terms of the Master Agreement. . . ." To render a decision in favor of the board would be to grant the board and principal discretionary powers not provided by the master agreement. The "need" of the teachers is to have the aides "take care of" bus duty. A ruling in favor of the board would allow the assignment of aides to meet the needs of the principal, not the teachers.

The School Board Prior to the 1980–1981 school year, two teachers supervised afternoon bus loading at the junior high school. About 300 junior high school students boarded buses on a city street in front of the school. When the students were released from school at 3:00 p.m., only four buses were waiting for them on the street. Many of the students would have to wait for the arrival of other buses. Between 3:00 and 3:15, buses continually arrived, loaded, and pulled away from the school. By 3:15, two-thirds of the students would have been picked up. Until the 1980–1981 school year, two teachers have been assigned to supervise the bus loading during this busy fifteen minute period.

In May, 1980, three teachers met with the junior high principal, Samson, to discuss the use of aides for the 1980–1981 school year. The teachers reported the results of a survey which indicated that the top priority for use of aides was afternoon bus duty. Principal Samson told the teachers that he would attempt to replace one teacher, but not both, with an aide. He explained that it was essential that at least one teacher be present between 3:00 and 3:15 when the greatest number of students were loading, because a classroom teacher commands greater deference from students than an aide.

By the time school started in the fall, Samson had been unable to hire an aide. Even so, he fully intended to do so as soon as possible, and he developed a teacher bus duty roster for the 1980–1981 school year which included only one teacher per afternoon instead of the two which had historically been assigned. Samson took the aide's assignment himself until he was able to hire an aide.

The board argued that this dispute arose when the grievant told the principal that he did not think teachers should be required to serve bus duty. His grievance alleged that, "I am required to serve bus duty contrary to the provisions of Article VI, Section 13 of the Master Agreement." However, Article VI, Section 13 of the Master Agreement provides that the principal is to assign aides. Section 13 merely assures that teachers' wishes are taken into consideration when the assignment decision is made by requiring that the principal make his decision after ascertaining faculty sentiment. Section 13 does not require the principal to make aide assignments in strict accord with faculty sentiment. Principal Samson unquestionably complied with the agreement in assigning the aide to afternoon bus duty, even though he did not comply with faculty sentiment by completely eliminating faculty bus duty. He worked cooperatively with the faculty to determine their wants, as the agreement requires. Nothing in the agreement prohibits the principal from applying his own professional judgment to determine how aides and teachers are to be assigned. There is no doubt that the parties intended faculty desires to be influential, but there is no indication they are to be determinative. The parties intended to give final, unrestricted decision-making authority to the principal, as Section 13 provides: "The Principal shall assign the aide or aides to duties. . . ." David Hunt, who negotiated the 1980 agreement on behalf of the board, testified without contradiction that the parties recognized that there would be a variety of opinions among the teachers as to where aides were needed. Consistent with the traditional role of administrators to allocate resources, the parties intended to give the principal the final authority as to where aides would be assigned.

The board cautioned that the intent of the grievance is to have the arbitrator add to the agreement by placing a prohibition on the assignment of grievant to afternoon bus duty. Nothing in the agreement supports such a prohibition. Article VI, Section 13 is not intended to regulate the assignment of junior high teachers. It says absolutely nothing about the assignment of teachers. There is no language speaking of where or how teachers will be assigned.

It is clear that the teacher aide language in Article VI, Section 13 was not intended to regulate the assignments of teacher. Section 13 explicitly provides that lunchroom and restroom duty are not to be assigned to high school teachers on an involuntary basis unless no volunteers can be found. Other provisions provide that no teacher is to be assigned to responsibilities normally performed by the custodial staff and that no teacher shall be assigned the transportation of pupils in a private conveyance. Furthermore, there is no comparable restriction on assigning junior high school teachers to bus duty. Therefore, the absence of an explicit restriction on assigning bus duty or any other duty to teachers is a most deliberate indication that no such restriction was intended.

The board explained that teacher aides are assigned side-by-side with teachers for other duties, such as lunchroom supervisors and hall monitors. Thus, the fact that an aide has been assigned to bus duty, in itself, in no way restricts the assignment of a teacher to bus duty.

The board also pointed out that the arbitrator is expressly prohibited by Article IV, Section 2 of the agreement from making any decision which is contrary to law. The interpretation of Article VI, Section 13 which is sought by the grievant would remove from the superintendent and his administrative staff authority to assign teachers. Thus, it is inconsistent with other terms of the agreement.

Questions

1. What is a past practice?
2. How do the parties change a past practice?
3. In an arbitration case, which takes priority: contract language or past practice?
4. Why have both parties reminded the arbitrator that he has "no power to alter, add to, or subtract from the terms of the Master Agreement. . . ."?
5. How should the arbitrator rule? Why?

Case 14
Compensation and Past Practice

Issue

Did the company violate the agreement between the parties as well as past practice when it changed its accounting procedure relative to the drivers' responsibilities for "overages" and "shortages"?

Background

The Pop Cola Bottling Company is engaged in the manufacture, distribution, and sale of Pop Cola and affiliated soft drink products in the area surrounding Chicago. The company bottles or otherwise packages soft drinks

---

Pop Cola Bottling Co. and Soft Drink Allied Workers*

*The authors wish to express appreciation to Dr. Alex J. Simon, retired arbitrator and Professor emeritis, Port Neches, Texas, for providing this case.

and distributes them to outlets such as grocery markets, restaurants and other businesses which sell soft drinks on a retail basis. The bargaining unit employees are represented by Soft Drink Allied Workers.

The basic and pertinent facts in this matter of arbitration are uncontradicted. Under the previous agreement and for the first few months of the current agreement, a great majority of the bargaining unit employees, though identified as Drivers, were actually combination drivers–salesmen–collectors for the company's products that were delivered from their respective trucks. The company had, in effect, what is known as a "cash settlement" accounting procedure which had been used for several years. Under this cash settlement procedure, the company did not receive documentation for each and every sales transaction which occurred between the company's delivery personnel and the company's customers. For example, there was no auditing whatsoever with regard to "cash" transactions in instances when the delivery driver received a cash payment for products which he delivered.

Under the previous settlement procedure, each delivery driver "settled up" after the daily deliveries and, due to lack of documentation, no full audit of daily transactions was possible. Under that settlement procedure, if a driver failed to deliver enough products to a customer and returned to the company with some products still on his truck, the company could not detect the existence of surplus products or identify their rightful owner. Thus, a driver who returned to the company with surplus products was "on his honor" to voluntarily return the products to the company as an "overage." Alternatively, he could "pocket" the value of products by turning in only enough cash and other payments (vouchers, etc.) to account for the value of the products which had actually been removed from the truck. Stated another way, if, at the end of each day there were any "overages" (if a driver returned with a combination of more cash, checks, credit slips, or any other kind of payment, as well as products on his truck, than he was charged for at the beginning of the day, this was known as an overage), these overages were credited to the driver; the money or products were his. As admitted by both parties, a driver who delivered too few products to one of his customers ideally would have turned the products over to the company, but since the company's accounting procedure could not identify that surplus the company could not order the driver to do so. Thus, a driver could *pocket* the value of the overage and the company, typically, would not be able to determine what had occurred.

In late May, 1982, the company introduced what is known as a "full settlement" accounting system to replace the antiquated "cash settlements" system. The full settlement procedure determines precisely the exact amount of soft drink products loaded onto a delivery driver's truck when the driver begins his daily deliveries, the amount of soft drink products remaining on the truck when the day's deliveries have been completed, and the amount of money, checks, credit slips, or other payments received. It combines these figures with the value of the products removed from the truck during the day and determines whether the company has been paid for all of the products delivered. The amount of products remaining on the delivery truck at the end of the day should equal the amount of products loaded onto the truck at the beginning of the day minus the products which, according to the driver's delivery invoices, were delivered to the company's customers. If the product remaining on the truck is less than that, the driver has what is known as a "shortage."

The delivery driver has sole custody over the products on his truck and he is, and always has been, generally held responsible for the amount of each "shortage." However, if the driver can explain that the shortage was not his fault, such as when the driver reasonably believed products have been stolen or have fallen off the delivery truck and such fact can be proven, the driver is not held responsible. The objective of the "full settlement" procedure is to insure that the company receives payment for each case of product taken out of the warehouse.

The union filed a grievance on behalf of the drivers after this new "full settlement" procedure was installed. Under the new system, a driver had to pay for shortages that were unaccountable and, on the other hand, would not receive the overages that were unexplained, as was done under the old system. The union's claim is that under the old system the overages and shortages were balanced; by no longer allowing the driver to keep the overages under the new system, pay was actually decreased.

The parties were unable to resolve the problem by the negotiated grievance procedure and the parties proceeded to arbitration.

Pertinent Contractual Provisions

Article II—Management Rights

Except to the extent expressly abridged by a specific provision of this Agreement, the Employer reserves and retains, solely and exclusively, all of its inherent rights to manage the business.

Without limiting the foregoing, the sole and exclusive rights of Management which are not abridged by this Agreement include, but are not confined to, the right to hire, maintain order, efficiency and economy of operation; the right to discipline and discharge for just cause; the right to determine and from time to time redetermine the size and composition of the work force, and the type, extent and nature of all equipment used; the right to determine and from time to time redetermine the method of operating the business and the running of routes, including the order and frequency of servicing routes, merchandising, maintenance and promotion of dealer rela-

tions, the products to be manufactured, the methods, processes and material to be employed, the standards of workmanship, the work schedule of employees, and the business hours of the establishment; to schedule, determine and from time to time redetermine the number and types of employees required and to assign work to such employees; the right to require the observance of Company rules and regulations; and the right to discontinue products or operations in whole or in part, or to discontinue their performance by employees of the Company and to sell or otherwise dispose of its business in whole or in part.

Article XIX—General Provisions

Section 12. **The Union recognizes the Employer's right to establish policies and procedures not in conflict with the Agreement during the term of this Agreement in the exercise of its rights and responsibilities in managing the business. The Employer agrees to notify the Union in writing of any new policies or procedures or of any changes to existing policies or procedures two (2) weeks prior to their announcement and implementation.**

Article XXIII
Complete Agreement, Wrap-up and Waiver, Separately and Savings, and Termination of Agreement

Section 1. **This writing constitutes the complete Agreement of the parties and there are no collateral agreements or understandings between the parties. Any amendments to this contract or any interpretation differing from the language of this Contract shall be of no validity unless reduced to writing and signed by both of the parties.**

Union Position

The union's main argument is that the company violated the agreement (as well as past practice) when it unilaterally began to retain *unknown overages* and charged to the delivery driver the *unknown shortages*.

The union contended that this change was never negotiated and it was a past practice of this company, as well as other companies in the area, to allow driver–salesmen the right to apply unknown overages against unknown shortages. It is undisputed that this change was never negotiated nor was it ever mentioned during negotiations of the existing contract.

The action of the company has affected the employees' wages. The controller, George Spellings, did not state or even hazard a guess as to the amount of money which was available in the funds created by the company from these unknown overages, even though it is his responsibility to manage the funds of Pop Cola. Further, the company does not make available to the drivers the reconciliation sheet after all the figures are checked. This has the effect of hiding any overages from the driver and prevents the driver from checking on his own route to see who, if anyone, might have been shortchanged. The company has admitted that they make no effort to locate anybody who might have been shortchanged by the driver; they only correct mathematical mistakes which are obvious on the check-in sheet.

The union has made it quite clear that they are not looking for a windfall and have no claim on any overage which can be traced by the company to its rightful owner. However, based on the actions and company procedures, the company has now managed to find a windfall for themselves in this regard. The company changed its practice almost immediately after the signing of the present contract, indicating that management had already considered further reducing employees' wages in this fashion.

Because of the fact that it was a past practice to allow union members to take a credit for unknown overages, because the change was not negotiated, and because it would significantly lower the wage scales of the delivery personnel, the union contended that this was in violation of the contract and an unauthorized abridgement of their established rights.

Therefore, the union requested that the unknown overages be credited against the unknown shortages from the date that the present procedure was instituted and that the union members be given full credit for any overages from that time.

Company Position

The company argued that what was really at issue here was the management rights question, that is, whether the company may implement settlement and accounting procedures which encourage the honest and efficient performance of its employees and which prevent the drivers from receiving windfalls at the expense of the company's customers. In light of the broad management rights provision of the agreement and in light of the principles traditionally recognized in interpreting such management rights provisions, the company has the right to utilize the accounting procedure in question.

The union has attempted to characterize the treatment of overages as a wage issue and has suggested that the company's treatment of overages has effectively reduced the wages of delivery drivers. The company contended that this was an absurd characterization of the issue before the Arbitrator. The wages of the delivery drivers have been determined by contractual agreement, and the compensation structure of delivery drivers has been converted into an hourly wage scale. The current compensation of delivery drivers is at least as great as, if not greater, than the compensation of these individuals prior to the establishment of the hourly wage scale.

The drivers are responsible for delivering specified amounts of the company's products to customers and for collecting revenues in exchange for those products. While a driver is traveling along his delivery route for a given day, he alone is responsible for the products on his truck and the revenues collected. In fact, if the delivery driver performs his job correctly and efficiently, he would deliver only the amount of products shown on the sales invoices and would collect only the revenue shown on the same invoice. In that situation no "overage" or "shortage" will arise. Accordingly, there will be absolutely no impact upon the driver's income.

Under close examination, the company concluded that the union's position was untenable and unacceptable. It stated that the payments which the union wished to obtain for the drivers logically had nothing to do with the concept of wages, and only by the most absurd logic could one describe an overage payment (described by one company official as an "invitation to theft") as an aspect of wages. Such payments could not be construed as compensation but, instead, represent a windfall to which the driver was not properly entitled.

Questions

1. Is past practice relevant in this case?
2. Did the "cash settlement" encourage cheating of customers or the company? How?
3. Are the "cash settlements" considered "wages" under the law? Under the agreement?
4. May the company change a practice without negotiating the new practice during the life of an agreement? If so, under what labor relations principles? If not, what are the principles that apply?
5. If a contract violation were found, what would be an appropriate settlement?
6. If you were the arbitrator, how would you rule? Why?

Case 15

Promotion and Due Process

Facts and Background

This case arises under a provision in the personnel handbook of the East Side Medical Clinic. The grievant, James Hope, was employed on June 14, 1976, at the clinic in Fairfax, Virginia, as a food service worker I. The initial

---

James Hope versus East Side Medical Clinic*

*The authors express appreciation to Dr. Jerald F. Robinson, (arbitrator and Professor of Labor Relations), Virginia Polytechnic Institute and State University for providing this unpublished case. The names of people and places have been changed.

appointment was as a temporary replacement, full time, for another employee who was on leave. Hope was terminated on September 10, 1976, when the regular employee returned. On September 22, 1976, he returned to work on a part-time basis as a regular employee; on November 1 he was given full-time regular employee status.

During late February 1977, Hope ascertained that an employee in the department, Cathy Gant, would soon be taking a maternity leave. Discussion with the present supervisor, Allen Jackson, was held. On or about April 7, 1977, Gant resigned effective April 29, 1977. Hope and one other employee in the department applied for the higher level position of food preparation worker. The other employee, Renee Fulgham, was promoted on May 1, 1977, by the new supervisor, Daisy Pitts.

Hope filed his grievance under Section 16 (complaint and grievance procedure) of the East Side Clinic's current personnel handbook. The grievance was initiated on or about May 6, 1977, and was denied by the employer at each of the four steps in the establishment procedure.

Under the rules outlined in the handbook, the employee filed a demand for arbitration dated August 8, 1977, seeking employment as a food preparation worker retroactive to May 1, 1977, alleging that the rules of the personnel procedures were violated in his promotion case. On August 30, 1977, the employer answered the demand by denying that the rules of the personnel handbook procedures had been violated and that the grievant had not been wrongly denied an advancement.

Relevant Provisions of the Personnel Handbook

Section 13 Promotion and Transfer

The Personnel Office will make a continuing effort to assure that the filling of vacant or new positions by current employees shall take account of ability, skills, ingenuity, industry, seniority, and those other intangible factors which determine an employee's contribution to the Authority.

The Personnel Office shall *post open positions* and opportunities for promotion each week in conspicuous places for a period of one week. The posted positions shall contain the following information: Title of Job, Department, Schedule of Weekly Hours; Pay Grade; Minimum Qualifications; Date of Posting.

An employee who meets the minimum qualifications may apply for a position. The Personnel Office will interview all employee applicants who qualify.

Section 11 Confidentiality of and Access to Personnel Files

Letters of caution, consultation, warning, and reprimand shall be considered temporary contents of the personnel records and shall be removed and destroyed no later than two years after they have been placed in the records.

Position of the Employee

The employee, through his legal counsel, alleged that the employer's own rules of personnel procedure were violated by the employer's representatives and others so that he was improperly denied the promotion to food preparation worker. The rules violated included the rule on posting of open positions as well as the criteria for filling of vacant positions. Both of these policies are found in Section 13 of the personnel handbook. Further provisions of the same section, relating to the interviewing process and the notifiation of applicants after the selection has been made, were also violated.

Hope also charged that Pitts attempted to intimidate him and did, in fact, threaten to harm him if he discussed the promotion denial further. He further claimed that during the early stages of the grievance procedure, he was offered a raise if he did not pursue the remaining steps of the procedure. Finally, the grievant alleged that the failure of the clinic president to hear and respond personally to the step 4 grievance substantially violated his due process rights.

Specifically, the employee suggested that several categories of handbook rule violations damaged his promotion chances:

1. Procedural errors in the process
   a. The supervisor, Pitts, changed the job content and the hours of work. This should have been noted on the posting. However, no posting was made—a violation of handbook rules. If the posting had been made as required, the employee would have had the opportunity to respond in a more informed manner in the interview with the supervisor.
   b. The supervisor chose Fulgham for the position prior to gaining access to the personnel records that would have shown Hope to be the more senior employee.
   c. When the supervisor discussed the promotion question with the personnel director, James Lowrey, after she had conducted the interviews, a letter of "reprimand" or of "poor performance" or both (dated September 30, 1976) was used to damage the promotion chances of the grievant; the letter should have been disallowed as a promotion variable.
   d. The president's failure to hear the grievance as required by the handbook damaged the employee's due process rights.
   e. The personnel office is required to interview all applicants; it did not. This failure to follow the rules allowed the supervisor to show bias in her choice rather than being assured that all criteria were properly weighted.

2. Supervisor's selection criteria
   a. The job was being restructured by the supervisor without clearance from the personnel office, and such actions are not permitted by supervisors acting alone.
   b. The restructuring may actually have been a preselection technique.

3. Role of seniority
   The grievant had been employed longer than the promoted worker and met the minimum job requirements. His seniority was overlooked by the supervisor in the selection.

4. Intimidation and promises
   When the supervisor advised Hope that the promotion had been given to Fulgham, he was naturally disappointed. However, Pitts told him not to discuss the promotion further and that if he did, he "would be out the door." The grievant was offered a twenty-cent hourly increase on his present job if the other applicant were to be selected; after her selection, he was again offered the raise if he would stop the grievance.

Position of the Employer

The employer, through its legal counsel, argued that the mandates of the personnel handbook were followed to the extent that any minor technical violation did not prejudice Hope, the grievant, in any fashion.

According to the personnel director, Lowrey, it is the practice of the employer to post all open positions unless it is evident that a promotion will be made from within that particular department. Since the job in question was other than an entry level position within the dietary department, he did not feel that persons outside the department would be both qualified and interested. Thus, it was not unusual in his view for there to have been no formal job posting in this present situation. Most employees knew before the new supervisor, Pitts, that Cathy Gant was planning to resign and not merely take maternity leave. The fact that both Hope and Fulgham did apply for the job indicates that the grievant's position was not endangered due to the absence of formal posting; the vacancy was openly discussed in the department. Hope did not even raise this issue until an intermediate step of the procedure.

The testimony of the new supervisor, Pitts, indicates that she discussed the promotion at least two times with the personnel director. Lowrey discussed the personnel files of both applicants with her on the phone due to the different physical locations of their offices and the centralized nature of the personnel files. The September 30th letter of reprimand to the grievant from Allen Jackson is significant, shows the employee's work problems with his supervisor, is relevant to the case, and should not be disallowed by the arbitrator.

The employer contended that the procedural matter of who hears the grievance is really immaterial to the case. Although the procedure does designate the president as the management representative in step 4, the employer's efforts to respond as quickly as possible and not delay the process was proper. The vice-president for administration acted in the president's absence, and that was proper delegation. This was hardly a violation of the grievant's due process; if so, why then this arbitration hearing?

On the matter of the personnel office interviewing all applicants, the employee misread the policy statement. The requirement holds only in the case of transfers between departments. Otherwise, it would be impossible to talk with all applicants for promotion due to the personnel department's small staff size. The director of personnel indicated that he allows department heads to make the selection, as was done in this case. This is the practice within all parts of the employer's organization.

In regard to the selection criteria, Section 13 of the handbook lists seniority as only one of several factors to consider, certainly not the sole or dominant one. There is no policy or past practice that requires seniority to be the determining factor in promotions. In the interview, Pitts explained to each applicant that the job would be changed somewhat; Fulgham responded with enthusiasm and excitement to the challenge of the job, and the grievant showed no reaction and had few comments.

The employer argued that the role of the arbitrator, if he should decide that the procedures were not followed, would only be to require the employer to vacate the position and go through with the proper procedure. The arbitrator should not substitute his judgment of the relative merits of the two applicants for promotion for that of the employer.

Questions

1. Since there is no union, under what legal authority is this arbitration taking place?
2. Does this employee have the right to sue the employer because of alleged lack of due process?
3. Could the grievant pursue his grievance to the EEOC? Explain.
4. Should the grievance be upheld by the arbitrator? Why or why not?
5. How do the parties share the expenses of arbitration if there is no labor agreement specifying the rules?

Case 16
Union Organizing

Crunch

Joe Laurens, the election observer for the National Professors Association (NPA) union, listened as Hartsville University's tower clock struck 4:00. He saw the NLRB agent move to the door of the room in which the voting had taken place and turn the lock. The second day of voting by the faculty had ended; the election was over. Had the union won the right to represent Hartsville's faculty? The answer would come soon.

Joe looked down the list of eligible voters. Every name was initialed. All 117 members of the bargaining unit had voted! Was that good? Only time would tell.

The local chapter of the NPA had petitioned the NLRB for certification as the faculty's representative on November 20, 1979, and had accompanied the petition with seventy-two cards, signed by members of the faculty, requesting that the chapter be designated their bargaining agent. Now it was February 1, 1980. Like the rest of the organizing committee, Laurens knew that there had been some loss of zeal during the intervening time. Instead of the election being held before the Christmas break, as the NPA chapter had hoped, the university's attorney had successfully maneuvered to delay the balloting. Not only had he claimed that the NPA was not a union within the meaning of the Taft-Hartley Act (as amended), but he simultaneously had challenged the appropriateness of the bargaining unit as defined in the union's petition. Both motions were subsequently denied by the NLRB local examiner, and that decision was confirmed by the region; however, it resulted in the Direction of Election not being issued by the NLRB until January 2, 1980, and the voting dates being set for January 31 and February 1. "Contracts for the next academic year are due to be tendered next week, too," thought Laurens. "That isn't a plus for the union."

Frank Jeffries, the NLRB agent, took out the box in which the previous day's ballots had been sealed and began to cut away the tape that the administration's observer, Roger Beatty, and Laurens had carefully signed the previous day. He opened the box and began to tally the votes under the watchful eyes of both observers. "Union, no union, union, union, no union, no union," Jeffries intoned aloud. Laurens realized that the vote was going to be very, very close. The organizing committee had felt that it had at least 60 percent of the vote when the balloting started. Had something gone wrong? As the counting proceeded, Laurens' mind raced back over the events that had led to the organizing campaign.

The Organizing Campaign at Hartsville University*

*The authors thank Asa Gardiner for providing this case. The names of people and places have been changed.

Background

Hartsville University, a private university located in a suburb of a growing, busy product distribution center, is one of a number of small liberal arts colleges that dot the country. Attractively situated on a multi-acre wooded site with a lake view, the campus is a special point of interest to Hartsville visitors. HU's enrollment is larger than that of most "small" institutions. At the time of the organizing campaign, there were about 2,400 students, down from an all-time high of nearly 3,200 two years earlier.

HU was born during the Great Depression. Jules Perrot, one of the community's leading citizens, and some of his business friends started it as a two-year night college. It gradually increased in size but remained relatively undistinguished until the 1950s, when the purchase of a large tract of land by the trustees and generous financing from a local industrialist, enabled it to move to the present site and to expand into a full four-year accredited institution. The addition of a master of arts in teaching degree provided the basis for the university designation.

Programs of study leading to the bachelor's degree are offered in some thirty areas of the liberal arts, the fine arts, the sciences, premedicine, predentistry, prelaw, physical education, business administration, and education. Of the students receiving degrees, however, more than half come from the combined areas of business and education.

The student body is composed of two groups, about equally divided in number: Day students from the community are in the slight majority; the remainder are resident students drawn from some thirty states and a few foreign countries.

Administratively, HU is governed by a large board of trustees, the president, the vice-presidents of academic affairs and of financial affairs, the deans of the college of fine arts and of arts and sciences, and seven division chairpersons appointed by the president.

The faculty, including librarians, physical education instructors, and the seven division chairpersons (who teach only a half load) number 126. However, when administrators who hold faculty status are added, the number swells to 164. More than 60 percent of the faculty holds earned doctorates, a fact stressed frequently by the administration. Course loads are a minimum of twelve semester hours, with three class preparations being the norm. Some professors teach fifteen semester hours in fields where they feel that small class size is important to the learning process. The HU catalog emphasizes the faculty's concern with classroom teaching. In point of fact, there is virtually no time for research and publication. Only a very few of the faculty have produced any work of note. Salary levels, as reported by the NPA annually, are consistently in the lower quartile, and the university has not attracted any outstanding scholars. HU depends on student tuition and fees for about two-thirds of its income, and increases in faculty salaries are customarily coupled with higher tuition. HU's endowment is small; donors give buildings but not the funds to staff and maintain them.

The management style of the administration has tended strongly toward the autocratic. Tight control rests in the trustees and the president. University governance is nonparticipative. There existed at the time of the case a nineteen-member Faculty Administration Council on which six elected representatives of the faculty served. But the FAC's role is strictly advisory. It makes no decisions. In any case, the seven division chairpersons who serve automatically on the FAC weight the balance whenever issues about which the administration holds strong views arise.

Development of the Issues

HU's enrollment for the fall semester of 1979 was down about 15 percent from the previous year's. Administrative response was quick and sharp. Without prior consultation with the general faculty, but with the assistance of the seven division chairpersons, the number of teaching faculty for the next academic year was immediately reduced so as to bring the budget into balance. Several young, able faculty members who had been hired in 1977 were notified by the third week in September that their contracts would not be renewed. The administration announced that several existing vacancies would not be filled and that retirees would not be replaced. It became apparent that there would not be a proportionate cut in administrative staff.

Not only was the faculty aroused, but there was spontaneous student reaction. Resident students held mass meetings and demanded an evaluation of possible alternative courses of action. Concurrently, at a stormy faculty meeting, ten representatives were elected for a similar purpose. The groups then combined at a formal meeting on October 9, elected cochairpersons as their only officers, adopted the name "Student-Faculty Committee on Alternatives," and proceeded to establish fact-finding subcommittees: alternatives in budget, new sources of funds, student recruitment, student retention, and faculty workload.

These subcommittees worked diligently but unfruitfully. The trustees refused to provide any financial information, even after a two-hour meeting with representatives of the Committee on Alternatives. The committee's final report on October 27 was largely an exercise in futility. About the only tangible result was prompt administrative action to remove the garbage collecting bin from under the students' dormitory windows!

Many of the young faculty members whose contracts were not being renewed were active members of the NPA chapter, which now became the only organized change agent possible. For several years, the chapter had been urging the HU administration to enlarge the role of the faculty in university governance in accordance with long-standing principles of the national association. A faculty-administration-trustee committee had been named in 1975, had met spasmodically, and had been quietly placed in limbo by the administration in early 1977. Faculty representation on the FAC was increased from three to six members as a result of chapter pressure, and a committee was appointed in 1979 to revise the faculty bylaws, which were badly outdated. There was no other action.

Collective bargaining had been endorsed by the NPA national as an additional way of realizing the association's goals in higher education. It became a more and more appealing avenue of action as the days dragged on and the administration continued to ignore requests for a detailed explanation of the rationale for its action in reducing faculty size.

A meeting of all teaching and research faculty called by the leadership of the NPA chapter on November 1 provided a forum for discussion of the issues. The faculty members at a chapter meeting held the same day decided to test the will of the entire HU faculty in regard to collective bargaining. A broad-based organizing committee was quickly formed; representation authorization cards were obtained, and instructions for organizers (Exhibit 1) were prepared and distributed with the cards.

By November 4, more than half the faculty in the prospective bargaining unit had signed, 20 percent more than the minimum required by the Labor Management Relations (Taft-Hartley) Act (as amended). A special meeting of the chapter was therefore called for November 9, at which time the chapter would vote to offer itself to the teaching and research faculty as their collective bargaining representative.

More than two-thirds of the active members of the chapter attended the meeting. The vote was almost unanimous for the chapter to proceed with a collective bargaining effort. The organizing committee was officially named, and approval was given for it to contact the president of HU to inform him of the chapter's action.

The Campaign

The committee met with the president on November 10. It informed him about the chapter's action and told him that more than half the faculty had requested it to represent them. The president was polite but said he could make no reply until he had consulted with the trustees.

An official reply (Exhibit 2) was received on November 17. It dashed any hope of a consent election. Its phrasing, according to a professor who taught labor management relations, indicated that it had been dictated by an attorney specializing in labor law. The chapter accordingly filed a "Petition for Certification of Representative" with the local office of the NLRB on November 20. The definition of the proposed bargaining unit purposely excluded the seven appointed division chairpersons. Six members of the library staff were also left out of the unit, with the idea that they would be

Exhibit 1 Instructions for Organizers

Instructions for Organizers

1. *Here are ten (10) representation cards and envelopes. There are more where these came from, so don't hold back in your efforts.*

2. *The faculty member should make out his or her own card, place it in the envelope, and seal it. The envelope can then be opened only by an NLRB examiner.*

3. *Write the name of the faculty member very lightly in pencil in the upper right-hand corner of the envelope. It will be erased later so that the signer will remain anonymous.*

4. *DO NOT LET THE CARDS OUT OF YOUR HANDS EXCEPT FOR SIGNING.*

5. *Return the sealed envelopes to the organizer in your division who enlisted you.*

6. *It is necessary to obtain signatures from at least 50 percent (50%) of the faculty right now, so be your most persuasive.*

7. *Here are some arguments you may want to use if you encounter resistance:*

   a. *After the cards have been signed and an agreement has been reached, the faculty will be able to run its own affairs. Hence, organizing assures faculty freedom and participation in governance.*

   b. *Two styles of management are available to administrators:*

      1. *autocratic/dictatorial*
      2. *democratic/participative*

      If the faculty member recognizes our type of administration as being autocratic, then the only protection he or she has as an individual is to organize.

   c. *Faculty on tenure have much greater security than other faculty, but will they deny the benefits of solidarity to others by not signing?*

8. *Remember that any discussion initiated by any administrative personnel regarding the signing of representation authorization cards is an unfair labor practice under the Labor Management Relations (Taft-Hartley) Act. If anyone asks, "Are you planning to sign?" or "Have you signed?" or makes any similar inquiry, be sure to keep a record of the exact words used, the time and place they were used, and the name of the person making the inquiry.*

9. *Ask that your division meeting be terminated a few minutes early so you will be free to discuss the possibility of organizing. If the division chairperson refuses to leave the room, or if you move to another room and he or she follows you, this also is an unfair labor practice.*

10. *GO TO IT!*

Exhibit 2 President's Official Reply

17 November 1979

Dr. Duncan Black, President
Hartsville University Chapter
National Professors Association
Hartsville University

Dear Dr. Black:

The purpose of this letter is to respond to the comments you made to me during our meeting on November 10, 1979, in which you stated that on November 9, 1979, the Hartsville University chapter of the National Professors Association had taken action to form a collective bargaining unit, that 50 percent of the full-time teaching faculty had indicated their desire to form such a unit, and that the NPA wished to engage in collective bargaining.

We do not believe that you represent the faculty of Hartsville University, and thus we are unwilling to recognize you as their bargaining representative until your status is resolved by an election conducted by the National Labor Relations Board.

Whether or not it is ultimately determined that you are the representative of the faculty members of Hartsville University, we will, of course, respect our faculty members' rights under the National Labor Relations Act.

Very truly yours,

Thomas A. Daniels
President

TAD: B

included if the administration challenged the appropriateness of the unit. On the same day, the chapter organizing committee distributed a memorandum (Exhibit 3) to each member of the faculty; it gave the expected chronology of the collective bargaining election process.

A series of letters now flowed from the president of HU to each member of the faculty. The letters began on December 1 and continued through January 29. The December 1 letter explained the recognition process. It associated collective bargaining with "blue collar" activities and urged faculty members to learn all they could about the unionization of faculties. It suggested that any problems existing at HU could best be solved "without interjecting a union between the faculty and the administration."

Exhibit 3 Expected Chronology of the Election Process

DATE: November 20, 1979

TO: The Faculty of Hartsville University

FROM: HU Chapter NPA

SUBJECT: Chronology of Collective Bargaining Election

In accordance with an earlier memorandum, the NPA chapter now estimates that the collective bargaining election process will follow the approximate pattern shown below. Unopposed recognition of the chapter as bargaining agent will shorten the process, whereas determined opposition will stretch it out.

10 November: *NPA organizing committee asked President Daniels to recognize the chapter as the collective bargaining agent. No official reply was given.*

17 November: *President Daniels refused to recognize the chapter as agent.*

20 November: *Petition for Certification of Representative has been filed with the National Labor Relations Board (NLRB). The NLRB examiner privately checked the representation authorization cards signed by members of the faculty and submitted with the petition to make sure that more than 30 percent of the members of the prospective bargaining unit want the NPA chapter to represent them.*

December: *The NLRB will investigate the chapter's definition of the bargaining unit ("full-time teachers/researchers").*

The NLRB will decide on the bargaining unit and eligibility of voters.

The NLRB will set an election date, ballot, and place.

January: *A secret ballot election by members of the bargaining unit, as defined by the NLRB, will be held. The NLRB will conduct the election on campus in accordance with prior notice. A ballot booth will be set up, and balloting will be Secret. Ballots will be placed in a locked box and will remain in the possession of the NLRB. Only the voter will know how he or she votes. Results will be announced after the ballots have been counted by the NLRB.*

You will be kept informed about the progress.

THE ORGANIZING COMMITTEE

Duncan Black
Eugene Grady
Samuel Jacobs
Joseph Laurens
Arthur McDearmon

A longer letter, dated December 5, stressed the loss of the faculty member's individual rights should the NPA chapter become the bargaining representative. It stated that terms of faculty contracts could no longer reflect the individual professors' abilities and performance. Individual complaints, it said, might be compromised by the union grievance process no matter how meritorious they were. It claimed that collective bargaining would introduce "an adversary process which is wholly incompatible with the traditional university ideal of a community of scholars." Furthermore, it noted, the presence of a union on the campus would have an adverse effect on donations, contributions, and grants. The letter closed by asking each faculty member to give careful consideration to the question of whether a union would be in his or her best interest.

The chapter countered these two letters with a memorandum rebutting each point raised. It made frequent reference to the official publications of the NPA and to chapter statements on policy. The memo touched on two matters not covered in the president's letters: the adoption of new faculty bylaws as an alternative to collective bargaining and the decertification of the union if the faculty became disenchanted with collective bargaining.

During the next few weeks, there was a lull in the flow of written material. The administration's motion to dismiss the chapter's petition on the ground that the NPA was not a union and its challenge as to the appropriateness of the bargaining unit as defined by the union led to a day-long hearing before the local NLRB examiner. The motion to dismiss was denied. The chapter agreed to include the six librarians and succeeded in excluding the seven administration appointed division chairpersons, holding that they were in fact supervisors under the terms of the Labor Management Relations Act. NPA national provided skilled legal assistance for the hearing and for the subsequent preparation of briefs to be submitted to the regional director for review. The examiner's decision, confirmed by the region, was announced January 2, 1980, three weeks after the hearing.

In a letter dated January 3, the president responded to the basic questions raised at the hearing. He pointed out that whereas the NPA had long been a professional association, it was now a labor union, regardless of what the chapter might say. The letter reemphasized the question of the adversary relationship and deplored the fact that four administrative officers and five faculty members had been tied up for a whole day, noting that they could have made "much better use of their time by performing their normal duties." It stated again that collective bargaining simply did not fit the economic conditions existing at HU and invited faculty cooperation in overcoming the current problems.

This letter drew a sharply worded, one-page response from the chapter (Exhibit 4). It said that it was the administration which was to blame for having created an adversary relationship and for having wasted time at the hearing. The administration had failed to plan properly for declining enrollment. Collective bargaining was necessary to check the downward spiral.

Exhibit 4 NPA Response to January 3 Letter

HARTSVILLE UNIVERSITY

TO: The Faculty *January 10, 1979*

With reference to the president's letter to you of January 3, you may be interested in the following facts:

1. The regional director of the National Labor Relations Board on January 2, 1979, issued a decision denying the administration's contentions regarding the composition of the voting unit for collective bargaining at HU.

2. The "adversary" nature of the NLRB hearing was entirely the result of the administration's determination not to yield on any points at issue. Specifically, the administration insisted on trying to pack the voting unit with the division Chairpersons, although the NLRB position on division chairpersons voting in a faculty election had been clearly and repeatedly stated in a series of landmark decisions: Where the division Chairpersons "make recommendations on hiring and change of status" of faculty members, they are excluded from the voting unit. The NLRB decision to exclude such people from our voting unit was cut and dried. It merely recited the obvious fact that our division Chairpersons had made recommendations regarding termination of faculty and cited landmark cases. It was indeed a waste of time and money for the administration to argue the point. We could not agree more! Let us all hope that the administration will approach its obligations under the forthcoming election and ensuing events with greater concern for university resources and without further futile adversary action.

3. With respect to the statement, "Collective bargaining cannot make more funds available to the University," nothing is further from the truth. Many students have already left because of the administration's failure both to plan properly for declining enrollment and to permit full student and faculty participation in exploring and passing judgment on alternative solutions to the problems which continue to plague us. More students will leave unless full and genuine participation is implemented before the end of this term and unless better solutions than the simplistic ones of cutting off personnel and raising tuition are found. The Committee on Alternatives was a step in the right direction, but it was completely frustrated by the refusal of the administration and the trustees to cooperate. Short of collective bargaining, any further efforts to secure full faculty and student participation in university affairs which affect them will surely fail and will make bad matters worse. Only collective bargaining can bring about the balance between the administration on the one hand and students and faculty on the other which is absolutely necessary to check the downward spiral in enrollment.

THE ORGANIZING COMMITTEE

HU Chapter NPA

The chapter also put out a question-answer type memorandum on the same day, January 10, dealing mostly with the issues raised by the president's letter of December 5. It contained facts and made reference to a publication of the NLRB, *A Layman's Guide to Basic Law under the National Labor Relations Act*, published in 1976. It also quoted from the collective bargaining agreement which the faculty of St. Johns University, New York, had reached with its administration, copies of which had been distributed to each faculty member at HU.

A chapter memorandum of January 12 continued the question-answer response to the administration's statements. However, it went beyond response in two areas. It brought up the possibility of meaningful faculty bylaws as a substitute for collective bargaining, pointing out that they could be made part of the collective bargaining agreement. It also raised the question of voting at faculty meetings by thirty-two administrators who had no teaching, research, or library responsibilities.

The next letter from the president was dated January 18. It gave the administration's view of the December 11 NLRB hearing in response to the chapter's sharp criticism of January 10. "Any attempt on this campus to draw a rigid distinction between 'administration' and 'faculty' is artificial," the letter stated. The distinction, it claimed, was indicative of the harmful effects of possible faculty unionization. The letter expressed a desire for faculty participation in university problem solving and mentioned that the draft of new faculty bylaws was currently being discussed by the Faculty Administration Council. A union could well decrease the opportunity for meaningful faculty participation in governance, it added.

On January 19, the chapter answered questions about collective bargaining which had been asked during the intervening week—questions about the equality of women faculty, the recovery of "banked" teaching credit hours lost when HU had shifted from a teaching load of fifteen semester hours to that of twelve, and the possible future participation of division chairpersons in the bargaining unit.

The president's letter of January 26 seemed to take advantage of any derogatory information about the union which had been revealed in investigation or publicity. It gave excerpts from the speech of the outgoing NPA president, made at the 1979 annual meeting, in which he expressed serious reservations about the association's endorsement of collective bargaining. The letter also talked about the damage a faculty strike might cause to HU, as well as about the divisive nature of the collective bargaining process itself. It closed with the hope that the faculty members would vote "no union" at the election on January 31 and February 1.

The union's response came on January 29. It quoted NPA official policy relative to strikes. It focused attention on the administration's use of excerpts out of context, noting that, after debate, the NPA annual meeting had endorsed collective bargaining by a vote of 373 to 54. The letter stated that while collective bargaining could not have prevented the drop in enrollment, it could have prevented the administration's unilateral action in reducing faculty size. It asked the faculty to give serious consideration to how it would vote.

The last word came from the president. In a letter dated January 29 but distributed January 30, he repeated each of the major points made in the earlier communications. He pointed to the progress that was being made in increasing faculty participation in the governance of the university. He said that that goal could best be achieved by the adoption of reasonable bylaws. He explained that the presence of a union would reduce the responsiveness of the community to appeals for much needed gifts and bequests. "A vote for unionization will seriously impair our unity and weaken our financial base," the letter continued. "The decision is now yours. I know that you will consider it carefully and will vote your honest conviction about what is best for you and the university."

The Tally

Now they had cast their votes! Joe Laurens felt uneasy as Frank Jeffries opened the box in which today's ballots had been placed and continued to count. The numbers swung inexorably toward "no union"; when the last vote was tallied, it stood union 52, no union 65. The campaign was over. Twenty faculty members who had signed representation authorization cards had voted against the chapter!

Questions

1. What caused the faculty to initiate actions that eventually led to an NLRB election?
2. Under what authority does the NLRB have jurisdiction for accepting a petition for an election from faculty members?
3. Examine the administration's reaction to the campaign. Compare it to behavior at a local manufacturing plant.
4. Why was the union's organizing campaign a failure?

Collective Bargaining Negotiations Exercise

Learning Objectives

1. To gain an understanding of negotiation preparations, actual negotiations, and assessment of negotiations outcomes.
2. To develop an appreciation for the psychological influences and the realism of contract negotiations.
3. To learn the mechanics of give-and-take, compromise, and trading issues and to practice the art of negotiations.
4. To familiarize the participants with the issues in collective bargaining and the difficulty of writing provisions to the satisfaction of both parties.
5. To realize the importance of and problems associated with teamwork in a bargaining situation.
6. To gain an appreciation for the application of bargaining theories to negotiations.

Rules of the Negotiations Exercise

1. Participants must not discuss the exercise with anyone except team members.
2. Each participant will be assigned a role (organization position) by the instructor.
3. The negotiations must take place within the framework of the present company and union. Creativity is encouraged, but a realistic and pragmatic approach is recommended.
4. Data, materials, and information used for each position or argument on behalf of a proposal should not be falsified.
5. Each team may have as many meetings outside of class as are needed and desirable.
6. Team members must follow the instructions of their respective team leaders.
7. All activities of team members should be directed toward negotiating an agreement that is mutually acceptable and that the parties can live with for the next period.

Instructions to the Participant

1. Each participant will be assigned to either the management or the union team. An organization position will be assigned to each person.
2. The team leaders—the president of the Industrial Workers United (IWU), AFL-CIO and the industrial relations director of Quality Furniture Manufacturing Company (QFM)—will call separate meetings to discuss and

---

Collective Bargaining Negotiations Exercise: QFM Company and IWU

prepare for the upcoming negotiations and anticipate each other's proposals.

Major issues for negotiations should include:
a. Union security, dues checkoff, union shop
b. Wages, classes, premiums
c. Management's rights
d. Promotions and layoffs (use of seniority)
e. Grievance procedure and arbitration
f. Affirmative action plans
g. Pension plans
h. Supplemental unemployment benefits
i. Vacations
j. Holidays
k. Sick leave
l. Other issues allowed by instructor

3. In the preparatory meeting, each team will study the present agreement, identify its problems, and gather materials, data, and information to justify the team's proposals and positions.
4. Based on study, analysis, strategy, and plans, each team will complete Form I and give it to the instructor. (The form is not to be shown to anyone else.)
5. The union president and the industrial relations director and their respective teams will meet at a time specified by the instructor for the purpose of negotiating a new agreement. Union will present its proposals first. Then management will present its proposals and/or counterproposals.
6. Actual negotiations will begin after the proposals are exchanged and will continue until a new agreement is negotiated and signed or the present contract expires. (The instructor will specify time periods.)
7. Upon completion of the negotiations, each team will determine the total annual costs (anticipated) of the new agreement.
8. Additional instructions will be given the participants by the instructor.

Sources of Materials for Preparation

Government publications: U.S. Department of Labor, Bureau of Labor Statistics. *Area Wage Surveys, Employment and Earnings, Handbook of Labor Statistics*, and *Characteristics of Major Collective Bargaining Agreements.* (Washington, D.C.: Government Printing Office.)

Form 1

Bargaining Priority (1 = Most Important, 2 = Second Most Important, and so on)	Subject Area for Negotiations (Brief Description)	Proposals to Other Party (First Day)	Realistic Objective for Negotiations	Actual Accomplishment (to Be Completed after Negotiations)

Binder services of Bureau of National Affairs, Commerce Clearing House, and Prentice-Hall. Especially helpful is the BNA *Collective Bargaining Negotiations and Contracts.*

Business Publications: *Business Week* and *Wall Street Journal.*

Professional industrial relations journals: *American Federationist, Arbitration Journal, Employee Relations Law Journal, Industrial and Labor Relations Review, Industrial Relations, Industrial Relations Law Journal, Journal of Collective Negotiations in the Public Sector, Labor Law Journal,* and *Monthly Labor Review.*

Proceedings: Industrial Relations Research Association, Labor Law Developments, National Academy of Arbitrators, and NYU Conference on Labor.

Labor agreements between companies and labor unions (as available).

Furniture Manufacturing Industry

The furniture industry can be characterized as a "highly competitive, nonintegrative industry composed largely of small and medium-sized, family controlled business."[1] Although the industry consists of about 1,200 companies, only 50 are publicly held, and most of the others are family operated. The latter showed little inclination to adopt efficiencies already common in other manufacturing industries. Furniture manufacturers still operate only one shift and remain highly labor-intensive. High quality workmanship and craftsmanship have been their goal, and much of the work is still done by hand to give the products their distinctiveness.[2]

While plants are scattered throughout the United States, two-thirds are located in the Southeast, the Middle Atlantic, and the Great Lakes regions. Since the Pacific Coast has an ample supply of softwood and hardwood, more plants are currently locating there. Manufacturers using plastics and metals (rather than wood) in their furniture are able to locate more closely to their markets and have therefore spread throughout the country.

Products are distributed over fairly wide geographic areas, and 70 percent of the output is sold directly to retailers. Brand names and product line identity are important to some of the larger manufacturers, but there are problems of design copying and enormous pressures for frequent restyling.[3]

Sales are sensitive to economic conditions, and employment in 1982 was 7 percent below the 1979 level for the industry. During the last few years residential housing has experienced a decline, the cost of borrowing money has remained high, and consumer demand has continued to be sluggish. The demand for high quality furniture, such as the "Eagle" brand for Quality Furniture Manufacturing Company, has been recession-proof, but the demand for low and moderately priced furniture has dropped significantly. Prospects for the next several years depend on a recovery in residential housing, lower mortgage and consumer credit interest rates, rising personal disposal income, and changing patterns of consumer spending. In addition, this industry should benefit from the 40 million people who will be between the ages of thirty-five and forty-four by the end of the 1980s (compared to 30 million in the 1970s), and the growing number of single-person households and two-income families.[4] Other changes which will affect the furniture industry will be the changing lifestyles that have resulted from inflation and higher energy costs, which have started a trend toward more dining and entertaining at home. Shifts in geographic population centers toward the Sun Belt and West will have an effect on the furniture market as well as on the distribution and manufacture of the products.[5]

[1]Wickham Skinner and David C. D. Rogers, *Manufacturing Policy in the Furniture Industry*, 3rd. ed. (Homewood, Ill.: Richard D. Irwin, 1968), p. 1.

[2]"Why Furniture Makers Feel So Comfortable," *Business Week*, July 30, 1979, p. 76.

[3]Skinner and Rogers, *Manufacturing Policy*, pp. 2–12.

[4]Bureau of Industrial Economics, *1983 U.S. Industrial Outlook* (Washington, D.C.: U.S. Department of Commerce, 1983), pp. 42–7 to 42–9.

[5]Carl Anderson Shaw, *Home Furnishings* (New York: Standard and Poor's Industry Surveys, 1982), pp. H55–H59.

The QFM Company and the Union

QFM Company began in 1820 in Laconia, New Hampshire, as a family-owned and operated furniture manufacturer. It was headed by Herman Sweeny, one of the early settlers in Laconia. The company grew to 30 employees by 1920, but at that time B. F. Sweeny, Herman's son, decided to move the firm to St. Louis, Missouri—a location more central to the firm's market. Barely surviving the 1930s depression, QFM was one of the first companies to convert its manufacturing processes to the production of war materials. The company prospered during the war, and afterwards Sweeny decided to expand, sell stock publicly, and focus on producing metal and plastic-laminated furniture. With the production experience it had gained during the war and with its location some distance from the predominantly wood furniture manufacturers, QFM Company launched a new era for itself in 1946.

By 1970, the St. Louis plant of Quality Furniture Manufacturing Company had 1,300 employees and was producing 450 dinette sets, 200 sets of lawn tables and chairs, and 300 bar stools and miscellaneous furniture daily. Then came the 1971–1973 furniture boom, with its expectations of continuous growth. QFM's new president, Gerald Brooks, decided that a new, modern plant and more diversity in the product line were necessary to meet the expected demand. Taking into consideration location, material supply, transportation, markets, labor situations, and other factors, Brooks decided to build the new plant in Dallas, Texas. This plant was to specialize in the new product lines, and the St. Louis plant was to concentrate only on dinette sets. In 1972, 200 employees were transferred from St. Louis, and another 200 were hired from the Dallas–Fort Worth area. The Dallas plant started with no union and 400 employees. By 1983, it had grown to a 900-employee work force, still with no union. It pays its Dallas employees at least $1 less per hour than it pays the St. Louis workers in comparable jobs. The St. Louis plant continues to produce 450 dinette sets per day, mostly for chain retailers, and employs about 1,000 workers. No new product lines have been added at the St. Louis plant, and its employment level is the same as the pre-1970 days. The Dallas plant has started producing a new product line—dinette sets under the Eagle brand name. Consumer response has been positive, and the Dallas plant's future looks very promising.

Throughout its history, QFM Company has prided itself on being a progressive employer; however, recent events—building the Dallas plant, increasing employment in Dallas while lowering it in St. Louis, paying QFM workers in St. Louis less than comparable area wages—resulted in an NLRB representation election for the Industrial Workers United union in St. Louis in 1975. After a heated campaign by both management and the union, NLRB investigations of unfair labor practices, and challenged ballots, the union lost the election by a vote of 497 to 481. Two years later, the union returned and won the election by a vote of 611 to 375. The election campaign was bitter, and the negotiations that followed were even more bitter. After a six-week strike, a labor agreement was signed. There have been two negotiations since 1977 and no strikes have occurred. However, the current agreement is close to expiration. Although the company officials now express a commitment to return to the era where management and labor trusted each other, worked cooperatively, and shared mutual goals and benefits, the union leaders are reacting by waiting to see their deeds. The upcoming negotiations will determine the company's commitment.

Exhibit 1 QFM Company Balance Sheet, 1983

Assets	
Current Assets:	
Cash	$ 1,503,040
Notes and Accounts Receivable	34,754,720
Inventories	43,911,840
Prepaid Expenses	575,680
Total Current Assets	$ 80,745,280
Fixed Assets	
Land	7,000,000
Buildings	17,500,000
Machinery and Equipment	13,747,440
Total Fixed Assets	$ 38,247,440
Total Assets	$118,992,720
Liabilities and Stockholders' Investment	
Current Liabilities:	
Notes and Accounts Payable	$ 11,556,160
Accrued Payroll	4,620,000
Taxes (local, state, federal)	37,100,000
Total Current Liabilities	$ 53,276,160
Stockholders' Investment:	
Common Stock (common @ $20 per share)	$ 28,000,000
Earned Surplus	37,716,560
Total Stockholders' Investment and Earned Surplus	65,716,560
Total Liabilities and Stockholders' Investment	$118,992,720

Exhibit 2 QFM Company Income Statement

	1982	1983
Net Sales	$134,409,738	$147,850,850
Cost of Goods Sold:		
Production (labor, materials, overhead, etc.)	108,360,170	113,202,970
Administrative	9,100,280	9,814,560
Sales	4,480,000	5,880,000
Other	1,137,098	1,289,960
Total Cost of Goods Sold	$123,077,548	$130,187,490
Income before Taxes	11,332,190	17,663,360
Taxes (local, state, federal)	3,267,600	4,356,800
Net Income	$ 8,064,590	$ 13,306,560

Exhibit 3 QFM Company Net Sales and Earnings

	Net Sales	Net Earnings
1981	$126,801,640	$10,144,131
1982	134,409,738	8,064,590
1983	147,850,850	13,306,560
1984 (estimated)	153,686,350	18,568,586

Exhibit 4 Number of QFM Production and Maintenance Employees by Seniority in St. Louis and Dallas Plants

Years	St. Louis	Dallas
0–1	5	100
1–2	15	150
2–3	40	160
3–4	45	150
4–5	45	158
5–10	205	115
10–15	200	25
15–20	105	20
20–25	120	10
25–30	152	10
30 or more	68	2
	1,000	900[a]

[a]Includes those transferring from St. Louis.

Exhibit 5 Number of QFM Employees in Each Job Title, by Wage Grade

Wage Grade	Job Title	St. Louis	Dallas
1	Janitor	10	9
2	General Laborer	30	32
3	Materials Handler	45	48
4	Packer	36	35
	Machine Operator–B	120	120
	Utility Worker	38	20
	Interplant Truck Driver	16	18
	Sander	40	40
	Assembler	295	319
5	Welder	16	10
	Machine Operator–A	120	62
	Electrician–B	5	7
	Maintenance Worker–B	11	12
	Gluer	56	40
6	Mechanic	10	8
	Spray Painter	43	35
	Cutoff Saw Operator	25	18
7	Electrician–A	15	8
	Maintenance Worker–A	11	8
	Inspector	26	18
8	Tool Grinder–A	5	5
9	Tool and Die Maker–A	12	8
10	Leadman	25	20
		1010	900

Exhibit 6 Average Hourly Earnings, Excluding Overtime for All Manufacturing Employees

	Oct. 1981	Oct. 1982
Total	$ 7.42	$ 7.79
Durable Goods	8.73	9.13
Lumber and Wood Products	7.10	7.62
Furniture and Fixtures	6.06	6.43
Stone, Clay, and Glass Products	8.50	9.01
Primary Metal Industries	10.97	11.43
Fabricated Metal Products	8.39	8.90
Machinery, Except Electrical	9.04	9.40
Electric and Electronic Equipment	7.80	8.34
Transportation Equipment	10.74	11.24
Instruments and Related Products	7.60	8.48
Miscellaneous Manufacturing Industries	6.05	6.49
Nondurable Goods	7.33	7.80
Food and Kindred Products	7.51	7.86
Tobacco Manufacturers	8.67	9.56
Textile Mill Products	5.72	5.88
Apparel and Other Textile Products	5.05	5.20
Paper and Allied Products	8.82	9.63
Printing and Publishing	8.40	8.88
Chemicals and Allied Products	9.37	10.24
Petroleum and Coal Products	11.47	12.55
Rubber and Miscellaneous Plastic Products	7.30	7.72
Leather and Leather Products	5.09	5.39

Source: U.S. Department of Labor, Bureau of Labor Statistics, *Employment and Earnings, December 1982* (Washington, D.C.: Government Printing Office, December, 1982), pp. 70–80.

Exhibit 7 Average Earnings for Selected Occupations in St. Louis, Missouri, and Dallas, Texas

Occupation	St. Louis (March 1981)	Dallas (December 1981)
Automotive Mechanics	$ 9.87	$10.19
Carpenters	9.51	10.45
Electricians	10.98	11.42
Machine-tool Operators (toolroom)	10.70	11.18
Machinists	9.61	10.76
Painters	10.21	11.20
Forklift Operators	8.76	8.97
Janitors	4.67(?)	7.28
Tool and Die Makers	12.02	11.09

Sources: The St. Louis data are from U.S. Department of Labor, Bureau of Labor Statistics, *Area Wage Survey, St. Louis, Missouri–Illinois Metropolitan Area, March 1981* (Washington, D.C. Government Printing Office, 1981). The Dallas data are from U.S. Department of Labor, Bureau of Labor Statistics, *Area Wage Survey, Dallas-Fort Worth, Texas, Metropolitan Area, October 1981* (Washington, D.C.: Government Printing Office, 1981), pp. 20–24.

Exhibit 8 Average Gross Hours and Earnings of Production Workers on Manufacturing Payrolls, 1976–1982

	St. Louis			Dallas		
	Weekly Earnings	Weekly Hours	Hourly Earnings	Weekly Earnings	Weekly Hours	Hourly Earnings
1976	$243.05	40.4	$6.01	$189.60	40.6	$4.67
1977	268.79	41.4	6.54	205.44	40.6	5.06
1978 (Mar.)	283.46	41.2	6.89	218.65	41.1	5.32
1979 (Mar.)	303.97	40.7	7.36	236.96	40.3	5.88
1980 (Nov.)	331.63	39.2	8.46	293.34	41.2	7.12
1982 (Jan.)	361.82	39.2	9.23	306.71	38.1	8.05
1982 (Nov.)	385.34	39.2	9.83	353.57	40.5	8.73

U.S. Department of Labor, Bureau of Labor Statistics, *Employment and Earnings* (Washington, D.C.: Government Printing Office, Jan. 1983) pp. 129-131.

Exhibit 9 Consumer Price Index for Urban Wage Earners and Clerical Workers and Percent Changes, 1967–1982

Year	Index	Percent Change
1967	100	—
1968	104.2	4.2
1969	109.8	5.4
1970	116.3	5.9
1971	121.3	4.3
1972	125.3	3.3
1973	133.1	6.2
1974	147.7	11.0
1975	161.2	9.1
1976	170.5	5.8
1977	181.5	6.5
1978	195.3	7.6
1979	217.7	11.5
1980	247.0	13.5
1981	272.3	10.2
1982	288.6	6.0

Source: U.S. Department of Labor, Bureau of Labor Statistics, *Monthly Labor Review* 106 (April 1983), p. 66.

Exhibit 10 Average Gross Hours and Earnings of Manufacturing Production Workers and Furniture Production Workers, 1976–1982

	Manufacturing			Furniture		
	Weekly Earnings	Weekly Hours	Hourly Earnings	Weekly Earnings	Weekly Hours	Hourly Earnings
1976	$209.32	40.1	$5.02	—*	—	—
1977	228.90	40.3	5.44	—	—	—
1978	249.27	40.4	5.91	$167.91	38.7	$4.35
1979	268.94	40.2	6.43	209.87	39.5	5.26
1980 (Dec.)	315.70	41.5	7.40	268.77	39.7	6.77
1982 (Jan.)	312.01	37.1	8.41	209.50	33.9	6.13
1982 (Nov.)	337.90	39.5	8.62	246.77	38.2	6.46

*The dashes indicate that figures are not available.

Source: U.S. Department of Labor, Bureau of Labor Statistics, *Employment and Earnings* (Washington, D.C.: Government Printing Office, January 1983) pp. 70–77.

Exhibit 11 Average Hourly and Weekly Earnings for All Private Workers and for Manufacturing Workers

	1981 (Nov.)	1982 (Nov.)
Hourly Earnings		
Total Private	$7.47	$7.80
Manufacturing	8.20	8.62
Average Weekly Earnings		
Total Private	$262.20	$270.66
Manufacturing (1977 dollars)	169.71	167.59

Source: U.S. Department of Labor, Bureau of Labor Statistics, *Employment and Earnings, January 1983* (Washington, D.C.: Government Printing Office, January 1983) pp. 104–120.

The Labor Agreement between Quality Furniture Manufacturing Company (QFM) and Industrial Workers United (IWU), AFL-CIO

This agreement is entered into on ———— by the Quality Furniture Manufacturing Company (QFM), located in St. Louis, Missouri, and Industrial Workers United (IWU). This agreement covers employees at the St. Louis plant only.

Article I
Recognition The company recognizes the IWU as the sole and exclusive collective bargaining agent in all matters pertaining to rates of pay, wages, hours of employment, and other conditions of employment for all production and maintenance employees, excluding professional employees, storeroom employees, office clerical employees, guards, and supervisors, as defined in the National Labor Relations Act.

Article II
Union Security The company agrees not to interfere with the right of employees to join the Union and will not discriminate against employees who are Union members. Employees in the bargaining unit are completely free to participate in the affairs of the Union, provided that such activities do not interfere with their work duties and responsibilities.

While no employee will be required to join the Union as a condition of employment, union dues will be deducted from any bargaining unit employee's pay check, provided proper written notification is given to the Company. At the end of each pay period, the Company will forward the collected dues, minus a 5 percent administrative fee, to the Union.

Article III
Management Rights All management functions of the enterprise that are not specifically limited by the express language of this agreement are retained by the Company. The functions and rights listed here are examples of the exclusive responsibilities retained by the Company and are not intended as an all-inclusive list: to manage the manufacturing operations and methods of production; to direct the work force; to decide what work shall be performed in the plant by subcontractors or by employees; to schedule working hours (including overtime work); to hire, promote, demote, and transfer; to suspend, discipline, and discharge for cause; to relieve employees due to lack of work or for other legitimate reasons; to create and enforce reasonable shop rules and regulations; to establish production standards and rates for new or changed jobs; to introduce new and improved methods, materials, equipment, and facilities; to change or eliminate existing methods, materials, equipment, and facilities.

Article IV
No Strike and No Lockout The Company agrees that during the life of this agreement there shall be no lockout of bargaining unit employees.

The Union agrees that during the life of this agreement there shall be no strike, work stoppage, slowdown, work refusal, delay of work, refusal to report for work, or boycott.

Article V
Hours of Work The normal workweek shall consist of eight (8) hours per day, forty (40) hours per week, for a five (5) day week, from Monday to Friday. The starting time shall be made by the Company, and it can be changed by the Company to suit varying conditions of the business. Such changes in working schedules shall be made known to the Union representative in the plant as far in advance as possible. Employees shall be notified by a written bulletin or other communications medium.

Article VI
Grievances and Arbitration Procedures Grievances arising out of the operation and interpretation of this agreement shall be handled and settled in the following manner:

- *Step 1.* The aggrieved employee and/or shop steward shall discuss the grievance with his or her supervisor.
- *Step 2.* Should the answer provided by the supervisor not produce a satisfactory solution to the grievance, the grievance shall be reduced to writing and shall state the provision of the agreement which has been violated. The department head shall arrange for a meeting of the aggrieved employee, the shop steward, the supervisor, the employee relations supervisor, and himself or herself for the purpose of discussing the grievance. The department head shall provide a written answer to the grievance after the close of the meeting.
- *Step 3.* If a satisfactory conclusion is not reached, the grievance can be referred to the plant manager by the Union. The plant manager shall schedule a meeting to discuss the grievance with the Union. The local Union can bring in a representative of the international Union at this step, and the plant manager can bring in anyone who he or she feels may aid in the resolution of the grievance.
- *Step 4.* If a grievance is appealed to arbitration, the Company and the Union shall attempt to select an arbitrator. If this attempt fails, the company and/or Union shall ask the Federal Mediation and Conciliation Service to submit a list of seven (7) arbitrators. Each party shall eliminate three (3) names from the list by alternately striking one name at a time, and the person whose name remains shall serve as the arbitrator.

The arbitrator shall render a decision in writing that shall be final and binding upon the parties.

The arbitrator to whom any grievance is submitted shall have the authority to interpret and apply the provisions of this agreement, and the arbitrator's decision must be in accordance with and based upon the terms of this agreement or of any written amendment thereto. But the arbitrator shall have no jurisdiction or authority to add to, subcontract from, or modify any of the terms of this agreement.

The Company and local Union shall each pay its own expenses incurred in connection with the arbitration and one-half of the expenses and fees of the arbitrator and the facilities used in the arbitration hearing.

Article VII

Seniority "Seniority" as used in this agreement shall be the period of continuous service in the job or plant from the date of the employee's appointment.

"Probationary employment" consists of a period of one hundred twenty (120) days of employment.

Layoffs shall be made in the following order:

a. Probationary employees
b. Other employees in order of job seniority

Recall shall be made in the following order:

a. Employees in order of job seniority, given equal job ability
b. Probationary employees

Promotions shall be made on the basis of qualifications, merit, and seniority. Promotions out of the bargaining unit remain management's prerogative.

An employee who quits or is discharged for cause shall lose all seniority rights.

If the Company decides to terminate any operation or job and the employees remain on layoff for a period of twelve (12) months, the employees shall be considered to have been terminated for cause at the expiration of said twelve (12) month period.

Article VIII

Wages and Classifications Job classifications and a wage schedule setting forth the rates of pay of the various classifications are included in Schedule A and are hereby made part of this agreement.

If and when the Company creates a new job classification or modifies, alters, amends, or combines existing jobs, or revises the skills and responsibilities of a job, job descriptions will be drawn and a wage rate assigned. The Union shall have a maximum of five (5) working days to examine the job description to determine whether it accurately describes the principal functions and whether the pay range is consistent with established job classification pay ranges.

If the Union takes exception, it can review both factors with the Company. If the issue cannot be resolved, the Union can take the issue through the grievance procedure.

Job classifications are for pay purposes only and do not pertain to whoever might perform the work in that classification—unless modified by the terms of the agreement.

Article IX
Insurance An employee who has completed ninety (90) days of employment is eligible for enrollment in the company group insurance programs on the monthly premium date for each particular insurance coverage that next follows the completion of ninety (90) days of employment.

1. *Group Life Insurance.*

Group Life Insurance	Accidental Death and Dismemberment
$10,000	$10,000

2. *Accident and health insurance.* One-half of the employee's weekly pay up to a maximum of $130. It is understood and agreed that the cost of the hospitalization, medical and health insurance, major medical insurance, accident and health and life insurance will be borne 50 percent (50%) by the Company and 50 percent (50%) by the employee, when subscribed to by the employee. It is understood and agreed that in the event that the Company wishes to change carriers, there is no obligation to negotiate with the Union prior to instituting the change.

Employees on medical leave for a period in excess of ninety (90) consecutive days may continue to be covered under the group insurance program after the first ninety (90) days, providing the employee pays the total insurance premium.

Article X
Pension Plan A pension plan for bargaining unit employees of the Company is hereby incorporated as a part of this agreement.

As of October 6, 1977, the normal retirement benefit for all years of service continues to be $8 per month per year of service.

Article XI
Holidays All employees, after completing six (6) months of service with the Company, shall be paid seven (7) hours' pay for the following holidays:

- New Year's Day
- Independence Day
- Labor Day
- Thanksgiving Day
- Day after Thanksgiving Day
- Christmas Eve Day
- Christmas Day

To be eligible for holiday pay, the employee must have worked the days immediately preceding and following the holiday. Legitimate excuses for absences will be considered.

Article XII
Vacation Employees shall qualify for vacation with pay in accordance with the following (determined June 1 of each year):

Continuous Service	*Vacation with Pay*
More than 1 but less than 5 years	1 week
More than 5 but less than 10 years	2 weeks
More than 10 but less than 20 years	3 weeks
More than 20 years	4 weeks

Vacation pay shall be computed on the basis of each employee's average weekly earnings from June to June. Payment will be made on the work day prior to the vacation period.

Article XIII
Sick Leave A full-time employee is eligible for sick leave after completing six (6) months' service with the Company. An eligible employee will accumulate sick leave at the rate of one-half day per month of service from date of hire. Sick leave will not be carried over from one year (January 1 to December 31) to the next, and it can be used only for personal illness not covered by workmen's compensation. The Company retains the right to require a doctor's certificate as proof that absence was due to a legitimate injury or illness.

Schedule A Wages and Classifications

Wage Grade	Job Title	Wage Rates
1	Janitor	$6.30
2	General Laborer	7.00
3	Materials Handler	7.10
4	Packer	8.40
	Machine Operator–B	8.40
	Utility Worker	8.40
	Interplant Truck Driver	8.40
	Sander	8.40
	Assembler	8.40
5	Welder	9.10
	Machine Operator–A	9.10
	Electrician–B	9.10
	Maintenance Worker-B	9.10
	Gluer	9.10
6	Mechanic	9.80
	Spray Painter	9.80
	Cutoff Saw Operator	9.80
7	Electrician–A	10.50
	Maintenance Worker–A	10.50
	Inspector	10.50
8	Tool Grinder–A	11.20
9	Tool and Die Maker–A	11.90
10	Leadperson	12.60

Article XIV
Duration of Agreement **This agreement shall become effective as of ______, and shall continue in effect until 11:59 P.M., ______. Thereafter, it shall renew itself for yearly periods unless written notice of termination is given by one party to the other not less than sixty (60) nor more than ninety (90) days prior to the expiration date.**

Name Index

Subject Index

The MF
Answer Book

Solutions for Effective Visual C++ Applications

Eugène Kain

ADDISON–WESLEY

Boston • San Francisco • New York • Toronto • Montreal
London • Munich • Paris • Madrid
Capetown • Sydney • Tokyo • Singapore • Mexico City

The publisher offers discounts on this book when ordered in quantity for special sales. For more information, please contact:

U.S. Corporate and Government Sales
(800) 382-3419
corpsales@pearsontechgroup.com

For sales outside of the U.S., please contact:

International Sales
(317) 581-3793
international@pearsontechgroup.com

Visit us on the Web at www.awprofessional.com

Library of Congress Cataloging-in-Publication Data

Kain, Eugène.
The MFC answer book: solutions for effective visual C++ applications / Eugène Kain.
p. cm.
Includes bibliographical references and index.
ISBN 0-201-18537-7
1. Microcomputers—Programming 2. Microsoft foundation class
QA76.76.063 S3566 2003
005.2'4—dc21 98-18901
CIP

ISBN 0-201-18537-7
Text printed on recycled paper
7 8 9 10 11 12 13—MA—0706050403
Seventh printing, April 2003

Contents

Foreword

If you've ever scanned one of the Visual C++/MFC newsgroups or mailing lists, you have probably noticed that they are chock full of questions like:

- How to I make my splitter windows nonresizable?
- How do I put a button or a combo in my toolbar?
- How do I give my dialog a different background color?

Someone new to MFC might think that the product is very poorly documented. But the real problem is that the tools in Visual C++, such as AppWizard and ClassWizard, give most developers a false sense of security. What typically happens is that a developer new to MFC development runs AppWizard, selects some options, and within five minutes has a complete working application. MFC development *feels* so easy!

Problems start when you try and do something like customize the behavior of the splitter window, which—if you don't have any help—might require days of plowing through the monumental pile of MFC source code that ships with Visual C++. Doesn't this seem crazy, especially since you created the bulk of your application in just minutes?

Many people incorrectly blame the Visual C++ technical documentation for this situation. MFC, like any C++ class library, is designed to be extremely extensible. (Heck, Microsoft even gives you the source code, so you could argue that MFC is *infinitely* extensible.) Unfortunately, the developers at Microsoft cannot begin to guess how an MFC user might need to extend the library for their application; only the basic interfaces for the MFC classes are documented, and brave developers are left to figure out the extensibility details on their own.

In today's world of increasingly sophisticated graphical user interfaces, MFC extensibility is essential in order for an MFC-based application to be competitive. In other words, nobody creates a vanilla Scribble style application any more. Try running the Scribble example next to a copy of Quicken, Microsoft Outlook, CorelDRAW, Adobe Photoshop, Microsoft Office, or any other application released since 1997 and you will see literally months of potential additional GUI work that you will need to invest in order to rise up to today's user interface standards.

I have been working with MFC since its first version, and started the online version of the MFC FAQ to learn more about MFC and to help people succeed with this class library. About three years ago I started Stingray Software with the goal of creating products that make it easier to create MFC applications. George Shepherd and I cowrote the books *MFC Internals* and *Inside Visual C++*, Fifth Edition—along with tons of magazine articles—as we continued working toward the same goal.

In all of the years I've been working with MFC, I haven't found a book that is as indispensable a reference as the one you now hold in your hands. Reading this book from cover to cover will definitely help you learn more about MFC and become super-productive with this class library. What I suspect most readers will do is dive into the book for a week, come back with a much improved application GUI, receive a raise from their manager, and inspire awe in their MFC developer peers (until they find out how you created all of your amazing enhancements).

If you plan to do any serious application development with MFC, the FAQs collected in this book will literally save you months of source code digging and hair pulling. This book is a "must-have" reference for every MFC developer!

—Scot Wingo
Maintainer of the MFC FAQ,
VP of the Stingray Division of Rogue Wave,
Coauthor of *MFC Internals* and *Inside Visual C++*, Fifth Edition
http://www.stingray.com/mfc_faq
http://www.stingray.com

Preface

Why Another Book on Microsoft Foundation Classes Programming?

To answer this question, let us look at a typical MFC programming scenario. First, you attend an MFC training session or read some introductory books on MFC programming. You quickly become able to write and customize small tutorial applications. AppWizard and ClassWizard allow you reach an unprecedented level of productivity. Your applications support the multiple document interface (MDI) and have a professional-looking user interface with a floating toolbar, a status bar, printing and print preview, and so on.

You then go back to work and start using MFC to produce great-looking applications. Code flows freely from your keyboard, the wizards work hard at your side, and life looks great under the MFC sun.

One day, you start wondering about how to implement new features that were not explicitly covered in the training session. For example:

- Make your application remember the last active document and automatically reopen it.
- Support multiple kinds of views on the same document and allow the user to explicitly open any kind of view.
- Add ToolTips to the controls in a form view.
- Dynamically switch the view displayed in a window to replace it with another kind of view.

- Implement an expanding dialog box.
- Embed a property sheet (tabbed dialog box) inside another window, such as a form view, a dialog box, or a mini frame window.
- Display a progress indicator in a status bar pane.
- Have a menu pop up when the user clicks a button on a toolbar or in a dialog box.
- Support headers and footers in your print and print preview.
- Display a custom Printing . . . dialog box with a progress indicator.

You feel that implementing these features cannot be *that* difficult: after all, you have already seen them in other Windows applications. But where do you start looking for an answer?

The solution may be as easy as knowing the specific MFC virtual functions that you must override to produce the desired effect or knowing the Windows messages you should trap and handle appropriately. For some features, however, more involved techniques may be needed—even to the point of tracing into MFC's source code to understand just where and how you can act to modify your application's default behavior.

One infuriating fact of life is that the answer to your particular question may be lying around somewhere, buried in some MFC programming book or magazine article, on the Microsoft Developer's Network CD-ROM, in the Microsoft Knowledge Base, in the various threads and mailing lists maintained on the Internet, or even in the online books and samples contained on the Visual C++ CD-ROM. The problem is this: how are you going to locate the most relevant and reliable source of information among all these resources? How are you going to find the solution you need *right now*?

Introducing *The MFC Answer Book*

This book is intended to provide ready-to-use techniques that answer the most common real-world questions that typically confront MFC developers. The structure of this book is specifically designed to help you quickly locate the answers you're looking for and integrate the relevant solutions into your own programs.

The FAQ format of this book makes it ideally suited to the needs of the developer looking for a quick answer to a pressing question. At the same time, you will find that many techniques will give you a better understanding of the inner workings of MFC applications and more generally help you improve your MFC programming skills. In particular, the Explanations and Additional Comments sections often delve into the MFC source code or undocumented functions to explain how the techniques discussed work and how they differ from or integrate with MFC's default behavior.

Key Features of This Book

Although most books about Visual C++ and MFC programming answer valid questions about MFC programming and provide useful tips if you read them from cover to cover, most of them are not structured in a way that allows you to quickly find an answer to a given problem. Moreover, even if you find the answer, it is likely to be buried inside a larger discussion and not readily available as a step-by-step technique that you can simply incorporate into your current project to add a required feature.

In contrast, *The MFC Answer Book* is specifically designed to help MFC developers solve their programming problems in the most efficient way:

- This book is organized so that the table of contents will help you to quickly zoom in on the FAQs that answer your questions.
- I have made every effort to build a convenient and comprehensive index that will direct you to all the pages relating to any keyword or function referenced in this book.
- Each FAQ is written in a concise way that first gives you the step-by-step answer you need. Explanations and additional comments are deferred to later sections so that they do not get in the way of the solution but are readily available for those who want to go further than the cookbook recipe and wish to understand what goes on under the hood.
- Each explanation comes with tested and reusable sample code that you can plug into your MFC application in a few minutes to integrate the required functionality immediately.

To summarize: *The goal of this book is to offer you the shortest way from a problem to the corresponding step-by-step solution that you can integrate immediately into your current project.*

Who Should Read This Book

This book is written for all MFC developers who wish to solve their MFC-related problems and at the same time learn advanced MFC techniques that will allow them to add a range of sophisticated features to their applications.

This book assumes a basic proficiency both in the C++ language and in MFC programming as well as a knowledge of how to use the Visual C++ integrated development environment and tools such as AppWizard and ClassWizard. The Visual C++ wizards are discussed only when used in nonstandard ways to achieve a specific result.

To benefit fully from this book, you should already understand the basic MFC concepts presented in the Scribble tutorial described in the Visual C++ documentation: the document/view architecture, message maps, the *UPDATE_COMMAND_UI* mechanism, dialog data exchange (DDX), and so on. Typically, you will either have followed the Scribble tutorial, attended a training session in MFC programming, or read one of the many introductory books on this topic.

Of course, having a more extensive background in MFC programming will not hurt! Quite to the contrary. Based on feedback from reviewers and colleagues, I know that this book will also appeal to experienced MFC developers, who will find many useful techniques to add to their bag of MFC programming tricks.

Finally, reading this book will allow all MFC developers to improve their understanding of fundamental MFC concepts and sharpen their MFC programming skills.

How To Use This Book

This book focuses on the 32-bit MFC version 4.x for Windows 95 and Windows NT. However, most techniques and concepts discussed here also apply to older versions of MFC. They should also remain valid for future MFC versions, because they rely on core MFC classes and behaviors that are not likely to evolve in a way that breaks existing code.

I tried to write this book so that it will become a flexible tool that you can use as you want to. This means that you can either read this book from cover to cover—I would certainly appreciate it if you do—or use it as a reference to look up only the specific topics that interest you. Most FAQs are cross-referenced to help you locate all the relevant information you might need even if you jump into the middle of the book.

However, before you start hunting for answers to your MFC questions, I suggest that you take a few minutes to read Chapter 0 (Terminology and Conventions) and Chapter 1 (Document/View Architecture Backgrounder) to make sure that we start on the same ground with respect to terminology and fundamental document/view architecture concepts.

What Is on the CD-ROM

The companion CD-ROM contains source code and executables for all of the book's sample programs. The folder hierarchy is organized first by chapter number and then by project name. Thus, the AutoSaveDoc project for Chapter 2 is located in the d:\Chap02\AutoSaveDoc folder, where "d:" is your CD-ROM drive's letter.

All the executables are located under their respective chapter folders. For example, all the executable sample programs for Chapter 2 are located in the d:\Chap02 folder. The EkUtil.h and EkUtil.cpp files located at the root of the hierarchy contain the various helper *Ek*...... functions and classes that are presented throughout the book.

You can choose to copy the whole folder hierarchy from the CD-ROM to your hard disk, copy only the examples that are of interest to you, or access the files directly from the CD-ROM. If you copy files from the CD-ROM to your hard disk, remember to remove the read-only attribute from the files on your hard disk.

All sample programs have been compiled and tested under both Visual C++ 5.0 and Visual C++ 6.0. They will also work properly with Visual C++ 4.x, but you will have to manually create the appropriate .mdp project file. Note, however, that the .dsp project files on the CD-ROM have the Visual C++ 5.0 format: if you open them with Visual C++ 6.0, simply answer Yes to the dialog box asking whether you want to convert these files to the new format.

The CD-ROM also includes numerous compiled examples of Stingray Software's Microsoft Foundation Class extension libraries, which you can find in the Stingray Demos folder. The Stingray extension libraries are an ideal complement to the topics addressed in this book, since they are especially designed to address the needs of MFC developers. The Stingray extension libraries provide helper classes and fully object-oriented frameworks that significantly extend the functionality and capabilities of the core MFC classes. They allow MFC developers to build in a few days applications with a sophisticated user interface on par with those of successful current commercial products. For more information, please visit the Stingray Web site at http://www.stingray.com

Your Feedback Is Welcome

I have done my best to accurately present topics that I feel should be of interest to most MFC developers. However, if you think that a topic should be covered differently or should use another technique, don't hesitate to send me e-mail at ekain@awl.com. Also, e-mail me if you want to submit a topic idea or a technique of your own that solves a problem you have encountered, if you find an error or have any problem with this book, or if you have suggestions or want to discuss anything with me.

I can promise that I will read all e-mail messages, take them into account, and try to respond to each of them as soon as possible. Note, however, that I may not have the time to answer specific MFC programming questions. You can also visit my Web site at http://www.mfcfaq.com/ to get late-breaking information.

I hope that this book will make you enjoy MFC programming more than ever and help you deliver great applications.

Good luck with your MFC projects!

—Eugène Kain
July 1998

Acknowledgments

Before delving into the subject of this book, please let me take a moment to express my gratitude to the many people who contributed their efforts to bring this book into existence.

The reviewers helped raise the overall quality of this book by reading the draft manuscript and suggesting several improvements. I want to thank Desiree Christensen, Charles Couchoud, Jack Mathews, Monika Weikel, and Don Willits for agreeing to invest their time and energy on my behalf.

Special thanks go to my friend Christophe Nasarre, who gave many well-thought-out suggestions about almost every page of my draft manuscript. You are certainly the most thorough reviewer I have ever met!

I am also deeply indebted to the staff at Addison-Wesley, without whom this book would never have made it into the finished product that you are holding now. Ben Ryan initially trusted me enough to accept the challenge of publishing a book written by somebody he had never met and who lived on another continent. J. Carter Shanklin and Krysia Bebick took on the task of supervising the completion of this work after Ben left to pursue other ambitions. John Fuller and his staff translated my manuscript from electronic bits and bytes into a properly typeset and bound book. Copy editor Betsy Hardinger did an excellent job of editing my manuscript. Marketing issues were expertly addressed by Robin Bruce, Ben Ames, and Chanda Leary. And finally, Elizabeth Spainhour efficiently helped coordinate the efforts of all those people.

Last but not least, I want to thank my wife, Corinne, for enduring the loneliness of an author's wife and courageously managing our household and taking care of our two children while I spent my evenings and weekends at the computer. Special thanks go also to my parents and parents-in-law, who provided lots of support and relief during this adventure, and to my brother-in-law Hervé for visiting us frequently and entertaining us with his good humor.

0 TERMINOLOGY AND CONVENTIONS

Each technical domain gives rise to its own specialized jargon, and MFC programming is no exception. Although such jargon serves a useful purpose in allowing one to write concise yet precise explanations, it can also bring unnecessary trouble and misunderstandings if there is some doubt about the meaning of a particular word or expression.

Therefore, before delving into the following chapters, I suggest that you spend a few minutes to read the following short sections and make sure we agree on the terminology and coding conventions that are used throughout this book. Do not be afraid if some definitions seem quite terse: when used in the context of a practical technique, they will be much easier to understand and relate to your needs. Thus, you should not hesitate to come back to these sections later while reading the FAQs in the following chapters.

Terminology Used in This Book

Application class: the *CWinApp*-derived class that implements, at least, your application's start-up code in its *InitInstance()* function.

Application object: the global—and unique—instance of your application class.

Child frame class: one of the *CMDIChildWnd*-derived classes in your project associated with a view's frame window, at least for MDI applications.

(In an SDI application, the main application window is also the view's frame window.)

Child frame window: see "view's frame window."

Document class: one of the *CDocument*-derived classes in your project.

Document object: an instance of one of your document classes.

Document template object: an instance of either the *CMultiDocTemplate* or the *CSingleDocTemplate* class.

Document template resource ID: the resource ID that associates a document template object with three resources: a menu resource, an icon resource, and a complex string resource (the document template string). This item is discussed in *FAQ 1.8 What is the role of the document template resource ID?*

Document template string: the string resource—referenced by the document template resource ID—that defines the seven substrings associated with a document template object. This item is discussed in *FAQ 1.8 What is the role of the document template resource ID?*

Document window: broad term designating what the user perceives as one "view" on a document without explicitly indicating if we refer to the child frame window or to the actual view window.

Main application window: the Windows top-level window of the application. This window is usually associated with a C++ object that is an instance of either a *CMDIFrameWnd*-derived class (for an MDI application) or a *CFrameWnd*-derived class (for an SDI application).

Main frame window class: the *CMDIFrameWnd*-derived or *CFrameWnd*-derived class that manages the main frame window of your application.

Main frame window object: the (unique) C++ object associated with the main frame window of your application.

View class: one of the *CView*-derived classes in your project.

View object: an instance of one of your view classes.

View (window): either a C++ object that is an instance of one of the *CView*-derived classes in your project or the Windows window associated with such an object.

View's frame window: the caption-bearing window that hosts one or more views as well as optional control bars. In an SDI application, the main application window is also the view's frame window.

Conventions Used in the Sample Code in This Book

Application object: all sample projects use an *extern* declaration such as the following. This declaration allows my code to reference the application object (*theApp*) anywhere.

```
class CMDIApp : public CWinApp
{
// ...
};

// The one and only CMDIApp object
extern CMDIApp theApp;
```

Casting: I use the new C++ *static_cast< >* operator most of the time, as defined by the C++ ANSI committee. The *static_cast< >* operator is similar to the old-style (*newtype*) cast but has the advantages of allowing only reasonably safe casts and being easy to spot in source code. The *static_cast< >* operator has the following syntax: *static_cast< newtype > (expression)*. If you want to, you can mentally replace the preceding expression with an old-style cast: *(newtype) expression.* Here is an example of how to use the *static_cast< >* operator:

```
T1* p1;
T2* p2 = static_cast< T2* >( p1 );   // p2 = (T2*) p1;
```

For further information about the *static_cast< >* operator—as well as about the other new-style cast operators: *const_cast, reinterpret_cast,* and *dynamic_cast*—see the Visual C++ online help or a recent book on the C++ language.

Counter document: the Counter document manages a counter that is incremented or decremented either by left- or right-clicking on the Counter view, by using the Count menu, or by using the associated toolbar buttons.

Drawing document: the Drawing document manages a current point as well as a current shape. The current point is changed by left-clicking on the Drawing view; the shape is changed with the help of the "Draw" menu or the toolbar buttons.

Sample menus and buttons: when a specific menu command is needed in a sample program, the relevant menu appears immediately to the left of the "View" menu even if the standard Windows user-interface guidelines dictate that this menu command should be located elsewhere. This convention makes it easy to locate menu commands that are specific to a particular sample program. Similarly, the toolbar buttons associated with sample-specific menu commands are almost always located on the demo toolbar that appears on the left side of the main application window.

DOCUMENT/VIEW ARCHITECTURE BACKGROUNDER

This chapter is the only theoretical one in this book. It tries to present and clarify the main issues regarding one of the most mystifying aspects of MFC development: the document/view architecture. This architecture is a blessing to MFC developers who know how to take advantage of it, and it's a curse to those who do not understand its underpinnings.

Because the rest of this book—and especially Chapters 2 and 3—assumes some familiarity with MFC's document/view architecture, this chapter is designed to give you the minimum required background information needed to understand the techniques discussed in later chapters. I hope that you will also be able to take advantage of this chapter as a useful quick reference on document/view architecture fundamentals during your MFC developments.

Note that this chapter is not designed to be used as a tutorial for learning basic MFC mechanisms and structures. Although I tried to make this backgrounder as comprehensive and accurate as possible, it is certainly far too terse and concise to use as a learning tool. If you need such a tutorial, you should either attend an introductory MFC training session or read a good book on MFC programming—or even follow the Scribble tutorial in the online help—before reading this chapter.

Let us now try to answer some fundamental questions about the document/view architecture.

What is the document/view architecture?

The document/view architecture is one of the cornerstones of the MFC class library. This architecture aims to simplify the development of today's sophisticated graphical applications by providing a coherent framework for managing an application's data and user interface.

The most fundamental concept of the document/view architecture is the separation between an application's *data*, represented by a *document* object, and the *views* that can exist on this data. Each view is responsible for managing one *visual presentation*—or rendering—of the data of its associated document.

■

See Also

- *FAQ 1.2 What are the benefits of the document/view architecture?*
- *FAQ 1.3 What components make up the document/view architecture and how do they relate to each other?*

What are the benefits of the document/view architecture?

Even if critics sometimes argue against using the document/view architecture—at least for some highly specialized applications—it has been proven to present a powerful paradigm for developing Windows applications. This architecture also remains flexible enough to accommodate a wide range of application and user-interface needs, as you can see for yourself by browsing through the remainder of this book.

Although it takes some time to learn and use well, the document/view architecture actually simplifies application development because it enables you to leverage most of the supporting functionality provided "for free" by the MFC framework:

- Correct synchronization of multiple view windows attached to the same document object in an application that opens several documents and views simultaneously (i.e., that uses the MDI user-interface model)
- Automatic menu switching in the main frame window depending on the type of document associated with the active view (again, this applies only to MDI applications)
- Intelligent routing of menu and toolbar button commands, allowing any command to be handled by a function in almost any class that relates to the document/view architecture (see *FAQ 1.10 How does MFC route command messages?*)
- Intelligent visual updating of menu items, toolbar buttons, and status bar indicators—thanks to the *UPDATE_COMMAND_UI* mechanism—again allowing the updating to be handled by a function in almost any class
- Support for printing and print preview
- Reasonable default built-in behavior for many common situations, such as prompting the user to save a modified document when closing the last view on a document

Correctly taking advantage of the document/view architecture in your application can therefore allow you to reduce your implementation efforts while at the same time benefiting from increased functionality—all provided by the MFC framework. In other words, the document/view architecture allows you to write sophisticated applications while letting MFC take care of most of the drudge work of managing a modern user interface.

Finally, separating the data part of the application (the document) from the user-interface part (the view) increases the modularity and object-orientation of your development, thus allowing you to produce applications that are more maintainable, more flexible, and easier to extend.

■

See Also

- *FAQ 1.1 What is the document/view architecture?*
- *FAQ 1.3 What components make up the document/view architecture, and how do they relate to each other?*
- *FAQ 1.10 How does MFC route command messages?*

What components make up the document/view architecture, and how do they relate to each other?

The document/view architecture relies on the following MFC components:

- The *document*
- The *view*
- The *view's frame window*
- The *document template*
- The *document template resource ID*

Note that, unlike the other items, the document template resource ID is not an actual component represented by a C++ class. It nevertheless plays a crucial role in the document/view architecture, as explained in *FAQ 1.8 What is the role of the document template resource ID?*

These components are discussed in the following FAQs. The cohesive role played by these elements is best illustrated in the way they are referenced in the *InitInstance()* function of a typical AppWizard-generated application, as shown in Listing 1-1.

Listing 1-1. Standard AppWizard-generated code for the *InitInstance()* function, showcasing each component of the document/view architecture.

```
BOOL CMyApp::InitInstance()
{
// ...

   // Register the application's document templates.
   // Document templates serve as the connection between
   // documents, frame windows, and views.

CMultiDocTemplate* pDocTemplate;     // Document template
pDocTemplate = new CMultiDocTemplate(
     IDR_MYDOCTYPE,                  // Resource ID
     RUNTIME_CLASS(CMyDoc),          // Document
     RUNTIME_CLASS(CChildFrame),     // View's Frame Window
     RUNTIME_CLASS(CMyView));        // View
 AddDocTemplate(pDocTemplate);       // Add doc template
                                     // to app list

// ...
}
```

Although they are not usually considered part of the core document/view architecture, the following elements also play an essential role in most MFC applications:

- The application object
- The main application window (note that this is the same as the view frame window for an SDI application)
- The various user-interface control elements: menus, toolbars, and status bars

Figures 1-1 to 1-4 show different ways of looking at the fundamental components that make up the document/view architecture. I suggest that you review these figures until you understand how these components relate with one another and with the visible part of an MFC application.

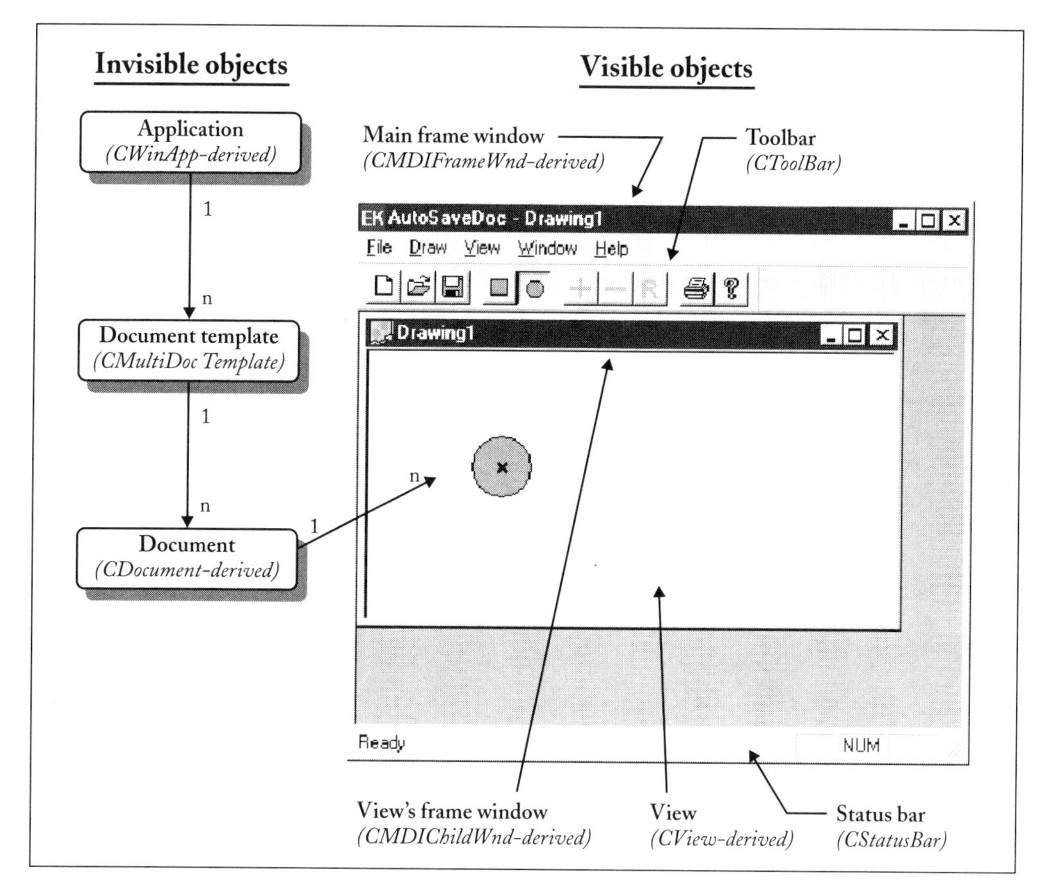

Figure 1-1. Runtime structure of a basic MFC application (MDI user-interface model, one document, and one view).

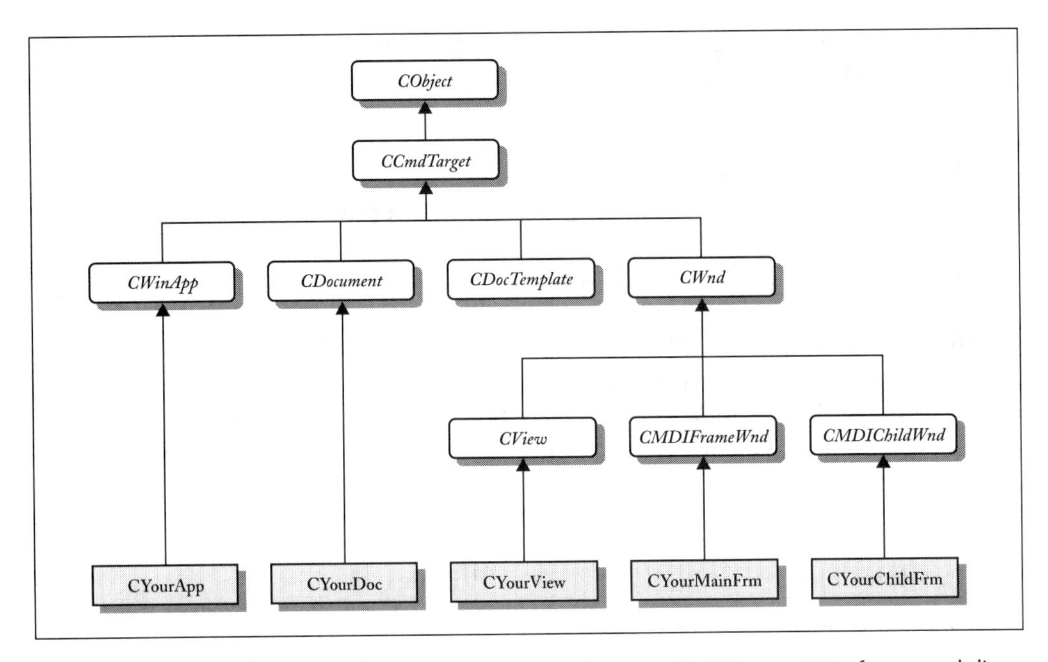

Figure 1-2. Class hierarchy for a basic MFC application (MDI user-interface model). The classes with a shaded background are the ones that AppWizard generates for you and that you customize in your application.

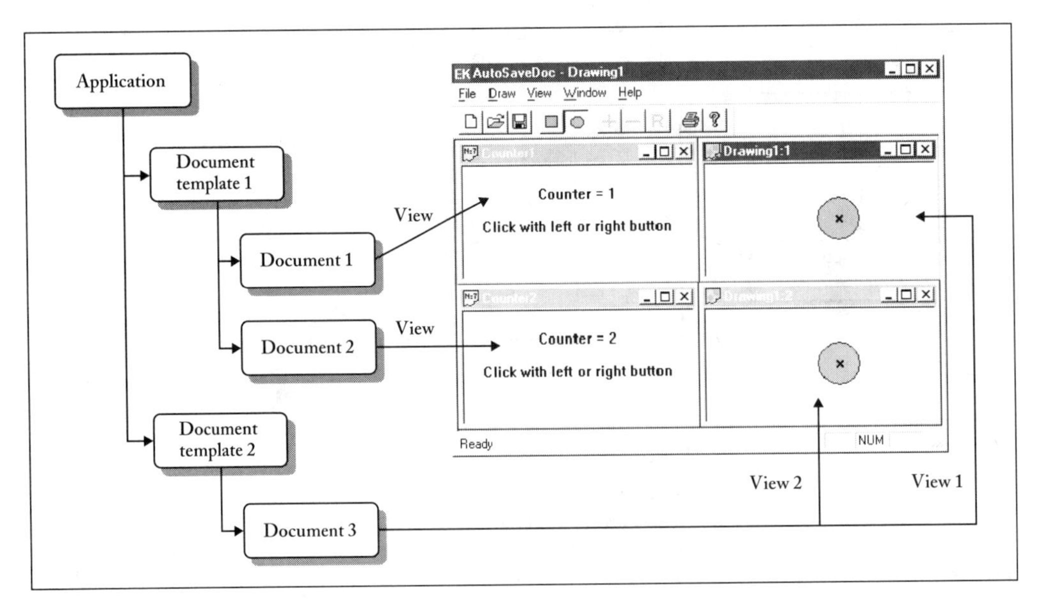

Figure 1-3. Runtime structure of a more complex MFC application (MDI user-interface model, two document templates, three documents, and four views).

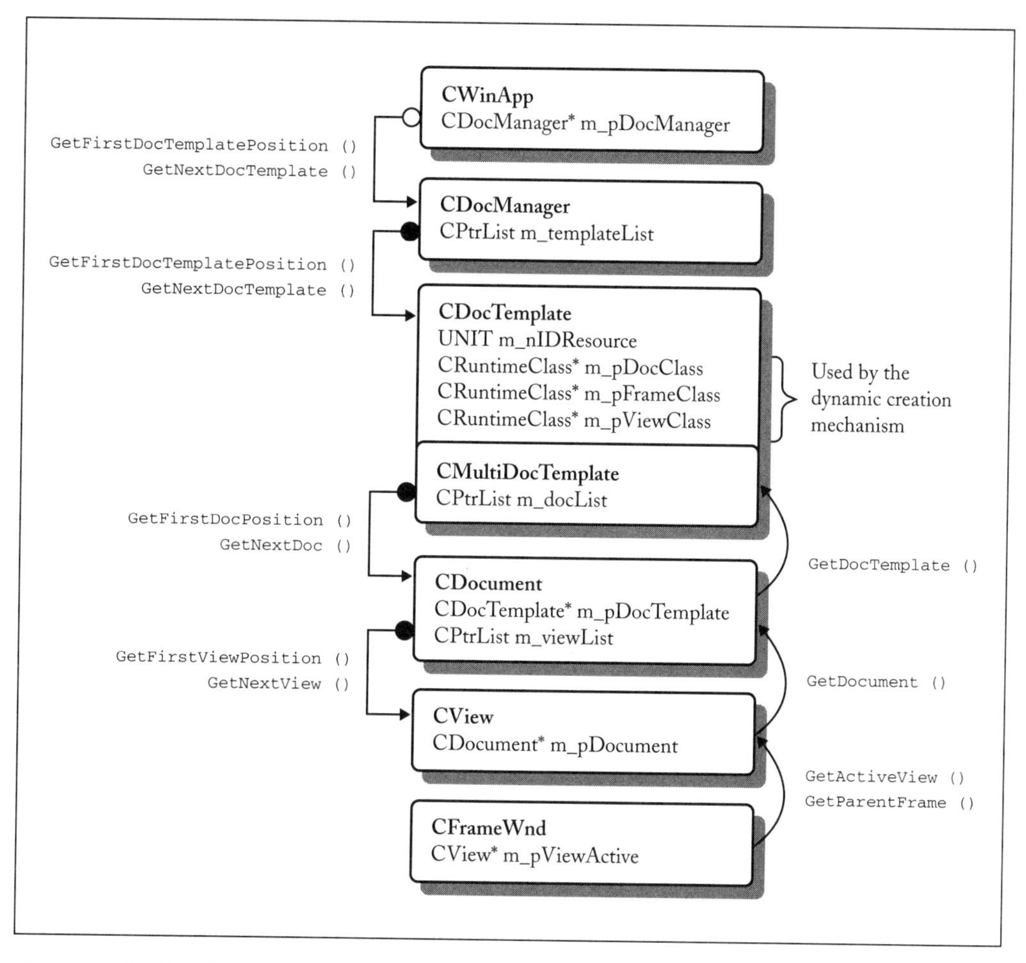

Figure 1-4. Relationships between the fundamental components of the document/view architecture.

■

See Also

- *FAQ 1.1 What is the document/view architecture?*
- *FAQ 1.2 What are the benefits of the document/view architecture?*
- *FAQ 1.4 What is the role of the document?*
- *FAQ 1.5 What is the role of the view?*
- *FAQ 1.6 What is the role of the view's frame window?*
- *FAQ 1.7 What is the role of the document template?*

- *FAQ 1.8 What is the role of the document template resource ID?*
- *FAQ 1.9 How do the document/view architecture component objects get created?*

FAQ 1.4 What is the role of the document?

The document has the following duties in the document/view architecture:

- *It conceptually contains the data upon which the application operates.* "Conceptually" means that the document object does not always need to store the actual data in its own data structure. For example, in a database application, the document object could store only the database connection and perhaps a handle to the result set associated with the last query. Similarly, in a messaging application, the document object could store the handle to the MAPI connection and maybe a pointer to an object representing the active message store. However, in all cases, the document object stores and manages the entry point to the relevant data, thereby conceptually representing the data.
- *It is responsible for storing and retrieving its data to a persistent medium.* This persistent medium is usually a disk file, and data storage and retrieval is usually done in the document's *Serialize()* member function, which MFC automatically calls during its processing of the "File, Open" and "File, Save" menu commands. However, many applications persist their data in a different medium, such as a relational database or a message store. Even in those cases, the data storage and retrieval is orchestrated by the document object, because it conceptually "owns" the data.
- *It acts as a synchronization agent for the various views that may be opened on the same document object.* This is usually the most visible part of the document's job. A document object performs this synchronization by keeping a list of all the views that are opened on it; when the document's *UpdateAllViews()* function is called, the document traverses this list and calls the *OnUpdate()* method on each view object—except the one referenced in the first argument to *OnUpdate()*—and that causes each view to refresh itself and display the current data from the document object.

■

See Also

- *FAQ 1.3 What components make up the document/view architecture, and how do they relate to each other?*
- *FAQ 1.5 What is the role of the view?*
- *FAQ 1.6 What is the role of the view's frame window?*
- *FAQ 1.7 What is the role of the document template?*
- *FAQ 1.8 What is the role of the document template resource ID?*
- *FAQ 1.9 How do the document/view architecture component objects get created?*

What is the role of the view?

The view is essentially an input-output device connecting the document to the end user:

- As an output device, the view extracts the relevant data from the document and draws, or renders, an appropriate representation of this data on its Windows window. Thus, the view presents the document's data—or at least part of it—to the user.
- As an input device, the view typically intercepts the user's actions with the mouse and the keyboard and updates the document object accordingly.

Note, however, that the main application window and the application's menus and toolbars may also participate in some user inputs and also give the user some feedback on the document's data.

■

Additional Comments

In an interesting and thought-provoking article printed in the August 1995 issue of the *Microsoft Systems Journal*, Allen Holub called his document and view classes *data_interface* and *user_interface*, respectively (see Appendix B).

Although you should read the whole article—as well as two other articles by the same author printed in the August 1996 and December 1996 issues of

Microsoft Systems Journal—to fully understand what those names stand for in the object-oriented design advocated by Holub, the *data_interface* and *user_interface* names convey concisely the essence of the respective roles played by the document and the view classes in the document/view architecture. Recalling those names can often help you decide whether a particular feature belongs in the document or in the view class.

See Also

- *FAQ 1.3 What components make up the document/view architecture, and how do they relate to each other?*
- *FAQ 1.4 What is the role of the document?*
- *FAQ 1.6 What is the role of the view's frame window?*
- *FAQ 1.7 What is the role of the document template?*
- *FAQ 1.8 What is the role of the document template resource ID?*
- *FAQ 1.9 How do the document/view architecture component objects get created?*

FAQ 1.6 What is the role of the view's frame window?

The main role of the view's frame window is to host one or more views—the latter with *splitter* frame windows—as well as various user-interface elements, collectively known as *control bars:* toolbars, status bars, and even dialog bars.

Uncoupling the view's frame window from the view itself allows for a much greater flexibility in user-interface design and makes it easy to mix and match various user-interface elements. For example, the same view class can usually work in either an MDI or an SDI application. Thanks to splitter windows, the view can live alone in its frame window or share it with other views. Toolbars and status bars can be added to the main application window or to child frame windows without the need to change the command-handling logic, and so on.

■

See Also

- *FAQ 1.3 What components make up the document/view architecture, and how do they relate to each other?*
- *FAQ 1.4 What is the role of the document?*
- *FAQ 1.5 What is the role of the view?*
- *FAQ 1.7 What is the role of the document template?*
- *FAQ 1.8 What is the role of the document template resource ID?*
- *FAQ 1.9 How do the document/view architecture component objects get created?*

1.7 What is the role of the document template?

The document template is a special object that helps MFC associate and create the previous three components: the document, the view, and the view's frame window. The document template also stores the resource ID, whose role is described in *FAQ 1.8 What is the role of the document template resource ID?*

To better understand the role of the document template, consider that when the user creates a new document or opens an existing one, MFC must dynamically create the following objects:

- The document object itself
- Its first view object and the associated Windows window
- The frame window hosting this view and the associated Windows window (except in an SDI application in which the view is hosted by the main application window; note that this frame is actually created before the view itself)

How does MFC know which classes it should use to instantiate these objects? Because MFC creates these objects through a document template object that in turn orchestrates—directly or indirectly—the creation of the other "real" objects. The document template object acts as a kind of bridge that enables MFC's code—written by Microsoft developers several years ago—to dynamically create instances of the document, view, and frame window classes that you define in your new code.

You may wish to refer to *FAQ 1.9 How do the document/view architecture component objects get created?* to better understand the role of the document template object and of its *CRuntimeClass* data members during the creation of document, frame window, and view objects.

■

Additional Comments

The kind of dynamic object creation referred to in the preceding section is made possible by a special dynamic creation mechanism provided by MFC's *CObject* class, with some additional help from the *CRuntimeClass* class.

The document template is able to perform this dynamic object creation because it stores pointers to the *CRuntimeClass* objects associated with each of your document, view, and frame window classes. Here is a quick overview of what goes on behind the scenes:

- Each of your document, view, and frame window classes has a *CRuntimeClass* object associated with it, because it derives from *CObject* and uses the *DECLARE_DYNCREATE()* and *IMPLEMENT_DYNCREATE()* macros.
- Each *CRuntimeClass* object can dynamically create a new object of its associated class through the *CRuntimeClass::CreateObject()* function.
- The *RUNTIME_CLASS()* macro used in Listing 1-1 returns a pointer to the *CRuntimeClass* object associated with a given class.
- The document template object contains pointers to the *CRuntimeClass* objects associated with your document, view, and frame window classes. When MFC code needs to create a new instance of one of your objects, it calls *CRuntimeClass::CreateObject()* on the appropriate pointer stored inside the document template object.

A complete discussion of the *CRuntimeClass* class and dynamic object creation is outside the scope of this book, but you can find additional information about this topic on pages 153 and 159 of *MFC Internals* (see Appendix B).

See Also

- *FAQ 1.3 What components make up the document/view architecture, and how do they relate to each other?*
- *FAQ 1.4 What is the role of the document?*
- *FAQ 1.5 What is the role of the view?*
- *FAQ 1.6 What is the role of the view's frame window?*
- *FAQ 1.8 What is the role of the document template resource ID?*
- *FAQ 1.9 How do the document/view architecture component objects get created?*

FAQ 1.8 What is the role of the document template resource ID?

The document template resource ID associates three specific resources with a given document template object:

- *An icon resource.* This icon shows up in the upper-left corner of each frame window object associated with this document template resource ID.
- *A menu resource.* When the user activates a particular frame window, MFC replaces the main application window menu with the menu resource associated with the document template resource ID of the active frame window object. Note that the main application window menu is totally replaced; there is no "merging" of menu commands similar to what happens with the OLE in-place editing feature. Therefore, if you want some menu commands always to appear, you must duplicate them on the individual menu resources associated with each document template resource ID (for MDI applications).
- *A string resource.* This string, called the *document template string*, is composed of seven substrings separated by "\n" characters. MFC uses these substrings on various occasions, as shown in Table 1-1.

Table 1-1. The seven fields of the document template string, for an actual string of "\nMyDoc\nMyDoc\nMyDoc Files (*.myd)\n.myd\nMyDoc.Document\nMyDoc.Document".

Document template string item	Example value	Description
windowTitle	"" (empty)	Frame window's title (used only in SDI applications, normally blank for MDI applications).
docName	"MyDoc"	Default name assigned to new documents of this type. Appears in the frame window's title and in the Save As dialog box (for new documents only).
fileNewName	"MyDoc"	Descriptive name for documents of this type. Appears in the File, New dialog box that MFC pops up when an application registers more than one document template.
filterName	"MyDoc Files (*.myd)"	Descriptive name for documents of this type and associated default file name extension. Appears in the "File type" field of the Open and Save As dialog boxes.
filterExt	".myd"	Default filename extension for documents of this type. *CWinApp::EnableShellOpen()* and *CWinApp::RegisterShellFileTypes()* register this extension with Windows Explorer to allow the user to open a file by double-clicking on it (see *FAQ 2.20*).
regFileTypeId	"MyDoc.Document"	Name that identifies this document type in the Registry (cannot contain spaces). Used by *CWinApp::RegisterShellFileTypes()* to associate the *filterExt* file extension with the application.
regFileTypeName	"MyDoc Document"	Descriptive name for documents of this type (can contain spaces). Appears as the human-readable name in Windows Explorer for files with the *filterExt* extension.

■

Additional Comments

Note that MFC uses the undocumented *AfxExtractSubString()* function to easily retrieve the appropriate part of the document template string. This function is discussed in *FAQ 4.7 How do I implement an expanding dialog box?*.

See Also

- *FAQ 1.3* *What components make up the document/view architecture, and how do they relate to each other?*
- *FAQ 1.4* *What is the role of the document?*
- *FAQ 1.5* *What is the role of the view?*
- *FAQ 1.6* *What is the role of the view's frame window?*
- *FAQ 1.7* *What is the role of the document template?*
- *FAQ 1.9* *How do the document/view architecture component objects get created?*
- *FAQ 2.20* *Why doesn't my application register its document files with Windows Explorer, and how do I correct this situation?*
- *FAQ 4.7* *How do I implement an expanding dialog box?*

FAQ 1.9 How do the document/view architecture component objects get created?

Once you understand the various components that make up the document/view architecture, you may wonder how all those objects get created. Here is a quick overview:

- The application object is a global object and is therefore created when your program starts.
- The application's *InitInstance()* function usually creates one or several document template objects.
- The document template's *OpenDocumentFile()* function creates a new document object, which either remains empty or is loaded from an existing file, as well as the associated frame window (see the later discussion of how and when this function usually gets called).

- When a view's frame window is created, its *OnCreate()* handler, called to process the *WM_CREATE* message, creates the associated view.

Listing 1-2 shows a simplified outline of the function calls that cause *CMultiDocTemplate::OpenDocumentFile()* to create the document, frame window, and view objects.

Listing 1-2. Simplified outline of the function calls that cause *CMultiDocTemplate::OpenDocumentFile()* to create the document, frame window, and view objects.

```
CMultiDocTemplate::OpenDocumentFile()

   CDocTemplate::CreateNewDocument()
      pDocumentClass->CreateObject() // create document

   CDocTemplate::CreateNewFrame()
      pFrameClass->CreateObject()    // create frame window

      CMDIChildWnd::LoadFrame()
         ...
         CMDIChildWnd::OnCreate()    // creating frame...
            ...
            CFrameWnd::OnCreateClient()

               CFrameWnd::CreateView()
                  pViewClass->CreateObject() // create view
```

Note that all the objects created through the document template rely on the dynamic object creation mechanism implemented by *CRuntimeClass::CreateObject()*.

Here are the major MFC functions that end up calling the document template's *OpenDocumentFile()* function:

- The *CWinApp::ProcessShellCommand()* function that is called by your application's *InitInstance()* function to process the potential command-line arguments. See *FAQ 2.6 How do I prevent an MDI application from opening a new (empty) document at start-up?* for a discussion of how a standard AppWizard application creates its initial (empty) document on start-up.
- The *CWinApp::OnFileNew()* and *CWinApp::OnFileOpen()* functions that are called when the user selects the "File, New" and "File, Open" menu commands. See *FAQ 1.11 How does MFC implement the standard menu commands?* for additional information on the program flow of these menu commands.

- The *CWinApp::OnOpenRecentFile()* function that is called when the user selects a file from the MRU (most recently used) file list.

■

See Also

- *FAQ 1.3 What components make up the document/view architecture, and how do they relate to each other?*
- *FAQ 1.7 What is the role of the document template?*
- *FAQ 1.11 How does MFC implement the standard menu commands?*
- *FAQ 2.6 How do I prevent an MDI application from opening a new (empty) document at start-up?*

FAQ 1.10 How does MFC route command messages?

One of the most perplexing things about MFC message routing is how *command messages* are handled—that is, the *WM_COMMAND* and *WM_NOTIFY* messages that are generated when the user selects a menu item or clicks on a toolbar button. Think about it: how does MFC manage to let you handle a command message in almost any class—document, view, frame window, application, and so on? For that matter, why do nonwindow objects such as documents and applications have message maps, and how do they receive a command message?

I will try to present the essential concepts needed to answer these questions. If you want to thoroughly understand the important and complex topic of MFC message and command routing, I urge you to read the article "Meandering Through the Maze of MFC Message and Command Routing" (see Appendix B).

The short answer to both of the preceding questions is that MFC provides a custom command routing mechanism that explicitly gives nonwindow classes a chance to handle command messages as long as these classes derive from *CCmdTarget*. Most of the logic for this command message routing is implemented through the virtual *CCmdTarget::OnCmdMsg()* function. This base class function searches the class's message map for a command handler, whereas derived classes—such as *CFrameWnd*, *CView*, and *CDocument*—override *OnCmdMsg()* to perform their custom command message routing. As an example, Listing 1-3 shows the pseudocode for the important *CFrameWnd::OnCmdMsg()* function (WinFrm.cpp).

Listing 1-3. Pseudocode for the *CFrameWnd::OnCmdMsg()* function (WinFrm.cpp).

```
BOOL CFrameWnd::OnCmdMsg(UINT nID, int nCode, void* pExtra,
                         AFX_CMDHANDLERINFO* pHandlerInfo)
{
   // 1 - Route command to active view FIRST
   CView* pView = GetActiveView();
   if (pView != NULL && pView->OnCmdMsg(nID, nCode, pExtra,
                                         pHandlerInfo))
      return TRUE;

   // 2 - Try to handle command ourselves
   if (CWnd::OnCmdMsg(nID, nCode, pExtra, pHandlerInfo))
      return TRUE;

   // 3 - Finally, route command to the application
   CWinApp* pApp = AfxGetApp();
   if (pApp != NULL && pApp->OnCmdMsg(nID, nCode, pExtra,
                                       pHandlerInfo))
      return TRUE;

   return FALSE;
}
```

As you can see in Listing 1-3, the frame window lets its active view try to handle the command; if the view does not handle the command, the frame window searches its own message map; if this search also fails to locate a handler, the frame window sends the message to the application object. Things are actually a little more complicated than this, because the view's *OnCmdMsg()* function also calls the document's *OnCmdMsg()* function, which in turn calls the document template's *OnCmdMsg()* function.

Figure 1-5 shows the complete command message dispatching through the various components of the document/view architecture. Listing 1-4 shows a simplified outline of the related function calls.

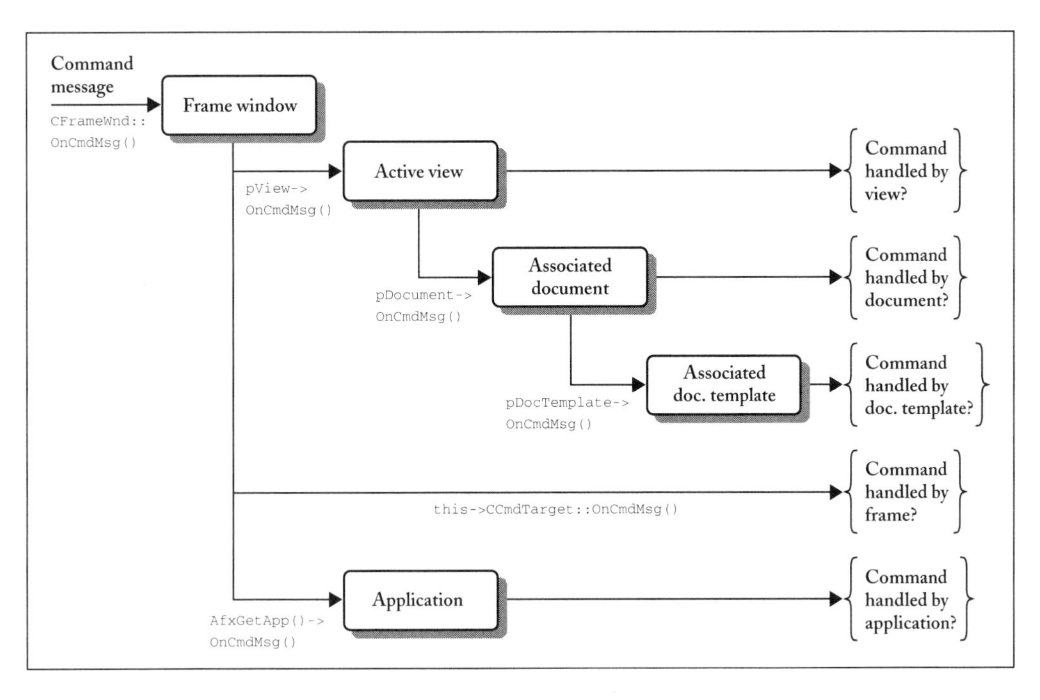

Figure 1-5. Command message dispatching through the various components of the document/view architecture. The right-hand column shows the priority order in which each command target gets a chance to handle a command message.

Listing 1-4. Simplified outline of the various function calls that dispatch a command message through the various components of the document/view architecture.

```
CWnd::WindowProc()
   CWnd::OnWndMsg()

      CWnd::OnCommand()  // special handling for
                         // command messages

         CFrameWnd::OnCmdMsg() // route to frame window

            CView::OnCmdMsg()  // route to active view
               CCmdTarget::OnCmdMsg()  // handled by view?

               CDocument::OnCmdMsg()   // route to document
                  CCmdTarget::OnCmdMsg() // handled by doc?
```

```
            CDocTemplate::OnCmdMsg()   // route to doc
                                       // template
              CCmdTarget::OnCmdMsg()   // handled by
                                       // doc template?

      CCmdTarget::OnCmdMsg()   // handled by frame?

      CWinApp::OnCmdMsg()   // route to application
```

As you can see in Listing 1-4, the command messages enjoy a special treatment early in MFC's message dispatching mechanism through the *CWnd::OnCommand()* function, which in turn starts the chain of calls to the various *OnCmdMsg()* functions.

Note that the *CMDIFrameWnd::OnCmdMsg()* function that gets called for the main frame window of an MDI application first calls its active MDI child frame window's *OnCmdMsg()* function before calling its own base class's *CFrameWnd::OnCmdMsg()* function. This arrangement gives the active MDI child frame window a chance to have its own command message handlers.

Finally, note that the exact same routing mechanism is used for the *UPDATE_COMMAND_UI* messages that you can handle to give the user visual feedback about the state of your application.

■

See Also

- *FAQ 1.11 How does MFC implement the standard menu commands?*

FAQ 1.11 How does MFC implement the standard menu commands?

Several techniques discussed in the following chapters show how to better control a specific user action, such as creating a new document, closing the active document, and opening a new window on a document. However, before modifying MFC's standard behavior, you should understand how MFC implements the standard menu commands. Table 1-2 provides a quick road map to the MFC code that handles the main standard menu commands, highlighting the most important overridable functions. Do not be afraid if some implementations, such as the "File, New" or "File, Open" menu commands, look rather daunting. You will understand them better after reading the related FAQs in the following chapters.

■

See Also

- *FAQ 1.3 What components make up the document/view architecture and how do they relate to each other?*
- *FAQ 1.9 How do the document/view architecture component objects get created?*
- *FAQ 1.10 How does MFC route command messages?*

Table 1-2. Overview of MFC's implementation of the main standard menu commands (for an MDI application).

Menu command	Command ID	Purpose	Implementation
File, New	ID_FILE_NEW	Create	**CWinApp::OnFileNew()**
		a new	CDocManager::OnFileNew()
		document	**CMultiDocTemplate::OpenDocumentFile(NULL)**
			CDocTemplate::CreateNewDocument()
			pDocumentClass->CreateObject()
			// document constructor called
			CMultiDocTemplate::AddDocument()
			CDocTemplate::CreateNewFrame()
			pFrameClass->CreateObject()
			// frame constructor called
			CMDIChildWnd::LoadFrame()
			CMDIChildWnd::Create()
			CMDIChildWnd::OnCreate()
			CFrameWnd::OnCreateHelper()
			CFrameWnd::OnCreateClient()
			CFrameWnd::CreateView()
			pViewClass->CreateObject()
			// view constructor called
			CWnd::Create()
			CDocument::OnNewDocument()
			CDocument::DeleteContents()
			CDocTemplate::InitialUpdateFrame()
			CFrameWnd::InitialUpdateFrame()
			CView::OnInitialUpdate()

Table 1-2. *(Cont.)*

Menu command	Command ID	Purpose	Implementation

File, Open	ID_FILE_OPEN	Open an existing document	`CWinApp::OnFileOpen()`
			`CDocManager::OnFileOpen()`
			`CDocManager::DoPromptFileName()`
			`CWinApp::OpenDocumentFile(lpszFileName)`
			`CDocManager::OpenDocumentFile(lpszFileName)`
			`CMultiDocTemplate::OpenDocumentFile(`
			`lpszFileName)`
			`CDocTemplate::CreateNewDocument()`
			`pDocumentClass->CreateObject()`
			`// document constructor called`
			`CMultiDocTemplate::AddDocument()`
			`CDocTemplate::CreateNewFrame()`
			`pFrameClass->CreateObject()`
			`// frame constructor called`
			`CMDIChildWnd::LoadFrame()`
			`CMDIChildWnd::Create()`
			`CMDIChildWnd::OnCreate()`
			`CFrameWnd::OnCreateHelper()`
			`CFrameWnd::OnCreateClient()`
			`CFrameWnd::CreateView()`
			`pViewClass->`
			`CreateObject()`
			`// view constructor called`
			`CWnd::Create()`
			`CDocument::OnOpenDocument()`
			`CDocument::DeleteContents()`
			`CDocument::Serialize()`
			`CDocTemplate::InitialUpdateFrame()`
			`CFrameWnd::InitialUpdateFrame()`
			`CView::OnInitialUpdate()`

File, Close	ID_FILE_CLOSE	Close the active document	`CDocument::OnFileClose()`
			`CDocument::SaveModified()`
			`CDocument::DoFileSave()`
			`CDocument::OnCloseDocument()`
			`// frame windows and views destroyed`
			`// document destructor called`

File, Save	ID_FILE_SAVE	Save the active document	`CDocument::OnFileSave()`
			`CDocument::DoFileSave()`
			`CDocument::DoSave(lpszPathName)`
			`CDocument::OnSaveDocument()`
			`CDocument::Serialize()`

Table 1-2. *(Cont.)*

Menu command	Command ID	Purpose	Implementation
File, Save As	ID_FILE_ SAVE_AS	Save the active document with a new name	**CDocument::OnFileSaveAs()** CDocument::DoSave(NULL) CWinApp::DoPromptFileName() **CDocument::OnSaveDocument()** **CDocument::Serialize()**
File, Print	ID_FILE_ PRINT	Print the active document	**CView::OnFilePrint()** **CView::OnPreparePrinting()** CView::DoPreparePrinting() **CView::OnBeginPrinting()** CDC::StartDoc() **CView::OnPrepareDC()** CDC::StartPage() **CView::OnPrepareDC()** **CView::OnPrint()** CDC::EndPage() CDC::EndDoc() **CView::OnEndPrinting()**
File, Print Preview	ID_FILE_ PRINT_ PREVIEW	Print preview the active document	**CView::OnFilePrintPreview()** CView::DoPrintPreview()
File, Print Setup	ID_FILE_ PRINT_ SETUP	Change the printer and printing options	**CWinApp::OnFilePrintSetup()** CWinApp::DoPrintDialog()
File, Recent File	ID_FILE_MRU_ FILE1 to ID_FILE_ MRU_FILE16	Open a recent document file	**CWinApp::OnOpenRecentFile()** **CWinApp::OpenDocumentFile(lpszFileName)** // same as File, Open

File, Exit	ID_APP_EXIT	Exit the application	**CWinApp::OnAppExit()**
			m_pMainWnd->SendMessage(WM_CLOSE)
			CFrameWnd::OnClose()
			CWinApp::SaveAllModified()
			CWinApp::CloseAllDocuments()
			CDocManager::CloseAllDocuments()
			CDocTemplate::CloseAllDocuments()
			CDocument::OnCloseDocument()
			// frame windows and views destroyed
			// document destructor called

Table 1-2. *(Cont.)*

Menu command	Command ID	Purpose	Implementation
View, Toolbar	ID_VIEW_ TOOLBAR	Show or hide the main frame toolbar	**CFrameWnd::OnBarCheck()** CFrameWnd::ShowControlBar()
View, Status Bar	ID_VIEW_ STATUS_BAR	Show or hide the main frame status bar	**CFrameWnd::OnBarCheck()** CFrameWnd::ShowControlBar()

Window, New Window	ID_ WINDOW_ NEW	Open another window for the active document	**CMDIFrameWnd::OnWindowNew()**
			   CDocTemplate::CreateNewFrame()
			      pFrameClass->CreateObject()
			         // frame constructor called
			      CMDIChildWnd::LoadFrame()
			         CMDIChildWnd::Create()
			            CMDIChildWnd::OnCreate()
			               CFrameWnd::OnCreateHelper()
			                  CFrameWnd::OnCreateClient()
			                     CFrameWnd::CreateView()
			                        pViewClass->CreateObject()
			                           // view constructor called
			                        CWnd::Create()
			   CDocTemplate::InitialUpdateFrame()
			      CFrameWnd::InitialUpdateFrame()

2 DOCUMENTS AND DOCUMENT TEMPLATES

Documents and document templates are two of the fundamental elements of the document/view architecture. The other elements, such as the view itself and its parent frame window, are the subject of Chapter 3.

The importance of correctly managing documents, especially multiple document templates, is often underestimated in the MFC documentation and in many books about MFC programming. As *FAQ 2.1 How should I create and reference multiple document templates in my application?* shows, even the standard AppWizard-generated code does not adequately address the issue of managing multiple document templates, although most MFC applications—all but the most basic ones—eventually end up using more than one document template.

The FAQs in this chapter address this issue and demonstrate many other useful techniques for dealing with documents and document templates and for adding useful features to your MFC applications.

Although these items may not be as visible to your application's users as those discussed in the following chapters—views, dialog boxes, control bars, and so on—they form the foundation for a large part of your application's functionality. Therefore, even if this chapter's topics do not seem as jazzy or cool as those presented later in this book, I advise you to take some time to understand the issues involved. This initial effort will pay back in the long run—and maybe even before!

Managing Document Templates

2.1 How should I create and reference multiple document templates in my application?

This problem usually shows up as soon as you discover the power of using multiple document template objects in your application. That will happen sooner than you might think, especially when you will try to apply some of the FAQs in this chapter and in the following one.

Unfortunately, the standard AppWizard-generated code shown in Listing 2-1 does not store the pointer to the document template object that is dynamically created in the *InitInstance()* function.

Listing 2-1. The AppWizard-generated code for the *InitInstance()* function does not store the pointer to the document template object.

```
BOOL CMyApp::InitInstance()
{
// ...

   // Register the application's document templates.
   // Document templates serve as the connection between
   // documents, frame windows, and views.

   // The pDocTemplate pointer is "lost" when the flow of
   // control leaves the InitInstance() function
   CMultiDocTemplate* pDocTemplate;
   pDocTemplate = new CMultiDocTemplate(
      IDR_MYDOCTYPE,
      RUNTIME_CLASS(CMyDoc),
      RUNTIME_CLASS(CChildFrame), // custom MDI child frame
      RUNTIME_CLASS(CMyView));
   AddDocTemplate(pDocTemplate);

// ...
}
```

If you follow the logic shown in Listing 2-1 when adding new document template objects to your application, you lose the ability to directly reference these objects in your code because the value stored in the *pDocTemplate* pointer is lost each time you create a new document template object. This is problematic, because several techniques shown elsewhere in this chapter rely on the ability to select a specific document template object and ask it to carry out some action—for example, to create a new document and its associated view and frame window.

Thus, you need to store pointers to your document template objects in a way that will make them readily accessible from any function in your project. The easiest solution is usually to store these pointers as *public* member variables in your application class, as shown in Listing 2-2.

Listing 2-2. Storing pointers to document template objects in your application class.

```
// ------------------------------------
// Class definition for CMyApp (MyApp.h)

class CMyApp : public CWinApp
{
// ...
public:
   // Member variables used to store the various
   // document templates objects that we create in
   // InitInstance()
   CMultiDocTemplate* m_ptTemplate1;
   CMultiDocTemplate* m_ptTemplate2;
   CMultiDocTemplate* m_ptTemplate3;

// ...
};

// ------------------------------------
// Implementation for CMyApp (MyApp.cpp)

BOOL CMyApp::InitInstance()
{
// ...

   // Create all our document template objects
   // and store pointers to them in our member
   // variables
```

```
    m_ptTemplate1 = new CMultiDocTemplate(
            IDR_MYDOCTYPE1,
            RUNTIME_CLASS(CMyDoc1),
            RUNTIME_CLASS(CMyChildFrame1),
            RUNTIME_CLASS(CMyView1));
    AddDocTemplate(m_ptTemplate1);

    m_ptTemplate2 = new CMultiDocTemplate(
            IDR_MYDOCTYPE2,
            RUNTIME_CLASS(CMyDoc2),
            RUNTIME_CLASS(CMyChildFrame2),
            RUNTIME_CLASS(CMyView2));
    AddDocTemplate(m_ptTemplate2);

    m_ptTemplate3 = new CMultiDocTemplate(
            IDR_MYDOCTYPE3,
            RUNTIME_CLASS(CMyDoc3),
            RUNTIME_CLASS(CMyChildFrame3),
            RUNTIME_CLASS(CMyView3));
    AddDocTemplate(m_ptTemplate3);

// ...
}
```

Then, in any function belonging to your project, you can easily reference one of your document template objects by using this syntax:

```
CDocTemplate* ptTemplate = theApp.m_ptTemplate1;
// (could have selected m_ptTemplate2 or m_ptTemplate3)
// ... Use ptTemplate ...
```

■

Additional Comments

Using multiple document templates in an MFC application usually means that you must be careful about some additional issues, such as those discussed in *FAQ 2.2 How do I manage multiple document templates without having a dialog box pop up each time the user tries to create a new document?* and *FAQ 2.4 How does MFC select the document template object to use when opening a file?*

Note that you do not need to apply the *delete* operator to the pointers that are passed to the *AddDocTemplate()* function: the standard *CWinApp* destructor will take care of deleting those objects.

Sample Code

There is no sample project for this FAQ.

See Also

- *FAQ 2.2 How do I manage multiple document templates without having a dialog box pop up each time the user tries to create a new document?*
- *FAQ 2.4 How does MFC select the document template object to use when opening a file?*

FAQ 2.2 How do I manage multiple document templates without having a dialog box pop up each time the user tries to create a new document?

As soon as you start to use more than one document template object, MFC pops up a New dialog box such as the one shown in Figure 2-1.

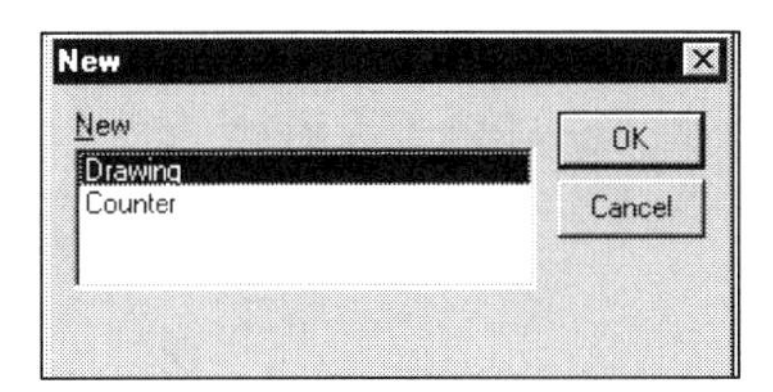

Figure 2-1. The standard MFC dialog box that prompts the user to select a document template object.

This dialog box is first shown when your application is started and afterward each time the user selects the "File, New" menu command.

Following these steps will help you replace the standard MFC behavior by the one that best suits your needs:

Step 1. Create the various document template objects in your application's *InitInstance()* function and store a pointer to each of those objects in a member variable of your application class (as explained in *FAQ 2.1 How should I create and reference multiple document templates in my application?*).

Step 2. Use ClassWizard to add a handler for the "File, New" menu command to your application class. In your handler, select among the pointer member variables stored in step 1 the one that points to the document template object that you want to use as your default template. Call the *OpenDocumentFile()* function through this pointer, passing a *NULL* parameter to request the creation of a new (empty) document, as shown in Listing 2-3.

Listing 2-3. Selecting the default document template in the *OnFileNew()* function.

```
void CMyApp::OnFileNew()
{
   // m_ptDefaultTemplate is the member variable pointing
   // to the document template object that you want to
   // use by default when the user selects the "File, New"
   // menu command
   m_ptDefaultTemplate->OpenDocumentFile( NULL );
}
```

Step 3. Make sure that the document template resource strings for all the document template objects *other* than your default one have an *empty fileNewName* substring. (The reason for this step is given in the Explanations section along with a way to skip this step.)

Now, when your application starts or when the user selects the "File, New" menu command, your default document template object—the one pointed to by *m_ptDefaultTemplate* in Listing 2-3—will be used to create the new document, without MFC showing any dialog box to the user.

Remember that you will probably have to program some alternate ways of using your other document template objects, because you have now bypassed the standard way provided by the New dialog box. For an explanation about how to implement this last step, refer to *FAQ 2.7 How do I programmatically create a new (empty) document?*

■

Explanations

When you register more than one document template object by calling *AddDocTemplate()* in your application's *InitInstance()* function, MFC has no way of knowing which of those document template objects it should use to fulfill the user's "File, New" request. Therefore, MFC pops up a dialog box listing the various registered document template objects to allow the user to indicate which one should be used to call *CDocTemplate::OpenDocumentFile()*. You can understand this logic by reading the source code for *CWinApp::OnFileNew()*, which is shown in Listing 2-4.

Listing 2-4. Pseudocode for the *CWinApp::OnFileNew()* function.

```
// ------------------------------------------------
// AppDlg.cpp

void CWinApp::OnFileNew()
{
   if (m_pDocManager != NULL)
      // 1 - Simply delegate call to
      // CDocManager::OnFileNew()
      m_pDocManager->OnFileNew();
}

// ------------------------------------------------
// DocMgr.cpp

void CDocManager::OnFileNew()
{
   if (m_templateList.IsEmpty())
   {
      TRACE0("Error: no document templates registered"
             "with CWinApp.\n");
      AfxMessageBox(AFX_IDP_FAILED_TO_CREATE_DOC);
      return;
   }

   // 2 - By default, select the first document template
   // object
   CDocTemplate* pTemplate =
         (CDocTemplate*)m_templateList.GetHead();

   // 3 - If more than one registered document template
   // object, pop up "New" dialog box
   if (m_templateList.GetCount() > 1)
   {
      // more than one document template to choose from
      // bring up dialog prompting user
```

```
        CNewTypeDlg dlg(&m_templateList);
        int nID = dlg.DoModal();
        if (nID == IDOK)
            // 4 - Store pointer to selected template object
            pTemplate = dlg.m_pSelectedTemplate;
        else
            return;      // none - cancel operation
    }

    // 5 - Use the selected document template object to
    // create the new document, frame window, and view
    pTemplate->OpenDocumentFile(NULL);
        // if returns NULL, the user has already been alerted
}
```

When you implement steps 1 and 2 of the preceding solution, the standard MFC message mapping mechanism ensures that your own handler will be called instead of the default *CWinApp::OnFileNew()* function when the user selects the "File, New" menu command.

Step 3 requires a little additional explanation: When your application is launched, the standard AppWizard-generated code in *InitInstance()* causes *CWinApp::OnFileNew()* to be called directly (by *ProcessShellCommand()*) without invoking the message mapping mechanism. Hence, without an additional precaution, your application would still display the New dialog box upon launch.

The trick lies in the fact that the *CNewTypeDlg* class used by the code in Listing 2-4 shows in its list only the document template objects that have a non-empty *fileNewName* substring in their associated document template resource string. If only one document template object satisfies this condition, this object is automatically returned as the "selected" one and the dialog box is not shown. To better understand this behavior, look at the pseudocode for *CNewTypeDlg::InitDialog()*, which is shown in Listing 2-5.

Listing 2-5. Pseudocode for the *CNewTypeDlg::InitDialog()* function (DocMgr.cpp).

```
BOOL CNewTypeDlg::OnInitDialog()
{
    // 1 - Get a pointer to the listbox on the dialog box
    CListBox* pListBox =
            (CListBox*)GetDlgItem(AFX_IDC_LISTBOX);

    // fill with document templates in list
    pListBox->ResetContent();
```

```
// 2 - Iterate through the application's document
// templates list
POSITION pos = m_pList->GetHeadPosition();
// add all the CDocTemplates in the list by name
while (pos != NULL)
{
   // 3 - For each document template object...
   CDocTemplate* pTemplate =
        (CDocTemplate*)m_pList->GetNext(pos);

   // 4 - Check if the "fileNewName" substring is
   // not empty before adding the string to the
   // listbox
   CString strTypeName;
   if (pTemplate->GetDocString(strTypeName,
                 CDocTemplate::fileNewName)
      && !strTypeName.IsEmpty())
   {
      // add it to the listbox
      int nIndex = pListBox->AddString(strTypeName);
      // ...
      pListBox->SetItemDataPtr(nIndex, pTemplate);
   }
}

int nTemplates = pListBox->GetCount();

if (nTemplates == 0)
{
   // 5 - If empty list => error !
   TRACE0("Error: no document templates to"
          "select from!\n");
   EndDialog(-1); // abort
}
else if (nTemplates == 1)
{
   // 6 - If only one item => automatically select
   // this document template object, and do NOT show
   // the dialog box
   m_pSelectedTemplate =
      (CDocTemplate*)pListBox->GetItemDataPtr(0);
   EndDialog(IDOK);    // done
```

```
    }
    else
    {
        // set selection to the first one (NOT SORTED)
        pListBox->SetCurSel(0);
    }

    // 7 - If we get here, the "New" dialog box will appear
    return CDialog::OnInitDialog();
}
```

Note that you can simply skip step 3 of the preceding solution if you use the technique shown in *FAQ 2.6 How do I prevent an MDI application from opening a new (empty) document at start-up?* to prevent your application from creating a new document at start-up.

■

Additional Comments

Another solution to avoid the New dialog box is to add only the default document template object to the list maintained by the application by calling *AddDocTemplate()* only for this object. In this case, remember to apply the *delete* operator on each pointer that you did *not* pass to *AddDocTemplate()*. Implement this cleanup in your application's *ExitInstance()* function, as shown in Listing 2-6.

Listing 2-6. Calling *AddDocTemplate()* only for one document template object.

```
BOOL CMyApp::InitInstance()
{
// ...

    // Create all our document template objects
    // and store pointers to them in our member
    // variables
    m_ptTemplate1 = new CMultiDocTemplate(
            IDR_MYDOCTYPE1,
            RUNTIME_CLASS(CMyDoc1),
            RUNTIME_CLASS(CMyChildFrame1),
            RUNTIME_CLASS(CMyView1));
    // Call AddDocTemplate() for only ONE document template
    // object
    AddDocTemplate(m_ptTemplate1);
```

```
    m_ptTemplate2 = new CMultiDocTemplate(
            IDR_MYDOCTYPE2,
            RUNTIME_CLASS(CMyDoc2),
            RUNTIME_CLASS(CMyChildFrame2),
            RUNTIME_CLASS(CMyView2));

    m_ptTemplate3 = new CMultiDocTemplate(
            IDR_MYDOCTYPE3,
            RUNTIME_CLASS(CMyDoc3),
            RUNTIME_CLASS(CMyChildFrame3),
            RUNTIME_CLASS(CMyView3));

// ...
}

int CMyApp::ExitInstance()
{
// ...

    // Destroy only the objects that were NOT passed to
    // AddDocTemplate()
    delete m_ptTemplate2;
    delete m_ptTemplate3;

// ...

}
```

If you decide to use this last method, you should note that it invalidates certain assumptions made by MFC with respect to the registration of all the document template objects. This situation may also break other techniques discussed elsewhere in this chapter, especially those that iterate through the list of document template objects maintained by the application: for example, *FAQ 2.11 How do I implement a "Save all documents" menu command that does not prompt the user before saving each modified document?; FAQ 2.13 How do I implement a "Close all documents" menu command?* and *FAQ 2.19 How do I iterate through the list of all the currently opened documents?*

Sample Code

There is no sample project for this FAQ.

See Also

- *FAQ 2.1 How should I create and reference multiple document templates in my application?*
- *FAQ 2.6 How do I prevent an MDI application from opening a new (empty) document at start-up?*
- *FAQ 2.7 How do I programmatically create a new (empty) document?*

FAQ 2.3 How do I create the resources associated with a new document template resource ID?

In MFC programming, you often need to create additional document template objects in order to reference and "glue together" different kinds of documents, views, or frame windows. When you create such a new document template object, you usually need to specify a new document template resource ID. Even if you do not need any specific menu, this resource ID is needed to define a new document template string that will prevent MFC from showing its New dialog box when the user invokes the "File, New" menu command. For a complete discussion of these issues, see *FAQ 2.1 How should I create and reference multiple document templates in my application?* and *FAQ 2.2 How do I manage several document templates without having a dialog box pop up each time the user tries to create a new document?*

To put the following steps into a meaningful context, we will assume that your application's *InitInstance()* function registers its default document template as shown in Listing 2-7.

Listing 2-7. Default document template registered in *CMDIApp::InitInstance()*.

```
BOOL CMDIApp::InitInstance()
{
// ...

    // 'Drawing' document template
    m_ptDrawView = new CMultiDocTemplate(
        IDR_DRAWTYPE,
```

```
        RUNTIME_CLASS(CDrawDoc),
        RUNTIME_CLASS(CChildFrame), // custom MDI child frame
        RUNTIME_CLASS(CDrawView));
    AddDocTemplate(m_ptDrawView);

// ...
}
```

In the preceding code fragment, the document class is called *CDrawDoc* and the default view class is called *CDrawView*. The document template whose address is stored in the *m_ptDrawView* variable has a resource ID called *IDR_DRAWTYPE*.

The following steps show how you can create the resources associated with a new document template resource ID that we will call *IDR_NEWDRAWTYPE* for these explanations.

Step 1. Create a new resource symbol with an ID called *IDR_NEWDRAWTYPE*. You can carry out this task in Developer Studio by selecting the "View, Resource Symbols" menu command and by clicking the New button on the dialog box that pops up, as shown in Figure 2-2.

Step 2. Copy the existing *IDR_DRAWTYPE* menu and icon resources: select each resource in the ResourceView pane of Developer Studio and then execute the "Edit, Copy" and "Edit, Paste" menu commands. Developer Studio will name your new resources with a new ID called *IDR_DRAWTYPE1*.

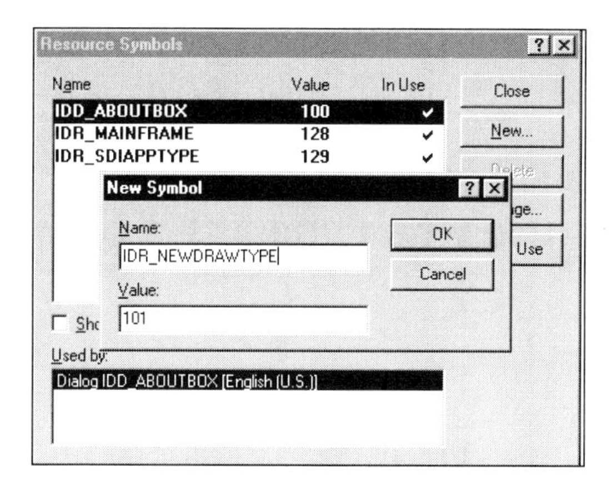

Figure 2-2. Creating a new resource symbol with Developer Studio.

Step 3. Change the ID of the new resources to *IDR_NEWDRAWTYPE*. Select each *IDR_DRAWTYPE1* resource in the ResourceView pane of Developer Studio and then execute the "Edit, Properties" menu command and replace the *IDR_DRAWTYPE1* resource ID with *IDR_NEWDRAWTYPE*.

Step 4. Create the new *IDR_NEWDRAWTYPE* resource template string. Open the String Table resource, select the existing *IDR_DRAWTYPE* string resource, and duplicate it with the "Edit, Copy" and "Edit, Paste" menu commands. Developer Studio creates a new string with an ID of *IDR_DRAWTYPE1*. Immediately select the "Edit, Properties" menu command and modify this string as follows:

Step 4a. Replace the *IDR_DRAWTYPE1* resource ID with *IDR_NEWDRAWTYPE*.

Step 4b. Edit the *IDR_NEWDRAWTYPE* resource template string and empty the *fileNewName* so that the additional document template that you are creating does not show up in the New dialog box that MFC may pop up. (For more information on this particular point, see *FAQ 2.2 How do I manage several document templates without having a dialog box pop up each time the user tries to create a new document?*)

■

Sample Code

There is no sample project for this FAQ.

FAQ 2.4 How does MFC select the document template object to use when opening a file?

When *CWinApp::OpenDocumentFile()* is called with a particular filename as an argument—either from your own code or because the user selected the "File, Open" menu command—how does MFC select the document template object to use for opening the given file?

You certainly understand that the file's extension and the *filterExt* substring of the document template string play a role here, but what happens if the user tries to open a file whose extension does not match any registered document template object's *filterExt* substring?

If you trace through a call to the *CWinApp::OpenDocumentFile()* function (AppUI.cpp), you will find that this function simply calls the *CDocManager::OpenDocumentFile()* function (DocMgr.cpp) through the *m_pDocManager* pointer stored in the application object. This last function does all the work of selecting the "best" document template object to use based on the file's extension.

To implement this selection process, *CDocManager::OpenDocumentFile()* iterates through its list of document template objects and calls the function *CDocTemplate::MatchDocType()* (DocTempl.cpp) for each member of this list, passing as an argument the filename of the document to be opened.

CDocTemplate::MatchDocType() in turn implements the following logic:

1. Iterate through the list of all the document objects opened with this particular document template and find whether one of them has the same filename as our argument. If it does, return a pointer to this document object along with a *confidence rating* of *yesAlreadyOpen*.
2. If the filename does not match any open document, check whether its extension matches the *filterExt* substring of the document template string. If it does, return a confidence rating of *yesAttemptNative*.
3. Otherwise, return a confidence rating of *yesAttemptForeign*.

During its iterations, *CDocManager::OpenDocumentFile()* keeps a pointer to the document template object that provided the best confidence rating. This best rating determines the action that *CDocManager::OpenDocumentFile()* will take next:

- If the filename argument matches an already opened document object (rating = *yesAlreadyOpen*), activate this document's frame window and view.
- Otherwise, if the filename extension matches the *filterExt* substring of one document template object (rating = *yesAttemptNative*), use this object as the best template candidate and call its *OpenDocumentFile()* function.
- If the filename extension does not match any document template object's *filterExt* substring (rating = *yesAttemptForeign*), arbitrarily select the first registered document template object as the best match and call its *OpenDocumentFile()* function. Note that this arbitrary choice may quite often be wrong. In this case, the document object's *Serialize()* function will

probably trigger an exception, which will be caught by the default handler in the *CDocument::OnOpenDocument()* function (DocCore.cpp) and display an error message.

You can deduce from the preceding discussion that if you want one of your document template objects to be used as the default template for any file whose extension does not match any particular *filterExt* substring, this default document template object should be the first one to be registered with *AddDocTemplate()*.

Listing 2-8 shows the pseudocode for the various functions involved in a call to *CWinApp::OpenDocumentFile()*.

Listing 2-8. Pseudocode for *CWinApp::OpenDocumentFile()*.

```
// ─────────────────────────
// AppUI.cpp

CDocument* CWinApp::OpenDocumentFile(LPCTSTR lpszFileName)
{
   ASSERT(m_pDocManager != NULL);
   // 1 - Simply delegate call to
   // CDocManager::OpenDocumentFile()
   return m_pDocManager->OpenDocumentFile(lpszFileName);
}

// ─────────────────────────
// DocMgr.cpp

CDocument* CDocManager::OpenDocumentFile(
                                    LPCTSTR lpszFileName)
{
   // 2 - Iterate through the application's document
   // templates list
   POSITION pos = m_templateList.GetHeadPosition();
   CDocTemplate::Confidence bestMatch =
                              CDocTemplate::noAttempt;
   CDocTemplate* pBestTemplate = NULL;
   CDocument* pOpenDocument = NULL;

   TCHAR szPath[_MAX_PATH];
   // ...
   // Make sure filename is correct, resolve shortcuts,
```

```
// etc. Store result in szPath.
// ...

while (pos != NULL)
{
   // 3 - For each document template object...
   CDocTemplate* pTemplate =
       (CDocTemplate*)m_templateList.GetNext(pos);

   // 4 - Caclulate "confidence rating" for this
   // document template object
   CDocTemplate::Confidence match;
   match = pTemplate->MatchDocType(szPath,
                                   pOpenDocument);

   // 5 - Store best match so far
   if (match > bestMatch)
   {
      bestMatch = match;
      pBestTemplate = pTemplate;
   }

   // 6 - Break out if the filename matches an already
   // opened document object
   if (match == CDocTemplate::yesAlreadyOpen)
      break;       // stop here
}

if (pOpenDocument != NULL)
{
   // 7 - If we found an already opened document object,
   // activate its frame window and view and return its
   // address

   // ...
   // Frame and view activation code omitted
   // ...

   return pOpenDocument;
}
```

```
   // 8 - No "best" template => error !
   if (pBestTemplate == NULL)
   {
      AfxMessageBox(AFX_IDP_FAILED_TO_OPEN_DOC);
      return NULL;
   }

   // 9 - Use the "best" document template object to open
   // the given filename
   return pBestTemplate->OpenDocumentFile(szPath);
}

// ----------------------------
// DocTempl.cpp

CDocTemplate::Confidence CDocTemplate::MatchDocType(
                                    LPCTSTR lpszPathName,
                                    CDocument*& rpDocMatch)
{
   rpDocMatch = NULL;

   // 10 - For each document object...
   POSITION pos = GetFirstDocPosition();
   while (pos != NULL)
   {
      CDocument* pDoc = GetNextDoc(pos);
      if (AfxComparePath(pDoc->GetPathName(),
                         lpszPathName))
      {
         // 11 - If the requested filename matches an
         // already opened document, return its address
         rpDocMatch = pDoc;
         return yesAlreadyOpen;
      }
   }

   // 12 - Get the default extension of the current
   // document object
   CString strFilterExt;
   if (GetDocString(strFilterExt, CDocTemplate::filterExt)
       && !strFilterExt.IsEmpty())
   {
```

```
        // see if extension matches
        LPCTSTR lpszDot = _tcsrchr(lpszPathName, '.');
        if (lpszDot != NULL && lstrcmpi(lpszDot,
                                        strFilterExt) == 0)
            // 13 - Extension matches!
            return yesAttemptNative;
    }

    // 14 - Extension does not match...
    return yesAttemptForeign;
}
```

■

Sample Code

There is no sample project for this FAQ.

How do I associate multiple file extensions with the same document or view class?

Sometimes, you would like your application to have one unique document class or view class (or both) associated with different file extensions. For example, a simple ASCII text file viewer should be able to read files with extensions such as .TXT, .ASC, or .INI. Any of these extensions should map to the same document and view class. How can we trick MFC into accepting this behavior?

As we explained in *FAQ 2.4 How does MFC select the document template object to use when opening a file?*, the algorithm used by MFC is essentially based on the file's extension, which gets compared with the *filterExt* substring of each registered document template's resource string.

However, each document template object can be associated with only *one* resource string and therefore with no more than one file extension—"no more than one" because the *filterExt* substring can be left empty. Therefore, you will need to create (usually in your application's *InitInstance()* function) one distinct document template object for each file extension that you want to use in your application. Remember that the document template constructor takes the following four arguments:

- A resource ID
- A document class
- A frame window class
- A view class

Each of the additional document template objects that you will create will share the *same* arguments as your initial document template object for the document, frame window, and view classes, because you want to handle the various file extensions using the same C++ classes. However, each of these document template objects will have a *distinct* resource ID. This arrangement will allow you to associate a different resource string—and in particular a different *filterExt* substring—with each document template object.

Following a simple example will help you better understand the necessary steps. We will assume that your application's *InitInstance()* function initially registers only one document template object for the .TXT file extension, using code similar to that shown in Listing 2-9.

Listing 2-9. *InitInstance()* function that initially registers only one document template object.

```
BOOL CMyApp::InitInstance()
{
// ...

   m_ptTemplateTXT = new CMultiDocTemplate(
            IDR_TXTDOCTYPE,
            RUNTIME_CLASS(CMyDoc),
            RUNTIME_CLASS(CMyChildFrame),
            RUNTIME_CLASS(CMyView));
   AddDocTemplate(m_ptTemplateTXT);

// ...
}
```

(The *m_ptTemplateTXT* pointer is a member variable of your application class. It is used to keep a handy reference to your document template object, as explained in *FAQ 2.1 How should I create and reference multiple document templates in my application?*)

The code in Listing 2-9 assumes that your resource file contains the following resources, all of which share the *IDR_TXTDOCTYPE* resource ID (as described in *FAQ 1.8 What is the role of the document template resource ID?*):

- An icon resource
- A menu resource
- A string resource: the famous document template string with its seven substrings

If the document template object created in Listing 2-9 is associated with the .TXT file extension, the *IDR_TXTDOCTYPE* document template string will contain substrings similar to the ones shown in Table 2-1.

Table 2-1. The seven substrings of the document template string for the *IDR_TXTDOCTYPE* document template string.

Document template substring	Example value
windowTitle	"" (empty string)
docName	"TextDoc"
fileNewName	"Text Document"
filterName	"Text Files (*.txt)"
filterExt	".txt"
regFileTypeId	"TextDoc.Document"
regFileTypeName	"TextDoc Document"

Let us follow the steps necessary to add support for the .ASC file extension to the preceding code. As you will see, most of the work involves your application's resources:

Step 1. Create a new document template resource ID called *IDR_ASCDOCTYPE* and copy the relevant resources from *IDR_TXTDOCTYPE:* menu, icon, and string. This technique is explained in *FAQ 2.3 How do I create the resources associated with a new document template resource ID?*

Step 2. Change the *filterName* and *filterExt* substrings of your *IDR_ASCDOCTYPE* string resource to read "ASCII Text Document (*.asc)" and ".asc", respectively. At this point, your project contains all the required *IDR_ASCDOCTYPE* resources (menu, icon, and string). You now need to "hook" these resources to a new document template object in your application class.

Step 3. Add a new *CMultiDocTemplate* pointer member variable to your application class, as shown in Listing 2-10.

Listing 2-10. The application class with a new *CMultiDocTemplate* pointer member variable added.

```
class CMyApp : public CWinApp
{
// ...

public:
   // Member variables used to store the various
   // document templates objects that we create in
   // InitInstance()
   CMultiDocTemplate* m_ptTemplateTXT;   // Initial pointer
   CMultiDocTemplate* m_ptTemplateASC;   // New pointer

// ...
};
```

Step 4. In your application's *InitInstance()* function, create the new "ASCII" document template object referencing the new *IDR_ASCDOCTYPE* resources, as shown in Listing 2-11.

Listing 2-11. Creating the new "ASCII" document template object in the application's *InitInstance()* function.

```
BOOL CMyApp::InitInstance()
{
// ...

   m_ptTemplateTXT = new CMultiDocTemplate(
           IDR_TXTDOCTYPE,
           RUNTIME_CLASS(CMyDoc),
           RUNTIME_CLASS(CMyChildFrame),
           RUNTIME_CLASS(CMyView));
   AddDocTemplate(m_ptTemplateTXT);
```

```
    m_ptTemplateASC = new CMultiDocTemplate(
            IDR_ASCDOCTYPE,          // Use our new resources
            RUNTIME_CLASS(CMyDoc),     // Same Document class
            RUNTIME_CLASS(CMyChildFrame),
            RUNTIME_CLASS(CMyView));  // Same View class
    AddDocTemplate(m_ptTemplateASC);

// ...
}
```

That's all there is to it! You can now open files with either the .TXT or the .ASC extension, and MFC will use the same document and view classes in each case. Of course, you can use the same technique again to associate other file extensions (such as .INI) to the same document and view classes.

■

Sample Code

- Project: MultiExt in the Chap02 subdirectory on the companion CD-ROM.
- Purpose: Implements a simple ASCII text file viewer that accepts multiple file extensions (.TXT, .ASC, .INI) and maps all of them to the same document, view, and frame window classes. Figure 2-3 shows the MultiExt application running with three files opened, each one having a distinct extension.

Implementation Highlights

- Resources: *IDR_TXTDOCTYPE, IDR_ASCDOCTYPE, IDR_INIDOCTYPE*
- *CWinApp::InitInstance()* function (MultiExt.cpp)

See Also

- *FAQ 2.1* *How should I create and reference multiple document templates in my application?*
- *FAQ 2.2* *How do I manage multiple document templates without having a dialog box pop up each time the user tries to create a new document?*

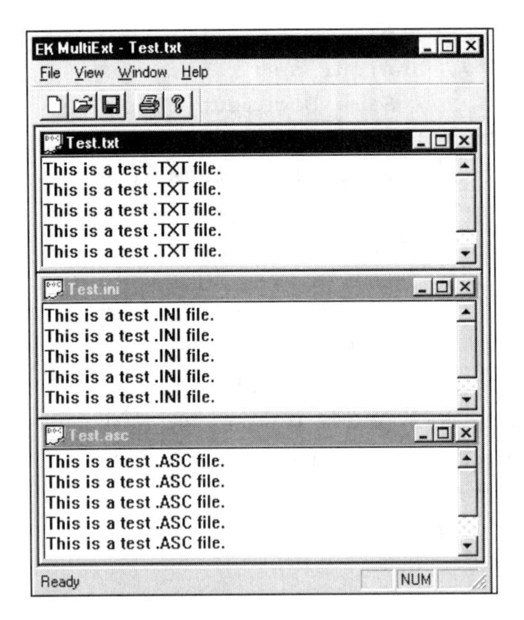

Figure 2-3. The MultiExt application running with three files opened having different extensions.

- *FAQ 2.3 How do I create the resources associated with a new document template resource ID?*
- *FAQ 2.20 Why doesn't my application register its document files with Windows Explorer, and how do I correct this situation?*
- *FAQ 1.8 What is the role of the document template resource ID?*

Managing Documents

FAQ 2.6 How do I prevent an MDI application from opening a new (empty) document at start-up?

Each time you launch a standard AppWizard-generated application, a new (empty) document is automatically created by MFC, as are the associated view and the view's frame window (see Figure 2-4). You can legitimately wonder where in your code this empty document gets created in the first place. Also, how can you make your application start without initially creating any document, as shown in Figure 2-5?

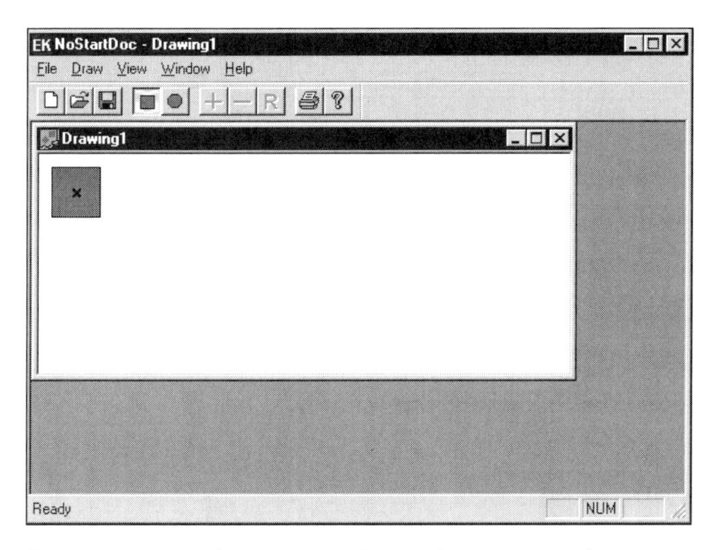

Figure 2-4. Application starting with an empty document automatically created by MFC.

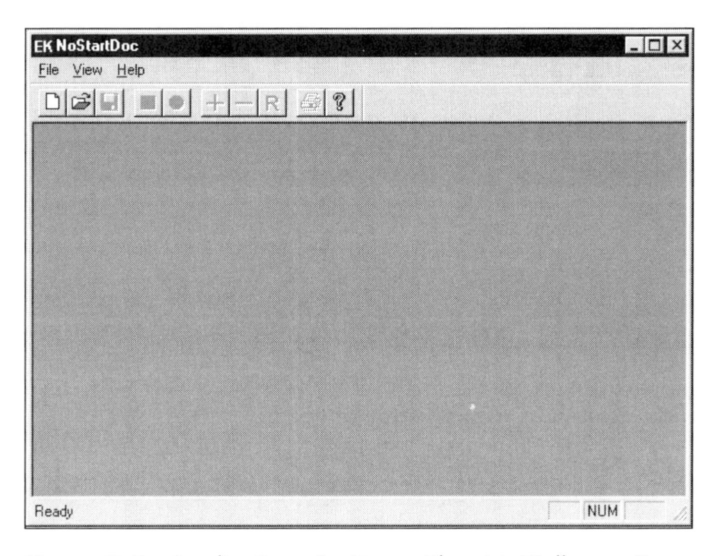

Figure 2-5. Application starting without initially creating any document.

Step 1. In your application's *InitInstance()* function, locate the block of code shown in Listing 2-12.

Listing 2-12. Default *InitInstance()* function generated by AppWizard.

```
BOOL CMyApp::InitInstance()
{
//    ...

   // Parse command line for standard shell commands,
   // DDE, file open
   CCommandLineInfo cmdInfo;
   ParseCommandLine(cmdInfo);

   // Dispatch commands specified on the command line
   if (!ProcessShellCommand(cmdInfo))
      return FALSE;
//    ...
}
```

Step 2. Modify this code by inserting the lines shown in Listing 2-13.

Listing 2-13. *InitInstance()* function that prevents the opening of a new document at start-up.

```
BOOL CMyApp::InitInstance()
{
//    ...

   // Parse command line for standard shell commands,
   // DDE, file open
   CCommandLineInfo cmdInfo;

   // ---------------------------------

   // Turn off default OnFileNew() call

   cmdInfo.m_nShellCommand = CCommandLineInfo::FileNothing;

   // ---------------------------------
```

```
    ParseCommandLine(cmdInfo);

    // Dispatch commands specified on the command line
    if (!ProcessShellCommand(cmdInfo))
       return FALSE;

//    ...
}
```

When you rebuild and launch your application, it will no longer create an initial empty document.

■

Explanations

Starting with MFC version 4.0, it is not very obvious where the new document gets instantiated during the application start-up. You may understand that *CWinApp::OnFileNew()* finally gets called, but where does this call come from?

In fact, all the processing leading to the call of *OnFileNew()* is hidden in the three lines of code shown in bold in Listing 2-13. Let us analyze what is happening behind the scenes:

1. A *CCommandLineInfo* object named *cmdInfo* is created on the stack. This object will be used by MFC functions to analyze the various switches that may be present on the application's command line and to store this information in a more useful form inside *public* member variables. Listing 2-14 shows the definition of these member variables.

Listing 2-14. Definition of class *CCommandLineInfo* member variables (AFXWIN.H).

```
class CCommandLineInfo
{
//    ...

    BOOL m_bShowSplash;      // Show splash screen?
    BOOL m_bRunEmbedded;     // OLE: /Embedding command
    BOOL m_bRunAutomated;    // OLE: /Automation command
```

```
    enum { FileNew, FileOpen, FilePrint, FilePrintTo,
           FileDDE, AppUnregister, FileNothing = -1 }
         m_nShellCommand;

    // m_nShellCommand indicates the shell command to be
    // processed:
    //    FileNew       -> Create a new document
    //    FileOpen      -> Open the file stored in
    //                     m_strFileName
    //    FilePrint     -> Print the file stored in
    //                     m_strFileName (/p command)
    //    FilePrintTo   -> Print the file stored in
    //                     m_strFileName (/pt command)
    //    FileDDE       -> DDE: /dde command
    //    AppUnregister -> OLE: /Unregister command
    //    FileNothing   -> Do nothing. This may be just what
    //                     we want!

    // not valid for FileNew
    CString m_strFileName;  // File to be opened or printed

    // valid only for FilePrintTo
    CString m_strPrinterName;
    CString m_strDriverName;
    CString m_strPortName;

//    ...
};
```

2. The *CCommandLineInfo* constructor (AppCore.cpp) is called for the *cmdInfo* object. Among other actions, this constructor initializes the *m_nShellCommand* member to the value *CCommandLineInfo::FileNew*.
3. The *CWinApp::ParseCommandLine()* function (AppCore.cpp) is called with the *cmdInfo* object as an argument. This function iterates over the command line looking for options starting with the characters "/" or "-". For each command-line argument found, *ParseCommandLine()* applies the *CCommandLineInfo::ParseParam()* method (AppCore.cpp) on the *cmdInfo* object.
4. The *CCommandLineInfo::ParseParam()* function in turn sets the member variables of the *cmdInfo* object according to the various command-line arguments that are transmitted by *ParseCommandLine()*. The value of the

m_nShellCommand member is changed only if an actual parameter is found on the command line. Otherwise, *m_nShellCommand* retains its last value—that is, *CCommandLineInfo::FileNew* as set in step 2 by the *cmdInfo* object constructor.

5. After *ParseCommandLine()* returns, the *cmdInfo* object is passed as an argument to the *CWinApp::ProcessShellCommand()* function (AppUI2.cpp). Using a *switch* statement, this function executes the appropriate action based on the value of *cmdInfo.m_nShellCommand.* The most frequent actions are shown in Table 2-2.

Table 2-2. Function calls made by *ProcessShellCommand()* for the main values of *cmdInfo.m_nShellCommand.*

Value of *cmdInfo.m_nShellCommand*	Function call made by *ProcessShellCommand()*
CCommandLineInfo::FileNew	*CWinApp::OnFileNew();* this function is *not virtual!*
CCommandLineInfo::FileOpen	*OpenDocumentFile(cmdInfo.m_strFileName)*
CCommandLineInfo::FilePrint, *CCommandLineInfo::FilePrintTo*	*m_pMainWnd->SendMessage (WM_COMMAND, ID_FILE_PRINT_DIRECT)*
CCommandLineInfo::FileNothing	*None*

Thus, you see that the default value to which the *cmdInfo* object constructor initializes the *m_nShellCommand* member in step 2 ultimately results in a call to *CWinApp::OnFileNew()* deep in the bowels of *ProcessShellCommand().* But when we take the opportunity to adjust the initial value of the *m_nShellCommand* member to *CCommandLineInfo::FileNothing,* no call to *OnFileNew()* will be made by *ProcessShellCommand()* and no new document will be created. That's just what we wanted in the first place.

Additional Comments

If you look up *m_nShellCommand* in the Visual C++ online help, you will find that Microsoft suggests that you use the code sample shown in Listing 2-15 to turn off the creation of an initial empty document.

Listing 2-15. Sample code from Visual C++ online help.

```
BOOL CMyWinApp::InitInstance()
{
//   ...

   // Parse command line for standard shell commands,
   // DDE, file open
   CCommandLineInfo cmdInfo;
   ParseCommandLine(cmdInfo);

// DON'T display a new MDI child window during startup!!!
   cmdInfo.m_nShellCommand = CCommandLineInfo::FileNothing;

// Dispatch commands specified on the command line
   if (!ProcessShellCommand(cmdInfo))
      return FALSE;

//   ...
};
```

Can you spot the difference between this code and the solution I gave you? Here is the answer: Microsoft's sample sets the *cmdInfo.m_nShellCommand* member to *CCommandLineInfo::FileNothing* *after* the call to *ParseCommandLine()*, whereas my sample implements the same operation *before* the call to *ParseCommandLine()*—in fact, just after the *cmdInfo* object is constructed.

What difference does this apparently minor detail make? My solution simply changes the default action from *CCommandLineInfo::FileNew* to *CCommandLineInfo::FileNothing*, but then it allows the normal command-line analysis to proceed. In contrast, Microsoft's sample code always overrides the normal command-line processing when it resets the *m_nShellCommand* field to *CCommandLineInfo::FileNothing*.

The net result is that Microsoft's sample code will not allow your application to process *any* command-line argument (such as launching the application with a specific document specified on the command line to be opened at start-up). With my solution, it is only the *default* behavior of the application that gets changed: if any command-line arguments are present, they will be processed normally. I leave it to you to decide which solution you prefer.

Older MFC Versions

If you use a version of MFC older than 4.0, your application's *InitInstance()* function will contain the block of code shown in Listing 2-16.

Listing 2-16. Default *InitInstance()* function generated by AppWizard for MFC versions older than 4.0.

```
BOOL CMyApp::InitInstance()
{
   ...

   // simple command line parsing
   if (m_lpCmdLine[0] == '\0')
   {
      // create a new (empty) document
      OnFileNew();   // <<== This is the call you may want
                     // to remove
   }
   else
   {
      // open an existing document
      OpenDocumentFile(m_lpCmdLine);
   }

   ...
}
```

In this case, it is much easier to see where the *OnFileNew()* function is called to instantiate a new document. Simply remove the explicit call to *OnFileNew()* shown in Listing 2-16, and you're finished!

Sample Code

- Project: NoStartDoc in the Chap02 subdirectory on the companion CD-ROM.
- Purpose: The application starts without initially creating any document, as shown in Figure 2-5.

Implementation Highlights

- *CMDIApp::InitInstance()* function (NoStartDoc.cpp)

2.7 How do I programmatically create a new (empty) document?

Some applications need to create a new (empty) document without forcing the user to explicitly select the "File, New" menu command. For example, a document could be created as the result of a specific user action in one of your application's windows or as an indirect consequence of another menu command. The following two techniques explain how you can achieve the desired behavior.

First Technique

If you want to exactly reproduce the "File, New" behavior, the easiest way is to simulate the choice of the "File, New" menu command by sending the appropriate *WM_COMMAND* message:

```
AfxGetMainWnd()->SendMessage( WM_COMMAND, ID_FILE_NEW );
   // Note: can use PostMessage() if you prefer
```

This instruction will indirectly call *CWinApp::OnFileNew()* through the normal MFC message map processing.

Second Technique

If your application creates multiple document template objects and you want to create a new document based on a specific template, you must explicitly select the document template object that you want to use and then call its own *CMultiDocTemplate::OpenDocumentFile()* function with a *NULL* argument:

```
CMultiDocTemplate* ptTemplate;
// ...
// Make ptTemplate point to the document template that you
// want to use
// ...
// Create a new document based on the document template
// pointed to by ptTemplate
ptTemplate->OpenDocumentFile( NULL );
```

You must find a way to store pointers to your various document template objects so that you can correctly set up the *ptTemplate* pointer in the preceding code. The easiest way is usually to store those pointers as member variables in your application class, as explained in *FAQ 2.1 How should I create and reference multiple document templates in my application?*

Then, to programmatically create a new document based on a specific template, you can simply issue the following call from anywhere in your code:

```
// Create new document, frame, and view using m_ptTemplate1
// (could use one of the other templates)
theApp.m_ptTemplate1->OpenDocumentFile( NULL );
```

■

Additional Comments

Both of the solutions create a new document object as well as a new view's frame window object and a new view object, using the normal MFC document template creation mechanism explained in *FAQ 1.9 How do the document/view architecture component objects get created?*

If your application has registered multiple document template objects (by passing them to the *CWinApp::AddDocTemplate()* function), the first solution will exactly reproduce the "File, New" behavior and will prompt the user for the document template to use—unless you have taken specific steps to avoid this prompt by using the technique described in *FAQ 2.2 How do I manage multiple document templates without having a dialog box pop up each time the user tries to create a new document?*

On the other hand, the second technique allows your code to explicitly select the document template object that will be used. In this way, you can precisely control the class of the document, view, and view's frame window objects that MFC will create.

If you want to use this last technique but do not wish to expose *public* member variables in your *CWinApp*-derived class, you can make those pointer members *protected* and instead encapsulate the document-creation logic in *public* member functions, as shown in Listing 2-17.

Listing 2-17. Encapsulating the document-creation logic in *public* member functions of the application class.

```
////////////////////////////////////////
// Class definition for CMyApp (MyApp.h)

class CMyApp : public CWinApp
```

```
{
// ...
public:
   // Wrapper functions for the document-creation logic
   CMyDoc1* CreateNewDoc1();
   CMyDoc2* CreateNewDoc2();
   CMyDoc3* CreateNewDoc3();

protected:  // These member variables are now 'protected'
   // Member variables used to store the various
   // document templates objects that we create in
   // InitInstance()
   CMultiDocTemplate* m_ptTemplate1;
   CMultiDocTemplate* m_ptTemplate2;
   CMultiDocTemplate* m_ptTemplate3;
// ...
};

/////////////////////////////////////////
// Implementation for CMyApp (MyApp.cpp)

BOOL CMyApp::InitInstance()
{
// ...
   // Create the document template objects and store
   // the pointers in our member variables as before
// ...
}

CMyDoc1* CMyApp::CreateNewDoc1()
{
   CDocument* pDoc = m_ptTemplate1->OpenDocumentFile(NULL);
   CMyDoc1* pDoc1 = static_cast< CMyDoc1* >( pDoc );
   ASSERT_VALID( pDoc1 );
   ASSERT_KINDOF( CMyDoc1, pDoc1 );
   return pDoc1;
}

CMyDoc2* CMyApp::CreateNewDoc2()
{
   CDocument* pDoc = m_ptTemplate2->OpenDocumentFile(NULL);
   CMyDoc2* pDoc2 = static_cast< CMyDoc2* >( pDoc );
```

```
    ASSERT_VALID( pDoc2 );
    ASSERT_KINDOF( CMyDoc2, pDoc2 );
    return pDoc2;
}

CMyDoc3* CMyApp::CreateNewDoc3()
{
    CDocument* pDoc = m_ptTemplate3->OpenDocumentFile(NULL);
    CMyDoc3* pDoc3 = static_cast< CMyDoc3* >( pDoc );
    ASSERT_VALID( pDoc3 );
    ASSERT_KINDOF( CMyDoc3, pDoc3 );
    return pDoc3;
}
```

With this last implementation, here is what the client code would look like to create a new document based on *m_ptTemplate1:*

```
// Create new document, frame, and view using m_ptTemplate1
// (could use one of the other templates)
CMyDoc1* pDoc1 = theApp.CreateNewDoc1();
```

One advantage of this implementation with wrapper functions is that we return a correctly typed pointer to the newly created document. Thus, the client code gets a "real" *CMyDoc1** pointer (or *CMyDoc2**, *CMyDoc3**, etc.) without the need for any further downcasting.

Sample Code

- Project: NewDoc in the Chap02 subdirectory on the companion CD-ROM.
- Purpose: Programmatically creates new documents.

Implementation Highlights

- *CMDIApp::OnNewdocFileNew()* function (NewDoc.cpp)
- *CMDIApp::OnNewdocDrawing()* function (NewDoc.cpp)
- *CMDIApp::OnNewdocCounter()* function (NewDoc.cpp)

Although this sample application implements all the preceding menu command handlers in its application class, those commands could be handled by any other class while using exactly the same code.

See Also

- *FAQ 2.2 How do I manage multiple document templates without having a dialog box pop up each time the user tries to create a new document?*
- *FAQ 1.9 How do the document/view architecture component objects get created?*

2.8 How do I programmatically open an existing document file?

Some applications need to open an existing document file without having the user explicitly select the "File, Open" menu command. For example, an existing document could be opened as the result of a specific user action in one of your application's windows or as an indirect consequence of another menu command. The following two techniques explain how you can achieve the desired behavior.

First Technique

If you want to reproduce the "File, Open" behavior that selects the document template object to use based on the file's extension, call *CWinApp::OpenDocumentFile()* and pass the desired filename as an argument, as shown in Listing 2-18.

Listing 2-18. Opening a document file and selecting the document template object to use based on the file's extension.

```
CString strFileName;
// ...
// Fill strFileName with the pathname of the document
// to open
// ...
// Open the document specified by strFileName, using
// the file's extension to select the document template
AfxGetApp()->OpenDocumentFile( strFileName );
```

Second Technique

If your application manages multiple document templates and you want to open a document file using a specific template without regard to the file's extension, you must explicitly select the document template that you want to use and then call its own *CMultiDocTemplate::OpenDocumentFile()* function with the desired filename as an argument, as shown in Listing 2-19.

Listing 2-19. Explicitly selecting the document template object to use for opening a document file.

```
CMultiDocTemplate* ptTemplate;
// ...
// Make ptTemplate point to the document template that you
// want to use
// ...
CString strFileName;
// ...
// Fill strFileName with the pathname of the document
// to open
// ...
// Open the document specified by strFileName, using
// the document template pointed to by ptTemplate
ptTemplate->OpenDocumentFile( strFileName );
```

You need a way to store pointers to your various document template objects so that you can correctly set up the *ptTemplate* pointer. The easiest way is usually to store those pointers as member variables in your application class, as explained in *FAQ 2.2 How do I manage multiple document templates without having a dialog box pop up each time the user tries to create a new document?*

■

Additional Comments

If you use the first technique and want to understand how MFC selects the document template object to use based on the filename you pass as an argument to the *CWinApp::OpenDocumentFile()* function, read *FAQ 2.4 How does MFC select the document template object to use when opening a file?*

If you use the second technique, you might find it useful to review the Additional Comments section of *FAQ 2.6 How do I prevent an MDI application from opening a new (empty) document at start-up?* This FAQ contains a complete discussion of how to store pointers to document template objects in your application class.

Sample Code

There is no sample project for this FAQ.

See Also

- *FAQ 2.2 How do I manage multiple document templates without having a dialog box pop up each time the user tries to create a new document?*
- *FAQ 2.4 How does MFC select the document template object to use when opening a file?*
- *FAQ 2.6 How do I prevent an MDI application from opening a new (empty) document at start-up?*
- *FAQ 1.9 How do the document/view architecture component objects get created?*

How do I make my application remember the last active document and automatically reopen it?

Solving this problem requires a two-step process. First, you store the filename of the active document when the application exits; then, when the user restarts the application, you reload this information and open the document referenced by the previously stored filename. Here's how:

Step 1. Save the filename of the active document. The best moment to save it is when the main frame window is about to close—that is, when it receives the *WM_CLOSE* message. Consequently, you must add a handler for the *WM_CLOSE* message to your main frame window class and insert the code shown in Listing 2-20 to save the active document's filename.

Listing 2-20. Saving the active document's filename in the *WM_CLOSE* message handler.

```
void CMainFrame::OnClose()
{
   // Save the active document's filename
   CString strDocName = "";

   // 1 - Get the active document object
   CMDIChildWnd* pChild = MDIGetActive();
   if( pChild )
   {
      CDocument* pDoc = pChild->GetActiveDocument();
      if( pDoc )
      {
         // 2 - Ensure the document has a name
         if( !pDoc->SaveModified() )
            return;
         pDoc->SetModifiedFlag( FALSE );

         // 3 - Get its complete filename
         strDocName = pDoc->GetPathName();
      }
   }

   // 4 - Store the filename in INI file or Registry
   AfxGetApp()->WriteProfileString( "Settings",
                                    "LastDocName",
                                    strDocName );

   // 5 - IMPORTANT: perform standard OnClose() processing
   CMDIFrameWnd::OnClose();
}
```

Step 2. Reload the information and open the appropriate document file. The best place to reload the previously saved document filename is in your application's *InitInstance()* function, as shown in Listing 2-21.

Listing 2-21. Opening the previously saved document filename in the *InitInstance()* function.

```
BOOL CMyApp::InitInstance()
{
// ...

   // Parse command line for standard shell commands, DDE,
   // file open
   CCommandLineInfo cmdInfo;
   ParseCommandLine(cmdInfo);

   // Restore the last active document
      // 1 - Only if no command-line argument
   if( cmdInfo.m_nShellCommand == CCommandLineInfo::FileNew
        || cmdInfo.m_nShellCommand ==
                                 CCommandLineInfo::FileNothing )
   {
      // 2 - Read last active document filename
      // from INI file or Registry
      CString strDocName = GetProfileString( "Settings",
                                             "LastDocName",
                                             "" );
      if( strDocName != "" )
      {
         // 3 - Reopen the last active document
         OpenDocumentFile( strDocName );
      }
   }
   else  // 4 - Perform standard command-line processing
   {
      // Dispatch commands specified on the command line
      if (!ProcessShellCommand(cmdInfo))
         return FALSE;
   }

   // The main window has been initialized, so show and
   // update it.
   pMainFrame->ShowWindow(m_nCmdShow);
   pMainFrame->UpdateWindow();

   return TRUE;
}
```

Note that *FAQ 2.17 How do I make my application automatically open the document that is at the top of the Recent Files list?* explains another way to achieve a similar—although slightly different—behavior.

■

Explanations

Although it took me some time to get everything working properly, the workings of the preceding technique are easy to follow for each step. The only block of code that may leave you wondering is the following excerpt from Listing 2-20:

```
// 2 - Ensure the document has a name
if( !pDoc->SaveModified() )
   return;
pDoc->SetModifiedFlag( FALSE );
```

This block of code solves one problem that initially caused me some grief: what would happen if the active document were untitled—that is, a new document that had never been saved? In this case, the *GetPathName()* call in Listing 2-20 would return an empty string, which would be then be written to the Registry or INI file. When the flow of execution fell through the *CMDIFrameWnd::OnClose()* call, the user would be given the opportunity to save the untitled document under a specific name. Unfortunately, our code would not be able to retrieve this name, and the subsequent launch of the application would not open *any* document.

The block of code excerpted from Listing 2-20 solves this problem by specifically asking the user to save the active document (only if needed, of course). If the user selects "Cancel," we just return from our message handler without closing any document. Otherwise, we mark the document as "not modified," which avoids having the same message pop up again later during the standard *CMDIFrameWnd::OnClose()* processing.

In case you are wondering, it would not be possible to store the document's name after the call to *CMDIFrameWnd::OnClose()*, because all the document objects are already destroyed when this function call returns (see Additional Comments).

Additional Comments

To better understand the frame shutdown process, you might be interested to read through the standard *CFrameWnd::OnClose()* implementation (WinFrm.cpp), whose pseudocode is shown in Listing 2-22.

Listing 2-22. Pseudocode for the *CFrameWnd::OnClose()* function (WinFrm.cpp).

```
void CFrameWnd::OnClose()
{
// ...

   // Note: only queries the active document
   CDocument* pDocument = GetActiveDocument();
   if (pDocument != NULL &&
      !pDocument->CanCloseFrame(this))
   {
      // document can't close right now — don't close it
      return;
   }

   CWinApp* pApp = AfxGetApp();

   // 1 - Check if the frame window about to close is in
   // fact the main frame window of the application
   if (pApp->m_pMainWnd == this)
   {
      // 2 - Attempt to save all documents
      if (pDocument == NULL && !pApp->SaveAllModified())
         return;     // don't close it

      // hide the application's windows before closing
      // all the documents
      pApp->HideApplication();

      // 3 - Close all documents
      pApp->CloseAllDocuments(FALSE);

      // ...
   }

   // 4 - If the frame window about to close is associated
   // with a particular document object, check if this is
   // the last frame on the document
   if (pDocument != NULL && pDocument->m_bAutoDelete)
```

```
    {
        BOOL bOtherFrame = FALSE;

        // 5 - Iterate through all the views connected to our
        // document object
        POSITION pos = pDocument->GetFirstViewPosition();
        while (pos != NULL)
        {
            CView* pView = pDocument->GetNextView(pos);
            ASSERT_VALID(pView);
            if (pView->GetParentFrame() != this)
            {
                // 6 - We found another frame window!
                bOtherFrame = TRUE;
                break;
            }
        }

        if (!bOtherFrame)
        {
            // 7 - We are the last frame window, so destroy
            // the document object
            pDocument->OnCloseDocument();
            return;
        }

        // allow the document to clean up before the window
        // is destroyed
        pDocument->PreCloseFrame(this);
    }

    // 8 - Finish by destroying the frame window itself
    DestroyWindow();
}
```

As the code in Listing 2-22 shows, all the document objects are still up and running when the main frame window starts to process the *WM_CLOSE* message, but they are destroyed in the *OnClose()* function. Therefore, trying to save the active document name in your application's *ExitInstance()* function would not work, because you can no longer access any document object at this time.

Sample Code

- Project: RememberDoc in the Chap02 subdirectory on the companion CD-ROM.
- Purpose: Remembers the name of the document (if any) that was active when the user closed the program and automatically reopens this document on the next execution.

Implementation Highlights

- *CMainFrame::OnClose()* function (MainFrm.cpp)
- *CMDIApp::InitInstance()* function (RememberDoc.cpp)

See Also

- *FAQ 2.8 How do I programmatically open an existing document file?*
- *FAQ 2.10 How do I make my documents autosave themselves without prompting the user?*
- *FAQ 2.11 How do I implement a "Save all documents" menu command that does not prompt the user before saving each modified document?*
- *FAQ 2.17 How do I make my application automatically open the document that is at the top of the Recent Files list?*

FAQ 2.10 How do I make my documents autosave themselves without prompting the user?

When a document is about to be closed and has been marked as "modified" (by a call to its *SetModifiedFlag()* function), the default MFC behavior is to show a message box asking the user whether to save the document (as shown in Figure 2-6).

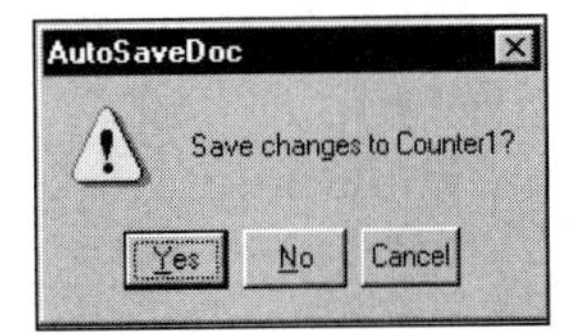

Figure 2-6. Standard MFC behavior asking the user whether to save a modified document.

However, it is sometimes desirable to have your modified documents save themselves automatically, without any user interaction, when they are about to be closed.

The function that implements the default MFC behavior is *CDocument::SaveModified()* (DocCore.cpp). This function is called by *CDocument::OnFileClose()* and *CDocument::CanCloseFrame()* when the user chooses the "File, Close" menu command or closes the last view on a particular document, respectively.

Fortunately, *SaveModified()* is defined as *virtual* in the *CDocument* base class, and that allows you to easily change its behavior: use ClassWizard to override this function in your own document class and implement it as shown in Listing 2-23.

Listing 2-23. *SaveModified()* function to make a document class autosaving.

```
BOOL CMyDoc::SaveModified()
{

    // Document with "autosave" feature
    if( !IsModified() )
        return TRUE;   // OK to destroy document

    // Actually save the document
    // (without prompting the user)
    return DoFileSave();
}
```

■

Explanations

MFC uses the return value of *SaveModified()* to know whether it's safe to destroy the document object. The code in Listing 2-23 returns *TRUE* either if the document does not need to be saved, or if the *DoFileSave()* function call is successful. This last function is the one that actually saves the document.

(To be honest, *DoFileSave()* first calls *DoSave()*, which in turn calls *OnSaveDocument()*, which sets up the document archive file and finally calls *Serialize()*! If you want to get to this level of implementation detail, feel free to read—or trace with the debugger—through the DocCore.cpp source code.)

Note that if the document has never been saved (it is still an untitled document), *DoFileSave()* will show a Save As dialog box so that the user can choose a filename for the document.

Sample Code

- Project: AutoSaveDoc in the Chap02 subdirectory on the companion CD-ROM
- Purpose: The Drawing document objects exhibit an autosaving behavior, whereas the Counter document objects keep the standard MFC behavior of asking the user whether to save a modified document.

Implementation Highlights

- *CDrawDoc::SaveModified()* function (DrawDoc.cpp)

FAQ 2.11 How do I implement a "Save all documents" menu command that does not prompt the user before saving each modified document?

Microsoft Visual C++ offers a useful "Save all documents" menu command. When the user selects this command, this application saves all its modified documents without any further user interaction (such as responding to a prompt like the one shown in Figure 2-6). Wouldn't it be nice if we could implement the same feature in our MFC application?

Knowing that MFC provides a *SaveAllModified()* member function in the *CWinApp* class, I first thought that this problem could be easily solved by making all documents autosaving using the technique explained in *FAQ 2.10 How do I make my documents autosave themselves without prompting the user?* However, this approach would require a modification of each document class in the application, and that does not seem a very elegant or object-oriented way of solving the problem. In addition, you might wish to implement a "Save all documents" command but still retain the normal MFC behavior of prompting users when they explicitly close a document. That is exactly how Microsoft Visual C++ behaves.

This last behavior is what the code shown in Listing 2-24 achieves. Better yet, this solution has the considerable advantage of being generic, because it requires absolutely no cooperation from the various document classes. In fact, this implementation is totally self-contained in the main frame window class. (Note that the same code could also reside in your application class without any problem. See the Additional Comments section.)

Listing 2-24. Implementing the "Save All Documents" menu command, which saves all the modified documents without prompting the user.

```
void CMainFrame::OnFileSaveAll()
{
   CWinApp* pApp = AfxGetApp();
   ASSERT_VALID( pApp );

   // 1 - Iterate through the application's document
   // templates list
   POSITION posTemplate =
                  pApp->GetFirstDocTemplatePosition();
   while( posTemplate != NULL )
   {
      // 2 - For each document template object...
      CDocTemplate* pTemplate =
         pApp->GetNextDocTemplate( posTemplate );
         ASSERT_VALID( pTemplate );
         ASSERT_KINDOF( CDocTemplate, pTemplate );

      // 3 - Iterate through the template's document list
      POSITION posDocument =
                  pTemplate->GetFirstDocPosition();
      while( posDocument != NULL )
      {
         // 4 - For each document object...
         CDocument* pDoc =
            pTemplate->GetNextDoc( posDocument );
         ASSERT_VALID( pDoc );
         ASSERT_KINDOF( CDocument, pDoc );

         // 5 - Save the document if necessary
         // (without prompting the user)
         if( pDoc->IsModified() )
            pDoc->DoFileSave();
      }
   }
}
```

■

Explanations

The technique shown in Listing 2-24 is easier to understand when you realize that I am combining two different techniques:

- First, I iterate through all the document objects in the application, using the code skeleton given in *FAQ 2.19 How do I iterate through the list of all the currently opened documents?*
- For each document object that I get hold of—that is, for each opened document from the user's point of view—I force the saving action to take place (if necessary) by calling *DoFileSave()* instead of *SaveModified()* (the latter function would prompt the user as shown in Figure 2-6). I am reusing the same technique that is given in *FAQ 2.10 How do I make my documents autosave themselves without prompting the user?*

With this explanation, the logic of the code shown in Listing 2-24 should be easier to follow.

Another way to understand this technique is to trace through the standard MFC implementation for the *CWinApp::SaveAllModified()* function (AppUI.cpp), which is shown in Listing 2-25.

Listing 2-25. Pseudocode for the *CWinApp::SaveAllModified()* function.

```
// ———————————————————————————
// AppUI.cpp

BOOL CWinApp::SaveAllModified()
{
    if (m_pDocManager != NULL)
        // 1 - Simply delegate call to
        // CDocManager::SaveAllModified()
        return m_pDocManager->SaveAllModified();
    return TRUE;
}

// ———————————————————————————
// DocMgr.cpp

BOOL CDocManager::SaveAllModified()
{
    // 2 - Iterate through the application's document
```

```
    // templates list
    POSITION pos = m_templateList.GetHeadPosition();
    while (pos != NULL)
    {
       // 3 - For each document template object...
       CDocTemplate* pTemplate =
               (CDocTemplate*)m_templateList.GetNext(pos);
       ASSERT_KINDOF(CDocTemplate, pTemplate);

       // 4 - Delegate call to
       // CDocTemplate::SaveAllModified()
       if (!pTemplate->SaveAllModified())
          return FALSE;
    }
    return TRUE;
}

// ______________________________
// DocTempl.cpp

BOOL CDocTemplate::SaveAllModified()
{
    // 5 - Iterate through the template's document list
    POSITION pos = GetFirstDocPosition();
    while (pos != NULL)
    {
       // 6 - For each document object...
       CDocument* pDoc = GetNextDoc(pos);

       // 7 - Save the document if necessary
       // (standard behavior prompts the user)
       if (!pDoc->SaveModified())
          return FALSE;
    }
    return TRUE;
}
```

As you can see by comparing the code in Listings 2-24 and 2-25, my implementation simply "folds" the three MFC *SaveAllModified()* functions into one (bigger) function in the main frame window class and replaces the *pDoc->SaveModified()* call with a call to *DoFileSave()* to avoid prompting the user.

Additional Comments

The "Save all documents" menu command could also be handled in your application class rather than in the main frame window class. Although you can keep the code in Listing 2-24 as is, handling the "Save all documents" menu command in your application class allows for a little simplification: you can omit the initial *AfxGetApp()* call and the *pApp->* prefix before the calls to *GetFirstDocTemplatePosition()* and *GetNextDocTemplate()*.

Should you implement your menu command handler in the main frame window or in the application class? That's largely a matter of personal taste and preference, although one could argue that the ability to save all the documents is more closely related to the application class than to the main frame window class. I leave this choice to your conscience.

Note that you can greatly simplify the code shown in Listing 2-24 if you use the *CEkDocList* class discussed in *FAQ 2.19* to relieve the burden of iterating through all the opened document objects. Listing 2-26 shows what the new *CMainFrame::OnFileSaveAll()* function looks like with the help of the *CEkDocList* class.

Listing 2-26. Implementing the "Save All Documents" menu command with the help of the *CEkDocList* class.

```
#include "EkDocList.h"  // For CEkDocList class

void CMainFrame::OnFileSaveAll()
{
   // 1 - Construct CEkDocList enumerator object
   CEkDocList DocList;

   // 2 - For each document object...
   CDocument* pDoc;
   while( pDoc = DocList.GetNextDoc() )
   {
      // 3 - Save the document if necessary
      // (without prompting the user)
      if( pDoc->IsModified() )
         pDoc->DoFileSave();
   }
}
```

As a final note, if you decide to make all your document classes autosaving by using the technique shown in *FAQ 2.10,* the problem almost goes away. You can simply call *CWinApp::SaveAllModified(),* which will no longer prompt the user.

Sample Code

- Project: SaveAllDocs in the Chap02 subdirectory on the companion CD-ROM.
- Purpose: Allows users to save all their modified documents without any prompting.

Implementation Highlights

- *CMainFrame::OnFileSaveAll()* function (MainFrm.cpp)

See Also

- *FAQ 2.10 How do I make my documents autosave themselves without prompting the user?*
- *FAQ 2.19 How do I iterate through the list of all the currently opened documents?*

2.12 How do I programmatically close a document?

Some applications need to close a document without having the user explicitly select the "File, Close" menu command. For example, a document might be destroyed as the result of a specific user action in one of your application's windows or as an indirect consequence of another menu command. The following techniques explain different ways of achieving the desired behavior.

First Technique

If you want to close the *active* document object by exactly reproducing the behavior of the "File, Close" menu command, the easiest way is to simulate the choice of the command by sending the appropriate *WM_COMMAND* message:

```
AfxGetMainWnd()->PostMessage( WM_COMMAND, ID_FILE_CLOSE );
```

This code will indirectly call the *CDocument::OnFileClose()* function through the normal MFC message map processing for the active document object, which will then go through its normal destruction process: asking the user whether to save a modified document, destroying all views and frame windows attached to this document object, and so on.

Second Technique

If you want to close a specific document object (not necessarily the active one) on which you have a pointer, simply call the *CDocument::OnCloseDocument()* function through the pointer:

```
CMyDoc* pDoc;
// Make pDoc point to the document object that you want
// to destroy
pDoc->OnCloseDocument();    // Destroy the document
                            // (and close its views)
```

Note that this solution will destroy the document object without trying to save it even if the document is marked as modified. To avoid this potentially dangerous behavior, use the third technique.

Third Technique

If you want to close a specific document object (not necessarily the active one) on which you have a pointer *and* you want to ask the user whether to save the document before closing it, you should write a generic function such as the one shown in Listing 2-27.

Listing 2-27. Generic function for closing a document object after saving it if necessary.

```
void EkCloseDocument( CDocument* pDoc )
{
   ASSERT_VALID( pDoc );
```

```
    // 1 - Give the user a chance to save the document
    if( !pDoc->SaveModified() )
       return;

    // 2 - Destroy the document object
    pDoc->OnCloseDocument();
}
```

This code snippet exactly mimics the implementation of the *CDocument::OnFileClose()* function (DocCore.cpp). However, because *CDocument::OnFileClose()* resides in the *protected* section of the *CDocument* class, you could not call it directly from anywhere in your code outside your own document classes. That's why you need a generic function such as the one shown in Listing 2-27.

■

Explanations

If you want to understand how a document object destroys its views and their associated frame windows and ultimately commits suicide, you will probably find the implementation of the standard *CDocument::OnCloseDocument()* function (DocCore.cpp) enlightening. This function is shown in Listing 2-28.

Listing 2-28. Pseudocode for the *CDocument::OnCloseDocument()* function (DocCore.cpp).

```
void CDocument::OnCloseDocument()
   // must close all views now (no prompting) -
   // usually destroys this
{
   // destroy all frames viewing this document
   // the last destroy may destroy us
   BOOL bAutoDelete = m_bAutoDelete;
   m_bAutoDelete = FALSE;  // don't destroy document
                           // while closing views
   while (!m_viewList.IsEmpty())
   {
      // get frame attached to the view
      CView* pView = (CView*)m_viewList.GetHead();
      CFrameWnd* pFrame = pView->GetParentFrame();

      // and close it
```

```
        PreCloseFrame(pFrame);
        pFrame->DestroyWindow();
            // will destroy the view as well
    }
    m_bAutoDelete = bAutoDelete;

    // clean up contents of document before destroying
    // the document itself
    DeleteContents();

    // delete the document if necessary
    if (m_bAutoDelete)
        delete this;
}
```

All the comments in Listing 2-28 are from the MFC team: for once, I did not think that any additional explanation was needed! Note, however, that the *m_bAutoDelete* member variable is set to *TRUE* in the constructor of the *CDocument* class; therefore, all document objects are self-destroying by default.

Sample Code

- Project: CloseDoc in the Chap02 subdirectory on the companion CD-ROM.
- Purpose: Programmatically closes document objects.

Implementation Highlights

- *EkGetActiveDocument()* function (CloseDoc.cpp)
- *EkCloseDocument()* function (CloseDoc.cpp)
- *CMDIApp::OnCloseDoc1()* function (CloseDoc.cpp)
- *CMDIApp::OnCloseDoc2()* function (CloseDoc.cpp)
- *CMDIApp::OnCloseDoc3()* function (CloseDoc.cpp)

Although this sample application implements all the preceding menu command handlers in its application class, these commands could be handled by any other class while using exactly the same code.

See Also

- *FAQ 2.10 How do I make my documents autosave themselves without prompting the user?*
- *FAQ 2.18 How do I get a pointer to the currently active document?*

How do I implement a "Close all documents" menu command?

Microsoft Visual C++ offers the useful "Close All Documents" menu command, which closes all the open documents and their views. You can implement the same feature in your MFC application with the help of two useful member functions offered by the *CWinApp* class: *CloseAllDocuments()* and *SaveAllModified()*.

First Technique

The *CloseAllDocuments()* function does exactly what its name implies: it destroys all the currently active document objects without any attempt at saving them. For this reason, it is strongly recommended that you first call *SaveAllModified()* to give users a chance to save their work before *CloseAllDocuments()* is called:

```
CWinApp* pApp = AfxGetApp();
if( pApp->SaveAllModified() )
   pApp->CloseAllDocuments( FALSE );
```

This code fragment will give your application the standard behavior of prompting the user to save each modified document before closing it.

Second Technique

If you want to save all the modified documents automatically without any user interaction, you can replace the *SaveAllModified()* function call by the technique shown in *FAQ 2.11 How do I implement a "Save all documents" menu command that does not prompt the user before saving each modified document?* The call to *CloseAllDocuments()* can simply be inserted at the end of the code that saves all the documents, as shown in Listing 2-29.

Listing 2-29. Implementing a "Close all documents" menu command that saves all the modified documents (without prompting the user) before closing them.

```
void CMainFrame::OnWindowCloseAll()
{
   CWinApp* pApp = AfxGetApp();
   ASSERT_VALID( pApp );
```

```
    // 1 - Iterate through the application's document
    // templates list
    POSITION posTemplate =
                    pApp->GetFirstDocTemplatePosition();
    while( posTemplate != NULL )
    {
       // 2 - For each document template object...
       CDocTemplate* pTemplate =
          pApp->GetNextDocTemplate( posTemplate );
       ASSERT_VALID( pTemplate );
       ASSERT_KINDOF( CDocTemplate, pTemplate );

       // 3 - Iterate through the template's document list
       POSITION posDocument =
                    pTemplate->GetFirstDocPosition();
       while( posDocument != NULL )
       {
          // 4 - For each document object...
          CDocument* pDoc =
             pTemplate->GetNextDoc( posDocument );
          ASSERT_VALID( pDoc );
          ASSERT_KINDOF( CDocument, pDoc );

          // 5 - Save the document if necessary
          // (without prompting the user)
          if( pDoc->IsModified() )
             pDoc->DoFileSave();
       }
    }

    // 6 - Now that all documents are saved, close them!
    pApp->CloseAllDocuments( FALSE );
}
```

■

Explanations

For a detailed discussion of *SaveAllModified()* and the code shown in Listing 2-29, see the Explanations section in *FAQ 2.11 How do I implement a "Save all documents" menu command that does not prompt the user before saving each modified document?*

If you want to understand how *CWinApp::CloseAllDocuments()* works, you can trace its execution through the MFC code, which is shown in Listing 2-30.

Listing 2-30. Pseudocode for *CWinApp::CloseAllDocuments()*.

```
// ———————————————————————
// AppUI.cpp

void CWinApp::CloseAllDocuments(BOOL bEndSession)
{
   if (m_pDocManager != NULL)
      // 1 - Simply delegate call to
      // CDocManager::CloseAllDocuments()
      m_pDocManager->CloseAllDocuments(bEndSession);
}

// ———————————————————————
// DocMgr.cpp

void CDocManager::CloseAllDocuments(BOOL bEndSession)
{
   // 2 - Iterate through the application's document
   // templates list
   POSITION pos = m_templateList.GetHeadPosition();
   while (pos != NULL)
   {
      // 3 - For each document template object...
      CDocTemplate* pTemplate =
              (CDocTemplate*)m_templateList.GetNext(pos);
      ASSERT_KINDOF(CDocTemplate, pTemplate);

      // 4 - Delegate call to
      // CDocTemplate::CloseAllDocuments()
      pTemplate->CloseAllDocuments(bEndSession);
   }
}

// ———————————————————————
// DocTempl.cpp
```

```
void CDocTemplate::CloseAllDocuments(BOOL bEndSession)
{
   // 5 - Iterate through the template's document list
   POSITION pos = GetFirstDocPosition();
   while (pos != NULL)
   {
      // 6 - For each document object...
      CDocument* pDoc = GetNextDoc(pos);
      if (bEndSession)
         pDoc->DisconnectViews();

      // 7 - Destroy the document object
      pDoc->OnCloseDocument();
   }
}
```

The implementation of *CDocument::OnCloseDocument()* is discussed in detail in *FAQ 2.12 How do I programmatically close a document?*

Additional Comments

Note that you can greatly simplify the code shown in Listing 2-29 if you use the *CEkDocList* class discussed in *FAQ 2.19 How do I iterate through the list of all the currently opened documents?* to relieve the burden of iterating through all the opened document objects. Listing 2-31 shows what the new *CMainFrame::OnWindowCloseAll()* function looks like with the help of the *CEkDocList* class.

Listing 2-31. Implementing the "Close all documents" menu command with the help of the *CEkDocList* class.

```
#include "EkDocList.h"  // For CEkDocList class

void CMainFrame::OnWindowCloseAll()
{
   // 1 - Construct CEkDocList enumerator object
   CEkDocList DocList;

   // 2 - For each document object...
   CDocument* pDoc;
   while( pDoc = DocList.GetNextDoc() )
   {
```

```
      // 3 - Save the document if necessary
      // (without prompting the user)
      if( pDoc->IsModified() )
         pDoc->DoFileSave();
   }

   // 4 - Now that all documents are saved, close them!
   pApp->CloseAllDocuments( FALSE );
}
```

Sample Code

- Project: CloseAllDocs in the Chap02 subdirectory on the companion CD-ROM.
- Purpose: Programmatically closes all the open documents and their associated views and frame windows.

Implementation Highlights

- *CMainFrame::OnWindowCloseAll1()* function (MainFrm.cpp)
- *CMainFrame::OnWindowCloseAll2()* function (MainFrm.cpp)

Although this sample application implements the preceding menu command handlers in its main frame window class, these commands could be handled by any other class while using exactly the same code.

See Also

- *FAQ 2.10 How do I make my documents "autosave" themselves without prompting the user?*
- *FAQ 2.11 How do I implement a "Save all documents" menu command that does not prompt the user before saving each modified document?*
- *FAQ 2.12 How do I programmatically close a document?*
- *FAQ 2.19 How do I iterate through the list of all the currently opened documents?*

Managing the Recent Files List (MRU)

FAQ 2.14 How do I customize the number of recent files shown in the "File" menu?

An MFC application automatically maintains a Recent Files list, which lists the most recently opened documents under the "File" menu. (This file list is also called the MRU list. MRU stands for "most recently used.") In a default AppWizard-generated application, this list holds exactly four elements.

You may wish to customize this feature in various ways. For some applications, the Recent Files list is irrelevant and should not be displayed. For other applications, the length of the list should be different from the default of four elements; for example, this length could be selected by the user in a Preferences dialog box.

The standard way to set the list length is by passing an explicit argument to the *LoadStdProfileSettings()* function, whose prototype is as follows:

```
void CWinApp::LoadStdProfileSettings(
                        UINT nMaxMRU = _AFX_MRU_COUNT );
```

By default, AppWizard generates code to call *LoadStdProfileSettings()* in your application's *InitInstance()* function, as shown in Listing 2-32.

Listing 2-32. The default call to *LoadStdProfileSettings()* generated by AppWizard in the application's *InitInstance()* function.

```
BOOL CMyApp::InitInstance()
{
// Standard initialization

// ...

#ifdef _AFXDLL
   Enable3dControls();
#else
   Enable3dControlsStatic();
#endif
```

```
    LoadStdProfileSettings();   // Load standard INI file
                                // options (including MRU)

    // Register the application's document templates.
    // Document templates serve as the connection between
    // documents, frame windows, and views.

    CMultiDocTemplate* pDocTemplate;

// ...
}
```

The AppWizard-generated call to *LoadStdProfileSettings()* shown in Listing 2-32 uses the default value for the *nMaxMRU* argument, which gives you a Recent Files list holding four elements (the *_AFX_MRU_COUNT* symbol is defined to be the value 4 in AFXWIN.H). Depending on the behavior that you need, you can use one of the two following techniques.

First Technique: No Recent Files List

If you do not want any Recent Files list to show up in your "File" menu, simply pass 0 (zero) as the argument when calling the *LoadStdProfileSettings()* function in your application's *InitInstance()* function, as shown in Listing 2-33.

Listing 2-33. Suppressing the Recent Files list.

```
BOOL CMyApp::InitInstance()
{
// ...

    LoadStdProfileSettings( 0 );   // No "Recent Files" list

// ...
}
```

You should also remove from all your menu resources the "File" menu item that reads "Recent File" and that has an ID value of *ID_FILE_MRU_FILE1*.

Note that it would not be a good idea to totally suppress the call to *LoadStdProfileSettings()*, because in future versions of MFC this function might well implement other initializations than loading the Recent Files list. In fact, in MFC 4.x, *LoadStdProfileSettings()* also retrieves the user's preference for the number of pages to show in Print Preview mode, as explained in the Additional Comments section.

Second Technique: Explicitly Setting the List Length

If you want to explicitly set the list length to a value different from the default of four elements, you must pass the desired length as an argument when calling *LoadStdProfileSettings()* in your application's *InitInstance()* function, as shown in Listing 2-34.

Listing 2-34. Explicitly setting the Recent Files list length.

```
BOOL CMyApp::InitInstance()
{
// ...

    // Retrieve the user's preferences
    // from INI file or Registry - default to 4
    UINT nMRULength = GetProfileInt( "Settings",
                                     "MRULength",
                                     4 );

    // Set correct MRU length
    LoadStdProfileSettings( nMRULength );

// ...
}
```

The *GetProfileInt()* call in Listing 2-34 assumes that your application somehow writes the user's preferences to an INI file or to the Registry by using the *WriteProfileInt()* function with the same *lpszSection* and *lpszEntry* arguments ("Settings" and "MRULength," respectively). See the Sample Code section for an example of how to implement this part.

Note that you should not try to set the length of the Recent Files list to a value greater than 16, which corresponds to the value of the *_AFX_MRU_MAX_COUNT* symbol (defined in AFXWIN.H). You can understand where this limit comes from by referring to Listing 2-40 in *FAQ 2.16 How do I intercept the selection of a Recent File item by the user?*

■

Additional Comments

You might think that you could dynamically change the length of the Recent Files list while the application is running simply by calling the *LoadStdProfileSettings()* function a second time. Unfortunately, this does not work. As shown in Listing 2-35, the *LoadStdProfileSettings()* function asserts if the *m_pRecentFileList* pointer is not *NULL* when you call it.

Listing 2-35. Standard implementation of the *LoadStdProfileSettings()* function (AppCore.cpp)

```
void CWinApp::LoadStdProfileSettings(UINT nMaxMRU)
{
   ASSERT_VALID(this);

   // The following assertion prevents calling
   // LoadStdProfileSettings() a second time without
   // first taking some precautions
   ASSERT(m_pRecentFileList == NULL);

   if (nMaxMRU != 0)
   {
      // create file MRU since nMaxMRU not zero
      m_pRecentFileList = new CRecentFileList(
                              0,
                              szFileSection, szFileEntry,
                              nMaxMRU);
      m_pRecentFileList->ReadList();
   }
   // 0 by default means not set
   m_nNumPreviewPages = GetProfileInt(
                                 szPreviewSection,
                                 szPreviewEntry,
                                 0);
}
```

To circumvent this problem, you could try to manipulate the *m_pRecentFileList* pointer before calling the *LoadStdProfileSettings()* function, as shown in Listing 2-36.

Listing 2-36. Manipulating the *m_pRecentFileList* pointer before calling the *LoadStdProfileSettings()* function.

```
#include <afxadv.h>  // For CRecentFileList definition

void CMyApp::SetMRULength( UINT nMaxMRU )
{
   ASSERT_VALID( this );

   if( m_pRecentFileList != NULL )
   {
      // Write current MRU list
      m_pRecentFileList->WriteList();

      // Free MRU object and set pointer to NULL
      delete m_pRecentFileList;
      m_pRecentFileList = NULL;
   }

   // Now call standard CWinApp function
   LoadStdProfileSettings( nMaxMRU );
}
```

Note that the code shown in Listing 2-36 must belong to a member function of your application class, because the *m_pRecentFileList* pointer is defined in the *protected* section of the *CWinApp* class and thus cannot be accessed from a class that is not derived from *CWinApp*.

Unfortunately—as I learned the hard way—being able to call the *LoadStdProfileSettings()* function repeatedly resolves only the easier half of the problem. The real difficulty comes from the items that the *CRecentFileList* class dynamically adds to the "file" menu. When your code changes the Recent Files list length, it must also delete those items. Although this may not seem a big deal at first, you must remember that an MDI application typically has one distinct menu resource for each document template as well as for the main frame window. You must update all these menus simultaneously; otherwise, prepare yourself to receive a handful of assertions!

Sample Code

- Project: MRULength in the Chap02 subdirectory on the companion CD-ROM.

- Purpose: Stores the user's preference regarding the Recent Files list length and sets this length correctly on the next execution. Figure 2-7 shows the MRULength application running with the length of its Recent Files list set to 6.

Implementation Highlights

- *CMDIApp::InitInstance()* function (MRULength.cpp)
- *CMDIApp::OnFileSetMRULength()* function (MRULength.cpp)

See Also

- *FAQ 2.15 How do I programmatically add a specific string to the Recent Files list?*
- *FAQ 2.16 How do I intercept the selection of a Recent File item by the user?*

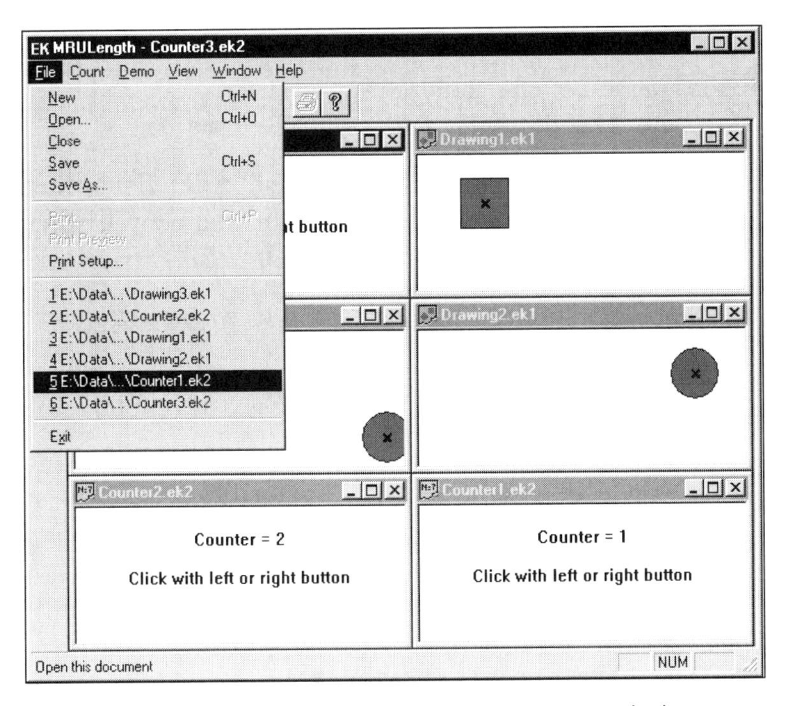

Figure 2-7. The MRULength application running with the length of its Recent Files list set to 6.

How do I programmatically add a specific string to the Recent Files list?

The Recent Files list contents are usually maintained automatically by MFC as the user opens and saves documents. However, it is sometimes useful to be able to programmatically add your own strings to this list. Use one of the following techniques.

First Technique

If the string that you want to add to the Recent Files list is actually a filename of one of your application's documents, you can call *CWinApp::AddToRecentFileList()* and pass it the desired filename:

```
CString strFilename;
// ...
// Fill strFilename with the desired filename
// ...
// Add strFilename to the Recent Files list
AfxGetApp()->AddToRecentFileList( strFilename );
```

Note that *CWinApp::AddToRecentFileList()* will call *AfxFullPath()* to obtain a full pathname to the filename that you passed as an argument. Listing 2-37 shows the pseudocode for *CWinApp::AddToRecentFileList()*.

Listing 2-37. Pseudocode for the *CWinApp::AddToRecentFileList()* function (AppUI.cpp).

```
void CWinApp::AddToRecentFileList(LPCTSTR lpszPathName)
{
// ...

   if (m_pRecentFileList != NULL)
   {
      // fully qualify the pathname
      TCHAR szTemp[_MAX_PATH];
      AfxFullPath(szTemp, lpszPathName);
      // then add to recent file list
      m_pRecentFileList->Add(szTemp);
   }
}
```

Because of this call to *AfxFullPath()*, you should pass only valid filenames to *CWinApp::AddToRecentFileList()*. Note, however, that MFC 4.x does not do anything with either the return value of *AfxFullPath()* or the *szTemp* buffer. Thus, any string that you pass to *CWinApp::AddToRecentFileList()* will get added to the Recent Files list.

To protect your code from changes in future versions of MFC, however, you should pass only valid filenames to *CWinApp::AddToRecentFileList()*. The second technique shows you how to write a generic *AddRecentString()* function that will safely add any string to the Recent Files list.

Second Technique

As explained in the first technique, if you want to add an arbitrary string to the Recent Files list I find it cleaner to write your own function to directly invoke *m_pRecentFileList->Add()* without calling *AfxFullPath()*, as *CWinApp::AddToRecentFileList()* does. Listing 2-38 shows an example.

Listing 2-38. Invoking *m_pRecentFileList->Add()* directly.

```
#include <afxadv.h>  // For CRecentFileList definition

void CMyApp::AddRecentString( LPCTSTR lpszString )
{
   ASSERT_VALID( this );
   ASSERT( lpszString != NULL );
   ASSERT( AfxIsValidString( lpszString ) );

   if (m_pRecentFileList != NULL)
   {
      // Directly add lpszString to the MRU list
      m_pRecentFileList->Add( lpszString );
   }
}
```

Note that the code shown in Listing 2-38 must belong to a member function of your application class, because the *m_pRecentFileList* pointer is defined in the *protected* section of the *CWinApp* class and thus cannot be accessed from a class that is not derived from *CWinApp*.

You can now call *AddRecentString()* from anywhere in your code to add a string to the top of the Recent Files list:

```
CString str;
// ...
// Fill str with the desired string
// ...
// Add str to the Recent Files list
theApp.AddRecentString( str );
```

■

Additional Comments

If you use the second technique and start adding strings to the Recent Files list that are not filenames, you must make sure that your code will intercept all selections made by the user in this list. Otherwise, the default MFC code will try to open a hypothetical document based on the selected "filename." This operation will probably fail, give the user a "<<<string>>> was not found" error message, and then remove the related entry from the Recent Files list.

See *FAQ 2.16 How do I intercept the selection of a Recent File item by the user?* for more explanation of intercepting the user's selections in the Recent Files list.

Sample Code

- Project: CustomMRU in the Chap02 subdirectory on the companion CD-ROM.
- Purpose: Programmatically adds strings to the Recent Files list. Figure 2-8 shows the CustomMRU application running with some arbitrary strings added to its Recent Files list.

Implementation Highlights

- *CMDIApp::AddRecentString()* function (CustomMRU.cpp)
- *CMDIApp::OnFileAddMRUString()* function (CustomMRU.cpp)

See Also

- *FAQ 2.16 How do I intercept the selection of a Recent File item by the user?*

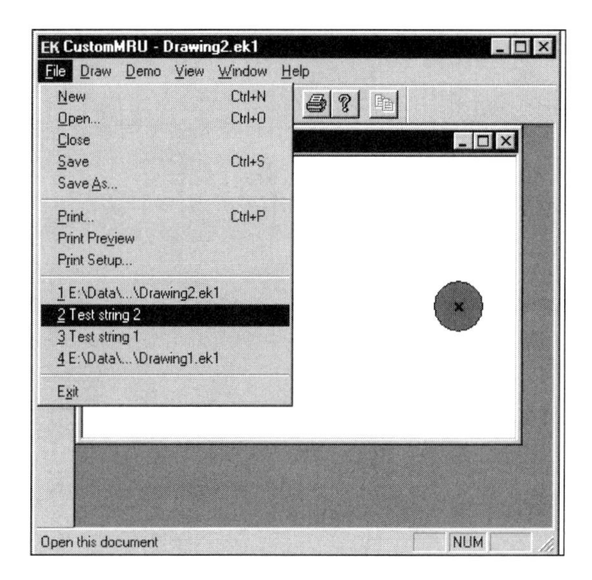

Figure 2-8. The CustomMRU application running with some arbitrary strings added to its Recent Files list.

FAQ 2.16 How do I intercept the selection of a Recent File item by the user?

It is sometimes necessary for your code to take control when the user of your application selects one item in the Recent Files list. For example, you may have used the technique shown in *FAQ 2.15 How do I programmatically add a specific string to the Recent Files list?* and you now need to take some special action when one of those strings is selected.

The best way to understand how you can intercept such a user selection is first to look at how MFC implements this same feature. MFC centralizes its handling of a user's selection in the Recent Files list in the *CWinApp::OnOpenRecentFile()* function (AppUI.cpp), whose pseudocode is shown in Listing 2-39.

Listing 2-39. Pseudocode for the *CWinApp::OnOpenRecentFile()* function (AppUI.cpp).

```
BOOL CWinApp::OnOpenRecentFile(UINT nID)
{
   ASSERT_VALID(this);
   ASSERT(m_pRecentFileList != NULL);
```

```
    ASSERT(nID >= ID_FILE_MRU_FILE1);
    ASSERT(nID < ID_FILE_MRU_FILE1 +
                 (UINT)m_pRecentFileList->GetSize());

    // Calculate index of selection in Recent Files list
    // (0 to 15)
    int nIndex = nID - ID_FILE_MRU_FILE1;

    ASSERT((*m_pRecentFileList)[nIndex].GetLength() != 0);

    TRACE2("MRU: open file (%d) '%s'.\n", (nIndex) + 1,
          (LPCTSTR)(*m_pRecentFileList)[nIndex]);

    // Retrieve the filename of the document stored at the
    // above index in the Recent Files list, and pass this
    // filename to the OpenDocumentFile() function
    if (OpenDocumentFile((*m_pRecentFileList)[nIndex])
                           == NULL)
       // If the document opening fails, remove the
       // corresponding entry from the Recent Files list
       m_pRecentFileList->Remove(nIndex);

    return TRUE;
}
```

CWinApp::OnOpenRecentFile() gets called through an almost normal message map processing. I say "almost normal" because MFC exploits the seldom-used *ON_COMMAND_EX_RANGE()* message map macro to map the range of valid Recent Files list entries (from *ID_FILE_MRU_FILE1* to *ID_FILE_MRU_FILE16*) to *OnOpenRecentFile()*. You can find the *ON_COMMAND_EX_RANGE()* macro in Listing 2-40, which shows *CWinApp*'s message map.

Listing 2-40. *CWinApp*'s message map (AppCore.cpp).

```
BEGIN_MESSAGE_MAP(CWinApp, CCmdTarget)
    //{{AFX_MSG_MAP(CWinApp)
    // Global File commands
    ON_COMMAND(ID_APP_EXIT, OnAppExit)
    // MRU - most recently used file menu
    ON_UPDATE_COMMAND_UI(ID_FILE_MRU_FILE1,
                         OnUpdateRecentFileMenu)
    ON_COMMAND_EX_RANGE(ID_FILE_MRU_FILE1,
```

```
                                    ID_FILE_MRU_FILE16,
                                    OnOpenRecentFile)
    //}}AFX_MSG_MAP
END_MESSAGE_MAP()
```

Now that you know how MFC handles the selection of a Recent File item by the user, the solution to the preceding problem statement must seem rather obvious:

Step 1. In your application class, add a prototype for your override of *OnOpenRecentFile():*

```
afx_msg BOOL OnOpenRecentFile(UINT nID);
```

You can choose a different name for this function if you want to, although I prefer to stick with *OnOpenRecentFile()* for this explanation.

Step 2. Add the following *ON_COMMAND_EX_RANGE()* macro to your application class's message map:

```
ON_COMMAND_EX_RANGE(ID_FILE_MRU_FILE1, ID_FILE_MRU_FILE16,
                    OnOpenRecentFile)
```

Note that you must type this entry manually, because ClassWizard does not support adding the *ON_COMMAND_EX_RANGE()* macro.

Step 3. Implement *CMyApp::OnOpenRecentFile()* and process the user's selection as needed. Listing 2-41 shows how you can retrieve the string associated with the Recent Files list item selected by the user.

Listing 2-41. Retrieving the string associated with the Recent Files list item selected by the user.

```
#include <afxadv.h>  // For CRecentFileList definition

BOOL CMyApp::OnOpenRecentFile(UINT nID)
{
// ...

    // Calculate index of selection in Recent Files list
    // (0 to 15)
    int nIndex = nID - ID_FILE_MRU_FILE1;
```

```
    // Retrieve the string stored at the
    // above index in the Recent Files list.
    CString strMRU = (*m_pRecentFileList)[nIndex];

// ...
    // ... Process strMRU as you like ...
// ...
}
```

Note that the code shown in Listing 2-41 must belong to a member function of your application class, because the *m_pRecentFileList* pointer is defined in the *protected* section of the *CWinApp* class and thus cannot be accessed from a class that is not derived from *CWinApp*.

■

Sample Code

- Project: CustomMRU in the Chap02 subdirectory on the companion CD-ROM.
- Purpose: Intercepts the selection of a Recent File item by the user, retrieves the associated string, and prompts whether to follow with the default processing. Figure 2-9 shows the dialog box that the CustomMRU application pops up when the user selects an item in the Recent Files list.

Implementation Highlights

- *CMDIApp::OnOpenRecentFile()* function (CustomMRU.cpp)

See Also

- *FAQ 2.15 How do I programmatically add a specific string to the Recent Files list?*

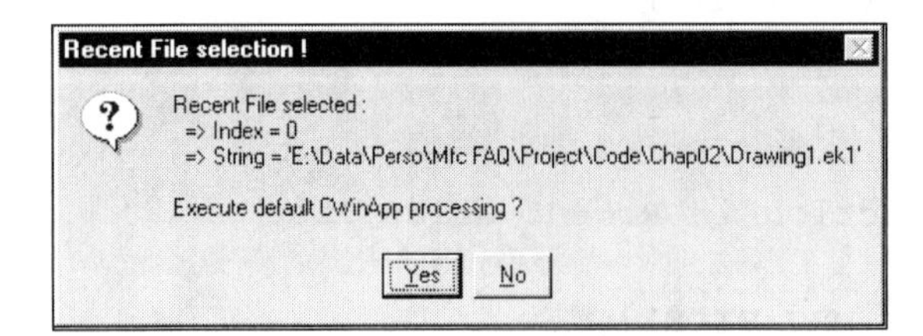

Figure 2-9. The dialog box that the CustomMRU application pops up when the user selects an item in the Recent Files list.

2.17 How do I make my application automatically open the document that is at the top of the Recent Files list?

This problem is similar to the one solved in *FAQ 2.9 How do I make my application remember the last active document and automatically reopen it?* However, the solution here will be even simpler, because the standard MFC Recent Files list mechanism will take care of storing and retrieving the list of recent documents. Thus, you need only implement the automatic opening of the document that is at the top of the list. This means adding some code to your application's *InitInstance()* function, as shown in Listing 2-42.

Listing 2-42. Opening the document at the top of the Recent Files list in the *InitInstance()* function.

```
#include <afxadv.h>  // For CRecentFileList definition

BOOL CMyApp::InitInstance()
{
// ...

   // Parse command line for standard shell commands, DDE,
   // file open
   CCommandLineInfo cmdInfo;
   ParseCommandLine(cmdInfo);

   // Restore the document at the top of the MRU list
     // 1 - Only if no command-line argument
   if( cmdInfo.m_nShellCommand == CCommandLineInfo::FileNew
      || cmdInfo.m_nShellCommand ==
                  CCommandLineInfo::FileNothing )
   {
      // 2 - Make sure that there is an MRU list
      if( m_pRecentFileList != NULL )
      {
         CString strMRU = (*m_pRecentFileList)[0];

         // 3 - Verify that the first MRU string is valid
         if( !strMRU.IsEmpty() )
```

```
            // 4 - Open this document file
            OpenDocumentFile( strMRU );
        }
    }
    else  // 5 - Perform standard command-line processing
    {
        // Dispatch commands specified on the command line
        if (!ProcessShellCommand(cmdInfo))
            return FALSE;
    }

    // The main window has been initialized, so show and
    // update it.
    pMainFrame->ShowWindow(m_nCmdShow);
    pMainFrame->UpdateWindow();

    return TRUE;
}
```

■

Sample Code

- Project: OpenMRUDoc in the Chap02 subdirectory on the companion CD-ROM.
- Purpose: When launched, the application automatically opens the document at the top of the Recent Files list.

Implementation Highlights

- *CMDIApp::InitInstance()* function (OpenMRUDoc.cpp)

See Also

- *FAQ 2.8 How do I programmatically open an existing document file?*
- *FAQ 2.9 How do I make my application remember the last active document and automatically reopen it?*

Miscellaneous Items

FAQ 2.18 How do I get a pointer to the currently active document?

The solution to this problem is not difficult in itself, but it requires a good understanding of the relationships among the various objects in an MFC application as well as knowledge of the functions that allow you to navigate among those objects. The technique shown in Listing 2-43 provides a generic, reusable way of obtaining a pointer to the currently active document object. You can call this function from anywhere in your code.

Listing 2-43. Getting a pointer to the active document object from anywhere in an MFC application.

```
CDocument* EkGetActiveDocument()
{
   // 1 - Get a pointer to the application's
   // main frame window
   CWnd* pWnd = AfxGetMainWnd();
   if( pWnd == NULL )
      return NULL;

   // 2 - Make sure the pointer is valid and more
   // strongly typed
   ASSERT_VALID( pWnd );
   ASSERT_KINDOF( CFrameWnd, pWnd );
   CFrameWnd* pMainFrame =
                    static_cast< CFrameWnd* >( pWnd );

   // 3 - Get a pointer to the active frame window
   // (may be 'this' for SDI application)
   CFrameWnd* pActiveFrame = pMainFrame->GetActiveFrame();
   if( pActiveFrame == NULL )
      return NULL;
```

```
    // 4 - Return a pointer to the active document object
    return pActiveFrame->GetActiveDocument();
}
```

Note that the implementation shown in Listing 2-43 works equally well for MDI and SDI applications. For an MDI application, the *GetActiveFrame()* function call will return a pointer to the active view's frame window (or *NULL* if none exists). For an SDI application, the *GetActiveFrame()* function simply returns the implicit *this* pointer, because the main frame window also plays the role of the view frame window.

■

Additional Comments

You should be aware that the function shown in Listing 2-43 may return a *NULL* pointer under some conditions. Consequently, you should design your code to account for this possibility.

Note also that the returned pointer is of the generic *CDocument** type. If you want to take an action based on the specific class of the active document object, you will have to rely on the runtime type information mechanism provided by MFC via the *CObject* class and the *CRuntimeClass* structure. Listing 2-44 shows how to check the class of the active document object in order to safely downcast the *CDocument** pointer returned by the *EkGetActiveDocument()* function to get a more strongly typed pointer.

Listing 2-44. Checking the class of the active document object and safely downcasting.

```
CDocument* pActiveDoc = EkGetActiveDocument();
if( pActiveDoc != NULL )
{
    if( pActiveDoc->IsKindOf( RUNTIME_CLASS( CMyDoc1 ) ) )
    {
        // Downcast is safe
        CMyDoc1* pMyDoc1 =
                    static_cast< CMyDoc1* >( pActiveDoc );

        // ... Use pMyDoc1 ...

    }
```

```
    else if( pActiveDoc->IsKindOf(
                              RUNTIME_CLASS( CMyDoc2 ) ) )
    {
       CMyDoc2* pMyDoc2 =
                    static_cast< CMyDoc2* >( pActiveDoc );

       // ... Use pMyDoc2 ...

    }
    else
    {
       // ...
    }
}
```

Listing 2-45 works in the same way as Listing 2-44 but uses the *DYNAMIC_DOWNCAST()* macro instead of *IsKindOf()* and *static_cast* for safe downcasting.

Listing 2-45. Using the *DYNAMIC_DOWNCAST()* macro for safe downcasting.

```
CDocument* pActiveDoc = EkGetActiveDocument();
if( pActiveDoc != NULL )
{
   CMyDoc1* pMyDoc1 = DYNAMIC_DOWNCAST(CMyDoc1,pActiveDoc);
   CMyDoc2* pMyDoc2 = DYNAMIC_DOWNCAST(CMyDoc2,pActiveDoc);
   if( pMyDoc1 != NULL )
   {
      // ... Use pMyDoc1 ...
   }
   else if( pMyDoc2 != NULL )
   {
      // ... Use pMyDoc2 ...
   }
   else
   {
      // ...
   }
}
```

Many readers will be eager to point out that the code structures shown in Listing 2-44 and 2-45 are not at all object-oriented and thus should be avoided whenever possible. I agree with this statement, and you must indeed be aware of the dangers of this code structure, especially regarding maintainability when the number of possible document types grows. However, this technique is sometimes the only (easy enough) way to get your work done.

Just be sure to use it only when you really cannot avoid it, and be conscious of the tradeoffs, and don't forget that overusing this technique probably means that your application's overall design needs to be reviewed and maybe reworked a bit.

Here's a crash course in object-oriented design. Look for the common operations that you expect to apply to each document class and create a base document class that declares these operations as virtual functions, maybe even as pure virtual functions. Each of your "real" document classes would inherit from this base class and implement each virtual operation appropriately. You would then call your virtual functions through the document pointers returned by *EkGetActiveDocument()* without needing to go through any of the contortions shown in Listing 2-44 or 2-45.

Sample Code

- Project: GetActiveDoc in the Chap02 subdirectory on the companion CD-ROM.
- Purpose: Gets a pointer to the active document object in an MDI application. Figure 2-10 shows the dialog box that the GetActiveDoc application pops up when the user selects the "Demo, Show Active Document Info" menu command.

Implementation Highlights

- *EkGetActiveDocument()* function (GetActiveDoc.cpp)
- *CMDIApp::OnFileActiveDocument()* function (GetActiveDoc.cpp)

Although this sample application implements the preceding menu command handler in its application class, this command could be handled by any other class while using exactly the same code.

See Also

- *FAQ 3.39 How do I get a pointer to the active view?*

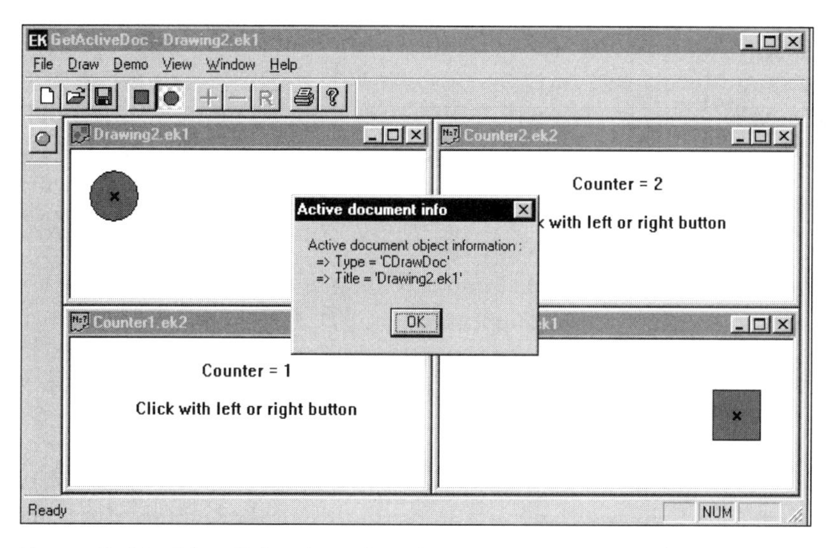

Figure 2-10. The dialog box that the GetActiveDoc application pops up when the user selects the "Demo, Show Active Document Info" menu command.

FAQ 2.19 How do I iterate through the list of all the currently opened documents?

You may sometimes need to iterate through the list of all the currently opened document objects—for example, to apply a specific operation to each document object. However, you may be baffled by the fact that the MFC documentation does not mention any list that would contain pointers to all the opened document objects.

Indeed, MFC does not maintain a global list of pointers to all the opened document objects. This information *is* accessible, however, albeit in a slightly more complex way:

- The application object stores a list of pointers to all the registered document template objects. You can traverse this first list by calling *CWinApp:: GetFirstDocTemplatePosition()* and *CWinApp:: GetNextDocTemplate()*. (These function calls delegate all the work to the *CDocManager* inner object, which actually manages the list of registered document templates.)

- Each document template object stores a list of pointers to all the document objects that have been created via its own *CDocTemplate::CreateNewDocument()* function (which always gets called at some point by *OpenDocumentFile()*). You can traverse this second list by calling *CDocTemplate::GetFirstDocPosition()* and *CDocTemplate::GetNextDoc()*.

Thus, by writing the necessary code to traverse this "list of list of" pointers to document objects structure, you can iterate through all the currently opened document objects. The first technique implements this traversal in a straightforward and explicit way, whereas the second technique shows how to design and use a *CEkDocList* helper class to ease the pain of enumerating your document objects.

First Technique

The most straightforward way to iterate through all the opened document objects is to explicitly write the code that will traverse the double-list structure explained earlier. Each iteration through the inner loop of this code returns a pointer to a document object, which you can then manipulate as you wish. Listing 2-46 shows how to implement this double-list traversal and where to insert your specific code.

Listing 2-46. Explicitly iterating through all the opened document objects.

```
CWinApp* pApp = AfxGetApp();
ASSERT_VALID( pApp );

// 1 - Iterate through the application's document
// templates list
POSITION posTemplate =
                pApp->GetFirstDocTemplatePosition();
while( posTemplate != NULL )
{
   // 2 - For each document template object...
   CDocTemplate* pTemplate =
      pApp->GetNextDocTemplate( posTemplate );
   ASSERT_VALID( pTemplate );
   ASSERT_KINDOF( CDocTemplate, pTemplate );

   // 3 - Iterate through the template's document list
   POSITION posDocument =
                pTemplate->GetFirstDocPosition();
   while( posDocument != NULL )
```

```
    {
        // 4 - For each document object...
        CDocument* pDoc =
            pTemplate->GetNextDoc( posDocument );
        ASSERT_VALID( pDoc );
        ASSERT_KINDOF( CDocument, pDoc );

        // ...
        // 5 - ==>> Work with pDoc HERE <<==
        // ...
    }
}
```

Second Technique

Although it is not a big deal to simply copy and paste the code shown in the first technique when and where you need it, you might—rightly—look for a more elegant and generic solution to this problem. The *CEkDocList* helper class whose implementation is shown in Listing 2-47 encapsulates all the double-list traversal code and presents you with a clean and easy-to-use interface.

Listing 2-47. Definition of the *CEkDocList* helper class for enumerating document objects.

```
// ————————————————————————————
// EkDocList.h: header file
//

#ifndef __EKDOCLIST_H__
#define __EKDOCLIST_H__

#include <afxtempl.h>    // For CTypedPtrList template

//////////////////////////////////////////////////////////////
// CEkDocList: enumerator class for the document objects
//             in an MDI application

class CEkDocList
{
public:
    // Constuction - Destruction
    CEkDocList();      // The constructor fills our internal
                       // list of pointer to document objects
```

```
    ~CEkDocList();

    // Operations
    CDocument* GetNextDoc();  // Gets next document object

    // Forbid copy and assignment of CEkDocList objects

private:
    CEkDocList( const CEkDocList& );
    const CEkDocList& operator = ( const CEkDocList& );

private:
    // Implementation

    // Internal list of pointers to document objects
    CTypedPtrList< CObList, CDocument* > m_DocList;

    // Current position in the above list
    POSITION m_posDocList;
};

#endif   // __EKDOCLIST_H__

// ----------------------------------
// EkDocList.cpp: implementation file
//

#include "stdafx.h"

#include "EkDocList.h"

////////////////////////////////////////////////////////////
// CEkDocList implementation

CEkDocList::CEkDocList()
{
    CWinApp* pApp = AfxGetApp();
    ASSERT_VALID( pApp );

    // 1 - Iterate through the application's document
```

```
   // templates list
   POSITION posTemplate =
               pApp->GetFirstDocTemplatePosition();
   while( posTemplate != NULL )
   {
      // 2 - For each document template object...
      CDocTemplate* pTemplate =
            pApp->GetNextDocTemplate( posTemplate );
      ASSERT_VALID( pTemplate );
      ASSERT_KINDOF( CDocTemplate, pTemplate );

      // 3 - Iterate through the template's document list
      POSITION posDocument =
               pTemplate->GetFirstDocPosition();
      while( posDocument != NULL )
      {
         // 4 - For each document object...
         CDocument* pDoc =
               pTemplate->GetNextDoc( posDocument );
         ASSERT_VALID( pDoc );
         ASSERT_KINDOF( CDocument, pDoc );

         // 5 - Add the document pointer to our
         // internal list
         m_DocList.AddTail( pDoc );
      }
   }

   // 6 - Initialize our POSITION member
   m_posDocList = m_DocList.GetHeadPosition();
}

CEkDocList::~CEkDocList()
{
   m_DocList.RemoveAll();
   m_posDocList = NULL;
}
CDocument* CEkDocList::GetNextDoc()
{
   if( m_posDocList == NULL )
      return NULL;
```

```
    CDocument* pDoc = m_DocList.GetNext( m_posDocList );
    ASSERT_VALID( pDoc );
    ASSERT_KINDOF( CDocument, pDoc );

    return pDoc;
}
```

Listing 2-48 shows how you might use the *CEkDocList* class in your code. Compare this code with the code shown in Listing 2-46, and I think that you will be convinced of the advantages provided by the *CEkDocList* class in terms of code clarity and maintainability.

Listing 2-48. Using the *CEkDocList* class to iterate through all the opened document objects.

```
#include "EkDocList.h"  // For CEkDocList class

// 1 - Construct CEkDocList enumerator object
CEkDocList DocList;

// 2 - For each document object...
CDocument* pDoc;
while( pDoc = DocList.GetNextDoc() )
{
    // ...
    // 3 - Work with pDoc HERE
    // ...
}
```

■

Additional Comments

Note that instances of the *CEkDocList* class should be short-lived, because the class initializes its document list only once, in its constructor. Therefore, the information maintained by the *CEkDocList* class remains current for only a short time. You should typically declare a *CEkDocList* object on the stack when you need one and use it only during the context of one message handler.

Note also that both techniques hand you pointers of the generic *CDocument** type. If you want to take an action based on the specific class of each document object, you will have to rely on the runtime type information mechanism provided by MFC via the *CObject* class and the *CRuntimeClass* structure. For a detailed discussion of this issue, see the Additional Comments section of *FAQ 2.18 How do I get a pointer to the currently active document?*

Sample Code

- Project: IterateDocs in the Chap02 subdirectory on the companion CD-ROM.
- Purpose: Iterates through the list of all the currently opened documents. Figure 2-11 shows the dialog box that the IterateDoc application pops up when the user selects either of the "Iterate..." menu commands.

Implementation Highlights

- *CEkDocList* class (EkDocList.h, EkDocList.cpp)
- *CDocListDlg::InitFirstTechnique()* function (DocListDlg.cpp)
- *CDocListDlg::InitSecondTechnique()* function (DocListDlg.cpp)

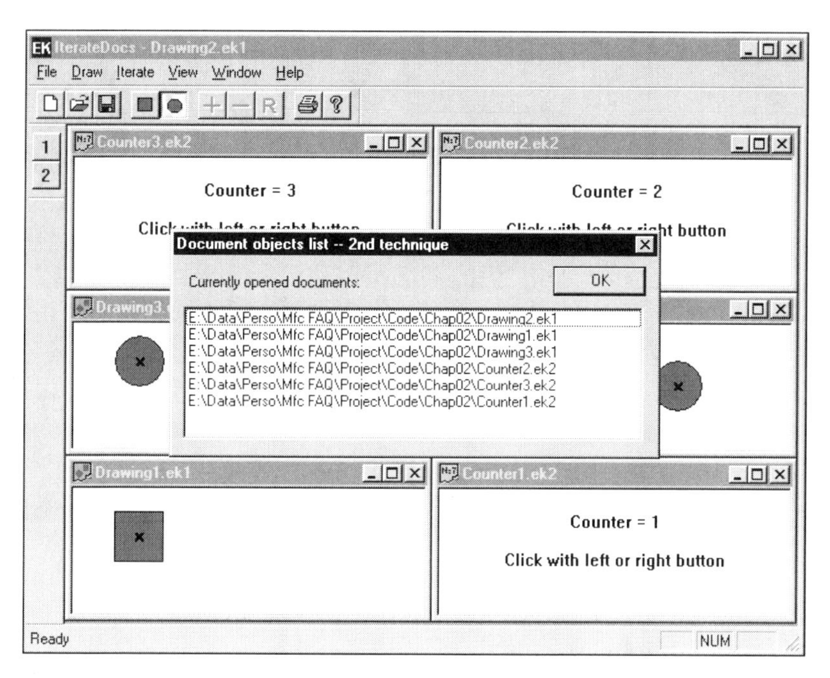

Figure 2-11. The dialog box that the IterateDocs application pops up when the user selects either of the "Iterate..." menu commands.

See Also

- *FAQ 2.11 How do I implement a "Save all documents" menu command that does not prompt the user before saving each modified document?*
- *FAQ 2.13 How do I implement a "Close all documents" menu command?*
- *FAQ 2.18 How do I get a pointer to the currently active document?*

2.20 Why doesn't my application register its document files with Windows Explorer, and how do I correct this situation?

An AppWizard-generated application usually registers itself automatically with Windows Explorer in order to function as a drop target for its document files and to allow the user to launch the application by double-clicking on a document file. However, you may come across some applications that do not behave in this way. Indeed, some AppWizard-generated applications seem not to register themselves at all with Windows Explorer. This problem usually shows up because you did not specify any extension string while using AppWizard to generate the skeleton of your application.

This situation can easily arise if you do not click the "Advanced..." button on AppWizard step 4. Clicking this button brings up the dialog box shown in Figure 2-12, where you can define the various parts of the document template string.

Note the "File extension" and "Filter name" edit boxes in Figure 2-12: both fields are empty by default. As soon as you type an extension in the "File extension" edit box, AppWizard supplies a guess for the "Filter name" string. You can override AppWizard's suggestion immediately, or change it later by editing the document template string in the ResourceView pane of Visual C++ Developer Studio.

The heart of the problem lies in the fact that AppWizard does not generate a particular block of code in your application's *InitInstance()* function when the "File extension" edit box is left blank, which is its default state if you don't explicitly click the "Advanced . . ." button in AppWizard step 4.

Listing 2-49 highlights the block of code that registers your application's document files with Windows Explorer.

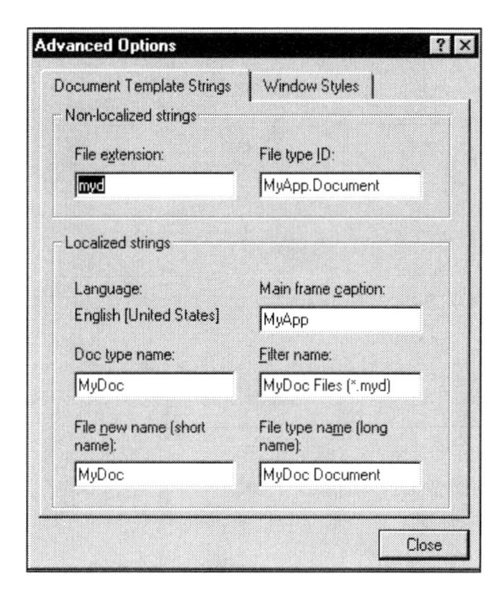

Figure 2-12. AppWizard Advanced Options dialog box for defining the various parts of the document template string.

Listing 2-49. The block of code that registers your application's document files with Windows Explorer.

```
BOOL CMyApp::InitInstance()
{
// ...

   CMultiDocTemplate* pDocTemplate;
   pDocTemplate = new CMultiDocTemplate(
      IDR_TESTTYPE,
      RUNTIME_CLASS(CMyDoc),
      RUNTIME_CLASS(CChildFrame), // custom MDI child frame
      RUNTIME_CLASS(CMyView));
   AddDocTemplate(pDocTemplate);

// ...
   // create main MDI Frame window
   CMainFrame* pMainFrame = new CMainFrame;
   if (!pMainFrame->LoadFrame(IDR_MAINFRAME))
      return FALSE;
   m_pMainWnd = pMainFrame;

   //---------------------------------
   // This block of code registers your document files
   // with Windows Explorer
```

```
    // Enable drag/drop open
    m_pMainWnd->DragAcceptFiles();

    // Allow Windows Explorer to open your application
    // by double-clicking on a document file
    EnableShellOpen();

    // Register your document files' extensions with
    // Windows Explorer
    RegisterShellFileTypes(TRUE);
    //------------------------------------

    // Parse command line for standard shell commands,
    // DDE, file open
    CCommandLineInfo cmdInfo;
    ParseCommandLine(cmdInfo);

// ...
}
```

If you do not find the preceding block of code in your own application's *InitInstance()* function, simply insert these lines at the appropriate location, as shown in Listing 2-49, and your application will now behave like a good Windows Explorer citizen! Just make sure that you have edited your document template string to add valid strings in the *filterExt, regFileTypeId,* and *regFileTypeName* fields.

■

Sample Code

There is no sample project for this FAQ.

See Also

- *FAQ 2.5 How do I associate multiple file extensions with the same document or view class?*
- *FAQ 1.8 What is the role of the document template resource ID?*

3 VIEWS AND FRAME WINDOWS

You might initially feel a little intimidated by this chapter, which is by far the longest in this book. There is, however, a reasonable explanation for its length: after all, views and frame windows are the central part of the user interface of most applications—the most notable exception being dialog-based applications—and everybody knows that the quality of the user interface can make or break an application.

Precise control of the behavior of views and frame windows in an MFC application is therefore essential if you are to craft a modern and sophisticated user interface that is both effective and attractive. This chapter's length reflects the many customizations that you can add to the default behavior of the standard MFC classes in order to design your own unique user interface.

I hope that this chapter will answer most of your user-interface questions as well as provide you with many cool features that you will be able to add to your application in a few minutes. Having used most of these features in several developments, I can testify to the "wow" effect that they have on many users—and on fellow developers, too!

Note that the FAQs in this chapter make liberal use of the word *view* to encompass the actual view object as well as the view's frame window, especially in the titles of several FAQs. For example, you will find FAQ titles referring to "opening a view," "closing a view," and so on. This imprecise wording is voluntary, because in many cases the desired behavior can be implemented either in the view's frame window or in the view class itself, as explained in *FAQ 3.2 How do I choose between implementing a specific behavior in the view class or in the view's frame window class?* Therefore, I decided to use the broader (and less precise) word *view* to refer to what the user perceives as a view on a document. I am careful, however, to differentiate between the view and its parent frame window in the technical explanations, where it matters most.

General Topics

3.1 How do I add a new kind of view or frame window to my application?

AppWizard and ClassWizard are certainly some of the coolest tools in the MFC developer's bag of tricks, but they do not help very much with certain simple tasks, such as adding another kind of view to your application. Although this task is basic in MFC programming, it already requires a good understanding of the various relationships among documents, document templates (and their associated resources), views, and a view's frame windows.

To put the following steps in a meaningful context, we will assume that your application's *InitInstance()* function already registers its default document template as shown in Listing 3-1.

Listing 3-1. Default document template registered in *CMDIApp::InitInstance()*.

```
BOOL CMDIApp::InitInstance()
{
// ...

   // 'Drawing' document template
   m_ptDrawView = new CMultiDocTemplate(
      IDR_DRAWTYPE,
      RUNTIME_CLASS(CDrawDoc),
      RUNTIME_CLASS(CChildFrame), // custom MDI child frame
      RUNTIME_CLASS(CDrawView));
   AddDocTemplate(m_ptDrawView);

// ...
}
```

In this code fragment, the document class is called *CDrawDoc* and the default view class is called *CDrawView*. The document template whose address is stored in the *m_ptDrawView* variable has a resource ID called *IDR_DRAWTYPE*.

The *m_ptDrawView* variable in the preceding code fragment is declared as a data member of type *CMultiDocTemplate* in your application's class. For an explanation of why and how you should store pointers to your document template objects in your application's class, refer to *FAQ 2.1 How should I create and reference multiple document templates in my application?*

We will also suppose that you have created a new view class called *CNewDrawView* and that you now want to hook this view class to your application:

Step 1. Create a new set of document template resources with an ID called *IDR_NEWDRAWTYPE* by following the explanations given in *FAQ 2.3 How do I create the resources associated with a new document template resource ID?*

Step 2. Add a new *CMultiDocTemplate* pointer member variable to your application class, as shown in Listing 3-2.

Listing 3-2. The application class with a new *CMultiDocTemplate* pointer member variable added.

```
class CMyApp : public CWinApp
{
// ...

public:
   // Member variables used to store the various
   // document templates objects that we create in
   // InitInstance()
   CMultiDocTemplate* m_ptDrawView;     // Initial pointer
   CMultiDocTemplate* m_ptNewDrawView;  // New pointer

// ...
};
```

Step 3. In your application's *InitInstance()* function, create a *NewDrawView* document template object that references the *IDR_NEWDRAWTYPE* resources and the *CNewDrawView* class. Listing 3-3 shows what the relevant fragment of your application's *InitInstance()* function should look like.

Listing 3-3. Creating the new *NewDrawView* document template object in the application's *InitInstance()* function.

```
BOOL CMyApp::InitInstance()
{
// ...

   // 'Drawing' document template
   m_ptDrawView = new CMultiDocTemplate(
      IDR_DRAWTYPE,
      RUNTIME_CLASS(CDrawDoc),
      RUNTIME_CLASS(CChildFrame), // custom MDI child frame
      RUNTIME_CLASS(CDrawView));
   AddDocTemplate(m_ptDrawView);

   // 'NewDrawView' document template
   m_ptNewDrawView = new CMultiDocTemplate(
      IDR_NEWDRAWTYPE,               // New resources
      RUNTIME_CLASS(CDrawDoc),       // Same document class
      RUNTIME_CLASS(CChildFrame),
      RUNTIME_CLASS(CNewDrawView)); // New view class
   AddDocTemplate(m_ptNewDrawView);

// ...
}
```

Step 4. Your new document template is now ready for use. To programmatically open a new window using the *m_ptNewDrawView* document template, use the *EkCreateNewWindow()* function discussed in *FAQ 3.3 How do I programmatically open a view based on a specific document template?* (I apologize for referring you to two other FAQs for the same problem here, but the only alternative I could think of would have been to duplicate the same text. So let's save some trees!)

If you want to add a new kind of frame window to your application (say, of class *CNewChildFrame*), follow the same steps but change step 2 so that your new document template references the *CNewChildFrame* class instead of the standard *CChildFrame* class (while keeping the same document and view classes).

Listing 3-4 shows the implementation of the *CMDIApp::InitInstance()* function for the MultiViews sample project for this FAQ. Each document template created in this function references the same *CDrawDoc* document class, but a different view's frame and view class as well as a different resource ID.

Listing 3-4. Implementing the *CMDIApp::InitInstance()* function to register multiple kinds of views and frame windows.

```
BOOL CMDIApp::InitInstance()
{
// ...

   // Register the application's document templates.
   // Document templates serve as the connection between
   // documents, frame windows, and views.

   // 'Drawing' document template
   m_ptDrawView = new CMultiDocTemplate(
      IDR_DRAWTYPE,
      RUNTIME_CLASS(CDrawDoc),      // DrawDoc document type
      RUNTIME_CLASS(CChildFrame), // standard view frame
      RUNTIME_CLASS(CDrawView));    // DrawView class
   AddDocTemplate(m_ptDrawView);

   m_ptDrawFormView = new CMultiDocTemplate(
      IDR_DRAWFORMTYPE,
      RUNTIME_CLASS(CDrawDoc),      // DrawDoc document type
      RUNTIME_CLASS(CEkFixedFormFrame), // "Fixed" frame
      RUNTIME_CLASS(CDrawFormView));     // Form View class
   AddDocTemplate(m_ptDrawFormView);

   m_ptSplitFrame = new CMultiDocTemplate(
      IDR_DRAWSPLITTERTYPE,
      RUNTIME_CLASS(CDrawDoc),      // DrawDoc document type
      RUNTIME_CLASS(CSplitFrame), // Splitter frame window
      NULL);                    // Views created by splitter
   AddDocTemplate(m_ptSplitFrame);

// ...
}
```

Listing 3-5 shows how the MultiViews sample project for this FAQ creates the various kinds of views when the user selects the corresponding menu command or toolbar button. I decided to handle these commands in the document class, a technique that makes it trivial to find the document with which the new view should be associated.

Listing 3-5. Creating multiple kinds of views in the MultiViews sample project.

```
void CDrawDoc::OnWindowNewView()
{
   EkCreateNewWindow( theApp.m_ptDrawView, this );
}

void CDrawDoc::OnWindowNewFormView()
{
   EkCreateNewWindow( theApp.m_ptDrawFormView, this );
}

void CDrawDoc::OnWindowNewSplitter()
{
   EkCreateNewWindow( theApp.m_ptSplitFrame, this );
}
```

■

Additional Comments

If the *CNewDrawView* class has a specific behavior for which you wish to display new menu commands, you can add these commands to the *IDR_NEWDRAWTYPE* menu resources that you created in step 1. MFC automatically swaps the menu to track the active view.

Sample Code

- Project: MultiViews in the Chap03 subdirectory on the companion CD-ROM.
- Purpose: Registers multiple document templates and opens different kinds of views on the same document (see Figure 3-1):
  - A standard drawing view
  - A form view
  - A three-way splitter window

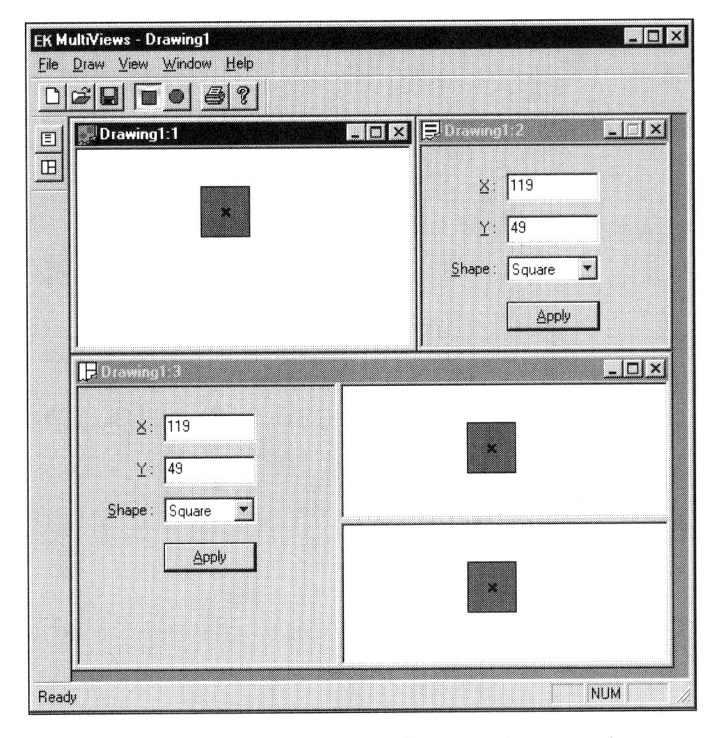

Figure 3-1. The MultiViews application showing the three different kinds of views it can open on the same document.

To create each kind of view, select the appropriate command from the "Window" menu or click on the associated toolbar button.

Implementation Highlights

- *CMDIApp::InitInstance()* function (MultiViews.cpp)
- *EkCreateNewWindow()* function (DrawDoc.cpp)
- *CDrawDoc::OnWindowNewView()* function (DrawDoc.cpp)
- *CDrawDoc::OnWindowNewFormView()* function (DrawDoc.cpp)
- *CDrawDoc::OnWindowNewSplitter()* function (DrawDoc.cpp)

See Also

- *FAQ 2.1 How should I create and reference multiple document templates in my application?*

- *FAQ 2.3 How do I create the resources associated with a new document template resource ID?*
- *FAQ 2.5 How do I associate multiple file extensions with the same document or view class?*
- *FAQ 3.3 How do I programmatically open a view based on a specific document template?*
- *FAQ 3.33 How do I program a window with both horizontal and vertical static splitter panes (three-way splitter)?*

3.2 How do I choose between implementing a specific behavior in the view class or in the view's frame window class?

As various FAQs in this chapter will show, some behaviors can be implemented either in the view class or in the view's frame window class. For example:

- *FAQ 3.7 How do I prevent a view from being closed by the user?*
- *FAQ 3.9 How do I set the initial position and size of a view?*
- *FAQ 3.11 How do I center a view?*
- *FAQ 3.15 How do I make a view initially appear minimized or maximized?*

To avoid repeating the same discussion, I will quickly compare the pros and cons of each technique here.

Choosing to implement a behavior *in the view class* has the following consequences:

- *Pros:* This design is usually the easiest to implement. In particular, there is no need to create a new view's frame class to implement a specific behavior.
- *Cons:* This design is not very clean, because it makes the view handle additional functionality that normally belongs to the view's frame class. This design may also create reusability problems. For example, what happens if you want to reuse the same view in another context, such as a splitter window? If one view implements an "open centered" behavior and the other one implements an "open at the upper-right corner" behavior, you will have to work hard to make them cooperate in a splitter window. Or suppose that you want to reuse the same behavior in another kind of view. Either you must factor this behavior in a common base class or you must duplicate the code.

Choosing to implement a behavior in the *view's frame window class* has the following consequences:

- *Pros:* This design is the cleanest one from an object-oriented perspective. It allows you to cleanly encapsulate the behavior in the view's frame window class and to freely associate this class with different kinds of views.
- *Cons:* Implementing this design is usually slightly more complex, because it typically requires the creation of a new view's frame window class that must subsequently be referenced in the appropriate document template(s). Although reusability is theoretically better with this design, you may find it necessary to create many distinct view's frame window classes (and the associated document template objects) to handle the various needs of your application. Imagine, for example, that you want some of your views to open centered, others to have a nonresizable frame window, and still others to be unavailable for closing by the user. Handling all the possible combinations of these behaviors means creating quite a few classes! Fortunately, most applications need only a few well-defined view's frame window behaviors.

■

Sample Code

There is no sample project for this FAQ.

Opening and Closing Views and Frame Windows

FAQ 3.3 How do I programmatically open a view based on a specific document template?

We will assume that you have stored pointers to your various document template objects in your application's class, as explained in *FAQ 2.1 How should I create and reference multiple document templates in my application?* and *FAQ 3.1 How do I add a new kind of view or frame window to my application?*

Here is how you can programmatically open a new view using the view's frame window and view classes specified in one of your document templates:

Step 1. Implement the *EkCreateNewWindow()* function as shown in Listing 3-6.

Listing 3-6. Implementing the *EkCreateNewWindow()* function to create a new view/frame pair on a document.

```
// Create a new view based on the pTemplate document
// template and associated with pDocument

CFrameWnd* EkCreateNewWindow( CDocTemplate* pTemplate,
                              CDocument* pDocument )
{
   ASSERT_VALID( pTemplate );
   ASSERT_VALID( pDocument );

   // 1 - Create the new frame window
   // (will in turn create the associated view)
   CFrameWnd* pFrame = pTemplate->CreateNewFrame(
                                       pDocument, NULL );
   if( pFrame == NULL )
   {
      // Window creation failed
      TRACE0( "Warning: failed to create new frame.\n" );
      return NULL;
   }
   ASSERT_KINDOF( CFrameWnd, pFrame );

   // 2 - Tell the frame to update itself
   // (and its child windows)
   pTemplate->InitialUpdateFrame( pFrame, pDocument );

   // 3 - Return a pointer to the new frame window object
   return pFrame;
}
```

Step 2. When you want to open a new view on an existing document object, use code similar to the following fragment:

```
CDocument* pDoc;

//...
// Make pDoc point to the document object
// on which you want to open the new view
//...

EkCreateNewWindow( theApp->m_ptYourTemplate, pDoc );
```

Listing 3-7 shows how the MultiViews sample project this FAQ creates the various kinds of views when the user selects the corresponding menu command or toolbar button. I decided to handle these commands in the document class, a technique that makes it trivial to find the document with which the new view should be associated.

Listing 3-7. Creating multiple kinds of views in the MultiViews sample project.

```
void CDrawDoc::OnWindowNewView()
{
   EkCreateNewWindow( theApp.m_ptDrawView, this );
}

void CDrawDoc::OnWindowNewFormView()
{
   EkCreateNewWindow( theApp.m_ptDrawFormView, this );
}

void CDrawDoc::OnWindowNewSplitter()
{
   EkCreateNewWindow( theApp.m_ptSplitFrame, this );
}
```

(The various document templates referenced in Listing 3-7 are defined in Listing 3-4 in *FAQ 3.1 How do I add a new kind of view or frame window to my application?*)

■

Additional Comments

Listing 3-8 shows the pseudocode for the *CDocTemplate::CreateNewFrame()* function (DocTempl.cpp), which is used by *EkCreateNewWindow()* to actually create the new frame/view pair.

Listing 3-8. Pseudocode for the *CDocTemplate::CreateNewFrame()* function (DocTempl.cpp).

```
CFrameWnd* CDocTemplate::CreateNewFrame(CDocument* pDoc,
                                        CFrameWnd* pOther)
{
   // 1 - Prepare context object
   CCreateContext context;
   context.m_pCurrentFrame = pOther;
   context.m_pCurrentDoc = pDoc;
   context.m_pNewViewClass = m_pViewClass;
   context.m_pNewDocTemplate = this;

   // 2 - Create frame window C++ object
   CFrameWnd* pFrame =
             (CFrameWnd*)m_pFrameClass->CreateObject();

   // 3 - Call LoadFrame()virtual function to create the
   // Windows window object and load the associated
   // resources
   pFrame->LoadFrame(m_nIDResource,
                     WS_OVERLAPPEDWINDOW | FWS_ADDTOTITLE,
                     NULL, &context))
   return pFrame;
}
```

The pseudocode for *CMDIChildWnd::LoadFrame()* is shown in Listing 3-16 in the Explanations section of *FAQ 3.7 How do I prevent a view from being closed by the user?*

Finally, if you want to create a new document—along with its frame/view pair—instead of opening a new view on an existing document, refer to *FAQ 2.7 How do I programmatically create a new (empty) document?*

Sample Code

- Project: MultiViews in the Chap03 subdirectory on the companion CD-ROM. This project is discussed in *FAQ 3.1*.

Implementation Highlights

- *CMDIApp::InitInstance()* function (MultiViews.cpp)
- *EkCreateNewWindow()* function (DrawDoc.cpp)
- *CDrawDoc::OnWindowNewView()* function (DrawDoc.cpp)
- *CDrawDoc::OnWindowNewFormView()* function (DrawDoc.cpp)
- *CDrawDoc::OnWindowNewSplitter()* function (DrawDoc.cpp)

See Also

- *FAQ 2.1 How should I create and reference multiple document templates in my application?*
- *FAQ 3.1 How do I add a new kind of view or frame window to my application?*
- *FAQ 3.7 How do I prevent a view from being closed by the user?*
- *FAQ 2.7 How do I programmatically create a new (empty) document?*

How do I open two (or more) specific views each time a new document is created?

I assume here that you have stored pointers to your various document template objects in your application's class, as explained in *FAQ 2.1 How should I create and reference multiple document templates in my application?* I also assume that you have read and understood *FAQ 3.1 How do I add a new kind of view or frame window to my application?* and *FAQ 3.3 How do I programmatically open a view based on a specific document template?*

First Technique: Behavior in the Document Class

Use ClassWizard to override the *OnNewDocument()* and *OnOpenDocument()* virtual functions in your document class. Implement those functions as shown in Listing 3-9.

Listing 3-9. Implementing *CDrawDoc::OnNewDocument()* and *CDrawDoc::OnOpenDocument()*.

```
BOOL CDrawDoc::OnNewDocument()
{
    // Create the new document—and the first view
    if (!CDocument::OnNewDocument())
        return FALSE;

    // Create the second view
    EkCreateNewWindow( theApp.m_ptDrawing2, this );

    return TRUE;
}

BOOL CDrawDoc::OnOpenDocument(LPCTSTR lpszPathName)
{
    // Open the new document—and the first view
    if (!CDocument::OnOpenDocument(lpszPathName))
        return FALSE;

    // Create the second view
    EkCreateNewWindow( theApp.m_ptDrawing2, this );

    return TRUE;
}
```

Second Technique: CEkMultiViewTemplate Class

Step 1. Implement the *CEkMultiViewTemplate* class as shown in Listing 3-10. This class maintains a list of *CMultiDocTemplate* pointers that reference the additional windows to be opened when MFC calls *CEkMultiViewTemplate::OpenDocumentFile()*. Additional document templates are added to the list by calling *CEkMultiViewTemplate::AddViewTemplate()*. When MFC calls

CEkMultiViewTemplate::OpenDocumentFile(), the *CEkMultiViewTemplate* class traverses its list of document templates and creates an additional view for each document template object in the list.

Listing 3-10. Implementing the *CEkMultiViewTemplate* class.

```
// ———————————————————————————
// Class definition for CEkMultiViewTemplate
// (EkMultiViewTemplate.h)

#include <afxtempl.h>   // For CTypedPtrList template

class CEkMultiViewTemplate : public CMultiDocTemplate
{
   DECLARE_DYNAMIC(CEkMultiViewTemplate)

// Constructors
public:
   CEkMultiViewTemplate(UINT nIDResource,
                        CRuntimeClass* pDocClass,
                        CRuntimeClass* pFrameClass,
                        CRuntimeClass* pViewClass);

// Operations
public:
   void AddViewTemplate(CMultiDocTemplate* pViewTemplate);

// Implementation
public:
   virtual CDocument* OpenDocumentFile(
      LPCTSTR lpszPathName, BOOL bMakeVisible = TRUE);

protected:
   // Internal list of pointers to additional "view"
   // document templates
   CTypedPtrList< CObList, CMultiDocTemplate* > m_ViewList;
};

// ———————————————————————————
// Implementation for CEkMultiViewTemplate
// (EkMultiViewTemplate.cpp)
```

```
IMPLEMENT_DYNAMIC(CEkMultiViewTemplate, CMultiDocTemplate)

CEkMultiViewTemplate::CEkMultiViewTemplate(
   UINT nIDResource, CRuntimeClass* pDocClass,
   CRuntimeClass* pFrameClass, CRuntimeClass* pViewClass)
: CMultiDocTemplate(nIDResource, pDocClass,
                  pFrameClass, pViewClass)
{ }

void CEkMultiViewTemplate::AddViewTemplate(
                      CMultiDocTemplate* pViewTemplate )
{
   ASSERT( pViewTemplate != NULL );
   ASSERT_VALID( pViewTemplate );

   // Add the doc template to our list
   m_ViewList.AddTail( pViewTemplate );
}

CDocument* CEkMultiViewTemplate::OpenDocumentFile(
      LPCTSTR lpszPathName, BOOL bMakeVisible )
{
   // 1 - First, let CMultiDocTemplate do its
   // standard thing
   CDocument* pDocument =
            CMultiDocTemplate::OpenDocumentFile(
                           lpszPathName, bMakeVisible );

   if( pDocument != NULL )
   {
      // 2 - Now open each additional view in our list
      POSITION pos = m_ViewList.GetHeadPosition();
      while( pos != NULL )
      {
         CMultiDocTemplate* pViewTemplate =
                              m_ViewList.GetNext( pos );
         EkCreateNewWindow( pViewTemplate, pDocument );
      }
   }

   return pDocument;
}
```

Step 2. In your application's *InitInstance()* function, create your "main" document template—the one that shows in MFC's New dialog box—by constructing an instance of the *CEkMultiViewTemplate* class instead of the standard *CMultiDocTemplate* class.

Step 3. In your application's *InitInstance()* function, create other *CMultiDocTemplate* objects as usual for each of your additional views, and call the *CEkMultiViewTemplate::AddViewTemplate()* to add those views to the *CEkMultiViewTemplate* object created in step 2. Listing 3-11 shows the relevant fragment of this FAQ's sample *InitInstance()* function.

Listing 3-11. Implementing the *InitInstance()* function to construct a *CEkMultiViewTemplate* object and add additional views to this object.

```
BOOL CMDIApp::InitInstance()
{
// ...

   // Register the application's document templates.
   // Document templates serve as the connection between
   // documents, frame windows, and views.

   // 'Counter' document templates

   // "Main" document template
   // (shows up in "New" dialog box)
   m_ptCounter1 = new CEkMultiViewTemplate(
      IDR_COUNTTYPE,
      RUNTIME_CLASS(CCountDoc),
      RUNTIME_CLASS(CChildFrame),
      RUNTIME_CLASS(CCountView));
   AddDocTemplate(m_ptCounter1);

   // Additional view(s)
   m_ptCounter2 = new CMultiDocTemplate(
      IDR_COUNTTYPE2,
      RUNTIME_CLASS(CCountDoc),
      RUNTIME_CLASS(CEkFixedFormFrame),
      RUNTIME_CLASS(CCountFormView));
   AddDocTemplate(m_ptCounter2);
```

```
    // Add second "Counter" view to m_ptCounter1
    // "MultiViews" document template
    m_ptCounter1->AddViewTemplate( m_ptCounter2 );

    // create main MDI Frame window

// ...
}
```

■

Additional Comments

The first technique discussed earlier is easy to implement and understand, but it has the drawback that the "original" view registered with the document template used to create the document will always be created last. Hence, this view always appears in front of the additional views that you create in *OnNewDocument()* and *OnOpenDocument()*.

On the other hand, the second technique needs a slightly more complex architecture, but the resulting design is much more object-oriented and reusable. You can simply plug the *CEkMultiViewTemplate* class into your project, so this last technique actually involves even less work for you than the first one.

Note that the implementation of the *EkCreateNewWindow()* function referenced in this FAQ was discussed in Listing 3-6 (see *FAQ 3.3 How do I programmatically open a view based on a specific document template?*).

Sample Code

- Project: TwoViews in the Chap03 subdirectory on the companion CD-ROM.
- Purpose: Opens two different views each time a new document is created (see Figure 3-2). The Drawing document-type class uses the first technique discussed in this FAQ in its *CDrawDoc* class, whereas the Counter document type uses the second technique with the *CEkMultiViewTemplate* class.

Implementation Highlights

- *CDrawDoc::OnNewDocument()* function (DrawDoc.cpp)
- *CDrawDoc::OnOpenDocument()* function (DrawDoc.cpp)

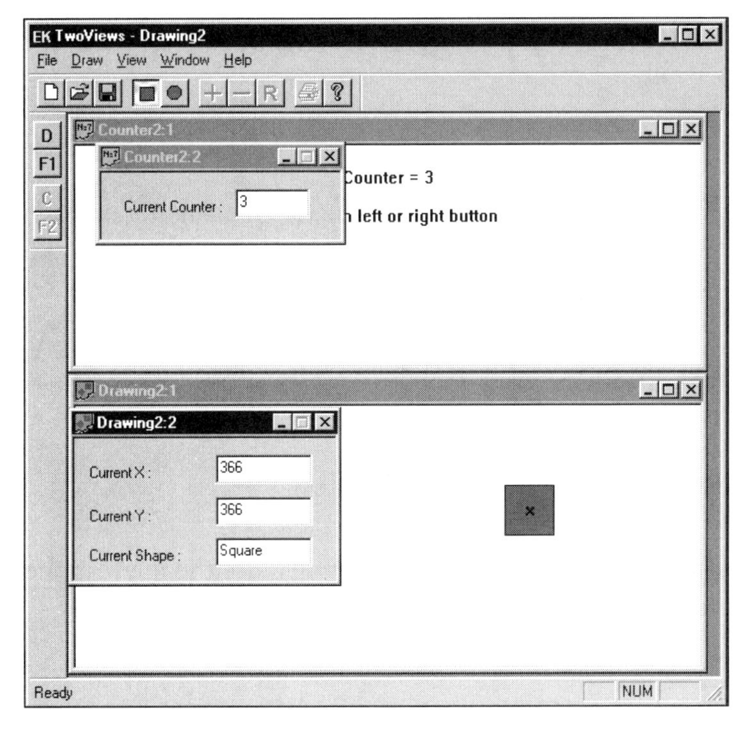

Figure 3-2. The TwoViews application opens two different views each time a new document is created.

- *CEkMultiViewTemplate* class (EkMultiViewTemplate.h, EkMultiViewTemplate.cpp)
- *CMDIApp::InitInstance()* function (TwoViews.cpp)

See Also

- *FAQ 2.1 How should I create and reference multiple document templates in my application?*
- *FAQ 3.1 How do I add a new kind of view or frame window to my application?*
- *FAQ 3.3 How do I programmatically open a view based on a specific document template?*
- *FAQ 3.9 How do I set the initial position and size of a view?*

How do I programmatically close a view?

Simply call *PostMessage()* to send a *WM_CLOSE* message to the view's parent frame window:

```
CFrameWnd* pFrame;
// ...
// Initialize pFrame to point to the frame window that
// you want to close
// ...

pFrame->PostMessage( WM_CLOSE );
```

Note that for an SDI application, this code will close the main application window and therefore shut down the application.

■

Sample Code

There is no sample project for this FAQ.

See Also

- *FAQ 3.7 How do I prevent a view from being closed by the user?*
- *FAQ 3.39 How do I get a pointer to the active view?*
- *FAQ 3.40 How do I get a pointer to the active frame window?*

How do I programmatically close all the views opened on a document?

The solution to this problem is an exercise in simplicity: when you close all views on a document, the document is destroyed, isn't it? Reversing this reasoning, you can conclude that destroying a document object will automatically close all its views.

When you want to close all the views associated with a particular document object, you need only close the document object itself. *FAQ 2.12 How do I programmatically close a document?* shows several techniques that you can use to this end.

■

Additional Comments

I first planned to include this topic in this book, but after some thought I decided to remove it, because I thought that the solution was so easy that anybody could think of it. However, while writing this book, I read at least twice about this "problem" in various magazines and newsgroups. The suggested answers were usually much too complicated. For example:

- Manually iterate through the list of all the views associated with the document object and post (or send) a *WM_CLOSE* message to each view's parent frame window.
- Call *UpdateAllViews()* on the document object, passing a specific *lHint* argument that tells each view to close itself. With this solution, you must override the *OnUpdate()* function for *each* view class and test for the specific *lHint* value that will cause the view object to commit suicide.

After reading these solutions, I decided to restore this topic to the book, if only to help readers avoid these less-than-optimal techniques.

Sample Code

There is no sample project for this FAQ.

See Also

- *FAQ 2.12 How do I programmatically close a document?*

3.7 How do I prevent a view from being closed by the user?

The two techniques discussed in this FAQ show how to create a view that has both its "Close" button and the associated system menu command disabled.

First Technique: Behavior in View's Frame Window Class

Step 1. Use ClassWizard to create a new *CMDIChildWnd*-derived class that will implement the "don't close" behavior.

Step 2. Use ClassWizard to override the *LoadFrame()* virtual function in the class created in step 1. Implement this function as shown in Listing 3-12 to disable the "Close" system menu command.

Listing 3-12. Implementing the *LoadFrame()* function to disable the "Close" system menu command.

```
BOOL CNoCloseFrame::LoadFrame( UINT nIDResource,
                               DWORD dwDefaultStyle,
                               CWnd* pParentWnd,
                               CCreateContext* pContext )
{
   // 1 - Call base class function
   BOOL bRet = CMDIChildWnd::LoadFrame( nIDResource,
                                         dwDefaultStyle,
                                         pParentWnd,
                                         pContext );

   if( bRet )
   {
      // 2 - Disable the "Close" command in the System menu
      CMenu* pMenu = GetSystemMenu( FALSE );
      pMenu->EnableMenuItem( SC_CLOSE,
                             MF_BYCOMMAND | MF_GRAYED );
   }

   return bRet;
}
```

Step 3. Don't forget to reference your view's frame class in the appropriate document templates in order to get the desired behavior (see *FAQ 3.1 How do I add a new kind of view or frame window to my application?*).

What if you sometimes *want* to explicitly close one of those view's frame windows? Simply call *PostMessage()* to send a *WM_CLOSE* message to the window, as shown in Listing 3-13.

Listing 3-13. Implementing the *OnCloseFrame()* function to programmatically close a frame window.

```
void CNoCloseFrame::OnCloseFrame()
{
    PostMessage( WM_CLOSE );
}
```

The standard MFC message-handling processing will then take care of closing the view's frame window and of destroying the associated document object if no other view exists on this document.

Second Technique: Behavior in View Class

Use ClassWizard to override the *OnInitialUpdate()* virtual function in your view class. Implement this function as shown in Listing 3-14 to disable the parent frame window's "Close" system menu command.

Listing 3-14. Implementing the *OnInitialUpdate()* function to disable the view's parent frame window's "Close" system menu command.

```
void CCountView::OnInitialUpdate()
{
    CView::OnInitialUpdate();

    // Disable the parent frame window's "Close" system menu
    // command
    CMenu* pMenu = GetParentFrame()->GetSystemMenu( FALSE );
    pMenu->EnableMenuItem( SC_CLOSE,
                           MF_BYCOMMAND | MF_GRAYED );
}
```

As explained in the first technique, you can explicitly close one of these views by calling *PostMessage()* to send a *WM_CLOSE* message to the view's parent frame window, as shown in Listing 3-15.

Listing 3-15. Implementing the *OnCloseFrame()* function to programmatically close the view's parent frame window.

```
void CCountView::OnCloseFrame()
{
    GetParentFrame()->PostMessage( WM_CLOSE );
}
```

■

Explanations

When does the *LoadFrame()* function get called, and what does this function really do? To answer these questions, we need to dig inside the MFC procedure for creating a frame window using a document template object. This procedure uses a four-step construction process to create the frame window C++ object and its associated Windows window:

1. MFC calls the document template object's *CreateNewFrame()* function.
2. *CreateNewFrame()* creates the correct frame window C++ object by calling the *CreateObject()* dynamic creation function.
3. *CreateNewFrame()* then calls the frame window's *LoadFrame()* function.
4. *LoadFrame()* creates the Windows window and attaches the associated resources (from the resource template ID).

Listing 3-16 shows the pseudocode for *CMDIChildWnd::LoadFrame()*. The pseudocode for *CDocTemplate::CreateNewFrame()* was shown in Listing 3-8 in the Additional Comments section of *FAQ 3.3 How do I programmatically open a view based on a specific document template?*

Listing 3-16. Pseudocode for the *CMDIChildWnd::LoadFrame()* function (WinMdi.cpp).

```
BOOL CMDIChildWnd::LoadFrame( UINT nIDResource,
                              DWORD dwDefaultStyle,
                              CWnd* pParentWnd,
                              CCreateContext* pContext )
{
   m_nIDHelp = nIDResource;      // ID for help context
                                 // (+HID_BASE_RESOURCE)

   // will be a child of MDIClient
   dwDefaultStyle |= WS_CHILD;

   // if available - get MDI child menus from doc template
   CMultiDocTemplate* pTemplate;
   pTemplate =
          (CMultiDocTemplate*)pContext->m_pNewDocTemplate)
```

```
    m_hMenuShared = pTemplate->m_hMenuShared;
    m_hAccelTable = pTemplate->m_hAccelTable;

    CString strFullString, strTitle;
    if (strFullString.LoadString(nIDResource))
       AfxExtractSubString(strTitle, strFullString, 0);
                                          // first sub-string

    // Create Windows window
    if (!Create(
            GetIconWndClass(dwDefaultStyle, nIDResource),
            strTitle, dwDefaultStyle, rectDefault,
            (CMDIFrameWnd*)pParentWnd, pContext))
    {
       return FALSE;    // will self destruct on failure
    }

    // it worked !
    return TRUE;
}
```

Keep in mind that Listing 3-16 shows only the *LoadFrame()* function for the *CMDIChildWnd* class, which is the most relevant function for our discussion. However, MFC also defines different implementations of *LoadFrame()* for the *CFrameWnd* and *CMDIFrameWnd* classes.

When you create a new document object using the standard "File, New" menu command, the chain of function calls leading to the *LoadFrame()* function is as follows:

```
CWinApp::OnFileNew() => CDocManager::OnFileNew() =>
CMultiDocTemplate::OpenDocumentFile() =>
CDocTemplate::CreateNewFrame() => CNoCloseFrame::LoadFrame()
```

If you create a new view on an existing document using the standard "Window, New Window" menu command, this chain of function calls becomes the following:

```
CMDIFrameWnd::OnWindowNew() => CDocTemplate::CreateNewFrame() =>
CNoCloseFrame::LoadFrame()
```

You may wish to refer to *FAQ 1.11 How does MFC implement the standard menu commands?* for a more thorough discussion of the standard implementation of the "File, New" and "Window, New Window" menu commands.

Additional Comments

Note that the preceding techniques are not aggressive enough to be totally bulletproof: if the user presses the Ctrl+F4 key combination or tries to exit the application, your view will still be closed. If you want to prevent this behavior at all costs or if you wish to leave the "Close" button enabled, you should consider using one of the following two techniques:

1. Handle the *WM_CLOSE* message in your view's frame window class and decide whether to allow the window to close, as shown in Listing 3-17.

Listing 3-17. Handling the *WM_CLOSE* message to decide whether to allow a frame window to close.

```
void CYourFrame::OnClose()
{
// ...

   if( /* Test if the frame should close */ )
   {
      // Do not close frame
      return;
   }

   // Close frame
   CMDIChildWnd::OnClose();
}
```

2. Use ClassWizard to override the *CDocument::CanCloseFrame()* function in your document class, as shown in Listing 3-18.

Listing 3-18. Overriding the *CanCloseFrame()* function to decide whether to allow a frame window to close.

```
BOOL CYourDoc::CanCloseFrame(CFrameWnd* pFrame)
{
// ...
```

```
    BOOL bRet = CDocument::CanCloseFrame(pFrame);
    if( /* Test if the frame should close */ )
    {
        // Do not close frame
        bRet = FALSE;
    }

    return bRet;
}
```

If you decide to try this last technique, you should be aware that *CDocument::CanCloseFrame()* is called just *before* the document will try to close the frame but *after* the normal document shutdown processing (if the frame happens to enclose the last view opened on this particular document). Therefore, when trying to close the last child window on a document, the user will be prompted to save the document *before* MFC calls your *CDocument::CanCloseFrame()* function. That may sometimes cause rather surprising behavior.

Sample Code

- Project: DontCloseView in the Chap03 subdirectory on the companion CD-ROM.
- Purpose: Disables the "Close" button and system menu command on child windows (see Figure 3-3). The Drawing document-type class uses the first technique discussed in this FAQ with the *CNoCloseFrame* view's frame window class, whereas the Counter document type uses the second technique inside its *CCountView* class.

Implementation Highlights

- *CNoCloseFrame::LoadFrame()* function (NoCloseFrame.cpp)
- *CNoCloseFrame::OnCloseFrame()* function (NoCloseFrame.cpp)
- *CCountView::OnInitialUpdate()* function (NoCloseFrame.cpp)
- *CCountView::OnCloseFrame()* function (CountView.cpp)
- *CMDIApp::InitInstance()* function (DontCloseView.cpp)

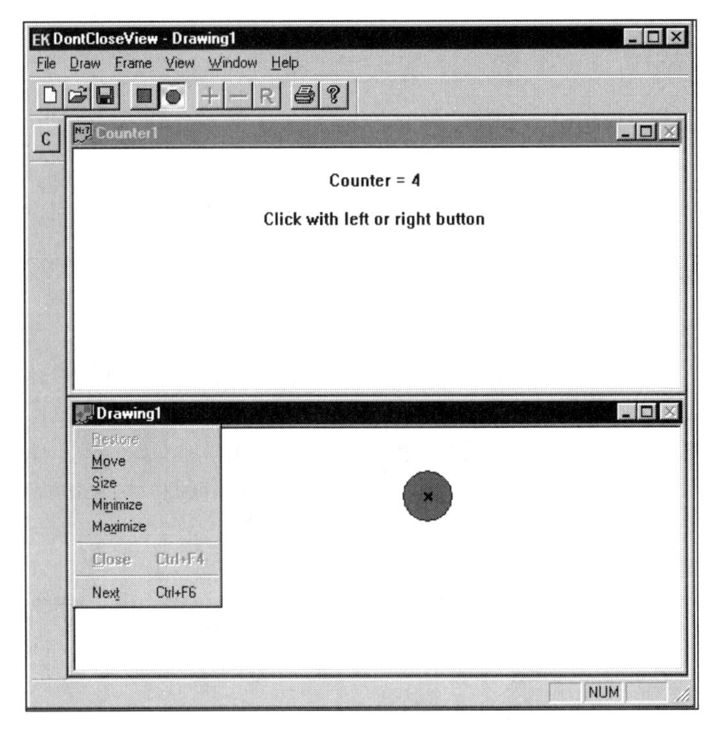

Figure 3-3. The DontCloseView application disables the "Close" button and system menu command on its child windows.

See Also

- *FAQ 3.1 How do I add a new kind of view or frame window to my application?*
- *FAQ 3.2 How do I choose between implementing a specific behavior in the view class or in the view's frame window class?*
- *FAQ 3.3 How do I programmatically open a view based on a specific document template?*
- *FAQ 3.5 How do I programmatically close a view?*
- *FAQ 1.11 How does MFC implement the standard menu commands?*

Managing Sizes and Positions

FAQ 3.8 How do I programmatically resize or reposition a view?

As you may already have found out by yourself, calling either the *MoveWindow()* or the *SetWindowsPos()* function *on the view object* does not work, because the "view" window is not an independent window but rather a child of its frame window. This latter window can be either the main application window of the application in an SDI model, or one of the MDI child windows in an MDI application.

When you want to move or resize a view, you actually must move or resize the *parent frame window* of the view. When it is moved or resized, this parent frame window will cause its child view window(s) to move or resize with it.

If you have a pointer to the view that you want to move or resize, you can get a pointer to its associated parent frame window by calling *GetParentFrame()*. Calling *MoveWindow()* or *SetWindowsPos()* through this last pointer will move or resize the parent frame window as desired, and the embedded view(s) will follow suit.

Listing 3-19 shows a sample function that moves the current view (actually, its parent frame window) to the upper-right corner of the main application window. This function is called when the user selects a menu command or clicks on a toolbar button.

Listing 3-19. Implementing *OnMoveUpperRight()*.

```
void CDrawView::OnMoveUpperRight()
{
   // 1 - Get pointer to parent frame window
   CFrameWnd* pParentFrame = GetParentFrame();
   ASSERT_VALID( pParentFrame );

   // 2 - Get pointer to MDI Client window
   CWnd* pMDIClient = pParentFrame->GetParent();
   ASSERT_VALID( pMDIClient );
```

```
    // 3 - Calculate client size of MDI Client window
    CRect rect;
    pMDIClient->GetClientRect( &rect );

    // 4 - Move the parent frame to the desired position
    pParentFrame->MoveWindow( rect.Width() / 2,
                              0,
                              rect.Width() / 2,
                              rect.Height() / 2 );
}
```

■

Additional Comments

It's up to you to decide where you want to move your view(s) according to your specific needs. The example shown in Listing 3-19 simply selects the position and size of the view's frame window relative to the main application window or, more precisely, in relation to the MDI client window, which entirely covers the client area of the main application window in an MDI application.

Sample Code

- Project: MoveView in the Chap03 subdirectory on the companion CD-ROM.
- Purpose: Demonstrates how to programmatically reposition and resize child windows (see Figure 3-4). The "Move" menu commands and the associated toolbar buttons allow the user to move the active view to any one of the four corners of the main application window.

Implementation Highlights

- *CDrawView::OnMoveUpperLeft()* function (DrawView.cpp)
- *CDrawView::OnMoveUpperRight()* function (DrawView.cpp)
- *CDrawView::OnMoveBottomLeft()* function (DrawView.cpp)
- *CDrawView::OnMoveBottomRight()* function (DrawView.cpp)

See Also

- *FAQ 3.9 How do I set the initial position and size of a view?*
- *FAQ 3.11 How do I center a view?*

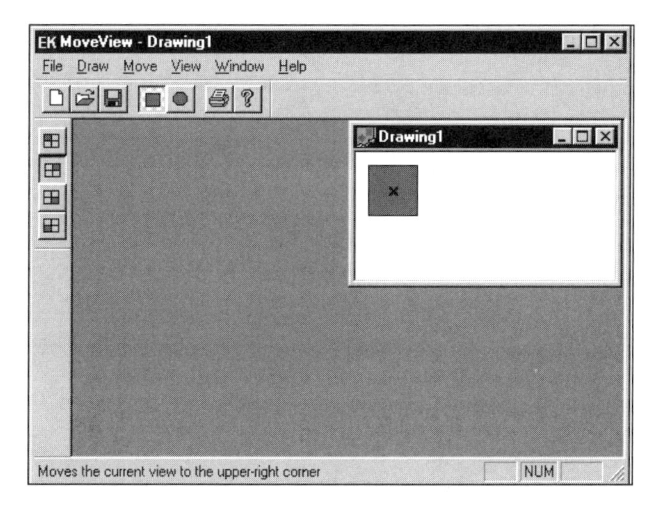

Figure 3-4. The MoveView application in action: moving a view to the upper-right corner of the main application window.

FAQ 3.9 How do I set the initial position and size of a view?

If you refer to *FAQ 3.8 How do I programmatically resize or reposition a view?* you will recall that moving or sizing a view actually involves moving its associated parent frame window. Therefore, the initial positioning behavior can be implemented either in the view's frame window class or in the view class. Those two techniques are described next.

First Technique: Behavior in View's Frame Window Class

Step 1. Use ClassWizard to create a new *CMDIChildWnd*-derived class that will implement the initial positioning behavior that you need.

Step 2. Use ClassWizard to add a handler in your *CMDIChildWnd*-derived class for the *WM_CREATE* message. Implement this handler as shown in Listing 3-20.

Listing 3-20. Handling the *WM_CREATE* message to select the initial position of a view's frame window.

```
int CCenterChildFrame::OnCreate(
                              LPCREATESTRUCT lpCreateStruct)
{
   if (CMDIChildWnd::OnCreate(lpCreateStruct) == -1)
      return -1;

   // Size the window to 1/4 of the main frame client
   // area size and center it
   CWnd* pMDIClient = GetParent();
   ASSERT_VALID( pMDIClient );

   CRect rect;
   pMDIClient->GetClientRect( &rect );

   MoveWindow( rect.Width() / 4, rect.Height() / 4,
               rect.Width() / 2, rect.Height() / 2 );

   return 0;
}
```

Step 3. Don't forget to reference your view's frame class in the appropriate document templates in order to get the desired behavior (see *FAQ 3.1 How do I add a new kind of view or frame window to my application?*).

Second Technique: Behavior in the View Class

Use ClassWizard to override the *OnInitialUpdate()* virtual function in your view class. Implement this function as shown in Listing 3-21 to move the parent frame window into the desired position each time a new view is created.

Listing 3-21. Implementing the *OnInitialUpdate()* function to select the initial position of the view's parent frame window.

```
void CDrawView::OnInitialUpdate()
{
   // Call base class first
   CView::OnInitialUpdate();

   // 1 - Get pointer to parent frame window
   CFrameWnd* pParentFrame = GetParentFrame();
```

```
    ASSERT_VALID( pParentFrame );

    // 2 - Get pointer to MDI Client window
    CWnd* pMDIClient = pParentFrame->GetParent();
    ASSERT_VALID( pMDIClient );

    // 3 - Calculate client size of MDI Client window
    CRect rect;
    pMDIClient->GetClientRect( &rect );

    // 4 - Move the parent frame to the desired position
    pParentFrame->MoveWindow( rect.Width() / 2,
                              0,
                              rect.Width() / 2,
                              rect.Height() / 2 );
}
```

■

Sample Code

- Project: PositionView in the Chap03 subdirectory on the companion CD-ROM.
- Purpose: Sets the initial position and size of child windows. Each new Counter view appears centered in the main application window client area, using the first technique discussed in this FAQ. Similarly, each new Drawing view appears in the upper-right corner of the main application window, using the second technique discussed in this FAQ (see Figure 3-5).

Implementation Highlights

- *CMDIApp::InitInstance()* function (PositionView.cpp)
- *CDrawView::OnInitialUpdate()* function (DrawView.cpp)
- *CCenterChildFrame::OnCreate()* function (CenterChildFrm.Cpp)

See Also

- *FAQ 3.1* *How do I add a new kind of view or frame window to my application?*
- *FAQ 3.2* *How do I choose between implementing a specific behavior in the view class or in the view's frame window class?*

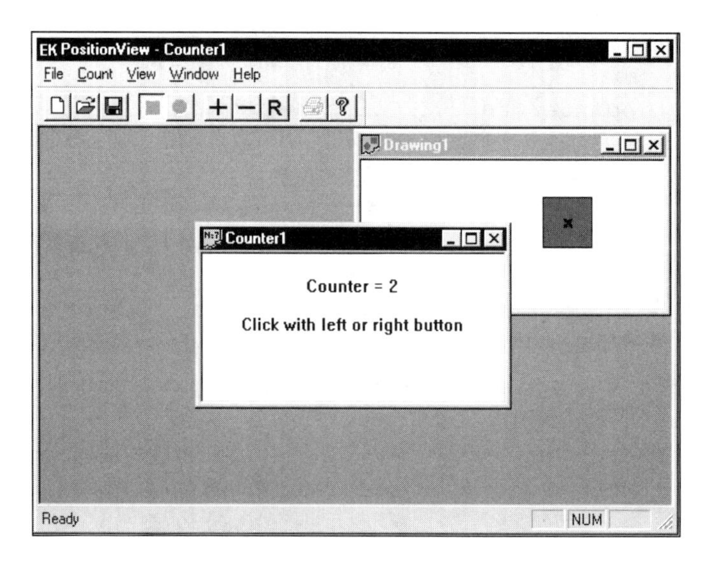

Figure 3-5. The PositionView application creates each new Counter view centered and each Drawing view in the upper-right corner of the main application window client area.

- *FAQ 3.8 How do I programmatically resize or reposition a view?*
- *FAQ 3.10 How do I center my main application window?*
- *FAQ 3.15 How do I make a view initially appear minimized or maximized?*

FAQ 3.10 How do I center my main application window?

MFC provides an easy way to center a window with the *CWnd::CenterWindow()* function, whose implementation is discussed in the Additional Comments section.

To have your main application window show up centered on the desktop, insert a call to *CenterWindow()* in your main application window's *OnCreate()* function, as shown in Listing 3-22.

Listing 3-22. Implementing *CMainFrame::OnCreate()* to center the main application window.

```
int CMainFrame::OnCreate(LPCREATESTRUCT lpCreateStruct)
{
   if (CMDIFrameWnd::OnCreate(lpCreateStruct) == -1)
      return -1;

   // Center the main frame window on the desktop
   // (the call to CWnd::GetDesktopWindow() is optional)
   CenterWindow( CWnd::GetDesktopWindow() );

// ...
}
```

■

Additional Comments

You might think that you could center a window in a few lines of code simply by computing the target position from the current window's rectangle and its parent's client area rectangle. This overall approach is certainly correct, but a robust implementation must take care of a few additional details, as you can see in the pseudocode for *CWnd::CenterWindow()*, which is shown in Listing 3-23.

Listing 3-23. Pseudocode for the *CWnd::CenterWindow()* function (WinCore.cpp).

```
void CWnd::CenterWindow(CWnd* pAlternateOwner)
{
   // Determine owner window to center against
   DWORD dwStyle = GetStyle();
   HWND hWndCenter = pAlternateOwner->GetSafeHwnd();
   if (pAlternateOwner == NULL)
   {
      if (dwStyle & WS_CHILD)
         hWndCenter = ::GetParent(m_hWnd);
      else
         hWndCenter = ::GetWindow(m_hWnd, GW_OWNER);
      if (hWndCenter != NULL)
      {
```

```
            // Let parent determine alternate center window
            HWND hWndTemp =
               (HWND)::SendMessage(hWndCenter,
                                   WM_QUERYCENTERWND, 0, 0);
            if (hWndTemp != NULL)
               hWndCenter = hWndTemp;
      }
   }
   // Get coordinates of the window relative to its parent
   CRect rcDlg;
   GetWindowRect(&rcDlg);
   CRect rcArea;
   CRect rcCenter;
   HWND hWndParent;
   if (!(dwStyle & WS_CHILD))
   {
      // Don't center against invisible or
      // minimized windows
      if (hWndCenter != NULL)
      {
         DWORD dwStyle = ::GetWindowLong(hWndCenter,
                                         GWL_STYLE);
         if (!(dwStyle & WS_VISIBLE) ||
              (dwStyle & WS_MINIMIZE))
            hWndCenter = NULL;
      }

      // Center within screen coordinates
      SystemParametersInfo(SPI_GETWORKAREA, NULL,
                           &rcArea, NULL);

      if (hWndCenter == NULL)
         rcCenter = rcArea;
      else
         ::GetWindowRect(hWndCenter, &rcCenter);
   }
   else
   {
      // Center within parent client coordinates
      hWndParent = ::GetParent(m_hWnd);
      ::GetClientRect(hWndParent, &rcArea);
      ::GetClientRect(hWndCenter, &rcCenter);
```

```
      ::MapWindowPoints(hWndCenter, hWndParent,
                        (POINT*)&rcCenter, 2);
   }

   // Find window's upper left based on rcCenter
   int xLeft = (rcCenter.left + rcCenter.right) / 2
              - rcDlg.Width() / 2;
   int yTop = (rcCenter.top + rcCenter.bottom) / 2
             - rcDlg.Height() / 2;

   // If the window is outside the screen, move it inside
   if (xLeft < rcArea.left)
      xLeft = rcArea.left;
   else if (xLeft + rcDlg.Width() > rcArea.right)
      xLeft = rcArea.right - rcDlg.Width();

   if (yTop < rcArea.top)
      yTop = rcArea.top;
   else if (yTop + rcDlg.Height() > rcArea.bottom)
      yTop = rcArea.bottom - rcDlg.Height();

   // Actually move the window!
   SetWindowPos(NULL, xLeft, yTop, -1, -1,
      SWP_NOSIZE | SWP_NOZORDER | SWP_NOACTIVATE);
}
```

Sample Code

- Project: CenterApp in the Chap03 subdirectory on the companion CD-ROM.
- Purpose: Makes the main application window appear centered on the desktop.

Implementation Highlights

- *CMainFrame::OnCreate()* function (MainFrm.cpp)

See Also

- *FAQ 3.9 How do I set the initial position and size of a view?*
- *FAQ 3.11 How do I center a view?*

How do I center a view?

As is often the case, the "open centered" behavior can be implemented either in the view's frame window class or in the view class. Those two techniques are described next.

First Technique: Behavior in View's Frame Window Class

Step 1. Use ClassWizard to create a new *CMDIChildWnd*-derived class that will implement the open centered behavior.

Step 2. Use ClassWizard to add a handler in your *CMDIChildWnd*-derived class for the *WM_CREATE* message. Implement this handler as shown in Listing 3-24.

Listing 3-24. Handling the *WM_CREATE* message to center a view's frame window.

```
int CChildFrame::OnCreate(LPCREATESTRUCT lpCreateStruct)
{
   if (CMDIChildWnd::OnCreate(lpCreateStruct) == -1)
      return -1;

   // Center the child frame window on its parent
   // (main frame) window
   CenterWindow();

   return 0;
}
```

Step 3. Don't forget to reference your view's frame class in the appropriate document templates in order to get the desired behavior (see *FAQ 3.1 How do I add a new kind of view or frame window to my application?*).

Second Technique: Behavior in View Class

Use ClassWizard to override the *OnInitialUpdate()* virtual function in your view class. Implement this function as shown in Listing 3-25 to center the parent frame window of the view each time a new view is created.

Listing 3-25. Implementing the *OnInitialUpdate()* function to center the view's parent frame window.

```
void CDrawFormView::OnInitialUpdate()
{
   CFormView::OnInitialUpdate();

   // Center the parent frame window on its parent
   // (main frame) window
   GetParentFrame()->CenterWindow();

}
```

■

Additional Comments

For a discussion of the *CenterWindow()* function, see *FAQ 3.10 How do I center my main application window?*

Sample Code

- Project: CenterView in the Chap03 subdirectory on the companion CD-ROM.
- Purpose: Centers new child windows when they are created. The standard drawing view uses the first technique discussed in this FAQ, whereas the form view uses the second technique (see Figure 3-6).

Implementation Highlights

- *CChildFrame::OnCreate()* function (ChildFrm.cpp)
- *CDrawFormView::OnInitialUpdate()* function (DrawFormView.cpp)

See Also

- *FAQ 3.1 How do I add a new kind of view or frame window to my application?*
- *FAQ 3.2 How do I choose between implementing a specific behavior in the view class or in the view's frame window class?*
- *FAQ 3.9 How do I set the initial position and size of a view?*
- *FAQ 3.10 How do I center my main application window?*

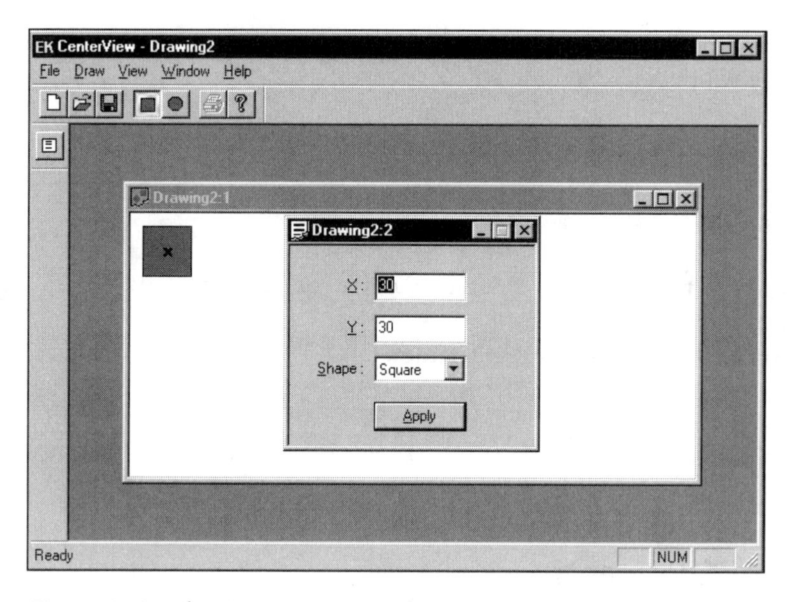

Figure 3-6. The CenterView application creates both its standard drawing view and its form view centered on the main application window.

FAQ 3.12 How do I make a frame window nonresizable?

The easiest way to prevent the user from resizing any kind of frame window—main application window or MDI view's frame window—is simply to remove the "resizable" style bit when creating the window, as explained in the following steps. (For a different technique for controlling the size of a view's frame window, please see *FAQ 3.13 How do I limit the maximum or minimum size of a view?*)

Step 1. Use ClassWizard to create a new *CMDIChildWnd*-derived class that will implement the "fixed frame" behavior.

Step 2. Use ClassWizard to override the *PreCreateWindow()* virtual function in your new *CMDIChildWnd*-derived class. Implement this function as shown in Listing 3-26.

Listing 3-26. Implementing the *PreCreateWindow()* function to make a frame window nonresizable.

```
BOOL CChildFrame::PreCreateWindow(CREATESTRUCT& cs)
{
    // Make the frame window nonresizable
    cs.style &= ~WS_THICKFRAME;

    // Optionally remove the 'Maximize' caption button
    // cs.style &= ~WS_MAXIMIZEBOX;

    return CMDIChildWnd::PreCreateWindow(cs);
}
```

Step 3. Don't forget to reference your view's frame class in the appropriate document templates in order to get the desired behavior (see *FAQ 3.1 How do I add a new kind of view or frame window to my application?*).

■

Sample Code

- Project: NoResize in the Chap03 subdirectory on the companion CD-ROM.
- Purpose: Implements nonresizable frame windows. Neither the main application window nor the drawing view's frame window can be resized by the user.

Implementation Highlights

- *CChildFrame::PreCreateWindow()* function (ChildFrm.cpp)
- *CChildFrame::OnCreate()* function (ChildFrm.cpp)
- *CMainFrame::PreCreateWindow()* function (MainFrm.cpp)

See Also

- *FAQ 3.1* *How do I add a new kind of view or frame window to my application?*
- *FAQ 3.9* *How do I set the initial position and size of a view?*
- *FAQ 3.13* *How do I limit the maximum or minimum size of a view?*
- *FAQ 3.29* *How do I make a form view initially appear with the exact size of the associated dialog resource?*

3.13 How do I limit the maximum or minimum size of a view?

In Windows programming, the best way to limit the size of a window is to handle the *WM_GETMINMAXINFO* message appropriately.

However, you must also remember that the window that the user resizes is not the view itself but rather the view's frame window—which is the parent frame window of the view. Therefore, you must handle this resizing issue in your view's parent frame window.

Step 1. Use ClassWizard to create a new *CMDIChildWnd*-derived class that will implement the desired size restrictions.

Step 2. Use ClassWizard to add a handler in your *CMDIChildWnd*-derived class for the *WM_GETMINMAXINFO* message. Implement this handler as shown in Listing 3-27, which limits the tracking size so that the client area of the frame windows stays between 200×50 and 400×200 pixels.

Listing 3-27. Handling the *WM_GETMINMAXINFO* message to limit the size of a view.

```
void CChildFrame::OnGetMinMaxInfo(MINMAXINFO FAR* lpMMI)
{
   // 1 - Let the default window proc fill the
   // MINMAXINFO structure
   CFrameWnd::OnGetMinMaxInfo(lpMMI);

   // Calculate the "nonclient overhead" of the
   // frame window
   CRect rectClient;
   GetClientRect( &rectClient );

   CRect rectWindow;
   GetWindowRect( &rectWindow );

   int nWidthOverhead = rectWindow.Width()
                              - rectClient.Width();
   int nHeightOverhead = rectWindow.Height()
                              - rectClient.Height();
```

```
    // 3 - Modify the MINMAXINFO structure to reflect our
    // size limits

    // Here we want a minimum CLIENT size of 200X50 pixels
    // and a maximum CLIENT size of 400X200 pixels

    lpMMI->ptMinTrackSize.x = 200 + nWidthOverhead;
    lpMMI->ptMinTrackSize.y = 50 + nHeightOverhead;

    lpMMI->ptMaxTrackSize.x = 400 + nWidthOverhead;
    lpMMI->ptMaxTrackSize.y = 200 + nHeightOverhead;
}
```

Step 3. Optionally use ClassWizard to override the *PreCreateWindow()* virtual function in your *CMDIChildWnd*-derived class. Implement this function as shown in Listing 3-28 to remove the *WS_MAXIMIZEBOX* style bit from the window's style.

Listing 3-28. Implementing the *PreCreateWindow()* function to remove the "Maximize" caption button.

```
BOOL CChildFrame::PreCreateWindow(CREATESTRUCT& cs)
{
    // Remove the 'Maximize' caption button
    cs.style &= ~WS_MAXIMIZEBOX;

    return CMDIChildWnd::PreCreateWindow(cs);
}
```

Step 4. Don't forget to reference your view's frame class in the appropriate document templates in order to get the desired behavior (see *FAQ 3.1 How do I add a new kind of view or frame window to my application?*).

■

Explanations

Windows sends the *WM_GETMINMAXINFO* message to a window when the size or position of the window is about to change. By handling this message and modifying various fields in the *MINMAXINFO* structure, you can explicitly override the window's default maximized size and position or override its default minimum or maximum tracking size.

When you use ClassWizard to handle the *WM_GETMINMAXINFO* message, ClassWizard generates a handler with the following prototype:

```
afx_msg void OnGetMinMaxInfo( MINMAXINFO FAR* lpMMI );
```

The *lpMMI* parameter points to the *MINMAXINFO* structure that initially contains information about the window's maximized size and position and its minimum and maximum tracking size:

```
typedef struct tagMINMAXINFO {
    POINT ptReserved;
    POINT ptMaxSize;       // Maximized size
    POINT ptMaxPosition;   // Maximized position
    POINT ptMinTrackSize; // Minimum tracking size
    POINT ptMaxTrackSize; // Maximum tracking size
} MINMAXINFO;
```

The maximized size and position fields control the size and position of the window when its state is set to "maximized." The minimum and maximum tracking sizes are, respectively, the smallest and largest window sizes that users can get by using the borders to size the window.

Each field is of type *POINT*, where *pt.x* and *pt.y* represent, respectively, the width and height of the given size. For example, *lpMMI->ptMinTrackSize.x* is the minimum allowable tracking width, and *lpMMI->ptMaxTrackSize.y* is the maximum allowable tracking height.

You might wonder why I advise you to remove the "Maximize" caption button in step 4. Here is the answer: If you do not remove this button while keeping the *WM_GETMINMAXINFO* message processing, your frame window will not behave properly when maximized, as you can see in Figure 3-7.

Additional Comments

The values that you assign to the *ptMinTrackSize* and *ptMaxTrackSize* fields of the *MINMAXINFO* structure set limits on the tracking size of the entire window and not only of its client area. Therefore, these values must take into account the various interface widgets—toolbars, scroll bars, and so on—as well as the nonclient elements: borders, caption, and so on. The code sample in Listing 3-27 shows how to calculate the overhead of those nonclient elements.

Note that most other solutions that try to use the traditional Windows messages—*WM_SIZE*, *WM_WINDOWPOSCHANGING*,

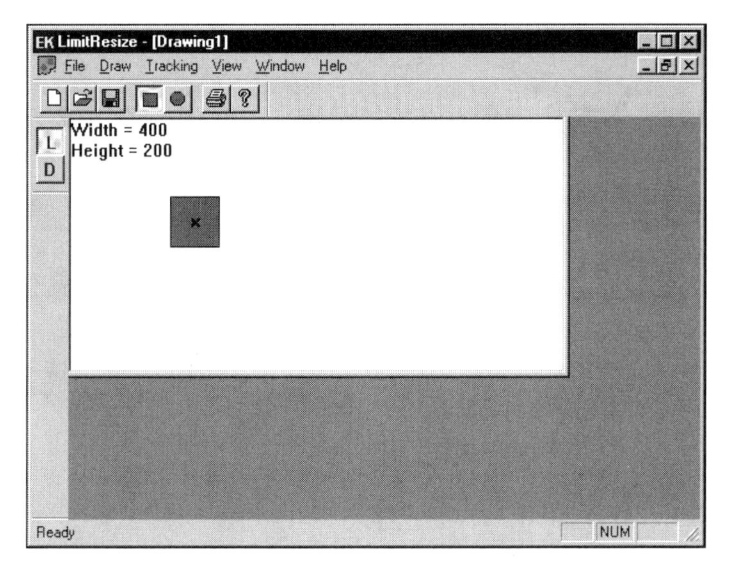

Figure 3-7. Bad behavior of a maximized view's frame window that limits its tracking size by processing the *WM_GETMINMAXINFO* message.

WM_WINDOWPOSCHANGED, and so on— to limit the size of a window usually do not give an ergonomically acceptable result. The *WM_GETMINMAXINFO* message *is* the best choice for this kind of functionality.

Sample Code

- Project: LimitResize in the Chap03 subdirectory on the companion CD-ROM.
- Purpose: Limits the size of child windows so that their client area stays between 200×50 and 400×200 pixels (see Figure 3-8).

Implementation Highlights

- *CChildFrame::OnGetMinMaxInfo()* function (ChildFrm.cpp)
- *CChildFrame::PreCreateWindow()* function (ChildFrm.cpp)

See Also

- *FAQ 3.1 How do I add a new kind of view or frame window to my application?*

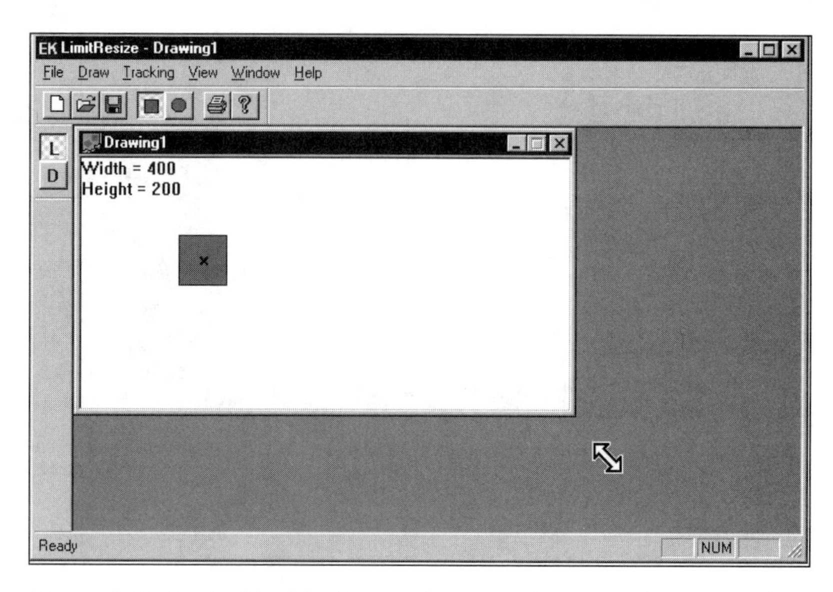

Figure 3-8. In the LimitResize application, the view's frame window can't grow larger than 400×200 pixels.

- *FAQ 3.12 How do I make a frame window nonresizable?*
- *FAQ 3.14 How do I limit the repositioning of a view?*
- *FAQ 3.19 How do I implement a full-screen view mode like the one in Visual C++ and Word?*

How do I limit the repositioning of a view?

In Windows programming, the best way to limit the repositioning of a window is to handle the *WM_WINDOWPOSCHANGING* message appropriately.

However, you must also remember that the window that the user moves is not the view itself but rather the view's frame window, which is the parent frame window of the view. Therefore, you need to handle repositioning in your view's parent frame window.

Step 1. Use ClassWizard to create a new *CMDIChildWnd*-derived class that will implement the desired positioning restrictions.

Step 2. Use ClassWizard to add a handler in your *CMDIChildWnd*-derived class for the *WM_WINDOWPOSCHANGING* message. Implement this handler as shown in Listing 3-29 to enforce your positioning restrictions. The code shown in Listing 3-29 ensures that each side of the frame window stays between the *XXX_MIN* and *XXX_MAX* limits (where *XXX* = *LEFT*, *TOP*, *RIGHT*, or *BOTTOM*). You must define the *XXX_MIN* and *XXX_MAX* constants inside your frame window class.

Listing 3-29. Handling the *WM_WINDOWPOSCHANGING* message to limit the repositioning of a view.

```
void CChildFrame::OnWindowPosChanging(
                              WINDOWPOS FAR* lpwndpos)
{
   CMDIChildWnd::OnWindowPosChanging(lpwndpos);

   if( !IsIconic() )
   {
      // Verify left side position
      if( lpwndpos->x < LEFT_MIN )
      {
         // Adjust horizontal size before left side
         lpwndpos->cx -= LEFT_MIN - lpwndpos->x;

         // Adjust left side
         lpwndpos->x = LEFT_MIN;
      }

      if( lpwndpos->x > LEFT_MAX )
      {
         // Adjust horizontal size before left side
         lpwndpos->cx += lpwndpos->x - LEFT_MAX;

         // Adjust left side
         lpwndpos->x = LEFT_MAX;
      }

      // Verify top side position
      if( lpwndpos->y < TOP_MIN )
      {
         // Adjust vertical size before top side
         lpwndpos->cy -= TOP_MIN - lpwndpos->y;
```

```
            // Adjust top side
            lpwndpos->y = TOP_MIN;
        }

        if( lpwndpos->y > TOP_MAX )
        {
            // Adjust vertical size before top side
            lpwndpos->cy += lpwndpos->y - TOP_MAX;

            // Adjust top side
            lpwndpos->y = TOP_MAX;
        }

        // Verify right side position
        if( lpwndpos->x + lpwndpos->cx < RIGHT_MIN )
        {
            lpwndpos->cx = RIGHT_MIN - lpwndpos->x;
        }

        if( lpwndpos->x + lpwndpos->cx > RIGHT_MAX )
        {
            lpwndpos->cx = RIGHT_MAX - lpwndpos->x;
        }

        // Verify bottom side position
        if( lpwndpos->y + lpwndpos->cy < BOTTOM_MIN )
        {
            lpwndpos->cy = BOTTOM_MIN - lpwndpos->y;
        }

        if( lpwndpos->y + lpwndpos->cy > BOTTOM_MAX )
        {
            lpwndpos->cy = BOTTOM_MAX - lpwndpos->y;
        }
    }
}
```

Step 3. Optionally use ClassWizard to override the *PreCreateWindow()* virtual function in your *CMDIChildWnd*-derived class. Implement this function as shown in Listing 3-30 to remove the *WS_MAXIMIZEBOX* style bit from the window's style.

Listing 3-30. Implementing the *PreCreateWindow()* function to remove the "Maximize" caption button.

```
BOOL CChildFrame::PreCreateWindow(CREATESTRUCT& cs)
{
   // Remove 'Maximize' caption button
   cs.style &= ~WS_MAXIMIZEBOX;

   // Enforce initial position
   cs.x = LEFT_MIN;
   cs.y = TOP_MIN;
   cs.cx = RIGHT_MIN - cs.x;
   cs.cy = BOTTOM_MIN - cs.y;
   return CMDIChildWnd::PreCreateWindow(cs);
}
```

Step 4. Don't forget to reference your view's frame class in the appropriate document templates in order to get the desired behavior (see *FAQ 3.1 How do I add a new kind of view or frame window to my application?*).

■

Explanations

Windows sends the *WM_WINDOWPOSCHANGING* message to a window when the position or size of the window is about to change. By handling this message and modifying various fields in the *WINDOWPOS* structure, you can explicitly override the window's default position and size.

When you use ClassWizard to handle the *WM_WINDOWPOSCHANGING* message, ClassWizard generates a handler with the following prototype:

```
afx_msg void OnWindowPosChanging( WINDOWPOS* lpwndpos );
```

The *lpwndpos* parameter points to the *WINDOWPOS* structure that initially contains information about the window's position and size:

```
typedef struct _WINDOWPOS { // wp
    HWND hwnd;
    HWND hwndInsertAfter;
    int  x;    // Position of window's left edge
    int  y;    // Position of window's top edge
```

```
    int  cx;  // Window's width  (pixels)
    int  cy;  // Window's height (pixels)
    UINT flags;
} WINDOWPOS;
```

For an explanation of why I advise you to remove the "Maximize" caption button, see the Explanations section of *FAQ 3.13 How do I limit the maximum or minimum size of a view?*

Additional Comments

Note that the technique used by the sample code to draw the pattern on the background of the main application window is described in *FAQ 3.27 How do I draw on the main application window background?*

Sample Code

- Project: LimitPosition in the Chap03 subdirectory on the companion CD-ROM.
- Purpose: Limits the repositioning of child windows (see Figure 3-9).

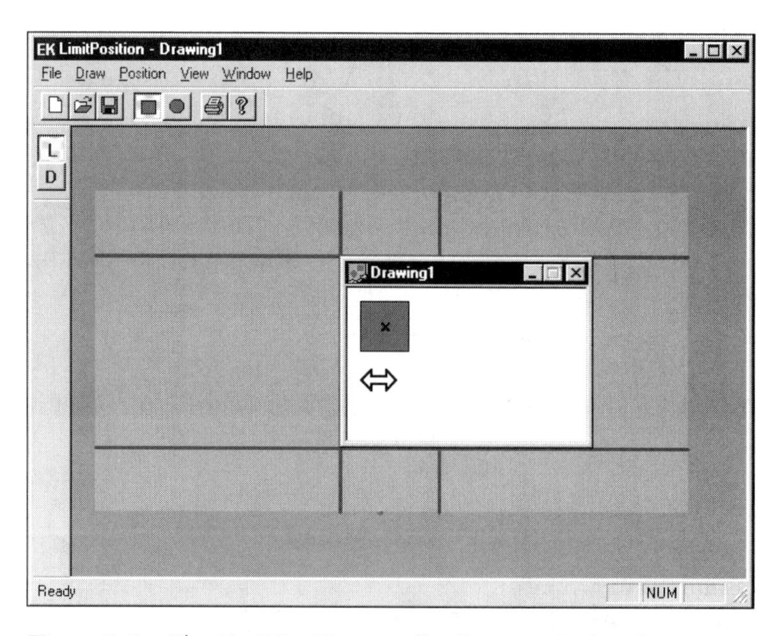

Figure 3-9. The LimitPosition application constrains the position of its view's frame window.

Implementation Highlights

- *CChildFrame:: OnWindowPosChanging()* function (ChildFrm.cpp)
- *CChildFrame::PreCreateWindow()* function (ChildFrm.cpp)
- *CMdiBackground::OnEraseBkgnd()* function (MdiBackground.cpp)
- *CMainFrame::OnCreate()* function (MainFrm.cpp)

See Also

- *FAQ 3.1 How do I add a new kind of view and/or frame window to my application?*
- *FAQ 3.13 How do I limit the maximum or minimum size of a view?*
- *FAQ 3.27 How do I draw on the main application window background?*

3.15 How do I make a view initially appear minimized or maximized?

If you refer to *FAQ 3.8 How do I programmatically resize or reposition a view?* you will recall that moving or sizing a view actually involves moving its associated parent frame window. Therefore, you can implement the "open maximized" behavior either in the view class or in the view's frame class. Those two techniques are described next.

First Technique: Behavior in View's Frame Window Class

Step 1. Use ClassWizard to create a new *CMDIChildWnd*-derived class that will implement the open maximized behavior.

Step 2. Add a Boolean member variable to your new view's frame class to keep track of the first time the frame window is activated. Initialize this variable in your class's constructor, as shown in Listing 3-31.

Listing 3-31. Implementing the *CMaximizeFrame* view's frame class to open in the maximized state.

```
// ——————————————————————————————
// Class definition for CMaximizeFrame (MaximizeFrame.h)
```

```
class CMaximizeFrame : public CMDIChildWnd
{

// ...

public:
// Overrides
   // ClassWizard generated virtual function overrides
   //{{AFX_VIRTUAL(CMaximizeFrame)
   public:
   virtual void ActivateFrame(int nCmdShow = -1);
   //}}AFX_VIRTUAL

// Implementation

// ...

private:
   BOOL m_bFirstTime;

// ...

};

// ————————————————————————————————
// Implementation for CMaximizeFrame (MaximizeFrame.cpp)

CMaximizeFrame::CMaximizeFrame()
{
   m_bFirstTime = TRUE;
}

void CMaximizeFrame::ActivateFrame(int nCmdShow)
{
   if( m_bFirstTime )
   {
      m_bFirstTime = FALSE;
      nCmdShow = SW_SHOWMAXIMIZED; // Force maximized state
   }

   CMDIChildWnd::ActivateFrame(nCmdShow);
}
```

Step 3. Use ClassWizard to override the *ActivateFrame()* virtual function in your *CMDIChildWnd*-derived class. Implement this function as shown in Listing 3-31: examine the Boolean member variable added in step 2 to determine whether this is the first time that the frame has been activated. In this case, change the *nCmdShow* parameter to the *SW_SHOWMAXIMIZED* value before calling the base class's *ActivateFrame()* function.

Step 4. Don't forget to reference your view's frame class in the appropriate document templates in order to get the desired behavior (see *FAQ 3.1 How do I add a new kind of view or frame window to my application?*).

If you wish your view's frame to open in the minimized state, simply replace the *SW_SHOWMAXIMIZED* with *SW_SHOWMINIMIZED* in Listing 3-31.

Second Technique: Behavior in View Class

Use ClassWizard to override the *OnInitialUpdate()* virtual function in your view class. Implement this function as shown in Listing 3-32 to call the *ShowWindow()* function with a *SW_SHOWMAXIMIZED* argument on your parent frame window.

Listing 3-32. Implementing the *OnInitialUpdate()* function to open the view's parent frame in the maximized state.

```
void CDrawView::OnInitialUpdate()
{
   CView::OnInitialUpdate();

   // Maximize parent frame window
   GetParentFrame()->ShowWindow( SW_SHOWMAXIMIZED );
}
```

Again, if you wish your view's frame to open in the minimized state, simply replace the *SW_SHOWMAXIMIZED* with *SW_SHOWMINIMIZED* in Listing 3-32.

■

Sample Code 1: Behavior in View's Frame Window Class

- Project: MinMaxFrame in the Chap03 subdirectory on the companion CD-ROM.
- Purpose: Makes child windows initially appear minimized or maximized. Each new drawing view appears maximized, and each counter view opens in the minimized state. This sample application uses the first technique discussed earlier to implement the opening behavior in two views' frame window classes.

Implementation Highlights

- *CMDIApp::InitInstance()* function (MinMaxFrame.cpp)
- *CMinimizeFrame::ActivateFrame()* function (MinimizeFrame.cpp)
- *CMaximizeFrame::ActivateFrame()* function (MaximizeFrame.cpp)

Sample Code 2: Behavior in View Class

- Project: MinMaxView in the Chap03 subdirectory on the companion CD-ROM.
- Purpose: Makes child windows initially appear minimized or maximized. Each new drawing view appears maximized, and each counter view opens in the minimized state. This sample application uses the second technique discussed earlier to implement the opening behavior in the drawing and counter view classes.

Implementation Highlights

- *CDrawView::OnInitialUpdate()* function (DrawView.cpp)
- *CCountView::OnInitialUpdate()* function (CountView.cpp)

See Also

- *FAQ 3.1 How do I add a new kind of view or frame window to my application?*
- *FAQ 3.2 How do I choose between implementing a specific behavior in the view class or in the view's frame window class?*
- *FAQ 3.8 How do I programmatically resize or reposition a view?*
- *FAQ 3.9 How do I set the initial position and size of a view?*

FAQ 3.16 How do I make my application start maximized or minimized?

All the work involved here takes place in your application's *InitInstance()* function, as explained in the following steps.

Step 1. In your application's *InitInstance()* function, locate the statement shown in bold in Listing 3-33.

Listing 3-33. Default *InitInstance()* function generated by AppWizard.

```
BOOL CMyApp::InitInstance()
{
// ...

   // Dispatch commands specified on the command line
   if (!ProcessShellCommand(cmdInfo))
      return FALSE;

   // The main window has been initialized, so show
   // and update it.
   pMainFrame->ShowWindow(m_nCmdShow);
   pMainFrame->UpdateWindow();

   return TRUE;
}
```

Step 2. Insert an instruction to set the *m_nCmdShow* member variable to the desired value—*SW_SHOWMAXIMIZED*, *SW_SHOWMINIMIZED*, or *SW_SHOWNORMAL*—before calling the *ShowWindow()* function, as shown in Listing 3-34.

Listing 3-34. Modifying the *InitInstance()* function to force the opening state of the application.

```
BOOL CMyApp::InitInstance()
{
// ...
```

```
    // Dispatch commands specified on the command line
    if (!ProcessShellCommand(cmdInfo))
        return FALSE;

    // ---------------------------------
    // Depending on your needs, insert one of the following
    // statements here:
    //    m_nCmdShow = SW_SHOWMAXIMIZED;   // Open "maximized"
    //    m_nCmdShow = SW_SHOWMINIMIZED;   // Open "minimized"
    //    m_nCmdShow = SW_SHOWNORMAL;      // Open "normal"
    // ---------------------------------

    // The main window has been initialized, so show
    // and update it.
    pMainFrame->ShowWindow(m_nCmdShow);
    pMainFrame->UpdateWindow();

    return TRUE;
}
```

■

Explanations

Do you remember the good old days of Windows programming without MFC, when you used only the bare SDK and your trusted C compiler? In those ancient times, your program would start with a *WinMain()* function that had the following prototype:

```
int WINAPI WinMain(
    HINSTANCE hInstance,      // handle to current instance
    HINSTANCE hPrevInstance,  // handle to previous instance
                              // (always NULL in Win32)
    LPSTR lpCmdLine,          // pointer to command line
    int nCmdShow              // show state of window
);
```

Windows handed down the *nCmdShow* parameter to your application to let it know in which state it should initially display its main window (normal, maximized, or minimized). Most well-behaved applications simply passed this parameter as is to the *ShowWindow()* function to initially display their main window in the correct state.

In modern times—that is, using MFC—you no longer write your own *WinMain()* function. However, MFC kindly stores in your application's object the parameters received in its *WinMain()* function, so that you can get to them later. Listing 3-35 shows a simplified view of MFC's initialization process to help you understand where all this magic happens.

Listing 3-35. Overview of MFC's initialization process.

```
// ─────────────────────────────
// AfxWinMain() function (WinMain.cpp)

int AFXAPI AfxWinMain (HINSTANCE hInstance,
                       HINSTANCE hPrevInstance,
                       LPTSTR lpCmdLine,
                       int nCmdShow)
{
   ASSERT(hPrevInstance == NULL);

   int nReturnCode = -1;
   CWinApp* pApp = AfxGetApp();

   // AFX internal initialization
   if (!AfxWinInit(hInstance, hPrevInstance,
                   lpCmdLine, nCmdShow))
      goto InitFailure;

   // App global initializations (rare)
   ASSERT_VALID(pApp);
   if (!pApp->InitApplication())
      goto InitFailure;
   ASSERT_VALID(pApp);

   // Perform specific initializations
   if (!pApp->InitInstance())
   {
      if (pApp->m_pMainWnd != NULL)
      {
         pApp->m_pMainWnd->DestroyWindow();
      }
      nReturnCode = pApp->ExitInstance();
      goto InitFailure;
   }
```

```
    ASSERT_VALID(pApp);

    nReturnCode = pApp->Run();
    ASSERT_VALID(pApp);

InitFailure:
    AfxWinTerm();
    return nReturnCode;
}

// ---------------------------------------------
// AfxWinInit() function (AppInit.cpp)

BOOL AFXAPI AfxWinInit(HINSTANCE hInstance,
                       HINSTANCE hPrevInstance,
                       LPTSTR lpCmdLine,
                       int nCmdShow)
{
    ASSERT(hPrevInstance == NULL);

    // handle critical errors and avoid Windows
    // message boxes
    SetErrorMode(SetErrorMode(0) |
        SEM_FAILCRITICALERRORS|SEM_NOOPENFILEERRORBOX);

    // set resource handles
    AFX_MODULE_STATE* pModuleState = AfxGetModuleState();
    pModuleState->m_hCurrentInstanceHandle = hInstance;
    pModuleState->m_hCurrentResourceHandle = hInstance;

    // fill in the initial state for the application
    CWinApp* pApp = AfxGetApp();
    if (pApp != NULL)
    {
        // Windows specific initialization (not done if
        // no CWinApp)
        pApp->m_hInstance = hInstance;
        pApp->m_hPrevInstance = hPrevInstance;
        pApp->m_lpCmdLine = lpCmdLine;
        pApp->m_nCmdShow = nCmdShow;
        pApp->SetCurrentHandles();
    }
```

```
    // initialize thread specific data (for main thread)
    if (!afxContextIsDLL)
        AfxInitThread();

    return TRUE;
}
```

As you can see from the bold lines in Listing 3-35, the parameters received from Windows in the *AfxWinMain()* function are stored in your application's object by *AfxWinInit()*. Therefore, when *AfxWinMain()* later calls your application's *InitInstance()* function, all these parameters—and especially *m_nCmdShow*—are available for your own use.

As we saw before, a well-behaved application usually displays its main window in the state asked for by Windows, and that is exactly what the AppWizard's generated *InitInstance()* function does by default. However, you still can explicitly control the starting state of your application's main window if you decide to do so by following the steps explained earlier.

Sample Code

- Project: MinMaxApp in the Chap03 subdirectory on the companion CD-ROM.
- Purpose: Explicitly selects the starting state of an application between the normal, maximized, and minimized states. A dialog box shown when the application is launched allows the user to select the state with which the main application window will open (see Figure 3-10).

Implementation Highlights

- *CMDIApp::InitInstance ()* function (MinMaxApp.cpp)

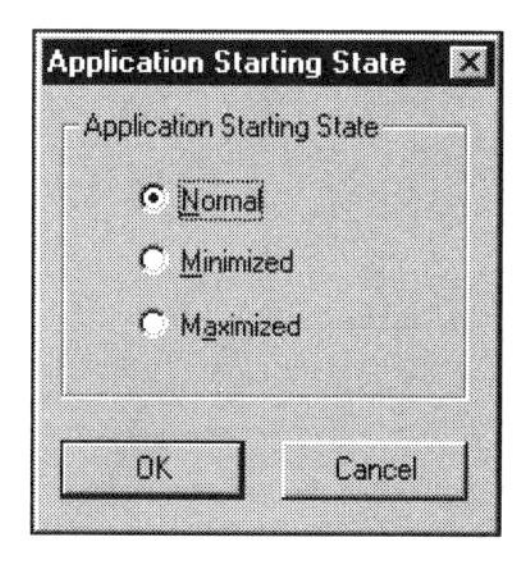

Figure 3-10. The starting dialog box of the MinMaxApp application allows the user to select the state in which the main application window will open.

How do I make my main application window stay always on top of other windows?

To make your main application window stay always on top of other windows, use code similar to the following fragment:

```
CWnd* pMainWnd = AfxGetMainWnd();
pMainWnd->SetWindowPos( &wndTopMost, 0, 0, 0, 0,
                        SWP_NOSIZE | SWP_NOMOVE );
```

If you need to bring back your main application window to normal mode, call *SetWindowPos()* again with the *wndNoTopMost* parameter:

```
pMainWnd->SetWindowPos( &wndNoTopMost, 0, 0, 0, 0,
                        SWP_NOSIZE | SWP_NOMOVE );
```

■

Additional Comments

Listing 3-36 shows an implementation of the *OnModeTopmost()* function, which toggles the main application window mode between always on top and normal.

Listing 3-36. Implementing the *OnModeTopmost()* function to toggle the main application window mode between "always on top" and "normal."

```
void CMainFrame::OnModeTopmost()
{
   if( GetExStyle() & WS_EX_TOPMOST )
   {
      // Go back to "normal" mode
      SetWindowPos( &wndNoTopMost, 0, 0, 0, 0,
                    SWP_NOSIZE | SWP_NOMOVE );
```

```
    }
    else
    {
        // Go into "always on top" mode
        SetWindowPos( &wndTopMost, 0, 0, 0, 0,
                      SWP_NOSIZE | SWP_NOMOVE );
    }
}
```

Note the *GetExStyle()* function call in Listing 3-36. This call relieves us from the need to maintain an additional Boolean member variable to remember whether the window is currently in the topmost state. It is usually a better design to avoid creating a member variable to duplicate state information that can be retrieved by some other means.

Note that the "Mode" menu should always appear, because the "Always On Top" property belongs to the main application window rather than to a specific document window. Therefore, this menu was first added to the *IDR_MAINFRAME* resource and then copied to the *IDR_DRAWTYPE* menu. If the application were to define additional document templates with specific menu resources, it would be necessary to copy the "Mode" menu to each specific resource to ensure the availability of this menu in all circumstances.

Sample Code

- Project: TopMostApp in the Chap03 subdirectory on the companion CD-ROM.
- Purpose: Makes the main application window stay always on top of other windows (see Figure 3-11).

Implementation Highlights

- *CMainFrame::OnModeTopmost()* function (MainFrm.cpp)

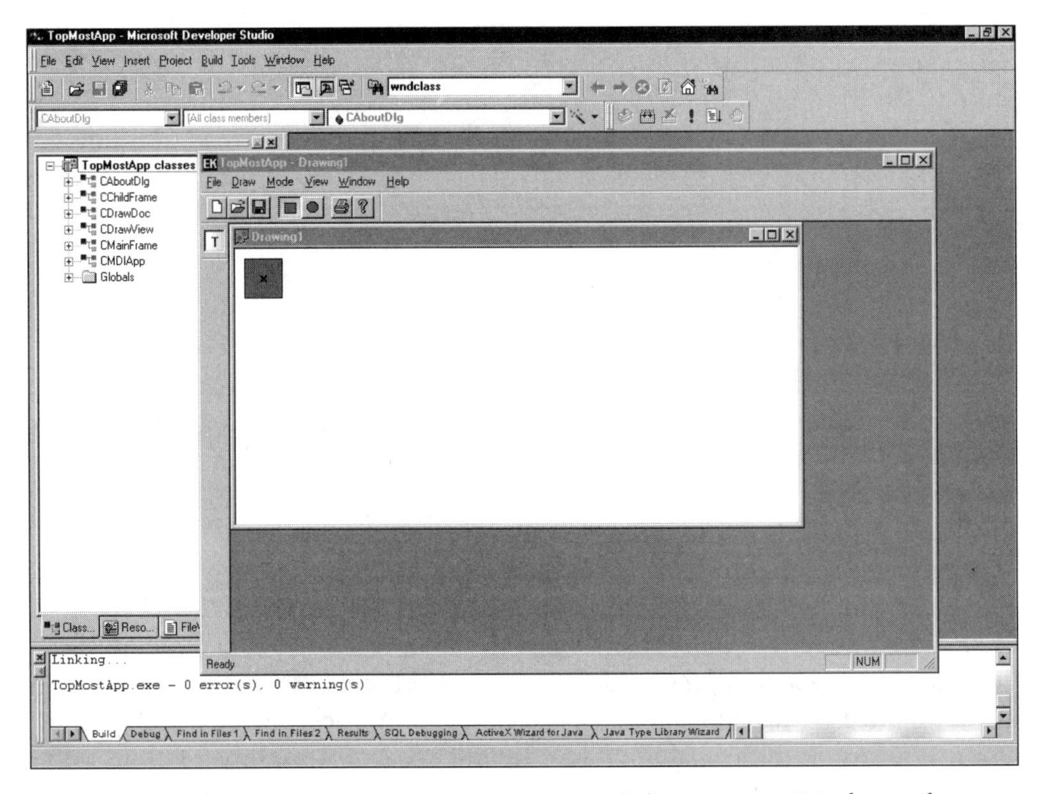

Figure 3-11. The TopMostApp application staying "always on top" in front of Developer Studio.

FAQ 3.18 How do I make one of my views stay always on top of other views?

Unfortunately, this problem does not lend itself to a solution as elegant—and as simple!—as the one discussed in *FAQ 3.17 How do I make my main application window stay always on top of other windows?* The best solution that I have been able to successfully implement uses the following hack:

- Create a timer that fires every 200 milliseconds. You can adjust this delay to your taste if you need to.
- When the timer fires, bring the selected document frame window in front of the other windows.

Because there are quite a few additional details to take care of, follow these steps (you should also refer to the complete implementation shown in Listing 3-37):

Step 1. Use ClassWizard to create a new *CMDIChildWnd*-derived class that will handle the always on top mode. Let us call this class *COnTopFrame* for the sake of the following discussion.

Step 2. Add a static member variable to *COnTopFrame:* a pointer to the currently topmost document frame window. This pointer is needed because no more than one *COnTopFrame* object can be in the topmost state at any given time. Without this pointer, a race condition could happen between several *COnTopFrame* objects that would compete for the topmost position. Therefore, this pointer either is *NULL* or points to the one and only topmost frame window object.

Step 3. Manually define the *COnTopFrame::SetModeTop()* and *COnTopFrame::SetModeNormal()* functions, which change the state of a *COnTopFrame* object while simultaneously managing the static pointer created in step 2.

Step 4. When setting a *COnTopFrame* object to the topmost state in the *COnTopFrame::SetModeTop()* function, call *SetTimer()* to create a Windows timer associated with the frame window and having a period of 200 milliseconds:

```
void COnTopFrame::SetModeTop()
{
// ...

   SetTimer( 1, 200, NULL );
}
```

Step 5. Use ClassWizard to add a handler in your *COnTopFrame* class for the *WM_TIMER* message. In this handler, call *SetWindowPos()* to bring the document frame window to the front each time the timer fires:

```
void COnTopFrame::OnTimer(UINT nIDEvent)
{
   SetWindowPos(&wndTop, 0,0,0,0,
                SWP_NOMOVE|SWP_NOSIZE|SWP_NOACTIVATE);
}
```

Step 6. Use ClassWizard to add a handler in your *COnTopFrame* class for the *WM_DESTROY* message. In this handler, call *SetModeNormal()* to correctly reset the static pointer created in step 2 and to destroy the timer created in step 4 (if needed):

```
void COnTopFrame::OnDestroy()
{
   SetModeNormal();
   CMDIChildWnd::OnDestroy();
}
```

Step 7. Don't forget to reference your view's frame class in the appropriate document templates in order to get the desired behavior (see *FAQ 3.1 How do I add a new kind of view or frame window to my application?*).

When your *COnTopFrame* class is fully operational and is hooked up to your document templates, you can then move any document frame window to the topmost position by calling *SetModeTop()* on the associated *COnTopFrame* object. You can make this function call either when the frame window is created or later in your application. For example, the sample project associated with this FAQ allows the user to designate any active view window as the topmost one by clicking on a toolbar button or by selecting the equivalent menu command.

Listing 3-37 shows the complete implementation of the *COnTopFrame* class to manage the always on top mode.

Listing 3-37. Implementing the *COnTopFrame* class to manage the always on top mode.

```
// ————————————————————————
// Class definition for COnTopFrame

class COnTopFrame : public CMDIChildWnd
{
// ...

public:
   void SetModeNormal();
   void SetModeTop();

private:
   static COnTopFrame* m_pTopFrame;    // The only top
                                       // frame window
```

```
// Generated message map functions
protected:
    //{{AFX_MSG(COnTopFrame)
    afx_msg void OnTimer(UINT nIDEvent);
    afx_msg void OnDestroy();
    //}}AFX_MSG

    DECLARE_MESSAGE_MAP()
};

// ----------------------------------
// Implementation for COnTopFrame

// ...

void COnTopFrame::SetModeNormal()
{
    if( m_pTopFrame == this )
    {
        KillTimer( 1 );
        m_pTopFrame = NULL;
    }
}

void COnTopFrame::SetModeTop()
{
    if( m_pTopFrame != NULL )
    {
        ASSERT_VALID( m_pTopFrame );
        ASSERT_KINDOF( COnTopFrame, m_pTopFrame );
        m_pTopFrame->SetModeNormal();
    }

    m_pTopFrame = this;

    SetTimer( 1, 200, NULL );
}

void COnTopFrame::OnTimer(UINT nIDEvent)
{
    ASSERT( nIDEvent == 1 );
    ASSERT( m_pTopFrame == this );
```

```
    SetWindowPos(&wndTop, 0,0,0,0,
                 SWP_NOMOVE|SWP_NOSIZE|SWP_NOACTIVATE);
}

void COnTopFrame::OnDestroy()
{
    SetModeNormal();
    CMDIChildWnd::OnDestroy();
}
```

■

Sample Code

- Project: TopMostView in the Chap03 subdirectory on the companion CD-ROM.
- Purpose: Makes a child window stay always on top of other views (see Figure 3-12).

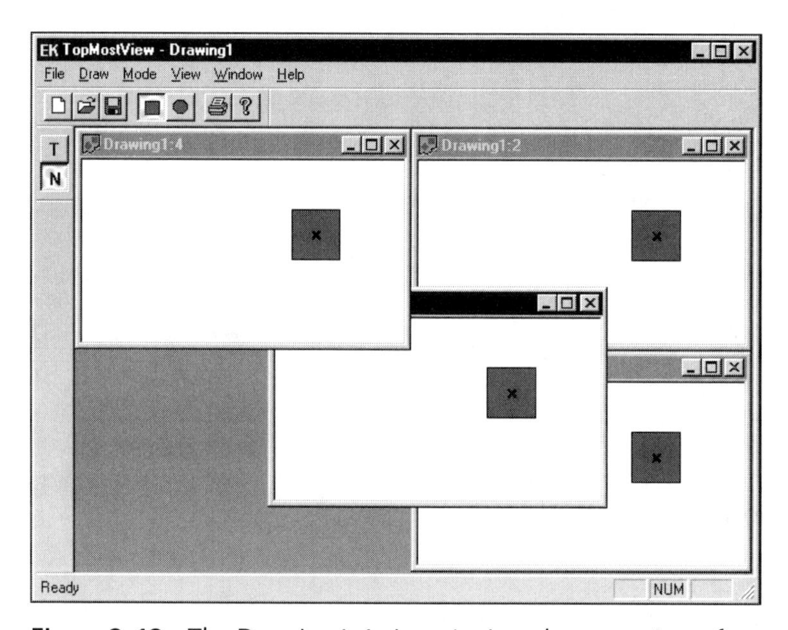

Figure 3-12. The Drawing1:4 view staying always on top of the other views.

Implementation Highlights

- *CChildFrame* class (ChildFrm.cpp)

See Also

- *FAQ 3.1 How do I add a new kind of view or frame window to my application?*

3.19 How do I implement a full-screen view mode like the one in Visual C++ and Word?

If you look closely at the way the full-screen view mode works in Microsoft Visual C++ and Microsoft Word, you will conclude that both applications implement this behavior in their main application window rather than in their view or view's frame windows. This fact is more easily revealed when you go into full-screen view with nonmaximized document windows. Note that the menu commands remain accessible either through the standard keyboard access keys (Alt+mnemonic) or through the keyboard accelerators.

The following technique works in the same way by adding the full-screen view mode to the main application window of an MFC application.

Step 1. Add two Boolean member variables to your main application window class:

```
class CMainFrame : public CMDIFrameWnd
{
// ...

// Implementation
protected:   // Full Screen view implementation
   BOOL m_bFullScreen;
   BOOL m_bWasZoomed;
};
```

Step 2. Add code to the constructor of your main application window class to initialize to *FALSE* the member variables added in step 1:

```
CMainFrame::CMainFrame()
{
   // ...

   m_bFullScreen = FALSE;
   m_bWasZoomed = FALSE;
}
```

Step 3. Add the "View, Full Screen" menu command to all your menu resources. Because this command is handled by the main application window, it should always be available whatever the currently active document or view type. Optionally add a toolbar button for the "View, Full Screen" command.

Step 4. Use ClassWizard to add an *ON_COMMAND* handler in your main application window class for the "View, Full Screen" menu command. Use ClassWizard again to add a handler for the *WM_GETMINMAX INFO* message to your main application window class. Implement those handlers as shown in Listing 3-38. Note that these two functions work in coordination to achieve the desired behavior.

Listing 3-38. Implementing *OnViewFullScreen()* and *OnGetMinMaxInfo()* to achieve the full-screen view behavior.

```
void CMainFrame::OnViewFullScreen()
{
   // 1 - Read the various system metrics
   int cyCaption = ::GetSystemMetrics( SM_CYCAPTION );
   int cxFrame = ::GetSystemMetrics( SM_CXFRAME );
   int cyFrame = ::GetSystemMetrics( SM_CYFRAME );
   int cxScreen = ::GetSystemMetrics( SM_CXSCREEN );
   int cyScreen = ::GetSystemMetrics( SM_CYSCREEN );
   int cyMenu = ::GetSystemMetrics( SM_CYMENU );

   // 2 - Toggle the current full-screen mode
   m_bFullScreen = !m_bFullScreen;

   // 3 - Go into full-screen mode or back into normal
   // Note: The following code works together with the
   // OnGetMinMaxInfo() function
```

```
if( m_bFullScreen )
{
   // 4 - Go from normal into full-screen mode

   m_bWasZoomed = IsZoomed();    // Store current state
   if( m_bWasZoomed )
   {
      // Go from maximized to full-screen mode
      // using SetWindowPos()
      SetWindowPos( NULL,
                    -cxFrame,
                    -(cyFrame+cyCaption+cyMenu),
                    cxScreen+2*cxFrame,
                    cyScreen+2*cyFrame+cyCaption+cyMenu,
                    SWP_NOZORDER );
   }
   else
   {
      // Go from normal to full-screen mode
      // using ShowWindow()
      ShowWindow( SW_SHOWMAXIMIZED );
   }
}
else
{
   // 5 - Restore the window to previous state
   // (can be either "normal" or "maximized")

   if( m_bWasZoomed )
   {
      // Restore to maximized state
      // using SetWindowPos()
      SetWindowPos( NULL,
                    -cxFrame, -cyFrame,
                    cxScreen+2*cxFrame,
                    cyScreen+2*cyFrame,
                    SWP_NOZORDER );
   }
   else
   {
      // Restore to normal state
      // using ShowWindow()
```

```
            ShowWindow( SW_RESTORE );
        }
    }
}

void CMainFrame::OnGetMinMaxInfo(MINMAXINFO FAR* lpMMI)
{
    // 1 - Read the various system metrics
    int cyCaption = ::GetSystemMetrics( SM_CYCAPTION );
    int cxFrame = ::GetSystemMetrics( SM_CXFRAME );
    int cyFrame = ::GetSystemMetrics( SM_CYFRAME );
    int cxScreen = ::GetSystemMetrics( SM_CXSCREEN );
    int cyScreen = ::GetSystemMetrics( SM_CYSCREEN );
    int cyMenu = ::GetSystemMetrics( SM_CYMENU );

    // 2 - Let the default window proc fill
    // the MINMAXINFO structure
    CFrameWnd::OnGetMinMaxInfo(lpMMI);

    if( m_bFullScreen )
    {
        // 3 - Full-screen MinMaxInfo
        lpMMI->ptMaxPosition.y = -(cyFrame+cyCaption+cyMenu);
        lpMMI->ptMaxSize.y = lpMMI->ptMaxTrackSize.y =
                        cyScreen+2*cyFrame+cyCaption+cyMenu;
    }
    else
    {
        // 4 - Normal MinMaxInfo
        lpMMI->ptMaxPosition.y = -cyFrame;
        lpMMI->ptMaxSize.y = lpMMI->ptMaxTrackSize.y =
                        cyScreen+2*cyFrame;
    }

    lpMMI->ptMaxPosition.x = -cxFrame;
    lpMMI->ptMaxSize.x = lpMMI->ptMaxTrackSize.x =
                        cxScreen+2*cxFrame;
}
```

At this point, your application already supports the full-screen view. However, you may wish to add a nice touch to the implementation by helping the user get back from the full-screen view to normal mode by simply pressing the Escape key. To do this, follow these additional steps:

Step 5. Create a new resource symbol called (for example) *ID_VIEW_BACK_TO_NORMAL*. To learn how to create a new resource symbol with Visual C++, see *FAQ 2.3 How do I create the resources associated with a new document template resource ID?*

Step 6. Use ClassWizard to add an *ON_COMMAND* handler in your main application window class for the *ID_VIEW_BACK_TO_NORMAL* symbol that you defined in step 5. Implement this handler:

```
void CMainFrame::OnViewBackToNormal()
{
   if( m_bFullScreen ) // Only if already in full-screen
   {
      // Toggle view back to normal mode
      OnViewFullScreen();
   }
}
```

Step 7. Edit your *IDR_MAINFRAME* accelerator table to define a new accelerator entry that associates the Escape key with the *ID_VIEW_BACK_TO_NORMAL* symbol that you created in step 5.

■

Explanations

This solution certainly warrants some explanations, as its workings are far from obvious.

Let's start with the *WM_GETMINMAXINFO* message, which we used in *FAQ 3.13 How do I limit the maximum or minimum size of a view?* Windows sends this message to a window when the size or position of the window is about to change. By handling this message and modifying various fields in the *MINMAXINFO* structure, we can explicitly override the window's default maximized size and position or its default minimum or maximum tracking size.

When you use ClassWizard to handle the *WM_GETMINMAXINFO* message, ClassWizard generates a handler with the following prototype:

```
afx_msg void OnGetMinMaxInfo( MINMAXINFO FAR* lpMMI );
```

The *lpMMI* parameter points to the *MINMAXINFO* structure that initially contains information about the window's maximized size and position and its minimum and maximum tracking size:

```
typedef struct tagMINMAXINFO {
    POINT ptReserved;
    POINT ptMaxSize;      // Maximized size
    POINT ptMaxPosition;  // Maximized position
    POINT ptMinTrackSize; // Minimum tracking size
    POINT ptMaxTrackSize; // Maximum tracking size
} MINMAXINFO;
```

The maximized size and position fields control the size and position of the window when its state is set to maximized. The minimum and maximum tracking sizes are, respectively, the smallest and largest window sizes that a user can display by using the borders to size the window.

Each field is of type *POINT*, where *pt.x* and *pt.y* represent, respectively, the width and height of the given size. For example, *lpMMI->ptMaxPosition.y* gives the vertical position of the upper-left corner of the maximized window, and *lpMMI->ptMaxSize.x* represents its width.

The code shown in Listing 3-38 for the *OnGetMinMaxInfo()* function uses the following algorithm to set the *ptMaxSize* and *ptMaxPosition* members of the *MINMAXINFO* structure:

- Call *CFrameWnd::OnGetMinMaxInfo(lpMMI)* to have the default window procedure initialize the *MINMAXINFO* structure. Note that all values in the *MINMAXINFO* structure are expressed in screen coordinates, where the upper-left corner of the screen is at (0,0).

- If the window is in full-screen mode, set the vertical position of the maximized window so that its top border frame, its caption, and its menu bar lie just above the visible screen area. Then set the height of the maximized window to the sum of the screen's height, the height of the window's caption and menu bar, and *twice* the height of the window's borders (to take into account both the top and bottom borders). This calculation ensures that the bottom border frame of the maximized window lies just under the visible screen area:

```
lpMMI->ptMaxPosition.y = -(cyFrame+cyCaption+cyMenu);
lpMMI->ptMaxSize.y = lpMMI->ptMaxTrackSize.y =
                          cyScreen+2*cyFrame+cyCaption+cyMenu;
```

- If the window is in normal mode, set the vertical position of the maximized window so that only its top border frame lies just above the visible screen area. Then set the height of the maximized window to the sum of the screen's height and *twice* the height of the window's borders (to take into account both the top and bottom borders). This calculation ensures that the bottom border frame of the maximized window lies just under the visible screen area:

```
lpMMI->ptMaxPosition.y = -cxFrame;
lpMMI->ptMaxSize.y = lpMMI->ptMaxTrackSize.y =
                         cyScreen+2*cyFrame;
```

- For both the full-screen and the normal modes, set the horizontal position of the maximized window so that its left border frame lies just to the left of the visible screen area. Then set the width of the maximized window to the sum of the screen's width and *twice* the width of the window's borders (to take into account both the left and right borders). This calculation ensures that the right border frame of the maximized window lies just to the right of the visible screen area:

```
lpMMI->ptMaxPosition.x = -cxFrame;
lpMMI->ptMaxSize.x = lpMMI->ptMaxTrackSize.x =
                         cxScreen+2*cxFrame;
```

Now that our *WM_GETMINMAXINFO* handler is ready, how do we trigger its execution from *OnViewFullScreen()*? All we do is maximize the window by calling *ShowWindow(SW_SHOWMAXIMIZED).* Windows will then send a *WM_GETMINMAXINFO* message to our window, and our handler will ensure that the maximized window is positioned to give the user the illusion of being in full-screen mode. We restore our window to normal mode by calling *ShowWindow(SW_RESTORE).*

This strategy works well most of the time. There is, however, a problem if the user tries to go into full-screen mode when the window is already in the maximized state. In this case, calling *ShowWindow(SW_SHOWMAXIMIZED)* does nothing, and that is understandable from Windows' point of view.

To solve this last problem, we must detect this situation and call *SetWindowPos()* instead of *ShowWindow()* both to go into full-screen mode and to come back to the maximized state. *SetWindowPos()* has the following prototype:

```
BOOL SetWindowPos( const CWnd* pWndInsertAfter,
                   int x, int y, int cx, int cy,
                   UINT nFlags );
```

We calculate the *x*, *y*, *cx*, and *cy* arguments using exactly the same formulas as discussed earlier for handling the *WM_GETMINMAXINFO* message. Finally, we use the *m_bWasZoomed* member variable to remember whether the window was initially in the maximized state and to choose between calling *ShowWindow()* or *SetWindowPos()* when escaping from full-screen back to normal mode.

Additional Comments

- While your main application window is in full-screen mode, the user can still access the menu commands by using the keyboard interface (ALT+key or direct accelerator key).
- You might wish to hide some toolbars and status bars while in full-screen mode. To do this, call *CFrameWnd::ShowControlBar()* (see also *FAQ 6.15 How do I programmatically show or hide a control bar?*).

Sample Code

- Project: FullScreen in the Chap03 subdirectory on the companion CD-ROM.
- Purpose: Implements a full-screen view mode (see Figure 3-13).

Implementation Highlights

- *CMainFrame::OnViewFullScreen()* function (MainFrm.cpp)
- *CMainFrame::OnGetMinMaxInfo()* function (MainFrm.cpp)
- *CMainFrame::OnViewBackToNormal()* function (MainFrm.cpp)

See Also

- *FAQ 3.13 How do I limit the maximum or minimum size of a view?*

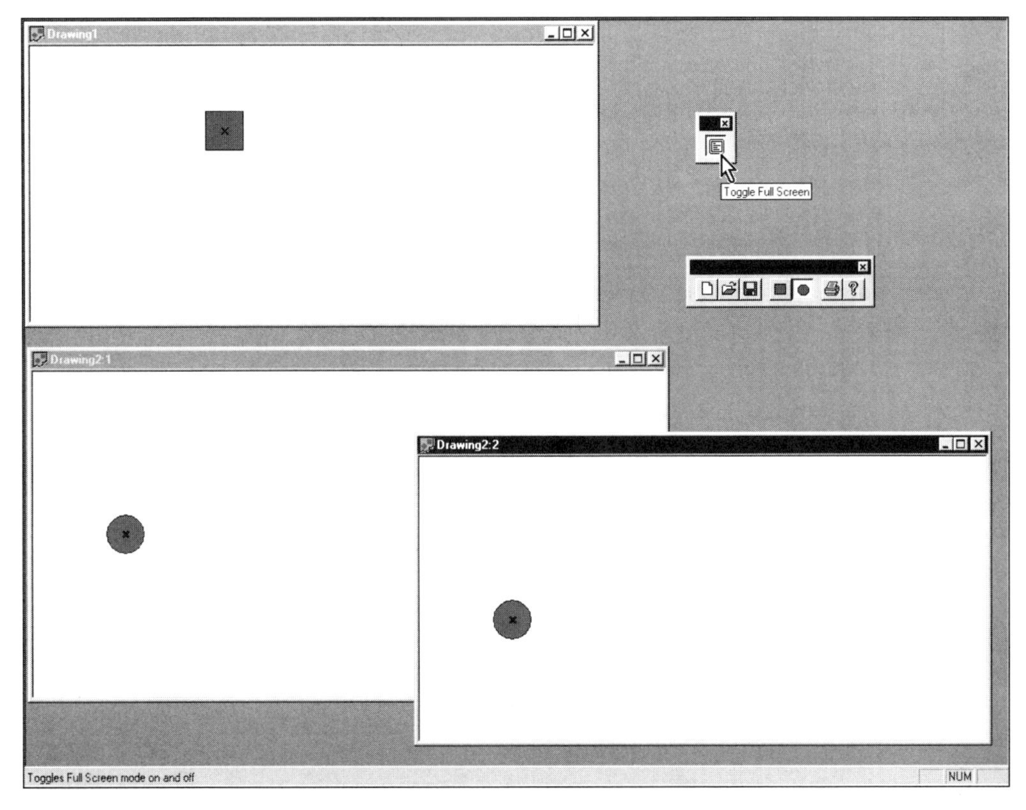

Figure 3-13. The FullScreen application in full-screen mode.

Managing Captions, Icons, Cursors, and Backgrounds

FAQ 3.20 How do I customize the captions of my views?

It is common to wish to customize the captions of your views—actually, of your views' frame windows. For example, you might wish to add some text to the standard caption to differentiate between the various views in your application.

You might also wish to remove the frame number that MFC appends to the document's name.

The answer lies in a little-known undocumented virtual function: *CFrameWnd::OnUpdateFrameTitle()*. This function can be overridden by each *CFrameWnd*-derived class so that you can customize the frame caption displayed. MFC calls this function each time a frame window needs to set its title.

If your frame window class overrides this function, you can have the final word on which caption you will display. Listings 3-39 and 3-40 show two different ways to customize these captions. These examples can serve as starting points to help you implement *OnUpdateFrameTitle()* to suit your needs.

Listing 3-39. Implementing *OnUpdateFrameTitle()* to customize the caption of a view's frame window: first example.

```
// ————————————————————————————
// Class definition for CChildFrame (ChildFrm.h)

class CChildFrame : public CMDIChildWnd
{

// ...

   // Undocumented overridable
   virtual void OnUpdateFrameTitle( BOOL bAddToTitle );

// ...
};

// ————————————————————————————
// Implementation for CChildFrame (ChildFrm.cpp)
void CChildFrame::OnUpdateFrameTitle( BOOL bAddToTitle )
{
   // 1 - First call default function
   CMDIChildWnd::OnUpdateFrameTitle( bAddToTitle );

   // 2 - Now adapt the title to our taste

   // 2a - Get the "standard" frame title
   CString strInitialTitle;
   GetWindowText( strInitialTitle );
```

```
   // 2b - Build our custom frame title
   CString strMyTitle = "Drawing View <"
                     + strInitialTitle + ">";
   SetWindowText( strMyTitle );
}
```

Listing 3-40. Implementing *OnUpdateFrameTitle()* to customize the caption of a view's frame window: second example.

```
// ____________________________
// Class definition for CEkFixedFormFrame
// (EkFixedFormFrame.h)

class CEkFixedFormFrame : public CMDIChildWnd
{

// ...

   // Undocumented overridable
   virtual void OnUpdateFrameTitle( BOOL bAddToTitle );

// ...

};

// ____________________________
// Implementation for CEkFixedFormFrame
// (EkFixedFormFrame.cpp)

void CEkFixedFormFrame::OnUpdateFrameTitle(
                                        BOOL bAddToTitle )
{
   // 1 - First call default function
   CMDIChildWnd::OnUpdateFrameTitle( bAddToTitle );

   // 2 - Now adapt the title to our taste

   // 2a - Get the document title
   CDocument* pDoc = GetActiveDocument();
   if( pDoc );
   {
      CString strDocTitle = pDoc->GetTitle();
```

```
        // 2b - Build our custom frame title
        CString strMyTitle = "Form - " + strDocTitle;
        SetWindowText( strMyTitle );
    }
}
```

Because *OnUpdateFrameTitle()* is an undocumented overridable function, you must add this function manually to your view's frame window class without any help from ClassWizard.

■

Explanations

Both examples shown in Listings 3-39 and 3-40 build their captions by prefixing the document name with the kind of view that the frame encloses ("Drawing View" and "Form," respectively). However, each example gets the document name in a slightly different way: Listing 3-39 retrieves the standard MFC frame caption using *CWnd::GetWindowText()*, whereas the code in Listing 3-40 gets the active document's title by calling *CDocument::GetTitle()*. The difference lies in the fact that the latter technique retrieves only the document's title (for example, "Drawing1.ek1"), whereas the former will get the entire standard MFC frame caption, which might include the frame count if many views are opened on the same document (for example, "Drawing1.ek1:2"). You can choose either technique depending on your exact needs.

Listing 3-41 shows how MFC implements the default behavior of *CMDIChildWnd::OnUpdateFrameTitle()*. When you override this function, this code can inspire you to customize your own frame captions, especially if you decide not to call the original function from your override.

Listing 3-41. Pseudocode for the *CMDIChildWnd::OnUpdateFrameTitle()* function (WinMdi.cpp).

```
void CMDIChildWnd::OnUpdateFrameTitle(BOOL bAddToTitle)
{
    // update our parent window first
    GetMDIFrame()->OnUpdateFrameTitle(bAddToTitle);

    // Suppressing the FWS_ADDTOTITLE style bit means
    // MFC will not alter the caption
```

```
    if ((GetStyle() & FWS_ADDTOTITLE) == 0)
        return;       // leave child window alone!

    CDocument* pDocument = GetActiveDocument();
    if (bAddToTitle && pDocument != NULL)
    {
        // Get the active document's title
        TCHAR szText[256+_MAX_PATH];
        lstrcpy(szText, pDocument->GetTitle());

        // Append the frame count if nonzero
        if (m_nWindow > 0)
            wsprintf(szText + lstrlen(szText), _T(":%d"),
                     m_nWindow);

        // Set the new window's title
        // set title if changed, but don't remove completely
        AfxSetWindowText(m_hWnd, szText);
    }
}
```

Additional Comments

In the Knowledge Base Article Q99182, Microsoft suggests that you use the following technique:

1. Modify the *PreCreateWindow()* function of your frame window class to remove the *FWS_ADDTOTITLE* style bit:

```
BOOL CChildFrame::PreCreateWindow(CREATESTRUCT& cs)
{
    cs.style &= ~FWS_ADDTOTITLE;

    return CMDIChildWnd::PreCreateWindow(cs);
}
```

2. Explicitly set the title of the frame window in your view's *OnInitialUpdate()* function:

```
void CDrawView::OnInitialUpdate()
{
    CView::OnInitialUpdate();
```

```
    CString strDocTitle = GetDocument()->GetTitle();
    CString strFrameTitle = "My own <" + strDocTitle + ">";
    GetParentFrame()->SetWindowText( strFrameTitle );
}
```

Note that you must implement the preceding code in your view class so that you can get at the associated document object and extract its title; the frame window has no direct knowledge about the document. This code must also reside in the view's *OnInitialUpdate()* function rather than in the *OnCreate()* function so that the document object can be correctly created and hooked to your view object.

This alternative method almost works. Its main shortcoming is that the frame window title is set only during the creation process. If the document name changes—for example, because the user executes the "File, Save As" command—the frame window keeps the old title. That is rather surprising!

Another drawback is that this technique requires both the view's frame window and the view classes to be modified in order to set the title, whereas my solution touches only the view's frame window class.

Sample Code

- Project: OwnCaption in the Chap03 subdirectory on the companion CD-ROM.
- Purpose: Customizes the caption of the MDI view's frame windows. Note that the standard drawing view title shows both the document title and the view number, whereas the form view title shows only the document title (see Figure 3-14).

Implementation Highlights

- *CChildFrame::OnUpdateFrameTitle()* function (ChildFrm.cpp)
- *CEkFixedFormFrame::OnUpdateFrameTitle()* function (EkFixedFormFrame.cpp)

See Also

- *FAQ 3.21 How do I show a "modified" indicator in the captions of the views associated with a "dirty" document?*

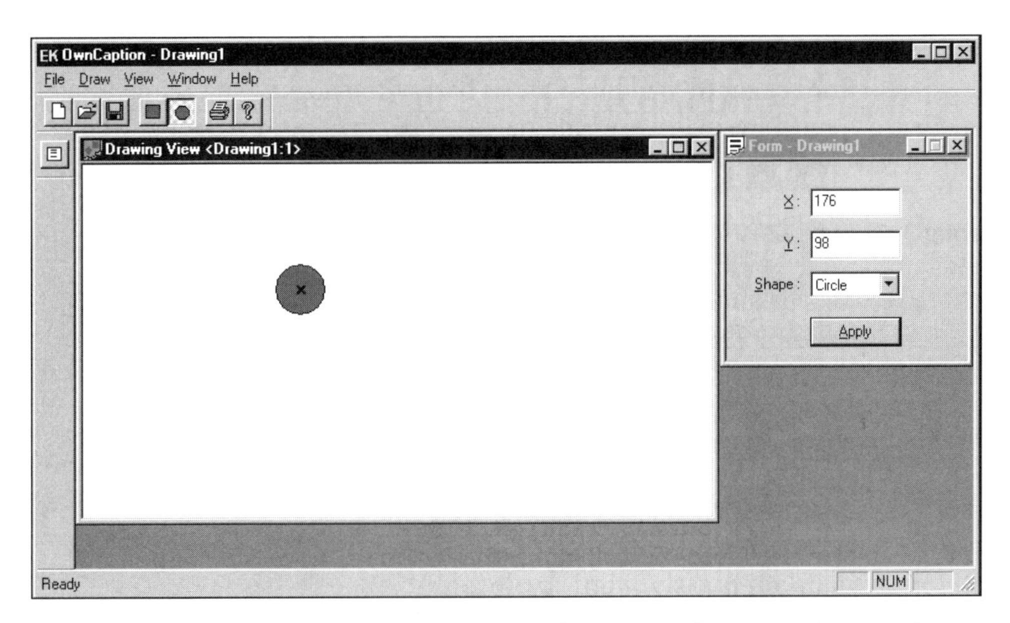

Figure 3-14. Note the customized captions of the view's frame windows in the OwnCaption application.

FAQ 3.21 How do I show a "modified" indicator in the captions of the views associated with a "dirty" document?

A general solution to this problem could be implemented as shown in *FAQ 3.20 How do I customize the captions of my views?* However, there is a simpler way if all you need is to display a simple "modified" indicator such as an asterisk ("*") in the caption of a "dirty" document: simply override the *CDocument::SetModifiedFlag()* function. You *do* call this function whenever the document object is modified, don't you?

We can safely override *SetModifiedFlag()*, because it is declared as *virtual* in the *CDocument* class even though the Visual C++ online help forgets to mention this fact.

Listing 3-42 shows an implementation of *SetModifiedFlag()* that modifies the title of the document to append an asterisk when the document becomes "dirty." The tricky part is to remove this asterisk whenever the document becomes "clean" again—usually because the user saved it.

Note also that the extra space added before the asterisk is necessary to prevent the asterisk from being treated by MFC as part of the document's name. Finally, note that you must manually override the *SetModifiedFlag()* without any help from ClassWizard.

Listing 3-42. Implementing *SetModifiedFlag()* to show a "modified" caption indicator.

```
// ————————————————————————
// Class definition for CDrawDoc (DrawDoc.h)

class CDrawDoc : public CDocument
{

// ...

   // Overriden to change the document's title
   virtual void SetModifiedFlag( BOOL bModified );

// ...

};

// ————————————————————————
// Implementation for CDrawDoc (DrawDoc.cpp)

// Overridden to change the document's title
void CDrawDoc::SetModifiedFlag( BOOL bModified )
{
   CString strTitle = GetTitle();

   // Note the space before the "modified" marker:
   // this prevents some problems with the document
   // name in the "Save As" dialog box
   CString strIndicator = " *";

   // 1 - Set the correct title depending on the new
   // state of our document object
   if( !IsModified() && bModified )
   {
      // 1a - Document was "clean", is now "dirty"
      SetTitle( strTitle + strIndicator );
```

```
    }
    else if( IsModified() && !bModified )
    {
        // 1b - Document was "dirty", is now "clean"
        SetTitle( strTitle.Left( strTitle.GetLength()
                        - strIndicator.GetLength() ) );
    }

    // 2 - Force update of the frame windows titles
    // (this will cause the frame windows to show our
    // new title)
    UpdateFrameCounts();

    // 3 - Finally, call the standard function
    CDocument::SetModifiedFlag( bModified );
}
```

■

Sample Code

- Project: ModifiedMark in the Chap03 subdirectory on the CD-ROM.
- Purpose: Shows a "modified" indicator in the captions of the child windows associated with a "dirty" document (see Figure 3-15).

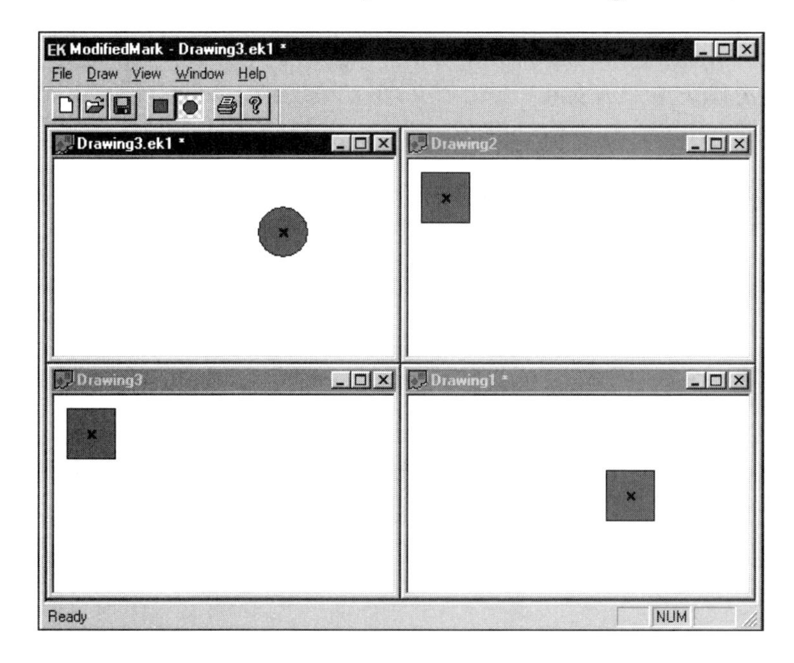

Figure 3-15. The ModifiedMark application in action. Can you spot which documents are currently dirty?

Implementation Highlights

- *CDrawDoc::SetModifiedFlag()* function (Drawdoc.cpp)

See Also

- *FAQ 3.20 How do I customize the captions of my views?*

FAQ 3.22 How do I modify the icons associated with each kind of window in my application?

To modify the icon associated with your main application window, simply change the icon associated with the *IDR_MAINFRAME* resource ID.

To modify the icon associated with each kind of document window in your application, follow these steps:

Step 1. Identify the document template resource ID associated with each kind of document window in your application. These document template objects are usually created in your application's *InitInstance()* function. Make sure that each of these document template objects is associated with a distinct template resource ID (see *FAQ 2.2 How do I manage multiple document templates without having a dialog box pop up each time the user tries to create a new document?* and *FAQ 3.1 How do I add a new kind of view or frame window to my application?*).

Step 2. Use Developer Studio's Resource Editor to change the icon associated with each document template resource ID identified in step 1.

■

Additional Comments

When you design icon resources, you need to create at least a standard 32×32 icon. However, I strongly advise that you also create a 16×16 icon for each kind of icon. Otherwise, Windows will create the 16×16 icon on the fly by shrinking the 32×32 icon, usually with disappointing results. Figure 3-16 shows where you select the kind of icon that you want to work on.

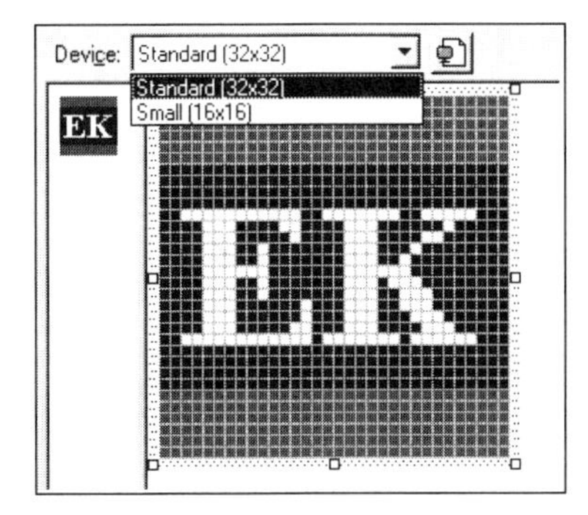

Figure 3-16. Selecting the 32×32 or 16×16 icon resource.

Sample Code

There is no sample project specifically developed for this FAQ. However, most sample applications for this chapter and Chapter 2 have custom icons for their main application window and for each type of document that they manipulate (Drawing or Counter documents).

Most sample applications in this chapter also have a custom icon for each type of document window that they can open on a Drawing document: normal drawing view, form view, or three-way splitter window. The MultiViews sample project provides a good example of these custom icons.

See Also

- *FAQ 3.23 How do I dynamically change the icon of my main application window?*

FAQ 3.23 How do I dynamically change the icon of my main application window?

Let us assume that you want the icon of your main application window to dynamically reflect the state of some part of your application. The following steps explain how you can implement this behavior.

Step 1. Find out the class that contains the state information you want to associate with the icon of your main application window (we will use the class *CDrawDoc* as an example in the following discussion).

Step 2. Add member variables of type *HICON* to the class that you identified in step 1. Create one variable for each icon that you want to display, as shown in Listing 3-43.

Listing 3-43. Adding member variables of type *HICON* to the *CDrawDoc* class.

```
class CDrawDoc : public CDocument
{
// ...

// Attributes
public:
    CPoint m_point;
    enum SHAPE { SQUARE = 0, CIRCLE = 1 } m_shape;

// ...

protected:
    void SetFrameIcon();
    HICON m_hIconSquare, m_hIconCircle;

// ...

};
```

Step 3. Add code to your class's constructor to initialize the *HICON* member variables declared in step 2 by loading the corresponding icons, as shown in Listing 3-44.

Listing 3-44. Initializing the *HICON* member variables in *CDrawDoc*'s constructor.

```
CDrawDoc::CDrawDoc()
{
// ...

    m_hIconSquare = AfxGetApp()->LoadIcon( IDI_SQUARE );
    ASSERT( m_hIconSquare != NULL );

    m_hIconCircle = AfxGetApp()->LoadIcon( IDI_CIRCLE );
    ASSERT( m_hIconCircle != NULL );
}
```

Step 4. Manually add the *SetFrameIcon()* member function to your class. This function is responsible for changing the main application window's icon as needed to reflect the state of your application. To change the icon, call the *::SetClassLong()* and *RedrawWindow()* functions on the main application window:

```
CWnd* pFrame = AfxGetMainWnd();
::SetClassLong( pFrame->GetSafeHwnd(), GCL_HICON,
                (long) hIcon );
pFrame->RedrawWindow( NULL, NULL,
                      RDW_FRAME | RDW_INVALIDATE );
```

Listing 3-45 shows a sample implementation of the *SetFrameIcon()* member function, which changes the main application window's icon to either the *IDI_SQUARE* or the *IDI_CIRCLE* icon resource depending on the current value of the *m_shape* member variable.

Listing 3-45. Implementing the *SetFrameIcon()* function to dynamically change the main application window's icon.

```
void CDrawDoc::SetFrameIcon()
{
   HICON hIcon = NULL;

   // 1 - Select the correct icon based on the state
   // of the application
   switch( m_shape )
   {
      default:
         ASSERT( FALSE );
         break;

      case CIRCLE:
         hIcon = m_hIconCircle;
         break;

      case SQUARE:
         hIcon = m_hIconSquare;
         break;
   }

   ASSERT( hIcon != NULL );
```

```
    CWnd* pFrame = AfxGetMainWnd();
    ASSERT_VALID( pFrame );

    // 2 - Retrieve the current icon
    HICON hCurrentIcon = (HICON) ::GetClassLong(
                        pFrame->GetSafeHwnd(), GCL_HICON );

    // 3 - Change the icon only if needed (avoid flicker)
    if( hCurrentIcon != hIcon )
    {
        ::SetClassLong( pFrame->GetSafeHwnd(), GCL_HICON,
                        (long) hIcon );
        pFrame->RedrawWindow( NULL, NULL,
                              RDW_FRAME | RDW_INVALIDATE );
    }
}
```

Step 5. Call *SetFrameIcon()* each time you want to update the main application window's icon—usually when the application's state, as reflected by your icon, has changed.

■

Additional Comments

In the sample code for this FAQ I am able to take an interesting shortcut with regard to step 5, because my application's icon reflects the currently selected shape (square or circle): I simply call *SetFrameIcon()* from the *UPDATE_COMMAND_UI* handlers for my "Square" and "Circle" toolbar buttons, as shown in Listing 3-46. MFC calls these handlers each time my application becomes idle, and I take advantage of this fact to update my main application window's icon.

Listing 3-46. Calling *SetFrameIcon()* from the *UPDATE_COMMAND_UI* handlers.

```
void CDrawDoc::OnUpdateDrawSquare(CCmdUI* pCmdUI)
{
    pCmdUI->SetCheck( m_shape == SQUARE );
    SetFrameIcon();
}

void CDrawDoc::OnUpdateDrawCircle(CCmdUI* pCmdUI)
{
```

```
    pCmdUI->SetCheck( m_shape == CIRCLE );
    SetFrameIcon();
}
```

Sample Code

- Project: DynamicIcon in the Chap03 subdirectory on the companion CD-ROM.
- Purpose: Dynamically changes the icon of the main application window (see Figure 3-17).

Implementation Highlights

- *CDrawDoc::SetFrameIcon()* function (DrawDoc.cpp)
- *CDrawDoc::OnUpdateDrawSquare()* function (DrawDoc.cpp)
- *CDrawDoc::OnUpdateDrawCircle()* function (DrawDoc.cpp)
- *CDrawDoc::CDrawDoc()* function (DrawDoc.cpp)

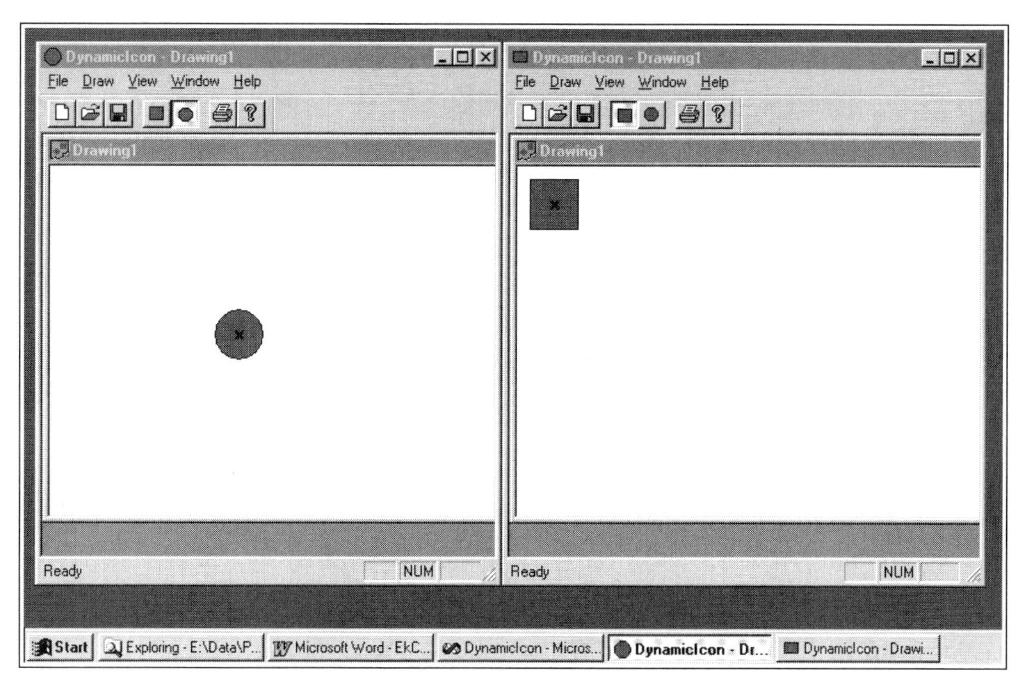

Figure 3-17. Running two different instances of the DynamicIcon application. Notice the icons on the main application window and on the taskbar.

See Also

- *FAQ 3.22 How do I modify the icons associated with each kind of window in my application?*

FAQ 3.24 How do I dynamically change the cursor for a view?

All the work here takes place inside the view class for which you want to dynamically change the cursor to reflect an application's state. This dynamic cursor usually reflects the value of a member variable belonging to either the view or the document class.

Step 1. Add member variables of type *HCURSOR* to the view class for which you want to dynamically change the cursor. Create one variable for each cursor that you want to display, as shown in Listing 3-47.

Listing 3-47. Adding member variables of type *HCURSOR* to the *CDrawView* class.

```
class CDrawView : public CView
{
// ...

// Implementation

protected:
   HCURSOR m_hcurSquare, m_hcurCircle;

// ...
};
```

Step 2. Add code to the constructor of the view class to initialize the *HCURSOR* member variables declared in step 1 by loading the corresponding cursors, as shown in Listing 3-48.

Listing 3-48. Initializing the *HCURSOR* member variables in *CDrawView*'s constructor.

```
CDrawView::CDrawView()
{
```

```
// ...
   m_hcurSquare = AfxGetApp()->LoadCursor( IDC_SQUARE );
   ASSERT( m_hcurSquare != NULL );

   m_hcurCircle = AfxGetApp()->LoadCursor( IDC_CIRCLE );
   ASSERT( m_hcurCircle != NULL );
}
```

Step 3. Use ClassWizard to add a handler for the *WM_SETCURSOR* message to your view class. Implement this handler as shown in Listing 3-49, calling *SetCursor()* to select the correct cursor depending on the state of your application. Return *TRUE* to indicate that the cursor was set by your handler. The sample implementation of the *OnSetCursor()* member function shown in Listing 3-49 changes the view's cursor to either the *IDC_SQUARE* or the *IDC_CIRCLE* cursor resource depending on the current value of the document's *m_shape* member variable.

Listing 3-49. Handling the *WM_SETCURSOR* message to dynamically change the view's cursor.

```
BOOL CDrawView::OnSetCursor(CWnd* pWnd, UINT nHitTest,
                            UINT message)
{
   // 1 - Use dynamic cursor only in client area
   if( nHitTest == HTCLIENT )
   {
      // 2 - Select correct dynamic cursor
      switch( GetDocument()->m_shape )
      {
         default:
            ASSERT( FALSE );
            break;

         case CDrawDoc::SQUARE:
            SetCursor( m_hcurSquare );
            return TRUE;   // Cursor was set

         case CDrawDoc::CIRCLE:
            SetCursor( m_hcurCircle );
            return TRUE;   // Cursor was set
      }
   }
```

```
    // 3 - Otherwise call base class to get standard cursor
    return CView::OnSetCursor(pWnd, nHitTest, message);
}
```

■

Explanations

Windows sends a *WM_SETCURSOR* message to the window under the mouse pointer each time the mouse pointer moves. When the *WM_SETCURSOR* message is not handled by the window, *DefWindowProc()* automatically sets the cursor in the following way:

- If the cursor is *outside* the window's client area (hit-test code != *HTCLIENT*), call *::SetCursor()* to set the cursor to the standard arrow (*IDC_ARROW*).
- If the cursor is *inside* the window's client area (hit-test code == *HTCLIENT*), call *::SetCursor()* to set the cursor to the *hCursor* field of the *WNDCLASS* structure associated with the window. (This *WNDCLASS* structure defines what is usually called the *window class;* it is first registered with Windows by calling *::RegisterClass()* and is then associated with a window via the first argument passed to the *::CreateWindow()* function.)

Thus, by handling the *WM_SETCURSOR* message in our own code, we are able to dynamically choose the shape of the cursor when the mouse pointer comes over our window's client area.

Additional Comments

When you design your own cursor, don't forget to set the correct *hotspot*, as shown in Figure 3-18.

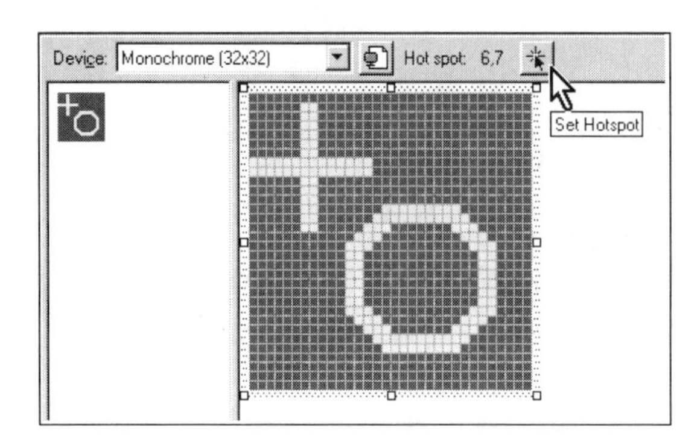

Figure 3-18. Setting the cursor hotspot.

Sample Code

- Project: DynamicCursor in the Chap03 subdirectory on the companion CD-ROM.
- Purpose: Dynamically changes the cursor for a view to reflect the application's current state (see Figure 3-19).

Implementation Highlights

- *CDrawView::OnSetCursor()* function (DrawView.cpp)
- *CDrawView::CDrawView()* function (DrawView.cpp)

See Also

- *FAQ 3.25 How do I display an hourglass cursor during a lengthy operation?*

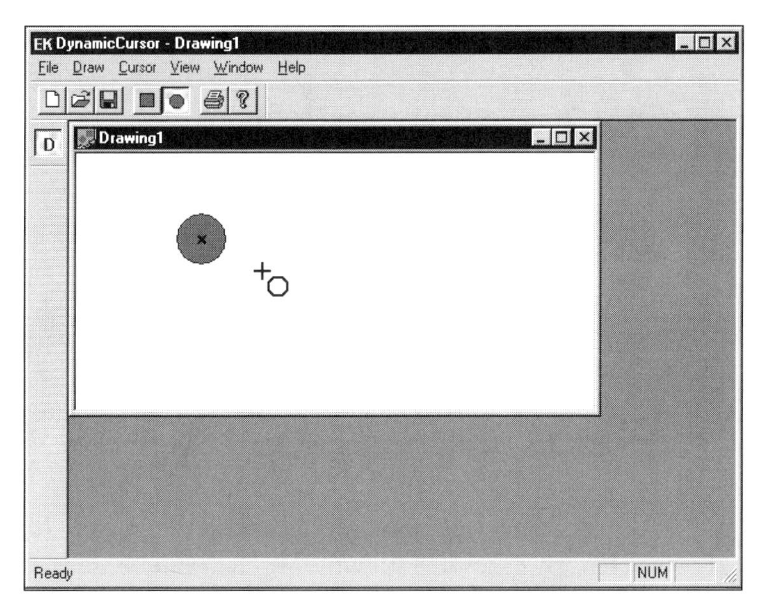

Figure 3-19. The DynamicCursor application showing a cursor that reflects the currently selected shape.

3.25 How do I display an hourglass cursor during a lengthy operation?

Choose between one of the following two techniques. One is easy, and the other even easier.

First Technique

Call *CCmdTarget::BeginWaitCursor()* to change the cursor to an hourglass, and call *CCmdTarget::EndWaitCursor()* to restore the cursor to its previous state. Note that these calls increment or decrement an internal reference count and that the hourglass cursor is removed only when this count reaches 0. In other words, if you call *BeginWaitCursor()* twice, you should also call *EndWaitCursor()* twice to restore the normal cursor. The following code fragment shows how to use these functions:

```
// ...

   // 1 - Start displaying hourglass cursor
   BeginWaitCursor();

   // ...
   // 2 - Do the work that takes a long time
   // ...

   // 3 - Stop displaying hourglass cursor
   EndWaitCursor();

// ...
```

Note that this technique can be used only in the context of a *CCmdTarget*-derived class. Fortunately, this includes all window classes—because class *CWnd* derives from CCmdTarget—as well as the classes derived from *CDocument* and *CWinApp*.

Second Technique

The *CWaitCursor* class provides an even easier way to display an hourglass cursor: the *CWaitCursor* constructor and destructor call *BeginWaitCursor()* and *EndWaitCursor()*, respectively, on the application object. Hence, simply instantiating a *CWaitCursor* object on the stack displays the hourglass cursor until the *CWaitCursor* variable goes out of scope:

```
// ...

   {
      // 1 - Display hourglass cursor from this point
      // to end of block
      CWaitCursor wait;

      // ...
      // 2 - Do the work that takes a long time
      // ...

   }
   // Normal cursor is automatically restored here

// ...
```

Using a *CWaitCursor* object instead of explicitly calling *BeginWaitCursor()* and *EndWaitCursor()* also results in more-robust code. The C++ language guarantees that the *CWaitCursor* destructor will be called in all situations, thereby restoring the cursor to its normal state.

■

Explanations

Do you wonder how the *CWaitCursor* class works? Listing 3-50 shows its entire implementation. As you can see, it is one of the smallest and simplest MFC classes!

Listing 3-50. Implementation of the *CWaitCursor* class.

```
// ——————————————————————————————
// Class definition for CWaitCursor (AfxWin.h)

class CWaitCursor
{
// Construction/Destruction
public:
   CWaitCursor();
   ~CWaitCursor();
```

```
// Operations
public:
    void Restore();
};

// ————————————————————————————
// Implementation for CWaitCursor (AfxWin2.inl)

_AFXWIN_INLINE CWaitCursor::CWaitCursor()
    { AfxGetApp()->BeginWaitCursor(); }

_AFXWIN_INLINE CWaitCursor::~CWaitCursor()
    { AfxGetApp()->EndWaitCursor(); }

_AFXWIN_INLINE void CWaitCursor::Restore()
    { AfxGetApp()->RestoreWaitCursor(); }
```

Sample Code

- Project: Hourglass in the Chap03 subdirectory on the companion CD-ROM.
- Purpose: Displays an hourglass cursor during a lengthy operation.

Implementation Highlights

- *CDrawView::OnLButtonDown()* function (DrawView.cpp)

See Also

- *FAQ 3.24 How do I dynamically change the cursor for a view?*

How do I change the background color of a view?

Use ClassWizard to add a handler in your view class for the *WM_ERASEBKGND* message. Implement this handler as shown in Listing 3-51.

Listing 3-51. Handling the *WM_ERASEBKGND* message to change the background color of a view.

```
BOOL CDrawView::OnEraseBkgnd(CDC* pDC)
{
   // 1 - Find out area to erase
   CRect rect;
   pDC->GetClipBox( &rect );

   // 2 - Create the correct brush and select into DC
   CBrush brush( m_crBackColor );
   CBrush* pOldBrush = pDC->SelectObject( &brush );

   // 3 - Erase the background
   pDC->PatBlt(   rect.left, rect.top,
                  rect.Width(), rect.Height(),
                  PATCOPY );

   pDC->SelectObject( pOldBrush );

   return TRUE;   // Background was erased
}
```

■

Explanations

Windows sends a *WM_ERASEBKGND* message to a window whenever an invalidated region of the window is prepared for repainting. When the *WM_ERASEBKGND* message is not handled by the window, *DefWindowProc()* automatically erases the window's background with the brush indicated by the *hbrBackground* field of the *WNDCLASS* structure associated with the window. (This *WNDCLASS* structure defines what is usually called the window class; it is first registered with Windows by calling *::RegisterClass()* and is then associated with a window via the first argument passed to the *::CreateWindow()* function.)

Thus, by handling the *WM_ERASEBKGND* message in our own code, we can dynamically choose the color of the window's background.

Sample Code

- Project: BackColor in the Chap03 subdirectory on the companion CD-ROM.
- Purpose: Dynamically changes the background color of a view (see Figure 3-20).

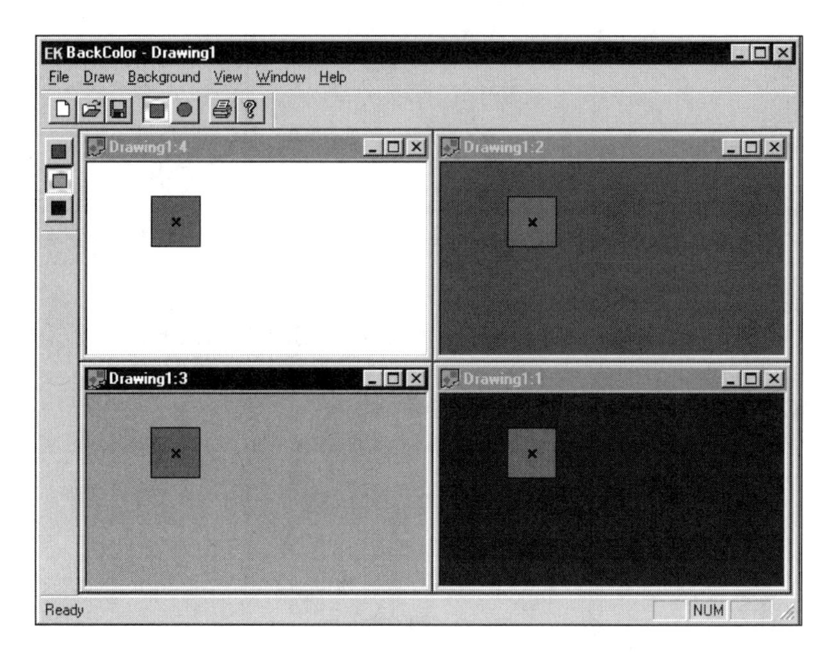

Figure 3-20. The BackColor application showing four views with different background colors (at least, this is the way it looks on a color monitor!).

Implementation Highlights

- *CDrawView::OnEraseBkgnd()* function (DrawView.cpp)

See Also

- *FAQ 3.31 How do I change the background color of a form view?*
- *FAQ 3.36 How do I visually show the user which splitter pane contains the active view?*

How do I draw on the main application window background?

Why settle for a dull dark gray MDI background like that of any AppWizard-generated application? (See Figure 3-21.) The following steps explain all you need to know to spice up your application with a flashier display, illustrated by Figures 3-22 and 3-23.

Step 1. Use ClassWizard to create a new *CWnd*-derived class (we will use the class *CMdiBackground* as an example in the following discussion). This class will be used to subclass the MDI Client window: the window that covers the client area of the main application window and that is the parent of all the document windows that the user can open.

Step 2. Use ClassWizard to add handlers for the *WM_ERASEBKGND* and *WM_SIZE* messages to the *CMdiBackground* class created in step 1.

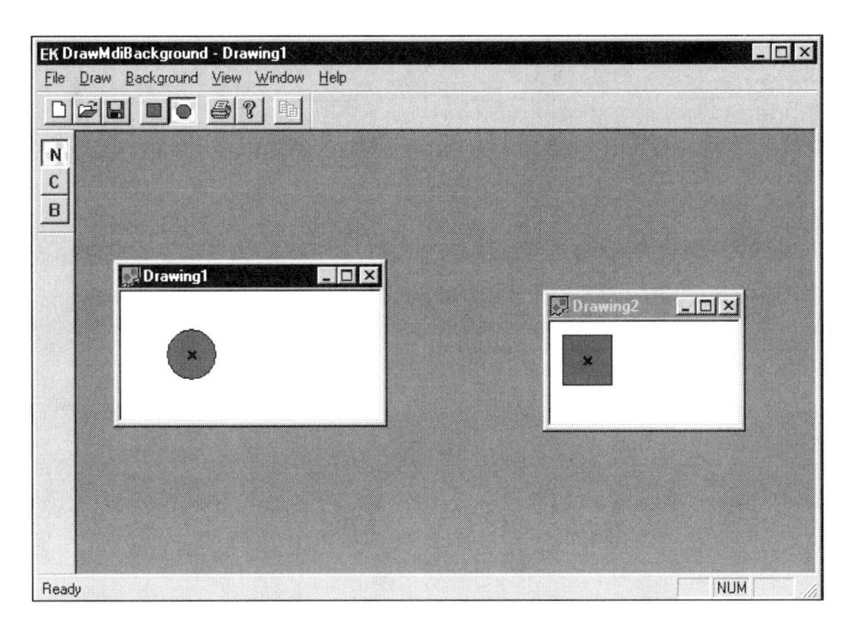

Figure 3-21. The DrawMdiBackground application drawing a normal MDI background.

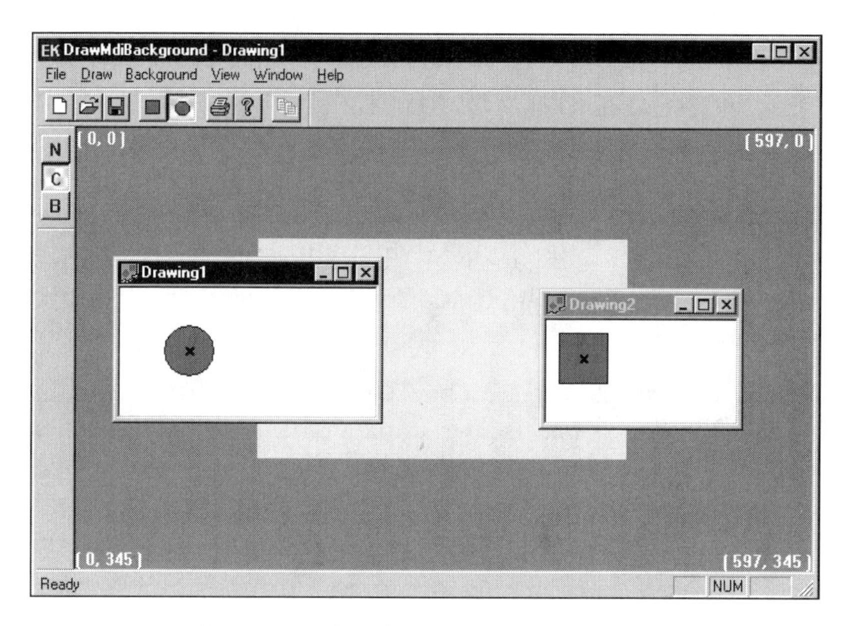

Figure 3-22. The DrawMdiBackground application drawing a custom MDI background.

Step 3. Implement the *OnEraseBkgnd()* function added in step 2 as shown either in Listing 3-52 or in Listing 3-53. The code in Listing 3-52 draws on the MDI background (see Figure 3-22), whereas the code in Listing 3-53 paints a bitmap image to cover the whole MDI background area (see Figure 3-23).

Listing 3-52. Handling the *WM_ERASEBKGND* message to draw on the main application window background: first example.

```
BOOL CMdiBackground::OnEraseBkgnd(CDC* pDC)
{
   // 1 - Draw the standard MDI background
   CWnd::OnEraseBkgnd( pDC );

   // 2 - Now draw a yellow rectangle (centered)
   CRect rect;
   GetClientRect( &rect );

   CBrush brYellow( RGB( 255, 255, 0 ) );
   CBrush* pOldBrush = pDC->SelectObject( &brYellow );
```

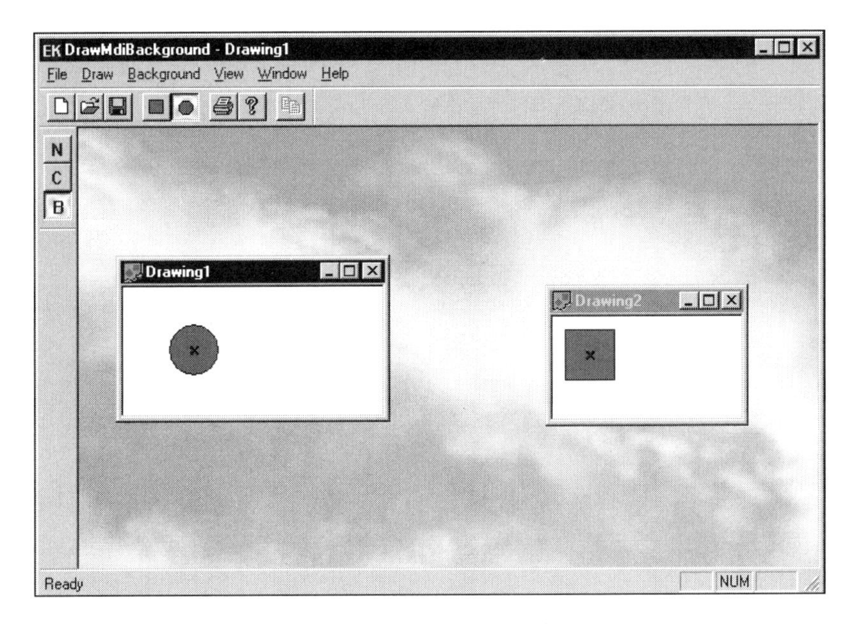

Figure 3-23. The DrawMdiBackground application painting a bitmap on the MDI background.

```
pDC->PatBlt( rect.left + rect.Width() / 4,
             rect.top + rect.Height() / 4,
             rect.Width() / 2,
             rect.Height() / 2,
             PATCOPY );

pDC->SelectObject( pOldBrush );

// 3 - Finally draw the coordinates of
// the window's corners
pDC->SetTextColor( RGB( 255, 255, 255 ) );
pDC->SetBkMode( TRANSPARENT );

CString s;

// 3a - Upper-left
pDC->SetTextAlign( TA_TOP | TA_LEFT );
s.Format( "( %ld, %ld )", rect.left, rect.top );
pDC->TextOut( rect.left, rect.top, s );
```

```
    // 3b - Bottom-left
    pDC->SetTextAlign( TA_BOTTOM | TA_LEFT );
    s.Format( "( %ld, %ld )", rect.left, rect.bottom );
    pDC->TextOut( rect.left, rect.bottom, s );

    // 3c - Upper-right
    pDC->SetTextAlign( TA_TOP | TA_RIGHT );
    s.Format( "( %ld, %ld )", rect.right, rect.top );
    pDC->TextOut( rect.right, rect.top, s );

    // 3d - Bottom-right
    pDC->SetTextAlign( TA_BOTTOM | TA_RIGHT );
    s.Format( "( %ld, %ld )", rect.right, rect.bottom );
    pDC->TextOut( rect.right, rect.bottom, s );

    return TRUE;    // Background was erased
}
```

Listing 3-53. Handling the *WM_ERASEBKGND* message to draw on the main application window background: second example.

```
BOOL CMdiBackground::OnEraseBkgnd(CDC* pDC)
{
    // 1 - Create a memory DC and select our bitmap into it
    CDC dcMem;
    dcMem.CreateCompatibleDC( pDC );
    CBitmap* pOldBitmap = dcMem.SelectObject( &m_bitmap );

    // NOTE: m_bitmap is a CBitmap member variable on which
    // the LoadBitmap() function was previously called
    // (for example in CMdiBackground's constructor)
    // in order to have the bitmap in memory ready
    // to be drawn

    // 2 - Retrieve the size of our bitmap...
    BITMAP bmp;
    m_bitmap.GetObject( sizeof( bmp ), &bmp );

    // 3 - ... and the size of our window's client area
    CRect rect;
    GetClientRect( &rect );
```

```
   // 4 - Fill the window's client area with our bitmap
   pDC->StretchBlt( rect.left, rect.top,
                    rect.Width(), rect.Height(),
                    &dcMem,
                    0, 0, bmp.bmWidth, bmp.bmHeight,
                    SRCCOPY );

   dcMem.SelectObject( pOldBitmap );

   return TRUE;    // Background was erased
}
```

Step 4. Implement the *OnSize()* function added in step 2 and call *Invalidate()* to force the MDI client window to repaint itself whenever its size changes:

```
void CMdiBackground::OnSize(UINT nType, int cx, int cy)
{
   CWnd::OnSize(nType, cx, cy);
   Invalidate( TRUE );
}
```

Step 5. Add a member variable of type *CMdiBackground* to your main application window class. This class is usually called *CMainFrame* if your application was generated by AppWizard (see Listing 3-54).

Step 6. Modify your main application window class's *OnCreate()* function to subclass the MDI client window by calling *SubclassWindow()* on the member variable added in step 5, as shown in Listing 3-54.

Listing 3-54. Modifying the main application window class to subclass the MDI client window.

```
// ——————————————————————————
// Class definition for CMainFrame(MainFrm.h)

#include "MdiBackground.h"

class CMainFrame : public CMDIFrameWnd
{
// ...
   // Implementation
protected:
```

```
   CMdiBackground   m_wndMdiBackground;  // MDI Background
                                         // Window
// ...
};

// ————————————————————————————
// Implementation for CMainFrame (MainFrm.cpp)

int CMainFrame::OnCreate(LPCREATESTRUCT lpCreateStruct)
{
   if (CMDIFrameWnd::OnCreate(lpCreateStruct) == -1)
      return -1;

// ...

   // Subclass MDI Client window
   ASSERT( m_hWndMDIClient != NULL );
   if( !m_wndMdiBackground.SubclassWindow(
                                   m_hWndMDIClient ) )
   {
      return -1;
   }

   return 0;
}
```

■

Explanations

The *m_hWndMDIClient* variable is an undocumented member of the *CMDI FrameWnd* class (defined in AfxWin.h). This variable is used by the implementations of the *CMDIFrameWnd* and *CMDIChildWnd* classes (WinMdi.cpp). Listing 3-55 shows how MFC creates the MDI client window and initializes the *m_hWndMDIClient* variable.

Listing 3-55. Creation of the MDI client window and initialization of the *m_hWndMDIClient* member variable (WinMdi.cpp).

```
CMDIFrameWnd::CMDIFrameWnd()
{
   m_hWndMDIClient = NULL;
```

```
}

BOOL CMDIFrameWnd::CreateClient(
                        LPCREATESTRUCT lpCreateStruct,
                        CMenu* pWindowMenu)
{
    ASSERT(m_hWnd != NULL);
    ASSERT(m_hWndMDIClient == NULL);
    DWORD dwStyle = WS_VISIBLE | WS_CHILD | WS_BORDER |
                    WS_CLIPCHILDREN | WS_CLIPSIBLINGS |
                    MDIS_ALLCHILDSTYLES;  // allow children to be
                                          // created invisible
    DWORD dwExStyle = 0;
    // will be inset by the frame

    if (afxData.bWin4)
    {
        // special styles for 3d effect on Win4
        dwStyle &= ~WS_BORDER;
        dwExStyle = WS_EX_CLIENTEDGE;
    }

    CLIENTCREATESTRUCT ccs;
    ccs.hWindowMenu = pWindowMenu->GetSafeHmenu();
        // set hWindowMenu for MFC V1 backward compatibility
        // for MFC V2, window menu will be set in
        // OnMDIActivate
    ccs.idFirstChild = AFX_IDM_FIRST_MDICHILD;

    if (lpCreateStruct->style & (WS_HSCROLL|WS_VSCROLL))
    {
        // parent MDIFrame's scroll styles move to the
        // MDICLIENT
        dwStyle |= (lpCreateStruct->style &
                           (WS_HSCROLL|WS_VSCROLL));

        // fast way to turn off the scrollbar bits
        // (without a resize)
        ModifyStyle(WS_HSCROLL|WS_VSCROLL, 0,
                    SWP_NOREDRAW|SWP_FRAMECHANGED);
    }
```

```
    // Create MDICLIENT control with special IDC
    if ((m_hWndMDIClient = ::CreateWindowEx(
            dwExStyle, _T("mdiclient"), NULL,
            dwStyle, 0, 0, 0, 0, m_hWnd,
            (HMENU)AFX_IDW_PANE_FIRST,
            AfxGetInstanceHandle(), (LPVOID)&ccs)) == NULL)
    {
        TRACE0("Warning: CMDIFrameWnd::OnCreateClient:"
              " failed to create MDICLIENT.\n");
        return FALSE;
    }
    // Move it to the top of z-order
    ::BringWindowToTop(m_hWndMDIClient);

    return TRUE;
}
```

In Listing 3-54, we use the *m_hWndMDIClient* variable in the following way:

```
if( !m_wndMdiBackground.SubclassWindow(
                                    m_hWndMDIClient ) )
// ...
```

The *SubclassWindow()* function call allows us to subclass the MDI client window. From this point on, all Windows messages normally directed to the MDI client window will instead be handled by our own *m_wndMdiBackground* object. This feature allows us to intercept the messages that we are interested in—*WM_ERASEBKGND* and *WM_SIZE*—and to handle them in our own way. Note that MFC automatically forwards all the messages that we do not handle to the original window procedure of the MDI client window. We can also choose to forward the messages that we handle by calling our base class's implementation.

Additional Comments

The DrawMdiBackground sample project allows the user to choose between three MDI backgrounds: standard background, custom-drawn background, or background filled with a bitmap image. This sample code implements all these variations in the *CMdiBackground::OnEraseBkgnd()* function

(MdiBackground.cpp). Although it's easy to understand, this solution has some shortcomings:

- *CMdiBackground::OnEraseBkgnd()* is implemented using a rather inelegant *switch* statement.
- The *CMdiBackground* class is tightly coupled to the *CMainFrame* class: the *CMdiBackground* class must "know" of all the possible drawing styles and must be able to find out the current drawing style from the main application window object.

These symptoms show that my *CMdiBackground* class does not conform to good object-oriented design methods. A more object-oriented design would define the *CMdiBackground* class as a base class and would implement each kind of drawing behavior in a specialized derived class. Each derived class would have its own *OnEraseBkgnd()* function to handle its own drawing.

With this design, the only class to know about all the drawing methods is the *CMainFrame* class, which must dynamically maintain the correct association between its *m_hWndMDIClient* member and the desired *CMdiBackground*-derived class.

Why did I not implement this scheme in the first place? Because most of the time, you will implement only one drawing method for your MDI background. In this situation, having to set up the class hierarchy as described is most likely overkill.

Sample Code

- Project: DrawMdiBackground in the Chap03 subdirectory on the companion CD-ROM.
- Purpose: Draws on the main application window background. (See Figures 3-21, 3-22, and 3-23 on pages 215–217.)

Implementation Highlights

- *CMainFrame::OnCreate()* function (MainFrm.cpp)
- *CMdiBackground::OnEraseBkgnd()* function (MdiBackground.cpp)
- *CMdiBackground::OnSize()* function (MdiBackground.cpp)

Form Views

FAQ 3.28 How do I keep my form views synchronized with my other views?

Like other kinds of views in the MFC document/view architecture, form views should always reflect the current state of their associated document object. However, if the synchronization feature of the document/view architecture works almost automatically for most kinds of views—provided that you remember to call *CDocument::UpdateAllViews()* whenever you update your document object—some additional work needs to be done to ensure a smooth synchronization of form views.

Step 1. Use ClassWizard to override the *OnUpdate()* virtual function in your form view class. Implement this function using code similar to Listing 3-56. The details of *OnUpdate()* will vary with the exact nature of your data structures, but the general idea will stay the same: first, "pull" the data you need from the document object into the form view's member variables; then, "push" the data from those member variables into the controls on the form view's window.

Listing 3-56. Implementing *OnUpdate()* to keep a form view's controls synchronized with its document.

```
void CDrawFormView::OnUpdate(CView* pSender,
                             LPARAM lHint, CObject* pHint)
{
   // 1 - Get the current data from our document
   CDrawDoc* pDoc = GetDocument();

   m_nX = pDoc->m_point.x;
   m_nY = pDoc->m_point.y;

   switch( pDoc->m_shape )
   {
   default :
```

```
      ASSERT( FALSE );   // This should never happen!
      break;

   case CDrawDoc::SQUARE :
      m_nShape = 0;
      break;

   case CDrawDoc::CIRCLE :
      m_nShape = 1;
      break;
   }

   // 2 - Show the current data in our controls
   UpdateData( FALSE );
}
```

Step 2. When you decide that you want to update your document—and other views—with the current data from the controls in the form view's window, use code similar to Listing 3-57. Again, the details of your functions will vary depending on your data structures, but the general idea will stay the same: first, pull the data from the controls on the form view's window into the form view's member variables; then push this data into the document's data structures; finally, call *CDocument::SetModifiedFlag()* and *CDocument::UpdateAllViews()* to, respectively, mark the document as dirty and force a global synchronization.

Listing 3-57. Implementing *OnApply()* for a form view.

```
void CDrawFormView::OnApply()
{
   // 1 - Get the data from our controls
   UpdateData( TRUE );

   // 2 - Update the document state
   CDrawDoc* pDoc = GetDocument();

   pDoc->m_point.x = m_nX;
   pDoc->m_point.y = m_nY;

   switch( m_nShape )
   {
   default:
```

```
            ASSERT( FALSE );        // This should never happen!
            break;

        case 0:
            pDoc->m_shape = CDrawDoc::SQUARE;
            break;

        case 1:
            pDoc->m_shape = CDrawDoc::CIRCLE;
            break;
    }

    // 3 - Tell the document something happened
    pDoc->SetModifiedFlag( TRUE );

    // 4 - Synchronize all other views
    pDoc->UpdateAllViews( this );
}
```

■

Explanations

The slight difference between form views and other kinds of views lies in the fact that form views maintain their own private data inside their member variables. Other views automatically stay synchronized in the following way:

1. A view modifies the document object and calls *CDocument::UpdateAllViews()*.
2. The implementation of *CDocument::UpdateAllViews()* traverses the list of views maintained by the document object and calls *OnUpdate()* for each view in this list except the one that can optionally be passed in the first parameter to *CDocument::UpdateAllViews()*.
3. The default implementation of *CView::OnUpdate()* simply invalidates each view's client area.
4. When each view receives the *WM_PAINT* message, MFC calls *OnDraw()*. Each view then redraws itself using the current data from its associated document object.

This standard MFC approach to view synchronization does not work automatically for form views, because step 4 will simply refresh the controls on the form view. And remember that a form view does not override *OnDraw()*. This function is implemented by the *CFormView* class, and it literally does nothing (because the controls simply paint themselves). This is why we need to work a little on our own and take advantage of the *OnUpdate()* function call in order to update our form view controls.

Sample Code

- Project: UpdateFormView in the Chap03 subdirectory on the companion CD-ROM.
- Purpose: Keeps form views synchronized with other views (see Figure 3-24).

Implementation Highlights

- *DrawFormView::OnUpdate()* function (DrawFormView.cpp)
- *DrawFormView::OnApply()* function (DrawFormView.cpp)

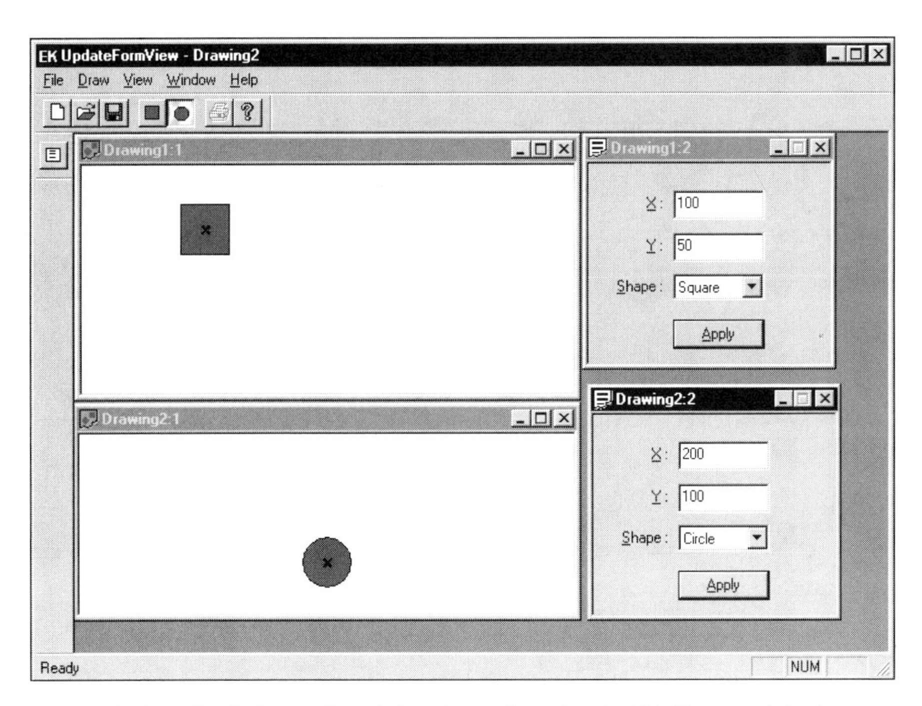

Figure 3-24. Each form view is kept synchronized with its associated document in the UpdateFormView application.

FAQ 3.29 How do I make a form view initially appear with the exact size of the associated dialog resource?

The user is—rightly—surprised when a form view pops up in a window that is either half as high as it should be or, conversely, takes twice the width of the underlying form view. Such a behavior can make your user interface look rather amateurish. Fortunately, the cure is easy: use ClassWizard to override the *OnInitialUpdate()* function in your form view class and implement this function as shown in Listing 3-58.

Listing 3-58. Implementing *OnInitialUpdate()* to make a form view's parent frame initially appear with the size of the associated dialog resource.

```
void CDrawFormView::OnInitialUpdate()
{
   // 1 - Let base class do default processing
   CFormView::OnInitialUpdate();

   // 2 - Resize parent frame to fit our Form View
   GetParentFrame()->RecalcLayout();
   ResizeParentToFit( FALSE );
   ResizeParentToFit( TRUE );
}
```

■

Sample Code

- Project: SizeFormView in the Chap03 subdirectory on the companion CD-ROM.
- Purpose: Makes a form view initially appear with the exact size of the associated dialog resource (see Figure 3-25).

Implementation Highlights

- *CDrawFormView::OnInitialUpdate()* function (DrawFormView.cpp)

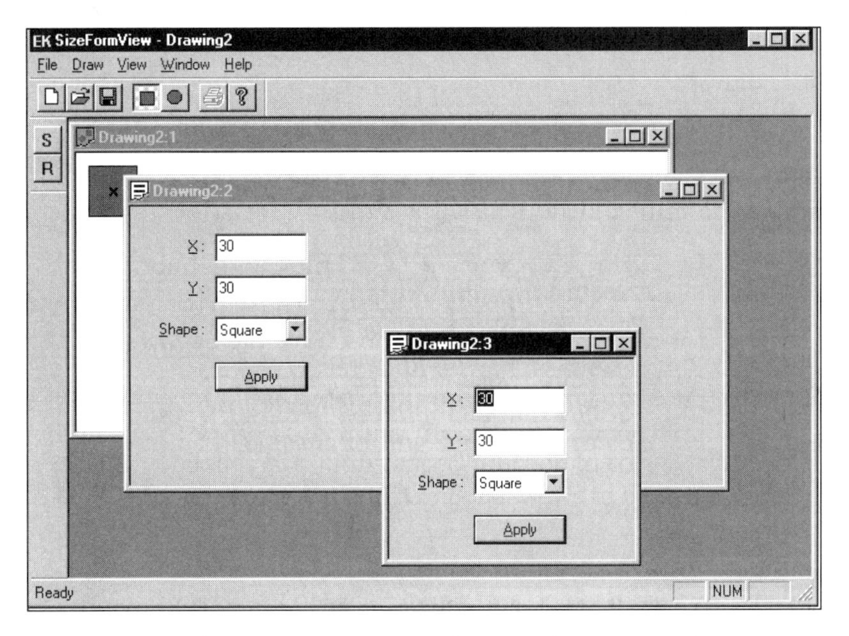

Figure 3-25. The SizeFormView application showing one form view opening with its default size and the other one resizing to fit the associated dialog resource.

See Also

- *FAQ 3.12 How do I make a frame window nonresizable?*

3.30 How do I use the *UPDATE_COMMAND_UI* mechanism in form views?

The *UPDATE_COMMAND_UI* mechanism is great for dynamically giving feedback to the user about the state of your application by checking, enabling, or disabling menu commands and toolbar buttons. Unfortunately, ClassWizard doesn't allow you to add *UPDATE_COMMAND_UI* handlers for your form view controls.

With a little work, however, you can also take advantage of the *UPDATE_COMMAND_UI* mechanism to dynamically update your form view controls (you may wish to refer to Listing 3-59 to put the following explanations in a meaningful context).

Step 1. Manually add a handler for the *WM_IDLEUPDATECMDUI* private MFC message to your form view class. To do this, you must execute the actions described in steps 1a through 1c.

Step 1a. Include the *<afxpriv.h>* MFC file that defines the *WM_IDLEUPDATECMDUI* private MFC message in your form view's implementation source file (.cpp).

Step 1b. Add the *OnIdleUpdateCmdUI()* function prototype to your form view's class definition:

```
class CDrawFormView : public CFormView
{
// ...
   afx_msg void OnIdleUpdateCmdUI();
// ...
};
```

Step 1c. Go to the message map of your form view class and add an *ON_MESSAGE_VOID()* macro entry that maps the *WM_ IDLEUPDATECMDUI* message to the *OnIdleUpdateCmdUI()* function:

```
BEGIN_MESSAGE_MAP(CDrawFormView, CFormView)
   //{{AFX_MSG_MAP(CDrawFormView)
   // ...
   ON_MESSAGE_VOID(WM_IDLEUPDATECMDUI, OnIdleUpdateCmdUI)
   // ...
   //}}AFX_MSG_MAP
END_MESSAGE_MAP()
```

Step 2. Implement the *OnIdleUpdateCmdUI()* function added in step 1b:

```
void CDrawFormView::OnIdleUpdateCmdUI()
{
   UpdateDialogControls( this, FALSE );
}
```

Step 3. Manually add *UPDATE_COMMAND_UI* handlers to your form view class. You will need a different handler for each control in your form view for which you wish to use the *UPDATE_COMMAND_UI* mechanism. For each handler that you want to add, execute the actions described in steps 3a and 3b.

Step 3a. Add your *UPDATE_COMMAND_UI* handler's function prototype to your form view's class definition:

```
class CDrawFormView : public CFormView
{
// ...
   afx_msg void OnUpdateEmpty( CCmdUI* pCmdUI );
// ...
};
```

Step 3b. Add an *ON_UPDATE_COMMAND_UI()* macro entry to the message map of your form view class:

```
BEGIN_MESSAGE_MAP(CDrawFormView, CFormView)
   //{{AFX_MSG_MAP(CDrawFormView)
   // ...
   ON_UPDATE_COMMAND_UI(IDC_EMPTY, OnUpdateEmpty)
   // ...
   //}}AFX_MSG_MAP
END_MESSAGE_MAP()
```

Step 4. Implement each *UPDATE_COMMAND_UI* handler added in step 3. These functions are standard *UPDATE_COMMAND_UI* handlers that accomplish their work as usual through the *pCmdUI* argument. For example:

```
void CDrawFormView::OnUpdateEmpty( CCmdUI* pCmdUI )
{
   pCmdUI->Enable(m_edtEdit.GetWindowTextLength() > 0 );
}
```

Listing 3-59 shows how those different pieces fit together in the sample code for this FAQ.

Listing 3-59. Implementing a form view class that uses the *UPDATE_COMMAND_UI* mechanism.

```
// ————————————————————————————
// Class definition for CDrawFormView (DrawFormView.h)

class CDrawFormView : public CFormView
{
// ...
// Implementation

   // Generated message map functions
   //{{AFX_MSG(CDrawFormView)
   afx_msg void OnApply();
   afx_msg void OnIdleUpdateCmdUI();
   afx_msg void OnUpdateChecked( CCmdUI* pCmdUI );
   afx_msg void OnUpdateEmpty( CCmdUI* pCmdUI );
   afx_msg void OnUpdateApply( CCmdUI* pCmdUI );
   //}}AFX_MSG

   DECLARE_MESSAGE_MAP()
};

// ————————————————————————————
// Implementation for CDrawFormView (DrawFormView.cpp)

BEGIN_MESSAGE_MAP(CDrawFormView, CFormView)
   //{{AFX_MSG_MAP(CDrawFormView)
   ON_BN_CLICKED(IDC_APPLY, OnApply)
   ON_MESSAGE_VOID(WM_IDLEUPDATECMDUI, OnIdleUpdateCmdUI)
   ON_UPDATE_COMMAND_UI(IDC_CHECKED, OnUpdateChecked)
   ON_UPDATE_COMMAND_UI(IDC_EMPTY, OnUpdateEmpty)
   ON_UPDATE_COMMAND_UI(IDC_APPLY, OnUpdateApply)
   //}}AFX_MSG_MAP
END_MESSAGE_MAP()

// ...

/////////////////////////////////////////////////////////////
// ON_UPDATE_COMMAND_UI handlers

void CDrawFormView::OnIdleUpdateCmdUI()
```

```
{
   UpdateDialogControls( this, FALSE );
}

void CDrawFormView::OnUpdateChecked( CCmdUI* pCmdUI )
{
   pCmdUI->Enable( m_chkCheck.GetCheck() == 1 );
}

void CDrawFormView::OnUpdateEmpty( CCmdUI* pCmdUI )
{
   pCmdUI->Enable( m_edtEdit.GetWindowTextLength() > 0 );
}

void CDrawFormView::OnUpdateApply( CCmdUI* pCmdUI )
{
   pCmdUI->Enable(   m_edtX.GetWindowTextLength() > 0
               && m_edtY.GetWindowTextLength() > 0 );
}
```

■

Explanations

For explanations regarding the *WM_IDLEUPDATECMDUI* message and the *ON_MESSAGE_VOID()* macro, please refer to *FAQ 4.12 How do I use the* UPDATE_COMMAND_UI *mechanism in dialog boxes?*

Sample Code

- Project: UpdateUIFormView in the Chap03 subdirectory on the companion CD-ROM.
- Purpose: Uses the *UPDATE_COMMAND_UI* mechanism in form views (see Figure 3-26).

Implementation Highlights

- *CDrawFormView* message map (DrawFormView.cpp)
- *CDrawFormView::OnIdleUpdateCmdUI()* function (DrawFormView.cpp)
- *CDrawFormView::OnUpdateXXX()* functions (DrawFormView.cpp)

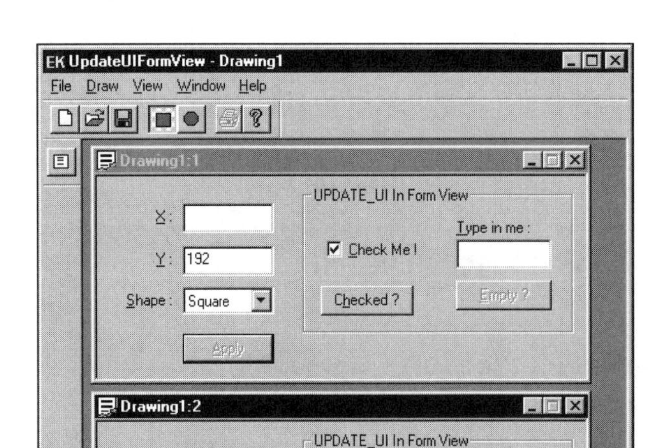

Figure 3-26. Using the *UPDATE_COMMAND_UI* mechanism in form views: compare the enabled or disabled state of the command buttons on the two form views in the UpdateUIFormView application.

See Also

- *FAQ 4.12 How do I use the* UPDATE_COMMAND_UI *mechanism in dialog boxes?*

3.31 How do I change the background color of a form view?

You might think that you could change the background color of a form view by simply using the technique explained in *FAQ 3.26 How do I change the background color of a view?* Unfortunately, this is not true. This surprising fact is the result of the peculiar way Windows handles dialog boxes, and a form view is a special kind of dialog box. Take heart and follow these steps if you wish to enliven your form view's backgrounds:

Step 1. Define and initialize a member variable of type *HBRUSH* in your form view class, as shown in Listing 3-60.

Listing 3-60. Definition and initialization of the *m_brBack* member variable.

```
// ─────────────────────────────
// Class definition for CDrawFormView (DrawFormView.h)

class CDrawFormView : public CFormView
{
// ...

// Implementation

private:
   COLORREF m_crBackColor;
   CBrush m_brBack;

// ...
};

// ─────────────────────────────
// Implementation for CDrawFormView (DrawFormView.cpp)

CDrawFormView::CDrawFormView()
   : CFormView(CDrawFormView::IDD)
{
// ...

   // Set initial background color
   m_crBackColor = ::GetSysColor( COLOR_BTNFACE ) );
   m_brBack.CreateSolidBrush( m_crBackColor );
}
```

Step 2. Use ClassWizard to add a handler for the *WM_CTLCOLOR* message to your form view class. Implement this handler as shown in Listing 3-61.

Listing 3-61. Handling the *WM_CTLCOLOR* message to change the background color of a form view.

```
HBRUSH CDrawFormView::OnCtlColor(CDC* pDC, CWnd* pWnd,
                                 UINT nCtlColor)
{
   switch( nCtlColor )
```

```
    {
    case CTLCOLOR_BTN:
    case CTLCOLOR_STATIC:
       pDC->SetBkMode( TRANSPARENT );
       // Fall through

    case CTLCOLOR_DLG:
       return (HBRUSH) m_brBack.GetSafeHandle();
    }

    return CFormView::OnCtlColor(pDC, pWnd, nCtlColor);
}
```

Step 3. To dynamically change the background color of the form view, use code similar to the following:

```
void CDrawFormView::OnBackgroundBlue()
{
   // 1 - Change the background color to blue
   m_crBackColor = RGB( 0, 0, 255 );
   m_brBack.DeleteObject();
   m_brBack.CreateSolidBrush( m_crBackColor );

   // 2 - Force the view to repaint
   Invalidate( TRUE );
}
```

■

Explanations

To allow a dialog box (or form view) to change the colors used to draw each control, Windows sends the *WM_CTLCOLOR* message for each control on the dialog box as well as for the dialog box itself. The handler for this message has the following prototype:

```
HBRUSH   CDrawFormView::OnCtlColor  (CDC* pDC,  CWnd* pWnd,
                                     UINT  nCtlColor);
```

The text color is set by calling *pDC->SetTextColor()*. The background color is set by returning a handle to the brush that is to be used for painting the control background. In this latter case, you must be careful to return a handle to a brush that will *not* be destroyed when leaving the *OnCtlColor()* function—that is, do not return a handle to a *CBrush* object created *on the stack* in the *OnCtlColor()* function.

The *pWnd* argument points to a (possibly temporary) *CWnd* object representing the control that is about to be drawn.

The *nCtlColor* argument indicates the type of control for which *OnCtlColor()* is called. This argument can take one of the following values:

- *CTLCOLOR_BTN*: button control
- *CTLCOLOR_DLG*: dialog box itself
- *CTLCOLOR_EDIT*: edit control
- *CTLCOLOR_LISTBOX*: listbox control
- *CTLCOLOR_MSGBOX*: message box
- *CTLCOLOR_SCROLLBAR*: scroll-bar control
- *CTLCOLOR_STATIC*: static control

Sample Code

- Project: BackColorFormView in the Chap03 subdirectory on the companion CD-ROM.
- Purpose: Dynamically changes the background color of a form view (see Figure 3-27).

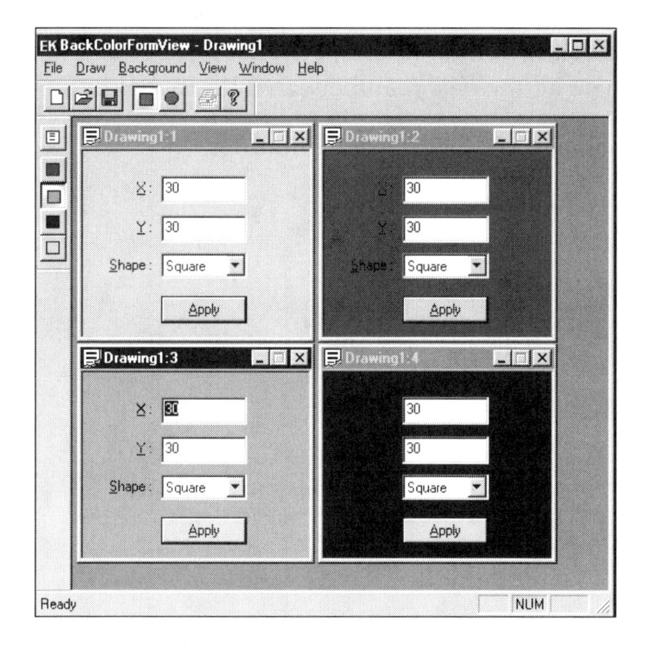

Figure 3-27. The BackColorFormView application showing four form views with different background colors (at least, this is the way it looks on a color monitor!).

Implementation Highlights

- *CDrawFormView::OnCtlColor()* function (DrawFormView.cpp)
- *CDrawFormView::CDrawFormView()* function (DrawFormView.cpp)
- *CDrawFormView::OnBackgroundXXX()* functions (DrawFormView.cpp)

See Also

- *FAQ 3.26 How do I change the background color of a view?*

How do I add ToolTips to the controls in a form view?

In addition to their classic use for toolbar buttons, ToolTips can also be useful for explaining the roles of various controls on a form view. This is a sure way to enhance the quality of your user interface, and it is not very complex, as the following steps show:

Step 1. Use ClassWizard to add a member variable of type "control" for each control on your form view.

Step 2. Manually add a member variable of type *CToolTipCtrl* to your form view class. The definition of your class should now look similar to the one shown in Listing 3-62, where all the new member variables are bold.

Listing 3-62. Adding new control member variables to handle ToolTips.

```
class CDrawFormView : public CFormView
{
// ...

// Form Data
public:
    //{{AFX_DATA(CDrawFormView)
    enum { IDD = IDD_FORMVIEW };
    CEdit       m_edtY;
    CEdit       m_edtX;
    CComboBox   m_cmbShape;
    CButton     m_cmdApply;
    int         m_nX;
```

```
    int         m_nY;
    int         m_nShape;
    //}}AFX_DATA

// ...

// Implementation

// ...

protected:
    CToolTipCtrl m_ToolTip;    // ToolTip control

// ...
};
```

Step 3. Use ClassWizard to add an override for *PreTranslateMessage()* in your form view class. Implement this function as shown in Listing 3-63 to relay messages to the ToolTip control.

Listing 3-63. Implementing *PreTranslateMessage()* to relay messages to the ToolTip control.

```
BOOL CDrawFormView::PreTranslateMessage(MSG* pMsg)
{
    // Relay events to the ToolTip control
    m_ToolTip.RelayEvent( pMsg );
    return CFormView::PreTranslateMessage(pMsg);
}
```

Step 4. Use ClassWizard to add an override for *OnInitialUpdate()* in your form view class. Implement this function as shown in Listing 3-64 to correctly create and initialize the ToolTip control.

Listing 3-64. Implementing *OnInitialUpdate()* to create and initialize the ToolTip control.

```
void CDrawFormView::OnInitialUpdate()
{
    CFormView::OnInitialUpdate();

    // 1 - Create the ToolTip control
    if( !m_ToolTip.Create( this ) )
```

```
    {
        TRACE0( "Unable to create ToolTip control\n" );
        return;
    }

    // 2 - Add the form view controls to the ToolTip
    m_ToolTip.AddTool( &m_edtX, IDS_TT_X );
    m_ToolTip.AddTool( &m_edtY, IDS_TT_Y );
    m_ToolTip.AddTool( &m_cmbShape, IDS_TT_SHAPE );
    m_ToolTip.AddTool( &m_cmdApply, IDS_TT_APPLY );

    // 3 - Activate the ToolTip control
    m_ToolTip.Activate( TRUE );
}
```

Step 5. Use the Visual C++ Resource Editor to define the string resources that the ToolTip control will display for each control on your form view. These strings are the same ones that were referenced in the calls to *AddTool()* in Listing 3-64 (such as *IDS_TT_X, IDS_TT_SHAPE*, etc.)

■

Additional Comments

If you wish to turn off the ToolTips—for example, because this is one of your configuration options—simply make the following call:

```
m_ToolTip.Activate( FALSE );
```

Sample Code

- Project: FormViewTooltips in the Chap03 subdirectory on the companion CD-ROM.
- Purpose: Adds ToolTips to the controls in a form view (see Figure 3-28).

Implementation Highlights

- *CDrawFormView::PreTranslateMessage()* function (DrawFormView.cpp)
- *CDrawFormView::OnInitialUpdate()* function (DrawFormView.cpp)

See Also

- *FAQ 4.13 How do I add ToolTips support to the controls in a dialog box?*

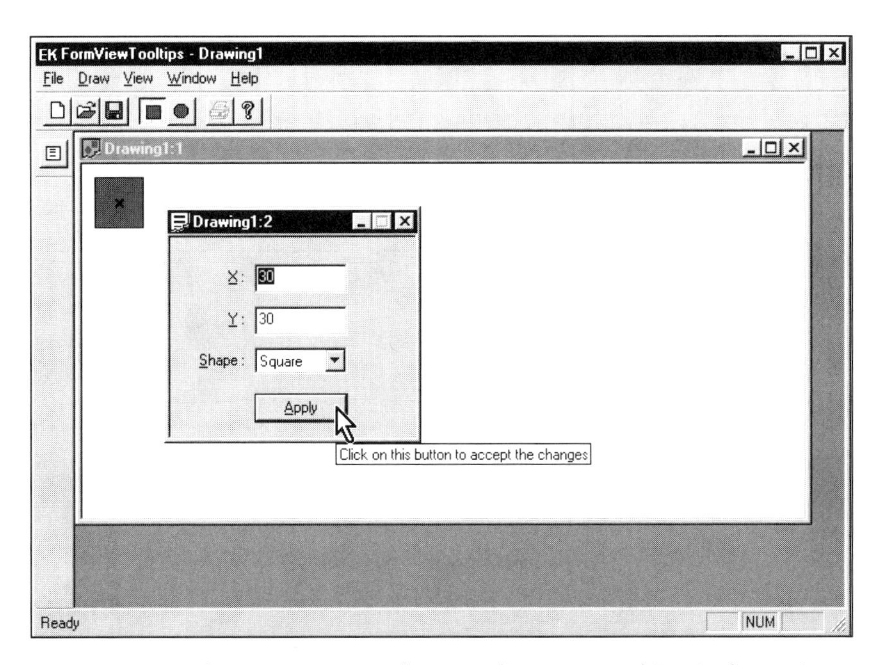

Figure 3-28. The FormViewTooltips application: ToolTips in form views are really cool!

Splitter Windows

FAQ 3.33 How do I program a window with both horizontal and vertical static splitter panes (three-way splitter)?

This problem is solved by creating *nested* splitter windows. Don't be afraid—it's not as difficult as it sounds. Because there are many possible layouts for those splitters, the following discussion will assume that you want to create a window that looks like the one shown in Figure 3-29. This window is split into two columns by a vertical splitter, and the right column is again split into two rows by a (nested) horizontal splitter.

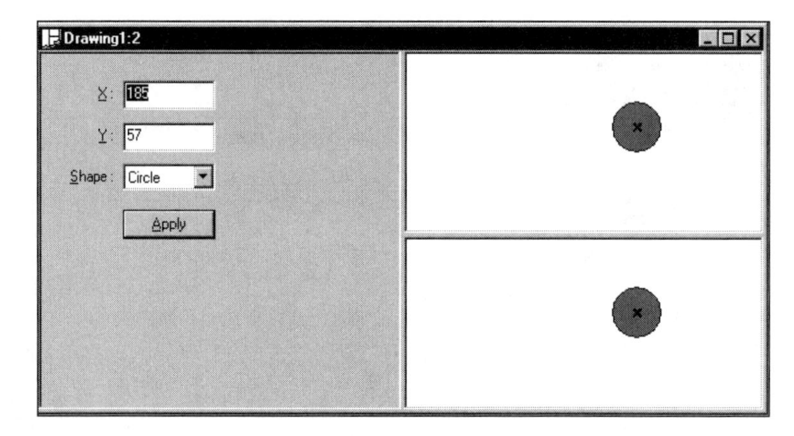

Figure 3-29. One possible layout for a three-way splitter window.

The following steps explain how to create the window shown in Figure 3-29:

Step 1. Use ClassWizard to create a new *CMDIChildWnd*-derived class that will host your splitter windows. Let's call this class *CSplitFrame*.

Step 2. Add two member variables of type *CSplitterWnd* to the *CSplitFrame* class that you created in step 1, as shown in Listing 3-65.

Listing 3-65. Adding *CSplitterWnd* member variables to the *CSplitFrame* class.

```
class CSplitFrame : public CMDIChildWnd
{
// ...

// Attributes
protected:
   CSplitterWnd    m_wndSplitter1; // Vertical splitter
   CSplitterWnd    m_wndSplitter2; // Horizontal splitter

// ...
};
```

Step 3. Use ClassWizard to add an override for the *OnCreateClient()* function in your *CSplitFrame* class. Implement this function as shown in Listing 3-66.

Listing 3-66. Implementing *OnCreateClient()* to create a three-way splitter window.

```
BOOL CSplitFrame::OnCreateClient(LPCREATESTRUCT /*lpcs*/,
                                 CCreateContext* pContext)
{
   CRect rect;
   GetClientRect( &rect );
   CSize size = rect.Size();
   size.cx /= 2;      // Initial column size
   size.cy /= 2;      // Initial row size

   // 1 - Create first static splitter (1 row, 2 cols)
   if( !m_wndSplitter1.CreateStatic( this, 1, 2 ) )
   {
      TRACE0( "Failed to create first static splitter\n" );
      return FALSE;
   }

   // 2 - Create left column view (row 0, col 0)
   if( !m_wndSplitter1.CreateView( 0, 0,
                  RUNTIME_CLASS( CDrawFormView ),
                  size, pContext ) )
   {
      TRACE0( "Failed to create left view\n" );
      return FALSE;
   }

   // 3 - Create nested static splitter (2 rows, 1 col)
   // in (row 0, col 1) of the first splitter
   if( !m_wndSplitter2.CreateStatic( &m_wndSplitter1, 2, 1,
                 WS_CHILD | WS_VISIBLE,
                 m_wndSplitter1.IdFromRowCol( 0, 1 ) ) )
   {
     TRACE0( "Failed to create nested static splitter\n" );
     return FALSE;
   }

   // 4 - Create top-right view (row 0, col 0)
   if( !m_wndSplitter2.CreateView( 0, 0,
                  RUNTIME_CLASS( CDrawView ),
                  size, pContext ) )
   {
```

```
        TRACE0( "Failed to create top-right view\n" );
        return FALSE;
    }

    // 5 - Create bottom-right view (row 1, col 0)
    if( !m_wndSplitter2.CreateView( 1, 0,
                        RUNTIME_CLASS( CDrawView ),
                        size, pContext ) )
    {
        TRACE0( "Failed to create bottom-right view\n" );
        return FALSE;
    }

    return TRUE;
}
```

Step 4. Don't forget to reference your *CSplitFrame* view's frame class in the appropriate document templates in order to get the desired behavior (see *FAQ 3.1 How do I add a new kind of view or frame window to my application?*). Note that because you are explicitly creating the view that goes inside each pane, the view type usually passed to the document template constructor becomes unnecessary. Therefore, you can pass *NULL* as the last argument to the document template constructor:

```
m_ptSplitFrame = new CMultiDocTemplate(
    IDR_DRAWSPLITTERTYPE,
    RUNTIME_CLASS(CDrawDoc),
    RUNTIME_CLASS(CSplitFrame),     // Splitter frame window
    NULL);
AddDocTemplate(m_ptSplitFrame);
```

■

Additional Comments

The *CSplitFrame2* class in the sample code for this FAQ shows how you can create another kind of layout (see Figure 3-30). The only difference between this and the preceding code lies in *CSplitFrame2::OnCreateClient()*, which creates the splitter windows in a different order: first the horizontal splitter and then the vertical one.

You can elaborate on the same technique to use more splitters and create more-complex layouts, but most applications are satisfied with the flexibility afforded by two- and three-way splitters—the notable exception being the famous dockable windows showcased in Visual C++ Developer Studio (but then those are not "real" splitters any more).

Sample Code

- Project: MultiSplit in the Chap03 subdirectory on the companion CD-ROM.
- Purpose: Creates three-way splitter windows with different layouts (see Figure 3-30).

Implementation Highlights

- *CSplitFrame1::OnCreateClient()* function (SplitFrame1.cpp)
- *CSplitFrame2::OnCreateClient()* function (SplitFrame2.cpp)
- *CMDIApp::InitInstance()* function (MultiSplit.cpp)
- *CDrawDoc::OnWindowNewSplitter1()* function (DrawDoc.cpp)
- *CDrawDoc::OnWindowNewSplitter2()* function (DrawDoc.cpp)

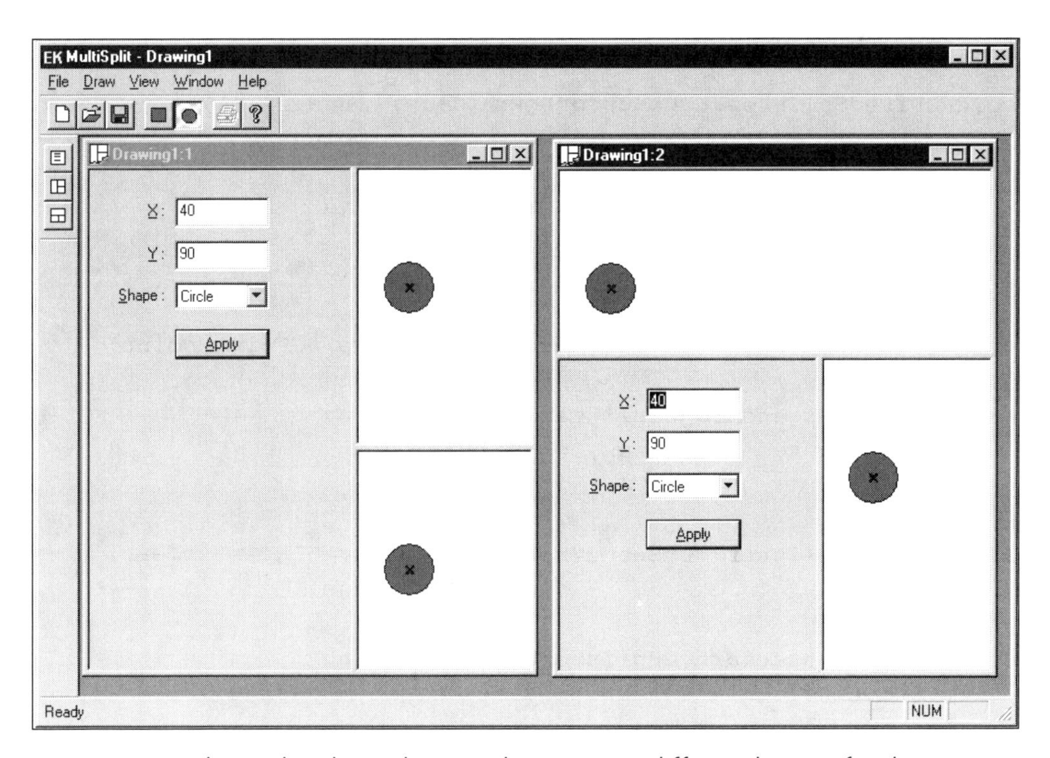

Figure 3-30. The MultiSplit application showing two different layouts for three-way splitter windows.

3.34 How do I lock a splitter window so that the user cannot move the divider line?

Sometimes you may wish to use a splitter window to structure your user interface without giving the user the ability to resize the different panes. The following steps show you how to attain this goal.

Step 1. Use ClassWizard to create a new *CSplitterWnd*-derived class that will implement the locked splitter behavior. Let's call this class *CFixedSplitter*.

Step 2. Use ClassWizard to add handlers for the *WM_LBUTTONDOWN*, *WM_MOUSEMOVE*, and *WM_SETCURSOR* messages to your *CFixedSplitter* class. Implement these handlers as shown in Listing 3-67 to achieve the locked splitter behavior.

Listing 3-67. Handling the *WM_LBUTTONDOWN*, *WM_MOUSEMOVE*, and *WM_SETCURSOR* messages to achieve the locked splitter behavior.

```
void CFixedSplitter::OnLButtonDown(UINT nFlags,
                                   CPoint point)
{
   // Bypass standard CSplitterWnd processing
   CWnd::OnLButtonDown(nFlags, point);
}

void CFixedSplitter::OnMouseMove(UINT nFlags, CPoint point)
{
   // Bypass standard CSplitterWnd processing
   CWnd::OnMouseMove(nFlags, point);
}

BOOL CFixedSplitter::OnSetCursor(CWnd* pWnd, UINT nHitTest,
                                 UINT message)
{
   // Bypass standard CSplitterWnd processing
   return CWnd::OnSetCursor(pWnd, nHitTest, message);
}
```

Step 3. In your view's frame window class, locate the definition of your splitter object(s). For each splitter that you want to exhibit the locked behavior, change the type of the member variable from *CSplitterWnd* to *CFixedSplitter:*

```
class CSplitFrame : public CMDIChildWnd
{
// ...
// Attributes
protected:
   CFixedSplitter    m_wndSplitter1; // Vertical splitter
   CFixedSplitter    m_wndSplitter2; // Horizontal splitter

// ...
};
```

■

Explanations

The preceding *CSplitterWnd*-derived class behaves like a locked splitter simply because it bypasses the standard *CSplitterWnd* handling of the *WM_LBUTTONDOWN* and *WM_MOUSEMOVE* messages. The *CSplitterWnd* class never sees any of those mouse messages and cannot get in resize mode, thereby giving the user the illusion of a locked splitter bar.

Our *CSplitterWnd*-derived class also bypasses the standard *WM_SETCURSOR* message to make sure that the cursor never changes to a "move splitter bar" shape when it passes over the splitter bar.

Additional Comments

The *CEkLockableSplitter* utility class uses the techniques discussed in this FAQ to implement a lockable splitter object. You can replace the standard *CSplitterWnd* object with *CEkLockableSplitter* in your own code. You can then control the splitter locked state with the member functions *SetLock()*, *GetLock()*, and *ToggleLock()*, which are defined as shown in Listing 3-68.

Listing 3-68. Definition of the *CEkLockableSplitter* utility class.

```
class CEkLockableSplitter : public CSplitterWnd
{
```

```
// ...

// Operations
public:
   void SetLock( BOOL bLock );
   BOOL GetLock() const;
   void ToggleLock();

// ...
};
```

Sample Code

- Project: LockSplitter in the Chap03 subdirectory on the companion CD-ROM.
- Purpose: Locks a splitter window so that the user cannot move the divider line. Note the "Splitter" menu when the splitter view's frame window has the focus (Figure 3-31).

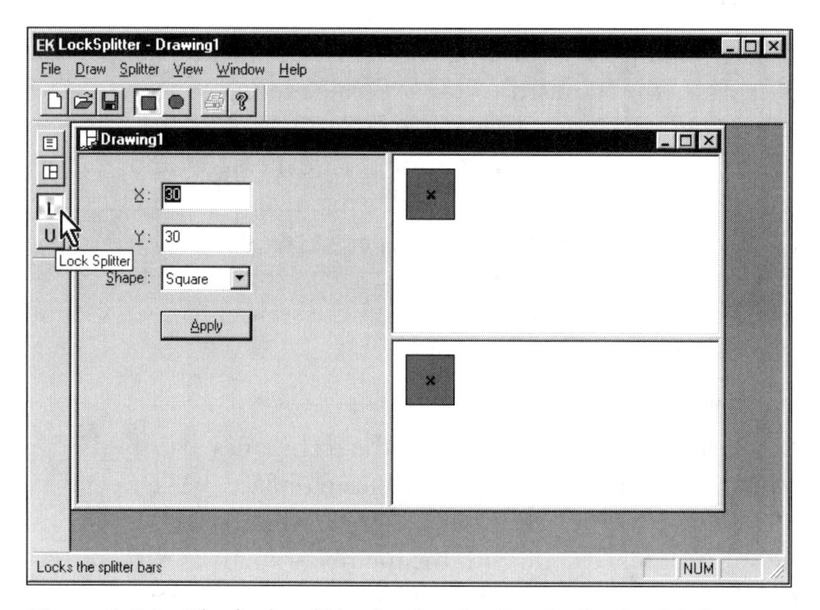

Figure 3-31. The lock splitter toolbar button in the LockSplitter sample application.

Implementation Highlights

- *CEkLockableSplitter* class (EkLockableSplitter.h, EkLockableSplitter.cpp)
- *CSplitFrame* class declaration (SplitFrame.h)
- *CSplitFrame::OnSplitterLock()* function (SplitFrame.cpp)
- *CSplitFrame::OnSplitterUnlock()* function (SplitFrame.cpp)

See Also

- *FAQ 3.35 How do I programmatically resize the panes in a splitter window?*

How do I programmatically resize the panes in a splitter window?

Just as you may need to programmatically resize some of your application's views, you may also wish to resize the panes in some of your splitter windows. However, calling the *MoveWindow()* or *SetWindowPos()* function will not do the job. Splitter panes must be handled in a different way. Here are the steps to follow if you want to implement a resize splitter pane function (you may wish to refer to Listing 3-69 to put the following explanations in a meaningful context):

Step 1. First, execute a sanity check—believe me, I learned about this the hard way! Retrieve the handle of the splitter window from the associated C++ object and check that this handle is valid:

```
HWND hWnd = m_wndSplitter.GetSafeHwnd();
if( hWnd == NULL || !::IsWindow( hWnd ) )
{
   return;
}
```

Step 2. Call either *GetColumnInfo()* or *GetRowInfo()* to get the current size of the views contained in each pane of your splitter window. Following each call to a *GetXXXInfo()* function, call the corresponding *SetXXXInfo()* function (*SetColumnInfo()* or *SetRowInfo()*, respectively) to change the size of each pane:

```
int cxCur, cxMin;

// Change size of first column to cxNewSize0
m_wndSplitter.GetColumnInfo( 0, cxCur, cxMin );
m_wndSplitter.SetColumnInfo( 0, cxNewSize0, cxMin );

// Change size of second column to cxNewSize1
m_wndSplitter.GetColumnInfo( 1, cxCur, cxMin );
m_wndSplitter.SetColumnInfo( 1, cxNewSize1, cxMin );
```

Step 3. When you have set the sizes of all the panes contained in your splitter, call *RecalcLayout()* to tell the splitter to finally update itself:

```
m_wndSplitter.RecalcLayout();
```

Listing 3-69 shows how these pieces fit together in the sample code for this FAQ. *CSplitFrame::OnResizeSplitters()* is called every time the three-way splitters in the sample application need to be resized. This function first resizes the outermost (vertical) splitter so that the client area of the frame window is divided into two panes of equal width. Then the function resizes the innermost (horizontal) splitter so that the rightmost column is divided into two horizontal panes of equal height.

Listing 3-69. Implementation of the *CSplitFrame::OnResizeSplitters()* from the sample code for this FAQ.

```
void CSplitFrame::OnResizeSplitters()
{
   // Sanity check - avoids exception because we receive
   // the first WM_SIZE before the splitter windows are
   // created
   HWND hWnd1 = m_wndSplitter1.GetSafeHwnd();
   HWND hWnd2 = m_wndSplitter2.GetSafeHwnd();

   if( hWnd1 == NULL || !::IsWindow( hWnd1 ) ||
       hWnd2 == NULL || !::IsWindow( hWnd2 ) )
   {
      return;
   }

   // 1 - Get the current client size for our entire
   // frame window
```

```
    CRect rect;
    GetClientRect( &rect );

    // 2 - Calculate the ideal row and column sizes
    CSize size = rect.Size();
    size.cx /= 2;       // Ideal column size
    size.cy /= 2;       // Ideal row size

    // 3 - Resize each column of the first splitter
    int cxCur, cxMin;
    m_wndSplitter1.GetColumnInfo( 0, cxCur, cxMin );
    m_wndSplitter1.SetColumnInfo( 0, size.cx, cxMin );

    m_wndSplitter1.GetColumnInfo( 1, cxCur, cxMin );
    m_wndSplitter1.SetColumnInfo( 1, size.cx, cxMin );

    // 4 - Resize each row of the second splitter
    int cyCur, cyMin;
    m_wndSplitter2.GetRowInfo( 0, cyCur, cyMin );
    m_wndSplitter2.SetRowInfo( 0, size.cy, cyMin );

    m_wndSplitter2.GetRowInfo( 1, cyCur, cyMin );
    m_wndSplitter2.SetRowInfo( 1, size.cy, cyMin );

    // 5 - Ask each splitter to recalculate its layout
    m_wndSplitter1.RecalcLayout();
    m_wndSplitter2.RecalcLayout();
}
```

■

Additional Comments

Don't forget the sanity check! It prevents an assertion that can be raised because Windows sends a *WM_SIZE* message during the creation of our frame window, before the splitter windows themselves have been created. Because my sample code tries to resize the splitter windows each time the parent frame window receives a *WM_SIZE* message, I must guard against this situation, and it is a good defensive programming technique anyway.

Sample Code

- Project: ResizeSplitter in the Chap03 subdirectory on the companion CD-ROM.
- Purpose: Programmatically resizes the panes in a splitter window every time the splitter frame window is resized (see Figure 3-32).

Implementation Highlights

- *CSplitFrame::OnResizeSplitters()* function (SplitFrame.cpp)
- *CSplitFrame::OnSize()* function (SplitFrame.cpp)

See Also

- *FAQ 3.33 How do I program a window with both horizontal and vertical static splitter panes (three-way splitter)?*

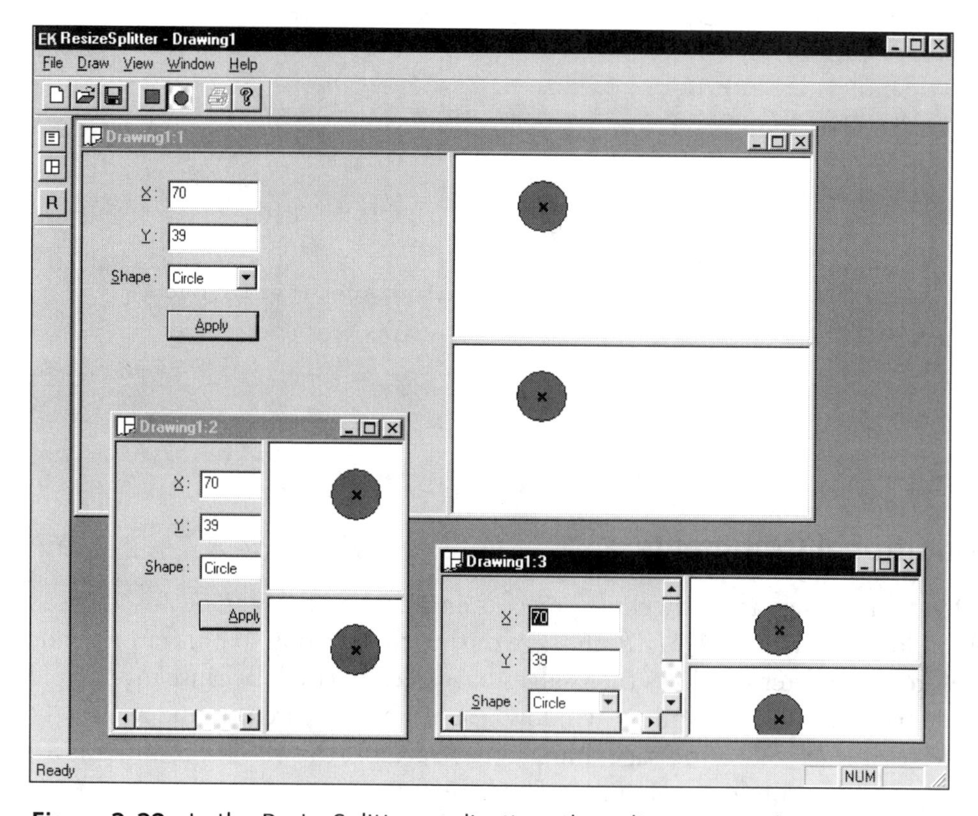

Figure 3-32. In the ResizeSplitter application, the splitter panes dynamically resize to keep the same proportions relative to the size of their parent frame window.

FAQ 3.36 How do I visually show the user which splitter pane contains the active view?

The only problem with splitter windows is that the user may lose track of which splitter pane contains the active view. To display that information, implement the following steps:

Step 1. Add a Boolean member variable to each view class for which you want to show the active state:

```
class CDrawView : public CView
{
// ...

// Implementation

protected:
   BOOL m_bActive;        // Does the view have the focus ?

// ...
};
```

Step 2. Add code to the constructor of each view class to set to *FALSE* the member variable added in step 1:

```
CDrawView::CDrawView()
{
   m_bActive = FALSE;
}
```

Step 3. Use ClassWizard to add an override for *OnActivateView()* in the view classes that you identified in step 1. Implement this function as shown in Listing 3-70 to detect when each view is activated or deactivated.

Listing 3-70. Implementing *OnActivateView()* to detect when a view is activated or deactivated.

```
void CDrawView::OnActivateView(BOOL bActivate,
                               CView* pActivateView,
                               CView* pDeactiveView)
```

```
{
   // 1 - Find out if the state of the view has changed
   BOOL bStateChanged = ( m_bActive != bActivate );
   m_bActive = bActivate;

   // 2 - If changed, trigger repaint
   if( bStateChanged )
   {
      RedrawWindow();
   }

   CView::OnActivateView(bActivate,
                         pActivateView,
                         pDeactiveView);
}
```

Step 4. Use the *m_bActive* member variable in your view's drawing code to draw the appropriate highlight clue when the view is active. For example, you can handle the *WM_ERASEBKGND* message and paint the background of the view with a different color depending on whether the view is active, as shown in Listing 3-71. Or you can simply modify your view's *OnDraw()* function to draw a highlight clue, as shown in Listing 3-72.

Listing 3-71. Handling the *WM_ERASEBKGND* message to change the background color when the view is in the active state.

```
BOOL CDrawView::OnEraseBkgnd(CDC* pDC)
{
   // If we don't have the focus, call the default
   // implementation
   if( !m_bActive )
   {
      return CView::OnEraseBkgnd(pDC);
   }

   // If we have the focus, draw our own background

   // 1 - Find out area to erase
   CRect rect;
   pDC->GetClipBox( &rect );

   // 2 - Create the correct brush and select into DC
```

```
    CBrush brush( RGB( 0, 255, 255 ) );   // Cyan
    CBrush* pOldBrush = pDC->SelectObject( &brush );

    // 3 - Erase the background
    pDC->PatBlt(   rect.left, rect.top,
                   rect.Width(), rect.Height(),
                   PATCOPY );

    pDC->SelectObject( pOldBrush );

    // 4 - Tell Windows that we erased the background
    return TRUE;
}
```

Listing 3-72. Adding code to *OnDraw()* to draw a highlight clue when the view is in the active state.

```
void CDrawView::OnDraw(CDC* pDC)
{
// ...
    // Standard drawing code
// ...

    // Draw "view highlight bar" when active
    if( m_bActive )
    {
        CRect rcClient;
        GetClientRect( rcClient );

        const int iBarWidth = 8;
        CPen penHighlight( PS_SOLID, iBarWidth,
                           RGB( 0, 0, 255 ) );   // Blue
        CPen* pOldPen = pDC->SelectObject( &penHighlight );

        pDC->MoveTo( rcClient.left,
                     rcClient.top + iBarWidth/2 );
        pDC->LineTo( rcClient.right,
                     rcClient.top + iBarWidth/2 );

        pDC->SelectObject( pOldPen );
    }
}
```

■

Explanations

MFC calls *OnActivateView()* each time a view is activated or deactivated. The following excerpt from the online help tells the whole story:

> The default implementation of this function sets the focus to the view being activated. Override this function if you want to perform special processing when a view is activated or deactivated. For example, if you want to provide special visual cues that distinguish the active view from the inactive views, you would examine the *bActivate* parameter and update the view's appearance accordingly.

Additional Comments

The sample code for this FAQ highlights the active view using two different methods: first by painting the background with a distinctive cyan color (in the *CDrawView::OnEraseBkgnd()* function) and then by drawing a blue bar at the top of the active view (in the *CDrawView::OnDraw()* function). Using both techniques simultaneously is probably overkill: a real application would probably display only one kind of cue.

Sample Code

- Project: HighlightView in the Chap03 subdirectory on the companion CD-ROM.
- Purpose: Highlights the active view (see Figure 3-33).

Implementation Highlights

- *CDrawView::OnActivateView()* function (DrawView.cpp)
- *CDrawView::OnEraseBkgnd()* function (DrawView.cpp)
- *CDrawView::OnDraw()* function (DrawView.cpp)

See Also

- *FAQ 3.26 How do I change the background color of a view?*
- *FAQ 3.33 How do I program a window with both horizontal and vertical static splitter panes (three-way splitter)?*

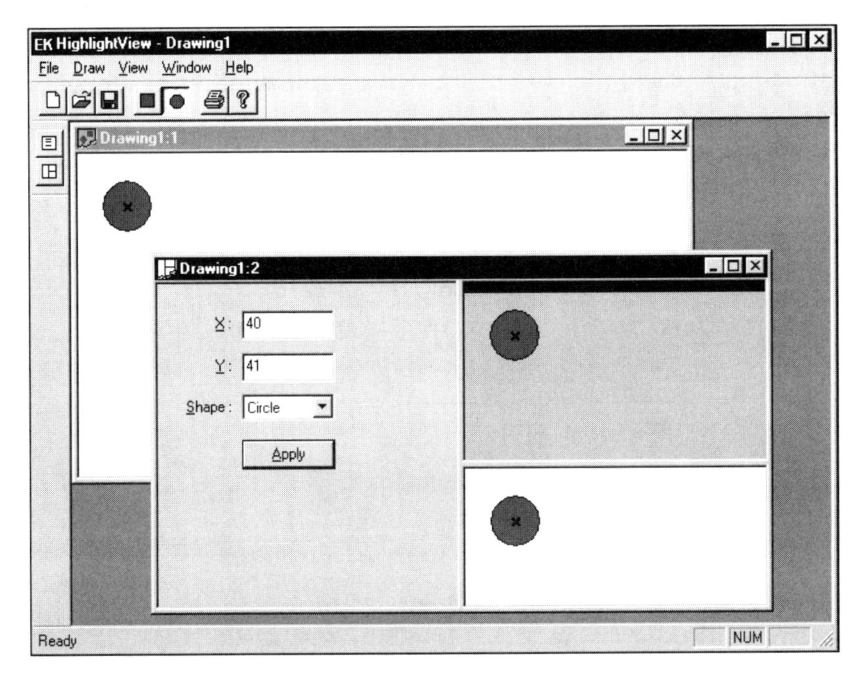

Figure 3-33. Notice that the active view is always highlighted in the HighlightView application.

Switching Views

FAQ 3.37 How do I dynamically switch the view displayed in an MDI child window or SDI main application window?

Who said that a frame window should stay bound to its associated view for its whole lifetime? Add some magic to your user interfaces by letting users dynamically choose the view they want *inside the same frame window*! With the *EkSwitchViewInFrame()* utility function, switching views is only a function call away.

Step 1. Implement *EkSwitchViewInFrame()* as shown in Listing 3-73. This function replaces the current view in a frame window by a new dynamically created view of the type you want.

Listing 3-73. Implementing *EkSwitchViewInFrame()* to dynamically replace a view in a frame window.

```
void EkSwitchViewInFrame( CFrameWnd* pFrame,
                          CRuntimeClass* pViewClass )
{
   ASSERT_VALID( pFrame );
   ASSERT( pViewClass != NULL );

   ASSERT( pViewClass->
           IsDerivedFrom( RUNTIME_CLASS( CView ) ) );

   // 1 - Find the currently active view
   CView* pActiveView = pFrame->GetActiveView();
   if( pActiveView == NULL )
   {
      TRACE0( "Unable to switch: no active view\n" );
      return;
   }

   if( pActiveView->IsKindOf( pViewClass ) )
   {
      // No need to switch for same view class
      return;
   }

   // 2 - Store current view position
   CRect rcView;
   pActiveView->GetWindowRect( &rcView );

   // 3 - Find the associated document
   CDocument* pDoc = pActiveView->GetDocument();
   ASSERT_VALID( pDoc );

   // 4 - Make sure the document won't self-destruct
   // when active view is destroyed
   BOOL bSaveAutoDelete = pDoc->m_bAutoDelete;
   pDoc->m_bAutoDelete = FALSE;
```

```
    // 5 - Destroy the active view
    pActiveView->DestroyWindow();

    // 6 - Restore document to initial state
    pDoc->m_bAutoDelete = bSaveAutoDelete;

    // 7 - Initialize creation context used by CreateView()
    CCreateContext context;
    context.m_pNewDocTemplate = NULL;
    context.m_pLastView = NULL;
    context.m_pCurrentFrame = NULL;

    context.m_pNewViewClass = pViewClass;
    context.m_pCurrentDoc = pDoc;

    // 8 - Create the new view
    CView* pNewView = static_cast<CView*>
                ( pFrame->CreateView( &context ) );

    ASSERT_VALID( pNewView );

    // 9 - Position the new view like the old one
    pFrame->ScreenToClient( &rcView );
    pNewView->MoveWindow( &rcView, TRUE );

    // 10 - Send WM_INITIALUPDATE to the view
    pFrame->InitialUpdateFrame( pDoc, TRUE );
}
```

Step 2. Call *EkSwitchViewInFrame()* when you want to switch a new view into a particular frame window (an MDI view's frame window or SDI main application window):

```
CFrameWnd* pFrame;

// ...
// Initialize pFrame to point to the relevant frame
// window object
// ...

// Switch a view of type "CMyView" into pFrame
EkSwitchViewInFrame( pFrame, RUNTIME_CLASS( CMyView ) );
```

Listing 3-74 shows how both sample code projects for this FAQ switch the active view when the user selects a menu command. This same code works for both MDI and SDI applications (in the SwitchViewMDI and SwitchViewSDI projects, respectively). The MDI application switches the view contained in the active view's frame window, whereas the SDI application switches the view contained in its main application window. (*EkGetActiveFrame()* is discussed in *FAQ 3.40 How do I get a pointer to the active frame window?*)

Listing 3-74. Sample code that switches the active view when the user selects a menu command. This code works for both MDI and SDI applications.

```
///////////////////////////////////////////////////////////////////
// Return the active frame window or NULL

CFrameWnd* EkGetActiveFrame()
{
   CWnd* pMainWnd = AfxGetMainWnd();
   ASSERT_VALID( pMainWnd );

   if( !pMainWnd->IsKindOf( RUNTIME_CLASS( CFrameWnd ) ) )
   {
      return NULL;
   }

   return static_cast<CFrameWnd*>( pMainWnd )
                                   ->GetActiveFrame();
}

///////////////////////////////////////////////////////////////////

#include "DrawView.h"
#include "DrawFormView.h"

void CDrawDoc::OnSwitchDrawView()
{
   CFrameWnd* pActiveFrame = EkGetActiveFrame();

   if( pActiveFrame )
   {
      EkSwitchViewInFrame( pActiveFrame,
                           RUNTIME_CLASS( CDrawView ) );
```

```
    }
}

void CDrawDoc::OnSwitchFormView()
{
    CFrameWnd* pActiveFrame = EkGetActiveFrame();

    if( pActiveFrame )
    {
        EkSwitchViewInFrame( pActiveFrame,
                             RUNTIME_CLASS( CDrawFormView ) );
    }
}
```

■

Additional Comments

Where should you handle the switch view command? This question can become controversial, because there are many good answers but no perfect one. Here are my thoughts on this matter:

- *In the application class.* Pros: this class already "knows" about all the views in the application. Cons: the command will always be available even when there is no active document; also, I wonder whether the switch view command should really be an applicationwide command.
- *In the main application window class.* Cons: handling the command there forces the main application window class to know about all the views it may switch to; and the command will always be available, even when there is no active document.
- *In the SDI frame window class.* Pros: with only one frame window, it's easy to find the correct frame MFC object in which the view will be replaced. Cons: handling the command there forces the SDI frame window class to know about all the views it may switch to.
- *In the view's frame window class.* Pros: in this case, it's easy to find the correct frame MFC object in which the view will be replaced; the switch view command is guaranteed to be available only when there is an active document object (with an active view). Cons: handling the command there forces the view's frame window class to know about all the views it may switch to; this solution can also lead to code duplication if you have multiple views' frame classes for which you want to switch views.

- *In the document class.* Pros: the switch view command is guaranteed to be available only when there is an active document object (with an active view); different kinds of documents can separately handle the switching to different kinds of views. Cons: handling the command there forces the document class to know about all the views it may switch to.

As you can see, there is no perfect answer to the question of where to handle the switch view command. I am inclined to opt for the last of these suggestions, because I find the document class to be the more logical place for handling this command—even if having the document class know about all the views it may switch to is not the prettiest design. As always, you must decide what is best for your application.

Sample Code (MDI and SDI applications)

- Projects: SwitchViewMDI and SwitchViewSDI in the Chap03 subdirectory on the companion CD-ROM.
- Purpose: These projects demonstrate how to dynamically switch the view contained in a frame window: either a view's frame window (Figure 3-34) or the SDI main frame window (Figure 3-35).

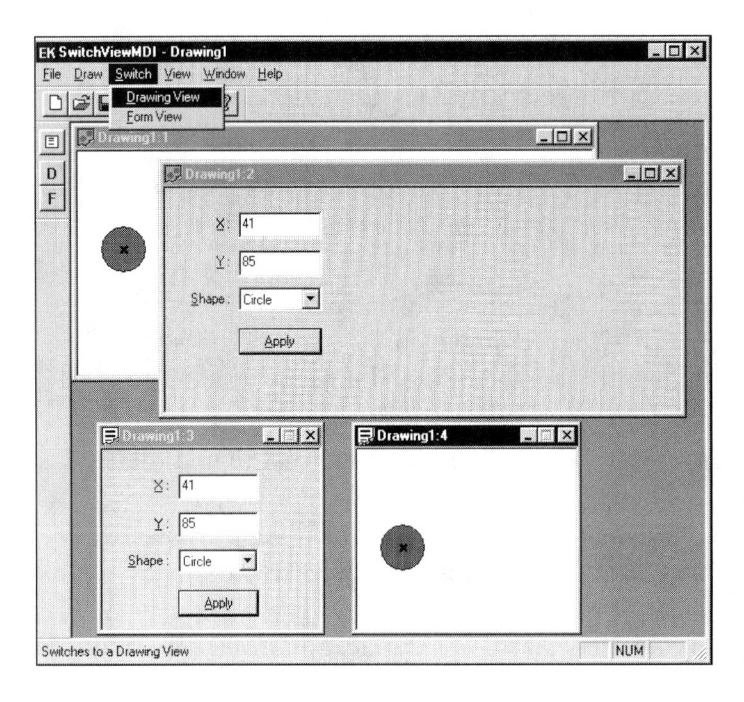

Figure 3-34. Switching views in an MDI application (SwitchViewMDI): two kinds of view frame windows, two kinds of views, four combinations.

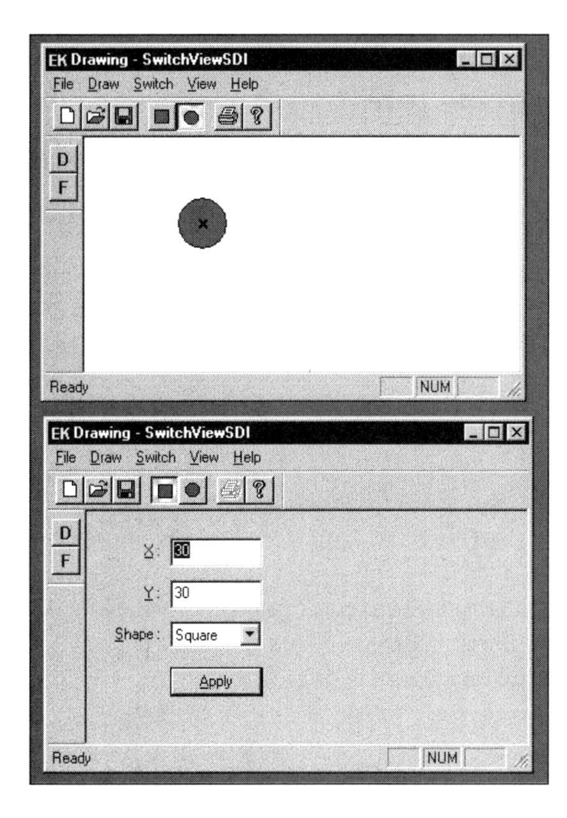

Figure 3-35. Switching views in an SDI application (SwitchViewSDI).

Implementation Highlights (Both Projects)

- *EkSwitchViewInFrame()* function (DrawDoc.cpp)
- *EkGetActiveFrame()* function (DrawDoc.cpp)
- *CDrawDoc::OnSwitchDrawView()* function (DrawDoc.cpp)
- *CDrawDoc::OnSwitchFormView()* function (DrawDoc.cpp)

See Also

- *FAQ 3.38 How do I dynamically switch the view displayed in a splitter window?*
- *FAQ 3.40 How do I get a pointer to the active frame window?*

How do I dynamically switch the view displayed in a splitter window?

At first sight, this question looks very similar to the one discussed in *FAQ 3.37 How do I dynamically switch the view displayed in an MDI child window or SDI main application window?* However, switching a view in a splitter window needs some special handling. Fortunately, the *EkSwitchViewInSplitter()* utility function will give you absolute switching power.

Step 1. Implement *EkSwitchViewInSplitter()* as shown in Listing 3-75.

Listing 3-75. Implementing *EkSwitchViewInSplitter()* to dynamically replace a view in a splitter window.

```
void EkSwitchViewInSplitter( CSplitterWnd* pSplitter,
                             int row, int col,
                             CRuntimeClass* pViewClass )
{
   ASSERT_VALID( pSplitter );
   ASSERT( pViewClass != NULL );

   ASSERT( pViewClass->
           IsDerivedFrom( RUNTIME_CLASS( CView ) ) );

   // 1 - Find the view to be replaced
   CWnd* pPaneWnd = pSplitter->GetPane( row, col );
   if( !pPaneWnd->IsKindOf( RUNTIME_CLASS( CView ) ) )
   {
      TRACE2(
         "Unable to switch: pane (%d,%d) is not a view\n",
         row, col );
      return;
   }

   CView* pCurrentView = static_cast<CView*>( pPaneWnd );
   ASSERT_VALID( pCurrentView );
   ASSERT_KINDOF( CView, pCurrentView );

   if( pCurrentView->IsKindOf( pViewClass ) )
   {
```

```
        // No need to switch for same view class
        return;
    }

    // 2 - Store current view position and activation state
    CRect rcView;
    pCurrentView->GetWindowRect( &rcView );

    CView* pActiveView = pSplitter->
                GetParentFrame()->GetActiveView();
    BOOL bSaveActive = ( pActiveView == NULL )
                    || ( pActiveView == pCurrentView );

    // 3 - Find the associated document
    CDocument* pDoc = pCurrentView->GetDocument();
    ASSERT_VALID( pDoc );

    // 4 - Make sure the document won't self-destruct
    // when current view is destroyed
    BOOL bSaveAutoDelete = pDoc->m_bAutoDelete;
    pDoc->m_bAutoDelete = FALSE;

    // 5 - Destroy the current view
    pCurrentView->DestroyWindow();

    // 6 - Restore document to initial state
    pDoc->m_bAutoDelete = bSaveAutoDelete;

    // 7 - Initialize creation context used by CreateView()
    CCreateContext context;
    context.m_pNewDocTemplate = NULL;
    context.m_pLastView = NULL;
    context.m_pCurrentFrame = NULL;

    context.m_pNewViewClass = pViewClass;
    context.m_pCurrentDoc = pDoc;

    // 8 - Create the new view
    pSplitter->CreateView(   row, col, pViewClass,
                             rcView.Size(), &context );
```

```
    CView* pNewView = static_cast<CView*>
                  ( pSplitter->GetPane( row, col ) );
    ASSERT_VALID( pNewView );
    ASSERT_KINDOF( CView, pNewView );

    // 9 - Position the new view like the old one and
    // activate it if needed
    pSplitter->ScreenToClient( &rcView );
    pNewView->MoveWindow( &rcView, TRUE );
    if( bSaveActive )
    {
       pSplitter->GetParentFrame()->SetActiveView(pNewView);
    }

    // 10 - Send WM_INITIALUPDATE to the view
    pNewView->GetParentFrame()->InitialUpdateFrame( pDoc,
                                                    TRUE );
}
```

Step 2. Call *EkSwitchViewInSplitter()* when you want to switch a new view into a particular splitter pane:

```
CSplitterWnd* pSplitter;

// ...
// Initialize pSplitter to point to the relevant splitter
// window object
// ...

// Switch a view of type "CMyView" into pane (row, col)
// of pSplitter
EkSwitchViewInSplitter( pSplitter, row, col,
                        RUNTIME_CLASS( CMyView ) );
```

Listing 3-76 shows how the sample code for this FAQ switches the view in the active splitter pane when the user selects a menu command. The logic of this code is more complex than usual, because my sample project uses a three-way splitter window that contains two nested splitters, as explained in *FAQ 3.33 How do I program a window with both horizontal and vertical static splitter panes (three-way splitter)?* Therefore, *OnSwitchDrawView()* and *OnSwitchDrawFormView()* must decide which of the two nested splitter windows contains the active view before calling *EkSwitchViewInSplitter()*.

Listing 3-76. Sample code to switch the view in the active splitter pane when the user selects a menu command (must decide between two nested splitters).

```
void CSplitFrame::OnSwitchDrawView()
{
   if( GetActiveView() == m_wndSplitter1.GetPane( 0, 0 ) )
   {
      // Active pane is leftmost in Splitter1
      EkSwitchViewInSplitter( &m_wndSplitter1, 0, 0,
                              RUNTIME_CLASS( CDrawView ) );
   }
   else
   {
      // Active pane is in Splitter2
      int row, col;
      m_wndSplitter2.GetActivePane( &row, &col );
      EkSwitchViewInSplitter( &m_wndSplitter2, row, col,
                              RUNTIME_CLASS( CDrawView ) );
   }
}

void CSplitFrame::OnSwitchFormView()
{
   if( GetActiveView() == m_wndSplitter1.GetPane( 0, 0 ) )
   {
      // Active pane is leftmost in Splitter1
      EkSwitchViewInSplitter( &m_wndSplitter1, 0, 0,
                          RUNTIME_CLASS( CDrawFormView ) );
   }
   else
   {
      // Active pane is in Splitter2
      int row, col;
      m_wndSplitter2.GetActivePane( &row, &col );
      EkSwitchViewInSplitter( &m_wndSplitter2, row, col,
                          RUNTIME_CLASS( CDrawFormView ) );
   }
}
```

■

Sample Code

- Project: SwitchViewSplitter in the Chap03 subdirectory on the companion CD-ROM.
- Purpose: Switches views inside splitter panes. Note the "Switch" menu when the splitter view's frame window has the focus (Figure 3-36).

Implementation Highlights

- *EkSwitchViewInSplitter()* function (SplitFrame.cpp)
- *CSplitFrame::OnSwitchDrawView()* function (SplitFrame.cpp)
- *CSplitFrame::OnSwitchFormView()* function (SplitFrame.cpp)

See Also

- *FAQ 3.37 How do I dynamically switch the view displayed in an MDI child window or SDI main application window?*

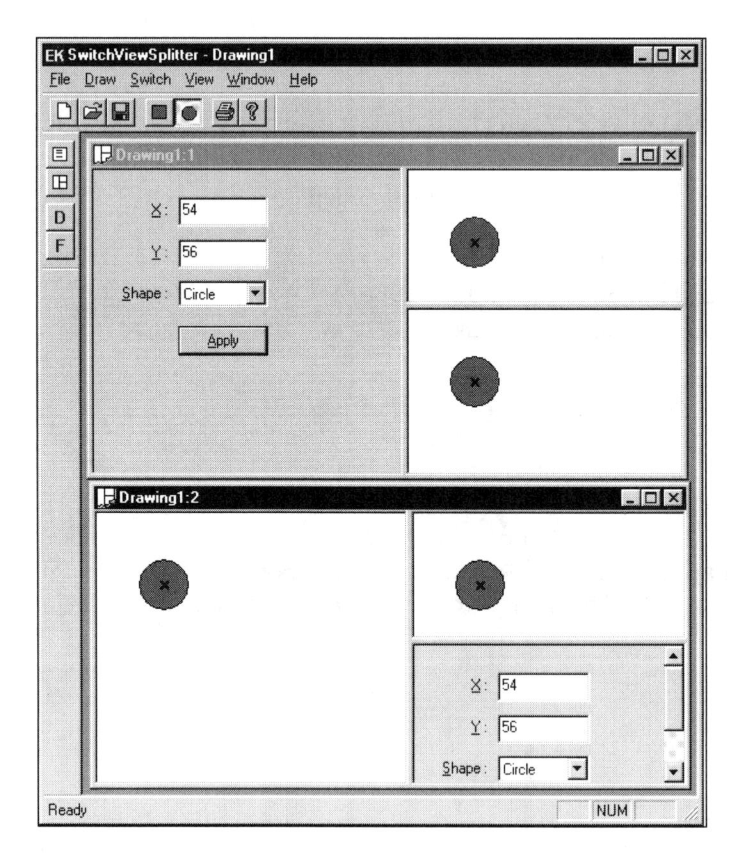

Figure 3-36. The SwitchViewSplitter application: switching views inside splitter panes.

Miscellaneous Items

How do I get a pointer to the active view?

Do you sometimes need to get a pointer to the active view from somewhere in your code? Follow these simple steps:

Step 1. Implement *EkGetActiveView()* as shown in Listing 3-77.

Listing 3-77. Implementing *EkGetActiveView()* to return a pointer to the active view.

```
// Return the active view window or NULL
CView* EkGetActiveView()
{
   CWnd* pMainWnd = AfxGetMainWnd();
   ASSERT_VALID( pMainWnd );

   if( !pMainWnd->IsKindOf( RUNTIME_CLASS( CFrameWnd ) ) )
   {
      return NULL;
   }

   return static_cast<CFrameWnd*>( pMainWnd )
                  ->GetActiveFrame()->GetActiveView();
}
```

Step 2. Call *EkGetActiveView()* whenever you want to retrieve a pointer to the active view:

```
CView* pView = EkGetActiveView();
if( pView != NULL )
{
   //...
   // Use pView
   //...
}
```

■

Additional Comments

Note that the *EkGetActiveView()* function shown in Listing 3-77 works for both MDI and SDI applications.

Sample Code

There is no sample project for this FAQ.

See Also

- *FAQ 2.18 How do I get a pointer to the currently active document?*
- *FAQ 3.40 How do I get a pointer to the active frame window?*

How do I get a pointer to the active frame window?

If we can get to the view (as shown in *FAQ 3.39 How do I get a pointer to the active view?*), we are certainly able to get a pointer to the active frame from anywhere in our code:

Step 1. Implement *EkGetActiveFrame()* as shown in Listing 3-78.

Listing 3-78. Implementing *EkGetActiveFrame()* to return a pointer to the active frame window.

```
// Return the active frame window or NULL
CFrameWnd* EkGetActiveFrame()
{
   CWnd* pMainWnd = AfxGetMainWnd();
   ASSERT_VALID( pMainWnd );

   if( !pMainWnd->IsKindOf( RUNTIME_CLASS( CFrameWnd ) ) )
   {
      return NULL;
   }

   return static_cast<CFrameWnd*>( pMainWnd )
                                    ->GetActiveFrame();
}
```

Step 2. Call *EkGetActiveFrame()* whenever you want to retrieve a pointer to the active frame window:

```
CFrameWnd* pFrame = EkGetActiveFrame();
if( pFrame != NULL )
{
    //...
    // Use pFrame
    //...
}
```

■

Additional Comments

Note that the *EkGetActiveFrame()* function shown in Listing 3-78 works for both MDI and SDI applications.

Sample Code

There is no sample project for this FAQ.

See Also

- *FAQ 3.39 How do I get a pointer to the active view?*

How do I iterate through the list of all the views associated with a document?

The code fragment shown in Listing 3-79 demonstrates how to iterate through the list of all the views associated with a document.

Listing 3-79. Iterating through the list of all the views associated with a document.

```
CDocument* pDoc;

// ...
// Initialize pDoc to point to the relevant document object
// ...
```

```
POSITION pos = pDoc->GetFirstViewPosition();
while( pos != NULL )
{
    CView* pView = pDoc->GetNextView( pos );
    ASSERT_VALID( pView );

    // ...
    // Use pView
    // ...
}
```

■

Sample Code

- Project: IterateViews in the Chap03 subdirectory on the companion CD-ROM.
- Purpose: Iterates through all the views associated with a document (see Figure 3-37).

Implementation Highlights

- *CViewListDlg::OnInitDialog()* function (ViewListDlg.cpp)

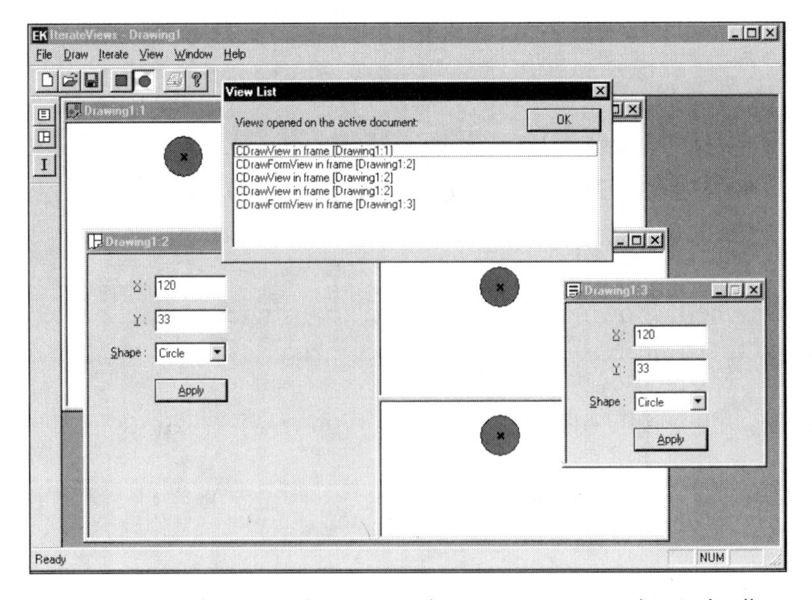

Figure 3-37. The IterateViews application: iterating through all the views associated with the active document.

4 DIALOG BOXES

Dialog boxes play an essential role in most Windows applications, mainly because they provide a convenient way to display values to the user and solicit input. Fortunately, MFC and ClassWizard cooperate to greatly simplify the process of adding dialog boxes to an application. These tools automatically generate the necessary code for binding the various dialog controls to associated C++ member variables, and that is a great improvement over the plain old C-SDK method of achieving the same results.

Even if the default MFC dialog box behavior usually satisfies the basic requirements of most Windows applications, the techniques described in this chapter show how you can further customize your dialog boxes to meet more-sophisticated needs. For example, you can implement an expanding dialog box (*FAQ 4.7*), add a toolbar to a dialog box (*FAQ 4.8*), or add ToolTips to the controls in your dialog box (*FAQ 4.13*).

General Topics

How do I set the initial position of a dialog box?

Most users are satisfied with the default location of dialog boxes in MFC applications; MFC ensures that these dialog boxes show up centered in the main application window. However, some applications can benefit from greater control over the initial position of at least some dialog boxes.

The initial impulse is usually to try to move the dialog box to the desired position in the "creating" code—the code that creates the C++ dialog box object and calls the *DoModal()* function—as shown in Listing 4-1.

Listing 4-1. Trying to set the initial position of a dialog box in the "creating" code. This does not work!

```
void CDrawDoc::OnDemoDialog()
{
   CDemoDlg dlg;

   // ...
   // Try to call dlg.MoveWindow(...)
   // or dlg.SetWindowPos(...)

   if( dlg.DoModal() == IDOK )
   {
      // ...
   }
}
```

Although the preceding code compiles without a hitch, executing the program in debug mode will trigger an assertion inside the call to *dlg.MoveWindow(...)* or *dlg.SetWindowPos(...)*. This is because the dialog's window is not created until the *dlg.DoModal()* call, and you cannot move a window that has not yet been created! (More precisely, the *m_hWnd* member of the *dlg* object is still *NULL*.) The correct solution is simply to have the dialog box reposition itself when it is created. To achieve this behavior, use ClassWizard to add a handler for the

WM_INITDIALOG message to your dialog box class, and implement this function as shown in Listing 4-2.

Listing 4-2. Handling the *WM_INITDIALOG* message to move the dialog box to the desired position.

```
BOOL CDemoDlg::OnInitDialog()
{
   CDialog::OnInitDialog();
   // ...
   // 1 - Compute x and y (in screen coordinates)
   // ...
   // 2 - Move the dialog to the desired position
   SetWindowPos(   NULL,
                   x,
                   y,
                   0, 0,
                   SWP_NOSIZE | SWP_NOZORDER );

   return TRUE;
}
```

■

Additional Comments

What if you absolutely need to determine the dialog box's initial position in the creating code rather than inside the dialog class itself? Here's an easy solution:

Step 1. Add a *public* member variable of type *CPoint* to your dialog class, as shown in Listing 4-3. We will name this member variable *m_point* in the following discussion, and it will hold the desired position for the upper-left corner of the dialog box.

Listing 4-3. The dialog class with a new *CPoint* member variable added.

```
class CDemoDlg : public CDialog
{
// ...
public:
   CPoint m_point;  // Initial dialog position
// ...
};
```

Step 2. Modify your dialog box's *OnInitialUpdate()* function to move the dialog box to the position indicated by the *m_point* member variable, as shown in Listing 4-4.

Listing 4-4. Moving the dialog box to the position indicated by the *m_point* member variable.

```
BOOL CDemoDlg::OnInitDialog()
{
   CDialog::OnInitDialog();

   // ...

   // Move the dialog to the desired position
   SetWindowPos(    NULL,
                    m_point.x,
                    m_point.y,
                    0, 0,
                    SWP_NOSIZE | SWP_NOZORDER );

   return TRUE;
}
```

Step 3. In the creating code, compute the desired dialog box position and set the *m_point* data member accordingly, as shown in Listing 4-5.

Listing 4-5. Setting the *m_point* member variable in the creating code.

```
void CDrawDoc::OnDemoDialog()
{
   // ...
   // Compute x and y (in screen coordinates)
   // ...
   CDemoDlg dlg;
   dlg.m_point = CPoint( x, y );
   // ...

   if( dlg.DoModal() == IDOK )
   {
      // ...
   }
}
```

Note that you can also choose to make the *m_point* member variable *protected* or *private* and instead pass the desired coordinates as additional arguments to your dialog's constructor, as shown in Listing 4-6.

Listing 4-6. Passing the desired coordinates as arguments to the dialog's constructor.

```
void CDrawDoc::OnDemoDialog()
{
   // ...
   // Compute x and y (in screen coordinates)
   // ...
   CDemoDlg dlg( x, y );

   // ...

   if( dlg.DoModal() == IDOK )
   {
      // ...
   }
}
```

Sample Code

- Project: InitialPosition in the Chap04 subdirectory on the companion CD-ROM.
- Purpose: Moves the Demo dialog box so that it appears with its upper-left corner positioned on the current point of the active view, as shown in Figure 4-1.

Implementation Highlights

- *CDemoDlg::OnInitDialog()* function (DemoDlg.cpp)

See Also

- *FAQ 4.2 How do I center a dialog box in relation to another window?*
- *FAQ 3.39 How do I get a pointer to the active view?*

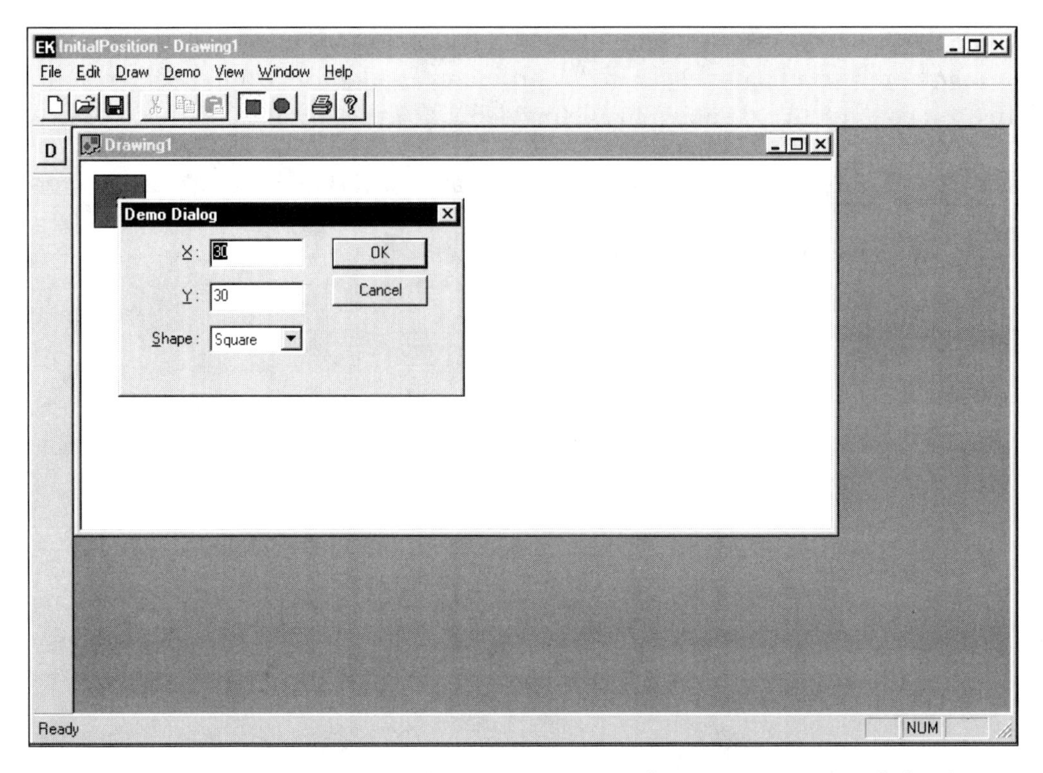

Figure 4-1. The InitialPosition application automatically moves its Demo dialog box so that it appears with its upper-left corner positioned on the current point of the active view.

FAQ 4.2 How do I center a dialog box in relation to another window?

This FAQ is a special version of the more general technique explained in *FAQ 4.1 How do I set the initial position of a dialog box?*

The default MFC implementation displays all dialog boxes centered in the main application window. For an explanation of how MFC achieves this behavior, see the Additional Comments section.

You can easily modify this default behavior to center your dialog box against any window. Call the *CenterWindow()* function in your dialog box's *OnInitDialog()* handler, as shown in Listing 4-7.

Listing 4-7. Handling the *WM_INITDIALOG* message to center a dialog box against the active frame window.

```
BOOL CDemoDlg::OnInitDialog()
{
   CDialog::OnInitDialog();

   // Center our dialog window relative to the active
   // frame window
   CWnd* pActiveFrame = EkGetActiveFrame();
   ASSERT_VALID( pActiveFrame );
   CenterWindow( pActiveFrame );

   return TRUE
}
```

If you want to center your dialog box against the whole desktop window, call the *CenterWindow()* function:

```
CenterWindow( CWnd::GetDesktopWindow() );
```

For a further discussion of *CenterWindow()*, see the Additional Comments section of *FAQ 3.10 How do I center my main application window?*

■

Additional Comments

How does MFC manage to center your application's dialog boxes? The answer to this question is found in the *_AfxPreInitDialog()* and *_AfxPostInitDialog()* functions, whose pseudocode is shown in Listing 4-8.

Listing 4-8. Pseudocode for the *_AfxPreInitDialog()* and *_AfxPostInitDialog()* functions (WinCore.cpp).

```
static void AFXAPI _AfxPreInitDialog(
   CWnd* pWnd, LPRECT lpRectOld, DWORD* pdwStyleOld)
{
   pWnd->GetWindowRect(lpRectOld);
   *pdwStyleOld = pWnd->GetStyle();
}
```

```
static void AFXAPI _AfxPostInitDialog(
   CWnd* pWnd, const RECT& rectOld, DWORD dwStyleOld)
{

   // Must be hidden to start with
   if (dwStyleOld & WS_VISIBLE)
      return;

   // Must not be visible after WM_INITDIALOG
   if (pWnd->GetStyle() & (WS_VISIBLE|WS_CHILD))
      return;

   // Must not move during WM_INITDIALOG
   CRect rect;
   pWnd->GetWindowRect(rect);
   if (rectOld.left != rect.left
         || rectOld.top != rect.top)
      return;

   // Must be unowned or owner disabled
   CWnd* pParent = pWnd->GetWindow(GW_OWNER);

   if (pParent != NULL && pParent->IsWindowEnabled())
      return;

   if (!pWnd->CheckAutoCenter())
      return;

   // Center modal dialog boxes/message boxes
   pWnd->CenterWindow();
}
```

As you can see from the code in Listing 4-8, *_AfxPreInitDialog()* simply stores the original position of the dialog box window along with its style attributes. The *_AfxPostInitDialog()* function then verifies certain assumptions about the dialog box—most notably that it did not move during the processing of the *WM_INITDIALOG* message—and finally calls *CenterWindow()* if and only if everything is OK.

_AfxPreInitDialog() and *_AfxPostInitDialog()* are themselves called by MFC's *_AfxActivationWndProc()* function while processing the *WM_INITDIALOG* message, as shown in Listing 4-9.

Listing 4-9. Pseudocode for the *_AfxActivationWndProc()* function (WinCore.cpp).

```
static const TCHAR szAfxOldWndProc[] = _T("AfxOldWndProc");

LRESULT CALLBACK _AfxActivationWndProc(HWND hWnd,
                    UINT nMsg, WPARAM wParam, LPARAM lParam)

{
   WNDPROC oldWndProc =
              (WNDPROC)::GetProp(hWnd, szAfxOldWndProc);

   LRESULT lResult = 0;
   TRY
   {
      BOOL bCallDefault = TRUE;
      switch (nMsg)
      {
      case WM_INITDIALOG:
         {
            DWORD dwStyle;
            CRect rectOld;
            CWnd* pWnd = CWnd::FromHandle(hWnd);
            _AfxPreInitDialog(pWnd, &rectOld, &dwStyle);
            bCallDefault = FALSE;
            lResult = CallWindowProc(oldWndProc, hWnd,
                                      nMsg, wParam, lParam);
            _AfxPostInitDialog(pWnd, rectOld, dwStyle);
         }
         break;

      // ...

   }
   CATCH_ALL(e)
   {
      // ...
   }
   END_CATCH_ALL

   return lResult;
}
```

Sample Code

- Project: CenterDialog in the Chap04 subdirectory on the companion CD-ROM.
- Purpose: The Demo dialog box appears centered relative to the active frame window, as shown in Figure 4-2.

Implementation Highlights

- *CDemoDlg::OnInitDialog()* function (DemoDlg.cpp)

See Also

- *FAQ 4.1 How do I set the initial position of a dialog box?*
- *FAQ 3.10 How do I center my main application window?*
- *FAQ 3.40 How do I get a pointer to the active frame window?*

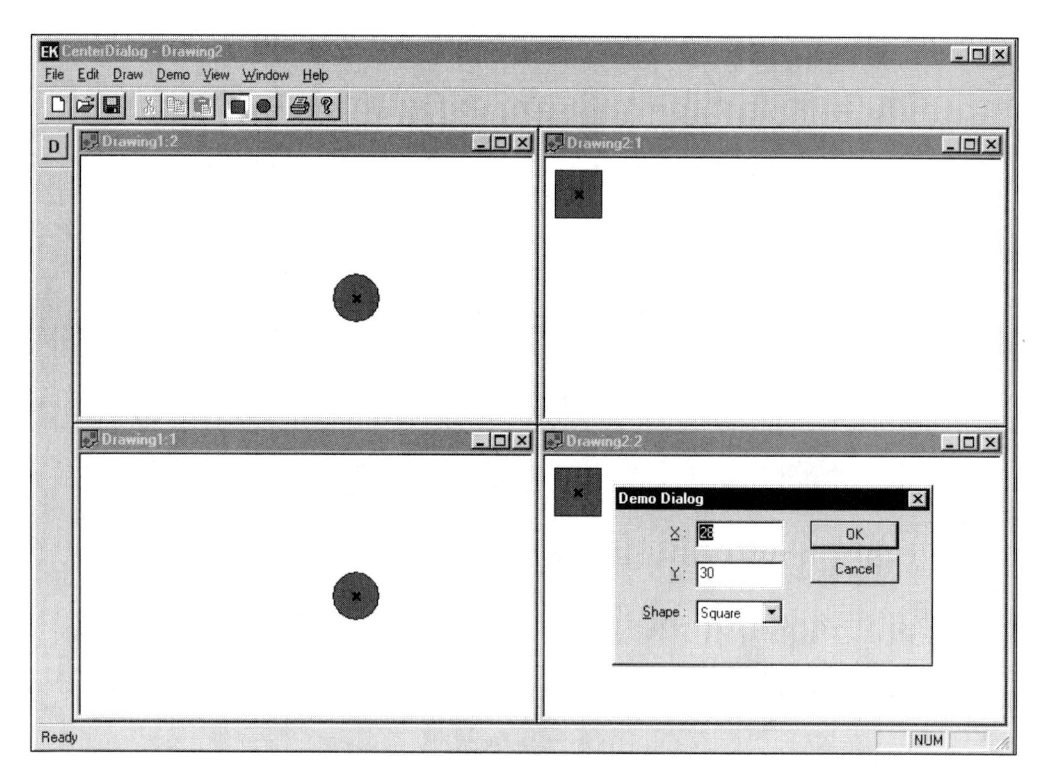

Figure 4-2. The Demo dialog box appears centered relative to the active frame window.

How can a dialog box access the active document (or view) object?

When you're handling commands in a document (or view) class, accessing the active document (or view) object is rather straightforward. Dialog boxes, however, are not directly hooked into MFC's document/view architecture and therefore cannot readily access the active document (or view) object.

Although the code invoking the dialog box can transfer the needed data back and forth between the document object and the dialog's member variables, manually coding these transfers can rapidly become cumbersome, especially when the dialog needs to read or update many fields in the document object. Therefore, it is sometimes desirable—and more elegant—to allow the dialog to directly access the document (or view) object to which the dialog box pertains.

The solution to this problem is almost trivial—once you have found it!

Step 1. Add a *protected* member variable of type *CYourDoc* to your dialog class, as shown in Listing 4-10. We will name this member variable *m_pDoc* in the following discussion.

Listing 4-10. The dialog class with a new *CYourDoc* member variable added.

```
class CDemoDlg : public CDialog
{

// Construction
public:
   CDemoDlg( CDrawDoc* pDoc, CWnd* pParent = NULL );

// ...

// Implementation
protected:
   CDrawDoc* m_pDoc;   // Pointer to our associated document

// ...

};
```

Step 2. Modify your dialog box's constructor to store the document pointer received as an argument in the *m_pDoc* member variable, as shown in Listing 4-11.

Listing 4-11. Storing the document pointer in the *m_pDoc* member variable.

```
CDemoDlg::CDemoDlg(CDrawDoc* pDoc, CWnd* pParent /*=NULL*/)
    : CDialog(CDemoDlg::IDD, pParent)
{

    ASSERT_VALID( pDoc );
    m_pDoc = pDoc;
    // ...
}
```

Step 3. Modify your dialog box's *DoDataExchange()* function to directly exchange data between your document object and the controls on the dialog box, as shown in Listing 4-12. Note that you no longer need to define member variables of types *CString*, *int*, and so on, associated with your dialog box's controls inside your dialog class, because you will directly fetch these values from your document object's data members.

Listing 4-12. Modifying the *DoDataExchange()* to directly exchange data between the document object and the dialog box's controls.

```
void CDemoDlg::DoDataExchange(CDataExchange* pDX)
{
    CDialog::DoDataExchange(pDX);

    // The m_shape variable needs special handling because
    // it is defined as an enumeration in the document class
    // as follows:
    // enum SHAPE { SQUARE = 0, CIRCLE = 1 } m_shape;
    int nShape = -1;
    if( !pDX->m_bSaveAndValidate )
    {
        nShape = m_pDoc->m_shape;
    }

    //{{AFX_DATA_MAP(CDemoDlg)
    DDX_Control(pDX, IDC_SHAPE, m_cmbShape);
    DDX_Control(pDX, IDC_Y, m_edtY);
```

```
    DDX_Control(pDX, IDC_X, m_edtX);
    DDX_Text(pDX, IDC_X, m_pDoc->m_point.x);
    DDX_Text(pDX, IDC_Y, m_pDoc->m_point.y);
    DDX_CBIndex(pDX, IDC_SHAPE, nShape);
    //}}AFX_DATA_MAP

    if( pDX->m_bSaveAndValidate )
    {
       m_pDoc->m_shape = static_cast< CDrawDoc::SHAPE >
                                                  ( nShape );

    }
}
```

Step 4. Pass the address of the document object that you want to associate with your dialog in the creating code, as shown in Listing 4-13. Note that the creating code no longer needs to transfer any data back and forth between the document object and the dialog's member variables.

Listing 4-13. Invoking the dialog and associating it with a document object.

```
void CDrawDoc::OnDemoDialog()
{
    CDemoDlg dlg( this );
    if( dlg.DoModal() == IDOK )
    {
       SetModifiedFlag( TRUE );
       UpdateAllViews( NULL );
    }
}
```

If you wanted to invoke the same dialog from a view, you would use code similar to the following fragment:

```
CDrawDoc* pDoc = GetDocument();
CDemoDlg dlg( pDoc );
if( dlg.DoModal() == IDOK )
{
    pDoc->SetModifiedFlag( TRUE );
    pDoc->UpdateAllViews( NULL );
}
```

Finally, note that the preceding explanations apply to the document object, but they can easily be adapted to handle a view instead.

■

Additional Comments

Instead of storing a pointer to the active document to the dialog object, this object could itself locate the active document by calling the *EkGetActiveDocument()* function discussed in *FAQ 2.18 How do I get a pointer to the currently active document?* Similarly, the active view can be located by calling the *EkGetActiveView()* function discussed in *FAQ 3.39 How do I get a pointer to the active view?*

Sample Code

- Project: GetActiveDoc in the Chap04 subdirectory on the companion CD-ROM.
- Purpose: Implements a dialog box that directly accesses the active document object.

Implementation Highlights

- *CDemoDlg::DoDataExchange()* function (DemoDlg.cpp)
- *CDrawDoc::OnDemoDialog()* function (DrawDoc.cpp)

See Also

- *FAQ 2.18 How do I get a pointer to the currently active document?*
- *FAQ 3.39 How do I get a pointer to the active view?*

How do I control the background color of a dialog box?

The answer to this question is almost identical to the solution given in *FAQ 3.31 How do I change the background color of a form view?*—and rightly so, because a form view is a special kind of dialog box.

Step 1. Define and initialize a member variable of type *CBRUSH* in your dialog box class, as shown in Listing 4-14.

Listing 4-14. Definition and initialization of the *m_brBack* member variable.

```
// ________________________________
// Class definition for CDemoDlg (DemoDlg.h)

class CDemoDlg : public CDialog
{
// ...

// Implementation

private:
   CBrush m_brBack;    // Background color brush

// ...
};

// ________________________________
// Implementation for CDemoDlg (DemoDlg.h)

CDemoDlg::CDemoDlg(CWnd* pParent /*=NULL*/)
   : CDialog(CDemoDlg::IDD, pParent)
{
   // ...

   // Set initial background color to cyan
   m_brBack.CreateSolidBrush( RGB( 0, 255, 255 ) );
}
```

Step 2. Use ClassWizard to add to your dialog box class a handler for the *WM_CTLCOLOR* message. Implement this handler as shown in Listing 4-15.

Listing 4-15. Handling the *WM_CTLCOLOR* message to change the background color of a dialog box.

```
HBRUSH CDemoDlg::OnCtlColor(CDC* pDC, CWnd* pWnd,
                            UINT nCtlColor)
```

```
{
   switch( nCtlColor )
   {
   case CTLCOLOR_BTN:
   case CTLCOLOR_STATIC:
      pDC->SetBkMode( TRANSPARENT );
      // Fall through

   case CTLCOLOR_DLG:
      return static_cast<HBRUSH>(
                                 m_brBack.GetSafeHandle() );
   }

   return CFormView::OnCtlColor(pDC, pWnd, nCtlColor);
}
```

Step 3. To dynamically change the background color of the dialog box, use code similar to the following:

```
void CDemoDlg::OnBackgroundYellow()
{
   // 1 - Change the background color to yellow
   m_brBack.DeleteObject();
   m_brBack.CreateSolidBrush( RGB( 255, 255, 0 ) );

   // 2 - Force the dialog to repaint
   Invalidate( TRUE );
}
```

■

Explanations

The *WM_CTLCOLOR* message is discussed in the Explanations section of *FAQ 3.31.*

Additional Comments

The technique explained in this FAQ allows you to select the color of any specific dialog box. However, MFC also provides an easy way to change the color of *all* your dialog boxes. Call the *SetDialogBkColor()* function in your application's *InitInstance()* function:

```
BOOL CMyApp::InitInstance()
{
  // ...

  COLORREF crBackground = RGB( 255, 255, 0 );
  COLORREF crText = RGB( 255, 0, 0 );

   // Set dialog color to red text on yellow background
   SetDialogBkColor( crBackground, crText );
   // ...
}
```

CWinApp::SetDialogBkColor() has the following prototype:

```
void SetDialogBkColor(
        COLORREF clrCtlBk = RGB(192, 192, 192),
        COLORREF clrCtlText = RGB(0, 0, 0) );
```

For more information about *CWinApp::SetDialogBkColor()*, see the online help.

Sample Code

- Project: BackColor in the Chap04 subdirectory on the companion CD-ROM.
- Purpose: The dialog box dynamically changes its background color, as shown in Figure 4-3.

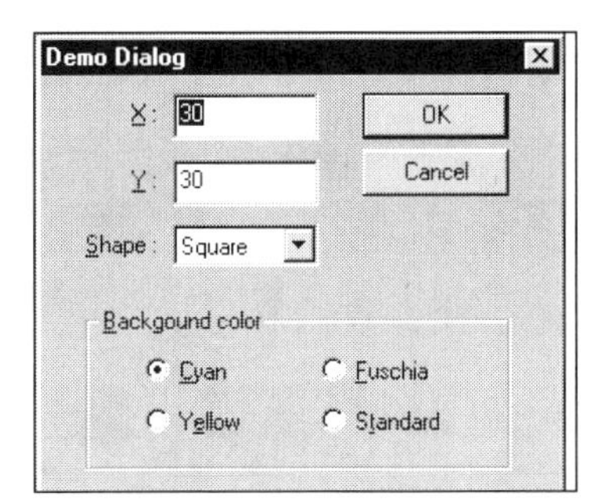

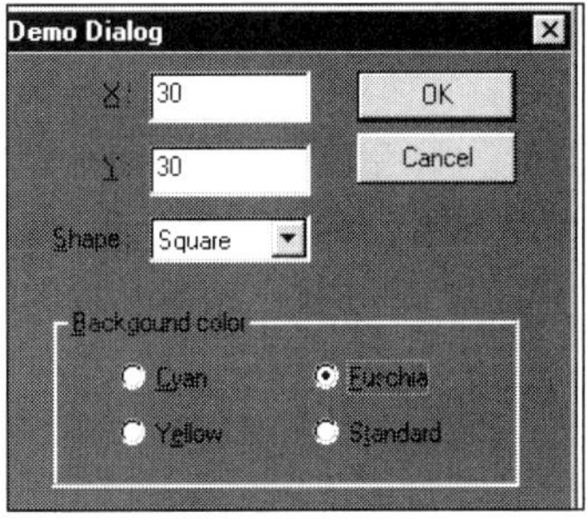

Figure 4-3 The dialog box dynamically changes its background color.

Implementation Highlights

- *CDemoDlg::OnCtlColor()* function (DemoDlg.cpp)
- *CDemoDlg:: CDemoDlg()* function (DemoDlg.cpp)
- *CDemoDlg::OnBackgroundXXX()* functions (DemoDlg.cpp)

See Also

- *FAQ 3.31 How do I change the background color of a form view?*

4.5 How do I add a preview area to (draw inside) a dialog box?

Having a dialog box show dynamically the consequences of a user's actions in a preview area is often a dramatic way to enhance the appeal of your application and to make it appear much more professional. Compare, for example, the two dialogs shown in Figures 4-4 and 4-5.

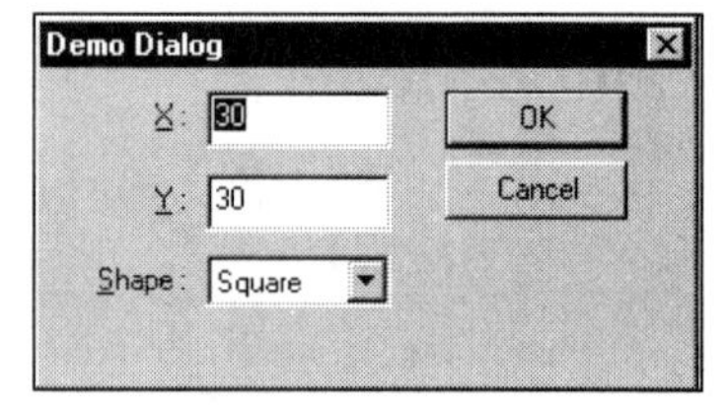

Figure 4-4. A dialog box without a preview area.

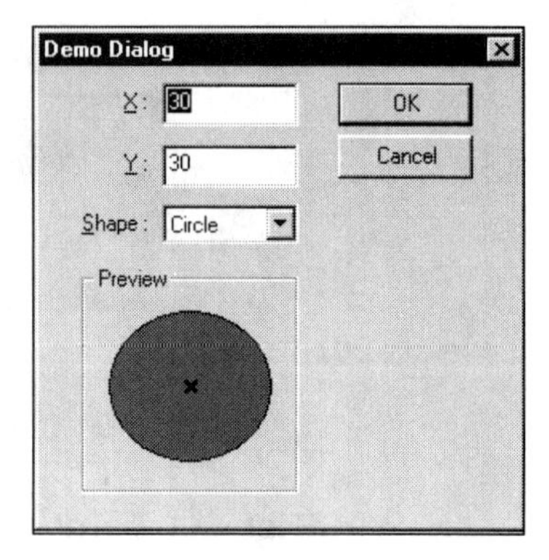

Figure 4-5. A much cooler dialog box with a preview area.

Step 1. Add a Picture control to your dialog box resource to mark the preview area. Set the styles of this Picture control to "Frame, Black, Not Visible," as shown in Figure 4-6.

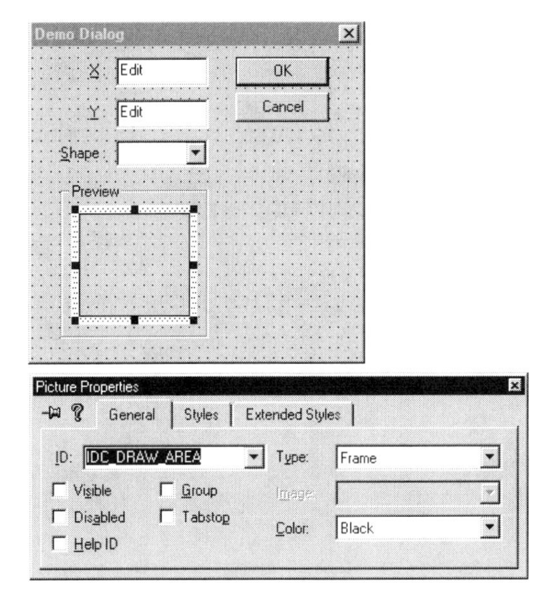

Figure 4-6. Adding a Picture control to a dialog box resource to mark the preview area.

Step 2. Use ClassWizard to add a variable of type *Control* to your dialog class. This variable is associated with the placeholder Picture control that you added in step 1, and it is named *m_DrawArea* in the code listings.

Step 3. Use ClassWizard to add a handler in your dialog class for the *WM_PAINT* message. Implement this handler as shown in Listing 4-16 to draw inside the preview area.

Listing 4-16. Handling the *WM_PAINT* message in a dialog box to draw inside the preview area.

```
void CDemoDlg::OnPaint()
{
   CPaintDC dc(this); // device context for painting

   // 1 - Get placeholder coordinates
   CRect rect;          // Placeholder rectangle
   m_DrawArea.GetWindowRect( &rect );
   ScreenToClient( &rect );
```

```
    // 2 - Draw inside placeholder rectangle
    // ...
    // Put your drawing code here
    // ...

    // Do not call CDialog::OnPaint() for painting messages
}
```

Step 4. Manually add a *RedrawArea()* helper function to force an update of the preview area. To avoid flicker, this function invalidates only the placeholder area rather than the entire dialog window. Implement *RedrawArea()* as shown in Listing 4-17.

Listing 4-17. Implementing *RedrawArea()* to force an update of the drawing area.

```
void CDemoDlg::RedrawArea()
{

    // 1 - Get placeholder coordinates
    CRect rect;        // Placeholder rectangle
    m_DrawArea.GetWindowRect( &rect );
    ScreenToClient( &rect );

    // 2 - Force update of the drawing area
    InvalidateRect( rect );
    UpdateWindow();
}
```

Step 5. To dynamically update your dialog's preview area, call *RedrawArea()* whenever the user changes relevant data in one of your dialog box controls.

■

Additional Comments

The sample code in the *CDemoDlg::OnPaint()* function uses classic Windows GDI functions such as *MoveTo()*, *LineTo()*, *Rectangle()*, and *Ellipse()* to draw inside the dialog's preview area. If you prefer to display a bitmap instead, use code similar to the *EkDrawBitmap()* function shown in Listing 4-18.

Listing 4-18. Drawing a bitmap on a device context.

```
void EkDrawBitmap( CDC* pDC, CBitmap* pBitmap, CRect rect,
                   BOOL bCenter = TRUE )
```

```
{
   ASSERT_VALID( pDC );
   ASSERT_VALID( pBitmap );

   // 1 - Create compatible memory DC
   CDC dcMem;
   dcMem.CreateCompatibleDC( pDC );

   // 2 - Select bitmap into memory DC
   CBitmap* pOldBitmap = dcMem.SelectObject( pBitmap );

   if( bCenter )
   {
      // 3 - Center bitmap in destination rectangle
      BITMAP bitmap;
      pBitmap->GetObject( sizeof( BITMAP ), &bitmap);
      CSize sizeBitmap( bitmap.bmWidth, bitmap.bmHeight );
      CSize diff = rect.Size() - sizeBitmap;
      rect.DeflateRect( diff.cx / 2, diff.cy / 2 );
   }

   // 4 - Blit the bitmap from the memory DC to the real DC
   pDC->BitBlt( rect.left, rect.top,
                rect.Width(), rect.Height(),
                &dcMem, 0, 0, SRCCOPY );

   // 5 - Deselect bitmap from memory DC
   dcMem.SelectObject( pOldBitmap );
}
```

The following code fragment shows how you can use *EkDrawBitmap()* to paint a bitmap on a device context:

```
CDC* pDC;
CRect rect;
// ... initialize pDC and rect ...
CBitmap bmp;
bmp.LoadBitmap( IDB_YOUR_BITMAP );

EkDrawBitmap( pDC, &bmp, rect );
```

Sample Code

- Project: DrawInDialog in the Chap04 subdirectory on the companion CD-ROM.

- Purpose: Displays a dialog box with a shape preview area that is dynamically updated to display the currently selected shape, as shown earlier in Figure 4-5.

Implementation Highlights

- *CDemoDlg::OnPaint()* function (DemoDlg.cpp)
- *CDemoDlg::RedrawArea()* function (DemoDlg.cpp)
- *CDemoDlg::OnSelchangeShape()* function (DemoDlg.cpp)

FAQ 4.6 How do I add an icon to a dialog box?

In a typical MFC application, most windows—except dialog boxes—display an icon in the left corner of their title bar (see Figure 4-7).

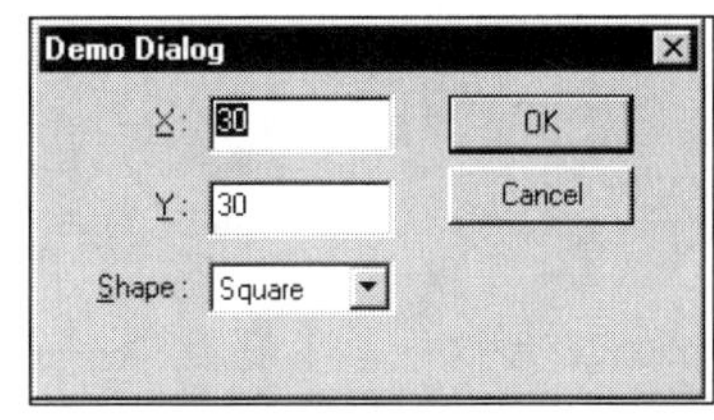

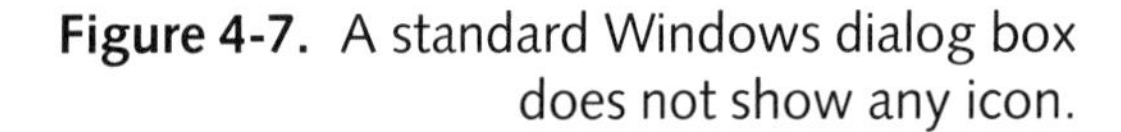

Figure 4-7. A standard Windows dialog box does not show any icon.

The following solution shows how you can easily allow your dialog boxes to display as shown in Figure 4-8.

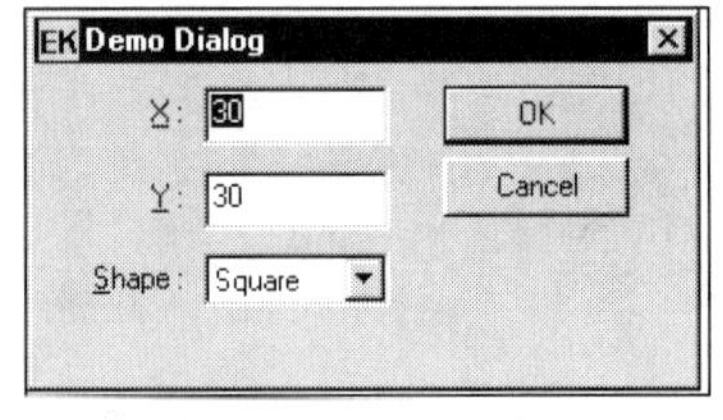

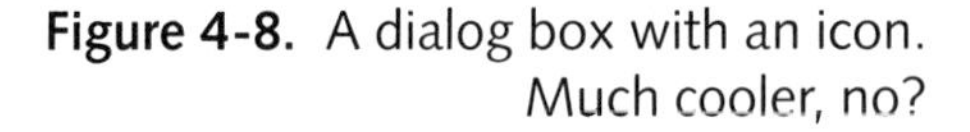

Figure 4-8. A dialog box with an icon. Much cooler, no?

Step 1. Use the Visual C++ Resource Editor to create your dialog box's icon. Note that the icon shown in your dialog's title bar will be the small (16 × 16) icon resource.

Step 2. Use ClassWizard add a handler for the *WM_INITDIALOG* message to your dialog class, and implement this function as shown in Listing 4-19.

Listing 4-19. Handling the *WM_INITDIALOG* message to add an icon to a dialog box.

```
BOOL CDemoDlg::OnInitDialog()
{
   CDialog::OnInitDialog();

   // 1 - Load the icon from the application's resources
   HICON hicon = AfxGetApp()->LoadIcon( IDI_DIALOG );
   ASSERT( hicon != NULL );

   // 2 - Associate the icon with the dialog box
   SetIcon( hicon, TRUE );

   return TRUE;
}
```

■

Sample Code

- Project: IconDialog in the Chap04 subdirectory on the companion CD-ROM.
- Purpose: Displays a dialog box with an icon, as shown earlier in Figure 4-8.

Implementation Highlights

- *CDemoDlg::OnInitDialog()* function (DemoDlg.cpp)

How do I implement an expanding dialog box?

Expanding dialog boxes allow your application to initially present the user with a restricted dialog box containing only the most essential controls and options while at the same time providing for easy access to more-advanced options.

Microsoft Word 97 provides a good example of an expanding dialog box in the Find dialog that is shown in Figures 4-9 and 4-10.

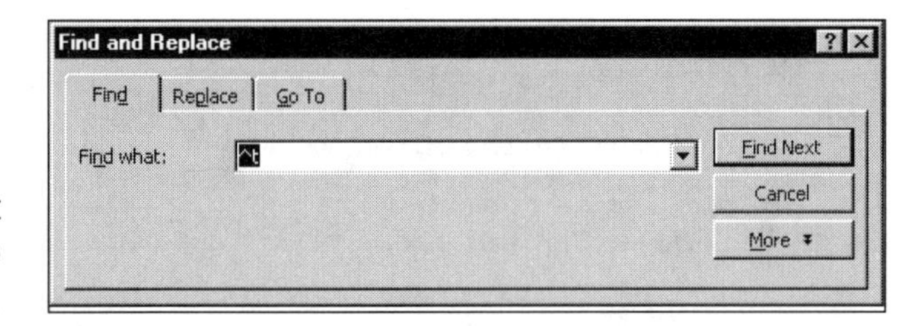

Figure 4-9. The Microsoft Word 97 Find dialog in the collapsed state.

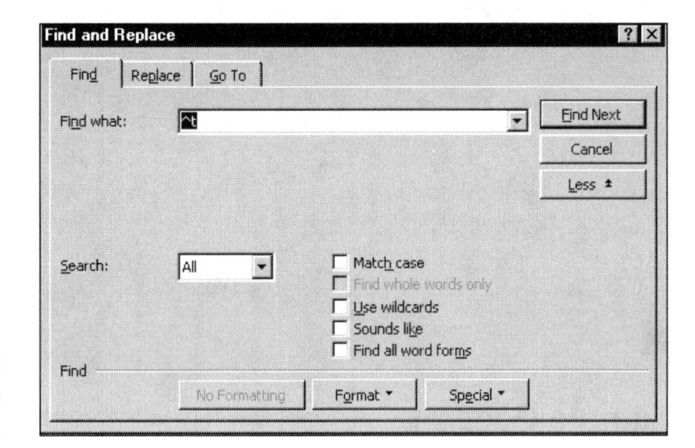

Figure 4-10. The Microsoft Word 97 Find dialog in the expanded state.

The following technique explains how you can achieve the same effect in your MFC application, as shown in Figures 4-11 and 4-12.

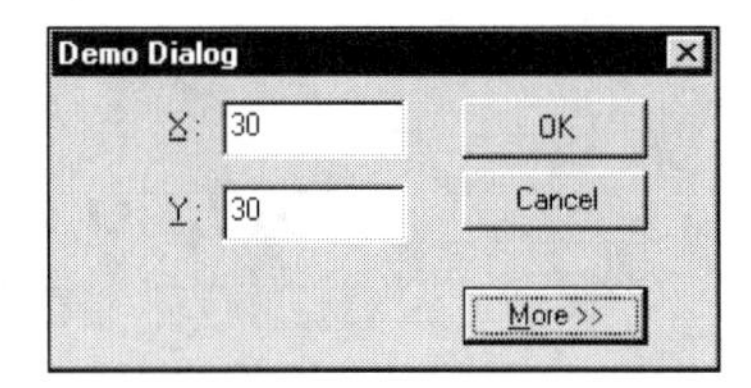

Figure 4-11. The Demo dialog in the collapsed state.

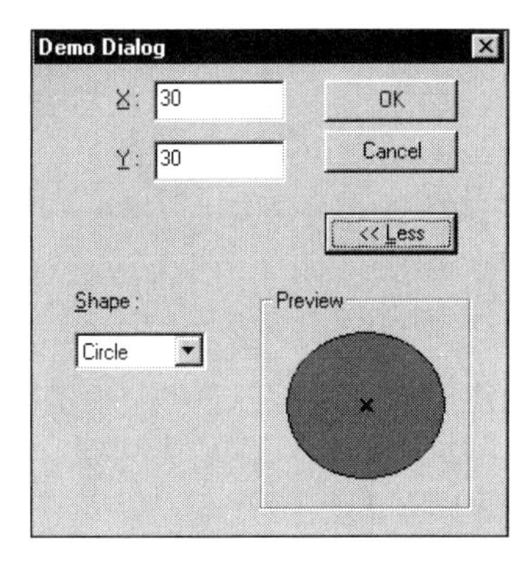

Figure 4-12. The Demo dialog in the expanded state.

Step 1. Create your expanded dialog box as usual using the Visual C++ Resource Editor. Prepare the dialog box by adding the following three special elements (see Figure 4-13):

- The More/Less command button (with an ID of *IDC_EXPAND* in the following discussion).
- The boundary of the collapsed dialog box (a Picture control with an ID of *IDC_SMALL* in the following discussion).
- The boundary of the expanded dialog box (a Picture control with an ID of *IDC_LARGE* in the following discussion).

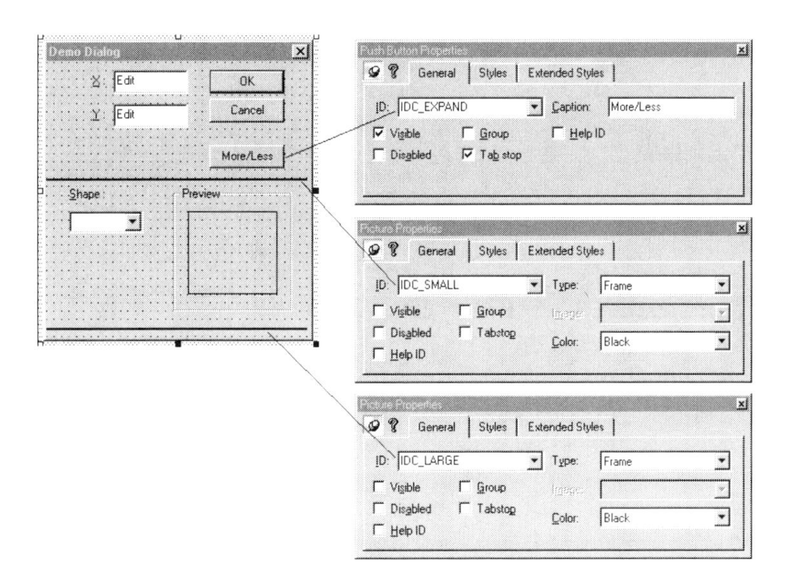

Figure 4-13. Designing an expanding dialog box.

Step 2. Create a string resource having the same ID as the More/Less command button. This string resource is made of two parts separated by the *"\n"* character. The first part of this string contains the "More" caption of the More/Less button, and the second part contains the "Less" caption of the same button. As an example, here is what this string looks like in the sample project for this FAQ: *"&More >>\n<< &Less".*

Step 3. Implement *EkExpandDialog()* as shown in Listing 4-20. You need only call this function whenever you wish to expand or collapse your dialog boxes, and it takes care of all the messy details for you.

Listing 4-20. Implementing *EkExpandDialog()* to expand or collapse a dialog box.

```
void EkExpandDialog( CDialog* pDlg,
                     UINT nSmallID, UINT nLargeID,
                     UINT nButtonID )
{
   ASSERT_VALID( pDlg );

   // 1 - Get the More/Less button control
   CWnd* pWndButton = pDlg->GetDlgItem( nButtonID );
   ASSERT_VALID( pWndButton );

   // 2 - Load button resource string and
   // parse More/Less parts
   CString strButton;
   VERIFY( strButton.LoadString( nButtonID ) );

   CString strMore, strLess;
   AfxExtractSubString( strMore, strButton, 0, _T('\n') );
   AfxExtractSubString( strLess, strButton, 1, _T('\n') );

   // 3 - Find out if we need to expand or
   // collapse the dialog
   CString strCaption;
   pWndButton->GetWindowText( strCaption );
   BOOL bExpand = ( strCaption == strMore );   // Collapse
                                               // by default

   // 4 - Get current dialog window rectangle
   CRect rcDialog;
   pDlg->GetWindowRect( &rcDialog );
   int nNewHeight = -1;
```

```
if( bExpand )
{
   // 5a - Change More/Less button caption
   pWndButton->SetWindowText( strLess );

   // 6a - Calculate new dialog height
   CWnd* pWndLarge = pDlg->GetDlgItem( nLargeID );
   ASSERT_VALID( pWndLarge );

   CRect rcLarge;
   pWndLarge->GetWindowRect( &rcLarge );

   nNewHeight = rcLarge.top-rcDialog.top;
}
else
{
   // 5b - Change More/Less button caption
   pWndButton->SetWindowText( strMore );

   // 6b - Calculate new dialog height
   CWnd* pWndSmall = pDlg->GetDlgItem( nSmallID );
   ASSERT_VALID( pWndSmall );

   CRect rcSmall;
   pWndSmall->GetWindowRect( &rcSmall );

   nNewHeight = rcSmall.top-rcDialog.top;
}

// 7 - Set new dialog height
ASSERT( nNewHeight > 0 );
pDlg->SetWindowPos( NULL, 0, 0,
                    rcDialog.Width(), nNewHeight,
                    SWP_NOMOVE | SWP_NOZORDER );

// 8 - Set the enabled state for each control depending
// on whether the control is currently visible or not
CWnd* pWndControl = pDlg->GetWindow( GW_CHILD );
while( pWndControl != NULL )
{
```

```
        CRect rcControl;
        pWndControl->GetWindowRect( &rcControl );
        pWndControl->EnableWindow(
                rcControl.top <= rcDialog.top + nNewHeight );
        pWndControl = pWndControl->GetWindow( GW_HWNDNEXT );
    }

    // 9 - Check if a control still has the focus
    // (can lose it if the active control becomes disabled)
    CWnd* pWndActiveControl = CWnd::GetFocus();
    if( pWndActiveControl == NULL )
    {

        // 10 - Set focus to "first" control on dialog
        CWnd* pWndFirstControl = pDlg->GetNextDlgTabItem(
                                                      NULL );
        ASSERT_VALID( pWndFirstControl );
        ASSERT( pWndFirstControl->IsWindowEnabled() );
        pWndFirstControl->SetFocus();
    }
}
```

Step 4. Use ClassWizard to add a handler in your dialog class for the *BN_CLICKED* message on the More/Less button. Implement this handler as shown in Listing 4-21 to automatically expand or collapse your dialog box.

Listing 4-21. Handling the *BN_CLICKED* message on the More/Less button to automatically expand or collapse your dialog box.

```
void CDemoDlg::OnExpand()
{
    // Expand or collapse the dialog box
    EkExpandDialog(this, IDC_SMALL, IDC_LARGE, IDC_EXPAND);
}
```

Step 5. Use ClassWizard to add a handler in your dialog class for the *WM_INITDIALOG* message. Implement this handler as shown in Listing 4-22 to have the dialog box initially appear collapsed.

Listing 4-22. Handling the *WM_INITDIALOG* message to have the dialog box initially appear collapsed.

```
BOOL CDemoDlg::OnInitDialog()
{
   CDialog::OnInitDialog();

   // Initially collapse the dialog box
   EkExpandDialog(this, IDC_SMALL, IDC_LARGE, IDC_EXPAND);

   return TRUE;
}
```

■

Explanations

As you can see, most of the interesting work is performed by *EkExpandDialog()*. I tried to design this function to be as flexible and general as possible while minimizing the work required to implement an expanding dialog box.

As a consequence, most of the work you have to do beyond implementing *EkExpandDialog()* itself—merely involves defining some resources and calling *EkExpandDialog()* once or twice from your own code.

EkExpandDialog() has the following commented prototype:

```
void EkExpandDialog(
        CDialog* pDlg,    // Dialog box to expand or collapse
        UINT nSmallID,    // "Collapsed" boundary control
        UINT nLargeID,    // "Expanded" boundary control
        UINT nButtonID    // "More/Less" button & string
                   );
```

Here is a broad overview of the steps this function goes through to accomplish its goal:

- Find out whether the dialog needs to be expanded or collapsed by comparing the current caption of the *nButtonID* control with the "More" part of the *nButtonID* string resource. If the button's caption currently matches the "More" string part, the dialog is expanded; otherwise, the dialog is collapsed.

- Change the caption of the *nButtonID* control to accurately reflect the new state of the dialog. Change the height of the dialog window to align its lower border on either the *nSmallID* or the *nLargeID* control.
- Iterate through all the controls on the dialog box and enable or disable each control depending on whether it is currently visible. This step ensures that the user cannot access a hidden control either with the Tab key or by using a keyboard shortcut.
- Last but not least, make sure that some visible control has the focus. Otherwise, the user can sometimes cause the control having the focus to become disabled by collapsing the dialog box by using the keyboard shortcut to the More/Less button while the focus is on a control that will be hidden in the collapsed state. This situation in turn disables all keyboard access to the dialog box until the user clicks on a visible control.

The body of *EkExpandDialog()* that is shown in Listing 4-20 contains detailed comments that explain the implementation of these operations.

Additional Comments

My implementation of *EkExpandDialog()* uses the undocumented *AfxExtractSubString()* function. You may find this last function useful each time you need to parse a string that is composed of various substrings separated by a special character. MFC internally calls this function to parse the famous document template string and the menu prompt (which has the form *"menu prompt \n tooltip"*).

Here is the commented prototype for *AfxExtractSubString()* (from AfxWin.h):

```
BOOL AFXAPI AfxExtractSubString(
        CString& rString,          // String to hold result
        LPCTSTR lpszFullString,    // String to extract from
        int iSubString,            // Index of substring
                                   // (zero-based)
        TCHAR chSep = '\n'         // Substring separator
                                  );
```

The pseudocode for *AfxExtractSubString()* is shown in Listing 4-23.

Listing 4-23. Pseudocode for the *AfxExtractSubString()* function (WinStr.cpp).

```
BOOL AFXAPI AfxExtractSubString(CString& rString,
                                LPCTSTR lpszFullString,
                                int iSubString,
                                TCHAR chSep)
{
   if (lpszFullString == NULL)
      return FALSE;

   // for each substring...
   while (iSubString—)
   {
      // advance pointer to next separator
      lpszFullString = _tcschr(lpszFullString, chSep);
      if (lpszFullString == NULL)
      {
         // if no separator found, return empty string
         rString.Empty();
         return FALSE;
      }
      lpszFullString++;     // point past the separator
   }

   // now find length of substring (may be last substring)
   LPCTSTR lpchEnd = _tcschr(lpszFullString, chSep);
   int nLen = (lpchEnd == NULL) ?
                  lstrlen(lpszFullString)
                : (int)(lpchEnd - lpszFullString);
   ASSERT(nLen >= 0);

   // copy substring into rString argument
   memcpy(rString.GetBufferSetLength(nLen), lpszFullString,
          nLen*sizeof(TCHAR));
   return TRUE;
}
```

Sample Code

- Project: ExpandingDialog in the Chap04 subdirectory on the companion CD-ROM.
- Purpose: Displays a dialog box that can be expanded to show a preview area or collapsed to show only the current coordinates, as shown earlier in Figures 4-11 and 4-12.

Implementation Highlights

- *EkExpandDialog()* function (DemoDlg.cpp)
- *CDemoDlg::OnExpand()* function (DemoDlg.cpp)
- *CDemoDlg::OnInitDialog()* function (DemoDlg.cpp)

See Also

- *FAQ 4.5 How do I add a preview area to (draw inside) a dialog box?*

4.8 How do I add a toolbar to a dialog box?

Even though toolbars are ubiquitous in most Windows applications, they usually show up only in the application's main window and not in any of its dialog boxes. As a result, adding a toolbar to an MFC dialog box is a little more involved than it should be.

The solution can be broken into two parts: first, add the toolbar to the dialog box; then add support for the *UPDATE_COMMAND_UI* mechanism to the toolbar. Note that you might not need to implement this second part if your toolbar does not need to display visual feedback to the user. However, in my experience this situation does not occur very frequently, and you will usually have to support the *UPDATE_COMMAND_UI* mechanism as explained on page 308.

Adding the Toolbar to the Dialog Box

Step 1. Use the Visual C++ Resource Editor to create the new toolbar resource corresponding to the toolbar that you want to add to your dialog box.

Step 2. Manually add a member variable of type *CToolBar* to your dialog class, as shown in Listing 4-24.

Listing 4-24. Adding a *CToolBar* member variable to your dialog class.

```
class CDemoDlg : public CDialog
{
// ...

// Implementation
protected:
   CToolBar    m_wndToolBar;  // dialog toolbar

// ...
};
```

Step 3. Use ClassWizard to add a handler in your dialog class for the *WM_INITDIALOG* message. Implement this handler as shown in Listing 4-25 to create the toolbar and correctly integrate it into the dialog box.

Listing 4-25. Handling the *WM_INITDIALOG* message to create the toolbar and integrate it into the dialog box.

```
BOOL CDemoDlg::OnInitDialog()
{
   CDialog::OnInitDialog();

   // 1 - Create the toolbar
   if (!m_wndToolBar.Create(this) ||
       !m_wndToolBar.LoadToolBar(IDR_DLG_TOOLBAR))
   {
      TRACE0("Failed to create dialog toolbar\n");
      EndDialog( IDCANCEL );
   }

   // 2 - Figure out how big the control bar(s) are.
   CRect rcClientStart;
   CRect rcClientNow;
   GetClientRect(rcClientStart);
```

```
    RepositionBars(AFX_IDW_CONTROLBAR_FIRST,
                   AFX_IDW_CONTROLBAR_LAST,
                   0, reposQuery, rcClientNow);

    // 3 - Move all the controls so they are in the same
    // relative position within the remaining client area as
    // they would be with no control bar(s).
    CPoint ptOffset(rcClientNow.left - rcClientStart.left,
                    rcClientNow.top - rcClientStart.top);

    CRect  rcChild;
    CWnd*  pwndChild = GetWindow(GW_CHILD);
    while (pwndChild)
    {
       pwndChild->GetWindowRect(rcChild);
       ScreenToClient(rcChild);
       rcChild.OffsetRect(ptOffset);
       pwndChild->MoveWindow(rcChild, FALSE);
       pwndChild = pwndChild->GetNextWindow();
    }

    // 4 - Adjust the dialog window dimensions to make room
    // for the control bar(s)
    CRect rcWindow;
    GetWindowRect(rcWindow);
    rcWindow.right += rcClientStart.Width() -
                            rcClientNow.Width();
    rcWindow.bottom += rcClientStart.Height() -
                            rcClientNow.Height();
    MoveWindow(rcWindow, FALSE);

    // 5 - Position the control bar(s)
    RepositionBars(AFX_IDW_CONTROLBAR_FIRST,
                   AFX_IDW_CONTROLBAR_LAST, 0);

    // 6 - Center the dialog on the screen
    // (this would not happen automatically because the
    // dialog window's size changed during the WM_INITDIALOG
    // processing)
    CenterWindow();

    return TRUE;
}
```

Step 4. Manually add handlers in your dialog class for the *WM_COMMAND* messages associated with your toolbar buttons. For each handler that you want to add, execute the actions described in steps 4a and 4b.

Step 4a. Add the function prototype of your *WM_COMMAND* handler to your dialog's class definition:

```
class CDemoDlg : public CDialog
{
// ...

   // Generated message map functions
   //{{AFX_MSG(CDemoDlg)
   // ...

   afx_msg void OnDrawSquare();
   afx_msg void OnDrawCircle();
   // ...
   //}}AFX_MSG
   DECLARE_MESSAGE_MAP()
};
```

Step 4b. Add an *ON_COMMAND()* macro entry to the message map of your dialog class:

```
BEGIN_MESSAGE_MAP(CDemoDlg, CDialog)
   //{{AFX_MSG_MAP(CDemoDlg)
   // ...
   ON_COMMAND(ID_DRAW_SQUARE, OnDrawSquare)
   ON_COMMAND(ID_DRAW_CIRCLE, OnDrawCircle)
   // ...
   //}}AFX_MSG_MAP
END_MESSAGE_MAP()
```

Step 5. Implement each *ON_COMMAND* handler added in step 4. For example:

```
void CDemoDlg::OnDrawSquare()
{
   m_cmbShape.SetCurSel( CDrawDoc::SQUARE );
}
```

```
void CDemoDlg::OnDrawCircle()
{
   m_cmbShape.SetCurSel( CDrawDoc::CIRCLE );
}
```

Adding support for the UPDATE_COMMAND_UI *mechanism*

Step 6. Manually create a *CDlgToolBar* class that is derived from the standard *CToolBar* class. Implement this class as shown in Listing 4-26 to handle the *WM_IDLEUPDATECMDUI* private MFC message correctly.

Listing 4-26. Implementation of the *CDlgToolBar* class to handle the *WM_IDLEUPDATECMDUI* private MFC message correctly.

```
// ————————————————————————————
// Class definition for CDlgToolBar (DlgToolBar.h)

class CDlgToolBar : public CToolBar
{
protected:
   // Generated message map functions
   //{{AFX_MSG(CDlgToolBar)

   afx_msg LRESULT OnIdleUpdateCmdUI(WPARAM wParam,LPARAM);
   //}}AFX_MSG
   DECLARE_MESSAGE_MAP()
};

// ————————————————————————————
// Implementation for CDlgToolBar (DlgToolBar.cpp)

#include "DlgToolBar.h"
#include <afxpriv.h>    // for WM_IDLEUPDATECMDUI

// ...

BEGIN_MESSAGE_MAP(CDlgToolBar, CToolBar)
   //{{AFX_MSG_MAP(CDlgToolBar)
   ON_MESSAGE(WM_IDLEUPDATECMDUI, OnIdleUpdateCmdUI)
   //}}AFX_MSG_MAP
END_MESSAGE_MAP()
```

```
// ...

///////////////////////////////////////////////////////////
// CDlgToolBar::OnIdleUpdateCmdUI
//   CToolBar::OnUpdateCmdUI() expects a CFrameWnd pointer
//   as its first parameter.  However, it passes this
//   parameter only to other functions that require only a
//   "plain" CCmdTarget pointer.
//   So, to make the compiler happy, we simply
//   cast our parent's CWnd pointer into a CFrameWnd
//   pointer before calling CToolBar::OnUpdateCmdUI().
//   This is certainly not elegant, but it works!

LRESULT CDlgToolBar::OnIdleUpdateCmdUI(
                              WPARAM wParam, LPARAM)
{
   if (IsWindowVisible())
   {
      CFrameWnd *pParent = (CFrameWnd *)GetParent();
      if (pParent)
         OnUpdateCmdUI(pParent, (BOOL)wParam);
   }
   return 0L;
}
```

Step 7. In your dialog class, change the declaration of the *CToolBar* member variable added in step 2 to make it a member variable of type *CDlgToolBar*:

```
class CDemoDlg : public CDialog
{
// ...
// Implementation
protected:
   CDlgToolBar    m_wndToolBar;  // dialog toolbar

// ...

};
```

Step 8. Manually add a handler for the *WM_KICKIDLE* private MFC message in your dialog class by executing the actions explained in steps 8a through 8c.

Step 8a. Include the *<afxpriv.h>* MFC file that defines the *WM_KICKIDLE* private MFC message in your dialog's implementation source file (.cpp).

Step 8b. Add the function prototype of your *WM_KICKIDLE* handler to your dialog's class definition:

```
class CDemoDlg : public CDialog
{

// ...

   // Generated message map functions
   //{{AFX_MSG(CDemoDlg)
   // ...
   afx_msg void OnKickIdle();
   // ...
   //}}AFX_MSG
   DECLARE_MESSAGE_MAP()
};
```

Step 8c. Add an *ON_MESSAGE_VOID()* macro entry to the message map of your dialog class:

```
BEGIN_MESSAGE_MAP(CDemoDlg, CDialog)
   //{{AFX_MSG_MAP(CDemoDlg)
   // ...
   ON_MESSAGE_VOID(WM_KICKIDLE, OnKickIdle)
   // ...
   //}}AFX_MSG_MAP
END_MESSAGE_MAP()
```

Step 9. Implement the *WM_KICKIDLE* message handler as shown in Listing 4-27 to send the *WM_IDLEUPDATECMDUI* message to all the child windows of your dialog box, including its toolbar.

Listing 4-27. Handling the *WM_KICKIDLE* private MFC message.

```
void CDemoDlg::OnKickIdle()
{
   SendMessageToDescendants( WM_IDLEUPDATECMDUI );
}
```

Step 10. Manually add *UPDATE_COMMAND_UI* handlers to your dialog class. You will need a different handler for each button in your toolbar for which you wish to use the *UPDATE_COMMAND_UI* mechanism. For each handler that you want to add, execute the actions described in steps 10a and 10b.

Step 10a. Add the function prototype of your *UPDATE_COMMAND_UI* handler to your dialog's class definition:

```
class CDemoDlg : public CDialog
{
   // ...

   // Generated message map functions
   //{{AFX_MSG(CDemoDlg)
   // ...
   afx_msg void OnUpdateDrawSquare(CCmdUI* pCmdUI);
   afx_msg void OnUpdateDrawCircle(CCmdUI* pCmdUI);
   // ...
   //}}AFX_MSG
   DECLARE_MESSAGE_MAP()
};
```

Step 10b. Add an *ON_UPDATE_COMMAND_UI()* macro entry to the message map of your dialog class:

```
BEGIN_MESSAGE_MAP(CDemoDlg, CDialog)
   //{{AFX_MSG_MAP(CDemoDlg)
   // ...
   ON_UPDATE_COMMAND_UI(ID_DRAW_SQUARE, OnUpdateDrawSquare)
   ON_UPDATE_COMMAND_UI(ID_DRAW_CIRCLE, OnUpdateDrawCircle)
   // ...
   //}}AFX_MSG_MAP
END_MESSAGE_MAP()
```

Step 11. Implement each *UPDATE_COMMAND_UI* handler added in step 10. These functions are standard *UPDATE_COMMAND_UI* handlers and accomplish their work as usual through the *pCmdUI* argument. For example:

```
void CDemoDlg::OnUpdateDrawSquare(CCmdUI* pCmdUI)
{
   pCmdUI->SetCheck( m_cmbShape.GetCurSel()
                              == CDrawDoc::SQUARE );
}

void CDemoDlg::OnUpdateDrawCircle(CCmdUI* pCmdUI)
{
   pCmdUI->SetCheck( m_cmbShape.GetCurSel()
                              == CDrawDoc::CIRCLE );
}
```

Listing 4-28 shows how these pieces fit together in the sample code for this FAQ.

Listing 4-28. Putting all the pieces together.

```
// ———————————————————————————————
// Class definition for CDemoDlg (DemoDlg.h)

#include "DlgToolBar.h"       // dialog toolbar

class CDemoDlg : public CDialog
{
// ...

// Implementation
protected:
   CDlgToolBar    m_wndToolBar;  // dialog toolbar

   // Generated message map functions
   //{{AFX_MSG(CDemoDlg)
   virtual BOOL OnInitDialog();
   afx_msg void OnDrawSquare();
   afx_msg void OnDrawCircle();
   afx_msg void OnKickIdle();
```

```
    afx_msg void OnUpdateDrawSquare(CCmdUI* pCmdUI);
    afx_msg void OnUpdateDrawCircle(CCmdUI* pCmdUI);
    //}}AFX_MSG
    DECLARE_MESSAGE_MAP()
};

// ___________________________________
// Implementation for CDemoDlg (DemoDlg.cpp)

#include <afxpriv.h>    // for WM_KICKIDLE
                        // and WM_IDLEUPDATECMDUI

// ...

BEGIN_MESSAGE_MAP(CDemoDlg, CDialog)
    //{{AFX_MSG_MAP(CDemoDlg)
    ON_COMMAND(ID_DRAW_SQUARE, OnDrawSquare)
    ON_COMMAND(ID_DRAW_CIRCLE, OnDrawCircle)
    ON_MESSAGE_VOID(WM_KICKIDLE, OnKickIdle)
    ON_UPDATE_COMMAND_UI(ID_DRAW_SQUARE, OnUpdateDrawSquare)
    ON_UPDATE_COMMAND_UI(ID_DRAW_CIRCLE, OnUpdateDrawCircle)
    //}}AFX_MSG_MAP
END_MESSAGE_MAP()

// ...

BOOL CDemoDlg::OnInitDialog()
{
    // Implementation omitted for brevity.
    // (see listing 4-25 on page 305)
}

void CDemoDlg::OnDrawSquare()
{
    m_cmbShape.SetCurSel( CDrawDoc::SQUARE );
}

void CDemoDlg::OnDrawCircle()
{
    m_cmbShape.SetCurSel( CDrawDoc::CIRCLE );
}
```

```
void CDemoDlg::OnKickIdle()
{
   SendMessageToDescendants( WM_IDLEUPDATECMDUI );
}

void CDemoDlg::OnUpdateDrawSquare(CCmdUI* pCmdUI)
{
   pCmdUI->SetCheck( m_cmbShape.GetCurSel()
                        == CDrawDoc::SQUARE );
}

void CDemoDlg::OnUpdateDrawCircle(CCmdUI* pCmdUI)
{
   pCmdUI->SetCheck( m_cmbShape.GetCurSel()
                        == CDrawDoc::CIRCLE );
}
```

■

Additional Comments

You may wonder why we need to define a special *CToolBar*-derived class to take advantage of the *UPDATE_COMMAND_UI* mechanism. The short answer is this: if we don't do it this way, it won't work!

The real reason has to do with the default handling of the *WM_IDLEUPDATECMDUI* message by the *CControlBar* class, whose implementation is shown in Listing 4-29.

Listing 4-29. Pseudocode for the *CControlBar::OnIdleUpdateCmdUI()* function (BarCore.cpp).

```
LRESULT CControlBar::OnIdleUpdateCmdUI(WPARAM wParam,
                                        LPARAM)
{

// ...

   // the style must be visible and if it is docked
   // the dockbar style must also be visible
   if ((GetStyle() & WS_VISIBLE) &&
      (m_pDockBar == NULL ||
```

```
                (m_pDockBar->GetStyle() & WS_VISIBLE)))
    {
        CFrameWnd* pTarget = (CFrameWnd*)GetOwner();
        if (pTarget == NULL || !pTarget->IsFrameWnd())
            pTarget = GetParentFrame();
        if (pTarget != NULL)
            OnUpdateCmdUI(pTarget, (BOOL)wParam);
    }
    return 0L;
}
```

As you can see from the highlighted lines in Listing 4-29, *CControlBar::OnIdleUpdateCmdUI()* explicitly looks for a *frame window*, which it will notify by calling *OnUpdateCmdUI()*. However, when the toolbar is part of a dialog box, this behavior causes the *WM_IDLEUPDATECMDUI* messages to be sent to the main application window, which then sends *UPDATE_COMMAND_UI* messages to its various documents, views, and frame windows. Unfortunately, dialog boxes are not included in this routing map and thus do not get a chance to process these *UPDATE_COMMAND_UI* messages.

Our override for *OnIdleUpdateCmdUI()* shown in Listing 4-26 simply ensures that our dialog box's *UPDATE_COMMAND_UI* handlers will be called to process the *UPDATE_COMMAND_UI* messages associated with our dialog box toolbar.

Sample Code

- Project: ToolbarDialog in the Chap04 subdirectory on the companion CD-ROM.
- Purpose: Displays a dialog box that contains a toolbar and handles the associated *UPDATE_COMMAND_UI* messages, as shown in Figure 4-14.

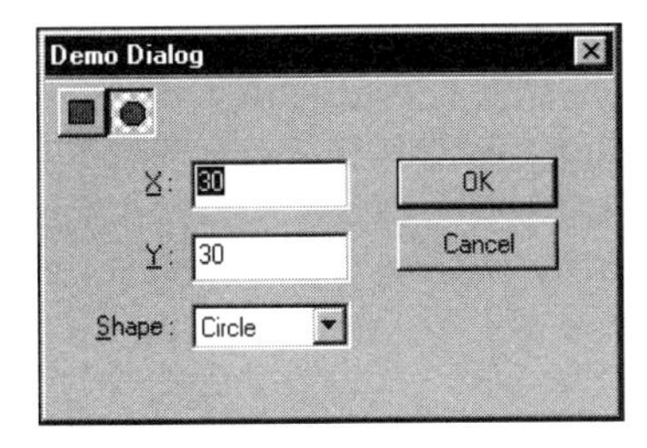

Figure 4-14. A dialog box that contains a toolbar and handles the associated *UPDATE_COMMAND_UI* messages.

Implementation Highlights

- *CDemoDlg::OnInitDialog()* function (DemoDlg.cpp)
- *CDlgToolBar* class (DlgToolBar.h, DlgToolBar.cpp)
- *CDemoDlg::OnKickIdle()* function (DemoDlg.cpp)
- *CDemoDlg::OnUpdateXXX()* functions (DemoDlg.cpp)

See Also

- *FAQ 4.12 How do I use the* UPDATE_COMMAND_UI *mechanism in dialog boxes?*

Managing Controls in a Dialog Box

4.9 How do I choose the control that will initially have the focus when a dialog box is displayed?

When a dialog box is created, Window's default behavior is to set the focus to the first control in the tab order that is capable of receiving the focus.

For some dialog boxes, you must bypass this standard behavior and instead explicitly choose which control will initially have the focus. For example, the first controls on your dialog box might be prefilled for the user by your application, and you wish to position the focus on the first control for which you do not supply a default value.

As with most dialog box initializations, the solution to this problem lies in your dialog box's *OnInitDialog()* function: simply apply *SetFocus()* to the control that you wish to receive the focus, as shown in Listing 4-30. Do not forget to return *FALSE* from your *OnInitDialog()* function to prevent Windows from applying its standard focus-setting behavior.

Listing 4-30. Explicitly setting the focus in *OnInitDialog()*.

```
BOOL CDemoDlg::OnInitDialog()
{
   CDialog::OnInitDialog();
```

```
    // ... other initializations, etc.

    // Case 1 : if you have a member variable of type
    // "control" associated with your control
    m_MyControlVariable.SetFocus();

    // Case 2 : directly access the control
    GetDlgItem( IDC_MYCONTROL )->SetFocus();

    return FALSE;  // prevent Windows from setting the focus
}
```

■

Sample Code

There is no sample project for this FAQ.

FAQ 4.10 How do I implement custom validation rules in a dialog box?

Although MFC's support for dialog data exchange and validation (DDX / DDV) greatly simplifies the display and input of data via dialog boxes, the standard validation rules supported by ClassWizard and the *DDV_xxx()* functions are often too simplistic for real-life applications. Shortcomings of these standard validation rules include the following:

- The validation code generated by ClassWizard is based entirely on static values. However, in many applications some numerical limits may vary depending on the current context. For example, the maximum discount percentage that can be applied to an item in a sales management application may vary depending on the authority level of the currently logged-on user.
- Each *DDV_xxx()* validation rule looks at only one individual control to decide whether its value is appropriate. In contrast, many real-life validation rules must check the consistency of some control values depending on their relationships with the values of other controls. For example, a discount percentage might be limited to different discount values depending on the chosen payment method, which might be indicated by a selection in another control on the same dialog box.

As you may know, the dialog data exchange and validation mechanism is orchestrated by the *DoDataExchange()* member function of your dialog class. Usually, ClassWizard writes all the code inside this function as you bind your dialog's controls to member variables. As is often the case with MFC, all it takes to replace the default behavior with the one you need is to write the correct code yourself.

For example, let us take the standard Demo dialog featured in most sample projects for this chapter and implement the following "business rules":

- If the chosen shape is square, then the values for *X* and *Y* must each lie between 100 and 300.
- If the chosen shape is circle, then the values for *X* and *Y* must each lie between 0 and 100 *and Y* must be greater than (or equal to) *X*.

(By the way, do not search for any meaning in these rules: I know that they are perfectly silly, but they allow me to show various kinds of validation rules. The concepts are important here and not the rules themselves.)

Listing 4-31 shows how to modify *CDemoDlg::DoDataExchange()* to implement the validation rules.

Listing 4-31. Modifying *CDemoDlg::DoDataExchange()* to implement specific validation rules.

```
void CDemoDlg::DoDataExchange(CDataExchange* pDX)
{
   // 1 - Standard Class Wizard-generated stuff

   CDialog::DoDataExchange(pDX);
   //{{AFX_DATA_MAP(CDemoDlg)
   DDX_Control(pDX, IDC_SHAPE, m_cmbShape);
   DDX_Control(pDX, IDC_Y, m_edtY);
   DDX_Control(pDX, IDC_X, m_edtX);
   DDX_Text(pDX, IDC_X, m_nX);
   DDX_Text(pDX, IDC_Y, m_nY);
   DDX_CBIndex(pDX, IDC_SHAPE, m_nShape);
   //}}AFX_DATA_MAP

   // 2 - Here come our custom validation rules
   if( m_nShape == CDrawDoc::SQUARE )
   {
```

```
        // 3 - Validate "100 < X < 300"
        pDX->PrepareEditCtrl( IDC_X );
        DDV_MinMaxInt( pDX, m_nX, 100, 300 );

        // 4 - Validate "100 < Y < 300"
        pDX->PrepareEditCtrl( IDC_Y );
        DDV_MinMaxInt( pDX, m_nY, 100, 300 );
    }
    else
    {

        // 5 - Validate "0 < X < 100"
        pDX->PrepareEditCtrl( IDC_X );
        DDV_MinMaxInt( pDX, m_nX, 0, 100 );

        // 6 - Validate "0 < Y < 100"
        pDX->PrepareEditCtrl( IDC_Y );
        DDV_MinMaxInt( pDX, m_nY, 0, 100 );

        // 7 - Validate "Y >= X" (custom validation)
        pDX->PrepareEditCtrl( IDC_Y );
        if( pDX->m_bSaveAndValidate && m_nY < m_nX )
        {

            // 8 - Display error message to the user
            CString prompt;
            prompt.Format(
                "Error: Y (%d) should be greater than X (%d).",
                 m_nY, m_nX );
            AfxMessageBox( prompt, MB_ICONEXCLAMATION );
            prompt.Empty(); // exception prep

            // 9 - Fail the validation
            pDX->Fail();   // note: throws a CUserException
        }
    }
}
```

■

Explanations

The code shown in Listing 4-31 illustrates the main points of custom validation rules:

- Before validating a control, call either *pDX->PrepareEditCtrl()* or *pDX->PrepareCtrl()*, depending on whether the control is an edit control. This is necessary so that the focus can return to the correct control in the event of a validation failure.
- You can call the standard *DDV_xxx()* functions with your own arguments to perform some kinds of validations. For example, you could validate that one field's value is in the range of two other controls by writing a call such as *DDV_MinMaxInt(pDX, m_nFieldToValidate, m_nMinField, m_nMaxField)*.
- When writing a custom validation block (such as block 7 in Listing 4-31), always start by checking the value of *pDX->m_bSaveAndValidate*. Execute your validation code only if this variable is set to *TRUE*. Remember that the *DoDataExchange()* function is also called with *pDX->m_bSaveAndValidate* set to *FALSE* to copy values from your C++ dialog object's data members into the Windows dialog's controls.
- To fail a validation, simply call *pDX->Fail()*. Be warned that this function throws an exception of type *CUserException*, which is normally caught by the *CWnd::UpdateData()* function that called your *DoDataExchange()* function in the first place. Therefore, the flow of control will not return to the line following the *pDX->Fail()* function call.

Additional Comments

If you are curious about the DDX / DDV functions and the *CDataExchange* member functions, you can find their implementations inside the DlgData.cpp file.

Sample Code

- Project: ValidationRules in the Chap04 subdirectory on the companion CD-ROM.
- Purpose: Implements a dialog box with custom validation rules.

Implementation Highlights

- *CDemoDlg::DoDataExchange()* function (DemoDlg.cpp)

How do I change the font and color of controls in a dialog box?

Even though the standard *Windows User Interface Guidelines* does not mandate it, it sometimes makes sense to change the font and color of some controls on your dialog boxes. One good reason for this might be to visually differentiate between required, calculated, and normal fields on a data-entry dialog box. You can achieve this goal with the following techniques, which can be used independently or together.

Changing the Color of Dialog Box Controls

To manage the color of the controls on your dialog box, use ClassWizard to add a handler in your dialog class for the *WM_CTLCOLOR* message. Implement this handler as shown in Listing 4-32.

Listing 4-32. Handling the *WM_CTLCOLOR* message to manage the color of the controls on a dialog box.

```
HBRUSH CDemoDlg::OnCtlColor(CDC* pDC, CWnd* pWnd,
                            UINT nCtlColor)
{
   HBRUSH hbr = CDialog::OnCtlColor(pDC, pWnd, nCtlColor);

   // IDC_STATIC_X and IDC_STATIC_Y controls
   // draw their text in BLUE
   if( pWnd->GetDlgCtrlID() == IDC_STATIC_X
       || pWnd->GetDlgCtrlID() == IDC_STATIC_Y )
   {
      pDC->SetTextColor( RGB( 0, 0, 255 ) );  //  BLUE
   }

   // IDC_X and IDC_Y controls draw their text in RED
   if( pWnd->GetDlgCtrlID() == IDC_X
       || pWnd->GetDlgCtrlID() == IDC_Y )
   {
      pDC->SetTextColor( RGB( 255, 0, 0 ) );  // RED
   }

   return hbr;
}
```

Changing the Font of Dialog Box Controls

Step 1. For each custom font that you will need, define a member variable of type *CFont* in your dialog box class:

```
class CDemoDlg : public CDialog
{
// ...

// Implementation
protected:
   CFont m_font1, m_font2;       // Custom fonts

// ...

};
```

Step 2. In your dialog box's *OnInitDialog()* function, create each of the fonts that you declared in step 1 and use *CWnd::SetFont()* to apply the new fonts to the appropriate controls, as shown in Listing 4-33.

Listing 4-33. Creating custom fonts and applying them to dialog controls.

```
BOOL CDemoDlg::OnInitDialog()
{
   CDialog::OnInitDialog();
   // ...

   CClientDC dc( this );      // need a DC for
                              // GetDeviceCaps() below

   LOGFONT lf;    // logical font structure
   ::ZeroMemory( &lf, sizeof( lf ) );

   // 12 point Times bold
   lf.lfHeight = - MulDiv( 12,
                           dc.GetDeviceCaps( LOGPIXELSX ),
                           72 );
   lf.lfWidth            = 0;
   lf.lfEscapement       = 0;
   lf.lfOrientation      = 0;
   lf.lfWeight           = FW_BOLD;
   lf.lfItalic           = FALSE;
   lf.lfUnderline        = FALSE;
```

```
    lf.lfStrikeOut       = FALSE;
    lf.lfCharSet         = DEFAULT_CHARSET;
    lf.lfOutPrecision    = OUT_DEFAULT_PRECIS;
    lf.lfClipPrecision   = CLIP_DEFAULT_PRECIS;
    lf.lfQuality         = DEFAULT_QUALITY;
    lf.lfPitchAndFamily = VARIABLE_PITCH | FF_ROMAN;

    // Create font
    m_font1.CreateFontIndirect( &lf );

    // Set control font
    GetDlgItem( IDC_STATIC_X )->SetFont( &m_font1 );
    GetDlgItem( IDC_STATIC_Y )->SetFont( &m_font1 );

    // 12 point Arial bold italic
    lf.lfItalic          = TRUE;
    lf.lfPitchAndFamily = VARIABLE_PITCH | FF_SWISS;

    // Create font
    m_font2.CreateFontIndirect( &lf );

    // Set control font
    GetDlgItem( IDC_X )->SetFont( &m_font2 );
    GetDlgItem( IDC_Y )->SetFont( &m_font2 );

    // ...
}
```

■

Explanations

The *WM_CTLCOLOR* message is discussed in the Explanations section of *FAQ 3.31 How do I change the background color of a form view?*

Sample Code

- Project: CustomControlDlg in the Chap04 subdirectory on the companion CD-ROM.
- Purpose: Displays a dialog box with custom fonts and colors for the X and Y labels and edit boxes, as shown in Figure 4-15.

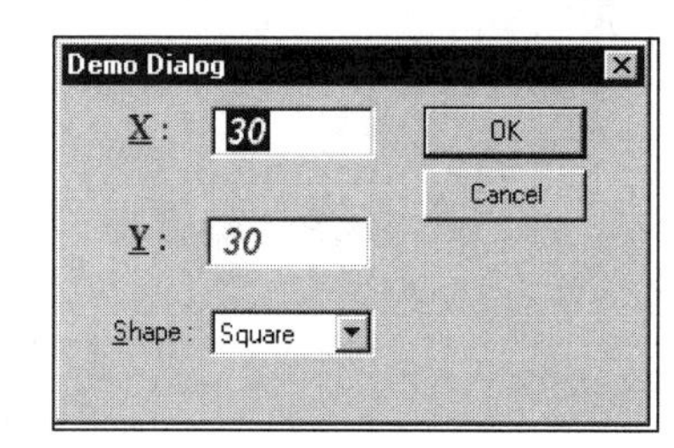

Figure 4-15. A dialog box with custom fonts and colors for the X and Y labels and edit boxes.

Implementation Highlights

- *CDemoDlg::OnCtlColor()* function (DemoDlg.cpp)
- *CDemoDlg::OnInitDialog()* function (DemoDlg.cpp)

See Also

- *FAQ 3.31 How do I change the background color of a form view?*

FAQ 4.12 How do I use the *UPDATE_COMMAND_UI* mechanism in dialog boxes?

The *UPDATE_COMMAND_UI* mechanism is great for dynamically giving feedback to the user about the state of your application by checking or by enabling or disabling menu commands and toolbar buttons. Unfortunately, ClassWizard doesn't allow you to add *UPDATE_COMMAND_UI* handlers for your dialog controls.

With a little work, however, you can also take advantage of the *UPDATE_COMMAND_UI* mechanism to dynamically update your dialog controls (you may wish to refer to Listing 4-34 to put the following explanations in a meaningful context).

Step 1. Manually add a handler for the *WM_KICKIDLE* private MFC message to your dialog class. To do this, you must execute the actions described in steps 1a through 1c.

Step 1a. Include the *<afxpriv.h>* MFC file that defines the WM_KICKIDLE private MFC message in your dialog's implementation source file (.cpp)

Step 1b. Add the *OnKickIdle()* function prototype to your dialog's class definition:

```
class CDemoDlg : public CDialog
{
// ...
   afx_msg void OnKickIdle();
// ...
};
```

Step 1c. Go to the message map of your dialog class and add an *ON_MESSAGE_VOID()* macro entry that maps the *WM_KICKIDLE* message to *OnKickIdle()*:

```
BEGIN_MESSAGE_MAP(CDemoDlg, CDialog)
   //{{AFX_MSG_MAP(CDemoDlg)
   // ...
   ON_MESSAGE_VOID(WM_KICKIDLE, OnKickIdle)
   // ...
   //}}AFX_MSG_MAP
END_MESSAGE_MAP()
```

Step 2. Implement the *OnKickIdle()* function added in step 1b:

```
void CDemoDlg::OnKickIdle()
{
   UpdateDialogControls( this, FALSE );
}
```

Step 3. Manually add *UPDATE_COMMAND_UI* handlers to your dialog class. You will need a different handler for each control in your dialog box for which you wish to use the *UPDATE_COMMAND_UI* mechanism. For each handler that you want to add, execute the actions described in steps 3a and 3b. In this example, we add an *OnUpdateEmpty()* function that conditionally enables or disables a button depending on whether an edit box is empty.

Step 3a. Add the function prototype of your *UPDATE_COMMAND_UI* handler to your dialog's class definition:

```
class CDemoDlg : public CDialog
{
```

```
// ...
   afx_msg void OnUpdateEmpty( CCmdUI* pCmdUI );
// ...
};
```

Step 3b. Add an *ON_UPDATE_COMMAND_UI()* macro entry to the message map of your dialog class:

```
BEGIN_MESSAGE_MAP(CDemoDlg, CDialog)
   //{{AFX_MSG_MAP(CDemoDlg)
   // ...
   ON_UPDATE_COMMAND_UI(IDC_EMPTY, OnUpdateEmpty)
   // ...
   //}}AFX_MSG_MAP
END_MESSAGE_MAP()
```

Step 4. Implement each *UPDATE_COMMAND_UI* handler added in step 3. These functions are standard *UPDATE_COMMAND_UI* handlers and accomplish their work as usual through the *pCmdUI* argument. For example:

```
void CDemoDlg::OnUpdateEmpty( CCmdUI* pCmdUI )
{
   pCmdUI->Enable( m_edtEdit.GetWindowTextLength() > 0 );
}
```

Listing 4-34 shows how these different pieces fit together in the sample code for this FAQ.

Listing 4-34. Implementing a dialog class that uses the *UPDATE_COMMAND_UI* mechanism.

```
// ——————————————————————————————————
// Class definition for CDemoDlg (DemoDlg.h)

class CDemoDlg : public CDialog
{

// ...

// Implementation
protected:
```

```
    // Generated message map functions
    //{{AFX_MSG(CDemoDlg)
    afx_msg void OnKickIdle();
    afx_msg void OnUpdateChecked( CCmdUI* pCmdUI );
    afx_msg void OnUpdateEmpty( CCmdUI* pCmdUI );
    afx_msg void OnUpdateOK( CCmdUI* pCmdUI );
    //}}AFX_MSG

    DECLARE_MESSAGE_MAP()
};

// ———————————————————————————
// Implementation for CDemoDlg (DemoDlg.cpp)

BEGIN_MESSAGE_MAP(CDemoDlg, CDialog)
    //{{AFX_MSG_MAP(CDemoDlg)
    ON_MESSAGE_VOID(WM_KICKIDLE, OnKickIdle)
    ON_UPDATE_COMMAND_UI(IDC_CHECKED, OnUpdateChecked)
    ON_UPDATE_COMMAND_UI(IDC_EMPTY, OnUpdateEmpty)
    ON_UPDATE_COMMAND_UI(IDOK, OnUpdateOK)
    //}}AFX_MSG_MAP
END_MESSAGE_MAP()

// ...

//////////////////////////////////////////////////////////////
// ON_UPDATE_COMMAND_UI handlers

void CDemoDlg::OnKickIdle()
{
    UpdateDialogControls( this, FALSE );
}

void CDemoDlg::OnUpdateChecked( CCmdUI* pCmdUI )
{
    pCmdUI->Enable( m_chkCheck.GetCheck() == 1 );
}

void CDemoDlg::OnUpdateEmpty( CCmdUI* pCmdUI )
{
    pCmdUI->Enable( m_edtEdit.GetWindowTextLength() > 0 );
}
```

```
void CDemoDlg::OnUpdateOK( CCmdUI* pCmdUI )
{
   pCmdUI->Enable(   m_edtX.GetWindowTextLength() > 0
                     && m_edtY.GetWindowTextLength() > 0 );
}
```

■

Explanations

During idle processing, MFC sends the *WM_IDLEUPDATECMDUI* message to the main frame window and to its direct child windows—toolbars, status bars, and views—which in turn update themselves by using the *CN_UPDATE_COMMAND_UI* message. However, because dialog boxes are not children of the main frame window, they do not get the *WM_IDLEUPDATECMDUI* message to begin with.

To give a dialog box a chance to implement its own idle processing, the MFC team defined the (private) *WM_KICKIDLE* message, which is sent automatically to any MFC dialog box when it gets idle— as soon as there are no more messages waiting in its message queue.

We can take advantage of the *WM_KICKIDLE* message to call *UpdateDialogControls()*, which in turn sends *CN_UPDATE_COMMAND_UI* notifications to all the controls on the dialog box. Here is the prototype of *UpdateDialogControls()*:

```
void CWnd::UpdateDialogControls( CCmdTarget* pTarget,
                                 BOOL bDisableIfNoHndler );
```

The *pTarget* argument identifies the window that will handle the *CN_UPDATE_COMMAND_UI* messages—that is, the C++ class whose message map contains the *ON_UPDATE_COMMAND_UI()* macros associated with the dialog box controls whose state you wish to manage. Because these update handlers are usually implemented in the C++ class associated with the dialog box itself, you usually pass *this* as the *pTarget* argument. However, if you wished to alter the state of the dialog box controls according to the data contained in another C++ object of your application—such as the active document or view—you would simply pass a pointer to this object in the *pTarget* argument. This assumes that you have added the update handlers for the dialog controls in this object's message map.

The *bDisableIfNoHndler* argument controls the behavior of *UpdateDialogControls()* with respect to the eventual absence of

UPDATE_COMMAND_UI handlers: if this argument is set to *TRUE*, any control that does not have an explicit *UPDATE_COMMAND_UI* handler will be disabled, much in the same way that MFC normally disables menu items that do not have associated command handlers. If *bDisableIfNoHndler* is set to *FALSE*, no action at all is taken for controls that do not have an explicit *UPDATE_COMMAND_UI* handler. You usually pass *FALSE* for the *bDisableIfNoHndler* argument unless you want to write update handlers for all the controls on your dialog box.

Additional Comments

In the code shown in Listing 4-34, note the use of the undocumented *ON_MESSAGE_VOID()* macro. This macro allows us to handle the *WM_KICKIDLE* message without having to worry about *wParam* and *lParam* arguments, because these arguments are not used by *WM_KICKIDLE*. This macro makes for somewhat simpler and cleaner code than the more general *ON_MESSAGE()* macro, and I encourage you to use it each time you need to handle a private message that does not use the *wParam* and *lParam* arguments and that does not have a return value.

Sample Code

- Project: UpdateUIDialog in the Chap04 subdirectory on the companion CD-ROM.
- Purpose: Uses the *UPDATE_COMMAND_UI* mechanism in a dialog box, as shown in Figure 4-16.

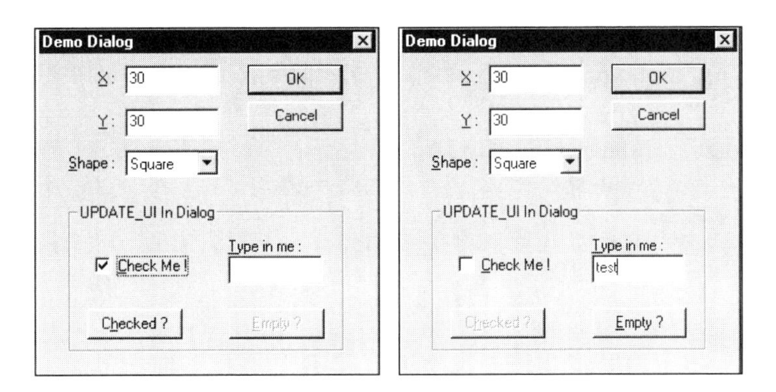

Figure 4-16. Using the *UPDATE_COMMAND_UI* mechanism in a dialog box: compare the enabled/disabled state of the command buttons on the two dialog boxes.

Implementation Highlights

- *CDemoDlg* message map (DemoDlg.cpp)
- *CDemoDlg::OnKickIdle()* function (DemoDlg.cpp)
- *CDemoDlg::OnUpdateXXX()* functions (DemoDlg.cpp)

See Also

- *FAQ 3.30 How do I use the* UPDATE_COMMAND_UI *mechanism in form views?*

4.13 How do I add ToolTips support to the controls in a dialog box?

In addition to their classic use for toolbar buttons, ToolTips can also be useful for explaining the roles of various controls on a dialog box. This is a sure way to enhance the quality of your user interface, and it is not very complex, as the following steps will show.

Step 1. Use ClassWizard to add a member variable of type *Control* for each control on your dialog box.

Step 2. Manually add a member variable of type *CToolTipCtrl* to your dialog class. The definition of your class should now look similar to the one shown in Listing 4-35, where all the new member variables are bold.

Listing 4-35. Adding new control member variables to handle ToolTips.

```
class CDemoDlg : public CDialog
{
// ...

// Dialog Data
    //{{AFX_DATA(CDemoDlg)
    enum { IDD = IDD_DEMO_DIALOG };
    CButton      m_cmdCancel;
    CButton      m_cmdOK;
    CComboBox    m_cmbShape;
```

```
   CEdit        m_edtY;
   CEdit        m_edtX;
   int          m_nX;
   int          m_nY;
   int          m_nShape;
   //}}AFX_DATA

// ...

// Implementation
protected:
   CToolTipCtrl m_ToolTip;    // Tooltip control

// ...
};
```

Step 3. Use ClassWizard to add an override for the *PreTranslateMessage()* function in your dialog class. Implement this function as shown in Listing 4-36 to relay messages to the ToolTip control.

Listing 4-36. Implementing *PreTranslateMessage()* to relay messages to the ToolTip control.

```
BOOL CDemoDlg::PreTranslateMessage(MSG* pMsg)
{
   // Relay events to the ToolTip control
   m_ToolTip.RelayEvent( pMsg );
   return CDialog::PreTranslateMessage(pMsg);
}
```

Step 4. Use ClassWizard to add a handler for the *WM_INITDIALOG* message in your dialog class. Implement this handler as shown in Listing 4-37 to correctly create and initialize the ToolTip control.

Listing 4-37. Handling the *WM_INITDIALOG* message to create and initialize the ToolTip control.

```
BOOL CDemoDlg::OnInitDialog()
{
   CDialog::OnInitDialog();

   // 1 - Create the ToolTip control
   if( !m_ToolTip.Create( this ) )
```

```
    {
      TRACE0( "Unable to create ToolTip control\n" );
    }
    else
    {

       // 2 - Add the dialog box's controls to the ToolTip
       m_ToolTip.AddTool( &m_edtX, IDS_TT_X );
       m_ToolTip.AddTool( &m_edtY, IDS_TT_Y );
       m_ToolTip.AddTool( &m_cmbShape, IDS_TT_SHAPE );
       m_ToolTip.AddTool( &m_cmdOK, IDS_TT_OK );
       m_ToolTip.AddTool( &m_cmdCancel, IDS_TT_CANCEL );

       // 3 - Activate the ToolTip control
       m_ToolTip.Activate( TRUE );
    }

    return TRUE;
}
```

Step 5. Use the Visual C++ Resource Editor to define the string resources that the ToolTip control will display for each control on your dialog box. These strings are the same ones that were referenced in the calls to *AddTool()* in Listing 4-37 (*IDS_TT_X, IDS_TT_SHAPE*, and so forth).

■

Additional Comments

If you wish to turn off the ToolTips—for example, because this is one of your configuration options—simply make the following call:

```
m_ToolTip.Activate( FALSE );
```

Sample Code

- Project: DialogTooltips in the Chap04 subdirectory on the companion CD-ROM.
- Purpose: Adds ToolTips to the controls in a dialog box (see Figure 4-17).

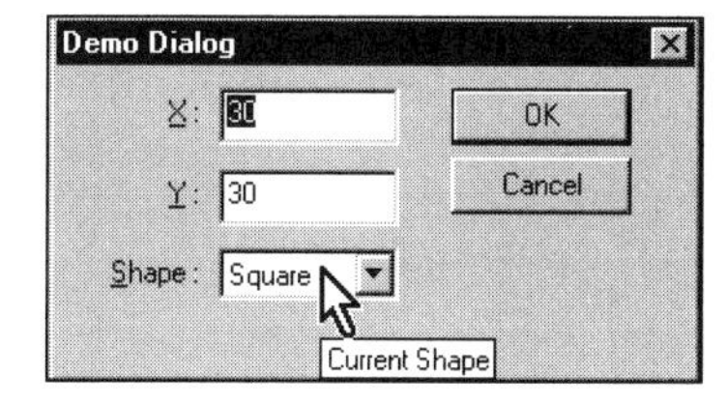

Figure 4-17. ToolTips in dialog boxes are really cool!

Implementation Highlights

- *CDemoDlg::PreTranslateMessage()* function (DemoDlg.cpp)
- *CDemoDlg::OnInitialUpdate()* function (DemoDlg.cpp)

See Also

- *FAQ 3.32 How do I add ToolTips to the controls in a form view?*

5 PROPERTY SHEETS

One dialog box, two dialog boxes, three dialog boxes. . . . Although dialog boxes are useful, users quickly become frustrated when an application forces them to navigate through many dialogs to accomplish what seems to be a single logical task, such as selecting various configuration options or entering complex data.

Property sheets, also called multipage or tabbed dialog boxes, have become a standard way of grouping several dialog boxes inside one window. The user can easily "flip" to one page or another without closing the main dialog window or losing track of the context. As with dialog boxes, MFC and ClassWizard provide an infrastructure that greatly simplifies the process of building property sheets. This chapter addresses some of the rough edges that remain in the everyday use of property sheets, such as *FAQ 5.2 How do I manage the Apply button in a property sheet?*, *FAQ 5.4 How do I customize the standard property sheet buttons?*, and *FAQ 5.8 How do I add icons to the tabs of my property pages?*

Finally, the techniques described in *FAQs 5.9* to *5.12* provide an important—but often overlooked—way of using property sheets that greatly increases their usefulness: as child windows embedded in other windows, such as dialog boxes, form views, splitter windows, and miniframe windows. Be sure to take a look at these FAQs and associated sample programs.

General Topics

How do I build and use a property sheet?

MFC offers very good support for property sheets and property pages through the *CPropertySheet* and *CPropertyPage* classes, but many developers have expressed the need for information about how to use these classes efficiently.

A little background information will clarify the terminology here: the *property sheet* is the outside window that contains a number of *property pages* among which the user can flip by clicking on the *tab control* that is also hosted by the property sheet (see Figures 5-1 and 5-2). Thanks to MFC's support, using property sheets in your application is similar to using plain dialog boxes, and it's almost as easy, especially if you follow the steps explained next.

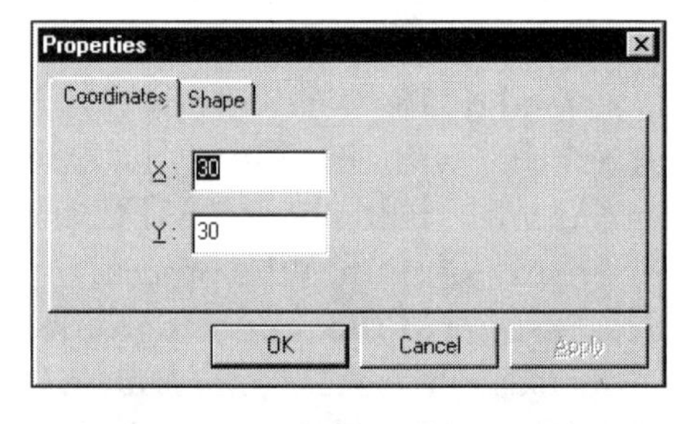

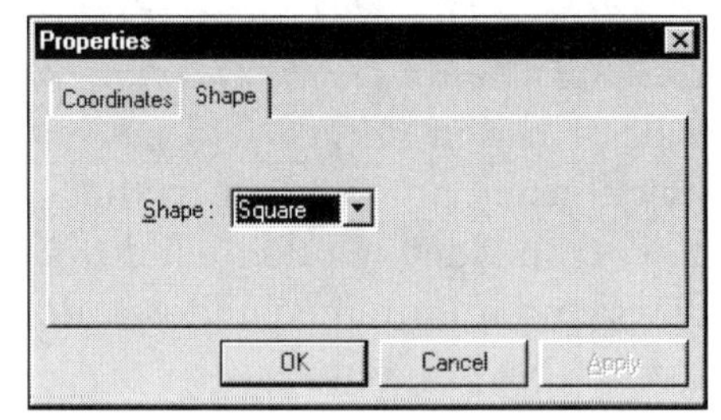

Figure 5-1. The simple property sheet used in most sample projects for this chapter.

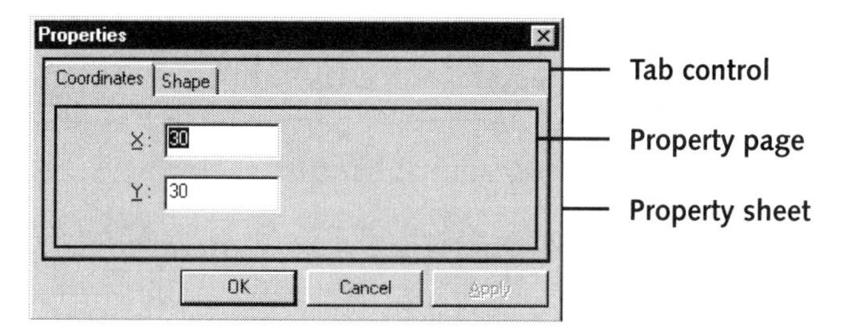

Figure 5-2. Anatomy of a property sheet.

Creating the Property Pages

Step 1. Use the Visual C++ Resource Editor to create a new property page resource: select the "Insert, Resource" menu command, expand the "Dialog" node, select one of the *IDD_PROPPAGE_xxxxx* choices, and finally click on the New button (see Figure 5-3).

Step 2. Lay out the controls on your property page as you would do for a dialog box; however, you do not need to include OK and Cancel buttons, because they will be provided by the property sheet that will contain your property pages. Set the "Caption" property of your property page to the label that you want to show on the associated tab in your finished property sheet.

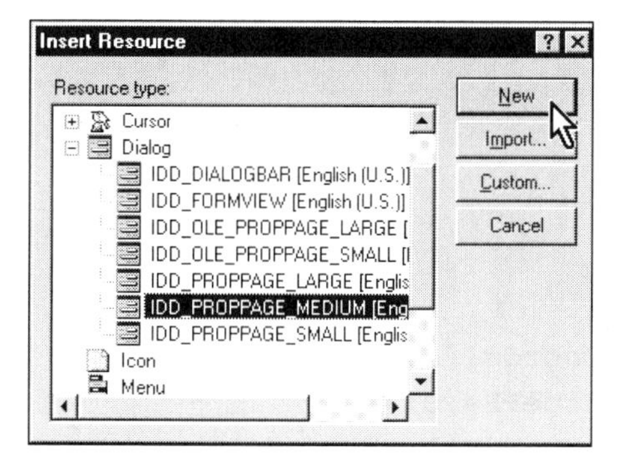

Figure 5-3. Creating a new property page resource.

Step 3. Use ClassWizard to create a new *CPropertyPage*-derived class associated with your property page resource ID. The easiest way to do this is to invoke ClassWizard while your property page resource is opened for editing in the Visual C++ Resource Editor.

Step 4. Use ClassWizard to add member variables to your *CPropertyPage*-derived class, associated with the controls on your property page resource, just as you would do for a standard dialog box.

Step 5. If you want your property page to exhibit dynamic behavior in response to user actions, add the necessary message handlers just as you would do for a standard dialog box. Repeat steps 1–5 for each property page that you want to show in your property sheet.

Creating the Property Sheet

Step 6. Use ClassWizard to create a new *CPropertySheet*-derived class.

Step 7. For each property page that you want to show in your property sheet, add a corresponding member variable to your *CPropertySheet*-derived class, as shown in Listing 5-1.

Listing 5-1. Adding property page member variables to your *CPropertySheet*-derived class.

```
class CCoordsPPage : public CPropertyPage
{ /* ... */ };

class CShapePPage : public CPropertyPage
{ /* ... */ };

class CDemoPSheet : public CPropertySheet
{
// ...
// Attributes
public:
   CCoordsPPage m_CoordsPPage;
   CShapePPage m_ShapePPage;

// ...
};
```

Step 8. Modify the constructor of your property sheet class to call *AddPage()* for each property page variable that you added in step 7, as shown in Listing 5-2. Your property sheet will show its pages in the same order that you use in calling *AddPage()*.

Listing 5-2. Adding the property page to your property sheet in your property sheet class's constructor.

```
CDemoPSheet::CDemoPSheet(UINT nIDCaption, CWnd* pParentWnd,
                         UINT iSelectPage)
   :CPropertySheet(nIDCaption, pParentWnd, iSelectPage)
{
   AddPage( &m_CoordsPPage );   // First page
   AddPage( &m_ShapePPage );    // Second page
}
```

Your property sheet class is now ready to be used.

Using a Property Sheet

You use a property sheet almost like you would use a dialog box, as shown in Listing 5-3. The main difference lies in the fact that the various member variables are not contained directly inside the property sheet class but rather are inside each property page member of the property sheet class.

Listing 5-3. Using a property sheet.

```
void CDrawDoc::OnDemoPSheet()
{
   // 1 - Create the property sheet object
   CDemoPSheet psheet;

   // 2 - Initialize the pages' member variables
   psheet.m_CoordsPPage.m_nX = m_point.x;
   psheet.m_CoordsPPage.m_nY = m_point.y;
   psheet.m_ShapePPage.m_nShape = m_shape;

   // 3 - Show the property sheet to the user
   if( psheet.DoModal() == IDOK )
   {
      // 4 - Read the new values from the
      // pages' member variables
```

```
        m_point.x = psheet.m_CoordsPPage.m_nX;
        m_point.y = psheet.m_CoordsPPage.m_nY;
        m_shape = static_cast< SHAPE >
                          ( psheet.m_ShapePPage.m_nShape );

        SetModifiedFlag( TRUE );
        UpdateAllViews( NULL );
    }
}
```

■

Additional Comments

When it created your property sheet class in step 6, ClassWizard generated the two constructors shown in Listing 5-4. Most of the time, your property sheet class will be easier to use if you remove the second constructor and modify the first one as shown in Listing 5-5, where *IDS_MY_PSHEET_CAPTION* is a string resource that contains the caption of your property sheet. This modification takes into account the fact that a given property sheet will usually keep the same caption, so the corresponding string resource ID can be embedded inside the class.

Listing 5-4. Standard ClassWizard-generated constructors for a property sheet class.

```
// ————————————————————————————
// Class definition for CMyPSheet (MyPSheet.h)

class CMyPSheet : public CPropertySheet
{
    DECLARE_DYNAMIC(CMyPSheet)

// Construction
public:
    CMyPSheet(UINT nIDCaption, CWnd* pParentWnd = NULL,
              UINT iSelectPage = 0);
    CMyPSheet(LPCTSTR pszCaption, CWnd* pParentWnd = NULL,
              UINT iSelectPage = 0);

// ...
};

// ————————————————————————————
// Implementation for CMyPSheet (MyPSheet.cpp)
```

```
CMyPSheet::CMyPSheet(UINT nIDCaption, CWnd* pParentWnd,
                     UINT iSelectPage)
   :CPropertySheet(nIDCaption, pParentWnd, iSelectPage)
{
}

CMyPSheet::CMyPSheet(LPCTSTR pszCaption, CWnd* pParentWnd,
                     UINT iSelectPage)
   :CPropertySheet(pszCaption, pParentWnd, iSelectPage)
{
}
```

Listing 5-5. An easier-to-use property sheet class.

```
// ------------------------------------------
// Class definition for CMyPSheet (MyPSheet.h)

class CMyPSheet : public CPropertySheet
{
   DECLARE_DYNAMIC(CMyPSheet)

// Construction
public:

   CMyPSheet(CWnd* pParentWnd = NULL,
             UINT iSelectPage = 0);

// ...
};

// ------------------------------------------
// Implementation for CMyPSheet (MyPSheet.cpp)

CMyPSheet:: CMyPSheet(CWnd* pParentWnd,
                      UINT iSelectPage)

   :CPropertySheet(IDS_MY_PSHEET_CAPTION, pParentWnd,
                   iSelectPage)

{

   // ... Add your property pages here ...
}
```

If you initially created a plain dialog box resource that you later decide to turn into a property page, you should be careful to apply the correct styles to the resource if you want everything to work properly. Here are the standard property page styles using the Visual C++ Resource Editor:

- Style = Child ("Styles" property page)
- Border = Thin ("Styles" property page)
- Title bar = checked ("Styles" property page)
- System menu = unchecked ("Styles" property page)
- Visible = unchecked ("More Styles" property page)
- Disabled = checked ("More Styles" property page)

If you prefer to edit the .RC resource file directly, modify the *STYLE* line of the script for your dialog resource to read as follows: *STYLE WS_CHILD | WS_DISABLED | WS_CAPTION.*

Sample Code

- Project: PropertySheet in the Chap05 subdirectory on the companion CD-ROM.
- Purpose: Demonstrates how to build and use a simple property sheet, as shown earlier in Figure 5-1.

Implementation Highlights

- *CDemoPSheet* class (DemoPSheet.h, DemoPSheet.cpp)
- *CCoordsPPage* class (CoordsPPage.h, CoordsPPage.cpp)
- *CShapePPage* class (ShapePPage.h, ShapePPage.cpp)
- *CDrawDoc::OnDemoPSheet()* function (DrawDoc.cpp)

FAQ 5.2 How do I manage the Apply button in a property sheet?

Even if it is not rocket science, correctly handling the Apply button for a property sheet can be tricky if you are not careful. The following explanations will clarify the ins and outs of this issue.

Enabling the Apply Button

When a property sheet appears, its Apply button is initially disabled. To enable this button, call the *CPropertyPage::SetModified()* function from each of your property page classes as soon as the user changes any setting, as shown in Listing 5-6.

Listing 5-6. Enabling the Apply button.

```
// ——————————————————————————————
// Class definition for CCoordsPPage (CoordsPPage.h)

class CCoordsPPage : public CPropertyPage
{

// ...

// Implementation
protected:
   // Generated message map functions
   //{{AFX_MSG(CCoordsPPage)
      afx_msg void OnChange();
   //}}AFX_MSG
   DECLARE_MESSAGE_MAP()
};

// ——————————————————————————————
// Implementation for CCoordsPPage (CoordsPPage.cpp)

BEGIN_MESSAGE_MAP(CCoordsPPage, CPropertyPage)
   //{{AFX_MSG_MAP(CCoordsPPage)
   ON_CONTROL_RANGE( EN_CHANGE, IDC_X, IDC_Y, OnChange )
   //}}AFX_MSG_MAP
END_MESSAGE_MAP()

// ...

void CCoordsPPage::OnChange()
{
   SetModified( TRUE );    // Enable "Apply" button
}
```

```
// ———————————————————————————————
// Class definition for CShapePPage (ShapePPage.h)

class CShapePPage : public CPropertyPage
{

// ...

// Implementation
protected:
   // Generated message map functions
   //{{AFX_MSG(CShapePPage)
   afx_msg void OnChange();
   //}}AFX_MSG
   DECLARE_MESSAGE_MAP()
};

// ———————————————————————————————
// Implementation for CShapePPage (ShapePPage.cpp)

BEGIN_MESSAGE_MAP(CShapePPage, CPropertyPage)
   //{{AFX_MSG_MAP(CShapePPage)
   ON_CBN_SELCHANGE(IDC_SHAPE, OnChange)
   //}}AFX_MSG_MAP
END_MESSAGE_MAP()

// ...

void CShapePPage::OnChange()
{
   SetModified( TRUE );    // Enable "Apply" button
}
```

In Listing 5-6, note the use of the *ON_CONTROL_RANGE* message map macro: this macro allows us to use a single function to handle the notifications issued by several controls. This may not seem very important for our sample Coordinates property page, which contains only two edit controls, but recall that real property pages can have a much larger number of edit controls (or option buttons, check boxes, combo boxes, and so on).

Handling the Apply Button

Now that you know how to enable the Apply button, how do you handle the user's click on this button? You handle it by writing a handler in your property sheet class for the *BN_CLICKED* message on the *ID_APPLY_NOW* button (this is a predefined standard ID). However, some details must be worked out so that your property sheet class can correctly notify the application of the user's action.

Step 1. Add a *protected* member variable of type *CYourDoc* to your property sheet class, as shown in Listing 5-7. We will name this member variable *m_pDoc* in the following discussion.

Listing 5-7. The property sheet class with a new *CYourDoc* member variable added.

```
class CDrawDoc;       // Forward declaration

class CDemoPSheet : public CPropertySheet
{
// Construction
public:
   CDemoPSheet(CDrawDoc* pDoc, CWnd* pParentWnd = NULL,
               UINT iSelectPage = 0);

// ...

protected:
   CDrawDoc* m_pDoc; // Pointer to our associated document

// ...

};
```

Step 2. Modify your property sheet's constructor to store the document pointer received as an argument in the *m_pDoc* member variable, as shown in Listing 5-8.

Listing 5-8. Storing the document pointer in the *m_pDoc* member variable.

```
CDemoPSheet::CDemoPSheet(CDrawDoc* pDoc, CWnd* pParentWnd,
                         UINT iSelectPage)
   :CPropertySheet(IDS_PSHEET_CAPTION, pParentWnd,
                   iSelectPage)
```

```
{
   ASSERT_VALID( pDoc );
   m_pDoc = pDoc;

   AddPage( &m_CoordsPPage );    // First page
   AddPage( &m_ShapePPage );     // Second page
}
```

Step 3. Manually add a handler for the *BN_CLICKED* message on the *ID_APPLY_NOW* button in your property sheet class. Implement this function as shown in Listing 5-9. Note that *UpdateData()* is called only for the *active* property page: MFC automatically calls this function when a page is about to be deactivated—because the user switches to another page—so you need update only the variables on the active property page.

Listing 5-9. Implementation of *OnApplyNow()*.

```
void CDemoPSheet::OnApplyNow()
{

   // 1 - Update data for the active property page
   GetActivePage()->UpdateData( TRUE );

   // 2 - Notify document of the user's click
   m_pDoc->OnApply( this );

   // 3 - Reset the "modified" flag for each property page
   for( int i = 0; i < GetPageCount(); ++i )
   {
      GetPage( i )->SetModified( FALSE );
   }
}
```

Step 4. Manually add *OnApply()* in your document class. Implement this function as shown in Listing 5-10.

Listing 5-10. Implementation of *OnApply()*.

```
void CDrawDoc::OnApply( CDemoPSheet* psheet )
{
   ASSERT_VALID( psheet );
```

```
    // 1 - Read the new values from the pages'
    // member variables
    m_point.x = psheet->m_CoordsPPage.m_nX;
    m_point.y = psheet->m_CoordsPPage.m_nY;
    m_shape = static_cast< SHAPE >(
                        psheet->m_ShapePPage.m_nShape );

    // 2 - Update all views
    SetModifiedFlag( TRUE );
    UpdateAllViews( NULL );
}
```

Step 5. Modify your document's function that creates and displays the property sheet to pass the *this* pointer—that points to the active document—to the property sheet constructor and to call *OnApply()*, as shown in Listing 5-11.

Listing 5-11. Passing a pointer to the active document to the property sheet object and calling *OnApply()*.

```
void CDrawDoc::OnDemoPSheet()
{

    // 1 - Create the property sheet object
    CDemoPSheet psheet( this );

    // 2 - Initialize the pages' member variables
    psheet.m_CoordsPPage.m_nX = m_point.x;
    psheet.m_CoordsPPage.m_nY = m_point.y;
    psheet.m_ShapePPage.m_nShape = m_shape;

    // 3 - Show the property sheet to the user
    if( psheet.DoModal() == IDOK )
    {
        // 4 - Apply changes
        OnApply( &psheet );
    }
}
```

Your property sheet's Apply button should now work correctly.

Hiding the Apply Button

If you do not wish to take the trouble to enable and handle the Apply button, you may prefer to hide it rather than leave it disabled. To do this, add the following line to your property sheet constructor:

```
m_psh.dwFlags |= PSH_NOAPPLYNOW;
```

The *m_psh* member of the *CPropertySheet* class is a *PROPSHEETHEADER* structure whose flags control the appearance and behavior of the property sheet window. As its name implies, the *PSH_NOAPPLYNOW* flag removes the Apply button from the property sheet window.

■

Sample Code

- Project: ApplyButton in the Chap05 subdirectory on the companion CD-ROM.
- Purpose: Enables and correctly handles the Apply button on the "demo" property sheet.

Implementation Highlights

- *CCoordsPPage::OnChange()* function (CoordsPPage.cpp)
- *CShapePPage::OnChange()* function (ShapesPPage.cpp)
- *CDemoPSheet::CDemoPSheet()* function (DemoPSheet.cpp)
- *CDemoPSheet::OnApplyNow()* function (DemoPSheet.cpp)
- *CDrawDoc::OnApply()* function (DrawDoc.cpp)
- *CDrawDoc::OnDemoPSheet()* function (DrawDoc.cpp)

See Also

- *FAQ 4.3 How can a dialog box access the active document (or view) object?*
- *FAQ 5.4 How do I customize the standard property sheet buttons?*

How do I programmatically change the active page in a property sheet?

To select the *initially* active page of a property sheet, call *CPropertySheet::SetActivePage()* either in the constructor of your property sheet class or in the code creating the property sheet object—before calling *DoModal()*—as shown in Listing 5-12.

Listing 5-12. Calling *CPropertySheet::SetActivePage()* to change the active page.

```
void CDrawDoc::OnDemoPSheet()
{
   // 1 - Create the property sheet object
   CDemoPSheet psheet;
   // 2 - Initialize the pages' member variables
   psheet.m_CoordsPPage.m_nX = m_point.x;
   psheet.m_CoordsPPage.m_nY = m_point.y;
   psheet.m_ShapePPage.m_nShape = m_shape;

   // 3 -Initially show the 2nd page (index from zero)
   psheet.SetActivePage( 1 );

   // 4 - Show the property sheet to the user
   if( psheet.DoModal() == IDOK )
   {
      // ...
   }
}
```

You can also use *CPropertySheet::SetActivePage()* to programmatically change the active page in response to a user action on another property page. However, you need to go from the context of your property page to the property sheet—that is, the property page's parent window, as shown in Listing 5-13.

Listing 5-13. Programmatically changing the active page inside a property page.

```
void CCoordsPPage::OnGotoShape()
{
   CPropertySheet* pParent = DYNAMIC_DOWNCAST(
```

```
                                CPropertySheet, GetParent() );
    if( pParent )
    {
        pParent->SetActivePage( 1 );  // 2nd page
    }
}
```

■

Additional Comments

The source code for *CPropertySheet::SetActivePage()* is shown in Listing 5-14. As you can see, this function is designed to have the correct behavior when called for either an active or an inactive property sheet.

Listing 5-14. Pseudocode for the *CPropertySheet::SetActivePage()* function (DlgProp.cpp).

```
BOOL CPropertySheet::SetActivePage(int nPage)
{
    if (m_hWnd == NULL)
    {
        // Property sheet not created yet
        m_psh.nStartPage = nPage;
        return TRUE;
    }

    // Send message to property sheet window
    return (BOOL)SendMessage(PSM_SETCURSEL, nPage);
}
```

Sample Code

- Project: SetActivePage in the Chap05 subdirectory on the companion CD-ROM.
- Purpose: Implements a property sheet that demonstrates how to programmatically change the active page when the user clicks on the Coords or Shape button.

Implementation Highlights

- *CDrawDoc::OnDemoPSheet()* function (DrawDoc.cpp)
- *CCoordsPPage::OnGotoShape()* function (CoordsPPage.cpp)
- *CShapePPage::OnGotoCoords()* function (ShapePPage.cpp)

5.4 How do I customize the standard property sheet buttons?

There are two popular ways to customize the standard property sheet buttons:

- Modify the captions of the standard buttons.
- Hide the standard buttons and center the remaining buttons on the property sheet window.

Each of these needs is addressed by the techniques explained next.

Modifying the Captions of the Standard Property Sheet Buttons

When you think about it, the standard property sheet buttons are bona fide child windows of the property sheet window, just like any control you put on a dialog box. Even if you do not explicitly create these buttons, you can manipulate them as you would any window in your property sheet class's *OnInitDialog()* function, provided that you know their IDs: *IDOK*, *IDCANCEL*, and *ID_APPLY_NOW*. Therefore, you can easily modify the captions of the standard property sheet buttons: use ClassWizard to add a handler in your property sheet class for the *WM_INITDIALOG* message, and implement this handler as shown in Listing 5-15.

Listing 5-15. Handling the *WM_INITDIALOG* message to modify the captions of the standard property sheet buttons.

```
BOOL CDemoPSheet::OnInitDialog()
{
   BOOL bResult = CPropertySheet::OnInitDialog();

   // Change "OK" button caption
   CWnd* pWnd = GetDlgItem( IDOK );
```

```
    ASSERT( pWnd != NULL );
    pWnd->SetWindowText( _T( "Accept" ) );

    // Change "Cancel" button caption
    pWnd = GetDlgItem( IDCANCEL );
    ASSERT( pWnd != NULL );
    pWnd->SetWindowText( _T( "Revert" ) );


    // Change "Apply" button caption
    pWnd = GetDlgItem( ID_APPLY_NOW );
    ASSERT( pWnd != NULL );
    pWnd->SetWindowText( _T( "Apply Now" ) );

    return bResult;
}
```

Of course, the new captions need not be hard-coded like the ones shown in Listing 5-15. You can easily refer to string resources or even have these strings (or string resource IDs) passed as arguments to your property sheet class.

Hiding the Standard Property Sheet Buttons

If you can get hold of the windows of the standard property sheet buttons to call *SetWindowText()* on them, you can use the same technique to call *ShowWindow (SW_HIDE)* on these windows. To save you some repetitive typing, Listing 5-16 shows the *EkHidePropertySheetButtons()* function, which conditionally hides any (or all) of the standard property sheet buttons.

Listing 5-16. Implementation of *EkHidePropertySheetButtons()* to conditionally hide any (or all) of the standard property sheet buttons.

```
void EkHidePropertySheetButtons(
                                CPropertySheet* pPSheet,
                                BOOL bHideOK,
                                BOOL bHideCancel,
                                BOOL bHideApply )
{
    ASSERT_VALID( pPSheet );

    // Hide "OK" button
    if( bHideOK )
    {
```

```
      CWnd* pWnd = pPSheet->GetDlgItem( IDOK );
      ASSERT( pWnd != NULL );
      pWnd->ShowWindow( SW_HIDE );
   }

   // Hide "Cancel" button
   if( bHideCancel )
   {
      CWnd* pWnd = pPSheet->GetDlgItem( IDCANCEL );
      ASSERT( pWnd != NULL );
      pWnd->ShowWindow( SW_HIDE );
   }

   // Hide "Apply" button
   if( bHideApply )
   {
      CWnd* pWnd = pPSheet->GetDlgItem( ID_APPLY_NOW );
      ASSERT( pWnd != NULL );
      pWnd->ShowWindow( SW_HIDE );
   }
}
```

Once you start to hide standard property sheet buttons, it is usually a good idea to center the remaining buttons on your property sheet window if you want to preserve the esthetic balance of your property sheet. This is exactly what *EkCenterPropertySheetButtons()*, shown in Listing 5-17, does.

Listing 5-17. Implementation of *EkCenterPropertySheetButtons()* to conditionally center the remaining standard property sheet buttons.

```
void EkCenterPropertySheetButtons(
                           CPropertySheet* pPSheet,
                           BOOL bCenterOK,
                           BOOL bCenterCancel,
                           BOOL bCenterApply )
{
   ASSERT_VALID( pPSheet );
   ASSERT( bCenterOK || bCenterCancel || bCenterApply );

   // Find "OK" button rectangle
   CWnd* pWndOK = pPSheet->GetDlgItem( IDOK );
   ASSERT( pWndOK != NULL );
   CRect rcOK;
```

```
pWndOK->GetWindowRect( &rcOK );
pPSheet->ScreenToClient( &rcOK );

// Find "Cancel" button rectangle
CWnd* pWndCancel = pPSheet->GetDlgItem( IDCANCEL );
ASSERT( pWndCancel != NULL );
CRect rcCancel;
pWndCancel->GetWindowRect( &rcCancel );
pPSheet->ScreenToClient( &rcCancel );

// Find "Apply" button rectangle
CWnd* pWndApply = pPSheet->GetDlgItem( ID_APPLY_NOW );
ASSERT( pWndApply != NULL );
CRect rcApply;
pWndApply->GetWindowRect( &rcApply );
pPSheet->ScreenToClient( &rcApply );

// Find property sheet client rectangle
CRect rcClient;
pPSheet->GetClientRect( &rcClient );

// Compute layout values
int nButtonWidth = rcOK.Width();
int nButtonMargin = rcCancel.left - rcOK.right;
int nButtons = (bCenterOK ? 1 : 0)
             + (bCenterCancel ? 1 : 0)
             + (bCenterApply ? 1 : 0);
int nGlobalWidth = nButtonWidth * nButtons;
if( nButtons > 1 )
{
   nGlobalWidth += nButtonMargin * (nButtons - 1);
}

int nCurrentX = ( rcClient.left + rcClient.right
                                - nGlobalWidth ) / 2;
int nTop = rcOK.top;

// Center "OK" button
if( bCenterOK )
{
   pWndOK->SetWindowPos( NULL,
                         nCurrentX,
```

```
                                   nTop,
                                   0, 0,
                                   SWP_NOSIZE | SWP_NOZORDER
                                              | SWP_NOACTIVATE );

      nCurrentX += nButtonWidth + nButtonMargin;
   }

   // Center "Cancel" button
   if( bCenterCancel )
   {
      pWndCancel->SetWindowPos( NULL,
                                nCurrentX,
                                nTop,
                                0, 0,
                                SWP_NOSIZE | SWP_NOZORDER
                                           | SWP_NOACTIVATE );

      nCurrentX += nButtonWidth + nButtonMargin;
   }

   // Center "Apply" button
   if( bCenterApply )
   {
      pWndApply->SetWindowPos( NULL,
                               nCurrentX,
                               nTop,
                               0, 0,
                               SWP_NOSIZE | SWP_NOZORDER
                                          | SWP_NOACTIVATE );
   }
}
```

These two functions should be called inside your property sheet class's *OnInitDialog()* function, as shown in Listing 5-18.

Listing 5-18. Calling *EkHidePropertySheetButtons()* and *EkCenterPropertySheetButtons()* from your property sheet class's *OnInitDialog()* function.

```
BOOL CDemoPSheet::OnInitDialog()
{
   BOOL bResult = CPropertySheet::OnInitDialog();
```

```
    // Hide "Cancel" and "Apply" buttons
    EkHidePropertySheetButtons( this, FALSE, TRUE, TRUE );

    // Center "OK" button in property sheet
    EkCenterPropertySheetButtons(this, TRUE, FALSE, FALSE);

    return bResult;
}
```

■

Additional Comments

As we explained in *FAQ 5.2 How do I manage the Apply button in a property sheet?* you can hide the Apply button by setting the special *PSH_NOAPPLYNOW* flag before the property sheet window is created. To do this, add the following line to your property sheet constructor:

```
m_psh.dwFlags |= PSH_NOAPPLYNOW;
```

The *m_psh* member of the *CPropertySheet* class is a *PROPSHEETHEADER* structure whose flags control the appearance and behavior of the property sheet window. As its name implies, the *PSH_NOAPPLYNOW* flag removes the Apply button from the property sheet window.

Sample Code

- Project: ManageButtons in the Chap05 subdirectory on the companion CD-ROM.
- Purpose: Demonstrates how to modify the captions of the standard property sheet buttons or hide all buttons except OK, as shown in Figure 5-4.

Implementation Highlights

- *EkHidePropertySheetButtons()* function (DemoPSheet.cpp)
- *EkCenterPropertySheetButtons()* function (DemoPSheet.cpp)
- *CDemoPSheet::OnInitDialog()* function (DemoPSheet.cpp).

See Also

- *FAQ 5.2 How do I manage the Apply button in a property sheet?*
- *FAQ 5.5 How do I control the size of my property sheet window?*

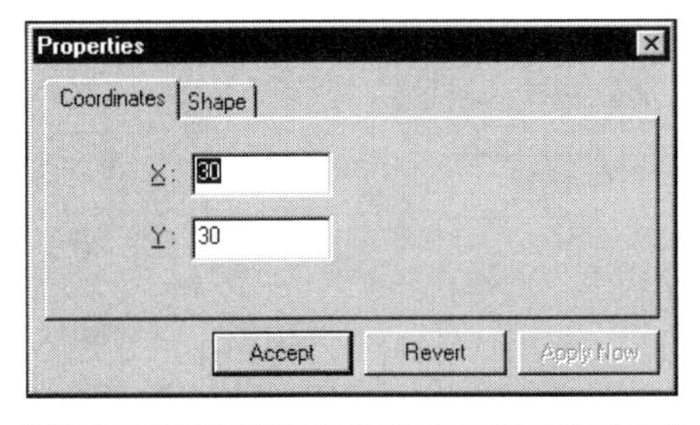

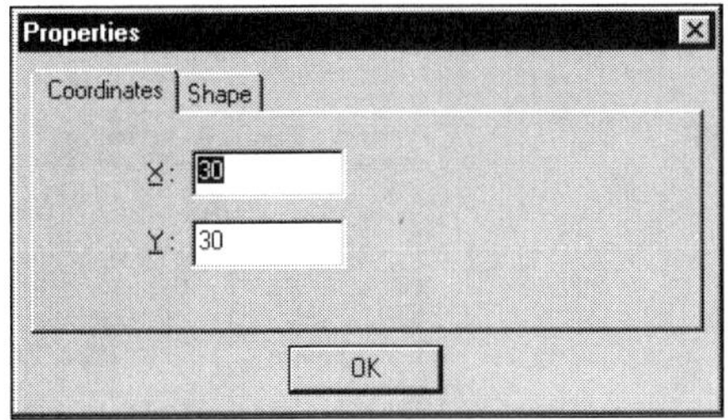

Figure 5-4. The same property sheet can either modify the captions of its standard buttons or hide all buttons except OK.

FAQ 5.5 How do I control the size of my property sheet window?

Usually, you do not need to worry about the size of your property sheet window: simply designing your property pages and adding them to your property sheet—as explained in *FAQ 5.1 How do I build and use a property sheet?*—is enough to make everything work correctly. Of course, this works because the property sheet window automatically resizes itself to accommodate the largest of your property pages as well as the standard buttons: OK, Cancel, and Apply (and optionally Help). Sometimes, however, you may wish to explicitly control the size of your property sheet window. For example, if you want to hide some of the standard buttons—as was explained in *FAQ 5.4 How do I customize the standard property sheet buttons?*—it often does not make sense to keep a wider than necessary property sheet window, especially if your property pages are rather narrow (see Figures 5-5 and 5-6).

The following technique shows you how to resize your property sheet window to suit your needs.

Step 1. Implement *EkResizePropertySheet()* as shown in Listing 5-19. This function manages the messy details of resizing both the property sheet window and the associated tab control.

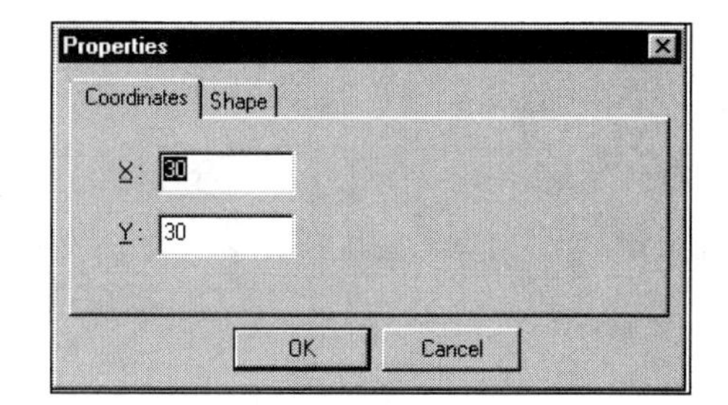

Figure 5-5. The default property sheet window is wide enough to hold the standard buttons—even if some of them are hidden.

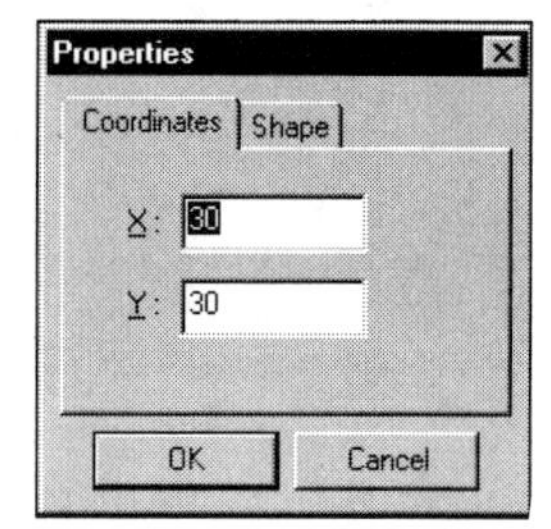

Figure 5-6. Resizing the property sheet window gives a more polished look to the application.

Listing 5-19. Implementing *EkResizePropertySheet()* to resize a property sheet.

```
void EkResizePropertySheet( CPropertySheet* pPSheet,
                            int nWidth )

{
   ASSERT_VALID( pPSheet );

   // 1 - Get current dimensions of tab control
   // and property sheet window
   CTabCtrl* pTabCtrl = pPSheet->GetTabControl();
   ASSERT( pTabCtrl != NULL );

   CRect rcTabCtrl;
   pTabCtrl->GetWindowRect( &rcTabCtrl );
   pPSheet->ScreenToClient( &rcTabCtrl );

   CRect rcPSheet;
   pPSheet->GetWindowRect( &rcPSheet );

   // 2 - Compute resizing offset
   int dcx = rcPSheet.Width() - nWidth;
```

```
    // 3 - Resize property sheet window
    pPSheet->SetWindowPos(   NULL,
                             0, 0,
                             nWidth,
                             rcPSheet.Height(),
                             SWP_NOZORDER | SWP_NOMOVE
                                          | SWP_NOACTIVATE );

    // 4 - Resize tab control window to restore
    // right margin
    pTabCtrl->SetWindowPos(   NULL,
                              0, 0,
                              rcTabCtrl.Width() - dcx,
                              rcTabCtrl.Height(),
                              SWP_NOZORDER | SWP_NOMOVE
                                           | SWP_NOACTIVATE );

    // 5 - Activate each property page to prevent drawing
    // problem
    int nCurrentPage = pPSheet->GetActiveIndex();
    for( int i = 0; i < pPSheet->GetPageCount(); ++i )
    {
       pPSheet->SetActivePage( i );
    }

    pPSheet->SetActivePage( nCurrentPage );
}
```

Step 2. Use ClassWizard to add a handler in your property sheet class for the *WM_INITDIALOG* message. Implement this handler as shown in Listing 5-20 to call *EkResizePropertySheet()*. Note that the rest of the code in Listing 5-20 uses the *EkHidePropertySheetButtons()* and *EkCenterPropertySheetButtons()* functions introduced in *FAQ 5.4* to manage the property sheet buttons. I left this code in the listing because I thought that you might find some use for it in your own applications.

Listing 5-20. Handling the *WM_INITDIALOG* message to resize the property sheet window and manage the property sheet buttons.

```
BOOL CDemoPSheet::OnInitDialog()
{
    BOOL bResult = CPropertySheet::OnInitDialog();
```

```
    EkResizePropertySheet( this, 200 );
       // Note : 200 width determined by trial and error

    // Hide "Apply" button
    EkHidePropertySheetButtons( this, FALSE, FALSE, TRUE );

    // Center "OK" and "Cancel" buttons in property sheet
    EkCenterPropertySheetButtons( this, TRUE, TRUE, FALSE );

    return bResult;
}
```

■

Additional Comments

You might wonder why I have not written a more general *EkResizePropertySheet()* function that would allow you to resize both the property sheet tab control and the property sheet window independently. In this way, you could put additional controls on your property sheet window outside the tab control—for example, a preview window or fields that should be shared between the various property pages.

Unfortunately, this approach does not fit well with the support currently provided by MFC and ClassWizard. This means that you would have to type a lot of code to make it work correctly. You can, however, get the same behavior by embedding a property sheet inside a dialog box, a topic that is fully explained in *FAQ 5.9 How do I embed a property sheet inside a dialog box?* Read this FAQ, and I think that you will no longer miss a more general *EkResizePropertySheet()* function.

Also, *EkResizePropertySheet()* resizes the property sheet window only in the horizontal direction; this is because the standard property sheet behavior automatically adapts the height of the property sheet window depending on the heights of your property pages. Therefore, there is rarely—never?—a need to modify a property sheet's height.

Sample Code

- Project: ResizePropertySheet in the Chap05 subdirectory on the companion CD-ROM.
- Purpose: Demonstrates how to programmatically resize a property sheet window, as shown earlier in Figure 5-6.

Implementation Highlights

- *EkResizePropertySheet()* function (DemoPSheet.cpp)
- *CDemoPSheet::OnInitDialog()* function (DemoPSheet.cpp)

See Also

- *FAQ 5.4 How do I customize the standard property sheet buttons?*
- *FAQ 5.9 How do I embed a property sheet inside a dialog box?*

Managing Tabs

FAQ 5.6 How do I choose between a stacked row of tabs and a single row of scrolling tabs?

If your property sheet begins to contain so many property pages that the tabs no longer fit on one row, the default behavior is to stack the tabs, as shown in Figure 5-7. This arrangement is much like the Tools, Options property sheet in Microsoft Word 97 and 95. However, you might prefer to have all your tabs appear on the same row, along with scrolling arrows, as shown in Figure 5-8. This is the approach taken in the Project, Settings property sheet in Developer Studio. Fortunately, the *CPropertySheet* class provides an undocumented *public* method that allows you to choose exactly the behavior you want. Here is its prototype:

```
void CPropertySheet::EnableStackedTabs(BOOL bStacked);
```

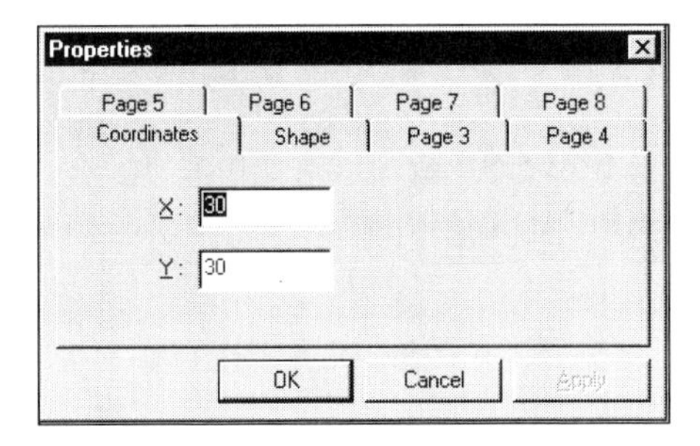

Figure 5-7. The default behavior stacks the tabs.

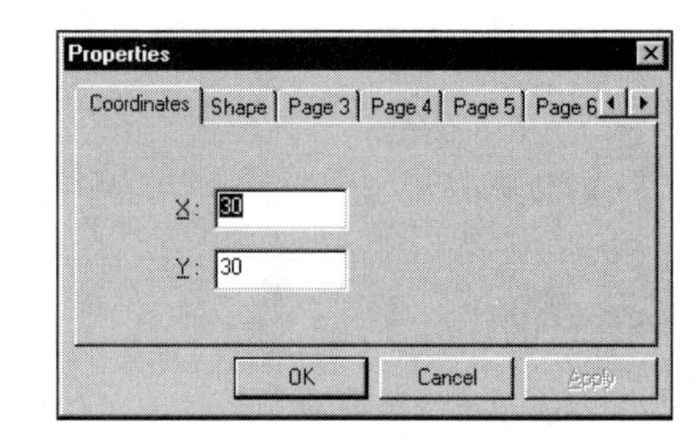

Figure 5-8. A property sheet with scrolling tabs.

Call *EnableStackedTabs()* in your property sheet's constructor, as shown in Listing 5-21—before *DoModal()* actually creates the Windows property sheet—to ensure that you get the tabs you want. Calling *EnableStackedTabs(TRUE)* gives you the default stacked tabs behavior, whereas calling *EnableStackedTabs(FALSE)* provides you with scrolling tabs.

Listing 5-21. Creating a property sheet with a single row of scrolling tabs.

```
CDemoPSheet::CDemoPSheet(CWnd* pParentWnd,
                         UINT iSelectPage)
   :CPropertySheet(IDS_PSHEET_CAPTION, pParentWnd,
                   iSelectPage)
{
   AddPage( &m_CoordsPPage );    // First page
   AddPage( &m_ShapePPage );     // Second page

   // ...

   EnableStackedTabs( FALSE );   // Scrolling tabs
}
```

■

Sample Code

- Project: StackedTabs in the Chap05 subdirectory on the companion CD-ROM.
- Purpose: Implements a property sheet that shows either stacked tabs or scrolling tabs on the same line, as shown earlier in Figures 5-7 and 5-8.

Implementation Highlights

- *CDrawDoc::OnDemoPSheet()* function (DrawDoc.cpp)

How do I change the captions of the tabs of my property pages?

Usually, you set the caption of each tab by setting the "Caption" property of each property page to the appropriate label, as explained in *FAQ 5.1 How do I build and use a property sheet?* This technique is appropriate for most applications, where the label of each tab is known at compile time. However, you may sometimes wish to dynamically modify the labels of some tabs, for example to display context information. The following explanations show how.

Step 1. Manually add a *SetTabCaption()* function to your property sheet class. Implement this function as shown in Listing 5-22.

Listing 5-22. Implementation of *SetTabCaption()*.

```
void CDemoPSheet::SetTabCaption( int nIndex,
                                 LPCTSTR szCaption )
{
   ASSERT( nIndex >= 0 && nIndex < GetPageCount() );

   CPropertyPage* pPage = GetPage( nIndex );
   pPage->m_psp.pszTitle = szCaption;
   pPage->m_psp.dwFlags |= PSP_USETITLE;
}
```

Step 2. After creating your property sheet object but before calling *DoModal()*, call your *SetTabCaption()* function for each property page whose label you want to set explicitly, as shown in Listing 5-23.

Listing 5-23. Calling *SetTabCaption()* to explicitly set tab labels.

```
void CDrawDoc::OnDemoPSheet()
{
   // 1 - Create the property sheet object
   CDemoPSheet psheet;

   // 2 - Initialize the pages' member variables
   psheet.m_CoordsPPage.m_nX = m_point.x;
```

```
    psheet.m_CoordsPPage.m_nY = m_point.y;
    psheet.m_ShapePPage.m_nShape = m_shape;

    // ** Change the pages' captions **
    CString strPage1;
    strPage1.Format(    "Coordinates (%d, %d)",
                    m_point.x, m_point.y );
    psheet.SetTabCaption( 0, strPage1 );

    CString strPage2;
    strPage2.Format(    "Shape (%s)",
                        (m_shape == SQUARE ? "Square" :
                         "Circle" ) );
    psheet.SetTabCaption( 1, strPage2 );

    // 3 - Show the property sheet to the user
    if( psheet.DoModal() == IDOK )
    {
        // ...
    }
}
```

Note that *SetTabCaption()* does not copy its string argument but rather stores the address of this string in the *PROPSHEETPAGE* structure associated with the desired property page. Therefore, you must ensure that the string that you pass to *SetTabCaption()* has a lifetime that extends at least until the call to *DoModal()*. Also, you must not change the strings passed to *SetTabCaption()* before the call to *DoModal()*; otherwise, the tab label will become incorrect.

■

Additional Comments

The preceding technique is not perfect, especially given the constraints on the lifetimes of the strings passed to *SetTabCaption()*.

The best solution would have been to store each string directly in the *CPropertyPage::m_strCaption* member variable. But because this variable is defined as *protected* in the property page class, you cannot access it from any class that does not derive from *CPropertyPage*. Either of the following two options could be used to solve this problem:

- Modify each property page class to add a new *SetCaption()* function with *public* access.
- Derive each property page class from a custom property page base class that provides a *public SetCaption()* function.

I find both options less than perfect, because they ask you to modify each of your property page classes. On the other hand, the technique explained earlier adds only one function to the property sheet class, independently of the number of property pages.

Sample Code

- Project: ChangeTabCaption in the Chap05 subdirectory on the companion CD-ROM.
- Purpose: Implements a property sheet that dynamically modifies the caption of its property page tabs to reflect the current state of the application, as shown in Figure 5-9.

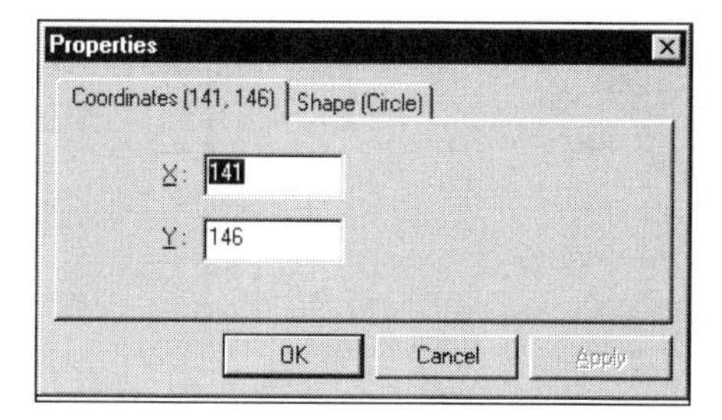

Figure 5-9. A property sheet that dynamically modifies the caption of its property page tabs to reflect the current state of the application.

Implementation Highlights

- *CDemoPSheet::SetTabCaption()* function (DemoPSheet.cpp)
- *CDrawDoc::OnDemoPSheet()* function (DrawDoc.cpp)

How do I add icons to the tabs of my property pages?

The property sheets used by most applications have only text labels on their tabs. But did you know that you can easily add icons to those tabs to make them more appealing? Here's how:

Step 1. Use the Visual C++ Resource Editor to create icons for your property pages. Note that these icons should be drawn in the small (16 × 16) icon resource.

Step 2. Modify the constructor of each of your property page classes to load the specific icon that you want to associate with each tab, as shown in Listing 5-24.

Listing 5-24. Adding an icon to a property page tab.

```
CCoordsPPage::CCoordsPPage()
   : CPropertyPage(CCoordsPPage::IDD)
{
   //{{AFX_DATA_INIT(CCoordsPPage)
   m_nX = 0;
   m_nY = 0;
   //}}AFX_DATA_INIT

   // Set tab icon
   HICON hIcon = AfxGetApp()->LoadIcon( IDI_PPAGE_COORDS );
   ASSERT( hIcon != NULL );
   m_psp.hIcon = hIcon;
   m_psp.dwFlags &= ~PSP_USEICONID;
   m_psp.dwFlags |= PSP_USEHICON;
}
```

That's all there is to it! Your property pages will now show a nice-looking icon.

■

Sample Code

- Project: TabIcons in the Chap05 subdirectory on the companion CD-ROM.
- Purpose: Implements a property sheet that displays icons on its property page tabs, as shown in Figure 5-10.

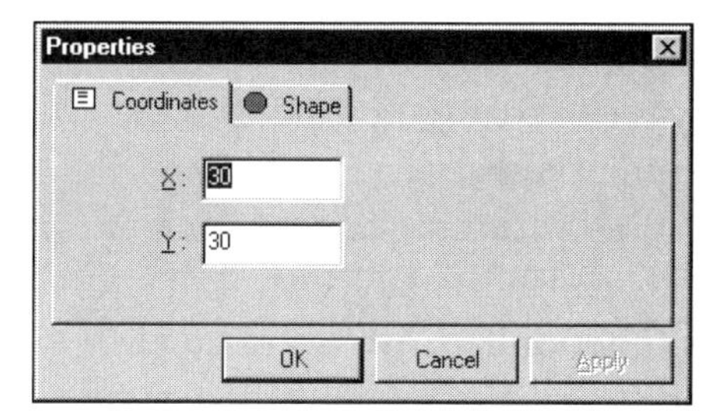

Figure 5-10. Icons on property page tabs are cool!

Implementation Highlights

- *CCoordsPPage::CCoordsPPage()* function (CoordsPPage.cpp)
- *CShapePPage::CShapePPage()* function (ShapePPage.cpp)

Embedding Property Sheets

5.9 How do I embed a property sheet inside a dialog box?

When you need to customize the behavior of a property sheet in a significant way—for example, to add other controls outside the property pages, such as a preview window or shared fields—you will usually find that embedding the property sheet in another window is the easiest and most flexible solution. By following the explanations given in this FAQ and in the following ones, you will be able to embed a property sheet in almost any kind of container window: a dialog box, a form view, a splitter window, a miniframe window, and so on.

These techniques give you the utmost in flexibility:

- You can add any number or kind of controls in your container window.
- You can lay out your container window in any way you like.

- You can embed several property sheets in the same container window.
- There will be no visible evidence that the property sheet window is nested inside another window.

Best of all, embedding a property sheet inside another window is easy to implement, thanks to the generic functions shown in Listings 5-25 and 5-26. *EkCreateEmbeddedPropertySheet()* creates an embedded property sheet and ensures that the window styles are correctly set so that the property sheet and the parent window cooperate in handling the Tab key correctly. *EkPositionEmbeddedPropertySheet()* takes care of repositioning and resizing an embedded property sheet. The trick is to correctly resize the tab control that is itself embedded inside the property sheet. This function has two overloaded forms that differ only in the way the property sheet's position is specified: the first overload takes a *CRect* argument, whereas the second overload takes the resource ID of a (hidden) Picture control that represents the desired property sheet position on the container window.

Listing 5-25. Implementing *EkCreateEmbeddedPropertySheet()* to create an embedded property sheet.

```
BOOL EkCreateEmbeddedPropertySheet(
                  CWnd* pParent,
                  CPropertySheet* pPSheet,
                  DWORD dwStyle = WS_CHILD | WS_VISIBLE,
                  DWORD dwExStyle = 0 )
{
   ASSERT_VALID( pParent );
   ASSERT_VALID( pPSheet );

   // 1 - Create the embedded property sheet window
   if( !pPSheet->Create( pParent,  dwStyle, dwExStyle ) )
   {
      TRACE0("Embedded property sheet creation failed\n");
      return FALSE;
   }

   // 2 - Add WS_TABSTOP and WS_EX_CONTROLPARENT to
   // the property sheet styles
   pPSheet->ModifyStyle( 0, WS_TABSTOP );
   pPSheet->ModifyStyleEx ( 0, WS_EX_CONTROLPARENT );
```

```
    // 3 - Add WS_EX_CONTROLPARENT to the parent window
    // styles
    pParent->ModifyStyleEx ( 0, WS_EX_CONTROLPARENT );

    return TRUE;
}
```

Listing 5-26. Implementing *EkPositionEmbeddedPropertySheet()* to position and resize an embedded property sheet.

```
void EkPositionEmbeddedPropertySheet(
                              CWnd* pParent,
                              CPropertySheet* pPSheet,
                              CRect rcNewPosition )
{
    ASSERT_VALID( pParent );
    ASSERT_VALID( pPSheet );

    // 1 - Get current coordinates of tab control
    // and property sheet window
    CTabCtrl* pTabCtrl = pPSheet->GetTabControl();
    ASSERT( pTabCtrl != NULL );

    CRect rcTabCtrl;
    pTabCtrl->GetWindowRect( &rcTabCtrl );
    pParent->ScreenToClient( &rcTabCtrl );

    CRect rcPSheet;
    pPSheet->GetWindowRect( &rcPSheet );
    pParent->ScreenToClient( &rcPSheet );

    // 2 - Calculate margin between property sheet
    // and tab control
    int dcx = rcPSheet.Width() - rcTabCtrl.Width();
    int dcy = rcPSheet.Height() - rcTabCtrl.Height();

    // 3 - Move and resize property sheet window
    // (also moves the tab window because it is a child
    // of the property sheet window)
    pPSheet->MoveWindow( rcNewPosition .left,
                         rcNewPosition.top,
```

```
                              rcNewPosition .Width(),
                              rcNewPosition.Height() );

   // 4 - Resize tab control window to restore
   // right / bottom margins
   pTabCtrl->SetWindowPos( NULL,
                           0, 0,
                           rcNewPosition.Width() - dcx,
                           rcNewPosition.Height() - dcy,
                           SWP_NOZORDER | SWP_NOMOVE
                                        | SWP_NOACTIVATE );

   // 5 - Activate each property page to prevent drawing
   // problem
   int nCurrentPage = pPSheet->GetActiveIndex();
   for( int i = 0; i < pPSheet->GetPageCount(); ++i )
   {
      pPSheet->SetActivePage( i );
   }

   pPSheet->SetActivePage( nCurrentPage );
}

void EkPositionEmbeddedPropertySheet(
                              CWnd* pParent,
                              CPropertySheet* pPSheet,
                              UINT nIDPSheetArea )
{
   ASSERT_VALID( pParent );
   ASSERT_VALID( pPSheet );

   // 1 - Retrieve property sheet destination position
   CRect rcNewPosition;
   CWnd* pWndNewArea = pParent->GetDlgItem(nIDPSheetArea);
   if( pWndNewArea == NULL )
   {
      ASSERT( FALSE );   // Invalid nIDPSheetArea
      return;
   }
```

```
    pWndNewArea->GetWindowRect( &rcNewPosition );
    pParent->ScreenToClient( &rcNewPosition );

    // 2 - Call overloaded function
    EkPositionEmbeddedPropertySheet( pParent, pPSheet,
                                     rcNewPosition );
}
```

Here is how you can use these two functions to embed a property sheet inside a dialog box:

Step 1. Add a Picture control to your dialog box resource to mark the area where you want your property sheet to appear, as shown in Figure 5-11. Set the styles of this Picture control to "Frame, Black, Not Visible," as we explained in *FAQ 4.5 How do I add a preview area to (draw inside) a dialog box?* Give this control an ID similar to *IDC_PSHEET_AREA*.

Step 2. Manually add a *public* member variable of type *CYourPropertySheet* to your dialog class, as shown in Listing 5-27.

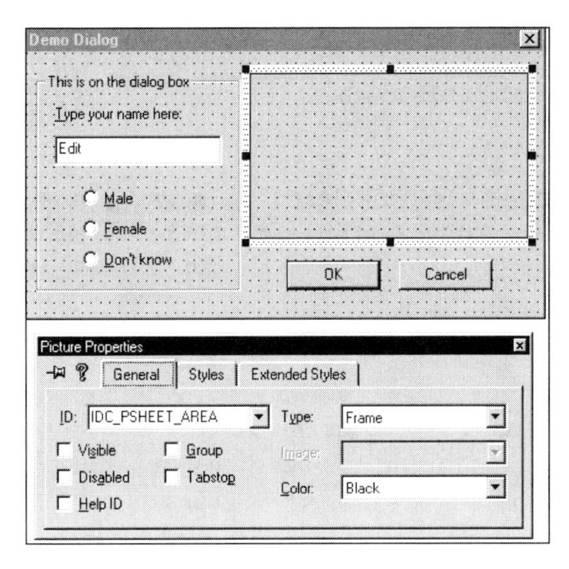

Figure 5-11. Creating a placeholder on the dialog box for the embedded property sheet.

Listing 5-27. Adding a *public* member variable of type *CYourPropertySheet* to your dialog class.

```
#include "DemoPSheet.h"

class CDemoDlg : public CDialog
{
// ...

public:
   CDemoPSheet m_psheet;    // Embedded property sheet

// ...
};
```

Step 3. Use ClassWizard to add a handler in your dialog class for the *WM_INITDIALOG* message. Implement this handler as shown in Listing 5-28 to create and position the embedded property sheet.

Listing 5-28. Handling the *WM_INITDIALOG* message to create and position the embedded property sheet.

```
BOOL CDemoDlg::OnInitDialog()
{
   CDialog::OnInitDialog();
   EkCreateEmbeddedPropertySheet( this, &m_psheet );
   EkPositionEmbeddedPropertySheet( this, &m_psheet,
                                    IDC_PSHEET_AREA );

   return TRUE;
}
```

Step 4. Use ClassWizard to override the *OnOK()* virtual function in your dialog class. Implement this function as shown in Listing 5-29 to correctly pull the data from the active property page inside the associated member variables when the dialog box is dismissed. (MFC automatically calls *UpdateData()* for each property page when the user switches to another page, but you need to call this function yourself for the last active page to correctly retrieve the associated data.)

Listing 5-29. Implementing the *OnOK()* virtual function to retrieve the data on the active property page.

```
void CDemoDlg::OnOK()
{
   m_psheet.GetActivePage()->UpdateData( TRUE );

   CDialog::OnOK();
}
```

Step 5. Create your dialog box and call its *DoModal()* function as usual, as shown in Listing 5-30. Just remember that some data members are not direct members of your dialog class but rather are members of the pages of the embedded property sheet. This arrangement makes for some interesting multilevel object nesting.

Listing 5-30. Creating a dialog box with an embedded property sheet.

```
void CDrawDoc::OnDemoPSheet()
{
   CDemoDlg dlg;

   dlg.m_psheet.m_CoordsPPage.m_nX = m_point.x;
   dlg.m_psheet.m_CoordsPPage.m_nY = m_point.y;
   dlg.m_psheet.m_ShapePPage.m_nShape = m_shape;

   if( dlg.DoModal() == IDOK )
   {
      m_point.x = dlg.m_psheet.m_CoordsPPage.m_nX;
      m_point.y = dlg.m_psheet.m_CoordsPPage.m_nY;
      m_shape = static_cast< SHAPE >(
                   dlg.m_psheet.m_ShapePPage.m_nShape );

      SetModifiedFlag( TRUE );
      UpdateAllViews( NULL );
   }
}
```

You should now have a superb dialog box with a fully functional embedded property sheet, as shown in Figure 5-12.

■

Sample Code

- Project: PropertySheetInDialog in the Chap05 subdirectory on the companion CD-ROM.
- Purpose: Implements a dialog box with an embedded property sheet, as shown in Figure 5-12.

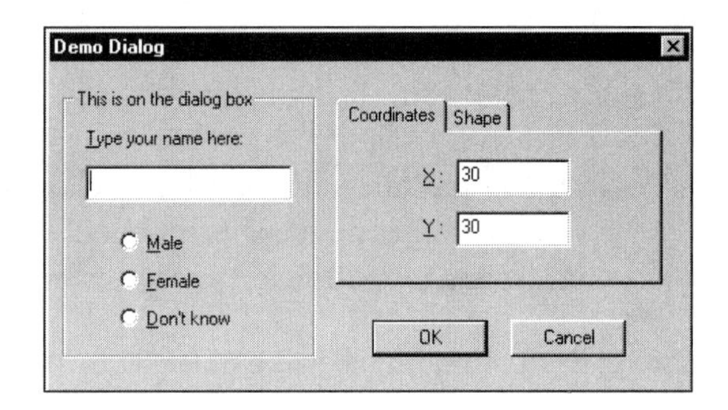

Figure 5-12. A property sheet embedded inside a dialog box.

Implementation Highlights

- *EkCreateEmbeddedPropertySheet()* function (DemoDlg.cpp)
- *EkPositionEmbeddedPropertySheet()* function (DemoDlg.cpp)
- *CDemoDlg::OnInitDialog()* function (DemoDlg.cpp)
- *CDemoDlg::OnOK()* function (DemoDlg.cpp)
- *CDrawDoc::OnDemoPSheet()* function (DemoDoc.cpp)

See Also

- *FAQ 4.5 How do I add a preview area to (draw inside) a dialog box?*
- *FAQ 5.10 How do I embed a property sheet inside a form view?*
- *FAQ 5.11 How do I embed a property sheet inside a splitter window pane?*
- *FAQ 5.12 How do I embed a property sheet inside a miniframe window?*

FAQ 5.10 How do I embed a property sheet inside a form view?

Because a form view is rather similar to a dialog box, you probably will not be surprised to learn that the technique for embedding a property sheet inside a form view is also quite similar to the one described in *FAQ 5.9 How do I embed a property sheet inside a dialog box?* Some details differ in the case of a form view:

Step 1. Follow steps 1 and 2 of *FAQ 5.9* to create a placeholder on the dialog resource associated with your form view and to add a member variable of type *CYourPropertySheet* to your form view class.

Step 2. Use ClassWizard to override the *OnInitialUpdate()* virtual function in your form view class. Implement this function as shown in Listing 5-31 to create and position the embedded property sheet.

Listing 5-31. Implementation of *OnInitialUpdate()* to create and position the embedded property sheet.

```
void CPSheetFormView::OnInitialUpdate()
{
   // 1 - Let base class do default processing
   CFormView::OnInitialUpdate();

   // 2 - Create and position embedded property sheet
   EkCreateEmbeddedPropertySheet( this, &m_psheet );
   EkPositionEmbeddedPropertySheet( this, &m_psheet,
                                    IDC_PSHEET_AREA );

   // 3 - Resize parent frame to fit the Form View dialog
   // template
   GetParentFrame()->RecalcLayout();
   ResizeParentToFit( FALSE );
   ResizeParentToFit( TRUE );

   // 4 - Set focus to first control with WS_TABSTOP style
   // on form view
   CWnd* pChild = GetWindow( GW_CHILD );
   while( pChild != NULL &&
           ( pChild->GetStyle() & WS_TABSTOP ) == 0 )
   {
```

```
        pChild = pChild->GetNextWindow( GW_HWNDNEXT );
    }

    if( pChild != NULL )
    {
        pChild->SetFocus();
    }
}
```

Step 3. Modify your form view's *OnUpdate()* and *OnApply()* functions to take into account the presence of the embedded property sheet, as shown in Listing 5-32.

Listing 5-32. Modifying *OnUpdate()* and *OnApply()* to take into account the presence of the embedded property sheet.

```
void CPSheetFormView::OnUpdate(CView* pSender,
                               LPARAM lHint,
                               CObject* pHint)
{

    // 1 - Get the current data from our document
    CDrawDoc* pDoc = GetDocument();

    m_psheet.m_CoordsPPage.m_nX = pDoc->m_point.x;
    m_psheet.m_CoordsPPage.m_nY = pDoc->m_point.y;
    m_psheet.m_ShapePPage.m_nShape = pDoc->m_shape;

    // 2 - Show the current data in the form view controls
    UpdateData( FALSE );

    // 3 - Show the current data in the active
    // property page
    if( m_psheet.GetSafeHwnd() != NULL )
    {
        m_psheet.GetActivePage()->UpdateData( FALSE );
    }
}

void CPSheetFormView::OnApply()
{
    // 1 - Get the data from our form view controls
    UpdateData( TRUE );
```

```
    // 2 - Get the data from the active property page
    m_psheet.GetActivePage()->UpdateData( TRUE );

    // 3 - Update the document state
    CDrawDoc* pDoc = GetDocument();

    pDoc->m_point.x = m_psheet.m_CoordsPPage.m_nX;
    pDoc->m_point.y = m_psheet.m_CoordsPPage.m_nY;
    pDoc->m_shape = static_cast< CDrawDoc::SHAPE >
                        ( m_psheet.m_ShapePPage.m_nShape );

    // 4 - Tell the document something happened
    pDoc->SetModifiedFlag( TRUE );

    // 5 - Synchronize all other views
    pDoc->UpdateAllViews( this );
}
```

■

Sample Code

- Project: PropertySheetInFormView in the Chap05 subdirectory on the companion CD-ROM.
- Purpose: Implements a form view with an embedded property sheet, as shown in Figure 5-13.

Implementation Highlights

- *CPSheetFormView::OnInitialUpdate()* function (PSheetFormView.cpp)
- *CPSheetFormView::OnUpdate()* function (PSheetFormView.cpp)
- *CPSheetFormView::OnApply()* function (PSheetFormView.cpp)

See Also

- *FAQ 3.29 How do I make a form view initially appear with the exact size of the associated dialog resource?*
- *FAQ 5.9 How do I embed a property sheet inside a dialog box?*
- *FAQ 5.11 How do I embed a property sheet inside a splitter window pane?*
- *FAQ 5.12 How do I embed a property sheet inside a miniframe window?*

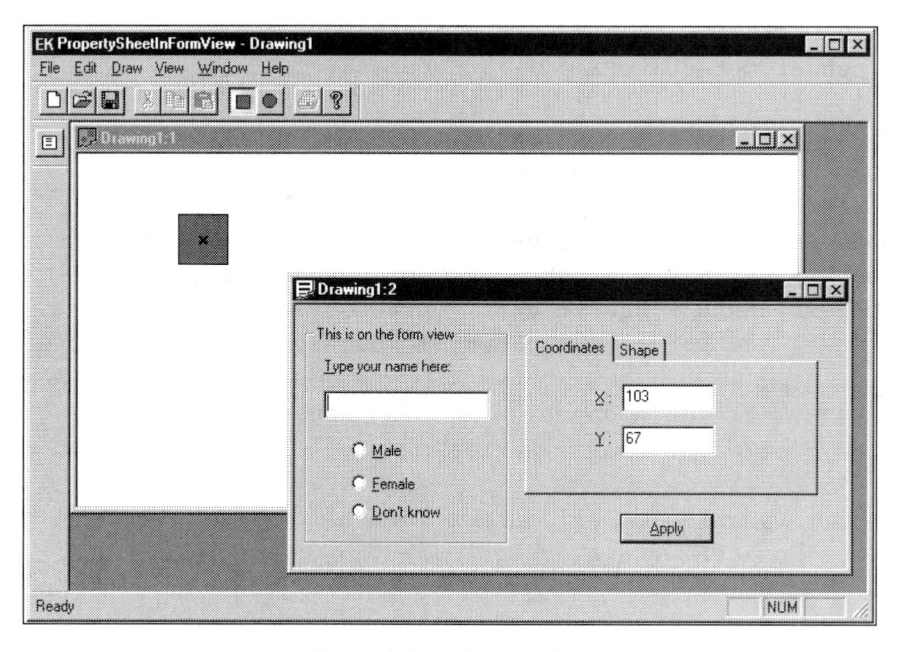

Figure 5-13. A property sheet embedded inside a form view.

How do I embed a property sheet inside a splitter window pane?

Embedding a property sheet inside a splitter window pane is almost trivial when you already know how to embed a property sheet inside a form view (see *FAQ 5.10 How do I embed a property sheet inside a form view?*): simply reference the form view class that contains your embedded property sheet when creating your splitter panes, as shown in Listing 5-33.

Listing 5-33. Creating splitter panes that contain a form view with an embedded property sheet.

```
BOOL CSplitFrame::OnCreateClient(LPCREATESTRUCT /*lpcs*/,
                                 CCreateContext* pContext)
{
   CRect rect;
   GetClientRect( &rect );
```

```
    CSize size = rect.Size();
    size.cy /= 2;        // Initial row size

    // 1 - Create static splitter
    if( !m_wndSplitter.CreateStatic( this, 2, 1 ) )
                                          // 2 rows, 1 col
    {
       TRACE0( "Failed to create static splitter\n" );
       return FALSE;
    }

    // 2 - Create top view
    if( !m_wndSplitter.CreateView( 0, 0, // row 0, col 0
                                        RUNTIME_CLASS( CDrawView ),
                                        size, pContext ) )
    {
       TRACE0( "Failed to create top view\n" );
       return FALSE;
    }

    // 3 - Create bottom view
    if( !m_wndSplitter.CreateView( 1, 0, // row 1, col 0
                            RUNTIME_CLASS( CPSheetFormView ),
                            size, pContext ) )
    {
       TRACE0( "Failed to create bottom view\n" );
       return FALSE;
    }

    return TRUE;
}
```

■

Sample Code

- Project: PropertySheetInSplitter in the Chap05 subdirectory on the companion CD-ROM.
- Purpose: Implements a splitter window pane with an embedded property sheet, as shown in Figure 5-14.

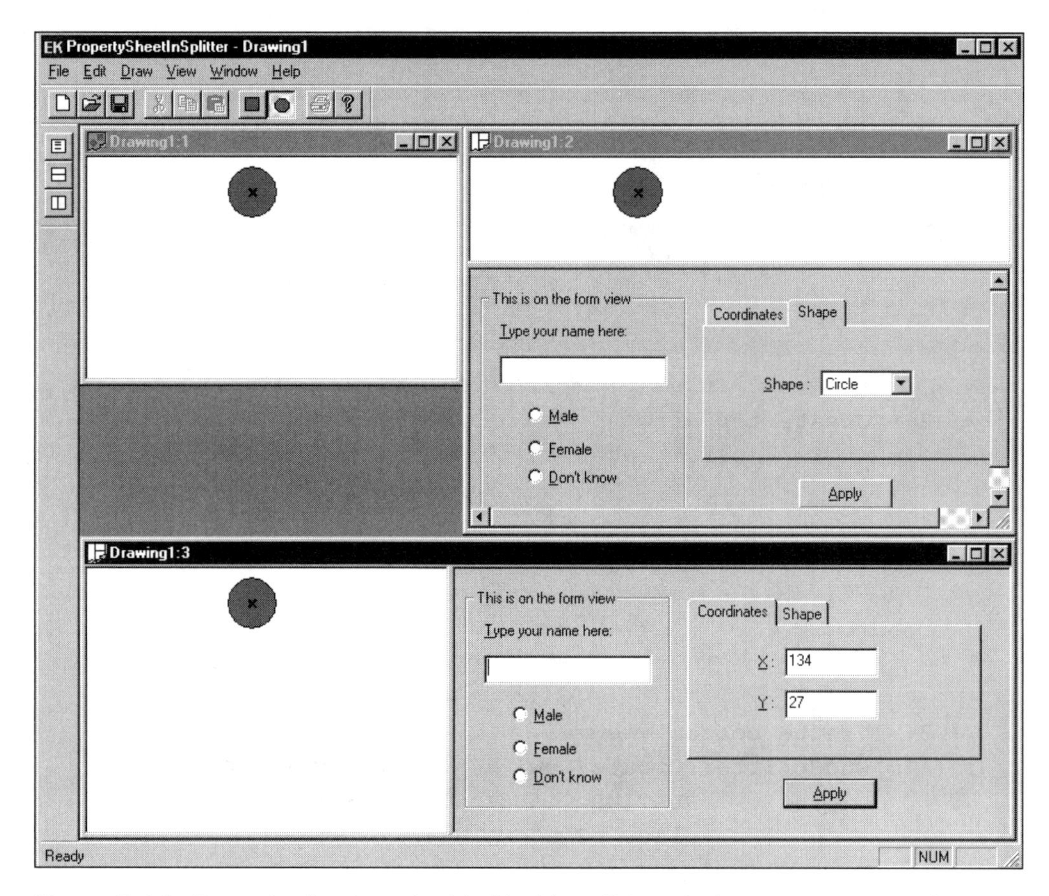

Figure 5-14. Property sheets embedded inside splitter window panes can work wonders!

Implementation Highlights

- *CSplitFrame::OnCreateClient()* function (SplitFrame.cpp)
- *CSplitFrame2::OnCreateClient()* function (SplitFrame2.cpp)

See Also

- *FAQ 5.9 How do I embed a property sheet inside a dialog box?*
- *FAQ 5.10 How do I embed a property sheet inside a form view?*
- *FAQ 5.12 How do I embed a property sheet inside a miniframe window?*

FAQ 5.12 How do I embed a property sheet inside a miniframe window?

Have you ever wanted to include in your application a floating palette similar to the Properties window of Developer Studio? Embedding a property sheet inside a miniframe window allows you to achieve this cool visual effect, as shown in Figure 5-15.

Step 1. Use ClassWizard to create a new *CMiniFrameWnd*-derived class.

Step 2. Change the access of the generated constructor access to *public*—instead of *protected*—and manually add a *public* member variable of type *CYourPropertySheet* to your miniframe class, as shown in Listing 5-34.

Listing 5-34. Adding a *public* member variable of type *CYourPropertySheet* to your miniframe class.

```
class CPSheetMiniFrameWnd : public CMiniFrameWnd
{
   DECLARE_DYNCREATE(CPSheetMiniFrameWnd)
```

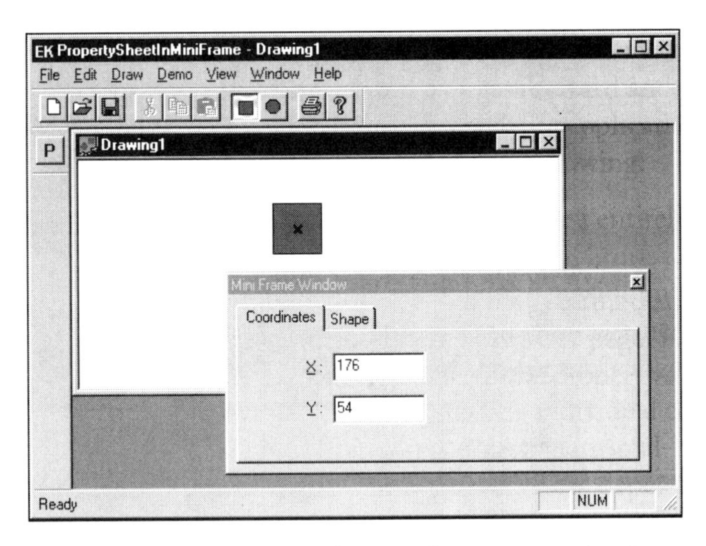

Figure 5-15. A floating palette with a property sheet embedded inside a miniframe window.

```
public:      // change constructor access to public
   CPSheetMiniFrameWnd();

// Attributes
public:
   CDemoPSheet m_psheet;    // embedded property sheet

// ...

};
```

Step 3. Use ClassWizard to add a handler in your miniframe class for the *WM_CREATE* message. Implement this handler as shown in Listing 5-35 to create the embedded property sheet.

Listing 5-35. Handling the *WM_CREATE* message to create the embedded property sheet.

```
int CPSheetMiniFrameWnd::OnCreate(
                              LPCREATESTRUCT lpCreateStruct)
{
   // 1 - Call base class to create the miniframe window
   if (CMiniFrameWnd::OnCreate(lpCreateStruct) == -1)
      return -1;

   // 2 - Create the embedded property sheet
   if( !EkCreateEmbeddedPropertySheet( this, &m_psheet ) )
   {
      return -1;
   }

   // 3 - Resize the miniframe window to fit the
   // property sheet
   CRect rcSheet;
   m_psheet.GetWindowRect( &rcSheet );

   CRect rcMiniFrame( rcSheet );
   CalcWindowRect( &rcMiniFrame );
   SetWindowPos( NULL, 0, 0,
                 rcMiniFrame.Width(), rcMiniFrame.Height(),
                 SWP_NOZORDER | SWP_NOMOVE | SWP_NOACTIVATE );
```

```
    // 4 - Center the miniframe window on the screen
    CenterWindow();
    ShowWindow( SW_SHOW );

    return 0;
}
```

Step 4. When you want to create and show the miniframe window, use code similar to that shown in Listing 5-36.

Listing 5-36. Creating and showing the miniframe window.

```
void CDrawDoc::OnDemoPSheet()
{
    // 1 - Create the miniframe window C++ object
    // (C++ object is deleted when window is destroyed)
    CPSheetMiniFrameWnd* pMiniFrameWnd =
                            new CPSheetMiniFrameWnd;

    // 2 - Initialize the pages' member variables
    pMiniFrameWnd->m_psheet.m_CoordsPPage.m_nX = m_point.x;
    pMiniFrameWnd->m_psheet.m_CoordsPPage.m_nY = m_point.y;
    pMiniFrameWnd->m_psheet.m_ShapePPage.m_nShape = m_shape;

    // 3 - Create the miniframe Windows window and show it
    // to the user
    pMiniFrameWnd->Create( NULL, _T( "Mini Frame Window" ),
                           WS_POPUP|WS_CAPTION|WS_SYSMENU,
                           CRect( 0, 0, 0, 0 ),
                           AfxGetMainWnd() );
}
```

■

Sample Code

- Project: PropertySheetInMiniFrame in the Chap05 subdirectory on the companion CD-ROM.
- Purpose: Demonstrates how to implement a floating palette with a property sheet embedded inside a miniframe window.

Implementation Highlights

- *CPSheetMiniFrameWnd* class (PSheetMiniFrameWnd.h)
- *CPSheetMiniFrameWnd::OnCreate()* function (PSheetMiniFrameWnd.cpp)
- *CDrawDoc::OnDemoPSheet()* function (DrawDoc.cpp)

See Also

- *FAQ 5.9 How do I embed a property sheet inside a dialog box?*
- *FAQ 5.10 How do I embed a property sheet inside a form view?*
- *FAQ 5.11 How do I embed a property sheet inside a splitter window pane?*

6 TOOLBARS AND STATUS BARS

Toolbars and status bars have become so ubiquitous that you would be hard-pressed to find any successful program that does not use any of these interface adornments, and for good reason: these widgets are truly useful and make good sense from a user-interface design point of view.

As is often the case with MFC, AppWizard gives you a good start by attaching a standard toolbar and status bar to your application's main frame window. However, as your application design evolves, you will quickly outgrow the basic AppWizard-generated features if you want to provide an efficient and ergonomic user interface.

The techniques presented in this chapter will enable you to dramatically expand the standard AppWizard-generated code in many ways. You will learn how to add several toolbars to your frame windows and control their position (*FAQs 6.1* to *6.3*), add another control, such as a combo box, to your toolbar (*FAQ 6.4*), allow the users to select the toolbars they need by right-clicking on a docking zone (*FAQ 6.7*), and so on.

Status bars are not forgotten. Various techniques demonstrate how to add custom status bars to frame windows and correctly manage the updating of indicators (*FAQs 6.9* and *6.10*), how to draw in a status bar pane (*FAQ 6.12*), and how to display a progress indicator in a status bar (*FAQ 6.14*).

Finally, be sure to take a look at *FAQ 6.18* to find out how to create a custom control bar. You'll gain a good understanding of the *UPDATE_COMMAND_UI* architecture at the same time.

Toolbars

6.1 How do I add one or more toolbars to my main frame window or to a view's frame window?

When AppWizard generates your skeleton MFC application, it dutifully provides one default toolbar that is attached to the main frame window. However, you will most likely need to add other toolbars either to your main frame window or to some of your view's frame windows if you want to provide a user interface that is rich as well as highly customizable.

The key idea is that by providing several toolbars instead of grouping all buttons on one monolithic toolbar, you give users the opportunity to select the toolbars they want to show or hide and to organize their workspace to suit their needs and tastes. Fortunately, the MFC framework makes it easy to add new toolbars to any frame window, and the two helper functions provided in the Additional Comments section will make this task even easier.

The following steps explain how you can add a new toolbar to one of your application's frame windows. These explanations apply either to your application's main frame window or to any of your view's frame windows.

Step 1. Create a toolbar resource using the Visual Studio Resource Editor. The following discussion assumes that this toolbar resource has an ID of *IDR_NEW_TOOLBAR*.

Step 2. Add a member variable of type *CToolBar* to the frame window class to which you want to add a toolbar, as shown in Listing 6-1.

Listing 6-1. Adding a member variable of type *CToolBar* to the frame window class.

```
class CMainFrame : public CMDIFrameWnd
{
// ...
```

```
// Implementation
protected:
   CToolBar    m_wndNewToolbar; // new toolbar

// ...
};
```

Step 3. If your frame window class does not yet have a handler for the *WM_CREATE* message, use ClassWizard to add such a handler.

Step 4. Modify your frame window class's *OnCreate()* function to correctly create the toolbar, load its resources, set its styles and docking attributes, and decide whether the toolbar should initially appear docked or floating, as shown in Listing 6-2. (Do not forget to look in the Additional Comments section for a way to drastically reduce the number of lines of code that you have to type to create and configure a new toolbar.)

Listing 6-2. Adding code to *OnCreate()* to create the toolbar and set its various attributes.

```
int CMainFrame::OnCreate(LPCREATESTRUCT lpCreateStruct)
{
   if (CMDIFrameWnd::OnCreate(lpCreateStruct) == -1)
      return -1;

   // ...

   // 1 - Create the new toolbar window
   if (!m_wndNewToolbar.Create( this,
                          WS_CHILD | WS_VISIBLE | CBRS_TOP,
                          IDR_NEW_TOOLBAR ) ||
       // 2 - Load the toolbar resources
       !m_wndNewToolbar.LoadToolBar(IDR_NEW_TOOLBAR))
   {
      TRACE0("Failed to create new toolbar\n");
      return -1;      // fail to create
   }

   // ...
```

```
    // 3 - Define the frame window docking behavior
    // (do this only once for the frame, independently of
    // the number of toolbars)
    EnableDocking(CBRS_ALIGN_ANY);

    // 4 - Define the new toolbar styles
    m_wndNewToolbar.SetBarStyle(
                        m_wndNewToolbar.GetBarStyle()
                        | CBRS_TOOLTIPS | CBRS_FLYBY
                        | CBRS_SIZE_DYNAMIC);

    // 5 - Define the new toolbar docking behavior
    m_wndNewToolbar.EnableDocking(CBRS_ALIGN_ANY);

    // 6 - Make the new toolbar initially appear docked
    // (call FloatControlBar() to have it appear floating)
    DockControlBar(&m_wndNewToolbar, AFX_IDW_DOCKBAR_LEFT);

    // ...

    return 0;
}
```

If you want to add other toolbars to the same frame window, simply repeat the preceding steps for each new toolbar.

■

Additional Comments

Given the ubiquity of toolbars in most MFC applications, it is tempting to try to simplify the way you create these user-interface elements in your code. Because the preceding steps are usually the same for each toolbar that you will create in an MFC application, I have abstracted them into two general-purpose functions—*EkCreateToolBar()* and *EkDockToolBar()*—which are shown in Listings 6-3 and 6-4. Each of these functions combines several steps. To further reduce the code clutter, these functions also take advantage of default arguments that provide a reasonable behavior in most cases and save you from having to specify each parameter explicitly.

Listing 6-3. Implementation of *EkCreateToolBar()*.

```
BOOL EkCreateToolBar( CFrameWnd* pParentFrame,
          CToolBar* pBar,
          UINT nIDBar,
          UINT nIDResource = 0,
          DWORD dwStyle1 = WS_CHILD | WS_VISIBLE | CBRS_TOP,
          DWORD dwStyle2 = CBRS_TOOLTIPS | CBRS_FLYBY |
                           CBRS_SIZE_DYNAMIC )
{
   ASSERT_VALID( pParentFrame );
   ASSERT_VALID( pBar );

   // 1 - No IDResource means resource ID is same as bar ID
   if( nIDResource == 0 )
   {
      nIDResource = nIDBar;
   }

   // 2 - Create toolbar and load resources
   if( !pBar->Create( pParentFrame, dwStyle1, nIDBar ) ||
       !pBar->LoadToolBar( nIDResource ) )
   {
      TRACE1( "Failed to create toolbar with ID=%d\n",
              nIDBar );
      return FALSE;      // fail to create
   }

   // 3 - Define toolbar styles
   pBar->SetBarStyle( pBar->GetBarStyle() | dwStyle2 );

   return TRUE;
}
```

Listing 6-4. Implementation of *EkDockToolBar()*.

```
void EkDockToolBar( CFrameWnd* pParentFrame,
                    CToolBar* pBar,
                    UINT nDockBarID = AFX_IDW_DOCKBAR_TOP,
                    CControlBar* pBarNextTo = NULL,
                    DWORD dwStyleDocking = CBRS_ALIGN_ANY )
{
```

```
    ASSERT_VALID( pParentFrame );
    ASSERT_VALID( pBar );

    ASSERT( ::IsWindow( pBar->GetSafeHwnd() ) );

    // 1 - Define toolbar docking behavior
    pBar->EnableDocking( dwStyleDocking );

    if( pBarNextTo != NULL )
    {
        // 2a - Dock toolbar next to an existing bar
        EkDockBarNextTo( pBar, pBarNextTo, nDockBarID );
    }
    else
    {
        // 2b - Dock toolbar on its own dockbar
        pParentFrame->DockControlBar( pBar, nDockBarID );
    }
}
```

Note that the *EkDockBarNextTo()* function used in Listing 6-4 is described in *FAQ 6.3 How do I programmatically dock a toolbar next to another one?*

Using the two helper functions *EkCreateToolBar()* and *EkDockToolBar()* makes the code sample shown in Listing 6-2 significantly more compact, as shown in Listing 6-5.

Listing 6-5. Creating a new toolbar with the helper functions *EkCreateToolBar()* and *EkDockToolBar()*.

```
int CMainFrame::OnCreate(LPCREATESTRUCT lpCreateStruct)
{
    if (CMDIFrameWnd::OnCreate(lpCreateStruct) == -1)
        return -1;

    // 1 - Create new toolbar, load resources, define styles
    if( !EkCreateToolBar( this, &m_wndNewToolbar,
                          AFX_IDW_TOOLBAR, IDR_MAINFRAME ) )
    {
        return -1;    // fail to create
    }

    // 2 - Define main frame window docking behavior
    EnableDocking(CBRS_ALIGN_ANY);
```

```
   // 3 - Define new toolbar docking behavior, dock toolbar
   EkDockToolBar( this, &m_wndNewToolbar,
                  AFX_IDW_DOCKBAR_LEFT );

   return 0;
}
```

The more toolbars you create, the more useful these two helper functions become. Listing 6-6 shows the *CChildFrm::OnCreate()* function for this FAQ's sample project: this function adds seven toolbars to the view's frame window. Notice that the code stays clean and compact, thanks to the helper functions.

Listing 6-6. The *CChildFrm::OnCreate()* function from this FAQ's sample project adds seven toolbars to the view's frame window.

```
int CChildFrame::OnCreate(LPCREATESTRUCT lpCreateStruct)
{
   if (CMDIChildWnd::OnCreate(lpCreateStruct) == -1)
      return -1;

   // 1 - Create toolbars
   if( !EkCreateToolBar( this, &m_wndShapes1, IDR_SHAPES )
    || !EkCreateToolBar( this, &m_wndColors1, IDR_COLORS )
    || !EkCreateToolBar( this, &m_wndDemo1,
                              IDR_DEMO_TOOLBAR2 )
    || !EkCreateToolBar( this, &m_wndColors2, IDR_COLORS )
    || !EkCreateToolBar( this, &m_wndDemo2,
                              IDR_DEMO_TOOLBAR2 )
    || !EkCreateToolBar( this, &m_wndColors3, IDR_COLORS )
    || !EkCreateToolBar( this, &m_wndShapes2, IDR_SHAPES ))
   {
      return -1;    // fail to create
   }

   // 2 - Define main frame window docking behavior
   EnableDocking(CBRS_ALIGN_ANY);

   // 3 - Define toolbar docking behavior, dock toolbars
   EkDockToolBar( this, &m_wndShapes1 );
   EkDockToolBar( this, &m_wndColors1,
                  AFX_IDW_DOCKBAR_TOP, &m_wndShapes1 );
   EkDockToolBar( this, &m_wndDemo1,
```

```
                    AFX_IDW_DOCKBAR_LEFT );
    EkDockToolBar( this, &m_wndColors2,
                   AFX_IDW_DOCKBAR_RIGHT );
    EkDockToolBar( this, &m_wndDemo2,
                   AFX_IDW_DOCKBAR_RIGHT, &m_wndColors2 );
    EkDockToolBar( this, &m_wndColors3,
                   AFX_IDW_DOCKBAR_BOTTOM );
    EkDockToolBar( this, &m_wndShapes2,
                   AFX_IDW_DOCKBAR_BOTTOM, &m_wndColors3 );

    return 0;
}
```

Sample Code

- Project: AddToolbars in the Chap06 subdirectory on the companion CD-ROM.
- Purpose: Demonstrates how to add several toolbars to the main frame window and to a view's frame window, as shown in Figure 6-1.

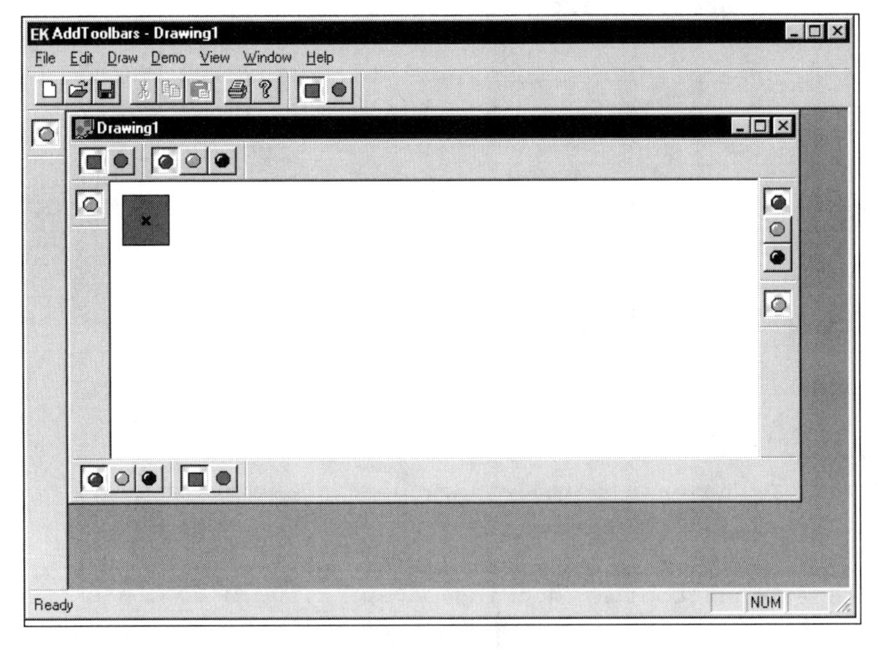

Figure 6-1. The AddToolbars sample application adds two toolbars to the main frame window and seven toolbars to the view's frame window. All the toolbars can be docked or floated.

Implementation Highlights

- *EkCreateToolBar()* function (MainFrm.cpp)
- *EkDockToolBar()* function (MainFrm.cpp)
- *CMainFrame::OnCreate()* function (MainFrm.cpp)
- *CChildFrame::OnCreate()* function (ChildFrm.cpp)

See Also

- *FAQ 6.2 What are the various options available for controlling the position, orientation, and general behavior of my toolbars?*
- *FAQ 6.3 How do I programmatically dock a toolbar next to another one?*
- *FAQ 6.9 How do I add a custom status bar to a view's frame window?*

What are the various options available for controlling the position, orientation, and general behavior of my toolbars?

Now that you know how to easily add new toolbars to your application by following the explanations given in *FAQ 6.1 How do I add one or more toolbars to my main frame window or to a view's frame window?* you will probably want to control precisely where those toolbars appear, what orientation they assume, and more generally how they react to the user's actions. For example, you might wish your toolbars to remain attached to their frame window or to appear only as a floating palette, or perhaps you want to enable the user to choose whether to float or dock a toolbar.

Using the following explanations, you will understand how to select the appropriate behavior for each of your toolbars. You might also wish to try this FAQ's sample project, SelectToolbarOptions, which will allow you to try the various available options and observe the result for yourself. You will quickly find out that some options cannot be arbitrarily combined.

Figure 6-2 shows the Toolbar Properties dialog box from the SelectToolbar Options sample project.

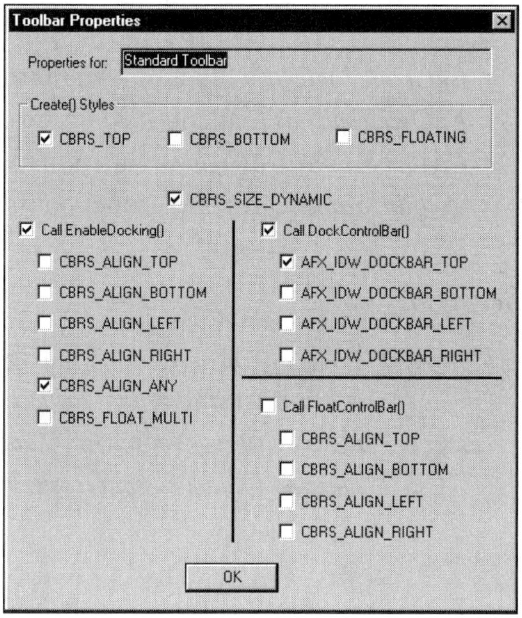

Figure 6-2. The Toolbar Properties dialog box from the SelectToolbar Options sample project allows you to experiment with the various options available for customizing a toolbar's behavior, initial position, and orientation.

The MFC framework determines the behavior and initial position and orientation of a toolbar depending on the following factors:

- The *CBRS_xxx* style that you pass to *CToolBar::Create()*.
- Whether or not you call *CControlBar::EnableDocking()* and which *CBRS_ALIGN_xxx* style(s) you pass to it.
- Whether or not you call either *CFrameWnd::DockControlBar()* or *CFrameWnd::FloatControlBar()* for your toolbar.

The *CBRS_xxx* style that you pass to *CToolBar::Create()* determines the default toolbar position: at the top or bottom of the frame window (*CBRS_TOP* and *CBRS_BOTTOM*, respectively) or floating (*CBRS_FLOATING*). Note, however, that the *CBRS_FLOATING* style did not seem to work properly with my MFC toolbar classes. You must call *CControlBar::EnableDocking()* and *CFrameWnd::FloatControlBar()* to obtain a floating toolbar.

Your toolbar will appear in the position corresponding to the *CBRS_xxx* style that you pass to *CToolBar::Create()* only if you do *not* call either *CFrameWnd::DockControlBar()* or *CFrameWnd::FloatControlBar()* for your toolbar—that is, if your toolbar will not be a docking toolbar but rather a fixed toolbar that will be attached permanently to its frame window.

If you want your toolbar to have a docking behavior or to appear as a floating toolbar, call *CControlBar::EnableDocking()* and pass a combination of *CBRS_ALIGN_xxx* style(s). These styles allow you to select the frame window sides on which your toolbar can be docked. Note that the actual sides available to the user for docking will be those for which the frame window decided to accept docking—by calling its own *EnableDocking()* function—and those on which the toolbar is willing to dock. Finally, note that MFC allows you to programmatically dock a toolbar to a side that was not specified in the flags passed to *CControlBar::EnableDocking()*; however, once the user floats the toolbar, it cannot be docked again in the same position—a surprising behavior, don't you think?

After you have called *CControlBar::EnableDocking()*, you must still call either *CFrameWnd::DockControlBar()* or *CFrameWnd::FloatControlBar()* to define your toolbar's initial position and orientation, with the adequate parameters as follows:

- If you want your toolbar to appear in the docked state, call *CFrameWnd::DockControlBar()* and specify the *AFX_IDW_DOCKBAR_xxx* flag that corresponds to the side of the frame window to which you want to dock. Docking on the top or bottom side orients your toolbar horizontally, whereas docking on the left or right side orients it vertically. The optional *lpRect* parameter of *CFrameWnd::DockControlBar()* allows you to specify more precisely the position of your toolbar on its docking area, as explained in the later section about the *EkDockBarNextTo()* function.
- If you want your toolbar to appear in the floating state, call *CFrameWnd::FloatControlBar()*. The *point* parameter gives—in screen coordinates—the position of the upper-left corner of your floating toolbar, whereas the *dwStyle* parameter allows you to choose your toolbar's orientation: *CBRS_ALIGN_TOP* and *CBRS_ALIGN_BOTTOM* give your toolbar a horizontal orientation, and *CBRS_ALIGN_LEFT* and *CBRS_ALIGN_RIGHT* orient it vertically.

Note that you can call *CControlBar::SetBarStyle()*—usually right after the *Create()* call—to select additional behavior options for your toolbar, such as the following:

- Whether your toolbar will support ToolTips: *CBRS_TOOLTIPS*
- Whether your toolbar will cause help prompts to appear when the user pauses the mouse on a button: *CBRS_FLYBY*

- Whether your toolbar can be dynamically resized by the user while in the floating state: *CBRS_SIZE_DYNAMIC*

Finally, if you want to precisely dock a toolbar next to another one, be sure to look at the *EkDockBarNextTo()* function discussed in *FAQ 6.3 How do I programmatically dock a toolbar next to another one?*

■

Additional Comments

Listing 6-7 shows the function in the SelectToolbarOptions sample project that creates a toolbar according to the various options selected in the Toolbar Properties dialog box.

Listing 6-7. The *CreateToolBarWithOptions()* function.

```
BOOL CMainFrame::CreateToolBarWithOptions(
                                    CToolBar* pBar,
                                    UINT nIDBar,
                                    UINT nIDResource,
                                    CDemoDlg* pDlg,
                                    LPCTSTR lpszName )
{
   ASSERT_VALID( pBar );
   pDlg->m_strName = lpszName;
   pDlg->DoModal();

   // 1 - Create toolbar
   {
      DWORD dwStyle = WS_CHILD | WS_VISIBLE;
      dwStyle |= ( pDlg->m_bCreateTop ? CBRS_TOP : 0 );
      dwStyle |= ( pDlg->m_bCreateBottom ?
                           CBRS_BOTTOM : 0 );
      dwStyle |= ( pDlg->m_bCreateFloating ?
                           CBRS_FLOATING : 0 );

      if( !pBar->Create(this, dwStyle, nIDBar ) ||
          !pBar->LoadToolBar( nIDResource ) )
      {
         TRACE1( "Failed to create '%s' toolbar\n",
                 lpszName );
```

```
      return FALSE;      // fail to create
   }
}

// 2 - Set additional toolbar style
pBar->SetBarStyle( pBar->GetBarStyle() |
            CBRS_TOOLTIPS | CBRS_FLYBY |
            ( pDlg->m_bSizeDynamic ?
                       CBRS_SIZE_DYNAMIC : 0 ) );

// 3 - Enable toolbar docking
if( pDlg->m_bEnableDocking )
{
   DWORD dwStyle = 0;
   dwStyle |= ( pDlg->m_bEnableTop ?
                         CBRS_ALIGN_TOP : 0 );
   dwStyle |= ( pDlg->m_bEnableBottom ?
                         CBRS_ALIGN_BOTTOM : 0 );
   dwStyle |= ( pDlg->m_bEnableLeft ?
                         CBRS_ALIGN_LEFT : 0 );
   dwStyle |= ( pDlg->m_bEnableRight ?
                         CBRS_ALIGN_RIGHT : 0 );
   dwStyle |= ( pDlg->m_bEnableAny ?
                         CBRS_ALIGN_ANY : 0 );
   dwStyle |= ( pDlg->m_bEnableFloatMulti ?
                      CBRS_FLOAT_MULTI : 0 );

   pBar->EnableDocking( dwStyle );

}

// 4 - Dock toolbar
if( pDlg->m_bDockControlBar )
{
   DWORD dwStyle = 0;
   dwStyle |= ( pDlg->m_bDockbarTop ?
                         AFX_IDW_DOCKBAR_TOP : 0 );
   dwStyle |= ( pDlg->m_bDockbarBottom ?
                         AFX_IDW_DOCKBAR_BOTTOM : 0 );
   dwStyle |= ( pDlg->m_bDockbarLeft ?
                         AFX_IDW_DOCKBAR_LEFT : 0 );
   dwStyle |= ( pDlg->m_bDockbarRight ?
```

```
                                    AFX_IDW_DOCKBAR_RIGHT : 0 );

        DockControlBar( pBar, dwStyle );
    }

    // 5 - Float toolbar
    if( pDlg->m_bFloatControlBar )
    {
        DWORD dwStyle = 0;
        dwStyle |= ( pDlg->m_bFloatTop ?
                                    CBRS_ALIGN_TOP : 0 );
        dwStyle |= ( pDlg->m_bFloatBottom ?
                                    CBRS_ALIGN_BOTTOM : 0 );
        dwStyle |= ( pDlg->m_bFloatLeft ?
                                    CBRS_ALIGN_LEFT : 0 );
        dwStyle |= ( pDlg->m_bFloatRight ?
                                    CBRS_ALIGN_RIGHT : 0 );

        CRect rect;
        GetWindowRect( &rect );
        CPoint point( rect.left + 100, rect.top + 100 );

        FloatControlBar( pBar, point, dwStyle );
    }

    return TRUE;
}
```

Sample Code

- Project: SelectToolbarOptions in the Chap06 subdirectory on the companion CD-ROM.
- Purpose: Implements a dialog box that allows you to experiment with the various options available for customizing a toolbar's behavior and initial position and orientation, as shown earlier in Figure 6-2.

Implementation Highlights

- *CMainFrame::CreateToolBarWithOptions()* function (MainFrm.cpp)
- *CMainFrame::OnCreateStandardToolbar()* function (MainFrm.cpp)
- *CMainFrame:: OnCreateShapesToolbar()* function (MainFrm.cpp)

See Also

- *FAQ 6.1 How do I add one or more toolbars to my main frame window or to a view's frame window?*
- *FAQ 6.3 How do I programmatically dock a toolbar next to another one?*

How do I programmatically dock a toolbar next to another one?

If you start to add several toolbars to your application, you will rapidly need a means of controlling their initial docked position. Repeatedly calling *CFrameWnd::DockControlBar()* with an ID such as *AFX_IDW_DOCKBAR_TOP* often will not do the trick, because the standard MFC layout algorithm will make each of your toolbars appear on a different docking band, as shown in Figure 6-3.

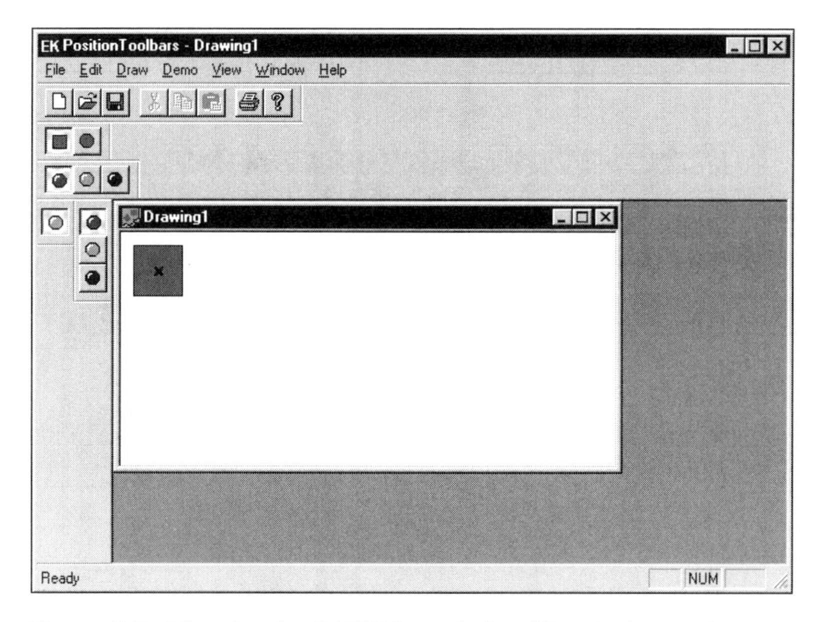

Figure 6-3. The standard MFC layout algorithm makes each toolbar appear on a different docking band.

You would probably prefer to lay out your toolbars on the same docking band, as shown in Figure 6-4.

The implementation of *EkDockBarNextTo()* is shown in Listing 6-8.

Listing 6-8. Implementation of *EkDockBarNextTo()*.

```
void EkDockBarNextTo( CControlBar* pNewBar,
                      CControlBar* pDockedBar,
                      UINT nDockBarID=AFX_IDW_DOCKBAR_TOP )
{
   ASSERT_VALID( pDockedBar );
   ASSERT_VALID( pNewBar );

   // 1 - Find the frame where we will dock
   CFrameWnd* pFrame = pDockedBar->GetDockingFrame();

   // 2 - Force MFC to compute the positions
   // of the docked control bar(s)
   pFrame->RecalcLayout();

   // 3 - Compute rectangle of already "docked" bar
   CRect rect;
   pDockedBar->GetWindowRect( &rect );
```

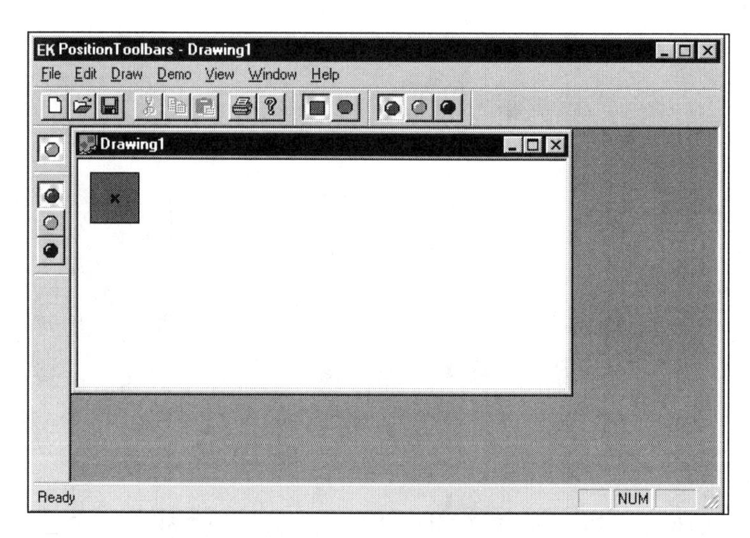

Figure 6-4. The *EkDockBarNextTo()* function allows you to lay out your toolbars next to each other on the same docking band, either horizontally or vertically.

```
   // 4 - Offset the rectangle slightly to the bottom right
   // so that the new bar will dock either to the right or
   // to the bottom of the existing bar (depending on the
   // side where this last bar is already docked)
   rect.OffsetRect(1,1);

   // 5 - Dock new bar to specified position
   pFrame->DockControlBar( pNewBar, nDockBarID, &rect );
}
```

Listing 6-9 shows how the code in sample project PositionToolbars calls *EkDockBarNextTo()* to lay out the child frame toolbars as shown in Figure 6-4.

Listing 6-9. Calling *EkDockBarNextTo()* to lay out your toolbars as shown in Figure 6-4.

```
int CMainFrame::OnCreate(LPCREATESTRUCT lpCreateStruct)
{
   if (CMDIFrameWnd::OnCreate(lpCreateStruct) == -1)
      return -1;

   // ...
   // Create toolbars and status bar
   // ...

   // Mainframe docking
   EnableDocking(CBRS_ALIGN_ANY);

   // Standard toolbar docking: top band, left position
   m_wndToolBar.EnableDocking(CBRS_ALIGN_ANY);
   DockControlBar( &m_wndToolBar, AFX_IDW_DOCKBAR_TOP );

   // Shapes toolbar docking: top band, next to standard
   // toolbar
   m_wndTBshapes.EnableDocking(CBRS_ALIGN_ANY);
   EkDockBarNextTo( &m_wndTBshapes, &m_wndToolBar,
                    AFX_IDW_DOCKBAR_TOP );

   // Colors1 toolbar docking: top band, next to shapes
   // toolbar
   m_wndTBcolors1.EnableDocking(CBRS_ALIGN_ANY);
   EkDockBarNextTo( &m_wndTBcolors1, &m_wndTBshapes,
                   AFX_IDW_DOCKBAR_TOP );
```

```
    // Demo toolbar docking: left band
    m_wndTBdemo.EnableDocking(CBRS_ALIGN_ANY);
    DockControlBar( &m_wndTBdemo, AFX_IDW_DOCKBAR_LEFT );

    // Colors2 toolbar docking: left band, next to demo
    // toolbar
    m_wndTBcolors2.EnableDocking(CBRS_ALIGN_ANY);
    EkDockBarNextTo( &m_wndTBcolors2, &m_wndTBdemo,
                     AFX_IDW_DOCKBAR_LEFT );

    return 0;
}
```

Note that the helper *EkDockToolBar()* function (described in *FAQ 6.1 How do I add one or more toolbars to my main frame window or to a view's frame window?*) also allows you to dock a toolbar next to another one, thanks to its *pBarNextTo* argument. This helper function actually calls *EkDockBarNextTo()* to implement this docking behavior.

■

Sample Code

- Project: PositionToolbars in the Chap06 subdirectory on the companion CD-ROM.
- Purpose: Demonstrates how to call *EkDockBarNextTo()* to lay out toolbars next to each other on the same docking band, as shown earlier in Figure 6-4.

Implementation Highlights

- *EkDockBarNextTo()* function (MainFrm.cpp)
- *CMainFrame::OnCreate()* function (MainFrm.cpp)

See Also

- FAQ 6.1 *How do I add one or more toolbars to my main frame window or to a view's frame window?*
- FAQ 6.2 *What are the various options available for controlling the position, orientation, and general behavior of my toolbars?*

How do I add a combo box to a toolbar?

There is no denying that buttons-only toolbars can significantly enhance many applications. However, adding other kinds of controls, such as combo boxes, to a toolbar can also significantly enhance its usefulness in many cases. You have only to look at the standard toolbars of Microsoft Word, Developer Studio, or even the standard Windows Explorer to understand what I mean.

Fortunately, adding a combo box to an existing MFC toolbar is not too tricky if you follow the explanations in this FAQ. Figure 6-5 shows the look of this FAQ's sample application. Note the combo boxes in the main frame and view's frame windows. Although it is not apparent on the screen capture, the behavior of this combo box is perfectly synchronized with the standard toolbar buttons and menu items.

Adding the Combo Box to the Toolbar

Step 1. Open your .rc resource file in an ASCII text editor—or in Developer Studio while specifying "As Text" in the Open File dialog box—and

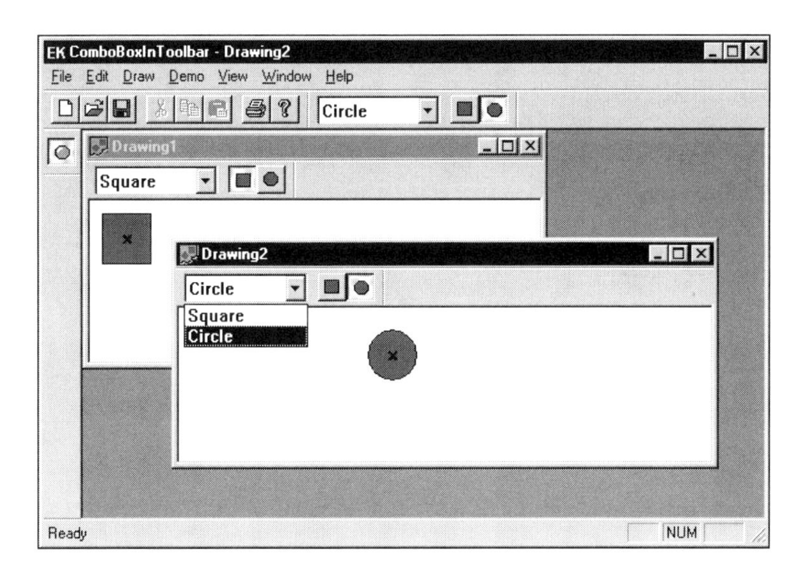

Figure 6-5. The ComboBoxInToolbar sample application features a combo box toolbar both in its main frame and in the view's frame windows.

locate your toolbar resource definition. Edit this definition to add *two* separators to your toolbar resource in the position where you want to create your combo box control. Listing 6-10 shows the edited resource for the Shapes toolbar in this FAQ's sample code.

Listing 6-10. The Shapes toolbar resource in this FAQ's sample code edited to add the two *SEPARATOR* entries.

```
IDR_SHAPES TOOLBAR DISCARDABLE  16, 15
BEGIN
    SEPARATOR
    SEPARATOR
    BUTTON          ID_DRAW_SQUARE
    BUTTON          ID_DRAW_CIRCLE
END
```

Step 2. Create a resource ID for your combo box control, such as *IDC_SHAPES_COMBO_BOX*. Make a good note of this ID, because it will be referenced several times in the following steps.

Step 3. Use ClassWizard to create a new *CToolBar*-derived class. Because ClassWizard does not explicitly support the creation of a *CToolBar*-derived class, you must select the "generic *CWnd*" type, let ClassWizard generate its code, and then edit this code to replace the references to *CWnd* with *CToolBar* both in the class definition and in the *BEGIN_MESSAGE_MAP* macro.

Step 4. Add a member variable of type *CComboBox* to your new toolbar class, as shown in Listing 6-11.

Listing 6-11. Adding a member variable of type *CComboBox* to the new toolbar class.

```
class CShapesToolBar : public CToolBar
{
// ...

// Attributes
public:
   CComboBox   m_cmbShapes;    // toolbar combo box

// ...
};
```

Step 5. Manually override the *CToolBar::Create()* virtual function in your toolbar class. Implement this function as shown in Listing 6-12 to create the embedded combo box when the host toolbar gets created. Note that step 6 in Listing 6-12 could be implemented in the frame window class that hosts the toolbar instead of inside the toolbar class.

LISTING 6-12. Implementation of the *Create()* virtual function in the toolbar class.

```
// ————————————————————————————————
// Class definition for CShapesToolBar (ShapesToolBar.h)

class CShapesToolBar : public CToolBar
{
// ...
public:
   BOOL Create( CWnd* pParentWnd,
                DWORD dwStyle = WS_CHILD | WS_VISIBLE |
                                           CBRS_TOP,
                UINT nID = AFX_IDW_TOOLBAR );

// ...
};

// ————————————————————————————————
// Implementation for CShapesToolBar (ShapesToolBar.cpp)

BOOL CShapesToolBar::Create( CWnd* pParentWnd,
                             DWORD dwStyle, UINT nID )
{
   // 1 - Create toolbar and load related resources
   if( !CToolBar::Create( pParentWnd, dwStyle, nID ) ||
       !LoadToolBar(IDR_SHAPES) )
   {
      return FALSE;
   }

   // 2 - Enlarge placeholder
   SetButtonInfo( 0, IDC_SHAPES_COMBO_BOX,
                  TBBS_SEPARATOR, 100 );

   // 3 - Retrieve destination coordinates
   CRect rect;
   GetItemRect( 0, &rect );
```

```
    // 4 - Enlarge rectangle to account for drop height
    rect.bottom = rect.top + 100;

    // 5 - Create toolbar combo box
    m_cmbShapes.Create( WS_CHILD | WS_VISIBLE | WS_VSCROLL |
                                                     CBS_DROPDOWNLIST,
                          rect, this, IDC_SHAPES_COMBO_BOX );

    // 6 - Add some entries to the combo box
    m_cmbShapes.AddString( _T( "Square" ) );
    m_cmbShapes.AddString( _T( "Circle" ) );

    return TRUE;
}
```

Step 6. Modify your frame window class to reference your new toolbar class instead of the classic *CToolBar* class, as shown in Listing 6-13.

Listing 6-13. Modifying the frame window class to reference the new toolbar class.

```
class CMainFrame : public CMDIFrameWnd
{
// ...

protected:  // control bar embedded members
    CStatusBar  m_wndStatusBar;
    CToolBar    m_wndToolBar;
    CShapesToolBar    m_wndTBshapes;  // combo box toolbar
    CToolBar    m_wndTBdemo;

// ...
};
```

Step 7. Create a string resource having the same ID as your combo box control (*IDC_SHAPES_COMBO_BOX* in the preceding discussion) to define both the prompt and the ToolTip associated with your combo box control; use the MFC standard "*Prompt text\nToolTip*" string format.

Your toolbar should now create itself correctly along with its embedded combo box control. However, creating the toolbar is only half the work: we still need to handle the *CBN_SELCHANGE* and *UPDATE_COMMAND_UI* messages for the combo box control if we expect it to become useful. How to do this is the subject of the next section.

Handling the CBN_SELCHANGE *and* UPDATE_COMMAND_UI *Messages*

To become fully functional, your toolbar combo box should do the following:

- Propagate the *CBN_SELCHANGE* message—indicating that the user has just selected a new item in the list—so that your code can handle this message in the most convenient place, just as if the user had clicked on a toolbar button
- Automatically update itself using the standard MFC *UPDATE_COMMAND_UI* mechanism

Believe it or not, solving these two issues was not as easy as you might think, especially because the handlers for the *CBN_SELCHANGE* and *UPDATE_COMMAND_UI* messages can easily step on each other's toes and result in an incorrect behavior.

Step 1. Manually add a handler in your new toolbar class for the *CBN_SELCHANGE* message. Implement this handler as shown in Listing 6-14 to repackage the *CBN_SELCHANGE* message in a custom *WM_COMMAND* message and send this last message on MFC's message-routing highway.

Listing 6-14. Handling the *CBN_SELCHANGE* message.

```
// ————————————————————————————
// Class definition for CShapesToolBar (ShapesToolBar.h)

class CShapesToolBar : public CToolBar
{
// ...
protected:
   //{{AFX_MSG(CShapesToolBar)
   afx_msg void OnSelChangeShapesComboBox();
                                  // toolbar combo box
   //}}AFX_MSG
   DECLARE_MESSAGE_MAP()
// ...
};

// ————————————————————————————
// Implementation for CShapesToolBar (ShapesToolBar.cpp)
```

```
BEGIN_MESSAGE_MAP(CShapesToolBar, CToolBar)
   //{{AFX_MSG_MAP(CShapesToolBar)
   ON_CBN_SELCHANGE(IDC_SHAPES_COMBO_BOX,
                                    OnSelChangeShapesComboBox)
   //}}AFX_MSG_MAP
END_MESSAGE_MAP()

// ...

void CShapesToolBar::OnSelChangeShapesComboBox()
{

   // Transform CBN_SELCHANGE message into WM_COMMAND
   // with combo box HWND into LPARAM
   AfxGetMainWnd()->PostMessage(
      WM_COMMAND, MAKEWPARAM( IDC_SHAPES_COMBO_BOX, 0 ),
      reinterpret_cast<LPARAM>(m_cmbShapes.GetSafeHwnd()));
}
```

Step 2. Manually add handlers for the *WM_COMMAND(IDC_SHAPES_COMBO_BOX)* and *UPDATE_COMMAND_UI(IDC_SHAPES_COMBO_BOX)* messages in the appropriate class—usually the class that manages the data (or state) related to the various combo box items. In the case of this project's sample FAQ, the combo box represents the currently selected shape, which is stored and managed by the *CDrawDoc* class; therefore, the *WM_COMMAND* and *UPDATE_COMMAND_UI* handlers are implemented in this class, as shown in Listing 6-15.

Listing 6-15. Implementation of the handlers for the *WM_COMMAND(IDC_SHAPES_COMBO_BOX)* and *UPDATE_COMMAND_UI(IDC_SHAPES_COMBO_BOX)* messages in the *CDrawDoc* class.

```
// ———————————————————————————
// Class definition for CDrawDoc (DrawDoc.h)

class CDrawDoc : public CDocument
{
// ...

protected:
   //{{AFX_MSG(CDrawDoc)
```

```
    // ...

    // Toolbar combo box
    afx_msg void OnSelChangeTBComboBox();
    afx_msg void OnUpdateTBComboBox(CCmdUI* pCmdUI);

    // ...
    //}}AFX_MSG
    DECLARE_MESSAGE_MAP()
};

// ___________________________________
// Implementation for CDrawDoc (DrawDoc.cpp)

BEGIN_MESSAGE_MAP(CDrawDoc, CDocument)
    //{{AFX_MSG_MAP(CDrawDoc)
    // ...

    // Toolbar combo box
    ON_COMMAND(IDC_SHAPES_COMBO_BOX, OnSelChangeTBComboBox)
    ON_UPDATE_COMMAND_UI(IDC_SHAPES_COMBO_BOX,
                                     OnUpdateTBComboBox)

    // ...
    //}}AFX_MSG_MAP
END_MESSAGE_MAP()

// ...

void CDrawDoc::OnSelChangeTBComboBox()
{
    // Find combo box from LPARAM
    HWND hWnd = reinterpret_cast<HWND>(
                        AfxGetApp()->m_msgCur.lParam );

    ASSERT( ::IsWindow( hWnd ) );

    CComboBox* pCB = static_cast<CComboBox*>(
                        CWnd::FromHandle( hWnd ) );

    ASSERT_VALID( pCB );
    ASSERT( pCB->GetDlgCtrlID() == IDC_SHAPES_COMBO_BOX );
```

```
    // Update document
    m_shape = static_cast< SHAPE >( pCB->GetCurSel() );
    UpdateAllViews( NULL );
    SetModifiedFlag( TRUE );
}

void CDrawDoc::OnUpdateTBComboBox(CCmdUI* pCmdUI)
{
    // Find combo box from pCmdUI
    CComboBox* pCB = static_cast<CComboBox*>(
                                pCmdUI->m_pOther );

    ASSERT( ::IsWindow( pCB->GetSafeHwnd() ) );
    ASSERT( pCB->GetDlgCtrlID() == IDC_SHAPES_COMBO_BOX );

    // Test to prevent flicker
    if( m_shape != pCB->GetCurSel() &&
        !pCB->GetDroppedState() )
    {
        pCB->SetCurSel( m_shape );
    }
}
```

Your toolbar combo box should now be fully functional.

■

Explanations

Although the first part of the preceding technique is not hard to understand, correctly handling the *CBN_SELCHANGE* and *UPDATE_COMMAND_UI* messages requires more exotic code. The main idea in the *CBN_SELCHANGE* handler shown in Listing 6-14 is to convert the *CBN_SELCHANGE* message into a custom *WM_COMMAND* message that will automatically be routed by the MFC architecture to the correct handler. This approach gives you the flexibility of implementing this *WM_COMMAND* handler as usual in the appropriate class for your application.

I had to solve two problems to ensure the success of this technique:

- Ensure that the technique still works correctly with multiple combo boxes that can be embedded inside either the same or different toolbars.

- Provide a means for the *WM_COMMAND* handler to access the combo box that generated the initial *CBN_SELCHANGE* message—because this code typically needs to retrieve the index of the newly selected item.

The implementation for the *CBN_SELCHANGE* shown in Listing 6-14 solves both problems by packaging custom parameters inside the *wParam* and *lParam* attributes of the *WM_COMMAND* message:

```
AfxGetMainWnd()->PostMessage(
        WM_COMMAND,
        MAKEWPARAM( IDC_SHAPES_COMBO_BOX, 0 ),
        reinterpret_cast<LPARAM>(m_cmbShapes.GetSafeHwnd()));
```

The *wParam* attribute is set to the ID of the combo box control, which was created in step 2 in the earlier section called Adding the Combo Box to the Toolbar. Provided that this ID is unique—such as a menu item ID—the MFC message-routing mechanism ensures that notifications originating from multiple combo boxes can be handled safely and easily by coding the appropriate *ON_COMMAND* message map entry.

The *lParam* attribute is set to the *hWnd* of the combo box control. This trick allows the code that handles the *WM_COMMAND* message to retrieve this handle and thus to manipulate the combo box control as it needs to, as shown in the following excerpt from Listing 6-15:

```
void CDrawDoc::OnSelChangeTBComboBox()
{
    // Find combo box from LPARAM
    HWND hwnd = reinterpret_cast<HWND>(
                              AfxGetApp()->m_msgCur.lParam );
    CComboBox* pCB = static_cast<CComboBox*>(
                              CWnd::FromHandle( hwnd ) );
    // ...
}
```

In the preceding code fragment, note the use of the undocumented *CWinThread::m_msgCur* public member variable. This member is an *MSG* structure that contains the Windows message that is currently being processed. This knowledge enables our code to extract the combo box's *hWnd* from the *lParam* field that was previously initialized by the *CBN_SELCHANGE* handler.

The *UPDATE_COMMAND_UI* handler has an easier way to obtain the combo box control, thanks to the *CCmdUI::m_pOther* member variable. This member is a pointer to the *CWnd* object for which the *UPDATE_*

COMMAND_UI message was generated. This should be our combo box control, just what we need!

Additional Comments

Once the appropriate command-handling code is in place, you can attach your new toolbar class to any frame window. As an example, this FAQ's sample project features the same Shapes toolbar both in its main frame window and in the view's frame window, as shown earlier in Figure 6-5.

Sample Code

- Project: ComboBoxInToolbar in the Chap06 subdirectory on the companion CD-ROM.
- Purpose: Implements a toolbar with an embedded combo box control that is synchronized with the standard toolbar buttons and menu items (see Figure 6-5, shown earlier).

Implementation Highlights

- *CShapesToolBar* class (ShapesToolBar.h, ShapesToolBar.cpp)
- *CShapesToolBar::Create()* function (ShapesToolBar.cpp)
- *CShapesToolBar::OnSelChangeShapesComboBox()* function (ShapesToolBar.cpp)
- *CDrawDoc::OnSelChangeTBComboBox()* function (DrawDoc.cpp)
- *CDrawDoc::OnUpdateTBComboBox()* function (DrawDoc.cpp)

How do I add text labels to my toolbar buttons?

Some users might find your toolbars easier to use if their buttons display not only an icon but also a short text label, as do the default buttons in, for example, Internet Explorer.

The *CToolBar* class provides the *SetButtonText()* function, which allows you to set the text of an individual toolbar button:

```
BOOL CToolBar::SetButtonText( int nIndex,
                              LPCTSTR lpszText );
```

However, if you decide to add text labels to your buttons, you will usually want to do so for all the buttons on a given toolbar, and calling *CToolBar::SetButtonText()* once for each button will quickly become tedious. This is why I have designed the *EkSetToolBarButtonText()* function, whose implementation is shown in Listing 6-16. This function allows you to set the text labels of all the buttons on a given toolbar with a single function call.

Listing 6-16. Implementation of *EkSetToolBarButtonText()* to set the text labels of all the buttons on a given toolbar.

```
void EkSetToolBarButtonText( CToolBar* pBar,
                             UINT nIDStrings,
                             TCHAR chSep = _T( '\n' ) )
{
   ASSERT_VALID( pBar );

   // 1 - Load string from resource
   CString strButtons;
   VERIFY( strButtons.LoadString( nIDStrings ) );

   // 2 - Start at beginning of string
   int nIndex = 0;
   LPCTSTR pszStart = strButtons;
   LPCTSTR pszEnd = NULL;

   // 3 - Isolate each substring and set button text
   do
   {
      // 4 - Find next separator
      pszEnd = _tcschr( pszStart, chSep );

      int nLen = ( pszEnd == NULL ) ?
                 _tcslen( pszStart ) :
                 (int)( pszEnd - pszStart );
      ASSERT( nLen >= 0 );

      // 5 - Create CString from substring
      CString strSubString;
      memcpy(   strSubString.GetBufferSetLength( nLen ),
                pszStart, nLen * sizeof( TCHAR ) );

      // 6 - Set button text, bump index
      pBar->SetButtonText( nIndex++, strSubString );
```

```
        // 7 - Skip separator
        pszStart += nLen + 1;
    }
    while( pszEnd != NULL );
}
```

To use *EkSetToolBarButtonText()* on a given toolbar, you should first create a string resource containing the text labels associated with each button on your toolbar, in the same order as your toolbar buttons: from left to right or top to bottom. Use a character of your choice as a separator between each label. I suggest using the "\n" character, because this is the default value for the *chSep* argument of *EkSetToolBarButtonText()*. Finally, don't forget to include empty string entries for the toolbar separator buttons. Here is a sample string resource for the standard AppWizard-generated toolbar:

```
"New\nOpen\nSave\n\nCut\nCopy\nPaste\n\nPrint\nAbout"
```

Once you have created the various string resources associated with your toolbars, do the following:

- Call *EkSetToolBarButtonText()* to set the text labels of each toolbar.
- Call *CToolBar::SetSizes()* to resize each toolbar to accommodate the new button size.

Listing 6-17 shows how this FAQ's sample project adds text labels to the standard toolbar and Shapes toolbar.

Listing 6-17. Calling *EkSetToolBarButtonText()* and *CToolBar::SetSizes()* to add text labels to toolbar buttons.

```
int CMainFrame::OnCreate(LPCREATESTRUCT lpCreateStruct)
{
    if (CMDIFrameWnd::OnCreate(lpCreateStruct) == -1)
        return -1;

    if (!m_wndToolBar.Create(this) ||
         !m_wndToolBar.LoadToolBar(IDR_MAINFRAME))
    {
        TRACE0("Failed to create standard toolbar\n");
        return -1;      // fail to create
    }
```

```
    EkSetToolBarButtonText( &m_wndToolBar,
                            IDS_BUTTONS_STANDARD );
    m_wndToolBar.SetSizes(CSize( 48, 35 ), CSize( 16, 15 ));
    if (!m_wndTBshapes.Create(this, WS_CHILD | WS_VISIBLE |
                              CBRS_TOP, IDR_SHAPES) ||
        !m_wndTBshapes.LoadToolBar(IDR_SHAPES))
    {
        TRACE0("Failed to create shapes toolbar\n");
        return -1;      // fail to create
    }

    EkSetToolBarButtonText( &m_wndTBshapes,
                            IDS_BUTTONS_SHAPES );
    m_wndTBshapes.SetSizes(CSize(48, 35), CSize(16, 15));

    // ...
}
```

■

Additional Comments

If you want to learn how your application can give its users the option of showing a toolbar with or without text labels, be sure to check the sample project for *FAQ 6.8 How do I dynamically switch between different toolbars?*

Sample Code

- Project: ButtonText in the Chap06 subdirectory on the companion CD-ROM.
- Purpose: Demonstrates how to add text labels to toolbar buttons, as shown in Figure 6-6.

Implementation Highlights

- *EkSetToolBarButtonText()* function (MainFrm.cpp)
- *CMainFrame::OnCreate()* function (MainFrm.cpp)

See Also

- *FAQ 6.8 How do I dynamically switch between different toolbars?*

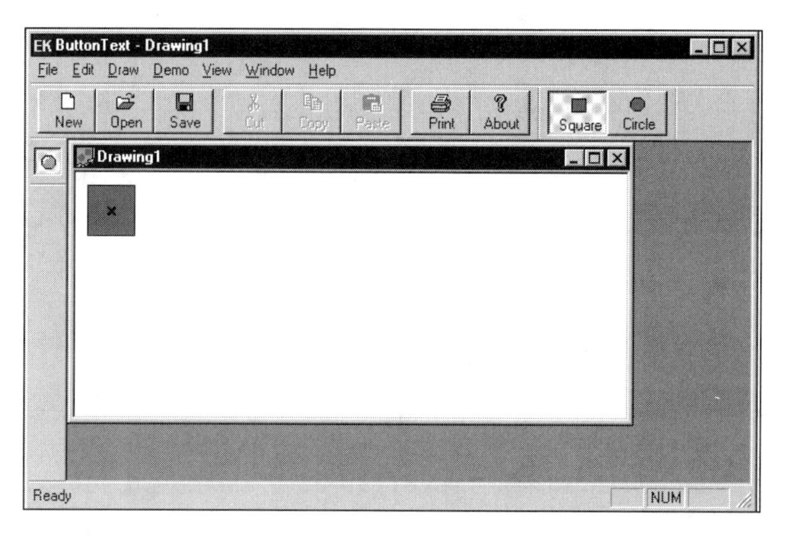

Figure 6-6. Text labels take the mystery out of toolbar buttons.

FAQ 6.6 How do I implement a menu that allows users to select the toolbars they want to see?

If you follow the explanations given in *FAQ 6.1 How do I add one or more toolbars to my main frame window or to a view's frame window?* to create several additional toolbars, it becomes mandatory to let users select the toolbars they want to see.

One standard way of providing this option is to build a menu that lists each of your toolbars, perhaps similar to the "View, Toolbars" menu of Microsoft Word 97. Users can then use this menu to select a toolbar they need or recall a toolbar that was inadvertently closed.

You could build this menu and handle its commands in the classic MFC way: by writing separate *ON_COMMAND* and *ON_UPDATE_COMMAND_UI* handlers for each entry in your menu. However, this approach is not very elegant nor easy to maintain if you want to offer a lot of toolbars in your application.

If you follow the technique explained here, all the code that handles the state of your toolbars will be condensed into two functions, and you will be able to hook additional toolbars into this mechanism by sticking to a simple convention and adding two message map macros for each toolbar. What could be easier and more maintainable?

Step 1. Create your "View, Toolbars" menu using the Visual Studio Resource Editor. Create a menu entry for each of your toolbars, and give each menu entry a distinct ID, such as *ID_VIEW_MY_FIRST_TOOLBAR*, *ID_VIEW_MY_SECOND_TOOLBAR*, and so on.

Step 2. Modify your toolbar creation code so that each toolbar has the same ID as the corresponding "View, Toolbars" menu item. You typically do this by changing the last argument of the *CToolbar::Create()* function when you create your toolbars in your frame window's *OnCreate()* function:

```
if (!m_wndTBshapes.Create( this,
                           WS_CHILD|WS_VISIBLE|CBRS_TOP,
                           ID_VIEW_SHAPES_TOOLBAR )
          // same ID as corresponding menu entry
 || !m_wndTBshapes.LoadToolBar(IDR_SHAPES))
   {
     TRACE0("Failed to create shapes toolbar\n");
     return -1;      // fail to create
   }
```

Step 3. Manually add *OnToggleBar()* and *OnUpdateBarMenu()* to your frame window class, and implement these functions as shown in Listing 6-18. These two functions will handle the menu commands and the *UPDATE_COMMAND_UI* feedback for all the toolbars hosted by your frame window class, thanks to the message map entries that we will add in step 4. Note that these functions use the *EkIsBarVisible()* helper function that is discussed in *FAQ 6.15 How do I programmatically show or hide a control bar?*

Listing 6-18. Implementation of *OnToggleBar()* and *OnUpdateBarMenu()*.

```
// ————————————————————————————
// Class definition for CMainFrame (MainFrm.h)

class CMainFrame : public CMDIFrameWnd
{
// ...

// Generated message map functions
protected:
   //{{AFX_MSG(CMainFrame)
   // ...
```

```
    afx_msg BOOL OnToggleBar(UINT nID);
    afx_msg void OnUpdateBarMenu(CCmdUI* pCmdUI);
    // ...
    //}}AFX_MSG
    DECLARE_MESSAGE_MAP()
};

// ______________________________
// Implementation for CMainFrame (MainFrm.cpp)

BOOL CMainFrame::OnToggleBar(UINT nID)
{
    // 1 - Find the control bar that we should show or hide
    CControlBar* pBar = GetControlBar( nID );

    if( pBar != NULL )
    {
        // 2 - Toggle the control bar "visible" state
        ShowControlBar( pBar, !EkIsBarVisible(pBar), FALSE );
        return TRUE;    // Command handled
    }
    return FALSE;       // Command not handled
}

void CMainFrame::OnUpdateBarMenu(CCmdUI* pCmdUI)
{
    // 1 - Find the control bar for which we are called
    CControlBar* pBar = GetControlBar( pCmdUI->m_nID );

    if( pBar != NULL )
    {
        // 2 - Set "checked" state depending on
        // "visible" state
        pCmdUI->SetCheck( EkIsBarVisible( pBar ) );
        return;                     // Command handled
    }

    pCmdUI->ContinueRouting();    // Command not handled
}
```

Step 4. For each toolbar hosted by your frame window, manually add the following two entries to your frame window class message map:

- An *ON_COMMAND_EX* entry that maps to *OnToggleBar()*
- An *ON_UPDATE_COMMAND_UI* entry that maps to *OnUpdateBarMenu()*

Listing 6-19 shows what the message map looks like for this FAQ's sample project, which handles the "visible" state of the standard MFC toolbar and status bar—see the Additional Comments section for more explanations on handling these standard control bars—as well as two additional custom toolbars.

Listing 6-19. Adding *ON_COMMAND_EX* and *ON_UPDATE_COMMAND_UI* entries to your frame window class message map.

```
BEGIN_MESSAGE_MAP(CMainFrame, CMDIFrameWnd)
    //{{AFX_MSG_MAP(CMainFrame)

    // ...

    // Standard toolbar
    ON_COMMAND_EX(ID_VIEW_TOOLBAR, OnToggleBar)
    ON_UPDATE_COMMAND_UI(ID_VIEW_TOOLBAR,
                         OnUpdateBarMenu)

    // Shapes toolbar
    ON_COMMAND_EX(ID_VIEW_SHAPES_TOOLBAR, OnToggleBar)
    ON_UPDATE_COMMAND_UI(ID_VIEW_SHAPES_TOOLBAR,
                         OnUpdateBarMenu)

    // Demo toolbar
    ON_COMMAND_EX(ID_VIEW_DEMO_TOOLBAR, OnToggleBar)
    ON_UPDATE_COMMAND_UI(ID_VIEW_DEMO_TOOLBAR,
                         OnUpdateBarMenu)

    // Standard status bar
    ON_COMMAND_EX(ID_VIEW_STATUS_BAR, OnToggleBar)
    ON_UPDATE_COMMAND_UI(ID_VIEW_STATUS_BAR,
                         OnUpdateBarMenu)

    // ...

    //}}AFX_MSG_MAP
END_MESSAGE_MAP()
```

■

Explanations

For more explanation about the *ON_COMMAND_EX* macro, please refer to *FAQ 7.1 How do I handle several distinct menu commands with a single function?*

Additional Comments

You need to be careful if you want to apply the preceding technique to the standard MFC toolbar and status bar. These two control bars work best within the MFC framework if you leave them with their default IDs: *AFX_IDW_TOOLBAR* and *AFX_IDW_STATUS_BAR*, respectively.

Fortunately, MFC defines—in AfxRes.h—the menu command IDs *ID_VIEW_TOOLBAR* and *ID_VIEW_STATUS_BAR* to have the same values as the corresponding control bar IDs. Therefore, you can take advantage of the preceding technique in the following way:

- Keep the standard IDs for your main toolbar and status bar by creating them as usual with AppWizard-generated code:

```
int CMainFrame::OnCreate(LPCREATESTRUCT lpCreateStruct)
{
    if (CMDIFrameWnd::OnCreate(lpCreateStruct) == -1)
        return -1;

    if (!m_wndToolBar.Create(this) ||
        !m_wndToolBar.LoadToolBar(IDR_MAINFRAME))
    {
        TRACE0("Failed to create standard toolbar\n");
        return -1;      // fail to create
    }

    // ...

    if (!m_wndStatusBar.Create(this) ||
        !m_wndStatusBar.SetIndicators(indicators,
              sizeof(indicators)/sizeof(UINT)))
    {
        TRACE0("Failed to create status bar\n");
        return -1;      // fail to create
    }

    // ...
}
```

- Define associated menu entries with IDs of *ID_VIEW_TOOLBAR* and *ID_VIEW_STATUS_BAR*.
- Create the message map entries for these two control bars as explained in step 4 (see Listing 6-19).

Sample Code

- Project: SelectToolbars in the Chap06 subdirectory on the companion CD-ROM.
- Purpose: Implements a "View" menu that allows the user to select toolbars for viewing, as shown in Figure 6-7.

Implementation Highlights

- *CMainFrame::OnToggleBar()* function (MainFrm.cpp)
- *CMainFrame::OnUpdateBarMenu()* function (MainFrm.cpp)
- *CMainFrame::OnContextMenu()* function (MainFrm.cpp)

See Also

- *FAQ 6.1* *How do I add one or more toolbars to my mainframe window or to a view's frame window?*
- *FAQ 6.7* *How do I allow users to choose the toolbars they want to see by selecting them in a popup menu that appears when they right-click on a docking zone?*
- *FAQ 6.15* *How do I programmatically show or hide a control bar?*
- *FAQ 7.1* *How do I handle several distinct menu commands with a single function?*

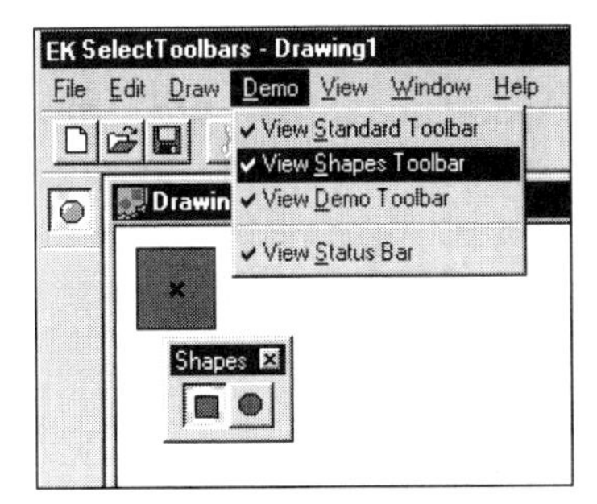

Figure 6-7. Providing a menu that allows the user to select toolbars for viewing.

6.7 How do I allow users to choose the toolbars they want to see by selecting them in a popup menu that appears when they right-click on a docking zone?

This FAQ explains how you can provide the functionality shown in *FAQ 6.6 How do I implement a menu that allows users to select the toolbars they want to see?* while at the same time adding an interesting twist: by right-clicking on any toolbar docking zone, users will see a popup menu that allows them to select the toolbars they want to see, as shown in Figure 6-8.

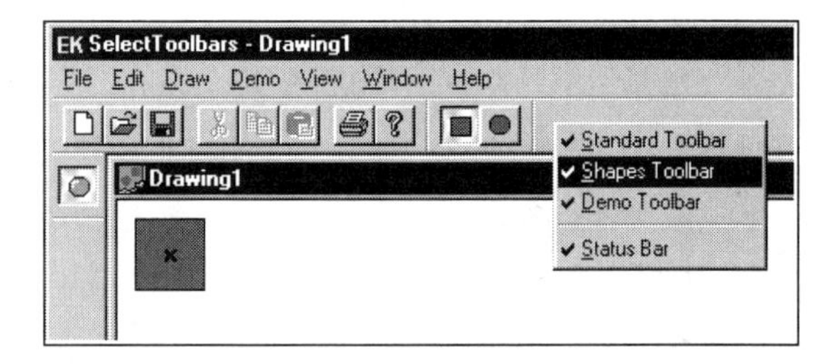

Figure 6-8. The SelectToolbars sample application allows users to select toolbars by right-clicking on any docking zone.

This behavior closely mirrors that of the Office 97 and Visual Studio applications and can therefore be considered almost a new user-interface standard for simplifying toolbar management. Fortunately, it's easy to add this nice touch to your application, thanks to the following explanations.

Step 1. Make sure that you have implemented all the steps shown in *FAQ 6.6* and that everything works properly with a standard "View, Toolbars" menu.

Step 2. Use the Visual Studio Resource Editor to create a new menu resource that corresponds to the popup menu that you want to display when the user right-clicks on a docking zone. Give this menu resource an ID similar to *IDR_POPUP_MENU.* Copy the entries from your "View, Toolbars" menu, as shown in Figure 6-9, thereby ensuring that your popup menu entries have exactly the same command IDs as your regular "View, Toolbars" menu items. The caption of your popup menu's top-level item will never be displayed, so you can give this item any label you like (see Figure 6-9).

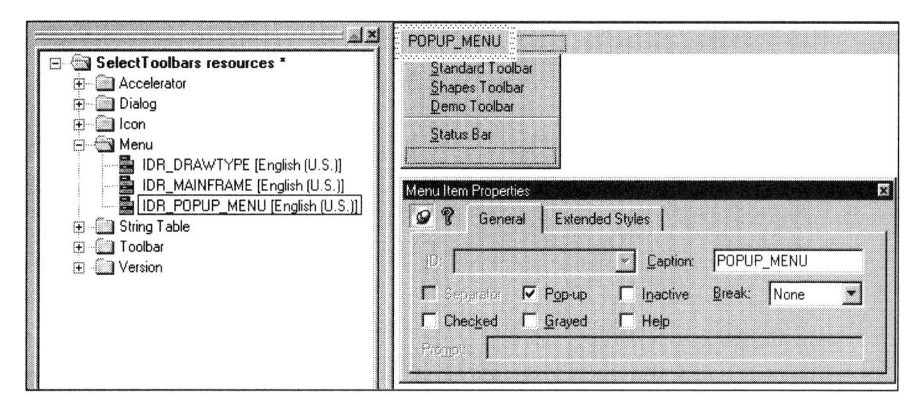

Figure 6-9. Creating the popup menu resource.

Step 3. Use ClassWizard to add a handler in your frame window class for the *WM_CONTEXTMENU* message. Implement this handler as shown in Listing 6-20 to display the popup menu.

Listing 6-20. Handling the *WM_CONTEXTMENU* message to display the popup menu.

```
#include <afxpriv.h>  // for CDockBar

void CMainFrame::OnContextMenu(CWnd* pWnd, CPoint point)
{
   // 1 - Ensure right-click was on a docking area
   if( pWnd->IsKindOf( RUNTIME_CLASS( CDockBar ) ) )
   {
      // 2 - Load top-level menu from resource
      CMenu mnuTop;
      mnuTop.LoadMenu( IDR_POPUP_MENU );

      // 3 - Get popup menu from first submenu
      CMenu* pPopup = mnuTop.GetSubMenu( 0 );
      ASSERT_VALID( pPopup );

      // Checked state for popup menu items is
      // automatically managed by standard MFC
      // UPDATE_COMMAND_UI mechanism!

      // 4 - Display popup menu
      pPopup->TrackPopupMenu( TPM_LEFTALIGN |
```

```
                                      TPM_LEFTBUTTON,
                                   point.x, point.y,
                                   this, NULL );

        // Popup menu commands are automatically handled
        // by standard MFC command-routing mechanism!

        return;

    }
}
```

That's all you need to make your popup menu work. Enjoy!

■

Additional Comments

Windows sends the *WM_CONTEXTMENU* message whenever the user clicks the right mouse button—provided that the mouse buttons have not been switched—in a window. If the window does not handle this message, as is usually the case, it is propagated up the parent window chain until it reaches the main frame window.

We would therefore receive the *WM_CONTEXTMENU* message whenever the user right-clicked on almost any window belonging to our application, be it a view, a status bar, the MDI client background, and so on. This is why our *WM_CONTEXTMENU* handler first checks whether the user actually right-clicked on a toolbar docking area before building and showing our context menu.

Note that the standard MFC *UPDATE_COMMAND_UI* and command-routing mechanisms elegantly free us from having to write any special code to manage the checked/unchecked state of our popup menu items or handle the user's final selection in this menu. We need only trap the *WM_CONTEXTMENU* message and build our popup menu, and MFC takes care of all the messy details. (OK, it is our code that ultimately handles the *UPDATE_COMMAND_UI* and *WM_COMMAND* messages, but you must admit that MFC message-routing architecture really shines here.)

Sample Code

- Project: SelectToolbars in the Chap06 subdirectory on the companion CD-ROM.
- Purpose: Implements a popup menu that appears when users right-click on a docking zone, where they can select the toolbars they want to see.

Implementation Highlights

- *CMainFrame::OnContextMenu()* function (MainFrm.cpp)

See Also

- *FAQ 6.6 How do I implement a menu that allows users to select the toolbars they want to see?*
- *FAQ 6.15 How do I programmatically show or hide a control bar?*
- *FAQ 7.2 How do I implement a right-button popup menu (context menu)?*

6.8 How do I dynamically switch between different toolbars?

Hiding and showing toolbars—as explained in *FAQ 6.6 How do I implement a menu that allows users to select the toolbars they want to see?* and *FAQ 6.7 How do I allow users to choose the toolbars they want to see by selecting them in a popup menu that appears when they right-click on a docking zone?*—covers the needs of most applications.

In some cases, however, you might wish to dynamically switch toolbars—that is, substitute one toolbar for another while your program is running. For example, this functionality would allow you to offer several toolbar designs for users to choose from. This behavior is implemented in this FAQ's sample project, which allows the user to switch between toolbars with buttons displaying only icons or icons and text labels, as shown in Figures 6-10 and 6-11.

Step 1. Implement *EkSwitchBars()* as shown in Listing 6-21. This helper function takes care of hiding or showing the correct toolbar in a pair while preserving the toolbar's child window ID. Note that this function uses the *EkIsBarVisible()* helper function that is discussed in *FAQ 6.15 How do I programmatically show or hide a control bar?*

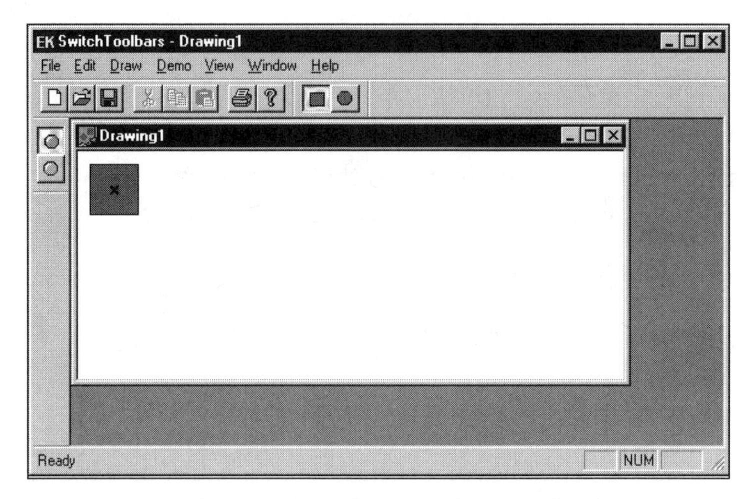

Figure 6-10. The SwitchToolbars application displaying its standard toolbar.

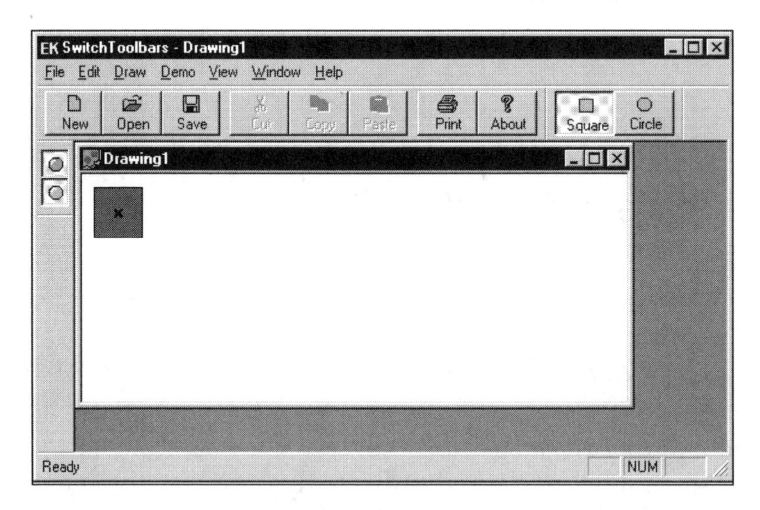

Figure 6-11. The SwitchToolbars application displaying its alternate toolbar.

Listing 6-21. Implementation of *EkSwitchBars()* to take care of hiding or showing the correct toolbar in a pair while preserving the toolbar's child window ID.

```
void EkSwitchBars( CFrameWnd* pFrame,
                   CControlBar* pBar1,
                   CControlBar* pBar2,
                   BOOL bShowBar2,
                   BOOL bDelay = TRUE )
{
```

```
    ASSERT_VALID( pFrame );
    ASSERT_VALID( pBar1 );
    ASSERT_VALID( pBar2 );

    // 1 - Compute "From" and "To" bars
    CControlBar* pBarFrom = bShowBar2 ? pBar1 : pBar2;
    CControlBar* pBarTo = bShowBar2 ? pBar2 : pBar1;
    BOOL bVisible = EkIsBarVisible( pBarFrom );

    // 2 - Exchange "From" and "To" window IDs
    UINT nIDFrom = ::GetWindowLong( pBarFrom->GetSafeHwnd(),
                                    GWL_ID );
    UINT nIDTo = ::GetWindowLong( pBarTo->GetSafeHwnd(),
                                  GWL_ID );

    ::SetWindowLong(pBarFrom->GetSafeHwnd(), GWL_ID, nIDTo);
    ::SetWindowLong(pBarTo->GetSafeHwnd(), GWL_ID, nIDFrom);

    // 3 - Hide "From" bar, show "To" bar if "From" bar
    // was visible
    pFrame->ShowControlBar( pBarFrom, FALSE, bDelay );
    pFrame->ShowControlBar( pBarTo, bVisible, bDelay );
}
```

Step 2. Create a duplicate toolbar resource for each toolbar that you want to switch, and edit the alternate toolbar to suit your needs.

Step 3. Add duplicate member variables of type *CToolBar* to your frame window class, as shown in Listing 6-22.

Listing 6-22. Adding duplicate member variables of type *CToolBar* to the frame window class.

```
class CMainFrame : public CMDIFrameWnd
{
// ...

protected:  // control bar embedded members
    CStatusBar  m_wndStatusBar;

    CToolBar    m_wndToolBar, m_wndToolBar2;
    CToolBar    m_wndTBshapes, m_wndTBshapes2;
    CToolBar    m_wndTBdemo;

// ...
};
```

Step 4. Manually define and implement *PositionToolbars()* as shown in Listing 6-23. This function should correctly lay out either the standard toolbars or the alternate ones depending on its *bAlternate* argument.

Listing 6-23. Implementing *PositionToolbars()* to correctly lay out either the standard toolbars or the alternate ones.

```
void CMainFrame::PositionToolBars( BOOL bAlternate )
{
    if( !bAlternate )
    {
        // Lay out "standard" toolbars
        EkDockToolBar( this, &m_wndToolBar );
        EkDockToolBar( this, &m_wndTBshapes,
                       AFX_IDW_DOCKBAR_TOP, &m_wndToolBar );
    }
    else
    {
        // Lay out "alternate" toolbars
        EkDockToolBar( this, &m_wndToolBar2 );
        EkDockToolBar( this, &m_wndTBshapes2,
                       AFX_IDW_DOCKBAR_TOP, &m_wndToolBar2 );
    }
}
```

Step 5. Modify your frame window's *OnCreate()* function as shown in Listing 6-24 to create the new duplicate toolbars, set their styles, call *Position-Toolbars()*, and initially hide the alternate toolbars.

Listing 6-24. Modifying the frame window's *OnCreate()* function to create the new duplicate toolbars, set their styles, call *PositionToolbars()*, and initially hide the alternate toolbars.

```
int CMainFrame::OnCreate(LPCREATESTRUCT lpCreateStruct)
{
    if (CMDIFrameWnd::OnCreate(lpCreateStruct) == -1)
        return -1;

    // Create standard toolbars
    if( !EkCreateToolBar( this, &m_wndToolBar,
                          AFX_IDW_TOOLBAR, IDR_MAINFRAME )
```

```
   || !EkCreateToolBar( this, &m_wndTBshapes,
                        IDR_SHAPES )
   || !EkCreateToolBar( this, &m_wndTBdemo,
                        IDR_DEMO_TOOLBAR ) )
{
   return -1;
}
m_wndTBshapes.SetWindowText(
                 CString( LPCSTR( IDR_SHAPES ) ) );

// Create alternate toolbars
if( !EkCreateToolBar( this, &m_wndToolBar2,
                      IDR_MAINFRAME2 )
   || !EkCreateToolBar( this, &m_wndTBshapes2,
                        IDR_SHAPES2 ) )
{
   return -1;
}

EkSetToolBarButtonText( &m_wndToolBar2,
                        IDS_BUTTONS_STANDARD );
m_wndToolBar2.SetSizes(CSize(48, 35), CSize(16, 15));

EkSetToolBarButtonText( &m_wndTBshapes2,
                        IDS_BUTTONS_SHAPES );
m_wndTBshapes2.SetSizes(CSize(48, 35), CSize(16, 15));

m_wndTBshapes2.SetWindowText(
                 CString( LPCSTR( IDR_SHAPES ) ) );

if (!m_wndStatusBar.Create(this) ||
    !m_wndStatusBar.SetIndicators(indicators,
           sizeof(indicators)/sizeof(UINT)))
{
   TRACE0("Failed to create status bar\n");
   return -1;      // fail to create

}

// Mainframe docking
EnableDocking(CBRS_ALIGN_ANY);
```

```
    // Toolbar docking
    PositionToolBars( FALSE );
    PositionToolBars( TRUE );
    EkDockToolBar( this, &m_wndTBdemo,
                   AFX_IDW_DOCKBAR_LEFT );

    // Initially hide alternate toolbars
    ShowControlBar( &m_wndToolBar2, FALSE, TRUE );
    ShowControlBar( &m_wndTBshapes2, FALSE, TRUE );

    return 0;
}
```

Step 6. Add a menu command or toolbar button (or both) to allow the user to toggle between the standard and alternate toolbars.

Step 7. Use ClassWizard to add handlers in your frame window class for the menu command added in step 6 and for the associated *UPDATE_COMMAND_UI* message. Implement these handlers as shown in Listing 6-25.

Listing 6-25. Switching the toolbars and updating the user interface.

```
void CMainFrame::OnViewAlternateToolbars()
{
    m_bAlternateToolBars = !m_bAlternateToolBars;

    EkSwitchBars( this, &m_wndToolBar, &m_wndToolBar2,
                  m_bAlternateToolBars );
    EkSwitchBars( this, &m_wndTBshapes, &m_wndTBshapes2,
                  m_bAlternateToolBars );

    // Reposition toolbars
    PositionToolBars( m_bAlternateToolBars );
}

void CMainFrame::OnUpdateViewAlternateToolbars(
                                        CCmdUI* pCmdUI)
{
    pCmdUI->SetCheck( m_bAlternateToolBars );
}
```

Step 8. Modify the functions that directly accessed your frame window's *CToolBar* member variables to instead call *CFrameWnd::GetControlBar()* to get a pointer to the correct *CToolBar* C++ object. Because *EkSwitchBars()* is designed to preserve the child window ID of the active toolbar, this technique allows your functions to work correctly with the active toolbar independently of the corresponding C++ object. Listing 6-26 shows both the old and the new implementations of *OnViewShapesToolbar()* and *OnUpdateViewShapesToolbar()*, which handle toggling the visible state of the Shapes toolbar.

Listing 6-26. Calling *CFrameWnd::GetControlBar()* instead of directly accessing the frame window's *CToolBar* member variables.

```
// ------------------------------
// OLD VERSION: directly accesses the CToolBar member
// variables

void CMainFrame::OnViewShapesToolbar()
{
   ShowControlBar( &m_wndTBshapes,
                   !EkIsBarVisible( &m_wndTBshapes ),
                   FALSE );
}

void CMainFrame::OnUpdateViewShapesToolbar(CCmdUI* pCmdUI)
{
   pCmdUI->SetCheck( EkIsBarVisible( &m_wndTBshapes ) );
}

// ------------------------------
// NEW VERSION: calls GetControlBar() to get the
// C++ CToolBar object by window ID

void CMainFrame::OnViewShapesToolbar()
{
   CControlBar* pBar = GetControlBar( IDR_SHAPES );
   if (pBar != NULL)
   {
      ShowControlBar( pBar, !EkIsBarVisible( pBar ),
                      FALSE);
   }
}
```

```
void CMainFrame::OnUpdateViewShapesToolbar(CCmdUI* pCmdUI)
{
   CControlBar* pBar = GetControlBar( IDR_SHAPES );
   if (pBar != NULL)
   {
      pCmdUI->SetCheck( EkIsBarVisible( pBar ) );
   }
}
```

■

Additional Comments

The design of *EkSwitchBars()* is a little more complex than you might have thought strictly necessary, but this added internal complexity makes for easier management of the associated toolbar pairs:

- *EkSwitchBars()* switches the toolbar's child window ID so that the active toolbar's ID always stays the same. This arrangement allows you to implement menu commands that work correctly on the active toolbar regardless of the corresponding C++ toolbar object. To take advantage of this feature, your menu commands should call *GetControlBar(IDR_TOOLBAR)* to get a pointer to the correct *CToolBar* C++ object, as explained earlier in step 8.
- *EkSwitchBars()* also takes care of *not* displaying the new active toolbar if its mate was hidden before the switch. This means that the global toolbar state is more easily preserved when you switch toolbars. However, the toolbars actually get switched, and the new active toolbar is the one that will appear when the user toggles its visible state.

You might have thought that calling *CToolBar::LoadToolBar()* would allow you to easily switch between different toolbar bitmaps. Unfortunately, this approach does not work well if your toolbars have different sizes, because the toolbar control will not resize itself to accommodate the new bitmap.

I thought about providing a data structure with an associated helper function that would allow you to build a list of associated toolbar pairs and automatically switch all toolbars in the list instead of calling *EkSwitchBars()* for each toolbar. However, I was not sure that the added complexity was needed in this case.

Note that the sample project for this FAQ restores the switched toolbars to their default (docked) position. I leave it as an exercise for you to modify *EkSwitchBars()* to restore the switched bar at the same position that was previously occupied by its mate.

Sample Code

- Project: SwitchToolbars in the Chap06 subdirectory on the companion CD-ROM.
- Purpose: Demonstrates how to dynamically switch between different toolbars while the program is running, as shown earlier in Figures 6-10 and 6-11.

Implementation Highlights

- *EkSwitchBars()* function (MainFrm.cpp)
- *CMainFrame::OnCreate()* function (MainFrm.cpp)
- *CMainFrame::PositionToolBars()* function (MainFrm.cpp)
- *CMainFrame::OnViewAlternateToolbars()* function (MainFrm.cpp)
- *CMainFrame::OnViewShapesToolbar()* function (MainFrm.cpp)
- *CMainFrame::OnUpdateViewShapesToolbar()* function (MainFrm.cpp)

See Also

- *FAQ 6.6* *How do I implement a menu that allows users to select the toolbars they want to see?*
- *FAQ 6.7* *How do I allow users to choose the toolbars they want to see by selecting them in a popup menu that appears when they right-click on a docking zone?*
- *FAQ 6.15* *How do I programmatically show or hide a control bar?*

Status Bars

6.9 How do I add a custom status bar to a view's frame window?

Many Windows applications are satisfied with having only one status bar attached to their main frame window. In some cases, however, you will find it useful to provide an additional status bar with some view's frame windows, for example to give the user dynamic feedback about key application variables.

The general technique for adding a status bar is similar to the one for adding a toolbar, as was described in *FAQ 6.1 How do I add one or more toolbars to my main frame window or to a view's frame window?* Follow these steps:

Step 1. Add a member variable of type *CStatusBar* to the view's frame window class to which you want to add a status bar, as shown in Listing 6-27.

Listing 6-27. Adding a member variable of type *CStatusBar* to the view's frame window class.

```
class CChildFrame : public CMDIChildWnd
{
// ...

protected:
   CStatusBar  m_wndStatusBar;    // additional status bar

// ...
};
```

Step 2. Create a new resource ID for your status bar—for example, *IDW_CHILD_STATUS_BAR*.

Step 3. Create new string resources for your status bar indicators (the panes that your status bar will display). Later you will dynamically update the text displayed in each pane, but the MFC *CStatusBar* class will use only the initial string resource to compute the width of each pane. Therefore, you should define each string resource to be long enough to accommodate the largest string that you plan to display. For example, if you want to display the current x-coordinate of the mouse in one pane, you could define the associated string resource as "*x=0000*" if you do not anticipate coordinates to exceed four digits.

Step 4. In the implementation file of your view's frame window class, define the *indicators* array, as shown in Listing 6-28. This array contains one entry for each pane in your status bar and is used to associate an ID with each pane (from left to right). Note that you can use a special ID of *ID_SEPARATOR* to define a stretching pane that will dynamically resize itself to cover all the remaining width of the status bar. This entry should be either the first or the last one in the *indicators* array.

Listing 6-28. Defining the *indicators* array.

```
// ————————————————————————————————
// Implementation for CChildFrame (ChildFrm.cpp)

static UINT indicators[] =
{
    ID_INDICATOR_X,
    ID_INDICATOR_Y,
    ID_INDICATOR_SHAPE
};
```

Step 5. If your view's frame window class does not yet have a handler for the *WM_CREATE* message, use ClassWizard to add such a handler.

Step 6. Modify your frame window class *OnCreate()* function to create the status bar and associate it with the *indicators* array, as shown in Listing 6-29.

Listing 6-29. Adding code to *OnCreate()* to create the status bar and associate it with the *indicators* array.

```
int CChildFrame::OnCreate(LPCREATESTRUCT lpCreateStruct)
{
   if (CMDIChildWnd::OnCreate(lpCreateStruct) == -1)
      return -1;

   // ...

   // Create the status bar
   if (!m_wndStatusBar.Create( this,
                        WS_CHILD | WS_VISIBLE | CBRS_BOTTOM,
                        IDW_CHILD_STATUS_BAR ) ||
           !m_wndStatusBar.SetIndicators(indicators,
           sizeof(indicators)/sizeof(UINT)))
   {
      TRACE0("Failed to create status bar\n");
      return -1;      // fail to create
   }

   // ...

   return 0;
}
```

Your status bar should now appear as expected in your view's frame window. However, it is not yet functional, because none of its panes displays anything meaningful. To enable the correct behavior, refer to *FAQ 6.10 How do I update the text of my status bar panes?*

■

Sample Code

- Project: AddStatusBar in the Chap06 subdirectory on the companion CD-ROM.
- Purpose: Demonstrates how to add a status bar to a view's frame window, as shown in Figure 6-12.

Implementation Highlights

- *CChildFrame::OnCreate()* function (ChildFrm.cpp)

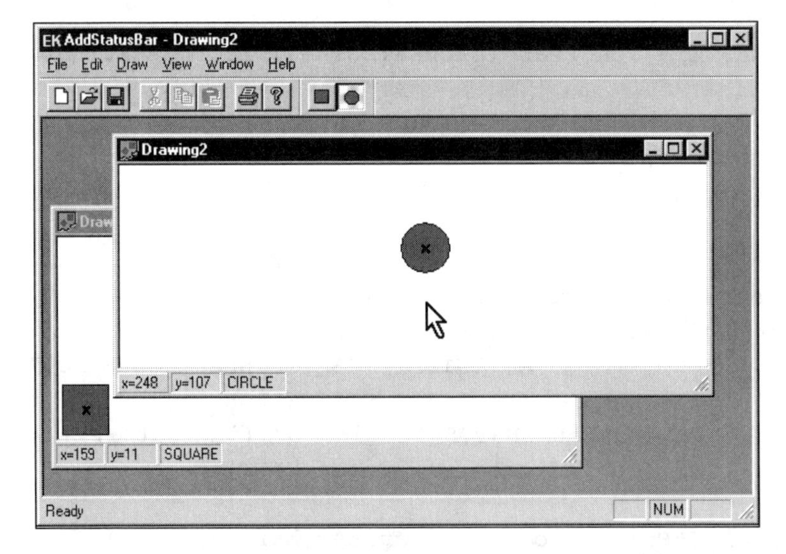

Figure 6-12. The AddStatusBar sample application adds a status bar to its view's frame window and dynamically updates the contents of the new indicators to reflect the current shape and the cursor position. Each coordinate indicator is checked (pops out) if the associated coordinate becomes greater than 200.

See Also

- *FAQ 6.1 How do I add one or more toolbars to my main frame window or to a view's frame window?*
- *FAQ 6.10 How do I update the text of my status bar panes?*

How do I update the text of my status bar panes?

After following the explanations given in *FAQ 6.9 How do I add a custom status bar to a view's frame window?* to create a new status bar or to add custom panes to an existing status bar, you probably want to be able to update the text of your status bar panes, also called status bar *indicators*. Fortunately, this functionality is easy to achieve even though the solution may not be very obvious at first.

Many MFC developers initially approach this problem from the wrong side, thinking that to act on the status bar they should call a function such as *CStatusBar::SetPaneText()*. Although you can manage to make this technique work, it is not the recommended way of updating the text of status bar panes, for a number of reasons:

- The code needing to update the text must access the status bar object directly. This object belongs to the frame window, but the code needing to update the text can be anywhere, such as in a document or view class.
- Each time the program state that is reflected in the various status bar panes is updated, you must write special code to update the text of the corresponding pane(s). This means that the code that accesses and updates the status bar may well become scattered in various unrelated places in your application.
- How would you write the code to update multiple status bars? This situation can easily arise if several view's frame windows are displayed simultaneously, each containing its own status bar.
- If your user-interface design wizards decide to shuffle some panes between the main frame status bar and your view's frame status bar, you will have to find and update all the code that called *CStatusBar::SetPaneText()*. The same problem shows up again if you change the order of the panes on your status bar, because *CStatusBar::SetPaneText()* works by pane position—unless you take care to always call *CStatusBar::CommandToIndex()* first.

The correct way of updating the text in your status bar panes is to write an *UPDATE_COMMAND_UI* handler for each pane. You read this right: MFC allows you—even encourages you—to treat each status bar pane in the same way that you treat menu items and toolbar buttons. Therefore, to update the text in a particular status bar indicator, simply write an *UPDATE_COMMAND_UI* handler associated with the ID of this pane. As with menu and toolbar button commands, you can and should write this handler in the class that is logically related to your status bar indicator—that is, the class that manages the state that is reflected in this pane, be it document, view, frame window, or whatever. The standard MFC message-routing architecture then ensures that your handler will be called as needed in the correct context during idle processing.

Note that you must write this handler and the corresponding message map entry manually without any help from ClassWizard. Listings 6-30 and 6-31 show how the AddStatusBar sample project for this FAQ implements *UPDATE_COMMAND_UI* handlers for its view's frame window custom status bar. The indicators *ID_INDICATOR_X* and *ID_INDICATOR_Y* show the current cursor coordinates, which are received by the view object in the *WM_MOUSEMOVE* message; therefore, the *UPDATE_COMMAND_UI* handlers for those indicators belong to the view class, as shown in Listing 6-30. On the other hand, the pane *ID_INDICATOR_SHAPE* displays the currently selected shape, which is managed by the document object; hence, the *UPDATE_COMMAND_UI* handler for this indicator is defined as a member function of the document class, as shown in Listing 6-31.

As you look at these sample code listings, note that updating our status bar indicators by using the MFC *UPDATE_COMMAND_UI* mechanism avoids the pitfalls enumerated earlier.

Listing 6-30. Handling the *UPDATE_COMMAND_UI* message in the view class to update the *ID_INDICATOR_X* and *ID_INDICATOR_Y* indicators.

```
// ——————————————————————————
// Class definition for CDrawView (DrawView.h)

class CDrawView : public CView
{
// ...

protected:
   CPoint m_ptLast;
```

```
// Generated message map functions
protected:
   //{{AFX_MSG(CDrawView)
   afx_msg void OnLButtonDown(UINT nFlags, CPoint point);
   afx_msg void OnMouseMove(UINT nFlags, CPoint point);

   // Update status bar indicators
   afx_msg void OnUpdateIndicatorX(CCmdUI* pCmdUI);
   afx_msg void OnUpdateIndicatorY(CCmdUI* pCmdUI);
   //}}AFX_MSG
   DECLARE_MESSAGE_MAP()
};

// ————————————————————————————
// Implementation for CDrawView (DrawView.cpp)

// ...

BEGIN_MESSAGE_MAP(CDrawView, CView)
   //{{AFX_MSG_MAP(CDrawView)
   ON_WM_LBUTTONDOWN()
   ON_WM_MOUSEMOVE()

   // Update status bar indicators
   ON_UPDATE_COMMAND_UI(ID_INDICATOR_X, OnUpdateIndicatorX)
   ON_UPDATE_COMMAND_UI(ID_INDICATOR_Y, OnUpdateIndicatorY)
   //}}AFX_MSG_MAP
   // Standard printing commands
   ON_COMMAND(ID_FILE_PRINT, CView::OnFilePrint)
   ON_COMMAND(ID_FILE_PRINT_DIRECT, CView::OnFilePrint)
   ON_COMMAND(ID_FILE_PRINT_PREVIEW,
                                CView::OnFilePrintPreview)

END_MESSAGE_MAP()

// ...

void CDrawView::OnUpdateIndicatorX(CCmdUI* pCmdUI)
{
   CString s;
   s.Format( _T("x=%d"), m_ptLast.x );
   pCmdUI->SetText( s );
```

```
    pCmdUI->SetCheck( m_ptLast.x > 200 );

    pCmdUI->Enable( TRUE );
}

void CDrawView::OnUpdateIndicatorY(CCmdUI* pCmdUI)
{
    CString s;
    s.Format( _T("y=%d"), m_ptLast.y );
    pCmdUI->SetText( s );

    pCmdUI->SetCheck( m_ptLast.y > 200 );

    pCmdUI->Enable( TRUE );
}
```

Listing 6-31. Handling the *UPDATE_COMMAND_UI* message in the document class to update the *ID_INDICATOR_SHAPE* indicator.

```
// ──────────────────────────────────
// Class definition for CDrawDoc (DrawDoc.h)

class CDrawDoc : public CDocument
{
// ...

// Attributes
public:
    CPoint m_point;
    enum SHAPE { SQUARE = 0, CIRCLE = 1 } m_shape;

// ...

// Generated message map functions
protected:
    //{{AFX_MSG(CDrawDoc)
    afx_msg void OnDrawSquare();
    afx_msg void OnDrawCircle();
    afx_msg void OnUpdateDrawSquare(CCmdUI* pCmdUI);
    afx_msg void OnUpdateDrawCircle(CCmdUI* pCmdUI);
```

```
    // Update status bar indicator
    afx_msg void OnUpdateIndicatorShape(CCmdUI* pCmdUI);
    //}}AFX_MSG
    DECLARE_MESSAGE_MAP()
};

// ________________________________________
// Implementation for CDrawDoc (DrawDoc.cpp)

// ...

BEGIN_MESSAGE_MAP(CDrawDoc, CDocument)
    //{{AFX_MSG_MAP(CDrawDoc)
    ON_COMMAND(ID_DRAW_SQUARE, OnDrawSquare)
    ON_COMMAND(ID_DRAW_CIRCLE, OnDrawCircle)
    ON_UPDATE_COMMAND_UI(ID_DRAW_SQUARE, OnUpdateDrawSquare)
    ON_UPDATE_COMMAND_UI(ID_DRAW_CIRCLE, OnUpdateDrawCircle)

    // Update status bar indicator
    ON_UPDATE_COMMAND_UI(ID_INDICATOR_SHAPE,
                                    OnUpdateIndicatorShape)
    //}}AFX_MSG_MAP
END_MESSAGE_MAP()

// ...

void CDrawDoc::OnUpdateIndicatorShape(CCmdUI* pCmdUI)
{
    pCmdUI->SetText( ( m_shape == SQUARE ) ?
                        _T( "SQUARE" ) : _T( "CIRCLE" ) );

    pCmdUI->Enable( TRUE );
}
```

■

Explanations

Here are the various operations that you can apply to the *CCmdUI* object associated with a status bar pane:

- *Enable(BOOL bOn = TRUE)* activates or disables the indicator—that is, it causes its contents to actually appear or not to appear. Note that older versions of MFC used to set the *SBPS_DISABLED* style by default on all status bar panes; therefore, if you did not write an explicit *UPDATE_COMMAND_UI* handler to call *pCmdUI->Enable(TRUE)* for each of your indicators, they would remain empty.
- *SetText(LPCTSTR lpszText)* sets the text that you want to display in the indicator. This is the recommended way of updating the text of a status bar pane.
- *SetCheck(int nCheck = 1)* allows you to check the indicator, which causes it to pop out of the status bar, thanks to the *SBPS_POPOUT* style, as can be seen in Figure 6-12 in *FAQ 6.9 How do I add a custom status bar to a view's frame window?*

Additional Comments

If you want to better understand how MFC works its *UPDATE_COMMAND_UI* magic on status bar panes, take a look at Listing 6-32, which shows the pseudocode for the *CStatusCmdUI* class. This class defines the behavior of the objects that actually get sent to your *UPDATE_COMMAND_UI* handlers for status bar indicators—the objects that you access through the *pCmdUI* pointer.

Listing 6-32. Pseudocode for the *CStatusCmdUI* class (BarStat.cpp).

```
// CStatusBar idle update through CStatusCmdUI class

class CStatusCmdUI : public CCmdUI      // class private
                                        // to this file!
{
public: // re-implementations only
   virtual void Enable(BOOL bOn);
   virtual void SetCheck(int nCheck);
   virtual void SetText(LPCTSTR lpszText);
};

void CStatusCmdUI::Enable(BOOL bOn)
{
   m_bEnableChanged = TRUE;
   CStatusBar* pStatusBar = (CStatusBar*)m_pOther;
   UINT nNewStyle = pStatusBar->GetPaneStyle(m_nIndex)
                                          & ~SBPS_DISABLED;
   if (!bOn)
```

```
      nNewStyle |= SBPS_DISABLED;
   pStatusBar->SetPaneStyle(m_nIndex, nNewStyle);
}

void CStatusCmdUI::SetCheck(int nCheck) // "checking" will
                                        // pop out the text
{
   CStatusBar* pStatusBar = (CStatusBar*)m_pOther;
   UINT nNewStyle = pStatusBar->GetPaneStyle(m_nIndex)
                                 & ~SBPS_POPOUT;
   if (nCheck != 0)
      nNewStyle |= SBPS_POPOUT;
   pStatusBar->SetPaneStyle(m_nIndex, nNewStyle);
}

void CStatusCmdUI::SetText(LPCTSTR lpszText)
{
   CStatusBar* pStatusBar = (CStatusBar*)m_pOther;
   pStatusBar->SetPaneText(m_nIndex, lpszText);
}
```

Sample Code

- Project: AddStatusBar in the Chap06 subdirectory on the companion CD-ROM.
- Purpose: Demonstrates how to dynamically update status bar indicators by using the MFC *UPDATE_COMMAND_UI* mechanism. The view's frame window contains a custom status bar that dynamically indicates the current cursor position as well as the currently selected shape (see Figure 6-12 in *FAQ 6.9 How do I add a custom status bar to a view's frame window?*).

Implementation Highlights

- *CDrawView::OnUpdateIndicatorX()* function (DrawView.cpp)
- *CDrawView::OnUpdateIndicatorY()* function (DrawView.cpp)
- *CDrawDoc::OnUpdateIndicatorShape()* function (DrawDoc.cpp)

See Also

- *FAQ 6.9 How do I add a custom status bar to a view's frame window?*

How do I customize my status bar font?

You might sometimes wish a status bar to have a splashier font than the default MFC proposition. Here is how to go about it.

Step 1. Add a member variable of type *CFont* to the frame window class that contains the *CStatusBar* object whose font you want to change, as shown in Listing 6-33. This member variable will store the new font for the lifetime of the frame window object and therefore the lifetime of the associated status bar.

Listing 6-33. Adding a member variable of type *CFont* to your frame window class.

```
class CChildFrame : public CMDIChildWnd
{
// ...

protected:
   CStatusBar  m_wndStatusBar;    // additional status bar

protected:

   CFont m_StatusBarFont;    // special font for status bar
   BOOL SetStatusBarFont(CStatusBar* pStatusBar );
                            // helper function

// ...
};
```

Step 2. Manually create the *CYourFrame::SetStatusBarFont()* helper function, as shown in Listing 6-34. This function first creates the desired font and then assigns it to the status bar window by calling *CWnd::SetFont()*.

Listing 6-34. Implementation of the *SetStatusBarFont()* helper function to create the desired font and assign it to the status bar window.

```
BOOL CChildFrame::SetStatusBarFont(CStatusBar* pStatusBar)
{
   ASSERT_VALID( pStatusBar );
```

```
    // 1 - Prepare LOGFONT structure
    CClientDC dc( this );    // need a DC for GetDeviceCaps()
                             // below

    LOGFONT lf;             // logical font structure
    ::ZeroMemory( &lf, sizeof( lf ) );

    // 12 point Times bold
    lf.lfHeight = - MulDiv( 12,
                            dc.GetDeviceCaps( LOGPIXELSX ),
                            72 );
    lf.lfWidth          = 0;
    lf.lfEscapement     = 0;
    lf.lfOrientation    = 0;
    lf.lfWeight         = FW_BOLD;
    lf.lfItalic         = FALSE;
    lf.lfUnderline      = FALSE;
    lf.lfStrikeOut      = FALSE;
    lf.lfCharSet        = DEFAULT_CHARSET;
    lf.lfOutPrecision   = OUT_DEFAULT_PRECIS;
    lf.lfClipPrecision  = CLIP_DEFAULT_PRECIS;
    lf.lfQuality        = DEFAULT_QUALITY;
    lf.lfPitchAndFamily = VARIABLE_PITCH | FF_ROMAN;

    // 2 - Create font
    if( !m_StatusBarFont.CreateFontIndirect( &lf ) )
    {
       return FALSE;
    }

    // 3 - Set status bar font
    pStatusBar->SetFont( &m_StatusBarFont );
    return TRUE;
}
```

Step 3. Call *SetStatusBarFont()* in your frame window class's *OnCreate()* function as shown in Listing 6-35. You should call *SetStatusBarFont()* *after* calling *CStatusBar::Create()* to create the status bar window but *before* calling *CStatusBar::SetIndicators()*. The *SetStatusBarFont()* function must be called before *CStatusBar::SetIndicators()*, because this last function uses the current status bar font to compute the size of the status bar window and of each status bar pane.

Listing 6-35. Calling *SetStatusBarFont()*.

```
int CChildFrame::OnCreate(LPCREATESTRUCT lpCreateStruct)
{
   if (CMDIChildWnd::OnCreate(lpCreateStruct) == -1)
      return -1;

   // Create the status bar
   if (!m_wndStatusBar.Create( this,
                               WS_CHILD | WS_VISIBLE
                                        | CBRS_BOTTOM,
                               IDW_CHILD_STATUS_BAR ) ||

        !SetStatusBarFont( &m_wndStatusBar ) ||
        !m_wndStatusBar.SetIndicators(indicators,
          sizeof(indicators)/sizeof(UINT)))
   {
      TRACE0("Failed to create status bar\n");
      return -1;      // fail to create
   }

   return 0;
}
```

■

Sample Code

- Project: StatusBarFont in the Chap06 subdirectory on the companion CD-ROM.
- Purpose: Implements a status bar that uses a custom font, as shown in Figure 6-13.

Implementation Highlights

- *CChildFrame::SetStatusBarFont()* function (ChildFrm.cpp)
- *CChildFrame::OnCreate()* function (ChildFrm.cpp)

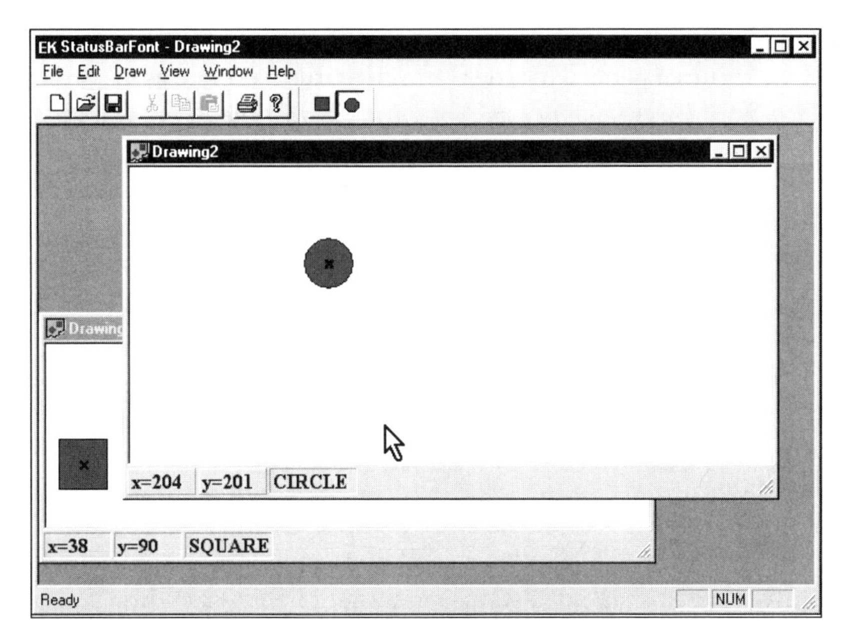

Figure 6-13. Compare the standard font of the main frame window's status bar with the custom font of the status bar in the view's frame window. Can you spot the difference?

FAQ 6.12 How do I draw in a status bar pane?

Although most status bar panes usually display only text indicators, some applications benefit from displaying a graphical indicator in some of their status bar panes. Examples of popular applications that draw in their status bars include Microsoft Word 97 and the popular WinZip shareware, as you can see in Figure 6-14.

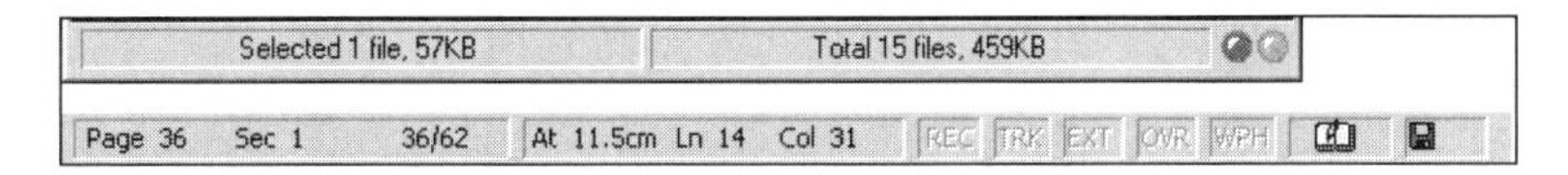

Figure 6-14. Status bars with graphical indicators: the top status bar is from Nico Mak Computing's WinZip 6.3; the bottom one comes from Microsoft Word 97.

Fortunately, drawing in a status bar pane is not fundamentally different from updating the text in a pane: First, define your status bar pane as explained in step 3 of *FAQ 6.9 How do I add a custom status bar to a view's frame window?*; Be sure to define and then set your pane's width by either associating it with a wide enough string—I like to use strings made of "@" characters to remind me that they will not actually be displayed—or by calling *CStatusBar::SetPaneInfo()* to resize your pane after creating the status bar.

You can and should implement the drawing behavior in an *UPDATE_COMMAND_UI* handler, for the reasons given in *FAQ 6.10 How do I update the text of my status bar panes?* Instead of calling *CCmdUI::SetText()* to display a string in the pane, your *UPDATE_COMMAND_UI* handler will draw directly inside the pane, which is, after all, nothing more exotic than a rectangle on the status bar window.

Listings 6-36 and 6-37 show the two graphical *UPDATE_COMMAND_UI* handlers for this FAQ's sample project. Both functions graphically display the currently selected shape in a status bar pane. The *CDrawDoc::OnUpdateIndicatorShapeBitmap()* function shown in Listing 6-36 simply displays a bitmap in the pane—using the *EkDrawBitmap()* function that was discussed in the Additional Comments section of *FAQ 4.5 How do I add a preview area to (draw inside) a dialog box?*—whereas the *CDrawDoc::OnUpdateIndicatorShapeDraw()* function shown in Listing 6-37 actually draws inside the pane. Note again that, thanks to the *UPDATE_COMMAND_UI* mechanism, these handlers can be written where they most logically belong. In this case, they're member functions of the *CDrawDoc* class, which manages the currently selected shape that these handler functions display.

Listing 6-36. Implementation of *CDrawDoc::OnUpdateIndicatorShapeBitmap()* to display a bitmap in an indicator pane.

```
void CDrawDoc::OnUpdateIndicatorShapeBitmap(CCmdUI* pCmdUI)
{
   // 1 - Prevent status bar from drawing text
   pCmdUI->SetText( _T( "" ) );
   pCmdUI->Enable( TRUE );

   // 2 - Retrieve pointer to status bar object
   CStatusBar* psb = static_cast<CStatusBar*>(
                                        pCmdUI->m_pOther );
   ASSERT_KINDOF( CStatusBar, psb );
   ASSERT_VALID( psb );
```

```
   // 3 - Compute drawing zone rectangle
   CRect rect;
   psb->GetItemRect( pCmdUI->m_nIndex, &rect );
   rect.DeflateRect( 2, 2 );

   // 4 - Draw current shape in pane
   CClientDC dc( psb );

   CBitmap bmp;
   bmp.LoadBitmap( m_shape == SQUARE ?
                              IDB_SQUARE : IDB_CIRCLE );

   EkDrawBitmap( &dc, &bmp, rect );
}
```

Listing 6-37. Implementation of *CDrawDoc::OnUpdateIndicatorShapeDraw()* to draw in an indicator pane.

```
void CDrawDoc::OnUpdateIndicatorShapeDraw(CCmdUI* pCmdUI)
{
   // 1 - Prevent status bar from drawing text
   pCmdUI->SetText( _T( "" ) );
   pCmdUI->Enable( TRUE );

   // 2 - Retrieve pointer to status bar object
    CStatusBar* psb = static_cast<CStatusBar*>(
                                   pCmdUI->m_pOther );
   ASSERT_KINDOF( CStatusBar, psb );
   ASSERT_VALID( psb );

   // 3 - Compute drawing zone rectangle
   CRect rect;
   psb->GetItemRect( pCmdUI->m_nIndex, &rect );
   rect.DeflateRect( 2, 2 );

   // 4 - Draw current shape in pane
   CClientDC dc( psb );

   // Erase destination rectangle
   CBrush brBack( ::GetSysColor( COLOR_3DFACE ) );
   CBrush* pOldBrush = dc.SelectObject( &brBack );

   dc.PatBlt( rect.left, rect.top,
              rect.Width(), rect.Height(), PATCOPY );
```

```
    // Draw shape
    CBrush brShape( RGB( 255, 0, 255 ) );
    dc.SelectObject( &brShape );

    switch( m_shape )
    {
    default :
       ASSERT( FALSE );   // We should never get here !
       break;

    case SQUARE :
       dc.Rectangle( &rect );
       break;

    case CIRCLE :
       dc.Ellipse( &rect );
       break;
    }

    dc.SelectObject( pOldBrush );
}
```

At this point, you should be able to compile your code and verify that your graphical status bar indicators work as expected. However, one little glitch still needs to be fixed: suppose that you cause your status bar to repaint—for example, by horizontally resizing its frame window or by moving another window in front of your own application's window. In that case, you will find that your graphical indicators end up empty! This comes from the fact that the standard status bar does not trigger the *UPDATE_COMMAND_UI* mechanism when it receives a *WM_PAINT* message; therefore, the status bar repaints itself normally but does not give us a chance to refresh our graphical indicators.

Fortunately, solving this problem is not very difficult, thanks to the *CEkDrawStatusBar* class, whose implementation is shown in Listing 6-38.

Listing 6-38. Definition of the *CEkDrawStatusBar* class that triggers the *UPDATE_COMMAND_UI* message when repainting.

```
// ------------------------------------
// Class definition for CEkDrawStatusBar
// (EkDrawStatusBar.cpp)
```

```
class CEkDrawStatusBar : public CStatusBar
{

// ...

// Implementation

   // Generated message map functions
protected:
   //{{AFX_MSG(CEkDrawStatusBar)
   afx_msg void OnPaint();
   //}}AFX_MSG
   DECLARE_MESSAGE_MAP()
};

// ——————————————————————————
// Implementation for CEkDrawStatusBar
// (EkDrawStatusBar.cpp)

#include <afxpriv.h>  // For WM_IDLEUPDATECMDUI message

// ...

BEGIN_MESSAGE_MAP(CEkDrawStatusBar, CStatusBar)
   //{{AFX_MSG_MAP(CEkDrawStatusBar)
   ON_WM_PAINT()
   //}}AFX_MSG_MAP
END_MESSAGE_MAP()

// ...

void CEkDrawStatusBar::OnPaint()
{
   // 1 - Let base class paint itself
   CStatusBar::OnPaint();

   // 2 - Send a WM_IDLEUPDATECMDUI message to ourselves
   // to ensure our "drawing" panes repaint correctly
   SendMessage( WM_IDLEUPDATECMDUI );
}
```

Finally, you need to modify your frame window class to reference *CEkDrawStatusBar* instead of the classic *CStatusBar* class, as shown in Listing 6-39.

Listing 6-39. Modifying the frame window class to reference the *CEkDrawStatusBar* class.

```
#include "EkDrawStatusBar.h"

class CChildFrame : public CMDIChildWnd
{

// ...
protected:
   CEkDrawStatusBar  m_wndStatusBar;   // "Drawing" status
                                       // bar

// ...
};
```

■

Sample Code

- Project: DrawInStatusBarPane in the Chap06 subdirectory on the companion CD-ROM.
- Purpose: Demonstrates how to draw in status bar panes, as you can see in Figure 6-15.

Implementation Highlights

- *CDrawDoc::OnUpdateIndicatorShapeBitmap()* function (DrawDoc.cpp)
- *CDrawDoc::OnUpdateIndicatorShapeDraw()* function (DrawDoc.cpp)
- *CEkDrawStatusBar* class (EkDrawStatusBar.h, EkDrawStatusBar.cpp)

See Also

- *FAQ 6.9 How do I add a custom status bar to a view's frame window?*
- *FAQ 6.10 How do I update the text of my status bar panes?*

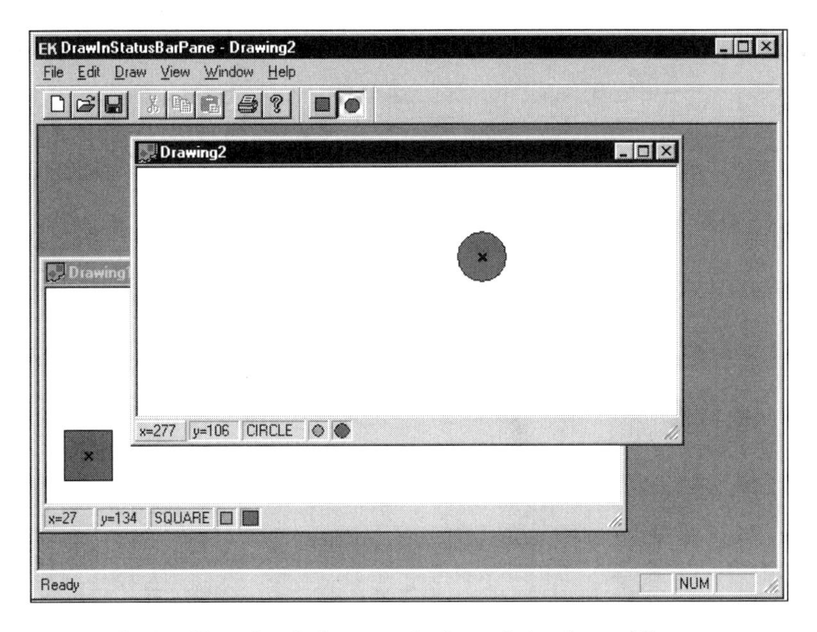

Figure 6-15. The view's frame window status bar of the DrawInStatusBarPane sample graphically displays the currently selected shape in two panes: the left pane displays bitmaps, and the rightmost one draws inside the pane.

FAQ 6.13 How do I maximize the message pane when displaying menu prompts?

As you load up your main frame window's status bar with indicator panes, the remaining space allotted to the message pane can become too small to display prompts for menu commands without truncating them. The following explanations show you how to overcome this problem by maximizing the message pane while a menu selection is in progress. By temporarily allowing the message pane to occupy the entire width of the status bar, this technique ensures that your menu prompts will not accidentally be clipped.

Microsoft Word 95 implemented this behavior, and Windows Explorer still behaves this way at the time of this writing, as you can see in Figures 6-16 and 6-17. Note, however, that Microsoft Word 97 "solves" this problem by no longer displaying any prompt for menu commands or toolbar buttons!

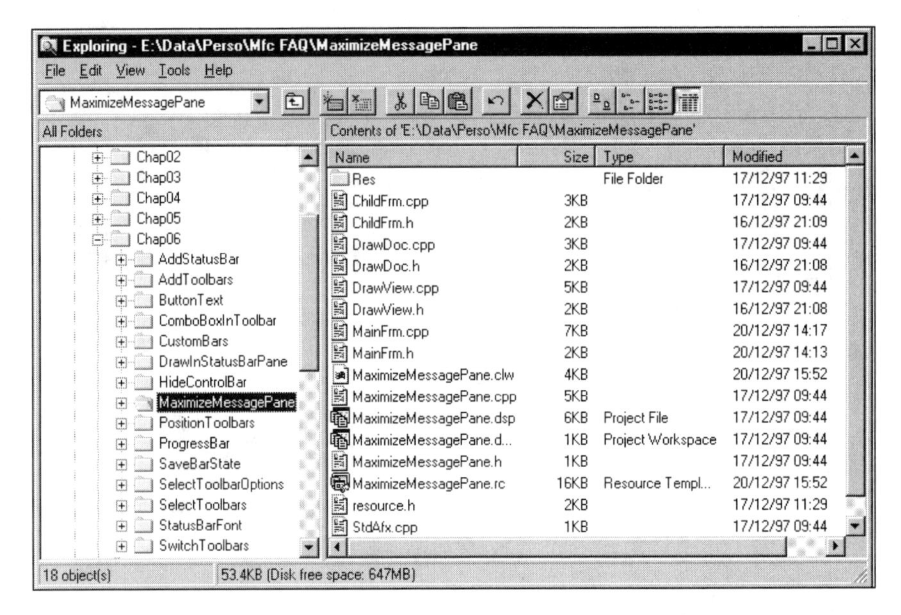

Figure 6-16. The standard Windows Explorer status bar has two indicator panes.

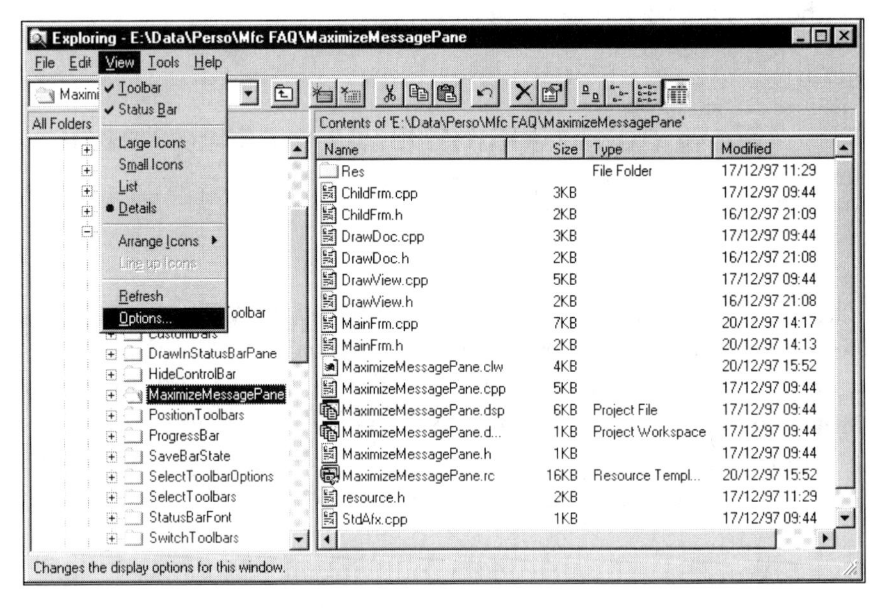

Figure 6-17. Windows Explorer maximizes its message pane to display menu prompts.

To correctly implement this behavior, add special message handlers to your main frame window for the *WM_INITMENUPOPUP* and *WM_MENUSELECT* messages:

Step 1. Manually add member variables to your main frame window class to manage the maximize message pane behavior, as shown in Listing 6-40.

Listing 6-40. Adding member variables to the main frame window class to manage the maximize message pane behavior.

```
class CMainFrame : public CMDIFrameWnd
{
// ...
protected:    // "Maximize message pane" behavior
   UINT m_nMessagePaneID;       // Save message pane ID
   UINT m_nMessagePaneStyle;    // Save message pane style
   INT  m_cxMessagePaneWidth;   // Save message pane width
   BOOL m_bInMenuSelect;        // In "menu selection" mode?
// ...
};
```

Step 2. Add handlers to your main frame window class for the *WM_INITMENUPOPUP* and *WM_MENUSELECT* messages. Unfortunately, the default behavior of ClassWizard does not display the *WM_MENUSELECT* message for the main frame window class. To correct this problem, call up ClassWizard and click on the Class Info tab. Select your main frame window class in the "Class name" combo box. Change the "Message filter" selection to "Window." You can now go back to the Message Maps tab and find both *WM_INITMENUPOPUP* and *WM_MENUSELECT* messages in the "Messages" list box, as needed for step 3.

Step 3. Use ClassWizard to add handlers in your main frame window class for the *WM_INITMENUPOPUP* and *WM_MENUSELECT* messages. Implement these handlers as shown in Listings 6-41 and 6-42.

Listing 6-41. Handling the *WM_INITMENUPOPUP* message to maximize the message pane.

```
void CMainFrame::OnInitMenuPopup( CMenu* pPopupMenu,
                                  UINT nIndex,
                                  BOOL bSysMenu )
```

```
{
   CMDIFrameWnd::OnInitMenuPopup(pPopupMenu, nIndex,
                                 bSysMenu);

   // 1 - Check if in "menu selection" mode and message
   // pane not stretched
   if( m_cxMessagePaneWidth == -1 && m_bInMenuSelect )
   {

      // 2 - Retrieve "normal" message pane style and width
      m_wndStatusBar.GetPaneInfo(0, m_nMessagePaneID,
                                 m_nMessagePaneStyle,
                                 m_cxMessagePaneWidth);

      // 3 - Stretch message pane width to cover
      // entire status bar
      CRect rc;
      m_wndStatusBar.GetWindowRect( &rc );
      m_wndStatusBar.SetPaneInfo(0, m_nMessagePaneID,
           SBPS_NOBORDERS|SBPS_STRETCH, rc.Width() );
   }
}
```

Listing 6-42. Handling the *WM_MENUSELECT* message to restore the message pane width.

```
void CMainFrame::OnMenuSelect( UINT nItemID, UINT nFlags,
                               HMENU hSysMenu )
{
   CMDIFrameWnd::OnMenuSelect(nItemID, nFlags, hSysMenu);

   // 1 - Was the menu dismissed?
   BOOL bMenuCanceled = (nFlags==0xFFFF && hSysMenu==0);
   if( bMenuCanceled && m_cxMessagePaneWidth != -1 )
   {

      // 2a - Restore message pane style and width
      m_bInMenuSelect = FALSE;
      m_wndStatusBar.SetPaneInfo( 0,
                                  m_nMessagePaneID,
                                  m_nMessagePaneStyle,
                                  m_cxMessagePaneWidth );
      m_cxMessagePaneWidth = -1;   // Guard (illegal) value
```

```
    }
    else
    {
        // 2b - Go into "menu selection" mode
        m_bInMenuSelect = TRUE;
    }
}
```

■

Explanations

Windows sends the *WM_MENUSELECT* message to the main frame window (which owns the menu) each time the user selects any item in a menu, whether this item belongs to the menu bar or to a popup menu. If the item selected causes a popup menu to appear—as is usually the case for commands that belong to the menu bar—then Windows also sends the *WM_INITMENUPOPUP* message to the main frame window.

The *WM_INITMENUPOPUP* message is sent only once before a popup menu is displayed, whereas the *WM_MENUSELECT* message is sent repeatedly as the user selects various menu items. When the user clicks on a top-level menu item, Windows first sends a *WM_MENUSELECT* message and then a *WM_INITMENUPOPUP* message.

Windows also sends a special *WM_MENUSELECT* message to inform the main frame window that the menu was dismissed, whatever the reason: selecting a menu item, clicking outside the menu, pressing the Escape key, activating another application, and so on.

Understanding the behavior and timing of these two messages is key to understanding the implementation of the message handlers discussed in step 3 of the preceding section. Here is an explanation of the workings of these functions during a typical user interaction with your application's menu:

- When the user clicks on a menu bar item, the *WM_MENUSELECT* handler is called first and sets the *m_bInMenuSelect* member variable to *TRUE* to go into menu selection mode.
- The *WM_INITMENUPOPUP* handler is then called, sees that the *m_cxMessagePaneWidth* member variable is still set to −1, and therefore decides to stretch the message pane.
- While the user mouses around the menu after this first click, the *WM_MENUSELECT* and *WM_INITMENUPOPUP* handlers become

no-ops, the latter one because the *m_cxMessagePaneWidth* member variable is no longer set to −1.

- When the menu is finally dismissed, the *WM_MENUSELECT* handler restores the message pane to its initial width and sets the *m_bInMenuSelect* member variable to *FALSE* to exit the menu selection mode.

Additional Comments

Note that the MFC framework also processes *WM_INITMENUPOPUP* and *WM_MENUSELECT* for its own purposes. To be more precise, *WM_MENUSELECT* is handled by the *CFrameWnd* class to ensure the appropriate display of the menu prompts and idle message, as shown in Listing 6-43.

Listing 6-43. Pseudocode for the *CFrameWnd::OnMenuSelect()* function (WinFrm.cpp).

```
void CFrameWnd::OnMenuSelect(UINT nItemID, UINT nFlags,
                             HMENU /*hSysMenu*/)
{
   CFrameWnd* pFrameWnd = GetTopLevelFrame();
   ASSERT_VALID(pFrameWnd);

   if (nFlags == 0xFFFF)
   {
      // Menu canceled, display idle message
      m_nFlags &= ~WF_NOPOPMSG;

      // Select correct idle message in case "help mode"
      // is on
      if (!pFrameWnd->m_bHelpMode)
         m_nIDTracking = AFX_IDS_IDLEMESSAGE;
      else
         m_nIDTracking = AFX_IDS_HELPMODEMESSAGE;

      // Send private WM_SETMESSAGESTRING message to
      // display prompt in message bar
      SendMessage(WM_SETMESSAGESTRING,
                  (WPARAM)m_nIDTracking);

      // Update message bar now
      CWnd* pWnd = GetMessageBar();
```

```
        if (pWnd != NULL)
            pWnd->UpdateWindow();
    }
    else
    {
        if (nItemID == 0 || nFlags & (MF_SEPARATOR|MF_POPUP))
        {
            // Do not display prompt for separator or
            // popup item
            m_nIDTracking = 0;
        }
        // ... else clauses omitted ...
        else
        {
            // Prompt for current menu item has same
            // ID as menu item
            m_nIDTracking = nItemID;
        }
        pFrameWnd->m_nFlags |= WF_NOPOPMSG;
    }
    // ...
}
```

CFrameWnd also handles *WM_INITMENUPOPUP* to create the *CCmdUI* objects that get sent to each menu item for *UPDATE_COMMAND_UI* processing. The entire code for *CFrameWnd::OnInitMenuPopup()* is complex. Listing 6-44 shows an abbreviated version that illustrates how the *CCmdUI* objects get created and sent to your menu command *UPDATE_COMMAND_UI* handlers.

Listing 6-44. Pseudocode for the *CFrameWnd::OnInitMenuPopup()* function (WinFrm.cpp).

```
void CFrameWnd::OnInitMenuPopup(CMenu* pMenu, UINT,
                                BOOL bSysMenu)
{
    // ...
    // Create and initialize the famous CCmdUI object
    CCmdUI state;
    state.m_pMenu = pMenu;
    // ...
    state.m_nIndexMax = pMenu->GetMenuItemCount();
```

```
    // For each menu item...
    for (state.m_nIndex = 0;
         state.m_nIndex < state.m_nIndexMax;
         state.m_nIndex++)
    {
       // Get menu item ID
       state.m_nID = pMenu->GetMenuItemID(state.m_nIndex);
       // ...
       if (state.m_nID == (UINT)-1)
       {
          // Maybe a popup menu, route to first item of
          // that popup
          state.m_pSubMenu = pMenu->GetSubMenu(
                                      state.m_nIndex);
          // ...
          // Update menu item (don't auto-disable popups)
          state.DoUpdate(this, FALSE);
       }
       else
       {
          // Normal menu item:
          // Auto enable/disable if frame window has
          // 'm_bAutoMenuEnable' set and command is not a
          // system command
          state.m_pSubMenu = NULL;
          state.DoUpdate(this,
                         m_bAutoMenuEnable &&
                                state.m_nID < 0xF000);
       }
    // ...
}
```

Sample Code

- Project: MaximizeMessagePane in the Chap06 subdirectory on the companion CD-ROM.
- Purpose: Demonstrates how an application can dynamically maximize its message pane to more adequately display long menu prompts, as shown in Figures 6-18 and 6-19.

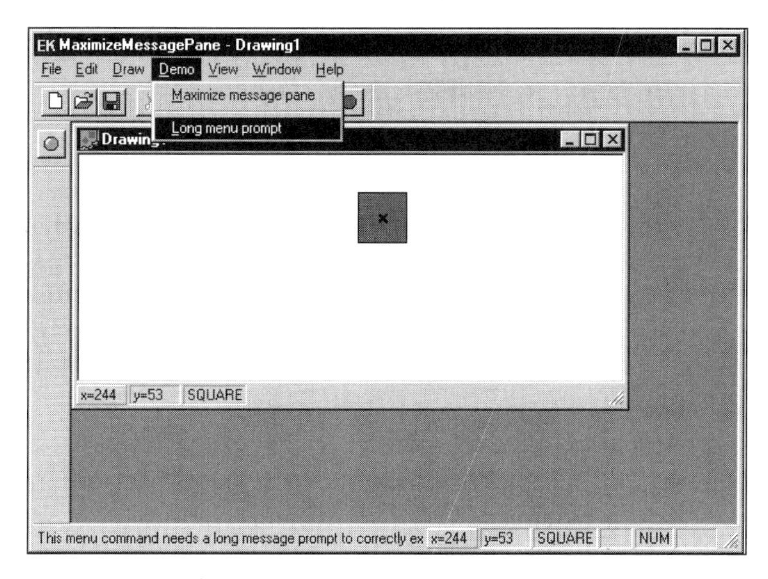

Figure 6-18. If the message pane is not maximized, the menu prompt is truncated.

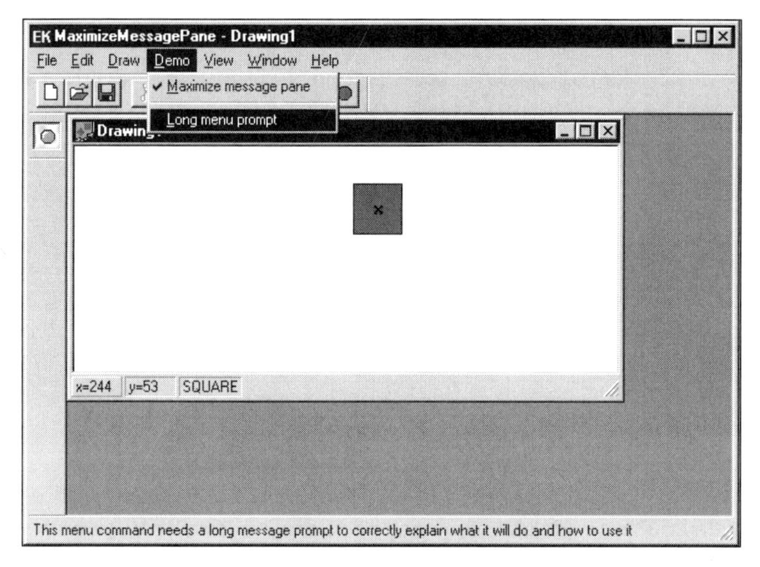

Figure 6-19. Maximizing the message pane to display menu prompts can make a significant difference.

Implementation Highlights

- *CMainFrame::OnInitMenuPopup()* function (MainFrm.cpp)
- *CMainFrame::OnMenuSelect()* function (MainFrm.cpp)

6.14 How do I display a progress indicator in a status bar?

Despite the tremendous improvements in raw computing performance experienced by the PC industry, some operations still manage to take long enough to test the user's patience. It is a well-known psychological trait of computer users that getting feedback about the progress of an operation significantly shortens the apparent subjective duration of the wait and therefore heightens the user's acceptance of the application.

Many popular applications satisfy their users' appetite for feedback by displaying and updating a progress indicator on the status bar during an operation. Examples include Microsoft Word 97 (when preparing for background printing) and Visual Studio (when opening a workspace).

Fortunately, it's easy to display a progress indicator in the status bar of an MFC application, thanks to the *EkCreateProgressBar()* function that is shown in Listing 6-45.

Listing 6-45. *EkCreateProgressBar()* creates a progress indicator inside a status bar.

```
BOOL EkCreateProgressBar( CProgressCtrl* pProgressCtrl,
                          CStatusBar* pStatusBar,
                          LPCTSTR szMessage = NULL,
                          int nPaneIndex = 0,
                          int cxMargin = 10,
                          int cxMaxWidth = -1,
                          UINT nIDControl = 1 )
{
   ASSERT_VALID( pProgressCtrl );
   ASSERT_VALID( pStatusBar );

   // 1 - Calculate destination rectangle for progress
   // control
   CRect rc;
   pStatusBar->GetItemRect( nPaneIndex, &rc );

   // 2 - Define progress bar horizontal offset
   if( szMessage != NULL )
   {
      // Compute message text extent
```

```
      CClientDC dc( pStatusBar );
      CFont* pFont = pStatusBar->GetFont();
      CFont* pOldFont = dc.SelectObject( pFont );
      CSize sizeText = dc.GetTextExtent( szMessage );
      dc.SelectObject( pOldFont );

      rc.left += sizeText.cx + cxMargin;
   }

   // 3 - Compute progress bar width
   if( cxMaxWidth != -1 )
   {
      rc.right = rc.left + min( cxMaxWidth, rc.Width() );
   }

   // 4 - Display message text
   pStatusBar->SetPaneText( nPaneIndex, szMessage );
   pStatusBar->RedrawWindow();

   // 5 - Create progress control
   return pProgressCtrl->Create( WS_CHILD | WS_VISIBLE,
                                 rc, pStatusBar, nIDControl );
}
```

Here is a detailed explanation of the various arguments of *EkCreateProgressBar()*:

- *pProgressCtrl* identifies the *CProgressCtrl* C++ object associated with the progress control that will be created. Note that the lifetime of this C++ object is the responsibility of the *caller* of *EkCreateProgressBar()*. Usually, this C++ object is allocated on the stack, as shown in Listing 6-46.
- *pStatusBar* is the status bar on which the progress control will be created.
- *szMessage* is the pointer to the string that will be displayed in the status bar to the left of the progress control. A *NULL* value does not display any message.
- *nPaneIndex* is the zero-based index of the status bar pane on which to create the progress control. The default value of zero uses the standard leftmost message pane.
- *cxMargin* is the margin (in pixels) between the end of the *szMessage* text and the left side of the progress control. The default value is 10 pixels.

- *cxMaxWidth* is the maximum width (in pixels) of the progress control. The default value of –1 causes the progress control to stretch to cover all the remaining pane width.
- *nIDControl* is the child window ID of the Windows progress control that will be created. You do not need to worry about this ID in most cases.

You typically create a progress indicator with *EkCreateProgressBar()* by executing the following steps:

1. Define a C++ *CProgressCtrl* object.
2. Call *EkCreateProgressBar()* to create the progress bar.
3. Initialize your progress control's range and step size.
4. Perform your long task and periodically update the progress control by calling either *CProgressCtrl::StepIt()* or *CProgressCtrl::SetPos()*.
5. Optionally call *DestroyWindow()* on the *CProgressCtrl* object to hide—and destroy—the progress control (see the Additional Comments section next).

Listing 6-46 shows how the *CMainFrame::OnDemoLongTask1()* function from this FAQ's sample project creates and updates its progress bar.

Listing 6-46. Implementation of *CMainFrame::OnDemoLongTask1()* to create and update a progress bar.

```
#include <afxpriv.h>   // for WM_SETMESSAGESTRING message

void CMainFrame::OnDemoLongTask1()
{
   // 1 - Create "progress bar"
   // (default options)
   CProgressCtrl wndProgress;
   EkCreateProgressBar( &wndProgress, &m_wndStatusBar,
                        _T( "Executing a long task (1), "
                        "press Esc to cancel..." ) );

   // 2 - Initialize progress control range and step size
   wndProgress.SetRange( 0, 100 );
   wndProgress.SetStep( 1 );

   // 3 - Here is where you would perform your long task
   // and regularly call wndProgress.StepIt() to update the
   // progress control.
```

```
   // For this demonstration, we simulate the long task
   // with a for loop and the Sleep() function.
   srand( (unsigned)time( NULL ) );    // seed random number
                                       // generator
   for( int i = 0; i < 100; ++i )
   {

      // 4 - Test for "Esc" key
      if( ::GetAsyncKeyState( VK_ESCAPE ) < 0 )
      {
         break;
      }
      int nSleepTime = MulDiv( 100, rand(), RAND_MAX );
      Sleep( nSleepTime );

      // 5 - Update progress control
      wndProgress.StepIt();
   }

   // 6 - Ensures that idle message is displayed again
   PostMessage( WM_SETMESSAGESTRING,
                  (WPARAM) AFX_IDS_IDLEMESSAGE, 0L );
}
```

Here's how *CMainFrame::OnDemoLongTask2()* creates a progress bar with a maximum width of 200 pixels:

```
EkCreateProgressBar( &wndProgress, &m_wndStatusBar,
                     _T( "Executing a long task (2), "
                         "press Esc to cancel..." ),
                     0, 10, 200 );
```

Finally, here's how *CMainFrame::OnDemoLongTask3()* creates a progress bar in pane 1 of the status bar:

```
EkCreateProgressBar( &wndProgress, &m_wndStatusBar,
                     NULL, 1 );
```

■

Additional Comments

Note that the *CProgressCtrl* object's destructor that is called when your code returns from your long task function will automatically destroy the associated Windows progress control. However, you can explicitly call *CWnd::DestroyWindow()* on the *CProgressCtrl* object if you ever need to get rid of the progress control before returning from the your long task function.

Sample Code

- Project: ProgressBar in the Chap06 subdirectory on the companion CD-ROM.
- Purpose: Demonstrates how to display and update a progress control in a status bar pane with various options, as shown in Figure 6-20.

Implementation Highlights

- *EkCreateProgressBar()* function (MainFrm.cpp)
- *CMainFrame::OnDemoLongTask1()* function (MainFrm.cpp)
- *CMainFrame::OnDemoLongTask2()* function (MainFrm.cpp)
- *CMainFrame::OnDemoLongTask3()* function (MainFrm.cpp)

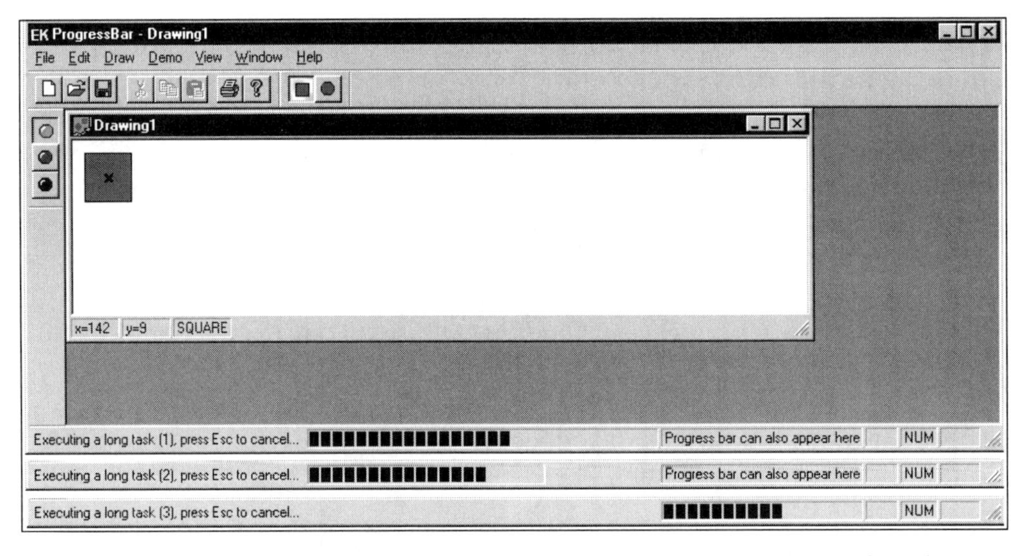

Figure 6-20. These three variants on the progress bar theme are executed by the ProgressBar sample.

General Control Bar Topics

How do I programmatically show or hide a control bar?

Simply call *CFrameWnd::ShowControlBar()* from the frame window class that contains the control bar that you want to show or hide, as shown in Listing 6-47.

Listing 6-47. Showing and hiding a toolbar.

```
void CMyFrameWnd::ShowToolBar()
{
    ShowControlBar( &m_wndMyToolBar, TRUE, FALSE );
}

void CMyFrameWnd::HideToolBar()
{
    ShowControlBar( &m_wndMyToolBar, FALSE, FALSE );
}
```

To check whether a control bar is currently visible, use the *EkIsBarVisible()* helper function, whose implementation is shown in Listing 6-48.

Listing 6-48. Implementation of *EkIsBarVisible()*.

```
BOOL EkIsBarVisible( CControlBar* pBar )
{
   ASSERT_VALID( pBar );

   return ( ( pBar->GetStyle() & WS_VISIBLE ) != 0 );
}
```

With the help of *EkIsBarVisible()*, you can easily toggle a control bar between the hidden and visible states and update the corresponding menu item or toolbar button accordingly, as shown in Listing 6-49.

Listing 6-49. Toggling a control bar between the hidden and visible states and updating the corresponding menu item or toolbar button.

```
void CMainFrame::OnViewShapesToolbar()
{
   ShowControlBar( &m_wndTBshapes,
                   !EkIsBarVisible( &m_wndTBshapes ),
                   FALSE );
}

void CMainFrame::OnUpdateViewShapesToolbar(CCmdUI* pCmdUI)
{
   pCmdUI->SetCheck( EkIsBarVisible( &m_wndTBshapes ) );
}
```

■

Additional Comments

CFrameWnd::ShowControlBar() has the following prototype:

```
void CFrameWnd::ShowControlBar( CControlBar* pBar,
                                BOOL bShow,
                                BOOL bDelay );
```

In case you wonder why I do not recommend that you simply call *ShowWindow (SW_HIDE)* on your toolbar, consider the implementation of the *CFrame Wnd::ShowControlBar()* function that is shown in Listing 6-50.

Listing 6-50. Pseudocode for the *CFrameWnd::ShowControlBar()* function (WinFrm.cpp).

```
void CFrameWnd::ShowControlBar(CControlBar* pBar,
                              BOOL bShow, BOOL bDelay)
{
   CFrameWnd* pParentFrame = pBar->GetDockingFrame();

   if (bDelay)
   {
      // Delay the operation
      pBar->DelayShow(bShow);
      pParentFrame->DelayRecalcLayout();
```

```
}
else
{
    // Immediately hide the control bar
    pBar->SetWindowPos(NULL, 0, 0, 0, 0,
        SWP_NOZORDER|SWP_NOMOVE|SWP_NOSIZE|SWP_NOACTIVATE|
        (bShow ? SWP_SHOWWINDOW : SWP_HIDEWINDOW));

    // Call DelayShow to clear any contradictory
    // DelayShow
    pBar->DelayShow(bShow);

    // Recalculate frame window layout
    if (bShow || !pBar->IsFloating())
        pParentFrame->RecalcLayout(FALSE);
}

// Show or hide the floating frame as appropriate
if (pBar->IsFloating())
{
    int nVisCount = pBar->m_pDockBar != NULL ?
            pBar->m_pDockBar->GetDockedVisibleCount()
            : bShow != FALSE;
    if (nVisCount == 1 && bShow)
    {
        pParentFrame->m_nShowDelay = -1;
        if (bDelay)
        {
            pParentFrame->m_nShowDelay = SW_SHOWNA;
            pParentFrame->RecalcLayout(FALSE);
        }
        else
            pParentFrame->ShowWindow(SW_SHOWNA);
    }
    else if (nVisCount == 0)
    {
        pParentFrame->m_nShowDelay = -1;
        if (bDelay)
            pParentFrame->m_nShowDelay = SW_HIDE;
        else
            pParentFrame->ShowWindow(SW_HIDE);
    }
```

```
        else if (!bDelay)
        {
            pParentFrame->RecalcLayout(FALSE);
        }
    }
}
```

As you can see, hiding a control bar involves quite a lot of additional work relating to the parent frame window layout and the floating frame window that may be present.

Sample Code

- Project: HideControlBar in the Chap06 subdirectory on the companion CD-ROM.
- Purpose: Demonstrates how to programmatically toggle a control bar between the hidden and visible states and update the corresponding menu item and toolbar button accordingly.

Implementation Highlights

- *CMainFrame::OnDemoViewShapesToolbar()* function (MainFrm.cpp)
- *CMainFrame::OnUpdateDemoViewShapesToolbar()* function (MainFrm.cpp)

See Also

- *FAQ 6.6 How do I implement a menu that allows users to select the toolbars they want to see?*
- *FAQ 6.7 How do I allow users to choose the toolbars they want to see by selecting them in a popup menu that appears when they right-click on a docking zone?*

6.16 How do I set the caption of a floating control bar?

This simple task should be simple to achieve—and so it is. But I included it in this book because many people have asked me this question or spent an inordinate amount of time looking in the wrong place for an answer.

The short answer is to call *SetWindowText()* on your control bar object whenever you want to set the caption of a control bar:

```
pBar->SetWindowText( szText );
```

The caption will show as soon as the control bar is floated. Just be sure to call the *SetWindowText()* function *after* the *Create()* function but *before* your control bar is floated. This last caveat reflects the fact that the miniframe window that hosts the floating control bar sets its own caption upon creation and does not update its caption if *SetWindowText()* is called after floating the control bar. Because most control bars that I have encountered have a static caption, accepting this restriction should not be a significant problem.

Listing 6-51 shows in a broader context how most of the FAQs in this chapter set the caption of their Shapes toolbar.

Listing 6-51. Setting the caption of a toolbar.

```
int CMainFrame::OnCreate(LPCREATESTRUCT lpCreateStruct)
{
   if (CMDIFrameWnd::OnCreate(lpCreateStruct) == -1)
      return -1;

   if (!m_wndToolBar.Create(this) ||
       !m_wndToolBar.LoadToolBar(IDR_MAINFRAME))
   {
      // ...
   }

   if (!m_wndTBshapes.Create(this, WS_CHILD | WS_VISIBLE
                              | CBRS_TOP, IDR_SHAPES) ||
       !m_wndTBshapes.LoadToolBar(IDR_SHAPES))
   {
      // ...
   }

   // ...

   // Mainframe docking
   EnableDocking(CBRS_ALIGN_ANY);

   // Standard toolbar docking
   m_wndToolBar.SetBarStyle(m_wndToolBar.GetBarStyle() |
```

```
        CBRS_TOOLTIPS | CBRS_FLYBY | CBRS_SIZE_DYNAMIC);
    m_wndToolBar.EnableDocking(CBRS_ALIGN_ANY);
    DockControlBar(&m_wndToolBar);

    // Shapes toolbar docking
    m_wndTBshapes.SetBarStyle(m_wndTBshapes.GetBarStyle() |
        CBRS_TOOLTIPS | CBRS_FLYBY | CBRS_SIZE_DYNAMIC);
    m_wndTBshapes.EnableDocking(CBRS_ALIGN_ANY);
    EkDockBarNextTo( &m_wndTBshapes, &m_wndToolBar,
                     AFX_IDW_DOCKBAR_TOP );

    // Set the caption of the "Shapes" toolbar
    m_wndTBshapes.SetWindowText(
                     CString( LPCSTR( IDR_SHAPES ) ) );

    // ...

    return 0;
}
```

■

Additional Comments

In Listing 6-51, you may wonder about the *CString* constructor call in the following statement:

```
    // Set the caption of the "Shapes" toolbar
    m_wndTBshapes.SetWindowText(
                     CString( LPCSTR( IDR_SHAPES ) ) );
```

This code fragment exploits a documented feature of the overloaded *CString::CString(LPCSTR)* constructor: if it receives a resource ID as argument, this constructor will automatically call *CString::LoadString()* to initialize the *CString* object by loading a string from the application's resources. Therefore, the preceding code fragment is roughly equivalent to this code:

```
    // Set the caption of the "Shapes" toolbar
    {  // dummy block to scope strTemp lifetime
       CString strTemp;
       strTemp.LoadString( IDR_SHAPES );
```

```
    m_wndTBshapes.SetWindowText( strTemp );
} // strTemp object automatically deleted here
```

Sample Code

There is no sample project for this FAQ. All sample projects for this chapter set the caption of their Shapes toolbar to "Shapes" in their *CMainFrame::OnCreate()* function.

How do I save and restore the position and state of my control bars?

Modern Windows applications are often chock-full of control bars: toolbars, status bars, dialog bars, custom bars, and so on. In this context, enabling your application to remember the position and state—visible or hidden, docked or floating, horizontal or vertical orientation—of each of these bars is a nice touch that most users will appreciate.

Fortunately, saving and restoring the context of your control bars is a simple matter of calling *CFrameWnd::SaveBarState()* and *CFrameWnd::LoadBarState()* at the appropriate time. Each function has a simple prototype:

```
void CFrameWnd::SaveBarState(
                        LPCTSTR lpszProfileName ) const;

void CFrameWnd::LoadBarState(
                        LPCTSTR lpszProfileName ) const;
```

The *lpszProfileName* argument is a simple string used by these functions to identify the context that is saved or restored. Remember that each one of several frame windows may have its own control bars whose layout it wants to save and restore. Depending on whether your application called *SetRegistryKey()* in its *InitInstance()* function, the *lpszProfileName* string serves either as the root name for several sections in your application's .INI file or as a subkey name in your application's registry settings, where *SaveBarState()* stores the relevant information.

To add a control bar persistence feature to your application, follow these simple steps for each frame window class that needs to save the state of its control bars:

Step 1. Use ClassWizard to add a handler in your frame window class for the *WM_CLOSE* message. Implement this handler as shown in Listing 6-52 to call *SaveBarState()*.

Listing 6-52. Calling *SaveBarState()* in the *WM_CLOSE* message handler.

```
const CString strBarState = _T( "MainFrameBarState" );

// ...

void CMainFrame::OnClose()
{
   // Save bar state
   SaveBarState( strBarState );

   CMDIFrameWnd::OnClose();
}
```

Step 2. Because your frame window class hosts some control bars—otherwise there is no point in trying to save them—it should already have a *WM_CREATE* message handler that creates them. Add a call to *LoadBarState()* at the end of this OnCreate() function after creating the control bars, as shown in Listing 6-53.

Listing 6-53. Calling the *LoadBarState()* function in the OnCreate() function.

```
int CMainFrame::OnCreate(LPCREATESTRUCT lpCreateStruct)
{

   if (CMDIFrameWnd::OnCreate(lpCreateStruct) == -1)
      return -1;

   if (!m_wndToolBar.Create(this) ||
      !m_wndToolBar.LoadToolBar(IDR_MAINFRAME))
   {
      //...
   }
```

```
    if (!m_wndTBshapes.Create(this, WS_CHILD | WS_VISIBLE
                              | CBRS_TOP, IDR_SHAPES) ||
        !m_wndTBshapes.LoadToolBar(IDR_SHAPES))
    {
        //...
    }

    if (!m_wndTBdemo.Create(this, WS_CHILD | WS_VISIBLE
                            | CBRS_TOP, IDR_DEMO_TOOLBAR) ||
        !m_wndTBdemo.LoadToolBar(IDR_DEMO_TOOLBAR))
    {
        //...
    }

    if (!m_wndStatusBar.Create(this) ||
        !m_wndStatusBar.SetIndicators(indicators,
              sizeof(indicators)/sizeof(UINT)))
    {
        //...
    }

    // Mainframe docking
    EnableDocking(CBRS_ALIGN_ANY);
    // Standard toolbar docking
    m_wndToolBar.SetBarStyle(m_wndToolBar.GetBarStyle() |
            CBRS_TOOLTIPS | CBRS_FLYBY | CBRS_SIZE_DYNAMIC);
    m_wndToolBar.EnableDocking(CBRS_ALIGN_ANY);
    DockControlBar(&m_wndToolBar);

    // Shapes toolbar docking
    // ...

    // Demo toolbar docking
    // ...

    // Restore saved bar state
    LoadBarState( strBarState );

    return 0;
}
```

Note that you can also call these functions at some other point in your code to explicitly save and restore your control bar context, as, for example, Visual C++ does when you switch from editing to debugging mode.

■

Additional Comments

If you want to understand how *CControlBar* persistence works, I advise you to read *MFC Internals* pp. 382–390 (see Appendix B). There you will learn about the many undocumented classes that make up the MFC control bar architecture, such as *CDockState*, *CControlBarInfo*, *CDockBar*, and *CMiniDockFrameWnd*.

Sample Code

- Project: SaveBarState in the Chap06 subdirectory on the CD-ROM.
- Purpose: The application automatically saves and restores the state of its control bars. The user can also explicitly save and restore the control bar context.

Implementation Highlights

- *CMainFrame::OnCreate()* function (MainFrm.cpp)
- *CMainFrame::OnClose()* function (MainFrm.cpp)
- *CMainFrame::OnDemoLoadBars()* function (MainFrm.cpp)
- *CMainFrame::OnDemoSaveBars()* function (MainFrm.cpp)

6.18 How do I create custom control bars?

For some applications, you need to be able to totally customize a control bar's behavior. Typically, this means that you want to take advantage of the ability to work with a child window that lies outside your frame window's client area and that is attached to one side of this same window. Taking advantage of this capability typically entails customizing the display of the control bar and sometimes even handling mouse messages.

Creating your own custom control bar is a powerful way to extend the functionality of your application's user interface to meet your needs, as you can see in the example shown in Figure 6-21. In this figure, the main frame window uses four custom border bars to get a cool chiseled border appearance, while each view's frame window contains a text bar that displays the current point coordinates.

To introduce you to the art of creating custom control bars, we will work through two examples. The first example explains how to create a border bar that displays a bitmap image; then we will move on to creating a text bar that takes advantage of the *UPDATE_COMMAND_UI* mechanism to handle its updating. During the following explanations, you may wish to refer to Figure 6-22 to understand how the various control bars are laid out in the CustomBars sample application.

Example 1: Border Bar, Simple Bitmap Painting

Step 1. Use ClassWizard to create a new *CControlBar*-derived class that we will call *CBorderBar*. Because ClassWizard does not explicitly support the

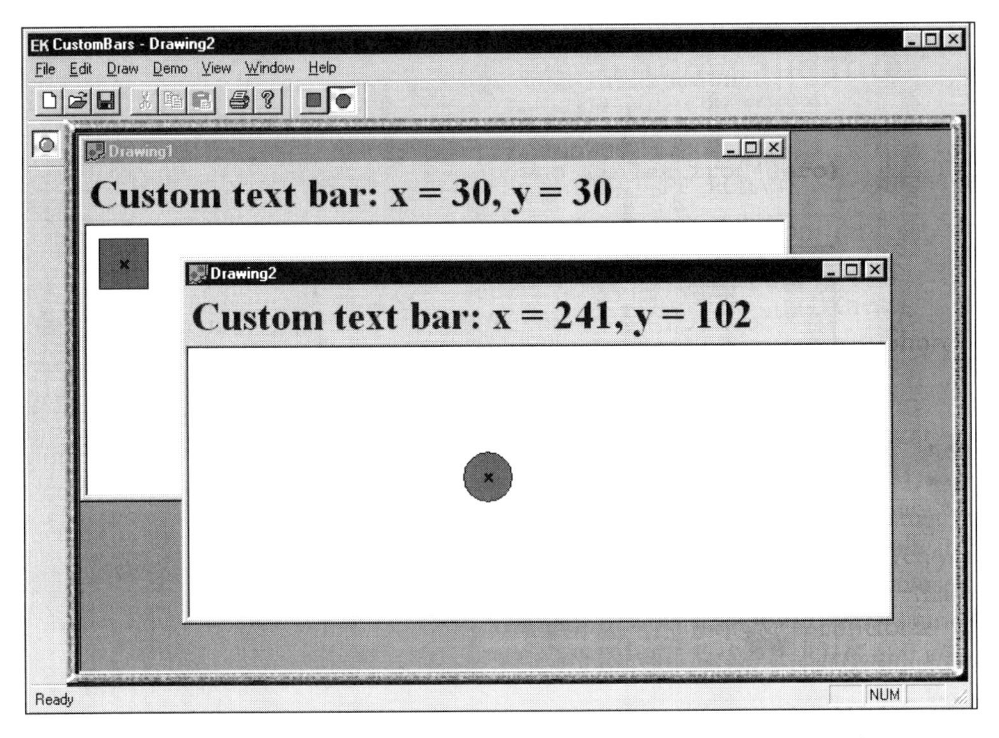

Figure 6-21. The CustomBars sample application: the main frame window uses four custom border bars to get a cool chiseled border appearance, while each view's frame window contains a text bar that displays the current point coordinates.

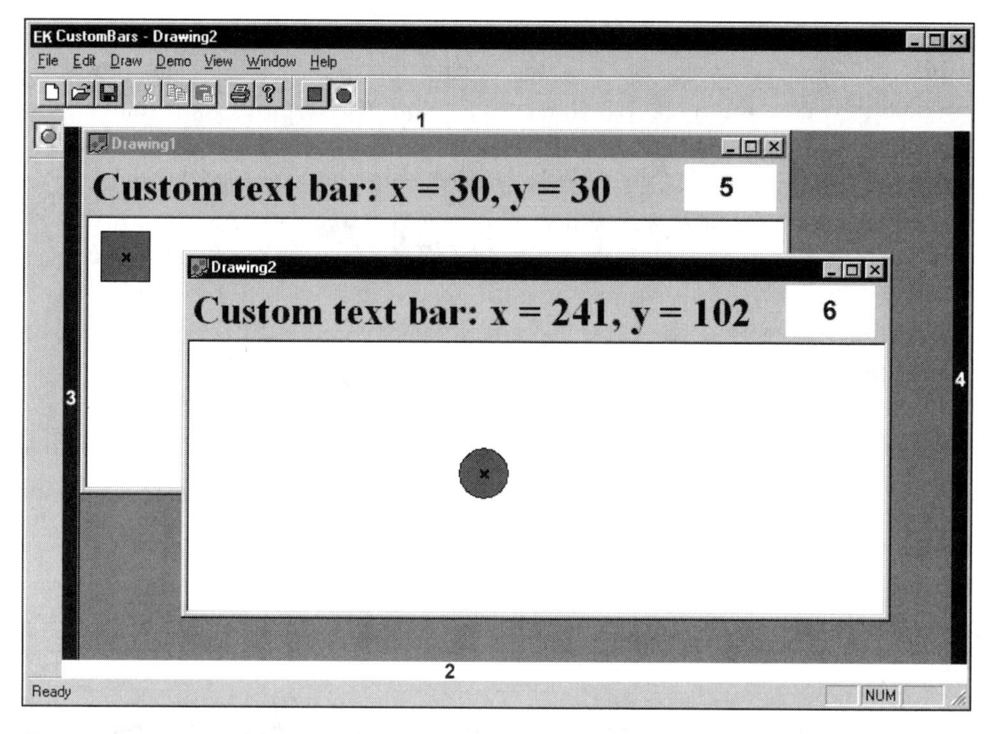

Figure 6-22. Actual layout of the various control bars of the CustomBars sample application.

creation of a *CControlBar*-derived class, you must select the "generic *CWnd*" type, let ClassWizard generate its code, and then edit this code to replace the references to *CWnd* with *CControlBar* both in the class definition and in the *BEGIN_MESSAGE_MAP* macro.

Step 2. Manually override the *CControlBar::CalcFixedLayout()* virtual function in *CBorderBar*. Implement this function as shown in Listing 6-54 to correctly tell MFC about your control bar's height and width.

Listing 6-54. Implementation of *CalcFixedLayout()* to tell MFC about your control bar's height and width.

```
// ———————————————————————————————
// Class definition for CBorderBar (BorderBar.h)
class CBorderBar : public CControlBar
{
// ...
```

```
// Implementation
// ...
protected:
   virtual CSize CalcFixedLayout(BOOL bStretch,
                                 BOOL bHorz);
};

// ____________________________________
// Implementation for CBorderBar (BorderBar.cpp)

CSize CBorderBar::CalcFixedLayout( BOOL bStretch,
                                   BOOL bHorz )
{
   CSize size = CControlBar::CalcFixedLayout( bStretch,
                                              bHorz );

   if( bHorz )
   {
      // Bar is horizontal, set height
      size.cy = HEIGHT;  // defined in CBorderBar class
   }
   else
   {
      // Bar is vertical, set width
      size.cx = WIDTH;   // defined in CBorderBar class
   }
   return size;
}
```

Step 3. Add the *m_nPosition* and *m_Bitmap* member variables to *CBorderBar*, as shown in Listing 6-55, to manage the bar's position and associated bitmap.

Listing 6-55. Adding the *m_nPosition* and *m_Bitmap* member variables to *CBorderBar*.

```
// ____________________________________
// Class definition for CBorderBar (BorderBar.h)

class CBorderBar : public CControlBar
{
// ...
```

```
// Implementation
// ...
protected:
   enum { WIDTH = 10, HEIGHT = 10 };
   int   m_nPosition;
   CBitmap m_Bitmap;
// ...
};

// ————————————————————————————
// Implementation for CBorderBar (BorderBar.cpp)

CBorderBar::CBorderBar()
{
   m_nPosition = 0;
}
```

Step 4. Manually define *CBorderBar::Create()* as shown in Listing 6-56. This function does the following:

- Initializes the *m_nPosition* variable depending on the *CBRS_xxx* style bit set in the *dwStyle* argument
- Saves the control bar style in the inherited *m_dwStyle* variable after ensuring that the *WS_CHILD*, *WS_VISIBLE*, and *CBRS_SIZE_FIXED* style bits are set
- Loads the bitmap resource specified in the *nIDBitmap* argument
- Creates the Windows child window associated with our control bar

Listing 6-56. Implementation of *CBorderBar::Create()*.

```
// ————————————————————————————
// Class definition for CBorderBar (BorderBar.h)

class CBorderBar : public CControlBar
{
// ...
// Operations
public:

   BOOL Create( CWnd* pParentWnd, DWORD dwStyle,
                UINT nIDBar, UINT nIDBitmap );
// ...
```

```
};

// ------------------------------------
// Implementation for CBorderBar (BorderBar.cpp)

BOOL CBorderBar::Create( CWnd* pParentWnd, DWORD dwStyle,
                         UINT nIDBar, UINT nIDBitmap )
{
   ASSERT_VALID(pParentWnd);   // must have a parent

   // 1 - Style must contain CBRS_TOP or CBRS_BOTTOM
   // or CBRS_LEFT or CBRS_RIGHT
   ASSERT((dwStyle & CBRS_TOP) || (dwStyle & CBRS_BOTTOM)
         || (dwStyle & CBRS_LEFT) || (dwStyle & CBRS_RIGHT));

   // 2 - Save bar position from style CBRS_xxx bits
   if( dwStyle & CBRS_TOP )
   {
      ASSERT( m_nPosition == 0 );
      m_nPosition = CBRS_TOP;
   }

   if( dwStyle & CBRS_BOTTOM )
   {
      ASSERT( m_nPosition == 0 );
      m_nPosition = CBRS_BOTTOM;
   }


   if( dwStyle & CBRS_LEFT )
   {
      ASSERT( m_nPosition == 0 );
      m_nPosition = CBRS_LEFT;
   }

   if( dwStyle & CBRS_RIGHT )
   {
      ASSERT( m_nPosition == 0 );
      m_nPosition = CBRS_RIGHT;
   }

   ASSERT( m_nPosition != 0 );
```

```
    // 3 - Save the style
    dwStyle |= WS_CHILD | WS_VISIBLE | CBRS_SIZE_FIXED;
    m_dwStyle = dwStyle;

    dwStyle &= ~CBRS_ALL;
    dwStyle |= CCS_NOPARENTALIGN | CCS_NOMOVEY |
                                  CCS_NODIVIDER | CCS_NORESIZE;

    // 4 - Load bitmap
    if( !m_Bitmap.LoadBitmap( nIDBitmap ) )
    {
       TRACE1( "Unable to load border bar bitmap "
                              "with ID = %d\n", nIDBitmap );
       return FALSE;
    }

    // 5 - Finally create the window
    CRect rc;
    rc.SetRectEmpty();
    if( !CWnd::Create( NULL, NULL, dwStyle, rc,
                       pParentWnd, nIDBar ) )
    {
       TRACE0( "Unable to create border bar window\n" );
       return FALSE;
    }

    return TRUE;
}
```

Step 5. Every *CControlBar*-derived class must implement the *OnUpdateCmdUI()* function that is declared as pure virtual in *CControlBar*. Our implementation of *OnUpdateCmdUI()* for *CBorderBar* is the barest minimum that we can get away with, as shown in Listing 6-57. For more explanation about this function, see the Explanations section.

Listing 6-57. Overriding the *OnUpdateCmdUI()* pure virtual function.

```
// ------------------------------------
// Class definition for CBorderBar (BorderBar.h)

class CBorderBar : public CControlBar
{
// ...
```

```
// Implementation
// ...
protected:
   void OnUpdateCmdUI(CFrameWnd* pTarget,
                      BOOL bDisableIfNoHndler);
// ...
};

// ________________________________
// Implementation for CBorderBar (BorderBar.cpp)

void CBorderBar::OnUpdateCmdUI(CFrameWnd* pTarget,
                               BOOL bDisableIfNoHndler)
{
   // Update the dialog controls added to the control bar
   // (if any)
   UpdateDialogControls(pTarget, bDisableIfNoHndler);
}
```

Step 6. The main reason for defining a custom control bar is to control the painting process of the new child window. So use ClassWizard to add a handler in *CBorderBar* for the *WM_PAINT* message. Implement this handler as shown in Listing 6-58 to display the bitmap image associated with the *CBorderBar* object. This function at last contains "standard" Windows code!

Listing 6-58. Handling the *WM_PAINT* message to display the bitmap image associated with the *CBorderBar* object.

```
void CBorderBar::OnPaint()
{
   CPaintDC dc(this); // device context for painting

   // 1 - Compute paint area
   CRect rc;
   GetClientRect( &rc );

   // 2 - Create compatible memory DC
   CDC dcMem;
   dcMem.CreateCompatibleDC( &dc );

   // 3 - Select bitmap into memory DC
   CBitmap* pOldBitmap = dcMem.SelectObject( &m_Bitmap );
```

```
    // 4 - Compute bitmap size
    BITMAP bitmap;
    m_Bitmap.GetObject( sizeof( BITMAP ), &bitmap);
    CSize sizeBitmap( bitmap.bmWidth, bitmap.bmHeight );

    // 5 - Blit the bitmap from the memory DC to the real DC
    dc.StretchBlt( rc.left, rc.top, rc.Width(), rc.Height(),
                   &dcMem, 0, 0, bitmap.bmWidth, bitmap.bmHeight,
                   SRCCOPY );

    // 6 - Deselect bitmap from memory DC
    dcMem.SelectObject( pOldBitmap );
}
```

The *CBorderBar* class is now operational, and we need to hook it up to a frame window host.

Step 7. Add four member variables of type *CBorderBar* to the *CMainFrame* class, as shown in Listing 6-59.

Listing 6-59. Adding member variables of type *CBorderBar* to the *CMainFrame* class.

```
#include "BorderBar.h"

class CMainFrame : public CMDIFrameWnd
{
// ...
// Implementation
// ...
protected:  // control bar embedded members
    CStatusBar  m_wndStatusBar;
    CToolBar    m_wndToolBar;
    CToolBar    m_wndTBshapes;
    CToolBar    m_wndTBdemo;

    CBorderBar  m_wndBorderTop, m_wndBorderLeft,
                      m_wndBorderBottom, m_wndBorderRight;
    enum
    {
          IDW_BORDER_TOP      = AFX_IDW_CONTROLBAR_LAST-1,
          IDW_BORDER_BOTTOM   = AFX_IDW_CONTROLBAR_LAST-2,
          IDW_BORDER_LEFT     = AFX_IDW_CONTROLBAR_LAST-3,
```

```
        IDW_BORDER_RIGHT     = AFX_IDW_CONTROLBAR_LAST-4
    };
// ...
};
```

Step 8. Modify *CMainFrame::OnCreate()* to create the new border bars, as shown in Listing 6-60. Note that the border bars must be created *after* the other control bars have been created and docked to ensure that the border bars appear toward the inside of the frame window. Notice in Figure 6-21 (shown earlier) that the other control bars lie outside the chiseled border delimited by the border bars.

Listing 6-60. Modify *CMainFrame::OnCreate()* to create the new border bars.

```
int CMainFrame::OnCreate(LPCREATESTRUCT lpCreateStruct)
{
   if (CMDIFrameWnd::OnCreate(lpCreateStruct) == -1)
      return -1;

   if (!m_wndToolBar.Create(this) ||
       !m_wndToolBar.LoadToolBar(IDR_MAINFRAME))
   {
      TRACE0("Failed to create standard toolbar\n");
      return -1;      // fail to create
   }

   // ...

   // Mainframe docking
   EnableDocking(CBRS_ALIGN_ANY);

   // Standard toolbar docking
   m_wndToolBar.SetBarStyle(m_wndToolBar.GetBarStyle() |
                            CBRS_TOOLTIPS | CBRS_FLYBY |
                            CBRS_SIZE_DYNAMIC);
   m_wndToolBar.EnableDocking(CBRS_ALIGN_ANY);
   DockControlBar(&m_wndToolBar);

   // ...

   // Create border bars
   if (  !m_wndBorderTop.Create( this, CBRS_TOP,
```

```
                        IDW_BORDER_TOP, IDB_BORDER_TOP )
        || !m_wndBorderBottom.Create( this, CBRS_BOTTOM,
                        IDW_BORDER_BOTTOM, IDB_BORDER_BOTTOM )
        || !m_wndBorderLeft.Create( this, CBRS_LEFT,
                        IDW_BORDER_LEFT, IDB_BORDER_LEFT )
        || !m_wndBorderRight.Create( this, CBRS_RIGHT,
                        IDW_BORDER_RIGHT, IDB_BORDER_RIGHT ) )
    {
        TRACE0("Unable to create border bars\n");
        return -1;      // fail to create
    }

    return 0;
}
```

That's it! Your main frame window should now sport a cool-looking chiseled inside border frame like the one shown earlier in Figure 6-21.

Example 2: Text Bar with UPDATE_COMMAND_UI Support

Step 1. Create a new *CControlBar*-derived class that we will call *CTextBar*, by following the explanations given in step 1 in the preceding section.

Step 2. Add the *m_Font* member variable to the *CTextBar* class, as shown in Listing 6-61, to store the bar's text font.

Listing 6-61. Adding the *m_Font* member variable to the *CTextBar* class.

```
class CTextBar : public CControlBar
{
// ...
// Implementation
// ...
protected:
    CFont m_Font;
    enum { LEFT_MARGIN = 5, TOP_MARGIN = 5 };
// ...
};
```

Step 3. Manually define the *CTextBar::Create()* function as shown in Listing 6-62. This function does the following:

- Saves the control bar style in the inherited *m_dwStyle* variable after ensuring that the *WS_CHILD*, *WS_VISIBLE*, and *CBRS_SIZE_FIXED* style bits are set
- Creates the Windows child window associated with our control bar

Listing 6-62. Implementation of *CTextBar::Create()*.

```
// ——————————————————————————
// Class definition for CTextBar (TextBar.h)

class CTextBar : public CControlBar
{
// ...
// Operations
public:

   BOOL Create( CWnd* pParentWnd, DWORD dwStyle,
                UINT nID );

// ...
};
// ——————————————————————————
// Implementation for CTextBar (TextBar.cpp)

BOOL CTextBar::Create( CWnd* pParentWnd, DWORD dwStyle,
                       UINT nID )
{
   ASSERT_VALID(pParentWnd);    // must have a parent

   // Style must contain CBRS_TOP or CBRS_BOTTOM
   ASSERT((dwStyle & CBRS_TOP) || (dwStyle & CBRS_BOTTOM));

   // 1 - Save the style
   dwStyle |= WS_CHILD | WS_VISIBLE | CBRS_SIZE_FIXED;
   m_dwStyle = dwStyle;

   dwStyle &= ~CBRS_ALL;
   dwStyle |= CCS_NOPARENTALIGN | CCS_NOMOVEY |
              CCS_NODIVIDER | CCS_NORESIZE;

   // 2 - Create the window
   CRect rc;
```

```
    rc.SetRectEmpty();
    if( !CWnd::Create( NULL, NULL, dwStyle, rc,
                       pParentWnd, nID ) )
    {
       return FALSE;
       TRACE0( "Unable to create text bar window\n" );
    }

    return TRUE;
}
```

Step 4. Use ClassWizard to add a handler in the *CTextBar* class for the *WM_CREATE* message. Implement this handler as shown in Listing 6-63 to properly initialize the *m_Font* variable.

Listing 6-63. Handling the *WM_CREATE* message to initialize the *m_Font* variable.

```
int CTextBar::OnCreate(LPCREATESTRUCT lpCreateStruct)
{
    if (CControlBar::OnCreate(lpCreateStruct) == -1)
       return -1;


    // 1 - Prepare LOGFONT structure
    CClientDC dc( this );    // need a DC for GetDeviceCaps()
                             // below

    LOGFONT lf;             // logical font structure
    ::ZeroMemory( &lf, sizeof( lf ) );

    // 24 point Times bold
    lf.lfHeight = - MulDiv( 24,
                            dc.GetDeviceCaps( LOGPIXELSX ),
                            72 );
    lf.lfWidth          = 0;
    lf.lfEscapement     = 0;
    lf.lfOrientation    = 0;
    lf.lfWeight         = FW_BOLD;
    lf.lfItalic         = FALSE;
    lf.lfUnderline      = FALSE;
    lf.lfStrikeOut      = FALSE;
    lf.lfCharSet        = DEFAULT_CHARSET;
```

```
   lf.lfOutPrecision   = OUT_DEFAULT_PRECIS;
   lf.lfClipPrecision  = CLIP_DEFAULT_PRECIS;
   lf.lfQuality        = DEFAULT_QUALITY;
   lf.lfPitchAndFamily = VARIABLE_PITCH | FF_ROMAN;

   // 2 - Create font
   if( !m_Font.CreateFontIndirect( &lf ) )
   {
      return FALSE;
   }

   return 0;
}
```

Step 5. Manually override the *CControlBar::CalcFixedLayout()* virtual function in *CTextBar*. Implement this function as shown in Listing 6-64 to correctly tell MFC about your control bar's height and width. This time, we base our width calculation on the width of the control bar's parent window; the height is determined based on the text extent of the selected font.

Listing 6-64. Implementation of *CalcFixedLayout()* to tell MFC about your control bar's height and width.

```
// ————————————————————————
// Class definition for CTextBar (TextBar.h)

class CTextBar : public CControlBar
{
// ...
// Implementation
// ...
protected:
   virtual CSize CalcFixedLayout(BOOL bStretch,
                                 BOOL bHorz);

// ...
};

// ————————————————————————
// Implementation for CTextBar (TextBar.cpp)
```

```
CSize CTextBar::CalcFixedLayout(BOOL bStretch, BOOL bHorz)
{
   CSize size = CControlBar::CalcFixedLayout( bStretch,
                                              bHorz );

   // Compute bar width
   CRect rc;
   GetParentFrame()->GetWindowRect( &rc );

   size.cx = rc.Width();   // should be more than
                           // wide enough...

   // Compute bar height
   CClientDC dc( this );

   CString strText = _T( "AaBcCcXxYyZz" );  // dummy string
                               // to compute text height

   CFont* pOldFont = dc.SelectObject( &m_Font );
   size.cy = dc.GetTextExtent( strText ).cy +
                       TOP_MARGIN * 2;

   dc.SelectObject( pOldFont );
   return size;
}
```

Step 6. Use ClassWizard to add handlers in *CTextBar* for the *WM_ERASEBKGND* and *WM_PAINT* messages. Implement these handlers as shown in Listing 6-65 to correctly paint the control bar's area.

Listing 6-65. Handling the *WM_ERASEBKGND* and *WM_PAINT* messages to correctly paint the control bar's area.

```
void CTextBar::OnPaint()
{
   CPaintDC dc(this); // device context for painting

   // 1 - Retrieve window text
   CString strText;
   GetWindowText( strText );

   // 2 - Select correct font
   CFont* pOldFont = dc.SelectObject( &m_Font );
```

```
    dc.SetBkMode( TRANSPARENT );

    // 3 - Draw text
    dc.TextOut( LEFT_MARGIN, TOP_MARGIN, strText );

    dc.SelectObject( pOldFont );

}

BOOL CTextBar::OnEraseBkgnd(CDC* pDC)
{
    // 1 - Find out area to erase
    CRect rc;
    pDC->GetClipBox( &rc );

    // 2 - Create the correct brush and select into DC
    CBrush brush( ::GetSysColor( COLOR_BTNFACE ) );
    CBrush* pOldBrush = pDC->SelectObject( &brush );

    // 3 - Erase the background
    pDC->PatBlt( rc.left, rc.top,
                 rc.Width(), rc.Height(),
                 PATCOPY );

    pDC->SelectObject( pOldBrush );

    return TRUE;   // Background was erased
}
```

Step 7. To enable *CTextBar* to benefit from the *UPDATE_COMMAND_UI* mechanism, we must define a special *CCmdUI*-derived class that overrides some *CCmdUI* virtual functions to execute the correct actions for a *CTextBar* object, as shown in Listing 6-66. In our case, the *CTextBarCmdUI* class overrides only the *CCmdUI::SetText()* function.

Listing 6-66. Defining the *CTextBarCmdUI* class that derives from *CCmdUI* and overrides the *CCmdUI::SetText()* function (TextBar.cpp).

```
// The CTextBarCmdUI is private to this file: its
// only purpose is to make sure that the SetText()
// function is defined to operate correctly on a
// CTextBar object
```

```
class CTextBarCmdUI : public CCmdUI
{
public: // re-implementations only
   virtual void SetText(LPCTSTR lpszText);
};

void CTextBarCmdUI::SetText(LPCTSTR lpszText)
{
   // 1 - Get a pointer to our CTextBar object
   CTextBar* pTextBar = (CTextBar*)m_pOther;
   ASSERT(pTextBar != NULL);
   ASSERT_KINDOF(CTextBar, pTextBar);
   ASSERT(m_nIndex < m_nIndexMax);

   // 2 - Change the text bar window's text
   CString strCurrentText;
   pTextBar->GetWindowText(strCurrentText);
   if( strCurrentText != lpszText )   // prevent flicker
   {
      pTextBar->SetWindowText(lpszText);
      pTextBar->Invalidate();
   }
}
```

Step 8. Finally—for the *CTextBar* class, that is—define the *OnUpdateCmdUI()* function that is declared as pure virtual in the *CControlBar* class. As shown in Listing 6-67, this function creates a *CTextBarCmdUI* object and uses it to send *CN_UPDATE_COMMAND_UI* messages to various potential targets. For more explanation about this function, see the Explanations section.

Listing 6-67. Overriding the *OnUpdateCmdUI()* pure virtual function to create a *CTextBarCmdUI* object and to send *CN_UPDATE_COMMAND_UI* messages to various potential targets.

```
// ―――――――――――――――――――――――――――――――
// Class definition for CTextBar (TextBar.h)

class CTextBar : public CControlBar
{
// ...
```

```
// Implementation
// ...
protected:
   void OnUpdateCmdUI(CFrameWnd* pTarget,
                      BOOL bDisableIfNoHndler);
// ...
};

// ——————————————————————————
// Implementation for CTextBar (TextBar.cpp)

void CTextBar::OnUpdateCmdUI(CFrameWnd* pTarget,
                             BOOL bDisableIfNoHndler)
{
   // 1 - Create the CCmdUI object, initialize its members
   CTextBarCmdUI state;
   state.m_pOther = this;
   state.m_nIndex = 0;
   state.m_nIndexMax = 1;   // only one element to update
   state.m_nID = GetDlgCtrlID();

   // 2 - Send CN_UPDATE_COMMAND_UI message to the text bar
   // itself
   if (CWnd::OnCmdMsg(state.m_nID, CN_UPDATE_COMMAND_UI,
                      &state, NULL))
      return;

   // 3 - Send CN_UPDATE_COMMAND_UI message to the owner
   // frame window
   state.DoUpdate(pTarget, FALSE);

   // 4 - Update the dialog controls added to the text bar
   UpdateDialogControls(pTarget, bDisableIfNoHndler);
}
```

Step 9. To associate our *CTextBar* class with a frame window host, add a member variable of type *CTextBar* to the *CChildFrame* class, as shown in Listing 6-68.

Listing 6-68. Adding a member variable of type *CTextBar* to the *CChildFrame* class.

```
class CChildFrame : public CMDIChildWnd
{
// ...
// Implementation
// ...
protected:
   CTextBar   m_wndTextBar;
// ...
};
```

Step 10. Manually define a new resource ID that will be used to identify your text bar control bar. In the following sample code, we use an ID named *IDW_TEXT_BAR*.

Step 11. Use ClassWizard to add a handler in your *CChildFrame* class for the *WM_CREATE* message. Implement this handler as shown in Listing 6-69 to create the embedded text bar.

Listing 6-69. Handling the *WM_CREATE* message to create an embedded text bar.

```
int CChildFrame::OnCreate(LPCREATESTRUCT lpCreateStruct)
{
   if (CMDIChildWnd::OnCreate(lpCreateStruct) == -1)
      return -1;

   // Create embedded "Text Bar"
   if( !m_wndTextBar.Create(this, CBRS_TOP, IDW_TEXT_BAR) )
   {
      TRACE0("Failed to create text bar\n");
      return -1;      // fail to create
   }

   return 0;
}
```

Step 12. The text bar is now ready to work inside the view's frame window. The only remaining work is to update its contents by writing an *UPDATE_COMMAND_UI* handler. As usual, this handler should be added to the class that is most logically related to the content that we want to display in the text bar. In our case, we want to display the current shape coordinates, which are stored inside the *CDrawDoc* class in the *m_point* member variable. Therefore, we will manually add a handler for the *UPDATE_COMMAND_UI(IDW_TEXT_BAR)* message in the *CDrawDoc* class and implement this handler as shown in Listing 6-70. Notice that our call to the standard *CCmdUI::SetText()* function will actually be routed to the *CTextBarCmdUI::SetText()* function, thanks to the magic of polymorphism and virtual functions.

Listing 6-70. Updating the text bar content in *CDrawDoc* by writing a handler for the *UPDATE_COMMAND_UI(IDW_TEXT_BAR)* message.

```
// ——————————————————————————————
// Class definition for CDrawDoc (DrawDoc.h)

class CDrawDoc : public CDocument
{
// ...
// Generated message map functions
protected:
   //{{AFX_MSG(CDrawDoc)
   afx_msg void OnDrawSquare();
   afx_msg void OnDrawCircle();
   afx_msg void OnUpdateDrawSquare(CCmdUI* pCmdUI);
   afx_msg void OnUpdateDrawCircle(CCmdUI* pCmdUI);
   afx_msg void OnUpdateTextBar(CCmdUI* pCmdUI);
   //}}AFX_MSG
   DECLARE_MESSAGE_MAP()
};

// ——————————————————————————————
// Implementation for CDrawDoc (DrawDoc.cpp)

BEGIN_MESSAGE_MAP(CDrawDoc, CDocument)
   //{{AFX_MSG_MAP(CDrawDoc)
   ON_COMMAND(ID_DRAW_SQUARE, OnDrawSquare)
   ON_COMMAND(ID_DRAW_CIRCLE, OnDrawCircle)
   ON_UPDATE_COMMAND_UI(ID_DRAW_SQUARE, OnUpdateDrawSquare)
   ON_UPDATE_COMMAND_UI(ID_DRAW_CIRCLE, OnUpdateDrawCircle)
   ON_UPDATE_COMMAND_UI(IDW_TEXT_BAR, OnUpdateTextBar)
   //}}AFX_MSG_MAP
END_MESSAGE_MAP()
```

```
// ...

void CDrawDoc::OnUpdateTextBar(CCmdUI* pCmdUI)

{

    CString s;

    s.Format( _T("Custom text bar: x = %d, y = %d"),
              m_point.x, m_point.y );

    pCmdUI->SetText( s );
}
```

Wow! There certainly is a lot to absorb in these explanations, but I hope that these two examples will give you a head start on implementing your own custom control bars. I think you will agree with me that it is preferable to read lengthy explanations than to try to discover for yourself how to make everything work properly.

■

Explanations

You might be wondering how the *OnUpdateCmdUI()* function that we defined in Listings 6-55 and 6-65 gets called—and by whom—and what its real purpose in life is.

The story starts when your MFC application becomes idle—that is, as soon as the *CWinThread::Run()* function (ThrdCore.cpp) finds that there is no longer any message to process in the application's message queue. *CWinThread::Run()* then calls *CWinThread::OnIdle()*, which in turn sends the *WM_IDLEUPDATECMDUI* MFC private message to the main frame window and to each of its children.

When *WM_IDLEUPDATECMDUI* reaches our control bar, the MFC standard routing architecture causes *CControlBar::OnIdleUpdateCmdUI()* to be called (BarCore.cpp). This function in turn calls *OnUpdateCmdUI()*, which must be overridden by each *CControlBar*-derived class because it is declared as pure virtual in the *CControlBar* class.

Now that we know how *OnUpdateCmdUI()* finally gets called, why did we define it as we did in Listing 6-67? The purpose of *OnUpdateCmdUI()* is to create an object of the appropriate *CCmdUI*-derived class for our particular control bar—*CTextBarCmdUI* in our case—and to send this object to the potential targets that may be interested in handling the *UPDATE_COMMAND_UI* message for one of our control bar's elements. These elements are individual buttons (for toolbars), and panes (for status bars). For the *CTextBar* class, our control bar contains only one element, so we set *state.m_nIndexMax* to 1 and do not need to loop through our elements as does *CToolBar::OnUpdateCmdUI()* (BarTool.cpp) or *CStatusBar::OnUpdateCmdUI()* (BarStat.cpp).

After creating the *CCmdUI*-derived object, we first send a *CN_UPDATE_COMMAND_UI* message to the control bar itself in case it has defined its own *UPDATE_COMMAND_UI* handlers. We then call the *CCmdUI::DoUpdate()* function (CmdTarg.cpp). This function in turn sends a *CN_UPDATE_COMMAND_UI* message to its *pTarget* argument and handles the automatic enabling or disabling of the current element if it does not find a handler for the *CN_UPDATE_COMMAND_UI* message.

Finally, calling the *CWnd::UpdateDialogControls()* function (WinCore.cpp) sends a *CN_UPDATE_COMMAND_UI* message to all children of our control bar. This allows these child windows to benefit from the *UPDATE_COMMAND_UI* mechanism and have their own *UPDATE_COMMAND_UI* handlers.

Additional Comments

Note that *CTextBar* could easily be made more generic and reusable, for example by defining additional member functions that would allow users to dynamically select the text font, or by handling the *CCmdUI::Enable()* function call to draw disabled text in gray. However, the goal of this FAQ is to focus on the fundamental techniques used in creating functional custom control bars, and limiting the functionality prevents us from getting buried in implementation details.

Similarly, there is little doubt that my implementation and use of the *CBorderBar* class could be enhanced. Most notably, the chiseled frame border looks good only in a certain range of main frame window sizes, especially if you look at the corners. This behavior is a side effect of using *StretchBlt()* rather simplistically and of using only four different bars to draw the entire frame. To get a more professional-looking result, we should separate the corners from the main body of each side and avoid stretching the corner bitmaps, as shown in Figure 6-23. However, for this approach we need at least eight bars to correctly model the chiseled frame, and again that would make it too complex for the explanatory purpose of this FAQ.

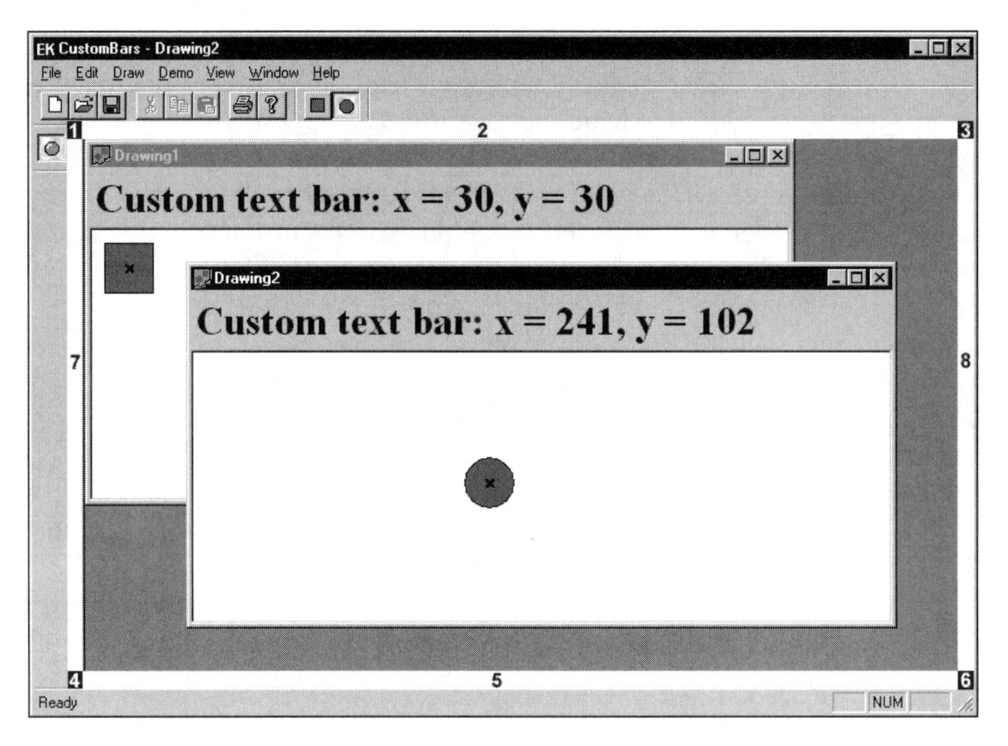

Figure 6-23. How to lay out the border bars to get a more professional-looking chiseled frame.

Sample Code

- Project: CustomBars in the Chap06 subdirectory on the companion CD-ROM.
- Purpose: Demonstrates how to implement two different kinds of custom control bars, as shown earlier in Figures 6-21 and 6-22. The border bar paints a custom bitmap, and the text bar correctly implements the *UPDATE_COMMAND_UI* mechanism to allow the application to easily update its contents.

Implementation Highlights

- *CBorderBar* class (BorderBar.h, BorderBar.cpp)
- *CTextBar* class (TextBar.h, TextBar.cpp)

7 MENUS

Like dialog boxes, menus play an essential role in most Windows applications. Menu commands are often one of the main ways, if not the only way, through which the basic application functionality is exposed to the user.

Although MFC and ClassWizard make it a snap to add menu command handlers, many applications need to go farther than this standard support to remain competitive in today's user-interface-driven battlefield. The FAQs in this chapter will show you how to write a single function that can handle several menu commands (*FAQ 7.1*), how to implement a variety of context menus that can pop up from toolbar buttons or dialog buttons (*FAQs 7.2* to *7.4*), and finally how to implement owner-drawn menus, which can dramatically enhance the effectiveness of your application's user interface by adding a nice graphical touch to the otherwise character-based world of menus (*FAQ 7.5*).

FAQ 7.1 How do I handle several distinct menu commands with a single function?

It is sometimes desirable to process several distinct—but related—menu commands with a single function. Classic examples include menus for selecting colors, patterns, zoom levels, and so on. We will base the following explanations on the color selection example that is implemented in the sample code for this FAQ, but the same principles can easily be adapted to other cases.

Let us imagine that you want to implement a "Color" menu or toolbar that allows the user to select among 16 colors. You could use ClassWizard in the usual way to add one standard *ON_COMMAND* handler for each of your menu items, as shown in Listing 7-1.

Listing 7-1. Adding multiple *ON_COMMAND* handlers for multiple menu commands.

```
BEGIN_MESSAGE_MAP(CDrawDoc, CDocument)
    //{{AFX_MSG_MAP(CDrawDoc)
    // ...
    ON_COMMAND(ID_COLOR0, OnColor0)
    ON_COMMAND(ID_COLOR1, OnColor1)
    ON_COMMAND(ID_COLOR2, OnColor2)
    // ...
    ON_COMMAND(ID_COLOR15, OnColor15)
    // ...
    //}}AFX_MSG_MAP
END_MESSAGE_MAP()

// ...

void CDrawDoc::OnColor0()
{
    m_crColor = GetColorRef( ID_COLOR0 );
    UpdateAllViews( NULL );
    SetModifiedFlag( TRUE );
}

void CDrawDoc::OnColor1()
{
    m_crColor = GetColorRef( ID_COLOR1 );
    UpdateAllViews( NULL );
    SetModifiedFlag( TRUE );
}

void CDrawDoc::OnColor2()
{
    m_crColor = GetColorRef( ID_COLOR2 );
    UpdateAllViews( NULL );
```

```
    SetModifiedFlag( TRUE );
}

// ...

void CDrawDoc::OnColor15()
{
    m_crColor = GetColorRef( ID_COLOR15 );
    UpdateAllViews( NULL );
    SetModifiedFlag( TRUE );
}
```

Although this solution would certainly work, it is neither elegant nor very maintainable: first, most of the code is redundant; second, if you want to change the action performed when the user selects a color, you must propagate this change through every individual *OnColorXX()* handler.

You might try to improve the situation by factoring the common code in a helper function, which you would then call from every *OnColorXX()* handler, as shown in Listing 7-2.

Listing 7-2. Factoring the common code in a helper function called by every *ON_COMMAND* handler.

```
// Helper function
void CDrawDoc::OnColorSelect( UINT nID )
{
    m_crColor = GetColorRef( nID );
    UpdateAllViews( NULL );
    SetModifiedFlag( TRUE );
}

void CDrawDoc::OnColor0()
{
    OnColorSelect( ID_COLOR0 );
}

void CDrawDoc::OnColor1()
{
    OnColorSelect( ID_COLOR1 );
}
```

```
void CDrawDoc::OnColor2()
{
   OnColorSelect( ID_COLOR2 );
}

// ...

void CDrawDoc::OnColor15()
{
   OnColorSelect( ID_COLOR15 );
}
```

Using the ON_COMMAND_RANGE *and* ON_UPDATE_COMMAND_UI_RANGE *Macros*

The code shown in Listing 7-2 improves significantly on Listing 7-1, but you can do even better by taking advantage of the *ON_COMMAND_RANGE* macro. This macro allows you to map a range of command IDs to a single handler function. The function handler for this macro has the following prototype:

```
afx_msg void memberFxn( UINT nID );
```

Here, the *nID* argument identifies the exact menu command that was selected by the user.

Our example becomes significantly more compact when we use the *ON_COMMAND_RANGE* macro and its companion *ON_UPDATE_COMMAND_UI_RANGE*, as you can see in Listing 7-3.

Listing 7-3. Using the *ON_COMMAND_RANGE* and *ON_UPDATE_COMMAND_UI_RANGE* macros to map a range of commands to a single handler function.

```
// ——————————————————————————
// Class definition for CDrawDoc (DrawDoc.h)

class CDrawDoc : public CDocument
{
// ...
// Generated message map functions
protected:
   //{{AFX_MSG(CDrawDoc)
   // ...
```

```
    //}}AFX_MSG

    // Color handling
    afx_msg void OnColor(UINT nID);
    afx_msg void OnUpdateColor(CCmdUI* pCmdUI);

    DECLARE_MESSAGE_MAP()
};

// ─────────────────────────────
// Implementation for CDrawDoc (DrawDoc.cpp)

BEGIN_MESSAGE_MAP(CDrawDoc, CDocument)
    //{{AFX_MSG_MAP(CDrawDoc)
    // ...
    //}}AFX_MSG_MAP
    // ...
    // Color handling
    ON_COMMAND_RANGE(ID_COLOR0, ID_COLOR15, OnColor)
    ON_UPDATE_COMMAND_UI_RANGE(ID_COLOR0, ID_COLOR15,
                                        OnUpdateColor)
END_MESSAGE_MAP()

// ...

void CDrawDoc::OnColor( UINT nID )
{
    m_crColor = GetColorRef( nID );
    UpdateAllViews( NULL );
    SetModifiedFlag( TRUE );
}

void CDrawDoc::OnUpdateColor(CCmdUI* pCmdUI)
{
    pCmdUI->SetCheck( GetColorRef( pCmdUI->m_nID ) ==
                                              m_crColor );
}
```

The code in Listing 7-3 supposes that the IDs *ID_COLOR0* to *ID_COLOR15* are defined as a contiguous range—that is, *ID_COLOR1 = ID_COLOR0 + 1*, *ID_COLOR2 = ID_COLOR0 + 2*, and so on. Note that you will have to add the

XXX_RANGE handlers as well as the related message map entries manually without any help from ClassWizard.

■

Additional Comments

MFC also provides the *ON_COMMAND_EX* macro, which allows you to map several distinct menu commands to the same handler without constraining their respective IDs. The function handler for this macro has the following prototype:

```
afx_msg BOOL memberFxn(UINT nID);
```

Inside your handler, you can use the *nID* argument to determine the exact menu command that caused your function to be called. Your function should return *TRUE* to indicate that the command was handled or return *FALSE* to ask MFC to continue routing the command and look for another handler. The behavior of the *ON_COMMAND_EX* macro is quite similar to that of the *ON_COMMAND_RANGE* macro, but using *ON_COMMAND_EX* does not restrict you to contiguous command IDs. On the other hand, a single *ON_COMMAND_RANGE* message map entry maps a whole range of command IDs to a handler function, whereas you need an explicit *ON_COMMAND_EX* message map entry for each command that you want to handle.

FAQ 6.6 How do I implement a menu that allows users to select the toolbars they want to see? shows an example of using the *ON_COMMAND_EX* macro to map several distinct menu commands to the same handler.

Note that there is no need for an *ON_UPDATE_COMMAND_UI_EX* macro. First, ClassWizard allows you to map several *UPDATE_COMMAND_UI* entries with distinct command IDs to the same handler; second, your *UPDATE_COMMAND_UI* handler can find out the item for which it is called by examining the *CCmdUI::m_nID* field of the *pCmdUI* argument that MFC passes to the handler. This was done, for example, in the *CDrawDoc::OnUpdateColor()* function shown in Listing 7-3.

If you need more flexibility in handling your menu commands—for example, to handle dynamic menu commands whose IDs are not known at compile time—you can use ClassWizard to override the *CWnd::OnCommand()* virtual function. This function is called each time a *WM_COMMAND* message should be processed either because the user selected a menu command, because a child control sent a notification message, or because an accelerator keystroke got translated. Listing 7-4 shows the skeleton of an *OnCommand()* handler function.

Listing 7-4. Skeleton of an *OnCommand()* handler function.

```
BOOL CYourWindow::OnCommand( WPARAM wParam, LPARAM lParam )
{
   if( CYourBaseClass::OnCommand( wParam, lParam ) )
   {
      // Command handled by base class
      return TRUE;
   }

   UINT nID = LOWORD( wParam );    // menu command ID

   UINT nCode = HIWORD( wParam ); // notification code
                                  // (0 for menu command)

   if( nCode == 0 )   // it *is* a menu command
   {
      // ... check if nID is one of your menu items ...
      // ... handle the menu command ...
   }

   /* return TRUE if command handled, FALSE otherwise */
}
```

Note that overriding the *CCmdTarget::OnCmdMsg()* virtual function can also give you yet another level of flexibility by allowing you to add some of your classes to MFC's command dispatch mechanism. For more information about this last topic, see the online help for the *CCmdTarget::OnCmdMsg()* function or read Paul DiLascia's excellent article "Meandering Through the Maze of MFC Message and Command Routing," in the July 1995 issue of *Microsoft Systems Journal* (see Appendix B).

Sample Code

- Project: MultiCommands in the Chap07 subdirectory on the companion CD-ROM.
- Purpose: Demonstrates how to associate a range of "Color" menu commands to a single *ON_COMMAND* and *ON_COMMAND_UI* handler (see Figure 7-1).

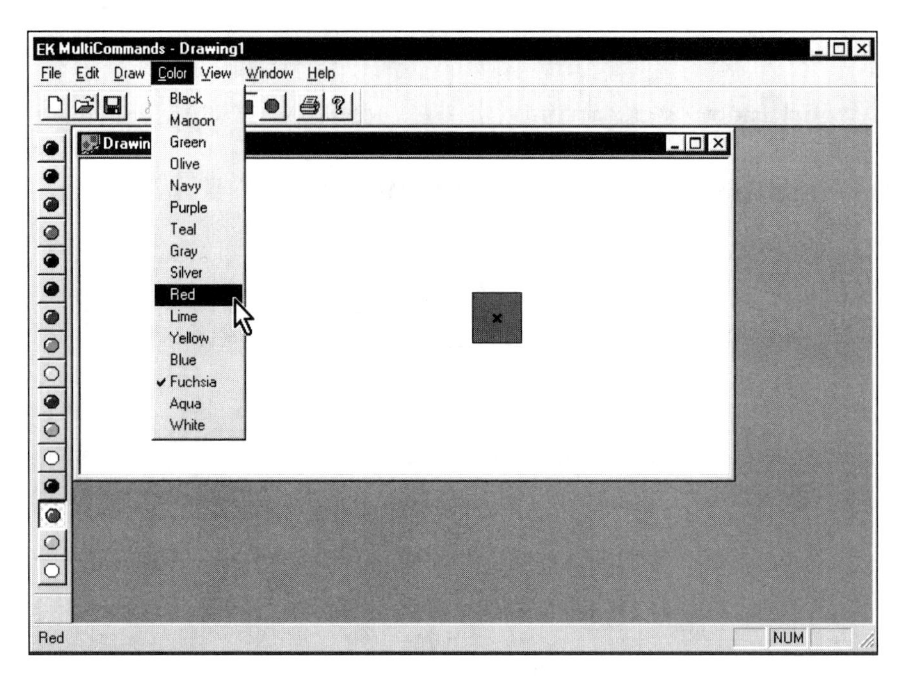

Figure 7-1. The MultiCommands sample application has only one handler function for all its "Color" menu items and toolbar buttons.

Implementation Highlights

- *CDrawDoc::OnColor()* function (DrawDoc.cpp)
- *CDrawDoc::OnUpdateColor()* function (DrawDoc.cpp)

FAQ 7.2 How do I implement a right-button popup menu (context menu)?

Context menus—popup menus that appear when the user right-clicks on an object—have become very popular during the past few years, all the more so since the "new" Windows 95 and Windows NT 4.0 shell make extensive use of them.

Fortunately, adding a context menu to an MFC application is quite easy:

Step 1. Use the Visual Studio Resource Editor to create a new menu resource that corresponds to the popup menu that you want to display, as shown in Figure 7-2. The caption of your popup menu's top-level item will never be displayed, so you can give this item any label you like. I like to use a distinctive label such as *COLOR_POPUP* for the top-level item to remind me that it is a special menu.

Step 2. Use ClassWizard to add a handler in your window class for the *WM_CONTEXTMENU* message, and implement this handler as shown in Listing 7-5 to display the popup menu. You can handle the *WM_CONTEXTMENU* message in any *CWnd*-derived class in your application. However, the most usual case is to handle this message in one of your view classes, as is done in Listing 7-5. Notice the use of *AfxGetMainWnd()* as the fourth argument in the call to *CMenu::TrackPopupMenu()*: this technique ensures that the various messages generated by the popup menu will be sent to our application's main frame window, and these messages will then be routed as usual by the MFC command-handling architecture.

Listing 7-5. Handling the *WM_CONTEXTMENU* message to display a popup menu.

```
void CDrawView::OnContextMenu(CWnd* pWnd, CPoint point)
{
   // 1 - Adjust point if needed
   // (for keyboard context menu)
   if( point.x == -1 && point.y == -1 )
   {
      CRect rect;
      GetClientRect( &rect );
      point = rect.TopLeft();
```

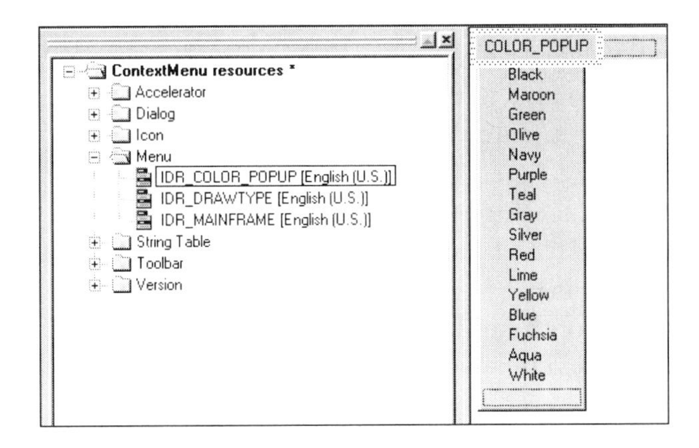

Figure 7-2. Creating the popup menu resource.

```
        point.Offset( 5, 5 );
        ClientToScreen( &point );
    }

    // 2 - Load top-level menu from resource
    CMenu mnuTop;
    mnuTop.LoadMenu( IDR_COLOR_POPUP );

    // 3 - Get popup menu from first submenu
    CMenu* pPopup = mnuTop.GetSubMenu( 0 );
    ASSERT_VALID( pPopup );

    // Checked state for popup menu items is automatically
    // managed by standard MFC UPDATE_COMMAND_UI mechanism!

    // 4 - Display popup menu
    pPopup->TrackPopupMenu( TPM_LEFTALIGN | TPM_LEFTBUTTON,
                            point.x, point.y,
                            AfxGetMainWnd(), NULL );

    // Popup menu commands are automatically handled
    // by standard MFC command-routing mechanism!
}
```

■

Additional Comments

Note that the standard MFC *UPDATE_COMMAND_UI* and command-routing mechanisms elegantly free us from having to write any special code to manage the checked/unchecked state of our popup menu items or handle the user's final selection in this menu. We need only trap the *WM_CONTEXTMENU* message and build our popup menu, and MFC takes care of all the messy details. (OK, it is our code that ultimately handles the *UPDATE_COMMAND_UI* and *WM_COMMAND* messages, but you must admit that MFC message-routing architecture really shines here.)

Finally, you should know that, in contrast to most other mouse messages, if the *WM_CONTEXTMENU* message is not handled by the exact window on which the user clicked, the message propagates up the parent window chain until it reaches the main frame window. This means that if your view contains child window(s) and the user right-clicks on one of them, your view will get the

WM_CONTEXTMENU message after all, with the *pWnd* argument indicating which window the user clicked on. If your view class does not handle the *WM_CONTEXTMENU* message, it will be propagated to the view's frame window and from there finally to the application's main frame window.

What is the reason for this surprising behavior, which is seemingly at odds with the way MFC handles other mouse messages? Quite simply, the *WM_CONTEXTMENU* message is not a "true" mouse message like *WM_RBUTTONDOWN* but rather is a command that the user sends to the application. This command can also be sent using the Shift+F10 keyboard combination or the dedicated Context Menu key on the new 105-key keyboards.

Sample Code

- Project: ContextMenu in the Chap07 subdirectory on the companion CD-ROM.
- Purpose: Implements a context menu that allows the user to quickly select a color, as shown in Figure 7-3.

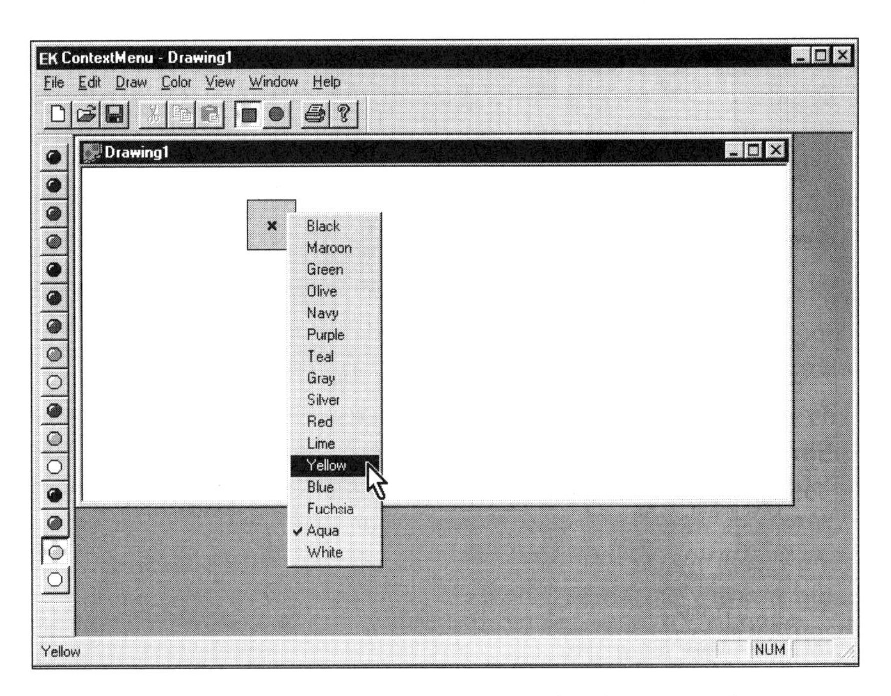

Figure 7-3. Displaying a context menu provides the user with a convenient shortcut.

Implementation Highlights

- *CDrawView::OnContextMenu()* function (DrawView.cpp)

See Also

- *FAQ 6.7 How do I allow users to choose the toolbars they want to see by selecting them in a popup menu that appears when they right-click on a docking zone?*

7.3 How do I display a popup menu when the user clicks a button on a toolbar?

Displaying a popup menu when the user clicks a button on a toolbar is similar to handling the *WM_CONTEXTMENU* message, as was discussed in *FAQ 7.2 How do I implement a right-button popup menu (context menu)?* The main difference lies in the fact that the popup menu will be displayed in answer to a *WM_COMMAND* message—when the user clicks on a toolbar button—rather than to the *WM_CONTEXTMENU* message. Furthermore, we must explicitly position the popup menu under the associated toolbar button.

Step 1. Create a menu resource associated with the popup menu that you want to display, as explained in step 1 of *FAQ 7.2.*

Step 2. Create the toolbar button that you want to use to call up your popup menu (see Figure 7-4). Give this button a distinctive ID.

Step 3. Use ClassWizard to add a handler for the *WM_COMMAND* message associated with the toolbar button created in step 2. For an easier implementation, you should add this handler in the frame window class that hosts the toolbar—usually the main frame window class—and implement it as shown in Listing 7-6 to display the popup menu positioned under the associated toolbar button.

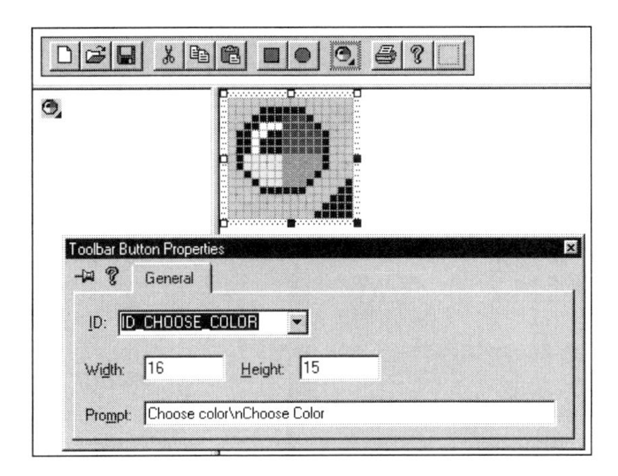

Figure 7-4. Creating the toolbar button that will call up the popup menu.

Listing 7-6. Handling the *WM_COMMAND* message to display a popup menu positioned under the associated toolbar button.

```
void CMainFrame::OnChooseColor()
{
    // 1 - Load top-level menu from resource
    CMenu mnuTop;
    mnuTop.LoadMenu( IDR_COLOR_POPUP );

    // 2 - Get popup menu from first submenu
    CMenu* pPopup = mnuTop.GetSubMenu( 0 );
    ASSERT_VALID( pPopup );

    // 3 - Find position of associated toolbar button
    CRect rc;
    int nIndex = m_wndToolBar.CommandToIndex(
                                        ID_CHOOSE_COLOR );

    ASSERT( nIndex >= 0 );

    m_wndToolBar.GetItemRect( nIndex, &rc );
    m_wndToolBar.ClientToScreen( &rc );

    // Checked state for popup menu items is automatically
    // managed by standard MFC UPDATE_COMMAND_UI mechanism!
```

```
    // 4 - Display popup menu
    pPopup->TrackPopupMenu( TPM_LEFTALIGN | TPM_LEFTBUTTON,
                            rc.left, rc.bottom,
                            this, NULL );
    // Popup menu commands are automatically handled
    // by standard MFC command-routing mechanism!
}
```

■

Sample Code

- Project: ToolbarMenu in the Chap07 subdirectory on the CD-ROM.
- Purpose: Implements a popup menu associated with a toolbar button, as shown in Figure 7-5.

Implementation Highlights

- *CMainFrame::OnChooseColor()* function (MainFrm.cpp)

See Also

- *FAQ 7.2 How do I implement a right-button popup menu (context menu)?*

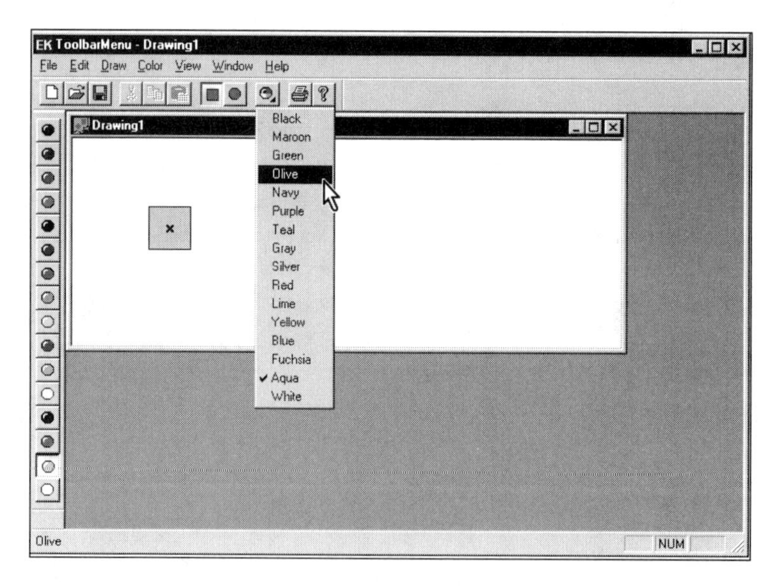

Figure 7-5. Displaying a popup menu associated with a toolbar button.

7.4 How do I display a popup menu when the user clicks a button in a dialog box?

It sometimes makes sense to display a popup menu when the user clicks a button in a dialog box. For an example of this behavior, look at the Find dialog box in Microsoft Word 97, shown in Figure 7-6.

You can implement a similar behavior in an MFC application by following steps similar to those explained in *FAQ 7.3 How do I display a popup menu when the user clicks a button on a toolbar?* There is, however, an interesting twist that you should care about if you want your dialog popup menu to benefit from the *UPDATE_COMMAND_UI* mechanism. Read on.

Implementing the Dialog Popup Menu

Step 1. Create a menu resource associated with the popup menu that you want to display, as explained in step 1 of *FAQ 7.2 How do I implement a right-button popup menu (context menu)?*

Step 2. Add to your dialog box the command button that you want to use to call up your popup menu. Use ClassWizard to associate a C++ member variable of type *CButton* to this control.

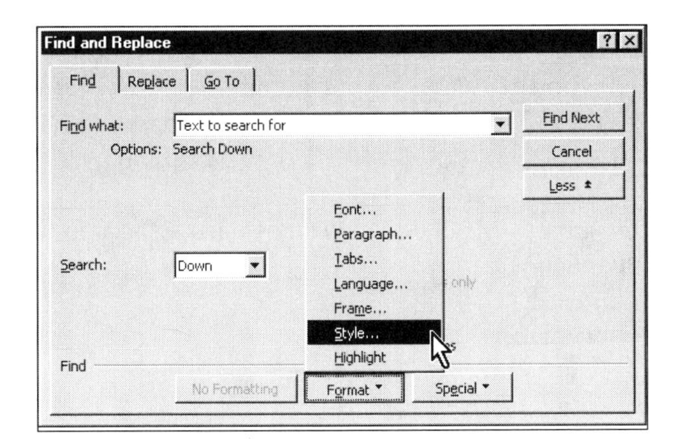

Figure 7-6. Microsoft Word 97 displays a popup menu when you click on either the Format or the Special button.

Step 3. Use ClassWizard to add a handler in your dialog class for the *BN_CLICKED* message on the command button that you created in step 2. Implement this handler as shown in Listing 7-7 to display the popup menu positioned under the associated command button.

Listing 7-7. Handling the *BN_CLICKED* message to display a popup menu positioned under the associated command button.

```
void CDemoDlg::OnChooseColor()
{
    // 1 - Load top-level menu from resource
    CMenu mnuTop;
    mnuTop.LoadMenu( IDR_COLOR_POPUP );

    // 2 - Get popup menu from first submenu
    CMenu* pPopup = mnuTop.GetSubMenu( 0 );
    ASSERT_VALID( pPopup );

    // 3 - Display popup menu under button
    CRect rc;
    m_btnChooseColor.GetWindowRect( &rc );
    pPopup->TrackPopupMenu( TPM_LEFTALIGN | TPM_LEFTBUTTON,
                            rc.left, rc.bottom,
                            this, NULL );
}
```

Step 4. Add handlers in your dialog class for the *WM_COMMAND* messages associated with the items on your popup menu. My sample code for this FAQ uses the *ON_COMMAND_RANGE* macro to handle all the "Color" choices with the same function, as shown in Listing 7-8.

Listing 7-8. Handling the *WM_COMMAND* messages associated with the "Color" items on the popup menu.

```
void CDemoDlg::OnColor( UINT nID )
{
    // 1 - Store new color
    m_crColor = CDrawDoc::GetColorRef( nID );

    // 2 - Repaint affected area
    CRect rc;       // Placeholder rectangle
```

```
    m_FillArea.GetWindowRect( &rc );
    ScreenToClient( &rc );
    InvalidateRect( &rc );
}
```

Note that my sample dialog box class uses the technique described in *FAQ 4.5 How do I add a preview area to (draw inside) a dialog box?* to show the currently selected color by drawing a rectangle in the dialog box, as shown in Figure 7-7. Your popup menu should be useful for generating *WM_COMMAND* messages by now, and you can stop reading here if you don't need to update the state of your popup menu items.

However, if you want to have checked or disabled items on your popup menu, don't miss the next section. (You may find it useful to read this section even if you don't need to apply this technique right now, because it might well be handy in the future.)

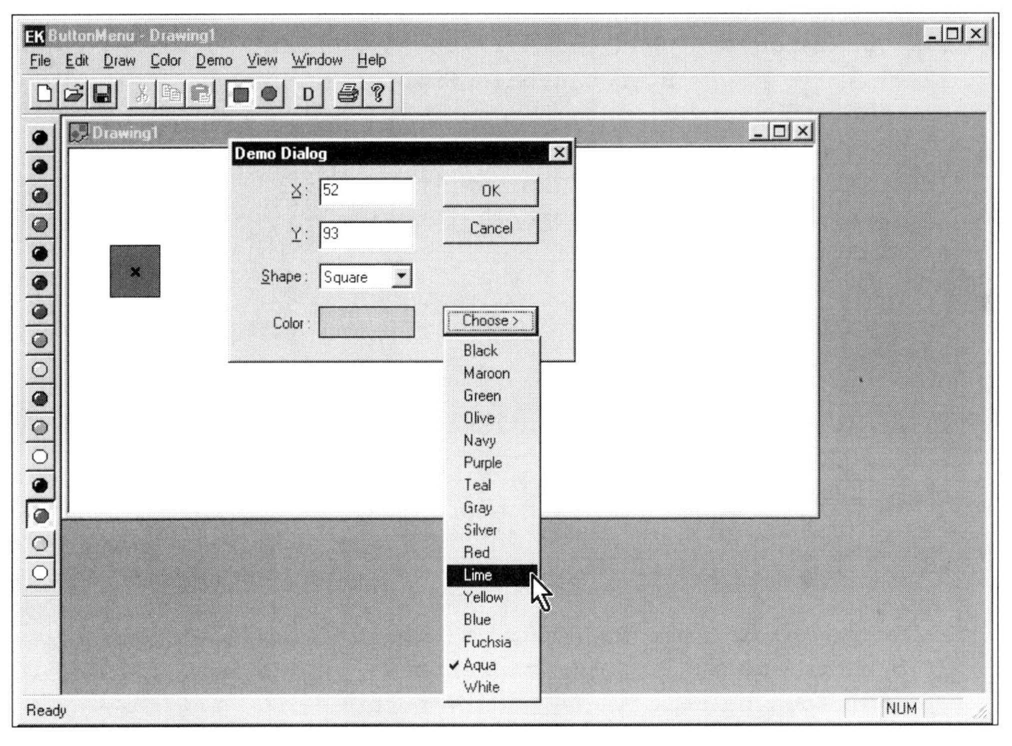

Figure 7-7. The dialog box for this FAQ's sample project displays a popup menu and shows the currently selected color by drawing a rectangle in the dialog box.

Adding UPDATE_COMMAND_UI *Handling to the Dialog Box*

If you have read some of the preceding chapters, you have probably noticed that I am fond of the *UPDATE_COMMAND_UI* mechanism. Alas, our dialog popup menu currently cannot benefit from this mechanism, because MFC dialog boxes do not implement the underlying logic as the *CFrameWnd* class does.

More specifically, we must handle the *WM_INITMENUPOPUP* message and send a *CCmdUI* object for each menu item to give a chance to potential *UPDATE_COMMAND_UI* handlers. The bad news is that the underlying logic is convoluted. The good news is that I have extracted this logic from the *CFrameWnd::OnInitMenuPopup()* function (WinFrm.cpp) that was discussed in *FAQ 6.13 How do I maximize the message pane when displaying menu prompts?* This logic is now available "for free" in the *EkUpdateMenuUI()* function that is shown in Listing 7-9.

Listing 7-9. The *EkUpdateMenuUI()* function that implements the *UPDATE_COMMAND_UI* mechanism for dynamic popup menus.

```
void EkUpdateMenuUI( CWnd* pOwner, CMenu* pMenu,
                     BOOL bAutoMenuEnable = TRUE )
{
   // Checks the enabled/checked state of various menu
   // items (adapted from MFC's own
   // CFrameWnd::OnInitMenuPopup() function -
   // WinFrm.cpp)

   ASSERT_VALID( pOwner );
   ASSERT( pMenu != NULL );

   // Create and initialize the famous CCmdUI object
   CCmdUI state;
   state.m_pMenu = pMenu;
   ASSERT(state.m_pOther == NULL);
   ASSERT(state.m_pParentMenu == NULL);

   // determine if menu is popup in top-level menu and set
   // m_pOther to it if so (m_pParentMenu == NULL
   // indicates that it is secondary popup)
   HMENU hParentMenu;
   if (AfxGetThreadState()->m_hTrackingMenu ==
                                    pMenu->m_hMenu)
      state.m_pParentMenu = pMenu;    // parent == child
```

```
                                            // for tracking popup
else if ((hParentMenu=::GetMenu(pOwner->m_hWnd))!=NULL)
{
   CWnd* pParent = pOwner->GetTopLevelParent();
      // child windows don't have menus — need to go to
      // the top!
   if (pParent != NULL &&
      (hParentMenu = ::GetMenu(pParent->m_hWnd))!=NULL)
   {
      int nIndexMax = ::GetMenuItemCount(hParentMenu);
      for (int nIndex = 0; nIndex < nIndexMax; nIndex++)
      {
         if (::GetSubMenu(hParentMenu, nIndex) ==
                                          pMenu->m_hMenu)
         {
            // when popup is found, m_pParentMenu is
            // containing menu
            state.m_pParentMenu =
                       CMenu::FromHandle(hParentMenu);
            break;
         }
      }
   }
}

state.m_nIndexMax = pMenu->GetMenuItemCount();

// For each menu item...
for (state.m_nIndex = 0;
     state.m_nIndex < state.m_nIndexMax;
     state.m_nIndex++)
{
   // Get menu item ID
   state.m_nID = pMenu->GetMenuItemID(state.m_nIndex);
   if (state.m_nID == 0)
      continue; // menu separator or invalid cmd
                // - ignore it

   ASSERT(state.m_pOther == NULL);
   ASSERT(state.m_pMenu != NULL);
   if (state.m_nID == (UINT)-1)
   {
```

```
            // Maybe a popup menu, route to first item of
            // that popup
            state.m_pSubMenu = pMenu->
                                  GetSubMenu(state.m_nIndex);
            if (state.m_pSubMenu == NULL ||
               (state.m_nID = state.m_pSubMenu->
                                  GetMenuItemID(0)) == 0 ||
               state.m_nID == (UINT)-1)
            {
               continue; // first item of popup can't be
                         // routed to
            }
            state.DoUpdate(pOwner, FALSE);  // popups are
                                    // never auto disabled
         }
         else
         {
            // Normal menu item:
            // Auto enable/disable if 'bAutoMenuEnable'
            // argument is set and command is _not_ a
            // system command
            state.m_pSubMenu = NULL;
            state.DoUpdate(pOwner,
                           bAutoMenuEnable &&
                                state.m_nID < 0xF000);
         }

         // adjust for menu deletions and additions
         UINT nCount = pMenu->GetMenuItemCount();
         if (nCount < state.m_nIndexMax)
         {
            state.m_nIndex -= (state.m_nIndexMax - nCount);
            while (state.m_nIndex < nCount &&
               pMenu->GetMenuItemID(state.m_nIndex) ==
                                             state.m_nID)
            {
               state.m_nIndex++;
            }
         }
         state.m_nIndexMax = nCount;
      }
}
```

Now let's pick up the technique where we left off earlier:

Step 5. You now need to add a handler to your dialog class for the *WM_INITMENUPOPUP* message. Unfortunately, the default behavior of ClassWizard does not display the *WM_INITMENUPOPUP* message for dialog boxes. To correct this problem, call up ClassWizard and click on the Class Info tab. Select your dialog class in the "Class name" combo box, and change the "Message filter" selection to "Window." You can now go back to the Message Maps tab and find the *WM_INITMENUPOPUP* messages in the "Message" list box, as needed for step 7.

Step 6. Use ClassWizard to add a handler in your dialog class for the *WM_INITMENUPOPUP* message. Implement this handler as shown in Listing 7-10 to hook up the *UPDATE_COMMAND_UI* mechanism to your dialog class.

Listing 7-10. Handling the *WM_INITMENUPOPUP* message to hook up the *UPDATE_COMMAND_UI* mechanism to a dialog class.

```
void CDemoDlg::OnInitMenuPopup(CMenu* pPopupMenu,
                               UINT nIndex, BOOL bSysMenu)
{
   CDialog::OnInitMenuPopup(pPopupMenu, nIndex, bSysMenu);

   // Delegate the real work to the EkUpdateMenuUI()
   // function
   EkUpdateMenuUI( this, pPopupMenu );
}
```

Step 8. Add handlers in your dialog class for the *UPDATE_COMMAND_UI* messages associated with the items in your dialog popup menu. My sample code for this FAQ uses the *ON_UPDATE_COMMAND_UI_RANGE* macro to handle all the "Color" choices with the same function, as shown in Listing 7-11.

Listing 7-11. Handling the *UPDATE_COMMAND_UI* messages associated with the "Color" items on the popup menu.

```
void CDemoDlg::OnUpdateColor(CCmdUI* pCmdUI)
{
   pCmdUI->SetCheck(
```

```
                CDrawDoc::GetColorRef( pCmdUI->m_nID ) ==
                                                    m_crColor );
}
```

Notice once again how the *UPDATE_COMMAND_UI* code stays clean and elegant, thanks to the *EkUpdateMenuUI()* function, which allows us to easily hook this powerful mechanism to our dialog box.

■

Additional Comments

Note that the implementation shown in Listing 7-7 is not very sophisticated in determining the position of the dialog popup menu: if the menu does not fit under the dialog button without extending past the bottom of the screen, Windows will simply move the menu position up until it fits on the screen. This action is likely to hide the command button that caused the menu to appear in the first place.

Although this behavior does not limit the functionality of the application, it is less convenient than the one used by Microsoft Word 97: if the menu does not fit under the button, Word will try to show it directly *above* the button, an approach that is without a doubt more pleasant to the eye. Feel free to modify the preceding implementation if you wish to implement this subtle behavior.

Finally, you might wish to use the *CBitmapButton* class to define a graphical button that displays a small triangle—as in Microsoft Word 97—to hint that clicking on the button shows a popup menu. *CBitmapButton* is easy to use and is well documented in the Visual C++ online help, so I will not discuss it further here.

Sample Code

- Project: ButtonMenu in the Chap07 subdirectory on the companion CD-ROM.
- Purpose: Implements a popup menu associated with a command button on a dialog box, as shown earlier in Figure 7-7.

Implementation Highlights

- *CDemoDlg::OnChooseColor()* function (DemoDlg.cpp)
- *CDemoDlg::OnColor()* function (DemoDlg.cpp)
- *EkUpdateMenuUI()* function (DemoDlg.cpp)

- *CDemoDlg::OnInitMenuPopup()* function (DemoDlg.cpp)
- *CDemoDlg::OnUpdateColor()* function (DemoDlg.cpp)

See Also

- *FAQ 7.1 How do I handle several distinct menu commands with a single function?*
- *FAQ 7.2 How do I implement a right-button popup menu (context menu)?*
- *FAQ 7.3 How do I display a popup menu when the user clicks a button on a toolbar?*
- *FAQ 4.5 How do I add a preview area to (draw inside) a dialog box?*
- *FAQ 6.13 How do I maximize the message pane when displaying menu prompts?*

How do I implement an owner-drawn menu?

Standard text menus are fine for most applications, but the ability to display graphical items can sometimes dramatically improve the quality of a menu. The "Color" menu that has been used in most sample projects for this chapter illustrates this point quite well, as you can see in Figure 7-8.

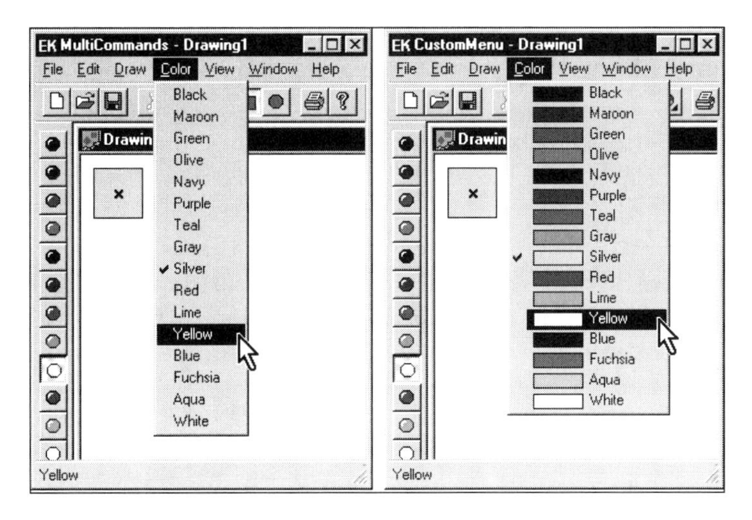

Figure 7-8. Which of the two "Color" menus do you think users would find more explicit and easier to use?

Fortunately, Windows supports the ability of an application to draw its own menu items. This kind of menu is called an *owner-drawn* menu, because the owner of the menu—that is, the window to which the menu is attached—is responsible for drawing the items instead of leaving this task to Windows.

To get the opportunity to paint your menu items, you must work a little harder than for standard menu items. Here are the general steps to implement an owner-drawn menu in standard Windows programming:

1. Mark your menu items with the *MF_OWNERDRAW* flag. This flag is set on an item-by-item basis, and a menu can have both owner-drawn and standard items. Unfortunately, the *MF_OWNERDRAW* flag cannot be specified at design time in the menu resource; you must programmatically create your owner-drawn menu items using *AppendMenu()* and *InsertMenu()* or use *ModifyMenu()* to add the *MF_OWNERDRAW* flag to existing menu items. Note that a menu item created with the *MF_OWNERDRAW* flag does not store a string caption as a standard item does. Instead, you get the opportunity to associate a 32-bit value with your item, which your application can use to maintain additional data associated with each menu item.
2. Handle the *WM_MEASUREITEM* message. Windows will send this message to the owner of the menu once for each owner-drawn item before the menu is displayed. To correctly process this message, the application should compute the size of the relevant menu item in pixels and fill accordingly the *itemWidth* and *itemHeight* fields of the *MEASUREITEMSTRUCT* structure that Windows passes as an argument with the *WM_MEASUREITEM* message:

```
typedef struct tagMEASUREITEMSTRUCT {
    UINT   CtlType;
    UINT   CtlID;
    UINT   itemID;      // ID of the menu item
    UINT   itemWidth;   // width of the menu item
    UINT   itemHeight;  // height of the menu item
    DWORD  itemData     // 32-bit value associated with item
} MEASUREITEMSTRUCT;
```

3. Handle the *WM_DRAWITEM* message. Windows sends this message to the owner of the menu every time an owner-drawn menu item should be drawn: the first time the menu is displayed as well as each time the user changes the highlighted state of an item. This message is accompanied by

a *DRAWITEMSTRUCT* structure that contains most of the necessary information for correctly drawing the menu item depending on its various possible states, as you can see in the following bold fields:

```
typedef struct tagDRAWITEMSTRUCT {
    UINT  CtlType;
    UINT  CtlID;
    UINT  itemID;      // ID of the menu item
    UINT  itemAction;
    UINT  itemState;   // state of the menu item:
                       // ODS_SELECTED, ODS_CHECKED,
                       // ODS_DISABLED, ODS_GRAYED
    HWND  hwndItem;
    HDC   hDC;         // device context where to draw
    RECT  rcItem;      // rectangle where to draw
    DWORD itemData;    // 32-bit value associated with item
} DRAWITEMSTRUCT;
```

Note that ClassWizard will show the *WM_MEASUREITEM* and *WM_DRAWITEM* messages in its "Messages" list only if you select the "Window" option in the "Message filter" combo box on the Class Info page.

Creating a Self-Drawn Menu Class

In standard Windows programming, as explained earlier, the window that owns the menu is responsible for handling the *WM_MEASUREITEM* and *WM_DRAWITEM* messages. This arrangement can be problematic if you want to reuse your owner-drawn menu in several windows.

Fortunately, MFC provides a more elegant and object-oriented alternative with what are called *self-drawn* menus. To implement a self-drawn menu, simply create a class derived from *CMenu* and override the *MeasureItem()* and *DrawItem()* virtual functions. You can then create an instance of your *CMenu*-derived class any time you need to display your owner-drawn menu. Your code becomes cleaner and more object-oriented, because all the details of drawing the owner-drawn items are encapsulated inside your *CMenu*-derived class.

Listing 7-12 shows the implementation of the *CColorMenu* class, which implements the self-drawn "Color" menu for this FAQ's sample application. Pay close attention to the *CColorMenu::MeasureItem()* and *CColorMenu::DrawItem()* functions in this code, because they are where most of the interesting action happens.

Listing 7-12. Implementation of the *CColorMenu* class to implement a self-drawn "Color" menu.

```
// ——————————————————————————————
// Class definition for CColorMenu (ColorMenu.h)

class CColorMenu : public CMenu
{
// Construction
public:
   CColorMenu();

// Attributes
public:

// Operations
public:
   static COLORREF GetColorRef( UINT nID );

// Implementation
protected:
   virtual void DrawItem( LPDRAWITEMSTRUCT lpDIS );
   virtual void MeasureItem( LPMEASUREITEMSTRUCT lpMIS );

   static int s_ColorMap[ 16 ];
   enum { CX_COLOR = 40, CX_COLOR_LEFT_MARGIN = 5,
           CX_COLOR_RIGHT_MARGIN = 5, CY_COLOR_MARGIN = 2 };
};

// ——————————————————————————————
// Implementation for CColorMenu (ColorMenu.cpp)
int CColorMenu::s_ColorMap[ 16 ] =
               {
                  0,        //black
                  1,        //dark red
                  2,        //dark green
                  3,        //light brown
                  4,        //dark blue
                  5,        //purple
                  6,        //dark cyan
                  12,       //gray
                  7,        //light gray
```

```
                    13,      //red
                    14,      //green
                    15,      //yellow
                    16,      //blue
                    17,      //magenta
                    18,      //cyan
                    19       //white
                };

CColorMenu::CColorMenu()
{

   // 1 - Create the popup menu and add owner-drawn items
   VERIFY( CreatePopupMenu() );
   ASSERT( GetMenuItemCount() == 0 );

   // 2 - Add items
   // (item data is set to item ID to provide a
   // consistency check in OnMeasureItem and OnDrawItem)
   for( int i = 0; i <= 15; ++i )
   {
      // ID_COLOR0 to ID_COLOR15 are consecutive IDs that
      // have associated string resources containing the
      // text for each menu item (like toolbar buttons)
      VERIFY( AppendMenu( MF_OWNERDRAW,
                          ID_COLOR0 + i,
                          (LPCTSTR)(ID_COLOR0 + i) ) );
   }
}

COLORREF CColorMenu::GetColorRef( UINT nID )
{
   // Find COLORREF from menu item ID
   ASSERT( nID >= ID_COLOR0 );
   ASSERT( nID <= ID_COLOR15 );

   // 1 - Get standard color palette
   CPalette* pPal = CPalette::FromHandle(
                  (HPALETTE) GetStockObject(
                                     DEFAULT_PALETTE ) );
   ASSERT( pPal != NULL );
   PALETTEENTRY pe;
```

```
   // 2 - Find color map entry in palette
   if( pPal->GetPaletteEntries(
               s_ColorMap[ nID-ID_COLOR0 ], 1, &pe ) != 0 )
   {
      return RGB( pe.peRed, pe.peGreen, pe.peBlue );
   }
   else
   {
      TRACE1( "Unable to find palette color entry for "
              "ID=%d\n", nID );
      return ::GetSysColor( COLOR_WINDOWTEXT );
   }
}

void CColorMenu::MeasureItem( LPMEASUREITEMSTRUCT lpMIS )
{
   ASSERT(lpMIS->CtlType == ODT_MENU);

   // 1 - Get menu item ID
   UINT id = (UINT) (WORD) lpMIS->itemID;

   // Consistency checks
   ASSERT( id == lpMIS->itemData );
   ASSERT( id >= ID_COLOR0 );
   ASSERT( id <= ID_COLOR15 );

   // 2 - Load item string
   CString strColor;
   AfxExtractSubString( strColor, CString(LPCSTR(id)), 0 );

   // 3 - Compute item text extent
   CDC* pdc = AfxGetMainWnd()->GetDC();
   CSize sizeText = pdc->GetTextExtent( strColor,
                                 strColor.GetLength() );
   AfxGetMainWnd()->ReleaseDC( pdc );

   // 4 - Compute check mark dimensions
   int cxCheckMark = ::GetSystemMetrics( SM_CXMENUCHECK );
   int cyCheckMark = ::GetSystemMetrics( SM_CYMENUCHECK );

   // 5 - Define final item size
   lpMIS->itemWidth = cxCheckMark + CX_COLOR_LEFT_MARGIN +
```

```
                           CX_COLOR + CX_COLOR_RIGHT_MARGIN +
                           sizeText.cx;
   lpMIS->itemHeight = max( sizeText.cy, cyCheckMark );
}

void CColorMenu::DrawItem( LPDRAWITEMSTRUCT lpDIS )
{
   ASSERT( lpDIS->CtlType == ODT_MENU );

   // 1 - Get menu item ID
   UINT id = (UINT) (WORD) lpDIS->itemID;

   // Consistency checks
   ASSERT( id == lpDIS->itemData );
   ASSERT( id >= ID_COLOR0 );
   ASSERT( id <= ID_COLOR15 );

   // 2 - Get device context & item rectangle
   CDC dc;
   dc.Attach( lpDIS->hDC );

   CRect rcItem( lpDIS->rcItem );
   int nCurrentX = rcItem.left;   // current position

   // 3 - Select background and foreground colors depending
   // on item selected state
   COLORREF crBack, crFore;
   if( lpDIS->itemState & ODS_SELECTED )
   {
      crBack = ::GetSysColor( COLOR_HIGHLIGHT );
      crFore = ::GetSysColor( COLOR_HIGHLIGHTTEXT );
   }
   else
   {
      crBack = ::GetSysColor( COLOR_MENU );
      crFore = ::GetSysColor( COLOR_MENUTEXT );
   }

   // 4 - Draw optional check mark
   if( lpDIS->itemState & ODS_CHECKED )
   {
      // Load check mark bitmap
```

```
    // (#define OEMRESOURCE before including Windows.h,
    // *OR* #define OBM_CHECK 32760)
    CBitmap bmCheck;
    bmCheck.LoadOEMBitmap( OBM_CHECK );

    // Compute bitmap size
    BITMAP bmStruct;
    bmCheck.GetObject( sizeof( BITMAP ), &bmStruct );
    CSize sizeBitmap(bmStruct.bmWidth,bmStruct.bmHeight);

    // Draw bitmap on menu DC
    CDC dcMem;
    dcMem.CreateCompatibleDC( &dc );
    CBitmap* pOldBitmap = dcMem.SelectObject( &bmCheck );

    dc.BitBlt( rcItem.left,
                ( rcItem.top + rcItem.bottom -
                                   sizeBitmap.cy ) / 2,
               sizeBitmap.cx, sizeBitmap.cy,
               &dcMem, 0, 0, SRCCOPY );

    dcMem.SelectObject( pOldBitmap );
}

nCurrentX += ::GetSystemMetrics( SM_CXMENUCHECK );

// 5 - Fill item background
CRect rcBack( nCurrentX, rcItem.top, rcItem.right,
                                     rcItem.bottom );
CBrush brFill( crBack );
dc.FillRect( &rcBack, &brFill );

nCurrentX += CX_COLOR_LEFT_MARGIN;

// 6 - Draw item color rectangle
CBrush brColor( GetColorRef( id ) );
CBrush* pOldBrush = dc.SelectObject( &brColor );
CRect rcColor( nCurrentX, rcItem.top + CY_COLOR_MARGIN,
               nCurrentX + CX_COLOR,
               rcItem.bottom - CY_COLOR_MARGIN );
dc.Rectangle( rcColor );
```

```
    dc.SelectObject( pOldBrush );

    nCurrentX += CX_COLOR + CX_COLOR_RIGHT_MARGIN;

    // 7 - Draw item text
    COLORREF crOldTextColor = dc.SetTextColor( crFore );
    int nOldBkMode = dc.SetBkMode( TRANSPARENT );
    CString strColor;
    AfxExtractSubString( strColor, CString(LPCSTR(id)), 0 );

    dc.TextOut( nCurrentX, rcItem.top, strColor,
                                   strColor.GetLength() );

    dc.SetTextColor( crOldTextColor );
    dc.SetBkMode( nOldBkMode );

    dc.Detach();
}
```

Note that the *AfxExtractSubString()* function used in *CColorMenu::MeasureItem()* and *CColorMenu::DrawItem()* in Listing 7-12 is discussed in the Additional Comments section of *FAQ 4.7 How do I implement an expanding dialog box?*

Displaying an Owner-Drawn Popup Menu

After you have created your self-drawn class, you can use it to display your owner-drawn menu as a popup menu that appears when the user either clicks the right mouse button or clicks on a toolbar button.

The techniques for each case are similar to the ones discussed in *FAQ 7.2 How do I implement a right-button popup menu (context menu)?* and *FAQ 7.3 How do I display a popup menu when the user clicks a button on a toolbar?* However, as you can see in Listings 7-13 and 7-14, the code here is actually simpler, because the self-drawn class takes care of dynamically creating the popup menu.

Listing 7-13. Displaying an owner-drawn popup menu when the user clicks the right mouse button.

```
void CDrawView::OnContextMenu(CWnd* pWnd, CPointpoint)
{
    // 1 - Adjust point if needed
    // (for keyboard context menu)
```

```
    if( point.x == -1 && point.y == -1 )
    {
        CRect rect;
        GetClientRect( &rect );
        point = rect.TopLeft();
        point.Offset( 5, 5 );
        ClientToScreen( &point );
    }

    // 2 - Display self-drawn popup menu
    CColorMenu menu;
    menu.TrackPopupMenu(    TPM_LEFTALIGN | TPM_LEFTBUTTON,
                            point.x, point.y,
                            AfxGetMainWnd(), NULL );

    // Popup menu commands are automatically handled
    // by standard MFC command-routing mechanism!
}
```

Listing 7-14. Displaying an owner-drawn popup menu when the user clicks on a toolbar button.

```
void CMainFrame::OnChooseColor()
{
    // 1 - Create self-drawn popup menu
    CColorMenu menu;

    // 2 - Find toolbar button position
    CRect rc;
    int nIndex = m_wndToolBar.CommandToIndex(
                                        ID_CHOOSE_COLOR );
    ASSERT( nIndex >= 0 );

    m_wndToolBar.GetItemRect( nIndex, &rc );
    m_wndToolBar.ClientToScreen( &rc );

    // 3 - Display popup menu
    menu.TrackPopupMenu(    TPM_LEFTALIGN | TPM_LEFTBUTTON,
                            rc.left, rc.bottom,
                            this, NULL );
```

```
    // Popup menu commands are automatically handled
    // by standard MFC command-routing mechanism!
}
```

Adding an Owner-Drawn Menu to the Menu Bar

Adding an owner-drawn menu to your application's menu bar is, paradoxically, more involved than creating a popup menu on-the-fly:

Step 1. Remove the standard "Color" menu from your menu resource.

Step 2. Add a member variable of type *CColorMenu* to your view's frame class, as shown in Listing 7-15. This variable must be added to the view's frame class because the menu that is displayed by the MDI main frame window actually belongs to the view's frame window associated with the active view. If your application supports multiple document templates, you might need to create a specific view's frame window class to customize its behavior with respect to the owner-drawn menu.

Listing 7-15. Add a member variable of type *CColorMenu* to the view's frame class.

```
class CChildFrame : public CMDIChildWnd
{
// ...
// Implementation
// ...
protected:
    CColorMenu    m_ColorMenu;        // self-drawn menu
    enum { POS_COLOR_MENU = 3 };      // zero-based from left

// ...
};
```

Step 3. Use ClassWizard to override the *LoadFrame()* virtual function in your view's frame class. Implement this function as shown in Listing 7-16 to dynamically add the owner-drawn menu to the menu bar of the view's frame window.

Listing 7-16. Implementation of the *LoadFrame()* virtual function to dynamically add the owner-drawn menu to the menu bar of the view's frame window.

```
BOOL CChildFrame::LoadFrame(UINT nIDResource,
                            DWORD dwDefaultStyle,
```

```
                                  CWnd* pParentWnd,
                                  CCreateContext* pContext)
{
   // 1 - Let base class load everything properly,
    // more particularly our own menu
   if( !CMDIChildWnd::LoadFrame( nIDResource,
                    dwDefaultStyle, pParentWnd, pContext ) )
   {
      return FALSE;
   }

   ASSERT( m_hMenuShared != NULL );

   // 2 - Get a pointer to our associated menu bar
   CMenu* pMenuBar = CMenu::FromHandle( m_hMenuShared );
   ASSERT_VALID( pMenuBar );

   // 3 - Check if popup was already inserted
   CString strItem;
   pMenuBar->GetMenuString( POS_COLOR_MENU, strItem,
                                          MF_BYPOSITION );
   if( strItem != _T( "&Color" ) )
   {
      // 4 - Insert custom menu in our menu bar
      pMenuBar->InsertMenu( POS_COLOR_MENU,
                            MF_POPUP | MF_BYPOSITION,
                            (UINT) m_ColorMenu.GetSafeHmenu(),
                            _T( "&Color" ) );
   }
   return TRUE;
}
```

■

Additional Comments

If you want to add your owner-drawn menu to the menu bar of the main frame window, do the following:

- Modify the preceding steps to reference your main frame window class instead of the view's frame class.

- Replace the reference to the *m_hMenuShared* variable with *m_hMenuDefault* in Listing 7-16.

Sample Code

- Project: CustomMenu in the Chap07 subdirectory on the companion CD-ROM.
- Purpose: Creates a self-drawn menu class and demonstrates three ways of displaying an owner-drawn menu, as shown in Figure 7-9.

Implementation Highlights

- *CColorMenu* class (ColorMenu.h, ColorMenu.cpp)
- *CDrawView::OnContextMenu()* function (DrawView.cpp)

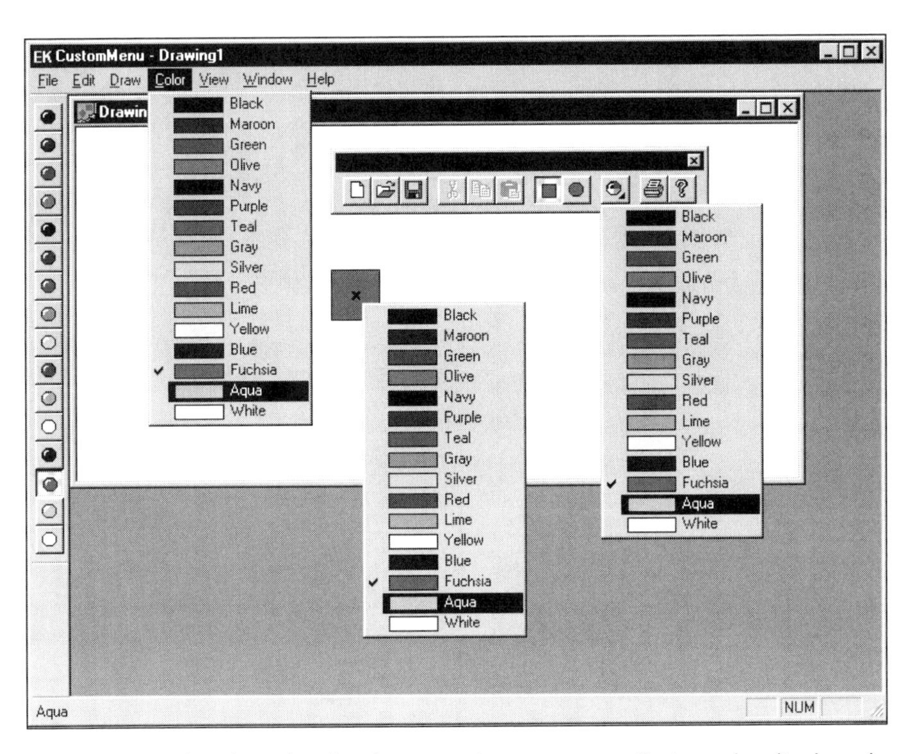

Figure 7-9. The three kinds of owner-drawn menus that can be displayed by the CustomMenu application (from left to right): menu bar menu, context menu, and toolbar menu.

- *CMainFrame::OnChooseColor()* function (MainFrm.cpp)
- *CChildFrame::LoadFrame()* function (ChildFrm.cpp)

See Also

- FAQ 7.2 *How do I implement a right-button popup menu (context menu)?*
- FAQ 7.3 *How do I display a popup menu when the user clicks a button on a toolbar?*
- FAQ 4.7 *How do I implement an expanding dialog box?*

8 PRINTING AND PRINT PREVIEW

Even with the growing popularity of e-mail and the Internet, the paperless office is not quite here. Most applications still must provide some means of committing their output to paper. Fortunately, adopting MFC and the document/view architecture gives you a head start in the printing race: your applications get basic printing and print preview support almost for free. You need only write your view's *OnDraw()* function and select the "Printing and print preview" check box in AppWizard's options.

However, applications that provide in-depth support for printing and print preview must go further than the standard functionality provided by MFC's printing architecture. The good news is that this same architecture effectively shields you from much of the complexity of the Windows printing process yet remains flexible enough to accommodate the customization needs of most applications.

After taking a quick tour of MFC's printing architecture in *FAQ 8.1, FAQ 8.2* will give you a hands-on explanation of how to add complete printing and print preview support to your application, including page headers and footers. Each of the following FAQs then covers a puzzling aspect of printing and print preview, such as how to predict page breaks (*FAQ 8.4*), how to change the printing orientation on-the-fly (*FAQ 8.5*), how to customize the Printing... dialog box (*FAQ 8.8*), and how to stop or abort a print job (*FAQ 8.9*).

A Word about This Chapter's Sample Projects

To show you how to print something meaningful, the sample projects for this chapter have been enhanced to offer more functionality than the applications used in the previous chapters. Here is a quick tour of the main functions provided by this chapter's sample projects:

- They allow the user to build a drawing made of individual shapes. The attributes of each shape are the position of its center point, its fill color, and the shape type itself: square or circle.
- The document maintains an array of pointers to the individual shape objects—implemented as a *CTypedPtrArray< CObArray, CShape* >* member—and allows the whole drawing to be persisted to disk, using MFC's serialization mechanism (see the *CDrawDoc::Serialize()* function).
- Printing and print preview do not print the current "drawing" but rather print a list of the shapes that make up the drawing. Each shape is drawn, and some information about it is printed, such as the shape type, its coordinates, and its color in RGB format. The list of shapes is printed by chunks of four elements per page, with a page header that prints the name of the current document and a page footer that shows the current page number as well as the total page number ("Page x of y"), as shown in Figure 8-1.

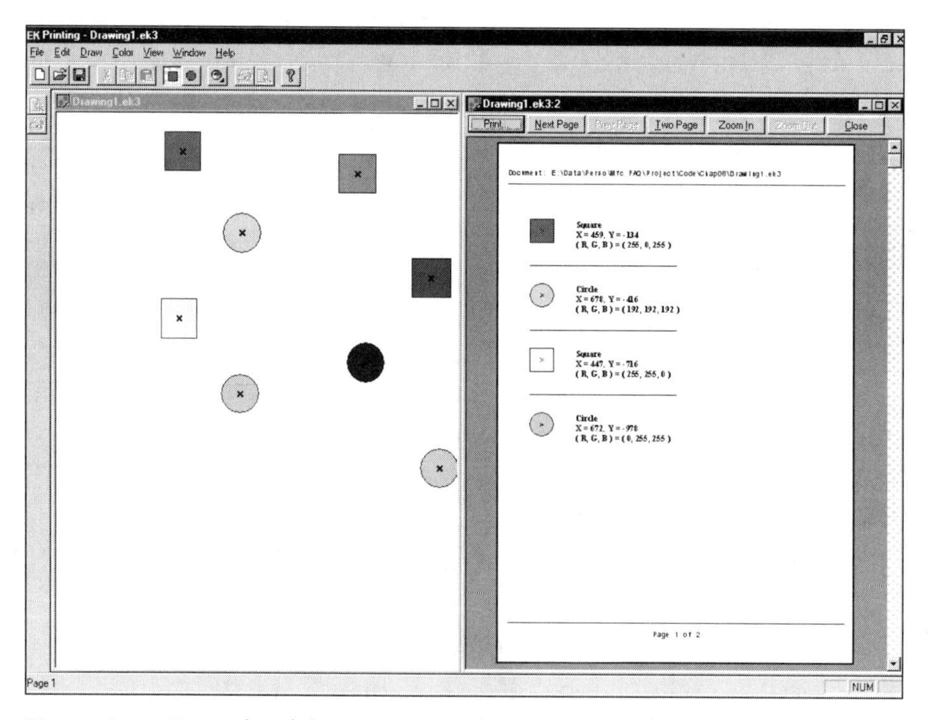

Figure 8-1. Example of the printing and print preview support implemented by this chapter's sample projects.

What is the MFC printing architecture?

Printing has been traditionally—and justly—considered as a necessary but complex feature of most Windows applications. Fortunately, MFC offers an architecture that saves developers most of the trouble of understanding tedious details such as printer device contexts, abort procedures, abort dialogs, and so on.

MFC's printing architecture builds on the abstraction provided by the "view" concept in the document/view architecture. As we explained in Chapter 1, the view can be considered an output device responsible for extracting the relevant data from the document and for drawing, or *rendering*, an appropriate representation of the data. Because the process for rendering data on a printed page is often quite similar to drawing inside a window, the MFC printing architecture makes the view responsible for managing the printing process.

More precisely, MFC manages printing via the *CView::OnFilePrint()* function (ViewPrnt.cpp) and calls various virtual functions that you should override in your view class to customize the printing process. These functions are described in Table 8-1. For more in-depth explanations and sample code, see *FAQ 8.2 How do I implement printing and print preview in my MFC application?*

Most of what is explained in this FAQ applies to print preview as well as to printing; MFC manages successfully to hide the difference between those two behaviors from your code. For more information on how print preview actually works, see *MFC Internals*, pp. 307–316 (see Appendix B).

Table 8-1. The *CView* virtual functions that should be overridden to control printing and print preview.

Function	Called when	Main goal
OnPreparePrinting()	When the user has just selected the "File, Print" (or "File, Print Preview") command	Call *pInfo->SetMaxPages()* to inform MFC of the document's page length (see *FAQ 8.4 How do I predict page breaks as Microsoft Word does*) and of other information about the print job. Call *DoPreparePrinting()* to show the Print dialog box.

Table 8-1 *(Cont.)*

Function	Called when	Main goal
OnBeginPrinting()	When the user has clicked the OK button on the Print dialog box and the printing job is about to start	Allocate GDI resources (such as fonts) and other resources (such as temporary files or memory buffers) that will be needed during the printing process.
OnPrepareDC()	Before each page is printed	If necessary, call *pDC->SetMapMode()* to select the correct mapping mode for the device context (see *FAQ 8.2 How do I implement printing and print preview in my MFC application?*). If doing on-the-fly pagination, find out whether there is something left to print and set the *pInfo->m_bContinuePrinting* flag accordingly (see *FAQ 8.3 How do I print a document whose page length is not known in advance (on-the-fly pagination)?*). If the *OnDraw()* function is used for printing, set up the viewport origin to draw the correct page.
OnPrint()	When each page is printed	Print the current page along with headers, footers, etc. Can either do its own rendering for printing—which I recommend—or call your view's *OnDraw()* function.
OnEndPrinting()	When the print job has ended	Clean up the resources allocated by *OnBeginPrinting()*.

Note that all the functions described in Table 8-1 receive as an argument a pointer to a *CPrintInfo* object—created and managed by MFC—that is used to pass information about the print job in progress between MFC and your own code. For example, your code should call *pInfo->SetMaxPage()* in the *OnPreparePrinting()* function to inform MFC of your document's page length. To retrieve the page range selected by the user, call *pInfo->GetFromPage()* and *pInfo->GetToPage()*. The current page is then stored in the *CPrintInfo::m_nCurPage* data member.

All the functions described in Table 8-1 except *OnPreparePrinting()* receive as an argument a pointer to a device context created and managed by MFC. This device context should be used by all functions to render their output. This device context will be associated with either the selected printer or the print preview window, but this situation is usually transparent for the application code (see *FAQ 8.11 How do I distinguish between drawing, print preview, and actual printing in my code?*).

Many applications do not need to override *OnPrepareDC()* for printing or print preview. If you do not need to set a specific mapping mode, if you do not perform on-the-fly pagination, and if you do not rely on your view's *OnDraw()* function for printing and print preview, you might very well be able to leave *OnPrepareDC()* alone. On the other hand, if you override this function, be sure to call the corresponding base class function in your override, especially if your view class derives from *CScrollView*.

Figure 8-2 shows a graphical overview of the MFC printing architecture.

■

Additional Comments

Looking inside the source code is sometimes the best way to understand what actually goes on. Listing 8-1 shows the pseudocode for the *CView::OnFilePrint()* function (ViewPrnt.cpp).

Listing 8-1. Pseudocode for the *CView::OnFilePrint()* function (ViewPrnt.cpp).

```
void CView::OnFilePrint()
{
   // get default print info
   CPrintInfo printInfo;

   // ... stuff to handle ID_FILE_PRINT_DIRECT ...

   // Call OnPreparePrinting(); this function in turn
   // usually calls DoPreparePrinting(), which displays the
   // "Print" dialog box
   if (OnPreparePrinting(&printInfo))
   {
      // ... stuff to prompt for file if print-to-file
      // selected ...
```

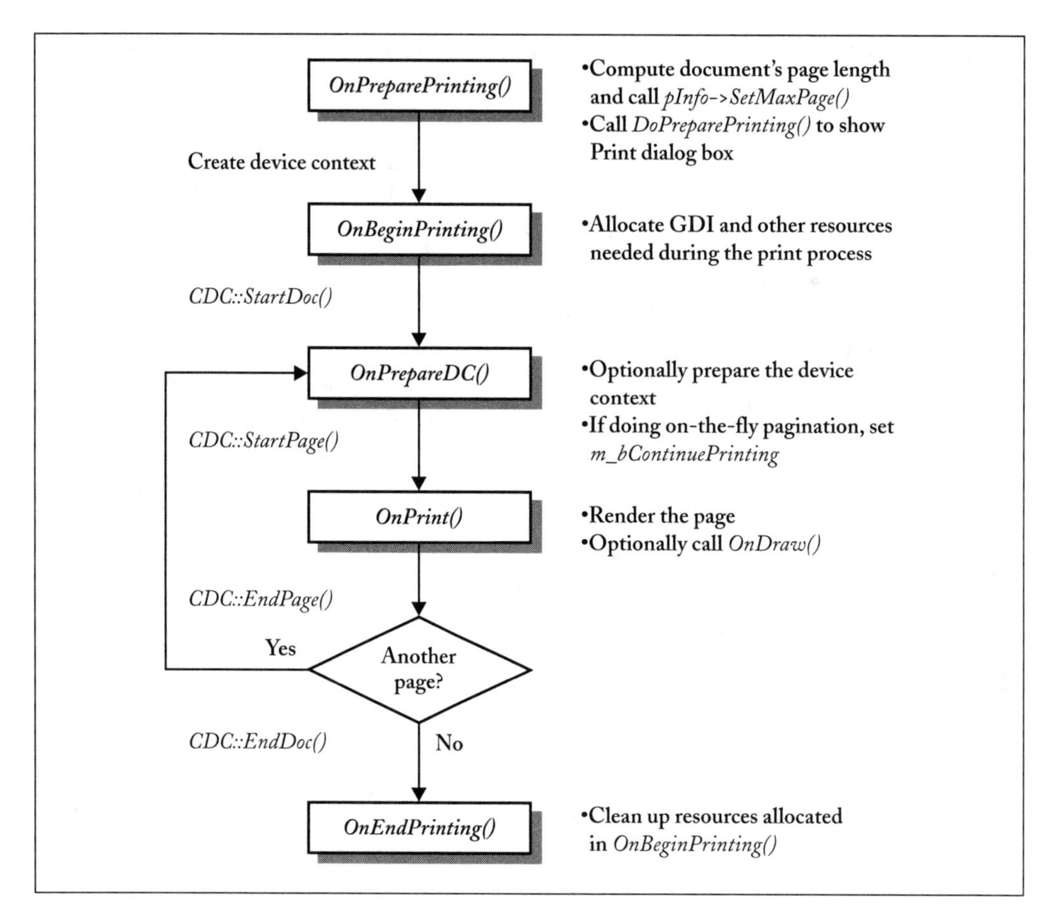

Figure 8-2. Overview of the MFC printing architecture.

```
// ... stuff to set up document info and start the
// document printing process ...

// setup the printing DC
CDC dcPrint;
dcPrint.Attach(printInfo.m_pPD->m_pd.hDC);
                                  // attach printer dc
dcPrint.m_bPrinting = TRUE;

// Let the view initialize the printing process
OnBeginPrinting(&dcPrint, &printInfo);
```

```
dcPrint.SetAbortProc(_AfxAbortProc);

// disable main window while printing & init printing
// status dialog
AfxGetMainWnd()->EnableWindow(FALSE);
CPrintingDialog dlgPrintStatus(this);

CString strTemp;
dlgPrintStatus.SetDlgItemText(AFX_IDC_PRINT_DOCNAME,
                              strTitle);
dlgPrintStatus.SetDlgItemText(
                AFX_IDC_PRINT_PRINTERNAME,
                printInfo.m_pPD->GetDeviceName());
AfxFormatString1(strTemp, nFormatID, strPortName);
dlgPrintStatus.SetDlgItemText(AFX_IDC_PRINT_PORTNAME,
                              strTemp);
dlgPrintStatus.ShowWindow(SW_SHOW);
dlgPrintStatus.UpdateWindow();

// start document printing process
if (dcPrint.StartDoc(&docInfo) == SP_ERROR)
{
   // ... error on StartDoc(): clean up and restore
   // initial state ...
}

UINT nEndPage = printInfo.GetToPage();
UINT nStartPage = printInfo.GetFromPage();
// ... stuff to ensure that nEndPage and nStartPage
// fall between printInfo.GetMinPage() and
// printInfo.GetMaxPage() ...

int nStep = (nEndPage >= nStartPage) ? 1 : -1;
nEndPage = (nEndPage == 0xffff) ? 0xffff : nEndPage +
                                             nStep;

strTemp.LoadString(AFX_IDS_PRINTPAGENUM);

// Here is the main page printing loop
BOOL bError = FALSE;
for (printInfo.m_nCurPage = nStartPage;
```

```
        printInfo.m_nCurPage != nEndPage;
        printInfo.m_nCurPage += nStep)
{
    OnPrepareDC(&dcPrint, &printInfo);

    // check for end of print
    if (!printInfo.m_bContinuePrinting)
        break;

    // write current page in "Printing" dialog
    TCHAR szBuf[80];
    wsprintf(szBuf, strTemp, printInfo.m_nCurPage);
    dlgPrintStatus.SetDlgItemText(
                                AFX_IDC_PRINT_PAGENUM,
                                szBuf);

    // set up drawing rect to entire page
    // (in logical coordinates)
    printInfo.m_rectDraw.SetRect(0, 0,
                dcPrint.GetDeviceCaps(HORZRES),
                dcPrint.GetDeviceCaps(VERTRES));
    dcPrint.DPtoLP(&printInfo.m_rectDraw);

    // attempt to start the current page
    if (dcPrint.StartPage() < 0)
    {
        bError = TRUE;
        break;
    }

    // must call OnPrepareDC on newer versions of
    // Windows because StartPage now resets the device
    // attributes.
    if (afxData.bMarked4)
        OnPrepareDC(&dcPrint, &printInfo);

    // page successfully started, so call OnPrint()
    // to render the page
    OnPrint(&dcPrint, &printInfo);

    if (dcPrint.EndPage() < 0 ||
            !_AfxAbortProc(dcPrint.m_hDC, 0))
```

```
         {
            bError = TRUE;
            break;
         }
      } // for (...) page printing loop

      // Now that we got out of the main page printing
      // loop, we must clean up the document printing
      // process

      if (!bError)
         dcPrint.EndDoc();
      else
         dcPrint.AbortDoc();

      // Re-enable main window
      AfxGetMainWnd()->EnableWindow();

      // Let the view clean up after printing
      OnEndPrinting(&dcPrint, &printInfo);

      dlgPrintStatus.DestroyWindow();

      dcPrint.Detach();    // will be cleaned up by
                           // CPrintInfo destructor
   } // if (OnPreparePrinting(&printInfo))
}
```

Sample Code

There is no sample project for this FAQ.

See Also

- *FAQ 8.2* *How do I implement printing and print preview in my MFC application?*
- *FAQ 8.3* *How do I print a document whose page length is not page known in advance (on-the-fly pagination)?*
- *FAQ 8.4* *How do I predict page breaks as Microsoft Word does?*
- *FAQ 8.11* *How do I distinguish between drawing, print preview, and actual printing in my code?*

FAQ 8.2 How do I implement printing and print preview in my MFC application?

After having read *FAQ 8.1 What is the MFC printing architecture?* you should have a good idea of the MFC printing architecture and of the interactions between MFC and your own code. The following steps show how to translate this knowledge into code to implement printing and print preview, complete with header and footer support, as you can see in Figure 8-3.

Step 1. Use ClassWizard to override the *OnPreparePrinting()* virtual function in your view class. The main goal of this function is usually to compute the page count of the document and to call *pInfo->SetMaxPage()* accordingly, as shown in Listing 8-2. More generally, this function

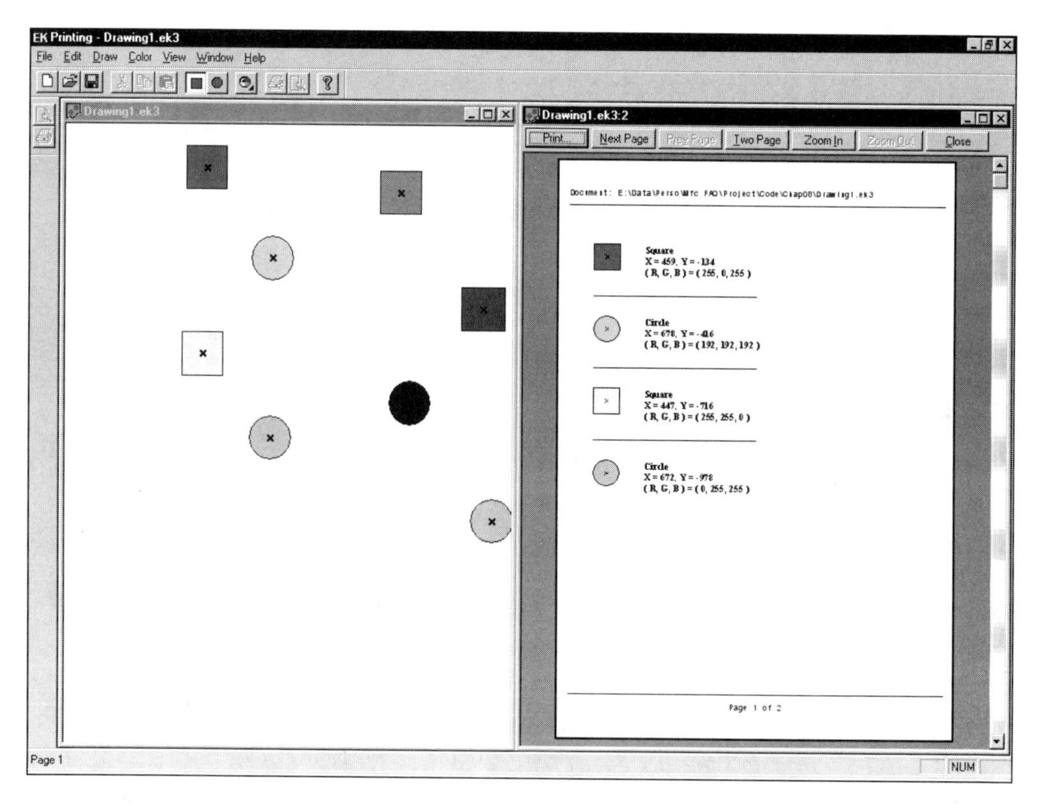

Figure 8-3. The Printing sample project implements printing and print preview with header and footer support.

should set up the various options of the Print dialog box, as explained in *FAQ 8.7 How do I customize the standard Print dialog box and retrieve the options selected by the user?* Be sure to check *FAQ 8.3 How do I print a document whose page length is not known in advance (on-the-fly pagination)?* if you do not know in advance the number of pages of your document, and *FAQ 8.4 How do I predict page breaks as Microsoft Word does?* if you need additional help in computing this number of pages in *OnPreparePrinting()*.

Listing 8-2. Implementation of the *OnPreparePrinting()* virtual function to compute the page count of the document.

```
BOOL CDrawView::OnPreparePrinting(CPrintInfo* pInfo)
{
   // Compute document page length
   CDrawDoc* pDoc = GetDocument();
   int nPages = pDoc->m_Shapes.GetSize() /
                                  ELEMENTS_PER_PAGE;
   if( (pDoc->m_Shapes.GetSize() % ELEMENTS_PER_PAGE) > 0 )
   {
      ++nPages;
   }
   pInfo->SetMaxPage( nPages );

   // default preparation (shows the "Print" dialog box)
   return DoPreparePrinting(pInfo);
}
```

Step 2. Use ClassWizard to override the *OnBeginPrinting()* and *OnEndPrinting()* virtual functions in your view class. The goal of these functions is typically to allocate and clean up resources that will be needed during the printing process—for example, special fonts used during printing—as shown in Listing 8-3. Note that the *m_PrintFont* variable that is used to hold the font during the printing process is declared with type *CFont* inside the *CDrawView* class.

Listing 8-3. Implementation of the *OnBeginPrinting()* and *OnEndPrinting()* virtual functions to create and clean up the font resource used during printing.

```
void CDrawView::OnBeginPrinting(CDC* pDC,
                                CPrintInfo* /*pInfo*/)
```

```
{
   // Create special font for printing
   // ...prepare LOGFONT structure
   LOGFONT lf;             // logical font structure
   ::ZeroMemory( &lf, sizeof( lf ) );

   // ...12 point Times bold
   lf.lfHeight = - MulDiv( 12,
                           pDC->GetDeviceCaps(LOGPIXELSX),
                           72 );
   lf.lfWidth          = 0;
   lf.lfEscapement     = 0;
   lf.lfOrientation    = 0;
   lf.lfWeight         = FW_BOLD;
   lf.lfItalic         = FALSE;
   lf.lfUnderline      = FALSE;
   lf.lfStrikeOut      = FALSE;
   lf.lfCharSet        = DEFAULT_CHARSET;
   lf.lfOutPrecision   = OUT_DEFAULT_PRECIS;
   lf.lfClipPrecision  = CLIP_DEFAULT_PRECIS;
   lf.lfQuality        = DEFAULT_QUALITY;
   lf.lfPitchAndFamily = VARIABLE_PITCH | FF_ROMAN;

   // ...create printing font
   m_PrintFont.CreateFontIndirect( &lf );
}

void CDrawView::OnEndPrinting(CDC* /*pDC*/,
                              CPrintInfo* /*pInfo*/)
{
   // Release the printing font
   m_PrintFont.DeleteObject();
}
```

Step 3. Manually define the *PrintPageHeader()*, *PrintPageFooter()*, and *PrintPageBody()* helper functions in your view class, as shown in Listing 8-4. These functions do exactly what their name suggests. Be aware that most of the complexity of supporting printing and print preview in an MFC application is usually concentrated in these functions. Note also that these functions expect the positive y-axis to be directed toward the top of the page, because my view uses the *MM_LOMETRIC* mapping mode (see the Additional Comments section for more details).

Listing 8-4. Implementation of the *PrintPageHeader()*, *PrintPageFooter()*, and *PrintPageBody()* helper functions.

```
// ───────────────────────────────
// Class definition for CDrawView (DrawView.h)

class CDrawView : public CView
{
// ...
// Implementation
// ...
protected:      // Printing and print preview
   enum { ELEMENTS_PER_PAGE = 4, TOP_MARGIN = 100,
          BOTTOM_MARGIN = 100, LEFT_MARGIN = 200 };
   void PrintPageHeader( CDC* pDC, CPrintInfo* pInfo );
   void PrintPageFooter( CDC* pDC, CPrintInfo* pInfo );
   void PrintPageBody( CDC* pDC, CPrintInfo* pInfo );
   CFont m_PrintFont;    // special font for printing

// ...
};

// ───────────────────────────────
// Implementation for CDrawView (DrawView.cpp)

void CDrawView::PrintPageHeader( CDC* pDC,
                                 CPrintInfo* pInfo )
{
   CRect& rcPage = pInfo->m_rectDraw;

   // 1 - Prepare page header
   CString strHeader = _T( "Document: " );
   strHeader += GetDocument()->GetPathName();
   CSize sizeHeader = pDC->GetTextExtent( strHeader );

   // 2 - Draw header
   int nCurrentY = rcPage.top - TOP_MARGIN;
   pDC->TextOut( 0, nCurrentY, strHeader );
   nCurrentY -= sizeHeader.cy * 2;

   // 3 - Draw line
   pDC->MoveTo( 0, nCurrentY );
```

```
    pDC->LineTo( rcPage.right, nCurrentY );

    // 4 - Adjust remaining printable area
    rcPage.top = nCurrentY;
}

void CDrawView::PrintPageFooter( CDC* pDC,
                                 CPrintInfo* pInfo )
{
    CRect& rcPage = pInfo->m_rectDraw;

    // 1 - Prepare page footer
    CString strFooter;
    int nPageCount = pInfo->GetToPage() -
                         pInfo->GetFromPage() + 1;
    strFooter.Format( _T( "Page %d of %d" ),
                      pInfo->m_nCurPage, nPageCount );
    CSize sizeFooter = pDC->GetTextExtent( strFooter );

    // 2 - Draw line
    int nBottomY = rcPage.bottom + BOTTOM_MARGIN +
                                 sizeFooter.cy * 2;
    int nCurrentY = nBottomY;
    pDC->MoveTo( 0, nCurrentY );
    pDC->LineTo( rcPage.right, nCurrentY );
    nCurrentY -= sizeFooter.cy;

    // 3 - Draw footer
    pDC->TextOut( rcPage.left + ( rcPage.Width() -
                                  sizeFooter.cx ) / 2,
                  nCurrentY,
                  strFooter );

    // 4 - Adjust remaining printable area
    rcPage.bottom = nBottomY;
}

void CDrawView::PrintPageBody( CDC* pDC,
                               CPrintInfo* pInfo )
{
    CFont* pOldFont = pDC->SelectObject( &m_PrintFont );

    // 1 - Compute which elements we will print on this page
    CDrawDoc* pDoc = GetDocument();
```

```
int nStart = ( pInfo->m_nCurPage - 1 ) *
                ELEMENTS_PER_PAGE;
int nEnd = min( nStart + ELEMENTS_PER_PAGE,
               pDoc->m_Shapes.GetSize() );

// 2 - Print each element
int nCurrentY = pInfo->m_rectDraw.top - 200;
for( int i = nStart; i < nEnd; ++i )
{
   // 3 - Draw shape
   CShape* pShape = pDoc->m_Shapes.GetAt( i );
   pShape->DrawAt( pDC, LEFT_MARGIN,
                  nCurrentY - CShape::HALF_SIZE );

   // 4 - Draw shape name
   CString strName = pShape->GetShapeName();
   pDC->TextOut( LEFT_MARGIN+200, nCurrentY, strName );
   nCurrentY -= pDC->GetTextExtent( strName ).cy;

   // 5 - Draw coordinates
   CString strCoords;
   strCoords.Format( _T( "X = %d, Y = %d" ),
                    pShape->m_ptCenter.x,
                    pShape->m_ptCenter.y );
   pDC->TextOut(LEFT_MARGIN+200, nCurrentY, strCoords);
   nCurrentY -= pDC->GetTextExtent( strCoords ).cy;

   // 6 - Draw color
   CString strColor;
   strColor.Format( _T("( R, G, B ) = ( %d, %d, %d )"),
                   GetRValue( pShape->m_crColor ),
                   GetGValue( pShape->m_crColor ),
                   GetBValue( pShape->m_crColor ) );
   pDC->TextOut( LEFT_MARGIN+200, nCurrentY, strColor );
   nCurrentY -= pDC->GetTextExtent( strColor ).cy;

   // 7 - Draw separator line (if needed)
   if( i < nEnd-1 )
   {
      pDC->MoveTo( LEFT_MARGIN-CShape::HALF_SIZE,
                  nCurrentY - 100 );
      pDC->LineTo( 1000, nCurrentY - 100 );
```

```
            nCurrentY -= 200;
        }
    }

    // 8 - Clean up
    pDC->SelectObject( pOldFont );
}
```

Step 4. Use ClassWizard to override the *OnPrint()* virtual function in your view class. Implement this function as shown in Listing 8-5 to print the page header, footer, and body for each page by calling the helper functions defined in step 3.

Listing 8-5. Implementation of the *OnPrint()* virtual function to print the page header, footer, and body for each page.

```
void CDrawView::OnPrint(CDC* pDC, CPrintInfo* pInfo)
{
    // The PrintPageHeader() and PrintPageFooter() functions
    // *must* be called before PrintPageBody(), because they
    // adjust pInfo->m_rectDraw to take into account the
    // space occupied by the header and footer
    PrintPageHeader( pDC, pInfo );
    PrintPageFooter( pDC, pInfo );

    PrintPageBody( pDC, pInfo );
}
```

■

Additional Comments

You will quickly notice that the Printing project is not a WYSIWYG (what you see is what you get) application, at least in the area of printing. Actually, the printed output is not at all related to the screen display except that both of them are constructed from the same data.

In most real-life applications, however, there is much more similarity between the screen display and the printed output than in this sample project. Even MFC's default implementation for *CView::OnPrint()* emphasizes this similarity by simply mapping to *OnDraw()*, as you can see in Listing 8-6.

Listing 8-6. Implementation of the *CView::OnPrint()* function (ViewCore.cpp).

```
void CView::OnPrint(CDC* pDC, CPrintInfo*)
{
   ASSERT_VALID(pDC);
   OnDraw(pDC);    // Call Draw
}
```

Calling *OnDraw()* from *OnPrint()* ensures that you have only one drawing code to maintain and that your application is WYSIWYG.

In my experience, however, I have always found it easier and cleaner to implement separate *OnPrint()* and *OnDraw()* functions to account for the differences that always crop up between screen display and printed output. For example, headers and footers should usually only be printed, whereas page breaks should only be displayed, paper size should be taken into account, and so on. If *OnDraw()* must evolve to implement the specific needs of both drawing and printing, it rapidly becomes complex and difficult to maintain, which is why I recommend separating the work of displaying and printing into two separate functions. You can, however, factor out large chunks of common drawing code inside helper functions that you can call from the *OnDraw()*, *OnPrint()*, and *PrintPageBody()* functions.

One last note about mapping modes: although you can implement separate mapping modes for displaying and printing, your code will usually be cleaner if you use the same mapping mode in both cases and if this mode is different from *MM_TEXT*. Using another mapping mode is important to ensure that the coordinates and sizes that you store in your document will be rendered at the right position and size on paper regardless of the resolution and paper size of the selected printer. Further information about mapping modes is outside the scope of this book, and I encourage you to look at the online help for a more thorough explanation of this subject.

To correctly set the mapping mode for your view, use ClassWizard to override the *OnPrepareDC()* virtual function and then call *SetMapMode()*, as shown in Listing 8-7.

Listing 8-7. Implementing the *OnPrepareDC()* virtual function to correctly set the mapping mode.

```
void CDrawView::OnPrepareDC(CDC* pDC, CPrintInfo* pInfo)
{
   CView::OnPrepareDC(pDC, pInfo);
```

```
    pDC->SetMapMode( MM_LOMETRIC );
}
```

MFC calls the *OnPrepareDC()* function to prepare the device context before calling *OnDraw()* and *OnPrint()*.

Note that if your view derives from *CScrollView* instead of *CView*, you should not override *OnPrepareDC()* as explained earlier. Instead, set your view's mapping mode by calling *SetScrollSizes()* in your view's *OnInitialUpdate()* function. *CScrollView::OnPrepareDC()* will then take care of setting the correct mapping mode for your device context.

Sample Code

- Project: Printing in the Chap08 subdirectory on the companion CD-ROM.
- Purpose: Implements a view class that supports printing and print preview, complete with header and footer support, as shown earlier in Figure 8-3.

Implementation Highlights

- *CDrawView::OnPreparePrinting()* function (DrawView.cpp)
- *CDrawView::OnBeginPrinting()* function (DrawView.cpp)
- *CDrawView::OnEndPrinting()* function (DrawView.cpp)
- *CDrawView::PrintPageHeader()* function (DrawView.cpp)
- *CDrawView::PrintPageFooter()* function (DrawView.cpp)
- *CDrawView::PrintPageBody()* function (DrawView.cpp)
- *CDrawView::OnPrint()* function (DrawView.cpp)
- *CDrawView::OnPrepareDC()* function (DrawView.cpp)

See Also

- *FAQ 8.1 What is the MFC printing architecture?*
- *FAQ 8.3 How do I print a document whose page length is not known in advance (on-the-fly pagination)?*
- *FAQ 8.4 How do I predict page breaks as Microsoft Word does?*
- *FAQ 8.7 How do I customize the standard Print dialog box and retrieve the options selected by the user?*

How do I print a document whose page length is not known in advance (on-the-fly pagination)?

The code discussed in *FAQ 8.2 How do I implement printing and print preview in my MFC application?* covers one important category of applications: those that can compute in advance—or at least in the *OnPreparePrinting()* function—the number of printed pages they will need to output.

However, another important category of applications contains those programs for which you cannot accurately predict the number of printed pages that you will need without actually performing the printing process. A classic example of this kind of application involves printing the results of a query against a database: you will typically fetch and format each record while printing, and it is impossible, or at least very difficult, to accurately predict the page length of the final document before reading through the entire result set.

Fortunately, MFC's printing architecture supports on-the-fly pagination with the help of the *CPrintInfo::m_bContinuePrinting* member variable. The main idea is that you do not compute the total page length of your document in *OnPreparePrinting()*. Instead, you tell MFC whether you have something left to print by dynamically setting the *CPrintInfo::m_bContinuePrinting* member variable in the *OnPrepareDC()* function, which is called before each page is printed.

To help you better understand the following explanations, take a quick look at Listing 8-8, which shows the simple protocol defined by the document class for this FAQ's sample project to simulate the fetching of data just as if we were retrieving the next record from a database query.

Listing 8-8. The document class for this FAQ's sample project defines a simple protocol that simulates the dynamic fetching of data.

```
class CDrawDoc : public CDocument
{
// ...

// Simulate on-the-fly "queries"
public:
```

```
    void InitQuery();
    const CShape* GetNextElement();
    BOOL IsQueryEnded();

// ...
};
```

Step 1. In your view's *OnPreparePrinting()* function, do not set the maximum page number of the document—that is, do *not* call the *pInfo->SetMaxPage()* function, as shown in Listing 8-9.

Listing 8-9. Implementation of the *OnPreparePrinting()* function that does *not* set the maximum page number of the document.

```
BOOL CDrawView::OnPreparePrinting(CPrintInfo* pInfo)
{
    // Note: *no* advance page computation here!

    // default preparation (shows the "Print" dialog box)
    return DoPreparePrinting(pInfo);
}
```

Step 2. In your view's *OnPrepareDC()* function, find out whether you still have something to print and set the *pInfo->m_bContinuePrinting* variable accordingly, as shown in Listing 8-10. Setting this variable to *TRUE* means that you want to print something on the current page; setting it to *FALSE* means that you have nothing left to print and that the print job is now over. Note that you must set this variable *after* calling the base class's *OnPrepareDC()* function, because the default behavior of *CView::OnPrepareDC()* forces *pInfo->m_bContinuePrinting* to *FALSE* after the first page of an unknown-length document, as you can see in Listing 8-11.

Listing 8-10. Implementing the *OnPrepareDC()* function to dynamically set the *pInfo->m_bContinuePrinting* variable.

```
void CDrawView::OnPrepareDC(CDC* pDC, CPrintInfo* pInfo)
{
    CView::OnPrepareDC(pDC, pInfo);

    pDC->SetMapMode( MM_LOMETRIC );

    if( pInfo != NULL )
```

```
    {
        // Continue printing only if there are some elements
        // left to print!
        pInfo->m_bContinuePrinting =
                            !GetDocument()->IsQueryEnded();
    }
}
```

Listing 8-11. Pseudocode for the *CView::OnPrepareDC()* function (ViewCore.cpp).

```
void CView::OnPrepareDC(CDC* pDC, CPrintInfo* pInfo)
{
    // ...
    // Default to one page printing if doc length not known
    if (pInfo != NULL)
        pInfo->m_bContinuePrinting =
            (pInfo->GetMaxPage() != 0xffff ||
                        (pInfo->m_nCurPage == 1));
}
```

Step 3. Implement your view's *OnPrint()* function to dynamically retrieve your data and print it. Listing 8-12 shows the implementation of the *CDrawView::PrintPageBody()* function for this FAQ's sample project. You may find it interesting to compare this implementation with the one given in Listing 8-4, where the number of elements printed on each page is a hard-coded value.

Listing 8-12. Implementation of the *CDrawView::PrintPageBody()* function for this FAQ's sample project

```
void CDrawView::PrintPageBody(CDC* pDC, CPrintInfo* pInfo)
{
    CFont* pOldFont = pDC->SelectObject( &m_PrintFont );

    CDrawDoc* pDoc = GetDocument();
    ASSERT( !pDoc->IsQueryEnded() );

    int nCurrentY = pInfo->m_rectDraw.top - 200;
    int nBottom = pInfo->m_rectDraw.bottom + m_nBlockHeight;
          // m_nBlockHeight is computed in
          // CDrawView::OnBeginPrinting()
```

```
// 1 - Print each element, as many as will fit on the
// page
while( !pDoc->IsQueryEnded() && (nCurrentY > nBottom) )
{

   // 2 - Draw shape
   const CShape* pShape = pDoc->GetNextElement();
   pShape->DrawAt( pDC, LEFT_MARGIN,
                   nCurrentY - CShape::HALF_SIZE );

   // 3 - Draw shape name
   CString strName = pShape->GetShapeName();
   pDC->TextOut(LEFT_MARGIN + 200, nCurrentY, strName);
   nCurrentY -= pDC->GetTextExtent( strName ).cy;

   // 4 - Draw coordinates
   CString strCoords;
   strCoords.Format( _T( "X = %d, Y = %d" ),
                     pShape->m_ptCenter.x,
                     pShape->m_ptCenter.y );
   pDC->TextOut( LEFT_MARGIN + 200, nCurrentY,
                 strCoords );
   nCurrentY -= pDC->GetTextExtent( strCoords ).cy;

   // 5 - Draw color
   CString strColor;
   strColor.Format( _T("( R, G, B ) = ( %d, %d, %d )"),
                    GetRValue( pShape->m_crColor ),
                    GetGValue( pShape->m_crColor ),
                    GetBValue( pShape->m_crColor ) );
   pDC->TextOut(LEFT_MARGIN + 200, nCurrentY, strColor);
   nCurrentY -= pDC->GetTextExtent( strColor ).cy;

   // 6 - Draw separator line (if needed)
   if( !pDoc->IsQueryEnded() &&
         ( nCurrentY - 200 > nBottom ) )
   {
      pDC->MoveTo( LEFT_MARGIN-CShape::HALF_SIZE,
                   nCurrentY - 100 );
      pDC->LineTo( 1000, nCurrentY - 100 );
   }
```

```
        nCurrentY -= 200;
    }

    // 7 - Clean up
    pDC->SelectObject( pOldFont );
}
```

■

Additional Comments

You should be fully aware that supporting on-the-fly pagination adds significant complexity to your printing code. Furthermore, this feature does not get along very well with several aspects of print preview and even of standard printing. Think about the following issues, which this FAQ's sample project does not even try to solve:

- If the user tries to print only selected pages from the document—say, pages 2 to 4 of a 10-page document—MFC will call your view's *OnPrepareDC()* and *OnPrint()* functions starting with page 2 (*pInfo->m_nCurPage==2*). How will your code compute the first element that should get printed?
- In print preview, how do you handle the case in which the user tries to go back to a previous page? How does your code get the correct data? The same problem occurs if the print preview window is invalidated and must be repainted either because it got covered by another window or because the user tried to change its size. MFC will call your view's *OnPrepareDC()* and *OnPrint()* functions again for the same page(s): how do you handle this case?

If you want to get perfect behavior in these cases, you will usually have to implement some kind of cache in your application. Your view's *OnPrepareDC()* and *OnPrint()* functions will then check the requested page number—in *pInfo->m_nCurPage*—and decide whether to request additional data or to print or draw the page from the cache.

You may find it easier to attack this problem by turning the unknown number of pages into a known quantity. To do this, you would probably prepare a cached image of all your pages and then implement your view's *OnPrint()* function to simply serve the requested page from your cache.

Sample Code

- Project: DynamicPagination in the Chap08 subdirectory on the companion CD-ROM.
- Purpose: Demonstrates how to implement on-the-fly pagination to print a document whose length is not computed in advance. You can see this behavior by toggling between portrait and landscape orientation, as shown in Figures 8-4 and 8-5.

Implementation Highlights

- *CDrawView::OnPreparePrinting()* function (DrawView.cpp)
- *CDrawView::OnPrepareDC()* function (DrawView.cpp)

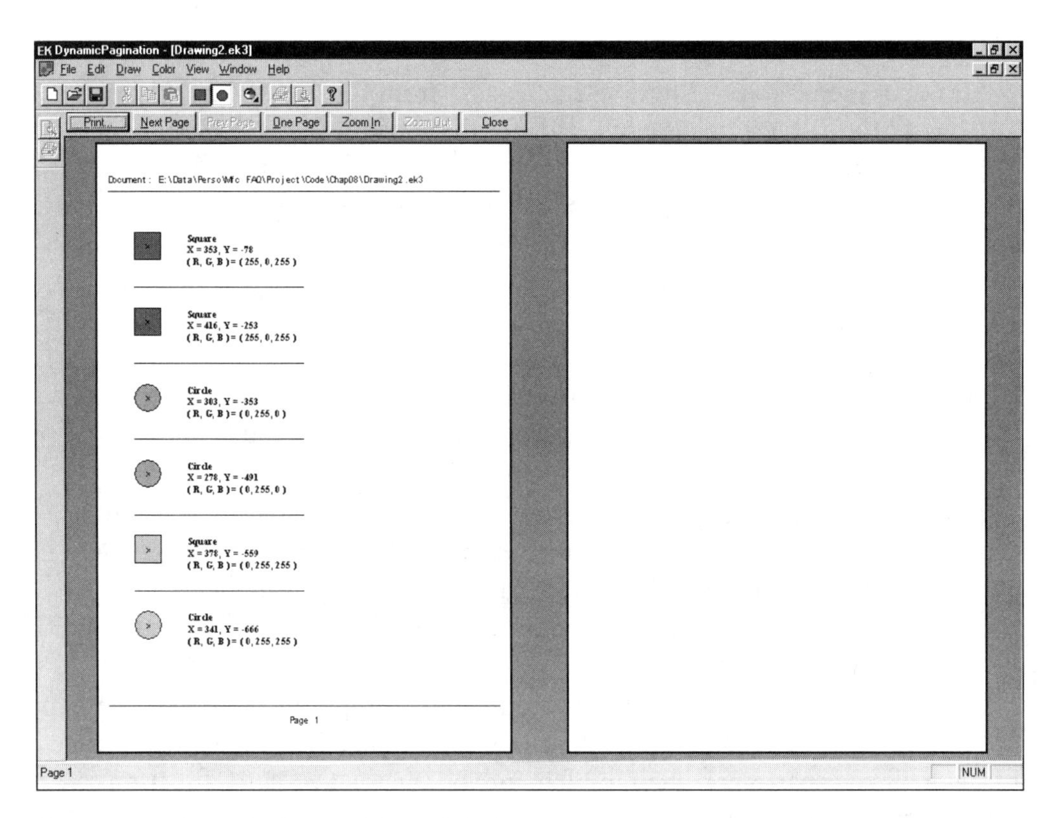

Figure 8-4. In portrait orientation, this document is only one page long.

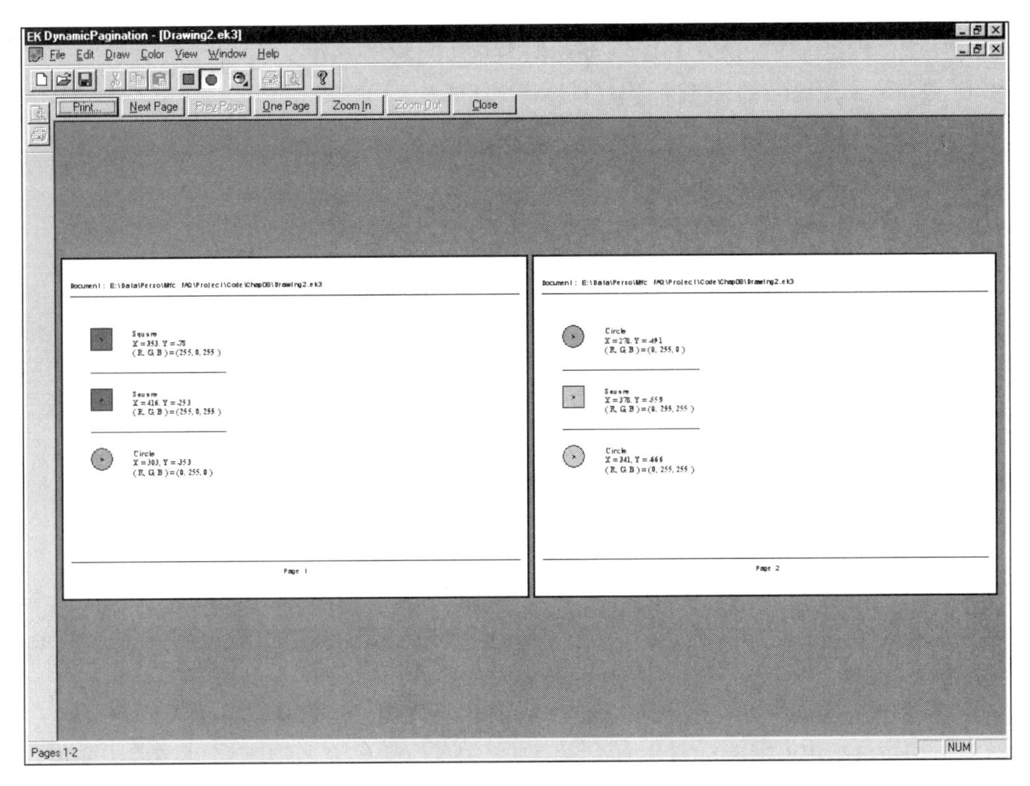

Figure 8-5. The same document needs two pages to print properly in landscape orientation.

- *CDrawView::PrintPageBody()* function (DrawView.cpp)
- *CDrawView::PrintPageHeader()* function (DrawView.cpp)
- *CDrawView::PrintPageFooter()* function (DrawView.cpp)
- *CDrawView::OnPrint()* function (DrawView.cpp)
- *CDrawView::OnBeginPrinting()* function (DrawView.cpp)
- *CDrawView::OnEndPrinting()* function (DrawView.cpp)

See Also

- *FAQ 8.2 How do I implement printing and print preview in my MFC application?*
- *FAQ 8.4 How do I predict page breaks as Microsoft Word does?*

How do I predict page breaks as Microsoft Word does?

The following questions come up quite frequently when you start to support printing in your application:

- How do I show page breaks inside my normal view drawing code as Microsoft Word does?
- How do I show the current page number when the user moves around in the document?
- How do I calculate the total page count of my document in the *OnPreparePrinting()* function, inasmuch as at this stage I do not have an available printer device context that I can query for the printable area dimensions?

To answer these questions, you usually need to know the height and width of the printable area so that you can compute how much of the data will fit on one page. You can easily retrieve these dimensions by calling *CDC::GetDeviceCaps()* with an argument of either *HORZRES* or *VERTRES* to retrieve the width and height, respectively, of the printable area (in pixels). But where do you get the printer device context object to begin with?

While your application is printing or in print preview mode, it receives this device context as an argument in the *OnBeginPrinting()*, *OnEndPrinting()*, *OnPrepareDC()*, and *OnPrint()* functions. However, *OnPreparePrinting()* does not receive such a device context argument, which it would need to be able to accurately call *CPrintInfo::SetMaxPage()*.

There is a good reason why MFC's printing architecture is set up this way: until the user has selected the desired printer in the Print dialog box, there is no way to know accurately the size of the printable area. But then how are you supposed to call *CPrintInfo::SetMaxPage()* in the *OnPreparePrinting()* function to fill the "To" field in the Print dialog box? How do commercial applications such as Microsoft Word solve this problem? Moreover, how do they manage to predict page breaks and display them while the user is editing a document?

The answer is that those applications don't really know: after all, you could select a different printer or page orientation at any time. However, they try to make their best guess by relying on the currently selected printer and on the properties of the current page setup.

You can adopt the same strategy by calling the *EkCreateDefaultPrinterDC()* function—whose implementation is shown in Listing 8-13—to retrieve a device context associated with the currently selected printer. Once you have this printer device context, you can then call *CDC::GetDeviceCaps()* to compute the height and width of the printable area, as shown in Listing 8-14. You can call these functions at any time: in your *OnPreparePrinting()* function to fill the "To" field in the Print dialog box or during background processing to predict page breaks and display them while the user edits a document.

Listing 8-13. Implementation of the *EkCreateDefaultPrinterDC()* function to retrieve a device context associated with the currently selected printer.

```
BOOL EkCreateDefaultPrinterDC( CDC* pDC )
{
   ASSERT_VALID( pDC );

   PRINTDLG pd;
   AfxGetApp()->GetPrinterDeviceDefaults( &pd );
   return AfxGetApp()->CreatePrinterDC( *pDC );
}
```

Listing 8-14. Computing the height and width of the printable area at any time.

```
void CDrawView::OnDemoPageDimensions()
{
   CDC dc;  // automatically released upon exit
   if( EkCreateDefaultPrinterDC( &dc ) )
   {
      int nHorzSize = dc.GetDeviceCaps( HORZRES );
      int nVertSize = dc.GetDeviceCaps( VERTRES );

      CString strMessage;
      strMessage.Format( _T( "Page width = %d pixels\n"
                             "Page height = %d pixels" ),
                         nHorzSize, nVertSize );

      AfxMessageBox( strMessage );

   }
}
```

■

Sample Code

- Project: PageDimensions in the Chap08 subdirectory on the CD-ROM.
- Purpose: Demonstrates how to compute the printable page dimensions at any time for the currently selected printer and page setup. Use the "File, Print Setup" menu command to select any combination of printer, paper size, and orientation; then click on the "P" button to get the information shown in Figure 8-6.

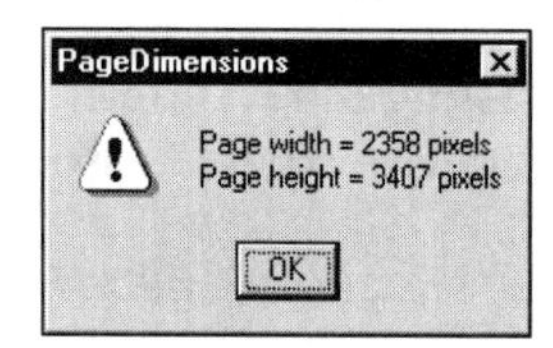

Figure 8-6. The PageDimensions sample project can compute the printable page dimensions at any time for the currently selected printer and page setup.

Implementation Highlights

- *EkCreateDefaultPrinterDC()* function (DrawView.cpp)
- *CDrawView::OnDemoPageDimensions()* function (DrawView.cpp)

How do I programmatically change the printing orientation (portrait versus landscape) on-the-fly?

For some applications, you need to be able to programmatically control the printing orientation and even change it on-the-fly during a print job. The *EkChangePrintingOrientation()* function, whose implementation is shown in Listing 8-15, takes care of the messy details. Just make sure that you call this function from your view's *OnPrepareDC()* function, as shown in Listing 8-16. Note that this solution works for both print preview and printing.

Listing 8-15. Implementation of *EkChangePrintingOrientation()* to dynamically change the printing orientation.

```
void EkPrintingChangeOrientation( CDC* pDC,
                                  CPrintInfo* pInfo,
                                  short NewOrientation )
```

```
{
   ASSERT_VALID( pDC );
   ASSERT( pInfo != NULL );
   DEVMODE* pDevMode = pInfo->m_pPD->GetDevMode();

   // Only change if new orientation is different
   if( pDevMode->dmOrientation != NewOrientation )
   {
      pDevMode->dmOrientation = NewOrientation;
      pDC->ResetDC( pDevMode );
   }
}
```

Listing 8-16. Calling *EkChangePrintingOrientation()* from the view's *OnPrepareDC()* function to have every third page print in landscape mode.

```
void CDrawView::OnPrepareDC(CDC* pDC, CPrintInfo* pInfo)
{
   // Programatically force the page's orientation
   if( pInfo != NULL )
   {
      // Find out the orientation we want: every third page
      // will print in "landscape" mode
      BOOL bLandscape = ( ( pInfo->m_nCurPage % 3 ) == 0 );
      short NewOrientation = bLandscape ?
                                DMORIENT_LANDSCAPE :
                                DMORIENT_PORTRAIT;

      EkChangePrintingOrientation( pDC, pInfo,
                                   NewOrientation );
   }

   CView::OnPrepareDC(pDC, pInfo);

   pDC->SetMapMode( MM_LOMETRIC );
}
```

■

Sample Code

- Project: ChangeOrientation in the Chap08 subdirectory on the companion CD-ROM.
- Purpose: Demonstrates how to change the printing orientation (portrait versus landscape) on-the-fly while printing. Every third page is printed in landscape mode, as you can see in Figure 8-7.

Implementation Highlights

- *EkChangePrintingOrientation()* function (DrawView.cpp)
- *CDrawView::OnPrepareDC()* function (DrawView.cpp)

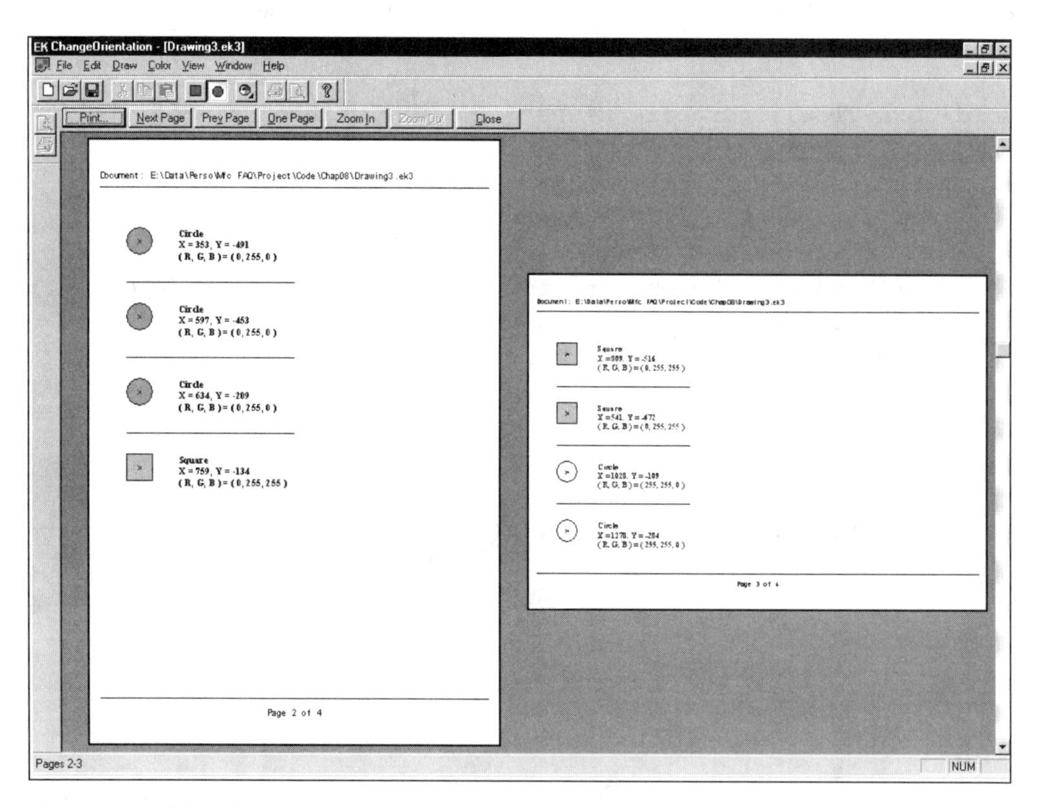

Figure 8-7. The ChangeOrientation project prints every third page in landscape mode.

How do I print without prompting the user with the standard Print dialog box?

In Microsoft Word 97, clicking on the Printer toolbar button immediately prints the current document without displaying the Print dialog box. In contrast, the Printer toolbar button in an AppWizard-generated MFC application maps to the *CView::OnFilePrint()* function, which displays the Print dialog box.

Fortunately, asking MFC to print while bypassing this dialog box is easy—once you know the answer! Simply post the *ID_FILE_PRINT_DIRECT* command to your application's main frame window:

```
AfxGetMainWnd()->PostMessage( WM_COMMAND,
                              ID_FILE_PRINT_DIRECT );
```

The MFC architecture will take care of everything else. (Read the Explanations section to understand what goes on under the hood.)

■

Explanations

Basically, the *ID_FILE_PRINT_DIRECT* message gets routed to the *CView::OnFilePrint()* function (ViewPrnt.cpp) just as the standard print command does. However, when processing the *ID_FILE_PRINT_DIRECT* message, *CView::OnFilePrint()* sets the *printInfo.m_bDirect* flag to *TRUE* before calling *OnPreparePrinting()*. This function usually ends up calling *DoPreparePrinting()*, which checks the *printInfo.m_bDirect* flag and does not show the Print dialog box if this flag is set to *TRUE*. Listing 8-17 shows an excerpt of the relevant code (from ViewPrnt.cpp).

Listing 8-17. Pseudocode for the *CView::OnFilePrint()* and *CView::DoPreparePrinting()* functions (ViewPrnt.cpp) showing the handling of the *ID_FILE_PRINT_DIRECT* message.

```
void CView::OnFilePrint()
{
   // get default print info
   CPrintInfo printInfo;
```

```
    // Specific handling for ID_FILE_PRINT_DIRECT
    if (LOWORD(GetCurrentMessage()->wParam) ==
                 ID_FILE_PRINT_DIRECT)
    {
       CCommandLineInfo* pCmdInfo = AfxGetApp()->m_pCmdInfo;

       if (pCmdInfo != NULL)
       {
          if (pCmdInfo->m_nShellCommand ==
                 CCommandLineInfo::FilePrintTo)
          {
             printInfo.m_pPD->m_pd.hDC =
                ::CreateDC(pCmdInfo->m_strDriverName,
                           pCmdInfo->m_strPrinterName,
                           pCmdInfo->m_strPortName, NULL);
             if (printInfo.m_pPD->m_pd.hDC == NULL)
             {
                AfxMessageBox(
                   AFX_IDP_FAILED_TO_START_PRINT);
                return;
             }
          }
       }

       // Prevent DoPreparePrinting() from displaying the
       // "Print" dialog box
       printInfo.m_bDirect = TRUE;
    }

    // Call OnPreparePrinting() function and start printing
    // process (OnPreparePrinting() must call
    // DoPreparePrinting())
    if (OnPreparePrinting(&printInfo))
    {
       // hDC must be set (did you remember to call
       // DoPreparePrinting?)
       ASSERT(printInfo.m_pPD->m_pd.hDC != NULL);

       // ... start printing process ...
    }
    // ...
}
```

```
BOOL CView::DoPreparePrinting(CPrintInfo* pInfo)
{
   // ...
   // don't prompt the user if we're doing print preview,
    // printing directly, or printing via IPrint and have
   // been instructed not to ask

   CWinApp* pApp = AfxGetApp();
   if (pInfo->m_bPreview || pInfo->m_bDirect ||
      (pInfo->m_bDocObject &&
         !(pInfo->m_dwFlags & PRINTFLAG_PROMPTUSER)))
   {
      if (pInfo->m_pPD->m_pd.hDC == NULL)
      {
         // Get default printer and create printer DC
         // without displaying "Print" dialog box
         if (!pApp->GetPrinterDeviceDefaults(
                                 &pInfo->m_pPD->m_pd))
         {
            // bring up dialog to alert the user they need
            // to install a printer.
            if (!pInfo->m_bDocObject || (pInfo->m_dwFlags &
                          PRINTFLAG_MAYBOTHERUSER))
               if (pApp->DoPrintDialog(pInfo->m_pPD) !=
                                                    IDOK)
                  return FALSE;
         }

         if (pInfo->m_pPD->m_pd.hDC == NULL)
         {
            // call CreatePrinterDC if DC was not created
            // by above
            if (pInfo->m_pPD->CreatePrinterDC() == NULL)
               return FALSE;
         }
      }

      // set up From and To page range from Min and Max
      pInfo->m_pPD->m_pd.nFromPage =
                           (WORD)pInfo->GetMinPage();
      pInfo->m_pPD->m_pd.nToPage =
                           (WORD)pInfo->GetMaxPage();
```

```
    }
    else
    {
        // Display the "Print" dialog box and allow
        // the user to change things

        // preset From-To range same as Min-Max range
        pInfo->m_pPD->m_pd.nFromPage =
                          (WORD)pInfo->GetMinPage();
        pInfo->m_pPD->m_pd.nToPage =
                          (WORD)pInfo->GetMaxPage();

        // The following call displays the "Print" dialog box
        if (pApp->DoPrintDialog(pInfo->m_pPD) != IDOK)
            return FALSE;        // do not print
    }

    // ...
    return TRUE;
}
```

Why does the *ID_FILE_PRINT_DIRECT* message exist in the first place? MFC uses this message to handle two kinds of special printing requests that your application may receive:

- The "Print File from Shell" request. If you right-click on one of your application's files in Windows Explorer and then select the "Print" command from the context menu, Windows will start your application with the *"-p"* or *"/p"* flag and the selected filename as command-line arguments. A well-behaved application should then print the given file without any user interaction. This case is handled by the *CWinApp::ParseCommandLine()*, *CCommandLineInfo::ParseParamFlag()*, and *CWinApp::ProcessShellCommand()* functions (AppCore.cpp and AppUi2.cpp).
- The "DDE Execute print" request. If your application receives a "DDE Execute" command containing a *"[print("...")]"* or *"[printto("...")]"* command, it should print its current document without displaying any dialog box. This case is handled by the *CDocManager::OnDDECommand()* function (DocMgr.cpp).

Whew! You now understand that the simple *AfxGetMainWnd()->PostMessage(WM_COMMAND, ID_FILE_PRINT_DIRECT)* call that I suggest you use to bypass the Print dialog box takes advantage of a significant infrastructure built into MFC for quite other purposes.

Additional Comments

Another way to bypass the standard Print dialog box is to set the *m_bDirect* flag of the *CPrintInfo* object to *TRUE* in your view's *OnPreparePrinting()* function before calling *DoPreparePrinting()*, as shown in Listing 8-18.

Listing 8-18. Another way to bypass the standard Print dialog box.

```
BOOL CDrawView::OnPreparePrinting(CPrintInfo* pInfo)
{
   // ... other OnPreparePrinting() stuff ...

   // Bypass the "Print" dialog box
   pInfo->m_bDirect = TRUE;

   // default preparation
   return DoPreparePrinting(pInfo);
}
```

Sample Code

- Project: PrintDirect in the Chap08 subdirectory on the companion CD-ROM.
- Purpose: Demonstrates how to print directly without displaying the standard Print dialog box.

Implementation Highlights

- *CDrawView::OnFilePrintDirectly()* function (DrawView.cpp)

8.7 How do I customize the standard Print dialog box and retrieve the options selected by the user?

Most applications let MFC take control of the standard Print dialog box. However, this dialog box offers several options that you might wish to customize for your own needs.

How to Customize the Standard Print Dialog Box

You should customize the standard Print dialog box in your view's *OnPreparePrinting()* function *before* calling *DoPreparePrinting()*, which will then display the Print dialog box. The customization happens through the *pInfo* argument (of type *CPrintInfo**) that MFC passes to *OnPreparePrinting()*.

The most basic customization involves calling *pInfo->SetMaxPage()* to define the number of printed pages of your document. If you do not know in advance the number of pages in your document, see *FAQ 8.3 How do I print a document whose page length is not known in advance (on-the-fly pagination)?*

Additional options are available through the *Flag* field of the *PRINTDLG* structure contained in *pInfo->m_pPD->m_pd*. By selectively setting or clearing the appropriate bit flags in this field, you can customize several options of the standard Print dialog box, as shown in Table 8-2.

Table 8-2. How to customize several options of the standard Print dialog box. In the code fragments, *pd.Flags* stands for *pInfo->m_pPD->m_pd.Flags*.

Option	Yes	No	Initially select or check
Enable "Print range, All" option button	(enabled by default)	(cannot be disabled)	*pd.Flags |= PD_ ALLPAGES*
Enable "Print range, Pages" option button	*pd.Flags &= ~PD_ NOPAGENUMS*	*pd.Flags |= PD_ NOPAGENUMS*	*pd.Flags |= PD_ PAGENUMS*
Enable "Print range, Selection" option button	*pd.Flags &= ~PD_ NOSELECTION*	*pd.Flags |= PD_ NOSELECTION*	*pd.Flags |= PD_ SELECTION*
Enable "Print to file" check box	*pd.Flags &= ~PD_ DISABLEPRINT-TOFILE*	*pd.Flags |= PD_ DISABLEPRINT-TOFILE*	*pd.Flags |= PD_ PRINTTOFILE*
Show "Print to file" check box	*pd.Flags &= ~PD_ HIDEPRINT-TOFILE*	*pd.Flags |=PD_ HIDEPRINT-TOFILE*	*pd.Flags |= PD_ PRINTTOFILE*

Retrieving the Options Selected by the User

After *DoPreparePrinting()* returns, you can retrieve the options selected by the user from the *pInfo* variable, as shown in Table 8-3.

Table 8-3. How to retrieve the options selected by the user from the *pInfo* variable.

Option	How to retrieve
Print the whole document ("Print range, Pages" option button)	*pInfo->m_pPD->PrintAll() == TRUE*
Print a page range ("Print range, Selection" option button)	*pInfo->m_pPD-> PrintRange() == TRUE*
Selected page range	*pInfo->GetFromPage()* *pInfo->GetToPage()*
Print current selection only ("Print range, Selection" option button)	*pInfo->m_pPD-> PrintSelection() == TRUE*
Print to file ("Print to file" check box)	*(pInfo->m_pPD->m_pd.Flags & PD_PRINTTOFILE) != 0*

■

Additional Comments

Listing 8-19 shows how the *OnPreparePrinting()* function for this FAQ's sample project first customizes the standard Print dialog box (depending on the options selected by the user in the dialog box shown below in Figure 8-8) and then displays the options finally selected in the standard Print dialog box.

Listing 8-19. Implementation of *OnPreparePrinting()* for this FAQ's sample project.

```
BOOL CDrawView::OnPreparePrinting(CPrintInfo* pInfo)
{
   // Compute document page length
   // ...

   pInfo->SetMaxPage( nPages );

   // Show the "Print Options" dialog box
   if( m_dlgPrintOptions.DoModal() != IDOK )
      return FALSE;

   // Setup the "Print" dialog box's options
   PRINTDLG& pd = pInfo->m_pPD->m_pd;
```

```
// ... enable print page range
if( m_dlgPrintOptions.m_bEnablePrintRange )
   pd.Flags &= ~PD_NOPAGENUMS;
else
   pd.Flags |= PD_NOPAGENUMS;

// ... enable print selection
if( m_dlgPrintOptions.m_bEnablePrintSelection )
   pd.Flags &= ~PD_NOSELECTION;
else
   pd.Flags |= PD_NOSELECTION;

// ... show print to file
if( m_dlgPrintOptions.m_bShowPrintToFile )
   pd.Flags &= ~PD_HIDEPRINTTOFILE;
else
   pd.Flags |= PD_HIDEPRINTTOFILE;

// ... enable print to file
if( m_dlgPrintOptions.m_bEnablePrintToFile )
   pd.Flags &= ~PD_DISABLEPRINTTOFILE;
else
   pd.Flags |= PD_DISABLEPRINTTOFILE;

// ... select default print range
switch( m_dlgPrintOptions.m_nDefaultRange )
{
default:
   ASSERT( FALSE );   // unknown case
   break;

case 0:   // print all pages
   pd.Flags |= PD_ALLPAGES;
   break;

case 1:   // print page range
   pd.Flags |= PD_PAGENUMS;
   break;

case 2:   // print selection
   pd.Flags |= PD_SELECTION;
```

```
      break;
   }

   // ... select print to file by default
   if( m_dlgPrintOptions.m_bDefaultPrintToFile )
      pd.Flags |= PD_PRINTTOFILE;

   // Default preparation (shows the "Print" dialog box)
   if( !DoPreparePrinting(pInfo) )
      return FALSE;

   // Retrieve and display the user's selections
   CPrintDialog* pPrintDlg = pInfo->m_pPD;
   CString strMessage( _T( "Options selected:\n" ) );

   // ... print all pages
   if( pPrintDlg->PrintAll() )
   {
      CString strRange;
      strRange.Format( _T( "\t- Print all pages: "
                           "%d to %d.\n" ),
                       pInfo->GetFromPage(),
                       pInfo->GetToPage() );
      strMessage += strRange;
   }

   // ... print page range
   if( pPrintDlg->PrintRange() )
   {
      CString strRange;
      strRange.Format( _T( "\t- Print page range: "
                           "%d to %d.\n" ),
                       pInfo->GetFromPage(),
                       pInfo->GetToPage() );
      strMessage += strRange;
   }

   // ... print selection
   if( pPrintDlg->PrintSelection() )
      strMessage += _T( "\t- Print selection.\n" );
```

```
    // ... print to file
    if( pd.Flags & PD_PRINTTOFILE )
        strMessage += _T( "\t- Print to file.\n" );

    if( AfxMessageBox( strMessage, MB_OKCANCEL ) != IDOK )
        return FALSE;

    return TRUE;
}
```

Sample Code

- Project: PrintOptions in the Chap08 subdirectory on the companion CD-ROM.
- Purpose: Displays the dialog box shown in Figure 8-8 and customizes the standard Print dialog box accordingly.

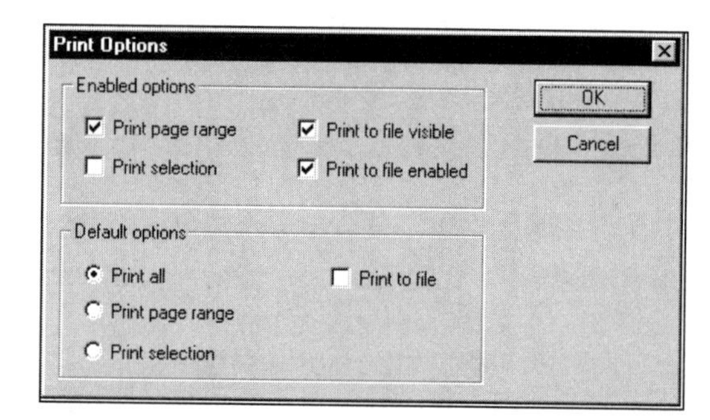

Figure 8-8. The PrintOptions sample project allows you to experiment with various options that affect the standard Print dialog box.

Implementation Highlights

- *CDrawView::OnPreparePrinting()* function (DrawView.cpp)

See Also

- *FAQ 8.3 How do I print a document whose page length is not known in advance (on-the-fly pagination)?*

FAQ 8.8 How do I customize the Printing . . . dialog box?

While a document is printing, *CView::OnFilePrint()* automatically displays a Printing . . . dialog box that shows useful information such as the following:

- The name of the document being printed
- The name of the selected printer
- The name of the printer port
- The current page number

Additionally, the Printing . . . dialog has a Cancel button that allows the user to abort the print job (see Figure 8-9).

Figure 8-9. MFC's standard Printing . . . dialog box.

Unfortunately, the MFC developers did not make any provision for easily replacing this standard Printing . . . dialog. This fact is apparent in the way that the *CPrintingDialog* class is intertwined with the *CView::OnFilePrint()* and the *_AfxAbortProc()* function (ViewPrnt.cpp). You can see for yourself how the *CPrintingDialog* object is created and referenced by *CView::OnFilePrint()* in Listing 8-1 on page 539.

But even if the MFC developers did not foresee it, you might need to replace the standard Printing . . . dialog with one of your own. For example, the custom Printing . . . dialog box of this FAQ's sample project indicates the current page number as well as the total number of pages ("Page x of y"). It also displays a graphical progress indicator, as you can see in Figure 8-10.

So how do we replace the standard Printing . . . dialog with our own? One radical approach would be to override the *OnFilePrint()* function in our view class, copy all the code from *CView::OnFilePrint()* into our own function, and

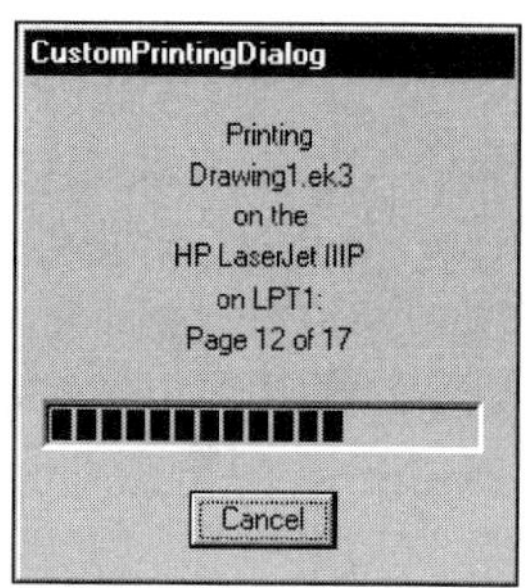

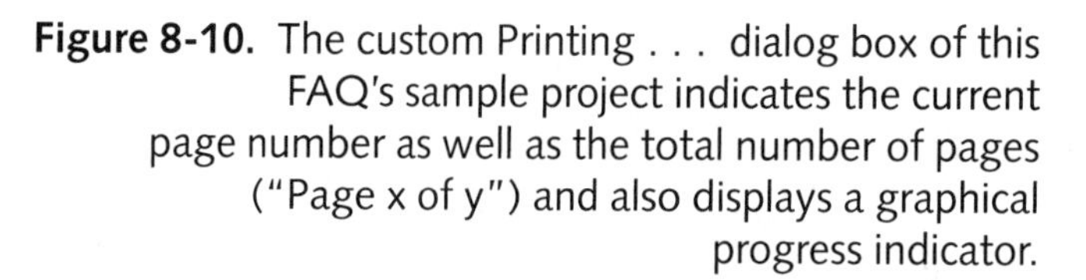

Figure 8-10. The custom Printing . . . dialog box of this FAQ's sample project indicates the current page number as well as the total number of pages ("Page x of y") and also displays a graphical progress indicator.

selectively modify this code to use our own Printing . . . dialog class instead of MFC's *CPrintingDialog*. Such an approach is not for the faint of heart, however, especially because *CView::OnFilePrint()* is more than 200 lines long! Moreover, we might need to propagate potential updates from MFC's code to our own upon each release of a new MFC version, and that is something I would rather avoid.

In contrast, the following technique keeps the original *CView::OnFilePrint()* function but works around MFC's standard Printing . . . dialog by taking advantage of the official *OnPrepareDC()* and *OnEndPrinting()* virtual functions.

Creating a Custom Printing . . . Dialog Class

Step 1. Use the Developer Studio Resource Editor to design your own Printing . . . dialog template. You might wish to model your dialog after the one in MFC, which can be found in the Mfc\Src\MfcDll.rc file with an ID of *AFX_IDD_PRINTDLG*. You can also add your own controls to this dialog resource, such as a progress control to indicate how the print job is going. Be sure to include the standard Cancel button on your dialog resource.

Step 2. Use ClassWizard to create a new *CDialog*-derived class associated with your dialog resource. Use ClassWizard again to associate member variables of category "Control" to your various controls. The resulting class definition is shown in Listing 8-20.

Listing 8-20. Associating member variables of category "Control" to controls on a custom Printing . . . dialog.

```
class CEkPrintingDlg : public CDialog
{
// ...
```

```
// Dialog Data
   //{{AFX_DATA(CEkPrintingDlg)
   enum { IDD = IDD_EK_PRINTING_DLG };
   CStatic   m_DocName;
   CStatic   m_PrinterName;
   CStatic   m_PortName;
   CStatic   m_PageNum;
   CProgressCtrl   m_Progress;
   //}}AFX_DATA

// ...
};
```

Step 3. Add a member variable of type *CWnd** to your custom Printing . . . dialog class, and modify this class's constructor to take a *CWnd** and store it in this member variable, as shown in Listing 8-21. This variable will hold a pointer to MFC's standard Printing . . . dialog object, with which we will need to communicate to correctly implement the Cancel button. Call *CDialog::Create()* from your class's constructor to create the Windows dialog box.

Listing 8-21. Adding a member variable of type *CWnd** to the custom Printing . . . dialog class and modifying the class's constructor to create the Windows dialog box.

```
// ——————————————————————————————
// Class definition for CEkPrintingDlg
// (EkPrintingDlg.h)

class CEkPrintingDlg : public CDialog
{
// Construction
public:
   CEkPrintingDlg(CWnd* pParent, CWnd* pStandardDialog);

// ...

// Dialog Data
   //{{AFX_DATA(CEkPrintingDlg)
   enum { IDD = IDD_EK_PRINTING_DLG };
   CStatic   m_DocName;
   CStatic   m_PrinterName;
   CStatic   m_PortName;
```

```
    CStatic    m_PageNum;
    CProgressCtrl    m_Progress;
    //}}AFX_DATA

// ...

// Implementation
protected:
    CWnd* m_pStandardDialog;   // Pointer to MFC's
                               // "Printing..." dialog

// ...

};

// ______________________________
// Implementation for CEkPrintingDlg
// (EkPrintingDlg.cpp)

CEkPrintingDlg::CEkPrintingDlg(CWnd* pParent,
                               CWnd* pStandardDialog)
    : CDialog(CEkPrintingDlg::IDD, pParent)
{
    //{{AFX_DATA_INIT(CEkPrintingDlg)
    //}}AFX_DATA_INIT

    ASSERT_VALID( pStandardDialog );
    m_pStandardDialog = pStandardDialog;

    // Create modeless dialog box
    // (MFC automatically disables the application's
    // main window while printing)

    Create(CEkPrintingDlg::IDD, pParent);
}
```

Step 4. Use ClassWizard to add handlers in your Printing . . . dialog class for the *WM_INITIDIALOG* and *BN_CLICKED(IDCANCEL)* messages. Implement these handlers as shown in Listing 8-22.

Listing 8-22. Implementation of *OnInitDialog()* and *OnCancel()*.

```
BOOL CEkPrintingDlg::OnInitDialog()
{
   SetWindowText( AfxGetAppName() );
   CenterWindow();

   return CDialog::OnInitDialog();
}

void CEkPrintingDlg::OnCancel()
{
   ASSERT_VALID( m_pStandardDialog );
   ASSERT( ::IsWindow(m_pStandardDialog->GetSafeHwnd()) );

   // Ask MFC's "Printing..." dialog to cancel
   // the printing process
   m_pStandardDialog->SendMessage(WM_COMMAND, IDCANCEL, 0);

   // Dialog is destroyed in view's OnEndPrinting()
   // function
}
```

Hooking the Custom Printing . . . Dialog Class into the Print Process

Step 5. Modify your view's *OnPrepareDC()* function as shown in Listing 8-23. When this function is called for the first time—*pInfo->m_lpUserData == NULL*—it hides MFC's standard Printing . . . dialog, creates the custom dialog, initializes its constant fields from MFC's own dialog, and finally shows the dialog. Afterward, *OnPrepareDC()* simply updates our custom dialog's controls to reflect the progress of the current print job. Note that the address of the C++ object associated with MFC's standard Printing . . . dialog is stored in the *pInfo->m_lpUserData* field, which then acts as an indicator of whether this is the first time that *OnPrepareDC()* is called for the current print job.

Listing 8-23. Implementation of *CDrawView::OnPrepareDC()* to manage the custom Printing . . . dialog.

```
void CDrawView::OnPrepareDC(CDC* pDC, CPrintInfo* pInfo)
{
   CView::OnPrepareDC(pDC, pInfo);
```

```
// ... other OnPrepareDC() stuff ...

// 1 - Only when actually printing
if( pInfo != NULL && !pInfo->m_bPreview )
{
   // 2 - Check for first time through
   if( pInfo->m_lpUserData == NULL )
   {
      // 3 - Get hold of MFC's "Printing..." dialog
      CWnd* pActiveWnd = CWnd::GetActiveWindow();
      ASSERT_VALID( pActiveWnd );
      ASSERT_KINDOF( CDialog, pActiveWnd );

      // 4 - Hide MFC's "Printing..." dialog
      pInfo->m_lpUserData = pActiveWnd;
      pActiveWnd->ShowWindow( SW_HIDE );

      // 5 - Create custom "Printing..." dialog and
      // initialize its fields from MFC's own dialog
      ASSERT( m_pPrintingDlg == NULL );
      m_pPrintingDlg = new CEkPrintingDlg( this,
                                           pActiveWnd );
         // dialog class calls Create() in its constructor

      // ... document name
      CString strDocName;
      pActiveWnd->GetDlgItemText( AFX_IDC_PRINT_DOCNAME,
                                  strDocName );
      m_pPrintingDlg->m_DocName.SetWindowText(
                                  strDocName );

      // ... printer name
      CString strPrinterName;
      pActiveWnd->GetDlgItemText(
                             AFX_IDC_PRINT_PRINTERNAME,
                             strPrinterName );
      m_pPrintingDlg->m_PrinterName.SetWindowText(
                             strPrinterName );

      // ... port name
      CString strPortName;
      pActiveWnd->GetDlgItemText(
```

```
                                AFX_IDC_PRINT_PORTNAME,
                                strPortName );
        m_pPrintingDlg->m_PortName.SetWindowText(
                                strPortName );

        // ... progress control
        m_pPrintingDlg->m_Progress.SetRange(
                                    pInfo->GetFromPage(),
                                    pInfo->GetToPage() );
        m_pPrintingDlg->m_Progress.SetPos(
                                    pInfo->m_nCurPage );

        // 6 - Show dialog window
        m_pPrintingDlg->ShowWindow( SW_SHOW );
      }

      // 7 - Update "Printing..." dialog

      // ... current page number
      CString strPageNum;
      strPageNum.Format( _T( "Page %d of %d" ),
                        pInfo->m_nCurPage,
                        pInfo->GetMaxPage() );

      m_pPrintingDlg->m_PageNum.SetWindowText(strPageNum);

      // ... progress indicator
      m_pPrintingDlg->m_Progress.SetPos(pInfo->m_nCurPage);
   }
}
```

Step 6. Modify your view's *OnEndPrinting()* function as shown in Listing 8-24 to destroy your custom dialog if it was created. This may not always be the case, because the custom dialog will not be created for print preview.

Listing 8-24. Implementation of *OnEndPrinting()* to destroy the custom dialog.

```
void CDrawView::OnEndPrinting(CDC* /*pDC*/,
                              CPrintInfo* /*pInfo*/)
{
   // ... other OnEndPrinting() stuff ...
```

```
    if( m_pPrintingDlg != NULL )
    {
       // Destroy your custom printing dialog
       m_pPrintingDlg->DestroyWindow();
       delete m_pPrintingDlg;
       m_pPrintingDlg = NULL;
    }
}
```

■

Additional Comments

Maybe you wonder why I create the custom Printing . . . dialog in the *OnPrepareDC()* function rather than in the *OnBeginPrinting()* function; the latter would certainly result in somewhat cleaner code. I made this choice because *CView::OnFilePrint()* calls *OnBeginPrinting() before* creating and showing the standard MFC Printing . . . dialog, and that means that we cannot get hold of this dialog and hide it in *OnBeginPrinting()*. Well, that's life!

Finally, note that the *CDrawView::OnPrint()* function in this FAQ's sample project calls *Sleep()* to simulate a lengthy processing while each page is printed, giving you a better chance to appreciate the custom Printing . . . dialog box.

Sample Code

- Project: CustomPrintingDialog in the Chap08 subdirectory on the companion CD-ROM.
- Purpose: Implements a custom Printing . . . dialog box that displays information about the current print job in "Pages x of y" form with an additional graphical progress control, as shown earlier in Figure 8-10.

Implementation Highlights

- *CEkPrintingDlg* class (EkPrintingDlg.h, EkPrintingDlg.cpp)
- *CDrawView::OnPrepareDC()* function (DrawView.cpp)
- *CDrawView::OnEndPrinting()* function (DrawView.cpp)

See Also

- *FAQ 8.1 What is the MFC printing architecture?*

How do I stop or abort a print job?

It is sometimes necessary to be able to abort a print job; for example, an unexpected error, such as a "Disk Full," might prevent your application from completing the rendering of its pages. Fortunately, MFC's printing architecture makes it easy to either stop or abort a print job. Stopping means that the pages that you have already rendered will be printed, whereas aborting tells Windows to cancel the whole print job.

- In your view's *OnPrepareDC()* function, you can set the *pInfo->m_bContinuePrinting* flag to *FALSE*—*after* calling your base class's *OnPrepareDC()*—to explicitly ask MFC to stop the print job immediately (the current page will not be printed). If you want to abort the current print job, set the *pInfo->m_bContinuePrinting* flag to *FALSE* and call the *pDC->AbortDoc()* function, as shown in Listing 8-25.

Listing 8-25. Stopping or aborting a print job in the view's *OnPrepareDC()* function.

```
void CMyView::OnPrepareDC(CDC* pDC, CPrintInfo* pInfo)
{
   CView::OnPrepareDC(pDC, pInfo);

   // ... other OnPrepareDC stuff() ...
   if( pInfo != NULL )
   {
      if( /* ... check for stop/abort condition ... */ )
      {
         // Ask MFC to stop the current print job
         pInfo->m_bContinuePrinting = FALSE;

         // Optionally abort the current print job
         pDC->AbortDoc();
      }
   }
}
```

- In your view's *OnPrint()* function, you can call either *pDC->StopDoc()* or *pDC->AbortDoc()* at any time to stop or abort the current print job, as shown in Listing 8-26.

Listing 8-26. Stopping or aborting a print job in the view's *OnPrint()* function.

```
void CMyView::OnPrint(CDC* pDC, CPrintInfo* pInfo)
{
   // ... other OnPrint() stuff ...

   if( /* ... check for stop/abort condition ... */ )
   {
      // Stop (1) or abort (2) the current print job
      pDC->EndDoc();        // (1)
      pDC->AbortDoc();      // (2)
   }
}
```

■

Sample Code

There is no sample project for this FAQ.

How do I implement print preview in shades of gray for a monochrome printer?

Many applications try to reuse as much code as possible between their drawing and printing routines. That is a noble goal. However, users might be surprised when they find out that your application's print preview functionality shows the "printed" document in full color even when they have only a monochrome printer!

If the goal of print preview is to give a realistic image of the printed result, the application should render its print preview in shades of gray when the selected printer is monochrome. Fortunately, such behavior is easy to implement: simply modify your drawing routines so that they check for the "print preview on a monochrome printer" condition and select gray-scale colors in this case. I provide the *EkIsMonoPreview()* and *EkColorRefToGray()* helper functions, whose implementations are shown in Listings 8-27 and 8-28, to make such an implementation even easier.

Listing 8-27. Implementation of *EkIsMonoPreview()*.

```
BOOL EkIsMonoPreview( CDC* pDC )
{
   ASSERT_VALID( pDC );

   // Check for monochrome device context
   BOOL bMono = ( pDC->GetDeviceCaps( NUMCOLORS ) == 2 );

   // Check for print preview mode
   BOOL bPreview = ( pDC->m_hDC != pDC->m_hAttribDC );

   return( bMono && bPreview );
}
```

Listing 8-28. Implementation of *EkColorRefToGray()*.

```
COLORREF EkColorRefToGray( COLORREF crColor )
{
   // Extract (r, g, b) factors from COLORREF
   BYTE red = GetRValue( crColor );
   BYTE green = GetGValue( crColor );
   BYTE blue = GetBValue( crColor );

   // Convert (r, g, b) to gray using standard formula
   BYTE gray = static_cast< BYTE >(
               ( red*30 + green*59 + blue*11 ) / 100 );
   return RGB( gray, gray, gray );
}
```

Listing 8-29 shows how the drawing code for this FAQ's sample project calls *EkIsMonoPreview()* and *EkColorRefToGray()* to properly set up its drawing color.

Listing 8-29. Drawing code for this FAQ's sample project to call *EkIsMonoPreview()* and *EkColorRefToGray()* to properly set up its drawing color.

```
void CShape::DrawAt( CDC* pDC, int x, int y ) const
{
   ASSERT_VALID( pDC );
   // Select optional gray fill color for print preview
   // on monochrome printer
   COLORREF crFill = EkIsMonoPreview( pDC ) ?
```

```
                                    EkColorRefToGray( m_crColor ) :
                                    m_crColor;

    CBrush brFill( crFill );
    CBrush* pOldBrush = pDC->SelectObject( &brFill );

    // ... other drawing code ...
}
```

■

Sample Code

- Project: PrintMono in the Chap08 subdirectory on the companion CD-ROM.
- Purpose: Demonstrates how to implement print preview in shades of gray for a monochrome printer.

Implementation Highlights

- *EkIsMonoPreview()* function (Shape.cpp)
- *EkColorRefToGray()* function (Shape.cpp)
- *CShape::DrawAt()* function (Shape.cpp)

See Also

- *FAQ 8.11 How do I distinguish between drawing, print preview, and actual printing in my code?*

How do I distinguish between drawing, print preview, and actual printing in my code?

Most developers will try to share as much code as possible between their drawing and printing routines. However, to take care of the differences that always crop up between standard drawing, print preview, and actual printing you must be able to easily distinguish the context in which your code is called.

Here is a quick checklist you can use to find out your current context from anywhere in your code:

- In functions that receive a pointer to a *CPrintInfo* object, such as *OnPrepareDC()*. If this pointer is *NULL*, you are in standard drawing mode. If the pointer is not *NULL*, you are either printing or are in print preview mode. Find out by checking the *CPrintInfo::m_bPreview* field. If this field is set to *TRUE*, you are in print preview mode; if it is *FALSE*, you are actually printing.
- In functions that do not receive a pointer to a *CPrintInfo* object, such as *OnDraw()*. You must at least have a pointer to a device context object; otherwise, how are you going to draw anything? If *CDC::IsPrinting()* returns *FALSE*, you are in standard drawing mode. If this function returns *TRUE*, you are either in print preview mode or are actually printing. Another indicator can be derived by comparing the values of the *CDC::m_hDC* and *CDC::m_hAttribDC* fields. If these handles are not the same, you are in print preview mode; otherwise, you are either in standard drawing mode or are actually printing.

Listing 8-30 shows the preceding algorithms translated into code in two overloaded versions of *EkGetPrintMode()* that find out the current mode when given a pointer to either a *CPrintInfo* or a device context object.

Listing 8-30. Implementation of two overloaded versions of *EkGetPrintMode()* to find out the current mode when given a pointer to either a *CPrintInfo* or a device context object.

```
enum EK_PRINT_MODE { DISPLAYING, PRINTING, PREVIEWING };

EK_PRINT_MODE EkGetPrintMode( CPrintInfo* pInfo )
{
   if( pInfo == NULL )
   {
      return DISPLAYING;
   }

   if( pInfo->m_bPreview )
   {
      return PREVIEWING;
   }

   return PRINTING;
}

EK_PRINT_MODE EkGetPrintMode( CDC* pDC )
```

```
{
   ASSERT_VALID( pDC );
   if( !pDC->IsPrinting() )
   {
      return DISPLAYING;
   }

   if( pDC->m_hDC != pDC->m_hAttribDC )
   {
      return PREVIEWING;
   }

   return PRINTING;
}
```

The appropriate *EkGetPrintMode()* function is called from both *CDrawView::OnDraw()* and *CDrawView::OnPrint()* to print a short string identifying the current mode, as you can see in Figure 8-11.

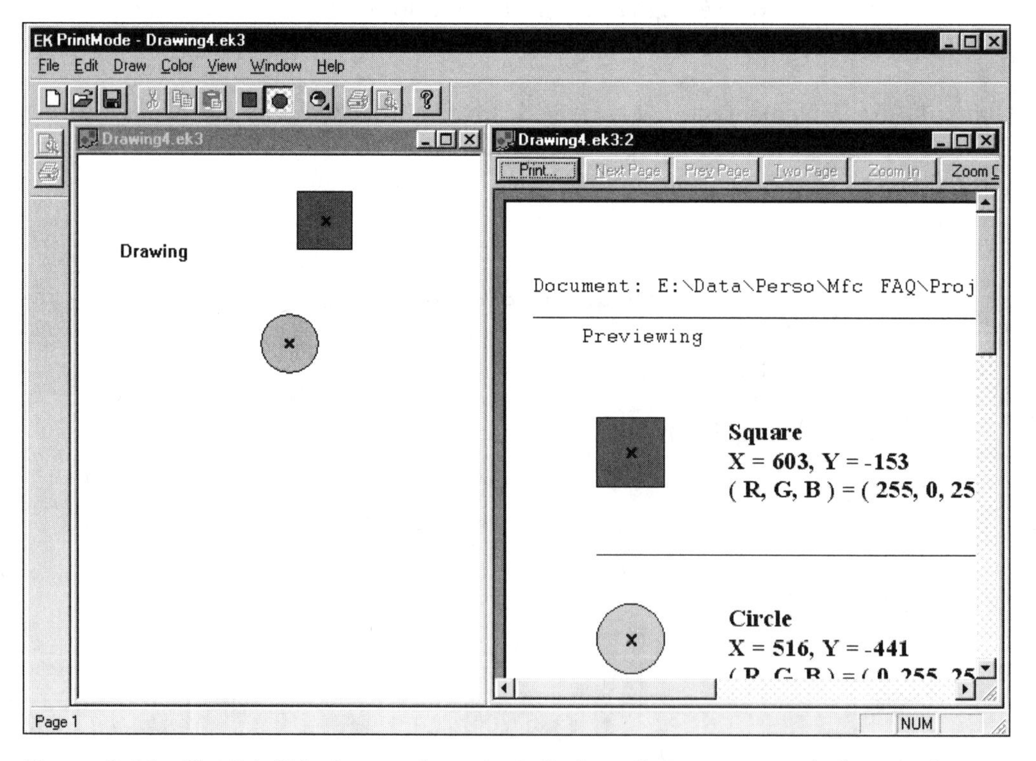

Figure 8-11. The PrintMode sample project displays the current mode for which its *OnDraw()* and *OnPrint()* functions are called.

Sample Code

- Project: PrintMode in the Chap08 subdirectory on the companion CD-ROM.
- Purpose: Demonstrates how to find out the current print mode in several functions—whether standard drawing, print preview mode, or actual printing—as shown in Figure 8-11.

Implementation Highlights

- *EkGetPrintMode()* function (DrawView.cpp)
- *CDrawView::OnDraw()* function (DrawView.cpp)
- *CDrawView::OnPrint()* function (DrawView.cpp)

See Also

- *FAQ 8.10 How do I implement print preview in shades of gray for a monochrome printer?*

APPENDIX A

UTILITY FUNCTIONS AND CLASSES

This appendix provides a one-stop place where you can find all the *Ek* . . . utility functions and classes discussed elsewhere in this book. The functions and classes are ordered first by chapter and inside each chapter by alphabetical order.

All these functions and classes are available in the EkUtil.h and EkUtil.cpp files located in the root folder of the companion CD-ROM.

Chapter 2: Documents and Document Templates

CEkDocList class

Purpose: Enumerate the document objects in an MDI application.
Discussed in: *FAQ 2.19 How do I iterate through the list of all the currently opened documents?*

CEkDocList: declaration

```
#include <afxtempl.h>   // For CTypedPtrList template

class CEkDocList
{
public:
   // Constuction - Destruction
```

```
   CEkDocList();     // The constructor fills our internal
                     // list of pointer to document objects
   ~CEkDocList();
   // Operations
   CDocument* GetNextDoc();  // Gets next document object

   // Forbid copy and assignment of CEkDocList objects
private:
   CEkDocList( const CEkDocList& );
   const CEkDocList& operator = ( const CEkDocList& );

   // Implementation
private:
   // Internal list of pointers to document objects
   CTypedPtrList< CObList, CDocument* > m_DocList;

   // Current position in the above list
   POSITION m_posDocList;
};
```

CEkDocList: implementation

```
CEkDocList::CEkDocList()
{
   CWinApp* pApp = AfxGetApp();
   ASSERT_VALID( pApp );
   // 1 - Iterate through the application's document
   // templates list
   POSITION posTemplate =
                     pApp->GetFirstDocTemplatePosition();
   while( posTemplate != NULL )
   {
      // 2 - For each document template object...
      CDocTemplate* pTemplate =
                     pApp->GetNextDocTemplate( posTemplate );
      ASSERT_VALID( pTemplate );
      ASSERT_KINDOF( CDocTemplate, pTemplate );
      // 3 - Iterate through the template's document list
      POSITION posDocument =
                     pTemplate->GetFirstDocPosition();
      while( posDocument != NULL )
      {
         // 4 - For each document object...
```

```
            CDocument* pDoc =
                  pTemplate->GetNextDoc( posDocument );
            ASSERT_VALID( pDoc );
            ASSERT_KINDOF( CDocument, pDoc );
            // 5 - Add the document pointer to our
            // internal list
            m_DocList.AddTail( pDoc );
         }
      }
   // 6 - Initialize our POSITION member
   m_posDocList = m_DocList.GetHeadPosition();
}

CEkDocList::~CEkDocList()
{
   m_DocList.RemoveAll();
   m_posDocList = NULL;
}

CDocument* CEkDocList::GetNextDoc()
{
   if( m_posDocList == NULL )
      return NULL;

   CDocument* pDoc = m_DocList.GetNext( m_posDocList );
   ASSERT_VALID( pDoc );
   ASSERT_KINDOF( CDocument, pDoc );

   return pDoc;
}
```

■

EkCloseDocument() function

Prototype:	`void EkCloseDocument( CDocument* pDoc );`
Purpose:	Close a document object after prompting the user to save the document if it was modified.
Discussed in:	*FAQ 2.12 How do I programmatically close a document?*
Parameters:	*pDoc*: pointer to the document object to be closed.
Return value:	None.

EkCloseDocument(): implementation

```
void EkCloseDocument( CDocument* pDoc )
{
   ASSERT_VALID( pDoc );

   // 1 - Give the user a chance to save the document
   if( !pDoc->SaveModified() )
      return;

   // 2 - Destroy the document object
   pDoc->OnCloseDocument();
}
```

■

EkGetActiveDocument() function

Prototype:	`CDocument* EkGetActiveDocument();`
Purpose:	Get a pointer to the active document object or *NULL*.
Discussed in:	*FAQ 2.18 How do I get a pointer to the currently active document?*
Parameters:	None.
Return value:	Pointer to the active document object or *NULL* if unsuccessful.

EkGetActiveDocument(): implementation

```
CDocument* EkGetActiveDocument()
{
   // 1 - Get a pointer to the application's
   // main frame window
   CWnd* pWnd = AfxGetMainWnd();
   if( pWnd == NULL )
      return NULL;

   // 2 - Make sure the pointer is valid and more
   // strongly typed
   ASSERT_VALID( pWnd );
   ASSERT_KINDOF( CFrameWnd, pWnd );
   CFrameWnd* pMainFrame = static_cast< CFrameWnd* >( pWnd );

   // 3 - Get a pointer to the active frame window
   // (may be 'this' for SDI application)
   CFrameWnd* pActiveFrame = pMainFrame->GetActiveFrame();
   if( pActiveFrame == NULL )
      return NULL;
```

```
   // 4 - Return a pointer to the active document object
   return pActiveFrame->GetActiveDocument();
}
```

Chapter 3: Views and Frame Windows

CEkFixedFormFrame class

Purpose: Frame window for a form view. The frame window is not resizable by the user, but it initially sizes itself to fit its associated form view.

CEkFixedFormFrame class: declaration

```
class CEkFixedFormFrame : public CMDIChildWnd
{
   DECLARE_DYNCREATE(CEkFixedFormFrame)
protected:
   CEkFixedFormFrame();

// Attributes
public:

// Operations
public:

// Overrides
   // ClassWizard generated virtual function overrides
   //{{AFX_VIRTUAL(CEkFixedFormFrame)
   protected:
   virtual BOOL PreCreateWindow(CREATESTRUCT& cs);
   //}}AFX_VIRTUAL

// Implementation
protected:
   virtual ~CEkFixedFormFrame();

   // Generated message map functions
   //{{AFX_MSG(CEkFixedFormFrame)
   afx_msg int OnCreate(LPCREATESTRUCT lpCreateStruct);
```

```
    //}}AFX_MSG
    DECLARE_MESSAGE_MAP()
};
```

CEkFixedFormFrame class: implementation

```
IMPLEMENT_DYNCREATE(CEkFixedFormFrame, CMDIChildWnd)

CEkFixedFormFrame::CEkFixedFormFrame()
{
}

CEkFixedFormFrame::~CEkFixedFormFrame()
{
}

BEGIN_MESSAGE_MAP(CEkFixedFormFrame, CMDIChildWnd)
    //{{AFX_MSG_MAP(CEkFixedFormFrame)
    ON_WM_CREATE()
    //}}AFX_MSG_MAP
END_MESSAGE_MAP()

BOOL CEkFixedFormFrame::PreCreateWindow(CREATESTRUCT& cs)
{
    // Make the frame window nonresizable
    cs.style &= ~WS_THICKFRAME;
    cs.style &= ~WS_MAXIMIZEBOX;

    return CMDIChildWnd::PreCreateWindow(cs);
}

int CEkFixedFormFrame::OnCreate(
                              LPCREATESTRUCT lpCreateStruct)
{
    if (CMDIChildWnd::OnCreate(lpCreateStruct) == -1)
       return -1;

    // The child FormView should already have been created
    // by the call to CMDIChildWnd::OnCreate()
    CFormView* pFormView = static_cast< CFormView* >
                           ( GetDescendantWindow(
                                AFX_IDW_PANE_FIRST, TRUE ) );
```

```
    ASSERT_VALID( pFormView );
    ASSERT_KINDOF( CFormView, pFormView );

    // Make sure that the view window size is correctly set
    RecalcLayout();

    // Make the view resize its parent frame - that is
    // "us", normally !
    pFormView->ResizeParentToFit( FALSE );
    pFormView->ResizeParentToFit( TRUE );

    return 0;
}
```

■

CEkLockableSplitter class

Purpose:	Splitter window that can be "locked."
Discussed in:	*FAQ 3.34 How do I lock a splitter window so that the user cannot move the divider line?*

CEkLockableSplitter class: declaration

```
class CEkLockableSplitter : public CSplitterWnd
{
// Construction
public:
    CEkLockableSplitter();

// Attributes
public:

// Operations
public:
    void SetLock( BOOL bLock );
    BOOL GetLock() const;
    void ToggleLock();

// Overrides
    // ClassWizard generated virtual function overrides
    //{{AFX_VIRTUAL(CEkLockableSplitter)
    //}}AFX_VIRTUAL
```

```
// Implementation
public:
   virtual ~CEkLockableSplitter();

protected:
   BOOL m_bLocked;

   // Generated message map functions
protected:
   //{{AFX_MSG(CEkLockableSplitter)
   afx_msg void OnLButtonDown(UINT nFlags, CPoint point);
   afx_msg void OnMouseMove(UINT nFlags, CPoint point);
   afx_msg BOOL OnSetCursor(CWnd* pWnd, UINT nHitTest, UINT
message);
   //}}AFX_MSG
   DECLARE_MESSAGE_MAP()
};
```

CEkLockableSplitter class: implementation

```
CEkLockableSplitter::CEkLockableSplitter()
{
   m_bLocked = FALSE;
}

CEkLockableSplitter::~CEkLockableSplitter()
{
}

BEGIN_MESSAGE_MAP(CEkLockableSplitter, CSplitterWnd)
   //{{AFX_MSG_MAP(CEkLockableSplitter)
   ON_WM_LBUTTONDOWN()
   ON_WM_MOUSEMOVE()
   ON_WM_SETCURSOR()
   //}}AFX_MSG_MAP
END_MESSAGE_MAP()

void CEkLockableSplitter::SetLock( BOOL bLock )
{
   m_bLocked = bLock;
}
```

```
BOOL CEkLockableSplitter::GetLock() const
{
   return m_bLocked;
}

void CEkLockableSplitter::ToggleLock()
{
   m_bLocked = !m_bLocked;
}

void CEkLockableSplitter::OnLButtonDown(UINT nFlags,
                                        CPoint point)
{
   if( m_bLocked )
   {
      // Bypass standard CSplitterWnd processing
      CWnd::OnLButtonDown(nFlags, point);
   }
   else
   {
      CSplitterWnd::OnLButtonDown(nFlags, point);
   }
}

void CEkLockableSplitter::OnMouseMove(UINT nFlags,
                                      CPoint point)
{
   if( m_bLocked )
   {
      // Bypass standard CSplitterWnd processing
      CWnd::OnMouseMove(nFlags, point);
   }
   else
   {
      CSplitterWnd::OnMouseMove(nFlags, point);
   }
}

BOOL CEkLockableSplitter::OnSetCursor(CWnd* pWnd,
                                      UINT nHitTest,
                                      UINT message)
{
```

```
    if( m_bLocked )
    {
        // Bypass standard CSplitterWnd processing
        return CWnd::OnSetCursor(pWnd, nHitTest, message);
    }
    else
    {
        return CSplitterWnd::OnSetCursor(pWnd, nHitTest,
                                         message);
    }
}
```

■

EkCreateNewWindow() function

Prototype:	`CFrameWnd* EkCreateNewWindow( CDocTemplate* pTemplate, CDocument* pDocument );`
Purpose:	Create a new "window" on a document—that is, a new child frame window with a new view inside it.
Discussed in:	*FAQ 3.3 How do I programmatically open a view based on a specific document template?*
Parameters:	*pTemplate*: pointer to the document template to use for creating the new view and frame window *pDocument*: pointer to the document object on which to open the new "window"
Return value:	Pointer to the newly created frame window or *NULL* if unsuccessful

EkCreateNewWindow(): implementation

```
CFrameWnd* EkCreateNewWindow( CDocTemplate* pTemplate,
                              CDocument* pDocument )
{
    ASSERT_VALID( pTemplate );
    ASSERT_VALID( pDocument );

    // 1 - Create the new frame window
    // (will in turn create the associated view)
    CFrameWnd* pFrame = pTemplate->CreateNewFrame(
                              pDocument, NULL );
```

```
    if( pFrame == NULL )
    {
       // Window creation failed
       TRACE0( "Warning: failed to create new frame.\n" );
       return NULL;
    }
    ASSERT_KINDOF( CFrameWnd, pFrame );

    // 2 - Tell the frame to update itself
    // (and its child windows)
    pTemplate->InitialUpdateFrame( pFrame, pDocument );

    // 3 - Return a pointer to the new frame window object
    return pFrame;
}
```

■

EkGetActiveFrame() function

Prototype:	`CFrameWnd* EkGetActiveFrame();`
Purpose:	Get a pointer to the active frame window or *NULL*.
Discussed in:	*FAQ 3.40 How do I get a pointer to the active frame window?*
Parameters:	None.
Return value:	Pointer to the active frame window or *NULL* if unsuccessful.

EkGetActiveFrame(): implementation

```
CFrameWnd* EkGetActiveFrame()
{
    CWnd* pMainWnd = AfxGetMainWnd();
    ASSERT_VALID( pMainWnd );

    if( !pMainWnd->IsKindOf( RUNTIME_CLASS( CFrameWnd ) ) )
    {
       return NULL;
    }

    return static_cast<CFrameWnd*>( pMainWnd )
                               ->GetActiveFrame();
}
```

■

EkGetActiveView() function

Prototype: `CView* EkGetActiveView();`
Purpose: Get a pointer to the active view or *NULL*.
Discussed in: *FAQ 3.39 How do I get a pointer to the active view?*
Parameters: None.
Return value: Pointer to the active view or *NULL* if unsuccessful.

EkGetActiveView(): implementation

```
CView* EkGetActiveView()
{
   CWnd* pMainWnd = AfxGetMainWnd();
   ASSERT_VALID( pMainWnd );
   if( !pMainWnd->IsKindOf( RUNTIME_CLASS( CFrameWnd ) ) )
   {
      return NULL;
   }

   return static_cast<CFrameWnd*>( pMainWnd )
               ->GetActiveFrame()->GetActiveView();
}
```

■

EkSwitchViewInFrame() function

Prototype:
```
void EkSwitchViewInFrame
                 ( CFrameWnd* pFrame,
                   CRuntimeClass* pViewClass );
```
Purpose: Replace the current view in a frame window by another view.
Discussed in: *FAQ 3.37 How do I dynamically switch the view displayed in an MDI child window or SDI main application window?*
Parameters: *pFrame*: pointer to the frame window containing the view to be replaced
pViewClass: pointer to the *CRuntimeClass* structure that identifies the class of the view object that will be created inside the frame window
Return value: None.

EkSwitchViewInFrame(): implementation

```
void EkSwitchViewInFrame( CFrameWnd* pFrame,
                          CRuntimeClass* pViewClass )
```

```
{
   ASSERT_VALID( pFrame );
   ASSERT( pViewClass != NULL );
   ASSERT( pViewClass->IsDerivedFrom(
                        RUNTIME_CLASS( CView ) ) );

   // 1 - Find the currently active view
   CView* pActiveView = pFrame->GetActiveView();
   if( pActiveView == NULL )
   {
      TRACE0( "Unable to switch: no active view\n" );
      return;
   }

   if( pActiveView->IsKindOf( pViewClass ) )
   {
      // No need to switch for same view class
      return;
   }

   // 2 - Store current view position
   CRect rcView;
   pActiveView->GetWindowRect( &rcView );

   // 3 - Find the associated document
   CDocument* pDoc = pActiveView->GetDocument();
   ASSERT_VALID( pDoc );

   // 4 - Make sure the document won't self-destruct
   // when active view is destroyed
   BOOL bSaveAutoDelete = pDoc->m_bAutoDelete;
   pDoc->m_bAutoDelete = FALSE;

   // 5 - Destroy the active view
   pActiveView->DestroyWindow();

   // 6 - Restore document to initial state
   pDoc->m_bAutoDelete = bSaveAutoDelete;

   // 7 - Initialize creation context used by CreateView()
   CCreateContext context;
   context.m_pNewDocTemplate = NULL;
   context.m_pLastView = NULL;
   context.m_pCurrentFrame = NULL;
```

```
    context.m_pNewViewClass = pViewClass;
    context.m_pCurrentDoc = pDoc;

    // 8 - Create the new view
    CView* pNewView = static_cast<CView*>
                ( pFrame->CreateView( &context ) );

    ASSERT_VALID( pNewView );

    // 9 - Position the new view like the old one
    pFrame->ScreenToClient( &rcView );
    pNewView->MoveWindow( &rcView, TRUE );

    // 10 - Send WM_INITIALUPDATE to the view
    pFrame->InitialUpdateFrame( pDoc, TRUE );
}
```

■

EkSwitchViewInSplitter() function

Prototype:

```
void EkSwitchViewInSplitter
                ( CSplitterWnd* pSplitter,
                  int row,
                  int col,
                  CRuntimeClass* pViewClass );
```

Purpose: Replace the current view inside a splitter window pane by another view.

Discussed in: *FAQ 3.38 How do I dynamically switch the view displayed in a splitter window?*

Parameters: *pSplitter*: pointer to the splitter window containing the view to be replaced
row, col: coordinates of the pane containing the view to be replaced
pViewClass: pointer to the *CRuntimeClass* structure that identifies the class of the view object that will be created inside the splitter window pane

Return value: None.

EkSwitchViewInSplitter(): implementation

```
void EkSwitchViewInSplitter( CSplitterWnd* pSplitter,
                             int row, int col,
                             CRuntimeClass* pViewClass )
```

```
{
   ASSERT_VALID( pSplitter );
   ASSERT( pViewClass != NULL );

   ASSERT( pViewClass->
            IsDerivedFrom( RUNTIME_CLASS( CView ) ) );

   // 1 - Find the view to be replaced
   CWnd* pPaneWnd = pSplitter->GetPane( row, col );
   if( !pPaneWnd->IsKindOf( RUNTIME_CLASS( CView ) ) )
   {
      TRACE2(
         "Unable to switch: pane (%d,%d) is not a view\n",
          row, col );
      return;
   }

   CView* pCurrentView = static_cast<CView*>( pPaneWnd );
   ASSERT_VALID( pCurrentView );
   ASSERT_KINDOF( CView, pCurrentView );

   if( pCurrentView->IsKindOf( pViewClass ) )
   {
      // No need to switch for same view class
      return;
   }

   // 2 - Store current view position and activation state
   CRect rcView;
   pCurrentView->GetWindowRect( &rcView );

   CView* pActiveView = pSplitter->
               GetParentFrame()->GetActiveView();
   BOOL bSaveActive = ( pActiveView == NULL )
               || ( pActiveView == pCurrentView );

   // 3 - Find the associated document
   CDocument* pDoc = pCurrentView->GetDocument();
   ASSERT_VALID( pDoc );

   // 4 - Make sure the document won't self-destruct
   // when current view is destroyed
```

```
    BOOL bSaveAutoDelete = pDoc->m_bAutoDelete;
    pDoc->m_bAutoDelete = FALSE;

    // 5 - Destroy the current view
    pCurrentView->DestroyWindow();

    // 6 - Restore document to initial state
    pDoc->m_bAutoDelete = bSaveAutoDelete;

    // 7 - Initialize creation context used by CreateView()
    CCreateContext context;
    context.m_pNewDocTemplate = NULL;
    context.m_pLastView = NULL;
    context.m_pCurrentFrame = NULL;

    context.m_pNewViewClass = pViewClass;
    context.m_pCurrentDoc = pDoc;

    // 8 - Create the new view
    pSplitter->CreateView(   row, col, pViewClass,
                             rcView.Size(), &context );

    CView* pNewView = static_cast<CView*>
                ( pSplitter->GetPane( row, col ) );
    ASSERT_VALID( pNewView );
    ASSERT_KINDOF( CView, pNewView );

    // 9 - Position the new view like the old one and
    // activate it if needed
    pSplitter->ScreenToClient( &rcView );
    pNewView->MoveWindow( &rcView, TRUE );
    if( bSaveActive )
    {
       pSplitter->GetParentFrame()->SetActiveView(pNewView);
    }

    // 10 - Send WM_INITIALUPDATE to the view
    pNewView->GetParentFrame()->InitialUpdateFrame( pDoc,
                                                     TRUE );
}
```

Chapter 4: Dialog Boxes

EkDrawBitmap() function

Prototype:
```
void EkDrawBitmap( CDC* pDC,
                   CBitmap* pBitmap,
                   CRect rect,
                   BOOL bCenter = TRUE );
```

Purpose: Draw a bitmap inside a device context.

Discussed in: *FAQ 4.5 How do I add a preview area to (draw inside) a dialog box?*

Parameters: *pDC*: pointer to the (window) device context into which to render the bitmap
pBitmap: pointer to the bitmap object that should be rendered
rect: location of the bitmap inside the destination device context
bCenter: *TRUE* if the bitmap should be centered inside the *rect* rectangle, *FALSE* otherwise

Return value: None.

EkDrawBitmap(): implementation

```
void EkDrawBitmap( CDC* pDC, CBitmap* pBitmap, CRect rect,
                   BOOL bCenter = TRUE )
{
   ASSERT_VALID( pDC );
   ASSERT_VALID( pBitmap );

   // 1 - Create compatible memory DC
   CDC dcMem;
   dcMem.CreateCompatibleDC( pDC );

   // 2 - Select bitmap into memory DC
   CBitmap* pOldBitmap = dcMem.SelectObject( pBitmap );

   if( bCenter )
   {
      // 3 - Center bitmap in destination rectangle
      BITMAP bitmap;
      pBitmap->GetObject( sizeof( BITMAP ), &bitmap);
      CSize sizeBitmap( bitmap.bmWidth, bitmap.bmHeight );
      CSize diff = rect.Size() - sizeBitmap;
      rect.DeflateRect( diff.cx / 2, diff.cy / 2 );
   }
```

```
    // 4 - Blit the bitmap from the memory DC to the real DC
    pDC->BitBlt( rect.left, rect.top,
                 rect.Width(), rect.Height(),
                 &dcMem, 0, 0, SRCCOPY );

    // 5 - Deselect bitmap from memory DC
    dcMem.SelectObject( pOldBitmap );
}
```

■

EkExpandDialog() function

Prototype: `void EkExpandDialog( CDialog* pDlg, UINT nSmallID, UINT nLargeID, UINT nButtonID );`

Purpose: Expand or contract an expanding dialog box.

Discussed in: *FAQ 4.7 How do I implement an expanding dialog box?*

Parameters: *pDlg*: pointer to the dialog to expand or contract
nSmallID: ID of the Picture control that defines the boundary of the collapsed dialog box
nLargeID: ID of the Picture control that defines the boundary of the expanded dialog box
nButtonID: ID of the Button control that toggles the state of the dialog box, and of the associated string resource

Return value: None.

EkExpandDialog(): implementation

```
void EkExpandDialog( CDialog* pDlg,
                     UINT nSmallID, UINT nLargeID,
                     UINT nButtonID )
{
    ASSERT_VALID( pDlg );

    // 1 - Get the More/Less button control
    CWnd* pWndButton = pDlg->GetDlgItem( nButtonID );
    ASSERT_VALID( pWndButton );

    // 2 - Load button resource string and
    // parse More/Less parts
```

```
CString strButton;
VERIFY( strButton.LoadString( nButtonID ) );

CString strMore, strLess;
AfxExtractSubString( strMore, strButton, 0, _T('\n') );
AfxExtractSubString( strLess, strButton, 1, _T('\n') );

// 3 - Find out if we need to expand or
// collapse the dialog
CString strCaption;
pWndButton->GetWindowText( strCaption );
BOOL bExpand = ( strCaption == strMore );  // Collapse
                                            // by default

// 4 - Get current dialog window rectangle
CRect rcDialog;
pDlg->GetWindowRect( &rcDialog );

int nNewHeight = -1;

if( bExpand )
{

   // 5a - Change More/Less button caption
   pWndButton->SetWindowText( strLess );

   // 6a - Calculate new dialog height
   CWnd* pWndLarge = pDlg->GetDlgItem( nLargeID );
   ASSERT_VALID( pWndLarge );

   CRect rcLarge;
   pWndLarge->GetWindowRect( &rcLarge );

   nNewHeight = rcLarge.top-rcDialog.top;
}
else
{

   // 5b - Change More/Less button caption
   pWndButton->SetWindowText( strMore );

   // 6b - Calculate new dialog height
```

```
        CWnd* pWndSmall = pDlg->GetDlgItem( nSmallID );
        ASSERT_VALID( pWndSmall );

        CRect rcSmall;
        pWndSmall->GetWindowRect( &rcSmall );

        nNewHeight = rcSmall.top-rcDialog.top;
    }

    // 7 - Set new dialog height
    ASSERT( nNewHeight > 0 );
    pDlg->SetWindowPos( NULL, 0, 0,
                        rcDialog.Width(), nNewHeight,
                        SWP_NOMOVE | SWP_NOZORDER );

    // 8 - Set the enabled state for each control depending
    // on whether the control is currently visible or not
    CWnd* pWndControl = pDlg->GetWindow( GW_CHILD );
    while( pWndControl != NULL )
    {
        CRect rcControl;
        pWndControl->GetWindowRect( &rcControl );
        pWndControl->EnableWindow(
                rcControl.top <= rcDialog.top + nNewHeight );
        pWndControl = pWndControl->GetWindow( GW_HWNDNEXT );
    }

    // 9 - Check if a control still has the focus
    // (can lose it if the active control becomes disabled)
    CWnd* pWndActiveControl = CWnd::GetFocus();
    if( pWndActiveControl == NULL )
    {
        // 10 - Set focus to "first" control on dialog
        CWnd* pWndFirstControl = pDlg->GetNextDlgTabItem(
                                                    NULL );
        ASSERT_VALID( pWndFirstControl );
        ASSERT( pWndFirstControl->IsWindowEnabled() );
        pWndFirstControl->SetFocus();
    }
}
```

Chapter 5: Property Sheets

EkCenterPropertySheetButtons() function

Prototype:

```
void EkCenterPropertySheetButtons(
                              CPropertySheet* pPSheet,
                              BOOL bCenterOK,
                              BOOL bCenterCancel,
                              BOOL bCenterApply );
```

Purpose: Conditionally center standard property sheet buttons (useful when some buttons are hidden).

Discussed in: *FAQ 5.4 How do I customize the standard property sheet buttons?*

Parameters: *pPSheet*: pointer to the property sheet that contains the buttons to center
bCenterOK: is the OK button included in the layout calculation?
bCenterCancel: is the Cancel button included in the layout calculation?
bCenterApply: is the Apply button included in the layout calculation?

Return value: None.

EkCenterPropertySheetButtons(): implementation

```
void EkCenterPropertySheetButtons(
                              CPropertySheet* pPSheet,
                              BOOL bCenterOK,
                              BOOL bCenterCancel,
                              BOOL bCenterApply )
{
   ASSERT_VALID( pPSheet );
   ASSERT( bCenterOK || bCenterCancel || bCenterApply );

   // Find "OK" button rectangle
   CWnd* pWndOK = pPSheet->GetDlgItem( IDOK );
   ASSERT( pWndOK != NULL );
   CRect rcOK;
   pWndOK->GetWindowRect( &rcOK );
   pPSheet->ScreenToClient( &rcOK );

   // Find "Cancel" button rectangle
   CWnd* pWndCancel = pPSheet->GetDlgItem( IDCANCEL );
```

```
ASSERT( pWndCancel != NULL );
CRect rcCancel;
pWndCancel->GetWindowRect( &rcCancel );
pPSheet->ScreenToClient( &rcCancel );

// Find "Apply" button rectangle
CWnd* pWndApply = pPSheet->GetDlgItem( ID_APPLY_NOW );
ASSERT( pWndApply != NULL );
CRect rcApply;
pWndApply->GetWindowRect( &rcApply );
pPSheet->ScreenToClient( &rcApply );

// Find property sheet client rectangle
CRect rcClient;
pPSheet->GetClientRect( &rcClient );

// Compute layout values
int nButtonWidth = rcOK.Width();
int nButtonMargin = rcCancel.left - rcOK.right;
int nButtons = (bCenterOK ? 1 : 0)
               + (bCenterCancel ? 1 : 0)
               + (bCenterApply ? 1 : 0);
int nGlobalWidth = nButtonWidth * nButtons;
if( nButtons > 1 )
{
   nGlobalWidth += nButtonMargin * (nButtons - 1);
}

int nCurrentX = ( rcClient.left + rcClient.right
                             - nGlobalWidth ) / 2;
int nTop = rcOK.top;

// Center "OK" button
if( bCenterOK )
{
   pWndOK->SetWindowPos( NULL,
                         nCurrentX,
                         nTop,
                         0, 0,
                         SWP_NOSIZE | SWP_NOZORDER
                                    | SWP_NOACTIVATE );

   nCurrentX += nButtonWidth + nButtonMargin;
}
```

```
    // Center "Cancel" button
    if( bCenterCancel )
    {
        pWndCancel->SetWindowPos( NULL,
                                  nCurrentX,
                                  nTop,
                                  0, 0,
                                  SWP_NOSIZE | SWP_NOZORDER
                                             | SWP_NOACTIVATE );

        nCurrentX += nButtonWidth + nButtonMargin;
    }

    // Center "Apply" button
    if( bCenterApply )
    {
        pWndApply->SetWindowPos( NULL,
                                 nCurrentX,
                                 nTop,
                                 0, 0,
                                 SWP_NOSIZE | SWP_NOZORDER
                                            | SWP_NOACTIVATE );
    }
}
```

■

EkCreateEmbeddedPropertySheet() function

Prototype:

```
BOOL EkCreateEmbeddedPropertySheet(
            CWnd* pParent,
            CPropertySheet* pPSheet,
            DWORD dwStyle = WS_CHILD | WS_VISIBLE,
            DWORD dwExStyle = 0 );
```

Purpose: Create a property sheet that is embedded inside another window.

Discussed in: *FAQ 5.9 How do I embed a property sheet inside a dialog box?*

Parameters: *pParent*: pointer to the parent window inside which the property sheet should be embedded

pPSheet: pointer to the *CPropertySheet* object associated with the Windows property sheet that will be created

dwStyle: window styles for the new property sheet window

dwExStyle: extended window styles for the new property sheet window

Return value: *TRUE* if successful, *FALSE* otherwise.

EkCreateEmbeddedPropertySheet(): implementation

```
BOOL EkCreateEmbeddedPropertySheet(
                  CWnd* pParent,
                  CPropertySheet* pPSheet,
                  DWORD dwStyle = WS_CHILD | WS_VISIBLE,
                  DWORD dwExStyle = 0 )
{
   ASSERT_VALID( pParent );
   ASSERT_VALID( pPSheet );

   // 1 - Create the embedded property sheet window
   if( !pPSheet->Create( pParent,  dwStyle, dwExStyle ) )
   {
      TRACE0("Embedded property sheet creation failed\n");
      return FALSE;
   }

   // 2 - Add WS_TABSTOP and WS_EX_CONTROLPARENT to
   // the property sheet styles
   pPSheet->ModifyStyle( 0, WS_TABSTOP );
   pPSheet->ModifyStyleEx ( 0, WS_EX_CONTROLPARENT );

   // 3 - Add WS_EX_CONTROLPARENT to the parent window
   // styles
   pParent->ModifyStyleEx ( 0, WS_EX_CONTROLPARENT );

   return TRUE;
}
```

■

EkHidePropertySheetButtons() function

Prototype:
```
void EkHidePropertySheetButtons(
                                CPropertySheet* pPSheet,
                                BOOL bHideOK,
                                BOOL bHideCancel,
                                BOOL bHideApply );
```

Purpose: Conditionally hide any (or all) of the standard property sheet buttons.

Discussed in: *FAQ 5.4 How do I customize the standard property sheet buttons?*

Parameters: *pPSheet*: pointer to the property sheet that contains the buttons to hide
bHideOK: hide the OK button?
bHideCancel: hide the Cancel button?
bHideApply: hide the Apply button?

Return value: None.

EkHidePropertySheetButtons(): implementation

```
void EkHidePropertySheetButtons(
                                CPropertySheet* pPSheet,
                                BOOL bHideOK,
                                BOOL bHideCancel,
                                BOOL bHideApply )
{
   ASSERT_VALID( pPSheet );

   // Hide "OK" button
   if( bHideOK )
   {
      CWnd* pWnd = pPSheet->GetDlgItem( IDOK );
      ASSERT( pWnd != NULL );
      pWnd->ShowWindow( SW_HIDE );
   }

   // Hide "Cancel" button
   if( bHideCancel )
   {
      CWnd* pWnd = pPSheet->GetDlgItem( IDCANCEL );
      ASSERT( pWnd != NULL );
      pWnd->ShowWindow( SW_HIDE );
   }
```

```
   // Hide "Apply" button
   if( bHideApply )
   {
      CWnd* pWnd = pPSheet->GetDlgItem( ID_APPLY_NOW );
      ASSERT( pWnd != NULL );
      pWnd->ShowWindow( SW_HIDE );
   }
}
```

■

EkPositionEmbeddedPropertySheet() function

Prototype:
```
void EkPositionEmbeddedPropertySheet
                ( CWnd* pParent,
                  CPropertySheet* pPSheet,
                  CRect rcNewPosition );
void EkPositionEmbeddedPropertySheet
                ( CWnd* pParent,
                  CPropertySheet* pPSheet,
                  UINT nIDPSheetArea );
```

Purpose: Position and resize an embedded property sheet.

Discussed in: *FAQ 5.9 How do I embed a property sheet inside a dialog box?*

Parameters:
pParent: pointer to the parent window that contains the embedded property sheet
pPSheet: pointer to the property sheet
rcNewPosition: new position of the embedded property sheet, in client coordinates of the parent window (pixels)
nIDPSheetArea: ID of a (hidden) Picture control that represents the desired property sheet position inside the parent window

Return value: None.

EkPositionEmbeddedPropertySheet(): implementation

```
void EkPositionEmbeddedPropertySheet(
                                     CWnd* pParent,
                                     CPropertySheet* pPSheet,
                                     CRect rcNewPosition )
{
```

```
ASSERT_VALID( pParent );
ASSERT_VALID( pPSheet );

// 1 - Get current coordinates of tab control
// and property sheet window
CTabCtrl* pTabCtrl = pPSheet->GetTabControl();
ASSERT( pTabCtrl != NULL );

CRect rcTabCtrl;
pTabCtrl->GetWindowRect( &rcTabCtrl );
pParent->ScreenToClient( &rcTabCtrl );

CRect rcPSheet;
pPSheet->GetWindowRect( &rcPSheet );
pParent->ScreenToClient( &rcPSheet );

// 2 - Calculate margin between property sheet
// and tab control
int dcx = rcPSheet.Width() - rcTabCtrl.Width();
int dcy = rcPSheet.Height() - rcTabCtrl.Height();

// 3 - Move and resize property sheet window
// (also moves the tab window because it is a child
// of the property sheet window)
pPSheet->MoveWindow( rcNewPosition .left,
                     rcNewPosition.top,
                     rcNewPosition .Width(),
                     rcNewPosition.Height() );

// 4 - Resize tab control window to restore
// right / bottom margins
pTabCtrl->SetWindowPos( NULL,
                        0, 0,
                        rcNewPosition.Width() - dcx,
                        rcNewPosition.Height() - dcy,
                        SWP_NOZORDER | SWP_NOMOVE
                                     | SWP_NOACTIVATE );

// 5 - Activate each property page to prevent drawing
// problem
int nCurrentPage = pPSheet->GetActiveIndex();
for( int i = 0; i < pPSheet->GetPageCount(); ++i )
{
```

```
      pPSheet->SetActivePage( i );
   }

   pPSheet->SetActivePage( nCurrentPage );
}

void EkPositionEmbeddedPropertySheet(
                              CWnd* pParent,
                              CPropertySheet* pPSheet,
                              UINT nIDPSheetArea )
{
   ASSERT_VALID( pParent );
   ASSERT_VALID( pPSheet );

   // 1 - Retrieve property sheet destination position
   CRect rcNewPosition;
   CWnd* pWndNewArea = pParent->GetDlgItem(nIDPSheetArea);
   if( pWndNewArea == NULL )
   {
      ASSERT( FALSE );   // Invalid nIDPSheetArea
      return;
   }

   pWndNewArea->GetWindowRect( &rcNewPosition );
   pParent->ScreenToClient( &rcNewPosition );

   // 2 - Call overloaded function
   EkPositionEmbeddedPropertySheet( pParent, pPSheet,
                                    rcNewPosition );
}
```

■

EkResizePropertySheet() function

Prototype: `void EkResizePropertySheet( CPropertySheet* pPSheet, int nWidth );`

Purpose: Horizontally resize a property sheet window along with the associated tab control.

Discussed in: *FAQ 5.5 How do I control the size of my property sheet window?*

Parameters: *pPSheet*: pointer to the property sheet to be resized
nWidth: new property sheet width (pixels)

Return value: None.

EkResizePropertySheet(): implementation

```
void EkResizePropertySheet( CPropertySheet* pPSheet,
                            int nWidth )
{
   ASSERT_VALID( pPSheet );

   // 1 - Get current dimensions of tab control
   // and property sheet window
   CTabCtrl* pTabCtrl = pPSheet->GetTabControl();
   ASSERT( pTabCtrl != NULL );

   CRect rcTabCtrl;
   pTabCtrl->GetWindowRect( &rcTabCtrl );
   pPSheet->ScreenToClient( &rcTabCtrl );

   CRect rcPSheet;
   pPSheet->GetWindowRect( &rcPSheet );

   // 2 - Compute resizing offset
   int dcx = rcPSheet.Width() - nWidth;

   // 3 - Resize property sheet window
   pPSheet->SetWindowPos(   NULL,
                            0, 0,
                            nWidth,
                            rcPSheet.Height(),
                            SWP_NOZORDER | SWP_NOMOVE
                                         | SWP_NOACTIVATE );

   // 4 - Resize tab control window to restore
   // right margin
   pTabCtrl->SetWindowPos(   NULL,
                             0, 0,
                             rcTabCtrl.Width() - dcx,
                             rcTabCtrl.Height(),
                             SWP_NOZORDER | SWP_NOMOVE
                                          | SWP_NOACTIVATE );

   // 5 - Activate each property page to prevent drawing
   // problem
   int nCurrentPage = pPSheet->GetActiveIndex();
   for( int i = 0; i < pPSheet->GetPageCount(); ++i )
   {
```

```
      pPSheet->SetActivePage( i );
   }

   pPSheet->SetActivePage( nCurrentPage );
}
```

Chapter 6: Toolbars and Status Bars

CEkDrawStatusBar class

Purpose:	Status bar class that triggers the *UPDATE_COMMAND_UI* message when repainting, ensuring that its drawing panes paint themselves correctly.
Discussed in:	*FAQ 6.12 How do I draw in a status bar pane?*

CEkDrawStatusBar: declaration

```
class CEkDrawStatusBar : public CStatusBar
{
// Construction
public:
   CEkDrawStatusBar();

// Attributes
public:

// Operations
public:

// Overrides
   // ClassWizard generated virtual function overrides
   //{{AFX_VIRTUAL(CEkDrawStatusBar)
   //}}AFX_VIRTUAL

// Implementation

   // Generated message map functions
protected:
   //{{AFX_MSG(CEkDrawStatusBar)
   afx_msg void OnPaint();
   //}}AFX_MSG
   DECLARE_MESSAGE_MAP()
};
```

CEkDrawStatusBar: implementation

```
#include <afxpriv.h>  // For WM_IDLEUPDATECMDUI message

// ...

CEkDrawStatusBar::CEkDrawStatusBar()
{
}

CEkDrawStatusBar::~CEkDrawStatusBar()
{
}

BEGIN_MESSAGE_MAP(CEkDrawStatusBar, CStatusBar)
   //{{AFX_MSG_MAP(CEkDrawStatusBar)
   ON_WM_PAINT()
   //}}AFX_MSG_MAP
END_MESSAGE_MAP()

void CEkDrawStatusBar::OnPaint()
{
   // 1 - Let base class paint itself
   CStatusBar::OnPaint();

   // 2 - Send a WM_IDLEUPDATECMDUI message to ourselves
   // to ensure our "drawing" panes repaint correctly
   SendMessage( WM_IDLEUPDATECMDUI );
}
```

■

EkCreateProgressBar() function

Prototype:
```
void EkCreateProgressBar( CProgressCtrl* pProgressCtrl,
                          CStatusBar* pStatusBar,
                          LPCTSTR szMessage = NULL,
                          int nPaneIndex = 0,
                          int cxMargin = 10,
                          int cxMaxWidth = -1,
                          UINT nIDControl = 1 );
```

Purpose: Create a progress indicator inside a status bar.
Discussed in: *FAQ 6.14 How do I display a progress indicator in a status bar?*
Parameters: *pProgressCtrl*: pointer to the *CProgressCtrl* C++ object associated with the Windows progress control to be created
pStatusBar: status bar on which the progress control will be created
szMessage: pointer to the string that will be displayed in the status bar, to the left of the progress control. A *NULL* value does not display any message
nPaneIndex: zero-based index of the status bar pane on which to create the progress control. Default value of zero uses the standard leftmost message pane
cxMargin: margin (in pixels) between the end of the *szMessage* text and the left side of the progress control
cxMaxWidth: maximum width (in pixels) of the progress control. Default value of –1 causes the progress control to stretch to cover all the remaining pane width
nIDControl: child window ID of the Windows progress control that will be created. The exact value of this ID is usually irrelevant
Return value: *TRUE* if successful, *FALSE* otherwise.

EkCreateProgressBar(): implementation

```
BOOL EkCreateProgressBar( CProgressCtrl* pProgressCtrl,
                          CStatusBar* pStatusBar,
                          LPCTSTR szMessage = NULL,
                          int nPaneIndex = 0,
                          int cxMargin = 10,
                          int cxMaxWidth = -1,
                          UINT nIDControl = 1 )
{
   ASSERT_VALID( pProgressCtrl );
   ASSERT_VALID( pStatusBar );

   // 1 - Calculate destination rectangle for progress
   // control
   CRect rc;
   pStatusBar->GetItemRect( nPaneIndex, &rc );

   // 2 - Define progress bar horizontal offset
   if( szMessage != NULL )
   {
```

```
        // Compute message text extent
        CClientDC dc( pStatusBar );
        CFont* pFont = pStatusBar->GetFont();
        CFont* pOldFont = dc.SelectObject( pFont );
        CSize sizeText = dc.GetTextExtent( szMessage );
        dc.SelectObject( pOldFont );

        rc.left += sizeText.cx + cxMargin;
    }

    // 3 - Compute progress bar width
    if( cxMaxWidth != -1 )
    {
        rc.right = rc.left + min( cxMaxWidth, rc.Width() );
    }

    // 4 - Display message text
    pStatusBar->SetPaneText( nPaneIndex, szMessage );
    pStatusBar->RedrawWindow();

    // 5 - Create progress control
    return pProgressCtrl->Create( WS_CHILD | WS_VISIBLE,
                                  rc, pStatusBar, nIDControl );
}
```

■

EkCreateToolBar() function

Prototype:

```
BOOL EkCreateToolBar( CFrameWnd* pParentFrame,
 CToolBar* pBar,
 UINT nIDBar,
 UINT nIDResource = 0,
 DWORD dwStyle1 = WS_CHILD |
                  WS_VISIBLE |
                  CBRS_TOP,
 DWORD dwStyle2 = CBRS_TOOLTIPS |
                  CBRS_FLYBY |
                  CBRS_SIZE_DYNAMIC );
```

Purpose: Create a toolbar window, load its associated resource, and define its styles.

Discussed in: *FAQ 6.1 How do I add one or more toolbars to my main frame window or to a view's frame window?*

Parameters: *pParentFrame*: pointer to the frame window that will be the toolbar's parent
pBar: pointer to the *CToolBar* object associated with the toolbar that will be created
nIDBar: child window ID of the toolbar window
nIDResource: of the toolbar resource to be loaded and associated with the new toolbar
dwStyle1: toolbar styles. See help for *CToolBar::Create()*
dwStyle2: additional toolbar styles. See help for *CControlBar::SetBarStyle()*

Return value: *TRUE* if successful, *FALSE* otherwise.

EkCreateToolBar(): implementation

```
BOOL EkCreateToolBar( CFrameWnd* pParentFrame,
                      CToolBar* pBar,
                      UINT nIDBar,
                      UINT nIDResource = 0,
                      DWORD dwStyle1 = WS_CHILD |
                                       WS_VISIBLE |
                                       CBRS_TOP,
                      DWORD dwStyle2 = CBRS_TOOLTIPS |
                                       CBRS_FLYBY |
                                       CBRS_SIZE_DYNAMIC )
{
   ASSERT_VALID( pParentFrame );
   ASSERT_VALID( pBar );

   // 1 - No IDResource means resource ID is same as bar ID
   if( nIDResource == 0 )
   {
      nIDResource = nIDBar;
   }

   // 2 - Create toolbar and load resources
   if( !pBar->Create( pParentFrame, dwStyle1, nIDBar ) ||
       !pBar->LoadToolBar( nIDResource ) )
   {
      TRACE1( "Failed to create toolbar with ID=%d\n",
              nIDBar );
```

```
        return FALSE;       // fail to create
    }

    // 3 - Define toolbar styles
    pBar->SetBarStyle( pBar->GetBarStyle() | dwStyle2 );

    return TRUE;
}
```

■

EkDockBarNextTo() function

Prototype:	`void EkDockBarNextTo( CControlBar* pNewBar, CControlBar* pDockedBar, UINT nDockBarID = AFX_IDW_DOCKBAR_TOP );`
Purpose:	Dock a toolbar next to an already docked toolbar on the same docking band.
Discussed in:	*FAQ 6.3 How do I programmatically dock a toolbar next to another one?*
Parameters:	*pNewBar*: pointer to the toolbar that should be docked *pDockedBar*: pointer to the already docked toolbar *nDockBarID*: side of the frame window that the new bar will be docked on (should be the same side on which the *pDockedBar* toolbar is already docked). See help for *CFrameWnd::DockControlBar()*
Return value:	None.

EkDockBarNextTo(): implementation

```
void EkDockBarNextTo( CControlBar* pNewBar,
                      CControlBar* pDockedBar,
                      UINT nDockBarID=AFX_IDW_DOCKBAR_TOP )
{
    ASSERT_VALID( pDockedBar );
    ASSERT_VALID( pNewBar );

    // 1 - Find the frame where we will dock
    CFrameWnd* pFrame = pDockedBar->GetDockingFrame();

    // 2 - Force MFC to compute the positions
    // of the docked control bar(s)
    pFrame->RecalcLayout();
```

```
    // 3 - Compute rectangle of already "docked" bar
    CRect rect;
    pDockedBar->GetWindowRect( &rect );

    // 4 - Offset the rectangle slightly to the bottom right
    // so that the new bar will dock either to the right or
    // to the bottom of the existing bar (depending on the
    // side where this last bar is already docked)
    rect.OffsetRect(1,1);

    // 5 - Dock new bar to specified position
    pFrame->DockControlBar( pNewBar, nDockBarID, &rect );
}
```

■

EkDockToolBar() function

Prototype:	`void EkDockToolBar( CFrameWnd* pParentFrame, CToolBar* pBar, UINT nDockBarID = AFX_IDW_DOCKBAR_TOP, CControlBar* pBarNextTo = NULL, DWORD dwStyleDocking = CBRS_ALIGN_ANY );`
Purpose:	Define a toolbar's docking behavior and dock the toolbar at the specified position.
Discussed in:	*FAQ 6.1 How do I add one or more toolbars to my main frame window or to a view's frame window?*
Parameters:	*pParentFrame*: pointer to the toolbar's parent frame window *pBar*: pointer to the toolbar to be docked *nDockBarID*: side of the frame window that the toolbar will be docked on (should be the same side on which the *pBarNextTo* toolbar is already docked). See help for *CFrameWnd::DockControlBar()* *pBarNextTo*: pointer to an already docked toolbar next to which *pBar* should be docked, or *NULL* *dwStyleDocking*: toolbar's docking behavior. See help for *CControlBar::EnableDocking()*
Return value:	None.

EkDockToolBar(): implementation

```
void EkDockToolBar( CFrameWnd* pParentFrame,
                    CToolBar* pBar,
                    UINT nDockBarID = AFX_IDW_DOCKBAR_TOP,
                    CControlBar* pBarNextTo = NULL,
                    DWORD dwStyleDocking = CBRS_ALIGN_ANY )
{
   ASSERT_VALID( pParentFrame );
   ASSERT_VALID( pBar );

   ASSERT( ::IsWindow( pBar->GetSafeHwnd() ) );

   // 1 - Define toolbar docking behavior
   pBar->EnableDocking( dwStyleDocking );
   if( pBarNextTo != NULL )
   {
      // 2a - Dock toolbar next to an existing bar
      EkDockBarNextTo( pBar, pBarNextTo, nDockBarID );
   }
   else
   {
      // 2b - Dock toolbar on its own dockbar
      pParentFrame->DockControlBar( pBar, nDockBarID );
   }
}
```

■

EkIsBarVisible() function

Prototype:	`BOOL EkIsBarVisible( CControlBar* pBar );`
Purpose:	Find out if a control bar is currently visible.
Discussed in:	*FAQ 6.15 How do I programmatically show or hide a control bar?*
Parameters:	*pBar*: pointer to the control bar whose current visibility state is checked
Return value:	*TRUE* if the control bar is currently visible, *FALSE* otherwise.

EkIsBarVisible(): implementation

```
BOOL EkIsBarVisible( CControlBar* pBar )
{
```

```
    ASSERT_VALID( pBar );

    return ( ( pBar->GetStyle() & WS_VISIBLE ) != 0 );
}
```

■

EkSetToolBarButtonText() function

Prototype:

```
void EkSetToolBarButtonText( CToolBar* pBar,
                             UINT nIDStrings,
                             TCHAR chSep = _T( '\n'
                                 ) );
```

Purpose: Set the text labels of the buttons on a toolbar.
Discussed in: *FAQ 6.5 How do I add text labels to my toolbar buttons?*
Parameters: *pBar*: pointer to the toolbar
nIDStrings: ID of the string resource that defines the labels associated with each toolbar button, in the same order as the toolbar buttons—from left to right or top to bottom
chSep: character used as separator in the *nIDStrings* string resource
Return value: None.

EkSetToolBarButtonText(): implementation

```
void EkSetToolBarButtonText( CToolBar* pBar,
                             UINT nIDStrings,
                             TCHAR chSep = _T( '\n' ) )
{
    ASSERT_VALID( pBar );

    // 1 - Load string from resource
    CString strButtons;
    VERIFY( strButtons.LoadString( nIDStrings ) );

    // 2 - Start at beginning of string
    int nIndex = 0;
    LPCTSTR pszStart = strButtons;
    LPCTSTR pszEnd = NULL;

    // 3 - Isolate each substring and set button text
    do
    {
```

```
        // 4 - Find next separator
        pszEnd = _tcschr( pszStart, chSep );
        int nLen = ( pszEnd == NULL ) ?
                        _tcslen( pszStart ) :
                        (int)( pszEnd - pszStart );
        ASSERT( nLen >= 0 );

        // 5 - Create CString from substring
        CString strSubString;
        memcpy(   strSubString.GetBufferSetLength( nLen ),
                  pszStart, nLen * sizeof( TCHAR ) );

        // 6 - Set button text, bump index
        pBar->SetButtonText( nIndex++, strSubString );

        // 7 - Skip separator
        pszStart += nLen + 1;
    }
    while( pszEnd != NULL );
}
```

■

EkSwitchBars() function

Prototype:

```
void EkSwitchBars( CFrameWnd* pFrame,
                   CControlBar* pBar1,
                   CControlBar* pBar2,
                   BOOL bShowBar2,
                   BOOL bDelay = TRUE );
```

Purpose: Hide or show the correct toolbar in a pair, while preserving the toolbar's child window ID.

Discussed in: *FAQ 6.8 How do I dynamically switch between different toolbars?*

Parameters: *pFrame*: pointer to the toolbar's parent frame window
pBar1: pointer to the first toolbar of the pair
pBar2: pointer to the second toolbar of the pair
bShowBar2: *TRUE* to show the second toolbar, *FALSE* to show the first toolbar
bDelay: if *TRUE*, delay showing/hiding the control bars. If *FALSE*, show/hide the control bars immediately. See help for *CFrameWnd::ShowControlBar()*

Return value: None.

EkSwitchBars(): implementation

```
void EkSwitchBars( CFrameWnd* pFrame,
                   CControlBar* pBar1,
                   CControlBar* pBar2,
                   BOOL bShowBar2,
                   BOOL bDelay = TRUE )
{
   ASSERT_VALID( pFrame );
   ASSERT_VALID( pBar1 );
   ASSERT_VALID( pBar2 );

   // 1 - Compute "From" and "To" bars
   CControlBar* pBarFrom = bShowBar2 ? pBar1 : pBar2;
   CControlBar* pBarTo = bShowBar2 ? pBar2 : pBar1;
   BOOL bVisible = EkIsBarVisible( pBarFrom );

   // 2 - Exchange "From" and "To" window IDs
   UINT nIDFrom = ::GetWindowLong( pBarFrom->GetSafeHwnd(),
                                   GWL_ID );
   UINT nIDTo = ::GetWindowLong( pBarTo->GetSafeHwnd(),
                                 GWL_ID );

   ::SetWindowLong(pBarFrom->GetSafeHwnd(), GWL_ID, nIDTo);
   ::SetWindowLong(pBarTo->GetSafeHwnd(), GWL_ID, nIDFrom);

   // 3 - Hide "From" bar, show "To" bar if "From" bar
   // was visible
   pFrame->ShowControlBar( pBarFrom, FALSE, bDelay );
   pFrame->ShowControlBar( pBarTo, bVisible, bDelay );
}
```

Chapter 7: Menus

EkUpdateMenuUI() function

Prototype:
```
void EkUpdateMenuUI( CWnd* pOwner,
                     CMenu* pMenu,
                     BOOL bAutoMenuEnable = TRUE );
```

Purpose: Implement the *UPDATE_COMMAND_UI* mechanism for dynamic popup menus.

Discussed in:	*FAQ 7.4 How do I display a popup menu when the user clicks a button in a dialog box?*
Parameters:	*pOwner*: pointer to the window that owns the menu and should receive the *UPDATE_COMMAND_UI* messages *pMenu*: pointer to the popup menu *bAutoMenuEnable*: *TRUE* if the menu items that have no associated command handler should automatically be disabled, *FALSE* otherwise
Return value:	None.

EkUpdateMenuUI(): implementation

```
void EkUpdateMenuUI( CWnd* pOwner,
                     CMenu* pMenu,
                     BOOL bAutoMenuEnable = TRUE )
{
   // Checks the enabled/checked state of various menu
   // items (adapted from MFC's own
   // CFrameWnd::OnInitMenuPopup() function --
   // WinFrm.cpp)

   ASSERT_VALID( pOwner );
   ASSERT( pMenu != NULL );

   // Create and initialize the famous CCmdUI object
   CCmdUI state;
   state.m_pMenu = pMenu;
   ASSERT(state.m_pOther == NULL);
   ASSERT(state.m_pParentMenu == NULL);

   // determine if menu is popup in top-level menu and set
   // m_pOther to it if so (m_pParentMenu == NULL
   // indicates that it is secondary popup)
   HMENU hParentMenu;
   if (AfxGetThreadState()->m_hTrackingMenu ==
                                      pMenu->m_hMenu)
      state.m_pParentMenu = pMenu;    // parent == child
                                      // for tracking popup
   else if ((hParentMenu=::GetMenu(pOwner->m_hWnd))!=NULL)
   {
      CWnd* pParent = pOwner->GetTopLevelParent();
         // child windows don't have menus — need to go to
```

```
            // the top!
        if (pParent != NULL &&
            (hParentMenu = ::GetMenu(pParent->m_hWnd))!=NULL)
        {
            int nIndexMax = ::GetMenuItemCount(hParentMenu);
            for (int nIndex = 0; nIndex < nIndexMax; nIndex++)
            {
                if (::GetSubMenu(hParentMenu, nIndex) ==
                                                pMenu->m_hMenu)
                {
                    // when popup is found, m_pParentMenu is
                    // containing menu
                    state.m_pParentMenu =
                              CMenu::FromHandle(hParentMenu);
                    break;
                }
            }
        }
    }

    state.m_nIndexMax = pMenu->GetMenuItemCount();

    // For each menu item...
    for (state.m_nIndex = 0;
         state.m_nIndex < state.m_nIndexMax;
         state.m_nIndex++)
    {

        // Get menu item ID
        state.m_nID = pMenu->GetMenuItemID(state.m_nIndex);
        if (state.m_nID == 0)
            continue; // menu separator or invalid cmd
                      // - ignore it

        ASSERT(state.m_pOther == NULL);
        ASSERT(state.m_pMenu != NULL);
        if (state.m_nID == (UINT)-1)
        {
            // Maybe a popup menu, route to first item of
            // that popup
            state.m_pSubMenu = pMenu->
                              GetSubMenu(state.m_nIndex);
```

```
            if (state.m_pSubMenu == NULL ||
                (state.m_nID = state.m_pSubMenu->
                        GetMenuItemID(0)) == 0 ||
                state.m_nID == (UINT)-1)
            {
                continue; // first item of popup can't be
                          // routed to
            }
            state.DoUpdate(pOwner, FALSE);  // popups are
                                   // never auto disabled
        }
        else
        {
            // Normal menu item:
            // Auto enable/disable if 'bAutoMenuEnable'
            // argument is set and command is _not_ a
            // system command
            state.m_pSubMenu = NULL;
            state.DoUpdate(pOwner,
                    bAutoMenuEnable &&
                        state.m_nID < 0xF000);
        }

        // adjust for menu deletions and additions
        UINT nCount = pMenu->GetMenuItemCount();
        if (nCount < state.m_nIndexMax)
        {
            state.m_nIndex -= (state.m_nIndexMax - nCount);
            while (state.m_nIndex < nCount &&
                pMenu->GetMenuItemID(state.m_nIndex) ==
                                    state.m_nID)
            {
                state.m_nIndex++;
            }
        }
        state.m_nIndexMax = nCount;
    }
}
```

Chapter 8: Printing and Print Preview

CEkPrintingDlg class

Purpose: Custom Printing . . . dialog box.
Discussed in: *FAQ 8.8 How do I customize the Printing . . . dialog box?*

CEkPrintingDlg: declaration

```
#include "EkResource.h"

class CEkPrintingDlg : public CDialog
{
// Construction
public:
   CEkPrintingDlg(CWnd* pParent, CWnd* pStandardDialog);

// ...

// Dialog Data
   //{{AFX_DATA(CEkPrintingDlg)
   enum { IDD = IDD_EK_PRINTING_DLG };
   CStatic    m_DocName;
   CStatic    m_PrinterName;
   CStatic    m_PortName;
   CStatic    m_PageNum;
   CProgressCtrl    m_Progress;
   //}}AFX_DATA

// ...

// Implementation
protected:
   CWnd* m_pStandardDialog;  // Pointer to MFC's
                             // "Printing..." dialog

// ...
};
```

CEkPrintingDlg: implementation

```
CEkPrintingDlg::CEkPrintingDlg(CWnd* pParent,
                               CWnd* pStandardDialog)
```

```
    : CDialog(CEkPrintingDlg::IDD, pParent)
{
    //{{AFX_DATA_INIT(CEkPrintingDlg)
    //}}AFX_DATA_INIT

    ASSERT_VALID( pStandardDialog );
    m_pStandardDialog = pStandardDialog;

    // Create modeless dialog box
    // (MFC automatically disables the application's
    // main window while printing)
    Create(CEkPrintingDlg::IDD, pParent);
}
void CEkPrintingDlg::DoDataExchange(CDataExchange* pDX)
{
    CDialog::DoDataExchange(pDX);
    //{{AFX_DATA_MAP(CEkPrintingDlg)
    DDX_Control(pDX, AFX_IDC_PRINT_DOCNAME, m_DocName);
    DDX_Control(pDX, AFX_IDC_PRINT_PRINTERNAME,
                                              m_PrinterName);
    DDX_Control(pDX, AFX_IDC_PRINT_PORTNAME, m_PortName);
    DDX_Control(pDX, AFX_IDC_PRINT_PAGENUM, m_PageNum);
    DDX_Control(pDX, IDC_PROGRESS, m_Progress);
    //}}AFX_DATA_MAP
}

BEGIN_MESSAGE_MAP(CEkPrintingDlg, CDialog)
    //{{AFX_MSG_MAP(CEkPrintingDlg)
    //}}AFX_MSG_MAP
END_MESSAGE_MAP()

BOOL CEkPrintingDlg::OnInitDialog()
{
    SetWindowText( AfxGetAppName() );
    CenterWindow();

    return CDialog::OnInitDialog();
}

void CEkPrintingDlg::OnCancel()
{
    ASSERT_VALID( m_pStandardDialog );
    ASSERT( ::IsWindow(m_pStandardDialog->GetSafeHwnd()) );
```

```
    // Ask MFC's "Printing..." dialog to cancel
    // the printing process
    m_pStandardDialog->SendMessage(WM_COMMAND, IDCANCEL, 0);
}
```

■

EkChangePrintingOrientation() function

Prototype:	`void EkChangePrintingOrientation ( CDC* pDC, CPrintInfo* pInfo, short NewOrientation );`
Purpose:	Dynamically change the printing orientation during a print job.
Discussed in:	*FAQ 8.5 How do I programmatically change the printing orientation (portrait versus landscape) on the fly?*
Parameters:	*pDC*: pointer to the device context whose orientation should be changed *pInfo*: pointer to the *CPrintInfo* structure associated with the current print job *NewOrientation*: select the new orientation of the paper. Can be either *DMORIENT_PORTRAIT* (1) or *DMORIENT_LANDSCAPE* (2). See help for the *DEVMODE* structure
Return value:	None.

EkChangeOrientation(): implementation

```
void EkChangePrintingOrientation( CDC* pDC,
                                  CPrintInfo* pInfo,
                                  short NewOrientation )
{
   ASSERT_VALID( pDC );
   ASSERT( pInfo != NULL );

   DEVMODE* pDevMode = pInfo->m_pPD->GetDevMode();

   // Only change if new orientation is different
   if( pDevMode->dmOrientation != NewOrientation )
   {
      pDevMode->dmOrientation = NewOrientation;
      pDC->ResetDC( pDevMode );
   }
}
```

■

EkColorRefToGray() function

Prototype: `COLORREF EkColorRefToGray( COLORREF crColor );`
Purpose: Convert a color to the corresponding gray shade.
Discussed in: *FAQ 8.10 How do I implement print preview in shades of gray for a monochrome printer?*
Parameters: *crColor*: color to convert
Return value: Corresponding gray shade.

EkColorRefToGray(): implementation

```
COLORREF EkColorRefToGray( COLORREF crColor )
{
   // Extract (r, g, b) factors from COLORREF
   BYTE red = GetRValue( crColor );
   BYTE green = GetGValue( crColor );
   BYTE blue = GetBValue( crColor );

   // Convert (r, g, b) to gray using standard formula
   BYTE gray = static_cast< BYTE >(
               ( red*30 + green*59 + blue*11 ) / 100 );
   return RGB( gray, gray, gray );
}
```

■

EkCreateDefaultPrinterDC() function

Prototype: `BOOL EkCreateDefaultPrinterDC( CDC* pDC );`
Purpose: Create a device context associated with the currently selected printer.
Discussed in: *FAQ 8.4 How do I predict page breaks as Microsoft Word does?*
Parameters: *pDC*: pointer to the *CDC* object that will be associated with the device context to be created
Return value: *TRUE* if successful, *FALSE* otherwise.

EkCreateDefaultPrinterDC(): implementation

```
BOOL EkCreateDefaultPrinterDC( CDC* pDC )
{
   ASSERT_VALID( pDC );

   PRINTDLG pd;
   AfxGetApp()->GetPrinterDeviceDefaults( &pd );
   return AfxGetApp()->CreatePrinterDC( *pDC );
}
```

■

EkGetPrintMode() function

Prototype:

```
enum EK_PRINT_MODE { DISPLAYING, PRINTING,
                     PREVIEWING };
EK_PRINT_MODE EkGetPrintMode( CPrintInfo* pInfo );
EK_PRINT_MODE EkGetPrintMode( CDC* pDC );
```

Purpose: Find out the current print mode given a pointer to either a *CPrintInfo* or a device context object.

Discussed in: *FAQ 8.11 How do I distinguish between drawing, print preview, and actual printing in my code?*

Parameters: *pInfo*: pointer to the *CPrintInfo* object associated with the current print job
pDC: pointer to the device context object associated with the current print job

Return value: Current print mode associated with the function parameter.

EkGetPrintMode(): implementation

```
enum EK_PRINT_MODE { DISPLAYING, PRINTING, PREVIEWING };

EK_PRINT_MODE EkGetPrintMode( CPrintInfo* pInfo )
{
   if( pInfo == NULL )
   {
      return DISPLAYING;
   }
   if( pInfo->m_bPreview )
```

```
    {
        return PREVIEWING;
    }

    return PRINTING;
}

EK_PRINT_MODE EkGetPrintMode( CDC* pDC )
{
    ASSERT_VALID( pDC );
    if( !pDC->IsPrinting() )
    {
        return DISPLAYING;
    }
    if( pDC->m_hDC != pDC->m_hAttribDC )
    {
        return PREVIEWING;
    }
    return PRINTING;
}
```

■

EkIsMonoPreview() function

Prototype: `BOOL EkIsMonoPreview( CDC* pDC );`
Purpose: Find out if a device context is currently used in print preview mode for a monochrome printer.
Discussed in: *FAQ 8.10 How do I implement print preview in shades of gray for a monochrome printer?*
Parameters: *pDC*: pointer to the device context to be checked for the "print preview on a monochrome printer" condition
Return value: *TRUE* if the device context is currently used in print preview mode for a monochrome printer, *FALSE* otherwise.

EkIsMonoPreview(): implementation

```
BOOL EkIsMonoPreview( CDC* pDC )
{
    ASSERT_VALID( pDC );
```

```
    // Check for monochrome device context
    BOOL bMono = ( pDC->GetDeviceCaps( NUMCOLORS ) == 2 );

    // Check for print preview mode
    BOOL bPreview = ( pDC->m_hDC != pDC->m_hAttribDC );

    return( bMono && bPreview );
}
```

APPENDIX B

BIBLIOGRAPHY AND ADDITIONAL RESOURCES

Here is my personal selection of books and articles about MFC programming. This list is short because it contains only items that I consider to be essential resources on the shelf of every MFC developer.

Note that I do not try here to address issues outside "pure" MFC development, such as COM, OLE, ActiveX, C++ language, object-oriented analysis and design, software project management, and so on. Although these topics are important to MFC developers, they lie outside the scope of this book.

Books

MFC Internals

George Shepherd and Scot Wingo, Addison-Wesley Developers Press, 1996
This book is neither a tutorial nor a how-to book but rather takes you for a guided tour inside MFC's undocumented—or poorly documented—aspects. The focus of this book is to answer the question "How does this feature work inside MFC?" for a great many features, including basic Windows support, message handling, document/view architecture, control bar architecture, printing and print preview, DLLs, threads, and COM and OLE support.

Although the style is intended for easy reading, this book's technical level makes it more suited for the serious MFC developer than for the beginner in this field. Strongly recommended.

Programming Windows 95 with MFC

Jeff Prosise, Microsoft Press, 1996

This is currently the best book for learning about Windows programming with MFC. Prosise presents most of the fundamental Windows and MFC concepts very clearly, and the book's structure closely reflects the way I like to teach MFC programming: first by writing all the code manually so that you really understand how things work together and then gradually introducing wizards to take care of the repetitive tasks. Globally, I find the progression between chapters very well thought out. Someone who reads this book from cover to cover will gain a solid understanding of both Windows programming and MFC fundamental concepts.

Although this book does not mention database access and COM and OLE programming with MFC, it covers some advanced topics, such as bitmaps, palettes and regions, the "new" Windows 95 common controls, and multithreaded programming. Strongly recommended.

Inside Visual C++

David J. Kruglinski, Microsoft Press, 1996

This book is also a good resource for learning about Windows programming with MFC, even if I tend to prefer the structure of Prosise's book for learning the fundamental concepts. On the other hand, *Inside Visual C++* includes a thorough treatment of advanced topics such as COM and OLE programming with MFC and database access via ODBC and DAO.

Professional MFC Programming with Visual C++ 5 (new edition of The Revolutionary Guide to MFC 4 Programming with Visual C++)

Mike Blaszczak, Wrox Press, 1996

Written by a member of the MFC development team, this book contains several useful tips and powerful techniques, and it addresses advanced topics such as threads, database access via ODBC and DAO, OLE containers and servers, and OLE controls. This book can sometimes be quite hard to follow for a beginner, but it provides a good way to extend one's knowledge of MFC programming.

Visual C++ Masterclass

Ramirez, Evans, Wingo, Li, Templeman, Fiol, Yuen, Alshibani, and Gillet, Wrox Press, 1996
This book is definitely not a tutorial but rather is a collection of techniques that touch various—and sometimes exotic—subjects, such as Windows 95 shell programming, Windows multimedia services, working with device-independent bitmaps (DIBs), the Windows 95 game SDK (DirectX), network programming, WinSock Internet programming, Internet programming with WinINet, and ActiveX documents.

Because this book's chapters are written by many different authors, they are of unequal depth and quality. However, you still might find this book useful because it touches unusual subjects that are seldom addressed in other MFC programming books.

Visual C++ 4 How-To

Scott Stanfield, Waite Group Press, 1996
This book is organized in a question-answer format similar to the one you are reading now, and you might at first consider the two books to be head-on competitors. However, comparing the contents of both books reveals only about a 20%–30% overlap. My book focuses squarely on MFC fundamentals, whereas I perceive the main strength of Stanfield's book to be on more advanced topics, such as multimedia, OLE and DDE, and system issues. Each book complements the other quite well, and buying both of them is a safe bet.

Articles

Meandering Through the Maze of MFC Message and Command Routing

Paul DiLascia*, Microsoft Systems Journal, *July 1995
To my knowledge, this article remains one of the best sources of information about the MFC message-routing mechanism. Although you should expect to read it twice before you assimilate its contents, this article will give you a thorough understanding of how MFC routes Windows messages and commands and how the *UPDATE_COMMAND_UI* mechanism *really* works. Thoroughly understanding this subject is not only interesting from a theoretical point of view but also will let you make use of this knowledge to create elegant

object-oriented designs that integrate new classes in MFC's command-routing mechanism. Strongly recommended.

Rewriting the MFC Scribble Program Using an Object-Oriented Design Approach

Allen Holub*, Microsoft Systems Journal, *August 1995
Although you may not always agree with the author on every point he tries to make about merging "pure" object-oriented design techniques with MFC's document/view architecture, this article will almost certainly cause you to think more deeply about design issues in your applications. It also judiciously introduces the *data_interface* and *user_interface* names to convey concisely the essence of the respective roles played by the document and the view classes inside the document/view architecture.

If you like this article, you may wish to follow up with two other articles written by the same author: "Hide Your Data" and "Make Objects Responsible for Their Own User Interfaces," *Microsoft Systems Journal,* August 1996 and December 1996.

Additional Internet Resources

Finally, here is a short list of Internet resources that you might find useful:

- *MFC FAQ* <http://www.mfcfaq.com/>: The companion Web site for this book. Check it out!
- *MFC Visual C++ FAQ* <http://www.stingsoft.com/mfc_faq/>: the original Internet MFC FAQ.
- *Visual C++ Developers Journal (VCDJ)* <http://www.vcdj.com/default.asp>: online Visual C++ magazine with several interesting articles.
- *MFC Programmer's Sourcebook* <http://www.codeguru.com/>: lots of short articles and tips.
- *MFC Professional* <http://www.visionx.com/mfcpro/>: the official MFC-L mailing list archive.
- *Visual C++ and MFC Internet Resources* <http://indigo.ie/~pjn/cplus.html>: list of links to Web sites, newsgroups, mailing lists, and resources devoted to Visual C++ and MFC programming.
- *Internet Resources for Windows Developers* <http://www.r2m.com/windev/>: even more links to resources devoted to Windows programming.

Index

A

B

C

D

E

F

G

N

O

P

R

S

T

U

V

W

MFC Programming

Alan R. Feuer

This book provides an in-depth introduction to writing 32-bit Windows applications using C++ and the Microsoft Foundation Class (MFC) library. The text builds from the ground up, first describing the Windows architecture and showing how MFC works with that architecture; then covering the document/view framework that simplifies the creation of industrial-strength programs; and finally illustrating advanced concepts like the usage of dynamic link libraries (DLL), creating Internet clients, and building form-based applications. *MFC Programming* answers the hard questions, diving below the surface presented in the Reference Manual by building comprehensive, detailed chapters on all types of controls, all of the common dialogs (along with the various methods of customization), serialization, printing and previewing, and customization of the Page Setup dialog. The accompanying CD-ROM contains source code for all programs in the book.

0-201-63358-2 • Hardcover • 480 pages • ©1997

Extending the MFC Library

Add Useful Reusable Features to the Microsoft® Foundation Class Library

David A. Schmitt

MFC allows you to code for new or customized capabilities by extending the application framework and creating your own reusable classes. *Extending the MFC Library* brings C and C++ programmers quickly up to speed on MFC's implementation of traditional C++ features, then presents numerous extension projects, discussing how they are created and used, and how to further customize them for use in your own projects. The extension projects are included ready-to-run on disk.

0-201-48946-5 • Paperback • 384 pages • ©1996

MFC Internals

Inside the Microsoft® Foundation Class Architecture

George Shepherd and Scot Wingo

According to Dean McCrory, Microsoft's MFC Development Lead, "Quite simply, this book is a must-have for any serious MFC developer." This guide to the inner workings of the Microsoft Foundation Classes gives you in-depth information on undocumented MFC classes, utility functions and data members, useful coding techniques, and analyses of the way MFC classes work together. The book covers both graphical user interface classes and extensions to the basic Windows support. You will learn about such specific topics as MFC's document/view architecture, undocumented aspects of MFC serialization and classes, how OLE controls are implemented, and more.

0-201-40721-3 • Paperback • 736 pages • ©1996

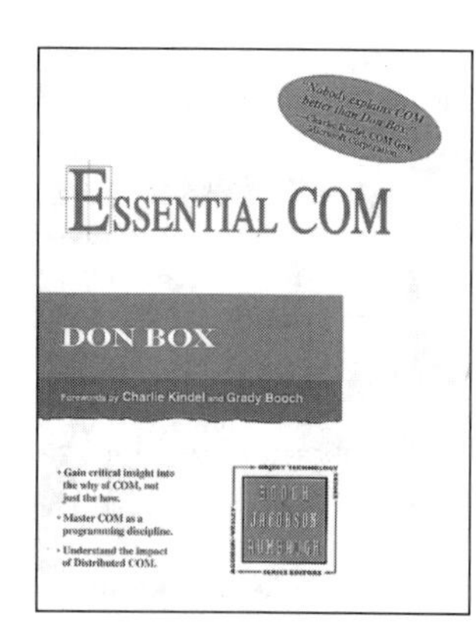

Essential COM

Don Box

Essential COM helps developers go beyond simplistic applications of COM and become truly effective COM programmers. You will find comprehensive coverage of the core concepts of Distributed COM (interfaces, classes, apartments, and applications), including detailed descriptions of COM theory, the C++ language mapping, COM IDL (Interface Definition Language), the remoting architecture, IUnknown, monikers, threads, marshalers, security, and more. Written by the premier authority on the COM architecture, this book offers a thorough explanation of COM's basic vocabulary, provides a complete Distributed COM application to illustrate programming techniques, and includes the author's test library of COM utility code. By showing you the why of COM, not just the how, Don Box enables you to apply the model creatively and effectively to everyday programming problems.

0-201-63446-5 • Paperback • 464 pages • ©1998

Effective COM

50 Ways to Improve Your COM and MTS-based Applications

Don Box, Keith Brown, Tim Ewald, and Chris Sells

Written by *Essential COM* author Don Box in conjunction with three other trainers at DevelopMentor, *Effective COM* offers fifty concrete guidelines for COM based on the communal wisdom that has formed over the past five years of COM-based development. This book is targeted at developers who are living and breathing COM, humbled by its complexity and challenged by the breadth of distributed object computing. Although the book is written for developers who work in C++, many of the topics (e.g., interface design, security) are approachable by developers who work in Visual Basic, Java, or Object Pascal. *Effective COM* takes a practical approach to COM, offering guidelines developers can use immediately to become more effective, efficient COM programmers.

0-201-37968-6 • Paperback • 208 pages • Available fall 1998

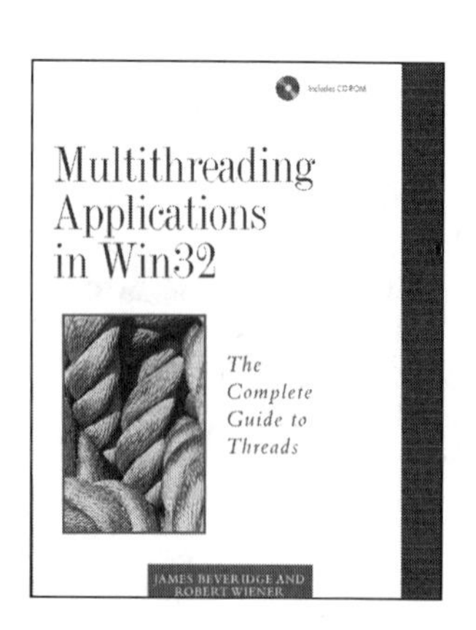

Multithreading Applications in Win32®

The Complete Guide to Threads

Jim Beveridge and Robert Wiener

Windows® 95 and Windows NT™ allow software developers to use the powerful programming technique of multithreading: dividing a single application into multiple "threads" that execute separately and get their own CPU time. This can result in significant performance gains, but also in programming headaches. Multithreading is difficult to do well, and previous coverage of the subject in Windows has been incomplete. In this book programmers will get hands-on experience about when and how to use multithreading, together with expert advice and working examples in C++ and MFC. The CD-ROM contains the code and sample applications from the book, including code that works with Internet Winsock.

0-201-44234-5 • Paperback • 400 pages • ©1997

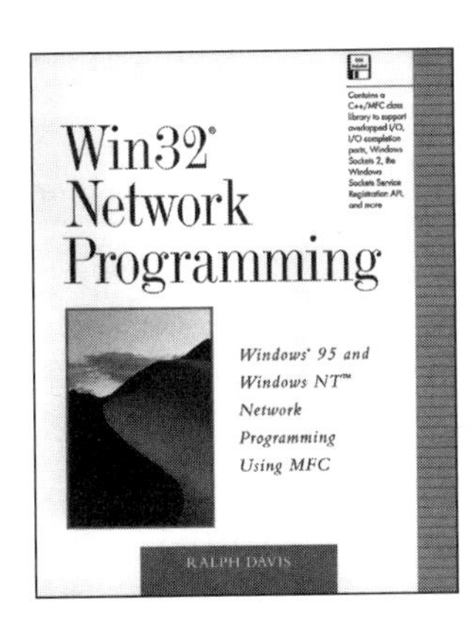

Win32® Network Programming

Windows® 95 and Windows NT™ Network Programming Using MFC

Ralph Davis

As a developer of applications that must communicate across Windows® 95 and Windows NT™, you need to know what network capabilities have been implemented across both platforms. *Win32® Network Programming* is a guide to building networked applications for both Windows 95 and Windows NT 4.0, focusing on overlapped I/O, Windows Sockets 2.0, the Registration Service API, RPC, and Named Pipes. The book's disk contains the example code cast as a C++/MFC class library that extends MFC to support overlapped I/O, I/O completion ports, the Windows Sockets Service Registration API, and related functionality.

0-201-48930-9 • Paperback • 832 pages • ©1996

Crafting Windows NT Device Drivers

The Developers Guide

Edward N. Dekker and Joseph M. Newcomer

Device drivers are a necessary evil, connecting the operating system with its peripherals. There is not always a need for a custom device driver, but it is difficult to determine when one is necessary until driver fundamentals are clear. This book emphasizes the core techniques of programming device drivers. Without this core knowledge, all of the "advanced" driver techniques (layered drivers, WDM, File System Filters, File System Drivers) are inaccessible. This book covers the components of a Kernel mode device driver for Windows NT. There is also background on the Bus Interfaces the Driver Programmer will use; the ISA and the PCI. The authors tackle both existing drivers (the ISA bus and the PCI bus, the primary buses in today's computers).

0-201-69590-1 • Hardcover • 704 pages • Available fall 1998

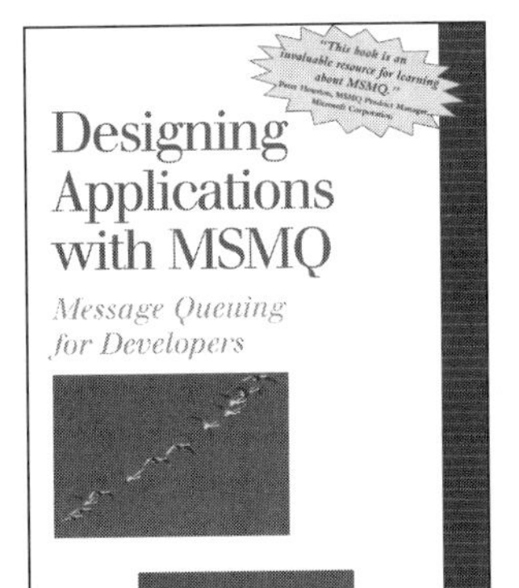

Designing Applications with MSMQ

Message Queuing for Developers

Alan Dickman

Using Web technology effectively to access a vast number of potential customers while keeping customer service levels high is a difficult task. MSMQ (Microsoft Message Queuing) works with MTS (Microsoft Transaction Server) to connect databases and automate responses to external customers (e.g., order processing, customer service issues via email). *Designing Applications with MSMQ* offers a resource for understanding the fundamentals of distributed transactional objects or components. Developing and deploying TP applications has historically been a highly complex task. Microsoft's transaction-processing products, now integrated with Windows NT, make development of mission-critical applications simpler. This book addresses the needs of both Window developers and UNIX TP developers, including software and examples to support the correct design of distributed transactional object systems using MS products, through detailed coverage of online retailing applications.

0-201-32581-0 • Paperback • 432 pages • Available fall 1998

Win32 System Programming

Johnson M. Hart

With this book you can capitalize on your knowledge of high-end operating systems such as Unix, MVS, or VMS to learn Windows system programming quickly. *Win32 System Programming* focuses on the core operating system services of Win32, the common API for the Windows 95 and Windows NT operating systems. The book offers extensive coverage of I/O, security, memory management, processes, threads, and synchronization. You will also find discussions of other advanced topics including file locking, DLLs, asynchronous I/O, fibers, and the registry. In addition, the book includes numerous practical examples and comparisons of Win32 and UNIX functions. The accompanying CD-ROM contains all of the code examples found in the text, a suite of programs for testing system performance, and a collection of UNIX-like utilities.

0-201-63465-1 • Hardcover • 384 pages • ©1997

Windows™ Sockets Network Programming

Bob Quinn and Dave Shute

Windows Sockets (WinSock), a standard network API for use with Windows®, UNIX®, and TCP/IP networking environments, is an extraordinary resource for network programmers. This book shows you how to reap WinSock's full benefits to create network-ready applications. In addition to comprehensive coverage of WinSock 1.1 and 2.0 function calls, you will find information on porting existing BSD Sockets source code to Windows, debugging techniques and tools, common traps and pitfalls to avoid, and the many different operating system platforms that currently incorporate WinSock.

0-201-63372-8 • Hardcover • 656 pages • ©1996

Win32 Programming

Brent E. Rector and Joseph M. Newcomer

This book covers all the material necessary to understand and write 32-bit Windows® applications for both Windows® 95 and Windows NT™ 3.5.1. The book details Win32 application programming concepts, approaches, and techniques for the common Application Programming Interface of Windows 95 and Windows NT. It covers basic methods of Windows message handling, advances in mouse and keyboard input handling, and graphical output using the Graphics Device Interface. The CD-ROM is a gold mine of useful programs, with a C template to create your own Windows applications and dozens of other programs.

0-201-63492-9 • Hardcover • 1568 pages • ©1997

Windows Telephony Programming

A Developer's Guide to TAPI

Chris Sells

TAPI has been called the "assembly language of telephony." TAPI has standardized the interface to telephony hardware under Windows and legitimized the computer telephony industry. In the process, however, TAPI has turned into one of the largest Application Programming Interfaces (APIs) available for Windows. This makes it general and flexible, requiring clear, concise instruction; otherwise it is difficult to learn. The goal of this book is to reduce the high learning curve associated with windows telephony. The book provides Windows C++ developers with a clear, concise TAPI tutorial, and offers several examples of popular telephony applications and a C++ class library to make Windows telephony more approachable.

0-201-63450-3 • Paperback • 320 pages • Available summer 1998

Windows NT™ Security Guide

Stephen A. Sutton

Weak links in a security system leave the door open to data tampering, virus attacks, and numerous other unpleasant scenarios. This book shows system administrators how to protect their networks from intruders. It contains information on critical security issues by providing practical examples and tutorials on configuring and managing a leak-proof network. *The Windows NT™ Security Guide* provides hands-on advice in the form of real life examples and tutorials for setting up and managing a secure network. Perhaps most crucial, it provides guidelines for assessing the effectiveness of a network's defense system.

0-201-41969-6 • Paperback • 384 pages • ©1997

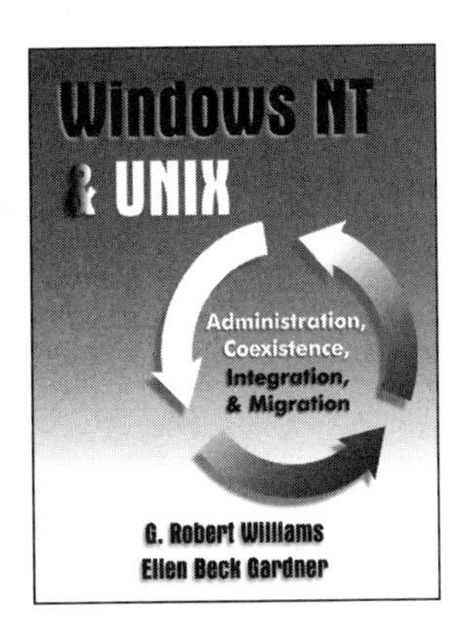

Windows NT & UNIX

Administration, Coexistence, Integration, & Migration

G. Robert Williams and Ellen Beck Gardner

This book will serve as a guidebook in your endeavor to manage a smoothly running system incorporating both UNIX and Windows NT. It clarifies the key issues you are likely to encounter in dealing with the two operating systems, focusing on the three specific areas of interaction: coexistence, integration, and migration. Planning and implementing the introduction of Windows NT into a UNIX environment is discussed in depth, from selecting a topological model and assessing hardware requirements through rollout and training. The book also addresses such topics as accessing data across platforms; user interface emulators; running Windows applications under UNIX and vice versa; ported POSIX commands and utilities; and SNMP. In addition, it presents available tools for porting UNIX applications to Win32, discusses retrofitting UNIX CPUs, and examines CORBA and DCOM interoperability issues.

0-201-18536-9 • Paperback • 768 pages • ©1998

CD-ROM License Agreement Notice

Addison-Wesley warrants the enclosed disc to be free of defects in materials and faulty workmanship under normal use for a period of ninety days after purchase. If a defect is discovered in the disc during this warranty period, a replacement disc can be obtained at no charge by sending the defective disc, postage prepaid, with proof of purchase to:

Addison-Wesley Professional
75 Arlington St., Suite 300
Boston, MA 02116

After the ninety-day period, a replacement will be sent upon receipt of the defective disc and a check or money order for $10.00, payable to Addison-Wesley.

This warranty applies only to the source code from the examples in the book. No warranty is expressed or implied with respect to the demos from Stingray Software. Addison-Wesley makes no warranty or representation, either expressed or implied, with respect to this software, its quality, performance, merchantability, or fitness for a particular purpose. In no event will Addison-Wesley, its distributors, or dealers be liable for direct, indirect, special, incidental, or consequential damages arising out of the use or inability to use the software. The exclusion of implied warranties is not permitted in some states. Therefore, the above exclusion may not apply to you. This warranty provides you with specific legal rights. There may be other rights that you may have that vary from state to state.

The contents of the CD-ROM are intended for personal use only. In case of code reuse in a commercial application, the following credit line must be included:

Segments of the code © 1998 Addison-Wesley Longman and Eugène Kain

More information and updates are available at: http://www.awl.com/cseng/titles/0-201-18537-7

CD-ROM System Requirements

The CD-ROM contains sample code and applications that run on any Windows 95 or Windows NT system with the MFC42.DLL file installed. The source code files will work with Visual C++ 4.0 or above. The included project files will open with Visual C++ 5.0 or above.